A NATURE
CONSERVATION REVIEW

VOLUME 1

The Pasque Flower, *Anemone pulsatilla*, a plant of chalk and limestone grasslands, now threatened through destruction of these habitats (approximately natural size).

Frontispiece

A NATURE
CONSERVATION REVIEW

The selection of biological sites of national importance to
nature conservation in Britain

EDITOR
DEREK RATCLIFFE
CHIEF SCIENTIST, THE NATURE CONSERVANCY COUNCIL

VOLUME 1

CAMBRIDGE UNIVERSITY PRESS

CAMBRIDGE

LONDON · NEW YORK · MELBOURNE

Published by the Syndics of the Cambridge University Press
The Pitt Building, Trumpington Street, Cambridge CB2 1RP
Bentley House, 200 Euston Road, London NW1 2DB
32 East 57th Street, New York, NY 10022, USA
296 Beaconsfield Parade, Middle Park, Melbourne 3206, Australia

First published 1977

Printed in Great Britain at the
University Press, Cambridge

Library of Congress Cataloguing in Publication Data

Main entry under title:

A Nature conservation review.

Published on behalf of the Nature Conservancy Council and the
Natural Environment Research Council.

Bibliography: v. 1, p.

Includes index.

1. Natural areas – Great Britain.   2.   Nature conservation –
Great Britain.
I.   Ratcliffe, Derek A.
II.   Great Britain. Nature Conservancy Council.
III.   Great Britain. Natural Environment Research Council.

QH77.G7N39   333.9'5'0941   76–11065

ISBN 0 521 21159 X

CONTENTS

ILLUSTRATIONS AND TABLES

TABLES

FOREWORD

By the Secretaries of State for Environment, and for Education and Science

A Nature Conservation Review is an account of the nation's heritage of wildlife and its habitats. It describes the biological features of more than 700 sites, classified in major habitat groups, and sets out criteria by which the importance of each site for nature conservation can be judged. The *Review* is a major addition to biological knowledge and reflects great credit on its authors.

Neither the Government nor landowners are committed to any action on particular sites mentioned in the text; but we believe that the *Review* will be a valuable aid to planners and managers in reaching decisions about the future use of rural land. With goodwill and co-operation the information embodied here can be translated into practical benefit for the nation.

We welcome this review and commend it to all who take an interest in natural history and nature conservation.

Shirley Williams

Peter Shore

PREFACE

This review was initiated in 1965 by the Nature Conservancy, then a component body of the Natural Environment Research Council but since 1973 an independent statutory Council. It is published on behalf of both Councils, who deeply appreciate the outstanding contributions made to this wide-ranging interdisciplinary project by their own officers and by individuals and bodies outside the Councils – in particular the universities and the voluntary societies.

They wish to pay a special tribute to Dr Derek Ratcliffe (now Chief Scientist of the Nature Conservancy Council) for the talent and dedication shown in carrying out his duties as Scientific Assessor for the review.

The selection of key sites is inevitably a continuing process, and the present list is open to revision in the light of subsequent events. It may not be possible for all those identified in the *Review* to be safeguarded. The limitations on the scope of the review (explained fully in the text) should, in time, be resolved; the concepts and methodology used will develop as scientific knowledge advances; and there is a continuing growth in professional and public concern about the environment. For all these reasons, the carrying out of periodic assessments of this kind is an essential base for the nation's policies for nature conservation.

The Councils wish to emphasise that this document does not imply any policy commitment by any person or organisation, public or private, to the ways in which the conservation of the sites to which it refers should be implemented.

AUTHORSHIP AND SOURCES

The authors indicated have primary responsibility for their sections, but in many cases they have used information and reports supplied by colleagues of both the Regional and Research staff of the former Nature Conservancy and by other contributors. All texts have been edited by D. A. Ratcliffe who has been responsible for compilation of the *Review*. The document as a whole is thus essentially a collective work, representing the efforts of many people, of whom the following are major contributors:

Introduction	D. A. Ratcliffe
Rationale of the review methods and results	D. A. Ratcliffe
The ecological background to site selection	D. A. Ratcliffe
Coastlands	D. S. Ranwell and D. A. Ratcliffe
Woodlands	R. C. Steele, G. F. Peterken and D. A. Ratcliffe, assisted by M. D. Barrow and A. D. Horrill
Lowland grasslands, heaths and scrub	
Acidic heaths, grasslands and scrub	S. B. Chapman
Calcareous grasslands	T. C. E. Wells
Calcareous scrub	L. K. Ward
Mixed heaths and rich grasslands	E. A. G. Duffey, P. A. Wright, T. C. E. Wells and D. A. Ratcliffe
Neutral grasslands	D. A. Wells
Open waters	N. C. Morgan and R. Britton
Peatlands	D. A. Goode and D. A. Ratcliffe

Upland grasslands and heaths	D. A. Ratcliffe
Artificial ecosystems	N. W. Moore, J. M. Way, M. D. Hooper, F. H. Perring and D. A. Ratcliffe
The conservation of flora	N. Hamilton and D. A. Ratcliffe
The conservation of fauna	D. A. Ratcliffe, J. L. F. Parslow, G. Atkinson-Willes, I. Prestt, P. S. Maitland, N. W. Moore, J. Heath, M. Skelton, P. Merrett, M. G. Morris and R. E. Stebbings

In general, the following were responsible for dealing with particular biological groups throughout the work:

Flowering plants, ferns, bryophytes and lichens	D. A. Ratcliffe
Mammals (general)	D. A. Ratcliffe
(Bats)	R. E. Stebbings
Birds (general)	D. A. Ratcliffe and J. L. F. Parslow
(Waders)	A. J. Prater and J. L. F. Parslow
(Wildfowl)	G. Atkinson-Willes
Reptiles and Amphibia	I. Prestt
Lepidoptera	J. Heath and M. Skelton
Coleoptera	M. G. Morris
Odonata	N. W. Moore and D. A. Ratcliffe
Arachnida	P. Merrett and E. A. G. Duffey

ACKNOWLEDGEMENTS

Staff of the Conservation Branch of the former Nature Conservancy (now the Nature Conservancy Council) were involved at various stages of the *Review*, in providing existing information on sites, in field survey and liaison with outside bodies and individuals in appraisal and choice of key sites, in preparation or revision of site accounts, and in subsequent revisions of the work. Their contribution is too large to be identified separately and, though it varied between individuals, any attempt to indicate differences would be invidious. Special tribute is made to the following for their invaluable help:

J. F. Archibald	G. Howells
M. E. Ball	I. Jones
R. N. Campbell	N. E. King
A. Currie	J. McCarthy
P. Walters Davies	E. M. Matthew
P. E. Davis	J. Mitchell
B. F. T. Ducker	Evan Roberts
B. E. Evans	R. Smith
H. M. T. Frankland	J. A. Thompson
P. A. Gay	C. R. Tubbs
M. George	D. A. White
R. Goodier	H. J. Williams
B. H. Green	R. Woods
P. Hope-Jones	P. A. Wright

In addition to those named under Authorship and sources, staff of the Research Branch of the former Nature Conservancy (now the Institute of Terrestrial Ecology) contributed substantially through field survey, site selection, providing information, and preparation of both background material and site accounts. Their criticism of various drafts was also of great value.

Grateful acknowledgement is made to A. H. F. Brown, R. G. H. Bunce, J. W. Kinnaird and M. W. Shaw (woodlands); F. H. Perring and M. H. Hamilton (flora and distribution of rare species); N. W. Moore (acidic heaths and coastlands, fauna); D. F. Perkins (uplands in Wales); D. Welch (uplands, mires, woodlands); P. S. Maitland and I. R. Smith (open waters) and S. E. Allen for chemical analyses of samples from open water sites.

Many people in universities, County Naturalists' Trusts, Society for the Promotion of Nature Reserves, Royal Society for the Protection of Birds, British Trust for Ornithology, and other bodies, or in an individual capacity, also gave great help.

Special tribute is paid to some outstandingly valuable external contributions. The national and international evaluations of the importance of wildfowl sites by George Atkinson-Willes, based on annual population counts for the Wildfowl Trust, have been used as the basis for selection of sites to represent this interest. The similar but more recent counts of wading birds, organised by A. J. Prater for the British Trust for Ornithology, were used for the evaluation of this element of faunal interest. The censuses of breeding seabird populations conducted under Operation Seafarer by W. R. P. Bourne, David Saunders and Stanley Cramp have strongly influenced the choice of coastal sites. All the data for these three surveys have been made freely available, and have provided one of the few quantitative bases for site selection in the *Review*. Valuable advice and comments on the selection of ornithological sites have also been received from W. R. P. Bourne, D. Nethersole-Thompson and J. T. R. Sharrock.

Many people contributed to the national woodland survey organised by the Nature Conservancy and the Society for the Promotion of Nature Reserves.

John and Hilary Birks have assisted with the choice of botanical sites and written the descriptions for a number of woodland and upland sites, in addition to providing much information on plant distribution, notably bryophytes, and Quaternary interest. Francis Rose has given generously of his encyclopaedic knowledge of the British flora, especially lichens and bryophytes, and advised particularly on the selection of woodland sites. A. J. C. Malloch wrote some of the background material on coastlands and recommended the choice of certain sea cliff sites. Some important salt marshes were identified and described in site accounts by P. Adam. The Breckland Conservation Committee gave guidance on the choice of sites, and A. S. Watt drew on his tremendous knowledge of the Breckland to help with the preparation of descriptive accounts of both district and sites. Sir Harry Godwin wrote the account of Wicken Fen based on his life-long association with the area, and D. E. Coombe gave similar assistance over the Lizard. C. D. Pigott kindly made available unpublished work on limestone grasslands, especially in Derbyshire; D. W. Shimwell allowed access to his data on the Magnesian Limestone and other grasslands; and J. Hope-Simpson lent his extensive and mostly unpublished studies of chalk grasslands.

Particular help, through information and advice, was also received for grasslands from E. Crackles and O. Gilbert; for calcareous heaths from P. J. Grubb; for woodlands from C. D. Pigott and O. Rackham; for open waters from A. V. Holden, C. Sinker, D. Le Cren and staff of both the River Station at East Stoke and the Windermere Laboratory of the Freshwater Biological Association, and J. W. G. Lund made helpful comments on the text; for mires from D. J. Bellamy, J. H. Tallis and M. C. Pearson; for flora from S. M. Walters, E. C. Wallace, P. W. James, J. G. Roger and T. D. V. Swinscow.

Earlier drafts of the *Review* were revised in the light of much helpful comment and criticism from Sir Harry Godwin, C. D. Pigott, J. L. Harper, and J. Phillipson, members of the Scientific Policy Committee of the former Nature Conservancy under the Natural Environment Research Council. Final revision of the document for publication was assisted by A. D. Bradshaw, D. A. Bassett and J. Phillipson, as members of the Nature Conservancy Council.

Finally D. A. Ratcliffe wishes to acknowledge with gratitude the immense amount of help received from colleagues, both within and outside the Nature Conservancy Council and the Institute of Terrestrial Ecology, and hopes there are no omissions from the lists of authors and sources. He would particularly like to thank R. E. Boote, M. E. D. Poore and M. W. Holdgate for their inspiration in launching the *Review* and for their constant encouragement during the work. In addition, he is grateful to Margaret Haas, who assisted in many ways with preparation of earlier drafts; to R. A. Fenton and G. W. Ledgard for producing the maps; to Peter Wakely for photographic assistance and to N. A. Bonnar, M. W. Henchman, A. H. Chapman and M. J. C. Streatfeild, who have contributed enormously to the final revision.

1 INTRODUCTION

A national strategy for nature conservation was formally prescribed in 1947 with the publication of the Government White Papers *Conservation of nature in England and Wales* (Cmd 7122) and *National Parks and the conservation of nature in Scotland* (Cmd 7235). These documents presented the basic philosophy that the practice of nature conservation in Britain should centre around the safeguarding of a fairly large number of key areas adequately representing all major types of natural and semi-natural vegetation, with their characteristic assemblages of plants and animals, and habitat conditions, of climate, topography, rocks and soils, and biotic influences. Geological and physiographic features were to be represented for their own intrinsic interest. Since such areas were intended to be set aside for a range of human uses in posterity, their selection had to be related to the variety of interests involved. In implementing nature conservation strategy, this key area concept has been expressed most significantly in the statutory declaration of a series of 150 National Nature Reserves, which provide the means of safeguarding many important sites, and in the notification of some 3500 Sites of Special Scientific Interest (SSSI). The growth of the voluntary conservation bodies movement has also led to the setting up of many nature reserves without statutory protection.

During the last two decades, human pressures on the land of Britain have caused a rate and scale of attrition of wildlife and habitat even greater than that foreseen in 1947. At the same time, growing interest in the biology and ecology of the natural environment has led to fuller survey and the identification of many more sites of high scientific value and importance to nature conservation. The Nature Conservancy therefore kept progress in the site conservation programme under periodic review, first in 1955, and then in 1965 when a still more comprehensive reappraisal of the situation was launched. This report presents the results of the last review, which has aimed at compiling a countrywide list of sites whose safeguarding is a matter of priority and urgency within the provisions for nature conservation in Britain.

This review has, however, been concerned essentially with biological features, and though these are considered in relation to the background of physical environment, the conservation of physical features other than soils (i.e. geological and physiographic features) has been left for separate, later assessment. Many important physical features are represented within biologically valuable key sites, but their inclusion is only incidental.

The key area concept itself is fairly straightforward, but the actual process of choosing sites and compiling a list to represent an adequate national sample of all major ecosystems[1] raises some extremely complex and difficult problems, both conceptual and practical. The earlier expositions of nature conservation requirements in Cmd 7122 did not dwell on these problems, but made recommendations intended to be taken as reasonable conclusions, having regard to the declared objectives, and the experience of those concerned with site selection.

It is now felt, however, that the case for safeguarding a national series of sites should explain why these key areas are important to nature conservation, and how the assessment of their quality is made. Considerable thought has therefore been given to the rationale behind the assessment and selection of key areas, and the next chapter spells out this thinking in some detail. This is a difficult field in which value judgements figure prominently and so a good deal of subjectivity of approach is inevitable. The valuation placed upon features of the ecosystem is to a large extent directly related to the fulfilment of some human purpose, be it scientific, educational, aesthetic or economic. There are profound philosophical problems in defining the ultimate purpose of nature conservation, and it is sufficient to say here that generally accepted criteria, relating to the range of human concern, have been defined and used in the evaluation of site features and therefore of overall site quality.

A four-point grading of quality has been devised for areas sufficiently important to be notified on SSSIs. Sites in the top two classes are regarded as of national importance to nature conservation; they exemplify the key area concept, and are termed 'key sites'. Each is described in vol. 2 of this report. Grade 1 sites are those of the highest importance; the safeguarding of these is regarded as essential to the success of nature conservation in Britain. Grade 2 sites are of almost equal importance, but either duplicate the features of related grade 1 sites or are of slightly lesser quality, or both. The conservation of grade 2 sites is a matter of less extreme urgency, but nevertheless requires considerable thought and effort.

The selection of key sites has required a systematic and comprehensive survey of areas of natural and semi-natural ecosystems over as much of Britain as could be covered in the time available. In general, the datum line is 1967, although revision to take account of subsequent develop-

---

[1] For an account of the concept of the ecosystem, and other ecological terms, the reader is referred to Tansley, 1939.

ments has been made wherever possible. The *Review* thus provides an extensive body of scientific data about our national capital of habitat and wildlife, and an inventory of sites graded according to their nature conservation value. 'Nature conservation value' expresses the range of human interest in wildlife and its habitat, and physical features. Wildlife is defined here as the sum total of the animals and plants of Britain, excluding domesticated or captive animals and introduced plants grown for human purposes; it thus embraces not only the native flora and fauna, but also introduced plant species which are not deliberately managed as a crop.

Vol. 1 of this report contains a synopsis of the choice of key sites and the reasons for their selection. It has seemed essential to present this choice in relation to a statement of the whole range of nature conservation interest in Britain, in the form of a background account of the range of natural and semi-natural ecosystems, with their physical features, flora and fauna. This account gives a framework of reference for the sites chosen and therefore contains a justification for their conservation, when read in conjunction with the site descriptions and the criteria for their assessment and selection. Vol. 1 is therefore written for a mixed audience, including landowners, administrators, planners and developers; and some sections presume little or no technical knowledge, though the need for scientific adequacy necessitates use of a certain number of technical terms and concepts, and scientific names. The background information accordingly includes an exposition of certain ecological principles at a fairly basic level, but the first part is intended also to contain sufficient detail to be of use to nature conservationists and others with technical knowledge. The difficulties of writing for an audience consisting of both laymen and experts have proved considerable, and there is a danger that the result will please neither, though it is hoped that both will find something of value. Vol. 1 can, if necessary, stand on its own as an exposition of the *Nature Conservation Review*. For those requiring fuller and more technical information about the character and interest of specific sites, vol. 2 provides the detailed descriptions. The document as a whole is intended to serve as a compendium of information and reference work on nature conservation interest in Britain, in which the sites of greatest importance are presented in relation to the wider background of wildlife and habitat over the country as a whole.

The present review is thus a presentation of material relating to the intrinsic scientific or nature conservation interest of these priority sites (including existing National Nature Reserves), but does not consider the methods by which they should be safeguarded. There have, moreover, been developments in the philosophy and practice of nature conservation in the last 20 years, notably in a reinforcement of the view that safeguarding key areas by no means satisfies the total requirement, and that there is a need to conserve the much greater part of the national capital of wildlife and habitat which lies outside this relatively small sample. There is a feeling too that arable farmland, derelict land and, to some extent, built-up areas, should be considered as well as less artificial habitats. The further requirements for nature conservation generated by this wider outlook are not specifically considered in the present review, but the background account of the whole field of interest gives some indication of what is involved, and some attempt is made to assess the contribution which the safeguarding of grade 1 and 2 sites would make to the conservation of Britain's flora and fauna.

This report is not intended to be a final, totally definitive statement on the subject, for field survey is still incomplete, and the methods of site assessment and selection are realistic rather than ideal. It is inevitable that, with further advances in basic knowledge and methods, and perhaps also through change of view and revision of needs, the present list of key sites will require amendment and/or addition. However, the list of sites now defined is presented as the best which can be achieved under the limitations of present circumstances, and as a recommended basis for early action in promoting conservation measures.

In the light of information received since preparation of the final draft, a few additions and a few regradings have been made to the list of key sites; details are given in the Appendix.

2 RATIONALE OF THE REVIEW, METHODS AND RESULTS

A. RATIONALE OF THE REVIEW

BASIC CONCEPTS

The key area concept in nature conservation has been admirably spelt out in Cmd 7122 (Ministry of Town and Country Planning, 1947) in a discussion of the main purposes of a series of National Nature Reserves (NNRs). The need to represent in such a series the countrywide diversity in nature conservation interest according to the range of human concern attaching to this is expressed as follows (*ibid.*, para. 50):

to preserve and maintain as part of the nation's natural heritage places which can be regarded as reservoirs for the main types of community and kinds of wild plants and animals represented in this country, both common and rare, typical and unusual, as well as places which contain physical features of special or outstanding interest. These places must be chosen so far as possible to enable comparisons to be made between primitive or relatively undisturbed communities and the modifications introduced by varying degrees of human interference; typical and atypical physical conditions; distinctive characteristics imposed upon communities and species by differences in geographical position, physiography, climate, geology and soil, both within the main physical regions and in the transitional zones between them; the behaviour of species or communities living within and at the margins of their geographical distribution or their ecological tolerance. The series as a whole should take fair account of the varied requirements and interests of the several different lines of scientific approach: the systematic study of particular groups of species; studies of communities or species in relation to their environment; of the rise and fall in population numbers; of breeding structures of populations and the way in which inherited variations are distributed; of geographical distribution; of plant and animal behaviour; of the climatic and microclimatic conditions which so largely govern the distribution of organisms; of soils; of the rocks and the fossils they hold; and of the physical forces which shape the surface of the land; as well as general evolutionary studies. Considered as a single system, the reserves should comprise as large a sample as possible of all the many different groups of living organisms, indigenous or established in this country as part of its natural flora and fauna; and within them the serious student, whatever his bent and whether he be professional or amateur, should be able to find a wealth of material and unfailing interest.

This lucid statement emphasised the range of scientific

value inherent in the features which were to be thus conserved and the exposition went on to elaborate the functions of the sites in providing for research, educational and 'amenity' use. It was stressed that such sites would usually need careful management if their scientific and nature conservation value was to be maintained, and that this in itself would often require research in depth. An extension of the 'open-air laboratory' notion was that some sites might have to be acquired specially as research areas, so that experiments of a kind destructive to other interests might be performed. Experimentation was envisaged as including the deliberate re-creation of new or lost habitats. The research was understood to serve the advancement of science, and the giving of advice on land management elsewhere (especially in National Parks). It should also serve as a means to an end in learning how to manage the sites themselves. The 'living-museum' concept was related more to the educational function and to provide 'for that considerable section of the public who without any scientific interests can derive great pleasure from the peaceful contemplation of nature'.

The above quotation makes it clear that the key areas were intended to cater for the wants of those with relatively simple interests in wildlife, as well as for the more esoteric needs of the scientist, and the aesthetic element is clearly stated. Within the range of broadly cultural functions, scientific purpose and maintenance of the 'natural heritage' were stressed above all. The conservation of key areas was thus held to be concerned especially with the advancement of knowledge and understanding, both in the individual and in society, and with human fulfilment in a non-material sense.

The present review accepts and endorses this rationale, but is concerned to examine in greater depth how it is translated in practice into criteria to guide the selection of the key sites.

It was emphasised further in Cmd 7122 that 'It has proved necessary under the conditions now obtaining in this country to concentrate in the first instance on *saving* places which are still known to possess high scientific value ...'. The experience of the last 25 years has reinforced this view. It is now accepted that human impact in Britain is so universal and pervasive that no area of land or water is safe from developments destructive or deleterious to their nature conservation interest, unless deliberate measures are taken to ensure that they remain unmodified. There is, in fact, an even stronger realisation now that, since many sites are both irreplaceable and severely at risk, serious and permanent loss is imminent if adequate safeguards are not taken or maintained.

Present concern in the *Review* has thus been to identify these irreplaceable sites before it is too late. The overall intention has been to delineate the most valuable and vulnerable part of the national capital of wildlife and habitat, plus an additional element which is adequately representative of other major semi-natural ecosystems. The process of selection presupposes that nature conservation interest is spread throughout Britain, but unevenly and discontinuously in a geographical sense, and variably also in terms of intrinsic quality. Graham (1944) first proposed a classification of land into categories of different quality according to its potential for agriculture, and the zoning of land according to its capability for one purpose or another is now widely accepted in planning. The *Nature Conservation Review* represents an attempt to identify the highest quality land of Britain in terms of nature conservation interest, but also indicates how the concept of differential quality could be made the basis for a more comprehensive zoning of this interest.

The term 'highest quality' obviously implies that the 'best' examples of the range of ecosystems should, by preference, be chosen for the national series of key sites. Yet the definition of 'best' in terms of specific, measurable qualities is an extremely difficult task, and often involves many-sided value judgements in which standards are essentially relative and not absolute. Moreover, the concepts of 'best' or 'most important' may involve a considerable degree of unusualness, since they connote the acme of quality. There is also some need to represent the typical or ordinary rather than the exceptional. The series of key sites will thus be a mixture of the scarce and unusual and the typical or common examples of ecosystems; moreover, there may be intermediate cases or both types may be represented within the same site.

While criteria for selection of sites must depend to a large extent on evaluation of their intrinsic qualities in relation to the range of human interest, there is an over-riding need to take account of the vulnerability of the features themselves. It is therefore necessary to consider where human impact bears most heavily on wildlife and its habitat; importance attaches especially to species, communities and habitats which have been most heavily reduced by past human influence, to those most likely to disappear if no remedial action is taken, and to those which are least readily replaced once they have been lost or badly damaged. The exceptional sites will thus tend to predominate in the selection, for these are the places whose destruction would cause the greatest loss to nature conservation. The typical sites are by definition usually more widespread than the exceptional, and there is more chance that examples will escape serious modification, or that they can be re-created elsewhere as opportunity allows. Even so, it is important that the national series of key sites contains major reference points within the field of ecological variation, as 'type' examples of significant ecosystems, communities and species aggregations. Where sites chosen for their special attributes do not also contain more ordinary and typical features, it is necessary to choose additional sites, to ensure that the whole series is adequately representative. The notion of a 'representative series' should not, however, be taken too far, for it could lead to the selection of sites which are unimportant in a national context.

The criteria for assessment of quality of an ecosystem must express the range of human concern contained within the whole concept of nature conservation. In other words, values have to be attached to ecosystem features according to their significance to definable human interests. Each criterion is thus a real attribute transformed by a value judgement about function into an abstract quality of dual character. As an example, *diversity* can be measured as an attribute, and as such has neutral value; but because high diversity usually has more interest to biologists than low diversity, the actual value measured can be used as an index of quality in this respect. But nature conservation is a complex subject, expressing a range of interests (see p. 3) each with its own scale of values, e.g. what is important to a geneticist may not be important to a field naturalist, and vice versa.

The requirements for the 'open-air laboratory' will often be different from those for the 'living museum'. Some criteria involve more subjective concepts of quality than others, and their attributes are less precisely quantifiable. An additional problem in the definition of criteria is that the human interests which they reflect not only cover a wide range of viewpoint, but also may undergo change in the future. Preferably they should therefore acknowledge potential as well as present values. These criteria, and the way in which they are applied, are discussed later.

The choice of key sites involves the comparative assessment of a large number of different examples of ecosystems, to identify those of high enough quality to be accepted for the national series. The process depends on an awareness of the range of variation in British ecosystems, within which certain 'types' can be identified. This in turn requires that the extensive knowledge of real plant and animal communities in the field be translated into some kind of abstract framework through a classification of data. Only through adequate field survey is it possible to be confident that this ecological framework of reference is reasonably complete, and that all the important sites are considered in making the selection of 'type' examples of natural and semi-natural ecosystems.

Sites of similar character, corresponding to a certain type or combination of types, are compared with each other and judged in terms of accepted criteria, so that relative status can be assigned to each. There is a steady process of sifting, to identify the most promising or obviously outstanding sites so that, finally, it is possible to decide that one site in particular is preferred above all others. Often, however, the type which is being considered for representation is so broad and variable that it can only be adequately represented by a series of specific sites. For instance, oakwood is an important semi-natural vegetation type in Britain, but woods with the common feature of oak dominance differ enormously in other ecological features according to differences in climate (on both a local and regional scale), topography, soil and management. It is therefore necessary to choose a series of different oakwood sites which adequately represent this range of variation.

A still more difficult aspect of the selection process concerns the extent and number of the preferred sites. In Cmd 7122 the highest importance was attached to safeguarding examples of major ecosystems as scientific study areas; it was felt that this selection, forming a NNR series, should include important 'museum-piece' examples of types not easily re-created or restored, but that the areas concerned should not be too large, nor the number of sites greater than a judiciously chosen minimum. It was, however, envisaged that important larger areas, e.g. of upland ecosystems, would be adequately safeguarded by other proposed measures which were not, in fact, later adopted. The failure to include in subsequent legislation the National Park Reserves, Scientific Areas and Conservation Areas proposed in Cmd 7122 at once made the original list of proposed NNRs inadequate.

Subsequent developments have involved a growing realisation that, on the one hand, the national strategy for nature conservation must consist of much more than the safeguarding of a hard core of key sites and, on the other, that wildlife and its habitats in Britain are under ever-growing pressure of an order greater than that envisaged a quarter of a century ago. It is therefore natural and desirable that the purpose of safeguarding key sites should have advanced beyond the idea of a minimum sample of relatively small areas to the notion that the series should be as large as can be allowed by available resources. Cmd 7122, para. 50, itself contains the statement that 'Considered as a single system, the reserves should comprise as large a sample as possible of all the many different groups of living organisms, indigenous or established in this country as part of its natural flora and fauna.' It is probable that 'reserves' here was intended to mean all categories of area safeguarded for their nature conservation interest, but the general view is clear and supports that just expressed.

The problems and decisions relating to 'as large a sample as possible' of key sites will be discussed in the following amplification of the selection process.

THE PROCESSES OF KEY SITE ASSESSMENT AND SELECTION

The objective of the *Review* has been to select according to established criteria of nature conservation value a series of sites which gives acceptable representation of all the more important features within the range of variation in natural and semi-natural ecosystems in Britain. The process of working towards this goal involves three distinct stages, though the second two are so interwoven that they tend to be thought of as one. These stages are as follows:

(i) Recording the intrinsic site features

This is the straightforward though usually laborious identification and recording of the primary scientific data for the site, to describe its range of ecosystem variation in terms of environmental and biological characteristics, which can be used to judge (ii).

(ii) Assessing comparative site quality

On the basis of the scientific record obtained in (i), the quality of each site is compared with that of other sites of similar type, so that there is a continual process of selection to identify the 'best' site within a related group.

(iii) Choosing the national series of key sites

This involves decision on which, how many and what extent of important sites should constitute the national series, and is the most difficult part of the whole process to rationalise satisfactorily, since it is essentially subjective, even when based on a consensus view.

These three phases will now be considered in detail.

Recording the intrinsic site features

For a review of this kind to be possible, there is a need for adequate knowledge of the range of natural and semi-natural ecosystems in Britain, at least qualitatively, and preferably quantitatively, in terms of habitat and associated organisms. The analytical description and hierarchical classification of the whole range of ecosystems represents a taxonomic framework which gives a basis for identifying and recording the variety of features at any site, and enables one to compare different sites, discern geographical trends and differences, and select sites according to properly defined criteria. Ideally, one would wish to consider in this way all the components of an ecosystem, including the inorganic factors, human influence, plants and animals. In practice, such are the imperfections of our knowledge and capacity for descriptive analysis that we have at present to limit our attention largely to the vegetational component of the ecosystem. This is, by general consent, the most useful parameter by which to characterise the ecosystem, for it is an integrated expression of a complex of interacting environmental influences, and at the same time is the major determinant of the animal component.

A hierarchical classification of vegetation which uses environmental and life-form criteria to separate the classes of higher rank is more useful for present purposes than one which relies on purely floristic (i.e. phytosociological) criteria. Accordingly, a primary separation has been made into the seven main ecosystem groups of Coastlands; Woodlands; Lowland Grasslands, Heaths and Scrub; Open Waters; Peatlands; Upland Grasslands and Heaths; and Artificial Ecosystems. These are regarded as formations (= major habitat grouping or ecosystem type).

These are intergrading or even overlapping classes, with arbitrary and artificial boundaries drawn between them, and two or more of them may be represented within the same site. Peatlands, for instance, are well represented within upland grassland and heath sites. Nevertheless, this has proved to be a convenient and practical subdivision into classes of first rank. Separation into classes of second and third rank has been according to life form and structure of the vegetation, physiography, or edaphic criteria, as seemed most convenient. The ideal would be to produce final classes of lowest rank determined essentially by floristic criteria (vegetation or community types, noda, associations), but only for upland grasslands and heaths are phytosociological data sufficient to allow this degree of definition. The whole task has, in fact, been greatly handicapped by the lack of a standard countrywide description and classification of British vegetation types. Dominant, constant and characteristic plant species have been used to define the upland vegetation types. Even at this finer level of analysis, there are few if any real discontinuities in vegetational variation, and the limits between related vegetation types are mostly arbitrarily drawn. For the formations other than the upland grasslands and heaths, the description of vegetation has been more flexible, according to present availability of knowledge.

The units of vegetational classification of any rank may be used as the basis for ecosystem recording on any site, but the lower the rank of unit employed, the more detailed and accurate does the record become. In this vegetational taxonomy, the units of 'nodum' (community type) rank, even if only provisional, may be regarded as equivalent to species in classical taxonomy, i.e. they represent a concept of parallel utility. The diagnosis of vegetation types thus gives a means of identifying plant communities encountered subsequently in the field, and of recording these simply, thereby providing a rapid but detailed description of the range of variation. It is, however, essential to characterise ecosystems in terms of as many features as possible, and supplementary information has been added, as available. Inventories of plant species have been compiled for as many sites as possible; vascular plants and bryophytes have been recorded most fully, lichens less so, whilst fungi and algae have received uneven and inadequate study, and have often been omitted. Species which are rare, local or decreasing are indicated in the lists, as are members of important phytogeographical elements.

The vegetation of open waters poses considerable problems of description, especially in terms of plant communities. Not only are there practical difficulties in examining and recording submerged vegetation, but the communities of aquatic plants are often open, heterogeneous and vertically stratified. Moreover, the algae, especially planktonic forms, are such an important component of the aquatic ecosystem that they must be considered as well, and the composition of the invertebrate fauna has also been used as an important criterion in the description and assessment of open water sites.

Apart from the open waters, it has not usually been possible to record animal communities as a parallel to vegetation types, and zoological records have consisted mainly of species inventories, with some indications of population size for certain vertebrates. Birds, mammals, reptiles and amphibia and freshwater fish have been fairly well recorded for most of the important sites. Recording of terrestrial and some aquatic invertebrates is still in a highly fragmentary and unsatisfactory state. Macrolepidoptera and Odonata are the best known taxonomic groups, but even here records are inadequate for many sites. Species lists for many groups of freshwater invertebrates, together with a measure of abundance, are available for most of the key open water sites. Specialist surveys of other invertebrate groups such as Curculionoidea (Coleoptera) and Arachnida, have given detailed knowledge for a limited number of sites, but patchy information of this kind is of mixed value, for it may lead to the overlooking or under-rating of unsurveyed but important sites. As with plants, efforts have been made to indicate occurrences of animal species which are rare, local, declining or of geographical importance. Knowledge of habitat and vegetation often makes it possible to predict the presence of characteristic animals with fair accuracy, and the various sections on fauna in vol. 1 follow an ecologically based treatment which indicates these relationships.

Climatic data of particular ecological relevance have been noted, especially rainfall, temperature and snow cover. The main geological and geomorphological features of sites have been recorded, with emphasis on lithology and especially the available lime content of the rock. Data on soil types and their chemical characteristics are available for some sites, but pedological information is rather uneven. Analyses of dissolved and particulate minerals are available for all open water sites. Biotic influences, especially those involving man, have been assessed and described whenever possible. Not only are past and present land use important because of their effects on the stability and present composition of the ecosystem, but some forms of land-use are also of intrinsic interest (e.g. coppice or water meadows). Even completely artificial sites with strong biological interest have been included in the survey. Detailed knowledge of the history of a site enhances its value, especially for teaching and research, so that relevant historical records have been included with site data whenever possible. The data for each defined area were entered on site record cards or check sheets and species record cards, boundaries selected and marked on a map, and an integrated statement prepared summarising the important environmental and biological features of the site.

The term 'site' has been used, for convenience, to refer to any surveyed area of land, large or small, for which prescribed boundaries can be drawn on a map to define a single geographical unit. There is a certain implication that these boundaries are clearly recognisable and self-defined on the ground, but this is often far from the case, especially in large continuous tracts of upland, where the limits to a site usually have to be arbitrarily defined. The problem is discussed in greater detail on pp. 16–17.

Assessing comparative site quality

CRITERIA FOR SITE ASSESSMENT AND SELECTION

A number of different criteria have, by general agreement and established practice, become accepted as a means of judging the nature conservation value of a defined area of land (= site); the following have been used in the *Review*.

Size (extent)

In the lowlands of Britain where semi-natural habitats tend to be highly fragmented, the importance of a site usually increases with size of area, and the concept of the 'viable unit' embodies the view that there is a minimum acceptable size for areas which need to be safeguarded in order to maintain their conservation interest. With woodlands or lowland grasslands and heaths, many of the best sites are undesirably small in their total area. Larger sites are not always valued more highly than smaller ones if other qualities are not equal, and minimum or optimum size for a key site varies according to the type of formation. With upland grasslands and heaths, and coastlands, the problem is often the converse one of having to restrict the choice to an area of reasonable size, i.e. not too large. In practice, the extent of a key site is determined by a variety of factors such as diversity, particular interest, and 'natural' boundaries. Size can also be taken as a mark of quality in terms of area of an especially interesting habitat or vegetation type within any formation, or of numbers (i.e. population size) of species of plant or animal. With species populations, an aggregation factor is often involved, notably with colonial animals in which a large proportion of the total British population is located within a relatively small number of sites, i.e. high density may be an important feature. A high proportion of a national, or still more, a world population of a species is regarded as very important. In the case of a wood, size can also refer to the actual stature of the trees, tall well-grown specimens being preferable to the small or poorly grown.

Diversity

One of the most important site attributes is variety in numbers of both communities and species, which are usually closely related and in turn depend largely on diversity of habitat. It is especially desirable to represent ranges of variation shown by important ecological gradients, e.g. catenas, altitudinal zonation, fading influence of salt spray and blown sand with distance from the sea, stages in podsolisation of soils, and effects of aspect on biological features. Site diversity is especially related to differences in local climate and micro-climate, topography (affecting drainage, exposure–shelter, aspect), parent rocks and derived soils. Variations in land-use and management practice are often related to these primary factors and have further important effects. Diversity is also related to extent, for the number of species of both plant and animal shows a marked tendency to increase with size of area (the species/area effect), quite apart from the probability that habitat variation will also increase. Diversity is sometimes related to habitat instability and may then give management problems. Often, instability or immaturity of habitat involves seral change, and there is need to represent particularly striking examples of vegetational succession, though many of these inevitably require continual or repeated intervention and management in order to preserve the early seral stages. Sometimes, however, seral changes may have to be allowed to run their course, and it is then important to ensure that earlier stages in the succession

are represented elsewhere in the area, i.e. the range of variation must not become depleted overall. Conversely, diversity of an area can often be increased by appropriate management. Areas containing high quality examples of more than one major formation, e.g. woodland and peatland, have especially strong claims to key site status. Very many sites rated as important mainly for one ecosystem contain lower grade examples of another type which can be regarded as a 'bonus', giving enhanced value.

Richness of flora and fauna, i.e. number of species, is an important criterion, and is partly related to extent, but also depends greatly on environmental diversity. Species diversity on areas of similar size is generally a reflection of habitat diversity. It is, however, usual in Britain for an area of calcareous rocks and soil to support a much richer flora than an otherwise similar area of non-calcareous substrata. Thus, areas of limestone tend to be highly rated. Similarly, as the Bryophyta are as a whole a moisture-loving group of plants, they tend always to be better represented in the more humid west of Britain than in the drier east. Many more species of bird are likely to occur within a square kilometre of woodland than within a comparable area of upland. In other words, species richness has to be treated as a factor of relative and not absolute importance.

Naturalness

It has been customary to use the term natural for vegetation or habitat which appears to be unmodified by human influence. This is a rare condition in Britain, where so much of the land surface has been profoundly altered from its original state by man's activities. Tansley (1939) gave the name semi-natural to modified types of vegetation in which the dominant and constant plant species are accepted natives to Britain, and structure of the community conforms to the range of natural types. For instance, many grasslands are semi-natural, whereas a hop-field or Sitka spruce plantation is artificial. Roadside and railway verges have a semi-natural character in floristics, but are regarded as artificial because of their linearity and setting. The distinction between natural, semi-natural and artificial cannot be rigidly defined, and the separations made in this review are somewhat arbitrary. Nature conservation interest is affected by the actual degree of modification, in both structure and species composition. An abundance or predominance of obviously introduced species usually, in fact, reduces the value of an area, though in moderation, non-indigenous species may add to diversity and interest.

This is a criterion which rates differently according to the formation concerned. For instance, unmodified vegetation is probably most consistently found in upland grasslands and heaths and coastlands whereas the whole of the chalk grassland is in some degree anthropogenic, and it is doubtful if any truly natural woodland remains in this country. Some wetlands have been much disturbed through peat-cutting or other activity, but natural processes of succession over a long period have subsequently restored a nearly original character to the vegetation and habitat, e.g. the Norfolk Broads. In general, this is a difficult criterion to apply: for one thing it is often not easy to judge accurately the degree of modification (especially since the nature of the truly natural ecosystem is often largely a matter of conjecture) and, for another, the realistic view of conservation nowadays results in a high value being placed upon some entirely artificial habitats. The bulk of ecosystems considered in the *Review* is semi-natural, but insofar as they are identifiable at all, the types least modified by man tend to be rated highly. Naturalness is perhaps of more concern to botanists than zoologists. It is a condition which management sometimes seeks to restore, and is often closely linked to rarity and fragility, i.e. its importance is partly that of scarcity value and dwindling or threatened habitat.

Rarity

To many people, one of the most important purposes of nature conservation is to protect rare or local species and communities. Rarity on the national scale has been given particular weight in the setting up of non-statutory 'species reserves' by bodies such as the Royal Society for Protection of Birds and local Naturalists' Trusts. In the present review, more emphasis has been given to the inclusion of rare communities, habitats or groups of species, and individual rare species have tended to be regarded as a bonus on sites selected for other reasons. The aggregation of several or many rare species to form a group within a single site, as in a plant refugium, is regarded as an important feature and has influenced the choice of certain key sites. Other things being equal, however, the presence of even one rare species on a site gives it higher value than another comparable site with no rarities.

The rare species which have received particular attention in the present choice of key sites are vascular plants, bryophytes, lichens, birds, mammals, Lepidoptera and dragonflies. Lack of knowledge or interest has led to the relative neglect of other groups, though some consideration has been given to fish, weevils and spiders. A recent examination of the status of rare British vascular plants (defined as species known to occur now in not more than 15 10-km grid squares of the *Atlas of the British Flora*, 1962) has given a more objective means of assessing needs and achievements in conserving this group (see Chapter 11). Comparable data for other groups are mostly lacking at present, but distribution mapping now in progress should in time remedy the deficiency.

Some species tend to be rare because they have extremely specialised habitat requirements, others have become rare because they are the focus of some direct human pressure, including collecting, or suffer indirectly by man's destruction of their habitat. Rarity of species is often obviously related to rarity of habitat, which again links with *extent*, but many rare species are relict, i.e. they have a discontinuous distribution, with a great many absences from apparently suitable localities, resulting from historical processes which have contracted and fragmented their range. A few rare species are recent arrivals which have not had a chance to spread, and others still (especially birds) are 'fringe' species which could apparently spread, but are at the limits of their climatic environment. Rare species and communities are often thus of great ecological and biogeographical significance, and their conservation is considered to be important. It is essential to understand as far as possible what makes a species rare, since this can affect management needs.

Rarity of habitat and community is closely connected with fragility, though it sometimes depends on the chance occurrence of unusual environmental conditions, singly or in combination, e.g. serpentine is an uncommon rock-type generally, whilst limestone is comparatively rare at high elevations.

Fragility

This criterion is complex but essentially it reflects the degree of sensitivity of habitats, communities and species to environmental change, and so involves a combination of intrinsic and extrinsic factors. Some ecosystems, such as certain seral vegetation types and associated animals, are inevitably unstable and ephemeral, and may require continuous management to maintain them in a desired state. Vegetational climaxes tend to be more inherently stable, but the natural, climatic types are necessarily more fragile than the biotic types. Intrinsic sensitivity to change varies considerably according to the organisms involved, e.g. during climatic shift, vegetation has a certain inertia of response, whereas certain insects may react very rapidly. Different species within the same taxonomic group can also vary widely in their resilience to adverse conditions.

Certain physical conditions besides climate may give an extrinsic disposition towards fragility, e.g. gravitational instability or a delicate balance in water table, but on the whole it is imminence of human impact, representing 'threat', which forms the main second element in this criterion. Virtually all natural and semi-natural habitats are sensitive to human impact of one kind or another, but there are geographical differences in vulnerability. Fragility rating for a particular ecosystem or site may also increase as land-use pressures intensify and spread. For instance, the great blanket bog 'flows' of east Sutherland and Caithness are easily damaged, but remain relatively safe unless there is increased interest in exploiting these peatlands for fuel or forestry. Some sites have escaped destruction largely by chance, e.g. certain chalk grasslands which, though fairly stable under the traditional grazing management regime, are extremely vulnerable to agro-economic trends. The nature conservation value of many important sites is therefore largely dependent on freedom from radical change in the established land-use pattern.

Fragility is thus a dual concept, but in practice the different elements have usually to be taken together. Fragile sites are usually highly valued, in that they so often represent ecosystems which are highly fragmented, dwindling rapidly, difficult to recreate, or perhaps threatened with total disappearance. Other criteria such as rarity obviously tend to enter this evaluation of survival risks. There are, however, cases where fragility is such that viability is also extremely doubtful, even under favourable conditions of management.

Fragility also applies to species of plant and animal, and especially includes relict or fringe species which maintain a foothold under marginal or suboptimal conditions; it is thus again linked with the criterion of rarity. A good example of a fragile species is the reintroduced large copper butterfly at Woodwalton Fen, for this would clearly die out rapidly but for careful management. Many of the rare British breeding birds, such as red kite, avocet and marsh warbler, are essentially fragile species, in that a small increase in adverse environmental pressure could easily tip the scales against their chances of survival.

The most fragile ecosystems and species have high value, but their conservation may be difficult and often requires relatively large resources.

Typicalness

While key sites, especially the 'living museum' kind, are usually chosen as the best examples of particular ecosystems, their quality may be determined by features which are in some degree unusual. This is valid but it is also necessary to represent the typical and commonplace within a field of ecological variation, insofar as this contains habitats, communities and species which occur extensively or commonly. Sites sometimes have to be selected for their characteristic and common habitats, communities and species, and it is then necessary to overlook the absence of special or rare features. This criterion links particularly with research needs for experimental areas, in which homogeneity may be a desirable feature, for a sufficiently extensive stand of a particular vegetation type is sometimes required, e.g. for plot replication is randomised treatments. The ordinary as well as the unusual attributes sometimes both occur within the same site, and a great many sites rated highly on other criteria take adequate account of typical and commonplace features. By definition, unusual communities or ecosystems may have only a few available samples, whereas there may be a much wider choice of those which are typical or common, and the actual selection may have to be somewhat arbitrary, or influenced by non-scientific factors.

Recorded history

The extent to which a site has been used for scientific study and research is a factor of some importance. The existence of a scientific record of long-standing adds considerably to the value of a site, and can elevate its rating above that of a site comparable in intrinsic quality, but about which little or nothing is known. For instance, the importance of Wicken Fen, Cambridgeshire, is enhanced considerably by the large body of biological and ecological data collected over several decades, giving a picture of the processes which mould and change the nature of the ecosystem in time. The detailed stratigraphical and pollen analytical studies made at Cors Goch glan Teifi show a classical developmental sequence from lake to raised mire and give this site an importance which could not be accorded simply from an examination of its present surface features. In some cases, sites form the location of long-term studies and experiments

whose value would be seriously damaged or destroyed if these study areas were no longer available.

This criterion should not, however, be over-rated. It is less important than the intrinsic features of the sites themselves, for in time the differences in amount of information about sites will tend to disappear, though there may well remain differences in historical value which are directly related to intrinsic site features (e.g. in the completeness of a stratigraphic sequence). Recorded history has not therefore been used as a criterion on its own, though there are instances, e.g. Kerloch Moor, Kincardineshire, where it gives added value to a typical ecosystem, and may with passage of time advance the claims of a site to key status. Where the research has revealed classical features of the site, it points to an important intrinsic feature, but research which is classical in the sense of revealing or extending ecological principles can also give added value to an area.

Position in an ecological/geographical unit

In the event of two sites representing a certain formation being of equivalent intrinsic value, contiguity of one site with a highly rated example of another formation is regarded as conferring superior quality. Where practicable, and without lowering the standards of selection, it has been felt desirable to include within a single geographical area as many as possible of the important and characteristic formations, communities and species of a district. Clearly, there are few areas where anything approaching a comprehensive representation could be made, and these are mainly in northern and upland districts, where fragmentation of semi-natural habitats is least. Such areas as the New Forest, Hampshire; the Isle of Rhum, Inverness-shire; Durness, Sutherland; Foinaven and Meall Horn, Sutherland; Inverpolly and Knockan, Ross–Sutherland; and Cairngorms, Inverness-shire, Banffshire, Aberdeenshire, illustrate the point. This criterion is obviously related to those of size and diversity. There is also a practical convenience in having two different key sites within a single geographical area.

Potential value

Certain sites could, through appropriate management or even natural change, eventually develop a nature conservation interest substantially greater than that obtaining at present. Sometimes a site once known to be of exceptional quality has deteriorated seriously in recent years through adverse treatment. This is especially true of certain woodlands which were spoiled by war-time timber extraction, and of some mires which have dried out through burning and/or draining. In such cases, it is sometimes probable that in time, and with suitable management – which depends partly on availability of adequate resources – the former quality of the ecosystem can be restored. When other high-quality examples of the ecosystems concerned cannot be found to take the place of those which have deteriorated, there is good reason for choosing the latter as key sites in the hope that restoration can be achieved through appropriate management. The potentiality for regeneration of high quality mire ecosystems in peat workings is shown by the

Norfolk Broads and Moorthwaite Moss, Cumberland, and it is hoped that the interest of Shapwick Heath, Somerset, and Thorne Waste, Yorkshire, will recover in some degree.

Similarly, when a particular ecosystem has been lost altogether, or when no viable examples remain, it may be best to attempt to re-create an example *de novo*, starting either from some quite different kind of formation, or from one with a closer relationship to that desired. As an instance, it would be possible to produce a woodland of desired type from a grassland or an area of scrub. If, as has been suggested, projected estuarine barrage schemes make provision for the development of completely new freshwater and other wildlife areas, it may be that sites of high quality will come to exist in places where conservation interest is at present quite different or merely negligible. Artificial reservoirs and flooded gravel workings are numbered among the high-quality open water sites, and the importance of other artificial habitats is an indication of the possibilities for creating sites of nature conservation interest. In many instances it would be advantageous to link potential value with the previous criterion, and to choose land contiguous with or part of a key site selected for its existing values.

Intrinsic appeal

There is finally the awkward philosophical point that different kinds of organism do not rate equally in value because of bias in human interest, as regards numbers of people concerned. There is no disputing that, for instance, birds as a group attract a great deal more interest in the public generally than do spiders or beetles. Similarly, colourful wild flowers and rare orchids arouse more enthusiasm than toadstools or minute liverworts. While science may view all creatures as equal, therefore, pragmatism dictates that in nature conservation it is realistic to give more weight to some groups than others. This view is supported by the fact that knowledge of the distribution and numbers of the 'popular' groups is often much greater than for obscure groups. The *Review* has thus given a good deal of weight to ornithological interest (apart from pest species such as the woodpigeon) and many wetlands and coastal sites have been rated highly for their concentrations of wildfowl, waders and seabirds. Nevertheless, within the limitations of available knowledge, an attempt has been made to ensure that the less popular groups of organisms are adequately represented in the key site series.

APPLICATION OF CRITERIA

These criteria tend in some instances to merge or even overlap with each other, and they often run parallel and so are additive; but sometimes there is mutual incompatibility, e.g. rarity is seldom compatible with typicalness or diversity with homogeneity, and while naturalness is usually rated highly, the Norfolk Broads are artificial in origin yet must be regarded as one of the most important wetland areas in Britain. The application of these criteria in site assessment is a complex matter, difficult to rationalise or explain simply. In general, for the first five, the larger the score the higher the quality. Large size does not necessarily confer high

quality if there are no other desirable features, but does so in combination with other attributes such as marked diversity or presence of rare communities/species. Conversely, marked diversity may not rate highly if the area involved is too small. However, a rare and fragile type of ecosystem can be extremely important, even if it is small and fairly uniform. Site assessment often involves variable weighting of criteria, i.e. they are not all of equal importance, nor everywhere of the same relative importance. Some criteria cannot be used on their own, and while some are independent others are inter-dependent. Ideally, to qualify as a key site, an area should rate highly according to as many criteria as possible, but few sites rate highly in all qualities; while a majority of key sites have been selected for a high quality conferred by a combination of features, some have been chosen for a single important attribute. Much depends on the choice available within any major ecosystem or community type.

The best way of discussing these criteria and their application is to take a specific example of a site which has long been accepted as a classic area of wildlife and habitat in Britain, and to analyse why it is so highly valued.

The North Norfolk Coast is a maritime ecosystem complex containing extensive examples of sand dunes, salt and brackish marshes, shingle beaches and inter-tidal flats, largely unmodified by man. The physical and biological processes involved in shore accretion and erosion are especially well demonstrated, and classical studies have been made of the dynamics of coastal physiography and plant succession, and of the relationships between the different habitats and their vegetation. The vegetation is rich in species, and there are especially large populations and extensive communities of certain plants which are characteristic of salt marshes in this part of Britain: a number of rare species occur, including some at the limits of their British range. This coast is an important breeding ground for certain coastal and brackish marsh birds which include big populations and interesting communities of rare species. In the autumn and winter, it is a major haunt of passage and wintering birds, especially waders and wildfowl. The invertebrate fauna is large and includes many rare species. Some of these features, such as the colonially breeding terns and the sheets of sea-lavender in flower are sufficiently spectacular to excite the lay public and the whole area serves an important educational function over a wide range and level of interest.

The aspects of importance are clearly inter-related, but there is an over-riding aspect, the total diversity of the area, which gives it an especially high value. This includes not only the diversity in range of major coastal features but also in species-richness of certain communities. The extent of the area and particular communities, the size of the populations of certain species, and the presence of many rare species are notable features. The natural state of the whole ecosystem is unusual and the range of variation also encompasses that characteristic of such coastal formations in this part of Britain, so that it may also be regarded as representing typical features. The research and educational value of the area is very high and the degree of documentation of many features of scientific interest over a long period gives an additional measure of importance. The physiographic interest of this coast is a further factor, although this aspect of nature conservation is not specifically considered in the present review.

These attributes of the North Norfolk Coast thus provide standards against which examples of similar ecosystems can be judged, and the *kinds* of values involved can be applied more widely to the assessment of other types of ecosystem. To continue the discussion in more general terms, similar sites are compared to see which scores most highly for particular features or combinations of features, the aim being to produce a final evaluation of the overall quality of each in relation to standards for its type, i.e. position in the abstract ecological classification. The judgements involved are comparative and therefore relative, and they concern what is available, which often falls well short of the ideal. The varying use and emphasis of different criteria according to formation are discussed under the accounts of the formations themselves.

The comparative assessment of sites could in theory be made more objective by applying a scoring system to the above criteria, so that the total score for a site would be a measure of its overall quality. While it was found possible to apply this procedure locally, or within a limited range of habitat (it was done in Coastlands) no attempt was made to develop a comprehensive scoring system to cover the whole range of British ecosystems. Not only are there complexities difficult to deal with, such as the frequent lack of independence of criteria, and the varying absolute and relative values of different criteria according to requirements, ecosystem group and locality, but basic information for different formations and sites is so variable at present that a scoring system could not be evenly applied throughout the country. Nor is there a satisfactory logical basis for allocating actual score values to different site features. While these problems may eventually be solved by careful study of conceptual difficulties and intensive collection of field data, at the moment any such attempt to quantify the process of selection for *all* key sites could only give a spurious objectivity. It is nevertheless sensible to follow a limited quantitative approach when this is feasible and valid as for example, by counting the number of communities or species in assessing such features as diversity. Recent studies, such as that by Helliwell (1973) indicate the kind of advances in approach which may lead to a more consistent and satisfactory methodology of evaluation of nature conservation interest.

Choosing the national series of key sites

So far, discussion has been limited to the processes whereby the respective merits of two or more sites of basically similar character are compared and the sites then arranged in order of relative importance. There remains the more difficult task of choosing a series of the most highly valued sites which will form an acceptable sample of the national range of variation in natural and semi-natural ecosystems. Part of the

problem may be approached reasonably objectively; given time and resources, the field of variation can be charted and samples (reference points) identified and described. The more intractable difficulty lies in the interpretation of the word 'acceptable' – for this interpretation must necessarily be subjective, since the ultimate purpose to be served is so broad and varied that no simple definition is possible, and it cannot be related to any absolute standards.

There is some analogy with the methods of taxonomy, for the taxonomic categories that are used to describe the field of ecosystem variation are also the abstract units on which the selection of a series of key sites is based. For instance, having grouped peatlands into six major classes of mire, it is a natural consequence to select key sites which will represent each class. And since each major class of mire is divided into a range of subclasses according to variations in climate, topography, hydrology and floristics, it follows that each of these subclasses should be represented in the series of key sites. The difficulty lies not in choosing between mire sites which are obviously different in major features but in deciding *how many* to choose from a number of mire sites which belong to the same major class but differ from each other in more minor features. This is reminiscent of the basic taxonomic problem of deciding on the spacing of the reference points within a field of continuous variation – should they be closer together or farther apart? At one extreme one could select virtually all sites with semi-natural or natural ecosystems, so that no possible minor variant could be omitted, while at the other extreme one could select so few sites that a great deal of the field of ecological variation was left out of the series. Clearly, something approaching the 'happy mean' is needed – but how does one strike the best point of balance?

The series of key sites to be presented represents the point of balance in the collective judgement of a number of people, just as an accepted taxonomic system tends to lie somewhere between the views of the 'splitters' and the 'lumpers'. A second major conceptual difficulty arising here is that there is not one basis but many for a taxonomy of ecosystems. There is general agreement that vegetation provides the best basis for such a system, but even vegetation may be looked at in different ways. For instance, woodland may be classified according to species-dominance within the tree layer, floristics of the subordinate layers, physical habitat factors (climate, topography, soil) or management/structural type. Often, these different parameters can be applied at different hierarchical levels within a single classification, and when this is both possible and convenient it seems a sensible practice to follow. These are different aspects of ecological diversity and, while they often show a degree of parallelism, each has claims to be considered separately when the choice of representative sites for the particular range of ecosystem variation is made. One is thus faced with further questions, namely, which and how many specific bases of ecosystem taxonomy shall be considered in selecting a series of key sites, and in what order of priority?

The actual selection of a national series of key sites

covering all natural and semi-natural ecosystems is in abstract a complex procedure, entailing in the choice of each site the appraisal of a body of recorded information and the application of various criteria for assessment in such a way that they become integrated as judgement is made. The description of the thought processes involved is a lengthy business, entailing various rationalisations and discussion of abstract concepts. Yet in reality, the procedure of site assessment and selection includes a number of steps which are taken almost automatically, in the same way that a person crossing a busy street makes numerous observations and calculations about his own motion and that of vehicles, without ever thinking consciously about the matter. Moreover, in analysing retrospectively the processes involved it is easy to claim a degree of logic and a sequential order of events which were not followed in practice. For instance, the comparative assessment of sites and determination of acceptable representation are not really separated in the manner indicated in this written presentation, but proceed together *pari-passu* as survey progresses and knowledge accumulates. And to a considerable degree, the criteria discussed under comparative assessment are also involved in the election of a site to the national series; when the application of these criteria indicates that a site is quite exceptional or unique, its selection automatically follows.

The position at the beginning of the present review was somewhat as follows. Over 100 NNRs representing the six major formations and various subdivisions of these were already declared. It is impressive that the original assessment of the great majority of sites proposed as NNRs in Cmd 7122 remains unchanged in the present review. It is, indeed, remarkable how consistently unanimous a view is to be found amongst experienced field ecologists and naturalists about the outstanding merits of many key sites. To the uninitiated it may seem that the manner of judgement is an art rather than a science but, whatever the case, the standards show a considerable degree of uniformity. The need for the *Review* grew not from any feeling that the established standards required re-judging, but from an increasing awareness that if these standards were to be applied consistently through the full range of ecosystems in Britain, a considerable number of other sites had equally strong claims for addition to the list of key areas. In other words, as knowledge of the range of ecosystems in this country increased, it became clear that there were many gaps in representation of important types. In some instances it was obvious that sites which had newly come to light were decidedly more valuable than certain others well known and already safeguarded.

People do not, in fact, usually go around thinking that this or that particular abstract type of ecosystem requires representation, but with the knowledge that, for example, *A*, *B* and *C* are outstandingly good upland sites of different kinds, but that there are other sites of unknown value which need examination. If upland site *D* is then found and looks good, the first question to be answered is whether it is broadly similar to or different from *A*, *B* or *C*. If *D* is similar to one of the others, a decision is needed as to whe-

ther it is inferior or superior, and this depends on evaluation of detailed differences. If *D* is markedly inferior it is dropped from further consideration as a key site, but if it is only just inferior, it may be included as an alternative to the other. Should *D* be superior to any other similar key site, it will automatically be included in the national series, and its rival will either be dropped or retained as an alternative. On the other hand, if *D* is quite different in main features from any other key site, one then has to judge whether it is sufficiently important in its new features to justify representation in the national series as a further type of upland. There is a continual and cumulative process of comparison and selection or rejection based on serial observations of a number of sites. It follows that those sites which one encounters first will tend to become standards, and this can be a source of bias. This kind of bias tends to diminish as experience of number and variety of sites grows.

The process is complex in practice and depends at the outset on a sufficiently wide knowledge of the detailed character and range of national variation in natural and semi-natural ecosystems – in short, an adequate field experience of vegetation and wild animals. This basic expertise naturally increases as survey progresses. The more there is background knowledge and experience on which to base the judgements involved in site selection, the more reliable and useful the process is likely to be. The pitfalls are sometimes unexpected. For instance, it might be thought that there are pedological and ecological grounds for representing all the major geological formations in the series of upland key sites. Only field experience can teach that the difference between, say, the Ordovician and Silurian formations *per se* is usually ecologically meaningless, and that it is far more important to differentiate between the calcareous and non-calcareous rocks within each of these formations.

While particular needs will be discussed under each major formation, the following general requirements for achieving the declared objective of the *Review* may be stated:

Selection of a series of sites adequately representing the national range of variation in the following ecological features:

Climatic

Biological features dependent on local and regional gradients of climate. Local gradients of climate are related especially to such topographical factors as altitude, aspect and proximity to water bodies; whereas regional gradients are concerned with larger scale tendencies such as the increase in oceanicity with distance west and decrease in mean temperature with distance north.

Physiographic

Biological features associated with major variations in land forms. Most diversity within this class may also be analysed in terms of climatic or edaphic variation, but it is often useful to consider physiography as an ecological factor in its own right.

Edaphic

Biological features associated with major variations in physical and chemical properties of soils and their parent materials, i.e. geological formations. Physical soil factors include especially wetness (determined by soil porosity, angle of slope, configuration of ground, water supply and evapotranspiration), while chemical factors include especially acidity–alkalinity (pH) and availability of important nutrients, notably calcium, potassium, nitrogen and phosphorus. There is a need to represent the complete range of soil types (identified in terms of physical/chemical profile characteristics) associated with the whole range of natural and semi-natural plant communities. Soil conservation is usually understood as concerned with maintenance of fertility and carrying capacity, and, while this may be an important requirement on some, it is not the case for every key site, and sometimes there is a need to prevent nutrient levels from increasing. The motives for soil management are different in nature conservation from those in agriculture.

Anthropogenic

Biological features associated with major variations in system of land management by man. These mostly represent varying degrees of modification of natural ecosystems by human influence, including clearing of woodland and scrub, burning, grazing and ploughing; they also include managed types of semi-natural ecosystems within woodland, grassland, heathland, upland, wetland and some coastland.

Some artificial ecosystems may have considerable conservation value, but it is usually felt that on their own these have no strong claims to representation in the national series of key areas, as in the case of plantations of alien conifers such as Sitka spruce. Sometimes an artificial habitat eventually develops a semi-natural character and may then have stronger claims to be considered in the selection of key sites, e.g. reservoirs, disused gravel pits and quarries. Other essentially artificial habitats which develop a semi-natural character may, from their very nature, be unsuitable for consideration as conservation sites on the national scale, e.g. hedges, roadside verges and railway embankments, yet they may have strong claims at the local level.

The biological features alluded to above include both communities and species of plants and animals. Ideally, at least one good example of every described plant community in Britain, and one viable population of every wild plant and animal species should be represented within at least one grade 1 or 2 site. It must at once be stated that achievement falls well short of this ideal. For one thing, vegetational taxonomy based on phytosociology is incomplete and many plant communities are not yet identified, while the description of animal communities has hardly begun and animal species are so numerous that the problem of their representation cannot possibly be tackled satisfactorily at the species level. Moreover, neither communities nor species are all of equal importance, but their varying value (and hence claims for representation) cannot yet be properly quantified.

At the risk of being repetitive, it is necessary to stress again that adequate representation is not synonymous with uniform or total representation of the field of variation. It is not the intention of the *Review* to advocate the safeguarding of every minor variant of habitat or community, especially when these are isolated from more important areas. The main need is to ensure that all major types are represented, and that all the really important sites are included. Sometimes, the philosophy of 'as large a sample as possible' has been applied to certain fragile and/or rare habitats, communities and species, especially when their international importance is high. This is especially the case with the major concentrations of wintering wildfowl and waders, and colonial breeding coastal birds, for which Britain has a strong international responsibility in conservation; virtually all the areas with numbers of these birds above certain levels have been included as key sites, though not all are grade 1. Every effort has been made to avoid extravagance in the compilation of the national series, and the final list of grade 1 and 2 sites is regarded as a reasonable minimum.

The choice of ordinary sites has been judiciously limited, and whilst the *Review* has taken some account of research needs, it has done so to a varying degree. Many of the key sites chosen have a known research value, which has been regarded as a significant attribute (see Recorded history, p. 9). Virtually all key sites have a potential research value, and the series as a whole would give a great deal of scope for research, but there has been no attempt to choose sites for a specialist research interest involving *experimentation*. Some sites with ordinary ecosystems which have been the location of long-term and intensive research projects may assume an increasing historical importance, e.g. Meathop Wood, Lancashire, for International Biological Programme studies and Kerloch Moor, Kincardineshire, for red grouse research. However, experimental research often places a premium on such attributes as uniformity (for work involving sampling and replication) and accessibility, and may involve considerable disturbance to the ecosystem, such as felling of trees or deliberate removal of species. Since these criteria and activities are usually difficult to reconcile with those discussed previously, it has been felt that the needs for research sites primarily of the experimental type should be dealt with as they arise, for they are often highly specific and relatively short term, as well as *ad hoc* and unpredictable. No attempt has therefore been made in the *Review* to cope with them, or to foresee all future research requirements relating to semi-natural and natural ecosystems.

Similar considerations apply to educational sites. For teaching purposes, convenience of access is often an important criterion, and these activities may create degrees of damage unacceptable within a classic 'living museum' site, e.g. through disturbance of rare and sensitive nesting birds or trampling of fragile plant communities. Many of these educational needs can be better met by sites of grade 3–4 or lesser importance, though features associated with diversity make many key sites especially valuable for teaching ecology, and sites showing various classical features are obviously the best demonstration areas for the phenomena in question. All sites are thus regarded as having potential educational value, but the degree to which this can be exploited will depend on various constraints, including both the requirements for management and the conditions of ownership.

Sites can be important in acting as reservoirs for species, including the genetic diversity of these. The general principle of selecting sites which include a range of phenotypic diversity in common and widespread organisms is likely to cater for many requirements for living material which may arise, ranging from the need for genotypically variable populations of species to parent stock for propagation work of various kinds. The degree to which key sites will serve as reservoirs for the natural dispersal of species must inevitably be variable and extremely difficult to assess, but the potential is probably considerable.

Conclusions

The comparative assessment of sites within a related group has been shown to present conceptual difficulties in regard to the relative weight that should be attached to the various intrinsic site features and to the different criteria which are applied in evaluating these features. The selection of key sites to give an adequate national series presents a still more difficult test of reason. There are problems in achieving consistency in choice of sites to form a series within a single formation type, e.g. woodlands, but it is still harder to prescribe the emphasis required in selecting one series of sites compared with another, e.g. a woodland series as compared with a coastal series. Similarly, how does one decide what weight to place on the representation of botanical and zoological features in relation to each other? What proportion of sites chosen should be of the classical and rare or typical and common types? How much prominence should be given to representation of rare species or groups of species? Should the disparity in total area between major formations influence the numbers of key sites chosen to represent these? For example, the combined area of upland key sites is far greater than the total area of chalk grassland remaining in Britain; should one therefore select a larger number of chalk sites to compensate for the larger area of upland sites?

There arise many questions which cannot be answered with any precision or according to clear-cut rules. The problems involved are a matter for careful thought and considered judgement, having regard to the need for a fair balance between the claims of the numerous and sometimes conflicting requirements involved in the assessment and selection of sites. It is possible to find a consensus of opinion on these matters amongst informed people working in this field who between them bring to bear an enormous body of knowledge, experience and wisdom. This consensus of view has repeatedly been sought, but the need for an adjudicator in cases of disagreement was realised and one of the functions of the Scientific Assessor (see p. 16) has been to

resolve such difficulties by a personal and often arbitrary decision.

In time, it may be possible to use more advanced techniques to achieve greater objectivity and consistency throughout in the selection of a national series of key sites. At present, the essential scientific data on which computer analysis is based are far too inadequate for such a treatment to give more than a biassed and provisional result, which could be misleading. Moreover, some aspects of the whole process of assessment and selection are not yet measurable. In the meantime, therefore, we have to rely on the computing and integrating abilities of the human mind, whatever the shortcomings in this procedure may be. Since the purpose of the *Review* is ultimately to satisfy a spectrum of human interests and activities, and is therefore heavily dependent on a series of value judgements, it is, in any case, difficult to see how this process can ever become completely objective. Some obvious forms of bias have to be eliminated as far as possible, as in the case of local or regional patriotisms, and personal preferences for certain criteria or features. However, it remains true that many of the judgements made are still subjective even when they are collective, and this is particularly so in deciding when the national series of sites is adequate. There is, in fact, no final way of answering this last kind of question, for it depends on values and factors which cannot be quantified on any satisfactory basis. In the last analysis, the inclusion or rejection of a site in the national series is based on informed opinion, and is thus open to argument and alteration. Values are also prone to change in time, and future generations may look at things rather differently. The present review is an attempt to prescribe the contemporaneous requirement for conservation of special sites according to current values, views, information and constraints. However elaborate the rationalisations which might be made to justify the way it has been done, it would be wrong to disclaim the element of intuition involved, though one hopes that this is built on awareness and experience.

The methods of evaluation and site selection used in the *Review* are therefore provisional and pragmatic, and dictated especially by incompleteness of survey information and the need to produce a working report within a reasonable time. Urgency and realism rather than theory and idealism have been the keynote of the operation. The issues involved are complex, and discussion is not made easier by the semantic confusion which has arisen over a long period through the habitually loose use of terms in ecology and nature conservation; these terms themselves now have such breadth of application that they are often virtually meaningless, and require further qualification. Within these limitations, an attempt has been made to explain the thinking behind the *Review*, and the guidelines which have been developed in relation to the situation in Britain. The results cannot be validated by reference to any absolute standards or economic base, but must be judged more broadly in terms of their eventual long-term contribution to nature conservation.

GRADING OF SITES

After examination and assessment, sites have been awarded a grading of quality on a four-point scale, as explained in the accompanying summary. Many important sites contain or adjoin areas where intrinsic nature conservation value is lower than the rest, rating around grade 4 or less. Often, these lower-grade areas contain different ecosystems from the more important parts of the site. Their inclusion with the site thus gives a bonus, enhancing the diversity and overall conservation value of the whole. This additional interest is mentioned and often described, but otherwise only key sites (grades 1 and 2) are the concern of the present report. Some sites contain high-quality examples of more than one major formation; in such cases the different main components are graded and described separately under different formations, though they lie together within a single continuous area. All sites have been assessed regardless of their existing conservation status, i.e. whether or not they are NNRs or any other category of reserve; this part of the *Review* has been concerned expressly with application of uniform standards in site assessment and selection according to intrinsic merits (except for the criterion of recorded history).

Grade 1

Sites of international or national (Great Britain) importance, equivalent to NNR in nature conservation value (many are already declared as NNRs); these are shown in capitals in the site indexes in vol. 1. Internationally important sites are denoted by asterisks. The safeguarding of all grade 1 sites is considered essential if there is to be an adequate basis for nature conservation in Britain, in terms of a balanced representation of ecosystems, and inclusion of the most important examples of wildlife or habitat.

Grade 2

Sites of equivalent or only slightly inferior merit to those in grade 1. These are thus also of prime importance but many duplicate the essential features of related grade 1 sites, which should have priority in conservation. Many can, however, be regarded as alternatives to grade 1 sites should it prove impossible to safeguard these.

Grade 1 and 2 sites are the actual places identified as exemplifying the abstract concept of key areas.

Grade 3

Sites of high regional importance, rated as high-quality Sites of Special Scientific Interest, but not of NNR standard. Regional, as distinct from national, criteria apply; some sites in this grade would receive a lower rating if located in a region with more extensive natural or semi-natural ecosystems, or a higher rating under converse circumstances.

Grade 4

Sites of lower regional importance, still rated as SSSI. Some such sites would not qualify if they were located in a region with more extensive representation of the particular ecosystem.

Grade 3 and 4 sites contribute to the total national requirement for key areas for conservation. Grade 1–4 sites cover a small part of Britain and the safeguarding of all grades is important for nature conservation. In the much larger proportion of ungraded land and water only a relatively small extent is virtually devoid of nature conservation interest, and consists mainly of urban and industrial areas covered by buildings or other man-made surfaces. The remaining very large total area of natural, semi-natural and artificial ecosystems has a variable nature conservation interest but is tremendously important in the aggregate. No attempt has been made in the *Review* to work out further gradations below grade 4, because an extension of this scale is inappropriate for land which cannot be scheduled within any one category. In the present system, the whole of a site is covered by its grading, though the subsidiary features of some composite sites have sometimes been given a lower grading under their own formation, in order to emphasise consistency of standards in assessment. For unscheduled land, a differential grading on a smaller scale is usually needed, but there are considerable difficulties in working out a system which could be applied throughout the country Such a system of evaluation is nevertheless urgently needed.

The assessment of *international* importance of sites involves application of the same criteria discussed previously, but the background scale becomes expanded to include the rest of Europe or even the whole world. In particular, high international importance is accorded to habitats, communities and species which are rare on the global scale. In Britain, sites thus designated are mostly high-quality examples of ecosystems and communities, and contain species with a very local occurrence in Europe, and some represent an endpoint to an ecological gradient of continental scale. The label 'international importance' given to some key sites is essentially subjective and arbitrary in most instances, and the category should be regarded as open to revision in the light of views from international bodies or experts with wide overseas experience. Only in the cases of wildfowl and waders have any quantitative yardsticks of assessment been followed, but in this review international status (grade 1*) is based on the total biological importance of a site.

It is obvious that within the list of grade 1 sites, there are varying shades of importance. The internationally important sites naturally take precedence on the whole, though any particular one is not necessarily more highly rated than any of those not given international status. The most outstandingly valuable sites are those which rate highly according to several major criteria, as in the case of the North Norfolk Coast discussed on pp. 10–11. In general, sites which are large, have high diversity (especially including more than one formation) and contain large populations of interesting species (especially rarities), rate very highly. However, the question of comparative importance between sites of disparate character, even within the same formation, leads to enormous conceptual and practical difficulties, and is not pursued further here.

B. METHODS AND RESULTS

OPERATIONAL PROCEDURE

An undertaking of this magnitude had to be tackled collectively, and involved the close co-operation of Conservation and Research staff of the Nature Conservancy, the former organised into regional groups (see map 2) with responsibility limited geographically but covering all habitats, and the latter organised into habitat survey teams with responsibility limited ecologically but covering the whole country. For each Region an inventory was compiled of all sites with noteworthy conservation value, arranged in grades of importance. This involved tapping as many sources of information as possible, both within and outside the Conservancy, literature search, and the organisation of field survey. In the South Region of England a complete survey of all semi-natural ecosystems has been made, the conservation value of each site mapped at the scale of 1:25000 and more detailed descriptions and records made for the most valuable sites. This ideal of complete coverage has not been achieved in other Regions, some of which have very large areas of semi-natural vegetation and thus present much more difficult problems for basic survey.

The habitat survey teams were provided by regional staff with the lists of the most important regional sites including existing NNRs, other categories of nature reserve, Sites of Special Scientific Interest, and unscheduled, recently discovered sites which appeared to be of a high quality. The habitat survey teams examined the most important sites, assessed their relative merits on the national scale and prepared recommendations for a final series of key sites for each habitat. In practice, regional staff and habitat teams worked in close conjunction, and were often involved in field survey at the same time. Habitat teams frequently undertook initial field survey to locate sites of importance in little known districts.

Such surveys were based on information about sites of known or suspected interest and on examination of 1 in. and 2½ in. Ordnance Survey maps. Knowledge of the range of variation of ecosystems within each region, in relation to that present on scheduled sites, focussed attention on filling obvious gaps in the representation of habitats. The surveys often involved prospecting, that is, examining areas of country more or less systematically to locate sites of interest and then making a more careful study of them. Student assistance was widely used in this field survey, especially in recording sites of known interest.

Both groups collected records of essential biological and environmental data for the more important sites, using prepared record cards and check sheets for convenience and uniformity in presenting data on location and size of site, physical features, climate, geology and soils, land-use, vegetation types, flora, fauna, and features of special ecological or biological interest. The Biological Records Centre at Monks Wood Experimental Station supplied record cards, or helped in their preparation, provided existing information on sites and ecosystem features, including species distribution, and processed and stored the recorded data.

Information on sites and ecosystem features has been gathered from a large number of professional and amateur biologists and other scientists outside the Conservancy. A considerable effort has been made to seek the advice and information of all individuals and bodies concerned with nature conservation, and in a position to help the *Review*. Non-statutory reserves established by other nature conservation bodies, notably the Royal Society for the Protection of Birds, Society for the Promotion of Nature Reserves, the National Trust and local Naturalists' Trusts, have been taken into account.

A Scientific Assessor, D. A. Ratcliffe, was appointed to the *Review*, to supervise and assist with various operations. His functions have been to assist in defining a descriptive framework of reference for ecosystem variation; to advise on field methodology and to formulate a rationale for the assessment of nature conservation value of sites and the needs for representation within a national key series; to help identify gaps in the existing NNR series; to approve key site selections, adjudicating when there was disagreement or doubt about the value of sites; and to compile and edit the final report.

DELINEATION OF SITE BOUNDARIES

Often, especially in lowland, agricultural country, the limits to a site are clearly defined on the map and on the ground by sharp, man-made boundaries which give a division between ground of high scientific interest and that with low or negligible scientific value. This is perhaps most obviously true of woodlands surrounded by farmland, but applies to most other formations. Such boundaries, defined by hedges, fences, walls or ditches are the obvious limits to draw for many key sites. Sometimes, however, there are no ready-made boundaries of this kind, especially in uplands, where areas of high scientific interest merge imperceptibly into less important ground.

In these cases, boundaries must usually be drawn arbitrarily though they may follow natural features such as streams, or artificial ones such as walls, fences, and roads. The principle followed here, though very largely subjective, is to define an area which is large enough to include the full range of diversity shown by the formation in the particular locality, but not so large as to give an unnecessarily extensive representation of certain features. This principle has some analogy with the concept of 'minimal area' in the plant community, i.e. the smallest area in which a particular community attains its full number of constant and characteristic species.

Sometimes it happens that an area is not of uniform quality, but the omission of the less valuable parts would create an unsatisfactory boundary, and perhaps cause later problems of management and protection. In such instances, areas which appear as natural units are often best treated as such in defining key sites. For some sites it is desirable to have a marginal or adjoining buffer zone to protect a vulnerable ecosystem, e.g. the hydrology of a valley or basin mire is particularly affected by changes in the catchment, and a measure of control over the latter is desirable. Similarly, it may not be possible to protect mobile creatures, notably birds, simply by safeguarding the place where they breed, e.g. species such as the red kite and osprey depend for their food supply on quite a large area beyond the confines of their nesting woods.

Where there is actual geographical continuity between high-quality examples of different formations, a boundary is drawn to include these within a single site. A single geographical unit containing examples of more than one major formation is known as a *composite site*. Where examples of the same formation lie close together but are separated by different land (especially farmland) of much lower quality, it is convenient to regard these as a single geographical and ecological unit, termed an *aggregate site*. Decisions on the particular clusters of sites which should be so treated are necessarily arbitrary. Conversely, within certain sites (mainly upland) which form single, continuous units, some parts are much less valuable than others, or certain vegetation types may be unnecessarily extensive. The implementation stage of the *Review* should consider how best to deal with these situations.

One of the disadvantages of carrying out the *Nature Conservation Review* according to subdivision into major formations is that geographical entities are often broken up and artificially compartmentalised, instead of being treated as integrated ecological units. As a result, the particular importance given by their diversity does not always emerge clearly from the separate assessments and descriptions. This applies especially to the New Forest, which is not simply an aggregation of important woodlands, acidic heaths and valley mires, but gains extra status as the largest continuous area of undeveloped land remaining in the whole of lowland England, i.e. its total value is greater than the sum of the individual parts. Some areas which once had this quality, e.g. Breckland and the Isle of Purbeck, have partly lost it through recent dissection and depletion by human activities, though their importance is still outstanding. In certain other districts, there are unusual concentrations of important sites, often covering a variety of formations, and these should be regarded as having special importance to nature conservation on this large scale.

PRESENTATION OF RESULTS

The *Nature Conservation Review* is presented in two parts. The first begins with a synoptic account of the field of ecological variation found in Britain, to provide a general background for the more detailed and separate treatment of the seven major formations of Coastlands; Woodlands; Lowland Grasslands, Heaths and Scrub; Open Waters; Peatlands; Upland Grasslands and Heaths; and Artificial Ecosystems. Treatment of each formation has varied according to the special features and problems associated with each. The formation sections begin with accounts of

habitat and vegetation, broadly following the lines of what seemed to be the most appropriate classification for each, with discussion of ecological and geographical relationships; where possible, vegetation types are named. The ensuing accounts of flora and fauna are again ecological and biogeographical, but deal also with abundance of species; much of this information is presented in tabular form. The purpose of this presentation of scientific information is to provide a framework of reference against which the selection of key sites can be viewed.

There is then a discussion of criteria for comparative site assessment which to some extent repeats what has already been said on this topic, but deals with the particular and varying emphasis required according to the particular formation. The special and general features of each formation needing representation in the national series are then enumerated.

Next in each formation section is a short review of the key sites chosen, following a somewhat elastic general plan and consisting of a résumé, in geographical order from south to north, of the sites and their position in the field of variation. There is often some discussion of the reasons for gradings given and indications of relative value of related sites, including alternative choices. Bonus habitats represented on sites chosen mainly to represent other formations are also mentioned. Each key site has a reference number, so that details of its scientific interest may be quickly obtained by consulting vol. 2. Under Upland Grasslands and Heaths and Coastlands, no subdivision of the formation has been made in the reviews of sites chosen, as the amount of diversity within many sites would lead to the same site being described under two or more categories. In the other formations, the geographical scan of key sites is made under several different subdivisions of the main type, e.g. in Peatlands, under the six different classes of mire. Cross-references are made when the same site is mentioned both under different major formations and under different subdivisions of these. Each formation section ends with an index of sites, giving grading, region, name of site, county and, in some cases, tabulated ecological information. The formation sections are followed by two separate sections which discuss the conservation of flora and fauna in relation to the series of sites.

In vol. 2 of the *Review*, key sites are listed in a standard geographical order under their formation (as in the Index of Sites for each formation in the first part) and for each there are details of relevant environmental factors, and notable ecological features, vegetation types, and selected species of plants and animal, including some rarities. The representation of features belonging to other formations is mentioned, and there are cross-references. Where relevant, relationships to other sites of similar character may be discussed. These accounts of key sites are, in fact, intended to provide a summary of their intrinsic scientific features and therefore of the case for their selection and grading.

Areas of sites are measured only approximately, unless they are already established as NNRs, in which case exact figures are given: the area quoted for coastal sites is confined to that part which lies above Mean Low Water. Grid references are of 4 or 6 figures, as is considered most appropriate to indicate the location of a site.

Scientific nomenclature is according to the standard systematic works listed in the Bibliography. English names for trees, shrubs, vertebrates, butterflies and moths have been generally used, though the scientific equivalents are all given somewhere in the text. Scientific names for other plants and animals are normally used throughout; for many lower organisms there is no accepted English name.

To save space, some common plant species which are the only representatives of their genus in Britain are referred to by their generic name only, after their full scientific name has been mentioned at least once. For the same reason the term Britain is used to denote Great Britain (England, Scotland and Wales).

All altitudes relate to height above Ordnance Datum (OD) unless otherwise stated. References to Nature Conservancy regions and to counties reflect the position in 1972. It is hoped that factual information is correct up to 1972, but environmental change is so rapid in many situations that some statements will inevitably become out of date in the period between final draft and publication.

3 THE ECOLOGICAL BACKGROUND TO SITE SELECTION

INTERNATIONAL SIGNIFICANCE

The special ecological features of Britain are related primarily to geographical and climatic position in the world. The British Isles as a whole lie in the temperate zone, but they differ from much of continental Europe in experiencing a strongly oceanic climate. A climatic regime of this kind is reflected in certain general ecological trends. The temperature range favours forest, composed largely of broad-leaved, relatively thermophilous trees, as the climax life-form over much of the country. The moisture balance, with a general excess of precipitation over evaporation, promotes leaching of nutrients from the soil, so that podsolisation is a widespread phenomenon, and there is a prevailing tendency towards development of acidic surface humus horizons. Where topography also contributes to waterlogging of the soil, peat mire inhibits tree growth and becomes the climax formation.

The high atmospheric humidity associated with an oceanic climate satisfies the needs of many hygrophilous plants; the fern, bryophyte and lichen floras are especially rich and the British Isles are the European headquarters of many Atlantic species, including some which have an interesting world disjunction. The equable temperatures of an oceanic climate also allow the survival locally of southern thermophilous plants, which reached their maximum extent at the Post-glacial Climatic Optimum, and also of a northern, montane element which cannot tolerate hot summers, and is a relict flora from the cold Late-glacial Period. Thus, although the insular position of the British Isles has resulted in a numerically poorer flora than many European countries, there is a unique blend of different phytogeographical elements which has given our flora an international distinction. Species of oceanic distribution which reach their greatest European abundance in Britain include a number of distinctive community dominants such as ash *Fraxinus excelsior*, heather *Calluna vulgaris*, bluebell *Endymion non-scriptus*, gorse *Ulex europaeus*, *U. gallii*, *U. minor* and heath rush *Juncus squarrosus*. Plant formations of strongly oceanic character, such as blanket mire and moss heath, are also more extensively developed in Britain and Ireland than in the rest of Europe, and some plant communities appear to be unique to this country, albeit usually recognisable as relatives of various continental types.

The Nature Conservancy's responsibilities did not extend to Ireland, but many of the important ecological features of Ireland are represented in the west of Britain, which has a strongly oceanic climate. There is a lesser representation in Britain of southern Atlantic and Lusitanian species, and no limestone karst country here is quite as fine and unspoiled as the Burren of County Clare, but on the whole the flora and fauna of Ireland are less rich than those of Britain.

Faunistically, the British Isles are internationally important for a number of insular races and subspecies which have diverged in isolation from the main European populations; as the breeding station for large populations of several globally rare and local birds, especially seabirds; and as the wintering haunts of a significant proportion of the total world or European population of certain wildfowl (Anatidae) and waders (shore-birds). The fauna also contains an interesting and diverse combination of different zoo-geographical elements. The mammal fauna of Britain is poor in species, partly as a result of extinctions caused by man, and the invertebrate fauna is much less rich than that of continental Europe.

Although relict elements of both flora and fauna are well represented, Britain has very few endemic species of either plant or animal. The British flora and fauna is, however, interesting for its ecological diversity, as the response to an unusual blend of climatic conditions within a small area. The particular combination of plant species in communities is, however, the most distinctive feature of this country, compared with the rest of Europe.

REGIONAL DIVERSITY

Within Britain there is a considerable range of geographical diversity in ecosystems, determined largely by major climatic gradients and geographical differences in physiography and geology, which in turn shape the pattern of variation in soil development, human activity and land use.

Climate

From south to north there is an overall latitudinal decrease in mean temperatures, and from east to west a general increase in oceanicity, i.e. decrease in temperature range, radiation and insolation, increase in precipitation, atmospheric humidity and wind speeds. These main gradients are complicated by the distribution of high land, which is concentrated in the north and west of Britain. High ground causes an increase in precipitation, atmospheric humidity, cloud cover and windiness, and decrease in mean temperature, giving local gradients which reinforce the major gradient of increasing oceanicity. The mountainous districts of western Britain, especially in Snowdonia, Lakeland, Galloway and the western Highlands and islands are thus extremely oceanic in terms of wetness, cloudiness and windiness. However, the latitudinal lapse in temperature results in a south to north gradient, from the warm oceanic climate of south-west England to the cool oceanic conditions of the north-west Highlands, Orkney and Shetland.

The warm and sunny south coast areas of England, especially in Dorset, Devon and Cornwall, give the nearest approach to a Mediterranean climate in Britain, whereas the most continental conditions are found in eastern districts which lie well away from the sea, from East Anglia to the north-east Highlands. While there is a general decrease in mean temperature with distance northwards, the coldest part of Britain in winter is not in the extreme north of Scotland, but in the central and eastern Highlands, which contain the largest mass of high mountain land. Duration of snow cover is a factor of increasing importance with increasing latitude and altitude on our mountains, and also attains its greatest influence in the central and eastern Highlands.

The major climatic gradients combine to give a general increase in severity of conditions for plant growth in a north-westerly direction. This tendency is reflected in the downward shift of the altitudinal zones of vegetation in upland country (forest and scrub, dwarf-shrub heath, montane grasslands and moss–lichen heaths) in the same direction. Over Britain as a whole, there is also a parallel between regional differences in climate and composition of the flora and fauna. One way of describing this is in terms of representation of the biogeographical groupings of species associated with different climatic regimes on a continental scale; another is according to changes in floristic composition of vegetation types, and their associated animal communities. Regional gradients in climate within Britain are reflected in the distribution of plant and animal species, both in presence/absence terms, and in abundance and performance. In general, there is a decrease in the number of species of flowering plants and animals with increasing distance northwards and, to a lesser degree, westwards. Some groups of invertebrates, notably those associated with sunny climates (e.g. butterflies, dragonflies) are especially poorly represented in the north of Britain. On the other hand, the cryptogamic flora of ferns, bryophytes and lichens is much richer in northern and western areas than in the south and east, for these plants are adapted to cool and humid conditions.

Geology and soils

Geological accidents have given a prevalence of younger, softer rocks and low-lying terrain in the south and east contrasting with older, harder rocks and mountainous country in the north and west. Calcareous rocks are likewise erratic-

ally distributed, consisting mainly of belts of Chalk and Jurassic limestone in the south and east, and tracts of Carboniferous and other limestone in the north and west. Non-calcareous rocks cover a much larger area of Britain. This is an important pedogenic factor since most naturally occurring British soils are characterised by having calcium (Ca^{2+}) as the predominant exchangeable cation (base), and therefore the main determinant of soil pH, but the nutrient quality of derived soils depends almost as much on topography and climate as on the original composition of the parent material. Except on local areas of acidic and porous sands and gravels, which often have deep podsols, the soils of the lowlands are mostly base-saturated and therefore usually fertile brown earth types with mull humus, even though free lime may not be present. Free lime is characteristic of soils formed from chalk and limestone but true rendzinas are very local in Britain. Whilst base-saturation and pH usually give a measure of overall soil fertility, and affect such processes as litter-decomposition and nitrification, some highly calcareous soils are relatively infertile through deficiency of available nutrients such as nitrogen and phosphorus. Raw soils with low nutrient exchange capacity occur on a variety of rocks and deposits, and in many different situations. Peats in the lowlands are mostly of a fen type, formed under the influence of base-rich ground water and a eutrophic vegetation. Only very locally are there lowland raised mires and valley mires with a base-poor peat developed under an acidophilous vegetation.

The lowlands also have a variety of alluvial soils which are usually base-rich. Coastal lands have moderately to strongly saline soils in a variety of situations, including not only stabilised marine sediment but also ground above high water swept by salt spray and solid particles. Spray and sand deposition can cause other mineral enrichment, and many coastal dune systems have highly calcareous deposits where there are numerous shell fragments in the sand.

Soils in northern and western Britain, especially the uplands, show a more marked bias towards podsolic types with mor humus, which on permanently waterlogged ground has characteristically developed into a thick layer of acidic blanket peat. Base-rich soils are often confined to flushed situations where there is a local downwash and deposition of particles and nutrients from above, and the heavy rainfall results in extensive occurrence of gley soils where lateral drainage waterlogs the surface layers especially of glacial drift covering the lower slopes and valleys. On the higher mountains there is a prevalence of skeletal and immature soils which reflect both climatic severity and gravitational instability, and the effects of solifluction are often pronounced.

In Britain, the flora of base-rich and especially calcareous substrata is almost invariably much richer in number of species than that of base-poor types; as the former are so much more local, and often subjected to selectively heavy exploitation, their conservation value is particularly high. Human influence has often been particularly marked on and through the soil. Deforestation, draining, ploughing, burning, grazing, peat-cutting and the addition of both natural and artificial fertilisers have all had a profound effect, in nearly all parts of the country. Their influence includes both reduction and enhancement of soil fertility.

History

The major and interacting environmental factors of climate and soil together determine the fundamental and original diversity of ecosystems which this country contains and which has to be provided for in our national series of sites requiring conservation. The present pattern of variation in ecosystems has, however, to be seen as the result of gross climatic changes during the period since the last advance of the Quaternary ice, modified increasingly during the last 2000 years by the impact of man. The general picture was of a slowly warming climate allowing the gradual spread of major plant formations and their associated fauna in a wave-like sequence to the north and west across Britain, as types with increasing warmth requirements and luxuriance successively replaced those adapted to cooler conditions but possessing less competitive power. The open fjaeldmark and tundra which first colonised ground freed from the ice were invaded by birch, juniper and willow scrub of the taiga type. Pine forest spread and took over from birch, but was itself later replaced by mixed deciduous forest, mainly of oak, ash, elm and hazel, but locally dominated by beech, alder, lime, hornbeam and yew. By migrating northwards and upwards, the earlier plant formations each survived where their optimum conditions remained, so that the time sequence of Late-glacial and Post-glacial vegetation types became zoned latitudinally and altitudinally within Britain.

The fjaeldmark and tundra complex became restricted to high levels of the mountains of northern and western Britain, though with lower-lying outposts in situations where closed woodland could not develop, as on exposed coasts and areas of bare rock and unstable, shallow soils; its limits are taken to define montane conditions. Below this on mountains were zoned submontane scrub and woodland, and the lowlands of the south and east were evidently covered with great tracts of forest. During the whole of the Post-glacial Period, woodland has thus been the climatic climax formation over most of Britain, and limited in its extent mainly by high altitude, severe wind exposure and waterlogging of the ground. Primitive man probably kept limited areas clear or thinly covered with trees, but populations were for a long time too sparse to have much effect in reducing forest cover. Woodland floristic composition varied according to geographical position and soil type but in general there was probably a greater diversity in age and size of the trees, and a more constant development of a shrub layer, than is usual in British woodlands of the present.

Around 5500 B.C. the climate became markedly wetter, and the widespread occurrence of buried tree stumps at the base of peat deposits suggests that, in the higher rainfall districts of western and northern Britain, the extent of forest became substantially reduced by the spread of mire vegetation over ground where drainage was poor. Yet, during this Atlantic Period, thermophilous trees and other plants probably reached their maximum extension and abundance in Britain. About this time, the rising sea-level cut the land bridge formerly connecting Britain with the rest of Europe, so that the immigration of new species was much curtailed for many groups of organisms.

Later still, around 500 B.C., the climate became cooler again, and this was followed by a slight downward and southward shift in the main climax vegetation zones. During this Sub-Atlantic Period, which has continued, with minor climatic fluctuation, up to the present day, human activity probably first began significantly to alter the general pattern of vegetation cover in Britain. Forests were destroyed on an increasing scale, to provide land for cultivation and grazing of domestic animals, and for fuel, including charcoal for smelting of iron. Woodland clearance, particularly rapid in Norman times, has only been compensated by extensive re-afforestation during the last 50 years. Animals dependent on the forest were either incidentally or deliberately eradicated or reduced, though new ecosystems, especially grasslands, were created, and some reached a fair measure of stability under the existing management practices. New species of plant and animal were introduced by man, either casually or purposely, and some of these arrived here so long ago that the concept of a native species is of doubtful validity.

Present-day changes

Climatically, edaphically and topographically, the southern and eastern lowlands of Britain, i.e. mainly England, is the region most suited to arable farming and human settlement, and it is this part of the country in which the original ecosystems have been most profoundly modified. Virtually all 'natural' habitat, unaffected by man, has gone and relatively little of even a semi-natural character remains. Woodland is still the major semi-natural habitat in the lowlands and its remnants from the main period of clearance were, until very recently, composed largely of native species, managed and cropped for their economic importance. Much forest land was also traditionally kept as sporting preserve, rather than for the value of its timber, and the creation of royal hunting reservations or chases has been instrumental in preserving large areas of forest land. The open park woodland associated with large country houses has also provided a particular type of wooded habitat which is largely confined to Britain. During the last few decades, a waning demand for slow-growing hardwoods, and an increasing need to manage all woodlands for an economic return, have contributed to the accelerating replacement of native tree species by alien conifers. These new woodland dominants profoundly alter the ecosystem in its subsidiary components, notably the field communities and dependent animals, and usually create a much impoverished type.

The sophistication of modern agricultural practice is leading to the steady eradication in arable areas of all habitats and higher forms of life extraneous to the crop itself, i.e. the destruction of hedges and hedgerow trees, elimination of weeds and filling-in of ponds. In some of the lowlands, large areas have been kept under permanent grassland as pasturage for domestic animals, especially cattle and sheep. While these are communities produced by man, some of the grasslands, especially on the Chalk, are long established ecosystems of considerable biological richness and value in their own right. Here, again, the last three decades have seen great inroads into the remaining area of semi-natural habitat. Many of the permanent pastures have been ploughed and converted to arable crops; even where they are retained as grassland there has often been fertilising and re-seeding, which has completely changed a botanical composition developed over centuries. Often, the only pastures to escape destruction or modification have been on ground too steep to plough, though with modern implements even steepness of slope is no longer such a limitation.

In the lowlands, areas of acidic sand and gravel have been sufficiently infertile to discourage attempts at farming, and so have tended to retain semi-natural acidic grassland, scrub and heath, notably with heather, bracken and gorse. Often this semi-natural complex, probably derived from original woodland, is associated also with common rights or maintenance of game preserves. Major areas of this kind occur in south-east England in a discontinuous belt from East Anglia to the New Forest and Isle of Purbeck. The area of such habitats has, however, contracted greatly since 1945, for the application of modern agricultural techniques can convert these types to farmland of reasonable productivity.

Rivers and streams are well represented all over Britain. Those of the uplands tend to be the eroding type, with swift-flowing turbulent and often rocky courses, whilst those of the lowlands are mainly the 'depositing' type, slower-moving through alluvial lands built up by their sediment over the ages. Upland open waters are also predominantly oligotrophic whereas many of those in the lowlands are eutrophic.

The major lake-forming processes in Britain were those of glacial erosion, and the mountain regions of north Wales, the Lake District, Galloway and the Scottish Highlands have large numbers of lakes and tarns. In the lowlands, glacial deposition was dominant and consequently fewer natural lakes were formed. South of the area covered by the ice at its maximum extent, natural bodies of standing water are scarce indeed. Because of the local scarcity of natural standing waters in the south, artificial lakes which have achieved a degree of naturalness (in certain cases, this can be a relatively rapid process) such as some gravel pits, reservoirs, ponds and especially the mediaeval peat diggings which form the Norfolk Broads are of considerable biological interest. Open waters, particularly rivers, in lowland areas are vulnerable to forms of disturbance not encountered in other habitats. Many lakes in lowland Britain have in recent years been receiving increasing amounts of nutrients from sewage effluents and from agricultural land and these have led to a number of adverse biological changes, especially in depletion of flora. Most lowland rivers are to some extent modified by the construction of artificial barriers and channels, and the abstraction of water, which affect the rates of flow and alter the natural substrate, or by the discharge of effluents including hot water, suspended solids, pesticides and other industrial toxins, domestic sewage and detergents.

Many of these forms of modification originate at points within the catchment remote from the scientifically important tracts of river or lake, and activities such as afforestation (involving extensive ploughing and fertilising), land improvement (also involving fertilising) and mining (with discharge of waste material) in hill areas can affect upland rivers markedly. On the whole modification is less severe in upland than lowland areas, but oligotrophic waters are intrinsically more fragile than eutrophic waters, and many of the finest oligotrophic lakes have been ruined by conversion to water supply and hydro-electric reservoirs. The proposed large-scale movement of water between catchments offers a new threat to the integrity of open waters. There is also a heavy and increasing pressure on open waters for recreational use, which can cause serious disturbance to marginal and submerged plant communities as well as to wildfowl.

Permanently wet ground with a vegetation cover (peatland) was formerly much more widespread in the lowlands, but has been greatly reduced in extent by drainage and conversion to farmland. The most notable examples are the Fenlands of Huntingdonshire and Cambridgeshire where the original expanse of swampland is now represented only by a few island remnants, maintained with difficulty in a somewhat modified state. Some ground has been difficult to drain, and locally there is deliberate maintenance of high water tables, as in water meadows. Shallow lakes and slow-flowing rivers often have a marginal fringe of swamp vegetation but, in general, there appears to be a tendency for drying out of such habitats, through falling water tables and hydroseral development, and many are progressing to carr woodland or wet meadow. The local areas of raised mire, developed on plains where the peat has been able to grow above the influence of mineral-rich water, are nearly all modified from their original condition and show varying degrees of drying out, with loss of *Sphagnum* cover. This kind of peat is valued as a source of moss litter and many of the deposits are being worked extensively; afforestation or reclamation for agriculture may then totally eradicate the original ecosystem.

In the north and west of Britain, the cool, cloudy and humid climate is physiologically unsuitable for many arable crop plants. Moreover, there is a prevalence of infertile, acidic soils which can be raised to a reasonable level of productivity only by considerable expense, and much of the ground is too steep, rocky or inaccessible to be cultivated. Arable farming is confined to the rather limited areas of fertile lowland on the plains adjoining the hills or in the upland valleys. The uplands themselves are used mainly as pasturage for herbivores, notably sheep, grouse and (mainly in Scotland) red deer. Cattle were formerly kept in much larger numbers than at present, and many areas once had considerable herds of goats. Pasturage for these animals was obtained by extensive clearance of the forests which formerly covered the uplands to varying altitude, depending on local and regional differences in climate, so that woodlands in the hill country are now fragmented remnants, modified by recent management and frequently by grazing of the field layer. Within the potential tree limit, British uplands are thus covered mainly by mixtures of derived grasslands and dwarf-shrub heaths (especially *Calluna* heath), subject to heavy grazing and repeated burning. Grassland predominates in the west and on the more basic soils, and heather moor in the east and on the more acidic soils.

While the differences between typical lowlands and typical uplands are fairly obvious, the dividing line between the two is extremely difficult to draw in general. As lowland–upland transition is recognised within most of the main formations, i.e. woodlands, grasslands and heaths, peatlands and open waters, and in the case of the grasslands and heaths it is made the basis of a separation into two different formations, the upland one representing the distinctive range of mountain communities. There are floral and faunal differences between lowland and upland zones, but they seldom, if ever, give a clear-cut boundary and there is usually a gradual transition from one to the other. In many hill areas, the upper limits of enclosed land give a useful, practical, though man-made boundary for delineating upland sites and habitats. This criterion has the advantage of being ecologically based, for it varies altitudinally according to regional differences in climate as do the natural vegetation zones – a feature which makes it impossible to define any one altitudinal boundary between lowland and upland. Nevertheless, this land-use separation is not always valid for, in the more southerly British hills, vegetation referable in floristics to lowland grassland and heath or peatland often lies above the limits of enclosed land, and grades into more distinctly upland communities only at higher levels.

Woodlands obviously belong mainly to the lowland zone, and the upper edge of a wood is sometimes used to define the boundary of an upland site. However, apart from the fact that woodland is usually patchy on lower hill slopes, with very variable upper limits, and often absent altogether, this formation is itself often separable into distinctive upland types at higher levels and/or in northern localities. In many hill areas, grassland, heath and peatland of upland type extends to well below the actual tree limit. The potential tree limit (which varies from over 610 m to near sea-level, according to geographical position) is regarded as the boundary between 'montane' (higher) and 'submontane' (lower) zones. The lower limits of the submontane zone correspond to the boundary between lowland and upland.

The submontane grassland and heath complex covers great areas of the British uplands, but on wetter ground grades into blanket mire, an acidic peat-forming ecosystem in which the vegetation receives nutrients largely from the atmosphere. Blanket mires cover large expanses of gently contoured land, even down to near sea-level, in districts of high precipitation/evaporation ratio, and are especially associated with the cool oceanic climate of northern and western Britain. They are variably modified by human influence and show all degrees of drying out and erosion, though some undisturbed areas remain. Though blanket mire was formerly too wet for tree growth, it has in recent years been extensively converted by draining and planting into coniferous forest, as have many areas of deforested grassland and heather moor. Large tracts of treeless upland up to 360–490 m have thus been given a forest cover but the plantations are largely of non-native softwoods, especially Sitka spruce and lodgepole pine.

The montane zone, restricted to the higher mountains and especially extensive in Scotland, contains a range of dwarf-shrub heaths, grasslands, peatlands, moss and lichen heaths and rock communities, which as a whole probably show a closer approach to natural climax vegetation than any other ecosystem in Britain now. Even these, however, have been modified, mainly by reduction of woody species and herbs, where grazing has been heavy and long established. Recreational developments, notably skiing, hill walking and rock climbing, have in recent years become a factor of some importance locally in mountain districts, and create their own kinds of disturbance to habitat and wildlife.

Coastal land also contains a good deal of habitat in a relatively undisturbed and original state. This is especially true of sea cliffs, which occupy a good deal of the British coast, but applies also to many sand-dune systems and shingle beaches. Stable dunes and machair have been long exploited as grazing or even arable land, and the higher, least sea-swept areas of salt marsh are used as pasturage, and former saltings behind sea walls are now being extensively converted to arable land. Coastlands are mostly unstable habitats in which development of climax woodland vegetation is limited or prevented and they are often subject to erosion and redistribution of water-borne material. The distribution of the different types of coastal habitat is irregular and determined by a combination of geology and geomorphological processes, but some, such as sand dune and salt marsh, are always limited in extent, and machair is confined to the windy coasts of the western Highlands and islands. With the exception of sea cliffs, much coastland is subject to considerable human pressure, whether for recreation or agricultural, urban and industrial development. If recent proposals for estuarine barrages and reservoirs come to fruition, they will affect salt marshes and offshore sand and mud flats particularly. Estuaries are especially under threat from urban–industrial development, e.g. deep-water ports and installations, and industrial complexes such as those associated with the exploitation of the North Sea oilfields. Coastal lowlands are also favoured sites for nuclear power stations, aluminium smelters and steel mills.

Many of the habitats and communities mentioned have been considerably modified by human influence, and in this sense are no longer natural. Some, such as the permanent grasslands of the lowlands, have been created by man from completely different types, yet are sufficiently similar to naturally occurring communities in other places to be regarded as semi-natural. The Norfolk Broads were almost completely artificial in origin, yet developed an almost completely natural character, and have become one of the most important wetland complexes in the country. In addition, the diversity of human activities has created numerous habitats and communities which, though often populated by naturally occurring species, have such artificial features that we cannot regard them as even semi-natural. This range of artificial ecosystems includes man-made habitats such as arable farmland, roadside and railway verges, ponds, derelict land, hedges and walls. These are in the aggregate of considerable importance to nature conservation, but are mostly too highly fragmented and dispersed to be dealt with in terms of the key area concept. The range of variation is nevertheless described, as an indication of the nature conservation interest, but specific sites of importance are not mentioned, except where they occur as a bonus interest in key sites chosen for their natural or semi-natural ecosystems.

CONCLUSION

The countrywide selection of key sites has thus to be made within a range of ecosystems which has been reduced in total area, greatly fragmented in distribution, and often depleted in quality, through human influence, but which may actually have become expanded in diversity by the same token. There is a contrast between the lowlands of the south and east with a large number of relatively small, diverse and scattered sites, and the uplands of the north and west with large, continuous masses of semi-natural habitat with rather less diversity in relation to the size of areas involved; both situations pose complex problems in survey and assessment. The limits of our sphere of interest in nature conservation are difficult to define as habitat passes from the semi-natural into the obviously artificial, and decisions here have necessarily to be subjective and arbitrary. The foregoing brief account of human impact on the original field of variation emphasises the difficulties of assessing and selecting sites within an ecosystem complex which is constantly changing, usually by loss of interest and area, but occasionally by the creation of new habitats. Values in this sphere are indeed relative, and future modifications to one site may change both its rating and that of other related sites.

4 COASTLANDS

RANGE OF ECOLOGICAL VARIATION

Habitat factors and vegetation

Coastal habitats may be regarded as belonging to one of four groups, as follows:

(i) Permanently submerged by the sea.

(ii) The inter-tidal zone.

(iii) Ground or water above Extreme High-Water Spring Tides but strongly affected by wind-blown material, i.e. salt spray and/or mineral particles.

(iv) Ground not markedly influenced edaphically by the sea, but subject to the special climatic conditions of the coast, i.e. windiness, small temperature range and high atmospheric humidity.

This review does not deal with (i) and no account is taken of the inter-tidal zone of rocky shores, though both these groups of habitat are represented incidentally in many of the sites discussed. The inter-tidal lands to be considered are essentially water-borne deposits ranging from clay and silt (= mud) through sand to shingle, which itself may vary from gravel to large boulders. Where these inter-tidal marine deposits are extensive and almost level, lying low in relation to Mean Sea Level (MSL) and therefore often remaining largely devoid of vascular plants, they are described as *flats*. Where similar deposits have been built up higher in relation to MSL and then colonised and stabilised by vascular plants, they are described as *salt marshes*. Where the inter-tidal mud, sand and shingle deposits slope more steeply from the sea to the land, and are exposed over only a rather narrow strip, they tend to remain unstable, with only an open vegetation cover; they are described as *beaches*.

The most distinctive habitat of group (iii) is the *sand-dune* system, in which deposits of wind-blown sand extend inland for varying distances beyond the upper edge of flats or beaches, and typically become shaped into series of ridges or mounds and hollows. Along the extremely windy coasts of western Scotland, sand may be blown longer distances inland and uphill, and salt spray deposition is likewise heavy over a zone lying well above high-tide mark. Where sand and salt spray are carried inland there is usually a range of coastal grasslands and heaths, and on otherwise poor soils this deposition causes marked enrichment in nutrient status. This influence may also affect wet ground of various kinds including open waters, giving brackish conditions. On coasts formed of hard rock the sea has usually cut back the land to give sheer *cliffs*, often with caves at their base.

There are, however, slopes of all degrees of steepness rising above the sea, and the less precipitous inclines naturally carry more vegetation. Cliffs and steep slopes are battered by huge waves during storms; severe up-currents of air are created and spray deposition is usually marked right up to the summits of these headlands.

Even where there is little deposition of mineral particles or spray, land on or close to the coast is influenced by the oceanic conditions. Greater than average wind speeds affect all but the most sheltered places, and the thermo-stabilising influence of the sea reduces the range of temperature, so that there is less frost than farther inland but cooler days in the height of summer. The proximity of a large body of water also tends to maintain high atmospheric humidity, and there are often coastal mists when inland areas are clear.

The landward limits of coastlands are difficult to define, for there is a continuous gradient from marine to non-marine conditions. The gradient is steeper in some places than others so that any boundary defined by an arbitrary distance is likely to be unsatisfactory. There is a loose but useful terminology to indicate relative position along this gradient: *maritime* refers to strong and direct influence of the sea, giving markedly saline soils; *submaritime* indicates less direct effect of the sea, though still with soils which are more saline than those far inland; and *paramaritime* describes the inner zone in which the special climatic conditions of the sea coast are influential but the soils are not obviously saline and halophytes are absent. If sufficient soil analytic and climatic data were available, these categories could be defined quantitatively, though their limits would have to be arbitrarily chosen. Coastlands are, however, best defined in terms of plant communities with a high frequency of species which have a more readily observable maritime, or submaritime distribution (see Table 1, p. 38). In practice, a full phytosociological treatment is not yet available and for convenience six distinctive physiographic categories have been recognised within the range of coastal habitats, and form the basis for the following detailed account of the range of variation in vegetation; these are *flats*, *salt marshes*, *sand dunes*, *vegetated shingle beaches*, *cliffs and related features*, and *coastal lagoons and swamps*.

FLATS

Although sand and mud flats form the most extensive coastal habitat in Britain, their lack of relief and the duration of tidal submergence greatly limit the total variety of life they can support. What they lack in overall variety is to some extent compensated by the abundance of *Zostera* spp., certain algae (notably *Enteromorpha*), and the richness of the invertebrate fauna (see p. 45), which all provide food for large populations of wildfowl and waders. These resources can, however, only be utilised when exposed at low water, and where there is a sufficient area for birds to be free of shoreline disturbance. Height of flats and their size are thus important factors determining the nature conservation value of this type of habitat. Flats are also important as roosts for coastal birds.

The flora and fauna are also much influenced by the physical and chemical composition of the sand and mud flats, which in turn depend on the nature of the parent material. In general, coarse-grained sands tend to be prevalent in the north and west, fine-grained muds in the south and east. The lime content of sand and mud is also important and is extremely variable.

The Scottish flats lie in tide ranges of less than 5 m and are generally coarse-grained, mobile sands supporting little life other than bacteria or diatoms. They vary from lime-rich sands with a high proportion of shell fragments on the coast of Sutherland at Durness and Invernaver; moderately lime-rich sands at St Cyrus in Kincardineshire; and lime-deficient sands at Culbin in Moray and Tentsmuir in Fife. These flats are mainly of incidental importance as sand feeder areas to adjoining dune systems, though they may provide important roosting areas for birds, e.g. eider duck at Tentsmuir and barnacle geese at Loch Gruinart, Islay.

Sheltered inlets such as the boulder-strewn flats of Loch an Duin, North Uist, and the Ruel Estuary, Argyll, support free-living macro-algal populations (notably fucoids). In their upper reaches small areas of silt contain northern forms or species of green algae; these are of considerable interest in comparison with their much more extensively developed counterparts in the big silt flat areas of England and Wales.

High-level silt flats are especially represented on the Solway Firth, Morecambe Bay, Dee Estuary in Cheshire, Humber Estuary, and Burry Inlet, Glamorgan. These are, however, still rather deficient in larger forms of plant life, and are most important as feeding grounds for wading birds, which flourish on their large invertebrate populations. Where the high-level silt flats are also lime-rich, and especially where they are overlain by a thin surface layer of clay, there is often an abundance of *Zostera* spp. (especially *Z. noltii*) and *Enteromorpha* spp. which form extensive swards and support large populations of herbivorous wildfowl, e.g. brent geese and wigeon, in addition to waders; examples are found at Maplin Sands in Essex, on the North Norfolk Coast and the Wash, and at Lindisfarne, Northumberland.

Fine-grained, lime-rich mud flats are well represented in southern England, at Chichester and Langstone Harbours on the Sussex–Hampshire coast, in the estuaries of the Essex coast, and at Bridgwater Bay in Somerset. They carry rich resources of mud-living invertebrates and additional species of blue-green algae and diatoms, and are especially attractive to waders. By contrast, Poole Harbour in Dorset is one of the best and most extensive examples of fine-grained mud flats deficient in free lime. The tidal range of these southern sites varies a great deal, e.g. from a minimum of 2 m (and double high-water peaks) at Poole Harbour, to a maximum of 12 m at Bridgwater Bay.

In a few places, notably the Dyfi estuary in west Wales and the Exe estuary in Devon, a wide range of estuarine deposits occurs within a single site. These places offer good opportunities for the study of variations in the flora and fauna of flats according to controlling differences in the substratum.

SALT MARSHES

The successional development of salt marsh, with formation of creeks and pans is well known (e.g. Tansley, 1939), and this account is concerned mainly with the geographical variations in this class of habitats.

Differences in physical and chemical composition of sand and mud flats are important in controlling the floristics of colonising vegetation composed of vascular plants. Variations in tidal range naturally control the vertical distance over which salt marsh can develop. In the minimum tide range of 2 m at Poole Harbour, salt marsh occurs in the vertical range of about 1 m; whereas in the maximum tide range of 12 m at Bridgwater Bay it develops over a vertical range of about 4 m. Another factor of some ecological significance is that spring tides recur at fixed periods in relation to daylight hours on particular parts of the coast, and these fixed periods differ from place to place.

The lateral relationship between land and sea is important to salt marsh development, and varies a good deal. Although open coast salt marshes occur in places, e.g. on the North Norfolk Coast and Bridgwater Bay, they are perhaps most characteristic of large estuaries, such as the Solway Firth, the Ribble Estuary, Morecambe Bay, the Wash and the Thames estuary. They occupy the edges of bays varying in depth, e.g. shallow at Arnside–Silverdale in Morecambe Bay to deep at Chichester and Langstone Harbours. Examples also occur behind spits, as at Lindisfarne (Holy Island) in Northumberland. Salt marshes can also occur at the head of sea lochs in mountainous country in Scotland, as in the Ruel estuary, Argyll, and at Burrafirth in Shetland.

Salt marshes vary in salinity according to their position in estuaries. Highland loch-head marshes are perhaps usually the least saline, for there is considerable subsurface flushing with land drainage water through generally porous substrata. There is often a transition from brackish upper estuary marshes to saline lower estuary marshes, but some estuarine salt marshes occur over a more limited sector. There may also be variations in mean particle size of substrata, and therefore in salt marsh development, according to position in an estuary, e.g. from panned marsh on sandy silt at the estuary mouth to level marsh on silty clay in upper estuary areas. The marshes of the Dyfi estuary in west Wales show particularly well the effect of lateral position on salinity and type of sediment.

In many places, salt marshes are associated with other coastal habitats, such as sand dune and shingle, and particularly good complexes of this kind occur on the North

Norfolk Coast, at Gibraltar Point and Saltfleetby in Lincolnshire, St Cyrus in Kincardineshire, Walney Island and Sandscale in Lancashire, Newborough on Anglesey, Burry–Whiteford in Glamorgan, and Dungeness in Kent.

A further factor of importance to development of salt marshes in general has been the tendency for the land surface of Britain to tilt slowly in relation to sea-level about a south-west to north-east axis. As a result, the salt marshes of the east and south coasts of England have formed on a sinking shore whereas those of the west and north lie on a rising coastline. Much of the extensive salt marsh of the Ribble Estuary, Morecambe Bay and the Solway Firth is high-lying in consequence, but also prone to spectacular marginal erosion, by undercutting along a brow edge, though this depends on proximity of adjacent river channels and their changes in position, and accretion usually proceeds on marsh edges farthest from the channels

The floristic details of salt marsh succession vary mainly according to the regional climate and the physical texture of the sediment. Climate affects maritime plant distribution (see Flora, p. 351) and hence the availability of species for colonisation. There is a steady diminution in number of salt marsh species with distance north, so that the most varied successions are those in southern England, while the most uniform occur in northern Scotland. Mean particle size of the substratum affects drainage, soil aeration and base-status, and hence the floristic composition of colonising vegetation; it appears that fewer species can grow on coarse sand than on silt and clay. Particle size tends to increase in a northerly and westerly direction. When these two factors are combined, they thus produce a marked geographical differentiation in the floristics of salt marsh succession.

In most parts of the country where fine-grained deposits prevail, the first colonists are *Salicornia* spp., which form an open growth on the mud flats. In nearly all areas *Puccinellia maritima* is an important early colonist of flats, forming patches which spread radially and join up to give a continuous sward. On muddy sediments this grass usually invades and eventually replaces the *Salicornia* but on sandy deposits in the west and north where *Salicornia* is sparse or absent it is the first of the pioneer salt marsh species. Other species which appear in this early stage of succession include *Cochlearia officinalis*, *Aster tripolium*, *Suaeda maritima*, *Plantago maritima* and *Triglochin maritima*. On the muddy coast of East Anglia, *A. tripolium* (mainly the var. *discoideus*) often becomes dominant at an early stage instead of *Puccinellia* and may be accompanied by abundance of *Salicornia*, *Suaeda maritima* and algae.

As accretion proceeds, other species appear in varying abundance, and there may be dominance of one of several species, or co-dominance of mixtures of these. Among the characteristic species of this 'middle marsh' are *Limonium vulgare*, *Spergularia media*, *S. marina*, *Triglochin maritima*, *Armeria maritima*, *Halimione portulacoides* and *Plantago maritima*. *Puccinellia maritima* often enters at this stage on some muddy east coast marshes and may persist in quantity when it has appeared earlier in the sequence. Other early pioneers such as *Salicornia* may also persist in some abun-

dance. Where *Limonium* and *Armeria* attain dominance, zoning tends to occur with *Limonium* to the seaward of *Armeria*. On the marshes of south-eastern England and East Anglia, *Halimione* often becomes dominant at this stage, reducing or suppressing completely the other species; and in this region *Inula crithmoides*, *Frankenia laevis* and *Limonium bellidifolium* are also locally abundant, but not together.

In the southern half of Britain the natural hybrid cord grass *Spartina anglica* has shown great vigour as a salt marsh pioneer, and in many places forms luxuriant swards which are extremely efficient at promoting accretion of sediment. The great competitive power of this plant tends to exclude all the previously mentioned pioneers from the *Salicornia* to the *Armeria* or mixed marsh stages, so that areas extensively invaded by *Spartina anglica* become impoverished floristically. Because of its efficiency as a sediment-binder, *S. anglica* is often planted to assist the development of marsh swards and reclamation of land from the sea – it is grazed by cattle and sheep – and has also rapidly spread naturally. Invasion by this species occurs as far north as the Mersey in the west and Holy Island in the east, but as it thrives best on muddy sediments, it may be somewhat limited northwards by the increasing sandiness of the substrata. While *Spartina anglica* has obvious economic importance, it is regarded by many ecologists as an undesirable 'weed' and one which should be controlled on botanically important salt marshes.

The salt marshes of eastern and south-eastern England are mostly abruptly delimited on their landward side by artificial embankments (sea walls) built to exclude the sea, so that former salt marsh could be reclaimed for agriculture. These sealed-off salt marshes first become converted to grazing marshes with neutral grasslands (probably produced mainly by the sowing of mixtures of grass seed) but it has been found economic to convert them to arable land, and this is taking place increasingly. The cut-off creeks behind the sea walls ('fleets') often remain brackish and carry relics of the original halophytic flora, especially *Scirpus maritimus*. The new salt marsh which has formed outside the sea walls is thus mostly of the early to middle stages, lacking the transition to non-halophytic vegetation. In western and northern Britain, sea walls are less typically present or are built at a higher level in relation to tides, so that salt marsh development to a more mature phase is commonly found, as on the Solway.

This later salt marsh succession proceeds with the appearance and increasing abundance of species such as *Festuca rubra*, *Glaux maritima*, *Juncus gerardii* and *Plantago coronopus*. Middle salt marsh species, especially *Puccinellia maritima* and *Armeria*, remain abundant but gradually disappear as the marsh level rises further and there is an increase of other less salt-tolerant species such as *Agrostis stolonifera*, *Leontodon autumnalis*, *Carex panicea*, *C. flacca*, *C. nigra*, *C. extensa* and *C. distans*. On some marshes the taller rush *Juncus maritimus* becomes locally dominant, forming a distinctive zone. The upper marsh communities are usually grazed by cattle and/or sheep, at least during part of the year. They develop into dense swards, completely covering the soil surface, and usually there is formation of a litter layer. Luxuriance of the sward and floristic composition vary according to grazing intensity, but the mature salt marsh community is essentially a type of grassland with varying abundance of forbs. Most of the true halophytes disappear or become scarce, but submaritime and paramaritime species may become abundant.

The creeks and pans which have developed during the upward and lateral growth of the salt marsh remain subject to more saline conditions and show plant communities characteristic of earlier stages in the succession. While creeks and pans may themselves show succession on a minor scale, they are often persistent features, and so may allow the survival of halophytic vegetation on parts of a marsh little subject to tidal influence and otherwise covered with a different vegetation.

The nature of the transition from salt marsh to ground no longer subject to tidal inundation varies greatly according to local conditions. There may be a change to sand dune or shingle, but where the ground remains low and waterlogged, there is often a change to brackish marsh in which *Phragmites communis* is especially characteristic, with *Carex otrubae, Sparganium ramosum, Iris pseudacorus, Scirpus maritimus, Oenanthe lachenalii, O. crocata, Eleocharis palustris, Juncus articulatus* and *Samolus valerandi. Althaea officinalis* and *C. divisa* are local southern brackish marsh species. This vegetation is close to eutrophic fen of the type associated with flood-plain mire, and it may grade into the freshwater type; this can be seen where maritime influence has become largely sealed-off from the land by either natural or artificial embankments, e.g. at Minsmere–Walberswick in Suffolk, and the Mound (Loch Fleet) in Sutherland. The west Highland coast often shows a transition to a zone of vegetation (just above high water mark) intermediate between eutrophic fen and damp meadow grassland, with much *Juncus articulatus* (or a presumed hybrid between this and *J. acutiflorus*), *Iris pseudacorus, Molinia caerulea* and many forbs including *Parnassia palustris, Pedicularis palustris, Caltha palustris, Lychnis floscuculi, Succisa pratensis, Anagallis tenella, Mentha aquatica* and *Carex nigra*.

Creeks or estuaries may lead back into freshwater channels or rivers, and the brackish zone often has abundance of *Phragmites, Phalaris arundinacea, Scirpus maritimus* and *Schoenoplectus tabernaemontani*. In brackish pools or ditches here, the fen species may occur with others associated with stagnant open water, such as *Ranunculus baudotii, Zannichellia palustris, Ruppia maritima, R. spiralis, Potamogeton pectinatus, P. filiformis* and *Eleocharis uniglumis*.

Where the ground remains dry and continues to rise slowly, there is often a transition to a kind of neutral or slightly acidic grassland which resembles that of some dry, grazed meadow grasslands. *Festuca rubra* may remain abundant but other halophytes are almost absent, and species such as *Juncus effusus* and *Deschampsia cespitosa* sometimes appear in quantity. This type of grassland is well developed on upper marsh levels on the Solway Firth, in a region where upward tilting of the land has gradually raised former salt marsh above the level of all but exceptionally high tides. Cultivation usually comes down to the lowest possible level, so that the inner edges of salt marshes mostly have an abrupt and artificial boundary. In the absence of man, the landward limit of salt marshes would presumably be grassland maintained by deer grazing, or some kind of woodland. There are very few places where gradual transition from salt marsh to woodland on level ground may be seen today. The extensive alder–willow woods at the Mound in Sutherland have developed on estuarine sediment, after the estuary was sealed off by an embankment. A similar transition in the upper reaches of the Fal–Ruan Estuary in Cornwall is an example of the final stage of marsh succession. Even oak trees occur at this site on river bank levels of tide-borne silt still subject to occasional tidal flooding and silting. Artificial banks on salt marshes readily become invaded by gorse above the level of highest tides.

SAND DUNES

Dune systems are the first of the submaritime coastal habitats in the sense that they are not subject to periodic inundation by the sea and are not strongly saline. They vary according to physiography and the nature of the colonising vegetation. Six main physiographic types are recognised, according to position of the system in relation to the shoreline. Three of these – offshore islands, spits and nesses – project into the sea and are generally of a prograding nature. They are more characteristic of the east coast, where the prevailing wind is not onshore. The other three types – bay dunes, hindshore dunes and machair – are increasingly driven back by wind action on to land behind the shore and are characteristic of western coasts where the prevailing wind is onshore. Dunes vary greatly in height (sand hills can exceed 30 m on large systems); in length and breadth of the system; in the orientation of the sandhills in distinct lines or other patterns; in the height and fluctuation of water tables in the intervening hollows to form wet slacks; and in the secondary redistribution of sand to give blow-outs or levelling down of the sandhills farther inland.

Spits are the commonest type of dune system and occur at the mouths of estuaries, bays or lakes in great variety of form, with or without slacks, often in association with shingle, and sometimes partially enclosing salt marsh. Such systems occur widely on all coasts and are represented by the South Haven peninsula in Purbeck, Dorset; Blakeney Point, Norfolk; Gibraltar Point, Lincolnshire; Tentsmuir Point, Fife; Sands of Forvie, Aberdeenshire; Loch Gruinart dunes, Islay; Walney and Sandscale Dunes, Lancashire; Morfa Harlech and Morfa Dyffryn, Merioneth; Ynyslas, Dyfi, Cardiganshire; Whiteford, Glamorgan; and Braunton Burrows, Devon. The ness type of dune system occurs at Winterton, Norfolk and Saltfleetby–Theddlethorpe, Lincolnshire, while offshore island dunes are represented by Holy Island, Northumberland; Scolt Head Island, Norfolk, and the Monach Isles, Outer Hebrides.

Bay dunes are widespread but have often been developed as holiday resorts or golf links, or form narrow systems lacking in variety. This type is represented in the Isles of Scilly, Strathbeg in Aberdeenshire, and Oxwich in Glamorgan. Hindshore dunes may originate by combination of some of the above forms, but are characterised by the extent to which they are blown back over the land; in the bigger systems alternating dune ridges and slacks develop and are perpetuated by wind action for some distance inland. Examples are the Culbin Sands, Morayshire; Ainsdale Dunes, Lancashire; Newborough Warren, Anglesey; and Braunton Burrows, Devon. Under extreme wind action in the far north and west of Scotland, dune growth is checked and sand is spread inland in a fan over low shores to form more or less level areas known as machair. This type of system is very local and found mainly in the Outer Hebridean islands of Barra, South Uist; Benbecula, North Uist; and the outlying Monach Isles. There is a great deal of machair on the southerly island of Tiree, rather less on Islay and relatively little on the Scottish mainland, though blown sand affects parts of the steep, rocky coast of Sutherland.

Dune vegetation varies according to stability, moisture content and calcium carbonate content of the sand. Stabilisation of dunes involves plant succession to form a closed vegetation, but the sequence varies according to moisture and lime status. Whereas the vegetation of the dry dunes shows affinities with lowland grassland or heath, that of the slacks is clearly related to marsh or fen.

Sand varies from highly base-deficient material composed largely of siliceous grains to strongly calcareous grains formed mainly of calcium carbonate. The first type is associated especially with occurrence of siliceous sandstones while the second occurs particularly where deposits of mollusc shells become comminuted by tidal movement. Both calcareous and non-calcareous sands occur widely and there appears to be no particular geographical pattern to their distribution. There is, naturally, a continuum of variation between the two, and moderately calcareous sand is probably the commonest type.

Above the sand or shingle beach of the foreshore there is often a seaward strip of low dunes with an open growth of plants tolerant of short immersion during especially high tides, e.g. *Agropyron junceiforme, Cakile maritima, Salsola kali* and *Honkenya peploides*. These fore-dunes grade into main dunes farther inland, where marram grass *Ammophila arenaria* is the main colonist, binding the sand with its roots and promoting the upward growth of the dunes. Marram occurs on virtually all dune systems, often forming luxuriant but open swards irrespective of the physical and chemical nature of the sand. A more local species occupying the same niche is the still more luxuriant lyme grass *Elymus arenarius*, which is locally abundant. These grasses are efficient dune builders, but do not form a layer of litter or bind the sand surface, so that subsequent erosion often occurs, with formation of blow-outs, causing disintegration of the dunes.

The bare sand between the marram tussocks is colonised by a variety of herbaceous plants. Among the most characteristic are maritime or submaritime species such as *Calystegia soldanella, Eryngium maritimum, Euphorbia paralias, E. portlandica* and *Phleum arenarium*. Many paramaritime species of plants which find a coastal niche also appear as open sand colonists, including *Senecio jacobaea, Carlina vulgaris, Ononis repens, Anthyllis vulneraria, Geranium sanguineum, Thalictrum minus, Vicia sepium, Plantago lanceolata, Echium vulgare, Cynoglossum officinale, Daucus carota, Achillea millefolium, Cirsium vulgare* and *C. arvense*. Some of these grow mainly on calcareous dunes, but the effect of varying lime content of the sand becomes more obvious as a closed vegetation develops and sand stabilisation is accompanied by leaching.

A closed vegetation develops, mainly of low-growing grasses, forbs, mosses and lichens. Where the sand is non-calcareous, the characteristic species which appear amongst the marram are *Festuca rubra, F. ovina, Agrostis tenuis, Carex arenaria, Thymus drucei, Hieracium pilosella, Galium verum, Sedum anglicum, Cerastium vulgatum, Veronica chamaedrys, Viola curtisii* (mainly in the west), *Trifolium repens* and *Ononis repens*, which form a thickening grassy sward. Less abundant or more local species include *Erodium cicutarium, Centaurium erythraea, Erophila verna, Cerastium arvense, Trifolium arvense, Filago minima, F. germanica, Jasione montana, Gentianella campestris, Polygala vulgaris* and *Euphrasia* spp. Mosses often appear in quantity, especially *Tortula ruraliformis* (an important sand stabiliser on many British dunes), *Ceratodon purpureus, Rhacomitrium canescens, Dicranum scoparium, Hylocomium splendens, Rhytidiadelphus squarrosus, R. triquetrus, Brachythecium albicans* and *Bryum* spp. Lichens such as *Cladonia impexa, C. sylvatica* and *Peltigera* spp. may become abundant.

The oldest and most stable parts of non-calcareous dunes are eventually invaded by dwarf shrubs, mainly *Calluna vulgaris* and *Erica cinerea*, to form a heath which approaches that of many inland lowland situations with podsolised, sandy soils. In the north, *Empetrum nigrum* often becomes abundant or even locally dominant, and other characteristic associates include *Rumex acetosella, Hypochoeris radicata, Luzula campestris* and *Festuca ovina*. Mosses such as *Hypnum cupressiforme, Pleurozium schreberi, Pseudoscleropodium purum* and *Dicranum scoparium* may be very abundant, but on some dunes, especially in the east, a lichen heath may develop with species such as *Cladonia impexa, C. sylvatica, Hypogymnia physodes* and *Cetraria aculeata* growing in great abundance amongst the dwarf shrubs. Bracken *Pteridium aquilinum* sometimes invades and large areas of it may develop.

During the early stages of closed sward formation, marram may remain very abundant, but with further development of the succession it gradually thins out and eventually disappears. The development of dwarf-shrub heath is also associated with marked leaching and acidification of the sand surface horizons, and the formation of an acidic mor humus layer.

On calcareous sand, the development of a closed grass–forb sward on the dry dunes differs largely in the presence of many additional species to those found on non-calcareous dunes, though a few calcifuge species (e.g. *Sedum anglicum*) are usually absent. The additional species include *Sedum acre*, *Lotus corniculatus*, *Campanula rotundifolia*, *Koeleria cristata*, *Ranunculus acris*, *R. bulbosus*, *Carex flacca*, *Bellis perennis*, *Plantago lanceolata*, *Leontodon hispidus*, *Thalictrum minus*, *Prunella vulgaris*, *Linum catharticum*, *Anthyllis vulneraria*, *Arenaria serpyllifolia*, *Holcus lanatus*, *Poa pratensis*, *Taraxacum laevigatum* and *Cerastium atrovirens*. Less abundant or more local species include *Astragalus danicus*, *Trifolium medium*, *T. striatum*, *Helianthemum chamaecistus*, *Fragaria vesca*, *Asperula cynanchica*, *Anacamptis pyramidalis*, *Primula vulgaris* and *P. veris*. The mossy facies of calcareous dunes again include usually an abundance of *Tortula ruraliformis*, and there are *Camptothecium lutescens*, *Hypnum cupressiforme* var. *elatum*, *Entodon concinnus*, *Ditrichum flexicaule*, *Encalypta streptocarpa*, *Thuidium tamariscinum*, *Trichostomum brachydontium* and *Barbula* spp. A lichen-rich facies includes species of *Cladonia*, *Peltigera*, *Parmelia*, *Collema* and *Leptogium*.

Further development involves a thickening of the grassy sward, extension of these herbs into the moss and lichen facies, and disappearance of the maritime or submaritime species such as marram and sand sedge *Carex arenaria*. Rabbits are, or were until recently, very numerous on many of these dune systems, and their grazing helped to produce a close-cropped species-rich *Festuca rubra*–*F. ovina* sward hardly distinguishable floristically from that on many inland grasslands on calcareous soils in the lowlands. Moss and lichen-rich facies sometimes persist in these stable dune grasslands. The calcium carbonate content and pH of calcareous dune sands gradually decrease with age, and organic content of the surface layers increases. Depending on the degree of loss of free lime and exchangeable bases, there may be further slow change towards a more acidophilous grassland with more *Agrostis* spp., *Holcus lanatus* and *Anthoxanthum odoratum*.

The foregoing refers to the parts of the dune system which remain well drained and dry. In the wet hollows between sand hills and ridges, a completely different kind of vegetation develops, varying according to the degree of waterlogging and the lime content of the sand.

The wetter kinds of *slack* amongst non-calcareous dunes have a range of communities showing some similarity to those found in certain types of acidophilous valley mire (poor-fen) with *Carex nigra*, *C. echinata*, *C. curta*, *C. rostrata*, *Agrostis stolonifera*, *Eleocharis palustris*, *Menyanthes trifoliata*, *Potentilla palustris*, *Galium palustre*, *Hydrocotyle vulgaris*, *Ranunculus flammula*, *Potamogeton polygonifolius*, *Juncus kochii*; there is a variable cover of *Sphagnum* spp., mainly *S. palustre*, *S. fimbriatum* and *S. recurvum*. Where the ground is less wet there is often a wet meadow community with *Agrostis* spp., *Molinia caerulea*, *Juncus effusus*, *J. acutiflorus*, *Rumex acetosa*, *Potentilla anserina*, *P. erecta*, *Ranunculus repens*, *Lotus uliginosus* and *Acrocladium cuspidatum*. These slacks show variable amounts of low-shrub growth with *Salix repens*, *S. aurita* and *Myrica gale*, and sometimes medium to tall willow scrub with other *Salix* spp. Some slacks show development towards still more acidophilous mire vegetation, with *Erica tetralix*, *Calluna* and *Molinia*. Between the wet slack and the dry dunes there is

often a transitional zone of damp, tussocky grassland, with *Agrostis stolonifera*, *A. tenuis*, *Holcus lanatus*, *Anthoxanthum odoratum*, *Festuca ovina* and *F. rubra*. Sand sedge may also be especially abundant on these soils of intermediate dampness.

On calcareous dunes, the vegetation of the slacks is usually quite different, except that *Salix repens* is often abundant (especially in the west) and its upward growth may produce a hummockiness within the slacks. In general, calcareous slack vegetation approaches that of eutrophic valley mire (rich-fen). A mixed sedge growth often occurs with *Carex nigra*, *C. flacca*, *C. panicea*, *C. pulicaris*, *C. demissa*, *Eleocharis quinqueflora*, *Triglochin palustris*, *Juncus articulatus*, *Equisetum palustre*, *Pedicularis palustris*, *Caltha palustris*, *Cardamine pratensis*, *Dactylorchis incarnata*, *D. fuchsii*, *Epipactis palustris*, *Parnassia palustris*, *Samolus valerandi* and *Iris pseudacorus*. Where water stands a good deal, especially in winter, a carpet of pleurocarpous 'brown mosses' may develop with *Drepanocladus revolvens*, *D. sendtneri* and its var. *wilsonii*, *D. lycopodioides*, *Campylium polygamum*, *C. elodes*, *C. stellatum*, *Scorpidium scorpioides* and *Acrocladium giganteum*.

In the less wet slacks the rather open sward may contain in addition such species as *Bellis perennis*, *Centaurium erythraea*, *Sagina nodosa*, *S. procumbens*, *Prunella vulgaris*, *Leontodon taraxacoides*, *Isolepis setacea*, *Agrostis stolonifera*, *Carex arenaria* and *Anagallis tenella*. The mosses in these places show a predominance of acrocarpous forms, e.g. *Barbula* spp., *Weissia* spp. and *Bryum* spp. This community in turn grades into those of the dry dunes. Where slacks show incipient acidification, *Potentilla anserina*, *Hydrocotyle vulgaris*, *Agrostis stolonifera* and *Acrocladium cuspidatum* are abundant. Where there is a saline influence, slack communities are intermediate between calcareous marsh and middle salt marsh, with species such as *Glaux maritima*, *Triglochin maritima*, *Juncus gerardii*, *Carex extensa*, *C. distans* and *Plantago maritima* growing alongside the freshwater plants.

The vegetation which eventually develops on fixed dunes varies from place to place. Heath and grassland may persist indefinitely, especially where grazing is heavy, but scrub of some kind often develops. On acidic dune heaths this is frequently of gorse *Ulex europaeus*, *U. gallii* (in the west), broom *Sarothamnus scoparius* or bramble *Rubus fruticosus* agg. On richer soils there is sometimes invasion by blackthorn *Prunus spinosa*, hawthorn *Crataegus monogyna*, and elder *Sambucus nigra*, and in some localities dense but low thickets of *Rosa pimpinellifolia* develop. The most characteristic dune scrub, however, is dominated by sea buckthorn *Hippophaë rhamnoides*, which is often bare beneath, except for growths of polypody *Polypodium vulgare* and a few other shade-tolerant species. The native range of this tall shrub has been much obscured by deliberate planting, and it is now a widespread dune species. Large, deep slacks may persist as permanent small basin mires, or there may be hydroseral development and redistribution of sand, leading to a drier type of stable dune vegetation. Damp situations often carry a tall grass 'dune meadow' sometimes with invasive scrub. There is evidence of local development of birch and even oakwood on the inner areas of dune systems, and this habitat has been extensively afforested with both native and alien conifers.

Dunes are in general a floristically rich habitat, and in one place or another there occur many rare or local species which favour sandy and/or calcareous soils. There are obvious regional differences in flora, but a considerable number of dune constants recur with remarkable consistency all over Britain. The tendency towards diminution of floristic richness with distance north is much less marked than in the case of salt marsh vegetation. The following are examples of regional floristic elements:

South

Dactylorchis praetermissa, Ophrys apifera, Anacamptis pyramidalis, Blackstonia perfoliata, Eryngium maritimum, Euphorbia portlandica, E. paralias, Vulpia membranacea, V. ambigua, Festuca juncifolia, Hordeum marinum, Medicago polymorpha, Trifolium subterraneum, T. ornithopodioides, T. glomeratum, T. suffocatum, Erodium moschatum, E. maritimum.

East

Corynephorus canescens; and a frequent development of lichen-rich facies in stable dune communities.

West

Viola tricolor ssp. *curtisii, Sedum anglicum, Rhynchosinapis monensis*; a frequent development of moss-rich facies in stable dune communities.

North

Dactylorchis purpurella, Corallorhiza trifida, Carex maritima, Blysmus rufus, Selaginella selaginoides, Equisetum variegatum and *Centaurium littorale.*

The only very rare species which appear to be confined to sand dunes are *Epipactis dunensis, Viola kitaibeliana, Festuca juncifolia* and *Corynephorus canescens*, but *Romulea columnae, Mibora minima* and *Cynodon dactylon* are confined to sandy places near the sea.

The machair of the far north-west of Britain varies more in form than in floristics from the other range of dune systems. Dry machair has a compact grass–forb sward essentially similar in floristics to stable calcareous dune grassland in other situations. The wet machair has merely a more extreme development of slack vegetation, since there is often a more permanently high water table and even lagoon formation; the resemblance to eutrophic flood-plain mire is often close. One floristic difference is the very local occurrence on blown-sand areas in northern Scotland of montane species such as *Dryas octopetala, Empetrum hermaphroditum, Arctostaphylos uva-ursi* and *Oxytropis halleri*. These are not usually on true machair, but occur where sand is blown on to rockier slopes and headlands.

VEGETATED SHINGLE BEACHES

In 1960, E. C. Willatts (unpublished data) estimated that one-third of the coastline of England and Wales was bordered by shingle. By far the greater part is almost or totally devoid of vegetation and these sterile deposits, though of interest to the physiographer and coastal engineer and to coastal protection in general, need no further consideration here. Vegetated shingle beaches are of particular scientific interest because of their scarcity, not only in Britain, but in Europe as a whole. Even in Britain there are only six really large examples (excluding Rye which is too close to Dungeness to be considered separately). These are confined to England (Chesil Beach, Dorset; Dungeness, Kent; Orford–Shingle Street, Suffolk; north Norfolk shingles; Walney, Lancashire; and Bridgwater Bay, Somerset). Two of these – Dungeness and Chesil Beach – are outstanding both for their size and for the range of pebble size found within them. Bridgwater Bay is notable for the high proportion of large limestone pebbles on parts of the beach, but also has a good range of pebble size. Apart from Culbin, Moray, which has quite extensive vegetated shingle, only small areas (less than 20 ha at a site) are known elsewhere in Britain, e.g. Beaulieu Warren, Hampshire. Shingle beaches carrying some vegetation are, however, widespread, and are often associated with other coastal habitats, especially sand dunes, which may be of much greater importance. In the Swale, Kent, and Maplin, Essex, shell accumulations carry a vestigial shingle beach flora.

Physiographic types include offshore island shingle (e.g. parts of the north Norfolk shingles), shingle bar (e.g. Chesil), ness type apposition beach series (e.g. Dungeness), main shore shingle spits varyingly associated with estuary, bay or lake mouths (e.g. Orford and Walney) or with open coast (e.g. Bridgwater Bay) and bay storm beaches often carrying only a sparse strandline shingle beach flora. Raised beaches carrying shingle beds occur locally, especially in western Scotland.

Ecologically, the most important factors in shingle beaches appear to be pebble size and position of the deposit in relation to tidal influence. The larger the pebbles the sparser the plant cover tends to be, but the characteristic feature of nearly all shingle communities is their openness, and this remains so as shingle grades into sand. Perhaps the most important factor affecting the degree of plant colonisation is the continuing influence of the sea, which tends to maintain instability, eroding and redistributing deposits of shingle according to vagaries of tide and weather. Only when stability is maintained sufficiently long for the shingle deposits to become sealed off from the direct influence of the sea is there a chance for completely closed communities to develop, and then they tend to have a paramaritime character, as over most of Dungeness. However, even disappearance of the direct impact of the sea is no guarantee that closed vegetation will develop: the shingle of some raised beaches bears closed heathy communities but on others (as on Jura, Argyll) is totally devoid of plant life except for lithophilous lichens.

Inter-tidal shingle in quiet inlets of the coast may support algal growths of *Fucus* spp. and *Enteromorpha* spp., and is usually associated with finer deposits as in Scottish lochs (e.g. Loch an Duin, North Uist, or Loch Gruinart, Islay).

These communities are transitional to those of rocky inter-tidal shores and have yet to be fully described. Above high-water mark spring tide, lichens (e.g. *Buellia* spp. and *Rhizocarpon* spp.) are the pioneer species on shingle and are one of the principal components of the shingle beach flora culminating in the epiphytes associated with scrub in fully stabilised shingle. There are distinctive regional variants of the lichen flora such as the south-western oceanic element found on the Isles of Scilly shingle and at Bridgwater Bay. Bryophytes are less well represented and then mostly by more generally abundant species, probably because damp habitats are either brackish, scarce or absent, and the polished surfaces of the pebbles do not form a good sub-stratum for lithophilous species.

Less than 20 species of flowering plant are more or less confined to shingle and most of these also occur occasionally on cliffs or stone embankments. Many which find their optimum habitat on sandy beaches or sand dunes may also grow on shingle, and the situation is complicated by the occurrence on many beaches of mixtures of sand and shingle. The typical and widespread shingle beach species include *Glaucium flavum, Crambe maritima, Honkenya peploides, Beta vulgaris* ssp. *maritima, Polygonum raii, Atriplex glabriuscula* and *Rumex crispus* var. *trigranulatus*; but equally common in this habitat are species of wider ecological range such as *Silene maritima, Armeria maritima, Plantago maritima, Festuca rubra, Agropyron junceiforme, A. pungens, Agrostis stolonifera, Trifolium scabrum* and *Catapodium marinum*. Common dune plants less often on shingle are *Eryngium maritimum, Calystegia soldanella, Carex arenaria* and *Elymus arenarius*; while salt marsh species include *Halimione portulacoides* and *Artemisia maritima*. A number of local coastal species are abundant on shingle within their geo-graphical ranges, e.g. *Frankenia laevis, Geranium purpureum, Raphanus maritimus, Suaeda fruticosa, Rumex rupestris* and *Lathyrus japonicus* in the south, and *Mertensia maritima* in the north.

Shingle beaches also support a large number of species which have no particular maritime bias (though they may have maritime ecotypes); among the most common are *Sedum acre, S. anglicum, Geranium robertianum, Lotus corniculatus, Plantago lanceolata, Galium verum, Rumex acetosella, Festuca ovina, Arrhenatherum elatius* and *Koeleria cristata*. Scottish loch shore beaches flushed by subsurface fresh drainage water carry a distinctive associes in which *Galium aparine, Polygonum persicaria, Tripleurospermum maritimum* and *Potentilla anserina* are abundant.

Shingle beaches show all stages in colonisation by these species, in many different combinations, with locally varying abundance and it is not easy to distinguish particular seral stages. On stable beaches succession tends to result in replacement of truly maritime species by others of wider ecological distribution, and the closed communities which eventually develop often approximate to a forb-rich grass-land not unlike that of cliff tops or stable dunes. Species often regarded as weeds may become abundant, e.g. *Senecio jacobaea, S. vulgaris, Sonchus oleraceus, S. arvensis* and *Stellaria media*. The species list of open shingle is often

very small; by contrast, that of stabilised banks may be very large. Eventually, further development to scrub may take place, through the invasion of such species as blackthorn, hawthorn, bramble and gorse. These form a low growth at first, and along the south coast a flattened form of broom occurs. *Rosa pimpinellifolia* is abundant on some shingle areas, and on parts of the south coast tamarisk (*Tamarix gallica*) has been extensively planted to stabilise shingle beaches. Some stable shingle banks develop into dwarf-shrub heath, with *Calluna vulgaris* and *Erica cinerea*, often rich in lichens, as at Dungeness. The apposition shingle system of Dungeness shows striking examples of differential succession, from depressions in which the shingle is colonised only by lithophilous lichens to ridges covered with heath; this site also has an unusual example of further seral development in the form of an open holly wood of considerable antiquity.

CLIFFS AND RELATED FEATURES

Only on the east coast of Britain between the Thames and Humber Estuaries are there long sections of shoreline devoid of cliffs. Even here, near Cromer, Norfolk, low cliffs of Pleistocene sands, gravels and boulder clays contain classic beds with subfossil material from this period. The form and height of sea cliffs depends on the nature (particularly structure) of the rocks. Soft materials, including relatively recent deposits such as those of the Norfolk coast, often give unstable, sloping cliffs which are being cut back relatively rapidly by the sea. Faces which are vertical or nearly so may be formed from a variety of rocks differing greatly in hardness. The Chalk of Kent, Sussex, the Isle of Wight, Dorset and east Yorkshire gives some particularly abrupt lines of precipice, but in places, as between Axmouth and Lyme Regis, south Devon, mixtures of Chalk, green-sand and clay have developed large landslips, giving steep, broken slopes. Most sections of coast with sheer cliff also have places where the abrupt rock walls give way to more broken faces and steep slopes, sometimes with litters of loose blocks (scree).

The average height for most sea cliffs in Britain probably lies between 45 and 90 m. The highest are in the islands off the north of Scotland. The granitic cliffs of St Kilda reach almost 430 m while the Old Red Sandstone precipice of Foula in the Shetland group is 370 m, and the same rock formation in Hoy, Orkney, gives the highest vertical wall at 335 m. The highest cliffs on the mainland are the 210 m Clo Mor, formed of Torridonian Sandstone on the coast of Sutherland, and 200 m Boulby Cliff, formed of Liassic shales and sandstones and boulder clay on the Yorkshire coast.

Many sections of cliff are notable for the number and size of caves cut into their base, and in places differential rates of erosion have given rise to isolated rock pillars or stacks lying out from the main cliffs. Occasionally, igneous masses of rock have given small and isolated islands almost completely bounded by cliffs, e.g. Bass Rock, Isle of May, and Ailsa Craig. Some cliffs fall to an undercliff lying partly above high-tide mark, and others drop to a storm beach swept by waves and spray during onshore gales; some sheer cliffs are accessible along their base only at low tide and others descend into deep water all the time. Land/sea movements, especially in western Scotland, have produced a series of raised beaches which are often overlooked by anciently cut cliffs now drawn back from the sea.

Cliff vegetation varies according to steepness of slope, i.e. gravitational instability, which affects degree of plant cover and depth of soil. There are also marked differences according to salinity which depends not only on height in relation to sea-level, but also on exposure to wind and hence to driven spray. Degree of shelter also affects the stature of vegetation on deeper soils above the strongly saline zone. Content of available lime in the parent rock is important, but less so within the zone where spray influence is strong, for this addition of sea water causes a certain degree of enrichment by calcium as well as by other nutrients, and may result in a relatively high base-status even on acidic rocks. Large seabird colonies cause other enrichment of cliff soils, especially by nitrogen and phosphorus, and it has been suggested that in these localities the high content of phosphate may be detrimental to the growth of many plant species by reducing the availability of calcium (by forming insoluble calcium phosphate); though the more obvious effects of seabird concentrations are mechanical damage and luxuriant growths of certain vigorously competitive plants.

Sea cliffs share with inland cliffs two important ecological effects, namely, that their steepness gives refuge to competition-sensitive plants which need an open, unstable substratum, and to species which cannot tolerate grazing by large herbivores. The vegetation of sea cliffs usually grades away from the sea into that of formations characteristic of uncultivated dry lowland habitats, i.e. into some form of grassland, heath, scrub or woodland. These submaritime or paramaritime examples of lowland formations form an essential part of the cliff habitat complex.

The pattern of vegetational variation on sea cliffs and slopes is determined primarily by degree of maritime influence and by variation in soil depth and moisture. Above the high spring tide level, usually characterised by a band of *Pelvetia canaliculata*, is a lichen-dominated zone with species such as *Ramalina scopulorum* and *Xanthoria parietina*. In crevices high in the lichen zone are the first individuals of a maritime crevice community characterised by widespread species such as *Armeria maritima*, *Plantago maritima*, *P. coronopus*, *Silene maritima* and *Festuca rubra*. In southern Britain, this open rock vegetation often includes *Crithmum maritimum*, *Inula crithmoides*, *Parapholis incurva*, *Spergularia rupicola* and *Limonium binervosum*, but these are replaced (with slight overlap) in Scotland by a northern element with *Ligusticum scoticum*, *Cochlearia scotica*, *Sedum rosea* and (in the far north) *Puccinellia capillaris*. The southern *Brassica oleracea* occurs on soft rocks such as chalk, whilst the halophytic moss *Grimmia maritima* is found mainly on the hard rocks of the north and west. *Cochlearia officinalis* grows in continually moist situations, especially on north aspects, *Glaux maritima* is mainly in waterlogged places on northern cliffs, and *Asplenium marinum* is a charac-

teristic crevice plant. Enrichment by bird excreta or algal debris is commonly marked by growths of *Lavatera arborea*, *Beta vulgaris* ssp. *maritima*, *Tripleurospermum maritimum* and *Atriplex hastata* agg.

Where conditions are favourable, a closed community develops above the zone of open rock vegetation. On ungrazed cliffs this is typically a mattress-like sward of *Festuca rubra*, with much *Armeria maritima*, *Silene maritima*, *Plantago maritima* and *Agrostis stolonifera*; in the south-west, *Daucus carota* ssp. *gummifer* is a characteristic associate.

Above this markedly spray-influenced zone, the influence of the bedrock begins to show. On steep, dry non-calcareous faces with only shallow pockets of soil, there is a characteristic maritime therophyte community with *Sedum anglicum*, (*S. acre* on more calcareous rocks), *Plantago coronopus*, *Armeria maritima*, *Festuca rubra*, *Cerastium atrovirens*, *Catapodium marinum*, *Aira praecox*, *A. caryophyllea*, *Anthyllis vulneraria*, *Cochlearia danica* and *Silene maritima*. More local species include *Jasione montana*, *Bromus ferronii*, *Spergularia rupicola*, *Umbilicus rupestris* and *Asplenium adiantum-nigrum*. With decreasing saline influence, species such as *Calluna vulgaris*, *Teucrium scorodonia* and *Hedera helix* appear, and there is often a transition to a closed, submaritime heath on the deeper soils of the exposed cliff top.

This submaritime heath is characterised by *Calluna vulgaris*, *Erica cinerea*, *Festuca ovina*, *Scilla verna*, *Hypochoeris radicata*, *Plantago maritima*, *Lotus corniculatus*, *Holcus lanatus*, *Anthyllis vulneraria* and *Thymus drucei*. Other less constant but typical species include *Salix repens*, *Potentilla erecta*, *Pedicularis sylvatica*, *Dactylorchis maculata* ssp. *ericetorum*, *Viola riviniana*, *Succisa pratensis*, *Anthoxanthum odoratum* and *Sieglingia decumbens*, and *Empetrum nigrum* is usually present in the north. Such heaths have a pH of 5.0–6.0 except over very acidic rocks, and often contain species more usually associated with calcareous habitats, e.g. *Polygala vulgaris*, *Filipendula vulgaris*, *Galium verum*, *Carex caryophyllea* and *Koeleria cristata*. Maritime species become progressively rarer with distance from the heavy spray zone, and this submaritime heath passes into the widespread *Calluna–Erica cinerea* type of lowland heath, or into the *Calluna–Ulex gallii* heath common in south-west England and Wales. On sheltered cliffs there may be a change from open rock communities direct to ordinary lowland heath. These dwarf-shrub communities in turn give way to other types: bracken stands, grassland, scrub or woodland.

Where non-calcareous cliffs have slopes and big ledges with deeper, moister soil, especially on north to east aspects, there is a characteristic herbaceous community with *Festuca rubra*, *Holcus lanatus*, *Dactylis glomerata*, *Armeria maritima*, *Cochlearia officinalis*, *Silene maritima*, *S. dioica*, *Rumex acetosa*, *Endymion non-scriptus*, *Heracleum sphondylium*, *Ranunculus ficaria*, *Primula vulgaris* and *Lotus corniculatus*. This community is especially a feature of western and northern Britain but, despite its obvious woodland affinities, evidence suggests that many of these sites have never borne woodland or even scrub. In north-west Scotland *Sedum rosea* is often present in this community. With decreasing influence of salt spray on non-calcareous rocks, these moist cliff slope soils change to mor humus with acidophilous woodland-type communities, often dominated by dense growth of *Luzula sylvatica*, but also with *Lonicera periclymenum, Rubus fruticosus, Calluna vulgaris, Polypodium vulgare, Blechnum spicant, Dryopteris dilatata, D. filix-mas, D. borreri, Athyrium filix-femina, Hedera helix* and *Chamaenerion angustifolium*. Ferns are usually well represented and in some west coast cliffs may include Atlantic species such as *D. aemula, Asplenium obovatum, Osmunda regalis, Hymenophyllum wilsonii* and *H. tunbrigense*.

Biotic influences, especially the manuring, treading, burrowing and grazing of birds and large mammals, can profoundly modify these closed cliff communities. Steep vegetated slopes are much used by nesting sea birds, sometimes in large concentrations (especially herring gulls and puffins) and their vegetation is often dominated by dense masses of *Cochlearia officinalis*, growing on a thick, rubbery layer of peaty soil; other abundant bird cliff and slope plant species are *Rumex acetosa, Stellaria media, Silene maritima, S. dioica, Holcus lanatus, Agrostis stolonifera, Poa annua, Anthoxanthum odoratum* and *Festuca rubra*. The vegetation of large seabird breeding colonies is nearly always much modified, limited in number of species and deficient in rare species, but has a considerable ecological interest. Where the cliff tops are grazed, the predominant vegetation in areas of high spray deposition such as St Kilda, many of the Atlantic cliffs of Scotland and the west coast of England and Wales, is a halophytic *Plantago* sward with a tight, close-grazed turf of *Plantago maritima, P. coronopus* and *P. lanceolata*, and an abundance of *Armeria maritima* and *Festuca rubra*. In northern Britain *P. maritima* is usually dominant and in the most waterlogged areas is accompanied by *Glaux maritima*. In southern Britain, *P. coronopus* is the dominant plantain and *P. maritima* is found chiefly in the wet areas on gleyed soils. Where cliff tops with moderately spray-influenced soils are heavily grazed by sheep, there is usually a grassland composed of species such as *Holcus lanatus, Festuca rubra, F. ovina, Anthoxanthum odoratum, Agrostis stolonifera, A. tenuis* and *Poa pratensis*. There may be an abundance of forbs such as *Leontodon autumnalis, Ranunculus acris* and *Trifolium repens*. Grassland of this kind, often showing a tussocky appearance, is well developed on many islands of the Scottish coast and is extensive on St Kilda. It is not necessarily associated with cliffs or steep ground, but is a submaritime community difficult to assign to one of the major habitats; there are certain affinities with grassland of mature salt marsh and damp machair in northern regions.

Where the rock is more basic, the cliff faces and slopes above the heavy spray zone have a greater variety of dwarf shrubs and herbs, with species such as *Anthyllis vulneraria, Achillea millefolium, Galium verum, Hieracium pilosella, Ononis repens, Helianthemum chamaecistus, Trifolium pratense, Pimpinella saxifraga, Carlina vulgaris, Daucus carota, Sedum acre, Verbascum thapsus, Geranium sanguineum, Gentianella campestris, Centaurea nigra, Centaurium erythraea, Chrysanthemum leucanthemum, Orchis mascula, Carex flacca, Dactylis glomerata, Brachypodium sylvaticum, Ar-*

rhenatherum elatius, Festuca arundinacea, F. gigantea and *Poa pratensis*. Where the slopes are sufficiently stable, these plants form a closed herb-dominated community on a fairly fertile brown loam, and there are obvious affinities with certain types of meadow grassland. On the cliff tops there is usually a forb-rich grassland more closely grazed, showing similarities to the species-rich grass heaths of more acidic soils, but with a larger proportion of basiphilous species.

On chalk and limestone the upper cliff faces and slopes support many of the species and communities which characterise these rock formations inland, and several coastal headlands are regarded as high quality examples of lowland calcareous grassland on rocky terrain, e.g. Tennyson Down and Compton Down, Isle of Wight (Chalk); Berry Head, Devon (Devonian limestone); Brean Down, Somerset; Gower coast, Glamorgan; Great Ormes Head, Caernarvonshire; and Humphrey Head, Lancashire (the last four are Carboniferous Limestone). The Avon Gorge, Gloucestershire, is best regarded as paramaritime. These calcareous coastal cliffs support a considerable number of rare and local plants, which are discussed more fully in the section on lowland calcareous grasslands; they include *Helianthemum apenninum, Koeleria vallesiana, Trinia glauca, Bupleurum baldense, Ononis reclinata, Draba aizoides, Cotoneaster integerrimus, Aster linosyris, Arabis stricta, Allium sphaerocephalon* and *Adiantum capillus-veneris*. These are paramaritime species confined to coastal stations in Britain, but the sea cliffs and their grasslands also support a number of rare calcicoles which occur inland, e.g. *Helianthemum canum, Veronica spicata* ssp. *hybrida, Cirsium tuberosum, Seseli libanotis, Ophrys fuciflora* and *O. sphegodes*. *Matthiola sinuata* and *M. incana* appear to be true maritime species of calcareous sea cliffs, but are both very rare.

With increasing shelter and soil moisture, these communities of base-rich sea cliffs gradually change to those characteristic of woodland mull soils, with a larger number of forbs, including *Angelica sylvestris, Primula vulgaris, Ajuga reptans, Valeriana officinalis, Filipendula ulmaria, Urtica dioica, Heracleum sphondylium, Geranium robertianum, Mercurialis perennis, Allium ursinum, Rubus fruticosus* and *Brachypodium sylvaticum*. Tall legumes such as *Vicia sylvatica, V. sepium, Lathyrus sylvestris* and *Astragalus glycyphyllos* are often represented, and contribute to the luxuriant, tangled state which the vegetation frequently shows. Basiphilous ferns are often in profusion, notably *Polystichum aculeatum, P. setiferum* and *Phyllitis scolopendrium*, and on wet, clayey soils there may be fragments of damp woodland communities, with *Equisetum telmateia, Eupatorium cannabinum, Carex sylvatica* and *C. pendula*.

Many sloping cliffs where the soil is too shallow or the exposure too great to allow tree growth have dense scrub, and this type of vegetation often occupies the crest of the cliff, where wind action is usually severe. Blackthorn is common, but there may be a good deal of hawthorn, hazel, elder, bramble and privet *Ligustrum vulgare*, with often a carpet of ivy *Hedera helix*. On western coasts, semi-prostrate forms of juniper often form a patchy fringe round cliff tops, and there may be a good deal of gorse and broom. Willows, especially *Salix cinerea*, are well represented in many damp places on cliffs, and *S. aurita* is common in Scotland.

Some cliff slopes and ledges support fragments of woodland, with the usual range of tree diversity according to soil type. Oak is usual on the acidic sites, along with variable amounts of birch, aspen and rowan; while ash and hazel are most prevalent on the more basic substrata. Although these cliff woodlands occur in relatively sheltered situations on exposed coasts they usually show severe wind pruning and dwarfing, or are restricted to places such as gullies. The tallest examples of cliff woodland are usually found on undercliffs (where shelter is greatest) as at Axmouth–Lyme Regis, Devon, and at Beast Cliff, near Whitby, Yorkshire. Good examples of west coast wind-pruned oakwood occur at Dizzard Point, Cornwall; Talbenny Woods, Pembrokeshire and on the steep coastal slopes north of Exmoor; in Scotland they are sometimes associated with raised beach and cliff systems, as on the Isle of Jura. Coastal ashwood is represented on a number of chalk and limestone areas on the south coast of England, the Gower peninsula and western Scotland, and hazel scrub is well developed on the basaltic cliff ranges of the coasts of Mull, Skye and Eigg, Inner Hebrides. The fragmentary cliff woods grade into more typical examples of woodland on seaward slopes; they are distinguished not so much by floristics *per se* as by the unusual forms of the trees and the general absence of grazing.

On western coasts, sea cliffs and their associated habitats are important stations for plants with an Atlantic distribution; some of the Atlantic flowering plants and ferns have already been mentioned, but they are greatly outnumbered by bryophytes and lichens. The moisture-loving species grow especially where the aspect is shaded, and tree growth, water seepage or stream gullies add to the diversity of conditions. Some cliffs and their caves associated with raised beaches are rich in these plants, and a cave of this type in Argyll provided the most northerly known locality for the rare frost-sensitive fern *Trichomanes speciosum*. By contrast, warmth-loving (as distinct from moisture-loving) Atlantic species grow in sun-exposed places, e.g. *Tuberaria guttata* and *Asparagus officinalis* ssp. *prostratus*. Mediterranean plants, e.g. *Scilla autumnalis* and *Brassica oleracea*, are also well represented on cliff habitats in southern England and Wales, often in sun-exposed situations.

On the serpentine and hornblende–schist of the Lizard, non-calcareous but base-rich soils on steep and rocky slopes by the sea have grasslands with an assemblage of Mediterranean and other southern European species unique in Britain, e.g. *Trifolium strictum*, *T. bocconei*, *T. incarnatum* ssp. *molinerii*, *Isoetes histrix* and *Herniaria ciliolata*. *Minuartia verna* is characteristic of the serpentine cliffs, whilst *T. occidentale* is plentiful, but found in such quantity elsewhere only at Land's End. These communities pass above into a varied complex of heath distinguished by great abundance of *Erica vagans* and *Schoenus nigricans*, and with a range of wet to intermittently wet habitats. The whole of this extremely interesting complex is described in detail in Chapter 6.

On the coasts of the northern and western Highlands, the open rocks of steep cliffs support a variety of montane species, especially where the rock is basic or influenced by blown shell sand. *Silene acaulis* is probably the commonest of these, but locally there are *Saxifraga oppositifolia*, *S. aizoides*, *Dryas octopetala*, *Thalictrum alpinum* and *Polygonum viviparum*. The northern *Oxytropis halleri* has more coastal than mountain stations in Britain, and grows in sand as well as on rocks, whilst *Primula scotica* occurs locally in submaritime cliff top swards. *Sedum rosea* grows abundantly and luxuriantly on many northern sea cliffs, and other species of damp, ungrazed mountain rock ledges, such as *Oxyria digyna* and *Saussurea alpina*, occur in places.

A large number of other species, of widely varying abundance and ecological/phytogeographical affinities, find a niche in sea cliffs and related habitats. These situations are also often the site of establishment of aliens, such as *Smyrnium olusatrum*, *Foeniculum vulgare*, *Allium triquetrum*, *Centranthus ruber* and *Carpobrotus edulis*, especially near sites of human habitation. A final noteworthy feature of sea cliff vegetation is that many species occur as dwarf ecotypes which remain small in cultivation, e.g. *Sarothamnus scoparius*, *Betonica officinalis*, *Serratula tinctoria*, *Chrysanthemum leucanthemum*, *Succisa pratensis* and *Genista tinctoria*.

COASTAL LAGOONS

These are shallow water bodies (generally less than 2 m deep) associated with the other classes of coastland habitat, varying from regularly tidal types (e.g. The Fleet in Dorset) to almost fresh water. The most typical coastal lagoons have formed behind sand or shingle deposits as at Slapton Ley, Devon, and the Loch of Strathbeg, Aberdeenshire. The lagoon of Little Sea at Studland, Dorset, was flooded at high tide in the eighteenth century but has since been sealed off from the sea by natural processes of marine deposition. In a few places, as at Minsmere and Walberswick on the Suffolk coast, lagoons have formed within the last 30 years as a result of valley flooding behind developing beaches. Other examples of coastal lagoons are the machair lochs of the Outer Hebrides, where shallow lochs have formed on the inner zones of these areas of blown sand. Large and permanent dune slacks with standing water, the pans of salt marshes and artificially sealed-off fleets of embanked former salt marshes in the south-east also qualify for inclusion within this category. On the whole, however, large lagoons are a relatively uncommon type of coastal feature.

The underlying bottom deposits of coastal lagoons vary, and range from peat at Benacre Broad, Suffolk; silt at Minsmere, Suffolk; sand in the Hebridean machair lochs; and shingle in the Oppen pits at Dungeness, Kent. Subsequently, the quiet waters invariably favour deposition of fine-grained material, i.e. clay or silt, as a superficial bottom layer in which submerged or emergent vegetation is rooted. This plant growth also adds a good deal of organic matter to the basal mud, which may become rather peaty at the surface. Superimposed on this general feature are directions of variation according to frequency and degree of tidal influence (affecting salinity), other variations in water chemistry according to nature of the substratum and water supply, and geographical location (i.e. climate). Incidence of grazing also affects the nature of the marginal vegetation.

A full description of the hydroseral sequence of vegetation in coastal lagoons belongs more properly to Chapter 7, and the present account is limited to those features which are especially associated with some degree of brackish influence. The planktonic and benthic micro-organisms have not been studied sufficiently for communities to be described, but they are known to be highly variable through the range of coastal lagoons in Britain.

Halophytic open water communities of *Zostera angustifolia*, *Z. noltii* and *Z. marina* are best represented in the fully tidal lagoon of The Fleet, Dorset. Brackish open water communities include growths of *Ruppia maritima*, *Zannichellia palustris*, *Myriophyllum alterniflorum*, *M. spicatum*, *Ceratophyllum demersum*, *Potamogeton pectinatus* and *Littorella uniflora* beneath the surface, while *Ranunculus baudotii* is a characteristic floating species, and there may be an abundance of *Polygonum amphibium*, *Menyanthes trifoliata* and *Nuphar lutea*. Emergent reed-swamp vegetation in deeper open water typically contains an abundance of *Phragmites communis* (often in large pure stands), *Scirpus maritimus* and *Schoenoplectus tabernaemontani*. Shallower water around the lagoon edge often has growths of *Eleocharis palustris*, *E. uniglumis*, *Iris pseudacorus*, *Sparganium erectum*, *Carex otrubae*, *C. acutiformis*, *C. acuta*, *C. distans*, *Schoenus nigricans*, *Glyceria maxima*, *G. fluitans*, *Ranunculus sceleratus*, *Oenanthe crocata*, *O. lachenalii* and *Samolus valerandi*. This mixed swamp may show invasion by species of willow, especially *Salix cinerea*, and alder, with progression towards a fringing carr woodland.

Regional variations in the floristics of this vegetational sequence rest mainly on the presence or absence of local brackish water species such as *Althaea officinalis*, *Carex divisa*, *Ruppia spiralis*, *Apium graveolens*, *Cyperus longus* and *Corrigiola litoralis* (very rare) in the south, and *Blysmus rufus*, *Potamogeton filiformis* and *Najas flexilis* in the north. Variations in distribution of freshwater species also add to this regional pattern.

Flora

The flora of coastlands consists ecologically of a mixture of species which appear to require saline soils (halophytes), others with an obvious preference for coastal conditions, and a third group of widespread species which include a coastal niche in their range of habitats. The number of species in the third group is very large, for a wide variety of non-saline (or only slightly saline) habitats is represented in coastal situations. Woodland, grassland, heathland and wetland habitats are all represented on the coast and show various transitions to the truly maritime habitats. Sand dunes often have a particularly rich flora, ranging from calcareous grassland to alkaline fen (in slacks) where the sand is rich in lime, and to acidic grassland/heath and poor-fen where the sand is non-calcareous. Sand-loving species of inland habitats flourish on dune systems, and many plants

which are sensitive to disturbance (e.g. grazing) find a niche on steep slopes and cliffs beside the sea.

An attempt is made to indicate the ecological range of each coastal species; four main classes of habitat (shingle, sandy shore and dunes, cliffs and related features, and salt marsh) are recognised in Table 1 (p. 38), plus a fifth, which comprises an ill-defined group of paramaritime grassy or heathy communities of waste ground, verges, banks and even fields, often on sandy soils. In addition, special preference for brackish and/or wet conditions is indicated. Relatively few species in Table 1 are highly specialised in their habitat requirements, and there is wide overlap between flora of the different habitats. Some species find their optimum in one habitat, and a few belong mainly to transition zones between two habitats. Species especially characteristic of open cliff faces are distinguished from those which occur in the more or less closed communities of large ledges, cliff slopes and summits. The most difficult to classify are species which belong to a rather nondescript range of lowland habitats lying close to the sea geographically but evidently little influenced by salt water.

Nearly all native species which have a coastal distribution in Britain are included in Table 1, regardless of whether they show this pattern on the continent, but only widespread species especially characteristic of markedly maritime communities are included. Many species have already been mentioned under their appropriate maritime habitat, and the following discussion of the coastal flora will concentrate on climatic and phytogeographical aspects.

Southern elements are much more strongly represented than northern elements, so that the British maritime flora decreases markedly in richness (i.e. number of species) from south to north. A good many species are widespread, occurring fairly evenly around the whole coastline, but some are limited by the availability of their particular habitat e.g. *Asplenium marinum* is absent from the eastern coast of England where there are no cliffs.

A strongly northern group of strictly maritime plants includes *Mertensia maritima*, *Cochlearia scotica*, *Ligusticum scoticum*, *Blysmus rufus*, *Carex maritima* and *C. recta*, and the northern species *Primula scotica*, *Centaurium littorale*, *Potamogeton filiformis* and *Juncus balticus* are best regarded as paramaritime, while the fern *Cystopteris dickieana* is known in Britain only in a sea cave in Kincardineshire. A group of montane species descends to coastal habitats such as sea cliffs and sand dunes in the west and north of Scotland, since the cool oceanic climate gives summer temperatures which are not too high for these plants, and excessive windiness restricts or prevents tree growth and helps to maintain bare, tree-less habitats on the exposed coasts. Montane species abundant close to or at sea-level in northern and western Scotland include *Dryas octopetala*, *Arctostaphylos uva-ursi*, *Saxifraga oppositifolia*, *S. aizoides*, *Silene acaulis*, *Sedum rosea*, *Oxyria digyna* and *Oxytropis halleri*; a few of these also occur on the east coast of Scotland. Many more species, although not reaching sea-level, occur within paramaritime habitats at much lower elevations in the far north than at their lowest limits in the central Highlands, e.g. *Salix herbacea*, *Arctous alpinus*, *Loiseleuria procumbens* and *Vaccinium uliginosum*. In addition, *Equisetum variegatum* and certain mosses (e.g. *Catoscopium nigritum*) which otherwise have a northern and montane distribution occur much farther south in calcareous dune slacks.

A group of generally southern maritime plants is spread through England and Wales, and many of its species reach southern parts of Scotland; this group includes *Inula crithmoides*, *Crithmum maritimum*, *Spergularia rupicola*, *Limonium binervosum*, *L. humile*, *Eryngium maritimum*, *Halimione portulacoides*, *Crambe maritima*, *Glaucium flavum*, *Euphorbia portlandica*, *E. paralias*, *Artemisia maritima*, *Calystegia soldanella*, *Beta vulgaris* ssp. *maritima*, *Ruppia spiralis*, *Carex punctata*, *Parapholis strigosa*, *Puccinellia rupestris*, *Agropyron pungens* and *Hordeum marinum*. Paramaritime species of similar distribution include *Erodium maritimum*, *Lepidium latifolium*, *Bupleurum tenuissimum*, *Parentucellia viscosa*, *Carex divisa*, *Vulpia membranacea* and *Isolepis cernua*. Another group is still more markedly southern, with few or no localities north of north Wales, and shows no strong bias towards either the east or west coasts; it includes *Brassica oleracea*, *Matthiola incana*, *Althaea officinalis*, *Geranium purpureum*, *Medicago polymorpha*, *Trifolium squamosum*, *Orobanche maritima*, *Otanthus maritimus* (formerly), *Juncus acutus*, *Cyperus longus*, *Festuca juncifolia*, *Puccinellia fasciculata*, *Parapholis incurva*, *Spartina maritima* and *S. alterniflora*. Paramaritime species of comparable distribution are *Erodium moschatum*, *Trifolium ornithopodioides*, *T. glomeratum*, *T. subterraneum*, *T. suffocatum*, *Scilla autumnalis*, *Bupleurum baldense*, *Orobanche hederae*, *O. purpurea*, *Vulpia ambigua* and *Poa bulbosa*.

A few species have a markedly south-eastern distribution in England, i.e. from the Wash to the Isle of Wight. This group includes *Frankenia laevis*, *Suaeda fruticosa*, *Limonium bellidifolium*, *Chenopodium botryodes* and *Peucedanum officinale*. By contrast, many more species are confined to south-western Britain, i.e. within the coastal belt from north Wales to the Isle of Wight. The strictly maritime species with this distribution are *Lavatera arborea*, *Polygonum maritimum*, *Rumex rupestris*, *Asparagus officinalis* ssp. *prostratus*, *Rhynchosinapis wrightii* and *Matthiola sinuata*. The still larger group of south-western paramaritime species includes *Lotus hispidus*, *L. angustissimus*, *Corrigiola litoralis*, *Centaurium tenuiflorum*, *Juncus capitatus*, *Eleocharis parvula*, *Polycarpon tetraphyllum*, *Herniaria ciliolata*, *Viola kitaibeliana*, *Helianthemum apenninum*, *Ononis reclinata*, *Trifolium strictum*, *T. incarnatum* ssp. *molinerii*, *T. bocconei*, *Aster linosyris*, *Trinia glauca*, *Rubia peregrina*, *Centaurium scilloides*, *Gentianella uliginosa*, *Echium lycopsis*, *Scrophularia scorodonia*, *Senecio integrifolius* var. *maritimus*, *Tuberaria guttata*, *Limosella subulata*, *Allium babingtonii*, *A. triquetrum*, *Romulea columnae*, *Koeleria vallesiana*, *Mibora minima*, *Isoetes histrix* and *Adiantum capillus-veneris*.

Many south-western species have a Mediterranean or oceanic southern distribution pattern in Europe as a whole, and their restriction to this part of Britain is explicable in terms of their need for an equable temperature regime with freedom from frost. The warm oceanic conditions of the south-western seaboard are particularly suited to the needs of species such as *Adiantum capillus-veneris*. Some paramaritime south-western species may well be associated largely with the coast in Britain because of their temperature requirements. A number of oceanic species which are fairly widespread inland in more southerly districts become increasingly restricted to coastal stations with distance north, e.g. *Dryopteris aemula*, *Asplenium obovatum*, *Polystichum setiferum*, *Phyllitis scolopendrium*, *Hymenophyllum tunbrigense*, *Equisetum telmateia*, *Sedum anglicum*, *Umbilicus rupestris*, *Hypericum androsaemum*, *H. elodes* and *Scutellaria minor*. This again indicates the thermo-stabilising effect of the sea in providing suitable conditions for plants beyond their general climatic limits. Proximity to the sea also gives relatively humid atmospheric conditions which some species need in addition to mildness of climate, and this combined temperature/humidity effect probably accounts for the occurrence of many Atlantic bryophytes and lichens along the coast of south-western Britain.

Some of the southern and south-western maritime and paramaritime species are rarities with a highly disjunct distribution. In the case of several calcicoles (e.g. *Helianthemum apenninum*, *Ononis reclinata*, *Trinia glauca*, *Aster linosyris*, *Bupleurum baldense* and *Koeleria vallesiana*) the association with the sea may be largely accidental, depending on the chance that in Britain these species have happened to find their required type of edaphic habitat (open, calcareous soils) only on scattered limestone headlands by the sea. The restriction of *Isoetes histrix*, *Trifolium strictum*, *T. incarnatum* ssp. *molinerii* and *T. bocconei* to a very few stations, mainly on the Lizard, may reflect a special combination of edaphic/climatic conditions, but the occurrence of *Tuberaria guttata* and *Senecio integrifolius* var. *maritimus* only in north Wales is likely to be a distributional accident.

A few maritime plants have distribution patterns which do not really fit any of those described. *Scilla verna* is a widespread western species whereas *Rhynchosinapis monesis* has a restricted western distribution between Wales and southern Scotland. *Vicia lutea* and *Corynephorus canescens* both have widely scattered and disjunct distributions.

Some coastal species have decreased greatly during the present century, especially on unstable habitats such as open sand and shingle. *Otanthus maritimus* is perhaps the most striking example, but *Matthiola sinuata*, *Polycarpon tetraphyllum*, *Polygonum maritimum*, *Vicia lutea*, *Lathyrus japonicus*, *Zostera marina*, *Ruppia spiralis*, *Asparagus officinalis* ssp. *prostratus*, *Juncus capitatus*, *Carex divisa*, *Puccinellia rupestris*, *Poa bulbosa*, *Hordeum marinum*, *Castridium ventricosum*, *Alopecurus bulbosus* and *Spartina maritima* all appear to have declined substantially. The northern species *Mertensia maritima* and *Blysmus rufus* have also decreased, but mainly in the southern part of their range. By contrast, the spontaneous polyploid hybrid *Spartina anglica* has spread enormously through Britain since its origin on Southampton Water around 1870, and in many places has become a dominant competitor with native salt marsh plants.

A few maritime plant species occur inland in Britain

Table 1. *Vascular plants of coastlands*

	Shingle	Sand dune & sandy shore	Cliffs & cliff grasslands or heaths	Salt marsh & estuarine grassland	Other habitats	Halophyte	Submaritime	Coastal niche	S.E. England	S.W. England	East Anglia	S. Wales	N. Wales	N. England	S. Scotland	W. Highlands	E. Highlands	Rare species	European distribution
	1	2	3	4	5	6	7	8	9	10	11	12	13	14	15	16	17	18	19
Isoetes histrix	—	—	—	—	L	—	+	—	+	—	—	—	—	—	—	—	—	+	—
Asplenium marinum	—	—	R	—	—	—	+	—	+	+	—	+	+	+	+	+	+	—	—
Adiantum capillus-veneris	—	—	R	—	—	—	+	—	+	+	—	+	—	+	—	—	—	—	—
Cystopteris dickieana	—	—	R	—	—	—	+	—	—	—	—	—	—	—	—	—	+	+	—
Ranunculus baudotii	—	—	—	—	W	—	B	—	+	+	+	+	+	+	+	+	+	—	OS
Thalictrum minus	—	+	R	—	—	—	—	+	—	+	+	+	+	+	+	+	+	—	—
Glaucium flavum	+	+	+	—	—	+	—	—	+	+	+	+	+	+	+	+	[+]	—	CS
Fumaria capreolata	—	—	+	—	U	—	+	—	+	+	+	+	+	+	+	+	+	—	—
Brassica oleracea	—	—	R	—	—	+	—	—	+	+	—	+	+	—	—	—	—	—	OW
Rhynchosinapis monensis	+	+	—	—	—	+	—	—	—	—	—	+	—	+	+	—	—	+	OW
R. wrightii	—	—	R	—	—	+	—	—	—	+	—	—	—	—	—	—	—	+	—
Raphanus maritimus	+	+	+	—	—	+	—	—	+	+	+	+	+	+	+	+	—	—	OW
Crambe maritima	+	+	R	—	—	+	—	—	+	+	+	+	+	+	+	—	—	—	OW
Cakile maritima	+	+	—	—	—	+	—	—	+	+	+	+	+	+	+	+	+	—	—
Draba aizoides	—	—	R	—	—	—	+	—	—	+	—	+	—	—	—	—	—	+	A
Lepidium latifolium	—	+	—	—	—	—	+	—	+	+	+	+	—	+	—	—	—	—	—
Cochlearia officinalis	—	—	+	+	—	+	—	—	+	+	+	+	+	+	+	+	+	—	ON
C. danica	—	+	+	+	—	+	—	—	+	+	+	+	+	+	+	+	+	—	ON
C. anglica	—	+	+	+	—	+	—	—	+	+	+	+	+	+	+	+	+	—	ON
C. scotica	+	+	+	—	—	+	—	—	—	—	—	—	—	+	+	+	+	—	—
Matthiola incana	—	—	R	—	—	+	—	—	+	+	—	—	—	—	—	—	—	+	M
M. sinuata	—	+	R	—	—	+	—	—	—	+	—	+	+	—	—	—	—	+	M
Viola tricolor ssp. *curtisii*	—	+	—	—	—	—	+	—	+	+	+	+	+	+	+	+	—	—	—
V. kitaibeliana	—	+	—	—	—	—	+	—	—	+	—	+	—	—	—	—	—	—	—
Helianthemum apenninum	—	—	R	—	—	—	+	—	—	+	—	—	—	—	—	—	—	+	OS
Tuberaria guttata	—	—	+	—	—	—	+	—	—	+	—	+	+	—	+	—	—	+	OS
Tamarix gallica	+	+	—	—	—	—	+	—	+	+	+	+	+	+	—	—	—	—	—
Frankenia laevis	+	+	+	+	—	+	—	—	+	+	+	+	—	—	—	—	—	—	M
Silene maritima	+	+	+	—	—	+	—	—	+	+	+	+	+	+	+	+	+	—	ON
Cerastium atrovirens	—	+	+	—	U	—	+	—	+	+	+	+	+	+	+	+	+	—	OW
Sagina maritima	+	+	+	+	—	+	—	—	+	+	+	+	+	+	+	+	+	—	OS
Honkenya peploides	+	+	—	—	—	+	—	—	+	+	+	+	+	+	+	+	+	—	OS
Spergularia rupicola	—	—	R	—	—	+	—	—	+	+	—	+	+	+	+	+	—	—	OW
S. media	—	—	—	+	—	+	—	—	+	+	+	+	+	+	+	+	+	—	—
S. marina	—	—	—	+	—	+	—	—	+	+	+	+	+	+	+	+	+	—	—
Corrigiola litoralis	—	—	—	—	W	—	B	—	—	+	—	—	—	—	—	—	—	+	CS
Polycarpon tetraphyllum	—	+	—	—	—	—	+	—	—	+	—	—	—	—	—	—	—	+	CS
Herniaria ciliolata	—	—	—	—	L	—	+	—	—	+	—	—	—	—	—	—	—	+	OW
Chenopodium botryodes	—	—	—	—	—	+	—	—	+	—	+	—	—	—	—	—	—	+	OW
Beta vulgaris ssp. *maritima*	+	—	+	—	—	+	—	—	+	+	+	+	+	+	+	+	+	—	OS
Atriplex littoralis	—	—	—	+	—	+	—	—	+	+	+	+	+	+	+	+	+	—	—
A. hastata	+	+	—	+	U	—	+	—	+	+	+	+	+	+	+	+	+	—	—
A. glabriuscula	+	+	—	+	—	+	—	—	+	+	+	+	+	+	+	+	+	—	ON
A. patula	+	+	—	—	U	—	+	—	+	+	+	+	+	+	+	+	+	—	—
A. laciniata	+	+	—	—	—	+	—	—	+	+	+	+	+	+	+	+	+	—	—
Halimione portulacoides	+	—	+	+	—	+	—	—	+	+	+	+	+	+	+	—	—	—	OS

Table 1 (contd.)

	1	2	3	4	5	6	7	8	9	10	11	12	13	14	15	16	17	18	19
Suaeda maritima	+	+	—	+	—	+	—	—	+	+	+	+	+	+	+	+	+	—	—
S. fruticosa	+	—	—	+	—	+	—	—	+	+	+	—	—	—	—	—	—	—	M
Salsola kali	+	+	—	—	—	+	—	—	+	+	+	+	+	+	+	+	+	—	—
Salicornia perennis	—	—	—	+	—	+	—	—	+	—	+	—	+	—	+	+	+	—	OW
S. dolichostachya	—	—	—	+	—	+	—	—	+	+	+	+	+	+	+	+	+	—	OW
S. pusilla	—	—	—	+	—	+	—	—	+	+	+	+	+	—	—	—	—	—	—
Lavatera arborea	—	—	R	—	—	+	—	—	+	—	+	—	+	+	+	—	—	—	M
Althaea officinalis	—	—	—	+	—	—	B	—	+	+	+	+	—	+	—	—	—	—	CS
Geranium sanguineum	—	+	+	—	U	—	—	+	—	+	—	+	+	+	+	+	+	—	—
G. purpureum	+	—	—	—	+	—	—	—	+	—	+	—	—	—	—	—	—	+	M
Erodium maritimum	—	+	+	—	—	—	+	—	+	+	+	—	+	+	+	—	—	—	OW
E. moschatum	—	+	+	—	—	—	+	—	+	+	+	—	+	+	+	—	—	—	CS
E. cicutarium	—	+	+	—	U	—	+	+	+	+	+	+	+	+	+	+	+	—	—
Medicago polymorpha	—	+	—	—	U	—	+	—	+	+	—	—	—	—	—	—	—	—	—
Trifolium squamosum	—	—	—	+	—	+	—	—	+	+	+	+	—	—	—	—	—	—	OS
T. ornithopodioides	—	—	+	—	U	—	+	—	+	+	+	+	—	—	—	—	—	—	OS
T. striatum	—	+	—	—	U	—	—	+	+	+	+	+	+	+	+	—	+	—	—
T. strictum	—	—	+	—	—	—	+	—	—	—	—	—	—	—	—	—	—	+	OS
T. incarnatum ssp. *molinerii*	—	—	+	—	—	—	+	—	—	—	—	—	—	—	—	—	—	+	OS
T. scabrum	+	+	—	—	U	—	—	+	+	+	+	+	+	+	+	—	+	—	CS
T. bocconei	—	—	+	—	—	—	+	—	—	—	—	—	—	—	—	—	—	+	OS
T. subterraneum	—	+	—	—	U	—	—	+	+	+	+	+	+	—	—	—	—	—	OS
T. glomeratum	—	+	—	—	U	—	+	—	+	+	+	+	—	—	+	—	—	—	OS
T. suffocatum	—	+	—	—	U	—	+	—	+	+	+	—	—	+	—	—	—	—	OS
T. occidentale	—	+	—	—	—	—	+	—	—	—	—	—	—	—	—	—	+	—	—
Ononis reclinata	—	+	—	—	—	—	+	—	—	—	+	—	—	[+]	—	—	+	—	OS
Anthyllis vulneraria	—	+	+	—	U	—	—	+	+	+	+	+	+	+	+	+	—	—	—
Lotus hispidus	—	—	—	—	U	—	+	—	+	+	—	+	—	—	—	—	—	—	OS
L. angustissimus	—	—	—	—	U	—	+	—	+	+	+	—	+	—	—	—	+	—	OS
Astragalus danicus	—	+	+	—	—	—	—	+	—	+	—	+	+	+	+	—	—	—	—
Oxytropis halleri	—	+	R	—	—	—	+	—	—	—	—	—	[+]	+	+	+	—	—	—
Vicia lutea	+	—	+	—	—	+	—	—	+	+	+	—	+	+	—	+	+	—	CS
V. lathyroides	—	+	+	—	U	—	—	+	+	+	+	+	+	+	+	—	—	—	—
V. bithynica	—	—	+	—	U	—	+	—	+	+	+	—	+	+	—	—	—	—	OS
Lathyrus japonicus	+	+	—	—	—	+	—	—	+	+	+	—	—	—	—	+	—	—	ON
L. sylvestris	—	—	+	—	U	—	—	+	+	+	+	+	+	+	+	—	—	—	—
Rosa pimpinellifolia	+	+	+	—	—	—	+	—	+	+	+	+	+	+	+	+	—	—	—
Sedum rosea	—	—	+	—	—	—	+	—	—	+	—	+	+	+	+	—	—	—	AA
S. anglicum	+	+	R	—	—	+	—	+	+	+	+	+	+	+	+	+	—	—	OW
S. acre	+	+	+	—	U	—	+	—	+	+	+	+	+	+	+	+	—	—	—
Hippophäe rhamnoides	+	—	+	—	—	—	+	—	+	+	+	+	+	+	+	+	—	—	—
Eryngium maritimum	+	+	—	—	—	+	—	—	+	+	+	+	+	+	+	[+]	—	—	OS
Smyrnium olusatrum	—	—	+	—	U	—	+	—	+	+	+	+	+	+	+	+	—	—	CS
Bupleurum baldense	—	+	+	—	—	—	+	—	+	—	—	—	—	—	—	—	—	+	OS
B. tenuissimum	—	—	—	+	—	+	—	+	+	+	+	—	—	—	—	—	—	—	—
Trinia glauca	—	—	+	—	—	—	+	—	+	—	+	—	—	—	—	—	—	+	CS
Apium graveolens	—	—	—	+	U	—	B	—	+	+	+	+	+	+	+	—	—	—	—
Crithmum maritimum	+	—	R	—	—	+	—	—	+	+	+	+	+	+	+	—	—	—	OS
Oenanthe lachenalii	—	—	+	—	—	—	B	—	+	+	+	+	+	+	+	—	—	—	CS
Foeniculum vulgare	—	—	+	—	—	—	+	—	+	+	+	+	+	+	—	+	—	—	CS
Ligusticum scoticum	—	—	+	—	—	+	—	—	—	—	—	+	+	+	+	—	—	—	AS
Peucedanum officinale	—	—	+	—	U	—	+	—	+	—	+	—	—	—	—	+	—	—	—
Daucus carota	—	+	+	—	U	—	—	+	+	+	+	+	+	+	+	+	—	—	—
D. carota ssp. *gummifer*	—	+	+	—	—	—	+	—	+	—	+	+	+	+	—	—	—	—	OS
Euphorbia portlandica	—	+	+	—	—	—	+	—	+	—	+	+	+	+	—	—	—	—	OW
E. paralias	—	+	—	—	—	—	+	—	+	+	+	+	+	+	—	—	—	—	OS
Polygonum raii	+	+	—	—	—	—	+	—	+	—	+	+	+	+	+	—	—	—	OS
P. maritimum	+	+	—	—	—	—	+	—	—	—	—	—	—	—	—	—	—	+	M
Rumex crispus	+	—	—	+	U	—	—	+	+	+	+	+	+	+	+	+	—	—	—
R. rupestris	+	+	+	—	—	+	—	—	+	+	+	—	—	—	—	+	—	—	—
R. acetosa	—	—	+	+	U	—	—	+	+	+	+	+	+	+	+	+	—	—	—

Table 1 (contd.)

	1	2	3	4	5	6	7	8	9	10	11	12	13	14	15	16	17	18	19
Salix repens	—	+	+	—	—	—	—	+	+	+	+	+	+	+	+	+	+	—	—
Limonium vulgare	—	—	—	+	—	+	—	—	+	+	+	+	+	+	+	+	—	—	OS
L. humile	—	—	—	+	—	+	—	—	+	+	+	+	+	+	+	—	—	—	ON
L. bellidifolium	+	—	—	+	—	+	—	—	—	—	+	—	—	—	—	—	—	+	M
L. binervosum	+	—	R	+	—	+	—	—	+	+	+	+	+	+	—	—	—	—	OW
Armeria maritima	+	—	+	+	—	+	—	—	+	+	+	+	+	+	+	+	+	+	ON
Primula scotica	—	—	+	+	—	—	+	—	+	+	+	+	+	+	+	+	+	—	—
Anagallis minima	—	+	—	—	U	—	—	+	+	+	+	+	+	+	+	+	+	+	—
Glaux maritima	+	—	+	+	—	+	—	—	+	+	+	+	+	+	+	+	+	—	—
Samolus valerandi	—	+	+	+	—	—	—	—	+	+	+	+	+	+	+	+	+	+	—
Centaurium tenuiflorum	—	—	—	—	U	—	+	—	—	+	—	—	—	—	—	—	—	+	OS
C. scilloides	—	—	+	—	—	—	+	—	—	+	—	+	—	—	—	—	—	+	—
C. capitatum	—	—	—	—	U	—	+	—	—	+	—	+	+	+	—	—	—	—	ON
C. pulchellum	—	+	+	+	U	—	+	—	+	+	+	+	+	+	—	—	—	—	—
C. littorale	—	+	—	+	—	+	—	—	—	+	—	+	+	+	+	+	+	—	ON
Mertensia maritima	+	+	—	—	—	+	—	—	—	—	[+]	—	[+]	+	+	+	+	—	AS
Echium lycopsis	—	+	+	—	—	—	+	—	—	+	—	—	—	—	—	—	—	+	M
Calystegia soldanella	+	—	—	—	+	—	—	—	+	+	+	+	+	+	+	+	+	—	—
Solanum dulcamara	+	—	—	+	—	—	—	+	+	+	+	+	+	+	+	+	+	—	—
Parentucellia viscosa	—	—	—	—	U	—	+	—	+	+	+	—	—	+	—	—	—	—	OS
Orobanche purpurea	—	—	+	—	—	—	+	—	—	+	—	+	—	—	—	—	—	+	CS
O. alba	—	—	+	—	—	—	+	—	—	+	—	—	+	+	+	—	—	—	CS
O. caryophyllacea	—	—	—	—	U	—	+	—	—	+	—	—	—	—	—	—	—	+	CS
O. hederae	—	—	+	—	U	—	+	—	—	+	—	+	—	—	—	—	—	—	OS
O. maritima	—	+	+	—	—	—	+	—	+	+	—	+	—	—	—	—	—	+	OS
Lamium molucellifolium	—	—	—	—	U	—	—	+	—	—	—	—	—	+	+	+	+	—	—
Plantago maritima	+	+	+	+	—	+	—	—	+	+	+	+	+	+	+	+	+	—	—
P. coronopus	—	+	+	+	U	—	+	—	+	+	+	+	+	+	+	+	+	+	CS
Rubia peregrina	—	—	+	—	—	—	+	—	+	+	—	+	+	—	—	—	—	—	OS
Senecio integrifolius var. *maritimus*	—	—	+	—	—	—	+	—	—	—	—	+	—	—	—	—	—	+	—
Inula crithmoides	+	—	R	+	—	+	—	—	+	+	+	+	+	+	—	+	—	—	—
Aster tripolium	—	—	+	+	—	+	—	—	+	+	+	+	+	+	+	+	+	—	—
A. linosyris	—	—	R	—	—	—	+	—	+	—	+	+	+	—	—	—	—	+	CS
Otanthus maritimus	+	—	R	—	—	+	—	—	[+]	[+]	[+]	—	—	—	—	—	—	+	M
Tripleurospermum maritimum	+	—	+	+	U	—	—	+	+	+	+	+	+	+	+	+	+	—	—
Artemisia maritima	+	—	+	+	—	+	—	—	+	+	+	+	+	+	+	—	+	—	ON
Carduus tenuiflorus	—	+	+	—	U	—	+	—	+	+	+	+	+	+	+	—	+	—	OS
C. pycnocephalus	—	—	?	—	—	—	+	—	—	—	—	—	—	—	—	—	—	—	—
Taraxacum laevigatum	—	+	+	—	—	—	+	—	+	+	+	+	+	+	+	+	+	—	—
Triglochin maritima	—	—	—	+	—	+	—	—	+	+	+	+	+	+	+	+	+	—	—
Zostera angustifolia	—	—	—	—	W	+	—	—	+	+	+	+	+	+	—	—	—	—	ON
Z. marina	—	—	—	—	W	+	—	+	+	+	+	+	+	+	+	+	—	—	—
Z. noltii	—	—	—	—	W	+	—	+	+	+	+	+	+	+	+	+	—	—	—
Potamogeton pectinatus	—	—	—	—	W	—	B	+	+	+	+	+	+	+	+	+	—	—	—
P. filiformis	—	—	—	—	W	—	B	+	—	+	+	—	+	—	+	+	+	—	CN
Zannichellia palustris	—	—	—	—	W	—	B	+	+	+	+	+	+	+	+	+	—	—	—
Ruppia spiralis	—	—	—	—	W	—	B	—	+	+	+	+	+	+	—	—	—	+	—
R. maritima	—	—	—	—	W	—	B	—	+	+	+	+	+	+	+	—	—	—	—
Asparagus officinalis ssp. *prostratus*	—	—	R	—	—	—	+	—	+	—	+	—	+	—	—	—	—	+	OW
Scilla verna	—	—	+	—	—	+	—	—	+	+	+	+	+	+	+	+	—	—	OW
S. autumnalis	—	—	+	—	—	—	+	—	+	+	+	—	—	—	—	—	—	—	OS
Allium babingtonii	—	—	—	—	U	—	—	—	—	+	—	—	—	—	—	—	—	+	—
Juncus gerardii	—	—	—	+	—	+	—	—	+	+	+	+	+	+	+	+	+	—	—
J. balticus	—	+	—	—	—	+	—	—	+	+	+	+	—	+	—	+	+	—	ON
J. maritimus	—	—	—	+	—	+	—	—	+	+	+	+	+	+	+	+	+	—	—
J. acutus	—	+	—	+	—	+	—	—	+	+	+	+	+	—	—	—	—	—	OS
J. capitatus	—	—	—	—	L	—	+	—	—	+	—	—	+	—	—	—	—	+	OS
Romulea columnae	—	+	—	—	—	—	+	—	—	+	—	—	—	—	—	—	—	+	OS
Epipactis dunensis	—	+	—	—	—	+	—	+	—	—	—	—	+	+	+	+	+	+	—
Scirpus maritimus	—	—	—	+	—	+	B	—	+	+	+	+	+	+	+	+	+	—	—

Table 1 (*contd.*)

	1	2	3	4	5	6	7	8	9	10	11	12	13	14	15	16	17	18	19
Schoenoplectus tabernaemontani	—	—	—	+	W	—	B	—	+	+	+	+	+	+	+	+	+	—	—
Isolepis cernua	—	+	—	+	—	—	+	—	+	+	+	+	+	+	+	—	+	—	OS
Eleocharis parvula	—	+	—	+	—	—	+	—	—	+	—	—	+	—	—	—	—	+	—
E. uniglumis	—	+	—	+	W	—	+	—	+	+	+	+	+	+	+	+	+	—	—
Blysmus rufus	—	—	—	+	—	+	—	—	—	—	+	+	+	+	+	+	+	—	ON
Cyperus longus	—	—	—	—	W	—	B	—	+	+	—	+	+	—	—	—	—	—	CS
Schoenus nigricans	—	+	+	+	—	—	B	+	+	+	+	+	+	+	+	+	+	—	—
Carex distans	—	—	R	+	—	+	—	—	+	+	+	+	+	+	+	+	+	—	CS
C. punctata	—	—	R	+	—	+	—	—	+	+	+	+	+	+	+	—	—	—	OS
C. extensa	—	—	—	+	—	+	—	—	+	+	+	+	+	+	+	+	+	—	OS
C. otrubae	—	—	—	+	—	—	B	+	+	+	+	+	+	+	+	+	+	—	—
C. arenaria	+	+	—	—	—	+	—	—	+	+	+	+	+	+	+	+	+	—	—
C. divisa	—	—	—	+	—	—	+	—	+	+	+	+	+	+	—	—	—	—	—
C. recta	—	—	—	+	+	—	B	—	—	—	—	—	—	—	—	—	+	+	AS
C. maritima	—	+	—	+	—	+	—	—	—	—	—	—	—	+	+	+	+	—	AA
Phragmites communis	—	—	—	+	—	—	B	+	+	+	+	+	+	+	+	+	+	—	—
Festuca rubra	+	+	+	+	—	+	—	—	+	+	+	+	+	+	+	+	+	—	—
F. juncifolia	—	+	—	—	—	+	—	—	+	+	+	—	—	—	+	—	—	+	OW
Vulpia membranacea	—	+	—	—	—	+	—	—	+	+	+	+	+	+	—	—	+	—	OS
V. ambigua	—	+	—	—	U	—	+	—	+	+	+	+	—	—	—	—	—	—	M
Puccinellia maritima	—	—	+	—	—	+	—	—	+	+	+	+	+	+	+	+	+	—	OW
P. distans	—	—	—	+	—	+	—	—	+	+	+	+	+	+	+	+	+	—	—
P. capillaris	—	—	R	—	—	+	—	—	—	—	—	—	—	—	+	+	+	—	—
P. fasciculata	—	—	—	+	—	+	—	—	+	+	+	+	—	—	—	—	—	—	OW
P. rupestris	—	—	—	+	—	+	—	—	+	+	+	+	+	+	+	—	+	—	OW
Gastridium ventricosum	—	+	—	—	U	—	+	—	+	+	+	+	—	—	—	—	—	—	M
Catapodium marinum	+	+	+	—	—	+	—	—	+	+	+	+	+	+	+	+	—	—	M
Poa bulbosa	—	+	+	—	—	+	—	+	+	+	+	—	—	—	—	—	—	—	—
Agropyron pungens	+	+	—	+	—	+	—	—	+	+	+	+	+	+	—	—	—	—	OS
A. junceiforme	+	+	—	—	—	+	—	—	+	+	+	+	+	+	+	+	+	—	—
Elymus arenarius	+	+	—	—	—	+	—	—	+	+	+	+	+	+	+	+	+	—	ON
Hordeum marinum	—	—	—	+	—	+	—	—	+	+	+	+	+	+	—	—	—	—	OS
Agrostis stolonifera	+	+	+	+	+	+	B	—	+	+	+	+	+	+	+	+	+	—	—
Koeleria cristata	—	+	+	—	—	—	—	+	+	+	+	+	+	+	+	+	+	—	—
K. vallesiana	—	—	R	—	—	—	+	—	+	—	—	—	—	—	—	—	—	+	OS
Ammophila arenaria	+	+	—	—	—	+	—	—	+	+	+	+	+	+	+	+	+	—	—
Phleum arenarium	—	+	—	—	—	+	—	—	+	+	+	+	+	+	+	—	+	—	OS
Alopecurus bulbosus	—	—	—	+	—	+	—	—	+	+	+	+	—	—	—	—	—	—	OS
Parapholis strigosa	+	—	—	+	—	+	—	—	+	+	+	+	+	+	+	—	—	—	OS
P. incurva	+	—	—	+	—	+	—	—	+	+	+	+	+	—	—	—	—	—	OS
Spartina maritima	—	—	—	+	—	+	—	—	+	+	—	—	—	—	—	—	—	—	OS
S. alterniflora	—	—	—	+	—	+	—	—	+	—	—	—	—	—	—	—	—	+	—
S. anglica	—	—	—	+	—	+	—	—	+	+	+	+	+	+	+	—	+	—	OW
Polypogon monspeliensis	—	—	—	+	U	+	—	—	+	+	+	—	—	—	—	—	—	+	CS
Mibora minima	—	+	—	—	U	—	+	—	—	—	—	—	+	—	—	—	—	+	OS
Cynodon dactylon	—	+	—	—	—	—	+	—	+	+	+	+	—	—	—	—	—	+	—
Hierochloe odorata	—	—	—	+	—	—	+	—	—	—	—	—	—	—	+	—	+	+	NM
Corynephorus canescens	+	+	—	—	—	—	+	—	—	—	+	[+]	—	+	—	—	+	+	C
Total 215	57	93	98	74	59	100	93	29	152 [1]	182 [1]	138 [2]	153 [1]	138 [1]	137	126 [2]	96	103 [2]	54	—

Notes

European distribution: M = Mediterranean; CS = continental southern; AA = Arctic–alpine; OS = oceanic southern; ON = oceanic northern; C = continental; A = Arctic; AS = Arctic–subarctic; OW = oceanic west European; NM = northern montane.

R = Especially associated with steep, open rocks.
B = Brackish habitat.
W = Open water habitat (river, ditch, lake, pool).
U = Uncultivated ground (bank, verge, waste ground, grassland).
L = Lizard heathland habitat.
[ ] = Extinct.

where natural salt deposits give a range of saline soils, e.g. *Glaux maritima* and *Aster tripolium*. Several others grow where there are extensive areas of non-saline sand, suggesting that these plants are not halophytic but arenicolous (sand-loving), e.g. *Carex arenaria*, *Ammophila arenaria*, *Corynephorus canescens* and *Phleum arenarium*.

Fauna

MAMMALS, REPTILES AND AMPHIBIANS

All British mammals occur somewhere, or at some time, within the range of coastland habitats. The two species which belong exclusively to the coast are the marine carnivores, the Atlantic (grey) seal *Halichoerus grypus* and common seal *Phoca vitulina*. These animals are associated with the land mainly during their breeding season, though they may haul out to rest on the shore at any time of the year (for the grey seal this is usually in places other than the breeding grounds). The grey seal is widely distributed around the coasts of Britain, but breeding colonies are relatively few; they include the Pembrokeshire coast and islands, Cardiganshire coast, Isles of Scilly, Lundy, Cornwall coast, Farne Islands, and coast of Scotland (especially the Hebrides, North Rona, Orkney and Shetland). The land habitat of this animal consists of rock slabs and platforms, cliff ledges, shingle and boulder beaches, and soil-covered slopes with a maritime sward. There the seals congregate in large numbers to mate and produce their pups. The breeding season is between August and December.

The common seal also occurs widely around the British coasts, and breeds in shallow waters of the Wash and East Anglian coast, Orkney, Shetland, east and west coasts of Scotland and the Hebrides. In the south, this species is associated especially with sand and mud banks, and estuarine flats, but in the north it occurs on various types of beach and rocky shore or island. The pups are born in the sea or within the inter-tidal zone, so that they take to the water earlier in life than pups of the grey seal. Mating takes place in late summer–early autumn, and the pups are born in early or mid summer the following year.

Of the other carnivores, the fox *Vulpes vulpes* has dens in many rocky coast areas, especially on block-littered steep slopes or broken cliffs, and on sand dunes. It ranges over all kinds of coastland in search of food, and often works beaches for birds washed up, and salt marshes and flats for injured wildfowl lost after being shot. The otter *Lutra lutra* often lives on the coast and feeds in the sea especially in the Scottish Highlands, and some individuals alternate between sea and fresh waters. In its Welsh haunts, the very local polecat *Mustela putorius* is also to be found in coastal habitats, as on the sand dunes and marshes of the Dyfi estuary. Stoats *Mustela erminea* and weasels *M. nivalis* occur in situations such as sand dunes and cliff or slope grasslands where there is plenty of cover and food for their prey.

In the western and northern Highlands, where the moors and mountains run down to sea, red deer *Cervus elaphus* feed a good deal on maritime swards, which are often nutritious 'greens' of greater feeding value than the acidophilous heath and mire vegetation farther away from the influence of the sea. Some deer descend at times to the actual shore to graze on seaweeds. Rabbits *Oryctolagus cuniculus* formerly found one of their optimum habitats on coastal dune systems, especially those formed of calcareous sand, and various types of coastal grassland also carried high densities in places. Since the myxomatosis epidemic of 1953 onwards, rabbits have been generally much fewer in these habitats except in certain localities, and their absence or scarcity has allowed the herbaceous vegetation to grow more luxuriantly and to become invaded by scrub species in many places. Brown hares *Lepus europaeus* occur in various types of grassy coastal habitat, and in common with other northern plants and animals, the blue hare *L. timidus* shows an altitudinal descent to within the coastal range of habitats in northern Scotland. Most of the small rodents occur within coastlands, but the short-tailed vole *Microtus agrestis* is the most widespread and numerous, thriving best where the vegetation is rank, as on some ungrazed cliff slopes. Some of the insular forms of small mammals in Britain necessarily belong to the paramaritime zone, e.g. the St Kilda mouse *Apodemus sylvaticus hirtensis* and Scilly shrew *Crocidura suaveolens*.

Hedgehogs *Erinaceus europaeus* occur on sand dunes and grassland or scrub on the less steep slopes above the sea, and moles *Talpa europaea* are often numerous on stabilised sand dunes or gently sloping grasslands near the sea. Sea cliffs with caves and clefts are locally important habitats for bats, which find sanctuary there for roosting, breeding and hibernating. The caves on the Dorset coast are especially important for the greater horseshoe bat *Rhinolophus ferrumequinum*, Bechstein's bat *Myotis bechsteini*, Natterer's bat *M. nattereri*, whiskered bat *M. mystacinus*, Daubenton's bat *M. daubentoni*, and the very rare mouse-eared bat *M. myotis*.

The British reptiles and amphibia probably all occur within a short distance of the sea, but only one species, the natterjack toad *Bufo calamita*, has a markedly coastal distribution. Although this amphibian was once more widespread inland in a few areas, it appears now to be restricted largely to the vicinity of the sea, where it lives and breeds in dune slacks or in pools and ditches which may sometimes be slightly brackish, as on the higher lying hinterland of some salt marshes. The common toad *Bufo bufo* and frog *Rana temporaria* are often common in these submaritime or paramaritime habitats, and evidently all three species of newt occur here in some parts of the country.

Broken cliffs, heathy slopes and stable dune areas are locally quite important habitats for the adder *Vipera berus*, common lizard *Lacerta vivipara* and slow worm *Anguis fragilis*. Sand dune systems are one of the two major habitats for the sand lizard *L. agilis*, and this species reaches its northern British limits on the Ainsdale Dunes in Lancashire; while on the dunes and coastal heaths at Studland in Dorset a large population of sand lizards is accompanied by the smooth snake *Coronella austriaca*.

BIRDS

Birds of the sea coast may be divided into summer breeding and winter populations, and both of these subdivided according to habitat. The coastal breeding birds fall into groups belonging to sea cliffs, offshore grassy/rocky islands, sand dunes, shingle beaches, machair and salt marshes. The winter populations are especially concentrated on tidal sand or mud flats and salt marshes, though a few sand dune systems are favoured, and coastal lagoons, inland lakes and seasonally-wet meadow grasslands are important alternative or additional habitats for some species.

BREEDING POPULATIONS

Sea cliffs and rocky slopes

Cliff breeding seabirds tend to occur in huge aggregations on certain favoured stretches of precipice. Sometimes this preference is related to certain species' needs, as with guillemots and razorbills, whose young jump into the sea before they are fledged and thus tend to favour cliffs which fall straight into the water, at least at high tide. High cliffs with undercliffs or storm beaches below are thus less usually occupied by these birds, which cannot necessarily move elsewhere if their traditional breeding haunts are disturbed or destroyed. Guillemots are famous for the way they pack in dense throngs on broad shelves of cliffs, among tumbled rocks, or on flat-topped stacks, but razorbills nest less densely and often in crannies as well as on open ledges. These auks lay their eggs on bare rock, but kittiwakes build nests and can do so on small or sloping ledges, so that quite large colonies of this gull sometimes occur on vertical or even overhanging cliffs. All three species nevertheless occur in greater numbers on cliffs and stacks which are steep but have an abundance of good ledges, a feature characteristic of many sandstone precipices. The puffin needs earthy slopes in which to burrow, and so is most abundant on the less sheer cliffs, though it will use rock crannies like those favoured by razorbills. The shag will use caves and deep crevices for its nest, but often builds on more open ledges, and the cormorant prefers exposed rock sites. The black guillemot is a crevice nester and finds its most suitable sites under large slabs on storm beaches. Fulmars favour small, soily ledges whilst gannets breed most densely on steep, rocky slopes, mainly on cliff-girt islands and rock stacks. Herring gulls breed in large numbers on many cliffs and use a wide variety of sites including steep broken slopes. Many of these birds are vulnerable to ground predators such as the fox, brown rat and, not least, man, and for this reason usually resort to the steepest cliffs or to rocky islands or stacks lying offshore.

The principal seafowl stations with the above species are scattered round our coasts and necessarily confined to the more precipitous sections; they are therefore represented mainly on the western and northern coasts of Britain, though there are several large colonies in the east. Some of the species in question spend much of their time on the open sea and are there especially susceptible to oil pollution hazards; some auk colonies along the western coasts have been much reduced in size during the last few decades, and losses of guillemots and razorbills have been especially severe from this and other causes during the last few years. The puffin has shown recent dramatic declines in many breeding stations, including such strongholds as St Kilda, the Shiants and the Clo Mor, but the causes are still a matter of debate. On the other hand the kittiwake, herring gull, great black-backed gull, fulmar and gannet have increased and extended their range. The spread of the fulmar, formerly with its original sole British locality at St Kilda, is one of the most spectacular recent changes in numbers and distribution of any bird species in Britain. The herring gull is extremely widespread on much of the rockier coastline and has reached high numbers locally; the degree of predation and disturbance by this species and the great black-backed is regarded by many people as an important factor locally in the decline of other bird populations, notably terns, and in the modification of habitat.

The Manx shearwater, storm petrel and Leach's petrel nest in burrows and crevices on rocky slopes, and are also extremely vulnerable to ground predators. All three are found almost entirely on the west coast, and mainly on rocky islands. The Manx shearwater nests up to considerable elevations on the mountains of Rhum, in the deep weathered soils on ultra-basic rocks. The rock pipit is a much more widespread species, occurring on grassy rocks and slopes all round our coasts. The eider duck is a widespread maritime Scottish bird, found also in north Northumberland and at Walney Island, Lancashire, which breeds on cliff slopes and summits as well as on low rocky and grassy shores, but nests in a variety of other habitats, including shingle and sand dune. Nearly all these sea birds have an extremely limited European or even world distribution, and for some the British Isles may be regarded as a key station or even headquarters. Their conservation is thus a matter of international importance.

A further group of non-maritime birds has a coastal niche. This consists of raptors and corvids which breed on coastal precipices and includes the peregrine, common buzzard, kestrel, golden eagle, raven, carrion crow, hooded crow, jackdaw and chough. Some of these are dealt with in Chapter 9, and the golden eagle is only a coastal bird in western Scotland where the moorlands run down to the cliff tops. The peregrine has decreased markedly in many coastal areas and has shown little tendency to recovery there; most of its sea cliff breeding population is now found in Scotland. The chough is now extinct as a breeding species in south-west England and has decreased in south Wales. It now occurs mainly in north Wales and the Isle of Man and a few pairs still nest in the Inner Hebrides and on the mainland coast of Argyll. The others are all widespread breeders on sea cliffs, though the hooded crow is confined to the Highlands and the Isle of Man. The rock dove is a widespread cliff nester, preferring caves, but the native stock is considerably hybridised with various forms of homing pigeon.

Sand dunes and shingle beaches

The breeding birds of these habitats include the ringed plover, oystercatcher, common tern, Arctic tern, roseate tern, little tern and Sandwich tern, black-headed gull, herring gull, lesser black-backed gull and, locally, common gull. The first two species and little tern are most usually on shingle, whilst the others are typically dune or sandy shore birds. The shelduck usually breeds where there are rabbit burrows amongst the dunes, but often has to go to farmland to find these, and a good many pairs nest locally under dense scrub such as gorse and bramble. The wheatear and stock dove are other burrow nesting species. In Britain, the terns are mostly concentrated in a small number of fairly large colonies, the Sandwich tern showing this tendency particularly. Tern colonies are, in general, prone to fluctuation and movement between alternative haunts, but the roseate tern has decreased recently and the little tern appears to be seriously declining, for it resorts to shingle beaches which are often much frequented by holiday-makers. The roseate and Arctic terns nest locally on low, rocky and often grassy islands, and the common tern breeds in this habitat, on salt marshes and on islands or tussocks in a few inland waters. The ringed plover, oystercatcher, shelduck, wheatear and stock dove are widespread species, but the others are local, though sometimes occurring in great numbers in their main colonies. The major tern colonies are well scattered round the coasts of Britain, though the Arctic tern is mainly a Scottish species. Their distribution is, however, irregular, and some large dune systems have few or none of these birds, perhaps as a result of disturbance.

Machair

The dry machairs of the Outer Hebrides have birds such as the lapwing, oystercatcher and ringed plover, but their avifauna is rather limited. Where the drainage deteriorates and there is a change to marshy vegetation with taller sedge–grass mixtures and shallow lagoons with fringing vegetation, other wading birds are well represented. In particular, dunlin reach a higher breeding density here than anywhere else in Britain, and are many times more numerous than on most of their moorland haunts. This is the classic British habitat of the red-necked phalarope, which feeds on the eutrophic lagoons and nests in the adjoining marsh, though only in very small numbers. There are also redshank, snipe, black-headed gulls, skylarks, corn buntings, hen harriers and short-eared owls.

Salt marshes

The more frequently inundated salt marshes are devoid of nesting birds. Where the ground level is high enough to escape immersion by all but exceptional spring tides, as on north-western marshes (e.g. the Solway) there is, however, a wide variety. Lapwing, skylark, redshank and oystercatcher are often at high density on these less saline marshes, where the vegetation is usually a grazed grassy sward; and locally, from the Ribble Estuary northwards, there are breeding dunlin. Colonies of black-headed gulls, lesser black-backed gulls and common terns with a few herring and great black-backed gulls breed on some of these marshes and they are the occasional nesting place of widespread birds such as moorhen, curlew, ringed plover, snipe, yellow wagtail, cuckoo, reed bunting and meadow pipit, and of rarities such as the black-tailed godwit. The present-day breeding haunts of avocets on the Suffolk coast are an unusual type of coastal habitat, consisting of brackish, shallow lagoons with sparsely vegetated mud flats on which the birds breed, and are maintained artificially by sea walls. Several species of duck nest at times on salt marshes, e.g. shelduck, mallard, teal, garganey and shoveler, but the numbers are usually small. Many species which breed on saltings also nest on the grazed grasslands of reclaimed marshes, and these may have still other species, such as corn bunting.

Paramaritime species

Some species have a looser attachment to the coast or coastal areas, often because of their food habits but sometimes for reasons not understood. The great and Arctic skuas are found mainly on moorlands and grassy hills next to the sea in a few remote islands in the far north and west of Scotland, because they depend for food partly on gulls and other seafowl which have a more direct connection with the sea. The great skua is globally a rare species and like the gannet shows an interesting bi-polar disjunction. The red-throated diver is most numerous on moorland lakes close to the sea, where it prefers to feed, but also occurs far inland. The whimbrel, which occurs mainly in Shetland as a breeding species, is a bird of somewhat maritime moorlands in Britain. Nowadays, the twite is most numerous in rocky coastal areas of the north-west Highlands and islands, and is curiously local as a moorland species. The stonechat is widespread but now more common in western coastal areas than elsewhere; a species badly hit by cold winters, its chances of survival are better under the equable coastal climate. The insular races of wren on St Kilda, the Outer Hebrides, Fair Isle and Shetland are best included here, as they live close to the sea and often nest on rocky coastal slopes and cliffs.

NON-BREEDING POPULATIONS

The coast is important to the winter population of wildfowl (ducks, geese and swans) and waders in providing both resting and feeding grounds. The British population of these groups of birds is augmented every autumn by large numbers from abroad, including some species which nest in Britain. Some autumnal arrivals are migrants on their way to other winter quarters; others are winter visitors which remain in this country until the spring. For many species, the numbers wintering in Britain are a significant proportion of the total European or even world population, so that conservation of their winter haunts is a matter of international concern.

Rocky coasts are little used by seabirds in winter, though guillemots may sometimes be seen sitting on their ledges, and cormorants, shags, and black guillemots remain throughout the year. The main haunts are the extensive areas of inter-tidal sand or mud flats in shallow coastal waters, the adjoining salt marshes and, locally, grazing marshes or arable land reclaimed from the sea by means of a sea wall. Many of the most extensive and important tidal flat–marsh systems are on river estuaries, and are thus particularly threatened by proposals to create freshwater reservoirs by means of tidal barrages across the estuaries.

Internationally, the most important winter coastland bird populations are of geese, notably the grey geese (grey lag, pink-footed and white-fronted) and also the barnacle and brent geese. Except the last, these species typically roost on the inter-tidal sands and mudflats of the coasts and estuaries, and flight to the salt marshes or farther inland to pastures or arable land on which to feed, usually during the day but sometimes at night. Of the grey geese, the pink-footed is now mainly a bird of northern England and Scotland, having declined greatly in East Anglia; and the grey lag is even more particularly Scottish. The European white-fronted is mainly in southern England and Wales, whilst the Greenland race winters in various parts of western Britain. The barnacle goose is a northern species and one of the few noteworthy birds of the Hebridean machair in winter, and in a few places it feeds on this type of maritime grassland in large numbers. The brent goose is mainly an east and south coast species, and is more exclusively maritime than the other geese, living and feeding on mud flats where there are extensive growths of *Zostera* spp. and *Enteromorpha* spp. The shelduck is another species almost confined to the sea shore in winter, especially on sand or mud flats.

The three species of swan occurring in Britain, the mute, whooper and Bewick's, may be found on some coastal waters and estuaries. Large numbers, however, are also common on inland waters and seasonally in flooded meadows.

The surface-feeding (dabbling) ducks of coasts and estuaries include wigeon, mallard, teal, pintail and shoveler. These duck, of which the first two are usually the most numerous, flight at dusk to the salt marshes or farmland farther inland and return at dawn to the coastal flats: they occur in numbers on paramaritime lakes and lagoons, which are also a favoured haunt of diving ducks such as pochard and tufted. Of the other coastal ducks, the goldeneye and scaup favour estuarine waters and bays, whereas eider, common and velvet scoter, and rarer long-tailed duck are more typical of the open sea or large firths. The scaup, eider and long-tailed duck are mainly northern species. The red-breasted merganser is mainly a bird of coastal bays and estuaries in winter, but the goosander is also found on inland waters.

The majority of our wading birds are found on the coast in winter and it is the mid-winter period for which Britain is mainly important. Unlike some wildfowl, they do not have regular daily flights between the coast and inland feeding grounds; they obtain their food by probing and picking at low water on the inter-tidal flats or among rocks on the shore. The coarser-grained sediments, such as those north of the Clyde–Tay line, have relatively little food value for waders, and the most productive flats seem to be fine sand

with a thin surface layer of sand–silt mixture which contain large populations of the 10–20 invertebrate species which form the principal food of these birds, e.g. *Arenicola marina, Cerastoderma edule, Corophium volutator, Gammarus* spp., *Hydrobia ulvae, Macoma balthica, Mytilus edulis, Nereis diversicolor, Tellina tenuis* and *Scrobicularia plana.* Most of the major estuaries of southern Scotland, England and Wales have extensive areas of inter-tidal silt flats which are important for waders in winter and during migration. A number of wader species also occur inland, at least on passage. Several species occur at this time of the year in vast numbers, representing a significant percentage of the total European or world population.

Waders especially associated with rocky shores with reefs, boulders and shingle flats or beaches, are the turnstone, purple sandpiper and oystercatcher. Most species favour the mud, silt and sand flats of the open coast and estuaries or the creeks and pools of the associated salt marshes; and include the black-tailed godwit, bar-tailed godwit, curlew, whimbrel, knot, dunlin, curlew sandpiper, little stint, sanderling, redshank, spotted redshank, greenshank, green sandpiper, ruff, ringed plover, grey plover and oystercatcher. Some of these birds rest on the salt marshes, especially at high tide, and curlew, whimbrel, lapwing and golden plover often occur in quite large flocks on these maritime grasslands. Many species also resort to grasslands and arable land farther inland, at least during exceptional tides.

Other birds of the estuarine and coastal flats, salt marshes and shingle beaches in winter include heron, cormorant, carrion crow, hooded crow, rock pipit, meadow pipit, twite and snow bunting. Raptors such as the peregrine and merlin often take up coastal territories during the winter, especially where there is a good supply of prey nearby. The coast also provides a landfall for many migrant species which are not maritime birds, but tend to appear mainly along the sea-shore of adjoining land during passage. Certain places are especially favoured in this way, and a chain of bird observatories and ringing stations has been established where valuable data are gathered on bird movements and migrations. Many rare birds appear on passage, and coastal habitats are one of the main haunts of the amateur ornithologist at all seasons of the year.

INSECTS

Only the Lepidoptera of coastlands are sufficiently well known to receive treatment here. A few species of dragonfly are present on dry coastal habitats during migration time but cannot properly be said to belong here, and the species which occur in dune slacks, brackish ponds and ditches or coastal lagoons are dealt with in Chapter 7.

Lepidoptera

The most conspicuous Lepidoptera of the coast, especially the southern coasts, are frequently migrant species such as the red admiral *Vanessa atalanta,* painted lady *Cynthia cardui* and silver Y *Plusia gamma.* These are not however confined to coastal habitats and certainly do not typify them.

Table 2. *Habitat and distribution of coastland Lepidoptera*[a]

		Salt marsh & reclaimed saltings	Sand dune	Shingle beach	Cliffs & grassy slopes	Dwarf shrubs	Forbs	Grasses	S. & S.E. England	East Anglia	S.W. England	Wales	N. England	S. Scotland	Highlands
		1	2	3	4	5	6	7	8	9	10	11	12	13	14
Butterflies															
Green-veined white	*Pieris napi*	+	+	—	—	—	+	—	+	+	+	+	+	+	—
Orange tip	*Anthocharis cardamines*	+	+	—	—	—	+	—	+	+	+	+	+	+	—
Grayling	*Hipparchia semele*	—	+	—	+	—	—	+	+	+	+	+	+	+	—
Marbled white	*Melanargia galathea*	—	—	—	+	—	—	+	+	—	+	+	—	—	—
Glanville fritillary	*Melitaea cinxia*	—	—	—	+	—	+	—	+	—	—	—	—	—	—
Green hairstreak	*Callophrys rubi*	—	—	—	+	+	+	—	+	+	+	+	—	—	—
Common blue	*Polyommatus icarus*	—	+	—	—	—	+	—	+	+	+	+	+	+	—
Chalk-hill blue	*Lysandra coridon*	—	—	—	+	—	+	—	+	—	+	—	—	—	—
Holly blue	*Celastrina argiolus*	—	—	—	+	+	—	—	+	—	+	—	—	—	—
Large blue	*Maculinea arion*	—	—	—	+	—	+	—	—	—	+	—	—	—	—
Lulworth skipper	*Thymelicus acteon*	—	—	—	+	—	—	—	+	—	+	—	—	—	—
Moths															
Ground lackey	*Malacosoma castrensis*	+	—	—	—	—	+	—	+	—	—	—	—	—	—
White satin moth	*Leucoma salicis*	—	+	+	—	+	—	—	+	+	—	—	+	+	—
Dark tussock	*Dasychira fascelina*	—	+	+	—	+	—	—	+	—	+	—	+	—	—
Cinnabar	*Tyria jacobaeae*	—	+	+	—	—	+	—	+	+	+	+	+	+	—
Brown-tail	*Euproctis chrysorrhoea*	—	—	+	—	+	—	—	+	—	—	—	—	—	—
Coast dart	*Euxoa cursoria*	—	+	—	—	—	+	—	+	+	+	+	+	+	—
White-line dart	*E. tritici*	—	+	—	+	—	+	—	+	+	+	+	+	+	—
Square-spot dart	*E. obelisca*	—	+	—	+	—	+	—	+	—	+	+	+	+	—
Crescent dart	*Agrotis trux*	—	+	—	—	—	+	—	+	—	+	+	—	+	+
Archer's dart	*A. vestigialis*	—	+	—	—	—	+	+	+	+	—	—	+	+	+
Sand dart	*A. ripae*	—	+	—	—	—	+	+	+	+	+	+	+	—	—
Portland moth	*Ochropleura praecox*	—	+	—	—	+	+	+	+	+	+	—	+	+	+
Dog's tooth	*Lacanobia suasa*	+	—	—	—	—	+	—	+	+	—	—	—	—	—
Grey	*Hadena caesia*	—	—	—	+	—	+	—	—	—	—	—	—	—	+
White spot	*H. albimacula*	—	—	—	+	—	+	—	+	—	+	—	—	—	—
Barrett's marbled coronet	*H. barrettii*	—	—	+	—	—	+	—	+	—	+	—	—	—	—
White colon	*Sideridis albicolon*	—	+	—	—	—	+	—	—	—	+	+	+	+	+
Southern wainscot	*Mythimna straminea*	+	—	—	—	—	+	+	+	+	+	+	+	—	—
Shore wainscot	*M. litoralis*	+	—	—	—	—	+	+	+	+	+	+	+	—	—
Toadflax brocade	*Calophasia lunula*	—	—	+	—	—	+	—	+	—	—	—	—	—	—
Beautiful gothic	*Leucochlaena oditis*	—	—	—	+	—	+	—	+	+	—	+	—	—	—
Feathered ranunculus	*Eumichtis lichenea*	+	—	—	—	—	+	—	+	—	+	+	+	—	—
Brindled ochre	*Dasypolia templi*	—	—	—	+	+	—	—	—	—	—	—	+	+	+
Black-banded	*Polymixis xanthomista*	—	—	—	+	—	+	—	—	—	+	—	—	—	—
Crescent striped	*Apamea oblonga*	+	—	—	—	—	—	+	+	+	—	—	+	—	+
Sandhill rustic	*Luperina nickerlii*	—	+	—	—	—	—	—	+	—	—	—	+	—	—
Saltern ear	*Amphipoea fucosa paludis*	+	+	—	—	—	—	+	+	+	+	+	+	+	+
Giant ear	*Hydraecia osseola hucherardi*	—	—	+	—	—	+	—	+	—	—	—	—	—	—
Morris's wainscot	*Photedes morrisii*	—	—	—	+	—	—	+	—	+	—	—	+	—	—
Lyme grass	*P. elymi*	+	—	—	—	—	+	+	+	—	—	+	—	+	—
Scarce blackneck	*Lygephila craccae*	—	—	—	+	—	+	—	—	—	+	+	—	—	—
Kent black arches	*Meganola albula*	+	—	—	—	—	+	—	+	+	—	—	—	—	—

Table 2 (*contd.*)

		1	2	3	4	5	6	7	8	9	10	11	12	13	14
Scarce black arches	*Nola aerugula*	—	—	—	+	—	+	—	+	+	—	—	—	—	—
Pigmy footman	*Eilema pygmaeola*	+	+	—	—	—	—	+	+	+	—	—	—	—	—
Dingy mocha	*Cyclophora pendularia*	—	—	—	+	+	—	—	+	—	—	—	—	—	—
Small grass emerald	*Chlorissa viridata*	—	—	—	+	+	—	—	—	—	—	+	—	—	—
Essex emerald	*Thetidia smaragdaria*	+	—	—	—	—	+	—	+	—	—	—	—	—	—
Sussex emerald	*Thalera fimbrialis*	—	—	—	+	—	+	—	+	—	+	—	—	—	—
Isle of Wight wave	*Idaea humiliata*	—	—	—	+	—	+	—	+	—	—	—	—	—	—
Portland ribbon wave	*I. degeneraria*	—	—	—	+	+	+	—	—	—	+	—	—	—	—
Cloaked pug	*Eupithecia abietaria*	—	—	—	+	+	—	—	+	—	—	—	+	—	—
Yarrow pug	*E. millefoliata*	—	—	+	—	—	+	—	+	—	—	—	—	—	—
Pinion-spotted pug	*E. insigniata*	+	—	—	—	+	—	—	—	+	—	—	—	—	—
Scarce pug	*E. extensaria*	+	—	—	—	—	+	—	+	+	—	—	—	—	—
Belted beauty	*Lycia zonaria*	—	+	—	—	+	+	—	—	—	—	+	—	—	—
Straw belle	*Aspitates gilvaria*	—	+	—	+	—	—	+	+	—	+	—	—	—	—
Narrow-bordered five-spot burnet	*Zygaena lonicerae*	+	+	—	+	—	+	—	+	+	+	+	+	—	—
Thrift clearwing	*Bembecia muscaeformis*	—	—	—	+	—	+	—	—	—	+	+	—	—	+
	Pedasia aridella	+	—	—	—	—	—	+	+	+	+	+	+	—	—
	P. contaminella	—	+	—	—	—	—	+	+	—	—	—	—	—	—
	Agriphila selasella	+	—	—	+	—	—	+	+	+	+	+	+	—	—
	Platytes alpinella	—	+	—	—	—	—	+	+	+	+	—	—	—	—
	Gymnancyla canella	—	—	+	—	—	+	—	+	+	+	—	—	—	—
	Epischnia banksiella	—	—	—	+	—	+	—	—	—	+	—	—	—	—
	Agdistis staticis	—	—	—	+	—	+	—	—	—	+	+	—	—	—
	A. bennetii	+	—	—	—	—	+	—	+	+	—	—	+	—	—
Total 93		19	23	9	29	12	42	19	50	28	41	25	27	16	9

Note

[a] The nomenclature of the Lepidoptera follows that of Kloet & Hincks (1972) but the arrangement follows the conventional order used by previous authors, viz. Butterflies, Macrolepidoptera and Microlepidoptera.

Salt marsh

Only two butterflies breed regularly, the green-veined white and orange tip (which occur widely in other habitats), but a number of moths are confined to salt marshes. These include the ground lackey confined to Essex and North Kent, the Essex emerald confined to Essex, the scarce pug associated with *Artemisia maritima* and more or less confined to the Norfolk salt marshes. More widely distributed salt marsh moths are the southern wainscot which occurs in all regions south of Scotland, and the shore wainscot which also extends into south Scotland.

Sand dunes

Two butterflies are particularly frequent on sand dunes, the grayling and common blue, both of which occur in this habitat throughout Britain. The widely distributed moths include coast dart, archer's dart, and white-line dart. More local species are the sandhill rustic only found in Lancashire, belted beauty confined to Wales and some Hebridean islands, and *Pedasia contaminella* only present in south-east England.

Shingle beach

Very few species can be said to belong to this habitat and these are associated with vegetation bordering the shingle.

They are the browntail, more or less confined to Kent and Essex, Barrett's marbled coronet, in the south-west and Wales, the giant ear, a species unknown in Britain until 1953 when it was discovered at Dungeness, to which area it is more or less confined, and the pyralid *Gymnancyla canella* (larva feeding on *Salsola kali*) which occurs on the south and south-east coast of England.

Cliffs and grassy slopes

The most notable butterflies are the Glanville fritillary, only found on the southern coast of the Isle of Wight; the large blue, confined in this habitat to the north Cornish and Devon coasts; and the Lulworth skipper which only occurs at Lulworth Cove and a few other places to the immediate east and west. Other coastal butterflies include the chalk-hill blue, the holly blue (frequently common in landslip areas) and the marbled white, found in such localities as the cliffs immediately to the east of Plymouth. Moths typical of cliffs include the grey coronet (confined to Rhum and Canna), beautiful gothic, found in a few places along the south-west coast, brindled ochre, occurring northwards from north-east England to north Scotland, black-banded, restricted to the north Cornish and Devon coasts from Land's End to Ilfracombe, and Isle of Wight wave, confined to the southern cliffs of the Isle of Wight.

SPIDERS

The spiders of some coastal habitats, notably sand dunes, shingle beaches, and salt marshes, have been well studied, particularly in southern England, East Anglia and Wales. A total of 40 typical coastal species is listed below, 28 of which have been found exclusively on coastlands in Britain, while the other 12 have been found mainly in coastal habitats but occasionally elsewhere. Many other species found commonly on coastlands also occur frequently inland, often in marshy or grassy habitats. It is noteworthy that relatively few of the exclusively coastal species are widespread and common.

Salt marshes

The two most widespread and characteristic salt-marsh spiders are *Pardosa purbeckensis* and *Erigone longipalpis*, neither of which occurs on other coastal habitats. The only other species confined to salt marshes are *Argenna patula*, which is frequent under salt marsh drift litter; *Arctosa fulvolineata*, also found mainly in litter but confined to the south and east of England; *Praestigia duffeyi*, abundant in a few sites from Kent to Suffolk; and *Acanthophyma gowerensis*, a recently described species which has been recorded only from Whiteford and Oxwich, south Wales, and one site in Ireland. *Enoplognatha schaufussi* is also restricted to salt marsh on the coast, but has been found occasionally in marshy habitats inland, as has *Erigone longipalpis*.

Sand dunes

The commonest and most widespread spiders associated with sand dunes are *Xerolycosa miniata*, *Zelotes electus* and *Arctosa perita*, the last two occurring in sandy habitats inland, e.g. in Breckland and on southern heaths. Other species confined to sand dunes but which have a more restricted distribution are *Clubiona similis*, known only from a number of sites in Norfolk and at Sandwich, Kent; *Agroeca lusatica*, found only at Sandwich; *Philodromus fallax*, frequent in England and Wales but not recorded from Scotland; *Phlegra fasciata*, known only from a few sites along the south coast; *Minyrioloides maritimus*, a species recently described from Winterton, the North Norfolk Coast and Gibraltar Point; *Silometopus incurvatus*, known from marram clumps in north England and south Scotland only; and *Ceratinopsis romanus*, a common species on English dunes but not recorded from Scotland. Other less exclusive sand dune species are *Argenna subnigra*, which also occurs occasionally in salt marshes and in sandy habitats inland and is widespread in England and Wales; *Hyctia nivoyi*, common on English dunes and rarely found inland in Britain although frequent inland on the Continent; *Attulus saltator*, common on southern English dunes and on a few sandy heaths inland; and *Synageles venator*, found exclusively on dunes in the south and west of Britain, but also well established at Woodwalton Fen, and frequent inland on the Continent. The two other dune species listed are *Clubiona juvenis*, known only from two sites in the British Isles, dunes in County Wicklow, Ireland, and brackish marsh at Poole Harbour and *Agroeca cuprea*, frequent on sand dunes in Kent and Sussex, but also found on sandy grassland in the Breck and in short grass and heather near Kynance Cove. *Clubiona juvenis* could perhaps equally well be classified as a salt marsh species.

Shingle beaches

The most widespread species of shingle beaches are *Pardosa arenicola*, *Halorates reprobus* and *Erigone arctica*, but all three are sometimes found elsewhere. Although *P. arenicola* has been reported from a few sites inland, this could be the result of mis-identification. *H. reprobus* is exclusively coastal, but is sometimes found also in drift litter on salt marsh or on sand dunes, while *E. arctica* is also sometimes found on salt-marsh drift and occasionally inland. It is interesting to note that *P. arenicola* and *E. arctica* on shingle appear to take the place of *P. purbeckensis* and *E. longipalpis* on salt marsh. Most species which are confined to shingle or most abundant on shingle are very local: *Haplodrassus minor* is known only from the Portland end of Chesil Beach, Colne Point and Havergate Island; *Heliophanus auratus* is known only from Colne Point; *Trichoncus hackmani* only from Colne Point and Needs Oar Point, Hampshire; *T. affinis* from Orfordness and Havergate and from Hayling Island (Hampshire), Dungeness (Kent) and Camber (Sussex); and *Trichopterna cito* from Colne Point and from an old sand dune at Camber. Slightly less rare species are *Euophrys browningi*, recorded from the north Kent coast, Colne Point, Shingle Street and Orfordness, and Blakeney Point, and *Sitticus rupicola*, recorded from Bridgwater Bay and a number of sites from Hampshire and the Isle of Wight round to Norfolk. These last two species are interesting in that both, and especially *E. browningi*, tend to occupy and lay their eggs in empty whelk shells if available.

Cliffs and grassy slopes

Only four species can be classified as characteristic of these habitats, all of them rare or of restricted range. The commonest is *Segestria bavarica*, which occupies cracks in sea cliffs and rocks near the sea throughout the west of England, but especially along the south coast of Cornwall and Dorset. The other three species are found on grassy slopes, on cliff tops or elsewhere near the sea. They are *Clubiona genevensis*, recorded from Scilly, the Lizard, Ringstead and Lulworth, and Skokholm; *Euophrys herbigrada*, found in several sites in Cornwall and south Devon; and the rarest, *Hahnia candida*, which has been recorded only from Portland and Chesil, Ringstead, and one inland site in Dorset.

There are three species which do not fit easily into any of the above categories. They are *Lathys stigmatisata*, known only from short vegetation on shingle at Dungeness and from among grass and heather at the Lizard and on Lundy, *Zelotes lutetianus*, found in litter and under stones in a variety of coastal habitats and sometimes inland, and *Silometopus ambiguus*, which is a typical inhabitant of drift litter, not usually as abundant as *Erigone arctica* in litter on shingle, but occupying a greater range of habitats.

Table 3. *Habitat and distribution of coastland spiders*

	Salt marsh	Sand dune	Shingle	Cliffs & grassy slopes	S. & S.E. England	East Anglia	S.W. England	Wales	N. England	S. Scotland	Highlands	Ireland
Lathys stigmatisata	—	—	+	+	+	—	+	—	—	—	—	—
Argenna subnigra	+	+	—	—	+	+	+	+	+	—	—	+
A. patula	+	—	—	—	+	+	—	+	+	—	—	—
Segestria bavarica	—	—	—	+	+	—	+	—	—	—	—	—
Haplodrassus minor	+	—	+	—	+	+	+	—	—	—	—	—
Zelotes lutetianus	+	—	+	—	+	+	—	—	—	+	—	+
Z. electus	—	+	—	—	+	+	+	+	+	+	—	+
Clubiona similis	—	+	—	—	+	+	—	—	—	—	—	—
C. juvenis	+	+	—	—	—	—	+	—	—	—	—	+
C. genevensis	—	—	—	+	—	—	+	+	—	—	—	—
Agroeca lusatica	—	+	—	—	+	—	—	—	—	—	—	—
A. cuprea	—	+	—	+	+	+	+	—	—	—	—	—
Philodromus fallax	—	+	—	—	+	+	+	+	+	—	—	—
Heliophanus auratus	—	—	+	—	—	+	—	—	—	—	—	—
Hyctia nivoyi	—	+	—	—	+	+	+	+	+	—	—	+
Euophrys herbigrada	—	—	—	+	—	—	+	—	+	—	—	—
E. browningi	—	—	+	—	+	+	—	—	—	—	—	—
Sitticus rupicola	—	—	+	—	+	+	—	—	—	—	—	—
Attulus saltator	—	+	—	—	+	+	+	+	+	—	—	—
Phlegra fasciata	—	+	—	—	+	—	+	—	—	—	—	—
Synageles venator	—	+	—	—	+	—	+	+	—	—	—	—
Pardosa arenicola	—	—	+	—	+	+	+	+	—	—	—	+
P. purbeckensis	+	—	—	—	+	+	+	+	+	+	+	+
Xerolycosa miniata	—	+	—	—	+	+	+	+	+	+	—	—
Arctosa perita	—	+	—	—	+	+	+	+	+	+	+	+
A. fulvolineata	+	—	—	—	+	+	—	—	—	—	—	—
Hahnia candida	—	—	—	+	—	—	+	—	—	—	—	—
Enoplognatha schaufussi	+	—	—	—	+	+	+	+	—	+	—	—
Praestigia duffeyi	+	—	—	—	+	+	—	—	—	—	—	+
Minyrioloides maritimus	—	+	—	—	—	+	—	—	—	—	—	—
Trichopterna cito	—	+	+	—	+	+	—	—	—	—	—	—
Silometopus incurvatus	—	+	—	—	—	—	—	—	+	+	+	—
S. ambiguus	+	+	+	—	+	+	—	+	+	+	+	+
Trichoncus affinis	+	—	+	—	+	+	—	—	—	—	—	—
T. hackmani	—	—	+	—	+	+	—	—	—	—	—	—
Acanthophyma gowerensis	+	—	—	—	—	—	—	+	—	—	—	+
Ceratinopsis romana	—	+	—	—	+	+	+	+	+	—	—	—
Erigone arctica	+	—	+	—	+	+	+	+	+	+	+	+
E. longipalpis	+	—	—	—	+	+	+	+	+	+	+	+
Halorates reprobus	+	+	+	—	+	+	+	+	+	+	+	+
Total = 40	15	19	13	6	32	29	25	19	16	11	7	14

CRITERIA FOR KEY SITE ASSESSMENT AND SELECTION

Comparative site evaluation

Some criteria have been regarded as having paramount importance through the whole range of coastal habitats, and have been applied throughout, namely:

1. *Size*. Large extent of habitat and size of populations are probably the most highly rated single criterion in coastlands as a whole.

2. *Diversity*. Both physiographic diversity *per se* and ecological diversity in terms of habitat and organisms is considered important within each major type of coastland. Floristic and faunal richness have been highly rated, including presence of rare species.

3. *Bird populations*. The breeding birds of coastlands and

the winter wildfowl and wader populations are one of the most important biological features of Britain on the international scale. The population size and species diversity of local concentrations of coastal birds, considered especially in relation to international rarity, thus weigh considerably in the comparative assessment of sites.

4. *Freedom from disturbance.* Many coastal habitats are particularly subject to disturbance by reclamation, building, industrial development, pollution, shipping and recreation. Sites where these forms of disturbance are least in evidence are the most highly regarded.

In addition, a somewhat different emphasis is needed in applying criteria for assessment between the different major types of coastal habitat, and these are considered separately.

Flats

The most highly rated flats are those of great extent, with large wildfowl/wader populations which depend on a copious food supply, and hence on a fine-grained sediment, i.e. on silt and clay flats. *Zostera*-grown flats are considered especially valuable.

Salt marshes

Perhaps the most valued feature here is the representation of the full range of seral stages in marsh development, including transition inland to brackish or completely non-saline habitats. Marshes in which the pioneer stages of growth have been severely truncated by subsequent erosion, or those in which the more mature stages have been lost by reclamation behind sea walls cannot be considered to be of the highest value vegetationally, although in association with adjoining flats they may be important for wildfowl and waders. Extensive development of creeks and pans adds diversity, other things being equal. Pioneer stages dominated by *Spartina anglica* are considered to be much less desirable than those with other species. In general, northern salt marshes are less valued botanically than those in the south, as they are distinctly poorer floristically, but the reverse applies in their interest for breeding birds. High-lying mature marsh is valuable for breeding bird populations.

Sand dunes

Diversity of dune topography and an extensive development of slacks are regarded as especially important attributes of a sand-dune system, and are usually accompanied by parallel diversity in plant communities and flora. Calcareous dunes are usually more valued botanically than non-calcareous types, because of their much greater floristic richness.

Vegetated shingle beaches

Physiographic diversity and range of successional stages are important features and are usually linked to the master criterion of size. Floristic richness is also related to geographical position, the most valuable sites botanically being in the south.

Cliffs and related features

Botanical and ornithological values tend to diverge within this habitat. Cliffs and slopes with large bird populations are usually spoiled botanically by the heavy manuring and trampling. The best bird cliffs are sheer, with many bare, flat ledges, and fall into deep water; islands are especially favoured because of their lack of disturbance. The best botanical cliffs are more broken, with soil-covered slopes as well as steep rocks. Landslip features and undercliffs are usually additionally diversifying for plants and invertebrates, and may give a range of vegetation including scrub and woodland. Calcareous cliffs are the richest floristically, and sites where the cliff top passes into unenclosed heath or grassland (instead of arable land) are especially valuable. Height of the cliff is important in giving a range of conditions from saline to non-saline, and the presence of ravines, streams or seepage areas down the cliff also enhances diversity.

Lagoons

These are the rarest type of coastal habitat, and the question of comparative assessment often does not arise. However, the most highly valued type is that showing markedly brackish conditions, since this is the rarest class of open water habitat.

In addition, many coastal sites contain more than one major habitat, so that the criterion of diversity often has to be applied on a broader scale, covering a wider range of features. When a site contains examples of shingle beach, dunes, flats and salt marsh, its aggregate value may be greater than that of a site which contains a better example of one or two habitats but lacks the others. Often, however, this kind of diversity is regarded as a bonus feature, i.e. many sites selected as especially good examples of one habitat incidentally contain average examples of one or more other habitats.

Requirements for the national series

In selecting the series of key coastland sites, an attempt has been made to include both outstanding and representative examples of the total range of variation within each of the six main types of coastal habitat. Two of these types are so local that the choice has necessarily been limited to a small number of sites; coastal lagoons are so scarce that all good examples have been included; and the only vegetated shingle beaches of great importance are the few really large areas and these have all been included too.

Sea cliffs and rocky slopes are so widely distributed that a primary concern has been to select examples of each to represent the wide range of geographical variation in physical and biological features. Some of this regional diversity is related to geological or physiographic differences, especially hardness and calcium carbonate content of the rock. The greater part is, however, related to the climatic gradients which profoundly affect the distribution of plant and animal species. The selection of cliff and rocky slope sites to give a fairly even distribution around the British coast takes account of this geographical variation.

Sand dunes and salt marshes are also widely distributed, but the large and important systems of both are somewhat localised and well defined. Dunes are rather fragile eco-systems with high nature conservation interest, and most of the larger areas, representing the range of climatic, physiographic and edaphic diversity, are regarded as nationally important. The really large areas of salt marsh are concentrated around a relatively few major estuaries, and the choice of key sites here has thus involved a still less regular geographical distribution than for dunes, though regional differences, such as differential tilting of the land surface in relation to sea-level, and changing mean particle size of sediments, have been fully taken into account. Salt marshes are mostly small and floristically poor in Scotland north of the Solway Firth, and the examples represented are mostly bonus inclusions within sites selected for dune or other interest. Similarly, while most shingle beaches around our coasts have little biological interest, many bonus examples occur within sites chosen for other reasons, and dunes are also often represented in this way.

From the international standpoint, the most outstandingly important feature of British wildlife is its coastal bird populations, especially the concentrations of breeding sea-fowl on the sea cliffs and rocky offshore islands, the tern colonies of dunes, shingle beaches and rocky islands, and the multitudes of waders and wildfowl which throng the estuaries and their flats in autumn and winter. Because of this especially high value to nature conservation, policy for site selection here has departed deliberately from the usual practice of choosing important sample areas of ecosystems. Virtually all sites with major concentrations of these bird groups, above a certain population size, have been rated as nationally important. These levels (counted independently) are waders – 20000 birds; wildfowl – 10000 birds; cliff-breeding seabirds – 20000 pairs; breeding terns – 1000 pairs.

In addition, a certain differential in grading has been applied between these bird groups according to the criterion of fragility. The important concentrations of breeding auks, petrels, kittiwakes and gannets are mainly on remote and/or inaccessible precipices and rocky islands in the north and west of Britain; direct disturbance to their breeding habitats is a smaller threat to these birds than various forms of marine pollution, so that safeguarding sites is a lesser need than broader environmental control. Although all the major stations have been identified as nationally important, the normal policy of regarding some as grade 2 alternatives to others has been applied. On the other hand, estuaries with their large wader and wildfowl populations represent a particularly fragile type of ecosystem, in which the wildlife interest can all too easily be damaged or destroyed: since the destruction of any major estuary as habitat for these birds would represent a serious loss to nature conservation not only in Britain but in the world as a whole, most of the nationally important estuaries have been rated grade 1. Tern colonies and their habitats are also fragile, but the important ones are few and mostly covered in the selection of dune and shingle grade 1 sites.

A further problem is that, in addition to the cliff-breeding seabirds which feed at sea and spend their lives there outside the breeding season, some ducks wintering around the British coasts are sea-going species. It is not normally practicable to identify areas of sea as requiring safeguards for wildlife, but an exception has been made in the case of a few large inlets, notably the Firth of Forth.

A general difficulty in dealing with the ornithological interest of coastlands is that it is by no means constant. The numbers of the various bird groups in many key sites have changed considerably over several decades or even within one decade, often showing long-term decreases or increases rather than temporary fluctuations. Tern colonies are notoriously prone to major fluctuations, with movement between different locations, and show a general impermanence. Many cliff-nesting stations and estuarine wintering grounds have shown marked changes in the numbers of some species during this century. The causes are various: increasing human disturbance and marine pollution are obviously important factors at some sites, but there may be more subtle and uncontrollable influences at work, such as climatic change, or adverse human impact may occur when some species are wintering or breeding away from Britain. There is thus a clear implication that the ornithological value of sites must be periodically re-assessed, and provision made for possible re-grading of some areas when status rests on this criterion.

Wintering wildfowl and waders often show large differences between one year and the next, though these are sometimes more apparent than real, and may result from change in distribution. The use of alternative haunts by these non-resident populations and the changes in these patterns, can confuse matters. The figures quoted for wildfowl and wader populations (except where otherwise stated) are thus averages of annual counts. In the case of wildfowl this is the average of the highest record obtained in each of the five most recent seasons for which adequate data are available. Wader populations are average numbers recorded during the 1969/70, 1970/71 seasons and to January 1972 of the 1971/72 season.

The number of species of coastal vascular plant increases with distance south, and is greatest in south-west England. The series of key sites requires adequate representation of the various phytogeographical elements, and a good deal of attention has been paid to the selection of floristically rich sites, especially in the south. Many sand-dune and sea cliff sites are included particularly for their floristic richness, and the representation of oceanic species rare in Europe as a whole has been considered especially important. Aggregations of nationally rare species have been included by choice, but individual rarities are represented largely incidentally.

In the case of habitats typically showing a seral development of vegetation, the range of variation between differing successions and within each of these needs to be represented, e.g. succession on dunes varies according to geographical position (affecting species available for colonisation), lime content of the sand, and wetness of the substratum. The series of key sites has been chosen to represent as much regional and local ecological diversity as possible.

The selection of coastal sites for other reasons automatically ensures the representation of a wide range of invertebrate interest, but in a few instances, sites have been chosen principally for their entomological importance. Knowledge of coastal invertebrates is at present insufficient to indicate whether this group of organisms is adequately represented as a whole within the national series of key sites.

Coastlands are of great physiographic importance and it is essential that an adequate range of diversity within this field be represented. The series of coastal land forms has thus been chosen partly for the range of features which illustrate the dynamic processes involved in their formation and continuing development. In this respect, sites which show the relationships between the different classes of coastland, e.g. flats, salt marsh, shingle and sand dune, are especially valuable and a number of sites have been chosen for this reason.

The larger estuaries present considerable problems for site selection. In the Wash, Morecambe Bay and the Solway, the distribution of ornithological interest is not uniform, and the areas involved are so large that it would be desirable to identify the more and less important parts within each and grade these independently. The extensive flats and their bird populations are, however, difficult to survey and are mobile systems in which the distribution of interest may change. It is thus difficult at present to support the application of a differential grading to these large flat systems; this may be possible in time or it may prove to be undesirable. The case for differential grading nevertheless applies more strongly to the salt marsh areas which border the estuarine flats. There are grounds for regarding these marshes with the flats as a single continuous ecosystem; they are used by many birds, especially waders, as feeding grounds or resting places during high tide, and so form an integral part of their whole habitat. However, some marshes are less used than others by wintering birds and, in general, salt-marsh interest centres more on vegetation and breeding birds. Although some marshes can be identified as having more interest than others within a large estuary, it has been considered desirable on balance to designate the whole complex of flats and marshes as one site with an overall grading. Where there is a differential, it is noted in the site accounts and should be borne in mind at the stage where consideration is being given to practical measures for safeguarding these sites.

REGIONAL DIVERSITY AND SELECTION OF KEY SITES

As the field of ecological variation in coastlands has been described in terms of six major habitat/vegetation types, it would be logical to discuss the selection of sites on the same basis. However, coastal sites usually contain at least two, and often more, of these habitat/vegetation types, and it is more convenient to discuss their selection in a simple geographical order, moving through the administrative Regions of the Nature Conservancy from south to north. This treatment avoids duplication. Any attempt to divide up the coast in a

more natural way (e.g. to separate the soft and hard coasts of southern England) would seem likely to create more problems than it solves.

SOUTH-EAST ENGLAND

The south coast of Kent and Sussex includes the five headlands of North and South Foreland, Dungeness, Beachy Head and Selsey Bill. It is an area mainly of Cretaceous rocks, of which the Chalk gives long lines of impressive sheer cliff between St Margaret's and Folkestone in Kent, and from Eastbourne to Brighton in Sussex. These Chalk precipices were famous as having, up to 1956, the densest population of peregrine falcons in Britain, and probably in the whole of Europe. The highest face, on Beachy Head, reaches an elevation of 170 m, and Cuckmere Haven to Beachy Head is regarded as a grade 1 site (C.1).[1] There are also examples of salt marsh, shingle and cliff-top calcareous grassland within the site, which has a rich flora and is of considerable physiographic interest. The much more broken and vegetated cliffs and undercliffs of the landslip system known as Folkestone Warren (C.2, gr. 1) are also important physiographically and for their flora and rich insect fauna.

Much of the lower-lying part of this coast has shingle beaches and sands which have been developed as holiday resorts and now have little nature conservation value. There is, however, one relatively undeveloped site of major importance. The great shingle spit of Dungeness (C.3, gr. 1*) is one of the largest and most valuable coastal sites in Britain, and has international fame as a classic system of shingle ridges. The construction of a nuclear power station has detracted little from this value either physiographically or biologically, and there are few coastal areas with a comparable range of ecological diversity. Dungeness has an extremely rich flora, and a wide range of communities from open growths of maritime plants to closed heath and scrub on shingle, open water and fringing fen (Oppen Pits, OW.1), and it is an important migration point for birds and insects. The related area of Romney Marsh, formed to the north of the Dungeness shingle, is cut-off from the sea by an embankment, and is now mainly an area of neutral grasslands or arable farmland, with few maritime associations. It is not regarded as a key coastal site, although it has considerable biological value and is rated grade 2 for its open water in the east (OW.4). From Deal to Sandwich and beyond to Pegwell Bay, a rather narrow strip of coastal sand dune and foreshore is much disturbed by recreation seekers, and consists partly of golf courses. It is, however, extraordinarily rich in coastal invertebrates and has a very varied flora; the Pegwell Bay end is also important for birds. For these reasons, it is regarded as a grade 1 site (C.4).

Between Portsmouth and Chichester a complex of indentations of the sea occupies the sites of drowned river valleys largely cut through relatively soft Eocene beds; in this they contrast with the drowned river valleys cut through hard rocks in Devon, Cornwall and Pembrokeshire. The two deep inlets of Chichester and Langstone Harbours (C.5,

[1] Cross references to key sites are identified by an initial letter (indicating habitat) and number.

gr. 1*) form part of a single inter-tidal system and are treated as such. With their extensive tidal mud flats and fringing marshes they are wildfowl and wader haunts of particular importance (notably for dark-bellied brent geese, shelduck and black-tailed godwits), and support a rich salt marsh flora in which southern species are well represented.

In north Kent, on the south side of the Thames mouth, the estuaries of the Swale and the Medway, separated by the Isle of Sheppey and lying over Eocene beds, have extensive areas of former saltings, now isolated by sea walls to form grazing marshes, but with brackish fleets remaining. Salt marsh has formed subsequently, but to a variable extent, outside the sea walls. This south side of the Thames estuary is extremely valuable as a winter haunt of wildfowl and waders, which find food and sanctuary on the great areas of mud flats. Four key sites are distinguished here, namely: The Swale (Isle of Sheppey) (C.6, gr. 1) which has the greatest all round interest, with fine salt marshes, grazing marshes and fleets, and flats which carry large wader populations; High Halstow/Cliffe Marshes (C.8, gr. 2); these are of less botanical interest than the Swale, but have larger wildfowl populations; Allhallows Marshes/Yantlet Creek (C.9, gr. 2), mainly fresh marshes of ornithological interest, but with good insect populations and dune flora; and the Medway marshes and estuary represented by Burntwick Island and Chetney Marshes (C.7, gr. 1) which have a considerable area of dissected salt marsh and large flats, and are the most important wildfowl site in north Kent. These sites have a good deal in common with the coastal flats and salt marsh systems of the Essex coast, and are complementary as wildfowl/wader wintering grounds. In common with all areas of marine alluvium in this part of Britain there is a fine-textured substratum, giving muds rather than sands, and a rate and extent of accumulation which have been affected by the general subsidence of land in relation to sea-level which has occurred in south-east England.

SOUTH ENGLAND

The coastlands of this region are confined to Hampshire and the Isle of Wight and lie mainly on Tertiary deposits, though there are Cretaceous beds (Chalk, greensands and clays) on the Isle of Wight. The mainland shore is largely low-lying, and is indented by several major river estuaries. Of these, Langstone Harbour belongs to the same system as Chichester Harbour and is described under the south-east Region. Southampton Water and Portsmouth Harbour have been developed for shipping and industry, and the most important area ecologically is that of the North Solent Marshes (C.11), which is relatively undisturbed, and has good examples of salt marsh and vegetated shingle. That site is, however, not sufficiently different in these features from Poole Harbour to the west or Chichester–Langstone Harbours to the east to be rated higher than grade 2 (see Appendix).

On the Isle of Wight, the north coast is low-lying and somewhat built up in places, but there is an interesting inlet with flats, shingle and fringing marshes on the north-west side at Newtown Harbour (C.12, gr. 2) and a varied

though rather small population of wildfowl occurs in winter. The south coast has a good deal of quite high sea cliff, mainly of Chalk and greensands, which is cut by deep ravines, locally called 'chines'. The assemblage ranging from Chalk through sandstone to shale and clay has very variable physical properties and the existence of this mixture of hard and soft materials has led to extensive land-slipping, and formation of tiers of cliff separated by sloping ground. At the western point, resistant beds of Chalk have given rise to the famous jagged rock stacks of the Needles. To the east lie Tennyson Down and Compton Down, which are nationally important in their own right for chalk scrub and chalk grassland respectively. Between Blackgang Chine and St Catherine's Point, landslips have produced much undercliff, with rough grassland, scrub and woodlands. This whole stretch has an extremely rich flora and insect fauna, and is a haunt of the rare Glanville fritillary. This site (C.10, gr. 1) is of considerable physiographic importance, with shingle beaches and various types of cliff structure well represented.

EAST ANGLIA

This long coastline stretching from the Thames to the Humber, is the flattest stretch of coast in Britain. The Essex shore, between the Thames estuary and Orfordness, lies on the London Clay, is much indented by other large estuaries, and bordered mainly by mud flats, salt marshes and shingle beaches. This soft coast is one of the most important areas in Britain for estuarine birds and salt marshes. The flats and salt marshes resemble those of the north Kent coast in being formed mainly of fine sediment (silt rather than sand) and in their somewhat uniform vegetational character. There has again been a great deal of marsh reclamation using sea walls, but a very high proportion of this reclaimed land is now arable, and little fresh grazing marsh remains on the Essex coast. There has been variable, but locally extensive, development of low- to medium-level new marsh on the large systems of sand and mud flats outside the sea walls. At the southern end of this coast, between the Thames and Crouch estuaries, the Foulness peninsula (especially Foulness Island) and its vast expanse of flats, the Maplin Sands (9100 ha), form the most outstanding of these estuarine systems in nature conservation interest (C.13, gr. 1*). These flats carry large amounts of eel grass (Zostera) which in winter provides food for one-fifth of the total world population of the dark-bellied brent goose (6000 birds); there are also large numbers of other wildfowl and an average wader population of some 20000 birds (which may reach considerably higher peak numbers). The importance is thus international.

The Essex salt marshes as a whole are important for their rich flora and fauna, both vertebrate and invertebrate, and three other Essex estuaries are given grade 1 status. Immediately north of Foulness is the Blackwater Estuary, with the adjoining flats and marshes of the Dengie Peninsula running southwards to the Crouch, and the subsidiary estuary of the Colne joining its mouth on the north side. This is regarded as one large grade 1* site (C.14), of considerable importance for its wildfowl and wader populations. Salt marsh is here much more extensive than on the Foulness peninsula, and the total numbers of birds approach those of Maplin Sands though there are fewer brent geese.

Farther north, just beyond Walton-on-the-Naze, the broad inlet of Hamford Water (C.15, gr. 1) has developed a complex of salt marsh islands surrounded by mud flats and some vegetated shingle, and is regarded as an important site with an especially rich salt marsh flora and fauna. A little farther north again, the large estuary of the Stour is joined by the Orwell at its mouth, near Harwich. This is an area with large numbers of wintering wildfowl, especially wigeon, and is regarded as a grade 1 site (C.16) on this account, though there is also salt marsh interest. This is the last of the major estuaries of the Essex coast, but in the extreme south, at the eastern side of Canvey Island on the Thames estuary, the smaller area of Leigh Marsh (C.22, gr. 2) has considerable interest and, despite its proximity to Southend, is much used as a feeding place at certain times by a substantial proportion of the Essex brent goose population.

Farther north, in Suffolk, the long shingle spit of Orford-ness (C.17, gr. 1) south of Aldeburgh is one of the largest and best examples of this habitat in Britain, with very good shingle communities with local plants, while the associated Havergate Island is an important ornithological site, noted for its breeding colony of avocets. The coast of Suffolk and Norfolk between Aldeburgh and a point west of Shering-ham is composed largely of Pleistocene beds which form the most important area of these young rocks in Britain. The low-lying coast north to Happisburgh is fringed mainly by shingle beaches and narrow sand-dune ridges, of which the system at Winterton (C.18) is sufficiently valuable to rate as a grade 1 site; this is an example of an acidic dune area with a continental element in its flora. The tidal inlet of Breydon Water at Yarmouth is important ornithologically, and is bordered by a large area of fresh marshes, consisting of neutral meadow grasslands on former marine sediment. On this coast, beach erosion and re-deposition continually tend to dam up the waters of some rivers draining to the sea by forming bars across their mouth. This process has been restrained by artificially clearing the bars, but during World War II, as a defence precaution, the two wide and shallow valleys at Minsmere and Walberswick were allowed to dam up and flood. Extensive areas of flood-plain mire, with brackish conditions at the seaward end, developed in consequence, and the two sites (described in Chapter 8) are now of such national ecological importance, especially for rare marsh birds, that the area is rated grade 1*.

Between Happisburgh and Weybourne the Pleistocene deposits form lines of low, crumbling cliff which undergo continual erosion. These exposed beds of glacial gravels, sands and clays form one of the most important sections of Quaternary deposits in the world. There is little biological interest, however, except an East Anglian breeding place of fulmars. West of Weybourne and extending along the North Norfolk Coast almost to Hunstanton is one of the most extensive and valuable salt marsh systems in Britain. It includes the well-studied examples on Scolt Head Island and Blakeney Point, with their associated dune and shingle ridges, the still more extensive area between Blakeney Harbour and Holkham, and the sections at Cley and Salthouse in the east and Brancaster to Holme in the west. These are regarded as a single aggregate site (C.19) with the grading 1*. The whole area is of great physiographic importance, has a rich maritime flora, and is famous for its large tern colonies and other bird populations, both breeding and migratory.

A 30 m cliff of Chalk at Hunstanton is the only exposure of bedrock on the whole remaining sector of the East Anglian coast. Almost the whole of the great sea inlet of the Wash is bordered by salt marsh, but this varies a good deal in width, and in places is only a narrow strip. The maritime influence is restricted by a sea wall system round the whole of the Wash, and behind this the former salt marsh has been reclaimed to give mainly arable land. The Wash was formerly continuous with the Fenlands which lie inland to the south and represents a gulf eroded in Jurassic and Cretaceous beds, overlain by boulder clay and later by marine sediments. There was originally presumably a gradual transition, through a brackish zone, from salt marsh to freshwater flood-plain mire.

The Wash flats cover an enormous area and, taken as a single system, are of international importance for their winter population of waders, which number 180 000 birds, and are the second largest concentration in Britain. The total numbers of knot (up to 100 000) are the biggest in the country, and the flocks of dunlin, curlew and oystercatcher are very large. The wader interest is well distributed, though current studies may show that some areas of the Wash flats are consistently more important than others for these birds. The Wash is also of great importance for wildfowl, but some areas are more valuable than others for this group. The flats from Gibraltar Point to Wrangle in the north-west have the main goose populations, with 3000 brent geese (the second biggest British flock) and up to 2000 pink-footed. The estuary of the Welland in the south-west is another notable area, with large numbers of wigeon and a great breeding colony of black-headed gulls on the north side; and the north-east coast is regarded as the third most important area. The Wash sandbanks are also the main breeding ground of the common seal in Britain.

The salt marshes fringing the Wash have not been surveyed in detail; they are clearly not of uniform interest, and in botanical features are different from those of the North Norfolk Coast, mainly in being poorer in species and community types. As a large area of salt marsh is already included within the latter grade 1 site, there is no good case for rating those of the Wash higher than grade 2 on botanical grounds. Yet the Wash marshes are an essential part of the inter-tidal ecosystem lying outside the sea walls, and some of them (e.g. Terrington Marsh in particular) are clearly important as part of the habitat of the wader and wildfowl populations. Provisionally, therefore, the Wash is regarded as a single, large grade 1* site (C.20) with various sectors which may eventually receive a differential grading. Impoundment schemes have been the subject of a Wash Feasibility Study; such developments could have a significant impact on nature conservation interest within the whole inlet. Other studies are in progress to predict these effects.

On the coast of Lincolnshire north of the Wash, the Chalk is overlain by marine deposits mainly forming flats, salt marshes and narrow dune ridges. The dune systems at Gibraltar Point and Saltfleetby/Theddlethorpe (C.21, gr.1) are wider and of considerable interest; the latter has highly calcareous dunes with an extensive slack system, associated with a large area of salt marsh. Northwards, sea walls again restrict the area of saltings.

SOUTH-WEST ENGLAND

Geologically this long coastline from Bournemouth to the head of the Severn Estuary is complex but mainly sedimentary. It is a rockier coast than those of the previous regions, with long lines of sea cliff and relatively little salt marsh and sand dune.

Although Bournemouth lies on its northern edge, the south side of the large maritime inlet known as Poole Harbour (C.23, gr. 1), Dorset, is an important area biologically for its flats, *Spartina* and other salt marsh communities, brackish marshes, acidic dunes, and coastal lagoon of Little Sea (OW.21). This diverse coastal complex grades into the Purbeck heathlands. The Isle of Purbeck with its varied range of coastal habitats and inland heath/mire complex is scientifically one of the outstandingly important areas in Britain. Between Swanage and Weymouth the coast is bounded mainly by sea cliffs of Jurassic and Cretaceous rocks, including limestone and Chalk. This is a scenically famous area, containing Lulworth Cove. The long section from Durlston Head to Ringstead Bay is regarded as a most valuable grade 1 site (C.24), markedly different physiographically (notably more sheer cliff and less undercliff), in fauna and flora, from the south coast of the Isle of Wight. The cliffs and calcareous grasslands above them have a rich flora and fauna, including many local and rare insects. From Portland, the celebrated shingle spit of Chesil Beach (C.25, gr. 1*) runs north-west for 9 km, impounding a lagoon, The Fleet. This is one of the three most important shingle beaches in Britain, and the associated lagoon has considerable wildfowl interest. Just inside Devon the coastal cliff landslip area between Lyme Regis and Axmouth, where there has been extensive seaward slipping of masses of rock from cliffs formed of Chalk, greensands and clay, is regarded as a grade 1* coastal site (C.26). The woodland which has developed is also rated as nationally important (W.67, gr. 1). Chalk cliffs also occur from Axmouth to Sidmouth.

The deep inlet of the Exe Estuary has moderately extensive flats, salt marsh and some sand dunes, but this part of the Devon coast has a heavy tourist pressure and is not of great biological importance, except for wildfowl and waders (C.36, gr. 2). South of Torquay, the very local Devonian limestone has a major outcrop at Berry Head (L.105), an important grassland locality with bonus maritime interest. Start Bay contains the coastal lagoon and retaining shingle beach at Slapton Ley. Although the complex is treated as an open water site (OW.22, gr. 1), there is a noteworthy coastal interest. From here westwards to Falmouth the much-indented coast is eroded mainly in Devonian strata, with cliffs in places and river estuaries bounded by low ground. This is a less studied stretch, and the only known areas of national importance are the Lynher Estuary and St John's Lake (C.37, gr. 2) Cornwall, a site of some importance for wildfowl, and the Fal–Ruan Estuary (C.38, gr. 2), near Truro, where the coastal woodlands (W.61, gr. 1) are of greater interest than the maritime habitats *per se*. The headlands from Start Point to Bolt Tail are composed of hard schists and gneiss, and the more westerly promontory of the Lizard (C.27, gr. 1*) is formed of serpentine and hornblende schist, which give a range of paramaritime heaths and a Mediterranean flora not found elsewhere in Britain. Ecologically, this is an area of first national importance. It is described in detail in Chapter 6 (L.95, gr. 1*).

The Isles of Scilly (C.28, gr. 1*), a cluster of small granite islands about 48 km west-south-west of Land's End, have a climate of the markedly warm oceanic type, contrasting with the cool oceanic conditions of northern island groups, e.g. St Kilda. They are internationally important for their rich flora of rocky shores (including many rare oceanic lichens), their paramaritime acidic heaths (L.93, gr. 1*) and their bird populations, especially during spring and autumn migration. The granite island of Lundy, 19 km north-west of Hartland Point, is famous for its seabirds, though these are fewer than formerly.

The coast from Land's End to Minehead has a frontage of cliff or steep slopes for most of its length. Though not surveyed in detail, this long rocky coast is of considerable interest and five sectors have been chosen to represent the range of features, especially in relation to the considerable geological diversity. The first, from Porthgwarra to Pordenack Point (C.39), lies on the granite of Land's End, but as its main features are represented on the Scilly granite, it is rated grade 2. The second, still on the Land's End peninsula, extends from Cape Cornwall to Clodgy Point by St Ives (C.29), and is on a complex mixture of sedimentary and intrusive igneous rocks. This is floristically much more diverse than the previous site, and is regarded as grade 1. Farther east, the Lower Devonian rocks from Godrevy Point to St Agnes Head (C.30) form a grade 1 stretch of cliff with interesting plant communities and flora; they are mostly on poor soils and include the lowland acidic heath site of Chapel Porth (L.94, gr. 1). The fourth, from Boscastle to Widemouth (C.31, gr. 1), is on the Culm Measures just south of Bude. The cliffs here are more broken and unstable in many places, and extensive steep slopes and undercliffs have a much wider range of paramaritime vegetation including scrubby, wind-pruned oakwood, than the previous Cornwall cliff sites. The Dizzard oakwood (W.62, gr. 1) is one of the best examples of this type in Britain. This relatively acidophilous undercliff vegetation complex contrasts with the calcicolous types at Axmouth–Lyme Regis. Another stretch of cliff on this geological formation has been chosen as grade 1: between Steeple Point and Black Church

Rock east of Hartland Point (C.32). The cliffs here are mostly steeper, but interrupted by the mouths of several deep, fairly sheltered valleys which drain to the sea. This is a faunally rich area, containing one of the few remaining haunts of the large blue butterfly, one of Britain's rarest insects, and a still declining species. The valleys contain complexes of paramaritime vegetation, i.e. grassland, heath, scrub and woodland. All these stretches of rocky coast have a rich cliff and cliff slope flora, with a strong representation of southern oceanic species. The precipices were formerly breeding strongholds of peregrines and choughs and still hold a good many pairs of ravens and buzzards.

Near Newquay, this rocky coast is interrupted by the large and interesting dune system of Penhale Sands and lower shores also break the continuity of the Culm Measure cliffs in Barnstaple Bay. At Braunton Burrows (C.33, gr. 1*) a large calcareous dune system forms the best example of this ecosystem within the region of warm oceanic climate. From Braunton to Minehead the coast lies almost entirely on Old Red Sandstone strata and there are cliffs or steep wooded slopes above the sea, especially between Coombe Martin and Minehead. From here to the Severn Estuary Triassic and Jurassic beds prevail and the shores are mostly low-lying, broken at Weston-super-Mare by the small but botanically important headland of Brean Down, where the Carboniferous Limestone projects westwards from the Mendip Hills; this is, however, of greater importance as a lowland grassland site (L.104, gr. 1). The most important coastal site in the Bristol Channel is Bridgwater Bay (C.34, gr. 1*), at the mouth of the River Parrett, where vast mud flats, with fringing marshes and shingle beaches, are a valuable wildfowl and wader haunt. The Severn Estuary (C.40, gr. 2) has wader populations of national importance and near its head the New Grounds at Slimbridge (C.35, gr. 1) are especially notable for their wildfowl and well-known as the headquarters of the Wildfowl Trust.

SOUTH WALES

The coast of south Wales is geologically complex, but sectors of importance to nature conservation are limited. The coasts of Monmouthshire and Glamorgan are formed mainly on sedimentary Carboniferous, Triassic and Jurassic rocks, and have been much industrialised. There is a botanically interesting stretch of Liassic limestone cliff coast west of Barry and much of the flatter shore between Porthcawl and Swansea was formerly fringed by sand dunes. Steel works at Port Talbot and Margam have spoiled some of these sandhills, but the large dune system at Kenfig (C.47) farther south is still an important site, though rated grade 2 by comparison with other dune areas in south Wales. On the inner side of the dunes is the large Kenfig Pool, a grade 2 open water site (OW.30).

West of Swansea, the Carboniferous Limestone peninsula of Gower has two important grade 1 sites. On the south side, stretching from Worms Head to Bishopston valley (C.41), is a varied complex of calcareous habitats, ranging from sea cliffs with maritime vegetation and birds, cliff top and slope paramaritime limestone grasslands, scrub and woodland, to the Oxwich dunes with their adjoining flats, salt marsh and rich-fen. This is an extremely diverse and floristically rich area and of great value educationally. On the north side of Gower, the broad and deep inlet of the Burry (C.42, gr. 1), has extensive flats with very large winter concentrations of waders; it is bordered on the south side by the important calcareous dune system of Whiteford, and farther east by a large area of salt marsh, while at the back of this soft coastal strip is a line of limestone cliff with scrub and woodland. North-west of the Burry Inlet a large dune area at Tywyn Gwendraeth (C.48, gr. 2), is considered another alternative site (besides Kenfig) to the combined Oxwich and Whiteford systems.

On the coast of Carmarthenshire, the long line of dunes between Laugharne and Pendine is considered to be of regional interest only. There are a few minor sea cliffs, but the next important stretch of coast begins in Pembrokeshire. Apart from the deep estuarine inlet of Milford Haven on Old Red Sandstone rocks and the head of St Bride's Bay on Coal Measures, much of the Pembrokeshire coast consists of cliff, which once supported a large breeding population of peregrines. They are still the nesting place of many ravens and buzzards and some choughs, but the mainland colonies of seabirds are far eclipsed by those of the offshore islands. Carboniferous Limestone stretches discontinuously westwards from Tenby to Linney Head. The section from Stackpole Head to Castlemartin, including the Flimston Stacks, has been rated grade 1 (C.43); it differs from the South Gower Coast in its more strongly maritime character, and is the best stretch of limestone cliff in Britain for maritime (as distinct from paramaritime) vegetation.

Milford Haven suffers pollution from its oil refinery and is now of relatively little biological interest. Farther north-west the rocky offshore islands of Skokholm, Skomer, Grassholm and Ramsey are composed of Old Red Sandstone and Ordovician rocks. They are the most important seabird stations in south-west Britain, with especially large numbers of Manx shearwaters and gannets. They are regarded as a single aggregate grade 1* site, the Ynysoedd Preseli (C.45). The coast from St David's to Fishguard is geologically complex, with Ordovician and Cambrian grits and shales much interrupted by igneous intrusions and extrusions, especially of dolerite. The section running 6.5 km south from Strumble Head (C.44) has been chosen as a grade 1 site for its cliff and cliff top vegetation, whilst the cliffs of St David's Head (C.49) are regarded as a grade 2 alternative.

From Fishguard eastwards along the coast of Cardigan Bay to Towyn, grits and shales of Ordovician and Silurian age prevail. The sea cliffs along much of the coast from Fishguard to Aberystwyth have not been properly surveyed, but no outstanding areas are known to exist. It is thought that the nature conservation interest is adequately represented by the Pembrokeshire cliff key sites named above.

North of Aberystwyth, in Cardiganshire, the large, deep inlet of the Dyfi estuary is an important coastal site (C.46, gr. 1), with a large system of flats, dunes, and salt marsh formed on the south side behind a protecting storm beach bar across the estuary mouth at Aberdyfi. Inland from the present maritime area is a large raised mire, Cors Fochno (Borth Bog) (P.29, gr. 1*), which has developed over former marine sediments. A submerged forest points to the origin of the estuary as involving the drowning of an earlier embayment.

NORTH WALES

A few kilometres north of Aberdyfi, the rock of the coast changes from Ordovician and Silurian to Cambrian in age, into which is cut the deep inlet of the Mawddach estuary, another drowned embayment of Cardigan Bay. The Mawddach has some fringing salt marsh, but there is no coastal site of great importance here. This long inland extension of an arm of the sea may, however, have some influence in maintaining extremely mild, oceanic conditions over the surrounding area which is noted for the richness of its Southern Atlantic bryophyte flora, especially in the numerous woods and rocky glens on the lower hill slopes close to the estuary. Cambrian beds extend in a continuous mass northwards, forming the Harlech Dome, and reach the area around Porthmadog in Caernarvonshire. Here, the twin arms of a deep inlet, the Traeth Mawr and Traeth Bach, have been reclaimed and former flats and saltings transformed into neutral grassland. On the Merioneth coast, on either side of Harlech, two important calcareous and floristically rich sand-dune systems (Morfa Harlech and Morfa Dyffryn) have formed; these are regarded as a single grade 1 site (C.50). The areas of flat still remaining in Traeth Bach, which are of some importance as a winter wildfowl haunt, are included within the Morfa Harlech sector.

The tip of the Lleyn peninsula has some high sea cliffs, formed by erosion of hard Ordovician and Precambrian beds and some dolerite intrusions. The rocky offshore island of Bardsey and the adjoining mainland cliffs near Aberdaron (C.53, gr. 2) are perhaps the most interesting part of this coast, though their main features probably duplicate those of the Ynysoedd Preseli (C.45) and Strumble Head (C.44) grade 1 sites in south Wales. There are several other cliff headlands and the lower islands of St Tudwals have ornithological value. Nearer Nefyn, the Bird Rock has a good cliff seabird colony and the granite and felsite mass of Yr Eifl forms a coastal mountain (U.15, L.122, gr. 2) which throws down a great escarpment to the sea and has good acidophilous heaths. From there to the Menai Straits, the coast is rather low-lying, with a small dune system at Morfa Dinlle. Much of the north coast of Wales is developed as holiday resort, and the most important site is where the Carboniferous Limestone runs out to form the two headlands of the Great and Little Orme. Both have high sea cliffs with bird colonies, but are regarded as lowland calcareous grassland rather than maritime sites. The Great Orme, in particular, has a rich calcicolous flora, and is rated as a grade 1 grassland (L.121) site; its maritime interest is rather less. The mud flats of the sheltered inlet of Conway Bay are also of considerable regional interest for their large populations of wintering waders.

A Carboniferous Limestone belt in the east of Anglesey gives rise to sea cliffs from Arthur's Table to Penmon Point and the adjoining Puffin Island. Although this is a floristically rich area, the limestone from Red Wharf Bay to Moelfre is not particularly noteworthy. There are modest seabird colonies but Puffin Island itself is now dominated by a huge herring gull colony. In the south-west, the large and botanically important calcareous sand-dune system of Newborough Warren, now partly afforested, lies over Precambrian metamorphic and igneous rocks, which are exposed as a ridge running out to Ynys Llanddwyn. The Malltraeth estuary to the north and the Braint estuary to the south have a good deal of salt and brackish marsh. This group of coastal habitats is regarded as a single grade 1 site (C.51), and the Malltraeth and Braint sections have wildfowl interest. Farther north-west the smaller calcareous dune system at Aberffraw (C.54, gr. 2), has interesting rare bryophytes. The northern and western coasts of Anglesey are mostly on ancient Precambrian rocks, extensively exposed as sea cliff. These reach the greatest height (137 m) at the North Stack on Holyhead Island, but the most interesting area biologically is from the South Stack to Penrhyn Mawr, where there are seabird cliffs, rare plants, good coastal dwarf-shrub heaths and interesting geological features. The Glannau Ynys Gybi is designated a coastal grade 1 site (C.52) and the cliff tops are a lowland acidic heathland grade 1 site (L.120). This sector probably includes most of the interesting features to be seen on the rugged north coast of Anglesey from Carmel Head to Point Lynas. The rocky island of Ynys Fenrig, off Rhosneiger has good tern colonies, but this interest is adequately represented elsewhere (e.g. Farne Islands).

MIDLANDS

This small stretch of coastline consists of the Wirral peninsula in Cheshire. On the west is the large estuary of the Dee, lying on its other shore in Flintshire; on the east, the Mersey, shared with Lancashire. The area is underlain by Triassic beds and Coal Measures, and the coast of both estuaries is almost entirely low lying. Although industrialised in part, the Dee Estuary (C.55, gr. 1*) with its large areas of flat and coastal salt marsh, is a site of high ornithological importance for its wader population, the third largest in Britain. Wildfowl numbers are smaller but of considerable interest. The small rocky island of Hilbre is much used as a resting place at high tides by large concentrations of waders. The upper Mersey above Liverpool has extensive flats but is important mainly for its large wintering population of duck – waders are much less numerous than on the Dee. It is rated as a grade 2 site (C.56). The projected road crossing and barrage scheme for the Dee may however lower the nature conservation value of that estuary and increase that of the Mersey, and the respective gradings of these two sites should be kept under review.

NORTH ENGLAND

This region has two coastal sectors; in the west, against the Irish Sea, from the Mersey to the head of the Solway; in the east bordering the North Sea from Spurn Head to Berwick on Tweed. On the west, low shores on Triassic beds occur between the Mersey and Heysham in Lancashire. The large calcareous sand-dune system of Ainsdale south of Southport (C.57, gr. 1), is a most important site botanically and zoologically, lately under heavy pressure from developers and recreation seekers. Between Southport and Blackpool lies the large series of flats, salt marshes and reclaimed marshes on the estuary of the Ribble (C.58, gr. 1*), mainly on its south side. The area is a major wildfowl and wader haunt and the complex of salt marshes and fresh marshes is an important example of the type characteristic of north-west England, with large and varied breeding bird populations in the spring and summer.

The hinterland of Morecambe Bay is composed mainly of Carboniferous Limestone rocks, exposed in places as low cliffs on the northern and eastern sides, and has some botanical interest, notably at Humphrey Head (L.133). The Bay contains four major estuaries, the Kent and Leven in the north, and the Lune and Wyre in the south, between Morecambe and Fleetwood. A vast system of sand–silt flats has developed which, in the aggregate, support in winter the largest population of wading birds in Britain, estimated at a peak of about 235 000 birds. Wildfowl are less important though numbers are considerable locally, especially in the Wyre–Lune area and there are up to 5000 shelduck on the Flookburgh to Carnforth Marshes in the late autumn/ winter. Salt marshes have developed in places around the Bay, but are less extensive and important than those of the Ribble or the Solway farther north. These marshes pass abruptly into oak or mixed deciduous woodland on more elevated ground in a few places, as at Silverdale and Roudsea Wood. Salt marsh also links up with the reconstituted brackish to fresh *Phragmites* swamps of Leighton Moss (P.51) at Silverdale. All the inter-tidal flats and marshes of Morecambe Bay are regarded as one large and outstanding grade 1* site (C.59); there is, however, a possibility of development, at least in part, for freshwater impoundments within the Bay.

The long, narrow Triassic island of Walney at the northern entrance to Morecambe Bay has small but faunally and floristically rich dune systems at its extremities, the northern one lying close to another rich dune area on limestone at Sandscale, on the mainland of Furness. The range of interest complements that of Ainsdale (the birds are much more important) and the three areas are treated as a single grade 1 site (C.60), which also includes quite extensive areas of shingle and sand flats and the small island of Foulney. Sandscale and north Walney border the deep inlet of the Duddon estuary which has fringing sand flats and salt marshes similar to those of the Leven, is important for its large wader population and is separately rated as a grade 2 site (C.66). On the coastal plains bordering the Duddon, Leven and Kent estuaries raised mires have developed on former marine sediments. Triassic rocks extend northwards up the Cumberland coast to Whitehaven. On the estuary of the Irt and Esk at Ravenglass are two systems of dunes; those of Drigg Point (C.67, gr. 2) to the north are famous ornithologically for breeding gulls and terns; those of

Eskmeals to the south are mainly of botanical interest. Most of this south-west coast of Cumberland is low, with boulder clay banks and shingle beaches, but at St Bees the Triassic sandstone is finely exposed in a cliff headland. St Bees Head has moderate-sized seabird colonies and a few notable plants, but has less all-round interest than some headlands on the Galloway coast opposite.

An industrialised coast on Coal Measures runs north to Maryport, and beyond this the Permo-Triassic sandstone extends to the Scottish border, at the head of the Solway Firth, though except for some small cliffs at Rockcliffe, the sandstone is not exposed. This section of the Cumberland coast is low lying, with shingle beaches and narrow dune systems to Grune Point, while beyond this to the point where the River Eden becomes tidal at Rockcliffe, the shore is fringed mainly by salt marshes of varying width. The Upper Solway (which has to be considered in relation to the northern, Scottish, as well as the southern, English, shore) is an area of outstanding ornithological importance. The vast system of inter-tidal sand flats is the haunt of great numbers of waders and wildfowl, with an especially valuable population of barnacle geese. Some of these birds frequent the adjoining salt marshes, high-lying grass plains which are the breeding place of large numbers of wading and other birds. Vegetationally, the salt marshes are interesting as examples of the more extreme type of north-western succession, with development on sand (rather than silt or mud) to a mature phase not found in the south-east. The flats and marshes of the Upper Solway as a whole are regarded as a site of international importance (C.61, gr. 1*). At the head of the Firth, the broad tongue of Rockcliffe Marsh between the estuaries of the Eden and the Esk, and the adjacent Burgh Marsh south of the Eden, rival the Ribble Marshes as the most important salt marsh system in north-west England. Between Drumburgh and Bowness-on-Solway the fringing marsh is extremely narrow, but farther west, on the Cardurnock peninsula, it widens and shows accretion, while in the deep inlet of Moricambe Bay, there is a fairly extensive system on Longnewton and Skinburness Marshes, though this is regarded as less important than Rockcliffe and Burgh Marshes.

There has apparently been a decline of interest in the Solway as a possible site for an estuarine barrage, and it may now be one of the least threatened of the major British estuaries.

On both sides of the Solway, large systems of raised mire have developed on sediments originally laid down by the sea. This coastline has risen relative to sea-level during the latter part of the Post-glacial Period, and the inner zones of some salt marshes are now so elevated that they are flooded only by exceptionally high tides. These Solway marshes are, conversely, vulnerable to marginal erosion, and this is a conspicuous feature on most sites.

The Humber (C.62, gr. 1*) has extensive inter-tidal flats with outstanding wildfowl and wader interest; they are divided into the lower Humber between Spurn Head and Hull, and the upper Humber between Hull and the Trent mouth. From Spurn to Flamborough the coast is bordered mainly by a narrow strip of sand and shingle beach, and the underlying Chalk has little influence. Between Flamborough Head and Filey, however, the Chalk is exposed in a long line of cliffs from Bempton to Buckton, ranging from 60 to 120 m high, and long famous for a great breeding colony of seabirds, the largest in England (C.63, gr. 1*) and formerly farmed for its eggs. The western, Speeton end of the cliffs has a more broken and vegetated escarpment with undercliffs.

Between Scarborough and Saltburn, the Jurassic rocks of the Cleveland Hills are extensively exposed along the coast as mainly broken stretches of cliff and steep slopes cut by deep and sometimes wooded gills well-known for their fossil-bearing beds. Near Robin Hood's Bay an extensive landslip area on these rather soft rocks at Beast Cliff (C.68, gr. 2) has a good example of coastal slope oakwood (W.160, gr. 2). To the west of Whitby they form the highest sea cliff in England at Boulby Cliff (200 m). The estuarine inlet of Teesmouth (C.69, gr. 2) formerly had good salt marshes, and the flats are still an important wader and wildfowl haunt, but the area has been so heavily industrialised that its interest is much depleted. The Magnesian Limestone occupies the Durham coast from Hartlepool to South Shields, and is exposed as low cliffs in places, as at the stack of Marsden. This sector is also somewhat spoiled by industrial development and has more geological than biological interest. The section from Hart Warren to Hawthorne Dene (C.70), which includes part of the wooded glen of Castle Eden Dene (W.162) is, however, rated as grade 2. The Coal Measure coast between Tynemouth and Amble in Northumberland is low and drift-covered and has no special interest apart from the low-lying Coquet Island off Amble, which is rated as grade 2 for its large tern colonies (C.71), though these are less valuable than those of the Farnes. The remaining sector, from Alnmouth to Berwick, on the Carboniferous Limestone Series and also partly drift obscured, has some important sites. The limestones are here secondary to sandstones and shales, but an interesting geological feature here is the exposure, on the coast, of the doleritic Whin Sill. This more resistant rock has given rise to the rather low cliffs at Bamburgh, Dunstanburgh and Lindisfarne (Holy Island) and is well seen in the cliffs near Craster; it forms the rocky offshore group of the Farne Islands (C.64, gr. 1*), noted for their great variety and numbers of breeding birds, and grey seals. Holy Island lies offshore, connected with the mainland by exposed sand banks at low tide. Between the island and the mainland shore the extensive Fenham Flats are a noted wildfowl and wader haunt. Holy Island has a long western ridge of calcareous dunes, contrasting with the more acidic and wider dune system of Ross Links on the opposite mainland shore. Budle Bay, south-east of Ross Links, also has wildfowl–wader interest. The whole complex here is regarded as a single grade 1 site (C.65).

SOUTH SCOTLAND

This region has a western coast extending from the head of the Solway at Sarkfoot to Arrochar at the head of Loch Long; and an eastern coast stretching from Berwick to the head of the Forth near Stirling. Triassic sandstones extending round the north side of the Solway to Annan then give way to a belt of Carboniferous sandstones and shales. At the Lochar mouth there is a further change to Permian sandstone which extends along the east shore of the Nith estuary, while the west shore is on Silurian beds, broken by the Criffel granite intrusion. Small fringing marshes along the north Solway shore widen considerably between the Lochar and Nith estuaries, giving the important salt marsh of Caerlaverock Merse and the smaller Kirkconnell Merse west of the Nith. Off Caerlaverock lie the great sand flats of the Blackshaw Bank. This estuarine complex is regarded as one of the two most important parts of the Upper Solway (C.61, gr. 1*) site, for its winter wildfowl and wader populations, and complements the Rockcliffe–Burgh Marsh system nearer the head of the Solway, especially as some of the birds move between the two sites. There are also important breeding bird populations, and a considerable vegetational interest.

Carboniferous rocks run out to Southerness Point and from there to Southwick Bay; this is a low shore with some minor salt marsh and sand dune areas. Silurian rocks give good cliffs to the west and there are scrubby growths of woodland on steep banks along this botanically interesting sector. The Criffel granite occupies most of Rough Firth and Auchencairn Bay, where there are low, wooded promontories and a few islands, but gives way to the Silurian at Balcary Head, where steep cliffs have breeding auks and other sea birds. Apart from a further occurrence of Carboniferous sandstones stretching to Abbey Head, most of the Galloway (Kirkcudbrightshire and Wigtownshire) coast lies on Silurian greywackes and shales, which give long sections of moderately high cliff, reaching c. 90 m at the Mull of Galloway at the far west end of this coast. In places steep banks hold wind-pruned woodland and scrub, as at Ravenshall (W.179, gr. 2), and this is a most interesting coastline botanically. The cliff coast of Galloway resembles that of Pembrokeshire and Devon–Cornwall in general character, but requires representation in a key site for its more northern features. The section of Wigtownshire cliff coast running several kilometres north-west from the Mull of Galloway itself has been chosen as having the greatest biological interest (C.73, gr. 1). There are modest-sized seabird colonies at the Mull, and the sector from here to Crammag Head, which has basic cliffs, is rich botanically, several southern maritime plants here reaching their northern limits, whilst cliff top and slope communities are very well developed. The Borgue coast in Kirkcudbrightshire (C.77, gr. 2) between Fleet and Kirkcudbright Bays has been chosen as an alternative, but lacks the same degree of ornithological interest as the Mull, and has lower cliffs.

This is an indented coast, with sandy estuaries between the major headlands. The Cree estuary at the head of Wigtown Bay has a moderately large system of sand flats rated as grade 2 (C.78) for their wildfowl–wader interest. The sands at the head of the much larger Luce Bay between Burrow Head and the Mull are smaller but feed a large and interesting acidic dune system, Torrs Warren (C.72, gr. 1), which has well-developed acidophilous slack vegetation and dune heath. The low stacks of the Scar Rocks, with a gannetry and guillemots, lie at the mouth of Luce Bay.

North of the Mull, the Rhinns of Galloway have a good deal of cliff along their west side, there being no change of topography where the Silurian gives way to Ordovician rocks, and the same kind of coastal terrain continues northwards into Ayrshire from the entrance to Loch Ryan. From Currarie Point northwards, the coast becomes geologically more complicated, and on the Coal Measures between Ayr and Ardrossan there is a good deal of urbanisation. The most important sectors of the mainland coast of southern Ayrshire are those south of Lendalfoot, and between the Maidens and the Heads of Ayr, both of which have moderately high cliffs and some coastal woodland. The latter is a woodland site (W.174, gr. 2). North of Ardrossan, the coast at Hunterston has cliffs of intrusive felsite and coastal woodland set back a little from the sea, and in the bay between Hunterston and Fairlie, at the entrance to the Clyde, an area of sand flats has large wader populations in winter.

About 18 km off the Ayrshire coast opposite Girvan is the great granite cone of Ailsa Craig (C.74, gr. 1*), with its huge seabird colonies, especially gannets, herring gulls, auks and kittiwakes, of considerable international importance. The larger islands of the Clyde are rather limited in their coastal interest. Arran has some raised beaches and sea cliffs, but probably the most important coastal feature of this geologically complex island is woodland and scrub on rocky slopes. The island of Bute has wildfowl interest, and there are some minor ranges of sea cliff here and on Little Cumbrae.

As northern Ayrshire passes into Renfrewshire, the coast lies on Old Red Sandstone, but is mostly bounded by the main road, and becomes increasingly influenced by urban–industrial development. The upper section of the Clyde estuary, above Port Glasgow, nevertheless has considerable conservation interest, in the Erskine mud flats, another area with a large winter population of waders. The north coast of the Clyde from Toward Point to Ardentinny is bounded by road, and the long sea-loch inlet of Loch Long has a mainly rocky shore, changing rapidly to sloping ground which has no maritime character and is extensively afforested.

On the east coast, sandstones and shales of the Lower Carboniferous extend from Berwick to Burnmouth and then give way to Silurian beds. Near St Abb's Head there is an outcrop of Old Red Sandstone with lavas of the same age forming the headland itself. A fine series of sea cliffs with large seabird colonies and a rich flora gives sections through all three of these geological systems (C.75, gr. 1). The bird populations are perhaps less important than at Bempton (C.63) or Fowlsheugh (C.85), but the botanical interest is greater. From the end of the cliffs beyond Fast Castle to the head of the Forth, the coast lies on an assemblage of sedimentary rocks in which there are numerous occurrences of both intrusive and extrusive igneous rocks. For the most part the coast is low-lying, and among the most interesting features is a string of small rocky volcanic islands. The best

known of these is the Bass Rock (C.79, gr. 2), off North Berwick, which has a large gannetry but is regarded as less important for breeding seabirds than Ailsa Craig (see Appendix). Nearer Edinburgh some small low islands in the Firth of Forth have large terneries (C.80, gr. 2). There is an interesting system of flats, salt marsh and sand dunes between Gullane and Aberlady Bay, and the sandflats, mussel beds and open waters of the upper Forth (C.76, gr. 1*) are a notable wildfowl and wader haunt in winter, with a huge population of scaup.

EAST SCOTLAND

The East Scotland Region has a long coast, stretching from the head of the Firth of Forth to Inverness, and including also the northern island groups of Orkney and Shetland. The north shore of the Forth, lying mainly in Fife, is on a varied assemblage of Carboniferous rocks, with numerous igneous masses. There are botanically interesting, rather low, basaltic cliffs and calcareous dunes at Kincraig, but much of this coast is developed and has relatively little nature conservation value. The wildfowl interest of the Forth extends to the north shore flats, but the most important site is the ecologically diverse Isle of May (C.81, gr. 1) with abrupt dolerite cliffs rising to a grassy plateau. This is a famous bird migration station, where this aspect of ornithology has been much studied, and a quite important breeding haunt of cliff seabirds; but a vast herring gull colony on the plateau has reduced other interest in recent years; the vegetation has been profoundly modified and four species of tern have ceased to nest. The Carboniferous rocks give way to Old Red Sandstone north of St Andrew's Bay, but the latter is obscured by drifted sand which gives the important acidic dune system of Tentsmuir Point (C.82, gr. 1) with its rich flora, and a continental character compared with Torrs Warren. The associated flats here and in the adjoining Eden estuary to the south (C.93, gr. 2) are of considerable importance for their wildfowl.

The deep inlet of the Firth of Tay (C.83, gr. 1*) has large sand flats and salt marshes along its northern shore above Dundee, and these are a wildfowl and wader haunt of considerable national importance. The Firth of Tay lies mainly on sediments of Old Red Sandstone-age with some andesite and basalt lavas, and alternating sequences of these two rocks extend up the Angus and Kincardineshire coasts to Stonehaven. The southern part of this coast is mostly low lying, and contains the deep natural inlet of the Montrose Basin, with its large flats which are a regionally important wildfowl and wader haunt. North of Montrose, the lavas outcrop as a series of cliffs at St Cyrus (C.84, gr. 1), and there is here a coastal sector of extraordinary ecological diversity and floristic richness, with base-rich cliffs, grasslands, sand dunes, salt marshes and flats. Immediately south of Stonehaven a long line of vertical cliffs has huge rock colonies of seabirds, especially kittiwakes and guillemots, and is known locally as Fowlsheugh (C.85, gr. 1*). This is an important site, with one of the three largest mainland breeding populations of seabirds, though there is little botanical interest.

North of Stonehaven the coast lies mainly on meta-morphic schists and grits of the Dalradian Series, and there are long stretches of rather low sea cliff. The most important site on this part of the eastern seaboard lies north of Aberdeen, at the mouth of the Ythan, where a large acidic dune system, the Sands of Forvie (C.86, gr. 1*), has developed. The Ythan estuary is quite small but has large and valuable wildfowl populations, while the dunes have great interest both botanically and in their breeding birds, and are regarded as the northernmost grade 1 example of lowland acidic heath (L.150, gr. 1). The granite sector either side of Peterhead has some extensive seabird cliffs. North-west of Rattray Head is the calcareous dune system and large coastal lagoon of Strathbeg (C.87, gr. 1), another important wildfowl site, and farther round on the marches of Aberdeenshire and Banffshire, the north coast has a fine series of high sea cliffs with large seafowl colonies from Macduff to Troup Head and Pennan Head (C.88, gr. 1). The rocks here are Old Red Sandstone lying on Dalradian meta-sediments, and there is a rich flora, with several montane species growing on sea cliffs. The range of interest is similar to that of the St Abb's coast, but this more northerly site is regarded as sufficiently important for grade 1 status also.

Much of the remaining south shore of the Moray Firth is low-lying, and on Dalradian rocks or Old Red and Permo-Triassic sandstones. The most important coastal site here is the Culbin Sands (C.89, gr. 1), with extensive flats and the largest dune system in Britain, now partly afforested and of importance both for coastal and northern woodland birds.

Orkney and Shetland are both archipelagos with a very long total extent of coast, most of which has not been examined for nature conservation interest. Only the more obviously important known sites can thus be discussed. In particular, these island groups are internationally important for their breeding seabirds. The total auk population (guillemot, razorbill, puffin) of Orkney approaches 200000 pairs, there are around 130000 pairs of kittiwakes, and the Arctic tern population exceeds 12000 pairs. The numbers of these species on Shetland are evidently not quite so great, but there are large numbers of gannets, and the bulk of the great and Arctic skuas nesting in Britain occur here.

The Orkneys are composed almost entirely of Old Red Sandstone, with numerous igneous dykes. On the island of Hoy, the sandstone gives one of the most formidable lines of vertical precipice in Britain, and St John's Head, reaching 335 m, is the highest truly vertical cliff in the country. This part of North Hoy is regarded as a grade 1 upland site (U.74) and has high quality montane heaths at an unusually low elevation; it is rated as a grade 2 coastal site for its cliff features and associated seabirds and vegetation (C.94). Elsewhere in Orkney, the coast varies from sea cliff to low sandy and shingly beaches. Botanically these shores are interesting, e.g. large colonies of *Mertensia maritima* and *Primula scotica*, and fuller survey could well reveal some sites of high quality. Westray and Papa Westray have very large colonies of guillemots, kittiwakes and Arctic terns, while the island of Copinsay and the Mainland cliff coast at Marwick Head are also large seabird breeding stations. The

two remote, rocky islands of Sule Skerry and Sule Stack off Orkney are important for their breeding seabirds (especially puffins and gannets, respectively).

Shetland is a complex assemblage of sedimentary, igneous and metamorphic rocks. The island of Noss on the east side is Old Red Sandstone and has high sea cliffs with large seafowl colonies (C.91, gr. 1*), including gannets, and important populations of great and Arctic skuas on its plateau. In the northernmost island, the Dalradian headland of Hermaness and the outlying stacks of Muckle Flugga form another important seabird station, at the most northerly point of Britain (C.92, gr. 1*). Hermaness also has an extensive area of peaty moorland, and carries large skua populations and other northern moorland birds. Although Noss and Hermaness are essentially similar, their bird populations are of such high international importance that both are rated as grade 1. A characteristic feature of the Shetland coast is the presence of numerous small islands, low-lying but with mostly rocky shores, which are so subject to salt spray that they are almost entirely covered with a maritime grassland. Most of these grassy 'holms' are grazed by sheep, but they support a characteristic flora and fauna of considerable interest. The small island of Haaf Gruney (C.95, gr. 2) between Unst and Fetlar is a good example, but there are others which are still largely unknown ecologically. Mousa (C.90, gr. 1) has this type of ecosystem but a larger range of grasslands which are less maritime in character, as it is big enough for the central parts to escape strong saline influence. Three upland sites in Shetland, namely the granite and diorite intrusion of Ronas Hill, and the serpentine exposures of Fetlar and the Keen of Hamar, are bounded in part by rocky coasts with cliffs, which represent bonus interest. The much indented shore of Shetland has a great extent of cliff coast and stony shore but little dune or flat. In south Mainland the now inland waters of Lochs of Spiggie and Brow (OW.85, gr. 2) were once connected with the sea, before the formation of dune bars.

The outlying islands of Foula and Fair Isle are both of great ecological interest, as oceanic islands with maritime grasslands and important cliff/slope bird populations. Foula (C.96, gr. 2) bears some resemblance to St Kilda and has cliffs almost as high, and Fair Isle (C.97, gr. 2) is famous as a bird migration study centre; both are important islands, especially as breeding stations for great seabird colonies and skuas, but as their main interest is strongly duplicated elsewhere, grade 2 status is felt to be appropriate (see Appendix).

WEST SCOTLAND

This coast, which extends from the Clyde round the north and west sides of Scotland to the Moray Firth, and includes the Hebrides, covers a greater extent than that of any other region. Much of the western Scottish coast and many of the smaller islands of the Hebrides remain unsurveyed, but it is hoped that the range of key sites chosen will adequately represent the field of variation. Geographical description will be limited to major features and well-known localities.

This coast lies north and west of the Highland Boundary

Fault, and thus forms the edge of a land mass composed of ancient metamorphic rocks, except in Caithness and the Moray Firth side of Sutherland and Ross, where Old Red Sandstone strata predominate. In the south-western coastal districts of Kintyre, Knapdale, Cowal and Lorne, and on the isles of Jura and Islay, the country rock is mainly the Dalradian Series, and consists of a range of types including mica schist, schistose grit, quartzite and altered impure limestone, though in Lorne there is an extensive spread of andesitic lavas of Old Red Sandstone age.

From Loch Linnhe at the southern end of the Great Glen northwards to Loch Alsh in Ross, the Moine Series prevails, with rock types varying from mica-schist, schistose grit to quartz-rich granulite. Between Loch Alsh and Enard Bay on the borders of Ross and Sutherland, the Precambrian Torridonian Sandstone occupies most of the coastal belt, but from here to Cape Wrath the Sandstone alternates with extensive tracts of Lewisian Gneiss. The geology of the Hebrides is very varied. In Skye and Mull, large areas of Tertiary basalt lava are intruded by intricate complexes of igneous rocks (similar complexes occur on Rhum, St Kilda and on the mainland peninsula of Ardnamurchan). Coll, Tiree and the whole of the Outer Hebrides are formed almost entirely of Lewisian Gneiss.

Along the north coast of Sutherland the Lewisian and Torridonian rocks give way to an important but limited area of dolomitic limestone on the east side of the Kyle of Durness, and this appears again on the east shore of Loch Eriboll. Cambrian Quartzite appears on the west side of Eriboll and at the tip of Whiten Head, but from there eastwards to near the Caithness border, the Moine Series takes over again. Caithness lies almost entirely on the Old Red Sandstone and, apart from a belt of Jurassic beds from Helmsdale to Golspie, the same is true of the east coast of Sutherland and Ross.

The greater part of all this long coastline is steep and rocky, with deep water close inshore, and only in the big inlets of the east coast cut in Old Red Sandstone (the Dornoch, Cromarty, Beauly and Moray Firths), are there significant areas of tidal flats and their associated landward accretions of salt marsh and sand dune. These firths are, however, important for their concentrations of wildfowl and waders in winter – especially the Cromarty Firth (C.112, gr. 1*), which has the largest populations of these birds in northern Scotland, especially in Nigg Bay, but is now likely to suffer loss of interest through industrial development. The Lower Dornoch Firth (C.123, gr. 2) at present has smaller wildfowl and wader populations. The third and smallest east coast inlet with large flats, Loch Fleet (C.110, gr. 1), has smaller bird populations, and is interesting mainly as one part of a composite site which also includes a large alder/willow swamp wood on former estuarine sediments behind an embankment (the Mound) which sealed off the upper estuary. The western Highlands and Islands are heavily glaciated country, and the cutting of numerous glacial valleys to below sea-level has produced many deep marine indentations. These sea lochs are mostly fringed by solid bed rock or boulder to large pebble beaches, and these

usually pass inland to hill slopes, which are sometimes so steeply inclined that they give a fjord-like appearance to the whole system. Examples of this type are Loch Etive in Argyll, Lochs Nevis and Hourn in west Inverness-shire, Loch Broom in west Ross, Lochs Glencoul and Glendhu in Sutherland, and Loch Seaforth between Harris and Lewis. At the other extreme are sea lochs with shores low and gentle enough to allow the formation of small areas of fringing salt marsh; these are exemplified by Loch Torridon in west Ross, and the Kyles of Durness and Tongue in Sutherland. Some sea lochs have islands sufficiently small and low to be influenced by waves and salt spray, and these are usually fertile and grassy, in contrast to the peaty and heathery character of bigger and higher islands. Good sea loch islands with a distinctive fauna occur in Loch Sunart, Argyll. Some sea lochs are extremely deep, and Lochs Eriboll and Ewe are among those which have been used as naval anchorages. On North Uist, Loch an Duin shows an interesting gradient from maritime to brackish conditions and has an extremely varied littoral flora; it has been classed as a key open water site (OW.87, gr. 1*).

Although so much of the western mainland coast is steep and rocky, there are relatively few large sea cliffs between the precipices at the Mull of Kintyre and those of the Cape Wrath headland. The north coast of Sutherland is different, and there are fine ranges of coastal cliff, including the Clo Mor (210 m) just east of Cape Wrath and Whiten Head. Caithness has a rugged coast with many lines of vertical cliffs on both the northern and eastern seaboards. The biggest coastal cliffs are, however, in the Hebrides. In Mull, the Tertiary basalt of the Ross and Ardmeanach peninsulas gives great crags, but these are exceeded in size by headlands carved out of the same rock series on Skye – Dunvegan, Waterstein and Talisker Heads are all around the 300 m mark and there are many lines of lesser cliff. The tallest precipices of all are on the St Kilda group of Hirta, Boreray and Soay, where sheer granophyre and gabbro rock walls reach 370–430 m and rock stacks are also the highest in Britain at 150–180 m.

This great extent of sea cliff harbours relatively few large colonies of seabirds, probably because they have too few good ledges or because they drop to a raised beach or storm beach. There are, however, some very large concentrations of seafowl, especially on the Torridonian and Old Red Sandstones, where favourable strata give numerous flat ledges, and on offshore islands where ground predators are absent. St Kilda, the Clo Mor, Handa, the Caithness cliffs and stacks, the Shiants, the Flannans, Mingulay, North Rona and Sula Sgeir are all important breeding stations. The grey seal has its headquarters in these western and northern coastal waters, and the lonely island of North Rona, off Cape Wrath, is an important pupping ground.

A selection of the most interesting sea cliffs and rocky islands has been made, and the ornithological interest has received especial emphasis. The St Kilda group (C.105, gr. 1*) is the most outstanding of these sites, with its huge colonies of gannets, puffins, other auks, kittiwakes and fulmars; Leach's petrels and endemic race of wrens; wild Soay sheep; and an interesting range of Atlantic maritime vegetation. The Clo Mor has similar cliff bird populations (but no gannets), and is identified as a grade 1* site (C.108) along with the Cape Wrath section, and the cliffs of Faraid Head farther east. The hill behind the Clo Mor, Sgribhis Bheinn, is part of a grade 1* upland site (U.68). North Rona has important sea bird interest besides its grey seals, and the outlying gannet stack of Sula Sgeir is included with it as another grade 1* site (C.106). The Shiants in the Minch (C.120, gr. 2) are another major seabird station, especially for puffins, but their interest is subsidiary to St Kilda (see Appendix); whilst Handa (C.121, gr. 2) close to the Sutherland coast, and the two contiguous islands of Mingulay and Berneray (C.117, gr. 2) at the southern tip of the Outer Hebrides, duplicate the features of other northern Scottish grade 1 seabird cliffs and islands. The remote rocky island group of the Flannans (C.122, gr. 2), north of Lewis, is included for its large auk colonies.

Other cliff sections chosen mainly for their botanical and invertebrate interest have fewer birds, and have broken slopes as well as sheer faces. The most important examples, representing different geological formations, are on Rhum (C.101, gr. 1*), Oldshore–Sandwood (C.107, gr. 1) and Ross of Mull (C.100, gr. 1); the first two of these represent the coastal sectors of two grade 1 upland sites (U.71 and U.69), and the third has been chosen as probably the most ecologically diverse of the coastal Tertiary basalt escarpments in the western Highlands. The coast of the Ardmeanach peninsula (C.116, gr. 2) has been regarded as an alternative to the Ross of Mull, and nearly equivalent in importance, while the cliff coasts of A'Mhoine (P.106, gr. 2) in Sutherland form an important bonus habitat.

Examples of rocky western coast with few or only low cliffs are included within the sections at Inverpolly, on the exposed seaboard of west Ross (described under U.66), and along the sheltered north shore of Loch Sunart forming the long sea inlet south of the Ardnamurchan peninsula in western Argyll (C.98, gr. 1).

Parts of the west Scottish coast show very fine series of raised beaches, with their associated inland cliffs and caves, and good examples are found on islands such as Islay, Jura and Rhum. When composed of large pebbles, some of these ancient beaches remain completely unvegetated, but others are colonised by vegetation of a semi-maritime character. Salt marsh has mostly a rather fragmentary occurrence in this region and is usually species-poor, but the Ruel Estuary (C.114), Argyll, is included as a grade 2 representative of this habitat at the head of a west coast sea loch. There are, however, two coastal influences which are very marked, and both are associated with the strong winds of this extremely oceanic region.

The first is the extensive deposition of blown sand, not only in fringing dune ridges, but also generally over land behind. Where the coast is low, with large tidal sand flats, quite extensive level areas of sand have built up behind the seaward dune ridges. As the sand in these situations usually contains a high proportion of shell fragments, the resulting landward deposits have a calcareous substratum, and they

develop a characteristic grass–forb sward, the whole system being known as machair. Shallow lagoons and fringing marshy ground have often formed on the inner side of the machair zone, and provide an extremely rich habitat for flora and fauna, especially birds. Machair land is best developed on the low-lying west coast of the southern Outer Hebrides, namely, Barra, South Uist, Benbecula and North Uist. Three grade 1 sites have been chosen here to represent the range of variation in the machair and its associated habitats: on South Uist, the areas around Grogarry and Loch Hallan (C.102, gr. 1); on North Uist, the Balranald area with its extensive machair marsh and loch (C.103, gr. 1) and the outlying group of the Monach Isles to the west (C.104, gr. 1). Whilst there is a good example of wet machair at Northton (C.119, gr. 2) in the south of Harris, there is very little machair ground in either Harris or Lewis. Farther south, Tiree has a high proportion of its total area covered by machair, and the area of Barrapol and Ballevullin (C.115) is regarded as a grade 2 example. There are more limited areas in Coll and Islay, and on most of the Inner Hebrides and the mainland west Highland coast this habitat is hardly represented at all.

In some places, as at Bettyhill and Durness, the blown shell sand is deposited on steeper and often rocky ground, and here the result is to produce a complex of enriched habitats from open rocks and flushes to sand banks and machair type deposits. With distance inland, the influence of the blown sand gradually disappears and in parallel there is a change to the acidic peaty soils and acidophilous vegetation of the interior moorlands. Both Bettyhill and Durness are important for the occurrence of varied calcicolous communities well behind their more typical fringing dune vegetation; they fall within the Invernaver (C.109, gr. 1*) and Cape Wrath coastal sites. The dune system at Baleshare–Kirkibost in North Uist (C.118, gr. 2) is a more typical area of western coastal sand hills, while that at Morrich More (C.111, gr. 1*) on the south side of the Dornoch Firth in east Ross is a fine north-east coast example of acidic and basic dunes. Good dune systems of the widespread type also occur at Luskentyre in Harris, Sandwood Bay in Sutherland (within site C.107), Dunnet Links in Caithness and there are small examples on Rhum. The sand flats, dunes and machair of Loch Gruinart–Loch Indaal on Islay (C.99, gr. 1*) are of international importance for their winter population of barnacle and Greenland white-fronted geese, and those on the Kintyre peninsula at Rhunahaorine (C.113, gr. 2) and Machrihanish and the Monach Isles also have some importance for wildfowl.

The second effect of this windy climate is to produce, by combination of heavy wave action and ferocious gusts, a landward deposition of salt spray as well as sand particles, and most of the vegetation of land bordering the Atlantic shows evidence of this influence. Salt spray is itself to some extent an enriching influence, adding calcium as well as sodium chloride to the soil, and the characteristic feature of the dwarf shrub heaths bordering the sea is their greater species richness, especially in mildly basiphilous herbs, compared with examples in similar situations farther inland.

There are obvious floristic relationships between these species-rich maritime heaths and the interesting ericoid heaths growing on calcareous soils far inland. On really exposed coasts, as on St Kilda, the spray drenching is so pronounced that completely halophytic plant communities resembling salt marsh swards occur on slopes at a considerable height above the sea, while species associated with saline or brackish conditions (and therefore normally found right beside the sea) grow abundantly for up to a kilometre or more from the sea.

The enriching influence of the sea has been put to good use by humans intent on making a living from these otherwise mainly sterile lands of the Atlantic coast of Scotland. Shell sand and seaweed have long been used as fertiliser here, and around long established crofting communities near the sea there are usually richer grasslands of a submaritime character. These are well developed on the lower parts of coastal islands, especially where the rock and soil give a natural tendency towards fertile conditions; they are well represented on Rhum, the Summer Isles, the Treshnish Isles, St Kilda, Foula and North Rona. Examples of oceanic islands, with their range of variation from maritime to submaritime grassland and then to heath, are represented in the national series by St Kilda, North Rona, Rhum, the Shiants, Foula, Fair Isle, Mingulay–Berneray and Handa.

The other important influence of the strongly oceanic climate is mentioned in Chapter 9, and concerns the gradual descent towards the west and north of altitudinal vegetation zones of the mountains. It is marked especially by the occurrence of otherwise montane (Arctic–alpine) plants close to sea-level. This effect may be seen as far south as the Mull of Kintyre, but it is most marked on the north coast of Sutherland, where extensive *Dryas* heaths occur on blown sand virtually down to sea-level, notably at Durness and Bettyhill (Invernaver), where there is a complete convergence of the montane and maritime habitats.

Table 4. INDEX OF COASTLAND SITES

* Internationally important sites

Region		Site	County	Flats 1	Salt marshes 2	Dunes 3	Lagoon & fen (brackish to fresh) 4	Vegetated shingle 5	Rocky shore & cliff habitats 6	Submaritime grassland & heath 7	Paramaritime habitats 8
South-east England											
GRADE 1	C.1	CUCKMERE HAVEN–BEACHY HEAD	SUSSEX	—	a	—	—	a	A	a	G
	C.2	FOLKESTONE WARREN	KENT	—	—	—	a	a	A	a	Gs
GRADE 1*	C.3	DUNGENESS	KENT	—	—	—	A	A	—	A	W
GRADE 1	C.4	SANDWICH/PEGWELL BAY	KENT	A	a	A	—	—	—	—	—
GRADE 1*	C.5	CHICHESTER/LANGSTONE HARBOURS (a) CHICHESTER HARBOUR (b) LANGSTONE HARBOUR	SUSSEX, HAMPSHIRE	A	A	—	—	—	—	—	—
GRADE 1	C.6	THE SWALE (ISLE OF SHEPPEY)	KENT	A	A	—	A	a	—	A	G
	C.7	BURNTWICK ISLAND/ CHETNEY MARSHES (MEDWAY MARSHES)	KENT	A	A	—	a	—	—	a	G
Grade 2	C.8	High Halstow/Cliffe Marshes	Kent	A	a	—	a	—	—	a	GW
	C.9	Allhallows Marshes/Yantlet Creek	Kent	A	a	a	a	a	—	—	G
South England											
GRADE 1*	C.5	CHICHESTER/LANGSTONE HARBOURS (PART)	HAMPSHIRE	See under South-east England							

Table 4 (*contd.*)

Region		Site	County	1	2	3	4	5	6	7	8
GRADE 1	C.10	NEEDLES–ST CATHERINE'S POINT, ISLE OF WIGHT	HAMPSHIRE	—	—	—	—	a	A	A	GS
Grade 2	C.11	North Solent Marshes*ᵃ*	Hampshire	A	A	—	a	A	—	A	gsw
	C.12	Newtown Harbour, Isle of Wight	Hampshire	A	A	—	—	a	—	a	g
East Anglia											
GRADE 1*	C.13	FOULNESS & MAPLIN SANDS	ESSEX	A	A	—	A	A	—	a	G
*	C.14	BLACKWATER FLATS & MARSHES (a) DENGIE PENINSULA (b) BLACKWATER ESTUARY (c) COLNE ESTUARY	ESSEX	A	A	—	A	a	—	a	G
GRADE 1	C.15	HAMFORD WATER	ESSEX	A	A	—	a	a	—	—	g
	C.16	STOUR ESTUARY	ESSEX	A	a	—	—	—	—	a	—
	C.17	ORFORDNESS/HAVERGATE	SUFFOLK	a	A	a	A	A	—	a	—
	C.18	WINTERTON DUNES	NORFOLK	—	—	A	—	—	—	A	G
GRADE 1*	C.19	NORTH NORFOLK COAST (a) HOLME–BRANCASTER (b) SCOLT HEAD ISLAND (c) OVERY–HOLKHAM (d) WELLS–MORSTON (e) BLAKENEY POINT (f) CLEY–SALTHOUSE	NORFOLK	A	A	A	A	A	—	a	—
*	C.20	THE WASH FLATS & MARSHES (a) GIBRALTAR POINT–WRANGLE (b) WRANGLE–WELLAND (c) WELLAND–NENE (d) NENE–OUSE (e) OUSE–HUNSTANTON	NORFOLK–LINCOLNSHIRE	A	A	a	a	a	—	a	a
GRADE 1	C.21	SALTFLEETBY/THEDDLETHORPE DUNES	LINCOLNSHIRE	A	A	A	A	—	—	A	S
GRADE 1*	C.62	HUMBER FLATS & MARSHES (PART)	LINCOLNSHIRE	See under North England							
Grade 2	C.22	Leigh Marsh	Essex	A	A	—	—	a	—	a	—
South-west England											
GRADE 1	C.23	POOLE HARBOUR	DORSET	A	A	A	A	a	—	a	H
	C.24	DURLSTON HEAD–RINGSTEAD BAY	DORSET	—	—	—	—	—	A	A	GSW
GRADE 1*	C.25	CHESIL BEACH/THE FLEET	DORSET	—	—	—	A	A	—	—	—
*	C.26	AXMOUTH–LYME REGIS UNDERCLIFFS	DEVON	—	—	—	—	—	A	a	W
*	C.27	THE LIZARD	CORNWALL	—	—	—	—	—	A	A	H
*	C.28	ISLES OF SCILLY	CORNWALL	a	—	a	a	a	A	A	HG
GRADE 1	C.29	CAPE CORNWALL–CLODGY POINT	CORNWALL	—	—	—	—	—	A	A	h
	C.30	GODREVY POINT–ST AGNES	CORNWALL	—	—	—	—	—	A	A	H
	C.31	BOSCASTLE–WIDEMOUTH	CORNWALL	—	—	—	—	—	A	A	WSHG
	C.32	STEEPLE POINT–BLACKCHURCH ROCK	CORNWALL–DEVON	—	—	—	—	—	A	A	WSHG
GRADE 1*	C.33	BRAUNTON BURROWS	DEVON	a	—	A	—	a	—	A	—
*	C.34	BRIDGWATER BAY	SOMERSET	A	A	—	—	A	a	A	—
GRADE 1	C.35	NEW GROUNDS, SLIMBRIDGE	GLOUCESTERSHIRE	A	A	—	—	—	—	A	—
Grade 2	C.36	Exe Estuary	Devon	A	A	a	—	—	—	a	—
	C.37	Lynher Estuary & St John's Lake	Cornwall	A	A	—	—	—	—	a	—
	C.38	Fal–Ruan Estuary	Cornwall	A	A	—	—	—	—	a	W
	C.39	Porthgwarra–Pordenack Point	Cornwall	—	—	—	—	—	A	A	H
	C.40	Severn Estuary: Aber Hafren	Somerset–Gloucestershire–Monmouthshire	A	a	—	—	—	—	a	—

Table 4 (*contd.*)

Region	Site		County	1	2	3	4	5	6	7	8
South Wales											
GRADE 1	C.41	SOUTH GOWER COAST: GLANNAU DE GŴYR	GLAMORGAN	a	a	A	A	—	A	A	WSG
	C.42	BURRY INLET	GLAMORGAN	A	A	A	—	a	a	a	wsg
	C.43	STACKPOLE HEAD–CASTLE-MARTIN CLIFFS: STACPOL-CLOGWYNI CASTELL MARTYN	PEMBROKESHIRE	—	—	a	—	—	A	A	GH
	C.44	STRUMBLE HEAD: PEN CAER– LLECHDAFAD	PEMBROKESHIRE	—	—	—	—	—	A	A	GH
GRADE 1*	C.45	YNYSOEDD PRESELI (a) SKOKHOLM (b) SKOMER (c) GRASSHOLM (d) RAMSEY: YNYS DEWI	PEMBROKESHIRE	—	—	—	—	—	A	A	G
GRADE 1	C.46	DYFI	CARDIGANSHIRE–MERIONETH–MONTGOMERYSHIRE	A	A	A	—	a	—	A	—
Grade 2	C.40	Severn Estuary (part)	Monmouthshire	See under South-west England							
	C.47	Kenfig Dunes: Tywyn Cynffig	Glamorgan	a	—	A	A	a	—	A	—
	C.48	Tywyn Gwendraeth: Towyn Burrows	Carmarthenshire	a	A	A	—	—	—	A	—
	C.49	St David's Head: Penmaendewi	Pembrokeshire	—	—	—	—	—	A	A	HG
North Wales											
GRADE 1	C.50	GLANNAU HARLECH (a) MORFA HARLECH & TRAETH BACH (b) MORFA DYFFRYN	MERIONETH	A	a	A	—	—	—	A	g
	C.51	NEWBOROUGH WARREN–YNYS LLANDDWYN	ANGLESEY	A	A	A	a	a	a	A	g
	C.52	GLANNAU YNYS GYBI: HOLY ISLAND COAST	ANGLESEY	—	—	—	—	—	A	A	H
GRADE 1*	C.55	ABER DYFRDWY: DEE ESTUARY (PART)	FLINTSHIRE	See under Midlands							
Grade 2	C.53	Ynys Enlli & Glannau Aberdaron: Bardsey Island & Aberdaron Coast	Caernarvonshire	—	—	A	—	—	A	A	GH
	C.54	Tywyn Aberffraw	Anglesey	a	—	A	—	—	—	a	—
Midlands											
GRADE 1*	C.55	ABER DYFRDWY: DEE ESTUARY	CHESHIRE–FLINTSHIRE	A	A	—	—	—	A	a	—
Grade 2	C.56	Mersey Estuary	Cheshire–Lancashire	A	A	—	—	—	—	a	G
North England											
GRADE 1	C.57	AINSDALE DUNES	LANCASHIRE	A	—	A	—	—	—	A	W
GRADE 1*	C.58	RIBBLE ESTUARY	LANCASHIRE	A	A	—	—	—	—	a	G
*	C.59	MORECAMBE BAY (including WYRE–LUNE)	LANCASHIRE	A	A	a	—	a	a	A	Gsw
GRADE 1	C.60	WALNEY & SANDSCALE DUNES	LANCASHIRE	A	a	A	—	A	—	A	—
GRADE 1*	C.61	UPPER SOLWAY FLATS & MARSHES	CUMBERLAND, DUMFRIES-SHIRE, KIRKCUDBRIGHTSHIRE	A	A	a	—	a	—	A	G
		(a) SARKFOOT–BOWNESS SHORE SARKFOOT–DORNOCK SHORE									

Table 4 (*contd.*)

Region		Site	County	1	2	3	4	5	6	7	8
		(b) GRUNE POINT–BOWNESS SHORE POWFOOT–DORNOCK SHORE									
		(c) LOCHAR–NITH SHORE									
	* C.62	HUMBER FLATS & MARSHES	YORKSHIRE–LINCOLNSHIRE	A	A	—	—	—	—	a	—
		(a) UPPER HUMBER FLATS (HULL–TRENT MOUTH)									
		(b) LOWER HUMBER FLATS (HULL–SPURN)									
	* C.63	BEMPTON/SPEETON CLIFFS	YORKSHIRE	—	—	—	—	—	A	a	g
	* C.64	FARNE ISLANDS	NORTHUMBERLAND	—	—	—	—	—	A	a	—
GRADE 1	C.65	LINDISFARNE–ROSS LINKS–BUDLE BAY	NORTHUMBERLAND	A	a	A	—	—	—	A	HG
Grade 2	C.56	Mersey Estuary (part)	Lancashire	See under Midlands							
	C.66	Duddon Sands	Lancashire–Cumberland	A	A	a	—	—	—	a	—
	C.67	Drigg Point	Cumberland	a	a	A	—	—	—	A	—
	C.68	Beast Cliff/Robin Hood's Bay	Yorkshire	—	—	—	—	—	A	A	WSG
	C.69	Teesmouth Flats & Marshes	Yorkshire–Durham	A	A	a	—	—	—	—	—
	C.70	Hart Warren–Hawthorn Dene Coast	Durham	—	—	A	—	—	A	A	WSG
	C.71	Coquet Island	Northumberland	—	—	—	—	—	A	A	—
South Scotland											
GRADE 1*	C.61	UPPER SOLWAY FLATS & MARSHES (PART)	DUMFRIES-SHIRE–KIRKCUDBRIGHTSHIRE	See under North England							
GRADE 1	C.72	TORRS WARREN	WIGTOWNSHIRE	A	—	A	A	—	—	A	H
	C.73	MULL OF GALLOWAY–CRAMMAG HEAD	WIGTOWNSHIRE	—	—	—	—	a	A	A	HGs
GRADE 1*	C.74	AILSA CRAIG	AYRSHIRE	—	—	—	—	—	A	A	G
GRADE 1	C.75	ST ABB'S HEAD	BERWICKSHIRE	—	—	—	—	—	A	A	HGs
GRADE 1*	C.76	FIRTH OF FORTH	FIFE, STIRLINGSHIRE, MID, EAST & WEST LOTHIAN	A	a	—	—	—	—	a	—
Grade 2	C.77	Borgue Coast	Kirkcudbrightshire	—	—	—	—	—	A	A	WHGS
	C.78	Wigtown Bay	Kirkcudbrightshire–Wigtownshire	A	A	—	—	—	—	a	—
	C.79	Bass Rock[a]	East Lothian	—	—	—	—	—	A	A	—
	C.80	Forth Islands	East & Mid-Lothian	—	—	—	—	—	A	a	—
East Scotland											
GRADE 1	C.81	ISLE OF MAY	FIFE	—	—	—	—	—	A	A	—
	C.82	TENTSMUIR POINT	FIFE	a	a	A	—	—	—	A	H
GRADE 1*	C.83	TAY ESTUARY	FIFE–PERTHSHIRE	A	A	—	—	—	—	a	—
GRADE 1	C.84	ST CYRUS	KINCARDINESHIRE	a	a	A	—	—	A	A	G
GRADE 1*	C.85	FOWLSHEUGH	KINCARDINESHIRE	—	—	—	—	—	A	a	a
	* C.86	SANDS OF FORVIE & YTHAN ESTUARY	ABERDEENSHIRE	A	a	A	—	—	a	A	H
GRADE 1	C.87	STRATHBEG	ABERDEENSHIRE	—	—	A	A	a	—	A	
	C.88	MACDUFF–PENNAN HEAD	ABERDEENSHIRE–BANFFSHIRE	—	—	—	—	a	A	A	HGs
	C.89	CULBIN SANDS	MORAY–NAIRN	A	A	A	—	A	—	A	—
	C.90	MOUSA	SHETLAND	—	—	—	—	—	A	A	HG
GRADE 1*	C.91	NOSS	SHETLAND	—	—	—	—	—	A	A	H
	* C.92	HERMANESS, UNST	SHETLAND	—	—	—	—	—	A	A	HG
Grade 2	C.93	Eden Estuary	Fife	A	a	—	—	—	—	a	—
	C.94	North Hoy	Orkney	—	—	—	—	—	A	A	H
	C.95	Haaf Gruney	Shetland	—	—	—	—	—	A	A	—
	C.96	Foula[a]	Shetland	—	—	—	—	—	A	A	HG
	C.97	Fair Isle	Shetland	—	—	—	—	—	A	A	HG

6-2

Table 4 (*contd.*)

Region	Site	County	1	2	3	4	5	6	7	8
West Scotland										
GRADE 1	C.98 SOUTH ARDNAMURCHAN COAST	ARGYLL	—	—	—	—	a	A	a	—
GRADE 1*	C.99 LOCH GRUINART–LOCH INDAAL, ISLAY	ARGYLL	A	a	A	—	—	—	A	GH
GRADE 1	C.100 ROSS OF MULL	ARGYLL	—	—	—	—	—	A	A	WSG
GRADE 1*	C.101 RHUM	INVERNESS-SHIRE	a	a	a	—	a	A	A	GH
GRADE 1	C.102 SOUTH UIST MACHAIR (a) GROGARRY (b) ASKERNISH COAST	INVERNESS-SHIRE	a	—	A	A	—	—	A	A
	C.103 BALRANALD, NORTH UIST	INVERNESS-SHIRE	a	—	A	A	—	—	A	—
	C.104 MONACH ISLES	INVERNESS-SHIRE	a	a	A	—	a	a	A	—
GRADE 1*	C.105 ST KILDA	INVERNESS-SHIRE	—	—	—	—	—	A	A	HG
*	C.106 NORTH RONA & SULA SGEIR	ROSS	—	—	—	—	—	A	A	—
GRADE 1	C.107 OLDSHORE–SANDWOOD COAST	SUTHERLAND	a	—	A	—	—	A	A	HG
GRADE 1*	C.108 CAPE WRATH–AODANN MHOR	SUTHERLAND	a	—	A	—	—	A	A	HG
*	C.109 INVERNAVER	SUTHERLAND	a	a	A	—	—	a	A	H
GRADE 1	C.110 LOCH FLEET	SUTHERLAND	A	a	a	A	—	—	A	WS
GRADE 1*	C.111 MORRICH MORE	ROSS	A	a	A	—	—	—	A	H
*	C.112 CROMARTY FIRTH	ROSS	A	a	—	—	—	—	a	—
Grade 2	C.113 Rhunahaorine	Argyll	—	—	—	a	—	—	—	A
	C.114 Ruel Estuary	Argyll	a	A	—	—	—	—	a	W
	C.115 Barrapol & Ballevullin, Tiree	Argyll	a	—	A	A	—	—	A	G
	C.116 Ardmeanach, Mull	Argyll	—	—	—	—	—	A	A	WSG
	C.117 Mingulay & Berneray	Inverness-shire	—	—	—	—	—	A	A	HG
	C.118 Baleshare/Kirkibost Dunes, North Uist	Inverness-shire	a	—	A	—	—	—	A	G
	C.119 Northton, Harris	Inverness-shire	a	a	A	—	—	—	a	—
	C.120 Shiant Isles[a]	Ross	—	—	—	—	—	A	A	HG
	C.121 Handa–Duartmore	Sutherland	—	—	—	—	—	A	A	HG
	C.122 Flannan Isles	Ross	—	—	—	—	—	A	—	—
	C.123 Lower Dornoch Firth	Ross–Sutherland	A	A	—	—	—	—	a	—

Notes

A = major occurrence of habitat; a = minor occurrence of habitat.
  Submaritime grassland and heath: includes communities with coastal species (e.g. stable dune and upper cliff swards).
  Paramaritime habitats (types of vegetation usually lacking coastal species).
W = woodland   H = heath
 S = scrub   G = grassland
(Capitals indicate major occurrence, lower case indicates minor occurrence.)

[a] See Appendix.

5 WOODLANDS

HISTORICAL ASPECTS OF BRITISH WOODLANDS

Human activity has had a particularly profound impact on the present character and distribution of woodland in Britain, and there is a considerable body of evidence to give a reasonably accurate picture of this influence and its effects. Of the major formations, only woodland has an extensive descriptive documentary record going back to mediaeval times. A brief account of these historical features is therefore helpful to an understanding of the present-day woodlands.

An outline of the prehistoric spread and development of woodland in Britain following the last Quaternary glaciation has been given in Chapter 2. By the time early man first began to have a significant influence, the general pattern was of a climax forest covering the greater part of the country up to 460–610 m (lower in western and northern Scotland) except on ground which was too wet, unstable or wind-exposed. Various types of broad-leaved woodland prevailed in the south but there were extensive pine forests in the Highlands. Much of the diversity of woodland type was then related to variations in soil conditions and climate on the local and regional scales.

Mesolithic man was not a cultivator and his numbers were too small to have much influence. The real impact of man on our forests began with the appearance of Neolithic agriculture around 3000 B.C. Clearance of woodland directly by cutting and burning and indirectly by grazing of domestic stock which prevented regeneration, and its replacement by cultivated land, began and grew on an ever-increasing scale. Areas cleared first were the most tractable for cultivation, mainly on well-drained sites of intermediate elevation rather than on wet valley bottoms. Steep and rocky ground tended to be avoided, and there was a distinct preference for the fertile soils on chalk and limestone. As clearance spread there was an avoidance of heavy clays, wet peats and acidic sands which were either difficult to work or of low fertility, so that extensive areas of woodland remained long after the appearance of Neolithic man.

The Iron Age created a need for fuel timber and saw an onslaught on remaining extensive forest lands which had escaped the attentions of cultivators. Smelting by charcoal led to clearance not only in southern areas such as the Weald, but also in remoter country such as the Lake District and western Highlands, where extensive tracts of primaeval forest were devastated. It is also believed that woodland was extensively burned *in situ* to remove refuges for undesirable creatures such as wolves.

In early mediaeval times, many of the remaining extensive tracts of woodland were set aside as Royal Forests, under whose laws the forests were kept as hunting preserves. The forests of some of these royal chases have survived until today as important areas of permanent woodland, the largest and best known being the New Forest in Hampshire. On a smaller scale, many areas were 'emparked' during mediaeval times for the holding of deer, and most of these appear to have incorporated remnants of the original forest. Moreover, all communities needed a supply of fuel and construction wood, and this, coupled with the difficulty of timber transportation, led to the retention of relatively small woods in every parish. Land closest to the village was cleared and cultivated first, and today many woods are adjacent to or astride parish boundaries. There is also a tendency for present-day woods to occupy the heaviest or poorest soil or steepest land in the parish.

The pattern of survival of land with a continuous Postglacial history of woodland cover ('permanent woodland') is thus largely the result of what might be termed ecological chance, i.e. the occurrence of conditions which discouraged forest clearance, in relation to developments in human needs. Moreover, although there is evidently a good deal of permanent woodland still left in Britain, very little, if any, of this remains in an original state. A great deal of re-planting has taken place, often using different species or proportions of species compared with the original, and nearly always there has been management which has resulted in some degree of modification. Natural re-establishment of woodland after clearance has often occurred when conditions allowed, and there has been extensive human re-establishment of tree cover on ground unwooded for varying periods. This is an additional complicating factor in understanding the present nature and distribution of woodland. Such re-development of woodland cover follows a change in land use, which often in turn results from economic change, but there is again a connection with the quality of land involved. Naturally re-established woodland is especially characteristic of such places as steep slopes in the Peak District and on the North and South Downs, and on former common grazings in infertile lowland areas. Large areas of moorland and sheep-walk which have become uneconomic as grazing land, and are unrewarding for other types of land-use, have been planted in recent years. The development of extensive ombrogenous mires from Atlantic times onwards reduced woodland cover in northern and western Britain but, with the recent drainage and drying out of these peatlands, conditions favourable to tree growth are returning over some of this ground, and birch is especially able to take advantage of this change by spreading onto the drying mire surfaces.

Woodlands offer special opportunities for studying the influence of man through the long-lasting effects of management practices inscribed in the living trees; in their form, their age-structure, and in the detailed distribution of species and individuals of particular ages and growth forms within individual woods. Some of these management practices have died out or have been so reduced in scale that their consequences and variability can no longer be observed, but in many woodlands the detailed effects of management can be reconstructed. Such sites are therefore of particular importance for reaching an ecological understanding of the present character of woodland and for studying woodland management. Woods for which there is in addition recorded information about past management and character are especially important.

Woodlands, together with grasslands and peatlands, have been an important semi-natural vegetation type in local economies. The location of woods is a reflection of local land-use history and settlement pattern. Their management in the past has reflected local patterns of ownership and rights, and the local and national requirements for wood and, to a limited extent, pasture. Many woods are, therefore, historical monuments whose significance ranks with that of the more obvious historical monuments such as churches, houses, bridges and earthworks.

Throughout lowland Britain all but the steepest and wettest ground has been ploughed at some time, or if there are any areas of ploughable land that have not been ploughed, it is very difficult to establish this fact with certainty. Ancient woodlands, however, once delimited during the land settlement process, have remained geographically stable, and until modern forestry techniques, including deep drainage, were introduced into some woods the soil in these woods was disturbed only on the surface. In lowland England, these woods are thus the only sites where guaranteed undisturbed soil profiles now occur. In the same way detailed pre-cultivation morphology of the ground surface has been preserved more or less undisturbed within these woods.

If truly natural woodland (i.e. that uninfluenced by man) now remains in Britain, it is as small fragments in uncultivable and inaccessible situations, such as steep screes, deep gorges and broken cliffs or on the islands of freshwater lakes (the smaller islands only; many of the larger wooded islands are or have been grazed, burned or deliberately managed). Although these natural fragments are especially interesting to the ecologist, we must accept that nearly all our woodlands are semi-natural or artificial. Different forms of management have affected species composition, stocking density, growth form and age class distribution of the trees themselves, and in consequence the composition of both plant and animal communities which depend upon the trees. Breaks in woodland continuity also have important

effects as many associated species of plant and animal appear to have an extremely limited capacity for spreading back to lost ground even when favourable conditions are restored. Plantations and other re-established woodlands are thus usually floristically and faunally impoverished by comparison with permanent woodlands in parallel ecological situations.

Traditional forms of management have declined in recent decades and have been replaced by practices which have very different ecological effects. Exotic species are widely planted, including conifers, most of which, in their dense, even-aged stands, cast a shade too heavy for many plants and animals. Broad-leaved trees are eliminated or reduced in number and variety and the field layer is now much more severely manipulated, often by the use of chemical herbicides. Drainage operations and soil disturbance occur on a larger scale than hitherto. These activities have led to substantial changes which have involved a marked decline in floristic and faunal richness in many woods.

PRESENT RANGE OF ECOLOGICAL VARIATION

Habitat factors and vegetation

A classification of British woodlands based on the dominant tree species is the most straightforward, and that adopted here. Tree dominance is, however, determined by climate, physical and chemical soil conditions, and past management, so that such a classification does not represent a simple ecological sequence. Woodland also has a greater degree of structural diversity than any other major ecosystem, and the separate layers of a woodland community can show a certain amount of independence in their relationships to each other. The orderly ecological descriptive treatment of woodland thus poses considerable conceptual problems, and probably no single approach is adequate. For this reason, the ecosystem will be described in terms of structure, with the ecological relationships of each layer considered separately; but no attempt will be made to unify these in a complete classification of woodland types.

THE TREE LAYER

This predominant structural component of woodland may be defined as the aggregation of woody species over 5 m in height and forming the canopy. Tree seedlings or saplings are best considered as part of whatever layer they belong to in stature. The original regional pattern of forest cover, as measured by the dominant trees, was determined primarily by range of climate, while the more local variations depended on soil conditions, both physical and chemical. In southern Britain, the temperate oceanic conditions give a western outpost of the broad-leaved mixed deciduous forest of continental central Europe, while in the north, the cool oceanic climate allows the survival of a south-westerly extension of the boreal coniferous forest of northern Europe. Although mixed woods are widespread, many British woodlands are now dominated by single tree species.

Woodlands are obviously much more than stands of trees, but the tree layer exerts a powerful influence on the whole complex of other plants and animals. Trees grow to maturity over a period measured in decades or even centuries, but unlike many smaller plants they have a finite life span, though this may be extended by such practices as coppicing. Typically, in a natural stand the cycle of death and regeneration is irregular in space and time, giving a varied structure and age distribution of the tree layer and often a great deal of dead and dying timber. The height and growth form of trees are much influenced by factors such as depth of soil, exposure to wind and density of individuals, and an examination of these characteristics often reveals the conditions under which the tree has grown. The age, growth form, stocking density and species characteristics of the trees help to determine the floristic composition of the subsidiary layers and the fauna of a woodland, and as the one changes in time, so do the others.

Probably most present-day British woodlands have a tree composition resulting from a combination of factors, including planting of seedlings and sowing of seed, natural regeneration, and selective elimination of certain species. Even when the same native tree species have been retained from the past, a present-day woodland owes much of its character to the silvicultural system in use. The stocking density of the trees, their size and shape, all depend on the nature of management. The coppice-with-standards system has been widely used in Britain, and gives a rather open canopy layer of large, spreading, standard trees, with a dense coppiced scrub layer, usually of tall shrubs (e.g. hazel) but sometimes of another tree (e.g. hornbeam, ash and sweet chestnut). Coppice may also be maintained without standards, and sometimes coppice of tree species (e.g. ash, hornbeam) is allowed to grow into taller canopy woodland. In park woodland widely scattered trees are maintained in a grassland community and often pollarded, so that they attain a squat, rounded and massive form, with short, thick trunks and a cluster of large, spreading limbs; regeneration is reduced or eliminated, the canopy kept open and the field layer changed by grazing. At the other end of the scale is high forest with trees which have tall, straight trunks, branching mainly in the high, rather compact crowns. The ecological consequences of these practices are markedly different. In coppices the field layer and woodland margin species are encouraged, but epiphytes reduced, whereas in park woodlands the field layer is impoverished and epiphytic lichens and bark-dwelling or wood-boring animals are encouraged.

The floristic composition of the tree layer has been much influenced by the species chosen for re-planting; these have variously been the original species, native trees other than the original species, and non-native species. Re-planting of the second type has especially confused the interpretation of factors controlling the distribution of native trees. Selective felling and other management intervention can also obscure the original pattern of woodland composition. It is now difficult to be sure of the details of the floristic composition of the woodland tree layer which once characterised any one set of site conditions. For instance, the pollen record repeatedly suggests that the Post-glacial forests of Britain contained a higher proportion of elm and alder, but less ash, than at present. Yet without knowledge of such factors as the differential pollen production and preservation between various trees during earlier periods, one cannot know how far inferences for present-day woodland composition may be drawn. It may be that reduction in elm and alder and increase in ash are partly due to man's influence. Some ecologists believe that single-tree species dominance is a recent and artificial condition in British woodlands, and that the original forest was everywhere characterised by species diversity in the tree layer. Problems such as these are not simply academic; they affect definition of a national range of scientifically important woodland types, and prescription for subsequent management. The matter is open to much speculation, but the simplest hypothesis is that consistent present relationships between habitat conditions and woodland composition also held in the past.

The most widespread type of British woodland composed of native trees is that dominated by oak. Despite many exceptions, there is a marked tendency for pedunculate oak *Quercus robur* to be dominant on base-rich soils in the south and east, and for sessile oak *Q. petraea* to prevail on base-poor soils in the north and west. Pedunculate oak is, however, often the sole dominant on woods on the less rich soils in southern England, and the high-level woods of Dartmoor are well-known examples of western and upland pedunculate oakwood on acidic soils. *Quercus robur* has been much more widely planted and used in forestry than *Q. petraea*, and this bias may have helped to obscure former, natural distribution patterns. Mixed populations of the two oaks, with all grades of intermediate or hybrid forms occur widely, and there is no simple pattern in their distribution. *Quercus robur* is regarded as more tolerant of wet soils than *Q. petraea*, and much pedunculate oakwood on heavy clays tends towards a moist character; however, as waterlogging of the ground becomes more severe, there is usually a change to alder or willow-dominated wood.

As soil base-status increases, especially in available calcium, other tree species appear in increasing abundance until the oaks are more or less completely replaced on highly calcareous soils. In many parts of Britain, ash *Fraxinus excelsior* and wych elm *Ulmus glabra* are trees which typically appear as soil base-status increases, at first sharing dominance with oak (though wych elm is consistently less abundant than ash), and then taking over completely on the most calcareous sites. On calcareous soils in the south and east of England, ash often appears abundantly after beech is cleared but the successional relationships between the two species are not entirely clear. Sometimes ash may persist as the climax woodland dominant, but in some places there is evidence that beech has replaced ash; the situation has probably been confused a good deal by management, including planting. In the west and north, ash certainly appears to persist as a climax woodland tree, as far north as west Ross and Skye, but is then replaced by birch or hazel in Sutherland. Ash is one of the most freely regenerating of our native trees.

In southern Britain, the mixed deciduous woods on basic soils may contain small-leaved lime *Tilia cordata*, but this species is regarded as native only as far north as Lakeland. In a few districts, such as parts of Lincolnshire, Northamptonshire and Gloucestershire, *Tilia cordata* is locally in quantity, even reaching dominance in parts of some woods. The much rarer *T. platyphyllos* occurs in such woods in scattered localities, mainly in the Welsh borders and Derbyshire. The wild service *Sorbus torminalis* is seldom present as more than thinly scattered trees, but is a characteristic species of some woods on the richer soils from Lincolnshire and the Welsh borders southwards. Wild cherry or gean *Prunus avium* is a widely distributed species in these mixed deciduous woodlands, but is not usually abundant. English elm *Ulmus procera* and smooth elm *U. carpinifolia* are plentiful in eastern and southern England, where they are more usually trees of hedgerows rather than woods, though they dominate some small woodlands. These species are believed to be introduced; the native elm is the wych elm *U. glabra*. Elms are declining severely in many southern districts because of the ravages of a severe epidemic of Dutch Elm Disease. Another alien species now characteristic of many mixed deciduous woods especially in south-eastern England is sweet chestnut *Castanea sativa*. Field maple *Acer campestre* is another typical member of mixed deciduous woods on the better soils in southern Britain, and beech *Fagus sylvatica* is often present, or sometimes abundant, in this region.

In the south and east of England, beech locally rivals oak as the principal woodland tree, but the relationships between the two species are not exactly understood. Both can grow on calcareous substrata, but it is believed that on thin soils over the Chalk and the Jurassic limestones, beech has a competitive advantage over oak and so becomes dominant, whereas on damper clay soils oak and ash have the advantage. The beechwoods of the Chilterns, Cotswolds and South Downs are regarded as particularly good examples of this forest type, but there are all transitions to the equally fine beechwoods on acidic sands and gravels in the New Forest, the Weald, Epping Forest and Burnham Beeches. Some of these are ancient beechwoods, but from historical evidence others are regarded as more recently established plantations on the site of former oakwood or even grassland. Beech is widespread in Britain as a planted tree, so that the status of particular populations and the limits of their native distribution are difficult to determine.

In the Scottish Highlands, especially in Inverness-shire, Aberdeenshire and Ross, Scots pine *Pinus sylvestris* locally replaces oak as the climax forest dominant. The pine forests of the Spey, Dee and Beauly catchments are probably the largest continuous areas of native, semi-natural woodland now left in Britain. Pine flourishes on strongly podsolised, acidic soils, and in places there are indications that pinewood is the climax on base-poor substrata, but is replaced by oak and/or birch on base-rich soils; these edaphic relationships are well illustrated around Loch Maree in west Ross. Scots pine is widely planted in southern Britain, especially on acidic sands and gravels, and regenerates

freely in places. It is not usually regarded as a native tree south of the Highlands, but some of the populations on or around lowland acidic mires in districts to the south have a natural appearance and regenerate well, e.g. on Kirkconnell Flow, Kirkcudbrightshire.

The two species of birch, *Betula pendula* (silver birch) and *B. pubescens* show inter-relationships similar to those found in the oaks. *Betula pendula* is more widespread and abundant in the east, whereas *B. pubescens* has a more western tendency, and the subspecies *odorata* is the only birch of the north-west Highlands. Intermediates are again common in many areas. Both species can grow on quite strongly basic soils but are more typical of base-poor substrata. South of the Highlands, birchwood (with either species) is evidently essentially a seral type. Birch regenerates freely and readily colonises the sites of felled woods, lowland heaths and the peat of drying mires. Many birchwoods become increasingly invaded by other trees, especially oak or beech, and so eventually pass over to climax woodland of another type. Birch is frequent in many mixed deciduous woodlands and both species, but especially *B. pubescens*, are also able to tolerate fairly wet soils, and occur in a range of damp woods, grading to carr with alder and willows.

Within the pine forest zone of the central Highlands, as on upper Speyside, birch may, however, represent a climax type on the better soils, for oak is here extremely sparse or absent as a native tree. Oak, pine and ash do not extend to the extreme north of Scotland, and in Sutherland, parts of Ross, and much of the Hebrides, birchwood is clearly the climax forest type under present conditions. Rowan *Sorbus aucuparia* is often abundant or even co-dominant in some of these northern birchwoods, though this is a widespread tree, occurring frequently in many different types of wood all over Britain. In some upland districts, scattered growths of rowan on elevated escarpments are all that is left to represent the upper forest limit.

Throughout Britain, alder *Alnus glutinosa* is the characteristic tree of waterlogged soils, over a wide range of elevation. It is locally dominant in the carrs which represent a late stage in hydroseral development, as in the Norfolk Broads, and in this situation, alder may share dominance with willows or birch (either species). On damp soils where drainage impedance is less marked, ash may be abundant in alderwoods, e.g. Carnach Wood, Argyll. Despite the apparent abundance of the species during much of the Postglacial Period, alderwood seldom covers large areas today, and it often occurs merely as patches or strips within larger woods dominated by other trees, or as a co-dominant with another species, e.g. oak in Coed Gorswen, Caernarvonshire. In northern England and Scotland, alder often forms small woods on wet hillsides, sometimes quite steeply sloping but usually drift covered, though it is more typical of flat ground at the foot of hill slopes. It also forms fringes on the alluvial banks of hill streams.

Of the other native trees, hornbeam *Carpinus betulus* is abundant in south-eastern England and parts of East Anglia, where it is usually associated with oakwoods and managed as coppice, so that the species often belongs more to the shrub than the tree layer. It grows on a variety of soils, but is most abundant on those of intermediate base-status. Yew *Taxus baccata* occurs locally as a dominant, forming dense dark woods with very few if any other plants. Yew woods are usually small in size, often being mere clumps of trees, and are best developed on the Chalk formations of the North and South Downs. Yew is common on Carboniferous Limestone, and it is also characteristic as a subsidiary component of Lakeland oak or oak–ash woods on the less calcareous Borrowdale Volcanic Series and Bannisdale Slates. Holly *Ilex aquifolium* is most usually a member of the woodland shrub layer, but in a few places, e.g. the New Forest, Hampshire, can attain a considerable size and occurs in fairly pure stands. In a few places in southern England, box *Buxus sempervirens* forms woods on calcareous soils.

The willows mostly belong to the shrub layer too, but *Salix cinerea* sometimes grows tall in carr with alder and has some claim to be considered as a woodland tree species. *Salix fragilis* and *S. alba* are fairly large trees, but are usually planted along river-sides and seldom occur as a wood. Of the poplars, only aspen *Populus tremula* is certainly native; this species is widely distributed in woods of various kinds, but seldom has a high cover and usually occurs as scattered clumps, because it commonly regenerates by suckering. Crab apple *Malus sylvestris* is frequent, but again usually occurs as scattered trees within woods or along their edges, and is equally common as a hedgerow tree.

The commonest non-indigenous trees in Britain are sweet-chestnut, horse-chestnut *Aesculus hippocastanum*, sycamore *Acer pseudoplatanus*, turkey oak *Quercus cerris*, larches *Larix* spp., Norway spruce *Picea abies*, Sitka spruce *P. sitchensis*, lodgepole pine *Pinus contorta*, Corsican pine *Pinus nigra* var. *calabrica*, Douglas fir *Pseudotsuga menziesii* and firs *Abies* spp. A sweet-chestnut facies of mixed deciduous woodland is recognised in south-east England and East Anglia, while sycamore has spread a great deal and dominates many small woods in various parts of Britain. The horse-chestnut and turkey oak *Q. cerris* are planted a good deal as ornamental trees but cannot be regarded as woodland species of any importance, except very locally. All the conifers except the *Abies* spp. are, by contrast, planted on a very extensive scale in commercial forestry, and woods of these species cover large areas, especially in western and northern Britain.

Both the amenity planting of alien broad-leaved species and commercial afforestation with conifers fall outside the scope of the *Review*, though the second activity is having an enormous impact on wildlife and habitat in Britain. Most of the above species nevertheless occur in varying abundance in semi-natural woodlands dominated by native trees, and here they often have the effect of enhancing ecological as well as floristic diversity. For the species which regenerate freely, such as sycamore and larch, present distribution is not necessarily an accurate indication of actual planting of the trees. The associated flora and fauna of the completely artificial woods composed of these alien species is not sufficiently outstanding or different from that of native woodlands to require special conservation measures at present.

In mountainous country, tree growth is increasingly inhibited above a certain altitude, and eventually gives way to less luxuriant life forms. The true altitudinal sequence from forest to montane vegetation is now very seldom found in Britain, so universally has woodland been destroyed by man towards its upper limit. Even so, it would seem probable that the original situation was a gradual diminution in height of the canopy-forming trees, as exposure increased with altitude, until a low scrubby growth marked the upper forest limit. This scrub evidently consisted of a depauperate growth of species such as oak, birch, ash and Scots pine, according to soil conditions, but mixed with tall shrubs such as hazel *Corylus avellana*, rowan, juniper *Juniperus communis* and willows. It is likely that this upper woodland fringe passed through tall growths of heather on acidic soils and smaller willows on basic soils as a zone transitional to the distinctly montane vegetation of really high ground. In many moorland areas, especially in Scotland, there are frequent patches of willow scrub, mainly of *Salix cinerea* and *S. aurita*, at elevations well below the tree limit, and these are often well developed beside streams. On the higher Scottish mountains there are still fragments of a montane willow (*Salix lapponum*, *S. lanata*) scrub which was probably once zoned above subalpine birchwoods, as it is in Scandinavia at the present day.

Actual altitudinal zonation of different woodland types is less clear. There are places where birchwood is zoned above either oakwood or pinewood, but as the reverse order sometimes holds, it may well be that the altitudinal distribution of woodland in Britain at present is more closely related to soil fertility or past management than to elevation *per se*. Because of the altitudinal descent of vegetation zones in a north-westerly direction, the actual upper limits of woodland vary according to geographical position in Britain. South of a line from the Humber to the Severn, it is very doubtful if the true potential upper limit of forest is ever reached, for there is no ground high enough. Tree growth on the higher parts of the Dartmoor plateau may have been inhibited by development of blanket mire since the Atlantic Period; elsewhere in southern England, at least on all but the wettest ground, it is likely that forest cover was once virtually continuous and that the present absence of tree growth is due to human influence.

In Brecknock, relict fragments of scrubby woodland still occur at 610 m and in north Wales the occurrence of scattered rowan and birch on high cliffs suggests that woodland may once have extended almost to this level, at least in sheltered places. In Lakeland, parallel observations suggest a rather lower upper limit, though the top of the Keskadale oakwood at 460 m may reflect the effects of insufficient soil rather than a true climatic limit. The best example of a true upper forest limit remaining in Britain is on the spur of Creag Fhiaclach in the western Cairngorms, Inverness-shire, where at 640 m a scrubby growth of gnarled Scots pine and juniper passes gradually into heather moor. With distance west in the Highlands there is a rapid descent of tree limits, and in north-west Sutherland it is probable that the potential upper tree limit lies at around 300 m. On the most wind-exposed western coasts, tree growth is in places virtually extinguished altogether, and is represented by pockets of scrub, mainly of hazel, aspen and willow, which survive in sheltered places. The tree-less nature of the Outer Hebrides, Orkney and Shetland may result from a combination of human influence and unfavourable climate. The surviving fragments of birchwood, hazel, aspen and willow scrub on the islands of some inland lochs here may be rather depauperate and atypical examples of former woodlands, but it is possible that the forest cover has always been patchy in these far northern and western parts of Scotland during the Post-glacial Period.

The following classification of major woodland types has been adopted in this work:

Oakwood
    Western facies
    Eastern facies

Mixed deciduous woodland
    Central facies
    Lime facies
    Hornbeam facies
    Sweet chestnut facies

Mixed deciduous woodland: ancient parks and overmature woodland
Beechwood
Ashwood
Pinewood
Birchwood
Alderwood

Other types of woodland
    Holly
    Yew
    Juniper
    Box
    Rare species

THE SHRUB LAYER

The presence or character of a woodland shrub layer (<5 m) depends on the influence of the dominant trees themselves, climate, soil conditions, and management practice. The heavy shade cast by a pure beechwood usually excludes undershrubs, and the heavy grazing to which many hill woods are subjected often results in their virtual absence, evidently by preventing regeneration. Upland woods of oak, birch and pine are commonly devoid of a shrub layer.

Hazel is probably the most widespread and abundant shrub layer species in Britain. There are indications that hazel can grow on fairly base-poor soils when grazing is absent, and may then form a patchy shrub layer in acidophilous oakwoods. This shrub is, however, characteristically most abundant in woods on base-rich and calcareous soils, where it is often coppiced and then forms a fairly dense shrub layer below or between the standard trees (usually oak). Hazel is especially associated with northern and western ashwoods, and sometimes remains after the dominant trees have died or been removed. Hazel scrub with few or no trees is widespread in coastal areas of the

western Highlands and is especially characteristic of exposed coastal ground on base-rich rocks in the Hebrides. In such situations, hazel scrub may locally represent a climatic climax, though it is possible that birch and perhaps ash and oak would also be present if there were no human disturbance.

On dry, fairly basic woodland soils, species such as hawthorn *Crataegus monogyna*, blackthorn *Prunus spinosa* and elder *Sambucus nigra* are often present in the shrub layer, and there are variable amounts of guelder rose *Viburnum opulus*, gooseberry *Ribes uva-crispa*, blackcurrant *R. nigrum*, wild roses *Rosa* spp., bramble *Rubus fruticosus* agg. and raspberry *R. idaeus*. Hawthorn scrub dominated by *Crataegus monogyna* is a characteristic seral scrub type on calcareous grassland where grazing has become too light to inhibit the growth of woody seedlings. Left to itself, this hawthorn scrub usually becomes invaded by trees such as oak and ash and is eventually converted to woodland. On the sheep-walks of the western and northern hills, especially in Wales and northern England, there are many examples of a more open and persistent hawthorn scrub which lies within the potential forest limit on more acid soils. This parkland type community may represent a period of recession in sheep farming, which reduced grazing temporarily and thereby allowed the invasion of grassland by hawthorn; subsequent restoration of sheep flocks would prevent further invasion of the shrub. Crab apple is sometimes represented in these hill hawthorn scrubs. Blackthorn often occurs in thickets both within the woodland and outside, and is found mainly on the better soils. It creates a deep shade and few other species are able to compete in well-established blackthorn scrub.

Scrub of gorse and broom belongs to the acidic heath ecosystem rather than to woodland and is not considered here. Roses and brambles are, on the other hand, abundant shrubs of woodland. *Rosa canina* is widespread, whereas *R. villosa* and *R. arvensis* are, respectively, somewhat northern and southern species. Roses as a whole, however, have a subsidiary role beneath the woodland canopy, and belong more to the woodland edge and hedges. Brambles are important low shrubs of woodland, and are often dominant almost to the exclusion of the field layer and may form dense, tangled, masses up to 2 m or more high. The ecology of the numerous micro-species has not been worked out, but brambles as a whole flourish best on soils of intermediate base-status, and in ungrazed woods, and they are evidently favoured by certain kinds of management. They are an important component of the woodland ecosystem for nesting birds and insects. A high cover of brambles is especially characteristic of oakwoods, but they can be found in association with almost any of the common woodland tree dominants, and may well be indicators of disturbance when dominant.

In England, the shrub layer of woodlands on calcareous soils is rich in species, which typically include Midland hawthorn *Crataegus oxyacanthoides*, privet *Ligustrum vulgare*, spindle *Euonymus europaeus*, whitebeam *Sorbus aria*, dogwood *Thelycrania sanguinea*, buckthorn *Rhamnus cath-*

articus and wayfaring tree *Viburnum lantana*. Most of these calcicolous shrubs have a southern distribution and reach their northern British limits on the limestone around the head of Morecambe Bay. Woods on basic soils from Norfolk northwards frequently have a good deal of bird-cherry *Prunus padus*, though this is usually patchy and seldom attains a high cover; while beechwoods on calcareous soils in southern England locally have an understorey of yew. Rare shrubs of calcicolous woodlands, especially ashwood on Carboniferous Limestone, include *Ribes alpinum*, *R. spicatum* and *Daphne mezereum*. *D. laureola* occurs more widely in calcicolous woodlands and can be abundant locally.

On base-rich rocks, mainly Carboniferous Limestone, in south-west England and Wales, are a number of rare or endemic whitebeams related to the more widespread *Sorbus aria* but now recognised as distinct species. This group is of special interest as it may have evolved since the last glaciation, and thus could represent a recent example of rapid evolutionary divergence and speciation. These species are *Sorbus minima*, *S. bristoliensis*, *S. leyana*, *S. anglica*, *S. subcuneata*, *S. devoniensis*, *S. porrigentiformis*, *S. vexans*, *S. leptophylla*, *S. wilmottiana* and *S. eminens*. A more widespread western and northern species is *S. rupicola*, and there is a local form of *S. aria*, *S. lancastriensis*, around the head of Morecambe Bay. In Arran, there are isolated occurrences of the two endemics, *S. arranensis* and *S. pseudofennica*, both confined to steep stream banks on granite. Most of these whitebeams occur in open, rocky habitats, where they are little subject to competition but some occur in the shrub layer of woodland, and a few attain the size of trees.

In woods on acidic soils (especially oakwoods), holly is one of the principal undershrubs and sometimes forms dense thickets. In the absence of grazing, holly would probably be a common or dominant understorey species in many hill oakwoods in western and northern Britain; in these districts it is often abundant on cliff faces and ravine sides. Holly is an oceanic species on the European scale, but is widespread in Britain and well represented in many parts of the east, though it is rare in the east Midlands from south Yorkshire to Northamptonshire. Rowan is also present in the shrub layer of many oakwoods on poor soils, and it often attains the size of a tree. Northern pine and birch woods often lack a shrub layer, but locally have an abundance of juniper *Juniperus communis* ssp. *communis*, mainly where the canopy is not too dense. Birchwoods on basic soils in north-west Scotland often have much hazel, which may share the rather low canopy and, under more natural conditions, holly, rowan and willows were probably also present. The remaining fragments of scrub woodland on islands in lakes probably give the closest approximation to original northern woodland, and typically show mixtures of these species.

Where the ground is moist, especially on clay soils, willows are usually represented, and include *Salix cinerea*, *S. pentandra*, *S. purpurea*, *S. triandra*, *S. viminalis* and *S. capraea*. These may reach dominance on really waterlogged ground and are then often mixed with alder and/or birch, to form carrs which may occur on their own or as patches within other woods. Such thickets are frequently associated with fen communities in valley mires and open water transition/flood-plain mires, and may overlie deep peat. Alder buckthorn *Frangula alnus*, is locally abundant in carrs, whilst tall bog myrtle *Myrica gale* sometimes occurs in the more open swamp woods and may then be regarded as part of the scrub. Carr is characteristically a late stage in hydroseral development, and may persist indefinitely or change to woodland, depending on the final relationship between water table and ground surface obtaining on a particular site.

Three of the four woody climbers, honeysuckle *Lonicera periclymenum*, ivy *Hedera helix* and woody nightshade *Solanum dulcamara*, belong in many respects to the field layer rather than the shrub layer. Both honeysuckle and ivy form low tangles or dense carpets on the ground as well as ascending trees. Both species occur most commonly on soil in the medium fertility range but honeysuckle can grow on fairly acid mor soils. Both are kept in check by grazing and so are often more characteristic of lowland than of upland woods. Ivy is an oceanic plant in Europe but is very characteristic of trees and woods of such dry districts as East Anglia in Britain. Woody nightshade is mainly a plant of swamp woods and carrs especially in the south. The fourth woody climber, old man's beard *Clematis vitalba*, is an indicator of calcareous soils and occurs mainly in southern England as a climber of scrub and woodland edges; it has increased since myxomatosis reduced rabbit populations.

In many woods, species such as *Mahonia aquifolium* and *Rhododendron ponticum* have been planted or are established as escapes. *Rhododendron* often becomes a pest from the ecological viewpoint as it spreads rapidly and creates such dense shade that the field and ground layer species beneath are killed. Dominance of certain shrubs, e.g. elder and perhaps holly, is sometimes the result of a wood having been used as a colonial roost or nesting place by berry-feeding birds.

Scrub is a seral development in other formations, such as grassland, heath or mire, so it is considered also in Chapter 6, and, more briefly, in Chapter 8.

THE FIELD LAYER

A woodland floor is typically covered by a dense growth of small shrubs, herbs and ferns usually less than 1 m in height, and termed the field layer. Some field communities of woodland occur with little variation from the extreme north to the extreme south of Britain and are thus of small value in identifying regional woodland types. Others contain groups of species with distinctive geographical distribution patterns which are of value in regional characterisation. The field layer varies in relation to chemical and physical soil differences, and variations in management, especially herbivore grazing. Field layer floristics are useful in characterising edaphic and biotic diversity within woodlands. The chief directions of variation in regard to soil conditions are base-status and degree of wetness. On the whole, field layer species have a need for the shade and humidity conferred by the tree and shrub layers, as is evidenced by the occurrence of many of the most characteristic species in the deep, vertical crevices of treeless limestone pavements, or on the moist ledges of elevated mountain cliffs. An important ecological separation of the woodland field layer is between grazed and ungrazed types.

Upland woods, especially of the hanging type, are typically unfenced above and are mostly heavily grazed, as they are often used as wintering places for the sheep pastured on the adjoining open hillsides. Only where enclosed farmland occurs above the woods, as in parts of Wales, are the woods fenced against the intrusion of grazing stock. On the other hand, most lowland woods are surrounded by agricultural land and are fenced, so that they are usually ungrazed, except sometimes by cattle or, less often, pigs. Some differences in the field layers between upland and lowland woods which were once attributed to the more obvious climatic differences between such sites, have been shown to result in part from this divergence in management.

The effect of heavy grazing by large herbivores in woodlands is to promote an increase of grass species at the expense of dicotyledonous herbs. A heavily grazed woodland thus has a generally grassy appearance, though the actual species vary according to soil conditions. On the dry, base-poor brown earths of upland oak and birchwoods, *Agrostis tenuis*, *A. canina*, *Anthoxanthum odoratum* and *Deschampsia flexuosa* are among the abundant grasses, whilst *Molinia caerulea* is often dominant in wetter situations. Bracken *Pteridium aquilinum* is often locally dominant in these upland woods, especially where the tree canopy is not dense, and may here be encouraged by grazing. Royal fern *Osmunda regalis* was once widespread in a variety of acidic woodland habitats, but has been much reduced by collecting and is now local and found especially in rocky situations, as in wooded ravines, or on islands in lochs.

The ungrazed counterparts of these acidic oak and birchwoods are much scarcer, and have field communities which are usually distinguished by a dominance of bilberry *Vaccinium myrtillus*, *Luzula sylvatica* or ferns such as *Dryopteris dilatata*, *D. filix-mas*, *D. borreri* and *Thelypteris limbosperma*. Bracken also flourishes in many ungrazed woods and evidently has an original niche in the woodland field layer; it is abundant or even dominant in such a wide range of woodland field communities that there are grounds for regarding it as a separate layer on its own, between the shrub and field layers in stature. Smaller ferns such as *Thelypteris dryopteris* and *T. phegopteris* also tend to be more abundant or luxuriant in ungrazed woods. *Lonicera periclymenum* is abundant in many of these ungrazed woods on poor soils, sometimes forming an important component of the field layer, and there is often an abundance of *Corydalis claviculata* in rocky places. Where the light intensity is high, *Calluna* and *Erica cinerea* may occur as members of the field layer in oak and birch woods. Whether grazed or ungrazed, the flora is usually poor in species and typical associates consist of *Potentilla erecta*, *Galium saxatile*, *Melampyrum pratense*, *Succisa pratensis*, *Digitalis purpurea*, *Luzula pilosa*, *Blechnum spicant*, *Dactylorchis maculata* and *Solidago*

virgaurea. Where soil conditions are rather less acidic and base-deficient, the field layer of oak and birch woods shows a greater variety of herbs. *Holcus mollis*, *Endymion non-scriptus*, *Anemone nemorosa* and *Oxalis acetosella* are locally dominant, and *Teucrium scorodonia*, *Viola riviniana*, *Veronica officinalis*, *Hypericum pulchrum*, *Lathyrus montanus*, *Stellaria holostea*, *Silene dioica*, *Galium aparine*, *Conopodium majus*, *Holcus lanatus*, *Poa trivialis* and *P. nemoralis* are characteristic of these less heavily podsolised soils. Some of these plants appear to thrive under grazing, whereas others do not, but there is always the tendency to a higher cover of grasses in heavily grazed woods. The various species of bramble may be regarded as belonging to either the field or shrub layers, or both, and flourish mainly on soils of intermediate fertility.

Oak, oak–ash or ash woods on base-rich soils have grasses such as *Brachypodium sylvaticum*, *Melica uniflora* and *Dactylis glomerata* on drier ground, and *Deschampsia cespitosa* in damper places. Forbs are abundant and typically include *Mercurialis perennis*, *Geranium robertianum*, *Primula vulgaris*, *Sanicula europaea*, *Fragaria vesca*, *Potentilla sterilis*, *Prunella vulgaris*, *Ajuga reptans*, *Ranunculus ficaria*, *Glechoma hederacea*, *Arum maculatum*, *Veronica chamaedrys* and *Circaea lutetiana*. Taller species include *Geum rivale*, *G. urbanum*, *Filipendula ulmaria*, *Allium ursinum*, *Urtica dioica*, *Valeriana officinalis*, *Listera ovata* and *Stachys sylvatica*. *Athyrium filix-femina* and *Carex sylvatica* are also usually present. Widespread but less constant forbs of these richer soils include *Mycelis muralis*, *Paris quadrifolia*, *Epipactis helleborine*, *Scrophularia nodosa*, *Carex laevigata* and the ferns *Phyllitis scolopendrium* and *Polystichum aculeatum*. Woods on basic substrata have many local or rare species, and those characteristic of the strongly calcareous formations include *Lithospermum purpurocaeruleum*, *Actaea spicata*, *Helleborus viridis*, *H. foetidus*, *Iris foetidissima*, *Polygonatum multiflorum*, *Atropa belladonna*, *Gagea lutea*, *Cephalanthera rubra*, *Orchis purpurea* and *Cypripedium calceolus*. Most of these rare and local basiphilous species occur in small quantity, but a few, e.g. oxlip *Primula elatior* in some Cambridgeshire woods, attain local dominance.

Heavily grazed woods on base-rich soils usually show dominance of grasses, with an abundance of grazed-down forbs. Ungrazed woodland field communities on basic soils have a lesser abundance of grasses and a higher cover of forbs and ferns, which attain a greater luxuriance and often have a larger number of species than in grazed woods. Tall forbs are especially sensitive to grazing, and ungrazed woods tend to have a higher representation of species than those which are heavily grazed.

As well as the range from acidic to basic and grazed to ungrazed, the woodland field communities show a gradient from dry to wet. The wet acidic type shows an approach to certain types of oligotrophic soligenous mire communities; there is typically an abundance of sedges such as *Carex echinata*, *C. nigra* and *C. rostrata*, and of other species such as *Juncus effusus*, *J. acutiflorus*, *Molinia caerulea*, *Agrostis stolonifera* and *Viola palustris*. Slightly richer wet soils have *Ranunculus repens*, *Chrysosplenium oppositifolium* and *Carex remota*, whilst the strongly basic wet mulls approach rich-fen, with *Carex paniculata, Caltha palustris, Cardamine amara, Oenanthe crocata, Senecio aquaticus, Crepis paludosa, Iris pseudacorus, Eupatorium cannabinum, Equisetum telmateia* and *Thelypteris palustris*. Grazing animals tend to avoid these wet woodland soils, so that there is usually less differentiation here between grazed and ungrazed communities. Since many of the basic woodland soils are clayey, some of the typical basiphilous field layer plants are species with a moderate moisture requirement and also occur in fen, e.g. *Filipendula ulmaria, Valeriana officinalis* and *Deschampsia cespitosa*.

The field communities described so far show only a limited degree of association with particular woodland tree dominants. The wettest types, both base-rich and base-poor, are usually found in alderwood, but oak, ash and birch all tolerate moderately wet soils and some of the relatively hydrophilous field communities can be associated with these trees. The dry acidophilous types occur mainly in association with oak and birch, while the dry basiphilous communities are found with these trees as well as with ash. The field layer of beechwood is usually a shade-impoverished derivative of one of the above communities, within the range of acidophilous to basiphilous dry types as beech does not grow on wet soils. Beechwoods often have a very poorly developed field layer, with little but saprophytes such as *Neottia nidus-avis* and *Monotropa hypopitys*, but they are the habitat of a few rare or very local orchids such as *Epipogium aphyllum, Cephalanthera rubra, C. damasonium* and *Epipactis purpurata*.

The woodland field layer may show little relationship to the particular tree species overhead, but its composition is greatly influenced by the intensity of shade cast by the canopy. Considerable changes in relative abundance of species follow thinning, coppicing or clearance of both the tree and shrub layers, and there are seral developments in the field layer as the overhead canopy is re-established. Many species spread rapidly, reach dominance in 'societies', and flower profusely when woodland is cleared. Some of these are wide amplitude species occurring commonly in treeless habitats, e.g. *Silene dioica, Filipendula ulmaria, Glechoma hederacea* and *Deschampsia cespitosa*, but others are typically woodland plants which flourish for a period under the abnormally high light intensities, e.g. oxlip. An abundance of *Digitalis purpurea* and *Chamaenerion angustifolium* is especially associated with burning of the brushwood. There are also important seasonal changes in floristic composition of the field layer between early spring and the middle of summer, which corresponds with decreasing light intensity as the canopy develops. Species such as *Endymion non-scriptus, Ranunculus ficaria, Anemone nemorosa* and *Allium ursinum* put on rapid vegetative growth and flower early in the year, then die down and almost disappear above ground. They are followed by later flowering species such as *Conopodium majus, Circaea lutetiana* and *Geum urbanum*. Some species flower early but persist vegetatively right through the summer, e.g. dog's mercury *Mercurialis perennis*. A few plants, such as the bluebell and the primrose,

are found mainly in woodland in the south and east, but are equally characteristic of tree-less habitats in the north and west.

The Scottish pinewoods have fairly distinctive field communities of two main types. The first, where the canopy is open and light intensity high, is a Callunetum which differs in only minor respects from that of the open moorland, while the second is a *Vaccinium* heath which resembles that of ungrazed oak and birchwoods but has typically an abundance of *V. vitis-idaea* as well as *V. myrtillus*. There is also a distinctive floral element of the pinewood communities which includes the northern species *Goodyera repens, Linnaea borealis, Pyrola minor, Orthilia secunda, Moneses uniflora, Listera cordata* and *Trientalis europaea*. Some of these plants are found in birchwood, and there is a good deal of overlap in the field layers of pine and birch wood in the Highlands. The abundance of *Molinia* in some wetter pinewoods may be partly a grazing effect.

Besides the examples mentioned under pinewood, certain floristic differences may be found in comparing southern with northern woods. On acidic soils, *Luzula forsteri* is a characteristic southern woodland species, whilst *Thelypteris phegopteris, T. dryopteris* and *Melampyrum sylvaticum* (rare) belong to the northern woods. Field layer composition shows greater divergence on basic soils, with *Lithospermum officinale, Galeobdolon luteum, Campanula trachelium, Cephalanthera damasonium, Epipactis purpurata, Ophrys insectifera, Arum maculatum, Carex strigosa, C. pendula* and *Polystichum setiferum* as geographically diagnostic (though seldom constant) species in the south, and *Stellaria nemorum, Rubus saxatilis, Crepis paludosa, Trollius europaeus, Cirsium heterophyllum, Geranium sylvaticum, Campanula latifolia, Festuca altissima* and *Melica nutans* in the north. Oceanic species particularly characteristic of woods along the Atlantic seaboard include *Dryopteris aemula, Polystichum setiferum* and *Hypericum androsaemum*, though these are also well represented in woods of the extreme south of England, especially Sussex and Kent.

Where rock outcrops and block-litters occur within woods, they often, or locally, have species of small shrub, herb and fern which are not regarded as woodland species, e.g. *Umbilicus rupestris, Sedum anglicum* and *Dryopteris abbreviata* on acidic rocks; and *Helianthemum chamaecistus, Sedum forsteranum, Saxifraga aizoides, Alchemilla alpina, Geranium lucidum, Arabis hirsuta, Pimpinella saxifraga, Orchis mascula, Carex flacca, Asplenium trichomanes, A. viride* and *A. adiantum-nigrum* on basic rocks. In addition, outcrops with big ledges and the precipitous sides of ravines often carry good examples of unmodified field communities which have been protected from grazing, and in some hill woods certain species of shrub, herb and fern may be confined to these habitats.

The definition of phytosociological units within the woodland field layer is difficult. Many species show a patchy abundance or dominance which makes for floristic heterogeneity, and the concept of the 'society' is particularly applicable to analysis of the pattern of variation. It therefore seems best to adhere to a small number of broadly-defined community units, within which separate societies can be recognised.

Some herbaceous plants of the field layer show a particular association with tree cover and are thus reliable indicators of permanent woodland, e.g. *Moneses uniflora*, *Primula elatior* and *Carex strigosa*. This should in theory be true of species with mycorrhizal and saprophytic associations with trees, such as *Goodyera repens*, *Neottia nidus-avis* and *Lathraea squamaria*, but it is always possible that these species may be transplanted along with tree seedlings and thus appear in recent plantations.

THE GROUND LAYER

The floor of a woodland may be covered largely with the litter of fallen leaves when canopy shade is intense, as in closed beech or yew woods, but where light intensity is higher, there is typically a carpet of bryophytes, and a lesser but varying abundance of lichens. On acidic soils, a characteristic group of species occurs with little variation over the whole country and includes *Hypnum cupressiforme*, *Pleurozium schreberi*, *Hylocomium splendens*, *Plagiothecium undulatum*, *Dicranum scoparium*, *Polytrichum formosum*, *Mnium hornum*, *Leucobryum glaucum*, *Campylopus flexuosus*, *Lophocolea bidentata*, *Calypogeia muellerana*, *Lepidozia reptans* and *Diplophyllum albicans*. On the more shaded and dry soils, this list may be only partly represented. The moss carpet may occur below a layer of species such as bilberry or in mixture with grasses, and it tends to be favoured by grazing, which reduces or suppresses the competition from vascular plants. In the western and northern woods, species such as *Rhytidiadelphus loreus*, *Dicranum majus*, *Isothecium myosuroides* and *Thuidium delicatulum* are often abundant.

Many of the western and northern woods are situated on the lower mountain slopes and frequently have a block-strewn floor and rock outcrops of varying size, including the walls of deep stream-cut ravines. The sides and crowns of larger blocks and sloping outcrops usually have carpets of the above-named bryophytes, with few vascular plants, and in the extreme west there is a strong representation of large and conspicuous bryophytes which have a markedly oceanic or Atlantic distribution in Europe. These include *Dicranodontium denudatum*, *Hylocomium umbratum*, *Sphagnum quinquefarium*, *Scapania gracilis*, *Plagiochila spinulosa*, *Mylia taylori*, *Saccogyna viticulosa*, *Bazzania trilobata*, *Lepidozia pinnata* and *Adelanthus decipiens*. These plants require a permanently humid atmosphere and thus flourish within the shade and shelter of woodlands in heavy rainfall areas of Britain. On acidic, exposed rocks the constant and abundant bryophytes include species such as *Sphagnum tenellum*, *Andreaea rupestris*, *A. rothii*, *Cynodontium bruntonii*, *Rhacomitrium aquaticum*, *R. heterostichum*, *Campylopus atrovirens*, *Hyocomium flagellare*, *Heterocladium heteropterum*, *Marsupella emarginata*, *Scapania undulata*, *Mylia taylori* and *Diplophyllum albicans*. These bare, rocky situations afford suitable habitats for a large number of other oceanic and Atlantic bryophytes, many of them small and rupestral, including many competition-intolerant species, and ranging from those which need permanently wet sites to

others which favour dry, but shady rocks. The ravine habitats in particular provide a diversity of conditions and are particularly rich in these plants. In the south-west, the Atlantic bryophyte flora contains a higher proportion of thermophilous species with tropical and Macaronesian connections, while in the north-west, montane oceanic species adapted to cool, humid conditions are correspondingly better represented.

Among the more notable of these rupestral oceanic and Atlantic bryophytes of acidic rocks are the mosses *Sematophyllum novae-caesareae*, *S. demissum*, *Daltonia splachnoides*, *Rhabdoweisia crenulata*, *Dicranum scottianum*, *Hypnum callichroum* and *Grimmia hartmanii*; and the liverworts *Cephaloziella pearsonii*, *Acrobolbus wilsonii*, *Radula carringtonii*, *R. aquilegia*, *Colura calyptrifolia*, *Aphanolejeunea microscopica*, *Drepanolejeunea hamatifolia*, *Harpalejeunea ovata*, *Lejeunea lamacerina*, *Frullania germana*, *F. microphylla*, *Lophocolea fragrans*, *Metzgeria hamata*, *Plagiochila tridenticulata*, *P. punctata*, *P. atlantica*, *Saccogyna viticulosa*, *Harpanthus scutatus*, *Jamesoniella autumnalis* and *Tritomaria exsecta*. Species associated with rocks in streams or water trickles include the mosses *Fissidens polyphyllus*, *F. serrulatus*, *Isothecium holtii* and *Eurhynchium alopecuroides*; and the liverworts *Jubula hutchinsiae*, *Porella pinnata*, *Radula voluta* and *Riccardia sinuata*. The two filmy ferns *Hymenophyllum tunbrigense* and *H. wilsonii* behave as bryophytes and grow on shaded mossy rocks and tree bases in the western woods and luxuriate on the walls of damp wooded ravines. A much rarer relative, the Killarney fern *Trichomanes speciosum* occurs in its few stations in Britain mainly in shady, damp or dripping caves and rock crannies in wooded ravines in the extreme west.

The Atlantic bryophyte flora consists mainly of calcifuge or indifferent species, and it is thus represented mainly in oak, oak-ash and birch woods on poor to moderately rich rocks and soils. The ground layer of woods on strongly basic soils has another distinctive group of bryophytes which includes *Rhytidiadelphus triquetrus*, *Eurhynchium striatum*, *E. praelongum*, *Brachythecium rutabulum*, *Ctenidium molluscum*, *Hylocomium brevirostre*, *Mnium undulatum*, *Atrichum undulatum*, *Fissidens taxifolius* and *Plagiochila asplenioides* var. *major*. *Thuidium tamariscinum* is usually abundant on soils of moderate base-status, and *H. splendens* is often more plentiful on these than on highly podsolised soils. Basic outcrops in woods and wooded ravines also have a characteristic bryophyte flora which includes *Neckera crispa*, *Tortella tortuosa*, *Grimmia apocarpa*, *Gymnostomum recurvirostrum*, *G. aeruginosum*, *Anoectangium aestivum*, *Orthothecium intricatum*, *Breutelia chrysocoma*, *Campylium protensum*, *Fissidens cristatus*, *F. osmundoides*, *Anomodon viticulosus*, *Distichium capillaceum*, *Brachythecium plumosum*, *Thamnium alopecurum*, *Ditrichum flexicaule*, *Bartramia hallerana*, *Preissia quadrata*, *Scapania aspera*, *Radula complanata*, *R. lindbergiana*, *Cololejeunea calcarea*, *Metzgeria pubescens*, *Leiocolea muelleri* and *L. turbinata*. Basiphilous Atlantic bryophytes include *Marchesinia mackaii* and the rare *Lejeunea mandonii*.

As drainage impedance increases at the acidic end of the

scale, Bryalean mosses are replaced by *Sphagnum* spp., including *S. palustre*, *S. recurvum*, *S. fimbriatum* and *S. capillaceum*, though *Polytrichum commune* often has a high cover in these damp woodlands, and *Acrocladium cordifolium* may be plentiful. Woodlands with wet soils of intermediate base-status may have other *Sphagnum* spp., such as *S. squarrosum*, *S. contortum*, *S. plumulosum* and *S. warnstorfianum*, but the richer wet woodland soils tend to be dominated by vascular plants with a poor development of a bryophyte carpet. Species such as *Cratoneuron commutatum*, *Pellia endiviifolia* and *Acrocladium giganteum* occur in these wet situations.

The ground layer also contains a number of lichens growing on soil, litter or rock surfaces, including common species of heaths and grasslands such as *Cladonia impexa*, *C. gracilis*, *C. cervicornis*, *C. rangiformis*, *Peltigera canina*, *P. polydactyla*, *P. horizontalis*, *Peltidea aphthosa*, *Parmelia saxatilis*, *P. omphalodes*, *Sphaerophorus fragilis* and *Stereocaulon vesuvianum*, and rarer, somewhat Atlantic species such as *Sphaerophorus melanocarpus* and *Nephromium lusitanicum*. Basidiomycete fungi are an important component of the woodland flora, but have not been studied in the *Review*.

The woodland bryophyte and lichen communities and flora are particularly sensitive to management effects. Many of the bryophytes, especially Atlantic species, need the shade and high atmospheric humidity conferred by an overhead canopy, and the more sensitive species rapidly die out when the tree or scrub cover is lost. For common and rapidly spreading species there is little or no problem – even after clear-felling of a wood, spores from other populations elsewhere in the district will recolonise the site, provided trees grow up again. However, for the rarer species, capacity for spread appears at present to be so limited that re-colonisation after complete clearance does not occur, and it is only when parent populations are allowed to persist continuously on the site (i.e. through avoidance of clear-felling) that the species in question survive. For similar reasons, re-established woods usually show an even greater scarcity of the kind of plants discussed above than those which have regenerated after clear-felling.

EPIPHYTES

A vascular epiphytic tree flora is very poorly represented in Britain. Ivy and honeysuckle have been noted as common climbing shrubs which also belong to the shrub and field layers, and mistletoe *Viscum album* is a local parasite of deciduous trees in southern Britain, but most commonly in orchards. In western Britain, oaks in particular often have vigorous growths of polypody *Polypodium vulgare*, but the bulk of the epiphytic flora consists of bryophytes and lichens. These increase in variety and luxuriance towards the west, and are best developed as communities under strongly oceanic conditions and where atmospheric pollution is least. Some genera of mosses, notably *Ulota* and *Orthotrichum* are largely arboreal, but in the western woods a large number of bryophyte species, including many with rock habitats, may be found growing on trees. Some of the larger species described as forming communities over stable block litters in western woods also grow over the surface roots and bases of trunks of larger trees and in especially shady, humid situations the filmy ferns behave similarly.

The most abundant epiphytic bryophytes in these woods are varieties of *Hypnum cupressiforme*, *Isothecium myosuroides*, *Dicranum scoparium*, *Ulota crispa* and *Frullania tamarisci*. Strongly Atlantic species especially characteristic of trees include *Ulota vittata* (mainly on hazel), *Frullania germana*, *Plagiochila punctata* and *Mylia cuneifolia*. A considerable number of arboreal bryophytes are characteristic of dry and even continental conditions, but many of these are local and some appear to be decreasing. They are usually associated more with single or scattered trees than with closed woodland, e.g. *Leucodon sciuroides*, *Tortula laevipila*, *T. tirescens*, *Pylaisia polyantha*, *Dicranum montanum*, *D. flagellare*, *D. strictum*, several *Orthotrichum* spp. and *Ptilidium pulcherrimum*. Some epiphytic bryophytes appear to grow mainly on trees on acidic soils, whereas others have an association with trees on basic soils.

Some bryophytes, mainly liverworts, are especially characteristic of dead fallen tree trunks which have been left to decay *in situ*; these include the conspicuous red *Nowellia curvifolia*, *Lophocolea cuspidata*, *L. heterophylla*, several species of *Cephalozia* and *Cephaloziella*, and rarities such as *Sphenolobus helleranus* and *Calypogeia suecica*.

In districts farthest from sources of atmospheric pollution, there is also a rich epiphytic lichen flora. Such communities are especially well developed in the west and include a number of species which are strongly Atlantic and others which flourish most abundantly in the west but are much less markedly Atlantic. These distinctive lichens include large foliose types such as *Lobaria pulmonaria*, *L. laetevirens*, *L. laciniata*, *Lobarina scrobiculata*, *Stictina sylvatica*, *S. limbata* and *S. fuliginosa*, and smaller species such as *Pannaria rubiginosa*, *Parmelia laevigata*, *Parmeliella plumbea* and *Normandina pulchella*. Rich lichen floras containing oceanic species are, however, by no means confined to the west, and numerous important outposts occur in eastern and southern England where rainfall is low. More widespread corticolous lichens include *Evernia prunastri*, *Hypogymnia physodes*, *Parmelia sulcata*, *P. caperata*, *P. saxatilis*, *Cetraria glauca*, *Ramalina farinacea*, *Alectoria* spp., *Usnea* spp. and *Physcia* spp. Many of these epiphytic lichens are associated with large, old trees, especially in the drier, eastern districts, and here they may be indicators of permanent woodland, or at least open tree growth. Epiphytic lichens are less tolerant of deep shade than many woodland bryophytes, and in England some of the richest areas for these lichens are park woodlands with their scattered growth of trees. Their connection with big, old trees is evidently related to a low capacity for spread, at least under present conditions. In western Scotland, however, some of the larger *Lobaria* spp. and *Sticta* spp. grow on a much wider variety of species and age classes of tree than in less oceanic districts. Conversely, some epiphytic species appear unable to withstand the high humidity of the extreme west and are absent from woods in the wettest areas.

The dependence of the less common arboreal bryophytes and lichens on continuity in time of tree cover is obvious. Some species need the shade and high humidity associated with a more or less closed canopy, but others grow in sun-exposed situations where it would seem that the permanence of the right substratum, i.e. tree bark, is more important than the micro-climate conferred by tree cover. The rarer species are again therefore good indicators of permanent woodland, or at least continuity of open tree growth.

Epiphytic bryophytes and lichens are believed to have declined considerably in districts subject to urban–industrial atmospheric pollution, and are very poorly represented, or even absent, within and around the larger cities. They increase in a fairly consistent manner with distance from these major sources of atmospheric pollution, so that concentric lichen zones can be distinguished, but it is possible that there may be adverse effects over considerable distances. Probably the outstanding richness of the western Highlands for lichens is a measure not only of favourable climate but also of remoteness from significant atmospheric pollution. The restriction of many species to older trees in some districts may reflect the inability of sporelings to establish on new host trees since pollution became significant at the beginning of the Industrial Revolution.

Flora

The flora of woodlands can be considered in different ways. In the previous subsection, woodland vegetation has been analysed into different layers, and some account given of the dominant, constant and characteristic species of each layer; to this extent, the flora of woodlands has been partially examined already. This description has, however, dealt adequately only with the rather limited range of species in the tree and tall-shrub layers, and the present subsection will deal explicitly with the very much larger number of species in the field and low-to-medium shrub layers. The field layer contains very many herbaceous species, both dicotyledons and monocotyledons, and is of especial interest to many botanists.

The woodland flora may be regarded as consisting of four main groups:

1 Species found exclusively or mainly in woodland.
2 Species of wider ecological amplitude, but with a strong representation in woodland.
3 Species belonging essentially to other habitats which sometimes occur within woodland, e.g. mires.
4 Species of communities such as grassland, heath and scrub which are seral to woodland and do not persist long when closed canopy has become established. The woodland edge and rides are included in this category.

Because of the very large number of vascular species involved in all four of these classes, only the first two will be dealt with here. The placing of species in the different classes has been a somewhat arbitrary procedure, based on the experience of a few people, and may be improved in the light of further knowledge. Table 5 (p. 82) lists all native vascular species of the field and low–medium shrub layers

which are judged to belong to categories 1 and 2 above; and the ecological and geographical distribution of these plants is indicated. This gives a basis for discussing various features of the woodland flora, though the tree and tall-shrub species will not be considered further.

Very few species or groups of species belong to a particular woodland type, as characterised by tree dominants. The main exception to this is the group of northern pinewood species already mentioned on p. 77 and including *Goodyera repens* and *Moneses uniflora*. Most of the other plants which are specific to a particular woodland type belong to a rather specialised habitat characterised also by a limited range of tree species, e.g. *Equisetum telmateia*, *Thelypteris palustris*, *Corallorhiza trifida* and *Pyrola rotundifolia* are associated with alder–willow woodland because they need moist conditions, and *Cypripedium calceolus*, *Carex digitata*, *Polygonatum odoratum* and *Polemonium caeruleum* tend to occur in ash wood because this is the usual type on the rocky limestone ground which they require.

The number of exclusively or even mainly woodland species in Table 5 is small – 76 out of a total of 236 species. Most of these are presumed to have a need for shade conditions in some degree, but for some of the mycorrhizal, saprophytic, semi-parasitic or parasitic species there is a more definite association with woody species or their litter, e.g. *Goodyera repens*, *Monotropa hypopitys*, *Neottia nidus-avis*, *Melampyrum pratense*, *Lathraea squamaria*, *Hedera helix* and *Viscum album*. Species certainly needing shade are the three members of the Hymenophyllaceae and many of the mosses and liverworts which form such a significant component of many western British woods. Nearly all these hygrophilous species can, however, grow in other shady habitats, as amongst rocks on north to east aspects where trees are absent.

Only 66 of the 236 species are associated with acidic, base-poor soils, and of these 15 are ferns and nine are grasses. It therefore follows that the richest woods floristically are those on base-rich or calcareous soils. Most of the basiphilous species grow over a wide range of base-rich substrata, but some are found mainly on highly calcareous rocks such as chalk and limestone, e.g. *Actaea spicata*, *Daphne mezereum*, *Polemonium caeruleum*, *Lithospermum purpurocaeruleum*, *Atropa belladonna*, *Cardamine impatiens*, *Phyteuma spicatum*, *Polygonatum odoratum*, *Cypripedium calceolus*, *Orchis purpurea*, *O. militaris*, *Ophrys insectifera*, *Helleborus viridis*, *H. foetidus* and *Cephalanthera rubra*. The northern calcicoles are often associated with limestone pavement and some species are able to grow in the deep clefts or 'grikes' even where there are no trees. Some woodland species have a preference for heavy, moist and base-rich clay soils, e.g. *Equisetum telmateia*, *Phyllitis scolopendrium*, *Polystichum setiferum*, *P. aculeatum*, *Ranunculus repens*, *Stellaria nemorum*, *Primula elatior*, *Glechoma hederacea*, *Ajuga reptans*, *Eupatorium cannabinum*, *Allium ursinum*, *Carex sylvatica* and *C. pendula*. Other species need soils rich in humus, either in the mull type with high base-status (e.g. *Crepis paludosa*, *Impatiens noli-tangere*, *Cardamine amara*) or with a mor surface horizon with low base-

Plate 1. *Chesil Beach, Dorset (C.25)* (see p. 55). This shingle beach, 22.5 km in total length, is one of the finest in Europe. A 14.5 km section consists of a narrow ridge, bounded on the inner side by a tidal lagoon, The Fleet, containing the Abbotsbury swannery. The pebble size increases from west to east, and the small pebbles at the west end have fine examples of shingle communities, with *Crambe maritima, Lathyrus japonicus, Silene maritima, Rumex crispus* and *Beta vulgaris* ssp. *maritima (see picture)*. There is a large colony of little terns. (Photo: D. A. Ratcliffe.)

Plate 2. *Scolt Head Island, Norfolk (C.19(b))* (see p. 54). A classic site on the North Norfolk Coast showing coastal accretion processes. The island consists of a main shingle beach with dunes running parallel to the sea, and a series of lateral ridges, partially dune covered, running landwards from the main ridge. The segments between the lateral ridges are filled with salt marshes formed by stabilisation of inter-tidal sand. The island has grown from the far (east) to the near (west) end. Its varied flora and fauna include large populations of rare species such as *Suaeda fruticosa* and breeding Sandwich tern. (Photo: Cambridge University Collection, copyright reserved.)

Plate 3. *Newborough Warren, Anglesey (C.51)* (see p. 57). This large sand dune system on Anglesey is now partly afforested with conifers. It shows especially fine stages in succession from mobile marram dunes to stabilised flats of blown sand with moss–lichen and herbaceous communities. Calcareous dune slacks with a rich flora are also well developed. The grade 2 lowland heath and upland site of Yr Eifl forms the skyline on the right. (Photo: courtesy of the Ministry of Defence: Crown copyright.)

Plate 4. *Sheepscombe Wood, Gloucestershire (W.72)* (see p. 117). The beechwoods of the Cotswold Oolitic limestone are famous for the quality of their trees. This is a particularly fine stand of straight-stemmed 30 m trees carefully managed for silviculture. The canopy is not as dense as in some beechwoods, and there are well-developed field communities besides good regeneration of the beech itself. (Photo: D. A. Ratcliffe.)

Plate 5. *Abernethy Forest, Inverness-shire* (W.187(e)) (see p. 120). The Scots pine forests of the Central Scottish Highlands are amongst the largest tracts of original woodland left in this country. They are extremely variable in structure, and the example shown is of a less common type, showing trees of uneven age and a patchy shrub layer of juniper. The clumps of heather belong to the more open phase, but bilberry and cowberry become dominant where the canopy is denser. (Photo: D. A. Ratcliffe.)

Plate 6. *Lodore Woods, Cumberland* (*W.133(d)*) (see p. 107). The steep slopes have 'hanging' woods of sessile oak on acidic rocks of the Borrowdale Volcanic Series, with mixed ash–oak–wych elm–hazel wood on the richer soils at the foot of the slope, passing to a fringe of alder and willow on the shore of Derwentwater. The scene is impressive in the blanket of trees extending to the skyline, conveying the appearance of continuous forest cover – a feature characteristic of lower hill slopes in bygone times but now usually represented only by fragmented woodland blocks. (Photo: D. A. Ratcliffe.)

Plate 7. *Bramshaw Wood, New Forest, Hampshire* (*W.26*) (see p. 116). This Ancient and Ornamental Woodland is dominated by a mixture of pedunculate oak and beech. The picture shows mainly oak, with a dense under-storey of hazel and holly. Many of the more heavily grazed areas of New Forest woodland are almost devoid of a tall-shrub layer. A characteristic feature of these woods (*see picture*) is the abundance of fallen dead timber, an important habitat for invertebrates. (Photo: D. A. Ratcliffe.)

Plate 8. *Lathkill Dale, Derbyshire (W.115(a))* (see p. 118). The Carboniferous Limestone dales of the Low Peak District have some of the finest ashwoods in Britain, and the ungrazed woods of Lathkill Dale are especially good examples. The picture shows the well-developed shrub and field layers containing a large variety of species. (Photo: D. A. Ratcliffe.)

status (e.g. *Goodyera repens, Trientalis europaea, Pyrola minor*). A few woodland species have an alternative habitat in calcareous dune slacks, e.g. *Monotropa hypopitys, Corallorhiza trifida, Pyrola rotundifolia, Epipactis leptochila* and *E. phyllanthes*.

There is a predominance of base-rich soils in the south and base-poor soils in the north, and this trend is paralleled by the tendency for southern species to be basiphilous and northern species acidophilous or indifferent to base-status. The number of woodland species is greater in the southern half of England than in the north (Table 5). This may be an expression of the greater extent of base-rich soils (with their richer flora) in the south, but it may also reflect the originally greater total area of woodland in this region. Species associated with rock habitats in woodland are absent from East Anglia and much of south-eastern England, as these habitats are missing (except in the Weald).

Another group (column 11 of Table 5) consists of species which show a wide distribution in Britain, except in the lowlands of central and eastern England. With some of these the scarcity or absence extends to the Welsh Borders, Gloucestershire, Hertfordshire, East Anglia and the East Riding of Yorkshire (cf. distribution maps of *Vaccinium myrtillus* and *Erica tetralix*). Most of these species are calcifuges and their scarcity matches the very limited occurrence of acidic soils in this part of Britain. They are not northern species, for they appear again in abundance on areas with a prevalence of base-deficient soils in the extreme south of England. Many species are necessarily scarce or absent in the Fenlands simply because there is so little woodland of any kind in this district.

Many species are widespread in Britain except in the north of Scotland (Table 5, column 10) but their scarcity or absence in this region is probably due to more than one factor. First, there is a general scarcity of woodland, and much of the far north is now virtually treeless moorland and mountain, so that extent of suitable habitat is limiting. In addition, there is the general decrease in floristic richness with distance north in British woodlands, and some of the species concerned may be at or near their northern limits in the Highlands.

Judged by British distribution, there are only eight markedly oceanic vascular species amongst the list in Table 5, and six of these are ferns. This is rather surprising in view of the large number of Atlantic bryophytes associated with British woodlands, but probably many of the vascular species with pronounced southern tendencies are oceanic in the sense of being thermophilous. J. R. Matthews (1937) lists 10 of the species (in Table 5) other than ferns in his oceanic southern and oceanic west European elements. *Physospermum cornubiense* is the only Mediterranean woodland species in Britain. Most of the 22 species which belong to the southern half of England fall within Matthews' continental, continental southern, oceanic southern and oceanic west European elements.

Many widespread and northern woodland herbs grow on basic cliff ledges up to 910–1070 m in the Scottish mountains, far above even the potential tree limit. In part, these herbaceous communities represent an upward extension of the field layer once characteristic of submontane woods on the better soils but now largely eradicated or severely modified by the heavy grazing which has affected all but a few of these hill woodlands. Communities of this type are well developed in the subalpine birchwoods of Scandinavia. The species commonly found in the tall-herb ledge communities include *Cirsium heterophyllum, Trollius europaeus, Geranium sylvaticum, Angelica sylvestris, Crepis paludosa, Silene dioica, Valeriana officinalis, Succisa pratensis, Filipendula ulmaria, Rubus saxatilis, Geum rivale, Luzula sylvatica* and *Deschampsia cespitosa*. Similar communities are also represented in ungrazed hay meadows in northern England and Scotland, and are dealt with in Chapter 6.

The acidophilous northern species are best represented in the pinewoods of the eastern Highlands, though some of the species concerned grow more widely in both pine and birch woods. A few species, notably *Actaea spicata, Ribes alpinum* and *Cypripedium calceolus* are in Britain confined to northern England, and *Impatiens noli-tangere* is found also in north Wales.

The 23 rare woodland species include one, *Euphorbia pilosa*, which is evidently extinct in Britain. Of the other 22, 12 are plants of basic soils in the southern half of England, and the remainder vary widely in distribution and soil requirements. Some rare woodland species may have become relict through destruction of the habitat and loss of many former localities, but probably others are rare because of an inability to spread from their few existing colonies, which became established largely through chance during favourable conditions.

Matthews' classification of geographical elements in the British flora includes only 68 flowering plants of the 236 woodland species in Table 5, the others being unclassified (presumably they are either widespread or irregularly distributed in Europe). Seven species of fern have also been classified using Matthews' system. The numbers of species in the different elements are as follows (the additional figures in parentheses are for tall shrubs and trees):

Total number of classified species	75 (15)
Mediterranean	1 (0)
Oceanic southern	7 (1)
Oceanic west European	10 (1)
Continental southern	15 (3)
Continental	12 (6)
Continental northern	22 (4)
Northern montane	7 (0)
Arctic–alpine	1 (0)

Some taxonomic groups are well represented in woodlands, especially ferns (19 species), and the families Ranunculaceae (10 species), Rosaceae (12 species), Scrophulariaceae (8 species), Liliaceae (10 species), Orchidaceae (20 species), Cyperaceae (9 species) and Gramineae (26 species). On the other hand, the Cruciferae, Caryophyllaceae, Chenopodiaceae, Papilionaceae, Umbelliferae and Compositae are poorly represented in proportion to their size.

Table 5. *Habitats and distribution of vascular plants of the woodland field–medium shrub layer*

	Amplitude	Acidic	Medium base	Calcareous	Moist-wet	Shade loving	Especially rock habitats	Widespread common	Widespread local	Widespread, except in N. Scotland	Widespread except in E. central England	Scattered very local	Oceanic	England & Wales	Southern	Northern	Rare species	European distribution
	1	2	3	4	5	6	7	8	9	10	11	12	13	14	15	16	17	18
Equisetum sylvaticum	2	—	+	—	(+)	—	—	—	—	—	—	—	—	—	—	+	—	—
E. telmateia	2	—	+	+	+	—	—	—	—	—	—	—	—	+	—	—	—	—
Osmunda regalis	2	+	+	—	(+)	—	(+)	—	—	—	—	—	+	—	—	—	—	OW
Trichomanes speciosum	2	+	—	—	+	+	+	—	—	—	—	—	+	—	—	—	+	OS
Hymenophyllum tunbrigense	2	+	—	—	—	+	+	—	—	—	—	—	+	—	—	—	—	OS
H. wilsonii	2	+	—	—	—	+	+	—	—	—	—	—	+	—	—	—	—	OW
Pteridium aquilinum	2	+	—	—	—	—	—	+	—	—	—	—	—	—	—	—	—	—
Blechnum spicant	2	+	—	—	—	—	(+)	—	—	—	+	—	—	—	—	—	—	OW
Phyllitis scolopendrium	2	—	+	+	—	+	+	—	—	+	—	—	—	—	—	—	—	—
Athyrium filix-femina	2	+	+	—	—	—	—	—	—	—	+	—	—	—	—	—	—	—
Dryopteris filix-mas	2	+	+	+	—	—	—	+	—	—	—	—	—	—	—	—	—	—
D. borreri	2	+	+	—	—	—	(+)	—	+	—	—	—	—	—	—	—	—	—
D. carthusiana	2	+	—	—	+	—	—	—	+	—	—	—	—	—	—	—	—	—
D. dilatata	2	+	—	—	—	—	(+)	+	—	—	—	—	—	—	—	—	—	—
D. aemula	2	+	—	—	—	+	+	—	—	—	—	—	+	—	—	—	—	OS
Polystichum setiferum	2	—	+	+	—	+	+	—	—	—	—	—	+	—	—	—	—	OS
P. aculeatum	2	—	+	+	—	(+)	+	—	+	—	—	—	—	—	—	—	—	—
Thelypteris palustris	2	—	+	+	+	—	—	—	—	—	—	—	—	+	—	—	—	—
T. dryopteris	2	+	—	—	—	(+)	+	—	—	—	—	—	—	—	—	+	—	—
T. phegopteris	2	+	—	—	—	(+)	+	—	—	—	—	—	—	—	—	+	—	—
Polypodium vulgare	2	+	+	—	—	—	(+)	—	—	—	+	—	—	—	—	—	—	—
Trollius europaeus	2	—	+	+	—	—	(+)	—	—	—	—	—	—	—	—	+	—	NM
Helleborus viridis	1	—	+	+	—	—	(+)	—	—	—	—	—	—	+	—	—	—	—
H. foetidus	1	—	+	+	—	—	(+)	—	—	—	—	—	—	+	—	—	—	—
Aconitum anglicum	2	—	+	+	(+)	—	—	—	—	—	—	—	—	+	—	—	—	—
Actaea spicata	2	—	—	+	—	+	(+)	—	—	—	—	—	—	—	—	+	+	CN
Anemone nemorosa	2	+	+	—	—	—	—	+	—	—	—	—	—	—	—	—	—	—
Ranunculus repens	2	—	+	+	(+)	—	—	+	—	—	—	—	—	—	—	—	—	—
R. auricomus	1	—	+	+	—	+	—	—	—	—	—	—	—	+	—	—	—	—
R. ficaria	2	—	+	+	—	—	—	+	—	—	—	—	—	—	—	—	—	—
Aquilegia vulgaris	2	—	+	+	—	—	(+)	—	—	—	—	—	—	+	—	—	—	—
Corydalis claviculata	2	+	—	—	+	(+)	—	+	—	—	—	—	—	—	—	—	—	OW
Cardamine amara	2	—	+	+	+	—	—	+	—	—	—	—	—	—	—	—	—	—
C. impatiens	2	—	—	+	—	—	+	—	—	—	—	+	—	—	—	—	—	—
C. flexuosa	2	—	+	+	—	—	+	+	—	—	—	—	—	—	—	—	—	—
Dentaria bulbifera	1	—	—	+	—	+	—	—	—	—	—	—	—	—	+	—	—	C
Viola odorata	2	—	+	+	—	+	—	—	—	—	—	—	—	+	—	—	—	—
V. hirta	2	—	+	+	—	—	(+)	—	—	—	—	—	—	+	—	—	—	—
V. riviniana	2	+	+	—	—	—	—	+	—	—	—	—	—	—	—	—	—	—
V. reichenbachiana	1	—	+	+	—	+	—	—	—	—	—	—	—	+	—	—	—	—
V. palustris	2	+	—	—	+	—	—	—	—	—	+	—	—	—	—	—	—	CN
Hypericum androsaemum	2	+	+	+	(+)	+	+	—	—	—	—	—	+	—	—	—	—	OS

Table 5 (*contd.*)

	1	2	3	4	5	6	7	8	9	10	11	12	13	14	15	16	17	18
H. pulchrum	2	+	−	−	−	−	(+)	−	−	−	−	+	−	−	−	−	−	−	
H. hirsutum	2	−	+	+	−	−	−	−	−	−	−	−	−	−	+	−	−	−	CN
H. maculatum	2	−	+	−	−	−	−	−	+	−	−	−	−	−	−	−	−	−	CN
Silene dioica	2	−	+	−	−	−	(+)	+	−	−	−	−	−	−	−	−	−	−	
Stellaria nemorum	1	−	+	−	+	+	−	−	−	−	−	−	−	−	−	−	+	−	
S. holostea	2	−	+	−	−	−	−	−	−	+	−	−	−	−	−	−	−	−	
Moehringia trinervia	2	−	+	−	−	−	−	−	−	+	−	−	−	−	−	−	−	−	
Geranium sylvaticum	2	−	+	+	−	−	(+)	−	−	−	−	−	−	−	−	−	+	−	
G. robertianum	2	−	+	+	−	−	(+)	+	−	−	−	−	−	−	−	−	−	−	
Oxalis acetosella	2	+	+	−	−	+	−	+	−	−	−	−	−	−	−	−	−	−	
Impatiens noli-tangere	1	−	+	−	(+)	+	−	−	−	−	−	−	−	−	−	−	+	−	−
Vicia sylvatica	2	−	+	+	−	+	(+)	−	−	−	−	+	−	−	−	−	−	−	CN
Lathyrus montanus	2	+	−	−	−	−	(+)	−	−	−	−	+	−	−	−	−	−	−	
Filipendula ulmaria	2	−	+	+	(+)	−	(+)	+	−	−	−	−	−	−	−	−	−	−	−
Rubus saxatilis	2	−	+	+	−	−	(+)	−	−	−	−	−	−	−	−	−	+	−	NM
R. idaeus	2	−	+	−	−	−	−	+	−	−	−	−	−	−	−	−	−	−	−
R. fruticosus agg.	2	−	+	+	−	−	−	+	−	−	−	−	−	−	−	−	−	−	−
Potentilla sterilis	2	−	+	+	−	−	−	−	−	−	+	−	−	−	−	−	−	−	−
P. erecta	2	+	−	−	−	−	−	+	−	−	−	−	−	−	−	−	−	−	−
Fragaria vesca	2	−	+	+	−	−	(+)	+	−	−	−	−	−	−	−	−	−	−	−
Geum urbanum	1	−	+	+	−	+	−	−	−	−	+	−	−	−	−	−	−	−	
G. rivale	2	−	+	+	(+)	−	(+)	+	−	−	−	−	−	−	−	−	−	−	
Rosa canina agg.	2	−	+	+	−	−	−	+	−	−	−	−	−	−	−	−	−	−	
R. villosa agg.	2	−	+	+	−	−	−	−	−	−	−	+	−	−	−	−	−	−	−
R. rubiginosa agg.	2	−	+	+	−	−	−	−	+	−	−	−	−	−	−	−	−	−	C
Chrysosplenium oppositifolium	2	−	+	−	+	−	−	−	−	−	−	+	−	−	−	−	−	−	
C. alternifolium	2	−	+	+	−	+	(+)	−	+	−	−	−	−	−	−	−	−	−	CN
Ribes sylvestre	1	−	+	+	(+)	−	−	−	−	−	−	−	−	−	+	−	−	−	−
R. spicatum	2	−	+	+	−	−	(+)	−	−	−	−	−	−	−	−	−	+	−	−
R. nigrum	1	−	+	+	(+)	−	−	+	−	−	−	−	−	−	−	−	−	−	−
R. alpinum	1	−	+	+	−	−	+	−	−	−	−	−	−	−	−	−	+	−	CN
R. uva-crispa	1	−	+	+	−	−	−	+	−	−	−	−	−	−	−	−	−	−	−
Daphne mezereum	1	−	−	+	−	−	+	−	−	−	−	−	−	−	+	−	−	+	−
D. laureola	1	−	+	+	−	−	−	−	−	−	−	−	−	−	+	−	−	−	CS
Epilobium montanum	2	−	+	+	−	−	(+)	+	−	−	−	−	−	−	−	−	−	−	
E. roseum	2	−	+	−	(+)	−	−	−	−	−	−	−	−	−	+	−	−	−	−
E. adenocaulon	2	−	+	−	(+)	−	−	−	−	−	+	−	−	−	+	−	−	−	−
E. tetragonum	2	−	+	−	(+)	−	−	−	−	−	−	−	−	−	+	−	−	−	
Circaea lutetiana	1	−	+	+	−	+	−	−	−	−	+	−	−	−	−	−	−	−	
C. × intermedia	2	−	+	+	−	+	(+)	−	−	−	−	−	−	−	−	−	+	−	CN
C. alpina	2	−	+	+	−	+	+	−	−	−	−	−	−	−	−	−	+	−	CN
Viscum album	1	−	+	−	−	−	−	−	−	−	−	−	−	−	+	−	−	−	−
Hedera helix	2	+	+	+	−	−	(+)	+	−	−	−	−	−	−	−	−	−	−	−
Sanicula europaea	1	−	+	+	−	+	(+)	+	−	−	−	−	−	−	−	−	−	−	
Conopodium majus	2	+	+	−	−	−	−	+	−	−	−	−	−	−	−	−	−	−	OW
Angelica sylvestris	2	−	+	+	(+)	−	(+)	+	−	−	−	−	−	−	−	−	−	−	CN
Physospermum cornubiense	1	−	+	−	−	+	−	−	−	−	−	−	−	−	−	+	−	+	M
Mercurialis perennis	2	−	+	+	−	+	(+)	−	−	+	−	−	−	−	−	−	−	−	
Euphorbia lathyrus	1	−	+	−	−	+	−	−	−	−	−	−	−	−	−	+	−	−	CS
E. pilosa	2	−	+	−	−	+	−	−	−	−	−	−	−	−	(+)	−	+	C	
E. hyberna	2	+	−	−	−	−	−	−	−	−	−	−	−	−	−	+	−	+	OW
E. stricta	2	−	−	+	−	+	−	−	−	−	−	−	−	−	−	+	−	+	C
E. esula	2	−	+	−	−	−	−	−	−	−	−	−	−	−	+	−	−	−	−
E. amygdaloides	1	+	+	+	−	−	−	−	−	−	−	−	−	−	+	−	−	−	CS
Urtica dioica	2	−	+	+	−	−	−	+	−	−	−	−	−	−	−	−	−	−	−
Erica tetralix	2	+	−	−	+	−	−	−	−	−	−	+	−	−	−	−	−	−	OW
Vaccinium vitis-idaea	2	+	−	−	−	−	(+)	−	−	−	−	−	−	−	−	−	+	−	AA
V. myrtillus	2	+	−	−	−	−	(+)	−	−	−	−	+	−	−	−	−	−	−	CN
V. oxycoccus	2	+	−	−	+	−	−	−	−	−	−	+	−	−	−	−	+	−	CN

Table 5 (*contd.*)

	1	2	3	4	5	6	7	8	9	10	11	12	13	14	15	16	17	18
Pyrola minor	2	+	+	—	—	+	—	—	—	—	—	+	—	—	—	—	—	—
P. media	2	+	+	—	—	—	—	—	—	—	—	—	—	—	—	+	—	CN
Orthilia secunda	2	+	—	—	—	+	(+)	—	—	—	—	—	—	—	—	+	—	CN
Moneses uniflora	1	+	—	—	—	+	—	—	—	—	—	—	—	—	—	+	+	CN
Monotropa hypopitys	1	—	+	+	—	—	—	—	—	—	—	—	—	+	—	—	—	—
Primula veris	2	—	+	+	—	—	—	—	—	—	—	—	—	+	—	—	—	—
P. elatior	1	—	+	+	—	+	—	—	—	—	—	—	—	—	+	—	—	—
P. vulgaris	2	—	+	+	—	—	—	+	—	—	—	—	—	—	—	—	—	—
Lysimachia nemorum	2	—	+	—	—	—	—	+	—	—	—	—	—	—	—	—	—	—
L. nummularia	2	—	+	+	—	—	—	—	—	—	—	—	—	+	—	—	—	—
Trientalis europaea	2	+	—	—	—	—	—	—	—	—	—	—	—	—	—	+	—	NM
Polemonium caeruleum	2	—	—	+	—	—	(+)	—	—	—	—	—	—	—	—	+	—	NM
Cynoglossum germanicum	1	—	+	—	—	+	—	—	—	—	—	—	—	—	+	—	+	C
Pulmonaria longifolia	2	—	+	—	—	+	—	—	—	—	—	—	—	—	+	—	—	OW
Myosotis sylvatica	2	—	+	+	—	+	(+)	—	+	—	—	—	—	—	—	—	—	—
Lithospermum purpurocaeruleum	2	—	—	+	—	—	—	—	—	—	—	—	+	—	—	—	+	CS
Atropa belladonna	2	—	—	+	—	—	(+)	—	—	—	—	+	—	—	—	—	—	CS
Solanum dulcamara	2	—	+	—	+	—	—	—	—	—	+	—	—	—	—	—	—	—
Scrophularia nodosa	2	—	+	+	—	—	—	—	—	—	+	—	—	—	—	—	—	—
S. umbrosa	2	—	+	—	+	—	—	—	—	—	—	—	+	—	—	—	—	CN
Digitalis purpurea	2	+	—	—	—	—	(+)	—	—	—	—	+	—	—	—	—	—	—
Veronica officinalis	2	+	+	—	—	—	(+)	+	—	—	—	—	—	—	—	—	—	—
V. montana	1	—	+	+	—	+	—	—	—	—	+	—	—	—	—	—	—	C
V. chamaedrys	2	—	+	+	—	—	—	—	+	—	—	—	—	—	—	—	—	—
Melampyrum pratense	2	+	—	—	(+)	+	—	—	—	—	—	+	—	—	—	—	—	—
M. sylvaticum	1	+	—	—	—	—	(+)	—	—	—	—	—	—	—	—	+	+	CN
Lathraea squamaria	1	—	+	+	—	—	—	—	+	—	—	—	—	—	—	—	—	—
Calamintha sylvatica	1	—	—	+	—	—	—	—	—	—	—	—	—	—	+	—	+	CS
Origanum vulgare	2	—	+	+	—	—	(+)	—	—	—	—	—	—	+	—	—	—	—
Clinopodium vulgare	2	—	+	+	—	—	—	—	—	—	—	—	—	+	—	—	—	—
Prunella vulgaris	2	—	+	+	—	—	—	+	—	—	—	—	—	—	—	—	—	—
Stachys sylvatica	2	—	+	+	—	—	—	+	—	—	—	—	—	—	—	—	—	—
Galeobdolon luteum	1	—	+	+	—	+	(+)	—	—	—	—	—	—	+	—	—	—	C
Glechoma hederacea	2	—	+	+	—	(+)	—	—	—	—	+	—	—	—	—	—	—	—
Teucrium scorodonia	2	+	+	+	—	—	—	—	+	—	—	—	—	—	—	—	—	—
Ajuga reptans	2	—	+	+	(+)	—	—	—	+	—	—	—	—	—	—	—	—	—
Campanula latifolia	1	—	+	+	—	+	—	—	+	—	—	—	—	—	—	—	—	—
C. trachelium	1	—	+	+	—	+	—	—	—	—	—	—	—	+	—	—	—	—
C. patula	1	—	+	—	—	+	—	—	—	—	—	—	—	+	—	—	—	—
Phyteuma spicatum	1	—	—	+	—	+	—	—	—	—	—	—	—	—	+	—	+	C
Galium odoratum	1	—	+	+	—	+	(+)	—	—	+	—	—	—	—	—	—	—	—
G. saxatile	2	+	—	—	—	—	—	—	—	—	+	—	—	—	—	—	—	—
G. aparine	2	—	+	—	—	—	—	—	+	—	—	—	—	—	—	—	—	—
Linnaea borealis	1	+	—	—	—	+	—	—	—	—	—	—	—	—	—	+	—	NM
Lonicera periclymenum	2	+	+	—	—	—	—	—	+	—	—	—	—	—	—	—	—	—
L. xylosteum	1	—	+	—	—	+	—	—	—	—	—	—	—	—	+	—	+	—
Adoxa moschatellina	2	—	+	+	—	+	—	—	—	—	+	—	—	—	—	—	—	—
Valeriana officinalis	2	—	+	+	(+)	—	(+)	+	—	—	—	—	—	—	—	—	—	—
Dipsacus fullonum	2	—	+	+	—	—	—	—	—	—	—	—	—	+	—	—	—	CS
Succisa pratensis	2	+	+	—	(+)	—	(+)	+	—	—	—	—	—	—	—	—	—	—
Solidago virgaurea	2	+	+	—	—	—	(+)	—	—	+	—	—	—	—	—	—	—	—
Eupatorium cannabinum	2	—	+	+	+	—	—	—	—	—	—	—	—	+	—	—	—	—
Arctium minus	2	—	+	—	—	—	—	—	+	—	—	—	—	—	—	—	—	—
Cirsium heterophyllum	2	—	+	+	—	—	(+)	—	—	—	—	—	—	—	—	+	—	CN
Lapsana communis	2	—	+	+	—	—	—	—	—	—	+	—	—	—	—	—	—	—
Mycelis muralis	2	—	+	+	—	—	(+)	—	—	—	—	—	—	+	—	—	—	—
Crepis mollis	2	—	—	+	—	—	—	—	—	—	—	—	—	—	—	+	—	C
C. paludosa	2	—	+	+	(+)	—	(+)	—	—	—	—	—	—	—	—	+	—	CN
Convallaria majalis	2	—	+	+	—	—	(+)	—	+	—	—	—	—	—	—	—	—	—

Table 5 (*contd.*)

	1	2	3	4	5	6	7	8	9	10	11	12	13	14	15	16	17	18
Polygonatum verticillatum	2	—	+	+	—	—	—	—	—	—	—	—	—	—	—	+	+	—
P. odoratum	2	—	—	+	—	—	+	—	—	—	—	+	—	—	—	—	—	—
P. multiflorum	1	—	+	+	—	—	—	—	—	—	—	—	—	+	—	—	—	—
Maianthemum bifolium	1	+	—	—	—	+	—	—	—	—	—	+	—	—	—	—	+	CN
Ruscus aculeatus	2	+	—	—	—	—	—	—	—	—	—	—	—	—	+	—	—	CS
Lilium martagon	1	+	—	—	—	—	—	—	—	—	—	+	—	—	—	—	—	—
Gagea lutea	2	+	+	—	(+)	—	—	—	—	—	—	+	—	—	—	—	—	C
Endymion non-scriptus	2	+	+	—	—	(+)	—	+	—	—	—	—	—	—	—	—	—	OW
Colchicum autumnale	2	+	+	—	(+)	—	—	—	—	—	—	—	—	+	—	—	—	CS
Paris quadrifolia	1	—	+	+	—	+	(+)	—	+	—	—	—	—	—	—	—	—	—
Luzula pilosa	1	+	+	—	—	—	—	—	—	—	+	—	—	—	—	—	—	—
L. sylvatica	2	+	+	—	—	—	(+)	—	—	—	+	—	—	—	—	—	—	—
L. forsteri	2	—	+	—	—	+	—	—	—	—	—	—	—	—	+	—	—	OS
L. multiflora	2	+	—	—	—	—	+	—	—	—	—	—	—	—	—	—	—	—
Allium ursinum	1	—	+	+	(+)	—	(+)	—	—	+	—	—	—	—	—	—	—	—
Galanthus nivalis	2	—	+	—	—	—	—	—	+	—	—	—	—	—	—	—	—	CS
Narcissus pseudo-narcissus	2	—	+	—	—	—	—	—	—	—	—	—	—	+	—	—	—	—
Iris pseudacorus	2	—	+	+	+	—	—	+	—	—	—	—	—	—	—	—	—	—
I. foetidissima	2	—	—	+	—	—	—	—	—	—	—	—	—	+	—	—	—	OS
Cypripedium calceolus	1	—	—	+	—	+	+	—	—	—	—	—	—	—	—	+	+	—
Cephalanthera damasonium	1	—	+	+	—	+	—	—	—	—	—	—	—	—	+	—	—	CS
C. longifolia	1	+	+	—	—	+	—	—	—	—	—	+	—	—	—	—	—	—
C. rubra	1	—	—	+	—	+	—	—	—	—	—	—	—	—	+	—	+	—
Epipactis helleborine	1	—	+	+	—	+	—	—	—	—	—	—	—	+	—	—	—	—
E. purpurata	1	—	+	+	—	+	—	—	—	—	—	—	—	—	+	—	—	—
E. leptochila	2	—	+	+	—	—	—	—	—	—	—	—	—	—	+	—	—	—
E. phyllanthes	2	—	+	+	—	+	—	—	—	—	—	—	—	+	—	—	—	—
Epipogium aphyllum	1	—	+	—	—	+	—	—	—	—	—	—	—	—	+	—	+	CN
Listera ovata	2	—	+	+	(+)	—	—	—	—	—	+	—	—	—	—	—	—	—
L. cordata	2	+	—	—	—	+	—	—	—	—	—	—	—	—	—	+	—	NM
Neottia nidus-avis	1	—	+	+	—	+	—	—	+	—	—	—	—	—	—	—	—	—
Goodyera repens	1	+	—	—	—	+	—	—	—	—	—	—	—	—	—	+	—	NM
Corallorhiza trifida	2	—	+	+	(+)	—	—	—	—	—	—	—	—	—	—	+	—	CN
Ophrys insectifera	2	—	+	—	—	+	—	—	—	—	—	—	—	+	—	—	—	C
Orchis purpurea	1	—	+	—	—	+	—	—	—	—	—	—	—	—	+	—	—	CS
O. mascula	2	—	+	+	—	—	(+)	+	—	—	—	—	—	—	—	—	—	—
O. maculata	2	+	—	—	(+)	—	—	—	—	—	+	—	—	—	—	—	—	—
O. militaris	1	—	+	—	—	—	—	—	—	—	—	—	—	—	+	—	+	C
Dactylorchis fuchsii	2	—	+	+	(+)	—	—	+	—	—	—	—	—	—	—	—	—	—
Arum maculatum	1	—	+	+	—	+	—	—	—	—	—	—	—	+	—	—	—	CS
Carex laevigata	2	—	+	—	(+)	—	—	—	+	—	—	—	—	—	—	—	—	—
C. binervis	2	+	—	—	—	(+)	—	—	—	—	+	—	—	—	—	—	—	OW
C. sylvatica	1	—	+	+	(+)	—	—	—	—	—	+	—	—	—	—	—	—	—
C. pendula	2	—	+	+	(+)	—	(+)	—	—	—	—	—	—	—	+	—	—	CS
C. depauperata	2	—	+	—	—	—	—	—	—	—	—	—	—	—	+	—	+	CS
C. strigosa	1	—	+	+	—	+	—	—	—	—	—	—	—	—	+	—	—	—
C. digitata	2	—	—	+	—	—	+	—	—	—	—	+	—	—	—	—	—	—
C. divulsa	2	—	+	—	—	—	—	—	—	—	—	—	—	—	+	—	—	—
C. remota	1	—	+	—	+	+	—	—	—	—	+	—	—	—	—	—	—	—
Molinia caerulea	2	+	—	—	(+)	—	—	—	—	—	+	—	—	—	—	—	—	—
Festuca arundinacea	2	—	+	+	—	—	—	—	—	—	+	—	—	—	—	—	—	—
F. gigantea	2	—	+	—	—	—	—	—	—	—	+	—	—	—	—	—	—	—
F. altissima	1	—	+	+	—	+	+	—	—	—	—	—	—	—	—	+	—	—
F. ovina	2	+	+	+	—	—	(+)	+	—	—	—	—	—	—	—	—	—	—
Poa nemoralis	2	—	+	+	—	+	(+)	—	+	—	—	—	—	—	—	—	—	—
P. trivialis	2	—	+	—	—	—	—	+	—	—	—	—	—	—	—	—	—	—
Dactylis glomerata	2	—	+	+	—	—	(+)	+	—	—	—	—	—	—	—	—	—	—
Melica uniflora	1	—	+	+	—	—	(+)	—	—	—	—	—	—	+	—	—	—	—
M. nutans	2	—	+	+	—	+	+	—	—	—	—	—	—	—	—	+	—	—

86 Woodlands

Table 5 (*contd.*)

	1	2	3	4	5	6	7	8	9	10	11	12	13	14	15	16	17	18
Zerna ramosa	1	—	+	+	—	—	—	—	—	+	—	—	—	—	—	—	—	—
Brachypodium sylvaticum	2	—	+	+	—	—	(+)	+	—	—	—	—	—	—	—	—	—	—
Agropyron caninum	1	—	+	+	—	—	+	—	+	—	—	—	—	—	—	—	—	—
Arrhenatherum elatius	2	—	+	+	—	—	—	+	—	—	—	—	—	—	—	—	—	—
Holcus lanatus	2	+	+	—	—	—	—	+	—	—	—	—	—	—	—	—	—	—
H. mollis	2	+	—	—	—	—	—	—	—	—	+	—	—	—	—	—	—	—
Deschampsia cespitosa	2	—	+	+	(+)	—	—	+	—	—	—	—	—	—	—	—	—	—
D. flexuosa	2	+	—	—	—	—	—	—	—	—	+	—	—	—	—	—	—	—
Calamagrostis epigejos	2	—	+	+	+	—	—	—	—	—	—	—	—	+	—	—	—	—
C. canescens	2	—	+	—	(+)	—	—	—	—	—	—	+	—	—	—	—	—	—
Agrostis canina	2	+	+	—	—	—	—	—	—	—	+	—	—	—	—	—	—	—
A. tenuis	2	+	+	—	—	—	—	+	—	—	—	—	—	—	—	—	—	—
A. stolonifera	2	—	+	+	(+)	—	—	+	—	—	—	—	—	—	—	—	—	—
Hordelymus europaeus	1	—	—	+	—	+	—	—	—	—	—	+	—	—	—	—	—	—
Milium effusum	1	—	+	—	—	+	—	—	—	—	—	—	—	+	—	—	—	—
Anthoxanthum odoratum	2	+	+	—	—	—	—	+	—	—	—	—	—	—	—	—	—	—
Total 236		65	177	137	16 (31)	70 (6)	21 (60)	53	19	22	22	13	8	45	22 (1)	32	21	

Notes

Categories

Amplitude
 1 = exclusively or mainly in woodland.
 2 = wider ecological range, but often in woodland.
Acidic: soil pH < 4.8, < 30 mg exchangeable calcium/100 g.
Medium base: soil pH 4.8–6.0, 30–300 mg exchangeable calcium/100 g.
Calcareous: soil pH 6.0, 300 mg exchangeable calcium/100 g.
Moist–wet:
Shade loving: } Subjectively assessed. Brackets indicate sometimes found under these conditions.
Especially rock habitats:
Widespread common: throughout Britain, in nearly all suitable habitats.
Widespread local: widely distributed in Britain but absent from some areas and suitable habitats.
Widespread except in northern Scotland: discussed in text.
Widespread except in east-central England: discussed in text.
Scattered very local: widely but discontinuously distributed, with many absences from suitable habitats.
Oceanic: mainly in southern and western coastal districts.
England and Wales: southern tendency in distribution but reaching to northern England and sometimes Scotland (very sparse and mainly in south).
Southern: confined to England south of grid northing 3/000.
Northern: mainly or entirely in northern England and Scotland.
Rare species: recorded in only 1–15 10-km squares since 1960.
European distribution: M = Mediterranean; OW = Oceanic west European; C = Continental; NM = Northern montane; OS = Oceanic southern; CS = Continental southern; CN = Continental northern; AA = Arctic–alpine.

Fauna

MAMMALS, REPTILES AND AMPHIBIANS

Many of the British mammals are associated with woodland in some degree, but few of our species are exclusively forest dwellers. All the British deer frequent woodland, although the native herds of red deer in England and Scotland have become adapted to treeless upland country and are mostly to be found within woodland only when the weather is severe. The introduced or escaped red deer of the English lowlands have, however, resumed the role of forest animals and in areas such as the Breckland they are seldom seen outside the woods. The roe deer *Capreolus capreolus* is more particularly a woodland species, favouring especially open areas, rides and wood margins, and has shown a general increase and expansion of range during recent decades, coincident with extensive re-afforestation of many parts of Britain. After suffering great restriction of range during the main period of forest clearance, it has now become a widespread species again in England and Scotland, but not Wales. Roe deer range over more open country around their forest haunts and often feed on grasslands, heaths and moorlands.

Feral herds of the introduced sika deer *Cervus nippon* are widespread but very local in England and Scotland, and live mainly in woodland, both broad-leaved and coniferous, favouring those where there is dense undergrowth. Fallow deer *Dama dama* are widespread but local and are either descended from possibly native stock (as in the ancient forests of Epping, Rockingham, Cannock Chase and the New Forest) or represent feral populations founded on escapes from deer parks. They frequent woodlands, mainly broad-leaved or mixed and preferably with thick shrub and field layer, and feed at night around the edges or on adjoining fields. The Chinese muntjac *Muntiacus reevesi* is another introduced species which is now widespread as a feral animal in the southern half of England, where, however, severe winters depress numbers periodically. Muntjac inhabit woods with dense shrub and field layers, and are relatively elusive animals whose presence may go undetected.

Deer can cause considerable damage in woodlands by nibbling or uprooting seedlings and rubbing or stripping the bark from saplings and young trees. Newly afforested ground may have to be enclosed with deer-proof fencing and efforts made to control the population in older forests by selective shooting. Uncontrolled heavy grazing by deer may also restrict or prevent natural regeneration of woodland. Locally, deer also cause damage on arable crops on farmland. Their activities may nevertheless have value to wildlife in checking the growth of some vigorous, competitive plants and in helping to prevent complete continuity of tree or shrub cover.

Carnivorous mammals are well represented in woodland. Badgers *Meles meles* are perhaps the most typical forest dwellers among the British species, and the majority of breeding places (setts) are in woods or copses, from which the animals forage over the surrounding countryside. The species is omnivorous and able to subsist in a wide variety of habitats; it is widespread in the British Isles and in the north often lives in treeless country. In some districts the badger is persecuted a good deal, usually needlessly, but the Forestry Commission encourage this animal and provide 'badger gates' in their rabbit-proof fences. The fox includes woodland among its haunts, and in the lowlands many 'earths' are inside woods, though these are simply refuges from which the animals range and feed over a wide area of surrounding country. This predator is ubiquitous in mainland Britain but absent from the Scottish islands except Skye. The strongly carnivorous habits of the fox bring it into general disrepute, but despite control measures, its numbers seem to be maintained remarkably well in most districts.

The wild cat *Felis silvestris* is partly a forest dweller within its range in the Scottish Highlands. Dens are in both broad-leaved and coniferous woods, but especially mountain woods where block litters provide safe refuges and breeding places. Wild cats have recently spread into coniferous plantations in the Campsie Fells in Stirlingshire, and the species seems to be increasing locally or holding its own elsewhere, despite local persecution by gamekeepers. The pine marten *Martes martes* is another predator of mountain woods in north Wales, Lakeland and the Highlands (more especially the north-west) but it can also live and breed in treeless country. Dens are usually deep in block litters or other holes, but occasionally disused tree nests of the larger birds are used. The pine marten is now rare outside the western Highlands, but does not appear to be much molested nowadays. It is an elusive and largely nocturnal animal and may easily escape notice.

The polecat was formerly widespread, but persecution reduced its range; some survivors hung on mainly in secluded parts of central Wales (a situation closely parallel to that of the red kite). Favoured situations for dens are in block litters, tree roots or rabbit holes within woods, including plantations. The polecat is increasing in Wales and quite numerous in some districts, but it is still destroyed where there is much rearing of poultry or preserving of game. The smaller mustelids, the stoat and weasel, both have a niche in woodlands where they feed mainly on small rodents or birds and their eggs and young. These are widespread species in Britain except in the Scottish islands, though a different subspecies of stoat *Mustela erminea ricinae* is recognised on Islay and Jura.

The wood mouse *Apodemus sylvaticus* is the most characteristic small rodent of woodland and lives in runs in and below the leaf litter. It is common over much of Britain, including many of the Scottish islands. The yellow-necked mouse *A. flavicollis* is another woodland species widespread in England and Wales, but apparently much less numerous than *A. sylvaticus*. The bank vole *Clethrionomys glareolus* is most abundant in woodland and scrub, and is widespread though absent from most of the Scottish islands. The short-tailed field vole occurs less commonly in woods than in more open habitats, but it is sometimes plentiful in clearings within woods or uncultivated rough ground around woodland edges. It often builds up to very high densities in recently afforested ground which has been fenced against sheep and deer and thus develops a rank growth of grasses, other herbs and dwarf shrubs, before the trees are tall enough to suppress this. The dormouse *Muscardinus avellanarius* is a local species found mainly in the south of England, where it is less numerous than formerly. It prefers dense woodland and scrub with an abundance of trees which produce edible seeds, e.g. beech, hazel, sweet chestnut.

The small rodents of woodland form an important food source for certain predators, including most of the mammalian species already mentioned, and certain birds, notably the owls. While the characteristic woodland rodents do not show the violent population fluctuations typical of *Microtus*, there are some changes in numbers according to season and year, and these may affect the breeding output of predators such as the tawny owl. These small animals may seriously reduce or prevent natural regeneration of native trees by eating the seeds and seedlings, and bank voles sometimes 'bark' small trees.

The mole is a widespread and common woodland dweller, although in upland districts it is found mainly in woods on the more base-rich soils, except where these are too shallow for burrowing. The common shrew *Sorex araneus* is also widespread in woodland and scrub (but absent from some of the Scottish islands): the pygmy shrew *S. minutus* and water shrew *Neomys fodiens* are, however, less numerous in these habitats, although they are equally widespread. In fact, the pygmy shrew, along with the wood mouse, is the most widely distributed mammal in Britain, and occurs in most of the larger Scottish islands. These four small mammals also form the prey of various woodland predators, notably the tawny owl.

The hedgehog occurs in woods over most of the British mainland, and on some of the Scottish islands where it has probably been introduced. It tends to avoid really dense wood and is most numerous in open woodland and scrub, though the nests are usually well hidden in undergrowth or burrows. The rabbit and brown hare include woodland among their range of habitats, though the rabbit is much sparser almost everywhere since myxomatosis appeared in 1954. Both species sometimes do considerable damage in young plantations by eating seedlings and 'barking' saplings. Woodland predators such as the buzzard, goshawk, fox, badger, stoat and weasel take both rabbits and brown hares (more especially the young) as prey.

Of all the British mammals, the red squirrel *Sciurus vulgaris* has the strongest association with woodland, and is more or less confined to this habitat. This animal has generally declined in numbers and retreated northwards during recent decades. It is locally plentiful in East Anglia, but is otherwise found mainly in northern and western Britain. The favourite habitat is coniferous woodland, but it also occurs widely in mixed and broad-leaved woodland. The dreys are usually placed high in trees or occasionally in tall hedges bounding a wood. The introduced grey squirrel *S. carolinensis* has largely replaced the red squirrel over much of southern Britain; sometimes there appears to have been competition but the red squirrel has also declined seriously in areas where the other species has not appeared. The grey squirrel is more a species of broad-leaved woodland, where its dreys are placed high in the trees and are conspicuous in winter. Both squirrels can do considerable damage in woodland, by eating seedlings and young shoots, and by 'barking' trees. The grey species is particularly harmful in this respect. They are also predators of birds' eggs and young and so may harm game interests.

Many species of bat have some association with woodland and roost and hibernate in hollow trees, and hunt insects over the canopy or along rides and edges. Some species appear to use hollow trees only during summer. Where there are no trees with suitable cavities, bats may use woodlands for feeding only. Most British species use hollow trees if available. They include the widespread whiskered bat *Myotis mystacinus*, Daubenton's bat *M. daubentoni*, noctule *Nyctalus noctula*, pipistrelle *Pipistrellus pipistrellus*, and long-eared bat *Plecotus auritus*; the more local (mainly England) barbastelle *Barbastella barbastellus* (also Wales), Natterer's bat *Myotis nattereri* (also Wales), serotine *Eptesicus serotinus* and Leisler's bat *Nyctalus leisleri*; and the rare Bechstein's bat *Myotis bechsteini* of southern England.

Woodland is not a particularly important habitat for reptiles and amphibia. Adders often lie up in the shade of woods during hot weather and may sometimes hibernate within woodland. This snake, with the grass snake *Natrix natrix* and smooth snake occur in open places and rides in woods and amongst open scrub. Common frogs *Rana temporaria* and toads *Bufo bufo* also frequent the more open and damper parts of woods and the more open habitats within woodland.

BIRDS

The breeding birds of woodland have been divided into two groups. The first consists of species which nest in closed woodland, and includes those whose major niche is non-arboreal as well as those which are confined to woodland. The second group consists of species which show some association with trees or tall shrubs but not with closed mature woodland. Data on habitat, distribution and population size for these two groups are presented in Tables 6 and 7.

The total list of woodland birds thus defined is quite long, with 92 species, a larger number than for any other major habitat group. Of these, only 35 species have an invariable association with woodland, trees or tall shrubs during the breeding season, but 23 other species belong mainly to these habitats. The passerines are especially well represented in woodland, and of the British breeding birds of prey, only two (the marsh harrier and peregrine) have no association with trees. The data for regional distribution do not indicate relative abundance within each region, but when taken in conjunction with the overall abundance class, they indicate which widespread species are common (e.g. woodpigeon) and which are local or rare (e.g. crossbill).

The preferences of birds for broad-leaved or coniferous woods are indicated and it will be clear from this that the first type tends to have the larger number of species. It follows that mixed woods containing both types often have the richest avifauna. However, much depends on other aspects of diversity, such as woodland structure and representation of transitional habitats, or on age of the trees, so that generalisations are often better avoided. It may nevertheless be said that maturing uniform conifer forests grown in dense canopy and often lacking any subsidiary layer (even bryophytes) are generally notable only for the relative poverty of their breeding bird fauna.

There is perhaps only one well-defined ecological–geographical group of woodland birds in Britain, namely that of the pine forests of the central Highlands, notably on Speyside. This group consists of the capercaillie, crossbill, siskin and crested tit, with a very few pairs of golden eagle, osprey, goshawk and, in 1969, wryneck. More widespread species showing a preference for coniferous woods or trees include long-eared owl, collared dove, coal tit, redpoll (in Wales and south-west England) and goldcrest. Birds especially associated with broad-leaved woodland are the three species of woodpecker, marsh tit, willow tit, nuthatch, tree creeper, redstart, nightingale, blackcap, garden warbler, willow warbler, chiffchaff, wood warbler, pied flycatcher, hawfinch and greenfinch.

The nightingale, blackcap, garden warbler, whitethroat, lesser whitethroat, wren, chiffchaff and long-tailed tit prefer woods and woodland clearings with a good deal of under growth, especially tangles of bramble, honeysuckle or tall herbs, in which they breed. By contrast, the wood warbler, and to a lesser extent the willow warbler, favour woodland with a rather bare floor. Other ground nesters such as the woodcock, mallard, capercaillie and robin, nest most often where there is moderate cover of low shrubs and herbs. The remaining species are tree nesters and the degree of cover in the field layer usually has little influence on these.

Species which breed within the tall shrub layer (e.g. hazel, blackthorn, hawthorn, holly, rhododendron, willows) below the main tree canopy include woodpigeon, turtle dove, collared dove, jay, song thrush, blackbird, hawfinch, greenfinch, redpoll and chaffinch. When mature woodland is available, many species nest by preference at a considerable height above the ground (i.e. more than 9 m) and are often in the canopy; these include all the predatory species, raven, carrion crow, hooded crow, rook, magpie, siskin and crossbill. Where only low trees are available, however, most of these species are sufficiently plastic in their requirements to breed much closer to the ground. Sparrowhawks, crows and magpies frequently nest in birch and willow scrub where taller trees are absent, and in the Highlands herons breed in low scrub on islands in lakes. The kestrel, hobby, merlin, tawny owl and long-eared owl use the old nests of other species, mainly crows, magpie and squirrels, and are limited by the choice of the actual nest builders.

Tree-hole breeders may be divided into those which utilise natural holes and those which excavate their own. The former group include goosander, kestrel, tawny owl, barn owl, little owl, stock dove, wryneck, jackdaw, great tit, blue tit, marsh tit, redstart, pied flycatcher, starling and tree sparrow, while the excavators are the three woodpeckers, crested tit and willow tit. The nuthatch takes over a natural or excavated hole, which it plasters over to its own size, and the tree creeper is a semi-hole nester, with its favourite nest site behind partially detached bark. The natural-hole nesters mostly need fairly mature timber in which cavities have had time to develop. Woodpeckers need dead or at least moribund trees, although the green woodpecker can dig holes in trees which appear healthy from the outside. The crested tit and willow tit depend on very soft, rotten wood or stumps in which to excavate their nests. Trees with holes and dying or dead trees are likely to be removed in normal forestry practice but the situation can be retrieved to some extent by the substitution of artificial nest boxes. In an area of the Forest of Dean, and in Yarner Wood, Devon, the populations of pied flycatchers have been boosted to very high levels by this means. Some tree-hole nesters also breed in holes in rock faces or masonry.

While the number of species breeding within a wood tends to increase with size of the wood, this is partly because diversity also often tends to increase with size. The honey buzzard probably needs large woods but may be limited mainly by the abundance of its main food source, wasps' nests. The large raptors often choose tree sites with a good look-out, and it may be for this reason that species such as the golden eagle and osprey tend to nest where trees are rather scattered or clumped and not in dense woodland.

In eastern Europe where the peregrine nests in trees, it is said often to choose the sharp cut edge to a tall wood, where the wall of trees is equivalent to a cliff face. A high proportion of sparrowhawk nests in large woods are placed close to the wood edge, a ride or some other break in continuity of the tree cover. This species is, however, one of the very few tree nesters which needs a wood as such and seldom nests in rows of trees or scattered trees. Of the birds classed as woodland species, some (such as the carrion crow, magpie, mistle thrush and crossbill) are locally found nesting more numerously in small clumps or rows of trees and in isolated trees (especially in hedgerows) than in large woods. The heron, raven, kestrel and hobby sometimes favour small woods and copses as nesting places, but are equally at home in large woods. The rook establishes its colonies in woods of all sizes or in groups of trees around houses, but is less inclined than some of its relatives to nest in low trees.

Among the species listed in Table 7 are those which have a decided preference for scattered trees, e.g. stock dove, barn owl, little owl, tree sparrow and merlin (insofar as this species nests in trees at all); these may nest also along a woodland edge, but seldom far inside a wood. A few birds from both groups often nest in orchards (which represent a rather open kind of woodland), e.g. magpie, jay, chaffinch, hawfinch, goldfinch and bullfinch, and, when old trees are present, various hole nesters such as the woodpeckers, wryneck and tits. Probably the majority of species which breed in hedges were originally scrubland and/or woodland breeders. The red-backed shrike, linnet and cirl bunting are birds of scrubland only, the first species in fairly tall scrub and the others in low–medium scrub.

Several birds belong to the ephemeral transitional stage between the clearance of a wood and its regeneration, or between the afforestation of unwooded ground and the formation of a more or less closed tree growth. The nightjar, which favours the barest ground, is the first to appear and disappear as the trees grow up. When the field layer becomes dense, often within a year or two of tree planting and fencing against stock (and sometimes rabbits), the pheasant, grasshopper warbler, whinchat, yellow-hammer and (more locally) stonechat often appear, along with birds such as the mallard, whitethroat and willow warbler. In the north, young conifer plantations often develop high densities of field voles and this usually draws short-eared owls to breed. These young plantations have been the refuge of the hen harrier, probably contributing significantly to the post World War II recovery and spread of this raptor. Black game also flourish in this habitat, and have recovered their numbers in many areas where they had declined. In the south, the Montagu's harrier has also colonised young conifer plantations in places.

These young conifer plantations support high densities of breeding birds, and for two species at least, the grasshopper warbler and Montagu's harrier, they probably represent the

Table 6. *Species of birds nesting in closed woodland*

	Broad-leaved woodland	Coniferous woodland	Scrubland	Hedges	Young plantation	Scattered trees	Clearings & rides	Dead or dying timber	Non-woodland habitat	S., S.E. & S.W. England	East Anglia	Midlands	Wales	N. England	S. Scotland	E. Highlands	W. Highlands	Abundance class
	1	2	3	4	5	6	7	8	9	10	11	12	13	14	15	16	17	18
Heron *Ardea cinerea*	X	X	—	—	—	—	—	—	+	X	X	X	X	X	X	+	X	4
Mallard *Anas platyrhynchos*	+	—	+	—	+	—	+	—	X	X	X	X	X	X	X	X	X	6
Golden Eagle *Aquila chrysaetos*	+	X	—	—	—	+	—	—	X	—	—	—	—	—	+	X	X	3
Common buzzard *Buteo buteo*	X	X	—	—	—	+	—	—	X	X	—	+	X	X	X	X	X	4
Sparrowhawk *Accipiter nisus*	X	X	+	—	—	—	—	—	—	X	+	+	X	X	X	X	X	4
Goshawk *A. gentilis*	X	X	—	—	—	—	—	—	—	+	—	+	+	+	—	+	—	1
Red kite *Milvus milvus*	X	—	—	—	—	—	—	—	—	—	—	—	X	—	—	—	—	2
Honey buzzard *Pernis apivorus*	X	+	—	—	—	—	—	—	—	X	—	—	—	—	—	—	—	1
Osprey *Pandion haliaetus*	—	X	—	—	—	+	—	+	—	—	—	—	—	—	—	X	+	1
Hobby *Falco subbuteo*	X	X	—	—	—	+	—	—	—	X	+	+	—	—	—	—	—	2
Kestrel *Falco tinnunculus*	X	X	—	—	—	+	—	—	X	X	X	X	X	X	X	X	X	5
Black grouse *Lyrurus tetrix*	+	X	+	—	X	+	—	—	+	+	—	+	X	X	X	X	X	5
Capercaillie *Tetrao urogallus*	+	X	—	—	—	—	—	—	—	—	—	—	—	—	X	X	+	5
Woodcock *Scolopax rusticola*	X	+	+	—	+	—	+	—	+	X	X	X	X	X	X	X	X	4
Woodpigeon *Columba palumbus*	X	X	X	X	—	+	—	—	+	X	X	X	X	X	X	X	X	7
Turtle dove *Streptopelia turtur*	+	—	X	+	—	—	—	—	—	X	X	X	+	+	+	—	—	5
Collared dove *S. decaocto*	+	X	+	+	—	X	—	—	—	X	X	+	X	X	X	X	X	4
Tawny owl *Strix aluco*	X	X	+	—	—	+	—	+	—	X	X	X	X	X	X	X	X	5
Long-eared owl *Asio otus*	+	X	+	—	—	—	—	—	—	+	+	+	+	X	X	X	X	4
Green woodpecker *Picus viridis*	X	—	—	—	—	+	—	X	—	X	X	X	X	X	+	—	—	5
Great-spotted woodpecker *Dendrocopos major*	X	+	—	—	—	+	—	X	—	X	X	X	X	X	X	X	X	5
Lesser-spotted woodpecker *D. minor*	X	—	—	—	—	+	—	X	—	X	X	X	X	X	+	—	—	4
Wryneck *Jynx torquilla*	+	—	—	—	—	X	—	X	—	X	—	—	—	—	—	—	—	1
Raven *Corvus corax*	+	+	—	—	—	+	—	—	X	+	—	+	X	X	X	X	X	4

Table 6 (*contd.*)

	1	2	3	4	5	6	7	8	9	10	11	12	13	14	15	16	17	18
Carrion crow *C. corone corone*	X	X	+	+	—	X	—	—	+	X	X	X	X	X	X	+	+	6
Hooded crow *C. c. cornix*	X	X	+	—	—	X	—	—	X	—	—	—	—	—	—	X	X	5
Rook *C. frugilegus*	X	X	—	—	—	X	—	—	—	X	X	X	X	X	X	X	X	7
Jackdaw *C. monedula*	X	+	—	—	—	X	—	+	X	X	X	X	X	X	X	X	X	6
Magpie *Pica pica*	X	+	X	X	—	+	—	—	X	X	X	X	X	X	X	+	—	5
Jay *Garrulus glandarius*	X	+	+	—	—	—	—	—	—	X	X	X	X	X	X	+	—	5
Great tit *Parus major*	X	+	+	—	—	+	—	+	+	X	X	X	X	X	X	X	X	7
Blue tit *P. caeruleus*	X	+	—	—	—	+	—	+	+	X	X	X	X	X	X	X	X	7
Coal tit *P. ater*	+	X	—	—	—	—	—	+	+	X	X	X	X	X	X	X	X	7
Crested tit *P. cristatus*	—	X	—	—	—	—	—	+	—	—	—	—	—	—	—	X	+	3
Marsh tit *P. palustris*	X	—	—	—	—	—	—	+	—	X	X	X	X	X	+	—	—	4
Willow tit *P. montanus*	X	—	—	—	—	—	—	X	—	X	X	X	X	X	+	—	—	4
Long-tailed tit *Aegithalos caudatus*	+	—	X	+	—	—	—	—	—	X	X	X	X	X	X	X	+	5
Nuthatch *Sitta europaea*	X	—	—	—	—	X	—	+	—	X	X	X	X	+	—	—	—	4
Tree creeper *Certhia familiaris*	X	+	—	—	—	+	—	+	—	X	X	X	X	X	X	X	X	5
Wren *Troglodytes troglodytes*	X	X	X	X	+	—	—	—	X	X	X	X	X	X	X	X	X	7
Mistle thrush *Turdus viscivorus*	X	X	—	—	—	+	—	—	—	X	X	X	X	X	X	X	X	5
Song thrush *T. philomelos*	X	+	X	X	—	—	—	—	—	X	X	X	X	X	X	X	X	7
Redwing *T. iliacus*	X	+	+	—	—	—	—	—	—	—	—	—	—	—	—	+	X	2
Blackbird *T. merula*	X	X	X	X	+	—	—	—	+	X	X	X	X	X	X	X	X	7
Redstart *Phoenicurus phoenicurus*	X	+	+	—	—	—	—	X	+	X	X	X	X	X	X	X	X	4
Nightingale *Luscinia megarhynchos*	X	—	+	—	—	—	—	—	—	X	X	+	—	—	—	—	—	4
Robin *Erithacus rubecula*	X	+	X	+	—	—	+	—	+	X	X	X	X	X	X	X	X	7
Blackcap *Sylvia atricapilla*	X	—	—	—	—	—	—	—	—	X	X	X	X	X	X	+	—	5
Garden warbler *S. borin*	X	—	+	—	—	—	—	—	—	X	X	X	X	X	X	+	—	5
Whitethroat *S. communis*	+	—	X	X	+	—	+	—	—	X	X	X	X	X	X	X	X	7
Lesser whitethroat *Sylvia curruca*	+	—	X	X	+	—	—	—	—	X	X	X	+	+	—	—	—	5
Willow warbler *Phylloscopus trochilis*	X	—	X	—	+	—	+	—	—	X	X	X	X	X	X	X	X	7
Chiffchaff *Phylloscopus collybita*	X	—	+	—	—	—	—	—	—	X	X	X	X	X	X	+	—	5
Wood warbler *P. sibilatrix*	X	—	—	—	—	—	—	—	—	X	+	X	X	X	X	+	X	4

Table 6 (*contd.*)

	1	2	3	4	5	6	7	8	9	10	11	12	13	14	15	16	17	18
Goldcrest *Regulus regulus*	—	X	+	—	—	—	—	—	—	X	X	X	X	X	X	X	X	5
Firecrest *R. ignicapillus*	—	X	—	—	—	—	—	—	—	X	—	—	—	—	—	—	—	1
Spotted flycatcher *Muscicapa striata*	X	+	—	—	—	+	—	—	+	X	X	X	X	X	X	X	X	5
Pied flycatcher *Ficedula hypoleuca*	X	—	—	—	—	—	—	+	—	+	—	+	X	X	+	+	—	4
Tree pipit *Anthus trivialis*	X	—	—	—	X	X	+	—	—	X	X	X	X	X	X	X	X	5
Starling *Sturnus vulgaris*	X	+	—	—	—	+	—	+	X	X	X	X	X	X	X	X	X	7
Hawfinch *Coccothraustes coccothraustes*	X	—	+	+	—	+	—	—	—	X	X	+	+	+	+	+	—	3
Greenfinch *Carduelis chloris*	X	+	X	X	—	—	—	—	—	X	X	X	X	X	X	X	X	6
Siskin *C. spinus*	—	X	—	—	—	—	—	—	—	+	+	—	+	+	+	X	+	3
Redpoll *Acanthis flammea*	X	X	+	+	—	—	—	—	—	+	+	+	X	X	X	X	X	5
Chaffinch *Fringilla coelebs*	X	+	+	+	—	+	—	—	—	X	X	X	X	X	X	X	X	7
Crossbill *Loxia curvirostra*	—	X	—	—	—	—	—	—	—	+	X	+	+	+	X	X	+	4
Total 66	60	45	32	16	9	29	6	18	22	59	51	55	55	54	52	53	45	

Notes

The symbol X denotes strong representation of a species, according to both habitat and regional distribution; + denotes scanty representation in these respects.

Column 6 includes orchards, park woodland, hedgerow and field trees.

Column 18, abundance class, uses the following notation:

Abundance class	Number of breeding pairs in Britain
1	1–10
2	10–100
3	100–1000
4	1000–10000
5	10000–100000
6	100000–1 million
7	1 million+

main habitat in Britain at the present time. For all the species named, except the black grouse which feeds on conifer shoots, the trees are incidental, and it is the luxuriant grass or low-shrub dominated vegetation which is the attraction, either in its food supply or cover for nesting. Some of the passerines use the trees as song or display flight posts, and two other species, the tree pipit and woodlark, have this particular association with trees and bushes in their grass-land and heathland nesting haunts.

Careful management of woods can obtain and maintain a generally rich avifauna, certain species individually or a group of species. Richness of species, however, also depends on geographical position and despite the special interest of the Highland pinewood birds, there is a distinct tendency for the number of woodland species to decrease with distance north. The New Forest is probably the most important woodland area for birds in Britain, in variety of species and size of their populations – a reflection of the diversity of habitat and large extent of this woodland. At least 75 of the species in Tables 6 and 7 breed in this district. By contrast, at the opposite end of Britain, the birchwoods of west Sutherland can together muster a total of only about 15 species.

Of the rare woodland birds, the red kite is a true relict species, confined to a limited area of central Wales, where it nests mainly in hanging oakwoods but hunts a great deal over open hillsides, moorlands and valley pastures. The rest may be regarded as fringe species which only just reach Britain from their European centres of distribution; this is true of the goshawk, honey buzzard, osprey, hobby, wryneck, redwing and firecrest. Four other sporadic woodland breeders in Britain, the hoopoe *Upupa epops*, golden oriole *Oriolus oriolus*, fieldfare *Turdus pilaris* and brambling *Fringilla montifringilla*, are also very much fringe species here. Conditions in this country may be marginal for some species such as the hobby, but some fringe birds may be in

Table 7. *The habitats and distribution of birds showing some association with trees*

	Woodland edge	Scrub	Hedge	Scattered trees	Young plantation	Trees as songposts only	Clearings & rides	Other non-arboreal habitats	S., S.E. & S.W. England	East Anglia	Midlands	Wales	N. England	S. Scotland	E. Highlands	W. Highlands	Abundance class
	1	2	3	4	5	6	7	8	9	10	11	12	13	14	15	16	17
Red-breasted merganser *Mergus serrator*	+	—	—	—	—	—	—	X	—	—	—	+	+	+	X	X	3
Goosander *M. merganser*	X	—	—	+	—	—	—	X	—	—	—	—	+	+	X	X	3
Hen harrier *Circus cyaneus*	—	—	—	X	—	—	—	X	—	—	—	+	+	+	X	X	3
Montagu's harrier *C. pygargus*	—	—	—	X	—	—	—	X	X	+	—	+	+	—	—	—	2
Merlin *Falco columbarius*	—	—	—	+	—	—	—	X	+	—	+	+	X	X	X	X	3
Pheasant *Phasianus colchicus*	+	—	—	—	+	—	+	X	X	X	X	X	X	X	X	X	6
Moorhen *Gallinula chloropus*	+	—	—	—	—	—	—	X	X	X	X	X	X	X	X	X	6
Stock dove *Columba oenas*	+	—	—	X	—	—	—	X	X	X	X	X	X	X	+	—	5
Cuckoo *Cuculus canorus*	+	+	+	—	+	—	+	X	X	X	X	X	X	X	X	X	4
Barn owl *Tyto alba*	+	—	—	X	—	—	—	X	X	X	X	X	X	X	+	+	4
Little owl *Athene noctua*	+	—	—	X	—	—	—	+	X	X	X	X	+	+	—	—	4
Short-eared owl *Asio flammeus*	—	—	—	—	X	—	—	X	+	+	—	+	X	X	X	X	4
Nightjar *Caprimulgus europaeus*	—	—	—	—	+	+	+	X	X	X	+	+	+	+	+	—	4
Woodlark *Lullula arborea*	—	—	—	—	—	+	—	X	X	X	+	+	—	—	—	—	3
Stonechat *Saxicola torquata*	—	—	—	—	+	+	—	X	X	+	—	X	+	X	+	X	4
Whinchat *S. rubetra*	—	—	—	—	+	+	—	X	+	+	+	X	X	X	X	X	5
Grasshopper warbler *Locustella naevia*	—	—	—	—	X	+	—	X	X	X	X	X	X	X	—	+	4
Hedge sparrow *Prunella modularis*	+	+	X	—	+	—	—	+	X	X	X	X	X	X	X	X	7
Red-backed shrike *Lanius collurio*	—	X	—	—	—	—	—	—	X	X	—	—	—	—	—	—	3
Goldfinch *Carduelis carduelis*	+	—	+	X	—	—	—	—	X	X	X	X	+	+	—	+	5
Linnet *Acanthis cannabina*	—	X	X	—	+	—	—	—	X	X	X	X	X	X	X	+	6
Bullfinch *Pyrrhula pyrrhula*	+	X	+	—	—	—	—	—	X	X	X	X	X	X	X	X	6
Yellowhammer *Emberiza citrinella*	+	X	X	—	X	—	+	+	X	X	X	X	X	X	X	X	7

Table 7 (*contd.*)

	1	2	3	4	5	6	7	8	9	10	11	12	13	14	15	16	17
Cirl bunting																	
E. cirlus	—	+	X	—	—	—	—	+	X	—	—	—	—	—	—	—	3
House sparrow																	
Passer domesticus	+	—	X	—	—	—	—	X	X	X	X	X	X	X	X	X	7
Tree sparrow																	
P. montanus	X	—	—	X	—	—	—	+	X	X	X	+	X	X	+	+	5
Total 26	14	7	8	7	12	5	4	22	23	21	18	23	23	22	19	19	

Notes

The symbol X denotes strong representation of a species, according to both habitat and regional distribution; + denotes scanty representation in these respects.

Column 4 includes orchards, park woodland, hedgerow and field trees and dead/dying trees.

Column 17, abundance class, uses the notation for Table 6.

the process of increasing and spreading. The appearance of the redwing has been associated with the recent trend towards colder springs, and the return of the osprey evidently reflects an overflow of population from southern Fennoscandia. Honey buzzard, red kite and goshawk were all formerly more widespread in Britain and may well be limited by persecution. This is clearly the reason for the common buzzard's absence from woods in eastern England. On the other hand, the sparrowhawk population withstood a great deal of destruction by gamekeepers, and this was an almost ubiquitous woodland species until the organochlorine pesticides caused its disappearance from much of southern and eastern England.

During autumn and winter, the bird fauna of woodland becomes impoverished by the loss of summer visitors, and these migrants contain a high proportion of insectivorous species. The numbers of a few species, such as the woodcock, are locally boosted by immigration, and flocks of starlings (which often roost in woodland) may reach enormous size. Many of the residents show a tendency to flock together for feeding, and roving bands of the smaller passerines such as finches, tits and thrushes are characteristic of woodlands in winter. Some of the corvids, especially rooks, jackdaws and carrion crows, roost communally in woodland during winter, and wood pigeons are usually found in flocks both for feeding and roosting. Many of the remaining species retain a normal dispersion in pairs, though in some the pairs break up and individuals lead a more or less solitary existence.

The woods which attract birds in autumn and winter are those with the most prolific food supply. For the vegetarians this means trees and shrubs which produce edible fruits and seeds (especially berries), e.g. oak, beech, alder, hazel, Scots pine, rowan, hawthorn, blackthorn, holly, yew, elder, cherries, crab apple, spindle, juniper, guelder rose, briars, brambles, currants and bilberry. The most attractive woodlands to birds at this time of year are thus those with a well-developed layer of underscrub, or edges, rides and clearings with an abundance of these shrubs; the least attractive are heavily grazed woods in which shrubs are poorly represented or absent. In good seed years, however,

even oak and beech woods with few shrubs become attractive to some species. It is interesting that the jay, which hides acorns in the ground, may be instrumental in promoting the regeneration of oak, sometimes at some distance from the parent trees. Crossbills follow the coniferous woods almost exclusively, and their numbers are influenced by the cone crop.

The insectivorous woodland birds, such as the tits and woodpeckers, are less dependent on a shrub layer, but need trees which provide a plentiful supply of insects, such as old trees with rough bark and dying or dead timber of all kinds. The predators mostly remain in their woodland haunts throughout the year, though some, such as the sparrowhawk and kestrel, do much of their hunting outside woods.

INSECTS

LEPIDOPTERA

Although not all directly associated with tree species, more lepidoptera occur in woodland than in any other major habitat. Probably more than half the British species are to be found in woodland. The trees themselves support a large proportion of these; for example, more than 100 species feed on oak, sallow, birch and hawthorn. Because of this abundance, the selection of species included in Table 8 is somewhat arbitrary, although all the woodland butterflies have been included.

Whilst many species are widely distributed geographically within a given woodland type, some are much more restricted in range. The butterflies with extremely restricted ranges include the heath fritillary, one of our rarest species, which is confined to a few woods in the extreme south-east and south-west of England; the black hairstreak – associated with old, large, blackthorn thickets – which is restricted to woods on the boulder clay in Huntingdonshire, Lincolnshire, Northamptonshire, Buckinghamshire and Oxfordshire; and the chequered skipper, which is exceedingly local, only occurring in a few woods in the east Midlands and the west Highlands. It is possible that two distinct subspecies are involved in this bicentric distribution of the chequered skipper. The purple emperor, a butterfly of oak and beech woods (the larva feeds on sallow), is probably not as rare as is supposed though it has declined during this century.

The two most widely distributed woodland butterflies are probably the purple hairstreak, an oak-feeding species, and the green-veined white, which is a common species in all woodlands although it occurs in most other habitat groups.

A post World War II feature of the woodlands in eastern England has been the decline in the *Viola*-feeding fritillaries. As the food plants have not shown a comparable decline, the decrease in these butterflies is at present unaccountable. There is some evidence that the fritillaries are recovering slowly in Yorkshire and at Monks Wood, Huntingdonshire.

Of the moths, some are also exceedingly local, e.g. the Kentish glory, a birch-feeding species only occurring in Wyre Forest in England and in apparently declining numbers in the eastern Highlands; the scarce hook-tip, with its larva feeding on the small-leaved lime and confined to the Forest of Dean area; and the netted carpet, restricted to a few places in the Lake District and north Wales where its very local larval food plant *Impatiens noli-tangere* occurs in quantity. This plant has special habitat requirements and needs moist, base-rich soils with deep shade and high rainfall, while the pupal stage of the moth itself appears to need flushed soils and a heavy rainfall as a protection against desiccation. Some species such as the Rannoch sprawler and the Saxon are Arctic–alpine, being only found in the extreme north of Britain.

Widely distributed moths include the poplar hawk, common lutestring, and mottled umber which occur throughout Britain in broad-leaved woodlands; and the pine beauty, pine carpet and bordered white are equally widely distributed in coniferous woodlands containing *Pinus* spp.

Generally speaking the lepidopterous fauna of the deciduous woodlands is much richer and quite distinct from that of coniferous woodlands. A few species, however, such as the black arches, the green-veined white and the pearl-bordered fritillary, occur in both where good rides exist.

The richness of a woodland lepidopterous fauna depends greatly on the structural and floristic diversity of this ecosystem, and thus on the management practices involved. Closed canopy woodland is much less rich in species than open woodland. Many species, especially of butterfly, are associated mainly with the transient, seral types of vegetation which form part of a woodland complex, i.e. the rides, edges, clearings and recent coppice, because the larval food plant of some species flourishes better under these more open conditions (e.g. *Viola* spp. for fritillaries), and shrubs and herbs with entomophilous flowers visited by the adults are similarly most abundant. Modern land-use methods accentuate the sharp boundaries between woodland and arable land in the agricultural lowlands. Butterflies and moths are most numerous in species and numbers where the woodland edge has a graded series of habitats, with tall shrubs, a rich field layer and an outer marginal strip of grassland with abundant dicotyledons. Woodland which changes suddenly to arable crop land is thus less valuable, but the more diverse conditions can be provided within the wood, e.g. along broad rides and on recently cleared or coppiced ground. Scrub, with its flora and fauna, is discussed more fully in Chapter 6, but it may be noted here that careful management is needed to maintain the entomological interest of scrub and other open habitats associated with woodland.

Well-developed hedgerows with herbaceous verges and scattered trees maintain some woodland butterflies and moths, but this habitat is being reduced at a considerable rate in the southern and eastern counties of England. The conservation of the right type of woodland in the right condition therefore becomes even more imperative for the maintenance of entomological interest. The extensive replacement of broad-leaved woodland by coniferous plantations has a considerable influence on the insect fauna and some woodland Lepidoptera are declining in consequence. However, if the conifer forests contain broad rides and do not develop too dense a canopy, many lepidotera can survive, and the planting of amenity fringes of broad-leaved trees and shrubs is also beneficial.

Certain woodland moths, whose larvae feed on the leaves of trees, can cause severe defoliation. Such moths include the oak roller moth (on oak), the mottled umber moth and the winter moth (on oak and other broad-leaved species), the northern winter moth (on birch) and the bordered white or pine looper (on pine).

ODONATA

Except where they contain aquatic habitats, such as streams, ponds and mires, woodlands are not the breeding place of dragonflies. Nevertheless, woodlands are much frequented by some species, both as feeding and resting places. The edges and rides are most favoured, and on warm, sunny days large species such as *Brachytron pratense*, *Aeshna cyanea* and *A. juncea* hawk up and down these situations and rest at times on the trees. In the south and east of England the migratory *A. mixta* is probably more common along woodland edges and rides than in any other habitat, and in the Highlands, the northern *A. caerulea* tends to frequent the open pine and birch woodland habitats adjoining its peatland breeding haunts. Among the smaller species, the darter dragonflies of the genus *Sympetrum* are also often associated with woodland edges. Where woods are close to their breeding places, most of the dragonfly species will be found at some time to resort to the trees, if only for resting, but there seems to be no species in Britain which is unable to exist without trees.

SPIDERS

Table 9 lists 59 species which are found exclusively in woodland or nearly so, and a further 46 species which are not so rigidly confined to woodland but are more plentiful there than in any other habitat. Many other species are also common in woodlands but may also occur abundantly elsewhere. Owing to the large numbers of species, and the fact that the spiders of woodlands have not been widely studied, it is not possible to describe them in so much detail as some other groups.

Table 8. *Habitat and distribution of woodland Lepidoptera**

	Trees, 5 m	Tall shrubs, 2–5 m	Dwarf shrubs & forbs	Grasses	Broad-leaved	Coniferous	Woodland type	S. & S.E. England	East Anglia	S.W. England	Wales	Midlands	N. England	S. Scotland	Highlands
	1	2	3	4	5	6	7	8	9	10	11	12	13	14	15
Butterflies															
Green-veined white *Pieris napi*	—	—	+	—	+	+	R	+	+	+	+	+	+	+	+
Wood white *Leptidea sinapis*	—	—	+	—	+	—	R	+	—	+	+	+	—	—	—
Brimstone *Gonepteryx rhamni*	—	+	—	—	+	—	R	+	+	+	+	+	+	—	—
Speckled wood *Pararge aegeria*	—	—	—	+	+	+	R	+	+	+	+	+	+	—	+
Ringlet *Aphantopus hyperantus*	—	—	—	+	+	—	R	+	+	+	+	+	+	+	+
Purple emperor *Apatura iris*	—	+	—	—	+	—	O&BeS	+	+	—	+	+	—	—	—
White admiral *Ladoga camilla*	—	—	+	—	+	—	R	+	+	+	+	+	—	—	—
Large tortoiseshell *Nymphalis polychloros*	+	—	—	—	+	—	E	+	+	?	+	?	—	—	—
Comma *Polygonia c-album*	—	—	+	—	+	+	R	+	+	+	+	+	—	—	—
Silver-washed fritillary *Argynnis paphia*	—	—	+	—	+	—	R	+	+	+	+	+	—	—	—
High brown fritillary *A. adippe*	—	—	+	—	+	—	R	+	—	+	+	+	+	—	—
Pearl-bordered fritillary *Boloria euphrosyne*	—	—	+	—	+	+	R	+	+	+	+	+	+	+	+
Small pearl-bordered fritillary *B. selene*	—	—	+	—	+	+	R	+	+	+	+	+	+	+	+
Heath fritillary *Mellicta athalia*	—	—	+	—	+	—	C	+	—	+	—	—	—	—	—
Marsh fritillary *Euphydryas aurinia*	—	—	+	—	+	—	R	+	—	+	+	+	—	—	—
Duke of Burgundy fritillary *Hamearis lucina*	—	—	+	—	+	—	R	+	+	—	—	+	+	—	—
Brown hairstreak *Thecla betulae*	—	+	+	—	+	—	B	+	+	+	+	+	—	—	—
Purple hairstreak *Quercusia quercus*	+	—	—	—	+	—	O	+	+	+	+	+	+	+	+
Black hairstreak *Strymonidia pruni*	—	+	—	—	+	—	B	—	+	—	—	+	—	—	—
White-letter hairstreak *S. w-album*	+	—	—	—	+	—	E	+	+	+	+	+	+	—	—
Holly blue *Celastrina argiolus*	—	+	—	—	+	—	H.I	+	+	+	+	+	+	—	—
Chequered skipper *Carterocephalus palaemon*	—	—	—	+	+	—	R	—	+	—	—	+	—	—	+
Moths															
Pine hawk *Hyloicus pinastri*	+	—	—	—	—	+	P	+	+	+	—	+	—	—	—

Table 8 (*contd.*)

	1	2	3	4	5	6	7	8	9	10	11	12	13	14	15
Lime hawk *Mimas tiliae*	+	—	—	—	+	—	L	+	+	+	?	+	—	—	—
Poplar hawk *Laothoe populi*	+	—	—	—	+	—	MD	+	+	+	+	+	+	+	+
Kentish glory *Endromis versicolora*	+	+	—	—	+	—	Bi	—	—	—	—	+	—	—	+
Lobster *Stauropus fagi*	+	—	—	—	+	—	Be	+	+	+	+	+	—	—	—
Great prominent *Peridea anceps*	+	—	—	—	+	—	O	+	+	+	+	+	+	+	—
Scarce prominent *Odontosia carmelita*	—	+	—	—	+	—	Bi	+	—	—	—	—	+	+	+
Common lutestring *Ochopacha duplaris*	—	+	—	—	+	—	Bi	+	+	+	+	+	+	+	+
Yellow horned *Achlya flavicornis*	+	+	—	—	+	—	Bi	+	+	+	+	+	+	+	+
Scarce hook-tip *Palaeodrepana harpagula*	+	+	—	—	+	—	L	—	—	—	+	+	—	—	—
Oak hook-tip *Drepana binaria*	+	—	—	—	+	—	O	+	+	+	+	+	+	—	—
Barred hook-tip *D. cultraria*	+	—	—	—	+	—	Be	+	+	+	?	+	—	—	—
Black arches *Lymantria monacha*	+	+	+	—	+	+	All	+	+	+	+	+	+	—	—
Plain clay *Eugnorisma depuncta*	—	—	+	—	+	—	MD	+	—	+	+	+	+	+	+
Double square-spot *Xestia triangulum*	—	+	+	—	+	—	MD	+	+	+	+	+	+	+	+
White-marked *Cerastis leucographa*	—	—	+	—	+	—	MD	+	—	—	—	+	+	—	—
Pine beauty *Panolis flammea*	+	—	—	—	—	+	P	+	+	+	+	+	+	+	+
Nut-tree tussock *Colocasia coryli*	+	+	—	—	+	—	MD	+	+	+	+	+	+	+	+
Rannoch sprawler *Brachionycha nubeculosa*	+	+	—	—	+	—	Bi	—	—	—	—	—	—	—	+
Conformist *Lithophane furcifera*	—	+	—	—	+	—	A	—	—	—	+	+	—	—	—
Orange sallow *Xanthia citrago*	+	—	—	—	+	—	L	+	+	+	+	+	+	+	—
Saxon *Hyppa rectilinea*	—	+	+	—	+	—	MD	—	—	—	—	—	+	+	+
Clay triple-lines *Cyclophora linearia*	+	—	—	—	+	—	Be	+	—	+	—	+	—	—	—
Orange underwing *Archiearis parthenias*	+	—	—	—	+	—	Bi	+	+	+	+	+	+	+	+
Large emerald *Geometra papilionaria*	—	+	—	—	+	—	Bi	+	+	+	+	+	+	+	+
Beech-green carpet *Colostygia olivata*	—	—	+	—	+	—	MD	+	—	+	+	+	+	+	+
Barred carpet *Perizoma taeniata*	—	—	+	—	—	+	Y	—	—	—	+	—	+	—	+
Netted carpet *Eustroma reticulatum*	—	—	+	—	+	—	MD	—	—	—	+	—	+	—	—
Juniper carpet *Thera juniperatum*	—	+	—	—	—	+	J	+	—	—	?	—	+	—	+
Chestnut-coloured carpet *T. cognata*	—	+	—	—	—	+	J	—	—	—	?	—	+	+	+
Pine carpet *T. firmata*	+	—	—	—	—	+	P	+	+	+	+	+	+	+	+

8

Table 8 (*contd.*)

	1	2	3	4	5	6	7	8	9	10	11	12	13	14	15
Lime pug *Eupithecia egenaria*	+	—	—	—	+	—	L	—	—	—	+	+	—	—	—
Juniper pug *E. pusillata*	—	+	—	—	—	+	J	+	—	—	+	—	+	+	+
Barred tooth-striped *Trichopteryx polycommata*	+	—	+	—	+	—	F	+	—	—	—	+	+	—	+
Winter *Operophtera brumata*	+	+	—	—	+	—	MD	+	+	+	+	+	+	+	+
Northern winter *O. fagata*	+	+	—	—	+	—	Bi	+	+	+	+	+	+	+	+
Drab looper *Minoa murinata*	—	—	+	—	+	—	MD	+	—	—	+	+	—	—	—
Dingy shell *Euchoeca nebulata*	—	+	—	—	—	—	A	+	+	+	+	+	+	—	—
Blomer's rivulet *Discoloxia blomeri*	+	—	—	—	+	—	E	+	—	+	+	+	+	—	—
Clouded magpie *Abraxas sylvata*	+	—	—	—	+	—	E	+	—	+	+	+	+	+	—
Barred red *Hylaea fasciaria*	+	—	—	—	—	+	P	+	+	+	+	+	+	+	+
Mottled umber *Erannis defoliaria*	+	—	—	—	+	—	MD	+	+	+	+	+	+	+	+
Brindled beauty *Lycia hirtaria*	+	+	—	—	+	—	MD	+	+	+	+	+	+	+	+
Oak beauty *Biston strataria*	+	—	—	—	+	—	O	+	+	+	+	+	+	?	?
Great oak beauty *Boarmia roboraria*	+	—	—	—	+	—	O	+	—	—	—	—	—	—	—
Grey birch *Aethalura punctulata*	+	—	—	—	+	—	Bi	+	+	+	+	+	+	+	+
Bordered white *Bupalus piniaria*	+	—	—	—	—	+	P	+	+	+	+	+	+	+	+
Festoon *Apoda avellana*	+	—	—	—	+	—	O	+	—	—	—	+	—	—	—
Triangle *Heterogenea asella*	+	—	—	—	+	—	O&Be	+	—	—	—	+	—	—	—
Oak roller *Totrix viridana*	+	+	—	—	+	—	MD	+	+	+	+	+	+	+	+
Total 72	37	25	22	3	62	15		61	43	49	53	61	47	31	35

Notes

Column 7, Woodland type:

R = Rides	O = Oak
S = Sallow	E = Elm
C = Cow-wheat	B = Blackthorn
H = Holly	I = Ivy
P = Pine	L = Lime
MD = Mixed deciduous	Bi = Birch
Be = Beech	Y = Yew
A = Alder	F = Ash
J = Juniper	

* The nomenclature of the Lepidoptera follows that of Kloet & Hincks (1972) but the arrangement follows the conventional order used by previous authors, viz. Butterflies, Macrolepidoptera and Microlepidoptera.

Table 9. *Habitat and distribution of woodland spiders*

(a) Almost exclusive woodland species

Species	Deciduous	Coniferous	Woodland type	Litter layer	Field layer	Shrub/tree layers	Under bark	Widespread, common	Widespread, local	Rare	Very rare	S. & S.E. England	East Anglia	S.W. England	Wales	Midlands	N. England	S. Scotland	Highlands	Ireland
	1	2	3	4	5	6	7	8	9	10	11	12	13	14	15	16	17	18	19	20
Hyptiotes paradoxus	—	+	Y,B	—	—	+	—	—	—	—	—	+	—	—	—	—	—	—	—	+
Haplodrassus silvestris	+	—	—	+	—	—	—	+	—	—	—	+	+	+	+	+	+	+	+	—
H. sörenseni	—	+	P	+	—	—	—	—	+	—	—	—	—	—	—	—	—	—	+	—
Micaria subopaca	+	+	—	—	+	+	—	—	+	—	—	+	—	—	—	—	—	—	—	—
Clubiona subsultans	—	+	P	+	—	—	—	—	—	—	—	—	—	—	—	—	—	—	+	—
C. compta	+	—	—	+	—	+	—	+	—	—	—	+	+	+	+	+	+	+	+	+
C. brevipes	+	—	esp.O	—	—	+	+	+	—	—	—	+	+	+	+	+	+	+	+	+
Anyphaena accentuata	+	—	—	—	—	+	—	+	—	—	—	+	+	+	+	+	+	+	+	+
Micrommata virescens	+	—	O	—	+	+	—	—	+	—	—	+	+	+	+	+	+	—	—	+
Diaea dorsata	+	+	Bo	—	—	+	—	—	+	—	—	+	+	+	+	+	+	—	—	—
Xysticus lanio	+	—	esp.O	—	—	+	—	—	+	—	—	+	+	+	+	+	+	—	+	+
Philodromus collinus	—	+	P	—	—	+	—	—	+	—	—	+	+	+	—	+	—	—	—	—
P. emarginatus	—	+	—	—	—	+	—	—	+	—	—	+	—	+	—	+	—	—	+	+
P. rufus	+	—	—	—	+	+	—	—	+	—	—	+	—	+	—	+	—	—	+	—
P. margaritatus	+	+	—	—	—	+	+	—	+	—	—	+	—	+	—	+	—	—	+	—
Salticus zebraneus	—	+	—	—	—	+	—	—	+	—	—	+	—	—	—	+	—	—	—	—
Ballus depressus	+	—	O	—	—	+	—	+	—	—	—	+	+	+	+	+	+	—	—	—
Evarcha falcata	+	—	—	—	+	—	—	+	—	—	—	+	+	+	+	+	+	+	+	+
Pardosa lugubris	+	+	—	+	—	—	—	+	—	—	—	+	+	+	+	+	+	+	+	+
Tegenaria silvestris	+	—	—	+	+	—	—	—	+	—	—	+	—	+	+	+	—	—	—	—
Tetrilus macrophthalmus	+	—	—	+	—	+	+	—	+	—	—	+	—	+	+	+	—	—	—	—
Tuberta maerens	+	—	—	—	—	+	+	—	—	+	—	+	—	+	—	—	—	—	—	—
Dipoena torva	—	+	P	—	—	+	+	—	—	+	—	—	—	—	—	—	—	—	+	—
Anelosimus vittatus	+	—	esp.O	—	—	+	—	+	—	—	—	+	+	+	—	+	+	+	—	+
Achaearanea lunata	+	+	—	—	—	+	—	—	+	—	—	+	+	+	+	+	—	—	—	+
A. simulans	+	—	—	—	—	+	—	—	+	—	—	+	+	+	—	—	—	—	—	—
Theridion pallens	+	+	—	+	+	+	—	+	—	—	—	+	+	+	+	+	+	+	+	+
Robertus scoticus	—	+	P	+	—	—	—	—	—	+	—	—	—	—	—	—	—	—	+	—
Tetragnatha pinicola	+	—	—	—	—	+	—	—	+	—	—	+	+	+	—	+	+	—	—	—
Araneus bituberculatus	+	—	B	—	—	+	—	—	—	+	+	+	+	+	—	—	—	—	—	—
A. gibbosus	+	—	—	—	—	+	—	—	+	—	—	+	+	+	+	+	+	+	—	+
A. angulatus	+	—	—	—	—	+	—	—	+	—	—	+	+	—	+	+	—	—	—	—
A. marmoreus	+	—	esp.Bi	—	—	+	—	—	+	—	—	+	+	—	+	+	+	+	—	—
A. alsine	+	—	—	—	+	+	—	—	+	—	—	+	+	+	—	+	—	—	—	—
A. sturmi	—	+	—	—	—	+	—	—	+	—	—	+	+	+	+	+	+	+	+	—
A. triguttatus	+	—	—	—	—	+	—	—	+	—	—	+	+	+	—	+	—	—	+	—
A. inconspicuus	+	—	—	—	—	+	—	—	—	+	—	+	+	+	—	+	—	—	—	—
A. alpicus	+	—	—	—	—	+	—	—	—	+	—	+	—	+	—	+	—	—	—	—
A. displicatus	—	+	—	—	—	+	—	—	—	+	+	—	—	—	—	—	—	—	—	—
Cyclosa conica	—	+	—	—	—	+	—	+	—	—	—	+	+	+	+	+	+	+	+	+
Walckenaera mitrata	+	—	—	—	—	—	—	—	—	+	—	+	—	—	—	—	—	—	—	—
Moebilia penicillata	—	+	—	—	—	+	+	—	+	—	—	+	+	+	+	+	—	—	+	+
Trematocephalus cristatus	+	—	—	—	—	+	—	—	+	—	—	+	+	—	—	—	—	—	—	—
Dismodicus elevatus	—	+	P	—	—	+	—	—	+	—	—	—	—	—	—	—	—	—	+	—
Gonatium rubellum	+	—	—	+	—	—	—	+	—	—	—	+	+	+	+	+	+	+	+	+
Pelecopsis elongata	+	+	—	+	—	—	—	—	+	—	—	+	—	—	—	+	—	—	+	—
Tapinocyba pallens	+	+	—	+	—	—	—	+	—	—	—	+	—	—	+	+	+	+	+	+
Asthenargus paganus	+	—	—	+	—	—	—	—	+	—	—	+	—	—	+	+	+	+	+	+
Syedrula innotabilis	+	+	—	—	+	+	+	—	—	—	—	+	+	—	+	+	+	+	+	+
Microneta viaria	+	—	—	+	—	—	—	+	—	—	—	+	+	+	+	+	+	+	+	+
Centromerus serratus	+	+	—	+	—	—	—	—	+	—	—	+	—	—	—	+	—	—	—	—
C. albidus	+	—	Be	+	—	—	—	—	+	—	—	+	—	—	—	—	—	—	—	—
C. cavernarum	+	—	Be	+	—	—	—	—	+	—	—	+	—	+	—	+	—	—	—	+
Drapetisca socialis	+	+	—	+	—	+	+	+	—	—	—	+	+	+	+	+	+	+	+	+

Table 9 (*contd.*)

	1	2	3	4	5	6	7	8	9	10	11	12	13	14	15	16	17	18	19	20
Labulla thoracica	+	—	—	+	+	—	+	+	—	—	—	+	+	+	+	+	+	+	+	+
Lepthyphantes expunctus	—	+	P	—	—	+	—	—	+	—	—	—	—	—	—	—	+	+	+	—
Helophora insignis	+	—	—	+	+	—	—	+	—	—	—	+	+	+	+	+	+	+	+	+
Linyphia peltata	+	—	—	—	+	+	—	+	—	—	—	+	+	+	+	+	+	+	+	+
L. hortensis	+	—	—	—	+	—	—	+	—	—	—	+	+	+	+	+	+	+	+	+

(b) Mainly woodland species which also occur in other habitats

	1	2	3	4	5	6	7	8	9	10	11	12	13	14	15	16	17	18	19	20
Lathys humilis	+	—	—	+	—	+	—	+	—	—	—	+	+	+	+	+	+	+	—	—
Clubiona corticalis	+	+	—	+	—	+	+	+	—	—	—	+	+	+	+	+	+	—	—	—
C. pallidula	+	—	—	+	+	+	+	+	—	—	—	+	+	+	+	+	+	+	+	+
C. terrestris	+	—	—	+	+	+	+	+	—	—	—	+	+	+	+	+	+	+	+	+
Scotina celans	—	+	—	+	—	—	—	+	—	—	—	+	+	+	+	+	+	+	—	+
Zora nemoralis	+	+	—	+	—	—	—	—	—	+	—	—	—	+	+	—	+	+	—	+
Xysticus luctuosus	+	—	—	+	—	—	—	—	+	—	—	+	+	+	+	+	—	+	+	+
Philodromus dispar	+	—	—	—	+	+	—	+	—	—	—	+	+	+	+	+	+	+	—	+
Marpissa muscosa	+	—	—	—	—	+	+	—	—	—	—	+	+	+	—	+	+	—	—	—
Coelotes terrestris	+	—	—	+	—	—	—	—	—	—	—	+	+	+	+	—	+	+	—	—
Cicurina cicur	+	—	—	+	—	—	—	—	—	—	—	+	+	+	—	+	+	—	—	—
Hahnia helveola	—	+	—	+	—	—	—	+	—	—	—	+	+	+	+	+	+	+	+	+
Crustulina guttata	—	+	—	+	—	—	—	—	—	—	—	+	+	+	+	+	+	+	—	+
Theridion mystaceum	+	+	—	—	—	+	+	+	—	—	—	+	+	+	+	+	+	+	+	+
T. tinctum	+	+	exp.Y,Bo	—	+	+	—	+	—	—	—	+	+	+	+	+	+	—	—	+
Tetragnatha obtusa	+	—	—	—	+	+	—	—	—	—	—	+	+	+	+	+	+	—	—	+
Pachygnatha listeri	+	—	—	+	—	—	—	—	—	—	—	+	+	+	+	+	+	+	+	+
Araneus marmoreus pyramidatus	+	—	—	—	+	+	—	—	—	—	—	+	+	+	+	+	+	+	+	+
A. patagiatus	+	—	—	—	+	+	—	+	—	—	—	+	+	+	+	+	+	+	+	+
A. umbraticus	+	+	—	—	—	+	+	+	—	—	—	+	+	+	+	+	+	+	+	+
A. cucurbitinus	+	—	—	—	+	+	—	+	—	—	—	+	+	+	+	+	+	+	+	+
A. opistographus	+	—	—	—	—	+	—	+	—	—	—	+	+	—	—	+	+	—	—	+
Zilla diodia	+	—	—	—	+	+	—	+	—	—	—	+	+	+	+	—	+	—	—	+
Zygiella stroemi	—	+	P	—	—	+	+	—	+	—	—	+	—	—	—	—	+	—	+	—
Ceratinella scabrosa	+	—	—	+	—	—	—	—	—	—	—	+	+	+	+	+	+	+	—	—
Walckenaera cucullata	—	+	—	+	—	—	—	+	—	—	—	+	+	+	+	+	+	+	+	+
W. obtusa	+	—	—	+	—	—	—	—	+	—	—	+	+	+	+	+	+	+	+	+
Erigonidium graminicola	+	—	—	—	+	+	—	—	—	—	—	+	+	+	+	+	+	+	—	+
Gongylidium rufipes	+	—	—	—	+	+	—	—	—	—	—	+	+	+	+	+	+	+	+	+
Hypomma cornutum	+	—	—	—	+	+	—	+	—	—	—	+	+	+	+	+	+	+	+	+
Hybocoptus decollatus	—	+	Y	—	—	+	—	—	—	+	—	—	—	+	—	—	—	—	—	+
Minyriolus pusillus	+	+	—	+	+	—	—	—	—	—	—	+	+	+	+	—	+	+	+	+
Tapinocyba insecta	+	—	—	+	—	—	—	—	+	—	—	+	+	+	—	—	+	+	+	+
Monocephalus fuscipes	+	+	—	+	—	—	—	+	—	—	—	+	+	+	+	+	+	+	+	+
Diplocephalus latifrons	+	—	—	+	—	—	—	+	—	—	—	+	+	+	+	+	+	+	+	+
Porrhomma oblitum	+	—	—	+	+	—	—	—	—	+	—	+	+	+	—	—	—	—	—	—
Centromerus dilutus	+	+	—	+	—	—	—	+	—	—	—	+	+	+	+	+	+	+	+	+
C. capucinus	+	—	—	+	—	—	—	—	—	+	—	+	+	+	—	—	+	+	—	—
Macrargus rufus	+	+	—	+	—	—	—	+	—	—	—	+	+	+	+	+	+	+	+	+
Lepthyphantes minutus	+	+	—	+	+	—	—	+	—	—	—	+	+	+	+	+	+	+	+	+
L. alacris	+	+	—	+	—	—	—	+	—	—	—	—	+	+	+	+	+	+	+	+
L. cristatus	+	—	—	+	—	—	—	—	+	—	—	+	+	+	+	+	+	+	+	+
L. flavipes	+	+	—	+	—	—	—	+	—	—	—	+	+	+	+	+	+	—	+	+
L. tenebricola	+	+	—	+	—	—	—	—	+	—	—	+	+	+	+	+	+	+	+	+
L. carri	+	—	—	+	—	—	—	—	—	—	+	+	—	—	—	+	—	—	—	—
Linyphia montana	+	—	—	+	+	+	—	+	—	—	—	+	+	+	+	+	+	+	+	+
Total 105	85	44	—	49	27	61	16	41	31	26	6	95	74	78	62	80	70	46	58	54

Note

Column 3, Woodland type: Y = Yew; Bo = Box; P = Pine; O = Oak; Be = Beech; Bi = Birch.

Woodland spiders fall into two broad categories, those which live in the litter layer and those which live on the undergrowth or on the trees. These categories overlap to some extent as some species which live high up on trees in the summer move down to the litter in winter. Some species are also specialised for living on or under bark or living on dead trees and these are also indicated in the table. The most widespread and characteristic bark species are *Clubiona brevipes*, *Moebilia penicillata*, *Syedrula innotabilis*, *Labulla thoracica*, *Drapetisca socialis*, *Clubiona corticalis*, *Theridion mystaceum* and *Araneus umbraticus*. Notably rare bark species are *Tetrilus macrophthalmus*, *Tuberta maerens*, which is known only from Bloxworth and Wytham, *Dipoena torva*, which is mentioned in Chapter 9, and *Zygiella stroemi*, known only from bark at the Black Wood of Rannoch and at Wytham, and in a hut at Leckford in Hampshire. Most species are found mainly in deciduous woodland but some are confined to, or show a marked preference for, coniferous woodland (usually pine). We cannot be sure that any species is confined to a particular type of woodland, but some species show a distinct preference for a certain type. *Hyptiotes paradoxus* is apparently confined to yew and box, and is known only from Box Hill, Bagley Wood, and several sites in the New Forest and elsewhere in Hampshire. Similarly, *Hybocoptus decollatus* is only known from yew in a few woods, including Box Hill and Kingley Vale, but has been found also on gorse in two sites on the south coast. Other more widespread species which show a preference for yew or box are *Diaea dorsata* and *Theridion tinctum*.

More species are characteristic of pinewoods. These include some found only in upland woods, namely *H. sörenseni*, *C. subsultans*, *D. torva*, *R. scoticus*, *D. elevatus*, *P. elongata* and *L. expunctus* (all also described in Chapter 9) which may be the only species strictly confined to pinewoods. The most widespread and abundant pinewood species are *Moebilia penicillata*, *Scotina celans*, *Hahnia helveola*, *Walckenaera cucullata* and *Araneus sturmi*. With the possible exception of the first named, all of these also occur less commonly in other habitats. Other characteristic pinewood species of more restricted range are *Philodromus collinus*, known only from a few sites in East Anglia and at Box Hill, *P. emarginatus*, *P. margaritatus*, *Salticus zebraneus*, *Cyclosa conica* and also *Araneus displicatus* known only from two sites in Surrey.

Among the predominantly deciduous woodland species, two small subgroups may be recognised – those which occur mainly in association with oak or beech. The most characteristic oakwood species are *Clubiona brevipes*, *Micrommata virescens*, *Xysticus lanio*, *Ballus depressus* and *Anelosimus vittatus*, and species found mainly in beech-woods are *Araneus bituberculatus*, which is known only from Burnham Beeches and one old record from Essex, *Centromerus albidus*, recorded from three sites including Box Hill, and *C. cavernarum*. The only species which is characteristic of birch is *Araneus marmoreus*, which occurs in a few sites in eastern and northern England, including Skipwith Common and Woodwalton Fen. *Helophora insignis* and *Linyphia*

hortensis are unusual in that they occur commonly in a wide variety of deciduous woodland, but nearly always in the field layer on *Mercurialis perennis*.

Among the most widespread and abundant species of deciduous woodland in general may be mentioned *Clubiona compta*, *Anyphaena accentuata*, *Pardosa lugubris*, *Theridion pallens*, *Gonatium rubellum*, *Microneta viaria*, *Linyphia peltata*, *Clubiona pallidula*, *Philodromus dispar*, *Araneus cucurbitinus*, *Erigonidium graminicola*, *Hypomma cornutum*, *Diplocephalus latifrons* and *Linyphia montana*.

Some species appear to be almost equally common in both deciduous and coniferous woodland. These include *Tapinocyba pallens* (only in the north), *Syedrula innotabilis*, *Drapetisca socialis*, *Theridion mystaceum*, *Araneus umbraticus*, *Minyriolus pusillus*, *Monocephalus fuscipes*, *Centromerus dilutus*, *Macrargus rufus*, *Lepthyphantes minutus*, *L. alacris*, *L. flavipes* and *L. tenebricola*.

Rarities not already mentioned are *Micaria subopaca*, known only from a few sites in Surrey and Sussex, including Ashdown Forest, *Achaearanea simulans*, recorded from three areas including Box Hill and the New Forest, *Araneus inconspicuus* and *A. alpicus* (records again include the New Forest and Box Hill), *Trematocephalus cristatus*, known from four sites in Surrey and Sussex including Box Hill, *Centromerus capucinus*, which has occurred in a few scattered localities including beechwoods in the Chilterns, *Lepthyphantes carri*, which has been recorded only from Sherwood Forest and Windsor Forest, and *Walckenaera mitrata*, which has recently been recorded for the first time in this country from Blean Wood.

Many of these woodland species occur also on or under isolated trees or clumps of trees or bushes and in hedgerows, and such habitats must be important for their conservation. Some species, especially those which are found mainly in the field layer or on low bushes, require fairly open conditions such as occur in rides or at the margins of woods. An example is *Micrommata virescens*, a local species which occurs on young oak trees or on *Molinia* tussocks below young oaks in damp areas.

CRITERIA FOR KEY SITE ASSESSMENT AND SELECTION

Background considerations

Woodlands are in some ways the most difficult of major ecosystems to deal with in the field of conservation. Although representing the climatic climax over much of Britain, woodland is now highly fragmented and woodlands of native species cover only a small fraction of the total land surface. Moreover, if any natural woodland remains, it is of very small extent. There has, nevertheless, been a great deal of concern about the structure and floristic composition of natural woodland, and many conservationists believe that this is an ideal condition which management should aim to restore on at least some of the important woodland sites. Thus sites which show the closest approach to the presumptive original state tend to be the most highly valued.

Woods have a dual nature; they are assemblages of trees with value and interest in their own right, and they are also the habitat of other organisms, including plants of quite different life-form and animals of many kinds. The conservationist is interested in both aspects of woodland, often on the same site, but sometimes separately. Given sufficient time, the tree component of the woodland ecosystem can be manipulated by management into almost any desired state, but the dependent organisms are less easily controlled at will. A desired tree structure and composition could eventually be obtained by planting an open field with appropriate species, but development *de novo* of the mature woodland with all its associated flora and fauna is likely to take centuries rather than decades, and is to be regarded more as a very long-term possibility.

Trees have a limited life span and unless there is adequate regeneration a wood will eventually die out. Woodland trees are seldom allowed to die of old age, and are usually cut for timber when mature. Coppicing of younger trees may prolong the life of individuals for a very long time, but usually there comes a point in the cycle when tree cover must be perpetuated by the growth of new individuals. In Britain, this regeneration is usually achieved by the planting of seedlings grown in nurseries. On nature reserves, natural regeneration is usually prescribed as a more desirable policy. There has thus been a tendency to rate highly those woods which show good natural regeneration and an uneven age structure of the dominant trees.

Areas where there has been continuity of woodland cover right through the Post-glacial Period are usually richer in dependent communities and organisms than sites where tree cover has been discontinuous during the last few centuries. The persistence of sensitive associates dependent on tree cover may well reflect a rotational cropping and regeneration within one woodland block, which has ensured that parent populations of the sensitive species were always at hand to supply new offspring to the regenerating forest. When species have been entirely lost from a site during a period of woodland clearance, their capacity for recolonisation of re-established forest clearly depends on their powers of spread and establishment. Mobile creatures such as birds, mammals and some insects most readily recolonise re-established woodland, but this ability varies from species to species. The crested tit is a British forest bird showing a very limited capacity for spread from its established Scottish haunts. Many insects, although theoretically mobile, appear to be remarkably sedentary in distribution over a period. Common plants are able to spread easily, and this is perhaps especially true in general of ferns, bryophytes, lichens and fungi with small, wind-dispersed spores. On the other hand, the rarer members of the flora (including these cryptogams) are usually characterised by an extremely limited capacity for spread, and once they have disappeared from a woodland site, perhaps during the unfavourable conditions of a clearance period, they have gone virtually forever unless they are deliberately reintroduced, and this may be difficult.

Because of their almost complete inability to spread and recover lost ground under the present, fragmented state of our woodlands, many vascular plants, ferns, bryophytes, lichens, fungi, insects, arachnids and molluscs are consistently absent from re-established woodland and are therefore reliable indicators of ancient, permanent woodland.

In general, therefore, re-established woodlands have a lower conservation value than permanent woodlands, in terms of richness of components other than the tree layer, as well as in the historical features discussed earlier. In both types, the tree layer itself may show all degrees of change in composition or reduction in diversity according to the conditions of management.

Woodlands have a great diversity of interest, so that the criteria of evaluation in assessment for conservation are necessarily numerous. They have the most complex organisation of any ecosystem and are the most luxuriant of all living communities; as such they have been a favourite focus for studies of the circulation of nutrients and energy, and of biological productivity. The economic values of trees cannot be divorced from nature conservation and the tree component of native woodland is commercially valuable, provides opportunities for silvicultural research and is an important source of genetic material. Woodlands are also important in demonstrating ecological relationships, including the response of vegetation to climatic change, the effects of spatial differences in soil conditions, plant succession, and the influence of man. Trees have a key position in the understanding of vegetational history, through pollen analysis, subfossil wood remains, dendrochronology, and the long-lasting effects of management practices inscribed in the living trees. Woodlands and trees are important features of the landscape and are of major recreational and educational value.

The nature conservation value of woods composed partly or wholly of alien species is a difficult subject. The present review is concerned essentially with assessing their value in relation to the selection of a series of nationally important woodland sites. The boundary between indigenous and non-indigenous species is not always clearly defined but, in general, it is accepted that alien trees have a lower conservation value than native species, both in themselves and with particular reference to invertebrates, as habitats for dependent organisms. However, well-established and freely regenerating aliens such as sycamore are of considerable ecological interest, and introduced poplars are important food plants for a number of interesting moths. Scots pine, outside its native range, is a common component of many woods dominated by deciduous trees, and is, for example, often preferred as a nest site by sparrowhawks. The pine rows and clumps are an artificial but characteristic feature of the East Anglian Breckland and are here largely responsible for the occurrence of the interesting population of breeding crossbills. The feeling that the purity and therefore quality of a native woodland is in some way diminished by the presence of alien trees cannot always be substantiated in reason. The presence of a certain proportion of non-native trees can add to the interest of a woodland, and may enhance the faunal diversity. The undesirable state is reached when alien trees cover such a large part of a wood that it cannot be regarded as a good example of the native type, or when vigorously competitive aliens are spreading at the expense of native species and creating unfavourable habitats for associated organisms. A good example of the second situation is the spread of rhododendron in some oak-woods, and the resulting virtual elimination of the field and ground layers.

Much depends on the species. Those which cast deep shade, such as rhododendron, sycamore and spruce tend to be regarded as undesirable, whereas Turkey oak, common lime and sweet chestnut are viewed with more favour. Some species are native in part of their range and introduced elsewhere (e.g. Scots pine, beech and hornbeam) and, while the presence of these is not regarded as objectionable, they are not usually rated so high in conservation interest in non-native localities. This does not always hold, as the entirely planted woods around Stornoway Castle, Lewis, are of very considerable regional interest. It is generally felt, however, that woods composed largely of introduced species do not merit grade 1 or 2 status. This is particularly so in the case of commercially grown species; it is pointless to give this grading to a wood of Sitka spruce or lodgepole pine at this time, when such large areas of these species are being planted every year.

Plantations of non-native trees, notably conifers, are of considerable conservation value. Especially in their younger stages, some have proved to be important habitats for rare breeding birds such as short-eared owl, hen harrier and Montagu's harrier (see subsection on birds, p. 89). These non-indigenous and recently created forests are so widespread and cover such a large total area that they are a major wildlife habitat in Britain. Nevertheless, most of these artificial forests, especially when mature, are so fundamentally different from the native woodlands that they can never represent the most important attributes of the latter or take their place as conservation sites. Much of the artificial woodland is re-established on ground which has had a long period without trees, and the associated communities which develop within, especially of plants and invertebrates, are usually of minor interest in that they are composed of common, rapidly spreading species, or those remaining from the treeless phase. Many conifer forests have such a high stocking density of trees that the subsidiary vegetational component is virtually eliminated and the fauna becomes greatly reduced, though some woodland birds thrive. Much can be done to improve the nature conservation value of commercial conifer forests by modifications in management, but it would be inappropriate to develop this theme here. Moreover, where native deciduous woodland is cleared and replanted with alien conifers, considerable subsequent impoverishment of the field and ground communities and the invertebrate fauna occurs, and this change in management involves greater conservation losses than gains. Native woodlands in Britain are a rapidly diminishing resource and the conservation of a representative series is a matter of the greatest urgency.

Comparative site evaluation

With these considerations in mind, the following attributes in particular are weighed in the comparative evaluation of the individual sites:

Size
The nature conservation value of a woodland tends to increase with size. Only in a large wood may it be possible to encompass the local range of diversity or to achieve diversity by means of different silvicultural systems or management practices. Large size is also a safeguard against accidental destruction, e.g. by fire. Experiments may need homogeneous conditions over an area of adequate size or they may be concerned with ecological diversity; both requirements are more likely to be satisfied in a large area than a small one. Some organisms, e.g. large birds, require a fairly large minimum area, depending on their territory size, so that a substantial area may be needed to contain a reasonable population.

Diversity
Diversity in woodland is of several kinds. There is structural diversity, including different age of the trees. Ecological diversity involves floristic and faunal variability within any part of a wood especially in response to varying soil conditions and topography, and also relationships in space and time such as the catena, seral stages and succession.

Permanence
A site which has been continuously occupied by woodland is usually more valuable than one where woodland has been re-established after a break in continuity, especially in regard to subsidiary elements of the flora and fauna. Its value will be further enhanced if a good historical record is available. Such woods are historical monuments, embodying many aspects of past rural life and organisation. Climax woodlands are to be preferred to seral types, for though examples of the latter are valuable in demonstrating dynamic processes, they can be more easily and rapidly created. The few examples of woodlands which appear to approach a 'natural' state are regarded as especially important, though they are usually fragments on islands, landslips, cliffs and ravine sides.

Lack of modification
While the tree layer usually reflects the silvicultural system used (and the range of system requires representation), the quality of the shrub and herb layers is particularly dependent on the absence of such influences as grazing by large herbivores. The permanence of tree cover may be especially important in maintaining the floristic richness of the subsidiary layers.

Rarity
The presence and abundance of rare species of trees, shrubs, herbs, pteridophytes, bryophytes and lichens, and of

animals, gives an added value to a woodland site selected on other criteria, but rarity is usually taken as a major criterion for selection only when a group of such species is involved. A very few sites are selected for the rarity of one species.

Requirements for the national series

Selection of the national series of key woodland sites has involved an attempt to represent adequately the most important types within the total field of variation. When the many directions of variation in woodlands are considered, especially in relation to the partial independence of the separate structural layers, the number of possible combinations of different character, i.e. the number of different woodland types, is extremely large. However, it is more realistic to lump small, closely related differences, and thus to reduce greatly the number of different woodland types required in the national series. Certain highly modified or degenerate types of woodland have deliberately been omitted, and a wide range of types with high nature conservation value has been included.

Choice of sites has been based first on the different major woodland types as identified by the dominant tree species (oakwood, pinewood and so on), and then on the range of diversity within the other components of the wood and ecosystem, i.e. the other layers, flora and fauna. Within each major woodland type the number of sites chosen has depended on the relative geographical extent and variability of the type. Mixed deciduous woodland is the most widespread and variable British woodland type and so is represented by the largest number of sites, whereas a local type such as pinewood is represented by a much smaller number. In addition, particular attention has been paid to representation of the following features.

1 Major silvicultural systems which influence the structural character of a woodland, especially in the tree and tall-shrub layers, e.g. high forest, coppice, coppice with standards, park woodland. These are represented under separate floristic woodland types, as relevant, e.g. oak high forest, oak–hazel coppice with standards, hornbeam coppice.

2 Other structural variations, related mainly to variations in development of the tall-shrub and field layers.

3 Topographic variations. These apply mainly in hilly country where differences in angle of slope, aspect and rockiness give different types of wood associated with plateaux, steep slopes (hanging woods), valley bottoms and river gorges. In some districts, e.g. the Vale of Ffestiniog, north Wales, and Borrowdale, Lakeland, the number of sites chosen within the same area is an attempt to represent this range of diversity, which seldom falls within the compass of a single woodland block, although it does so in the Wye valley, south Wales.

4 Local diversity in soil conditions. This is often associated with feature 3 above, especially in sites representing a catena, where both nutrient status and wetness of soil are affected by topography. Base-status is also strongly influenced by the nature of the parent rock and where there are non-calcareous and calcareous rocks within the same

wood or in the slope above, the effect on woodland floristic composition is usually very marked. Where this situation obtains, it is often possible to have good examples of different major woodland types represented within the same site. A classic case is Roudsea Wood, north Lancashire.

5 Woodland succession. Colonisation of acidic mire or heath by birch and pine, and of base-rich fen by alder and willow, is well represented on many peatland and heathland sites. There are also many examples of the changes associated with the coppice cycle. The replacement of one or more dominant tree species by others is a rarer condition, but examples have been chosen which may throw light on some species relationships not yet fully understood, e.g. oak–beech, beech–ash, birch–oak, birch–pine and oak–pine.

6 Natural woodland. This is so fragmentary that it has a considerable scarcity value and examples are difficult to find. Indeed, it has been said that there is no woodland in Britain completely unmodified by man. Woods which approach most closely to the presumptive original condition are in relatively inaccessible situations, and in remoter parts of Britain. A range of types has been included in the national series but none is extensive.

7 Floristic richness of the subsidiary layers. Selection for a wide range of tree and tall shrub species is implicit in what has been said above (except perhaps for rare and local shrubs such as *Sorbus* spp.), but this does not necessarily take equal account of variety in the field and ground layers. Care has been taken to represent the full range of floristic richness, especially on the calcareous rock formations, where the herbaceous component of the woodland flora is often very varied and rare species (e.g. certain orchids) are well represented. In a few instances woods which are of no particular interest for their tree and shrub component have been chosen for their rich herbaceous flora (e.g. Conistone Old Pasture and Bastow Wood, Yorkshire).

In western Britain many woods, especially those with rocky floors or stream ravines, are extremely rich in bryophytes, which grow in great abundance and luxuriance. There is a strong component of Atlantic mosses and liverworts forming an interesting phytogeographical element for which Britain and Ireland form the European headquarters. This Atlantic bryoflora changes somewhat in composition latitudinally, especially in representation of southern, thermophilous species, and there are also differences in richness according to degree of humidity. A series of sites (especially sessile oakwoods, since most Atlantic species are calcifuge) has been chosen to cover the range of variation in south-west England, west Wales, north-west England and western Scotland. Stream gorge woodlands are well represented.

Britain has a rich Atlantic lichen flora, in parallel with the bryophytes, though there is a different bias in habitat preference, and epiphytic lichen interest is only partly covered in the selection of woods rich in Atlantic bryophytes. Selection of additional sites for their rich lichen flora has thus paid special attention to the park woodlands which are an optimum habitat for some species and are so especially a feature of Britain.

8 Vertebrate interest. Selection of woodlands for botanical features automatically includes a wide range of variation in species of vertebrates, especially birds. Ornithological interest has often been used as a secondary criterion in the choice of woodland sites primarily for botanical reasons. In some instances, however, ornithological interest may rate more strongly. The important and distinctive avifauna of the central Scottish pinewoods, and the extremely diverse and large bird populations of the New Forest have already been mentioned.

9 Invertebrate interest. Several woodlands have been chosen especially for the richness of their insect fauna, notably the Lepidoptera, e.g. Monks Wood, Huntingdonshire; Waterperry Wood, Oxfordshire; and Craigellachie Wood, Inverness-shire. This has also been a strong supporting criterion in many other cases, e.g. the New Forest. The other groups of woodland invertebrates have been much less fully surveyed, and it is not known how adequate the present selection of sites will be for the conservation of this very large group of organisms.

10 Features of international importance. These are mainly floristic features associated with the strongly oceanic climate of Britain. Particularly noteworthy woodland species and communities in Britain are ash as a tree dominant, holly and various whitebeams in the tall-shrub layer, bluebells and various ferns as field layer dominants, bryophytes in general and Atlantic species in particular in the ground layer, and lichens (especially Atlantic species) as epiphytes. All these features are well represented in the selection of woodland sites now to be described.

Implications for conservation

A major problem in the conservation of woodlands is the high degree of fragmentation to which this ecosystem has been subjected. Ideally, one would wish to safeguard a large continuous block of woodland containing the whole range of local environmental diversity that is characteristic of the particular region. Separate blocks would then be chosen to represent the major regional environmental differences, which would be mainly climatic but partly geological. This ideal situation hardly exists anywhere in Britain at present, and it is usually necessary to select several discrete sites in attempting to conserve the woodland diversity characteristic of any particular district; sometimes these sites are not widely separated, however, and there is a case for treating them as a single aggregate site (e.g. Borrowdale Woods, Cumberland). Even the limited range of diversity peculiar to a single local woodland type (e.g. oak–lime woods in Lincolnshire) may not be represented in one site, and it is necessary to include two or more adjacent sites in order to encompass adequately this variability. The sites selected and delimited are often only part of a more extensive block of woodland, which also has features of ecological importance. Though every attempt has been made to delimit precisely the area of importance, the boundaries of some sites may, on further inspection, require alteration. Similarly, as our knowledge of the flora, and more particularly

the fauna, increases it may be necessary to revise this list of key sites.

In many cases where numerous woods of biological importance occur in a restricted geographical area it is perhaps inappropriate to select a few particular sites and more appropriate to achieve conservation through prescriptions aimed at the management of the woods as a whole. Examples of such areas are the western Weald, New Forest, Forest of Dean, Dartmoor woodlands, Wye valley, north Wales, Lincolnshire, Lake District, Loch Sunart and Spey–Dee Valleys (see also Chapter 13). Selection of separate sites in such areas is difficult, but an attempt has been made to do this, to maintain uniformity of treatment throughout the *Review*.

REGIONAL DIVERSITY AND SELECTION OF KEY SITES

Oakwood

Of the British woods composed of native trees, those with dominance or co-dominance of oak are by far the most widespread. Because of the large numbers of sites involved, it is best to deal with the purer oakwoods on their own, and to treat separately the mixed oakwoods which mostly belong to more base-rich soils in the edaphic series. The inconsistencies in ecological distribution pattern make it appropriate to deal with pedunculate and sessile oakwoods together, but the specific identity of the oak will be mentioned whenever it is clearly known.

The main directions of variation in oakwoods are climatic, and a separation can be made into western types in regions of humid climate, and eastern types existing under drier conditions. The western oakwoods are internationally important for their rich Atlantic flora, especially of bryophytes, which is more fully represented in some of the heavy rainfall districts than in any other part of Europe. Particular emphasis has been laid on identifying and selecting an adequate latitudinal series of western oakwoods, to cover the considerable south to north changes in this Atlantic flora. The eastern oakwoods show less varied floristic features, and a more widely spaced latitudinal series has been judged adequate. Considerable variations also occur according to differences in management, especially between grazed and ungrazed woods – the former tending to be upland and the latter lowland.

WESTERN OAKWOODS

Although many of the important woodlands in south-west England are in upland country, they differ from many hill woods farther north in being below the limits of enclosed land and thus mostly fenced against stock. Consequently there is often little disturbance, herbs are luxuriant, and the well-developed shrub layer includes many evergreens such as holly and ivy. The most important oakwoods of this region are on the flanks of the upland areas of Dartmoor and Exmoor. The Bovey Valley woodlands (W.63, gr. 1)[1]

---

[1] Cross-references to key sites are identified by an initial letter (indicating habitat) and number.

include Yarner Wood on the eastern edge of Dartmoor, which is mainly a plateau sessile oakwood with rather shallow gills, and the adjoining Becka Falls–Hound Tor woods on the steeper sides of a deep glen, but including river terrace with mixed woodland as well. The woods of Holne Chase (W.64, gr. 1*) a few kilometres farther south are another important complex of plateau and valley-side sessile oakwoods, but have a good deal of mixed deciduous woodland on richer soils. Dendles Wood (W.80, gr. 2) on the southern edge of Dartmoor is a pedunculate oakwood occupying a small hill valley, and contains a good deal of planted oak and conifers. Draynes Wood (W.78, gr. 2), on the south side of Bodmin Moor, is a gorge oakwood with a fairly rich bryophyte and fern flora, and a counterpart to the woods at Becka Falls in the Bovey Valley complex.

Wistman's Wood (W.65, gr. 1), Black Tor Copse (W.66, gr. 1) on northern Dartmoor, and Piles Copse (W.79, gr. 2) in the south are also of pedunculate oak, but are high-level woods on extremely rocky ground and lie in a heavy rainfall area; the depauperate, often contorted form of the trees is in contrast to the well-grown oaks of the lower woodlands. Black Tor Copse lies within the North Dartmoor grade 1 composite site (L.92).

Bryophytes and ferns are well represented in these Dartmoor woodlands, and the Holne Chase woods have some nationally rare Atlantic species. On the whole, however, the Atlantic flora here is less rich than in north Wales, Lakeland or the western Highlands, as the climate is less wet. South-west England is the warmest of the oceanic regions of Britain, but the less humid conditions also differentiate these Dartmoor woods from those of the Killarney area, in south-west Ireland, where a similarly equable temperature regime obtains.

On the north side of Exmoor, the woods of the Holnicote and Horner Water (W.69, gr. 1) are one of the largest continuous blocks of sessile oakwood in Britain, showing a great variety of slope and aspect, with a wide range of management types. Mixed deciduous woodland is also well represented here. Farther west on Exmoor, Watersmeet (W.68, gr. 1), above Lynton, is another complex of sessile oak and mixed deciduous woodland, and has an especially rich flora with good representation of thermophilous Atlantic species. The woods of Holford and Hodder's Combes (W.84, gr. 2) on the Quantocks, are somewhat similar to those of the Horner Water, and can be regarded as an alternative site, whilst the Heddon Valley Woods (W.82, gr. 2) west of Lynton are a second choice to Watersmeet. In Somerset, Great Breach and Copley Woods (W.86, gr. 2) form a large lowland oakwood on relatively fertile soils. Although western in geographical position, it has stronger affinities with some eastern oakwoods or mixed deciduous woods than most of those mentioned above, as has Ashen Copse (W.85, gr. 2).

The south-west peninsula has a number of coastal woods of distinctive character. On the extremely exposed and windswept north Cornish coast, steep slopes above the sea at Dizzard Point (W.62, gr. 1) have a dense, wind-pruned wood of pedunculate oak with luxuriant ungrazed field communities, forming one of the best examples of coastal scrub woodland in the country. Similar steep and rocky slopes above the sea at Woody Bay (W.81, gr. 2) and Hobby Woods at Clovelly (W.83, gr. 2), and Nance Wood (W.77, gr. 2) in Cornwall, have other examples of this maritime oakwood, regarded as alternative sites to the Dizzard Wood. A different type of coastal woodland is found in the deep, sheltered inlets of the sea which penetrate the south coast of Cornwall and Devon. At the head of the Fal Estuary (W.61, gr. 1), near Tregony, salt water backs up a low valley, creating salt marsh which passes through alder–willow carr into sessile oakwood on the drier valley sides. This is probably the best example of this kind of sequence known in Britain. Merthen Wood (W.76, gr. 2) on the estuary of the Helford River, is closer to the sea, but shows less varied stages of transition from saline habitats to oakwood.

In south Wales, the valleys of the headwaters of the River Tywi hold a number of hanging sessile oakwoods famous as the nesting haunt of the red kite in its last British refuge, amongst these sequestered hills. The most important of these woods in its own right is the Cothi Tywi (W.91, gr. 1: including Allt Rhyd y Groes), which partly belongs to the Royal Society for the Protection of Birds and forms an integral part of the complex of hill farmland, woodland and open moor constituting their Gwenffrwd reserve. The upland site of Nant Irfon (W.96, gr. 2) also contains sessile oakwoods which are the nesting place of kites. Farther north, the gorge of the River Rheidol at Devil's Bridge, Cardiganshire, is thickly wooded, mainly with sessile oak but with patches of mixed deciduous wood on richer soils. Unlike most of the Welsh oakwoods, Coed Rheidol (W.90, gr. 1) is ungrazed, and the field communities are less modified than usual. Alternative woodland sites to these are the oakwoods in the Elan Valley at Glannau (W.100, gr. 2) and Carn Gafallt (see Appendix) (W.97, gr. 2), both of which have mixed deciduous wood, and the latter an area of alderwood as well. Farther south, in Glamorgan, the valleys of Blaenau Nedd & Mellte (W.98, gr. 2) have mixtures of woodland which include stands of sessile oak, and the complex at Coed Aber Edw (W.101, gr. 2) in Radnor also has this type represented.

North Wales is especially rich in oakwoods and a choice of sites has been made from a large number. As this is a district of generally heavy rainfall and one of the richest parts of Britain for Atlantic ferns, bryophytes and lichens, considerable emphasis has been placed on the representation of this floral element. Moreover, Merioneth in particular contains an exceptionally fine series of gorge woodlands, and an adequate sample of these is needed. No single wood contains anything like the full range of ecological variation characteristic of the district, and a group of sites has been selected to give this range in the aggregate. The greatest range of oakwood types is found in the Coedydd Dyffryn Maentwrog (W.107, gr. 1*) in northern Merioneth. Here, Coedydd Maentwrog represents a hanging oakwood of southern aspect, but changing at its eastern end to the rather open gorge wood of Coed Cymerau. On the opposite side of the valley, a north- to north-west-facing hanging oakwood is represented by Coed Camlyn which bends round at its western end into the deep gorge of Ceunant Llennyrch, containing a mixture of oak, mixed deciduous and birch wood. Just beyond the head of this glen, above Trawsfynydd Reservoir, Coed y Rhygen is a rocky open bryophyte-rich hillside oak–birch wood on less steep slopes but at a higher level than Coed Camlyn, and facing north to north-east. Below Ffestiniog, a second deep gorge, Ceunant Cynfal carries a good fringe of oakwood and mixed woodland, and a third gorge, Ceunant Llechrwd below Gellilydan, is similar but less deep.

Farther south in Merioneth two oakwoods are of outstanding bryological interest. The Coed Ganllwyd (W.108, gr. 1*) north of Dolgellau surround the rather open waterfall gorge of Rhaiadr Du and have been famous for their rich Atlantic flora for over 100 years. On the opposite, western, side of the Rhinog Mountains, there are various oakwoods along the Artro valley; the best of these is Coed Crafnant (W.109, gr. 1*), one of the most natural looking of all the British oakwoods and another important Atlantic bryophyte and lichen locality. Near Harlech, Coed Llechwedd (W.114, gr. 2) is mainly a mixed deciduous wood but has oakwood represented.

Although this series of grade 1 Merioneth oakwoods includes 7 geographically distinct sites the total area covered by these is only 370 ha. This is felt to be a reasonable requirement for grade 1 status in view of the wide range of aspect, slope, altitude, geology and soil type encompassed therein.

In the far south of Caernarvonshire, the woods at Hafod Garegog (W.111, gr. 2) in the reclaimed estuary of the Traeth Mawr occupy low, rounded knolls virtually at sea-level. They are good stands of oak, but with relatively little interest in the associated communities, which are of widespread types. Coed Llety Walter (W.113, gr. 2) near Llanbedr is another Artro valley oakwood, but on less steep ground than Coed Crafnant. Near Llanberis, Coed Dinorwig (W.106, gr. 1) is a good example of the now rare type of ungrazed hill oakwood with unmodified field communities, and although this ecosystem is well represented in several oakwoods in south-west England and on the Loch Lomond islands, it is thought desirable to include a Welsh example. Other north Wales woods, such as Coedydd Aber (W.104, gr. 1), Coed Gorswen (part of W.103), and Coed Maes yr Helmau (W.112, gr. 2) are variable woodland complexes with good stands of sessile oak of equal merit with associated mixed deciduous woodland, and the Rhinog and Cader Idris grade 1 upland sites contain bonus fragments of sessile oakwood. The oak–birch woods of Cannock Chase in Staffordshire (W.122, gr. 2) are an easterly example of this western woodland type.

In north-west England, the Lake District has strong ecological similarity to north Wales, but has somewhat lower mean temperatures and thus has fewer and less abundant thermophilous organisms. The finest semi-natural upland woods, mainly of sessile oak, but usually containing some mixed deciduous species, are in Borrowdale, and here an aggregate series of sites (W.133, gr. 1*) has been selected, extending along almost the whole length of the valley

between Keswick and Seathwaite. Great Wood on a gentle slope beside Derwentwater, is important for its lichens, and is an example of valley bottom woodland on mull soils, while the Lodore–Troutdale Woods farther south have fine hanging oakwoods with seral birch, and contain the cascade ravine of Lodore Falls, famous for its Atlantic bryophytes. Castle Crag is a further example of hanging oakwoods. Johnny's Wood at Longthwaite has both north-east and south facing slopes which illustrate finely the effect of aspect on the hygrophilous component of the flora, while the Seatoller Wood still nearer the dale head demonstrates how, in favouring these plants, extreme rainfall can compensate for a sun-exposed aspect. This exceptional series of woodlands is completed by two other areas. Castle Head Wood lies at the drier end of the rainfall gradient and is well-developed sessile oak over hazel woodland. It is entirely surrounded by enclosed farmland which must have reduced the grazing pressure over a long period and enabled some natural regeneration to take place. The Ings is also ungrazed and is a very fine example of northern alderwood with a field layer which varies with the mineral/humus properties of the soil.

Elsewhere in Lakeland, Scales Wood (W.146, gr. 2) above Buttermere, and Low Wood (W.150, gr. 2) above Brotherswater, are, respectively, shaded and sun-exposed alternatives to the Borrowdale Woods, but bryologically are not in the same class. Naddle Low Forest (W.149, gr. 2) above Haweswater contains a variety of woodland, including sessile oakwood on both shaded and sun-exposed aspects, but most of the range of variation here is represented in the Borrowdale Woods, and the Atlantic bryophyte flora is also much less rich. Both the Roeburndale Woods (W.141, gr. 1) near Lancaster and the Lyne Woods (W.147, gr. 2) in north Cumberland contain examples of sessile oakwood in a lower rainfall district. Roudsea Wood (W.139, gr. 1) also contains sessile oakwood on acidic slates, contrasting with ash–oak wood on limestone and other examples of oakwood on drift covered limestone soils are Whitbarrow and Witherslack Woods (W.136, gr. 1) and Gait Barrows (W.140, gr. 1) in the Morecambe Bay area. In the Grasmoor group of fells in Cumberland, Keskadale and Birkrigg Oaks (W.134, gr. 1) are two essentially similar fragments of high-level oakwood on slate scree which have become celebrated along with the high Dartmoor oakwoods as surviving remnants of this forest type near its upper altitudinal limits. They have become classic sites, but their interest resides in the trees themselves and not in the associated flora. Both lie within Buttermere Fells grade 2 upland site (U.27).

The total area of grade 1 oakwood sites in Lakeland is 895 ha, a modest figure in view of their diversity and importance.

In south-west Scotland, few semi-natural oakwoods remain, and there are none of first national importance. The Wood of Cree (W.177, gr. 2) in Kirkcudbrightshire consists largely of coppiced oak and has minor bryological interest, while the Fleet Woodlands (W.178, gr. 2) include Castramont Wood and Killiegowan Wood, also coppiced in part and with mixtures of trees locally. A coastal cliff slope oakwood at Ravenshall (W.179, gr. 2), in the same district, is rather similar to some of the coastal woods of steep slopes in south-west England. While none of these three woods merits grade 1 status, they have some national importance as representatives of the regional forest types.

In the western Highlands, oakwood is a widespread type, but few extensive areas remain, and there is often a considerable mixture of birch with the oak. The islands of the Loch Lomond group (W.169, gr. 1*), especially Inchcailloch, have fine stands of sessile oak with ungrazed field communities which are much more luxuriant than those of most Scottish oakwoods, as on the eastern shore of the loch. There is a considerable range of aspect and soil type, and the varied history of management on the different islands is ecologically significant. Farther west, in Knapdale, the sheltered peninsula of Taynish in the sea inlet of Loch Sween has an extensive and diverse area of woodland. Taynish Wood (W.196, gr. 1*) shows a great variety of soil types and aspect, but sessile oakwood is one of the major woodland communities and rises straight from sea-level. There is a rich lichen flora, especially of arboreal species. On the east coast of Knapdale, the hanging woods overlooking Loch Fyne between Mealdarroch Point–Skipness (W.197, gr. 1*) have been chosen for their wealth of Atlantic bryophytes and ferns. They are oak–birch woods traversed by several deep ravines with cascading streams, and contain a greater abundance of certain thermophilous species than any woods seen outside south-west Ireland. At Coille Ardura (W.212, gr. 1), Mull, is the most extensive area of woodland of any western Scottish island. Here the complicated topographical pattern and the variations in geology and soil are reflected in the sessile oakwoods, ash–oak woods, ash and ash–hazel areas. The birch and oak woods at Kinuachdrach (W.218, gr. 2) on Jura are regarded as an alternative site in this respect. The oakwoods of Choille Mor (W.213, gr. 2), Colonsay, and Claggain–Ardmore (W.214, gr. 2), Islay, are not sufficiently outstanding to merit grade 1 status but are interesting as probably the most westerly examples of this woodland type in Britain. In the district of Lorne on the Argyll mainland, the woods at Clais Dhearg (W.219, gr. 2) are quite extensive stands of oak on fairly gentle slopes or flat ground, but have little interest apart from the trees themselves.

The deep, sheltered sea inlet of Loch Sunart (W.190, gr. 1*) in Argyll has a good deal of oak and birch wood, but this has been fragmented and impoverished by clearance and locally replaced by conifer plantations. The largest remaining oakwood at Ariundle lies back from the sea above Strontian. This is a fairly typical hill oakwood with grazed field communities and few undershrubs, but the bryophyte flora is rich, especially for a slope of south-east aspect, whilst the more open tree growth below the main woodland towards the river carries a rich lichen flora. On the north shore of Loch Sunart, the discontinuous areas of mainly oakwood with some birch between Salen and Strontian, and the birchwoods around Laudale, Glen Cripesdale and Creag Dubh on the south shore are of international importance for their extremely rich bryophyte and lichen floras. As this interest is spread over such a large area, there is a need here for a general policy of woodland conservation which pays heed to the requirements of the bryophytes and lichens. Farther north, fairly pure oakwoods near Arisaig have a limited range of interest in features other than the trees, and are not regarded as of national importance. The most northerly oakwood of any size in the western Highlands is at Letterewe on the north side of Loch Maree (W.206, gr. 1*) in Ross. This site is evidently close to the climatic limits of oak, and there are interesting ecological questions in the relationship between this type and birchwood on the richer soils of the Loch Maree area, and between oak and pine wood on the poorer soils. The Letterewe woods are good examples of sessile oakwood in their own right.

The series of grade 1 western oakwood sites mentioned covers a total of 6560 ha. From south to north these sites occur within a wide range of climate; in south-west England they are within the rainfall range of 140–180 'wet days'; in north Wales, Lakeland and the south-west Highlands from 180–220 wet days; while Arriundle and Letterewe Woods experience over 220 wet days annually, on average. They also show a fairly even spread within the mean annual temperature range of 11 °C in the south to 8 °C in the north. Geologically, the oakwood sites cover a wide variety of sedimentary, igneous and metamorphic rocks, differing considerably in hardness, physical structure and base-status.

EASTERN OAKWOOD

The oakwoods of lowland England overlap to a considerable extent with mixed deciduous woodland and in the majority of oakwoods the oak dominates as a result of coppice-with-standards management. The majority of such woods have been considered as mixed deciduous and only a residue of oak high forest, oak over oak and oak over hazel coppice-with-standards remain to be considered here. Furthermore, many ancient and over-mature oakwoods have been dealt with in that section, including for example Parham Park (W.18, gr. 2), Sussex; Savernake Forest (W.31, gr. 2), Wiltshire; Staverton Park (W.34, gr. 1), Suffolk; Sherwood Forest (W.130, gr. 2), Nottinghamshire; and the New Forest (W.26, gr. 1*), Hampshire. A number of sites chosen for other characteristics also contain a stand of oak, or oak–hazel, for example, Hatton Wood (W.45(i)(a), gr. 1) in Lincolnshire, and Ellenden Wood (W.16, gr. 2) in Kent. In the case of the chalk beechwoods, oak woodland is often included as a type characteristic of adjacent Clay-with-Flints oaks, as in Wouldham–Detling (W.7, gr. 1) in Kent, and Aston Rowant Woods (W.29, gr. 2) in Buckinghamshire–Oxfordshire.

The residue of oak high forest, oak over oak coppice-with-standards and oak over hazel woods are scattered through southern and eastern Britain, with a concentration in the south east and Midlands, where they are the prevalent type.

Oak–hazel woods are a product of intensive management and most are probably planted, even though many are on continuously wooded sites. A stand is included within Ham Street Woods (W.2, gr. 1), Kent, as well as a small stand in Hatton Wood. But perhaps the best example still managed actively is Long Itchington and Ufton Woods (W.120, gr. 1) in Warwickshire, in the central Midlands which are otherwise devoid of high grade woods. Pipewell Woods (W.128, gr. 2) in Northamptonshire are an alternative to Ufton.

Mature oak high forest is often a product of nineteenth-century planting, but stands are selected in areas with other features of interest. A stand in the Forest of Dean (W.73, gr. 1), Nagshead, represents the range of types in that area. Waterperry (W.25, gr. 1) and Windsor Forest (W.23, gr. 1) are examples in the south Midlands and south where the entomological interest is high. High Halstow (C.8, gr. 2) in Kent may be regarded as an oakwood modified by invasion of elm. Foxley Wood (W.47, gr. 2) in Norfolk has an area of disturbed oak high forest.

Oak coppice and coppice-with-standards occurs sparingly in eastern and southern Britain on more acid, well-drained soils. Scords Wood (W.4, gr. 1) is selected to represent this extensive Wealden type because in this site it is associated with other types of woodland. Likewise Swanton Novers Woods (W.39, gr. 1*) in Norfolk have a stand comprised of both species in a wood where two other important types occur. Wyre Forest (W.121, gr. 1), Worcestershire, is a special case, with both oak coppice and high forest, with floristic features linking north and south and an oak population said to be an intermediate in some features between the western sessile oaks and the eastern pedunculate oaks; Chaddesley–Randan Woods (W.132, gr. 2) can to some extent be regarded as an alternative to Wyre Forest. In the Habberley Valley (W.131, gr. 2) in Shropshire, and Downton Gorge (W.125, gr. 2) in Hereford, sessile oak woodland is one of the two contrasting types.

In the northern half of eastern Britain, oakwoods on acidic brown earths are fairly widespread, but show a rather limited range of variation. The grazed upland examples are usually devoid of a shrub layer, and even those in the lowlands which are enclosed often have only a sparse growth of tall shrubs. There are examples on the Millstone Grit of north Derbyshire and south Yorkshire, but these do not appear to be of national importance. In north Yorkshire, Raincliffe Wood (W.144, gr. 1) contains an example of pedunculate oakwood along with mixed deciduous woodland, and in the west, Burton Wood (W.154, gr. 2) near Lancaster is mainly a sessile oakwood which has affinities with eastern types, probably because it is in a low rainfall area compared with the Lakeland oakwoods. Near Carlisle, Orton Moss (W.135, gr. 1) is a complex of woodland on dried out peat-moss, and among the types represented is a small area of oakwood with an acidophilous flora. Holystone Woods (W.163, gr. 2) in the Cheviots, have a good example of upland eastern oakwood, but are hardly of grade 1 rank. Small areas of oakwood are represented in the glens of Monk Wood (W.164, gr. 2) and Hesleyside Park (W.165, gr. 2), Northumberland, but these are selected mainly for other features.

The hill valleys of the Southern Uplands in the eastern counties have a number of quite interesting small oakwoods, but none of national quality has yet been found, and most examples are rather like western oakwoods with a less rich bryophyte flora. In the eastern Highlands, two northern examples are regarded as worthy of grade 1 status. These are the woods of the Pass of Killiecrankie (W.185) where fairly pure sessile oakwood passes into mixed deciduous woodland in the glen of the River Garry, and the small and isolated but very fine example of both pedunculate and sessile oakwood at Dinnet (W.180) adjoining the great Glen Tanar pinewood (W.187(b)). In the far north east of Scotland, the Ledmore Wood, Spinningdale (W.227, gr. 2) in Sutherland has a pure stand of oak unusual in its heather-dominated field layer; it is evidently a planted wood but has considerable interest.

Mixed deciduous woodland

Mixed broad-leaved deciduous woodland occupies the median position in the field of variation in British woodland, and is the most widespread of all woodland types in this country, being especially characteristic of soil types which fall between the extremes of acidity and alkalinity, or dry skeletal brown earths and waterlogged peats. This woodland type probably comes closer than most others to primaeval woodland in floristic composition; this is especially true of woodlands on sites that have never been cleared.

These woodlands are extremely variable. Since this variation is continuous, however, only arbitrary subdivisions can be made within them. Some of this variation is structural and results from management; much of the diversity, however, is in the composition of the tree and shrub layers. High forest and park woodlands are widespread but the majority have been managed as coppice with or without standards; following neglect or as a result of deliberate management, many of the coppice woods, whilst retaining some of their coppice features, are developing towards high forest. Because oak was the normal standard, these may have been previously described as oakwoods. However, with changing forestry practices and the felling of the big timber during and since the World Wars, many have lost their dominant oak and it now seems more realistic to consider them as mixed deciduous.

The central floristic type consists of mixtures of oak, ash and hazel, usually also with wych elm and sometimes birch (particularly in northern and western areas) and field maple (in the south and east). There are woods in which one or more of these species is absent, or present in very small numbers but, with one exception, those with at least two of these species forming a significant proportion of the standing crop are treated as mixed deciduous woods. The exception is an oak–hazel mixture in which hazel forms a distinct layer beneath the oak, and which is therefore considered as oakwood. Mixed deciduous woods with more than 20 different native tree and shrub species are common, and many species normally present as a minority element may in some woods be dominant or co-dominant. In addition, woods in which more than five species are co-dominant, though uncommon, are widespread, and the number of possible combinations of species is very large. Three floristic variants from the central facies are considered sufficiently distinctive to justify separate consideration: these are mixed deciduous woodland in which small-leaved lime or horn-beam is abundant, and similar woodland in which sweet chestnut, an introduced species, is abundant as a result of management. Even so, many intermediates can be found between these and the central type.

Mixed deciduous woods contain, in aggregate, a very large number of herbaceous species in the field layer as well as a rich variety of native trees and shrubs. Those which have been managed as parkland are generally poorer, except in epiphytic lichens and wood-boring invertebrates. Conversely, woods managed as coppice, whilst rich in field layer species and bird and insect populations, are poor in epiphytes, and the bryophytes which need continuity of shade and humidity are generally of more limited interest. Even in the relatively dry and warm climate of East Anglia, however, a few rare and hygrophilous bryophyte species occur sparingly and coppice stools are important habitats for some mosses.

Mixed deciduous woodlands are prevalent in the English lowlands but, whilst they are much less extensive in the north and west, some important examples occur in these areas. The northern examples, from Lakeland northwards, are the most uniform in both structure and floristics. Many western oakwoods contain examples of oak–ash–wych elm woodland, varying in size from fragments of less than half a hectare along watercourses and in flushed situations to large stands of scores of acres. Except where these are large and well defined, they will not be mentioned again in the present section, as they have been treated in the account of oak-woods (pp. 105–9).

In the selection of sites containing mixed deciduous woodland an attempt has been made to reflect their wide geographical/climatic spread and the full range of associated soil types. The central type is included throughout its range, and examples of major variants (edaphic, biogeographic and management-induced) are selected in districts where these are particularly obvious. A number of examples have been selected in some districts, partly because individual woods are small and the full range of variation may not be present in one wood, but also because each separate wood exhibits different aspects of the impact of past and present management on the existing woodland. A relatively large number of sites is included in the south-west of England where there is a considerable range of soil types. In some areas these woods grow on fertile soils which, but for past land settlement and use factors, would be cultivated today. This is particularly so in arable eastern England where the permanent woods are almost the only sites in which undisturbed profiles of the widespread soil types can be studied, and where in consequence it is considered justifiable to select a relatively large number of sites. In situations where only one of a number of woods could justifiably be chosen to represent a variant, the final choice of site was determined by the presence of rare species or a relatively large number of species. Some sites are included because they exemplify certain particularly important special features.

THE CENTRAL FACIES

SOUTH AND EAST

In southern England, mainly in the south-east, there is an enormous variety of mixed deciduous woodland. Most types occur on sands, gravels and clays, but a particularly important type on Chalk has oak–ash–maple woodland with other species such as hornbeam but without beech, over a deep calcareous loam on the steep Chalk scarp. This is a situation normally covered by beech over a thin soil, and it is possible that these sites, Alkham Valley (W.3, gr. 1) in Kent, and Gopher Wood (see L.26) in Wiltshire, represent a soil condition pre-dating that associated with the widespread beechwoods. Woodland on Chalk at Wye and Crundale Downs (L.3) appears to represent a similar mixed type of a secondary nature.

In the High Weald outcrops of sandstone in wooded gills are associated with the occurrence of plants normally regarded as Atlantic in distribution, notably the ferns *Dryopteris aemula* and *Hymenophyllum tunbrigense* and certain bryophytes. These woods are normally oak, beech and ash with alder along springlines and on low ground, and often have mature trees and a rich flora. The best of these outcrops is in Wakehurst and Chiddingly Woods (W.12, gr. 1), and the Fairlight, Ecclesbourne and Warren Glens (W.14, gr. 1), also in Sussex, are almost as rich, the latter site having a number of rare bryophytes and a coastal situation rare in lowland English woods. Saxonbury Hill/Eridge Park (W.9, gr. 1*) also has an example of this community which grades into woodland with a rich ground flora over Wadhurst Clay.

The western Weald, one of the most densely wooded areas of Britain, has a distinctive type of mixed deciduous woodland characterised by oak standards over mixed coppice of hornbeam, ash and hazel. The ground flora is moderately rich, and there may be many tree and shrub species, though the commercial species are strongly dominant. Few of these woods are individually outstanding, but the area as a whole is extraordinarily rich, particularly in insect species. In these circumstances it is better to consider the area as a whole and, with few exceptions, make no attempt to select individual sites. Thus only Ebernoe Common (W.11, gr. 1) and The Mens and The Cut (W.13, gr. 1) have been listed, with the sole addition of Glover's Wood (W.21, gr. 2) which is both representative of the hornbeam and mixed coppice of this area, and has a complicated development.

One other mixed wood on Weald Clay, Staffhurst Wood (W.19, gr. 2), is included partly to enlarge the geographical coverage but mainly as a representative of a different structural type. It is a common wood of oak, beech, hornbeam and ash with a mixture of age classes, including large, ancient trees with rich epifloras, and a range of field layer communities.

The Gault Clay woodlands are a related type distinguished by the influence of rich calcareous downwash from the Chalk and consequent floristic differences. They are typically oak standards over ash–hazel–hornbeam coppice and, being fairly close ecologically to the western Weald Clay woods, only one site is included. This is Asholt Wood (W.5, gr. 1) in Kent, one of the most diverse of the type and probably the best remaining, now that Ryarsh Wood has been partly converted to conifers.

A distinctive feature of the Weald is the occurrence of alder on springlines and low-lying ground in mixed deciduous woodland, associated with a field community including both *Chrysosplenium* spp. This is represented in many sites chosen for other features, e.g. Wakehurst and Chiddingly Woods and Scords Wood. Nevertheless, an additional site, Colyers Hanger (W.20, gr. 2) in Surrey, is included partly because it has a good stand of alder but also because it is an excellent example of the zonation of woodland types determined by soil conditions: oakwood occurs on dry, sandy soil and mixed wych elm–ash–maple woodland on base rich soil. More extensive Wealden alder carrs occur elsewhere but the type is adequately represented by Colyers Hanger.

One other site in the Weald, Scords Wood (W.4) is included as a representative of oak woodland (discussed elsewhere), but it also has a variety of woodland types corresponding with differences in underlying geology. The valley contains mixed deciduous woodland of beech, ash, maple, wych elm and oak, and an alder carr on clay at the bottom. Corresponding changes in the field layer emphasise the close correlation with underlying geology, and it is mainly for the clarity of this relationship that this particular wood is selected.

The south Region contains few important mixed deciduous woodlands: much of the land is chalk and the main woodland types are beech, oak and oak–hazel. Selborne Common, with recently developed oak–ash–hawthorn–hazel woodland, is included in the Selborne Hanger (W.27, gr. 1) beechwood site to add diversity and a sample of plateau woodland. Cranborne Chase (W.32, gr. 2) in Wiltshire also includes chalk plateau woodland – mainly oak – but is selected to include an unusual ash–maple wood on Chalk, which has limited quantities of oak, beech, yew and holly and a rich epiphytic flora. A further site at Wychwood (W.24, gr. 1) in Oxfordshire is included (even though the present woodland is largely the product of planting in the last century) because it is a reasonably rich example of mixed deciduous woodland in an area otherwise almost devoid of scientifically valuable woodland. It also has an interesting range of other habitats including scrubby woodland edge, broad rides, springs and flushes, ponds and grassland. Waterperry Wood (W.25, gr. 1), although much of it has been felled and replanted, is also included as an example.

The mixed deciduous woodlands of East Anglia, Lincolnshire and the east Midlands are typically coppice-with-standards of oak, ash, hazel and maple on calcareous clay with a rich variety of shrubs and field–ground layer species. The field and ground flora varies according to soil base-status and drainage conditions but the tree and shrub layers are at least partly the product of past management. Clear geographical groups can be distinguished on the basis of certain species of local occurrence, e.g. hornbeam (treated as a separate type), oxlip in East Anglia, bird-cherry in Norfolk and, to some extent, lime in Lincolnshire (also treated separately).

Selection of sites here has to take into account a number of features, in addition to the need for geographical scatter. The average type must be well-represented, as well as the main variants, and woodlands intermediate between it and other types. Since their character has been modified by management, a range of past and present management types must be included and distinct phytogeographical types such as oxlip woods should also be represented.

The average type is represented by a series of sites. Monks Wood (W.42, gr. 1) and Castor Hanglands (W.44, gr. 1), are both rich floristically and faunally, the former showing a variety of management types and the latter crossing a series of geological boundaries. Sites which may be regarded as alternative to Monks Wood and Castor Hanglands are Whittlewood Forest (W.129, gr. 2) in Northamptonshire – an area of entomological importance – Leighfield Forest (W.127, gr. 2), Leicestershire, and the Kesteven group (W.58, gr. 2) of Dole Wood, Dunsby Wood, Kirton Wood and Sapperton–Pickworth Woods. Although alternative in general terms, these enlarge both the geographical range and the range of management variants in selected areas. The Kesteven Woods are included as a series to represent variation within a geographical group (cf. limewoods in central Lincolnshire, oakwoods in north Wales, Scottish pinewoods). King's Wood (W.51, gr. 2), Bedfordshire, is in part an alternative to the grade 1 sites here.

In many cases these woods are infiltrated by narrow-leaved elms to the extent that elm woodland is produced. This is often the case in re-established woods (a series of these is included at Hintlesham Woods) but also occurs in some permanent woods. Hayley Wood (W.40, gr. 1) in Cambridgeshire has small examples of this, but a further site is added at Overhall Grove (W.56, gr. 2) as an example of the advanced form of this change with many peculiar features. At Dunsby Wood a similar process is apparent, but the species here is English elm.

On the drier more sandy soils oak woodland may occur, but in some sites the mixed deciduous character is retained with abundant birch. Hintlesham Woods (W.33, gr. 1) in Suffolk exhibit this well, in addition to numerous other features. Similar effects are also represented in Foxley Wood (W.47, gr. 2), Norfolk, and Newball and Hardy Gang Woods (see W.45(i)(*b*), gr. 1), Lincolnshire. Although many sites have valuable features showing the interaction of past and present management with the natural flora and fauna, these features are of outstanding interest in only a few, notably Felshamhall and Monks Park Woods (W.35, gr. 1*), Hintlesham Woods, Swanton Novers Woods (W.39, gr. 1*) and Hardwick Wood (W.57, gr. 2).

Three important variants are recognised with, respectively, oxlip, alder and bird-cherry as important constituents. The oxlip woods selected cover a range of variants within the type: Hayley Wood and Felshamhall and Monks Park Woods are actively managed still, whilst Canfield Hart

Wood (W.53, gr. 2) in Essex is the most southerly and a good example of this variant. Overhall Grove has been mentioned as an example of narrow-leaved elm woodland and Hardwick Wood has an area of planted wych elm. Surprisingly for woods so commonly wet for long periods of each year, alder is often completely absent. Sites where it occurs may be of particular significance in understanding the management modifications resulting from many centuries of coppice management. Felshamhall and Monks Park Woods are the main representative, but it is also well developed in Foxley Wood and in parts of Swanton Novers Woods. Bird-cherry is more or less confined to Norfolk woods, where there is an outlying population from the centre of occurrence in north and western Britain. Wayland Wood (W.48, gr. 2) is selected because bird-cherry is an abundant component of the coppice layer. Likewise a small portion of Swanton Novers Woods has coppice of this species mixed with alder.

Three kinds of woodland intermediate between this central type and the oak, hornbeam and lime woods can be recognised. Some woods, though mainly mixed deciduous, have small stands of oak, e.g. Foxley Wood, whilst Wayland Wood differs from oak–hazel coppice-with-standards only in having a proportion of bird-cherry in the coppice layer. Four woods have small areas of lime; Felshamhall and Monks Park Woods, Hintlesham Woods, Kirton Wood and Dole Wood. Hatfield Forest (W.54, gr. 2) in Essex is included as both a variant of the basic type in which oak is unusually poorly represented and as a type intermediate with the hornbeam woods.

In Suffolk and Essex it is extremely difficult to define the boundaries between the central ranges of variation of oak, hazel, ash, maple and birch, and the hornbeam and lime facies. There are, however, still a large number of woods with a variety of these coppice types, and collectively these amount to a considerable range of more or less clear-cut types and intermediate combinations. Hintlesham Woods have been selected as a site with a wide range of variation in a relatively undamaged state, but many other woods exhibit other aspects of this variation. Had all these woods been surveyed in detail, further grade 1 or 2 sites might have been selected. The following woods are the most promising on present knowledge: Elmsett Park Wood in Suffolk, and, in Essex, Quendon Wood, Hempstead Wood, East End Wood, Coggeshall Woods and Hockley Wood. In addition, Hales Wood National Nature Reserve (NNR) is a relatively small piece of woodland which is only a small remnant of what was once a much larger wood whose chief features are better represented in, for example, Hayley Wood. However, for the time being Hales Wood is retained as a grade 2 site (W.52).

A group of sites is included to represent multiple mixtures of more than four main species of tree or shrub. Bedford Purlieus (W.43, gr. 1) and Swanton Novers Woods are of this type and also have numerous rare species. Felshamhall and Monks Park Woods can also be included here, as can the more mixed parts of Newball Wood and Wickenby Wood (see W.45(ii)).

WEST AND NORTH

Mixed deciduous woodlands in western and northern Britain occur in lowland country but are perhaps more characteristic of the lower hill slopes. They occur on a wide variety of parent materials, but notably on those which are moderately base-rich, such as calcareous igneous rocks, shales, grits and sandstones. Sometimes, on hillsides, they occupy the middle or lower enriched zone of a catena, or they may be associated with flush lines. They are also highly characteristic of stream ravines, but it is noticeable that, except on completely acidic rocks such as granite and quartzite, these stream gorges, very typically, have mixtures of both sessile oakwood on leached brown earths and mixed deciduous wood on more fertile mull soils.

Floristically, these western and northern mixed deciduous woods are poorer in tree and tall-shrub species than those of the south and east, and in particular the number of species representing these life forms decreases with distance north. Hornbeam, sweet chestnut, small-leaved lime, field maple and *Sorbus* spp. (except *S. aucuparia*) gradually drop out but gean remains widespread (though usually sparse) and bird-cherry is a species mainly found in the north and west. The number of field layer species also tends to decrease in the same directions, but bryophytes increase in number and luxuriance with distance west, and some extreme western mixed deciduous woods are rich in Atlantic species. The most typical examples have a near dominance of ash, with a variable understorey of hazel, and a constancy of oak, wych elm and birch. This grades into purer ashwood (often still with wych elm) on definitely calcareous soils, and into pure oakwood on markedly base-deficient soils. The field layer is composed largely of basiphilous species, but the upland woods are usually grazed and show predominance of grasses at the expense of forbs.

Numerous examples of mixed deciduous wood occur within woodlands chosen as representatives of oak or ash wood in the west and north, and in many districts there is no need to add further examples. In south-west England the Bovey Valley Woods (W.63, gr. 1), Holne Chase (W.64, gr. 1*) and Avon Gorge (Leigh Woods) (W.70, gr. 1) have mixed deciduous wood grading into oakwood, whereas Asham Wood (see W.71(b), gr. 1) grades from this type into ashwood. Weston Big Wood (W.87, gr. 2) is included as a mixed deciduous wood in its own right. In the hill country of south Wales, Coed y Cerrig (W.92, gr. 1), Coed Rheidol (W.90), Carn Gafallt (W.97) and Blaenau Nedd & Mellte (W.98) all have examples of the central type, while Tarren yr Esgob (see U.8, gr. 2) has an atypical high-level scrub woodland which includes ash, birch, willow, rowan and hawthorn.

In the west Midlands several mixed woods have been chosen which are intermediate in character between the lowland and upland types. These, which in places have affinity with ash–wych elm wood on calcareous soils, mostly occur on fairly steep slopes and they are floristically rich in both woody and herbaceous species. The sites, which themselves represent a range of variation are, Tick Wood (W.119

gr. 1), Halesend Wood (W.116, gr. 1), Hill Hole Dingle (see Appendix) (W.118, gr. 1), and Habberley Valley (W.131, gr. 2). The Wye valley on the borders of south Wales and Gloucestershire/Herefordshire has one of the most varied and important complexes of woodland in Britain, mainly on Carboniferous Limestone where soil conditions vary according to topography. In the Wye valley complex, mixed deciduous wood with little oak and a usual admixture of beech, small-leaved lime, ash and wych elm is represented within three separate sites, namely Blackcliff–Wyndcliff–Pierce Woods (W.94, gr. 1), Lady Park Wood (see W.95, gr. 1*) and Hudnalls (W.75, gr. 1). Four other sites in the same area, Coombe Woods (W.102, gr. 2), Dingle Wood (see W.73, gr. 1), Downton Gorge (W.125, gr. 2) and Bushy Hazels and Cwmma Moors (W.126, gr. 2) are of this type but with different structural and floristic features which merit their inclusion in the national series. Salisbury Wood (W.93, gr. 1) has a mixture of species and characteristics of both upland and lowland coppices.

In north Wales, the Conwy valley has good upland examples of mixed deciduous woodland on calcareous pumice tuffs, or mixed drifts giving fairly base-rich soils. These are of the hanging type at Coed Dolgarrog (see W.103, gr. 1), and the gorge type in the adjoining ravine of Ceunant Dulyn, while Coedydd Aber (W.104) has a combination of both types and Coed Gorswen (W.103(b)) is on gentle slopes and grades into alder–oak wood. The cliff fragment of this type at the existing NNR of Cwm Glas Crafnant is not considered to rate more highly than grade 3, but Coed Tremadog (W.105, gr. 1) is important and includes cliff, scree and scrub habitats. The Merioneth gorge woods of Ceunant Llennyrch (see W.107), Ceunant Cynfal (W.107(d)), Coed Ganllwyd (W.108), Coed Maes yr Helmau (W.112) and Ceunant Llechrwd, Gellilydan (W.107(e)) all have this kind of woodland as a bonus. On the Creuddyn limestone, Bryn Maelgwyn and Gloddaeth (W.110, gr. 2) is a western lowland example of mixed deciduous woodland with a rich flora.

In northern England many of the sessile oakwoods of Lakeland contain examples of oak–ash–wych elm–hazel wood, usually on base-rich beds in the predominantly acidic rocks, and especially where there is also flushing. The mixed type is, however, equally well represented with oakwood in Seatoller Wood (see W.133) and Low Wood (W.150) (in both there is a close approach to limestone ashwood); and in Lodore–Troutdale Woods (W.133(d)) and Naddle Low Forest (W.149), the mixed woodland occupies the more basic soils at the gentler foot of steep slopes with hanging oakwood. Two woods on limestone just south of Lakeland are intermediate between the richer kind of northern oak-wood and more typical mixed deciduous woodland; they are at Whitbarrow and Witherslack Woods (W.136) and Gait Barrows (W.140). Gowbarrow Park (W.148, gr. 2) includes a fine example of mixed woodland on the crags on the north side of Ullswater. Eaves Wood (W.153, gr. 2) in the same area has a rather artificial appearance with various non-native species, but is important for its rich field layer. Two rather similar complexes of sessile oak and mixed

deciduous wood in river glens south and north of Lakeland are Roeburndale Woods (W.141, gr. 1) and its alternative site Lyne Woods (W.147, gr. 2). Thornton and Twisleton Glens (W.157, gr. 2) have ashwood grading into a more mixed type.

The above woods are all in the west of northern England. In the centre, in Teesdale, Shipley Wood (W.145, gr. 1), is a fine example of mixed deciduous wood with a rich flora. The valleys of the North York Moors in the east of northern England have varied woodlands which range from oak to mixed types on fairly rich soils, and the best remaining examples are Raincliffe Wood (W.144), Ashberry and Reins Woods (W.158, gr. 2) and Beckhole Woods (W.159, gr. 2). This last group has stronger affinities than the other woods in northern England with the mixed deciduous woods of the south and east, but the sites mentioned are all valley-side woods. The once fine woods of Newtondale in the same area of Yorkshire were recently subjected to extensive felling and can no longer be considered. In Durham, Castle Eden Dene (W.162, gr. 2) is a good example of mixed deciduous wood in a glen of Magnesian Limestone. Beast Cliff (W.160, gr. 2) is an example of oak–ash wood that has developed on slipped Jurassic strata on the Yorkshire coast.

In southern Scotland, the prevailing Ordovician and Silurian greywackes and shales give a prevalence of base-rich soils well suited to the development of mixed deciduous woodland and this type is extremely widespread in the region, especially in stream gorges. Very few outstanding examples are known, however, and only one site has been rated as grade 1 for this woodland type. This is one of the Clyde valley ravine woods at Avondale (W.170), and the nearby sites of Hamilton High Park (W.175) and Nethan Gorge (W.176) are regarded as grade 2 alternatives. On the Scar Water in Dumfries-shire, Chanlock Foot (W.172) and Stenhouse Wood (W.173) are also rated as grade 2 to represent examples not in gorges; the first is on steep slopes and the second on gentler ground. The Maidens to Heads of Ayr (W.174, gr. 2) represent mixed deciduous woodland on coastal cliffs of Old Red Sandstone. It is possible that further survey in this region may disclose more valuable sites, but present views are that the range of variation is adequately represented in northern England and Avondale.

In the eastern Highlands, mixed deciduous woods appear to be few, and only three examples have been chosen, all in river gorges. The first, at Killiecrankie (W.185), occupies the rather open gorge of the River Garry, together with oakwood. The second, in Glen Tarff (W.184, gr. 1), lies in a deep, long glen on the Fort Augustus side of the Monadh-liath. The third clothes the precipitous sides of a cascading stream ravine at Keltney Burn (W.189, gr. 2) in the Breadalbane Hills.

Mixed deciduous woods are extremely widespread in the western Highlands, especially in river gorges, though they are replaced on exposed coasts of the west mainland and Hebrides by hazel scrub and in the far north by birchwood rich in herbs. Probably the best gorge wood of this type is on Inverneil Burn (W.198, gr. 1*) in Knapdale, a site also very rich in bryophytes. Other very fine gorge examples are

Allt nan Carnan (W.205, gr. 1), and Corrieshalloch W.209, gr. 1) in Ross, and Geary Ravine (W.202 gr. 1) in Skye. The Glasdrum Wood (W.193, gr. 1*) in Argyll grades from ash–hazel to more mixed wood with much oak, and the Doire Donn (W.216, gr. 2), Loch Linnhe, Loch Moidart (W.221, gr. 2), Ben Hiant (see W.190, gr. 1*) and Glendaruel Woods (W.217, gr. 2), Cowal, show some affinities to this same type, but are on less calcareous soils. The hazel scrub at Drimnin (W.192, gr. 1) in Morvern grades into taller woodland in sheltered places and is best placed in the present group; it has a rich and luxuriant field layer, an unusual feature in hill woods. Further good examples of this type of woodland probably remain to be discovered in the region, especially in river gorges, where survey is far from complete. There are numerous areas of hazel scrub on the Isle of Mull, and bonus examples are represented on the Ross of Mull (C.100) and Ardmeanach (U.95).

THE LIME FACIES

Woodlands in which lime is dominant occur in England and Wales where they are mostly confined to a broad belt from Lincolnshire, Nottinghamshire and Norfolk through the Midlands to the Welsh borderland, south Wales and parts of Gloucestershire and Somerset, with outlying concentrations in south Lakeland and the Pennines, Essex and Suffolk and north Wales, and only rare occurrences of no more than a few individuals in the south-east and southern counties. In all these areas *Tilia cordata* is the usual species and only rarely is *T. platyphyllos* present in significant quantities. *T. × europaea* occurs in small numbers in woods in which *T. cordata* is the most abundant lime, but in some woods it is the most abundant species. It is probable that many if not most occurrences of the hybrid are plantings, but the occurrence of natural hybrids is not fully understood.

The greatest concentration of almost pure limewoods is in Bardney Forest (W.45). These Lincolnshire Limewoods grow mainly on neutral or acid, poorly drained boulder clay, with some areas on Kimmeridge and Ampthill Clays or sandy gravels. Most appear to be primary woodland which has been managed as coppice-with-standards since at least the eleventh century, but many woods are now slightly larger than their minimum extent. In such expanded woods the primary woodland is often distinguished by the presence of lime and wild service tree, whilst the secondary woodland is generally dominated by ash and oak without lime. Although the general silvicultural system was pedunculate oak standards over lime coppice, there are areas where hazel, ash, maple and oak form the principal coppice species. Associated with these are numerous shrub and tree species, including Midland hawthorn, hawthorn, blackthorn, willow and holly. In some woods, exotic strains of *Ulmus* have become established.

The ground flora reflects the variation in the quantity of clay and sand in the soil. Where sand is prevalent, *Pteridium aquilinum*, *Convallaria majalis*, *Potentilla erecta*, *Corydalis claviculata*, *Succisa pratensis* and other species of well-drained soils are found. On clay soils, communities dominated by *Geum rivale* and *G. urbanum* occur, together with typical clay ground flora species such as *Primula vulgaris*, *Sanicula europaea*, *Platanthera chlorantha* and *Galeobdolon luteum*. *Mercurialis perennis* occurs in some woods, but is evidently absent from others. In areas apparently disturbed in the past, the ground flora is dominated by *Lonicera periclymenum* and *Rubus fruticosus*. The rides and the wood margins, which normally reveal a mediaeval bank and ditch, add appreciably to the floristic diversity.

The woods are noted entomologically, especially for their Lepidoptera. Marsh fritillary and purple emperor have occurred, and recent records include white admiral, comma and five fritillaries, the small pearl-bordered, pearl-bordered, dark green, high brown and silver-washed. There is a rich fauna of more common lepidopterae. Several woods or parts of woods are considered necessary to represent the full range of structural and floristic types, but survey is continuing to determine the final selection. The range of variation is provisionally covered by two aggregate samples comprising separate parts of four woods as grade 1 sites, and three more sites at grade 2. The latter enlarge the range of variation represented by the grade 1 sites, but can also be regarded as alternatives. Hatton Wood (W.45(i)(a)) is regarded as the best stand of high forest, particularly as parts are occupied by other woodland types, oak–ash and oak–hazel. Great West Wood and Stainton Wood are alternatives (W.45(ii)(a) and (b)). Newball and Hardy Gang Woods (W.45(i)(b)) are the best example of coppice, with a range of woodland types of which lime coppice is only one, and a range of soil conditions from wet clays to dry sands. It also includes a small area of coppice-with-standards. Wickenby Wood is regarded as an alternative site, but with a calcareous soil (W.45(ii)(c)). Fulnetby Wood (W.45(ii)(b)) is the best remaining stand of oak standards over lime coppice, but has a restricted flora. Stainfield and Scotgrove Woods (W.45(i)(c)) together represent the strongly acid end of the variation with poor drainage, whilst Potterhanworth Wood (W.45(i)(d)) is included as an example of the western group with species not found in the main group. Cocklode–Spring Woods (W.45(ii)(a)) is regarded as an alternative site, with features intermediate between Newball and Potterhanworth Woods.

At the other end of the main belt of limewoods, the southern Welsh borderlands, and Somerset, *Tilia* is especially characteristic of base-rich soils, where it is common as a minor constituent or dominant over small areas. Such occurrences are already represented in woods selected as characteristic of other woodland types, e.g. Salisbury Wood (W.93), Holne Chase (W.64), Avon Gorge (Leigh Woods) (W.70), Rodney Stoke (part of W.71) and Weston Big Wood (W.87). In the Wye valley area, though many of the woods are still unknown, two sites, Lady Park Wood (part of W.95) and Blackcliff–Wyndcliff–Pierce Woods (W.94), are selected. Both are floristically rich and include a number of woodland types. Lady Park is the only wood in which large-leaved lime *Tilia platyphyllos* forms an appreciable proportion of the canopy. In this area the contrasting Hudnalls (W.75) also has a good deal of lime but here it is on acidic soils. Collinpark Wood (W.74, gr. 1) is representative of sessile oak–lime woodland on poorly drained soils.

With the conversion of most of Shrawley Wood, Worcestershire, to conifers, what was the best area of oak–lime woodland in the Midlands is no longer worth including. No other comparable area of lime is known, but Habberley Valley (W.131) includes an area of large-leaved lime, and Halesend Wood (W.116) and Tick Wood (W.119) are mixed deciduous with lime one of the more abundant species. Halesend Wood is included in addition to Tick Wood partly because the lime there is *T. × europaea*.

Outside the main belt of limewoods, the species occurs as a minor constituent in woods selected mainly for other characteristics: e.g. Box Hill (L.7), Burton Wood (W.154), Coed Rheidol (W.90), Cressbrook Dale (W.115(*b*)), Felshamhall and Monks Park Woods (W.35); or as a constituent of mixed deciduous woodland, e.g. Swanton Novers Woods (W.39), Bedford Purlieus (W.43) and King's Wood (W.51).

THE HORNBEAM FACIES

Hornbeam, like beech, has been widely planted, but its native range is restricted to southern counties. Its centre of distribution as a native species is south-east England and the Home Counties, but it extends north to Norfolk and west to Monmouthshire. Through much of this range it is a minor constituent of, for example, Chiltern beechwoods some sites in the Wye valley and mixed East Anglian woods and Midlands woods such as Chaddesley. Only in a belt from south-east Norfolk through Essex to Hertfordshire and Middlesex, and thence to Surrey, Sussex and Kent is hornbeam a major constituent of the woodlands.

Typically, these woods constitute oak–hornbeam coppice-with-standards. At the centre of the distribution there is a clear separation into stands with mainly sessile oak standards and those with mainly pedunculate oak standards. Wormley Wood–Hoddesdon Park Wood (W.15, gr. 1) in Hertfordshire is considered to be the best remaining example of the former and King's Wood, Bedfordshire, is in part an alternative here. Parts of Epping Forest (W.55, gr. 2) have been selected to represent the latter. The grading of Epping Forest below Wormley Wood–Hoddesdon Park Wood is consistent with its grading as a beechwood site, and is justifiable because pedunculate oak–hornbeam woods are selected elsewhere at, for example, part of Ham Street Woods (W.2) in Kent. Sessile oak–hornbeam woodland is also included in Blean Woods (W.1, gr. 1) which is selected in addition as a representative of sweet chestnut coppice, and Ellenden Wood (W.16), an alternative to Blean. At the northern end of its native range (cf. Felbrigg Wood (W.50, gr. 2), Norfolk, for beech) and in the absence of information on the majority of possible sites, Sexton Wood (W.49, gr. 2) in Norfolk is provisionally selected.

Hornbeam occurs as one of the major constituents of a number of western Wealden sites, but Glover's Wood (W.21) is the only one selected.

THE SWEET CHESTNUT FACIES

Though it is an introduced species planted throughout most of Britain, woods of sweet chestnut have been present since the early Middle Ages, and in some areas, notably southeast England, this tree dominates a high proportion of broad-leaved woodlands. It is present as a minor constituent of many selected sites, but in view of its abundance and long period as a denizen, it is desirable to include small samples of sweet chestnut woodland. The sites selected – Wouldham–Detling (W.7), Blean Woods (W.1) and Ham Street Woods (W.2) – are all in the south-east. They have been chosen from a large number of possible sites because sweet chestnut is only one of the woodland types present and the woods as a whole are floristically rich.

Mixed deciduous woodland: ancient parks and overmature woodland

Mixed deciduous woodland varies not only in composition but also in structure. Structural variation is important in providing a range of habitats for various components of the fauna, but it is also significant floristically in that individual mature and overmature trees provide a habitat for epiphytes, and some stands give the richest occurrences of corticolous lichen communities in the country. Woodlands composed mainly of ancient, overmature trees occur throughout most of England. They are mostly survivals of mediaeval land-uses, such as deer parks and royal forests, which have persisted with little alteration in the subsequent centuries, and which may have been formed originally on the remnants of primaeval woodland. As such they are a biologically important component of deciduous woodland and are said to be better developed here than elsewhere in Europe. It is therefore considered important that a number of sites should be included in the selection.

The significance of these overmature woodlands is threefold. First, the tree species present, though undoubtedly influenced by centuries of management, may represent survivals of primaeval woodland. Secondly, the epiphytic lichen flora is usually rich, with far more species than occur in nearby plantations and secondary woodlands, ancient coppice and coppice-with-standards woodland: these lichen communities are regarded as survivals of similar communities in the primaeval woodland on the sites. Thirdly, by possessing large quantities of dead, dying and overmature timber, these woods often contain populations of local and rare wood-boring invertebrates. These too are regarded as relict populations whose survival has only been possible through continuity of habitat.

Until very recently only a few such woods had been studied in detail and even these are known only incompletely. As a result the significance of some sites is not fully appreciated and their relative importance changes as further sites are examined. In selecting sites on the basis of existing knowledge, an attempt has been made to include examples of the main combinations of tree species and sites with the richest epiflora. Furthermore, because of the biogeographical significance of the accompanying flora and fauna, sites have been selected to give a wide geographical coverage. Sites are considered here which are not strictly mixed deciduous: as a structural variant in the range of variation of British woodlands, these ancient woods do not fit easily into a species-based classification.

The south-east and south of England were richly endowed with mediaeval forests and parks, many of which survive with overmature woodland composed mainly of oak, beech, holly or some combination of these. The two sites with the richest epiflora, the New Forest (W.26) and Eridge Park (W.9), are of international importance. The former contains the typical oak–beech–holly composition, but the latter is somewhat richer in tree species, notably with field maple and ash as additions. In south-east England, Ashburnham Park (W.17, gr. 2) is mainly oak and mixed oak–beech, birch and holly. Parham Park (W.18) is included as an ancient oak woodland. In southern England two other sites in mediaeval royal forests are included, not so much as alternatives to the New Forest, but as sites of separate significance but less importance. Savernake Forest (W.31) is mainly oak, with a more continental epiflora and Windsor Forest (W.23, gr. 1) is mainly of oak and beech. Ebernoe Common (W.11), The Mens and The Cut (W.13), part of Bignor Hill (W.8, gr. 1) and Staffhurst Wood (W.19) also contain a few ancient beech and oak with a rich epiflora, but they are included mainly for other characteristics.

In East Anglia, mediaeval park woods are of particular importance biogeographically, containing in the most continental part of Britain species which are normally regarded as Atlantic in distribution. Three sites have been selected: Staverton Park (W.34) has one of the richest epifloras in East Anglia and one of the best stands of holly in Europe; Sotterley Park (W.37, gr. 1) is the richest East Anglian site for epiphytes, and is an excellent example of a mediaeval deer park; Benacre Park (W.46, gr. 2) is also rich in epiphytes and is complementary to Sotterley Park. Burnham Beeches (W.28, gr. 2) is a beech and mixed oak wood with numerous ancient trees and a rich epiflora for a site so close to London. Epping Forest (W.55) also includes some ancient oak–beech–hornbeam woodland, but its epiflora has been largely eliminated by pollution and it is in any case selected for other features.

In south-west England two ancient parks, Boconnoc (W.60, gr. 1*), Cornwall, and Melbury (W.59, gr. 1), Dorset, have been chosen for their outstanding epiphytic lichens; the trees of Boconnoc support at least 180 species, the largest number for an area of this size in western Europe.

In the west Midlands and west Gloucestershire a further concentration of ancient woodlands occurs. Three sites are selected but further research may show that this choice is inadequate. One site, Speech House (W.73(c), gr. 1), lies in the Forest of Dean: it is beech–oak–holly woodland, structurally very similar to parts of the New Forest but not as rich epiphytically. Moccas Park (W.117, gr. 1) has a rich variety of tree species and epiphyte lichens. It is similar to Brampton Bryan Park (W.124, gr. 2) which may on further examination be the better site. However, Moccas Park is

regarded as more important at this stage, because it has a greater variety of tree species and is known to be outstandingly rich faunally, while Brampton Bryan Park is virtually unexplored in this respect (see Appendix).

The epiphytic flora of the east and central Midlands is impoverished by pollution and the only known site of importance in other respects is Sherwood Forest (W.130). This is an oakwood, with the two species more or less equally abundant in a range of ages including saplings and very old individuals, and appears to be one of the few woods of any value in the area.

In northern England away from areas of high atmospheric pollution a number of mediaeval parklands have survived. The ancient woods are mainly oak, with ash, elm, yew or sycamore. Three sites have been chosen, all of which have the additional feature of floristically rich ravine or valley woodlands. Monk Wood (W.164) – part of Whitfield Park, Northumberland – has the richest epiphytes. Hesleyside Park (W.165) and Lowther Park (W.152, gr. 2) are also rich in epiphytes and extend the geographical coverage.

In Wales and Scotland these woods are both infrequent and differ less in their epiflora from other woods of younger trees. For this reason, no sites of ancient woodland have been selected in these areas.

Beechwood

Beechwoods occur in most parts of Britain, but the status of beech as a native tree has been much confused by widespread planting. Although there are good beechwoods which regenerate naturally in some northern districts, e.g. Aberdeenshire, this species is regarded as native only in the southern half of England and in south-east Wales. It is believed that the native range of beech once extended into Cornwall, north Wales and north Norfolk, and some present day occurrences in these districts may represent relict colonies. A valuable timber tree, beech has also been widely planted within its native range, and many existing beechwoods are the product of eighteenth- and nineteenth-century planting of sheep-walk. Nevertheless, many beechwoods occupy sites which have been wooded throughout historic times, although the woodland has often been modified considerably. Many were probably managed as coppice-with-standards, from which unproductive species were eliminated, but the majority have been converted to high forest, so that beech coppice is not a rare structural type.

Management has also obscured the ecological relationships of beech with other trees, especially oak, and the relationship of beechwood to other natural climax forest types in Britain is not clear; the relationship may vary according to conditions of soil and topography. For the purposes of the *Review*, some compromise in the treatment of beechwoods has been necessary, and it has been decided to select sites only from those districts where the species is likely to be native, but to choose here from the full range of variation, regardless of departures from the natural condition caused by management.

Beechwoods within the native range have been divided by

Tansley (1939) into five main types, according to under-lying soil type. These are rendzinas of softer Chalk and Jurassic limestones; shallow soils of harder limestones; slightly alkaline to acidic loams; unpodsolised sandy soils; and podsolised silts and sands. To some extent these edaphic differences correspond with the major geographical groupings of beechwoods, those of soft calcareous rocks being represented on the Chalk of the North Downs, South Downs, and Chilterns, and the Jurassic limestones of the Cotswolds; whilst those of hard limestones are exemplified by the beechwoods of the Wye valley and Brecknockshire. The middle range of beechwoods, on basic to acidic loams, occurs on the plateau soils of the Downs and Chiltern Chalk, and examples on unpodsolised sands are well represented in the Weald and the London Basin. Beech-woods on strongly podsolised sands are especially well developed on the Tertiary deposits of the New Forest and London Basin.

The choice of beechwood sites has been made with the two directions of variation in mind, and with special regard to floristic diversity associated with these edaphic and geo-graphical differences.

The beech 'hangers' at Selborne (W.27) at the western end of the South Downs, are especially good examples of scarp slope beechwoods on chalk rendzinas, and the Sel-borne site has plateau woodland in which beech is mixed with oak and ash over basic loam. Bignor Hill (W.8) is another Chalk scarp beechwood farther east on the South Downs and lies on a steep, north-facing slope, which gives it a damper aspect than the other beech hangers, with associated floristic differences. Perhaps because of their oceanic position, these South Down beechwoods contain a greater abundance of evergreen shrubs than other examples farther inland. Wouldham–Detling (W.7) has beechwood in a diverse woodland also noted for scrub. Old Winchester Hill (L.25) is another South Down site but with a rather small area of beechwood. On the North Downs, Crookhorn Wood (W.6, gr. 1) and Box Hill (L.7) have areas of beech-wood of both the scarp and plateau types.

There are many fine and large areas of beechwood in the Chiltern Hills of Oxfordshire and Buckinghamshire, ranging from the scarp woods with thin, highly calcareous soils and a sparse ground flora of calcicolous species, through plateau beechwoods on neutral Clay-with-Flints soils to mildly acidic sands on the dip slopes. This is an area where woodland conservation should not be confined to a few sites of high scientific value, but must become part of an overall management policy for the whole region. Three sites have been selected. The Bradenham Woods (W.22) represent the neutral and acidic soil types; Windsor Hill (W.30) is predominantly of the calcareous, scarp type. Aston Rowant Woods (W.29) cover both types, but have recently been modified by felling, thinning and replanting. Scarp beechwoods are represented well elsewhere, so only Bradenham Woods are graded as 1.

The south-western half of the Cotswold hills carries beech-woods, and forms one of the major areas dominated by this species on calcareous soils. They contrast strongly with the woodlands on the north-eastern half of the Cotswolds, which have been managed as mixed coppice-with-standards for many centuries, and whose affinities are towards the eastern coppice woodlands. Many of the beechwoods are undoubtedly of a secondary nature, having been planted on unprofitable sheep-walk, but some are certainly primary. The latter appear to be the woods with the richest ground flora, but this point requires further study. The dominance of beech, often to the exclusion of other species from the canopy, is a product of management. Clearings left in these woods are often filled with dense thickets of ash, a process which occurs throughout the natural range of beech in Britain. Floristically, these woods are believed to be more closely related to continental beechwoods: in particular the species *Cephalanthera rubra*, *Stachys alpina*, *Epipactis leptochila* and *Hordelymus europaeus* are very rare or re-stricted in this country but characteristic of that type of woodland on the continent.

Within this extensive and fairly uniform woodland type the selection of sites depends on minor qualitative differ-ences, mainly extent and floristics. The Cotswold Commons and Beechwoods (W.72, gr. 1) on the Jurassic limestones in Gloucestershire form an important complex, including both scarp and plateau beechwood, and containing considerable floristic diversity, in regard to composition of tree, shrub and field layers. The Birdlip–Painswick Woods are the most diverse single group, containing a rich flora and a range of structural types. They are nearly contiguous with Sheeps-combe Wood, another excellent beechwood with a wide variety of species. This is an area which, like the New Forest, Chilterns, Western Weald and elsewhere, should be considered as a whole. The beechwoods on harder lime-stones are represented by the gorge woodland of Cwm Clydach (W.88, gr. 1) in Brecknock, lying partly on Car-boniferous Limestone. Cwm Clydach is also interesting as one of the westernmost outliers of native beechwood, while the Wye beechwoods are an important component of a diverse range of woodland characteristic of this valley, where they also occur on the sandstone at Hudnalls (W.75).

The Weald of Sussex has beechwoods or mixed beech–oak woods on fairly base-rich clay loams and sands in plateau situations. The best of these woods located so far is on Ebernoe Common (W.11), where the beech is mixed with a good deal of oak. The Mens and The Cut in the same district is partly a mixed deciduous wood but has a good deal of beech, especially in the Bedham Escarpment area where there is a fine stand of beech on acidic strata. The best examples of the two beechwood types at the acidic end of the series, on non-podsolised (but acidic) and podsolised sands, are in the New Forest, and the London Basin. In the New Forest (W.26), Mark Ash and Denny Wood are among the many especially fine stands of beech, whilst Bramshaw Wood is an example of mixed beech–oak wood. A similar range of beechwoods occurs at Burnham Beeches (W.28), and Epping Forest (W.55). The New Forest woods have been preferred because they form part of the largest and most important semi-natural woodland area in southern Britain and because their epiphytic flora is much richer than in the other two areas. Epping Forest has areas with loam over heavy clay where beech is mixed with both oak and hornbeam. While all three areas contain a mixture of age classes, they all have a substantial proportion of mature and overmature timber, which creates a considerable management problem.

As a counterpart to Cwm Clydach, Felbrigg Woods (W.50) in north Norfolk is an eastern outlier at the probable native limits of beech. It has a good epiphytic lichen flora, but is so similar to the other southern beechwoods on acidic sands that it is not regarded as a grade 1 site.

Ashwood

Woodland dominated by ash represents a western and northern equivalent to beechwood, as an alternative end-point to the edaphic series beginning with pure oakwood on acidic soils and ending with a different dominant on calcareous soils. The intermediate type, mixed oak–ash wood, naturally grades imperceptibly into ashwood, and there are few ashwoods, even on the most calcareous substrata, which are without a small admixture of oak. Ashwood is a strongly oceanic forest type, better represented in Britain than in any other part of Europe, and therefore rates as an ecosystem of international importance. It is widespread but local, with a distribution determined largely by the occurrence of strongly calcareous rocks. There is considerable variation in the subsidiary elements of ashwood from south to north, but, compared with that needed for oak and mixed deciduous woods, a smaller series of sites adequately covers this range of diversity.

Climax ashwood occurs chiefly on the Carboniferous Limestone formation and has four main distribution centres, on the Mendips of Somerset; around the edges of the south Wales coalfield, in Glamorgan and Brecknock; in the Derbyshire Dales; and in the Craven and northern Pennines of Yorkshire and Westmorland.

In the Mendips (W.71, gr. 1) a group of three sites is regarded as necessary to represent variation at the southern limits of climax ashwood. Rodney Stoke is an example of the drier facies on mainly south-facing slopes, Ebbor Gorge includes the damp gorge facies, and Asham Wood represents the plateau type. These Mendip ashwoods have a well-developed, species-rich, calcicolous shrub layer containing most of the species characteristic of southern England, and there is a rich ungrazed field layer containing a number of thermophilous southern forbs. The Chalk of southern England has a number of ashwoods which may be a climax type, but here the relationships between ash and beech are not clear. Mostly these chalk ashwoods do not differ sufficiently from the limestone ashwoods, or from the oak–ash woods on Chalk, to have strong claims for inclusion in the national series, but the example at Wye and Crundale Downs (L.3) is regarded as a bonus and ashwood is well represented in the Wouldham–Detling Escarpment complex (W.7). Ashwood on Jurassic limestone is also well represented in the naturally regenerated woodland complex on the Axmouth–Lyme Regis Undercliffs (W.67, gr. 1), and

there is a bonus example in the Cotswold Commons and Beechwoods. Chippenham Fen (P.13) in Cambridgeshire also has enough ash to be regarded as a bonus site for this type of wood, and this species is locally abundant in the southern England woods of Blean, Bignor Hill, Chiddingly and Wakehurst and Fairlight Glen.

The Carboniferous Limestone in south Wales has only limited areas of ashwood and only two sites are regarded as nationally important. The small wood of Penmoelallt (W.89, gr. 1) in south Brecknock is unique for its populations of endemic or rare *Sorbus* spp., while Darren Fach (W.99) on the opposite side of the same valley is a grade 2 example. However, Craig y Rhiwarth has a good area of bonus ashwood within the open water grade 1* site of Ogof Ffynnon Ddu (OW.27), and the coast scrub woodland of Tor Gro on the Gower limestone is also worth including in this category (see C.42). In north Wales, Coed Tremadog (W.105) has stands of ash at the foot of cliffs.

The Derbyshire Dales (W.115, gr. 1*) contain probably the largest stands of ashwood in Great Britain. These deep, steep-sided limestone valleys have complexes of calcicolous grassland, scrub and woodland which evidently represent seral stages leading to the climax, and have to be considered as composite ecological units. Dove Dale has probably the finest example of ashwood in the district, from the structural point of view, with an uneven aged population of the dominant ash and a well-developed shrub layer rich in species, including both southern and northern elements; the opposed slopes give west- and east-facing aspects. Lathkill Dale has especially fine field communities rich in woodland forbs which show no sign of past disturbance by grazing, and the opposed slopes here give south- and north-facing aspects. The woods of Cressbrook Dale (W.115(*b*)) and Monks Dale (L.124(i)(*d*)) are on their own not as important as the two previous sites, but are each an integral part of limestone complexes regarded as having first national importance. They both show differences in representation of shrubs and herbs compared with Dove Dale and Lathkill Dale, and both have good examples of seral limestone scrub.

At least one of these sites should include plateau land with base-poor soils, on which acidophilous woodland could be re-established, to show the relationships between contrasting woodland types according to topographic and edaphic conditions. The bryophytes of ashwood are especially well represented in these Derbyshire Dales woods, but most of the less common species belong to the exposed rock habitats within the woods, though a few are corticolous. On the whole, ashwoods are, from the calcareous nature of the habitat, poor in Atlantic bryophytes, even when they lie close to the west coast. The ashwoods of the Hamps and Manifold Valleys in Staffordshire (W.123, gr. 2) are generally similar to the Derbyshire Dale ashwoods but exhibit unusual features in the presence of abundant holly and of well-grown trees of both species of oak.

The remaining ashwoods of the Craven and northern Pennines are mostly small, and, as they are nearly all situated on the lower slopes of hills, tend to be grazed by sheep. A small group of the Craven ashwoods, each in a different topographic situation, has been chosen to exemplify the range of northern ashwood, with a subalpine element in the field layer of the Ribblehead Woods (W.142, gr. 1). Colt Park Wood on the lower slopes of Ingleborough, represents the best example of ashwood on limestone pavement, while the nearby Ling Gill on one of the headstreams of the Ribble, is a limestone gorge ashwood. Both lie at just over 300 m and have field communities which owe their richness and luxuriance to the protection from grazing conferred by the peculiar topographic features. In Wharfedale, part of Bastow Wood (W.143, gr. 1) is regarded as nationally important for its field communities which contain a different blend of rare species from the previous sites, and lie in a different topographic situation, namely exposed scar and scree. The wood itself requires restoration and the herbaceous field layer needs protection against the increasing sheep grazing. In Littondale, Hawkswick Wood (W.155, gr. 2) and Scoska Wood (W.156, gr. 2) are similar to Bastow Wood, but are regarded as less important floristically and are also subject to moderate grazing. Several other ashwoods in Wharfedale and Littondale were once of high quality but have deteriorated during the last 20 years through heavy grazing. In the same middle section of the Pennines, two other river glen ashwoods of good quality are represented at Thornton and Twisleton Glens (W.157), Ingleton, and at Kisdon Force Woods (W.161) in Swaledale, but neither is considered to be sufficiently different from other ashwoods of this type to rate higher than grade 2.

On the limestone exposures around the head of Morecambe Bay, much of the remaining woodland is of the mixed deciduous type. Eaves Wood (W.153) near Silverdale is much modified by management and planting, but is important floristically for its field layers. Hutton Roof Crag wood (L.135) to the east has a grazed ashwood which may be regarded as a bonus to this important pavement site. The Roudsea (W.139) and Whitbarrow and Witherslack Woods (W.136) are mainly oak–ash, but contain patches of ashwood alone, and in the Lake District, the Seatoller Woods (W.133(g)) show alternation between ash–hazel and sessile oak as the rock varies between calcareous and non-calcareous beds of the Borrowdale Volcanic Series.

In the northern Pennines, above Brough, is the fine hill ashwood complex of Helbeck and Swindale Woods (W.138, gr. 1*). The Helbeck section lies on the Pennine scarp slope facing the Eden valley, while the Swindale portion occupies a deep glen with high cliffs in places. These woods have ungrazed areas and here show finely developed herbaceous field communities. In places the upper edge of the wood, which reaches 360 m, is fringed with rather open birch–hawthorn growths. Situated about 160 km north of the Derbyshire Dales ashwoods, these Brough woods are of high quality; they are particularly valuable as the best woodland component of the outstandingly important upland area which includes Upper Teesdale. A few kilometres west of Kirkby Stephen, the deep wooded glen of Smardale (W.151, gr. 2) provides an alternative though less varied and floristically rich ashwood site characteristic of northern England. The grassland complex of Crosby Gill (L.140)

near Shap also contains an interesting small fragment of herb-rich ashwood in a rocky valley. In east Yorkshire, stands of ash are represented in some of the mixed deciduous woods, e.g. Raincliffe Wood (W.144), and extend the diversity.

In southern Scotland, mixed deciduous woods on basic soils of the Ordovician and Silurian Series of rocks often show local dominance of ash, and a good example is represented at Chanlock Foot (W.172) on a tributary of the River Nith. Despite the extensive occurrence of mixed deciduous oak–ash wood on basic soils in Scotland, ash-dominated wood is rare and very fragmentary. Patches occur in many mixed woods in both the Southern Uplands and Highlands, but are seldom continuous over more than half a hectare. One of the best examples of Highland ashwoods occurs at the head of Loch Creran on the west coast of Argyll, not far north of Oban. This Glasdrum Wood (W.193, gr. 1*) lies on a south-east-facing slope of calcareous Dalradian schists and consists of an ash–hazel zone grading into alderwood below and oakwood above, as soil conditions change. It is lightly grazed and has well-developed field communities which show a considerable resemblance to those of more southerly regions, whereas the shrub layer lacks the species variety of that in southern ashwoods. There is a rich Atlantic flora of bryophytes and lichens, though this is more strongly represented in the upper oakwood zone. Above the village of Glencoe, on the north-facing side of the same massif, the corresponding woodland on a rather steeper calcareous schist slope has an unusual ash–alder mixture. This Carnach Wood (W.191, gr. 1) appears to owe its existence to the combination of moisture-retaining clay soils on a north aspect and an extremely heavy rainfall, which give conditions suitable for the growth of alder in an unusually steep situation.

The most northerly ashwood of any size in Britain is at Rassal (W.208, gr. 1), at the head of Loch Kishorn in west Ross, and lies on an outcrop of the dolomitic Durness Limestone. This wood had become a rather open stand of ash, with virtually no shrubs, on an area with fragmentary exposures of limestone pavement, but covered mainly with a heavily grazed grassland. Fencing has allowed both regeneration of the ash and vigorous growth of the field layer into a tall grass–forb community in which bryophytes are much reduced. Rassal ashwood is interesting as an example of woodland near its climatic limit. Fragmentary ashwood also occurs on outcrops of Durness Limestone on Skye and the species is represented at the north end of Tokavaig Wood (W.201, gr. 1*) and also in Coille Ardura (W.212), Mull.

Pinewood

Woods of truly native Scots pine are generally thought to occur only in the Scottish Highlands. It is, however, quite possible that some woods or more open growths of pine on lowland acidic mires or even heaths farther south could be fragmented remnants of a native population. Pine growths of this kind are well represented on Kirkconnell Flow

(W.168, gr. 1), Kirkcudbrightshire, which is also a key mire site; Wedholme Flow (P.62), Moorthwaite Moss (P.56), and Cumwhitton Moss (P.57), Cumberland; Cliburn Moss (P.66), Westmorland; Chartley Moss (P.42) and Cranberry Bog (P.45), Staffordshire; Llyn (P.33), Radnor; Cranesmoor (P.3(a)), New Forest, Hampshire; and Morden Bog (P.27), Dorset. Some of these pine areas are likely to be plantations, for this is a very widely planted tree in Britain. It regenerates well under favourable conditions and some pinewoods south of the Highlands are evidently sub-spontaneous (self-regenerated), e.g. at Orton Moss (W.135) in Cumberland where pinewood is one component of a mixed woodland complex on former raised mire. Pine rows, clumps and hedges form a characteristic habitat in the Breckland, and are represented on many of the sites selected in that important district.

The pinewoods of the Highlands represent a southern and western outlier of the boreal coniferous forest of northern Europe, and in this region Scots pine replaces oak to a large extent. The most extensive pine forests are in the more central parts of the Highlands, where they occupy the poorer, more base-deficient soils. On the north side of the Cairngorms, draining to the Spey Valley, pine forest covers the lower slopes and flats of granitic drift soils at 210–610 m in a discontinuous belt extending from Glen Feshie to Nethy Bridge in Inverness-shire. The main segments are the Invereshie, Inshriach and Rothiemurchus Forest (W.187(d)) and Abernethy Forest (W.187(e)). That within the Glen Feshie sector of the Cairngorms NNR is best regarded as a bonus. The woods of Invereshie and Inshriach consist mainly of hanging pinewoods on steep slopes, and include the important example, at 640 m on Creag Fhiachlach, of the natural upper limit to woodland which now hardly occurs elsewhere in Britain. Much of the Rothiemurchus area lies on gently sloping ground, and here the trees attain a larger size in places. Abernethy Forest is the largest continuous block of pinewood on Speyside, and lies mainly on level or gently sloping ground, and so has a good deal of peatland, including an interesting complex of valley and basin mires.

On Deeside in Aberdeenshire there are pinewoods in the glens on the south side of the Cairngorms, such as Glens Quoich, Lui and Derry (W.187(c)) but the more important forests lie south of the Dee. There are two main areas, the Ballochbuie Forest (W.187(a)) near Braemar and Glen Tanar (W.187(b)) near Aboyne. Crathie Wood (W.181, gr. 1) on the north side of the Dee is a mixed wood of pine, birch and juniper on richer soils than most pinewoods.

These Speyside and Deeside pinewoods (W.187, gr. 1*) are all of high conservation value, principally because of their large size, for they are the largest continuous areas of semi-natural woodland remaining in Britain. Each differs from the others in some respects, such as age class distribution and form of the trees, but all show a general similarity in field communities and flora. There are a few faunal differences, such as the abundance of the crested tit in some of the Speyside woods and their absence from Deeside. On the whole, however, it is difficult to choose between these

woods and they are all regarded as grade 1 in quality. Some of these woods, notably Abernethy, Ballochbuie and Glen Tanar, are so large that their management for commercial timber production need not necessarily detract in any appreciable way from their value as conservation areas – provided that cutting is on a rotational basis, that the total area under trees is maintained, and the native Scots pine is kept as the dominant tree. It would be desirable to preserve some of the remaining stands of really old trees, such as those in Glen Quoich, but for the rest there is every reason from a conservation viewpoint to have a wide distribution of age classes within a forest.

Although there are woods of Scots pine at Crannach (W.215, gr. 2) overlooking Rannoch Moor in Argyll, and at Cononish, near Tyndrum in Perthshire, the only large and important pinewood in the southern part of the Highlands is the Black Wood of Rannoch (W.186), overlooking Loch Rannoch, Perthshire, from the south side. The Black Wood also has areas of birch and there is oak on the opposite side of the lake, so that climatically this locality may be close to the natural limits of Scots pine. The large extent, southern position and entomological interest justify grade 1 status for the site.

North of the Great Glen, on the sides of the glens which feed the Beauly River in eastern Inverness-shire, is the second area of extensive pinewoods in the Highlands: Glens Guisachan, Affric (W.204, gr. 1), Cannich and Strathfarrar (W.203, gr. 1). These woods are mostly on slopes of moderate steepness and lie in an area of rather more oceanic climate than the forests of the Spey–Dee Valleys. A negative feature here is the general absence of natural regeneration of pine, perhaps due to heavy grazing by red deer. Much of this pine woodland has been affected recently by felling, and the best remaining area is that of Glen Strathfarrar, which is therefore proposed as the representative grade 1 site for this district, but also has a good deal of birchwood.

On the eastern side of the northern Highlands, the most northerly pinewood of relatively natural appearance is that at Amat Wood (W.224, gr. 2) in Strath Carron, east Ross, though there are more obviously planted pinewoods around Bonar Bridge and Rosehall in east Sutherland, such as the Migdale Woods (W.228, gr. 2) at Spinningdale. Much of the Amat pinewood has been felled and birchwood is now the more extensive type there. Farther south, in the Black Isle, the grade 1 peatland site of Monadh Mor has bonus pinewoods. In west Ross there are important western outliers of pinewood at Loch Maree (W.206) both on its larger islands and on the southern shore, on the lower slopes of Beinn Eighe. These Loch Maree pinewoods occur in a region of strongly oceanic climate, with a very heavy rainfall, and the associated communities, especially of bryophytes, have a strongly hygrophilous character. Natural regeneration is limited in these woods, evidently by a combination of deer-grazing and unfavourable soil conditions related to the humid climate. The Loch Maree woods are regarded as the best example of north-western pinewood. There are less extensive pinewoods in Coulin Forest and Shieldaig (see Appendix) (W.222, gr. 2) south of Loch Maree, and the most northerly example on the west side of the country is at Rhidorroch to the east of Ullapool. The mixed woods on the islands of Loch Morar (W.200, gr. 1) contain small stands of pine.

Some of the western pinewoods show interesting relationships with other woodland types. At Loch Maree, south-facing slopes around Letterewe are occupied mainly by oakwood, except on the shallow soil of precipitous slopes, and pine occurs on north-east aspects or more level ground where there is a layer of peat. In the Beinn Eighe wood, pine gives way to birch on an area of richer soil receiving drainage from calcareous mudstones. A zonation of birch above pine may be a natural altitudinal sequence in Crannach Wood, but the reverse order obtains at Rhidorroch, where it is evidently related to the change in soil conditions according to slope and altitude.

Birchwood

Birch is represented in a large number of woodland key sites scattered widely over Britain, and as a bonus within sites chosen for other formations. Acidic heathland in the lowlands is often subseral to birchwood and some sites show a marked tendency to change from the one to the other; sites selected for their heathland, but containing colonising birch in quantity, include Thursley and Hankley Commons, Surrey; New Forest, Hampshire; Tuddenham and Cavenham Heaths and Dunwich Heaths and Marshes, Suffolk; Skipwith Common, Yorkshire; and the Moor of Dinnet, Aberdeenshire. Birch, mainly *Betula pubescens*, also colonises lowland acidic mires, where the peat is drying around the edges, as on Dersingham Bog, Norfolk; Rhos Goch, Radnor; Glasson Moss, Bowness Common, and Wedholme Flow, Cumberland; and Kirkconnell Flow, Kirkcudbrightshire. In Orton Moss (W.135), Cumberland, a former peat mire is almost entirely covered by woodland in which birchwood is an important component in its own right; while at Holme Fen (W.41), Huntingdon, a raised mire developed over fen is covered by an almost pure wood of tall birch of both species regarded as grade 1. The mixed dune woods at Earlshall Muir (W.188, gr. 2) in Fife contain a good deal of both birch and alder. The ancient oakwoods of Sherwood Forest (W.130), Nottinghamshire, also contain some birch.

In the above localities, birch is itself probably a seral type which would in theory eventually be replaced by oak, or perhaps Scots pine in a few localities. In practice, however, further change would be unlikely until the birchwood began to die out from old age and, in some sites, parent oak is so scarce in the immediate area that it is not easy to envisage its spread onto the birchwood site. In some situations, poorly drained ground supports birch, but remains too wet to carry oak, e.g. in Johnny's Wood (W.133(*f*)), Cumberland. Besides these there are woodlands in which birch has become locally dominant, evidently as a seral stage, following thinning or more general removal of the dominant oak. This would seem to account for the abundance or local dominance of birch in Coed Camlyn–Ceunant Llennyrch and Coed y Rhygen (W.107(*a*)), Merioneth; Lodore–Troutdale

Woods (W.133(*d*)) and Scales Wood (W.146), Cumberland; Naddle Low Forest (W.149), Westmorland; Inverneil Burn (W.198), Mealdarroch Point–Skipness (W.197) and Glen Nant Woods (W.194, gr. 1) in Argyll. On Birk Fell (W.137, gr. 1), Westmorland, birch may have replaced oak, but much of the hillside is now covered with juniper and the relationships between these three species in the original woodland of the site are not clear. Co-dominance of birch and oak is also found in places, e.g. Roeburndale Woods (W.141), Lancashire, and here too relationships between these trees are sometimes obscure. There are in addition a large number of woods in which birch occurs as an abundant component tree, with a fairly stable (or at least 'steady state') role in the woodland ecosystem, but without ever becoming dominant. This is particularly true of mixed deciduous woods in northern and western Britain. Birchwood is sometimes a distinctive subsidiary component in hill ashwoods, such as the Helbeck and Swindale Woods (W.138), Westmorland. There are in fact few key woodlands from which birch is entirely absent.

In southern Scotland, birchwood is represented in the oakwoods of Wood of Cree (W.177) and the gorge woodland of Avondale (W.170).

Most of the key sites chosen as examples of birchwood lie in those parts of the Scottish Highlands where this type is likely to be a climax woodland. The selection is made to represent the main directions of variation in climate and soil type found within these largely upland (subalpine) birchwoods. The most southerly example of subalpine birchwood, possibly the remnant of a once more extensive climax forest of the same type, is the small wood at High Force in the Upper Teesdale upland grade 1* site in Yorkshire and Durham. This fragment is notable for its tall herb communities containing several northern species. Probably the finest example of subalpine birchwood in Britain is that on Morrone (W.182, gr. 1), Braemar, at 380–610 m, where a rather small juniper forms both an understorey beneath the birch and areas of treeless scrub. The site has calcareous soils and there is a range of subalpine grassland, marsh and flushes; the whole complex has strong Scandinavian affinities.

Also on Deeside, Crathie Wood (W.181) is a mixed birch, pine and juniper wood, again on rich soils, but the altitude is lower (270–400 m) and both birch and juniper are of larger growth form than in Morrone Wood. This wood has a diverse composition and age structure, whereas the rather similarly situated Craigellachie Wood part of the Aviemore birchwood complex (W.183, gr. 1) in the Spey Valley, is a mature, fairly even-aged birchwood, evidently representing the climax forest type on the more fertile soils in this district. Craigellachie is especially interesting for its rich insect fauna. The Torr Alvie birch woodlands of Kinrara contain areas of Scots pine and of oak (planted) with juniper occurring extensively as an understorey. The field layer is generally acidophilous but with a more pronounced basiphilous element on the north and east slopes. The fairly central area of the Highlands around Laggan and Loch Ness has a good deal of birchwood at still lower levels. The deep valley of Glen Tarff (W.184) draining from the Monadhliath to Fort Augustus is an example of a centrally situated birchwood but also contains a good deal of oak, ash and hazel, and is perhaps better regarded as a mixed deciduous woodland on fairly rich soils. Observations at this site would throw light on seral and climatic relationships of different woodland types in this area. There are also extensive pinewoods in the Beauly–Garve area, for example at Strathfarrar (W.203).

Both the southern-central Black Wood of Rannoch (W.186), and the north-western Loch Maree Woods (W.206) have been selected chiefly because of their pinewoods, but contain also areas of dominant birch on better soils. There is an even larger stand of birch at Shieldaig (W.222), also in west Ross, and at Amat Wood (W.224), east Ross, birchwood is now more extensive than pinewood. The birchwood components of woodlands selected on other grounds have a high bonus value and are interesting additions to the series of Highland climax birchwoods. In Taynish Wood (W.196), Knapdale, birchwood occupies the upper slopes and ridge tops instead of the oak and mixed deciduous wood prevailing below, and may here represent an edaphic climax. In the western Highlands, a final series has been chosen from south to north to represent the Atlantic facies of birchwood. North of Ullapool in west Ross, this is, in fact the only type of wood represented, discounting hazel and willow scrub, and it represents the closest approximation in Britain to the 'taiga' of the Arctic.

On the south side of Loch Sunart the steep, rocky and gully seamed hillsides around Laudale have birchwoods and are especially rich in oceanic bryophytes and lichens; this is the shade facies of this flora which is mentioned under the south-facing Salen–Strontian and Ariundle woods as being of great international importance (see W.190(a), (b), gr. 1*).

In the south-west, patches of birchwood on granite block scree on the lower slopes of Meall nan Gobhar (W.195, gr. 1), Argyll, may represent another kind of edaphic climax, in which the ground is too rocky and the soils too immature to support oak. These woods have extremely luxuriant growths of Atlantic bryophytes and ferns. Eighty km north-north-west, on the southern Sleat peninsula of Skye, Tokavaig Wood (W.201) represents another mixed wood mainly of birch, but also with some oak, which is evidently close to its climatic limits. This site is partly on limestone, and there is some ash, but perhaps the most notable feature is the rich Atlantic bryophyte flora, which contains several very rare species and rivals Coed Ganllwyd in Merioneth in this respect. The woods of Loch na Dal (W.220, gr. 2), also in Sleat, are similar to Tokavaig Wood, but rather less rich floristically and certainly a second choice. The rocky birchwoods at Kinuachdrach (W.218), Jura, are chosen mainly for their wealth of Atlantic bryophytes and ferns, and represent an alternative site to the oak–birch woods of Mealdarroch Point–Skipness.

On the Inverpolly NNR in west Ross close to the Sutherland border, the area of Lewisian Gneiss and Torridon Sandstone chosen mainly for its upland ecosystem complex, has several birchwoods, which can be regarded collectively as a grade 1 woodland site (W.207). They occur on a range of aspects and soil types and represent the typical climax birchwoods of the far north-west Highlands. Inverpolly includes the island birchwoods of Loch Sionascaig. Ardvar Woodlands (W.229), Sutherland, are included as a grade 2 alternative site. Other examples of mixed scrub woodland with birch (and also rowan) in the north-west are on the Fionn Loch Islands (W.223, gr. 2) in west Ross, and Eilean na Gartaig (W.225, gr. 2) near Elphin, Sutherland. There are other good areas of birchwood farther north; at Loch a' Mhuillin (W.226, gr. 2) near Scourie, on Ben Hope, Ben Loyal, the Kyle of Tongue, above Loch Naver, and south of Bettyhill. The most unusual of these is a wood in which rowan is co-dominant with birch on steep block scree in Strathbeag (W.211, gr. 1*) at the head of Loch Eriboll. The aspect is north-west so that the bryophyte flora is rich and luxuriant, and the wood has a generally undisturbed appearance.

Birchwoods occur widely in east Sutherland, but none is considered sufficiently important or different from the western examples to warrant national status. Compared with western birchwoods there are fewer Atlantic bryophytes, but no parallel gain in other plants.

Alderwood

Although alder itself is extremely widespread and represented in a great many key sites all over the country, woodland dominated by this species over a large area is rather rare, and the majority of alder stands are small or contain a mixture of other tree species. The best and most extensive alderwoods in Britain are probably the hydroseral carr woodlands developed from fen vegetation in the Norfolk Broads. The Bure Marshes (W.38, gr. 1) contain good and representative examples of alder–willow carr with well-developed field communities rich in hydrophilous species, and showing transitions to sedge swamp and open water. Chippenham Fen (P.13), Cambridgeshire, and Cothill Fen (P.4), Berkshire, have examples of similar alderwood as bonus elements in complexes important primarily for their mires, and the species is well-represented in carr associated with the richer lowland mires scattered widely over Britain. The estuarine transition from salt marsh to alderwood occurs on the Fal Estuary (W.61) in Cornwall, but by far the largest estuarine alderwood (with willows) yet found is on former tidal lands behind an artificial sea embankment at the Mound (W.210, gr. 1), on the east coast of Sutherland.

Alderwood is represented in many places as the basal part of catenas on hill slopes with other woodland types, but often forms a fairly narrow strip. The best examples of this kind are Coed y Cerrig (W.92), Monmouthshire; Carn Gafallt (W.97), Brecknockshire; Coedydd Aber (W.104), Caernarvonshire; Lodore–Troutdale, Great Wood and The Ings (see W.133) and Lyne Woods (W.147), Cumberland; Naddle Low Forest (W.149), Westmorland; Wood of Cree (W.177) and Ravenshall Woods (W.179), Kirkcudbrightshire; and Glasdrum Wood (W.193), Argyll. Alderwood on springlines is represented in Colyers Hanger (W.20),

Surrey, and in various parts of the New Forest, and examples in waterlogged hollows occur in Roudsea Wood (W.139), Lancashire, and at Earlshall Muir (W.188), Fifeshire.

Alder is also locally abundant in damper places in various situations within a variety of oak and mixed deciduous woodlands, spread widely over Britain, e.g. Scords Wood (W.4), Chiddingly Wood (W.12) and Wormley Wood–Hoddesdon Park Wood (W.15) in south-eastern England; Swanton Novers (W.39), Felshamhall and Monks Park (W.35) and Foxley Wood (W.47) in East Anglia; the Bovey Valley Woods (W.63) in Devon; Cwm Sere (see U.4) in Brecknock; Cannock Chase (W.122) in Staffordshire; Raincliffe (W.144) and Ashberry and Reins Woods (W.158) in east Yorkshire; and Claggain–Ardmore (W.214) on Islay.

Alderwood occurs in many places as a fringing growth along river and lake banks, but a more extensive stand occurs on the alluvium of a river delta at Urquhart Bay (W.199, gr. 1), Loch Ness. An extensive stand on flushed silty material occurs at Dobbins Wood, part of the Gowbarrow Park (W.148) site. On the uplands of the north, wet clayey soils and river alluvium often have patches or fringes of alderwood, but these are usually grazed heavily and show little or no regeneration. This hill alderwood is especially characteristic of the Borders of England and Scotland, and one of the most extensive examples is at Billsmoor Park (W.166, gr. 2) in Northumberland; there is a smaller example within the Harbottle Moors upland site (U.30). Two unusual mixed alderwoods, of high value in themselves, are Coed Gorswen (W.103(b)), Caernarvonshire, an oak–alder wood on rather wet drift soils; and Carnach Wood (W.191), Glencoe, Argyll, a hanging ash–alder wood on steep slopes of calcareous schist in a heavy rainfall district. A fairly high-level example of alderwood occurs in part of Coed Dolgarrog (W.103(a)) in Caernarvonshire.

This short series of selected alderwood sites is considered adequate in the light of present knowledge, but as this woodland type is so widespread yet local, it is possible that future survey may reveal still better examples which should take precedence over known sites.

Other types of wood

Under this heading are considered an assortment of woods which do not fall neatly into any of the preceding categories. They consist of woods with unusual tree dominants and those whose distinctive features result from unusual physiographic settings.

HOLLY WOOD

As an undershrub, holly is a widespread species occurring in abundance in many key woodland sites, but is unusual as a dominant in its own right. Staverton Park (W.34), Suffolk, contains one of the finest stands of holly in Europe, with trees of remarkable stature, but probably the best areas of holly wood in Britain are in the New Forest. Another interesting area with abundance of this species and actually known as The Hollies may be regarded as a bonus within the acidic heathland site of the Stiperstones (L.123) in Shropshire. An open growth of holly on shingle at Dungeness (C.3) is also regarded as a bonus, though it is arguable whether this can properly be termed a wood. A very different kind of holly scrub is represented on the Fionn Loch Islands (W.223) in west Ross.

YEW WOOD

Yew has two main centres of distribution as a native tree in Britain: on the Chalk of southern England and both Carboniferous Limestone and relatively non-calcareous rocks (both igneous and sedimentary) in northern England. In southern England, patches of yew wood are represented on various Chalk sites such as Old Winchester Hill (L.25), but the finest yew wood in this region is the famous example at Kingley Vale (W.10, gr. 1*). In northern England, yew is well-represented in the ash and mixed deciduous woods on limestone, such as Roudsea Wood and the Whitbarrow and Witherslack Woods, and is abundant in patchy mixed scrub on the limestone pavements of Gait Barrows and Hutton Roof Crag (L.135). In Scotland, native stands of yew are scarce, but there is a long established example on Inchlonaig, one of the Loch Lomond islands (W.169(f)).

JUNIPER WOOD

Juniper has a distribution showing some parallel to that of yew in Britain. It is widespread on the Chalk of southern England and the Carboniferous Limestone of northern England, but in the uplands of north Wales, northern England and Scotland it is widespread on a wide variety of rocks which give acidic soils. The chalk juniper is often a constituent of mixed scrubs and, as a convenience, this type has been described in Chapter 6, section C, while the northern types are dealt with here.

Juniper is represented again in several northern key sites. It occurs in the patchy scrub on the pavements of Gait Barrows, and Hutton Roof Crag, but by far the most extensive and luxuriant juniper scrubs in the north are on relatively base poor soils. The Lake District has many good examples, but the most extensive is on Birk Fell (W.137, gr. 1) above Ullswater, where it grades below into birchwood. Another fine stand is situated around High Force in Upper Teesdale and there contains an abundance of the rare shrub *Potentilla fruticosa* and is in part on fairly basic alluvial soils. Tynron Wood (W.167) is a very striking but completely isolated juniper wood in southern Scotland and, though probably planted, is of considerable interest and rated grade 1.

Juniper is widespread in the eastern Highlands and a characteristic though patchy shrub layer species of many pinewoods. Special mention may be made of Crathie Wood (W.181) on Deeside, where juniper is locally dominant in a mixed wood with birch and pine; and Morrone (W.182), higher up the Dee, at Braemar, where a more montane birchwood has a dense shrub layer of a smaller juniper. The Morrone Wood is especially interesting for its rich flora (on calcareous schist), and as a type intermediate between lowland juniper scrub and the true montane type of the north-west Highlands dominated by ssp. *nana*.

BOX WOOD

There are a very few woods in southern England with local dominance of box as a native species. Three examples have been rated as key sites. The finest is at Ellesborough Warren, others are at Box Hill, where the box forms a scrub with holly and yew under a canopy of beech or beech–oak on Chalk, and Boxwell in Gloucestershire where there is a dense box scrub with only open woodland on Oolitic limestone. These sites are described in Chapter 6.

RARE SPECIES

Included under this heading is the ravine wood of Glen Diomhan (W.171), Arran, Bute, rated as grade 1 for its two endemic *Sorbus* spp., *S. arranensis* and *S. pseudofennica*, which form an open tree growth along the sides of this granite and schistose glen, and are associated also with rowan, birch, holly and aspen.

Table 10. INDEX OF WOODLAND SITES

* Internationally important sites.

Woodland type (cols. 1, 2 oak; 3–6 mixed deciduous)

Region		Site	County	Western 1	Eastern 2	Central type 3	Lime facies 4	Hornbeam facies 5	Sweet chestnut facies 6	Ancient parks 7	Beech 8	Ash 9	Pine 10	Birch 11	Alder 12	Other 13
South-east England																
GRADE 1	W.1	BLEAN WOODS	KENT	—	a	a	—	A	A	—	—	a	—	—	—	—
	W.2	HAM STREET WOODS	KENT	—	A	—	—	A	A	—	—	a	—	—	—	—
	W.3	ALKHAM VALLEY WOODS	KENT	—	—	A	—	—	—	—	—	—	—	—	a	—
	W.4	SCORDS WOOD	KENT	—	A	A	—	—	—	—	—	—	—	—	—	—
	W.5	ASHOLT WOOD	KENT	—	—	A	—	a	—	—	A	—	—	—	a	—
	W.6	CROOKHORN WOOD	KENT	—	a	—	—	—	A	A	A	a	—	—	—	—
	W.7	WOULDHAM–DETLING ESCARPMENT	KENT	—	a	—	—	—	—	A	A	a	—	—	—	—
	W.8	BIGNOR HILL	SUSSEX	—	—	—	—	—	—	—	a	a	—	—	—	—
GRADE 1*	W.9	SAXONBURY HILL/ERIDGE PARK	SUSSEX	—	A	—	—	—	a	A	a	a	—	a	a	A
*	W.10	KINGLEY VALE	SUSSEX	—	—	—	—	—	—	—	A	—	—	—	—	—
GRADE 1	W.11	EBERNOE COMMON	SUSSEX	—	—	A	—	—	—	—	—	a	—	—	a	—
	W.12	WAKEHURST & CHIDDINGLY WOODS	SUSSEX	—	A	A	—	—	—	—	—	—	—	—	—	—
	W.13	THE MENS & THE CUT & BEDHAM ESCARPMENT	SUSSEX	—	A	—	—	—	—	—	A	—	—	—	—	—
	W.14	FAIRLIGHT, ECCLESBOURNE & WARREN GLENS	SUSSEX	—	—	A	—	—	—	—	—	a	—	—	a	—
	W.15	WORMLEY WOOD–HODDESDON PARK WOOD	HERTFORDSHIRE	—	—	—	—	A	—	—	—	a	—	—	—	—
Grade 2	W.16	Ellenden Wood	Kent	—	A	A	—	A	—	—	—	—	—	—	—	—
	W.17	Ashburnham Park	Sussex	—	—	a	—	—	—	A	—	—	—	—	—	—
	W.18	Parham Park	Sussex	—	—	—	—	—	—	A	—	—	—	—	—	—
	W.19	Staffhurst Wood	Surrey	—	—	A	—	—	—	—	—	—	—	—	—	—
	W.20	Colyers Hanger	Surrey	—	a	a	—	—	—	—	—	—	—	—	—	—
	W.21	Glover's Wood	Surrey	—	—	A	—	A	—	—	—	—	—	—	A	—
South England																
GRADE 1	W.22	BRADENHAM WOODS	BUCKINGHAMSHIRE	—	—	A	—	—	—	—	A	—	—	—	—	—
	W.23	WINDSOR FOREST	BERKSHIRE	—	A	A	—	—	—	A	A	—	—	—	—	—
	W.24	WYCHWOOD FOREST[a]	OXFORDSHIRE	—	A	A	—	—	—	—	A	a	A	A	A	A
	W.25	WATERPERRY WOOD	OXFORDSHIRE	—	A	—	—	—	—	A	A	—	A	A	A	A
GRADE 1*	W.26	NEW FOREST	HAMPSHIRE	—	—	a	—	—	—	A	A	—	A	A	A	—
GRADE 1	W.27	SELBORNE HANGER	HAMPSHIRE	—	—	—	—	—	—	A	A	—	A	A	A	—
Grade 2	W.28	Burnham Beeches	Buckinghamshire	—	a	—	—	—	—	A	A	a	—	A	A	—
	W.29	Aston Rowant Woods	Buckinghamshire/Oxfordshire	—	—	—	—	—	—	—	A	—	—	—	—	—
	W.30	Windsor Hill	Buckinghamshire	—	—	—	—	—	—	A	—	—	—	—	—	—
	W.31	Savernake Forest	Wiltshire	—	—	—	—	—	—	A	—	—	—	—	—	—
	W.32	Cranborne Chase	Wiltshire/Dorset	—	—	A	—	—	—	—	—	A	—	—	—	—

Table 10 (*contd.*)

				1	2	3	4	5	6	7	8	9	10	11	12	13
East Anglia																
GRADE 1	W.33	HINTLESHAM WOODS	SUFFOLK	—	—	A	a	A	—	—	—	—	—	—	—	a
		(a) HINTLESHAM & RAMSEY WOODS		—	A	a	—	—	—	—	—	—	—	a	—	—
		(b) WOLVES WOOD		—	a	—	—	—	—	—	—	—	—	A	A	A
	W.34	STAVERTON PARK	SUFFOLK	—	—	A	—	—	—	A	—	—	—	A	A	A
GRADE 1*	W.35	FELSHAMHALL & MONKS PARK WOODS	SUFFOLK	a	A	a	—	—	—	A	—	—	—	a	a	—
GRADE 1	W.36	CAVENHAM–TUDDENHAM WOODS	SUFFOLK	—	—	—	—	—	—	A	—	—	—	—	—	—
	W.37	SOTTERLEY PARK	SUFFOLK	—	—	A	—	—	—	A	—	—	—	—	—	—
	W.38	BURE MARSHES	NORFOLK	—	A	A	A	—	—	—	—	—	—	—	A	—
GRADE 1*	W.39	SWANTON NOVERS WOODS	NORFOLK	—	—	A	—	—	—	—	—	—	—	—	A	a
GRADE 1	W.40	HAYLEY WOOD	CAMBRIDGESHIRE	—	—	A	—	—	—	—	—	—	—	A	—	—
	W.41	HOLME FEN	HUNTINGDONSHIRE	—	—	—	—	—	—	—	—	—	—	—	—	—
	W.42	MONKS WOOD	HUNTINGDONSHIRE	—	—	A	—	—	—	—	—	—	—	A	—	a
	W.43	BEDFORD PURLIEUS GROUP	NORTHAMPTONSHIRE, HUNTINGDON & PETERBOROUGH	—	—	—	—	—	—	—	—	—	—	—	—	—
		(a) BEDFORD PURLIEUS		A	A	A	A	—	—	—	—	—	—	a	—	a
		(b) WITTERING COPPICE		—	—	—	—	—	—	—	—	—	—	—	—	—
		(c) EASTON HORNSTOCKS		—	—	—	—	—	—	—	—	—	—	—	—	—
		(d) COLLYWESTON GREAT WOOD		—	—	—	—	—	—	—	—	—	—	—	—	—
	W.44	CASTOR HANGLANDS	HUNTINGDON & PETERBOROUGH	—	—	A	—	—	—	—	—	—	—	—	—	—
	W.45	(i) BARDNEY FOREST (LINCOLNSHIRE LIMEWOODS)	LINCOLNSHIRE	—	—	—	—	—	—	—	—	—	—	—	—	—
		(a) HATTON WOOD		—	a	A	A	—	—	—	—	—	—	A	—	—
		(b) NEWBALL & HARDY GANG WOODS		—	A	A	A	—	—	—	A	—	—	A	a	—
		(c) STAINFIELD & SCOTGROVE WOODS		—	a	A	A	—	—	—	—	—	—	—	—	—
		(d) POTTERHANWORTH WOOD		—	—	A	A	—	—	—	—	—	—	—	—	—
Grade 2	W.45	(ii) Bardney Forest (Lincolnshire Limewoods)	Lincolnshire	—	—	A	A	—	—	—	—	—	—	—	—	—
		(a) Great West–Cocklode–Spring Woods		—	A	A	A	—	—	—	—	—	—	—	—	—
		(b) Stainton–Fulnetby Woods		—	A	A	A	—	—	—	—	—	—	—	—	—
		(c) Wickenby Wood		—	A	A	—	—	—	A	—	—	—	—	—	—
	W.46	Benacre Park	Suffolk	—	A	A	—	—	—	A	—	—	—	—	—	—
	W.47	Foxley Wood	Norfolk	—	A	A	—	—	—	—	—	—	—	—	A	—
	W.48	Wayland Wood	Norfolk	—	—	A	—	A	—	—	—	—	—	—	—	a
	W.49	Sexton Wood	Norfolk	—	—	—	—	A	—	—	—	—	—	—	—	—
	W.50	Felbrigg Woods	Norfolk	—	a	A	a	A	—	—	A	—	—	—	—	—
	W.51	King's & Baker's Woods	Bedfordshire	—	A	A	a	a	—	—	—	—	—	A	—	A
	W.52	Hales Wood	Essex	—	A	A	—	A	a	—	—	—	—	—	—	—
	W.53	Canfield Hart Wood	Essex	—	A	A	—	a	a	a	A	—	—	—	—	A
	W.54	Hatfield Forest	Essex	—	—	A	—	A	a	a	—	—	—	—	—	—
	W.55	Epping Forest	Essex	—	A	A	—	—	—	—	—	—	—	—	—	A
	W.56	Overhall Grove	Cambridgeshire	—	—	—	a	—	—	—	—	—	—	—	a	—
	W.57	Hardwick Wood	Cambridgeshire	—	A	A	a	—	—	—	—	—	—	—	—	A
	W.58	Kesteven Woods	Lincolnshire	—	—	A	—	—	—	—	—	—	—	—	—	—
		(a) Dole Wood		—	A	A	a	—	—	—	—	—	—	—	—	—
		(b) Dunsby Wood		—	A	A	—	—	—	—	—	—	—	—	a	a
		(c) Kirton Wood		—	A	a	a	—	—	—	—	—	—	—	—	—
		(d) Sapperton–Pickworth Woods		—	A	A	—	—	—	—	—	—	—	—	—	—

South-west England

Grade	No.	Site	County
GRADE 1	W.59	MELBURY PARK	DORSET
GRADE 1*	W.60	BOCONNOC PARK & WOODS	CORNWALL
GRADE 1	W.61	FAL ESTUARY	CORNWALL
	W.62	DIZZARD–MILLOOK CLIFFS	CORNWALL
	W.63	BOVEY VALLEY & YARNER WOODS	DEVON
GRADE 1*	W.64	HOLNE CHASE	DEVON
GRADE 1	W.65	WISTMAN'S WOOD	DEVON
	W.66	BLACK TOR COPSE	DEVON
	W.67	AXMOUTH–LYME REGIS UNDERCLIFFS	DEVON
	W.68	WATERSMEET	DEVON
	W.69	HOLNICOTE & HORNER WATER	SOMERSET
	W.70	AVON GORGE (LEIGH WOODS)	GLOUCESTERSHIRE, SOMERSET
	W.71	MENDIP WOODLANDS	SOMERSET
		(a) RODNEY STOKE	
		(b) ASHAM WOOD	
		(c) EBBOR GORGE	
	W.72	COTSWOLD COMMONS & BEECHWOODS	GLOUCESTERSHIRE
	W.73	FOREST OF DEAN	GLOUCESTERSHIRE
		(a) NAGSHEAD INCLOSURE	
		(b) DINGLE WOOD	
		(c) SPEECH HOUSE	
	W.74	COLLINPARK WOOD	GLOUCESTERSHIRE
	W.75	HUDNALLS	GLOUCESTERSHIRE
GRADE 1*	W.95	WYE GORGE (PART)	GLOUCESTERSHIRE — See under South Wales
Grade 2	W.76	Merthen Wood	Cornwall
	W.77	Nance Wood	Cornwall
	W.78	Draynes Wood	Cornwall
	W.79	Piles Copse	Devon
	W.80	Dendles Wood	Devon
	W.81	Woody Bay	Devon
	W.82	Heddon Valley Woods	Devon
	W.83	Hobby Woods	Devon
	W.84	Holford & Hodder's Combes	Somerset
	W.85	Ashen Copse	Somerset
	W.86	Great Breach & Copley Woods	Somerset
	W.87	Weston Big Wood	Somerset

South Wales

Grade	No.	Site	County
GRADE 1	W.88	CWM CLYDACH	BRECKNOCK
	W.89	PENMOELALLT	BRECKNOCK
	W.90	COED RHEIDOL	CARDIGANSHIRE
	W.91	COTHI TYWI	CARMARTHENSHIRE
	W.92	COED Y CERRIG	MONMOUTHSHIRE
	W.93	SALISBURY WOOD: COED SALSBRI	MONMOUTHSHIRE
	W.94	BLACKCLIFF–WYNDCLIFF–PIERCE WOODS: CLOGWYN DU–CLOGWYN GWYN–COED PYRS	MONMOUTHSHIRE
GRADE 1*	W.95	WYE GORGE: HAFAN GWY	MONMOUTHSHIRE–GLOUCESTERSHIRE–HEREFORDSHIRE
Grade 2	W.96	Nant Irfon	Brecknock
	W.97	Carn Gafallt[a]	Brecknock
	W.98	Blaenau Nedd & Mellte	Brecknock

Table 10 (contd.)

Grade 2

Site	County	1	2	3	4	5	6	7	8	9	10	11	12	13
W.99 Darren Fach	Brecknock	A	—	—	—	—	—	—	—	A	—	—	—	—
W.100 Glannau	Radnor	A	—	a	—	—	—	—	—	—	—	—	—	—
W.101 Coed Aber Edw	Radnor	A	—	A	—	—	—	—	—	—	—	—	—	—
W.102 Coombe Woods: Coed y Cwm	Monmouthshire	—	—	A	—	—	—	—	—	—	—	—	—	—

North Wales

GRADE 1

Site	County	1	2	3	4	5	6	7	8	9	10	11	12	13
W.103 COEDYDD DYFFRYN CONWY	CAERNARVONSHIRE													
(a) COED DOLGARROG		a	—	A	—	—	—	—	—	—	—	—	a	—
(b) COED GORSWEN		A	—	A	—	—	—	—	—	—	—	—	A	—
(c) CEUNANT DULYN		a	—	A	—	—	—	—	—	—	—	a	—	—
W.104 COEDYDD ABER	CAERNARVONSHIRE	A	—	A	—	—	—	—	—	—	—	—	a	—
W.105 COED TREMADOG	CAERNARVONSHIRE	a	—	A	—	—	—	—	—	—	—	—	—	—
W.106 COED DINORWIG	CAERNARVONSHIRE	A	—	A	—	—	—	—	—	—	—	—	—	—
W.107 COEDYDD DYFFRYN MAENTWROG	MERIONETH													
(a) COED CAMLYN–CEUNANT LLENNYRCH		A	—	A	—	—	—	—	—	—	—	A	—	—
(b) COEDYDD MAENTWROG–COED CYMERAU		A	—	—	—	—	—	—	—	—	—	—	—	—
(c) COED Y RHYGEN		A	—	A	—	—	—	—	—	—	—	A	—	—
(d) CEUNANT CYNFAL		A	—	a	—	—	—	—	—	—	—	—	—	—
(e) CEUNANT LLECHRWD, GELLILYDAN		A	—	a	—	—	—	—	—	—	—	—	—	—

GRADE 1*

Site	County	1	2	3	4	5	6	7	8	9	10	11	12	13
W.108 COED GANLLWYD	MERIONETH	A	—	A	—	—	—	—	—	—	—	—	—	—
* W.109 COED CRAFNANT	MERIONETH	A	—	A	—	—	—	—	—	—	—	—	a	—
** W.110 Bryn Maelgwyn & Gloddaeth	Caernarvonshire	—	—	A	—	—	—	—	—	—	—	—	a	—

Grade 2

Site	County	1	2	3	4	5	6	7	8	9	10	11	12	13
W.111 Hafod Garegog	Caernarvonshire	A	—	A	—	—	—	—	—	—	—	—	—	—
W.112 Coed Maes yr Helmau: Torrent Walk	Merioneth	A	—	a	—	—	—	—	—	—	—	—	—	—
W.113 Coed Llety Walter	Merioneth	A	—	—	—	—	—	—	—	—	—	—	—	—
W.114 Coed Llechwedd	Merioneth	A	—	a	—	—	—	—	—	—	—	—	—	—

Midland

GRADE 1

Site	County	1	2	3	4	5	6	7	8	9	10	11	12	13
W.43 BEDFORD PURLIEUS GROUP (PART)	NORTHAMPTONSHIRE	See under East Anglia												

GRADE 1*

Site	County	1	2	3	4	5	6	7	8	9	10	11	12	13
W.115 DERBYSHIRE DALES WOODLANDS	DERBYSHIRE/ STAFFORDSHIRE	—	—	—	—	—	—	—	—	—	—	—	—	—
(a) LATHKILL DALE		—	—	—	—	—	—	—	A	—	—	—	—	—
(b) CRESSBROOK DALE		—	—	a	a	—	—	—	A	—	—	—	—	—
(c) DOVE DALE ASHWOOD		—	—	—	—	—	—	—	A	—	—	—	—	—
* W.95 WYE GORGE (PART)	HEREFORDSHIRE	See under South Wales												

GRADE 1

Site	County	1	2	3	4	5	6	7	8	9	10	11	12	13
W.116 HALESEND WOOD	HEREFORDSHIRE	—	—	A	A	—	—	—	—	A	—	—	—	—
W.117 MOCCAS PARK	HEREFORDSHIRE	—	—	A	—	—	—	—	—	A	—	—	—	—
W.118 HILL HOLE DINGLE[a]	HEREFORDSHIRE	—	—	A	A	—	—	A	—	A	—	—	a	—
W.119 TICK WOOD	SHROPSHIRE	—	—	A	—	—	—	—	—	—	—	—	—	—
W.120 LONG ITCHINGTON & UFTON WOODS	WARWICKSHIRE	—	A	A	—	—	—	—	—	—	—	a	a	—
W.121 WYRE FOREST	WORCESTERSHIRE, SHROPSHIRE	A	—	A	—	—	—	A	—	A	—	—	—	—

Grade 2

Site	County	1	2	3	4	5	6	7	8	9	10	11	12	13
W.122 Cannock Chase	Staffordshire	A	A[b]	A	—	—	—	—	—	—	—	A	a	—
W.123 Hamps & Manifold Valleys	Staffordshire	—	A	A	—	—	—	—	—	A	—	A	a	—
W.124 Brampton Bryan Park[a]	Herefordshire	—	—	A	—	—	A	—	—	—	—	—	—	—
W.125 Downton Gorge	Herefordshire	—	—	A	—	—	—	A	—	A	—	—	—	—
W.126 Bushy Hazels & Cwmma Moors	Herefordshire	—	—	A	—	—	—	—	—	A	—	—	—	—
W.127 Leighfield Forest	Leicestershire	—	—	A	—	—	—	—	—	—	—	—	—	—
W.128 Pipewell Woods	Northamptonshire	—	A	A	—	—	—	—	—	—	—	—	a	—
W.129 Whittlewood Forest	Northamptonshire	—	A	A	—	—	—	A	—	A	—	—	—	—
W.130 Sherwood Forest	Nottinghamshire	—	A	A	—	—	—	—	—	—	—	—	—	—
W.131 Habberley Valley	Shropshire	—	—	a	—	—	—	—	—	—	—	a	—	—
W.132 Chaddesley–Randan Woods	Worcestershire	A	A[b]	A	a	—	—	—	—	—	—	a	a	—

Grade	No.	Site	County									
North England												
GRADE 1*	W.133	BORROWDALE WOODS	CUMBERLAND	A	—	—	—	—	—	—	—	—
	(a)	CASTLE HEAD WOOD		A	A	A	—	—	—	—	—	A
	(b)	THE INGS		A	A	A	A	a	a	—	—	—
	(c)	GREAT WOOD		A	A	A	a	a	a	—	—	A
	(d)	LODORE–TROUTDALE WOODS		A	A	A	A	a	a	—	—	—
	(e)	JOHNNY'S WOOD		A	A	A	—	A	A	—	—	—
	(f)	SEATOLLER WOOD		A	a	a	A	A	A	—	a	A
GRADE 1	W.134	KESKADALE & BIRKRIGG OAKS	CUMBERLAND	A	A	A	A	A	a	—	a	A
	W.135	ORTON MOSS	CUMBERLAND	A	A	A	a	a	a	—	a	—
	W.136	WHITBARROW & WITHERSLACK WOODS	WESTMORLAND	A	A	a	a	a	a	—	—	a
	W.137	BIRK FELL	WESTMORLAND	A	a	a	A	A	a	—	—	a
GRADE 1*	W.138	HELBECK & SWINDALE WOODS	WESTMORLAND	a	—	a	a	—	a	—	a	—
GRADE 1	W.139	ROUDSEA WOOD	LANCASHIRE	A	A	A	A	a	a	—	—	a
	W.140	GAIT BARROWS	LANCASHIRE	a	—	a	—	a	—	—	—	—
	W.141	ROEBURNDALE WOODS	LANCASHIRE	a	A	a	A	a	a	—	a	—
	W.142	RIBBLEHEAD WOODS	YORKSHIRE					A				
	(a)	COLT PARK		—	—	—	—	A				
	(b)	LING GILL		—	—	—	—	A	A			
	W.143	CONISTONE OLD PASTURE & BASTOW WOOD	YORKSHIRE	—	A	A	a	a	A			
	W.144	RAINCLIFFE WOOD	YORKSHIRE	—	A	A	—	A	A			
	W.145	SHIPLEY WOOD	DURHAM/YORKSHIRE	—	—	—	—	—	—			
Grade 2	W.146	Scales Wood	Cumberland	A	A	A	—	A	A			
	W.147	Lyne Woods	Cumberland	A	A	A	—	A	A			
	W.148	Gowbarrow Park	Cumberland	A	A	A	a	A	A			
	W.149	Naddle Low Forest	Westmorland	A	A	A	a	a	a	a		
	W.150	Low Wood, Hartsop	Westmorland	—	A	A	A	A	A			
	W.151	Smardale Woods	Westmorland	—	—	—	A	A	A			
	W.152	Lowther Park	Westmorland	—	—	A	A	—	—			
	W.153	Eaves Wood	Lancashire	—	A	A	a	A	A			
	W.154	Burton Wood	Lancashire	a	A	A	A	A	A			
	W.155	Hawkswick Wood	Yorkshire	—	A	A	A	A	A			
	W.156	Scoska Wood	Yorkshire	—	A	A	a	A	A			
	W.157	Thornton & Twisleton Glens	Yorkshire	—	a	a	—	a	—	a		
	W.158	Ashberry & Reins Woods	Yorkshire	—	A	A	a	A	A			
	W.159	Beckhole Woods	Yorkshire	—	A	A	A	A	A			
	W.160	Beast Cliff	Yorkshire	A	—	A	A	A	—			
	W.161	Kisdon Force Woods	Yorkshire	—	A	A	a	A	a	a		
	W.162	Castle Eden Dene	Durham	—	A	A	A	A	A		A	
	W.163	Holystone Woods	Northumberland	A	A	A	—	A	A	a		
	W.164	Monk Wood	Northumberland	A	A	A	—	—	—			
	W.165	Hesleyside Park & Hareshaw Linn	Northumberland	A	—	—	—	A	A	a		
	W.166	Billsmoor Park & Grasslees Wood	Northumberland	—	—	—	—	—	—			
South Scotland												
GRADE 1	W.167	TYNRON JUNIPER WOOD	DUMFRIES-SHIRE	—	—	—	—	—	A	—	—	A
	W.168	KIRKCONNELL FLOW	KIRKCUDBRIGHTSHIRE	—	a	a	A	a	—	a	—	—
GRADE 1*	W.169	LOCH LOMOND WOODS	DUNBARTONSHIRE/STIRLINGSHIRE									
	(a)	INCHCAILLOCH		A	A	A	a	—	—	—	—	—
	(b)	TORRINCH		A	a	a	a	a	—	—	—	a
	(c)	CLAIRINCH		A	a	A	a	a	—	—	—	A
	(d)	CREINCH		A	—	—	—	—	—	a	a	A
	(e)	ABER ISLE										
	(f)	INCHLONAIG		A	—	—	a	A	a	A	A	A
	(g)	MAINLAND WOODS										a

Table 10 (contd.)

	Site	County	1	2	3	4	5	6	7	8	9	10	11	12	13
GRADE 1	W.170 AVONDALE	LANARKSHIRE	—	—	A	—	—	—	—	—	—	—	a	—	A
	W.171 GLEN DIOMHAN, ARRAN	BUTESHIRE	—	—	—	—	—	—	—	—	—	—	—	—	A
Grade 2	W.172 Chanlock Foot	Dumfries-shire	—	—	A	—	—	—	—	—	a	—	—	—	—
	W.173 Stenhouse Wood	Dumfries-shire	—	—	A	—	—	—	—	—	—	—	—	—	—
	W.174 Maidens–Heads of Ayr	Ayrshire	—	—	A	—	—	—	—	—	—	—	—	—	—
	W.175 Hamilton High Park	Lanarkshire	—	—	A	—	—	—	—	—	—	—	—	—	—
	W.176 Nethan Gorge	Lanarkshire	—	—	A	—	—	—	—	—	—	—	—	—	—
	W.177 Wood of Cree	Kirkcudbrightshire	A	—	—	—	—	—	—	—	a	—	a	—	—
	W.178 Fleet Woodlands	Kirkcudbrightshire	A	—	—	—	—	—	—	—	—	—	—	—	—
	(a) Castramont Wood		A	—	—	—	—	—	—	—	—	—	—	—	—
	(b) Killiegowan Wood		A	—	—	—	—	—	—	—	—	—	a	a	a
	(c) Jennoch Wood		a	—	—	—	—	—	—	—	—	—	—	—	—
	(d) Craigy Braes Wood		A	—	—	—	—	—	—	—	—	—	a	—	—
	W.179 Ravenshall Wood	Kirkcudbrightshire	A	—	A	—	—	—	—	—	—	—	a	a	—
East Scotland															
GRADE 1	W.180 DINNET OAKWOOD	ABERDEENSHIRE	—	A	—	—	—	—	—	—	—	A	A	—	A
	W.181 CRATHIE WOOD	ABERDEENSHIRE	—	—	A	—	—	—	—	—	—	—	A	—	A
	W.182 MORRONE WOOD	ABERDEENSHIRE	—	—	A	—	—	—	—	—	—	—	A	—	—
	W.183 AVIEMORE WOODLANDS	INVERNESS-SHIRE	—	—	—	—	—	—	—	—	—	—	—	—	—
	(a) CRAIGELLACHIE		—	a	—	—	—	—	—	—	—	a	A	—	—
	(b) KINRARA WOODS (ALVIE)		—	—	—	—	—	—	—	—	—	—	a	—	—
	W.184 GLEN TARFF	INVERNESS-SHIRE	—	A	A	—	—	—	—	—	—	—	A	—	—
	W.185 PASS OF KILLIECRANKIE	PERTHSHIRE	—	A	A	—	—	—	—	—	—	—	—	—	—
	W.186 BLACK WOOD OF RANNOCH	PERTHSHIRE	—	—	—	—	—	—	—	—	—	A	A	—	A
GRADE 1*	W.187 SPEYSIDE–DEESIDE PINEWOODS	INVERNESS-SHIRE–ABERDEENSHIRE	—	—	—	—	—	—	—	—	—	—	—	—	—
	(a) BALLOCHBUIE FOREST	ABERDEENSHIRE	—	—	—	—	—	—	—	—	—	A	—	—	—
	(b) GLEN TANAR		—	—	—	—	—	—	—	—	—	A	—	—	—
	(c) GLENS QUOICH, LUI & DERRY		—	—	—	—	—	—	—	—	—	A	—	—	—
	(d) ROTHIEMURCHUS–INVERESHIE		—	—	—	—	—	—	—	—	—	A	—	—	—
	(e) ABERNETHY FOREST		—	—	—	—	—	—	—	—	—	A	—	—	—
Grade 2	W.188 Earlshall Muir	Fife	—	—	—	—	—	—	—	—	—	—	A	A	—
	W.189 Keltney Burn, Coshieville	Perthshire	—	—	A	—	—	—	—	—	—	—	—	—	—
West Scotland															
GRADE 1*	W.190 LOCH SUNART WOODLANDS	ARGYLL	A	—	—	—	—	—	—	—	—	—	—	—	—
	(a) ARIUNDLE		A	—	—	—	—	—	—	—	—	—	—	—	—
	(b) SALEN–STRONTIAN		A	—	a	—	—	—	—	—	—	—	A	—	—
	(c) LAUDALE–GLEN CRIPESDALE		—	—	a	—	—	—	—	—	—	—	A	—	—
	(d) BEN HIANT		—	—	A	—	—	—	—	—	—	—	—	A	—
GRADE 1	W.191 CARNACH WOOD	ARGYLL	—	—	—	—	—	—	—	A	—	—	—	—	A
	W.192 DRIMNIN	ARGYLL	—	—	—	—	—	—	—	—	—	—	—	—	—
GRADE 1*	W.193 GLASDRUM WOOD	ARGYLL	—	—	A	—	—	—	—	A	—	—	a	—	—
GRADE 1	W.194 GLEN NANT WOODS	ARGYLL	—	—	—	—	—	—	—	—	—	A	A	a	—
	W.195 MEALL NAN GOBHAR	ARGYLL	—	—	—	—	—	—	—	—	—	A	A	—	a
GRADE 1*	W.196 TAYNISH WOOD	ARGYLL	A	—	A	—	—	—	—	—	—	A	A	—	—
**	W.197 MEALLDARROCH POINT–SKIPNESS	ARGYLL	A	—	A	—	—	—	—	—	—	—	A	—	—
*	W.198 INVERNEIL BURN	ARGYLL	—	—	A	—	—	—	—	—	—	—	A	A	—
GRADE 1	W.199 URQUHART BAY	INVERNESS-SHIRE	—	—	—	—	—	—	—	—	—	—	—	—	—
	W.200 LOCH MORAR ISLANDS	INVERNESS-SHIRE	—	—	—	—	—	—	—	—	a	—	—	—	—

		County
GRADE 1*	W.201 TOKAVAIG WOOD, SKYE	INVERNESS-SHIRE
GRADE 1	W.202 GEARY RAVINE, SKYE	INVERNESS-SHIRE
	W.203 GLEN STRATHFARRAR	INVERNESS-SHIRE
	W.204 GLEN AFFRIC	INVERNESS-SHIRE
	W.205 ALLT NAN CARNAN	ROSS
GRADE 1*	W.206 LOCH MAREE WOODS	ROSS
	(a) BEINN EIGHE (COILLE NA GLAS-LEITIRE)	
	(b) LOCH MAREE ISLANDS	
	(c) LET'TEREWE OAKWOODS	
GRADE 1	W.207 INVERPOLLY WOODS	ROSS
	W.208 RASSAL ASHWOOD	ROSS
	W.209 CORRIESHALLOCH GORGE	ROSS
	W.210 MOUND ALDERWOODS	SUTHERLAND
GRADE 1*	W.211 STRATHBEAG	SUTHERLAND
GRADE 1	W.212 COILLE ARDURA, MULL	ARGYLL
Grade 2	W.213 Choille Mor, Colonsay	Argyll
	W.214 Claggain–Ardmore, Islay	Argyll
	W.215 Crannach Wood	Argyll
	W.216 Doire Donn	Argyll
	W.217 Glendaruel Wood	Argyll
	W.218 Kinuachdrach, Jura	Argyll
	W.219 Clais Dhearg	Argyll
	W.220 Loch na Dal, Skye	Inverness-shire
	W.221 Loch Moidart	Inverness-shire
	W.222 Shieldaig^a	Ross
	W.223 Fionn Loch Islands	Ross
	W.224 Amat Wood	Ross
	W.225 Eilean na Gartaig, Cam Loch	Sutherland
	W.226 Loch a' Mhuillin Wood, Scourie^a	Sutherland
	W.227 Ledmore Wood, Spinningdale	Sutherland
	W.228 Migdale Woods	Sutherland
	W.229 Ardvar Woodlands	Sutherland

Notes

A = major occurrence of habitat.
a = minor occurrence of habitat.
* See Appendix.
b Intermediate western/eastern oakwood.

6 LOWLAND GRASSLANDS, HEATHS AND SCRUB

The criteria for distinguishing between lowland and upland in Britain have been set out more fully in Chapter 3. No strict altitudinal separation is appropriate, and a more valid definition based on climatic parameters has not yet been attempted. The lowland grasslands, heaths and their scrub are defined here as an anthropogenic complex of plant communities characteristic of well-drained to damp soils at low levels, where recent land-use has been mainly limited to grazing. The category has been chosen to distinguish a series of vegetation types with their associated fauna, which are represented mainly in the southern half of England, and show a gradually decreasing extent with distance north. With increasing altitude and latitude there are transitions to corresponding upland and northern vegetation complexes on soils of equivalent type, involving a gradual replacement of the essentially lowland and southern species. The combination of increasing wetness of climate as well as decreasing temperature towards the north and west has caused a general development of ombrogenous peat in low-lying situations which would carry acidophilous heath or grassland in southern and eastern England.

The complex of lowland grassland, heath and scrub is mostly a derivative of original climax forest, and is maintained in a subclimax state by human intervention. In the absence of man, all three types would probably in most places revert to woodland, and scrub is itself usually a seral development of grassland and heath, formed by the natural invasion of medium and tall shrubs. Some grasslands have been produced by draining of flood-plain mires (fens) but the water tables may have been so permanently lowered that these too would change to woodland in the absence of management to maintain grassland. Grasslands and heaths are a closely related ecological group of formations essentially associated with man's use of land for providing fodder for herbivorous animals, now mainly cattle and sheep, but formerly also goats, horses and, locally, rabbits. Scrub is mainly a transient phase which develops on these types when management for grazing animals is reduced or abandoned.

In the lowlands, land with acidic soils which has been deforested but not recently cultivated is usually occupied by a mixture of dwarf shrub heath (mainly of *Calluna vulgaris*), grassland and scrub composed of acidophilous or acid-tolerant species. The dwarf-shrub heath is predominant and the acidophilous grasslands and scrub are usually so closely related spatially and in time to the heath communities that all are best considered together as a single complex, described for convenience as acidic heath.

Most of the lowland grasslands are situated on basic soils, though these vary from only moderately base rich to highly calcareous. Base-rich soils occur in a wide range of situations and on a variety of parent materials in the lowlands, but calcareous soils (i.e. those containing free lime) are confined to parent materials consisting largely of calcium carbonate, i.e. chalk, limestone and derived clays. The basic grasslands are of much higher nutritive value than the acidic complex, and are mostly used as grazing land for domestic animals. They are conveniently though arbitrarily divided into two main groups according to soil base-status. First are the calcareous grasslands on the calcareous rock formations, mainly Cretaceous Chalk, Jurassic limestone and Carboniferous Limestone; they are associated with brown earth or rendzina-type soils with pH usually above 7.0 and containing free calcium carbonate. Until quite recently, these were the most extensive of the lowland grasslands, forming large tracts of open downland on the low hills of southern England. Up to 1940, there were many areas measurable in hundreds of hectares, but subsequent agricultural changes have greatly reduced and fragmented their extent. Second are the neutral grasslands on a wide range of parent materials and superficial deposits, but usually with deep loams or even peaty soils of pH 5.5–7.0, deficient in free calcium carbonate. These include the grasslands of enclosed fields and meadows bounded by hedges, fences, walls or ditches at frequent intervals, so that individual areas are usually small, and an extent of over 40 ha is rather rare. Neutral grasslands are, however, more extensive than the calcareous types in the aggregate.

The calcareous grasslands naturally follow the distribution of the major calcareous rock formations, and are widespread in England, very local in Wales and rare in Scotland. Although base-rich soils show a general increase in prevalence in a southerly and easterly direction within Britain, the calcareous and neutral grasslands do not show an identical pattern because there is a trend towards increasing arable farming in the same direction. In particular, the neutral grasslands are most extensively represented in wetter districts where cattle- and sheep-rearing takes precedence over arable farming. Neutral grasslands are extremely widespread showing floristic differentiation into southern and northern types, and grading locally into grasslands associated with mature or reclaimed salt marshes, and with drained wetlands.

Both calcareous and neutral grasslands typically have floristically rich swards, with many species of grass, sedge and forb, which have developed during a long period of grazing. Some have considerable antiquity, where the management regime has been relatively stable over several centuries. Some of these ancient pastures have considerable interest and many of the calcareous examples are associated with distinctive archaeological features, such as various kinds of earthworks. Floristic composition and richness, on which the nature conservation interest depends, is dependent on the kind of grazing. The open chalk and limestone downs were traditionally grazed by sheep, and many also had large numbers of rabbits. The enclosed neutral grasslands were grazed by sheep, cattle and horses, but many were first allowed to grow for a hay crop, and only grazed later in the year after this had been cut. Floristic diversity can be reduced, through dominance of grasses and suppression of forbs, by grazing which is too heavy, too light, or too selective, but appropriate adjustment can usually restore the desired state.

Many of these old grasslands have either never been cultivated or have escaped ploughing for a long period. Their vegetation is composed almost entirely of native species, and although both created by and dependent on human influence, they may be regarded as semi-natural types. The present threat to their survival comes from the more radical modification caused by modern agricultural practice. Large areas of permanent grassland have been ploughed and converted to arable land, and even where grassland has been retained there has often been a drastic change, with ploughing, followed by re-sowing with grass seed mixtures of commercial species, and often heavy application of fertiliser. The resulting swards are completely artificial and almost devoid of nature conservation interest.

Some calcareous soils with semi-natural grassland are shallow and pose problems for the cultivator, but with modern agricultural techniques it has proved economic to plough and fertilise such ground, and to grow hay or arable crops. Old meadows have been equally subject to this kind of improvement, even in places such as river flood plains, where drainage was formerly regarded as unfavourable for growing crops. During the last 30 years, the permanent lowland grasslands of Britain, both enclosed and unenclosed, have suffered great attrition in this way. The chalk grasslands and old meadows, in particular, have lost much ground and are under such increasing pressure that they could foreseeably disappear altogether, except where deliberately protected. The survival of ancient lowland grasslands has so far depended mainly on chance factors, such as the occurrence of slopes too steep to plough, elderly farmers adhering to traditional methods of farming, common grazing rights and Ministry of Defence occupation.

Locally in the lowlands, diversity of soil conditions within a small space has produced various mixtures of acidic heath and basic grassland communities. The Breckland of East Anglia is the most important of these areas, with a complex of grasslands and heaths unique in Britain, though now greatly reduced and fragmented; much interest attaches here to the distinctive flora and fauna associated with the continental climate. Another interesting type is the range of com-

munities in which both calcifuges and calcicoles of the usually spatially separate heaths and grasslands grow together in intimate mixtures on calcareous or base-rich soils. These calcareous heaths are most usually herb-rich heather communities, and are widespread though seldom extensive. There is a floristic link here with submaritime heaths found especially on the top of western sea cliffs, where spray produces soil enrichment, and a much greater variety of herbs than in the typical acidic heaths of ground farther inland. Magnesium-rich soils derived from serpentine locally carry communities obviously referable to the grassland and heath complex, but with unusual floristic features. The most outstanding examples are the heaths of the Lizard in Cornwall, and these will be considered with the other mixed types.

A variety of scrub types develops naturally on both calcareous and neutral grasslands where grazing pressure has been reduced or removed, thus allowing seedlings of woody species to grow up unchecked and suppress the grasses and forbs. Scrub may itself be a relatively stable community, but often in turn shows invasion by tree species. As scrub on calcareous soils covers a variety of distinctive, floristically rich and sometimes extensive communities, the category calcareous scrub is recognised as a separate type from the associated grasslands.

Although grassland, heath and scrub are anthropogenic in a broad sense, many of the component stands are the product of a long period of equilibrium during which human influence has been of a rather casual nature. The regime of management has even been beneficial, promoting diversity within the former forest cover, allowing the spread of some species which need more open ground and introducing others from lands far away. Many old grasslands have probably existed in more or less their present condition for hundreds or even thousands of years, and they have acquired considerable importance as distinctive ecosystems in their own right. As a group, grasslands, heaths and scrubs of basic soils are notable for floristic richness, with a strong representation of rare species not found elsewhere, and as the habitat of a rich and diverse fauna, especially of invertebrates. Heaths and scrubs are also much subject to reclamation for forestry and agriculture, but heath is the more threatened type, for nowhere is it gaining ground, whereas scrub shows a good deal of spread locally. Scrub is itself actually a threat to grassland and heath in many places where myxomatosis has eradicated rabbits and domestic animals are no longer grazed.

The lowland grasslands, heaths and scrubs show associations with all the other main habitat formations, and the representation of these various types on sites chosen mainly for the present group of formations is summarised in Table 19, p. 195. The diversity and species-richness of acidic heaths, calcareous grasslands, mixed grasslands and heaths, calcareous scrub and neutral grasslands is such that they are treated here as separate formations, but a single composite Index of Sites is given.

Some sites within this grouping contain various types of rock habitat, especially on the coast, and in the west or north; and these habitats sometimes add significantly to the overall interest. Lowland acidic heaths have rock outcrops and detached blocks (either scattered or as scree) in western Britain, but these are interesting mainly for lithophilous bryophytes and lichens, except on sea cliffs, where there is a much greater variety of vascular plants. Although the Chalk presents some formidable vertical precipices and more broken cliffs to the sea, there are relatively few open rock habitats inland on this formation, with the exception of artificial chalk pits and quarries, and scattered Sarsen stones on some southern England sites. By contrast, the harder limestones, especially the Carboniferous, give rise not only to high sea cliffs, but also to extensive inland exposures as gorges, crags, screes, pavements and potholes, all important for their flora. In the north and west, these open calcareous rock habitats of karstic terrain are often associated with areas of grassland, heath and scrub, and such complexes are floristically the richest of all, giving refuge to numerous vascular species which are sensitive to heavy grazing or competition, and are the habitat of many bryophytes and lichens. Even where rock outcrops are extensive, there is usually at least some grassland and, to avoid duplication, these open habitats will be treated along with calcareous grasslands, though the relative importance of the two types will be indicated.

A. ACIDIC HEATHS, GRASSLANDS AND SCRUB

RANGE OF ECOLOGICAL VARIATION

Habitat factors and vegetation

Where areas of acidic soil have remained uncultivated and unwooded in lowland Britain, they are usually covered with a dwarf shrub community in which *Calluna vulgaris* is dominant, though on some areas *Erica cinerea* is also abundant. These soils are typically deep podsols developed on base-deficient sands, gravels or clays, and their low fertility has itself probably helped the heathland formation to survive, by discouraging cultivation. Some dry heaths are commons and owe their persistence to divided land tenure, under which there is less pressure for the kind of reclamation responsible elsewhere for conversion of many former heaths into arable land. Lowland heaths are in general under considerable threat nowadays, for the addition of suitable fertilisers can make them worth cultivating, and any waste land in the lowlands is likely to attract developers.

Lowland acidic heath and grassland has less diversity than many other vegetation formations. Major variations are related mainly to geographical position and so may be regarded primarily as a range of climatic types, though there is local variability in relation to wetness of soil, base-status of soil, altitude and management.

On the European scale, heather heath is an oceanic type of vegetation, but the species is widespread all over lowland Britain where soil conditions are favourable. Floristically, the lowland heaths are usually extremely poor. Gorse is often abundant, co-dominant or locally dominant with the heather(s), but the species varies, *Ulex europaeus* being widespread, *U. gallii* mainly in the south and west (especially Cornwall, Devon and west Wales), and *U. minor* mainly in the south and east (especially Dorset, the New Forest, Sussex and Surrey). From their position and nature, lowland heaths are vulnerable to fire and most areas suffer from periodic fires which probably help to impoverish the flora, reduce scrub and maintain a fire climax of heather and gorse. During regeneration after a fire *Erica cinerea*, *E. tetralix*, grasses or *Chamaenerion angustifolium* may show temporary abundance, and the open conditions may allow the spread of bracken, which is often locally dominant, forming dense stands on lowland heaths. Ling heather is somewhat frost-sensitive and may suffer die-back during a severe winter; at Cavenham Heath, Suffolk, much heather was killed by the frosts of early 1963, but there has been good regeneration from seed. It can also suffer from spring and summer drought in eastern districts. When undisturbed, heather has a natural cycle of maturation and decay, and as the older growth becomes leggy and open, new plants may appear.

The soil beneath heather typically has a layer of litter and mor humus, and in the more open places a growth of crustaceous lichens develops, with *Cladonia pyxidata*, *C. coccifera*, *C. floerkeana*, *C. fimbriata*, *C. gracilis* and *C. squamosa*. Where the heather is more patchy, the foliose species, such as *C. impexa*, *C. arbuscula*, *C. rangiformis* and *Cetraria aculeata* often form dense mats. *Parmelia physodes* is often abundant on moribund heather. Where the ground is not too dry or recently burned, a moss layer is usually present beneath the heather, and has *Hypnum cupressiforme*, *Pleurozium schreberi*, *Polytrichum commune*, *Dicranum scoparium* and *Campylopus flexuosus*, with *Polytrichum piliferum*, *P. juniperinum* and *Pohlia nutans* in open places. Grasses are plentiful and constant over some heaths but are seldom dominant except in rather limited patches, although where grazing is heavy they may locally replace the dwarf shrubs, and they may be encouraged by fire; the most abundant species are *Festuca ovina*, *Agrostis canina*, *A. tenuis*, *Deschampsia flexuosa* and *Molinia caerulea*. Common vascular plants of acidic heaths include *Rumex acetosella*, *Potentilla erecta*, *Galium saxatile*, *Veronica officinalis*, *Carex binervis* and *C. pilulifera*. Characteristic plants of dry heaths, not always present but occurring locally in abundance, include *Cuscuta epithymum* (parasitic mainly on *Calluna* but also on *Ulex minor* and *U. gallii*), *Genista anglica* and *Hypericum pulchrum*. Certain species of very local distribution in Britain occur abundantly in this community within their range, and thus give distinctive geographical facies: they include *Agrostis setacea* in south and south-west England; *Erica ciliaris*, mainly in Dorset; and *E. vagans* on the Lizard in Cornwall.

Lowland heaths show several directions of variation about the 'central' type described above. The most common is that found with increasing wetness of soil, which gives a gradient towards acidic mire. Southern British heathlands commonly occur on undulating terrain, with dry heath covering the well-drained convexities and plateaux, and mire occupying the valleys and depressions. Where the water table is permanently at the surface, the vegetation is mostly classed as valley mire and treated under that heading. Sometimes, however, transitional vegetation between the two extremes is well represented, and two intermediate types are recognised; a humid heath in which there is merely impeded drainage, and a wet heath in which the water table is near the soil surface for most of the year.

The humid heath is characterised by an abundance of *Erica tetralix*, but *Calluna* is still dominant. Within their geographical ranges, both *Erica ciliaris* and *E. vagans* belong typically to this situation, with the former replacing *E. tetralix* but the latter occurring more usually as co-dominant with *Schoenus nigricans*. The moss *Hypnum imponens* is highly characteristic. Wet heath consists essentially of the above communities (but not the *E. vagans* type) with the addition of more strongly hydrophilous species, notably *Sphagnum compactum*, *S. tenellum*, *S. molle*, *Odontoschisma sphagni*, *Mylia anomala*, *Gymnocolea inflata* and *Lepidozia setacea*, with vascular plants such as *Juncus squarrosus*, *J. acutiflorus*, *J. bulbosus*, *Molinia caerulea*, *Trichophorum cespitosum*, *Potentilla erecta*, *Carex panicea*, *Eriophorum angustifolium*, *Drosera rotundifolia*, *Polygala serpyllifolia*, *Pedicularis sylvatica* and *Narthecium ossifragum*. Among the characteristic local species of wet heath are *Gentiana pneumonanthe*, *Anagallis tenella*, *Pinguicula lusitanica*, *Lycopodium inundatum*, *Drosera intermedia* and the moss *Dicranum spurium*. Wet heath grades into acidophilous mire with the addition of such species as *Sphagnum papillosum*, *S. rubellum*, *Eriophorum vaginatum*, *Rhynchospora alba*, *Menyanthes trifoliata*, *Vaccinium oxycoccos*, *Utricularia minor*, and the oceanic plants *Hypericum elodes*, *Scutellaria minor* and (rarely) *Rhynchospora fusca*. There are grassy equivalents of these humid and wet heaths, with *Molinia caerulea*, *Agrostis stolonifera*, *Sieglingia decumbens*, *Nardus stricta* and *Anthoxanthum odoratum*, and a characteristic species of these communities in the south and west is *Wahlenbergia hederacea*.

Where they are present, the peatlands, generally in the form of valley mires, are an integral part of the heathland ecosystem and cannot be separated from the dry heathland in its assessment or study of its ecology. The conservation of these lowland acidic peat areas depends upon having a good surrounding catchment of heathland, especially where agricultural reclamation is taking place in the neighbourhood.

With increasing altitude and latitude, lowland heather heath grades imperceptibly into upland Callunetum of the grouse-moor type, and the boundary between these two can be drawn only very arbitrarily. The upland tendencies are often shown first by an increased proportion of grasses, this being mainly a reflection of the combined effect of sheepgrazing and moor-burning, which sway the competitive balance between dwarf shrubs and grasses. Other signs are the increased constancy and abundance of bilberry and a corresponding reduction in species such as *Ulex europaeus* and *U. gallii*. Submontane plants such as *Vaccinium vitis-idaea*, *Lycopodium clavatum* and *Empetrum nigrum* appear, and the moss layer gains in species and luxuriance. Good examples of the transition may be found on Exmoor and Dartmoor, the Bannau Preseli in Pembrokeshire, the Stiperstones in Shropshire, and the coastal hills of north Wales, such as Yr Eifl. In the north of Britain, the topographic situations of lowland heath are usually occupied by this submontane type of Callunetum, while in the humid west there is often a general covering of acidic blanket mire which extends over such ground. Dried-out raised and blanket mires may, however, develop a dry Callunetum similar to that of heathland.

There is also a gradient of variation from acidic heath to basic grassland as soil pH, base-status and fertility rise, on substrata derived from richer parent materials such as chalk, limestone, calcareous clays, shales and sandstones, and basic igneous rocks. Where intermediate communities are distinctive and more than fragmentary in occurrence, they are recognised as a separate grouping of mixed heaths and rich grasslands and treated in a later section. Some of the Breckland heaths are of the typical acidic type, but many are included in this intermediate group as are the chalk heaths and the unique heaths (including *Erica vagans* communities) of the Lizard serpentine.

Yet another spatial gradient is towards the essentially submaritime heather heaths which are so characteristic of headlands above the sea where the rock is acidic. This type occurs along a large part of the rocky west coast of Britain from Land's End to Cape Wrath and the Scottish islands. There is inevitably a strong influence of wind and salt spray, which adds other nutrients, including calcium and magnesium, to the soil and creates conditions which approach those of the base-rich soils. These submaritime heaths are typically dominated by rather dwarfed, compact ecotypes of heather but have a characteristic mixture of species such as *Salix repens*, *Festuca rubra*, *Agrostis stolonifera*, *Sieglingia decumbens*, *Plantago maritima*, *P. lanceolata*, *Erica cinerea*, *Potentilla erecta*, *Succisa pratensis*, *Galium saxatile*, *Polygala serpyllifolia*, *Dactylorchis maculata* ssp. *ericetorum*, *Pedicularis sylvatica*, *Lotus corniculatus*, *Hypericum pulchrum*, *Viola riviniana*, *Thymus drucei*, *Carex nigra*, *C. panicea*, *C. binervis*, *Hypnum cupressiforme*, *Eurhynchium praelongum* and *Frullania tamarisci*. In the extreme north of Scotland, these submaritime heaths grade into montane heaths of *Dryas octopetala*, *Arctostaphylos uva-ursi*, *Empetrum hermaphroditum* and *Juniperus communis* ssp. *nana* occurring on ground affected by blown shell sand, almost at sea-level, and in the Hebrides they show transitions to the rich calcicolous communities of the machair as the proportion of shell sand in the soil increases. On acidic sands, short heather heaths with *Empetrum nigrum* occupy stable areas of coastal dune, as at the Sands of Forvie.

Finally, the lowland heaths often show a tendency towards change through invasion by tree seedlings, mainly of birch and Scots pine, but locally by oak as well. Some of the southern heaths show all stages to the formation of closed woodland and this is a process which, if unchecked, could reduce still further the extent of heathland. Succession to woodland is, however, often resisted by heath fires which destroy the young trees and, in some localities, trees seem slow to regenerate, perhaps because of the density of the heather and bracken or the extreme acidity and aridity of the soil surface. In some areas such as the south east of England, grazing – especially by rabbits – may have been important, combined with burning, in preventing the establishment and spread of young trees.

The presence of some woodland and scrub nevertheless adds to the diversity of heathland, especially in extending the range of habitat for animals. The richest heaths biologically are those which also show transitions to mire vegetation and to calcareous soil as well. Physiognomically similar complexes of heather heath, colonising birchwood and mire occur throughout Britain, there being southern examples in the New Forest, at Thursley Common in Surrey, and Cavenham Heath in Suffolk; an intermediate at Skipwith Common in Yorkshire; and a northern variant at the Moor of Dinnet in Aberdeenshire. The different regional examples vary considerably in flora and fauna, but the overall ecological pattern of variation remains remarkably similar.

Flora

The habitats and geographical distribution of the vascular plant species are given in Table 11. An analysis of this flora tends to reflect the rather arbitrary and artificial limits which have been drawn for this formation. For instance, as heathy vegetation rich in montane and northern species has been classed as uplands, the lowland heaths are necessarily poor in northern species (only eight). Similarly, the deliberate exclusion of most of the characteristic Breckland grass–heath species and the species of specialised habitats on the Lizard serpentine has greatly reduced representation of the south-eastern element and the number of rare or local species; the floras of these two districts are dealt with in detail later. The limits of wet heath and mire are ill defined, and many species are common to both classes, so that there is overlap here in the separate account of the two floras, though strongly hydrophilous mire species have been excluded. On the other hand, the inclusion of plants of incompletely podsolised soils which occur on many otherwise acidic heathlands, appreciably increases the richness of the flora to be considered, and the species thereby added indicate relationships to the markedly base-rich grasslands.

It is clear that the majority of species recognised in the heathland flora (Table 11) are common and widespread wherever suitable habitats occur. An interesting phytogeographical feature nevertheless emerges – that there is a strong representation of oceanic species and out of a total of 22 such species, 12 may be termed southern oceanic. This is matched by the fact that lowland acidic heath is a formation characteristic of an oceanic climate. Rather few species show a marked degree of exclusiveness to lowland acidic heath; *Lycopodium inundatum*, *Ophioglossum lusitanicum*, *Cicendia filiformis*, *Gentiana pneumonanthe*, *Genista pilosa*, *Ulex gallii*, *U. minor*, *Erica ciliaris*, *E. vagans*, *Cuscuta*

epithymum, *Lobelia urens* and *Agrostis setacea* are the most characteristic and include all five of the really rare species of this ecosystem type.

The *Atlas of the British Flora* indicates that several local species of acidic lowland heath have become extinct in numerous localities, suggesting that adverse pressures on this kind of habitat are especially heavy. Much-decreased species include *Lycopodium inundatum*, *L. selago* (in the south), *Pilularia globulifera*, *Radiola linoides*, *Drosera intermedia*, *Gentiana pneumonanthe*, *Antennaria dioica* (in the south) and *Eleocharis multicaulis*. It is, however, possible that other factors could have been involved in some of these declines.

Rock habitats within acidic heath areas are found only in western and northern Britain, and are interesting mainly for bryophytes and lichens, though they support a few characteristic or even rare vascular plants, such as *Sedum anglicum*, *Umbilicus rupestris*, *Corydalis claviculata*, *Polypodium vulgare* agg., *Asplenium obovatum* and *Genista pilosa*.

Fauna

See under calcareous grasslands (p. 151).

CRITERIA FOR KEY SITE ASSESSMENT AND SELECTION

In many districts, the existing lowland heaths represent the fragmented remnants of much larger areas which have either been afforested or converted to farmland. This attrition of habitat continues and has been particularly severe in the Isle of Purbeck since 1945. The surviving areas of heathland are in general rather fragile ecosystems and urgently in need of conservation. Due regard has therefore been paid to factors which are directly concerned with the perpetuation of scientific quality, and emphasis was placed on the following criteria:

Comparative site evaluation

Size

An oligotrophic ecosystem surrounded by agricultural land is likely to suffer from the application of fertilisers to the surrounding area and subsequent modification of its vegetation. If it is surrounded by woodland plantations there is the problem of invasion by tree species. Small areas are more vulnerable in these respects than larger areas. Management requirements on the site itself, such as burning, will also be restricted by the proximity of woodland. Management of many heathland areas may require a rotational burning programme; if this is based on an approximately 15-year cycle, and peatland is present, an area of at least 200 ha is required. Acidic peatland sites also require an adequate acidic heathland catchment for their protection as they are even more sensitive to change than dry heath. These considerations, which emphasise the necessity of selecting a large enough area, are not so important for some special types such as coastal heathland.

Table 11. *Habitat and distribution of vascular plants of lowland acidic heath and grassland*

	Dry heath	Wet heath	Acidic	Weakly basic	Southern oceanic	Oceanic	South-eastern	Southern	Widespread common	Widespread local	Northern	Rare species	Continental distribution
	1	2	3	4	5	6	7	8	9	10	11	12	13
Lycopodium selago	+	+	+	—	—	—	—	—	—	—	+	—	—
L. inundatum	—	+	+	—	—	—	—	—	—	+	—	—	—
L. clavatum	+	—	+	—	—	—	—	—	—	—	+	—	—
Osmunda regalis	—	+	+	—	—	+	—	—	—	—	—	—	—
Pteridium aquilinum	+	—	+	—	—	—	—	—	—	+	—	—	—
Pilularia globulifera	—	+	+	—	—	—	—	—	—	+	—	—	—
Ophioglossum lusitanicum	+	—	—	+	+	—	—	—	—	—	—	+	—
Corydalis claviculata	+	—	+	—	—	—	—	—	—	+	—	—	OW
Teesdalia nudicaulis	+	—	+	—	—	—	—	—	—	+	—	—	C
Viola riviniana	+	—	—	+	—	—	—	—	+	—	—	—	—
Polygala vulgaris	+	—	—	+	—	—	—	—	+	—	—	—	—
P. serpyllifolia	+	—	+	—	—	—	—	—	+	—	—	—	—
Hypericum undulatum	—	+	+	—	+	—	—	—	—	—	—	—	OW
H. humifusum	+	—	+	—	—	—	—	—	—	+	—	—	—
H. pulchrum	+	—	+	—	—	—	—	—	+	—	—	—	—
H. elodes	—	+	+	+	+	—	—	—	—	—	—	—	OW
Radiola linoides	—	+	+	+	—	—	—	—	—	+	—	—	—
Genista anglica	+	—	+	—	—	—	—	—	—	+	—	—	OW
G. pilosa	+	—	+	—	—	—	—	+	—	—	—	+	—
Ulex europaeus	+	—	+	+	—	—	—	—	+	—	—	—	OW
U. gallii	+	—	+	—	+	—	—	—	—	—	—	—	OW
U. minor	+	—	+	—	—	—	+	—	—	—	—	—	OW
Ononis repens	+	—	—	+	—	—	—	+	—	—	—	—	—
Ornithopus perpusillus	+	—	—	+	—	—	—	+	—	—	—	—	OS
Potentilla erecta	+	+	+	—	—	—	—	—	+	—	—	—	—
Sedum anglicum	+	—	+	—	—	+	—	—	—	—	—	—	OW
Crassula tillaea	+	—	—	+	—	—	+	—	—	—	—	—	OS
Drosera rotundifolia	—	+	+	—	—	—	—	—	+	—	—	—	CN
D. intermedia	—	+	+	—	—	+	—	—	—	—	—	—	CN
Carum verticillatum	—	+	—	+	—	+	—	—	—	—	—	—	OW
Rumex acetosella	+	—	+	—	—	—	—	—	+	—	—	—	—
Salix repens	+	+	+	+	—	—	—	—	+	—	—	—	—
Calluna vulgaris	+	+	+	+	—	—	—	—	+	—	—	—	—
Erica tetralix	—	+	+	+	—	—	—	—	+	—	—	—	OW
E. ciliaris	+	+	+	—	+	—	—	—	—	—	—	+	OW
E. cinerea	+	—	+	—	—	—	—	—	+	—	—	—	OW
E. vagans	+	+	—	+	+	—	—	—	—	—	—	+	OW
Vaccinium vitis-idaea	+	+	+	—	—	—	—	—	—	—	+	—	AA
V. myrtillus	+	—	+	—	—	—	—	—	+	—	—	—	CN
V. oxycoccos	—	+	+	—	—	—	—	—	—	—	+	—	—
Empetrum nigrum	+	+	+	—	—	—	—	—	—	—	+	—	AA
Anagallis tenella	—	+	+	+	—	+	—	—	—	—	—	—	OS
Cicendia filiformis	—	+	+	—	+	—	—	—	—	—	—	—	OS
Gentiana pneumonanthe	—	+	+	—	—	—	—	+	—	—	—	—	CN
Echium vulgare	+	—	—	+	—	—	—	—	+	—	—	—	—
Cuscuta epithymum	+	—	+	—	—	—	—	—	+	—	—	—	—
Veronica officinalis	+	—	+	+	—	—	—	—	+	—	—	—	—
Pedicularis sylvatica	—	+	+	—	—	—	—	—	+	—	—	—	—
Pinguicula lusitanica	—	+	+	+	—	+	—	—	—	—	—	—	OW

Table 11 (*contd.*)

	1	2	3	4	5	6	7	8	9	10	11	12	13
P. vulgaris	—	+	+	+	—	—	—	—	—	—	+	—	CN
Scutellaria minor	—	+	—	+	+	—	—	—	—	—	—	—	OW
Plantago coronopus	+	—	+	—	—	—	—	—	—	+	—	—	CS
Wahlenbergia hederacea	—	+	+	—	+	—	—	—	—	—	—	—	OW
Campanula rotundifolia	+	—	—	+	—	—	—	—	+	—	—	—	—
Jasione montana	+	—	+	—	—	+	—	—	—	—	—	—	—
Lobelia urens	+	—	+	—	+	—	—	—	—	—	—	+	OW
Galium verum	+	—	—	+	—	—	—	—	+	—	—	—	—
G. saxatile	+	—	+	—	—	—	—	—	+	—	—	—	—
Succisa pratensis	—	+	+	+	—	—	—	—	+	—	—	—	—
Filago germanica	+	—	+	—	—	—	—	—	—	+	—	—	—
F. minima	+	—	+	—	—	—	—	—	—	+	—	—	—
Gnaphalium sylvaticum	+	—	+	—	—	—	—	—	—	+	—	—	—
Antennaria dioica	+	—	+	+	—	—	—	—	—	—	+	—	NM
Cirsium dissectum	—	+	—	+	—	—	—	+	—	—	—	—	OW
Hieracium pilosella	+	—	—	+	—	—	—	—	+	—	—	—	—
Narthecium ossifragum	—	+	+	—	—	—	—	—	+	—	—	—	OW
Juncus squarrosus	+	+	+	—	—	—	—	—	+	—	—	—	—
J. acutiflorus	—	+	+	+	—	—	—	—	+	—	—	—	—
J. effusus	+	+	+	+	—	—	—	—	+	—	—	—	—
J. bulbosus	—	+	+	+	—	—	—	—	+	—	—	—	—
Luzula campestris	+	—	+	+	—	—	—	—	+	—	—	—	—
L. multiflora	+	—	+	+	—	—	—	—	+	—	—	—	—
Dactylorchis maculata	+	+	+	+	—	—	—	—	+	—	—	—	—
Eriophorum angustifolium	—	+	+	+	—	—	—	—	+	—	—	—	CN
E. vaginatum	—	+	+	—	—	—	—	—	—	—	+	—	CN
Trichophorum cespitosum	—	+	+	—	—	—	—	—	+	—	—	—	CN
Eleocharis multicaulis	—	+	+	—	—	+	—	—	—	—	—	—	CN
Schoenus nigricans	—	+	—	+	—	+	—	—	—	—	—	—	—
Rhynchospora alba	—	+	+	—	—	+	—	—	—	—	—	—	—
R. fusca	—	+	+	—	+	—	—	—	—	—	—	—	CN
Carex binervis	+	+	+	—	—	—	—	—	+	—	—	—	OW
C. panicea	—	+	+	+	—	—	—	—	+	—	—	—	—
C. pilulifera	+	—	+	—	—	—	—	—	+	—	—	—	—
C. nigra	—	+	+	+	—	—	—	—	+	—	—	—	—
C. echinata	—	+	+	—	—	—	—	—	+	—	—	—	CN
Molinia caerulea	+	+	+	+	—	—	—	—	+	—	—	—	—
Festuca ovina	+	—	+	+	—	—	—	—	+	—	—	—	—
Holcus mollis	+	+	+	—	—	—	—	—	+	—	—	—	—
Deschampsia flexuosa	+	+	+	—	—	—	—	—	+	—	—	—	—
D. setacea	—	+	+	—	—	—	—	—	—	+	—	—	OW
Aira praecox	+	—	+	—	—	—	—	—	+	—	—	—	—
Agrostis setacea	+	+	+	—	+	—	—	—	—	—	—	—	OW
A. canina	+	+	+	+	—	—	—	—	+	—	—	—	—
A. tenuis	+	+	+	+	—	—	—	—	+	—	—	—	—
A. stolonifera	+	+	+	+	—	—	—	—	+	—	—	—	—
Nardus stricta	+	+	+	—	—	—	—	—	—	—	+	—	—
Sieglingia decumbens	+	—	—	+	—	—	—	—	+	—	—	—	—
Total 97	62	55	81	42	12	10	2	7	45	13	8	5	

Notes

European distribution:

OS = oceanic southern   OW = oceanic west European
 C = continental   CN = continental northern
NM = northern montane   AA = Arctic–alpine

Diversity

In the case of heathland, diversity often means physical diversity especially with respect to soil moisture, as this produces floristic (and faunal) diversity. Other vegetation types related to management effects, such as birch or gorse scrub, bracken and acidophilous grassland, add to diversity. Some heathland vegetation types can be regarded as having high scientific value (open dwarf-shrub heath and peatland) whereas others (bracken and birch scrub) may in some cases be considered of low value or even undesirable. Bare soil and sand are often important animal habitats and rock outcrops are important for bryophytes.

Ecological process

In most cases, dwarf-shrub heath is an artificial habitat maintained by fire or grazing, but some heathland is maintained by exposure and even when poor in species, assumes a special ecological interest. If grazing on the latter is prevented, an ecosystem approaching equilibrium, with production and breakdown in balance, may be achieved. The natural climax heathlands are regarded as having especially high scientific value.

Public pressure and land-use

Dwarf-shrub heath is not particularly amenable to heavy public pressure, as heather is not very resistant to trampling and there is always the risk of unintentional heath fires when the public have unrestricted access. Grazing, often by commoners' stock, is an important factor in many heathland areas. Removal of grazing may in some areas lead to invasion by scrub, especially birch and, if birch invasion passes a certain point, burning tends to increase it rather than control it. Grazing tends to increase the abundance of grass species. There is thus a preference for sites where access is limited and management can be controlled.

Requirements for the national series

The selection of key lowland heath sites has to be made mainly within southern England, where most of this formation is located. The field of variation is much more limited than that of the calcareous grasslands, and is accordingly represented adequately by a smaller number of sites. In particular, an attempt has been made to represent the following ecological features and directions of variation in lowland heathland.

1 The east to west gradient from continental to oceanic conditions.

2 The range of variation from dry heath to wet heath and then valley mire, as exemplified by the heathland complexes of the New Forest.

3 The range of variation from acidic heath to calcareous grassland, as exemplified by the Breckland, and including variants associated with unusual rocks, e.g. the Lizard serpentine.

4 The transition to northern and submontane heathland characteristic of the British uplands.

5 The maritime heaths characteristic especially of west coast headlands but also found on acidic dune systems.

6 Floristic variety, largely associated with 1–5 above.

7 Faunally rich heathlands which are not represented by sites selected according to the foregoing criteria.

REGIONAL DIVERSITY AND SELECTION OF KEY SITES

The most continental heathland area is the Breckland of south-west Norfolk and north-west Suffolk, where the underlying Cretaceous Chalk is variably obscured by sandy boulder clay and wind-blown sand, giving a vegetational sequence from calcareous grassland to acidic heathland as soil calcium status decreases. The Breckland grassland–heath complex is sufficiently important to be treated later on its own (p. 174), but among the most important acidic heathland sites may be mentioned Berner's, Horn and Weather Heaths (see L.62, gr. 1),[1] valuable as a large and secluded area, and Cavenham–Tuddenham Heaths (see L.61, gr. 1), valuable for their diversity. Bridgham and Brettenham Heaths (see L.60, gr. 1) are another large area of acidic Breckland heath; and this formation is also represented on Lakenheath Warren (see L.62), East Wretham Heath and Stanford Practical Training Area (L.60(a), gr. 1), Foxhole Heath (L.63, gr. 1) and Thetford Heath (L.65(a), gr. 1).

There are two other fairly extensive heathland areas in East Anglia – on the east Suffolk Sandlings, of Pleistocene sands and clays, and on the north Norfolk drift-covered Chalk and Greensand. In east Suffolk, Dunwich Heaths and Marshes (L.58, gr. 1) form an integral part of an important ecosystem complex which also includes woodland, scrub and flood-plain mire. Roydon Common (L.59, gr. 1) near King's Lynn is probably the best of the north Norfolk heaths, being fairly large and diverse, with transitions to wet heath and basiphilous valley mire. Other north Norfolk heaths such as Sandringham Warren (L.76, gr. 2), and Holt Lowes (L.75, gr. 2) are less diverse and suffer from heavy public pressure. As a whole, the East Anglian heathlands are not particularly distinguished floristically and, apart from *Calluna vulgaris*, *Ulex europaeus* is the commonest shrub.

In the southern and less continental counties of Surrey, Sussex and Hampshire, are large areas of acidic heathland on Cretaceous and Tertiary sands and gravels. The Surrey heaths are a good deal fragmented, and there are several interesting distinct sites, but probably the best is the combined area of Thursley and Hankley Commons (L.2, gr. 1) near Godalming, a large, little-disturbed complex with good valley mire. Ashdown Forest (L.1, gr. 1), Sussex, and the New Forest (L.20, gr. 1*), Hampshire, are two very large areas with mixtures of dry heathland, wet heathland, valley mire and woodland. Although these two areas lie in the same region of England and have a good deal in common, their great size (2600 and 16400 ha respectively) confers

---

[1] Cross references to key sites are identified by an initial letter (indicating habitat) and number.

high nature conservation value and requires that both be given grade 1 status. Grade 2 alternative sites are Iping and Ambersham Commons (L.13), Sussex, and Chobham Common (L.14), Surrey (see Appendix). Semi-natural eco-systems of such extent are now so rare in lowland Britain that their conservation is a matter of great importance and urgency. These southern England heaths are the main areas for *Ulex minor* communities, and they support a distinctive southern flora and fauna.

South-east Dorset, notably the Isle of Purbeck, has other important tracts of heathland, now considerably reduced and fragmented. These contain important complexes of valley mire and at their seaward edges merge into brackish communities and then salt marsh; they rate highly for their great ecological diversity and floral and faunal richness. Communities dominated by the very local *Erica ciliaris* are a distinctive feature here. As much as possible of the remaining parts of this once extensive heathland area should be conserved. The most important parts may be divided into two groups – the Hartland–Arne Heaths (L.88, gr. 1*) and the Studland–Godlingston Heaths (L.89, gr. 1*). The former contains the Hartland Moor National Nature Reserve (NNR) and the Royal Society for the Protection of Birds' Arne reserve, while the latter contains the Studland Heath NNR. The two key sites now recognised include considerably more ground than that already scheduled as nature reserves. The Creech–Grange–Povington Heaths (L.106, gr. 2) are also regarded as having considerable scientific value. To the north, Morden Bog (L.90) is an important outlying complex of heathland, valley mire and pinewood regarded as essential for inclusion in the series of grade 1 Dorset heathlands.

Farther west, in Devon and Cornwall, the climate is still milder and the more humid conditions, combined with a local prevalence of base-poor rocks, give considerable areas of acidic soils covered with heath vegetation. This is an extremely oceanic district, contrasting with Breckland at the opposite end of the east–west climatic gradient. There is a great abundance of *Ulex gallii* in the heaths here, and a strong representation of other oceanic species such as *Wahlenbergia hederacea*, *Hypericum elodes* and *Scutellaria minor*. Aylesbeare Common (L.91, gr. 1) in east Devon is regarded as the most important typical representative of these south-western heathlands and is a fairly low-level example overlying Triassic Pebble Beds. The south-west also contains the three more elevated moorland tracts of Dartmoor, Bodmin Moor and Exmoor, and here the heath-land vegetation characteristic of the lowlands shows a gradual transition to a distinctly upland complex with sub-montane heather moor, soligenous mire and blanket mire. An area of North Dartmoor (L.92, gr. 1) has been chosen to include lowland, intermediate and upland heaths, spread over the vertical range of 330 m, and lying on both the Culm Measures and granite. This site is also regarded as the southernmost occurrence in Britain of upland vegetation. Dunkery Beacon (L.107, gr. 2) on Exmoor in Somerset is an alternative but less varied complex of the same type, on Old Red Sandstone.

The windswept rocky coasts of the south-west peninsula carry the submaritime type of dwarf-shrub heath which is probably a climax type. The granite Isles of Scilly (L.93, gr. 1*) have a considerable extent and diversity of this extremely oceanic heathland, on thin peaty soils or variable depths of Pleistocene gravels. On the mainland, the north Cornwall coast, from Chapel Porth to St Agnes (L.94, gr. 1) on Devonian shales, has another area of submaritime heath of a more species-rich kind, and is regarded as part of an important rocky coast site (C.30).

The other major climatic gradient to be considered in relation to the selection of key heathland sites, is the south to north decrease in mean temperature; being almost by definition a southern formation, however, lowland heaths become fewer and smaller with distance north in Britain.

In the west, lowland type heaths are well represented on acidic headlands and coastal hills in both south and north Wales. An area of the Bannau Preseli (L.117), which lie farther inland, is regarded as a grade 2 example of acidic heath intermediate between lowland and upland. The heaths of the Glannau Ynys Gybi (L.120, gr. 1) on Anglesey have been chosen as the best example of this formation in Wales, but there are other good areas, grading into more distinctly upland-type heaths on the coastal massif of Yr Eifl (L.122, gr. 2) in Lleyn. Just outside Wales, the rather low hills of western Shropshire known as the Stiperstones (L.123, gr. 1) show a still more northern example of the transition from lowland to submontane heath. As in Wales, there is here an abundance of the oceanic *Ulex gallii* on lower ground, but *Vaccinium vitis-idaea* is abundant at higher levels. In north-west England, the western Lakeland fells have diminishing areas of *Calluna–Ulex gallii* heath on their lower slopes. In Cumberland, the low New Red Sandstone range of Lazonby and Wan Fells (L.146, gr. 2) north of Penrith has good areas of Callunetum intermediate between lowland and upland in type, and on the Solway Plain around Carlisle are small outposts of true lowland heath with *Ulex minor*.

In eastern England, north of Norfolk, there are now only very limited areas of heathland in the predominantly agricultural lowlands. Lincolnshire has several grassland and heath systems which have developed where a layer of acidic cover sand variably overlies Jurassic limestones. The most interesting of these heaths now remaining is Risby Warren (L.66, gr. 1) near Scunthorpe where, within the compass of a single site, there is much of the range of ecological diversity characteristic of the Breckland, i.e. from unstable dune to closed vegetation and from calcareous grassland to acidic heath. There is, however, not the species richness of the Breckland grasslands and heaths, either in flora or fauna. Nottinghamshire formerly had extensive areas of lowland heath, but these are much reduced in size, and the remaining tracts are insufficiently diverse to be regarded as nationally important. In the Vale of York still farther north there are much reduced remnants such as Allerthorpe and Strensall Commons (L.145, gr. 2), but the best remaining site is Skipwith Common (L.129, gr. 1), a good example of a northern continental heath. Some drier heather areas of the

North York Moors have affinities with lowland heath but
are better regarded as submontane types. Lowland heathland is rare in Scotland, where its place is taken largely by
vegetation of more obvious upland affinities, but the large
coastal dune system at the Sands of Forvie (L.150, gr. 1) in
Aberdeenshire has quite a large area of a heath which
represents a northern type of this formation. Torrs Warren
(C.72) in Wigtownshire is a west coast example of a similar
type. In the western Highlands, submaritime dwarf-shrub
heath is well developed on sea cliff tops and seaward slopes
throughout the region, and good examples occur on Rhum,
Inner Hebrides (C.101); around Loch Druidibeg, Outer
Hebrides (OW.88(a)); and on the Durness coast, Sutherland (C.108). At Invernaver, Sutherland (C.109), there is a
transition to montane dwarf-shrub heath almost at sea-level.

B. CALCAREOUS GRASSLANDS

RANGE OF ECOLOGICAL VARIATION

Habitat factors and vegetation

Variability in lowland calcareous grasslands will be discussed in terms of three main factors – rocks and soils,
climate and human influence.

ROCKS AND SOILS

Calcareous grasslands are distributed over a variety of geological formations, which are chemically all limestones,
ranging from the soft Cretaceous Chalk through the
moderately hard Jurassic examples to the hard rock of the
Carboniferous. Besides occurring over a range of limestone
rock varying physically, calcareous grasslands are also found
on limestone with large amounts of magnesium (the Magnesian Limestone and the dolomitic Durness Limestone),
and on calcareous igneous and metamorphic rocks, including
pumice tuff, dolerite, basalt, andesite, and certain schists and
gneisses. Related communities are also found on soils
derived from sand and chalky boulder clays in the Breckland, and there are close relationships with communities of
stable calcareous sand dunes on the coast, notably the shell
sand machair of the Outer Hebrides.

In spite of wide differences in the physical and litho-
logical nature of the underlying substratum, the soils
derived from these varied parent materials are relatively
similar chemically and this common factor gives the characteristic composition, both in terms of floristics and structure, to calcareous grasslands. These soils are characterised
by a high pH, usually in the range 6.5–8.5, a high available
calcium content, usually in the range 300–1000 mg calcium/
100 g, a high free calcium carbonate content (30–75%) and
often a high organic matter content (7–20%), the last being
associated with the permanent nature of these grasslands.
Rendzinas are well developed, especially on steeper ground,
and there is a wide range of brown earths.

Local variations in soil character may be caused by the
presence of variable superficial deposits, such as Clay-with-

Flints, glacial gravels and sand, or loess, which insulate the
vegetation from the country rock, or by different degrees of
leaching which may be attributed to varying aspect, precipitation and steepness of slope. The degree of variation in the
vegetation caused by these local differences in soils depends
largely on the extent to which lime-status is reduced in the
rooting horizon of the soil; thus a thick Clay-with-Flints
deposit over Chalk may support an acidic heath community
containing no calcicoles, while local leaching of a soil
derived from impure Carboniferous Limestone may create,
locally, conditions which enable a calcifuge species such as
Potentilla erecta to compete in an otherwise essentially
calcicolous community. In the north and west, peat often
forms over calcareous substrata in stable situations. Chalk
and limestone soils tend to be porous and therefore dry, but
where there is clay or compacted drift derived from calcareous rocks, marked drainage impedance may result and
give a transition from dry grassland to marsh or even mire
(fen). Minor spatial variations in soil moisture can also give
a good deal of floristic diversity. There are also transitions
from calcareous grasslands (including machair) to submaritime grasslands and heaths where salt spray enriches
the soil with other nutrients besides calcium.

Open rock habitats have extremely immature soils –
except on big ledges – and on cliffs, screes and pavements
they consist largely of variable pockets containing mixtures
of humus and downwashed or windblown mineral particles.
These vestigial soils have rendzina or brown earth affinities,
and are usually developed directly on the bedrock. The importance of open rocks is that they provide favourable
habitats for species which are suppressed by grazing, or
those which cannot tolerate competition in a closed community, especially one composed of more luxuriant species.
In wet climates, too, the instability of rock habitats resists
leaching and allows an intimate contact between plant roots
and a highly calcareous substratum. Thin, immature soils
over friable chalk or limestone, and shallow calcareous
sandy soils, are also prone to instability and erosion, again
giving a range of open habitats.

Geology is obviously important in producing variation in
the range from calcareous to non-calcareous grasslands, but
other factors are evidently responsible for much of the
variation in botanical composition within the range of calcareous grasslands. However, for convenience and ease of
reference, the lowland calcareous grasslands have been subdivided according to the major geological formations, i.e.
Chalk, Jurassic limestones, Carboniferous Limestone,
Devonian limestone, Magnesian Limestone and other calcareous rocks.

There is some parallelism between grassland floristics and
the nature of the soil parent material, though the relationship may be largely incidental, because the major calcareous
rock formations show a certain geographical/climatic separation within Britain, e.g. Chalk in the south and east, Carboniferous Limestone in the north and west. Hardness of
the parent rock and its effect on the physical nature of the
habitat and soil is evidently a factor of some importance
in determining vegetational differences between these cal-

careous formations. It is possible that more critical pedo-logical investigations may disclose other differences between the soils of these different geological formations which prove to be significant for differences between their associated grasslands. Until this has been shown, however, these floristic differences are best regarded as the result mainly of a combination of geographical/climatic, land-use and chance factors which have produced a variety of distribution patterns for many plant species of calcareous grassland.

The calcareous grasslands are characterised by great floristic diversity not only in grasses but also in forbs, and therein lies their special botanical interest. There is, however, growing evidence that this floristic richness is often associated with a poverty of major soil nutrients other than calcium, i.e. nitrogen, potassium and phosphorus, which limits the growth performance and competitive power of certain species (especially grasses). Addition of manure and fertilisers can upset this competitive balance and lead to sward impoverishment as some species increase in cover and stature.

Despite their wide geographical variations in floristics, lowland calcareous grasslands have a large enough number of constant vascular species to give a certain overall homogeneity and characteristic appearance to this broad class of vegetation. The constants are recognised from approximately 1500 1-m² sample quadrats, consisting of c. 1100 on Chalk, 184 on Jurassic limestones, 170 on Carboniferous Limestone, 39 on Devonian limestone and only 4 on Magnesian Limestone. These overall constants are: *Briza media, Festuca ovina, F. rubra, Carex flacca, Lotus corniculatus, Plantago lanceolata, Poterium sanguisorba* and *Thymus drucei*. Other species which reach high constancy through the range of lowland calcareous grasslands include *Carex caryophyllea, Koeleria cristata, Helictotrichon pratense, H. pubescens, Agrostis stolonifera, Trisetum flavescens, Orchis mascula, Leontodon hispidus, Scabiosa columbaria, Campanula rotundifolia, Helianthemum chamaecistus, Linum catharticum, Veronica chamaedrys, Ranunculus bulbosus* and *Polygala vulgaris*. Some less abundant species occur at lower frequency through most of the five classes of lowland calcareous grassland and so are characteristic of the formation as a whole; they include *Botrychium lunaria, Thalictrum minus* agg., *Arabis hirsuta, Viola hirta, Geranium lucidum, Anthyllis vulneraria, Sedum acre, Saxifraga tridactylites, Pimpinella saxifraga, Daucus carota, Gentianella amarella, Acinos arvensis, Calamintha ascendens, Plantago media, Carlina vulgaris, Coeloglossum viride, Gymnadenia conopsea, Ophrys apifera, Anacamptis pyramidalis*.

Other groups of local constants can be recognised and may be ecologically meaningful as well as useful in characterising associations within this grassland complex. For example, *Brachypodium pinnatum, Zerna erecta* and *Helianthemum chamaecistus* show higher constancy on Jurassic limestones than on Chalk, although all three are common in some chalk grasslands; while *Dactylis glomerata, Koeleria cristata* and *Prunella vulgaris* are constant on Chalk but less so on Jurassic limestones. A number of species of lower constancy and rare species belong mainly to one or other of the major calcareous rock formations and so have value as differentials for the various grassland associations.

CHALK GRASSLAND

Seven main types of chalk grassland are recognised according to differences in dominance of grass or sedge species, namely: *Festuca ovina–F. rubra, Carex humilis, Zerna erecta, Brachypodium pinnatum, Arrhenatherum elatius, Helictotrichon pubescens* and mixed Gramineae. The *Festuca* and *C. humilis* types are those which have come to be regarded as high quality chalk swards, on account of their floristic richness; the former is widespread on the Chalk formation but *C. humilis* swards are confined to the more westerly districts and are best developed in Wiltshire. Within these two associations various facies are recognised tentatively according to different consistent combinations of other locally constant species, as follows:

Sieglingia decumbens facies, best seen in the Isle of Wight and some of the westernmost chalk grasslands, e.g. at Long Knoll, Wiltshire.

Carex flacca–Poterium sanguisorba facies, widespread but characteristic of the *Festuca ovina* grasslands particularly in the Chilterns.

Poterium sanguisorba–Helianthemum chamaecistus facies, characteristic of south-facing slopes in the more continental areas, e.g. Chilterns, Kent, East Anglia.

Serratula tinctoria–Betonica officinalis–Succisa pratensis facies, a strikingly western facies, often associated with *Carex humilis* but also in *Festuca ovina* grasslands.

Scabiosa columbaria–Succisa pratensis facies, a local variant of the western chalk grasslands.

Poterium sanguisorba–Filipendula vulgaris facies, local in distribution.

Leontodon hispidus facies, widespread, but best developed in Wiltshire and Dorset.

Phyteuma tenerum–Scabiosa columbaria–Succisa pratensis facies, restricted to Hampshire and the South Downs.

Daucus carota facies, very local and associated with the *Poterium* facies.

Chrysanthemum leucanthemum facies, very local, and always associated with the *Festuca ovina* or *Carex humilis* main associations.

These facies or others as yet undescribed appear to have ecological significance, in being related to such factors as geographical position, aspect and slope. J. F. Hope-Simpson has emphasised that northernmost occurrences of chalk grassland, on the Yorkshire Wolds, are a special case which has to be considered on rather different grounds from the rest of the Chalk, for the following reasons: (i) the Wolds are widely separated from all other chalk grasslands; (ii) northerly aspects in the Wolds are steeper and more common than in the Downs and they have a 'poorer' flora; (iii) many species common on the southern Chalk are absent or at their northern limit on the Yorkshire Chalk (e.g. *Cirsium acaulon*); (iv) *Conopodium majus*, virtually unknown on the southern Chalk, is common on the Wolds and other species such as *Knautia arvensis* are regular members of the Wolds chalk grassland but only occasional members of the southern chalk grassland.

The *Zerna erecta* and *Brachypodium pinnatum* communities usually represent stages in the retrogression of chalk grassland following cessation of grazing, resulting both from the removal of sheep stocks and elimination of rabbits by myxomatosis. These vigorously competitive grasses spread or increase in luxuriance, thus suppressing the smaller herbs and reducing species diversity. A further stage is the invasion by medium- to tall-shrub species which grow into a dense scrub and eventually smother most of the grassland plants. These retrogressive changes have been widespread in the remaining chalk grasslands during the last 15 years, and have often produced communities greatly impoverished in both plants and associated animals. Such successional tendencies create management problems for downland areas which it is desired to retain in an original condition. On the other hand, the changes associated with reduction or cessation of grazing are not always detrimental; they may, for instance, allow the flowering and better performance of some species, and may lead to a different balance in which greater diversity of ecosystem is actually attained.

The *Arrhenatherum elatius* and mixed grass types of chalk sward are often associated with more fundamental disturbance, including heavy grazing and manuring, application of fertilisers, ploughing and even reseeding. These swards usually lack most of the more characteristic herbs of old chalk grassland and tend to be floristically poor; they show close relationships with the more modified types of lowland neutral grassland.

JURASSIC LIMESTONE GRASSLAND

The grasslands of the Jurassic limestones have been less closely studied than those of the Chalk, and a smaller number of associations has been recognised so far. The juxtaposition of the two geological formations (the Jurassic outcrop closely follows the northern boundary of the Chalk) leads to a certain correspondence in their major grassland types, but present data indicate that the Jurassic limestone grasslands are the less variable of the two, with a large number of plant species belonging to the higher constancy classes. Three main types are recognised, dominated by *Festuca ovina*, *Brachypodium pinnatum* and *Zerna erecta*, the last two species being often intermixed.

Floristic variation within these three associations is similar to that in the corresponding types described for the Chalk. The *Festuca* type is the high-quality Jurassic limestone sward and in it species such as *Helianthemum chamaecistus*, *Poterium sanguisorba* and *Cirsium acaulon* are often more abundant and show higher constancy than on the Chalk. The slightly more northerly position of the Jurassic probably accounts for the lesser overall floristic richness of its grasslands, especially in the lower representation of species with an essentially southern and/or oceanic distribution; there are few species which show a distribution related to that of the Jurassic limestones rather than to other cal-

careous formations. Many of the Jurassic limestone swards nevertheless show species totals as high as those of the Chalk, and the distinctive calcicolous herbs are often equally abundant. The *Brachypodium pinnatum* and *Zerna erecta* communities are again mostly derived from the *Festuca* type by invasion of the coarser species following reduction or cessation of grazing.

CARBONIFEROUS LIMESTONE GRASSLAND

This geological formation has a much more northerly and westerly bias in distribution than the Chalk and Jurassic limestones. The scattered southernmost occurrences are mainly coastal, around the Bristol Channel and are isolated from the major, mostly inland, outcrops in north Wales, the north Midlands and northern England. The variation in floristics resulting from this geographical and ecological separation is amplified by the uneven and often rocky nature of the Carboniferous Limestone terrain, which gives great diversity in edaphic and micro-climatic conditions. A final factor which makes for floristic heterogeneity within the grasslands of this rock formation is the relatively large number of locally abundant species with a disjunct distribution within the total extent of the Carboniferous Limestone.

Festuca ovina–F. rubra swards are again a common type of grassland association, but both *Zerna erecta* and *Brachypodium pinnatum* are southern species poorly represented on the Carboniferous Limestone. Other southern constants or characteristic species such as *Poterium sanguisorba*, *Helianthemum chamaecistus*, *Hippocrepis comosa*, *Filipendula vulgaris*, *Asperula cynanchica*, *Orchis morio* and *Cirsium acaulon* become increasingly discontinuous in distribution with distance north, and lose constancy, or even presence. The northern and mainly upland grass *Sesleria albicans* is usually constant and locally dominant in limestone grasslands reaching down to sea-level in northern England, and some of these swards are lowland in character. There are transitions in this region to submontane types of calcareous grassland with northern and upland species such as *Antennaria dioica*, *Saxifraga hypnoides*, *Potentilla crantzii*, *Galium boreale* and *Minuartia verna*. Farther inland, especially in the Pennines, these in turn assume a distinctly montane character by the addition, at higher levels, of *Polygonum viviparum*, *Cochlearia officinalis* ssp. *alpina*, *Draba incana* and, very locally, *Gentiana verna*, *Carex capillaris* and *Myosotis alpestris*.

The scars, screes and pavements of the Carboniferous Limestone in various regions carry distinctive assemblages of plants, including many which have a need for open, immature habitats with freedom from competition. As most of these species do not form communities, except in the loosest sense, they are best mentioned under the account of flora.

MAGNESIAN LIMESTONE GRASSLAND

The Magnesian Limestone extends as a narrow strip northwards from Nottingham to Durham which is nowhere more than a few kilometres wide. It is entirely lowland in altitude and reaches the coast in Durham. Lying as it does between the Jurassic limestones to the east and south and the Carboniferous Limestone to the west and north, the Magnesian Limestone has grasslands which show intermediate characteristics in floristics. It is sufficiently far south to support southern grassland dominants such as *Brachypodium pinnatum* and *Zerna erecta*, and characteristic species such as *Anemone pulsatilla* (formerly), *Linum anglicum*, *Blackstonia perfoliata*, *Inula conyza* and *Carex ericetorum*; while some of the exposures are far enough north to have northern plants such as *Sesleria albicans* and *Epipactis atrorubens*.

In general floristics, the Magnesian Limestone grasslands have a good deal in common with those of the Jurassic limestones. They are now extremely limited in area, since many of the original outcrops of this rock formation have been quarried virtually out of existence. The other magnesium-rich limestones of Scotland are best regarded as belonging to the upland group of ecosystems, and the best known exposures the Durness Limestone, are dealt with in Chapter 9.

DEVONIAN LIMESTONE GRASSLAND

The Devonian limestone outcrops in a number of areas in south Devon. Even the most important sites are small, and most are under heavy pressure from holiday makers. The coastal position of the most important sites ensures that a mixture of maritime species is present with the calcicoles, and the extremely mild, oceanic climate may account for the presence of a number of distinctive plants in both groups. The grasslands are in general similar floristically to those of southern coastal outcrops of Chalk and Jurassic limestones, and the more special features are the presence of various rare or local species, some of which are associated particularly with the open ground of rocky slopes and cliffs.

RELATED GRASSLANDS ON OTHER CALCAREOUS ROCKS

Though they are not classed as limestone, a number of other rock formations scattered over the lowlands of Britain give base-rich or even calcareous substrata which carry unenclosed grassland or open rock communities. Various types of sandstone, shale, greywacke, schist, gneiss, and igneous rock locally contain enough calcium carbonate to give soils which are calcareous, or at least base-saturated, and where these occur in lowland situations they frequently bear grasslands of obvious floristic affinity to those found on the real limestones, though not falling within the strict definition of 'calcareous'. The richer examples of these grasslands are similar in floristics to those of Chalk and Limestone, but some species are characteristic of soils with only moderate calcium status derived from less rich parent materials, e.g. *Ranunculus acris*, *Viola riviniana*, *Trifolium campestre*, *T. dubium*, *Fragaria vesca*, *Saxifraga granulata*, *Gentianella campestris*, *Galium verum*, *Bellis perennis*, *Achillea millefolium*, *Hieraceum pilosella* and *Agrostis tenuis*. Open places on dry basic soils in general have species such as *Arabidopsis thaliana*, *Arenaria serpyllifolia*, *Veronica arvensis* and *Sherardia arvensis*.

Often, on these other geological formations, the parent rock is not sufficiently calcareous to resist leaching, so that the areas of base-rich soil tend to be small and may be restricted to flushed ground. The most important examples are found in Scotland, on such formations as the Silurian greywackes and shales of the Southern Uplands, the Dalradian schists of the southern Highlands, the Old Red Sandstone of north-east Scotland and Orkney, and the Tertiary basalts of the western Highlands and islands. In a few places they include limited areas of a real limestone, such as that forming the island of Lismore in the Firth of Lorne.

Many of these northern occurrences of calcareous rock support communities which are of upland rather than lowland affinity. In places where there are grasslands of recognisably lowland character these seldom appear to be of sufficient importance to warrant separate consideration, and examples are usually represented within sites rated highly for their other formations. However, certain localities are of considerable interest for their flora. In particular, there are several occurrences of igneous rock, mainly dolerite, or related material, which support not only calcicolous plants but also others with evidently unusual mineral requirements. Stanner Rocks in Radnor and Breidden Hill on the borders of Montgomeryshire and Shropshire are among the best known of such outcrops. The second is famous for the very rare *Potentilla rupestris* and both have other rare species such as *Lychnis viscaria*, *Veronica spicata* ssp. *hybrida*, *Sedum forsteranum* and *Bartramia stricta*, mixed with more common calcicoles. Arthur's Seat, Salisbury Crags and Blackford Hill in Edinburgh have *L. viscaria*, *Vicia sylvatica*, *Dianthus deltoides*, *P. tabernaemontani* and *Asplenium septentrionale*, and Traprain Law in East Lothian has several rare mosses, especially of the genus *Grimmia*. The slopes adjoining some of these sites have species-rich grasslands, but they are seldom as varied as examples on real limestone. These igneous rocks often provide important quarry stone, and several of the best sites have been spoiled. Breidden Hill was probably the most important but has deteriorated greatly through quarrying. Both this site and Stanner Rocks also have woodland affinities (see Appendix).

Submaritime grasslands which have affinities with the lowland calcareous grasslands (e.g. the Hebridean machairs) are dealt with in Chapter 4.

CLIMATE

Climate is regarded as a major determinant of geographical differences in floristic composition of lowland calcareous grasslands, through its effect on the distribution of many characteristic species. Differences in species' distribution patterns according to climate are examined in greater detail under Flora, p. 146. To a large extent, total European species' distribution patterns are repeated on a smaller scale in Britain, but there are certain discrepancies. The overall constants of lowland calcareous grassland are assumed to be species of wide climatic tolerances, though different ecotypes may be involved in some instances.

The calcareous grasslands of south-western England contain several species with a southern oceanic distribution in Europe, such as *Helianthemum apenninum*, *Koeleria vallesiana, Ononis reclinata, Rubia peregrina* and *Polygala calcarea*, though the last species extends fairly well to the east in southern England. The oceanic west European *Thesium humifusum* is also better represented in the western Chalk and Jurassic areas of southern England than in the east.

The calcicolous grassland species in J. R. Matthews' (1937) continental southern element mostly show a southern bias (suggestive of a requirement for summer warmth and sunshine) in Britain. They vary, however, from species restricted to the extreme south of England (e.g. *Ophrys sphegodes, O. fuciflora, Orchis simia, Carex humilis, Trinia glauca* and *Ajuga chamaepitys*) to those which reach to the north of England (e.g. *Hippocrepis comosa, Ophrys apifera, Anacamptis pyramidalis, Asperula cynanchica, Spiranthes spiralis* and *Blackstonia perfoliata*). The continental element recognised by Matthews shows a similar range of distribution in Britain, from species confined to southern England (e.g. *Bunium bulbocastanum, Dianthus gratianopolitanus, Orchis militaris, Seseli libanotis* and *Phyteuma tenerum*) to those which extend to northern England (e.g. *Inula conyza, Ophrys insectifera, Cirsium acaulon, Carex ericetorum* and *Anemone pulsatilla* (formerly)). As an indication of its southern climatic requirements, *Cirsium acaulon* is confined to south- or south-western-facing slopes in its northernmost localities, in Derbyshire and Yorkshire.

In addition, a number of species of fairly widespread distribution on the continent have a markedly southern distribution pattern in Britain, and are commonest in the south of England, e.g. *Filipendula vulgaris, Campanula glomerata, Gentianella anglica, Pimpinella major, Galium pumilum, Cirsium eriophorum, Orchis morio, Zerna erecta* and *Brachypodium pinnatum*. A few such species are confined to the south of England, e.g. *Arabis stricta, Polygala austriaca, Bupleurum baldense, Cirsium tuberosum* and *Allium sphaerocephalon*. These plants may be limited in Britain by warmth requirements, but the second group are perhaps better regarded as disjunct species.

The northern and submontane element of lowland calcareous grasslands and open rocks is better represented in northern England than Scotland, probably because of the much greater extent of suitable habitat (Carboniferous Limestone) in the first region; several species are confined to northern England or have their headquarters there (e.g. *Epipactis atrorubens, Primula farinosa, Polemonium caeruleum, Sesleria albicans* and *Dryopteris villarii*). A few northern species reach south-western England or south Wales on Carboniferous Limestone (e.g. *Saxifraga hypnoides, Asplenium viride, Polygonatum odoratum*) but only *Antennaria dioica* reaches the Chalk of the south-east. In general, there is a decrease in floristic richness of lowland calcareous grasslands with distance north, and it is the *upland* types which are species-rich, containing a large number of montane species totally absent from southern Britain.

A number of species with fairly well-defined continental distribution patterns show highly disjunct distribution patterns in Britain (e.g. *Helianthemum canum, Hypochoeris maculata, Aster linosyris, Veronica spicata* ssp. *hybrida* and

Cirsium tuberosum). The stations of these species lie within certain overall climatic limits but their absence from a great number of apparently suitable localities is unaccountable in terms of present ecological conditions. The same is true of many locally abundant species (e.g. *Carex humilis, Gentianella germanica*) which seem not to occupy their potential climatic range in Britain.

Some of the above species with climatically restricted distribution patterns are so scarce that they play an insignificant part in the composition of vegetation even where they occur. Some of the more abundant species, however, are sufficiently plentiful to be recognised as regional or local constants in lowland calcareous grassland, and thus give a means of recognising noda with distinctive geographical/climatic relationships within this formation. Some species occurring at lower frequency have value as characteristic species in the same way.

HUMAN INFLUENCE

The effect of grazing on the competitive balance between calcicolous grassland species has been mentioned. The range of variation between the short mixed grass–forb community characteristic of heavily grazed chalk grassland, and the tall swards dominated by grasses such as *Zerna erecta* and *Brachypodium pinnatum* on ungrazed sites is one of the best examples of this differentiation. Still more marked divergence from the sward developed under a long history of grazing management is found when grassland has been ploughed in the past, and reseeded or even cultivated as arable land, and then allowed to revert. Such profound disturbance destroys many of the original chalk grassland species and produces a grassland community of completely different floristic composition, resembling that of many enclosed meadows. In time there is a slow re-adjustment, with reinvasion by some of the original species, and eventually the community may regain much of its original floristics.

However, the extent of recovery depends very greatly on the time over which it has taken place. Re-adjustment, through invasion and competition, is slow and it may take several centuries for anything approaching the original community to redevelop. A great deal depends on the ability of former species to spread back and recolonise the lost ground. This depends in turn not only on the intrinsic power of species for spread, but on other factors such as climate, soil conditions and size of parent populations to provide the seed. In general, species which were originally local or rare will not reappear, or will take longest, for their powers of spread under the prevailing conditions are very limited. It is the common and vigorous species which will reappear first and assume the most prominent place in the changing community. Recently reverted grasslands of this type are usually recognisable because they contain only the common species and lack those which are rare or local. From this, it is reasonable to suppose that calcareous grasslands with a large number of rare and local species are of considerable age, and have remained under a particular kind of grazing management, without other disturbance, over a long period. The idea also explains how local extinction of species may occur.

This factor thus has a powerful influence on the distribution of the local and rare species, and has to be considered in any discussion of phytogeography and local variations in community floristics. For instance, on a uniform chalk scarp, with the same geology, altitude, aspect and slope, it is not uncommon to find sections which differ considerably in floristic composition. These differences may be not only in the quantities of the species present, but may involve also the complete absence of two or three species which are abundant in another section. It is often found that these differences occur where adjacent areas are in different parishes and hence have belonged to different farm units or owners for many centuries. This suggests that differences in farming practice, perhaps over a long period, may be responsible for these floristic variations. Sometimes other factors, including chance, could be involved and convincing information on land-use history to support the above hypothesis is usually difficult to obtain.

Whatever the validity of this kind of historical inference about community variation, observation certainly shows that age and management of calcareous grassland is important to its quality, and that the essential character of key examples is something which cannot readily be recreated once it is destroyed. Although essentially anthropogenic, calcareous grassland has something of the character of natural vegetation, in that it is a climax type evolved during a long period of environmental stability, yet has a marked degree of fragility.

Flora

Some of the dominant, constant and characteristic vascular plant species of lowland calcareous grasslands have already been discussed under plant communities (p. 142). Table 12 presents a fuller analysis of this flora according to parent rock type and geographical distribution. In general, there appear to be no significant chemical differences (in relation to vegetation) between the five major calcareous rock formations, and such floristic differences as exist are more probably related to the different physical properties and geographical/climatic positions of these rock types. The data on geographical distribution also give some idea of climatic preferences between the different species. The flora of lowland calcareous grasslands and related habitats is large and the number of rare species is correspondingly high. The rarity of many species has, however, been considerably increased by the widespread destruction of their habitat.

Some species of wide ecological amplitude are well represented in other vegetation formations as well as in other types of lowland grassland and the selection of species in Table 12 is somewhat arbitrary. The flora of calcareous scrub necessarily has a good deal in common with the grasslands from which the scrub is derived, and some species also occur in woodland. There is also considerable overlap with the flora of neutral grasslands and related habitats such as roadside and railway verges. Even some

degree of overlap occurs with acidic grasslands and heaths in regard to species which are only moderately base-demanding or perhaps completely tolerant, such as *Viola riviniana, Ononis repens, Ornithopus perpusillus, Crassula tillaea, Campanula rotundifolia, Galium verum, Succisa pratensis, Antennaria dioica, Hieraceum pilosella, Carex panicea, Festuca ovina, Agrostis tenuis* and *A. stolonifera.* Different ecotypes may, however, be involved when a species grows on soils of widely differing base content.

Many plant species of calcareous grassland are well represented in maritime or paramaritime habitats with suitable soil conditions, e.g. calcareous dunes and slopes or headlands above the sea. Several species in Table 12 are, in fact, confined in Britain to coastal stations, and their association with the sea may reflect a need for a mild, oceanic climate as well as for calcareous soils. A few species may owe their coastal position simply to the chance that the only suitable calcareous habitats which they were able to reach, or survive in, during the Post-glacial Period, happened to be by the sea.

Within the calcareous grassland formation, a good many plant species are widespread, occurring on all the major calcareous rock formations, and in each geographical region where calcareous soils are well represented. These plants appear to react largely to high calcium status of the substratum and to be unspecialised in climatic requirements. They naturally include most of the general constants of the various calcareous grassland associations. Others show varying degrees of restriction ecologically and geographically, and there follows a discussion of this more specialised element according to their representation on the different geological formations and in the different regions of Britain.

The Chalk, as the most southerly and easterly of the calcareous rock formations, not surprisingly supports the largest number of calcicolous species in J. R. Matthews' (1937) continental southern element, though some of these plants belong to woodland. As the climate of some Chalk districts is fairly mild, especially in the west, there are also several species of markedly oceanic distribution which are particularly associated with this rock formation. The following vascular plants appear to be confined to the Chalk: *Iberis amara, Seseli libanotis, Bunium bulbocastanum, Gentianella germanica, Phyteuma tenerum, Veronica spicata* ssp. *spicata* (Breckland), *Ajuga chamaepitys, Ophrys fuciflora, Orchis militaris* and *O. simia.* Six of these are classed as nationally rare species. A number of other species are found mainly on the Chalk, but occur more sparingly on other calcareous formations, namely: *Polygala calcarea, Salvia pratensis, Teucrium botrys, Carex humilis, Thesium humifusum, Senecio integrifolius, Cirsium tuberosum, Herminium monorchis, Ophrys sphegodes, Aceras anthropophorum* and *Himantoglossum hircinum.*

The floristic richness of the Chalk is famous and the number of species of orchid especially noteworthy. To many botanists the great attractiveness of the chalk flora derives from the beauty of many of its species and there is a special aesthetic quality in the appearance of a rich chalk grassland. Some of the rarer species have declined greatly and the

Table 12. *Flora of lowland calcareous grasslands*

	Chalk	Jurassic limestone	Carboniferous Limestone	Magnesian Limestone	Devonian limestone	Other calcareous & base-rich soils	Only in open habitats (sandy or exposed rock)	Coastal occurrence	S.E. England	S. England	S.W. England	East Anglia	Wales	Midlands	N. England	Scotland	Rare species	European distribution
	1	2	3	4	5	6	7	8	9	10	11	12	13	14	15	16	17	18
Dryopteris villarii	—	—	+	—	—	—	+	—	—	—	—	—	+	—	+	—	—	—
Thelypteris robertiana	—	—	+	—	—	—	+	—	+	—	+	—	+	+	+	+	+	—
Botrychium lunaria	+	+	+	+	—	+	—	+	+	+	+	+	+	+	+	+	+	—
Anemone pulsatilla	+	+	+	[+]	—	—	—	—	—	+	+	+	—	—	—	—	—	C
Ranunculus acris	+	+	+	+	+	+	—	+	+	+	+	+	+	+	+	+	+	—
R. bulbosus	+	+	+	+	+	+	—	+	+	+	(+)	+	+	+	+	+	+	—
Thalictrum minus agg.	+	+	+	+	+	+	—	+	—	—	(+)	+	+	+	+	+	+	—
Iberis amara	+	—	—	—	—	+	—	—	+	+	—	+	—	—	—	—	—	CS
Thlaspi perfoliatum	—	+	—	—	—	+	—	—	—	+	—	—	—	—	—	—	+	—
Hornungia petraea	—	—	+	—	—	—	+	+	—	—	—	+	+	+	+	—	—	CS
Draba muralis	—	—	+	—	—	+	+	—	—	—	—	+	+	+	+	—	—	—
Cardamine impatiens	+	+	+	—	—	+	+	—	+	+	+	+	+	+	+	+	—	—
Arabis hirsuta	+	+	+	+	+	+	—	+	+	+	+	+	+	+	+	+	+	—
A. stricta	—	—	+	—	—	—	+	—	—	—	+	—	—	—	—	+	—	—
Arabidopsis thaliana	+	+	+	+	+	+	+	+	+	+	+	+	+	+	+	+	—	—
Viola hirta	+	+	+	+	+	+	—	+	+	+	+	+	+	+	+	+	(+)	—
V. riviniana	+	+	+	+	+	+	—	+	+	+	+	+	+	+	+	+	—	—
Polygala vulgaris	+	+	+	+	+	+	—	+	+	+	+	+	+	+	+	+	—	—
P. calcarea	+	+	—	—	—	—	+	+	+	+	+	+	—	—	—	—	—	OS
P. amara	+	—	—	—	—	—	—	+	—	—	—	—	—	—	—	—	+	—
Helianthemum chamaecistus	+	+	+	+	+	+	—	+	+	+	+	+	+	+	+	+	—	—
H. apenninum	—	—	+	—	+	—	+	+	—	—	+	—	+	—	+	—	+	OS
H. canum	—	—	+	—	—	—	+	+	—	—	—	—	+	—	+	—	+	CS
Silene nutans	—	—	+	+	—	+	—	+	+	+	+	—	+	+	+	+	—	—
Dianthus deltoides	—	—	—	—	+	—	—	+	—	—	—	+	+	+	+	+	—	C
D. gratianopolitanus	—	—	+	—	—	+	—	—	—	—	+	—	—	—	—	—	+	C
Cerastium pumilum	+	+	+	—	+	—	—	+	+	+	+	+	—	—	—	—	—	—
C. semidecandrum	+	+	+	+	+	+	+	+	+	+	+	+	+	+	+	+	—	—
Arenaria serpyllifolia	+	+	+	+	+	+	+	+	+	+	+	+	+	+	+	+	—	—
Linum anglicum	+	—	+	—	—	—	+	—	—	—	+	—	+	—	+	—	—	—
L. catharticum	+	+	+	+	+	+	—	+	+	+	+	+	+	+	+	+	—	—
Geranium sanguineum	+	+	+	+	—	+	—	+	—	—	+	+	+	+	+	—	—	—
G. lucidum	+	+	+	+	+	+	+	+	+	+	+	+	+	+	+	+	—	—
Ononis reclinata	—	—	+	—	+	—	+	+	—	—	+	—	—	—	—	—	+	OS
Trifolium campestre	+	+	+	+	+	+	—	+	+	+	+	+	+	+	+	+	—	—
T. dubium	+	+	+	+	+	+	+	+	+	+	+	+	+	+	+	+	—	—
Anthyllis vulneraria	+	+	+	+	+	—	+	+	+	+	+	+	+	+	+	+	—	—
Lotus corniculatus	+	+	+	+	+	+	—	+	+	+	+	+	+	+	+	+	—	—
Astragalus danicus	+	+	+	+	—	+	—	—	+	+	+	—	+	+	+	—	—	CN
Hippocrepis comosa	+	+	+	—	+	—	—	+	+	+	+	+	+	+	+	—	—	CS
Onobrychis viciifolia	+	+	—	+	—	—	—	+	+	+	+	+	—	—	+	—	—	CS

II-2

Table 12 (*contd.*)

	1	2	3	4	5	6	7	8	9	10	11	12	13	14	15	16	17	18
Filipendula vulgaris	+	+	+	+	+	+	—	+	+	+	+	+	+	+	+	+	—	—
Potentilla tabernaemontani	+	+	+	+	—	+	—	+	—	+	+	+	+	+	+	+	—	—
P. rupestris	—	—	—	—	—	+	+	—	—	—	—	—	+	—	—	+	+	NM
Fragaria vesca	+	+	+	+	—	+	—	+	+	+	+	+	+	+	+	+	—	—
Poterium sanguisorba	+	+	+	+	+	+	—	+	+	+	+	+	+	+	+	+	—	—
Sedum acre	+	+	+	+	+	+	+	+	+	+	+	+	+	+	+	+	—	—
Saxifraga granulata	+	+	+	+	—	+	—	+	+	+	+	+	+	+	+	+	—	—
S. tridactylites	+	+	+	+	+	+	+	+	+	+	+	+	+	+	+	+	—	—
Thesium humifusum	+	+	—	—	—	—	—	+	+	+	+	—	—	—	—	—	—	OW
Bupleurum baldense	+	—	—	—	+	—	+	+	+	—	+	—	—	—	—	—	+	—
Trinia glauca	—	—	+	—	+	—	+	+	—	—	+	—	—	—	—	—	+	CS
Bunium bulbocastanum	+	—	—	—	—	—	—	+	—	+	—	+	—	—	—	—	+	C
Pimpinella saxifraga	+	+	+	+	+	+	—	+	+	+	+	+	+	+	+	+	—	—
P. major	+	+	+	+	—	+	—	+	+	+	+	+	+	+	+	—	—	—
Seseli libanotis	+	—	—	—	—	—	—	+	+	—	—	+	—	—	—	—	+	C
Daucus carota	+	+	+	+	+	+	—	+	+	+	+	+	+	+	+	+	—	—
Euphorbia cyparissias	+	+	+	+	+	+	—	+	+	+	+	+	+	+	+	+	—	—
Blackstonia perfoliata	+	+	+	+	+	+	—	+	+	+	+	+	+	+	(+)	—	—	CS
Gentianella campestris	+	+	+	+	+	+	—	+	+	+	+	+	+	+	+	+	—	CN
G. germanica	+	—	—	—	—	—	—	—	+	—	+	—	+	—	—	—	+	C
G. amarella	+	+	+	+	+	+	—	+	+	+	+	+	+	+	+	+	—	CN
G. anglica	+	+	—	—	—	—	—	+	+	+	+	+	—	—	—	—	—	—
Polemonium caeruleum	—	—	+	—	—	—	—	—	—	—	—	—	—	+	+	—	—	NM
Veronica chamaedrys	+	+	+	+	+	+	—	+	+	+	+	+	+	+	+	+	—	—
V. spicata ssp. *hybrida*	—	—	+	—	—	—	—	—	—	—	+	—	+	—	+	—	—	C
V. spicata ssp. *spicata*	+	—	—	—	—	—	—	—	—	—	+	—	—	—	—	—	+	C
V. arvensis	+	+	+	+	+	+	+	+	+	+	+	+	+	+	+	+	—	—
Euphrasia officinalis	+	+	+	+	+	+	—	+	+	+	+	+	+	+	+	+	—	—
Primula farinosa	—	—	+	+	—	—	—	—	—	—	—	—	—	—	+	+	—	—
Orobanche alba	—	—	+	—	—	+	—	+	—	—	+	—	—	—	+	+	—	CS
O. reticulata	—	—	+	—	—	—	—	—	—	—	—	—	—	—	+	—	+	C
O. elatior	+	+	+	—	—	—	—	+	+	+	+	+	+	+	—	+	—	C
O. picridis	+	—	—	—	—	+	—	+	+	—	+	—	+	—	—	—	+	CS
Origanum vulgare	+	+	+	+	+	+	—	+	+	+	+	+	+	+	+	+	—	—
Thymus pulegioides	+	+	+	—	—	+	—	+	+	+	+	+	+	+	+	+	—	—
T. drucei	+	+	+	+	+	+	—	+	+	+	+	+	+	+	+	+	—	ON
Calamintha ascendens	+	+	+	+	+	+	—	+	+	+	+	+	+	+	+	+	—	CS
C. nepeta	+	+	+	—	—	—	—	+	+	+	—	+	—	+	—	—	—	CS
Acinos arvensis	+	+	+	+	+	+	—	+	+	+	+	+	+	+	+	+	—	—
Salvia pratensis	+	+	—	—	—	—	—	+	+	+	+	—	—	—	—	—	+	—
Stachys germanica	—	+	[+]	—	—	—	—	—	—	—	+	[+]	[+]	—	—	—	+	CS
Teucrium botrys	+	+	—	—	—	—	—	+	+	+	+	—	—	—	—	—	+	—
Ajuga chamaepitys	+	—	—	—	—	—	—	+	+	—	+	—	+	—	—	—	—	CS
Plantago media	+	+	+	+	+	+	—	+	+	+	—	+	+	+	+	(+)	—	—
P. lanceolata	+	+	+	+	+	+	—	+	+	+	+	+	+	+	+	+	—	—
Campanula glomerata	+	+	+	+	—	+	—	+	+	+	+	+	(+)	+	+	(+)	—	—
C. rotundifolia	+	+	+	+	+	+	—	+	+	+	+	+	+	+	+	+	—	—
Phyteuma tenerum	+	—	—	—	—	—	—	+	+	+	+	—	—	—	—	—	—	C
Sherardia arvensis	+	+	+	+	+	+	—	+	+	+	+	+	+	+	+	+	—	—
Asperula cynanchica	+	+	+	+	+	+	—	+	+	+	+	+	+	(+)	(+)	—	—	CS
Galium verum	+	+	+	+	+	+	—	+	+	+	+	+	+	+	+	+	—	—
G. pumilum	+	+	+	—	—	+	—	+	+	+	+	+	—	+	—	+	—	—
G. sterneri	—	—	+	—	—	+	—	+	—	—	—	—	+	+	+	+	—	—
Scabiosa columbaria	+	+	+	+	+	+	—	+	+	+	+	+	+	+	+	(+)	—	—
Succisa pratensis	+	+	+	+	+	+	—	+	+	+	+	+	+	+	+	+	—	—
Senecio integrifolius	+	+	+	—	—	—	—	+	+	+	+	+	(+)	—	(+)	—	—	C
Inula conyza	+	+	+	+	+	+	—	+	+	+	+	+	+	+	+	—	—	C
Antennaria dioica	+	+	+	+	—	+	—	+	—	—	+	+	+	+	+	+	—	NM
Aster linosyris	—	—	+	—	+	—	+	+	—	—	+	—	+	—	+	—	+	CS
Erigeron acer	+	+	+	+	—	+	—	+	+	+	+	+	+	+	+	(+)	—	—
Bellis perennis	+	+	+	+	+	+	—	+	+	+	+	+	+	+	+	+	—	—

Table 12 (*contd.*)

	1	2	3	4	5	6	7	8	9	10	11	12	13	14	15	16	17	18
Achillea millefolium	+	+	+	+	+	+	—	+	+	+	+	+	+	+	+	+	—	—
Carlina vulgaris	+	+	+	+	+	+	—	+	+	+	+	+	(+)	+	+	+	—	—
Cirsium acaulon	+	+	+	+	+	—	—	+	+	+	+	+	(+)	+	(+)	—	—	C
C. eriophorum	+	+	+	+	—	—	—	+	+	+	+	+	+	+	+	—	—	—
C. tuberosum	+	—	+	—	—	—	—	—	+	+	+	—	—	—	—	+	—	
Serratula tinctoria	+	+	+	+	+	+	—	+	+	+	+	+	+	+	+	(+)	—	C
Hypochoeris maculata	+	+	+	—	—	+	—	+	+	+	+	+	—	+	—	—	—	C
Leontodon hispidus	+	+	+	+	+	+	—	+	+	+	+	+	+	+	+	+	—	—
L. taraxacoides	+	+	+	+	+	+	—	+	+	+	+	+	+	+	+	(+)	—	—
Hieracium pilosella	+	+	+	+	+	+	—	+	+	+	+	+	+	+	+	+	—	—
Polygonatum odoratum	—	+	+	—	—	—	+	—	—	+	—	+	+	+	—	—	—	
Allium sphaerocephalon	—	—	+	—	—	—	+	—	—	+	—	—	—	—	—	+	—	
Epipactis atrorubens	—	—	+	+	—	—	+	—	—	—	—	+	+	+	+	—	—	
Spiranthes spiralis	+	+	+	+	+	+	—	+	+	+	+	+	+	+	+	—	—	CS
Herminium monorchis	+	+	—	—	—	—	—	+	+	+	+	+	(+)	—	—	—	—	CN
Coeloglossum viride	+	+	+	+	+	+	—	+	+	+	+	+	+	+	+	+	—	CN
Gymnadenia conopsea	+	+	+	+	+	+	—	+	+	+	+	+	+	+	+	+	—	—
Leucorchis albida	+	—	+	—	+	+	—	—	—	—	+	+	+	+	+	—	—	NM
Ophrys apifera	+	+	+	+	—	—	—	+	+	+	+	+	+	+	—	—	—	CS
O. fuciflora	+	—	—	—	—	—	—	+	—	—	—	—	—	—	—	+	—	CS
O. sphegodes	+	+	—	—	—	—	—	+	+	+	+	—	—	—	—	—	—	CS
O. insectifera	+	+	+	+	—	—	—	+	+	+	+	+	(+)	+	+	—	—	C
Himantoglossum hircinum	+	+	+	—	—	—	—	+	+	—	+	+	—	+	—	—	—	CS
Orchis militaris	+	—	—	—	—	—	—	+	—	+	—	+	—	—	—	—	+	C
O. simia	+	—	—	—	—	—	—	+	—	+	—	—	—	—	—	—	+	CS
O. ustulata	+	+	+	+	[+]	+	—	+	+	+	+	+	—	+	+	—	—	C
O. morio	+	+	+	+	—	+	—	+	+	+	+	+	+	+	+	(+)	—	—
O. mascula	+	+	+	+	+	+	—	+	+	+	+	+	+	+	+	+	—	—
Aceras anthropophorum	+	+	+	—	—	—	—	+	+	+	+	+	—	—	—	—	—	CS
Anacamptis pyramidalis	+	+	+	+	+	+	—	+	+	+	+	+	+	+	+	(+)	—	CS
Carex flacca	+	+	+	+	+	+	—	+	+	+	+	+	+	+	+	+	—	—
C. ericetorum	+	+	+	+	—	+	—	—	—	—	+	+	+	+	—	—	—	CN
C. caryophyllea	+	+	+	+	+	+	—	+	+	+	+	+	+	+	+	+	—	—
C. montana	+	+	+	+	—	—	—	+	+	+	+	—	+	+	—	—	+	CN
C. humilis	+	+	+	—	—	—	—	+	—	+	+	—	—	—	—	—	—	CS
C. ornithopoda	—	+	+	—	—	—	—	—	—	—	—	—	+	+	—	—	—	CN
C. pulicaris	+	+	+	—	+	—	+	+	+	+	+	+	+	+	+	—	—	—
Festuca rubra	+	+	+	+	+	+	—	+	+	+	+	+	+	+	+	+	—	—
F. ovina	+	+	+	+	+	+	—	+	+	+	+	+	+	+	+	+	—	—
Catapodium rigidum	+	+	+	+	+	+	—	+	+	+	+	+	+	+	+	(+)	—	CS
Nardurus maritimus	+	+	—	—	—	—	—	+	+	—	+	—	—	—	—	+	—	—
Briza media	+	+	+	+	+	+	—	+	+	+	+	+	+	+	+	+	—	—
Zerna erecta	+	+	+	+	+	+	—	+	+	+	+	+	(+)	+	+	(+)	—	—
Brachypodium pinnatum	+	+	+	+	+	+	—	+	+	+	+	+	(+)	+	+	(+)	—	—
Koeleria cristata	+	+	+	+	+	+	—	+	+	+	+	+	+	+	+	+	—	—
K. vallesiana	—	—	+	—	—	+	+	—	—	+	—	—	—	—	—	+		OS
Trisetum flavescens	+	+	+	+	+	+	—	+	+	+	+	+	+	+	+	+	—	
Helictotrichon pratense	+	+	+	+	+	+	—	+	+	+	+	+	+	+	+	+	—	
H. pubescens	+	+	+	+	+	+	—	+	+	+	+	+	+	+	+	+	—	
Agrostis tenuis	+	+	+	+	+	+	—	+	+	+	+	+	+	+	+	+	—	
A. stolonifera	+	+	+	+	+	+	—	+	+	+	+	+	+	+	+	+	—	
Sesleria albicans	—	—	+	+	—	+	—	—	—	—	—	—	—	—	+	+	—	
Total 154	126	114	128 [1]	95 [1]	77 [1]	99	26	129	114	114	126	117 [1]	108 [1]	105	116	88	28	

Notes

European distribution:

OS = oceanic southern ON = oceanic northern
CS = continental southern OW = oceanic west European
CN = continental northern C = continental
(+) = rare; [+] = extinct NM = northern montane

survival of a few is threatened as a result of the extensive ploughing and reseeding or arable cultivation of chalk downland during the last 30 years. Many species react adversely to the application of fertilisers, even when the ground is not otherwise disturbed. The post-myxomatosis changes in chalk grasslands, with rise to dominance of coarse and competitive grasses such as *Zerna erecta* and *Brachypodium pinnatum*, and the extensive encroachment of scrub, have been inimical to the survival of many species which flourish on close-cropped downland. The native flora of the Chalk is thus especially in need of conservation.

While the flora of the Jurassic limestone grassland has much in common with that of the Chalk, it has a smaller total number of species, and would appear to have only two, *Thlaspi perfoliatum* and *Stachys germanica*, which are confined to this rock formation. A few species, such as *Anemone pulsatilla*, *Cirsium eriophorum* and *Astragalus danicus* evidently occur more abundantly than on the Chalk. It is doubtful if there are any significant ecological differences between Chalk and Jurassic *per se*, and such differences in flora and vegetation as exist are probably attributable to the more northerly position and more limited total extent of the Jurassic limestones, and to chance factors which impinge on plant distribution generally.

The Carboniferous Limestone has a distinctive flora which appears to be associated with its westerly and northerly position and with its hardness, which gives a wide variety of open rock habitats. Distinctly southern and especially south-eastern plants are naturally less well represented than on the Chalk or Jurassic limestones. However, the southernmost occurrences of this rock, in the Mendips, Brean Down and Cheddar Gorge, Somerset; and Avon Gorge, Gloucestershire, have several very rare southern species, namely *Arabis stricta*, *Allium sphaerocephalon*, *Dianthus gratianopolitanus*, *Koeleria vallesiana*, *Trinia glauca* and *Helianthemum apenninum* (the last two species are also on Devonian limestone). Several other extremely local or rare species of wider distribution are found mainly or solely on the Carboniferous Limestone; they include *Dryopteris villarii*, *Thelypteris robertiana*, *Hornungia petraea*, *Draba muralis*, *Cardamine impatiens*, *Helianthemum canum*, *Veronica spicata* ssp. *hybrida*, *Aster linosyris*, *Polemonium caeruleum*, *Polygonatum odoratum* and *Carex ornithopoda*. Most of these species need open habitats, and are found mainly on scars, screes and pavements. Most of them also have a curiously restricted or scattered distribution, either concentrated in northern England or spread discontinuously over the whole extent of the Carboniferous Limestone. It is difficult to account for the absence or scarcity of these species on the hard Scottish limestones, but a few northern species, e.g. *Orobanche alba*, *Epipactis atrorubens* and *Sesleria albicans*, are well represented in both northern England and Scotland. Surprisingly, only a few lowland calcicoles reach their northern British limits on the Carboniferous Limestone of northern England, e.g. *Hippocrepis comosa*, *Hypochoeris maculata* and *Spiranthes spiralis*; and many species of this group occur well into Scotland on the eastern side.

The open rock habitats of the Carboniferous Limestone provide a wide variety of conditions, and in particular the limestone pavements of northern England often have a varied flora, including not only species of lowland grassland and open rock, but also those of woodland and scrub, which flourish in the deep crevices or grikes. The woodland species include common field layer plants such as *Mercurialis perennis*, *Allium ursinum*, *Mycelis muralis*, *Phyllitis scolopendrium*, *Dryopteris filix-mas*, *Polystichum aculeatum* and the rare *Actaea spicata*. In northern England, several distinctly upland species occur on limestone hills within the lowland zone (e.g. *Asplenium viride*, *Minuartia verna*, *Viola rupestris*, *Draba incana* and *Sesleria albicans*) and there are all transitions to higher-level limestone grasslands and rocks with a rich montane flora. It is, however, noteworthy that many species of the lowland calcareous grasslands remain abundant or even constant in their montane counterparts, e.g. *Festuca ovina*, *F. rubra*, *Thymus drucei*, *Plantago lanceolata*, *Campanula rotundifolia*, *Achillea millefolium*, *Ranunculus acris*, *Viola riviniana*, *Veronica chamaedrys*, *Linum catharticum*, *Lotus corniculatus* and *Carex flacca*. Several species common on chalk downs occur, often at altitudes around 900 m, with the Arctic–alpines of cliff faces and ledges, e.g. *Anthyllis vulneraria*, *Arabis hirsuta*, *Botrychium lunaria*, *Pimpinella saxifraga*, *Coeloglossum viride*, *Orchis mascula* and *Helictotrichon pratense*.

Only one species, *Orobanche reticulata*, is restricted to the Magnesian Limestone, and the high magnesium content of this rock (like that of calcareous serpentine) has no obvious effect on its flora, i.e. it appears to have much the same edaphic value as other calcareous rocks. The main significance of the Magnesian Limestone is that it is a lowland limestone stretching northwards from the Jurassic limestones and Chalk of eastern England and provides the most northerly stations for certain southerly species, such as *Cirsium eriophorum*, *Silene nutans*, *Carex montana* and formerly *Anemone pulsatilla*. Lousley (1969) has commented that, probably because of its lowland position, the Magnesian Limestone has a flora which shows more in common with that of the southern Chalk than with that of the geographically closer Carboniferous Limestone. There is a strong representation of orchids, notably *Ophrys apifera*, *O. insectifera*, *Anacamptis pyramidalis* and *Orchis ustulata*, and other southern species are locally abundant, e.g. *Pimpinella major*, *C. ericetorum*, *Campanula glomerata*, *Zerna erecta* and *Brachypodium pinnatum*.

The outcrops of Devonian limestone around Torquay and Brixham have some noteworthy rare plants. The best locality, Berry Head, has *Helianthemum apenninum*, *Ononis reclinata*, *Bupleurum baldense*, *Trinia glauca* and *Aster linosyris*. None of these species is confined to the Devonian limestone; the *Bupleurum* grows on coastal Chalk in Sussex and the other four on isolated headlands of Carboniferous Limestone on the west coast. The two stonecrops *Sedum album* and *S. forsteranum* may be native here. It is again doubtful if this particular type of limestone has any special pedological significance compared with other limestones, and the interesting flora of the Devonian limestone probably owes more to the geographical position of the outcrops. There are numerous widespread southern calcicoles, as well as other species not usually associated with limestone, such as *Umbilicus rupestris* and *Parietaria diffusa*.

Other calcareous rocks in the lowlands carry a calcicolous flora which varies in richness according to the calcium carbonate content of the parent material and the extent of its outcrop. Only one species, the very rare *Potentilla rupestris*, would seem to be confined to 'other calcareous rocks', and in general their flora is much less varied than that of real limestone. The constants of lowland calcareous grasslands are usually present, and among the more local species represented in one place or another are *Thalictrum minus, Cardamine impatiens, Dianthus deltoides, Astragalus danicus, Potentilla tabernaemontani, Polemonium caeruleum, Veronica spicata* ssp. *hybrida, Campanula glomerata, Leucorchis albida* and *Orchis ustulata*. Most of the important occurrences of other calcareous rocks in the lowlands are cliffs or steep rocks with a ledge and face vegetation, and with varying extent of associated grassland on steep slopes. Among the more celebrated localities are Stanner Rocks and Breidden Hill in Wales, Arthur's Seat and Salisbury Crags in Edinburgh, and St Cyrus on the east coast of Scotland. Some of these places also have species which apparently need an unusual balance of cations in the substratum, e.g. *Lychnis viscaria* and *Asplenium septentrionale*. Most of the uplands of England, Wales and Scotland have exposures of moderately calcareous rock at the lower levels, and these usually support assemblages of the common calcicoles but few or none of the rarer or more lime-demanding species; Eryri, Wasdale Screes and the Moffat Hills are examples of such places. Many calcicolous plants find a habitat on older mortared walls or dry-stone walls of limestone, and certain rock-dwelling ferns, such as *Asplenium trichomanes, A. ruta-muraria, A. adiantum-nigrum* and, more especially, *Ceterach officinarum*, are more abundant here than on natural rocks. The walls of older buildings are an important habitat for certain native or long-established plants such as *Parietaria diffusa, Erinus alpinus, Centranthus ruber* and *Cheiranthus cheiri*.

Fauna

For convenience, the mammals, reptiles and amphibians and birds of lowland acidic grasslands and heaths, calcareous grasslands, and neutral grasslands are described in a single account, though particular species' preferences are indicated.

MAMMALS, REPTILES AND AMPHIBIANS

The most important mammal of lowland grasslands and heaths is the rabbit. Since the advent of myxomatosis in 1953, the numbers of rabbits in most parts of Britain have generally been low compared with previous years, and only in a few places does this animal now occur at high density. The rabbit appears to flourish where the soils are calcareous or sandy, the high base-status evidently providing good productivity of fodder, while sandy substrata are most suitable for burrowing. Certain areas where the soils are both

calcareous and sandy thus had the densest rabbit populations of all, as in the Breckland and on certain coastal dune systems. Some lowland grassland and heath areas were once managed primarily as rabbit warrens, with a considerable crop of the animal removed annually for its flesh and fur, and the term 'warren' often figures in place names for such sites.

In recent years however, the rabbit has been widely regarded as a pest, and the myxomatosis epidemic has been followed by fairly intensive campaigns in many areas to prevent recovery in numbers. It is clear that the decline or virtual elimination of rabbits in many areas has had profound effects on semi-natural vegetation, especially in places where grazing by other herbivores such as sheep has also declined. The most obvious effects are on the vegetation of calcareous grasslands such as chalk and limestone downs and some of the richer Breckland grasslands, but the effects are also very marked on some of the more acidic heaths.

The first change on grasslands is the development of a luxuriant and often tussocky grass sward in which certain grasses become completely dominant and suppress many species of the original community, especially the smaller forbs needing a close-grazed turf and open soil. The next stage is usually the growth of shrubs whose seedlings would normally be grazed and eliminated by rabbits, and there is a progressive development of scrub which in time ousts even the luxuriant grasses and is accompanied by the appearance of woodland and woodland edge species. On the acidic heaths, disappearance of rabbits is followed by an increase in luxuriance of dwarf shrubs (especially heather) and grasses, reduction in bare ground, and the invasion of trees, particularly birch and Scots pine.

These vegetational changes have profound effects on the associated fauna. Species which need open ground with a sparse vegetation dwindle or disappear, as do those which actually breed in rabbit holes, such as the wheatear and stock dove (and the shelduck in coastal areas). There is a change in the balance of invertebrates, notably phytophagous insects, some species being favoured by the increased luxuriance of the sward, while others suffer from decrease in their food plants. Animals which need cover are favoured and there is an increase in small herbivorous rodents.

The rabbit thus exerts a powerful influence on the whole ecosystem, and its disappearance or decline on many grassland and heath areas has created considerable management problems. This is particularly so as there has also been a decrease in use of these habitats as sheep-walks. The rabbit is also an important prey species for some lowland carnivores such as fox, stoat and weasel, and these animals have had to turn increasingly to other prey as the rabbit declined. These three predators are widespread on lowland grasslands and heaths, although their numbers are limited by territorial demands and size of prey populations.

Brown hares are well represented on the lowland grasslands and, as with the rabbit, high densities are particularly associated with chalk and limestone areas. Roe deer commonly range over grassland and heath, where there are associated woodlands, and the other British species of deer all occur in these habitats at times.

The mole is a common animal of lowland grassland on richer soils, both in meadows and unenclosed grasslands, but is not usually found in the podsolised, base-poor soils of acidic heaths, which lack earthworms. The hedgehog is also numerous in these habitats, and where cover is dense there are large but fluctuating populations of short-tailed field voles. The common shrew, lesser shrew *Sorex minutus* and harvest mouse *Micromys minutus* are often quite plentiful in the taller grasslands, but the wood mouse and bank vole are less common in this habitat.

Most of the British species of bat feed over lowland grasslands and heaths as these produce large numbers of insects. The widespread conversion of these habitats into intensively managed farmland may have been a contributory factor in the general decline of bats, at least in southern England. Some of the important winter hibernation roosts of these mammals are in caves associated with limestone formations which support important areas of calcareous grassland and open rock habitat, e.g. the Mendip Hills and Cheddar Gorge.

The six species of British reptile are all found on lowland heaths (including heathy coastal dunes) and, with the exception of sand lizard and smooth snake, on grasslands as well. Their habitat requirements differ in detail so that the various species may occupy different niches within the heathland complex of habitats. The grass snake needs also the open water of ponds, dykes or rivers, while the adder (viper) hibernates in holes and recesses of various kinds in dry situations, and summers in wet, boggy areas or in dry places within reach of water. The smooth snake and sand lizard are evidently able to occupy dry, open heathland throughout the year, provided the heather is of the correct height. The common lizard and the slow worm occupy a wider range of habitat and can occur in hedgerows and woods, but favour dry heathland.

The smooth snake is confined to the extreme south of England and the sand lizard, although rather more widespread is an exceedingly local creature reaching its northern limit at Ainsdale on the Lancashire coast. The grass snake reaches Scotland but is rare north of the Midlands, and the slow worm is more common in the south than the north of Britain. The common lizard and adder are widespread species as characteristic of the northern moorlands as of the southern heaths. The adder, however, is curiously local and absent from many apparently suitable localities; the random occurrences of severe heath and moor fires may have something to do with the patchy distribution of this snake. The adder often appears to be scarce or absent from the calcareous rock formations, but it occurs on chalk grassland in places. The southern heaths of Dorset, Hampshire and Surrey are the best British localities for reptiles, and here all six species often occur on the same site.

The six species of reptile have declined to some extent through destruction of their heathland habitat. The smooth snake and sand lizard are particularly under threat, because their distribution is so limited and their habitat so vulnerable to modern pressures on uncultivated lowlands.

The common frog and common toad were until recently abundant and widespread over most of Britain, requiring open water of some kind in which to breed, but widely distributed through other associated habitats (including lowland heaths, grasslands and meadows) in their adult phase. Since 1950, both amphibians have declined greatly over much of lowland agricultural Britain, evidently as a result of widespread changes in land-use and human pressure within this environment, and they are now seldom to be seen in many such areas. The natterjack toad is mainly a coastal species and is found on sand dunes and their slacks, among other habitats. There were formerly inland colonies on some of the Surrey heaths, where the species bred in ponds, and these have only recently died out.

BIRDS

Few species are adapted to the lack of cover which characterises the once extensive Chalk downs of southern England and the flint-strewn brecks of East Anglia, but the stone curlew actually needs these conditions and has declined not only because much of the original habitat has been reclaimed, but also because the absence of rabbit-grazing since myxomatosis has led to an over-luxuriant vegetation cover on many of the former nesting grounds. The ringed plover has almost disappeared from its former Breckland nesting places probably for the same reasons, while wheatear and stock dove have decreased considerably. The lapwing breeds in short or open turf and has partly recovered its numbers in the low country since the hard winter of 1963. It is a bird of the cultivated fields as well as the untilled grasslands and heaths, and the same is true of the stone curlew (and to a lesser extent the ringed plover) on farmland which has been reclaimed from heaths where it has traditionally nested. The great bustard has long since disappeared from these open grass heaths and the stone curlew is a species whose survival in Britain is now threatened; it requires the maintenance of steppe-like conditions in those parts of southern and south-eastern England where it still remains. The oystercatcher is locally another bird of the short grasslands, whether ploughed or not.

The heather, gorse and bracken-clad heaths are the main haunt of the nightjar, especially where there is adjoining woodland or scattered trees. This species has declined greatly, and largely disappeared from the northern parts of its range, where it formerly nested widely on the lower moorlands and open wooded areas. It is still widespread in the southern half of England but much less numerous than formerly. The Dartford warbler is a much more local bird of heather- and gorse-grown heaths, mainly in the New Forest and Dorset, but also in Sussex and formerly in Surrey. Various types of heath and common, from the heather–bracken–gorse type to those with mainly tussocky grassland, are the habitat of curlew, stonechat, whinchat, meadow pipit, tree pipit (where trees or bushes occur), woodlark, cuckoo, linnet, willow warbler, yellowhammer, reed bunting, red-legged partridge, grey partridge and pheasant. The woodlark is one of the species most in need of conservation, its numbers having declined greatly in recent years. The grasshopper warbler breeds on those grasslands and heaths with tall grass or dwarf to medium shrubs, and both whitethroat and lesser whitethroat have niches here as well as in woodland. The corn bunting occurs in places on the grassier type of common, but is more a bird of hay meadows and cornfields. The red-backed shrike is particularly a bird of tall scrub of various kinds on heaths and commons, and is another much decreased species now restricted to East Anglia and a few southern counties of England. Montagu's harrier nests at times on heaths, and other predators such as the kestrel, sparrowhawk, hobby and tawny owl have a connection with this habitat for feeding, though they breed in trees. Many birds which nest on heaths and rough grasslands are found on ground which has been afforested and fenced against grazing animals, and they remain until the young trees reach such a height that the field layer becomes diminished and the habitat is no longer heath or grassland. Heathland with Scots pine in scattered clumps or fringing woodlands is regarded as the classic breeding habitat for the hobby in Britain.

The neutral grasslands at times have some of the above species, but are especially the breeding place of lapwing, skylark and game birds. The damper types with seasonally wet ground are the nesting haunt of snipe, redshank, yellow wagtail and reed bunting, and the recent nesting places of black-tailed godwits in Britain mostly appear to be of the seasonally flooded meadow type. In some parts of the country, curlews breed in both these permanent grasslands and in tilled fields. The corncrake resorts to crops of hay and cereal, as well as to rough meadow grasslands, and is now found most plentifully along the western seaboard of Scotland, where agriculture is least mechanised. Several of the other birds which breed in fields, such as the corn bunting, lapwing and snipe, have locally declined on farmland in recent years, probably as a result of changes in agricultural practice.

The farmland species which nest in hedges and trees are dealt with in Chapter 5, though many of these birds depend partly or wholly on the fields for food, e.g. chaffinch, blackbird, rook, barn owl and kestrel.

The winter bird populations of the lowland heaths are very limited in numbers of species, for many of the breeders are summer visitors. However, the resident predators continue to hunt over this habitat, and the hen harrier and short-eared owl are local additions to the winter fauna. The enclosed agricultural dry grasslands become wintering grounds for species such as lapwing, golden plover, fieldfare, redwing and brambling, which flock together sometimes in considerable numbers. A few favoured farmlands in East Anglia are time-honoured passage haunts of the dotterel but, on the whole, the bird fauna of farm grasslands from autumn to spring consists of a much depleted version of that found in summer and there are relatively few interesting passage migrants.

The lowland grasslands subject to wetness or flooding in autumn and winter are, however, extremely productive for birds at this time of year. The types known as washes, flood meadows, alluvial meadows and water meadows can all be good, but the first is outstanding; in particular the Ouse Washes (OW.17, gr. 1) north of Earith in the Fenlands are one of the most important winter wildfowl haunts in Europe.

In the south, the wildfowl of the seasonally wet grasslands consist mainly of the surface feeding ducks, mallard, teal, wigeon, pintail, shoveler and gadwall, and the three species of swan; in Scotland, the grey geese are often also included. The only regular haunts of the bean goose now known in Britain are meadowland in the Ken Valley, Galloway (where Greenland white-fronted also occur), and the Yare Marshes, Norfolk. Pink-footed and greylag geese occur in substantial numbers in such habitats in the fertile lowlands of southern and eastern Scotland. The various species of duck and geese often feed on arable land as well as permanent grasslands, and in some localities the geese are regarded as a nuisance by farmers.

Wading birds also frequent the seasonally wet meadowlands in some numbers and these habitats may hold large populations of lapwing and golden plover and smaller numbers of snipe and jack snipe.

INSECTS

This account is mainly of the Lepidoptera, as the best-known group of insects of lowland acidic and calcareous grasslands, heaths and scrub. There is also a brief report on a wider survey of the invertebrate fauna of lowland calcareous grassland giving some information on the occurrence, habitat and distribution of species in other taxonomic groups. The more significant data from the survey are incorporated in vol. 2.

LEPIDOPTERA

The two subdivisions of this formation complex with the most distinctive Lepidoptera are (1) calcareous grassland and (2) grass heaths of Breckland. Very few species seem to be associated with all four of the main types of grassland and heath but many occur in three out of four (Table 13). The small heath butterfly is distributed throughout all subdivisions and regions. Other widely distributed species include the meadow brown, grayling, small tortoiseshell and the large skipper, amongst the butterflies, and such moths as the drinker, the small square spot, the marbled minor and the antler. Some of the fritillary butterflies are commonly found as adults in a wide range of lowland habitats falling within this group, and the chalk grasslands of Porton Down support especially large numbers of dark green fritillaries.

The species especially associated with calcareous grassland can be divided into two groups – those of the Chalk and limestone of southern England and those of the Carboniferous Limestone of northern Britain. The distinctive chalk species are the widely distributed chalk-hill blue, the much more local Adonis blue, the small blue, and the silver-spotted skipper butterflies and such moths as Mother Shipton, burnet companion and six spot burnet all of which feed as larvae on papilionaceous plants. Rare species in this habitat are the large blue in the Cotswolds (formerly), and of the moths, the feathered ear on the North

Table 13. *Habitat and distribution of Lepidoptera[a] of lowland grasslands, heaths and scrub*

Column key: 1 Acidic heathland; 2 Chalk & limestone grassland; 3 Breckland grass heaths; 4 Neutral grasslands; 5 Scrub; 6 Dwarf shrubs; 7 Forbs[b]; 8 Grasses; 9 S. & S.E. England; 10 E. Anglia; 11 S.W. England; 12 Wales; 13 Midlands; 14 N. England; 15 S. Scotland; 16 Highlands

		1	2	3	4	5	6	7	8	9	10	11	12	13	14	15	16
Butterflies																	
Small white	*Pieris rapae*	—	—	—	+	—	—	+	—	+	+	+	+	+	+	+	—
Green-veined white	*Pieris napi*	—	—	—	+	—	—	+	—	+	+	+	+	+	+	+	—
Orange tip	*Anthocharis cardamines*	—	—	—	+	—	—	+	—	+	+	+	+	+	+	+	—
Brimstone	*Gonepteryx rhamni*	—	—	—	—	+	—	—	—	+	+	+	+	+	—	—	—
Wall brown	*Lasiommata megera*	—	+	+	—	—	—	+	—	+	+	+	+	+	+	+	—
Grayling	*Hipparchia semele*	+	+	+	—	—	—	—	—	+	+	+	+	+	+	+	—
Ringlet	*Aphantopus hyperantus*	—	+	+	+	—	—	—	—	+	+	+	+	+	+	+	—
Meadow brown	*Maniola jurtina*	—	+	+	+	+	—	—	—	+	+	+	+	+	+	+	—
Hedge brown	*Pyronia tithonus*	—	+	+	+	+	—	—	—	+	+	+	+	+	—	—	—
Small heath	*Coenonympha pamphilus*	+	+	+	+	—	—	—	—	+	+	+	+	+	+	+	—
Marbled white	*Melanargia galathea*	—	+	—	—	—	—	—	—	+	+	+	+	+	—	—	—
Peacock	*Inachis io*	—	+	+	+	—	—	+	—	+	+	+	+	+	+	+	—
Small tortoiseshell	*Aglais urticae*	—	+	+	+	—	—	+	—	+	+	+	+	+	+	+	+
Marsh fritillary	*Euphydryas aurinia*	—	+	—	+	—	—	+	—	+	—	+	+	+	—	+	—
Green hairstreak	*Callophrys rubi*	+	+	+	—	+	+	—	—	+	+	+	+	+	+	+	—
Small copper	*Lycaena phlaeas*	—	+	+	+	—	—	+	—	+	+	+	+	+	+	+	—
Silver-studded blue	*Plebejus argus*	+	+	+	—	+	—	P	—	+	+	+	+	+	?	—	—
Brown argus	*Aricia agestis*	—	+	+	—	—	—	+	—	+	+	+	+	+	—	—	—
Northern brown argus	*A. artaxerxes*	—	+	—	—	—	—	+	—	—	—	—	—	—	+	+	—
Common blue	*Polyommatus icarus*	—	+	+	—	—	—	P	—	+	+	+	+	+	+	+	—
Chalk-hill blue	*Lysandra coridon*	—	+	—	—	—	—	P	—	+	+	+	+	+	—	—	—
Adonis blue	*L. bellargus*	—	+	—	—	—	—	P	—	+	—	+	—	?	+	—	—
Small blue	*Cupido minimus*	—	+	—	—	—	—	P	—	+	+	+	+	—	+	+	—
Large blue	*Maculinea arion*	—	+	—	—	—	—	+	—	—	—	+	—	—	—	—	—
Brown hairstreak	*Thecla betulae*	—	—	—	—	+	—	—	—	+	+	+	+	—	+	—	—
Grizzled skipper	*Pyrgus malvae*	—	+	+	—	—	—	+	—	+	+	+	+	+	+	—	—
Dingy skipper	*Erynnis tages*	—	+	+	—	—	—	P	+	+	+	+	+	+	+	+	—
Small skipper	*Thymelicus sylvestris*	—	+	+	+	—	—	—	+	+	+	+	+	+	+	—	—
Essex skipper	*T. lineola*	—	+	+	—	—	—	—	+	+	+	+	+	+	—	—	—
Large skipper	*Ochlodes venata*	—	+	+	+	—	—	—	+	+	+	+	+	+	+	+	—
Silver-spotted skipper	*Hesperia comma*	—	+	—	—	—	—	P	+	+	—	+	+	—	—	—	—
Moths																	
Small elephant hawk	*Deilephila porcellus*	—	+	+	—	—	—	+	—	+	+	+	+	+	+	+	—
Elephant hawk	*D. elpenor*	—	+	+	—	—	—	+	—	+	+	+	+	+	+	+	—
Privet hawk	*Sphinx ligustri*	—	—	—	—	+	—	—	—	+	+	+	+	+	—	—	—
Oak eggar	*Lasiocampa quercus*	+	+	+	—	—	+	—	—	+	+	+	+	+	+	+	—
Emperor	*Saturnia pavonia*	+	—	—	—	—	+	—	—	+	+	+	+	+	+	+	+
Drinker	*Philudoria potatoria*	—	+	+	+	—	—	—	+	+	+	+	+	+	+	+	—
Cinnabar	*Tyria jacobaeae*	—	+	+	—	—	—	+c	—	+	+	+	+	+	+	+	—
Scarlet tiger	*Callimorpha dominula*	—	—	—	+	—	—	+	—	+	+	+	+	—	—	—	—
White-line dart	*Euxoa tritici*	—	—	+	—	—	—	+	—	+	+	+	—	+	+	+	—
Archer's dart	*Agrotis vestigialis*	—	—	+	—	—	—	+	—	+	+	+	—	—	—	—	—
Shuttle-shaped dart	*A. puta*	—	—	—	+	—	—	+	—	+	+	+	—	+	+	—	—
Hart and dart	*A. exclamationis*	—	—	—	+	—	—	+	—	+	+	+	+	+	+	+	—
True lover's knot	*Lycophotia porphyrea*	+	—	—	—	—	+	—	—	+	+	+	+	+	+	+	—
Small square spot	*Diarsia rubi*	+	+	+	—	—	—	+	—	+	+	+	+	+	+	+	—
Large yellow underwing	*Noctua pronuba*	—	+	+	+	—	—	+	—	+	+	+	+	+	+	+	—
Pale shining brown	*Polia bombycina*	—	+	—	—	—	+	+	—	+	+	—	—	+	—	+	—
Feathered ear	*Pachetra sagittigera*	—	+	—	—	—	—	—	+	+	—	—	—	—	—	—	—
Varied coronet	*Hadena compta*	—	+	+	—	—	—	+	—	+	+	—	—	+	—	—	—

Table 13 (*contd.*)

		1	2	3	4	5	6	7	8	9	10	11	12	13	14	15	16
Viper's bugloss	*H. irregularis*	—	—	+	—	—	—	+	—	—	+	—	—	—	—	—	—
White colon	*Sideridis albicolon*	—	—	+	—	—	—	+	—	—	+	—	—	—	—	—	—
Antler	*Cerapteryx graminis*	+	+	+	—	—	—	—	+	+	+	+	+	+	+	+	—
Striped lychnis	*Cucullia lychnitis*	—	+	+	—	—	—	+	—	+	+	—	—	+	—	—	—
Dark brocade	*Blepharita adusta*	+	+	—	—	—	—	+	+	+	+	+	+	+	+	+	—
Clouded bordered brindle	*Apamea crenata*	+	+	+	—	—	—	—	+	+	+	+	+	+	+	+	—
Marbled minor	*Oligia strigilis*	+	+	+	—	—	—	—	+	+	+	+	+	+	+	+	—
Least minor	*Photedes captiuncula*	—	+	—	—	—	—	—	+	—	—	—	—	—	+	—	—
Pale lemon swallow	*Xanthia ocellaris*	—	—	+	—	—	+	+	—	—	+	—	—	—	—	—	—
Marbled clover	*Heliothis viriplaca*	—	—	+	—	—	—	+	—	—	+	—	—	—	—	—	—
Spotted sulphur	*Emmelia trabealis*	—	—	+	—	—	—	+	—	—	+	—	—	—	—	—	—
Mother Shipton	*Callistege mi*	—	+	+	—	—	—	P	—	+	+	+	+	+	+	+	—
Burnet companion	*Euclidia glyphica*	—	+	+	—	—	—	P	—	+	+	+	+	+	+	+	—
Four-spotted	*Tyta luctuosa*	—	+	+	—	—	—	+	—	+	+	+	—	+	—	—	—
Beautiful snout	*Hypena crassalis*	+	—	—	—	—	+	—	—	+	+	+	+	+	+	—	—
Rest harrow	*Aplasta ononaria*	—	+	—	—	—	—	P	—	+	+	—	—	—	—	—	—
Tawny wave	*Scopula rubiginata*	—	—	+	—	—	—	+	+	—	+	—	—	—	—	—	—
Oblique carpet	*Orthonama vittata*	—	—	—	+	—	—	+	—	+	+	+	+	+	+	+	—
Heath rivulet	*Perizoma minorata*	+	—	—	—	—	—	+	—	—	—	—	—	—	+	+	—
Pretty chalk carpet	*Melanthia procellata*	—	+	—	—	—	—	+	—	+	+	—	—	+	—	—	—
Oblique striped	*Mesotype virgata*	—	+	+	—	—	—	+	—	+	+	—	—	—	—	—	—
Juniper carpet	*Thera juniperata*	—	—	—	+	—	—	—	—	+	+	—	+	—	+	+	+
Grey carpet	*Lithostege griseata*	—	—	+	—	—	—	+	—	—	+	—	—	—	—	—	—
Small waved umber	*Horisme vitalbata*	—	—	—	+	—	—	—	—	+	+	+	+	+	—	—	—
Fern	*H. tersata*	—	—	—	+	—	—	—	—	+	+	+	+	+	—	—	—
Juniper pug	*Eupithecia pusillata*	—	—	—	+	—	—	—	—	+	+	+	+	+	+	+	+
Triple spotted pug	*E. trisignaria*	—	+	—	—	—	—	+	—	+	—	+	—	—	—	—	—
Narrow-winged pug	*E. nanata*	+	—	—	—	—	+	+	—	+	+	+	+	+	+	+	—
Silky wave	*Idaea dilutaria*	—	+	—	—	—	—	+	—	+	—	+	—	—	—	—	—
Black-veined	*Siona lineata*	—	+	—	—	—	—	+	+	—	+	—	—	—	—	—	—
Six-spot burnet	*Zygaena filipendulae*	—	+	+	—	—	—	P	—	+	+	—	+	—	—	—	—
Scarce forester	*Adscita globulariae*	—	+	—	—	—	—	+	—	+	—	—	+	—	—	—	—
Ghost	*Hepialus humuli*	—	—	—	+	—	—	—	+	+	+	+	+	+	+	+	—
	Evergestis extimalis	—	—	+	—	—	—	+	—	—	+	—	—	—	—	—	—
	Margaritia sticticalis	—	—	+	—	—	—	+	—	—	+	—	—	—	—	—	—
	Crombrugghia distans	—	—	+	—	—	—	+	—	—	+	—	—	—	—	—	—
Total 85		15	53	47	19	12	8	53	22	69	72	59	51	57	47	40	2

Notes

[a] The nomenclature of the Lepidoptera follows that of Kloet & Hincks (1972), but the arrangement follows the conventional order used by previous authors, viz Butterflies, Macrolepidoptera and Microlepidoptera.

[b] P = Papilionaceae.

[c] Lichens found here.

Downs, and rest harrow on the South Downs. The marbled white butterfly also has an important niche in chalk grassland.

The Carboniferous Limestone of northern England is noted for the northern brown argus which occurs in the low hills of south Westmorland and north Lancashire as well as Durham, Northumberland and south Scotland. This single-brooded butterfly was until recently considered to be conspecific with the double-brooded brown argus which is widely distributed in southern England. The two English localities for the Scotch argus are both on Carboniferous Limestone. One moth, the least minor, is confined to the limestone extending eastwards from Morecambe Bay to the Craven district of Yorkshire.

Breckland is noted for the number of rare moths confined to the area and for coastal sand-dune species which have their only inland stations here. These dune moths include the white-line dart and archer's dart. Other species although widely distributed are particularly abundant in Breckland, notably the cinnabar moth, on its food plant *Senecio jacobaea*. Rarities of this area are the moths, viper's bugloss, white colon, pale lemon sallow (a unique Breckland form), marbled clover, spotted sulphur (may be extinct), four-spotted, tawny wave and the pyralids *Evergestis extimalis*, *Margaritia sticticalis* and *Crombrugghia distans*.

The acid heathland is typified by the butterflies, grayling, green hairstreak and silver-studded blue and the moths, oak eggar, emperor, beautiful yellow underwing, true lover's knot, beautiful snout (local, almost confined to the south, only occurring rarely in northern England), the narrow-winged pug and the heath rivulet which only occurs in northern England and Scotland. There is a considerable overlap in the Lepidoptera of lowland heaths and upland moors, many species being common to both.

Neutral grassland has a more restricted fauna. The typical butterflies are the small white, green-veined white, orange tip, meadow brown, ringlet, wall brown, large skipper and small skipper. The marsh fritillary which is much persecuted by collectors occurs in neutral grassland as well as on dry calcareous grassland. In most of its remaining stations, the large blue evidently frequents paramaritime grasslands with *Thymus* which are between neutral and calcareous in character. Some typical moths of neutral grassland are the drinker, oblique carpet, ghost and the rather local scarlet tiger.

Scrub naturally supports a mixture of some of the butterflies and moths of both grassland and woodland (especially the former), but certain species are particularly associated with this intermediate type of habitat. They include the brimstone and brown hairstreak among the butterflies, and a variety of moths such as the privet hawk, juniper carpet, small waved umber, fern, juniper pug, triple-spotted pug, silky wave and black-veined. The hedge brown butterfly especially favours bramble scrub as an adult.

DRAGONFLIES
See Chapters 7 and 12.

SPIDERS

In the present state of knowledge, it is only possible to describe the spiders of the Breckland grass heaths, and of acidic heaths and calcareous grasslands south of a line from the Bristol Channel to the Wash. The species listed are typical of these habitats in this region, but their occurrence in other parts of the country is also shown.

The most characteristic species of acidic heathland, i.e. those which are more or less restricted to this habitat, but widespread and frequent in it, are *Xysticus sabulosus*, *Philodromus histrio*, *Euophrys petrensis*, *Aelurillus v-insignitus*, *Ero tuberculata*, *Episinus truncatus*, *Araneus adiantus*, *Mangora acalypha*, *Walckenaera furcillata*, *Mecopisthes peusi*, *Micrargus laudatus* and *Linyphia furtiva*. Other rarer species exclusive to acid heath are *Thomisus onustus*, now frequent only in Dorset, Hampshire and Surrey; *Uloborus walckenaerius*, found in the same region but less common; *Oxyopes heterophthalmus*, known only from Chobham Common and an old record from the New Forest; *Xysticus luctator*, recorded only from Bloxworth Heath and the New Forest; *Alopecosa fabrilis*, known from several sites on Morden Heath and on Hankley Common, *Zelotes petrensis* and *Zora silvestris*, both confined to the south-east and Suffolk, and *Gonatium corallipes*, which is restricted to Ashdown Forest and a few sites in east Surrey and Kent.

A further group of acidic heathland species are also common on the Breckland heaths, the most widespread examples being *Zelotes pusillus*, *Cheiracanthium virescens*, *Scotina gracilipes*, *Euophrys aequipes*, *Hypsosinga albovittata* and *Typhochrestus digitatus*. More local species in this category are *Micaria silesiaca*, *Oxyptila scabricula*, *Steatoda albomaculata* and *Phaulothrix hardyi*, all of which are abundant locally on open sandy areas or recently burnt heathland in Dorset, the New Forest, Surrey and the Breck, the last named also occurring on moorland in upland regions.

Some other acidic heath species are commonly found in calcareous grassland. The burrowing species *Atypus affinis*, *Jacksonella falconeri* and *Wiehlea calcarifera* require well-drained slopes which can be found in both these habitat formations, while the lycosids *Pardosa hortensis* and *Xerolycosa nemoralis* require open stony conditions on heathland or chalk. *Trichoncus saxicola* and *Bathyphantes parvulus* occur mainly in grassy areas on acidic heath, and are also common in calcareous grassland.

Few widespread species are characteristic of calcareous grassland, the best examples probably being *Zelotes praeficus*, *Xysticus bifasciatus*, *Micrargus subaequalis*, *Panamomops sulcifrons* and *Diplostyla concolor*. Other species only frequent locally on southern Chalk and limestone are *Phrurolithus minimus*, *Oxyptila nigrita*, *Bianor aenescens* and *Lepthyphantes insignis*, while *Pelecopsis radicicola* has been recorded only from Heyshott Down and Rodney Stoke, and *Tapinocyboides pygmaea* from Heyshott Down and near Edinburgh. A number of other species are common on calcareous grassland but are also widespread in other habitats.

A small group of species found on calcareous grassland and on Breckland grass heaths, but absent from or very rare on southern acidic heathland, include *Zelotes pedestris*, *Clubiona diversa*, *Alopecosa cuneata*, *Hypsosinga pygmaea* and *Centromerus incilium*.

Only one species is known to be confined to the Breckland in Britain, namely *Walckenaera stylifrons*, recorded from Weeting Heath. There are, however, a number of mainly coastal species which occur also in sandy areas in the Breck, including *Agroeca cuprea*, *Zelotes electus*, *Attulus saltator* and *Arctosa perita*, the last two also sometimes occurring in open sandy areas in southern acidic heaths.

Finally, there is a small group of species which appear to be almost equally common on acidic heaths, calcareous grassland and on Breckland grass heaths. These include *Xysticus erraticus*, *Alopecosa accentuata*, *Hahnia nava*, *Walckenaera melanocephala* and *Tapinocyba praecox*.

Notes on surveys of invertebrate animals on lowland calcareous grasslands

Calcareous grasslands support several species of invertebrate animals of particular interest, many of which appear to be restricted to such habitats, in this country at least, or to be especially associated with them. They include species feeding on plants which are themselves restricted to, or particularly characteristic of, calcareous grassland, and also many other animals, for example snails and spiders.

Although it is evident that communities of invertebrate animals of calcareous grasslands show variation in response to differences in environmental factors such as climate, rock and soil type, floristics and vegetation structure, such variation cannot be fully assessed at present because the communities themselves have not yet been fully described and classified.

Table 14. *Spiders of heathlands and grasslands*

	Acid heath	Calcareous grassland	Breck grass heaths	S. & S.E. England	S.W. England	E. Anglia	Midlands	Wales	N. England	S. Scotland	Highlands	Ireland
	1	2	3	4	5	6	7	8	9	10	11	12
Atypus affinis	+	+	—	+	+	+	+	+	+	+	—	+
Dictyna latens	+	—	+	+	+	+	+	+	+	+	—	+
Uloborus walckenaerius	+	—	—	+	—	—	—	—	—	—	—	—
Drassodes lapidosus	—	+	—	+	+	+	+	+	+	+	+	+
D. cupreus	+	—	+	+	+	+	+	+	+	+	+	+
Haplodrassus dalmatensis	+	—	+	+	+	+	+	+	—	—	—	—
Phaeocedus braccatus	+	+	—	+	+	+	—	—	—	—	—	—
Zelotes pedestris	—	+	+	+	+	+	+	—	—	—	—	—
Z. pusillus	+	—	+	+	+	+	+	+	+	+	+	+
Z. praeficus	—	+	—	+	+	+	+	—	—	—	—	—
Z. serotinus	+	—	—	+	+	+	—	—	+	+	—	+
Z. petrensis	+	—	—	+	—	+	—	—	—	—	—	—
Micaria scintillans	—	+	—	+	+	—	—	—	—	—	—	—
M. silesiaca	+	—	+	+	+	+	—	—	—	—	—	—
Clubiona neglecta	—	+	—	+	+	+	+	+	+	+	+	+
C. trivialis	+	—	—	+	+	+	+	+	+	+	+	+
C. diversa	—	+	+	+	+	+	+	+	+	+	+	+
Cheiracanthium virescens	+	—	+	+	+	+	+	+	+	+	+	+
Scotina gracilipes	+	—	+	+	+	+	+	+	+	+	+	+
Zora silvestris	+	—	—	+	—	+	—	—	—	—	—	—
Phrurolithus minimus	—	+	—	+	+	—	—	—	—	—	—	—
Thomisus onustus	+	—	—	+	+	+	+	—	—	—	—	—
Xysticus erraticus	+	+	+	+	+	+	+	+	+	+	+	+
X. bifasciatus	—	+	—	+	+	—	+	+	+	+	+	—
X. luctator	+	—	—	+	—	—	—	—	—	—	—	—
X. sabulosus	+	—	—	+	+	+	+	+	+	+	+	+
X. robustus	+	—	—	+	+	—	—	—	—	—	—	—
Oxyptila scabricula	+	—	+	+	+	+	—	+	—	—	—	—
O. nigrita	—	+	—	+	+	—	+	—	—	—	—	—
O. brevipes	—	+	—	+	+	+	+	+	+	—	—	+
Philodromus histrio	+	—	—	+	+	+	+	+	+	—	+	—
Thanatus formicinus	+	—	—	+	—	—	—	—	—	—	—	—
Heliophanus flavipes	—	+	+	+	+	+	+	+	+	+	+	+
Bianor aenescens	—	+	—	+	—	+	+	—	+	—	—	—
Euophrys petrensis	+	—	—	+	+	—	—	—	+	—	—	+
E. aequipes	+	—	+	+	+	+	+	—	+	+	—	—
Aelurillus v-insignitus	+	—	—	+	+	+	—	+	—	—	+	—
Oxyopes heterophthalmus	+	—	—	+	+	—	—	—	—	—	—	—
Pardosa tarsalis	+	—	—	+	+	+	+	+	+	+	+	+
P. hortensis	+	+	+	+	+	+	+	—	+	+	—	—
Xerolycosa nemoralis	+	+	—	+	—	+	+	—	—	—	—	—
Alopecosa cuneata	—	+	+	+	+	+	+	—	+	—	—	—
A. accentuata	+	+	+	+	+	+	+	+	+	+	+	+
A. fabrilis	+	—	—	+	—	+	—	—	—	—	—	—
Hahnia nava	+	+	+	+	+	+	+	+	+	+	+	+
Ero tuberculata	+	—	—	+	+	+	+	—	—	—	—	—
Epsinus angulatus	+	+	—	+	+	+	+	+	+	+	+	+
E. truncatus	+	—	—	+	+	—	+	—	—	—	—	+
Dipoena prona	+	—	+	+	+	+	—	—	—	—	—	—
D. inornata	+	—	—	+	+	+	+	+	—	—	—	+
Steatoda albomaculata	+	—	+	+	+	+	—	—	—	—	—	—

Table 14 (*contd.*)

	1	2	3	4	5	6	7	8	9	10	11	12
Anelosimus aulicus	+	−	−	+	+	+	−	−	−	−	−	−
Achaearanea riparia	+	−	−	+	+	+	+	+	+	−	−	+
Theridion bimaculatum	−	+	+	+	+	+	+	+	+	+	+	+
Enoplognatha thoracica	+	−	−	+	+	+	+	+	+	+	−	+
Araneus redii	+	−	−	+	+	+	+	+	−	−	−	+
A. adiantus	+	−	−	+	+	+	+	+	−	−	−	+
Hyposinga albovittata	+	−	+	+	+	+	+	−	+	+	−	−
H. pygmaea	−	+	+	+	+	+	+	+	+	−	+	+
H. sanguinea	+	−	−	+	+	−	+	−	−	−	−	+
Cercidia prominens	−	+	−	+	+	+	+	+	+	+	−	−
Mangora acalypha	+	−	−	+	+	+	+	+	+	−	−	+
Walckenaera melanocephala	+	+	+	+	+	+	+	+	+	−	+	+
W. stylifrons	−	−	+	−	−	+	−	−	−	−	−	−
W. dysderoides	+	−	+	−	+	+	+	+	+	+	−	−
W. furcillata	+	−	−	+	+	+	+	−	+	−	−	−
W. incisa	+	+	+	+	+	+	−	+	+	−	−	−
Entelecara flavipes	−	+	−	+	+	−	+	−	+	+	−	−
Dismodicus bifrons	+	+	−	+	+	+	+	+	+	+	+	+
Metopobactrus prominulus	−	+	−	+	+	+	+	+	+	+	+	+
Gonatium corallipes	+	−	−	+	−	−	−	−	−	−	−	−
Pelecopsis radicicola	−	+	−	+	+	−	−	−	−	−	−	−
Mecopisthes peusi	+	−	−	+	+	−	−	+	+	−	−	−
Acartauchenius scurrilis	+	+	−	+	+	−	−	−	−	−	−	−
Trichoncus saxicola	+	+	−	+	+	−	+	−	−	−	−	+
Ceratinopsis stativa	−	+	−	+	+	−	+	+	+	−	−	+
Tapinocyba praecox	+	+	+	+	+	+	+	+	+	+	+	+
Tapinocyboides pygmaea	−	+	−	+	−	−	−	−	−	+	−	−
Jacksonella falconeri	+	+	−	+	+	−	+	+	−	−	+	−
Micrargus subaequalis	−	+	−	+	+	+	+	+	+	+	+	+
M. laudatus	+	+	−	+	+	−	+	−	+	−	−	−
Wiehlea calcarifera	+	+	−	+	+	−	−	−	−	−	−	−
Diplocephalus cristatus	−	+	−	+	+	+	+	+	+	+	+	+
Panamomops sulcifrons	−	+	−	+	+	+	+	−	+	−	−	−
Typhochrestus digitatus	+	−	+	+	+	+	+	+	+	+	+	+
Phaulothrix hardyi	+	−	+	+	+	+	+	+	+	+	+	+
Meioneta saxatilis	−	+	−	+	+	+	+	+	+	+	+	+
Centromerus incilium	−	+	+	+	−	+	−	−	−	+	−	−
Diplostyla concolor	−	+	−	+	+	+	+	+	+	+	+	+
Bathyphantes parvulus	+	+	−	+	+	+	+	+	+	+	+	+
Lepthyphantes pallidus	−	+	−	+	+	+	+	+	+	+	+	+
L. insignis	−	+	−	+	+	−	+	−	−	−	−	−
Linyphia furtiva	+	−	−	+	+	+	+	+	−	−	−	−
Total 93	63	46	26	92	81	67	66	50	53	40	33	44

Some indications of the range of variation shown by animal communities of calcareous grassland can be obtained from two types of information: (1) anecdotal records of particular species from particular sites. Such information is valuable, but limited, because it is often haphazard, and may be far from an expression of real distribution or abundance. It is sometimes possible to build up a picture of the occurrence of some species, such as butterflies, in a large number of sites, but only for groups of animals particularly popular with naturalists. Many sites have simply not been examined for more obscure groups; (2) the systematic information obtained from the programme of sampling for the *Review*.

In brief, standard vacuum net samples were taken from a number of key lowland calcareous grassland sites. The three groups Hemiptera–Heteroptera, Hemiptera–Auchenorhyncha and Coleoptera–Curculionoidea were chosen to represent the whole fauna. The samples were compared with those taken from a reference site (Barton Hills, Bedfordshire) where the fauna is well known.

Although rarity of particular species is an important criterion in assessing sites the programme of systematic sampling was unlikely to record many rare species. It is not always certain that measurements of diversity (e.g. Williams, 1964) are appropriate in conservation work and greater reliance has been placed initially on the number of species recorded as indicating diversity. For this purpose the Hemiptera–Auchenorhyncha are the most important group, as the mean number of individuals taken in the sample so far examined was 165 as against 33 Heteroptera and 15 Curculionoidea. Also, in two samples (chosen at random) from the reference site, 48 % of the known Auchenorhyncha from the site were recorded, compared with 35 % Heteroptera and 9 % Curculionoidea.

Vegetation structure is an important factor in determining the occurrence and abundance of invertebrate animals in different sites. It was found in assessing sites that allowance must be made at each site for the height of vegetation, i.e. almost any tall grassland will show a higher diversity of the recorded groups than the richest short grassland. It is only valid to compare diversity in sites of similar vegetation height, or against the mean value of diversity for grassland of that height. As vegetation height can be easily varied by management, it is therefore not a primary quality in the comparative assessment of sites.

Most other variations in the animal communities are probably caused by factors affecting variations in the composition of the plant communities. Geographical position is important and contributes to the richness of calcareous grasslands in south-east England, probably because this part of the country is nearest to the continent. Most probably, however, this factor is combined with micro-climatic effects in determining the distribution of animals in southern England, particularly those associated with open ground. The samples of Auchenorhyncha from the Yorkshire Wolds are particularly interesting as representing the most northerly type of chalk grassland fauna in Britain. Although having many similarities with the faunas of southern sites, these northern associations contain several species not found, or only rarely found, in the south and thus are particularly valuable in indicating the regional importance of the sites. Conversely, species of known southerly distribution are absent from the Wolds sites. Fewer Auchenorhyncha samples have been taken from the extreme westerly representative chalk grassland sites, and here, e.g. at Axmouth–Lyme Regis NNR, the fauna appears to be influenced by factors other than the purely geographical, particularly the proximity of the sea. Usually, but not always, samples of Auchenorhyncha taken near the sea, lack *Turrutus socialis*, the characteristically most numerous and dominant species in the chalk and limestone fauna generally. Only very rarely does *T. socialis* fail to appear in the samples from inland sites.

The information on fauna given in site accounts is that available, and in most cases is extremely scanty. Despite the limitations of anecdotal records, the known presence of rarities as breeding species, e.g. at Wye and Crundale Downs, is undoubtedly useful in assessing the nature conservation value of some sites. Even the systematic sampling, or rather the identification of the samples, is incomplete. For some sites the results of sampling on two occasions in high summer are known; for other sites, especially the large number in Wiltshire, only the results of sampling on one occasion are complete and can be included. It has been thought better to assess the sites on the basis of what is known (i.e. to include the results of sampling on both occasions where possible) rather than to attempt a standard assessment on the basis of the first round of sampling occasions.

CRITERIA FOR KEY SITE ASSESSMENT AND SELECTION

Comparative site evaluation

In assessing the relative merits of calcareous grassland sites to represent a particular type in the field of variation, the following criteria were given the greatest weight.

Size

As a result of the great inroads made by arable cultivation into the former extent of lowland calcareous grassland, many of the remaining areas are small in extent, so that large area is especially valued in this formation.

Lack of recent disturbance

Since, by definition, lowland calcareous grasslands are not natural, the criterion of naturalness does not normally apply. At the same time, it is clear that the highest-quality swards are those which have remained under an old-fashioned grazing regime for a very long time, and have acquired a particular range of floristic composition which is associated with lack of recent change in the management system, as by application of fertilisers, ploughing and re-seeding, or pig rearing. Selection has been very much for these ancient pastures. On the Carboniferous Limestone of northern England, karst features, especially pavement (clint and grike structure) have been included in this Chapter, and here the criterion of naturalness applies strongly, i.e. sites have been selected for lack of interference with physical structure (as by limestone winning and quarrying), and for relative freedom from sheep-grazing.

Lack of deterioration after myxomatosis

The rise to dominance of coarse, vigorously competitive grasses as a result of decline in rabbit-grazing has been stressed, and grasslands which have not been swamped by these dominants have been preferred. Some calcareous grasslands have likewise been heavily invaded by scrub, and these also have largely been ignored unless they had a particular value as examples of scrub in its own right.

Floristic richness

This is partly a measure of criterion 2 above. Swards with a large number of species have been rated highly, though the actual identity of the species is also important. This criterion was considered objectively, i.e. on the basis of 1-m^2 plot analyses. A sample plot of this size containing 38–45 species of flowering plants and mosses is regarded as indicative of a very rich grassland.

Presence of rare plant species

The lowland calcareous grasslands are a notable habitat for many rare vascular plants, especially orchids, and the presence of large populations of these, or combinations of species, has been judged important. The presence of species – not necessarily rarities – representative of particular phytogeographical elements has also been regarded as a valuable feature.

Habitat diversity

Because of the influence of aspect, slope, soil moisture and extent of bare rock in differentiating a range of communities within the calcareous grasslands, sites with high diversity in these physical features have been rated highly. On the Chalk, however, the ploughing of all but the steepest slopes has led to a preponderance of scarp slope grasslands, and on this rock formation the occurrence of substantial areas on the flat or on gentle slopes has been regarded as a desirable feature.

Vegetational diversity

Where an area contains a good example of calcareous grassland, and also has calcareous heath and/or scrub, it may be regarded as of better overall quality than a similar area of grassland without the other types. This is especially so if the heath and scrub are long established, and not of the recently invading type.

Entomological interest

As a result of entomological surveys, especially on the Chalk, certain sites could be identified as being rich in species of insects, or in having rarities. When such data were available, the criteria of faunal richness, and presence of rare species and distinctive zoogeographical elements were applied in the same way as for plants.

Archaeological interest

The presence of earthworks or other archaeological features is regarded as valuable, since evidence of history of a site and past land-use may have a considerable bearing on the vegetation, flora and fauna of the present day.

These criteria are not usually applied singly, but in various combinations, e.g. large size is of no value unless the particular grassland is of high quality in other respects, such as floristic richness. Conversely, high quality in other features is of little value if a site is too small, though in one case (Knocking Hoe) the extreme floristic richness and presence of rare species were considered to outweigh the disadvantage of small size. The selection of lowland calcareous grassland key sites was originally based on botanical criteria alone, but entomological data were later taken into account. Interest in these two fields was often found to run parallel. Entomological qualities were used to decide the choice between two sites of equivalent value botanically, and a few sites were chosen primarily for their insect interest.

Requirements for the national series

The main aim has been to select a series of lowland calcareous grassland sites which adequately represent the range of ecological variation according to:

1 The five major calcareous rock formations, Chalk, Jurassic limestones, Carboniferous Limestone, Magnesian Limestone and Devonian limestone.

2 The major climatic gradients within Britain, of oceanicity from east to west, and mean temperature from south to north.

It is important that the series thus chosen takes full account of the need to represent as much as possible of the rich chalk and limestone flora and fauna, which varies according to both geology and climate. The local variations which arise from differences in land-use and other biotic effects should be represented, but the central objective is to conserve a series of the rapidly dwindling high-quality swards (with their associated animals) found on calcareous soils. These local variations include transitions to calcareous heath, neutral grassland and scrub communities which are considered separately.

REGIONAL DIVERSITY AND SELECTION OF KEY SITES

CHALK GRASSLAND

Although the Cretaceous Chalk formation extends from Devon and Dorset in the south-west to the Yorkshire Wolds in the north-east, with easterly extensions into Kent and Sussex forming the North and South Downs, the total area occupied by chalk grassland is small and greatly dissected. In the first place, maps of solid geology give a misleading impression of the extent of chalk habitats, for the broad belts of this formation indicated in East Anglia and Lincolnshire are mostly obscured by drift. Where this superficial material is of chalky boulder clay, calcareous grassland is found on uncultivated areas, but where there is base-poor sand the effect of the underlying Chalk is obliterated.

The former area of chalk grassland has, moreover, been greatly reduced during the present century. Changing agricultural practice has resulted in the general removal of sheep flocks and the widespread conversion of open downland to arable land or, by ploughing and reseeding, to improved pasture. The great rolling expanses of short, grazed turf which characterised the North and South Downs in Sussex and Kent have now largely gone. In most places the fragmented downland remnants are on scarp slopes too steep to plough, and good chalk swards on level or gently sloping ground are now a rarity. In some areas, only the minor irregularities of ancient earthworks and tracks have allowed the survival of fragments of this habitat in a great expanse of agricultural land; the Devil's Dyke near Newmarket in Cambridgeshire is a good example. Conversely, certain areas of chalk grassland are regarded by archaeologists as of first importance in containing some of the best examples of the prehistoric activities of man.

Blackwood & Tubbs (1970) estimated that in 1966, of a

total of 1.3 million ha of land on Chalk, only about 44000 ha were still occupied by unenclosed and untilled chalk grassland, the remainder being arable land, reseeded pasture or woodland. Of the total remaining hectarage of chalk grassland, 80% occurs in the western half of southern England, mostly in Wiltshire, Dorset and Hampshire. The largest continuous areas of chalk grassland now left are in Wiltshire, namely, the military training area of Salisbury Plain, where security measures have debarred from agricultural use a relatively large tract of downland. However, because of access difficulties, this area is inadequately known, and it is anticipated that fuller survey here will reveal further sites with strong claims to consideration in the national series of important chalk grasslands. On the other defence establishment at Porton Down, a very large area of chalk grassland has survived for similar reasons, and may well be the most extensive continuous area of this vegetation left in England. Most of this is only lightly grazed by rabbits and hares, but the balance between grasses and forbs has remained favourable, and in summer there is a profusion of colourful flowers, and a spectacular abundance of butterflies. There is much open scrub and also an area of stony, lichen-rich chalk sward reminiscent of the East Anglian Breckland. Porton Down (L.36)[1] is regarded as one of the most important sites for nature conservation in the whole southern half of England, and is high on the list of grade 1 calcareous grassland sites in order of quality.

Still other parts of Wiltshire contribute strongly to the list of key sites. A group of grade 1 sites in the south-west of the county, along the valleys of the Rivers Wylye and Ebble includes Wylye Down (L.27), Prescombe Down (L.28), Knighton Downs (L.29), Steeple Langford Downs (L.30), Woodminton Down (L.31), Knapp Down (L.32), Starveall Down and Stony Hill (L.33), Parsonage Down (L.34) and Scratchbury Hill (L.35). All of these are characterised by abundance or dominance of *Carex humilis* and by extreme species-richness, but differ from each other in detailed floristics. Parsonage Down is outstanding as a large area of uniformly rich chalk sward entirely on level or gently sloping ground. A second, smaller group of chalk grasslands in this district is recognised as worthy of grade 2 status, and has similar floristic features to the above larger group. It includes Homington, Odstock and Coombe Bissett Downs (L.49), Throope Down (L.51), Trow Down (L.52) and Well Bottom, Upton Lovell (L.53). Conversely, in north Wiltshire, Pewsey Downs (L.26, gr. 1) on the escarpment of Pewsey Vale are characterised by absence of *C. humilis*, and grassland here is of the *Festuca ovina–F. rubra* type. Oldbury Castle and Cherhill Downs (L.42, gr. 1) is an example of a chalk grassland site which contains areas of floristically rich grassland interspersed with areas of coarse grassland, with a variety of aspects and slopes. Fyfield Down NNR (L.48, gr. 2) is a somewhat modified area of chalk grassland, and is not regarded as a grade 1 site on vegetational grounds, though it has considerable geological and archaeological interest.

[1] Cross references to key sites are identified by an initial letter (indicating habitat) and number.

In Hampshire, Martin Down (L.24, gr. 1) is an important site close to the borders of Dorset and Wiltshire, and has relatively large areas of chalk grassland on flat or gently sloping ground, extensive *Zerna erecta* sward, an interesting range of chalk heath, great species diversity, and a well-documented historical record. Noar Hill (L.50, gr. 2) is another floristically rich site of rather less overall importance. Old Winchester Hill NNR (L.25, gr. 1) is famous for its woods, scrub and herb-rich *Festuca ovina–F. rubra* grasslands and, on the Isle of Wight, Compton Down (L.23, gr. 1) is a good example of a paramaritime chalk grassland. A series of three areas in Dorset completes the western representation of the field of variation in chalk grassland. These are a group of three sites centred on Eggardon Hill (L.96, gr. 1), Hod and Hambledon Hills (L.97, gr. 1) and Park Bottom, Higher Houghton (L.108, gr. 2), all of which have considerable archaeological as well as botanical interest.

In the south-east, Wye and Crundale Downs NNR (L.3, gr. 1) in Kent is regarded as the best remaining example of the North Downs chalk grassland, characterised by abundance of *Brachypodium pinnatum* swards and the presence of a rich continental element in the flora, including several very rare orchids. Folkestone–Etchinghill Escarpment (L.15, gr. 2) is regarded as the best alternative site and is also rich in orchids, as are Purple Hill and Queendown Warren (L.17, gr. 2).

Three Sussex sites, Castle Hill, Balsdean (L.4, gr. 1), Mount Caburn (Lewes Downs) (L.5, gr. 1) and Heyshott Down (L.16, gr. 2), have been chosen to represent the South Downs, since it is felt that this district has grasslands sufficiently different from other chalk sites in Hampshire and Kent to merit representation. Lullington Heath NNR in Sussex is notable mainly for its good development of chalk heath and Kingley Vale NNR is more important for its yew wood and scrub than for grassland, which is rather small in extent. Box Hill (L.7, gr. 1) in Surrey is famous for its chalk flora but is regarded here as more important for its chalk heath and scrub.

In Berkshire, Aston Upthorpe Downs (L.22, gr. 1) has a complex of chalk grassland and scrub, and the Hertfordshire site of Therfield Heath (L.18, gr. 2) is floristically rich and representative of the East Anglian type of chalk grassland. Aston Rowant NNR (L.21, gr. 1) on the Chiltern scarp in Oxfordshire has good examples of *Festuca ovina–Carex flacca–Poterium sanguisorba* and *Helictotrichon pubescens* swards, and is a valuable research site. On the northward extension of the Chalk in southern England, the isolated fragment of untilled grassland at Knocking Hoe NNR (L.67, gr. 1), Bedfordshire, is one of the finest examples of this vegetation type and has an exceedingly rich floristic composition. Barton Hills (L.68, gr. 1) in the same county have well-developed *Zerna erecta* grassland and are an important research site for management studies of the chalk ecosystem.

The northern outpost of chalk grasslands, on the Yorkshire Wolds, is geographically isolated from the southern areas of this ecosystem, and shows interesting intermediate features between this type and the northern Carboniferous

Limestone grasslands. The southern *Brachypodium pinnatum* and *Zerna erecta* grasslands are well represented, but in *Festuca* swards there are marked species differences compared with southern chalk swards. The local features peculiar to the Yorkshire Wolds are well represented in a group of three grade 1 sites consisting of Waterdale (L.130), Duggleby High Barn Wold (L.131) and East Dale (L.132). The fragmentary grasslands of the East Anglian Chalk are represented mainly by the richer types of Breckland grass heath, which are considered separately elsewhere (see p. 174).

JURASSIC LIMESTONE GRASSLAND

The Jurassic system runs in a belt to the west and north of, but parallel with, the Chalk. It extends from Dorset through Wiltshire, Gloucestershire, Oxfordshire, Northamptonshire and Lincolnshire and has a northern projection in the North York Moors. As Lousley (1969) has pointed out, from its geographical position the Jurassic forms a link between the limestone floras of the west and east and also between those of the south and north. The Great Oolite Series is the rock underlying most of the important calcareous grasslands in this formation, although locally, as in the Isle of Purbeck, the Portland Series and Inferior Oolite Series support a calcareous grassland. By far the most extensive areas of Jurassic limestone grassland occur in the Gloucestershire Cotswolds, with smaller, more fragmented areas in Wiltshire, Northamptonshire and Lincolnshire, and very little elsewhere.

The best example of Cotswold Oolitic limestone grassland is Barnsley Warren (L.99, gr. 1), but two other sites, Rodborough Common (L.100) and Cleeve Hill (L.101), are sufficiently different and valuable to be included as grade 1. In addition, three less important sites, at Brassey (L.109), Hornsleasow Roughs (L.110) and Minchinhampton Common (L.111) are rated as grade 2. The complex of woodland and grassland at Painswick Hill also rates as a bonus for this type of grassland (see W.72). All these sites lie in Gloucestershire. Farther north-east at Barnack Hills and Holes (L.69, gr. 1) near Peterborough is a fine example of calcareous grassland, partly on old quarry workings and, in the same district, the grassland part of the woodland, scrub and grassland complex at Castor Hanglands (L.81, gr. 2) is of slightly less importance. Another grade 2 site is recognised in Lincolnshire at Holywell Mound (L.80).

LOWLAND CARBONIFEROUS LIMESTONE GRASSLANDS

Grasslands on Carboniferous Limestone at altitudes of less than 300 m are found in the Mendips and Bristol area, Glamorgan and Brecknock, Denbighshire and Caernarvonshire, the Low Peak of Derbyshire, and in the Pennines, Morecambe Bay and Shap Fells areas of northern England. Unlike the Chalk, which is massively exposed as bedrock only on coastal cliffs, this hard calcareous rock outcrops repeatedly as cliffs, both inland and coastal, screes, and level or gently inclined pavements usually riven by numerous vertical fissures. There are also features such as pot-holes, sink-holes, cave systems and disappearing streams, and

some districts, notably in south Wales and the Craven Pennines, have most of the characteristic features of typical karst country. Where these open rock habitats are extensive below 300 m, they are usually treated along with the lowland calcareous grasslands, but in the north of England certain areas below 300 m are so clearly associated with ground of higher elevation that it has seemed best to treat them as uplands.

In south-west England, the Carboniferous Limestone forms the east–west ridge of the Mendip Hills which terminate in the seaward promontory of Brean Down (L.104, gr. 1) at Weston-super-Mare, a famous botanical locality. Dolebury Warren (L.113, gr. 2), Crook Peak (L.112, gr. 2), and Purn Hill are other notable plant localities in this district. There are quite extensive grasslands, but the most notable feature is the great chasm of Cheddar Gorge (L.103, gr. 1), with its 120 m cliffs and screes below, another famous botanical locality. Equally celebrated is the more open gorge of the River Avon at Clifton, Bristol (L.102, gr. 1), with 60 m crags and an extremely rich flora.

The Carboniferous Limestone of south Wales occurs as a discontinuous ring surrounding the uplands of south Brecknock and Glamorgan, and outcrops extensively on the coasts of Glamorgan and Pembrokeshire. The exposures at Craig y Ciliau and Fforest Fawr are treated as upland, and the main lowland exposures and grasslands are on the rocky coasts of Gower (Glamorgan) and Stackpole-Flimston (Pembrokeshire), and the two grade 1 coastal sites (C.41 and C.43) have bonus interest in their limestone grasslands.

In north Wales, the Carboniferous Limestone occurs as coastal grassland and cliff at Penmon and Bwrdd Arthur in south-east Anglesey and the Great and Little Ormes Heads in Caernarvonshire. The Great Orme (L.121, gr. 1) is an important exposure, but much of the botanical interest is on the cliffs, and the grassland is mostly heavily grazed by sheep and trampled by visitors. In Denbighshire two fairly massive north–south inland ridges lie on both sides of the vale of Clwyd. The one to the west includes the well-known Cefn yr Ogof, and that to the east, overlapping into Flintshire, forms part of the Clwydian range. The latter has not been properly examined, but the only well-known site of botanical or other importance is Mynydd Eglwyseg (U.14) at the south end, treated as a grade 2 upland site.

The Derbyshire Dales (which extend into Staffordshire) include some of the most important Carboniferous Limestone exposures in Britain and consist mainly of steep-sided valleys cut to a depth of about 60–90 m in a plateau-land which lies at a general level of 300–360 m, so that they approach the upper limits of lowland. These valleys are variably lined with crag and scree, and some have no streams. The best-known is Dove Valley with its extension into Biggin Dale and Wolfscote Dale, but other important valleys rated as grade 1 (L.124(i)) include Lathkill Dale, Cressbrook Dale, Monks Dale, Long Dale and Gratton Dale. Miller's Dale, Deep Dale and Coombs Dale are rated grade 2 (L.124(ii)) and other important valleys are Monsal Dale, Raven's Dale, Chee Dale and the Winnats Pass. Many of these contain extensive woodland which is dealt with under that heading. Because of their general similarity and geographical proximity, these dales should be regarded as far as possible as a single geographical/ecological unit.

The most extensive occurrences of Carboniferous Limestone are in northern England, especially in the Craven Pennines, but much of this ground is upland. The upland sites of Malham–Arncliffe (U.24) and Appleby Fells (U.22) contain bonus areas of lowland limestone grassland, and some of the interesting communities of Bastow Wood and Dib Scar, Wharfedale (W.143), include grassland. The main lowland exposures are around the head of Morecambe Bay, in both Lancashire and Westmorland. Here, a botanically famous group of low hills around Arnside, Hutton Roof and Witherslack show large areas of limestone pavement, scar and scree. The pavements are especially important geomorphologically and floristically, and the best examples are at Gait Barrows (L.134, gr. 1), Underlaid Wood, Hutton Roof Crags and Farleton Knott (L.135, gr. 1). Cliff and scree are best represented at Whitbarrow Scar (L.136, gr. 1) and Scout Scar (L.137, gr. 1) and there is a small but important coastal headland at Humphrey Head (L.133, gr. 1) on Morecambe Bay. Extensive areas of limestone grassland occur at most of these sites, and also at Arnside Knott, Middlebarrow and Warton Crag (L.147, gr. 2), and many of these limestone hills also carry woodland.

Although a large area of Carboniferous rocks extends northwards across the Tyne Gap into Northumberland and the Scottish Borders, there are few limestone exposures of any size north of Westmorland, and none appears to be of high nature conservation value.

MAGNESIAN LIMESTONE GRASSLANDS

The Magnesian Limestone, of Permian age, extends as a narrow strip nowhere more than a few kilometres wide, from Nottingham northwards to Durham. On account of its use by the steel industry, most of the exposures have been or are being quarried. Although small areas of the Magnesian Limestone grassland are known to persist in Nottinghamshire, Derbyshire and Yorkshire, the only extensive areas (and even these are limited) occur in Durham. A conservation survey of this formation made by Shimwell (1968) indicated that only two areas were worthy of consideration as possible key sites and our attention has been directed to these alone. Thrislington Plantation (L.138, gr. 1) is regarded as the more important, and Cassop Vale (L.148, gr. 2) as an alternative site.

DEVONIAN LIMESTONE GRASSLANDS

The Devonian limestone outcrops in a number of very limited areas in south Devon. The main exposures are at Walls Hill, Ansteys Cove, Daddyhole Plain and Berry Head (L.105). All these sites are small, under heavy pressure from holiday-makers, and have a mixture of maritime species in addition to those associated with inland limestones. Berry Head is regarded as the most important, and is rated as a grade 1 site to represent this formation.

C. CALCAREOUS SCRUB

RANGE OF ECOLOGICAL VARIATION

Habitat factors and vegetation

Lowland scrub is widespread in Britain as a seral community which develops spontaneously through the invasion of tall and medium shrubs on any grassland under suitable conditions, potentially as a stage in succession to a woodland climax, although it may remain as a climax of scrub under conditions which inhibit tree growth. In lowland situations, development of woodland is limited principally by extreme maritime exposure, and by instability of habitat or immaturity of soils as on rock habitats such as cliffs, screes and pavements. In northern and western Scotland the altitudinal limits of tree growth are much lower than in southern Britain, and scrub locally forms a climax community at much lower levels than in the south. Scrub can be artificially maintained but restricted from further spread or development by man, as in the case of hedgerows, coppiced areas and woodland edges. These types of habitat are common in the agricultural and silvicultural landscape of lowland Britain, so that many of the scrub species are relatively familiar. Scrub which occurs as the tall–medium shrub layer within woodland, or is derived from such an ecosystem by loss of the tree layer, is more properly considered under the section on woodlands (Chapter 5). Similarly, coppice or regenerating woodland composed of young trees passes through a scrub phase but, when tree species are involved, e.g. oak, ash, hornbeam, the system clearly belongs to woodland.

Scrub is especially well developed and varied on the calcareous soils of the Chalk and limestone formations, and emphasis has been placed on this range of types in field survey and selection of key sites. Some of these scrub types, however, are also well developed on a wider range of lowland soils lacking free calcium carbonate; these include the fertile loams of neutral grasslands.

The presence of colonising scrub in the lowlands is strongly related to the economics of land-use and, on the steep escarpments of the chalk downs of southern England where it is no longer economic to graze sheep, and rabbits are now scarce, grassland areas are changing to scrub. The past and present influence of man's activities has produced some regional variation in the presence of scrub species; for example, juniper has almost disappeared from the Cotswold grasslands although there are many past records of the species there.

Where scrub is developing anew, hawthorn is usually the predominant species, and others such as yew and juniper do not appear readily. This may be partly a matter of abundance of seed-producing parents, hawthorn being a common shrub, especially in hedges, but it may also depend on interspecific differences in capacity for spread and establishment. Thus, although in theory many scrub types could be produced *de novo* by suitable management, it is necessary to select for conservation the best areas where there is good local balance of seed parents. Otherwise, a great deal of deliberate planting of species would be required. In addition, in the case of species such as juniper, conservation in the sense of preservation of present stands may be necessary.

The seral character of scrub imposes changes in the vegetation with time, and some of these changes occurring in southern Britain have been studied. In the early stages of colonisation by woody plants the predominating influence is that of the existing community, and descriptions of the types of calcareous grasslands are given on pp. 142–4. Of the woody species, juniper and roses (particularly *Rosa rubiginosa* agg.) are more common in the early stages of succession. Juniper is in fact one of the best adapted of the woody plants to grazing, as stands apparently regenerate under grazed conditions, and can be subsequently managed under the same regime. Many other woody species can be found as very short coppiced plants cropped by grazing animals, and these shoot up unchecked when the grazing pressure is relaxed. Other species enter the sere in later stages. Reversion to scrub may occur without any intervening period of grazing, as when ploughed land is abandoned, and this may allow different species to invade.

As litter accumulates and the woody plants grow and produce a mosaic of shade patterns, plants regarded as typical of wood margins, clearings and rides become established. At the same time plants characteristic of woodland itself also begin to colonise the area. Typical herbaceous plants of this stage are *Arrhenatherum elatius, Dactylis glomerata, Holcus lanatus, Trisetum flavescens, Achillea millefolium, Agrimonia eupatoria, Centaurea nigra, C. scabiosa, Chamaenerion angustifolium, Clinopodium vulgare, Eupatorium cannabinum, Galium aparine, G. mollugo, Heracleum sphondylium, Hypericum hirsutum, H. perforatum, Inula conyza, Origanum vulgare, Pastinaca sativa, Rubia peregrina, Scrophularia nodosa, Senecio jacobaea, Sonchus arvensis, Teucrium scorodonia, Torilis japonica, T. arvensis, Tragopogon pratensis, Valeriana officinalis, Verbascum nigrum, Vicia cracca* and *V. sepium*, and also the climbers *Clematis vitalba, Bryonia dioica,* and *Tamus communis.*

A list of the principal woody species is given under the classification of scrub types.

The mosaic of grassland and scrub can persist in balance for a long period when there is grazing pressure of the right intensity, which is generally light or intermittent. Good examples of this are found in the Derbyshire Dales, e.g. Cressbrook Dale and Monks Dale. In the absence of such control by grazing, a closed canopy eventually develops and almost completely suppresses the original flora of the open scrub and grassland. Of the scrub woody species, some such as juniper and blackthorn (and on coastal dune areas sea buckthorn *Hippophaë rhamnoides*) are particularly light-demanding and die out when shaded. On the other hand, species such as *Rubus caesius, Daphne laureola* and *Hedera helix* enter as the scrub thickens. Field layer species of the more dense and shady calcareous scrub in southern Britain are *Brachypodium sylvaticum, Poa trivialis, Ajuga reptans, Arum maculatum, Campanula trachelium, Circaea lutetiana, Fragaria vesca, Geum urbanum, Iris foetidissima, Mercurialis*

perennis, Ophrys insectifera, Sanicula europaea, Solanum dulcamara, Stachys sylvatica and *Urtica dioica.*

Invasion by tree species throughout the succession depends on a number of circumstances, especially the proximity of seed parents, and occurrence of suitable conditions for germination. Thus, the succession may pass directly to mature closed woodland, with the former scrub now forming the shrub layer, or there may be various degrees of dominance by scrub species such as hawthorn. In the latter event it is not known how long such conditions may persist before the woodland climax is attained. Examples of such dense scrub are sometimes found on commons, and are considered by Salisbury (1918) as 'thicket scrub' produced by intermittent grazing, burning and coppicing. Where seral development proceeds to woodland, this may be dominated by oak, ash, beech or various mixtures of these species with others such as wych elm, common elm and hornbeam.

Although the herb layers are often very interesting, they can be relatively ephemeral, and the principal feature in the classification of scrub types is therefore the dominant woody species or mixture of species, although the presence of associated herbs may support the classification. In the chalk and limestone scrubs there are a number of woody species which are positively associated when a series of quadrats is compared. These are *Corylus avellana, Euonymus europaeus, Fagus sylvatica, Fraxinus excelsior, Ilex aquifolium, Juniperus communis, Ligustrum vulgare, Rhamnus catharticus, Rosa rubiginosa* agg., *Sorbus* spp., *Taxus baccata, Thelycrania sanguinea* and *Viburnum lantana.* In addition *Crataegus monogyna, Rubus* spp., *Prunus spinosa, Rosa* spp., and *Sambucus nigra* may be present either scattered or even dominant, but even so they are not so positively associated with the species of the first group. A range of mixtures of all these species can be found together with other less common species, and hazel, hawthorn, ash, juniper, privet, rose, bramble, yew, dogwood and *Viburnum* can be dominant or co-dominant.

The classification of calcareous scrub is still tentative because survey was strongly biased to the southern Chalk and further comparison of northern and southern scrub types is required. However some attempt is made to produce a classification of the various mixtures.

Juniperus communis *ssp.* communis

This scrub type is associated with shallow dry soils, and open habitats on chalk and limestone soils, although it is almost absent now from the south-west region of England. Common associates of this scrub type in the south are *Sorbus aria, Viburnum lantana* and *Taxus baccata,* although almost all the other woody plants can be present. Succession is frequently to *Taxus* dominance, although it can also be to *Fraxinus excelsior.* The field layer is characteristically of the older grassland type, often of the *Festuca rubra–F. ovina,* and may be grazed. The taller forbs are less common. Occasionally juniper occurs in association with *Sambucus* and the ground flora is more nitrophilous, as described under the *Sambucus* type. There is some indication that the longevity of the juniper is increased under such conditions.

In the north of England and Scotland, juniper often occurs as an undershrub with birch and pine, and extensive juniper scrub also occurs here on more acidic soils, forming a type floristically distinct from that of calcareous soils. Juniper scrub on non-calcareous soils is well represented in the Lake District (e.g. Birk Fell, W.137) and an extensive stand occurs in Upper Teesdale (U.21). The Tynron Juniper Wood (W.167) is an isolated example in the Southern Uplands. In the eastern and central Highlands, juniper scrub is widespread both on treeless moorland and as a component of birch and pine wood, but in the north and west, most juniper belongs to ssp. *nana*.

Taxus baccata

This type of scrub is closely related to the juniper type, and juniper is frequently present, but it can be entirely absent, especially in areas where juniper is no longer present in the district to colonise a site in the early stages. Most of the other scrub woody species can also occur, In the south the ground flora in the open glades between bushes is of the shorter grassland type, and although taller forbs invade on the edges of the woody plants, they are less numerous than in many of the other scrub types. Eventually the dense shade of the evergreen yew suppresses almost all the field and ground layers, only a few species such as *Mercurialis perennis*, *Fragaria vesca*, *Brachypodium sylvaticum* and *Urtica dioica* persisting in the lighter areas. The purest yew-woods are characteristic of the Chalk of southern England, but fragments occur on the Carboniferous Limestone of northern England (e.g. Roudsea Wood, W.139) and on Inchlonaig in Loch Lomond. Mixed scrub of yew and juniper occurs on both Chalk and limestone. In Lakeland, yew is a characteristic component also of woods and juniper scrub on soils derived from the Borrowdale Volcanic Series and from Silurian sedimentary rocks which, at best, are only moderately base-rich.

Corylus avellana

This type is commoner in the north and on the limestones than on the southern Chalk. It is important in the Derbyshire Dales where it forms so-called 'retrogressive scrub' which can have a very rich herb flora including the local or rare species *Melica nutans*, *Convallaria majalis*, *Silene nutans* and *Geranium sanguineum*. It also occurs on limestone pavements. In the Highlands, hazel scrub is a widespread and characteristic scrub type of many western coastal areas, especially on basalt and other basic rocks. Sometimes it has been derived from woodland by loss of the dominant trees, especially ash, and it is often the nearest approach to woodland on ground where exposure to onshore winds is extreme. These northern and western hazel scrubs often have rich field layers and they may be bryophyte-rich, especially on block-strewn ground.

In the south, hazel scrub is often a remnant of coppiced areas. Although *Corylus* can occasionally be the dominant species of invasive scrub on chalk grassland it is usually present in less abundance. It tends to have associated with it a tall-herb field community containing various woodland margin species.

Southern mixed scrub

This is an interesting association occurring on calcareous soils in the south, especially on the Chalk. A range of mixtures of species occurs with *Ligustrum*, *Thelycrania*, *Clematis*, *Crataegus monogyna*, *Euonymus*, *Rhamnus catharticus*, *Rosa* spp., *Rubus* spp. and *Viburnum lantana* as the commonest species. Other species such as *Juniperus*, *Taxus* and *Acer campestre* can be present also. As one proceeds north, various species disappear on reaching their climatic limit: *Viburnum lantana* in Derbyshire, *Clematis* in southwest Yorkshire, *Rhamnus catharticus* and *Thelycrania* in Cumberland and Durham, *Euonymus* in south Scotland. *Ligustrum* occurs further north, but it is thought that it is not native in Scotland. In the south, the ground flora in the open stages has many of the marginal species, while in damper places the marginal herbs include *Arctium minus*, *Eupatorium cannabinum*, *Succisa pratensis* and *Valeriana officinalis*. However, dense canopies can be formed and little survives beneath, although on the edges *Brachypodium sylvaticum*, *Fragaria vesca*, *Mercurialis perennis*, *Galium aparine*, *Teucrium scorodonia*, *Daphne laureola* and *Iris foetidissima* may occur.

Thelycrania

This type is a variant of southern mixed scrub and is dominated by *Thelycrania*, with some *Crataegus monogyna*, *Clematis* and *Rosa* spp. It occurs on the Chalk and is said to be associated with regeneration on ploughed arable land. Typical associated herbaceous plants are *Arrhenatherum elatius*, *Brachypodium sylvaticum*, *Festuca rubra*, *Holcus lanatus*, *Agrimonia eupatoria*, *Clinopodium vulgare*, *Fragaria vesca*, *Galium mollugo*, *Hypericum perforatum*, *Leontodon hispidus*, *Lotus corniculatus*, *Origanum vulgare*, *Teucrium scorodonia* and *Viola hirta*. *Thelycrania* can also form a similar association on limestone screes in the Cotswolds and in Derbyshire.

Crataegus monogyna

This is the commonest species of scrub plant and often the dominant member on both Chalk and limestone, and on many other soils besides. It can apparently invade most types of grassland but is perhaps more frequent on the deeper soils, and there is some indication of dwarfing on very shallow chalk soils. Many marginal species occur in the open scrub, and the most frequent woody associates are species of bramble and wild rose, although practically any woody species can be present in the mixtures. Succession occurs to ash, pedunculate oak and occasionally to beech, but hawthorn alone may form a closed canopy. In the south, *Brachypodium sylvaticum*, *Poa trivialis*, *Galium aparine*, *Geranium robertianum*, *Geum urbanum* and *Urtica dioica* are commonest below the closed canopy. In upland districts of England and Wales there is also locally an open scrub of hawthorn on lower hill slopes, in which this shrub is scattered in heavily grazed *Festuca–Agrostis* grassland on relatively base-poor soils. These hill hawthorn scrubs are often even-aged and it has been suggested that they date from a period of depression in hill farming when a substantial reduction in sheep numbers allowed the establishment of hawthorn in the previously heavily grazed grasslands. A dense example of this scrub occurs at Craig y Ciliau, Brecknock.

Buxus

This is a very distinct type of scrub in which box *Buxus sempervirens* forms the dominant or co-dominant species and may represent a climax community; it is found on the Chalk, and on the Jurassic limestone of the Cotswolds. Of the only three stands thought to be native in origin, the species is the dominant in two; at Ellesborough Warren, Buckinghamshire, it is a co-dominant with *Sambucus*, while at Box Hill it also forms an understorey to *Taxus* in places. On sites where it is thought to have been introduced it occurs with *Fraxinus* and other woody plants. It tends to form a rather dense canopy and typical associated plants are *Arctium minus, Chamaenerion angustifolium, Glechoma hederacea, Mercurialis perennis* and *Urtica dioica*.

Sambucus

This is a specialised scrub type tending to occur only in relatively small areas in disturbed situations or sites high in nitrogen. On the Chalk it typically marks the site of old rabbit warrens, although this may also reflect its high resistance to rabbit-grazing. Frequent woody associates are hawthorn, bramble and wild rose. The canopy tends to be rather dense and the situation moist, and common ground flora plants are *Arrhenatherum elatius, Poa trivialis, Dryopteris filix-mas, Arctium minus, Arum maculatum, Chamaenerion angustifolium, Galium aparine, Geum urbanum, Glechoma hederacea, Mercurialis perennis, Myosotis arvensis, Solanum dulcamara* and *Urtica dioica*. Elder is important locally as the habitat of various epiphytic mosses.

Prunus spinosa

This type of scrub is common on many different kinds of soils although it is perhaps more typical of the deeper more acid soils with some clay. Although it occurs on the Chalk it rarely forms the dominant species except on the clay cappings or valley bottoms, and in chalk heaths. Elsewhere it is commoner on limestones and in the coastal situations.

Coastal scrub on calcareous soils

This type has not been examined, so little information is available on its place in scrub classification. Blackthorn is often dominant, but there may be a variety of shrubs. It is typically developed on the sloping crest of cliffs and steep slopes running down to the sea. Interesting examples occur at Oxwich point, Glamorgan, at Axmouth–Lyme Regis, Devon, and at Great Ormes Head, Caernarvonshire, where there is the only native station for *Cotoneaster integerrimus*. Also included here is scrub dominated by sea buckthorn usually on moderately basic to calcareous dune systems, and the lower and less dense communities of *Rosa pimpinellifolia* in similar habitats.

Non-native species

On calcareous soils, stands of non-native species occur occasionally, usually regenerating from nearby seed sources. The commonest species are sycamore and evergreen oak.

Flora

As scrub so often represents a seral and transitory type of vegetation, its flora tends to be composed of a mixture of species from other types of vegetation related in the succession, i.e. from grassland and woodland.

Scrub consists essentially of dominant medium to tall shrubs and herbaceous associates; the herbs are either residual species from the original community or colonists which are favoured by the conditions which the shrubs create. Scrub typically develops on grassland, so that it contains grassland species which can withstand the degree of shade and competition which the shrubs create; and since it is a kind of incipient woodland, there is invasion by species which need a moderate amount of shade, or have other dependence on taller, woody plants. The list of species in Table 15 is arbitrarily chosen, and includes the species most characteristic of scrub, and those which are commonly found there as well as in other habitats. In consequence, relatively few rare species are included. A great many more species have occurrences in scrub, but most of these are not characteristic of this class of vegetation and have their main niches in other habitats. Table 12 (p. 147) indicates the range of species likely to be found in the early stages of scrub development.

As will be seen from Table 15, many scrub plants occur also in hedgerows and related habitats, and some of them grow in the heterogeneous herb communities of waste ground. For some species, as for the shrubs themselves, the absence of grazing is the critical factor which allows them to become established; once well grown, the scrub then forms a further barrier against large herbivores. Climbers need the woody shrubs on which to grow upwards, e.g. *Clematis vitalba, Tamus communis, Bryonia dioica, Calystegia sepium* and *Convolvulus arvensis*. Some legumes are semi-climbers and grow more luxuriantly when there are bushes or tall herbage for support. The herbaceous species growing between the bushes are mostly tall, and the smaller plants either form a separate field layer or are associated with open rocky ground.

The more important of the shrubs which form scrub have been included in Table 15, but the various species of the *Sorbus aria* agg. have been dealt with in Chapter 5. *S. aria* (*sensu strictu*) is a fairly frequent member of scrub in southern England, and *S. rupicola* occurs in the northern limestone scrubs, but most of the other *Sorbus* spp. are rare or very local shrubs of crags and rocky woods.

The flora of scrub varies somewhat according to the nature of the underlying substratum, and is usually richest on Chalk and limestone. The list in Table 15 may, however, be somewhat biassed by the fact that most of the survey work so far has been confined to scrub found on these rock formations. There has also been bias towards study of

Table 15. *Flora of lowland calcareous scrub*

	Woodland	Grassland	Rocky terrain	Coastal scrub	Hedges, banks & verges	S. & S.E. England	S.W. England	E. Anglia	S. Wales	N. Wales	Midlands	N. England	S. Scotland	E. Highlands	W. Highlands	Rare species	European distribution
	1	2	3	4	5	6	7	8	9	10	11	12	13	14	15	16	17
Juniperus communis	+	+	+	+	—	+	+	+	+	+	—	+	+	+	+	—	—
Taxus baccata	+	+	+	—	+	+	+	—	+	+	+	+	(+)	—	—	—	—
Helleborus foetidus	+	—	+	—	—	+	+	+	+	+	+	+	—	—	—	—	—
H. viridis	+	—	+	—	—	+	+	+	+	+	—	+	—	—	—	—	—
Clematis vitalba	—	—	—	+	+	+	+	+	+	+	+	+	—	—	—	—	CS
Aquilegia vulgaris	+	+	+	—	—	+	+	+	+	+	+	+	+	+	—	—	—
Berberis vulgaris	—	—	+	—	+	+	+	+	+	+	+	+	+	+	+	—	—
Hypericum perforatum	—	+	—	+	+	+	+	+	+	+	+	+	+	+	(+)	—	—
H. maculatum	—	+	—	+	+	+	+	+	+	+	+	+	+	+	(+)	—	—
H. hirsutum	+	+	+	+	+	+	+	+	+	+	+	+	+	+	—	—	CN
H. montanum	—	+	+	—	—	+	+	+	+	+	+	+	—	—	—	—	C
Geranium sanguineum	—	+	+	+	+	—	+	(+)	+	+	+	+	+	+	(+)	—	—
G. columbinum	—	+	—	+	+	+	+	+	+	+	+	+	(+)	(+)	—	—	—
Ilex aquifolium	+	+	+	+	+	+	+	+	+	+	+	+	+	+	+	—	OS
Acer campestre	+	—	—	+	+	+	+	+	+	+	+	+	—	—	—	—	CS
Euonymus europaeus	+	—	+	+	+	+	+	+	+	+	+	+	—	—	—	—	—
Buxus sempervirens	+	—	—	—	+	+	+	—	—	—	—	—	—	—	—	+	—
Rhamnus catharticus	+	+	—	+	+	+	+	+	+	+	+	+	—	—	—	—	—
Astragalus glycyphyllos	—	+	+	+	+	+	+	+	(+)	—	+	+	(+)	(+)	—	—	C
Vicia cracca	—	+	+	+	+	+	+	+	+	+	+	+	+	+	+	—	—
V. sepium	+	+	+	+	+	+	+	+	+	+	+	+	+	+	+	—	—
V. bithynica	—	—	—	—	—	+	+	+	+	—	(+)	(+)	(+)	—	—	—	—
Lathyrus nissolia	—	+	—	+	+	+	+	+	(+)	—	+	—	—	—	—	—	CS
L. sylvestris	—	+	—	+	+	+	+	+	+	+	+	(+)	(+)	(+)	—	—	—
Rubus caesius	+	+	—	+	+	+	+	+	+	+	+	+	+	(+)	—	—	—
R. fruticosus agg.	+	+	+	+	+	+	+	+	+	+	+	+	+	+	+	—	—
R. idaeus	+	+	+	+	+	+	+	+	+	+	+	+	+	+	+	—	—
Agrimonia eupatoria	—	+	—	+	+	+	+	+	+	+	+	+	+	+	—	—	—
Potentilla sterilis	+	+	+	+	+	+	+	+	+	+	+	+	+	+	—	—	—
P. anglica	—	+	—	+	+	+	+	+	+	+	+	+	+	(+)	(+)	—	—
Fragaria vesca	+	+	+	+	+	+	+	+	+	+	+	+	+	+	+	—	—
Geum urbanum	+	+	—	+	+	+	+	+	+	+	+	+	+	+	—	—	—
Rosa canina agg.	+	+	—	+	+	+	+	+	+	+	+	+	+	+	—	—	—
R. villosa agg.	+	+	+	+	+	+	+	+	+	+	+	+	+	+	+	—	C
R. rubiginosa	+	+	—	+	+	+	+	+	+	+	+	+	+	+	—	—	C
R. pimpinellifolia	—	+	+	—	+	+	+	+	+	+	+	+	+	+	—	—	—
Prunus spinosa	+	+	+	+	+	+	+	+	+	+	+	+	+	+	—	—	—
P. padus	+	—	+	+	—	+	+	+	+	+	+	+	+	—	—	—	—
Cotoneaster integerrimus	—	—	+	—	—	—	—	—	—	+	—	—	—	—	—	+	—
Crataegus monogyna	+	+	+	+	+	+	+	+	+	+	+	+	+	+	+	—	—
C. oxyacanthoides	+	—	—	—	+	(+)	+	(+)	—	+	(+)	—	—	—	—	—	—
Sorbus aucuparia	+	+	+	+	+	+	+	+	+	+	+	+	+	+	+	—	—
S. aria agg.	+	+	+	+	+	+	+	+	+	+	+	+	+	+	+	—	—
Malus sylvestris	+	—	—	+	+	+	+	+	+	+	+	+	+	+	(+)	—	—
Ribes nigrum	+	—	—	—	+	+	+	+	+	+	+	+	+	+	—	—	—
R. spicatum	+	+	+	—	—	—	—	—	—	—	—	+	(+)	+	(+)	—	—
R. alpinum	+	—	+	—	—	—	—	—	—	+	+	+	—	—	—	—	CN
R. uva-crispa	+	—	—	+	+	+	+	+	+	+	+	+	+	+	+	—	—
Daphne laureola	+	—	—	—	+	+	+	+	+	+	+	+	—	—	—	—	CS

Table 15 (*contd.*)

	1	2	3	4	5	6	7	8	9	10	11	12	13	14	15	16	17
D. mezereum	+	−	+	−	−	(+)	(+)	−	−	−	(+)	(+)	−	−	−	+	−
Hippophae rhamnoides	−	−	−	+	−	+	+	+	+	+	+	+	+	+	+	−	−
Chamaenerion angustifolium	+	+	+	+	+	+	+	+	+	+	+	+	+	+	+	−	−
Circaea lutetiana	+	+	+	+	+	+	+	+	+	+	+	+	+	+	+	−	−
Thelycrania sanguinea	+	+	+	+	+	+	+	+	+	+	+	+	+	−	−	−	−
Hedera helix	+	−	+	+	+	+	+	+	+	+	+	+	+	+	+	−	−
Heracleum sphondylium	+	+	+	+	+	+	+	+	+	+	+	+	+	+	+	−	−
Pastinaca sativa	−	+	−	+	+	+	+	+	+	(+)	+	+	−	−	−	−	−
Torilis japonica	+	+	−	+	+	+	+	+	+	+	+	+	+	+	(+)	−	−
T. arvensis	−	+	−	−	+	+	+	+	(+)	−	+	(+)	(+)	−	−	−	CS
Sanicula europaea	+	−	+	+	+	+	+	+	+	+	+	+	+	+	+	−	−
Chaerophyllum temulentum	+	+	−	−	+	+	+	+	+	+	+	+	+	+	(+)	−	−
Anthriscus sylvestris	+	+	+	+	+	+	+	+	+	+	+	+	+	+	+	−	−
Bryonia dioica	−	−	−	−	+	+	+	+	+	+	+	−	−	−	−	−	−
Mercurialis perennis	+	+	+	+	+	+	+	+	+	+	+	+	+	+	+	−	−
Euphorbia cyparissias	−	+	−	+	+	+	+	+	+	(+)	+	+	−	(+)	(+)	−	−
Polygonum dumetorum	−	−	−	+	+	+	+	−	−	(+)	−	−	−	−	−	−	−
P. convolvulus	−	−	−	−	+	+	+	+	+	+	+	+	+	+	+	−	−
Urtica dioica	+	+	+	+	+	+	+	+	+	+	+	+	+	+	+	−	−
Salix cinerea	+	−	+	+	+	+	+	+	+	+	+	+	+	+	+	−	−
S. caprea	+	−	+	+	+	+	+	+	+	+	+	+	+	+	+	−	−
S. aurita	−	−	+	+	−	+	+	+	+	+	+	+	+	+	+	−	−
S. repens	−	+	+	+	−	+	+	+	+	+	+	+	+	+	+	−	−
Primula vulgaris	+	+	+	+	+	+	+	+	+	+	+	+	+	+	+	−	−
Fraxinus excelsior	+	+	+	+	+	+	+	+	+	+	+	+	+	+	+	−	−
Ligustrum vulgare	+	+	−	+	+	+	+	+	+	+	+	+	+	+	+	−	−
Cynoglossum officinale	−	+	−	+	−	+	+	+	+	+	−	+	(+)	(+)	(+)	−	C
Lithospermum officinale	+	−	−	−	+	+	+	+	+	+	+	+	−	(+)	−	−	−
L. purpurocaeruleum	+	−	−	−	−	−	+	−	(+)	(+)	−	−	−	−	−	+	CS
Convolvulus arvensis	−	−	−	+	+	+	+	+	+	+	+	+	+	(+)	−	−	−
Calystegia sepium	+	−	−	+	+	+	+	+	+	+	+	+	+	+	−	−	−
Atropa bella-donna	+	−	−	+	+	+	+	+	(+)	(+)	+	+	(+)	(+)	−	−	−
Solanum dulcamara	+	−	−	+	+	+	+	+	+	+	+	+	+	+	(+)	−	−
Verbascum thapsus	−	+	+	+	+	+	+	+	+	+	+	+	+	+	(+)	−	−
V. nigrum	−	+	−	+	+	+	+	+	+	+	+	−	−	−	−	−	−
Melampyrum cristatum	−	+	−	−	+	−	+	+	−	−	−	−	−	−	−	−	−
Orobanche rapum-genistae	−	−	−	−	−	(+)	(+)	(+)	(+)	(+)	(+)	(+)	(+)	−	−	−	−
Scrophularia nodosa	+	+	+	+	+	+	+	+	+	+	+	+	+	+	−	−	−
Origanum vulgare	+	+	+	+	+	+	+	+	+	+	+	+	+	+	(+)	−	−
Stachys sylvatica	+	+	−	+	+	+	+	+	+	+	+	+	+	+	+	−	−
Ajuga reptans	+	−	+	+	+	+	+	+	+	+	+	+	+	+	+	−	−
Teucrium scorodonia	+	+	+	+	+	+	+	+	+	+	+	+	+	+	+	−	−
Clinopodium vulgare	+	+	+	+	+	+	+	+	+	+	+	+	+	+	−	−	−
Galium cruciata	−	+	−	+	+	+	+	+	+	+	+	+	+	+	(+)	−	−
G. aparine	+	+	−	+	+	+	+	+	+	+	+	+	+	+	+	−	−
G. mollugo	−	+	−	+	+	+	+	+	+	+	+	+	+	+	(+)	−	−
Campanula patula	+	−	−	+	+	+	(+)	+	−	+	−	−	−	−	−	−	−
C. trachelium	+	−	−	−	+	+	+	+	+	+	−	−	−	−	−	−	−
Rubia peregrina	−	+	+	+	−	+	+	(+)	+	+	−	−	−	−	−	−	OS
Sambucus nigra	+	+	−	+	+	+	+	+	+	+	+	+	+	+	+	−	−
Viburnum lantana	+	+	−	+	+	+	+	+	+	(+)	(+)	−	−	−	−	−	CS
V. opulus	+	−	−	+	+	+	+	+	+	+	+	+	+	+	+	−	−
Adoxa moschatellina	+	−	+	−	+	+	+	+	+	+	+	+	+	+	(+)	−	−
Valeriana officinalis	+	+	+	+	+	+	+	+	+	+	+	+	+	+	+	−	−
Inula conyza	−	+	−	+	+	+	+	+	+	+	+	+	−	−	−	−	C
Eupatorium cannabinum	+	−	+	+	+	+	+	+	+	+	+	+	+	+	+	−	−
Senecio jacobaea	−	+	+	+	+	+	+	+	+	+	+	+	+	+	+	−	−
Sonchus arvensis	−	+	−	−	+	+	+	+	+	+	+	+	+	+	+	−	−
Centaurea nigra	+	+	+	+	+	+	+	+	+	+	+	+	+	+	+	−	−
C. scabiosa	−	+	−	−	+	+	+	+	+	+	+	+	(+)	(+)	(+)	−	−

Table 15 (contd.)

	1	2	3	4	5	6	7	8	9	10	11	12	13	14	15	16	17
Tragopogon pratensis	—	+	—	—	+	+	+	+	+	+	+	+	+	+	(+)	—	—
Cirsium eriophorum	—	+	—	—	+	+	+	+	+	+	+	+	—	—	—	—	—
Convallaria majalis	+	—	+	—	+	+	+	+	+	+	+	+	(+)	(+)	—	—	—
Ornithogalum pyrenaicum	+	—	—	—	—	+	+	+	—	—	—	—	—	—	—	—	—
Leucojum aestivum	—	—	—	—	—	+	+	—	—	—	—	—	—	—	—	+	—
Iris foetidissima	+	—	+	+	—	+	+	+	+	+	+	—	—	—	—	—	OS
Tamus communis	—	—	—	—	+	+	+	+	+	+	+	+	—	—	—	—	CS
Ophrys insectifera	+	+	—	—	+	+	+	+	(+)	(+)	+	+	—	—	—	—	C
Himantoglossum hircinum	—	+	—	—	—	+	+	+	—	—	—	—	—	—	—	+	CS
Orchis simia	—	+	—	—	—	+	—	—	—	—	—	—	—	—	—	+	CS
O. mascula	+	+	+	+	+	+	+	+	+	+	+	+	+	+	+	—	—
Carex digitata	+	—	+	—	—	—	+	—	—	—	+	+	—	—	—	+	—
C. divulsa	+	+	—	—	+	+	+	+	+	+	+	+	—	—	—	—	—
Hordelymus europaeus	+	—	—	—	—	+	+	+	—	+	+	+	—	—	—	—	—
Arrhenatherum elatius	+	+	+	+	+	+	+	+	+	+	+	+	+	+	+	—	—
Dactylis glomerata	+	+	+	+	+	+	+	+	+	+	+	+	+	+	+	—	—
Brachypodium sylvaticum	+	+	+	+	+	+	+	+	+	+	+	+	+	+	+	—	—
Poa trivialis	+	+	—	+	+	+	+	+	+	+	+	+	+	+	+	—	—
Holcus lanatus	+	+	—	+	+	+	+	+	+	+	+	+	+	+	+	—	—
Trisetum flavescens	—	+	—	+	+	+	+	+	+	+	+	+	+	+	(+)	—	—
Total 129	84	82	61	87	102	121	123	118	116	113	117	113	91	88	78	8	

Notes

European distribution:
OS = oceanic southern   CS = continental southern
 C = continental   CN = continental northern
(+) = rare

southern localities. Table 15 shows a preponderance of species with a southern distribution in Britain, and many of those which reach Scotland are rare or very local there. In particular, several of the shrubs which characterise calcareous scrub belong mainly to England from the Midlands southwards.

Plants with a northern tendency include *Prunus padus*, *Ribes spicatum* and *R. alpinum*. In Scotland there are occasional examples of juniper scrub, such as that on Morrone (W.182) in Aberdeenshire, which contain northern or montane herbs, such as *Alchemilla alpina*, *Polygonum viviparum*, *Potentilla crantzii* and *Galium boreale*. Examples of hazel scrub or growths of willows on river banks in northern England and Scotland also have species such as *Geranium sylvaticum*, *Cirsium heterophyllum*, *Trollius europaeus* and *Crepis paludosa*.

Most of the species listed in Table 15 are widespread in Europe and do not fall into any one of J. R. Matthews' (1937) phytogeographical elements.

Fauna

VERTEBRATES

The vertebrate animals of scrub consist largely of a mixture of species characteristic of woodland or grassland, and of ecotones between the two, e.g woodland edges, rides and glades. For some mammals, scrub is an important habitat, but probably no species belongs to scrub in preference to other major habitats. Carnivores such as the fox, badger, stoat and weasel thrive here, because the luxuriance of the grass–forb component of the scrub gives good cover and abundant food for the herbivores on which they feed. Rabbits and brown hares are sometimes numerous in scrub, and there can be dense populations of small mammals such as the short-tailed vole, wood mouse, bank vole and common shrew. Moles and hedgehogs are also usually well represented. Various species of deer frequent scrub, especially roe, sika and muntjac, and often produce their young in the dense cover which it provides.

Of the reptiles, the grass snake and slow-worm often occur in the grassier and more open parts of scrub systems, and the adder and common lizard are sometimes to be found. The frog and common toad occur here where there is sufficient water for breeding nearby.

The bird populations of scrub are often large and varied, since there is a great deal of cover for nesting and a copious food supply from the large numbers of invertebrates. The red-backed shrike is the scrub species *par excellence*, finding its optimum habitat in this kind of vegetation, the nest being placed in the taller bushes. Many small species build in the dense growths of herbaceous vegetation which scrub usually contains, or in the lower parts of overgrown bushes; these include the whitethroat, lesser whitethroat, whinchat, stonechat, robin, willow warbler, grasshopper warbler, tree pipit, yellowhammer, blackcap, garden warbler, nightingale and dunnock. The cuckoo is often numerous as it parasitises

Table 16. *The approximate number of species of the principal phytophagous insect groups associated with genera of scrub woody plants*

Plant genus	Macrolepidoptera	Microlepidoptera	Heteroptera	Homoptera Aphididae	Psyllidae	Coccidae	Aleyrodidae	Hymenoptera Symphyta	Cynipidae	Coleoptera	Thysanoptera	Diptera Cecidomyidae	Agromyzidae	Total
Acer	7	12	3	7	0	2	0	3	0	2	1	4	0	41
Buxus	0	0	2	0	1	0	0	0	0	0	0	1	1	5
Clematis	13	0	0	0	0	0	0	0	0	2	0	0	3	18
Corylus	28	28	16	4	0	1	2	10	0	9	3	6	0	107
Crataegus	88	53	14	12	3	5	1	12	0	33	2	6	1	230
Euonymus	2	9	0	2	1	5	0	0	0	0	0	0	0	19
Ilex	3	2	0	2	0	2	0	0	0	3	0	0	1	13
Juniperus	5	8	6	1	0	2	0	1	0	2	1	1	0	27
Ligustrum	17	10	0	1	0	1	0	2	0	1	1	2	0	35
Lonicera	20	12	0	2	0	0	1	5	0	1	1	2	4	48
Malus	34	43	15	11	3	4	0	2	0	16	2	2	1	133
Prunus	57	43	5	6	2	4	0	13	0	17	4	6	0	157
Rhamnus	6	11	2	2	3	1	0	0	0	0	0	2	0	27
Rosa	27	25	2	10	0	4	0	22	10	3	1	3	0	107
Rubus	45	18	3	4	0	2	3	16	1	6	3	5	1	107
Sambucus	4	3	1	4	0	0	0	2	0	1	1	2	1	19
Sorbus	2	4	1	1	0	3	0	13	0	11	0	1	0	36
Taxus	2	2	0	0	0	1	0	0	0	0	0	0	0	6
Thelycrania	6	7	0	2	0	1	0	1	0	0	0	1	0	18
Ulex	9	12	6	2	2	2	0	0	0	12	7	0	0	52
Viburnum	3	3	0	4	0	1	1	3	0	1	0	1	0	17
Total 21	378	305	76	77	15	41	8	105	11	120	27	46	13	1222

some of these species. Birds which nest more usually in the shrubs are the blackbird, song thrush, bullfinch, chaffinch, greenfinch, goldfinch, redpoll, turtle dove, collared dove, woodpigeon, magpie, jay, carrion crow, chiffchaff, long-tailed tit and house sparrow. Linnets have a particular association with gorse scrub and goldcrests quite frequently nest in taller junipers. Where scattered taller trees occur in scrub, they attract other woodland species for breeding, including hole nesters, such as the three woodpeckers, various tits and redstarts. In areas where taller woodland is lacking, even species such as the sparrowhawk, buzzard and rook will nest in tall scrub. Larger ground nesters such as the grey partridge, red-legged partridge, pheasant and mallard are well represented in this habitat, and occasionally there are species such as the nightjar and woodcock.

INVERTEBRATES

Although the invertebrate fauna of scrub is known to be rich there has been relatively little work on this subject from the conservation angle. The Lepidoptera have been considered briefly in the account given under lowland grasslands (p. 153); they contain a large number of species represented in grassland or woodland, and relatively few which belong primarily to scrub. Work has begun on other insect groups found in scrub, but is at present only in a preliminary phase.

Some idea of the approximate numbers of the principal groups of phytophagous insects associated with the genera of scrub woody plants can be obtained from Table 16, which has been compiled from the literature. The animals listed are the relatively specific species in most of the phytophagous groups. (A very few groups are not covered in this table.) Although the insect species are not necessarily very closely restricted to one host plant, they are not polyphagous (here arbitrarily defined as feeding on more than eight host species). The importance of the Rosaceae as insect hosts stands out in this table, but it is to be noted that quite a number of these species will feed on more than one genus in that family.

Parasites and predators are associated with these phytophagous species and the numbers of these can be quite high. Again there is practically no work on the subject but an indication is obtained from work at Silwood, Berks, by Imperial College, showing that on broom some 70 parasites

Table 17. *Phytophagous invertebrates associated with juniper in Britain*

	Juniperus communis	Other *Juniperus* spp.	Other conifers	Hertfordshire	Kent	Surrey	Sussex	Hampshire	Wiltshire	Berkshire	Buckinghamshire	Oxfordshire	East Anglia	S.W. England	Wales	N. England	Scotland	On NNR	On key sites
				S.E.				S.											
Arceuthomyia valerii Dipt.	+	−	−	−	−	−	−	−	−	−	−	−	−	−	−	+	−	?	−
Argyresthia abdominalis Lep.	+	−	−	−	−	+	−	−	−	+	+	+	−	−	−	+	−	?	+
A. arceuthina	+	−	−	−	+	−	−	−	−	+	−	−	−	−	−	+	+	+	+
A. aurulentella	+	−	−	−	+	−	−	−	−	−	−	−	−	+	+	−	−	?	−
A. dilectella	+	+	−	+	+	+	+	+	+	+	+	+	+	−	−	+	−	+	+
A. praecocella	+	−	−	−	−	−	−	−	?	−	?	−	−	−	−	+	+	+	−
Carulaspis juniperi Hom.	+	+	+	−	−	+	−	−	−	+	−	−	−	−	−	−	−	−	+
Cinara juniperi Hom.	+	+	+	+	+	+	+	+	+	+	+	+	+	+	+	+	+	+	+
Cyphostethus tristriatus Het.	+	−	−	+	−	+	+	+	+	+	+	+	−	−	−	−	−	+	+
Dichomeris juniperella Lep.	+	−	−	−	−	−	−	−	−	−	−	−	−	−	−	−	(+)	+	−
D. marginella	+	+	−	−	+	+	−	−	+	+	−	+	−	−	+	−	−	?	+
Dichrooscytus valesianus Het.	+	−	−	−	+	+	+	+	+	+	+	−	−	−	−	−	−	+	+
Eremocoris abietus Heter.	+	−	+	−	−	−	−	−	−	−	−	−	−	−	−	+	−	+	−
E. fenestratus	+	−	−	−	−	−	−	−	−	−	(+)	−	−	−	−	−	−	−	+
Eupithecia intricata Lep.	+	+	+	−	−	−	−	−	−	−	−	−	−	?	+	+	?	−	
E. pusillata	+	+	−	+	+	+	+	+	+	+	+	+	+	−	+	+	+	+	−
Megastigmus bipunctatus Hym.	+	−	−	−	?	+	−	+	+	+	+	−	−	−	?	?	+	−	
Monoctenus juniperi Hym.	+	−	−	−	−	−	−	−	−	−	−	−	−	−	−	(+)	+	−	
Oligonychus ununguis Acar.	+	+	+	+	+	+	+	+	+	+	+	+	+	?	?	?	?	+	−
Oligotrophus juniperinus Dip.	+	+	−	−	−	−	−	−	−	−	−	−	−	−	−	+	−	?	−
O. panteli	+	+	−	−	−	−	−	−	−	−	−	−	−	−	−	+	−	?	−
O. schmidti	+	+	−	−	−	−	−	−	−	−	−	−	−	−	−	+	−	?	−
Phalonia rutilana Lep.	+	−	−	−	−	−	−	−	−	+	−	−	−	−	−	−	−	−	?
Schmidtiella gemmarum Dipt.	+	−	−	+	−	+	−	+	+	(+)	+	+	−	−	−	−	−	+	−
T. cognata	+	−	−	−	−	−	−	−	−	−	−	−	−	−	+	+	+	+	−
Thera juniperata Lep.	+	−	−	+	+	+	+	+	+	+	+	+	−	−	+	+	+	+	−
Thrips juniperi Thys.	−	−	−	−	−	−	−	−	−	−	−	−	−	−	−	?	+	+	−
Trisetacus quadrisetus Acar.	+	−	−	+	+	+	+	+	+	+	+	+	?	?	?	?	?	+	−
Zygimus nigriceps Het.	+	−	−	−	−	−	−	−	−	−	−	−	−	−	−	−	(+)	+	−
Total 29	28	7	5	8	9	12	9	9	11	15	12	11	5	1	4	14	12	18	9

Notes

+ = present.

(+) = rare.

? = probable (not included in totals).

and 60 common predatory species were associated with 23 phytophagous species.

Work is in progress on the fauna of juniper in Britain, and Table 17 shows the known phytophagous species. From the conservation point of view the specific insects and their distribution are particularly important, and some information is accumulating on this aspect. Table 17 gives some indication of specificity to juniper and geographical distribution where known. There is some division into southern and northern elements in the fauna, and it is probably the southern fauna that is in greatest need of protection because of its fast diminishing habitat. One species has already been lost, *Pitedia juniperina* (Heteroptera), a fruit feeder on the North Downs, not collected since the turn of the century. Some of the southern species are very restricted, *Eremocoris fenestratus* having been found only at Coombe Hill, Buckinghamshire, and *Phalonia rutilana* in Berkshire. It is thought that in the south the minimum numbers of fruiting bushes for conservation of the fauna in an isolated juniper colony is 1000. The Spey Valley, Inverness-shire, also has a particularly interesting fauna with three species not yet found elsewhere.

CRITERIA FOR KEY SITE ASSESSMENT AND SELECTION

Comparative site assessment

Size

As scrub is usually of small extent and often highly fragmented, high value is attached to the larger and more continuous stands. Large size is also desirable from a management point of view, for the unstable, seral nature of scrub may necessitate the creation of a mosaic pattern of different developmental stages on a rotational basis, and for this it would be desirable to have an area above a minimum size.

Diversity

On the whole, a wide range of shrubs has been regarded as a desirable feature, but good examples of scrubs with a single dominant have also been chosen. Diversity in the sense of different scrub types, and a range of seral development from grassland through scrub to woodland, are considered valuable when represented on the same site. Floristic diversity in the field layer is a feature of some importance, though it may be a somewhat ephemeral condition.

Stability

While all scrub may in theory be a seral stage, some examples are in a less active state of change than others, and have a greater appearance of permanence, at least under existing conditions (which may include a certain grazing regime). The more stable types of scrub are valued more highly than those which are obviously changing rapidly, and juniper scrub often appears to be of the former type.

Faunal richness

Assessment of scrub has been largely according to botanical characteristics, as zoological knowledge is usually very limited. However, sites known to be important for their bird or invertebrate faunas have been rated highly.

Rare species

The presence of rare or local species, whether of the shrubs themselves, or associated herbs and animals, has sometimes been taken into account in the selection of scrub sites.

Fragility

Many types of scrub are easily destroyed by fire, and it is clear that juniper regenerates much less readily than many dominant shrubs, so that there is an additional need to conserve this species.

Requirements for the national series

The primary aim has been to select a series of scrub sites which give adequate representation of the range of types distinguished according to dominant shrubs, i.e. the 11 scrub types named on pp. 164–6. In particular, juniper and southern mixed scrubs on Chalk cover a wide range of variation, and selection has aimed at representing these fairly fully. The more widespread hazel and hawthorn scrubs are inevitably represented on a large number of sites selected for other reasons, and the choice has favoured examples of scrub which are important in their own right. Examples of scrub dominated by unusual species, such as box, have been included, but in proportion to their frequency of occurrence.

It is desirable to spread the distribution of key sites over the range of edaphic and climatic variation but, as much of the diversity of scrub is related to varying land use and other biotic factors (such as rabbit-grazing), the representation of biotic diversity has taken precedence. The change, mainly in associated field layer species, which takes place from east to west is well represented in the series of sites chosen within the southern half of England. Change with distance north involves a decrease in number of scrub species and northern calcareous scrub is generally less diverse and extensive than that in the south.

The edaphic gradient from highly calcareous to acidic soils is reflected in a parallel range of scrub types and, in particular, an attempt has been made to represent the interesting intermediate types which are often associated with chalk heath. The range of scrubs associated with open rock habitats is incidentally well represented on the Carboniferous Limestone key sites chosen primarily for other features.

Scrub is an important faunal habitat, especially for insects, but basic information about the range of interest within this field is insufficient at present for a judgement to be made on the adequacy of representation on key sites. It is likely that much of the faunal variation on the southern Chalk is included, but this may not be true for other calcareous rock formations and other parts of Britain.

The national series of key scrub sites together with the sites which have a bonus scrub interest probably includes examples of all the main types of succession in which this community is an integral part and also has representatives of the more important kinds of stable scrub.

REGIONAL DIVERSITY AND SELECTION OF KEY SITES

The study of scrub for conservation purposes had been relatively neglected before the present review began, and survey to date has concentrated on the Chalk of southern England. It is felt that, apart from Dorset and the Yorkshire Wolds, scrub on the Chalk has been fairly adequately surveyed, but knowledge of this type of vegetation on the other calcareous rock formations farther north is much more patchy and incomplete, and further additions to the list of key sites may be indicated by new survey information.

A great many sites chosen as calcareous grasslands also contain examples of scrub, so that a considerable amount of the field of variation in scrub is thus represented incidentally. Selection for scrub in particular has accordingly concentrated on major types not represented as bonus occurrences. A series of the important and distinctive juniper scrubs on the Chalk has been chosen; on the South Downs of Sussex it includes an example of young growth at Harting Down (L.8, gr. 1)[1] and older, partly senescent, juniper mixed with the yew woodland at Kingley Vale (L.9, gr. 1*). Farther west on the South Downs, in Hampshire, the grassland site of Old Winchester Hill (L.25) also has juniper and yew thickets, in addition to areas of more mixed scrub. In Berkshire, Aston Upthorpe Downs (L.22) is the best remaining example of juniper scrub, and is associated with good grassland.

The best area for juniper scrub on Chalk lies farther west on Salisbury Plain in Wiltshire. Bulford Downs (L.41, gr. 1) has been chosen as an especially fine and extensive example of this type in an early stage of succession, associated with a species-rich grassland. The extensive chalk grasslands of Porton Down (L.36) also in Wiltshire, have probably the largest remaining total area of juniper on this rock formation, with both young and old stands well represented, and this important site has a variety of other scrub types. In Hampshire, Burghclere Beacon (L.39, gr. 1) has another good area of juniper scrub, at a later stage in the succession than Bulford Downs, and on Rushmore Down (L.40, gr. 1) in the same district there is juniper scrub of advanced age, together with a good variety of other scrub types. Stockbridge Down (L.54, gr. 2) is a less important example of this range of scrub in Hampshire. Finally, to complete the series of southern juniper scrubs, Aston Rowant (L.21) has been chosen as a Chiltern example and is important also for its mixed scrub and rich chalk grassland; juniper here shows regeneration, a relatively local phenomenon. Coombe Hill, Wendover (L.56, gr. 2), has a similar range of vegetation but with a lesser extent.

The mixed calcareous scrub, so widespread in southern England, is extensively represented on the North Downs at Wouldham–Detling Escarpment (L.10, gr. 1) and Halling–Trottiscliffe (L.11, gr. 1). Farther west White Downs (L.12, gr. 1) and Box Hill–Headley (L.7) have good examples of mixed scrub. This type is less well developed on the South Downs, where much of the scrub is dominated by hawthorn, but it is represented, along with juniper, on Newtimber Hill (L.19, gr. 2). Heyshott Down (L.16) in Sussex is important mainly for its grassland, but has a large number of scrub species, with much *Rosa rubiginosa*. A good mixed coastal scrub of this type occurs as a bonus at Folkestone Warren (C.2), Kent. As a northerly site, Aston Rowant has good mixed scrub as well as juniper scrub. Elsewhere in the Chilterns, mixed scrub is less prominent and hawthorn is the main scrub-forming species, as at Barton Hills (L.68) and a less important site, Ivinghoe Hills, Steps Hill and Pitstone Hill (L.55, gr. 2). Barton Hills also have good hazel scrub, a type not common on the Chalk.

More acidophilous scrub, developed often in association with chalk heath, and containing an abundance of gorse and *Rosa pimpinellifolia* is extensively represented on Lullington Heath (L.6, gr. 1) and on the eastern South Downs of

[1] Cross references to key sites are identified by an initial letter (indicating habitat) and number.

Sussex and further bonus examples occur at Castle Hill (L.4) and Fulking Escarpment/Newtimber Hill (L.19) in Sussex and Folkestone–Etchinghill Escarpment (L.15) in Kent. Tennyson Down (L.37, gr. 1) in the Isle of Wight has another good example of chalk heath scrub, in a more advanced state of seral development than at Lullington Heath, and lies in a coastal situation. Martin Down (L.24) in Hampshire is a very varied site with quite extensive development of chalk heath scrub.

Scrub dominated by box *Buxus sempervirens* is best developed at Ellesborough Warren (L.38, gr. 1) in Buckinghamshire where there are both young and old stands, the latter mixed with elder. An almost pure stand of box occurs at Boxwell (L.98, gr. 1), on Jurassic limestone, in Gloucestershire. Box Hill and Headley Heath in Surrey is another but less important example, where the box is mixed with other scrub types and woodland.

Up to the present, a less extensive exploration of the Jurassic limestone formation has produced relatively few good scrub sites. One of the best examples is at Castor Hanglands (L.81) near Peterborough, where mixed scrub has extensively invaded limestone grassland, and grades also into oak–ash woodland. Another is at Bredon Hill (L.127, gr. 2) in Worcestershire, where the scrub is mainly of hawthorn and elder.

The Carboniferous Limestone carries a good deal of calcareous scrub, and in some of the rockier situations such as cliffs, screes and pavements this may be of a relatively stable, possibly climax, type. Good examples are represented on a number of sites chosen primarily for their grassland and/or rich flora of open rock habitats. In south-west England, limestone scrub is well developed in the Avon Gorge (L.102), Cheddar Gorge (L.103), Brean Down and Uphill Cliff (L.104), Crook Peak (L.112) and Dolebury Warren (L.113). These localities experience an oceanic climate (Brean Down is actually coastal) and this is reflected by their floristics, and by the occurrence in the Mendip sites of a variant of calcareous heath and scrub with abundance of gorse. These Gloucestershire and Somerset sites are in general floristically rich, with a relatively large number of rare species.

In Wales, the coastal Carboniferous Limestone in the south and north has examples of calcareous scrub on the South Gower Coast: Glannau de Gŵyr (C.41) and Great Ormes Head: Pen y Gogarth (L.121).

In the Midlands, the Carboniferous Limestone dales of Derbyshire nearly all have well-developed scrub represented as bonus examples in the key grassland sites. Mostly this is the so-called retrogressive scrub dominated by hazel, and this usually grades into ash woodland, as in Cressbrook Dale, Lathkill Dale and Monks Dale (L.124(i)(*c*)(*b*)(*d*)), Coombs Dale and Miller's Dale (L.124(ii)(*a*)(*b*)). Most of the shrubs of southern calcareous scrub are still abundant as far north as this, and in places there is an approach to southern mixed scrub. In addition, Dove Valley (L.124(i)(*a*)) has a gorse–hawthorn scrub and Coombs Dale a dense *Ulex europaeus* scrub. Long Dale (L.124(i)(*e*)) has a scrub of *U. gallii* developed in association with limestone heath, while Topley

Pike and Deep Dale (L.124(ii)(c)) has a scrub of hazel with much bird-cherry.

In northern England, the group of key Carboniferous Limestone sites around the head of Morecambe Bay, selected for their lowland grassland and open rock habitats, all have good bonus examples of scrub. On the limestone pavement areas of Gait Barrows (L.134) and Hutton Roof Crags (L.135) there is a mixed scrub with juniper, yew, hazel and young ash, while on Whitbarrow Scar (L.136), Scout and Cunswick Scars (L.137), Arnside Knott and Warton Crag (L.147) and Humphrey Head (L.133) a wide variety of species contribute to the development of mixed scrubs on screes, cliffs and grassland slopes.

The representation of the more particularly coastal types of scrub on base-rich soils is indicated in Chapter 4, but it may be noted here that a wide range of types occurs on the coastal key sites.

D. MIXED HEATHS AND RICH GRASSLANDS

This is a rather heterogeneous assemblage of heath and grassland types which do not fit easily into either the acidic or calcareous groupings, but combine certain features of both. Three main groups are recognised. The first is where a range of communities from acidic heaths to calcareous grassland occurs within a single site in all combinations from large stands of different 'pure' types to complex mixtures of these and intermediates, as a result of irregular diversity in soil conditions. The Breckland of Norfolk and Suffolk is the main district for this group, but there are small areas in Lincolnshire. The second group is of communities composed of intimate mixtures of calcifuge and calcicolous species, growing on base-rich soils which allow this unusual blending of contrasting ecological elements. These are widespread and occur on most of the main calcareous rock formations, but are seldom extensive. The third group occurs on unusual kinds of rock (mainly serpentine) giving rise to soils which are base-rich, but low in available calcium. The communities of these magnesium-rich soils are particularly distinctive in the area of the Lizard, Cornwall, but most of the other main occurrences of serpentine are in upland situations, in Scotland. The other rocks which yield soils with an unusual balance of cations, such as gabbro and peridotite, occur mainly in the Hebrides, and also in places where conditions are upland in character.

D.1 BRECKLAND GRASSLANDS AND HEATHS

Breckland is a low-lying (6–60 m) dissected plateau forming a flat to gently undulating landscape which is crossed by four main rivers (Lark, Wissey, Thet and Little Ouse) and their tributaries, flowing westwards to the Fenland Basin.

The district extends from Swaffham in the north to Bury St Edmunds in the south and from Garboldisham in the east to the margin of the Fenland Basin in the west, an area of approximately 900 km².

RANGE OF ECOLOGICAL VARIATION

Habitat factors and vegetation

The range of scientific, cultural and historical interest of the Breckland is outstanding, and in nature conservation value it rates highly. The biological importance of the district lies especially in the once extensive area of grassland and heath which carries a semi-continental, steppe type of flora and fauna, better represented here than anywhere else in Britain (Clarke, 1925).

Through the ages man has had an especially profound effect on the ecological character of the Breckland, and the diversity of archaeological remains from the Mesolithic, Neolithic, Bronze Age, Roman and Anglo-Saxon periods is a notable feature. Pollen analysis suggests that the grasslands and heaths so characteristic of recent times gradually replaced forest, a process initiated by Neolithic clearance of earlier mixed oak forest; and some of the distinctive annual plants are weeds of cultivation. Whether or not some treeless heathland always persisted through the Post-glacial Period, one of the most remarkable features of Breckland is the survival of ancient solifluction patterns which could only have developed under periglacial climatic conditions. On several heaths there are well-developed fossil soil networks and stripes which are revealed the more clearly by associated patterning of the vegetation, notably in the distribution of heather, and sometimes in the density of plant cover.

The steppe component of the flora and fauna is a result, not only of the extensive occurrence of open, sandy soils but also reflects the semi-continental climate, with its low rainfall (c. 53 cm annually), hot summers and cold winters. Vegetational diversity within the Breckland was first interpreted by A. S. Watt (1936–40) as the result primarily of variations in soil conditions from place to place, but Farrow's (1941) and his emphasis on the importance of rabbit influence has been underlined by the profound changes which have taken place since the myxomatosis epidemic of 1953–55. The present composition of the Breckland grasslands and heaths is thus the expression of a long history of heavy but changing biotic influence, superimposed on the effects of edaphic diversity and operating within a special climatic regime.

The soils of Breckland are formed from superficial deposits of varying depth of chalky till and cover sands overlying a foundation of Chalk. Depending on the depth of the superficial deposits and the proportions of chalk fragments and sand which they contain, soil conditions range from highly calcareous (pH 8.0) to strongly acidic (pH 3.6), even within the space of a few centimetres. Though there are complex variations, the soils of the district may be regarded as a graded series which range from raw chalk debris and rendzina-like calcareous types, through acidic brown earths, incipient and shallow podsols to deep, heavily podsolised deposits of acidic sand with a well-developed humus iron pan. Locally, where the sands were deep and infertile, and where the vegetation cover was broken by overgrazing or cultivation, wind erosion formerly resulted in severe sand storms and in the formation of blow-outs. Extensive sand drift took place from time to time and formed mobile dunes with depths of sand over 4.5 m above original soil level. Such changes could either expose or bury chalky material, and give an added element of variability to soil conditions within the district. The activities of rabbits and moles, especially heavy on the more calcareous soils, also help to maintain disturbance and instability without necessarily causing large scale erosion.

Watt also described in parallel with the soil series an associated sequence of types of grassland, which at the time and for centuries previously, had been grazed by rabbits and sheep. Although post-myxomatosis changes have greatly altered the composition and luxuriance of many of the remaining examples of these grasslands, they represent the most distinctive of the Breckland vegetation types and are an important ecological feature which conservation measures should aim to maintain. They will therefore be described in terms of their pre-myxomatosis condition, and subsequent changes will be indicated.

The beginning of the series (Grassland A) is represented by raw, shallow, highly calcareous soils, carrying an open growth of calcicolous plants, including abundant but small *Festuca ovina, Minuartia hybrida, Galium parisiense, Arabidopsis thaliana, Carlina vulgaris, Sedum acre, Asperula cynanchica, Leontodon hispidus, Erigeron acer, Linum catharticum, Botrychium lunaria, Ditrichum flexicaule, Camptothecium lutescens, Pleurochaete squarrosa, Encalypta vulgaris* and lichens. It should, perhaps, be regarded merely as an open facies of the next stage (Grassland B) which is a closed sward with strong resemblance to *F. ovina* chalk grassland; it contains several of the above species, especially *Festuca*, together with *Koeleria cristata, Briza media, Helictotrichon pratense, Phleum phleoides, Carex caryophyllea, C. ericetorum, Thymus* spp., *Hieracium pilosella, G. verum, Silene otites, Gentianella amarella, A. cynanchica, Saxifraga tridactylites, Cirsium acaulon, Lotus corniculatus, Daucus carota* and *Rhytidium rugosum*. At least 80 vascular species have been recorded from this type, which grows on slightly deeper chalk soils showing similarities to chalk rendzinas. There are also both moss-rich and lichen-rich facies of this closed calcareous grassland.

The next stage (Grassland C), shows incipient acidity, and the soils are deeper and less base rich. The grasses are mostly the same as in B, but denser, and strongly calcicolous associates are sparse or absent. Calcifuges, such as *Galium saxatile* and *Pleurozium schreberi* begin to appear. There is a gradation to dense *Festuca–Agrostis* sward decidedly lacking in calcicoles, and containing abundance of *Rumex acetosella, Teesdalia nudicaulis, Luzula campestris* and patchy lichen (*Cladonia impexa, C. arbuscula, C. rangiformis, Cetraria aculeata*) (Grassland D). These soils are quite deep and acidic

with low base-status. This community passes into types dominated by lichen carpets containing sparse growths of a few highly tolerant vascular species on strongly podsolised sandy soil (Grasslands E–G). To some extent these communities stand in edaphic seral relationship, and erosion can return the system to any of the earlier stages, depending on how much surface soil is removed.

Three other species, heather, bracken and *Carex arenaria* attain dominance locally to give a range of communities additional to the grassland sequence A–G. All three can grow on a wide range of soils, but become dominant on the more acidic types. Heather heath occurs especially on the deeper podsols, bracken on deeper soils of moderate to high acidity, and *Carex arenaria* is associated especially with blown sand. All three communities are floristically poor, except where they grade into one or other of the grassland types. As a community dominant of inland heaths, *Carex arenaria* is confined to the Breckland, but the heather and bracken communities are virtually identical botanically with those of acidic heaths in other lowland districts in the southern half of England, though their invertebrate fauna is much more distinctive. All three of these communities and the grassland series may be invaded by gorse, birch (mainly *Betula pendula*) or Scots pine and so be converted into scrub or woodland. The plant communities of Breckland thus span the general range of variation between calcareous grassland and acidic heath, and in such a way that they are best treated as a single complex.

Although the characteristic Grasslands A–G of the open brecks probably originated through cultivation of these sandy soils, their ancient character is suggested by a comparison with brecks of superficially similar appearance but recent origin. Within the Stanford Practical Training Area (PTA) areas of breck have reverted from arable land since 1939 and are physiognomically similar to Grasslands B–D in their sandy, stony and sparsely vegetated appearance, but a closer comparison shows wide differences in floristics. The recent brecks characteristically have a high cover of *Hieracium pilosella* and *Agrostis stolonifera*, and an abundance of *Erodium cicutarium, Cerastium arvense, Sedum acre, Taraxacum officinale* agg. and *Hypnum cupressiforme*, but contain few of the most characteristic species of Grasslands B–D. Ground ploughed around 1960–63 on Thetford Heath shows even less similarity to the older brecks. These comparisons suggest that once the notable Breckland plants have lost ground they do not spread back rapidly even where conditions are suitable, and their ability to do so probably depends on the persistence of adequate parent populations in the vicinity of any favourable habitat created recently. A number of the most distinctive Breckland flowering plants, mostly annuals, appear to be associated with the long history of cultivation in this district, and their survival may now be linked with the maintenance of open ground by such artificial methods as ploughing in the areas where they have persisted (see also pp. 177–8).

The dry and often acidic soils of Breckland are now marginal land in the agricultural sense and in the past the area under crops has fluctuated according to economic conditions. Many of the brecks were, in fact, managed as vast rabbit warrens and sheep-walks. Scattered coverts and pine hedges were planted in the nineteenth century as wind-breaks to stabilise the soil, check wind erosion and provide cover for game. Around 1900, the characteristic Breckland scene was of large flat or gently undulating expanses of short grassland, flint-strewn and sandy, and grown with heather and bracken in places, but broken only by well-spaced pine rows and occasional larger woods. Contemporary descriptions (e.g. Dutt, 1906; Clark, 1925) vividly portray the district as an empty, primitive wilderness akin to semi-desert or steppe, where the evidence of human presence was much more ancient than recent, in the form of numerous earthworks and flint artefacts. After the creation of the Forestry Commission in 1919, the need arose to find large areas of cheap, agriculturally unproductive land on which conifers would nevertheless flourish, and some of the earliest large scale afforestation by the Commission was carried out in this district. Today, the Breckland has some of Britain's largest forests, especially of Scots and Corsican pine, amounting to a total of 18 600 ha. Modern farming techniques, with liberal application of fertilisers and the use of lucerne, have also made possible the continued cropping of these previously unprofitable soils, and large areas of former breck are now arable land. Expansion of towns and construction of airfields have made further inroads into the original area of heathland, and the processes of attrition continue.

The uncultivated Breckland has thus been greatly reduced and fragmented during the last 50 years, and to a large extent has lost its former wilderness character. Apart from the 6070 ha of the Stanford PTA, no really large grasslands and heaths now survive, and the remaining total of this habitat is only about 2000 ha, fragmented into 50–60 separate parts. In spite of extensive reclamation, good areas of Breckland showing the full range of ecological variation still remained after World War II in different localities, and mobile sand areas, although diminished in extent, occurred in places. In 1954, myxomatosis reached Breckland, virtually destroyed the rabbit population and thus profoundly changed the general character of the vegetation. Only Grassland A and some areas of Grassland B have remained largely unchanged, probably owing to dryness or rawness of soil, but A is now an extremely local type, found mainly in a few small areas on Lakenheath Warren. The greatest post-myxomatosis change has taken place on the Grasslands B, C and D, which are by far the most widespread. As on the chalk grasslands of southern England, there has been a great increase in stature and luxuriance of grasses, especially *Festuca* spp., *Agrostis* spp., *Arrhenatherum elatius* and, locally, *Deschampsia flexuosa*, which have grown into rank, tussocky mats, with dense litter, smothering the smaller forbs and preventing establishment of many species. Several species, especially annuals, characteristic of the calcareous to mildly acidic grasslands have declined considerably as a result, and the importance of various types of disturbed ground in providing habitats for some of these plants has increased. On the other hand some taller forbs

suffered from heavy grazing by rabbits, and benefited from myxomatosis, e.g. *Silene otites* and *Dianthus deltoides* flowered with unusual vigour, but have since declined in some places as the dominant grasses grew taller and denser.

The more acidic grasslands have retained much the same floristics as before, with lichens dominant and grasses sparser, but here the low fertility of the soil probably limits plant production. Heather heaths, by contrast, have changed strikingly in appearance, with the heather forming tall, bushy growths instead of the former tight, rounded cushions. The remaining areas of mobile dune, as at Icklingham Plains, have nearly all become vegetated and stabilised, and this once characteristic feature of Breckland is now represented only at Wangford Warren. By allowing seedling survival, reduced grazing pressure has promoted the invasion of trees and tall shrubs, and this is further reducing the area of grass heath. In some areas a type of scrubby woodland, mainly of birch and Scots pine, has developed and provides a habitat for roe deer and some rare invertebrates. Elsewhere gorse and hawthorn scrub is found and gives breeding sites for the red-backed shrike, though this is a declining species. Today, 15 years after the advent of myxomatosis, very little of the former close-grazed grassland and heath remain, most of the uncultivated ground having progressed to tall grassland or heather, and scrub. Compared even with its state in 1939, the district has been transformed and greatly reduced in nature conservation interest.

The loss of the open, somewhat disturbed and sparsely vegetated habitats both on the open calcareous soils and deep sands has caused a decrease in the number of rare animal species as well as plants. Some, such as the stone curlew, are much less common, while the ringed plover is now found mainly on ploughed farmland, and some ground-living invertebrate animals have become very scarce, particularly the spiders *Arctosa perita*, *Attulus saltator*, *Oxyptila scabricula* and *Micaria silesiaca*. This change has emphasised the importance of artificial habitats such as roadside verges, waste land, rough corners and field margins where some of the rare annual plants and insects are now found. An extreme pre-myxomatosis condition on Grassland B has been restored at Weeting Heath by enclosing a rabbit population with fence and wire-netting, and allowing numbers to build up to a high level. This experiment in management has been very successful in improving both the vegetational interest and the breeding bird populations, and indicates how easily natural succession could be reversed in other areas. The rabbit population has also increased markedly on the remaining part of this heath, and reduced dense, tussocky grassland to a short, mossy sward.

The complex of habitats in Breckland includes far more than variants of dry grasslands and heaths. The 18 400 ha of planted forest constitute an important new habitat whose interest should increase as the plantations mature and become more diverse. Many of the different forest sections have special features of interest such as small areas of heath and deciduous woodland, wide rides where the stone curlew and nightjar still nest, meres, marshes and artefacts such as sand, gravel and chalk pits, and collectively these are of growing significance to wildlife conservation in Breckland. There are also older semi-natural woods of oak and planted Scots pine rows or clumps, as well as seral birch and pine which are important for their invertebrate fauna and flora.

Also forming an integral part of the Breckland is an important complex of wetlands of four types: valley (eutrophic) mires by the rivers Lark, Wissey and Ouse; the Breckland meres, land-locked lakes with fringing and aquatic vegetation, showing a fluctuating water table; mesotrophic basin mires developed on extinct meres; and ancient, probably artificial meres and mires which may have formed in flint and chalk pits, although their origin is uncertain. The valley mires perhaps show the greatest floristic diversity although most are too small to be considered as key sites on their own.

Flora

Breckland has a distinctive flora, with a group of species which has a continental distribution in Europe and contains a high proportion of annuals dependent on open soils for survival. This important phytogeographical element includes a number of species which in Britain are either confined to the Breckland or have their headquarters here, namely, *Artemisia campestris, Veronica spicata* ssp. *spicata, V. verna, V. praecox, V. triphyllos, Silene otites, S. conica, Herniaria glabra, Phleum phleoides, Medicago falcata, M. minima, Galium parisiense, Ornithogalum umbellatum, Thymus serpyllum* ssp. *serpyllum, Scleranthus perennis* ssp. *prostratus, Crassula tillaea, Carex ericetorum, Vulpia ambigua, Apera spica-venti, A. interrupta* and *Muscari atlanticum. Holosteum umbellatum* is regarded as long extinct, and the rare *Gnaphalium luteoalbum* is of uncertain status as a native plant. There are also forms, varieties and subspecies of more widespread vascular plants which are especially characteristic of, or belong to, this district.

This characteristic phytogeographical group occurs widely under similar edaphic conditions on heaths in continental Europe, but is in fact ecologically diverse, with the various species occupying a rather wide range of niches. Some are regarded as long-established weeds of ancient cultivation, whose presence here has depended on the persistence of open soils broken periodically by the plough or other disturbance. The group shows a wide range of sensitivity to both grazing and competition, though most species will grow in soils of the grassland B type. *Medicago falcata, Silene otites* and *Artemisia campestris* are sensitive to rabbit-grazing, and the first two thrive best in the closed vegetation of roadside verges. Although closed, Grassland B has some of the group, at least under moderate grazing, but several competition-intolerant species occur nowadays not in the semi-natural grass–heaths but in the more open and ephemeral habitats associated with agriculture or other disturbance. *Veronica praecox* and *V. triphyllos* are almost exclusively on the soils of cultivated or only recently abandoned fields, *Vulpia ambigua* particularly favours recently ploughed ground, and several species show some association

with trackways, notably *Crassula tillaea.* From the combined influence of recent changes mentioned above, some of these plants have become much restricted in both habitat and distribution.

Where disturbed, as by cultivation, trampling and rabbit burrowing, the sandy soils of the area also carry an abundance of more widely distributed large weeds of open, base-rich soils such as *Carduus nutans, Reseda luteola, R. lutea, Senecio jacobaea, Verbascum nigrum, V. thapsus, Cynoglossum officinale, Echium vulgare* and *Artemisia vulgaris.* Smaller herbs of these open, sandy soils include *Sedum acre, Filago germanica, F. minima, Veronica agrestis, Cerastium arvense, C. semidecandrum, Myosotis ramosissima, Erodium cicutarium, Trifolium arvense, T. striatum, Vicia lathyroides, V. angustifolia, Ornithopus perpusillus, Spergularia rubra, Erophila verna, Arabidopsis thaliana* and *Saxifraga tridactylites.* Fields left fallow and permanent waste ground are especially productive for plants of this kind, whilst sandy cart-tracks and their verges are quite important habitats.

The more calcareous of the grasslands have strong affinities with other chalk grassland of southern England, and their distinctive species include *Astragalus danicus, Lotus corniculatus, Carlina vulgaris, Cirsium acaulon, Gentianella amarella, Asperula cynanchica, Thymus drucei, Sagina nodosa, Koeleria cristata* and *Carex ericetorum.* Certain characteristic calcicoles, such as *Poterium sanguisorba, Hippocrepis comosa* and *Helianthemum chamaecistus* are decidedly local in Breckland; others such as *Thesium humifusum, Orchis ustulata* and *Linum anglicum* are now very rare; and *Anemone pulsatilla* has disappeared. The occurrence of the very rare *O. militaris* in a single wooded chalk-pit is puzzling, and the possibility of deliberate introduction cannot be ruled out. In the acidic range of grasslands and lichen heaths, *Teesdalia nudicaulis* is perhaps the most distinctive of the more local vascular plants, whilst *Dianthus deltoides* is characteristic of grassland on intermediate soils. The rare dwarf shrub *Genista pilosa,* which was probably associated with *Calluna* heaths, is now extinct.

The occurrence of coastal plants far inland here is well known, the best example being the sand-dune sedge *Carex arenaria* which is a widespread and locally dominant plant of the sandy heathlands. The characteristic dune grass *Phleum arenarium,* the pansy *Viola tricolor* ssp. *curtisii* and moss *Tortula ruraliformis* are also locally abundant. The very local coastal grass *Corynephorus canescens* still occurs in small quantity, and the uncommon moss *Pleurochaete squarrosa* is present in a few places. As with the several coastal animals which occur in Breckland, these are best regarded as sand-loving species which here find (or rather found) a large area of suitable habitat. The Breckland has another interesting phytogeographical feature, in that it is the southernmost British outpost for several northern plants. Only one, the moss *Rhytidium rugosum,* grows in the calcareous brecks, and it is here locally abundant in Grassland B. The others, *Goodyera repens, Dicranum polysetum* and *Ptilium crista-castrensis* are mainly plants of northern pinewood and grow here in the recently planted conifer woods, though the last species grows also under heather on Caven-ham Heath.

The occurrence of well-developed lichen heaths on some brecks is an interesting feature, perhaps connected with the continental climate, but these communities are composed mainly of widespread species. There is a small and distinctive group of rare lichens found mainly on the open soils of Grassland A, and including *Fulgensia fulgens, Lecidea decipiens, Buellia epigaea, Squamaria lentigera* and *Toximia lobulata* as faithful species; and *T. caerulea* var. *nigricans, Diploschistes scruposus* var. *bryophilus* and *Bacidia muscorum* as characteristic species.

The floristic richness of the Breckland thus depends on the extremely wide diversity of habitat represented in this district, only part of which falls under the heading of mixed grassland and heath. Some species clearly belong to artificial ecosystems (see Chapter 10) and are considered under that heading. Watt (1971) has given a detailed account of the Breckland flora and the habitat requirements of the various species.

Fauna

MAMMALS, REPTILES AND AMPHIBIANS

The coniferous plantations of Breckland have become a haunt of red deer, though this animal is not now native here. It is almost exclusively a forest dweller and tends to be little seen. The roe deer is widespread and fairly numerous in the woods, and ranges also over the grasslands and heaths, where it feeds a good deal. The woods and rows of trees also have a substantial population of the red squirrel, and the Breckland is now one of the few strongholds of this species in southern Britain.

The importance of the rabbit in Breckland has already been stressed. On many of the remaining heaths and breck grasslands the numbers of this animal are now low. By far the greatest density occurs within the southern enclosure on Weeting Heath, and numbers here may even exceed those found on some former warrens during the pre-myxomatosis era. The effect of high rabbit density on the general composition of the vegetation and on the numbers of breeding birds is here very strikingly shown. Rabbit numbers are also probably higher on the northern part of Weeting Heath than on any other Breckland site, but in most places there has been no appreciable tendency towards recovery. On a few sites, such as Stanford PTA and Deadman's Grave, sheep-grazing is sufficient to maintain ground in a fairly open condition and to prevent the formation of a tall, dense grassland sward, though the dryness and low nutrient status of the soil may also have a part in this inhibition of plant growth. Brown hares are common but never in sufficient numbers to have much effect on the vegetation, and the more luxuriant grasslands do not appear to encourage any great increase in small rodent populations. Moles are abundant on the more calcareous brecks, and their activities contribute to the open, unstable nature of these sandy soils.

The adder occurs in a number of places, especially on acidic heaths which adjoin wetlands, and on some heaths it is accompanied by the grass snake. The common lizard is surprisingly scarce in the Breckland, though widespread in other parts of East Anglia. There is an old record of the sand lizard from the southern fringe of the district, but this species has not been seen recently. The slow worm is sparse though again widely spread through East Anglia. The common amphibians, frog, toad and smooth newt are all well represented in the wetland areas.

BIRDS

As a haunt of breeding birds, Breckland has suffered a decline in recent years. The great bustard, which formerly bred here, disappeared over a century ago, but the other notable steppe bird, the stone curlew, was abundant until 30 years ago. The district is still the British headquarters of the stone curlew, but the species has declined greatly through human encroachment and post-myxomatosis vegetation changes, which have all reduced the area of its breeding grounds, i.e. sandy, stony and sparsely vegetated brecks. The species has shown some degree of adaptation, breeding in places on farmland, broad forest rides, and both used and disused airfields. Its density is now very variable from place to place, some suitable-looking sites having few or none, and only in two localities are numbers at a high level, judged by pre-World War II standards; the reasons for this patchy distribution are not understood, but the species may still be declining, and the available habitat does not seem to be fully occupied. Of the other birds of the open, rabbit-infested brecks, the wheatear and stock dove have declined and the ringed plover (interesting as a coastal bird here inland) has almost disappeared; the remaining breeding stations of the last species are probably on ploughed land.

Decline of ornithological interest is not confined to the open sandy warrens, as birds characteristic of the closed grasslands, heaths and even scrub areas have diminished in numbers too. The nightjar, red-backed shrike and woodlark have all decreased substantially, and the stonechat has become very rare, though there is no shortage of suitable habitat for all these species. On the credit side, however, the area has gained the common curlew, which is now quite widespread on the rougher grasslands and heaths, and the Breckland is a stronghold of the mistle thrush. The crossbill breeds every year, though its numbers fluctuate, and the siskin has nested in recent years, whilst woodland species especially associated with the recent conifer forests are the coal tit and goldcrest. Skylarks are common on the grasslands everywhere, the lapwing is widespread and locally plentiful, and the tree pipit occurs on many heaths. Sparrowhawks have declined seriously in the woodlands, evidently as a result of pesticidal effects, but the kestrel is still fairly widespread as a nesting bird. The hobby and Montagu's harrier formerly bred sparingly and perhaps may still do so sporadically. The raven was once a tree nester in the Breckland but disappeared about a hundred years ago.

The bird life of the mires and meres is a good deal richer than that of the dry grasslands and heaths, but descriptions are given under the accounts of these wetland formations. While not all the species of the Norfolk Broads are represented, the Breckland meres have seven species of breeding duck, including the gadwall and garganey.

INVERTEBRATES

The ecological interest of the invertebrate fauna of Breckland is also very great, but much less well-known and documented, than the flora and avifauna. It is derived, to a considerable extent, from the wide range of habitats which still occur, including marshes, scrub, woodland and disturbed sites as well as the surviving heathland. The heaths such as Foxhole, Lakenheath, Weeting and similar areas are generally poorer in species than other habitats, particularly if the vegetation is short and patchy. However, this specialised and rigorous environment may include a number of species of considerable conservation and ecological interest. The very rare scarabaeid beetle *Diastictus vulneratus* has been taken in some numbers in the very short vegetation of Foxhole Heath, the bug *Arenocoris waltlii* and the beetle *Phytonomus dauci* both feed on *Erodium cicutarium* (a common plant on coastal dunes). Both are uncommon, but neither is confined to Breckland. The staphylinid beetle *Ocypus cupreus* has been frequently taken in traps on Foxhole Heath, while the closely related *O. aeneocephalus* occurs on the calcareous grassland at Weeting Heath but on neither heath have both species been recorded. The heathland spider fauna is remarkably distinct and includes several species local or rare outside Breckland. In open stony areas with little vegetation *Oxyptila scabicula* is probably the commonest crab spider, although elsewhere in Britain it is known from only a few southern heaths. In the same habitat is found the ant mimic *Micaria silesiaca*, *Lithyphantes albomaculatus*, *Agroeca cuprea* and the widespread coastal species *Arctosa perita*, and *Attulus saltator*. Wangford Warren, which still has areas of open mobile sand, is one of the few places where these species are still relatively common. Where a grass turf is well developed as on Grasslands B and C, and the growth generally short, other species occur including *Wideria stylifrons* (Weeting Heath is the only known British locality), *Centromerus incilium* and *Wideria incisa* (only eight localities known in Britain). Interesting Coleoptera include the staphylinid *Ocypus ophthalmicus* and the carabid *Panagaeus bipustulatus*, but the decrease in open sandy habitats needed by 'coastal' species may have caused the disappearance of *Broscus cephalotes*. The cicadellid bug *Hardya melanopsis* also occurs in this type of grassland at Weeting Heath. The *Carex arenaria* community on such heaths, for example at Lakenheath Warren, includes some notable species of Hemiptera, especially *Kelisia pannonica* (form *sabulicola*) and *Xanthodelphax flaveola*, the last known from only two other stations in Britain.

One of the distinctive features of the Breckland fauna which is of particular conservation importance is the association of interesting and rare insects with common plants, as already mentioned in the case of *Erodium cicu-*

tarium. Many occur on the weeds of abandoned fields and disturbed roadside verges or rubbish heaps, while others live on planted trees such as *Populus* spp. Examples include the moth *Lithostege griseata*, confined to Breckland but feeding on *Descurainia sophia* and other crucifers; the very local moth *Xanthia ocellaris*, whose larvae feed on *Populus* sp.; the rare weevils *Dorytomus tremulae* and *D. filirostris* also on poplars, the weevil *Tychius venustus* on *Sarothamnus* and *Brachonyx pineti* on *Pinus sylvestris*. On roadside verges the weevil *Ceuthorhynchus unguicularis* occurs on *Arabis hirsuta* and is known from only three localities in England. The related species *C. pulvinatus* is restricted to Breckland and occurs on the crucifer *Descurainia sophia*, and another weevil *Sitona griseus*, usually coastal, feeds on various Leguminosae. The moth *Emmelia trabealis* feeds on the common plant *Convolvulus arvensis* but has seldom been taken outside Breckland. Some rare plants also have interesting species associated with them, as in the case of the moth *Hadena irregularis*, which feeds on *Silene otites*, which was first recorded in 1868, and has never been taken outside Breckland. The butterflies are not of special interest, though the grayling is a characteristic species.

CRITERIA FOR EVALUATION AND SELECTION OF KEY SITES

Only 50 years ago, Breckland was one of the largest areas of uncultivated, semi-natural habitat in the southern half of England, covering approximately 60 000 ha. It formed the nearest equivalent, and the only one of its kind in Britain, to the steppe country of continental Europe, with a flora and fauna which were rich, distinctive and, in the aggregate, unique in this country. Today, only fragmented remnants of this earlier Breckland remain, and the situation is far from being stabilised. The pressures generated by an ever-growing need for land in this district, for building, farming and forestry, result in a continuing process of attrition which could foreseeably consume all that remains, were there no constraints. The undeveloped areas of Breckland are virtually all of high scientific importance as the dwindling remnants of a rapidly disappearing ecosystem peculiar to this part of Britain.

The remaining fragments are thus to be regarded as collectively representing a barely adequate sample of the Breckland of 50 years ago, and there is a clear need to safeguard all the more important remnants. The majority of the larger Breckland sites are therefore placed in grade 1, and only a few smaller ones treated as alternatives. The acidic heathland areas appear to be the most uniform, but even here the faunal interest is felt to be sufficiently outstanding to warrant the selection of several different areas in the grade 1 series. The areas of predominantly heather heath can, however, be regarded also as part of the national series of lowland acidic heaths.

While the dry grasslands and heaths are the best known and most distinctive of the Breckland habitats, the others such as woodland and mire form an integral part of this whole ecosystem, and should be represented in the selection of key sites. Moreover, cultivation has played an important part in determining the characteristic flora and fauna of the district, and it is desirable, in seeking adequate representation of a range of habitats for conservation, to include various types of disturbed ground and stages in the dereliction of arable land which has been abandoned to revert towards uncultivated breck. This is especially important for the conservation of the rare plants which are not, or no longer, found on the main remaining areas of grass heath, but belong to more recently disturbed and artificial habitats.

The invertebrate fauna of the Breckland has been surveyed in much greater depth than that of many habitats and areas, and some sites which appear to be similar vegetationally prove to be quite different faunally. Zoological criteria have thus had greater weight than usual in site evaluation and selection in this region. As human historical factors concerned with land-use have been so important in this district, thought has been given to the need for deliberate management of land in order to re-create the range of conditions which are essential to the survival of many members of the characteristic flora and fauna of the Breckland. Species not represented within key sites mostly belong to miscellaneous disturbed habitats of a kind which could be created as desired within a safeguarded area, though the organisms concerned might have to be deliberately reintroduced to these places.

DISTRIBUTION OF BRECKLAND GRASSLANDS AND HEATHS, AND SELECTION OF KEY SITES

By far the largest remaining single expanse of grassland and heath is the Stanford PTA, of some 6070 ha, lying several kilometres north of Thetford. Until 30 years ago, when it was requisitioned for military training purposes, this land consisted mainly of arable farmland, enclosed permanent pasture and woodland, with several meres (Fowl Mere, Home Mere, West Mere, Stanford Water, Thompson Water) and fen systems. Since it was thus taken over, most of the arable land has been allowed to revert slowly to uncultivated breck, and sheep have been pastured over most of the ground. Hedges have grown tall, and boundary fences within the Training Area have mostly disappeared. This is the one remaining piece of Breckland large enough to give the essential character of the district as it was before twentieth century reclamation began – large unenclosed tracts of gently undulating, untilled, sandy and flint-strewn prairie extending to the horizon and broken only by the occasional row of trees or larger wood. The uncultivated and un-afforested areas contain examples of nearly all the main types of Breckland grassland and heath, as well as the other habitats mentioned – woodland, meadow, fen and open water. Because of the very recent character of many of the brecks here, however, there is not the full range of biological interest, especially in terms of species representation, for which the district is famous.

Several other noteworthy sites in the Wretham area link up with the Stanford PTA and are thus regarded with this

as forming a single aggregate site (L.60, gr. 1). To the southeast there is East Wretham Heath with its two small lakes, Lang Mere and Ring Mere, clumps of old pines and *Deschampsia flexuosa* grassland. This passes southwards into the large expanse of acidophilous grassland and heath (heather, bracken, rank *Festuca–Agrostis*) known as Bridgham and Brettenham Heaths. To the east of Stanford PTA is the eutrophic and faunally rich basin mire of Cranberry Rough (P.19, gr. 2) and north of this lies Thompson Common, an interesting complex of eutrophic fen, calcareous and neutral grassland (L.71, gr. 1).

Centred on Icklingham, in Suffolk, is a group of sites which either link up or are separated from each other by only short distances (mostly a few hundred metres), and are regarded as another single large aggregate site (L.61, gr. 1). Cavenham and Tuddenham Heaths have mainly heather- and bracken-dominated heath, with good areas of *Carex arenaria*, all showing colonisation by birch and passing into closed birchwood with both dry and wet facies. On Cavenham Heath there is a transition from acidic heath to calcareous grassland, and then a change to valley mire of a relatively eutrophic kind, beside the River Lark. Adjoining this site is a good deal of former arable land recently gone out of cultivation and covered with large populations of weeds; this would make an ideal experimental management area, and some of this ground is therefore included within the site boundaries. Icklingham Plains and Triangle across the Lark, contain good examples of unstable or disturbed habitats, especially sand dunes and roadside verges, which act as a refuge for certain Breckland plants and animals. A little farther to the north, the area around Deadman's Grave has especially fine and extensive examples of chalk Grassland B and is of high faunal importance.

Another group of Breckland sites is centred on Lakenheath and Elveden and includes Lakenheath Warren (L.62, gr. 1) where Watt's (1936–40) classic studies of grass heath vegetation were made. This is the only site with a good example of Grassland A (*c.* 0.5 ha), and has virtually the whole range of grass heath types recognised in the district, though these have been much affected by post-myxomatosis changes. Lakenheath Warren is, after the Stanford PTA, the largest remaining tract of Breckland grass heath. Eriswell High and Low Warrens are similar vegetationally to Lakenheath Warren which they adjoin on the south side and of which they are essential parts. Berner's, Horn and Weather Heaths, a little farther south-east than Lakenheath Warren, form a continuous extent of acidic heathland, mainly with Callunetum, but showing faunal differences compared with Cavenham–Tuddenham Heaths. Adjoining Lakenheath Warren on the north side, Wangford Warren has the only mobile dune area surviving in Breckland, and the breck at Airfield Lights is an extension of this system with closed grass heaths. Wangford Carr contains another area of wind-blown sand, now mainly stabilised by vegetation. Maidscross Hill and Lord's Well Field near Lakenheath are important sites for annual plants of disturbed ground included within the Lakenheath grade 1 aggregate site, while Chalk Hill (L.79, gr. 2) to the south of Barton

Mills is regarded as a lower grade alternative to the Ickling-ham calcareous grasslands. Foxhole Heath (L.63) is an isolated area of breck midway between Barton Mills and Lakenheath Warren, with good examples of lichen-rich basic and acidic grasslands and a rich invertebrate fauna.

Weeting Heath (L.64) is an isolated area of breck which must be considered on its own. It has an extensive area of Grassland B restored to its former condition by fencing and heavy rabbit-grazing and supports a rich flora and fauna. Weeting Heath is sufficiently different from the other brecks, and valuable as probably the largest single area of calcareous grassland, to rate as grade 1, though it shows less habitat diversity, and only clumps of large pines, and patches of willowherb and bracken to add variation to the grassland. This site is already a NNR, and a small enclosure nearby is managed as an arable weed reserve.

The final complex of Breckland sites lies just to the south of Thetford. Though fragmented into separate pieces, the contiguous areas of Thetford Heath, Sketchvar Heath, RAF Barnham, Barnhamcross Common and Little Heath are best regarded as a single site (L.65, gr. 1). The vegetation here is mainly of luxuriant *Festuca–Agrostis* grassland, and *Calluna* heath with gorse scrub and colonising pines. There are small areas of open grassland of both calcareous and acidic types, and fossil soil nets and stripes are finely revealed by the vegetational pattern. This aggregate site contains little which is not represented on the three large grade 1 sites, but it considerably extends the representation of certain communities and species. Little Heath is a relatively small site on which a patchy stand of Grassland A has been formed in recent years through removal of surface soil. Barnham Heath (L.77, gr. 2) to the east has a range of communities from dense acidic grassland and bracken to colonising birch, oak and pine – an ecosystem complex well represented on other sites. Thetford Warren (L.78, gr. 2) is a golf course with a wide range of Breckland communities from calcareous to acidic, and wet to dry, but is similar to certain other sites, e.g. Cavenham–Tuddenham Heaths.

The only other mixed heath–grassland site approaching the Breckland type and sufficiently important to be rated as grade 1 is Risby Warren (L.66) on the cover sands of north Lincolnshire; this site is more important for its acidic heath component however. Coastal sand-dune systems sometimes show a sequence from calcareous to acidic, associated with increasing age and stability, but these are dealt with in Chapter 4.

D.2 CALCAREOUS HEATHS

RANGE OF ECOLOGICAL VARIATION

Habitat factors and vegetation

Calcareous heath consists of a community in which elements of both calcareous grassland and acidic heath are intimately mixed. It can occur on any of the major calcareous rock formations, but is always rather local and small in extent, as the soils which allow its development are similarly limited in their occurrence. These soils sometimes have base-poor surface horizons grading to base-rich lower horizons, or they may simply be brown earths intermediate between rend-zinas and calcareous loams on the one hand and base-deficient podsols on the other. Such soils may be produced by processes such as fluvio-glacial deposition or loess formation, in combination with surface leaching. Essentially, these are originally calcareous soils in which secondary processes have variably reduced base-status below saturation point. The best known of these systems is the chalk heath of southern England.

Chalk heath has been defined by Grubb *et al.* (1969) as 'a plant community over chalk in which *Calluna vulgaris* or *Erica cinerea* is mixed with the usual chalk grassland species'. A broader view of chalk heath is taken here and includes communities in which *Ulex europaeus* or *U. gallii* are the dominants, because both of these communities are developed under the same conditions as the chalk heath in the narrow sense, and it may be that *Calluna* or *Erica* may have been eliminated by competition at some time in the past. This process can be seen occurring at Lullington Heath, Kingley Vale and elsewhere and it therefore seems more logical to use the term 'chalk heath' to include any mixtures of acidophilous and calcicolous species occurring on the Chalk, whatever their precise composition. Recent research by Grubb and his colleagues has indicated that succession in the community can result in acidification of the soil by *Calluna* and *Ulex* leaflets. In addition, their work makes it clear that the concept of stratification in the community with deep-rooting calcicoles and shallow rooting calcifuges certainly does not apply, at least at Lullington Heath. The calcifuges most often met on chalk heaths are: *Calluna vulgaris*, *Erica cinerea*, *Potentilla erecta*, *Ulex europaeus* and *U. gallii*. The most frequent calcicoles are: *Poterium sanguisorba*, *Filipendula vulgaris*, *Cirsium acaulon*, *Leontodon hispidus* and *Helictotrichon pratense*. Chalk heath occurs on plateaux, on dip-slopes and on coombe bottoms. The soil is most often derived from Clay-with-Flints, but other superficial deposits or loess may underlie the chalk heath community. All types are extremely readily ploughed and only small areas remain.

Calcareous heath similar in floristic composition to chalk heath has been noted on Devonian limestone at Berry Head, on Jurassic limestones in the Cotswolds, on Carboniferous Limestone in the Mendips, Wales and northern England, and on calcareous rocks of various kinds in Scotland. The lowland occurrences of calcareous heath on these other geological formations differ increasingly in floristics from those on the Chalk with increasing altitude and distance north. Those on Carboniferous Limestone in northern England usually contain *Sesleria albicans*, and in Upper Teesdale they also have species such as *Gentiana verna*, *Galium boreale* and *Viola lutea*. Scottish examples often contain grazed-down submontane herbs such as *Trollius europaeus* and *Cirsium heterophyllum* and at high levels they have montane species. Northern calcareous heaths in general often contain *Empetrum nigrum*, and at higher levels there are transitions to a distinct type in which this species or the more montane *E. hermaphroditum* replace the other ericoids as the dominant dwarf shrub. In Perthshire and in north Sutherland examples have been found of a montane calcareous dwarf-shrub heath dominated by *E. hermaphroditum* and *Dryas octopetala*.

In the uplands, calcareous heath is now rare but may once have been much more widespread on soils of intermediate base-status. Its rarity is to be explained partly by the selectively heavy sheep- and deer-grazing pressure which all base-rich soils receive in these predominantly acidic areas. As the acidophilous dwarf shrubs are soon eliminated by heavy grazing, it is likely that these preferentially grazed sites have nearly all lost these plants and now appear just as grasslands, of a type intermediate between basiphilous and acidophilous.

There are related submaritime grass heaths in many places on the western Scottish seaboard, and these grade into more acidophilous submaritime heaths of which examples are described on p. 135.

Flora and fauna

These consist so essentially of a mixture of elements of acidic heaths/grasslands and calcareous grasslands that it is unnecessary to describe them again. The number of species of plants and animals occurring in chalk heath is far more limited than in the two separate formations, since chalk heath covers only a small area in aggregate. The characteristic species tend to be those common and widespread in the acidic heaths/grasslands and calcareous grasslands.

CRITERIA FOR KEY SITE ASSESSMENT AND SELECTION

Comparative site evaluation

Good examples of calcareous heath are so few and local that assessment is relatively simple, the main criteria being size and species-richness. Most examples of this vegetation type are too small to be considered. Stands which form part of larger areas of calcareous grassland have been preferred, and a high proportion of the examples included fall into the category of bonus interest.

Requirements for the national series

Again, the limited occurrence and variety of this vegetation type limits the choice available. The major need is to represent the full range of floristic and faunal variation, and to include examples from different parts of the total geographical area, and from all the major rock formations on which this type occurs.

REGIONAL DIVERSITY AND SELECTION OF KEY SITES

The major occurrences of calcareous heath examined so far are all on the Chalk of south and south-eastern England.

One of the largest areas is at Lullington Heath (L.6)[1] in Sussex, where there were until recently about 40 ha of chalk heath of the *Erica cinerea–Festuca ovina* type. This has become extensively invaded by gorse, to give a different type of heath, and also a considerable management problem, as this taller shrub could completely dominate the site and destroy its other interest. Box Hill–Headley (L.7) in Surrey is now important as one of the best remaining areas of *Erica cinerea* chalk heath, though this is of rather limited extent. Fulking Escarpment/Newtimber Hill (L.19) is a less important area showing evidence of seral change and increasing soil acidification within chalk heath. Bonus examples of chalk heath occur in Sussex at Kingley Vale (L.9), Castle Hill (L.4) and Heyshott Down (L.16).

In southern England, the important chalk downland site of Martin Down (L.24) contains examples of chalk heath which rate highly in their own right. These include plateau and valley types and are richer floristically than the chalk heath at Lullington. Tennyson Down (L.37) on the Isle of Wight is a good example of coastal chalk heath, and grades into chalk grassland and into submaritime cliff and slope communities. In south-west England bonus stands of calcareous heath occur on Carboniferous Limestone at Crook Peak (L.112) and Dolebury Warren (L.113) both in Somerset. Carboniferous Limestone in the Midlands and northern England also gives several bonus examples of little-studied calcareous heath within grade 1 calcareous grassland systems. These are on plateau edge soils in Derbyshire at Lathkill Dale and at Long Dale and Gratton Dale (see L.124(i)), and in complexes of limestone pavement and grassland in south Westmorland at Hutton Roof Crags and Farleton Knott (L.135), Whitbarrow Scar (L.136) and Scout and Cunswick Scars (L.137).

D.3 LIZARD SERPENTINE HEATHS

The serpentine of the Lizard peninsula in south Cornwall gives extensive areas of base-rich soil in which magnesium replaces calcium as the predominant cation. The combination of unusual soil conditions (from dry to wet) and a mild, somewhat Mediterranean climate, has given a range of vegetation unique in Britain in its floristics. This is described in detail in the account of the most important serpentine areas, which are identified as a single aggregate grade 1 Lizard site (L.95). These Lizard heaths have the strongest affinities to the acidic lowland heaths and grasslands, as is shown by the prominence of *Calluna vulgaris*, *Erica vagans*, *E. cinerea*. *E. tetralix*, *Ulex europaeus*, *U. gallii*, *Genista pilosa*, *Molinia caerulea* and *Agrostis setacea*. On the other hand, the occurrence of grassland rich in species of *Trifolium*, and of species such as *Anthyllis vulneraria*, *Serratula tinctoria*, *Filipendula vulgaris*, *Campanula rotundifolia*, *Chrysanthemum leucanthemum*, *Betonica officinalis* and *Succisa pratensis* indicates relationships with both calcareous and neutral grasslands. The unusual drier *Schoenus nigri-*

[1] Cross references to key sites are identified by an initial letter (indicating habitat) and number.

cans communities are different from those of rich-fen, but there are mixtures of this species and others such as *Cladium mariscus* which show some resemblance to eutrophic valley mire. The complex as a whole has obvious submaritime or even maritime affinities, though it is different from the other coastal Cornish heath key sites, on the Isles of Scilly (L.93) and Chapel Porth–St Agnes (L.94).

E. NEUTRAL GRASSLANDS

RANGE OF ECOLOGICAL VARIATION

Habitat factors and vegetation

Tansley (1939) used the term 'neutral grasslands' to include 'semi-natural grasslands whose soil is not markedly alkaline nor very acid, mostly developed on the clays and loams'. In this review, the term includes certain communities transitional between neutral grasslands and other vegetational formations. Other more extreme transitional types are dealt with under the appropriate formations, as follows: (1) *Molinia* grasslands with *Sphagnum* are dealt with in Chapter 8; (2) wet grasslands and freshwater marshes with *Phragmites communis* are dealt with in Chapter 7; (3) estuarine grasslands with salt marsh species such as *Puccinellia maritima* and *Glaux maritima* fall within Chapter 4.

Few data on the location of possible sites were available initially and there is no general assessment, and very little specific work, on neutral grasslands in Britain. Survey therefore aimed at recording botanical composition and soil conditions of neutral grasslands and from the results an ecological classification into 14 main groups has been derived (see pp. 185–8). Neutral grasslands occur throughout Britain mainly below 300 m but since they are associated chiefly with grazing and/or hay-making, they have decreased greatly in extent in southern and eastern England as a result of recent trends in agriculture, which have involved the conversion of much permanent pasture to arable land. Some of the southern and eastern examples thus have a special scarcity value.

Four main factors determine the botanical composition of neutral grasslands, namely, water regime, management, soil and location.

WATER REGIME

The composition of the vegetation depends on differential tolerances of various species to inundation or, conversely, desiccation, at certain periods of the year. Thus, *Sanguisorba officinalis*, a common plant of flood meadows, is absent from the much longer-inundated washes, while the cowslip *Primula veris* occurs in many permanent grasslands but is absent from flood meadows.

Increasing soil moisture results in a change through groups of characteristic species in the following order:

1 *Festuca rubra, Anthoxanthum odoratum, Primula veris, Orchis morio*;

2 *Holcus lanatus, Alopecurus pratensis, Poa trivialis, Sanguisorba officinalis, Cardamine pratensis*;

3 *Carex panicea, Carex disticha, Juncus articulatus, Dactylorchis incarnata, Lychnis flos-cuculi*;

4 *Carex acutiformis, Juncus effusus, Caltha palustris, Galium palustre*;

5 *Phragmites communis* or *Glyceria maxima*.

Only the first two groups can strictly be regarded as grassland, and the other three grade into fen.

MANAGEMENT

The two major forms of management are grazing and cutting. Their main ecological effects are as follows.

Summer grazing

Animals are turned out in spring and remain until the end of the growing season, producing a patchwork of communities and structure. Floristic composition is affected by factors such as palatability, resistance to grazing, and ability to colonise a sward opened up by grazing. *Agrostis* spp. and *Festuca* spp. are more palatable than *Deschampsia cespitosa* and are more resistant to grazing than *Arrhenatherum elatius*. Continued grazing of a sward containing these species will therefore eventually eliminate *A. elatius* and leave a sward of *Agrostis–Festuca* interspersed with tussocks of *D. cespitosa*. Grazing can open a sward either by overgrazing or by excessive treading under wet conditions (poaching). The grazing allows colonisation by species such as *Senecio jacobaea* and *Cirsium arvense*, and treading is beneficial locally to *Bartsia alpina, Blysmus compressus* and *Anagallis tenella*, though its effects are often destructive when trampling is really heavy. The concentration of nutrients combined with treading around feeding areas and gateways favours *Polygonum aviculare* and other ruderal species.

If the grazing is carefully managed – animals not turned out too early in spring and controlled throughout the season so that overgrazing does not occur – an entirely different grassland is formed, dominated by *Lolium perenne* and *Trifolium repens*, which has little conservation value but considerable agricultural interest.

Grazed grasslands form a valuable breeding habitat for many birds, particularly waders, certain duck and passerines such as skylark, meadow pipit and yellow wagtail.

Hay-cutting

Hay-making removes most of the aerial portion of the plant and therefore favours species such as *Fritillaria meleagris* and *Orchis morio* which mature early, and annuals (e.g. *Bromus commutatus*) that require to set seed which can then fall into a relatively open sward. The tall herbage resulting from a hay crop is less attractive to nesting birds, though the common partridge, corn bunting and corncrake favour this habitat. Intensive cutting can also affect wetter areas, e.g. reed-cutting eliminates species such as *Carex paniculata*.

Early spring grazing followed by hay-cutting

This is a common form of management for grassland groups

6 and 10, neither of which has early flowering species, unlike group 7 where early spring grazing prevents the seeding of *F. meleagris* and to a lesser extent *O. morio*. The effect of this form of management on early breeding birds like black-tailed godwit is not known, but it is occasionally practised on those meadows in groups 3 and 4 which are a habitat for this species.

Burning, a form of management on certain Jurassic limestone grasslands, is rarely practised on neutral grasslands.

Irrigation is a feature of grassland group 6 and is discussed in more detail later. A form of irrigation is also practised in the washlands (which form part of groups 3 and 4) whereby water is allowed to flood the areas in winter, at times of maximum water levels in the associated river, and is held there until drained off the meadows by a series of ditches in early spring, when water levels in the river are normally low. These ditches, together with the meadows and surrounding banks, provide a wide range of habitats from aquatic to dry grasslands.

Meadows managed for hay and/or grazing were at one time an integral part of the rural economy of this country, and some, such as Lammas lands, had their management prescribed by law long ago. Management was of such a kind that over centuries it developed and maintained grasslands with high nature conservation interest; the vegetation had a stable, subclimax character, and a large measure of floristic richness. Recent shifts in agricultural economics and techniques, especially during the last three decades, have caused radical changes, and the old style meadows with their characteristic range of neutral grasslands are fast disappearing. Efforts to obtain greater production have involved a generally heavy application of artificial fertilisers, often preceded by ploughing of the sward, and sowing of commercial grass seed mixtures. Wetter pastures have been extensively drained, and herbicides applied freely. This produces uniform and ecologically dull pastures in which the sensitive plants are eliminated, though some forbs such as *Ranunculus acris* and *Cirsium arvense* may become abundant. In many instances, grasslands have been converted to arable land and the original interest totally lost.

SOIL

Unlike dry calcareous grasslands formed directly on the parent rock, e.g. Chalk and Jurassic limestones, most neutral grasslands occur on glacial drift or riverine sediment. The usually strong and direct association between grassland floristics and the underlying rock formation is thus much less evident in neutral grasslands, for the physical and chemical properties of these soils depend on the nature of the transported material and on the processes of deposition. Variation in physical constitution is much greater in these derived soils and accounts for some of the floristic differences within the neutral grasslands, especially through effects on drainage.

Several plant genera show species differences in preference for soils of varying physical type within this complex. *Juncus inflexus* occurs on heavy clay soils, *J. effusus* on lighter soils and often on more peaty ground, and *J.*

conglomeratus on soils with a high silt content. *Carex disticha* is common on soils with a high humus content, whilst *C. otrubae* occurs on heavy clay soils.

There are also the familiar differences in floristics associated with varying base-status (especially calcium) of neutral grassland soils. Species such as *Conopodium majus*, *Centaurea nigra*, *Filipendula ulmaria*, *Lychnis flos-cuculi*, *Betonica officinalis*, *Meum athamanticum*, *Carex nigra* and *Arrhenatherum elatius* occur on the least basic soils, whereas others such as *Orchis morio*, *O. mascula*, *Listera ovata*, *Coeloglossum viride*, *Poterium sanguisorba*, *Primula veris*, *P. farinosa*, *Silaum silaus*, *Filipendula vulgaris*, *Carex flacca* and *Briza media* are confined to the more calcareous substrata. Many neutral grassland species are, however, tolerant of a fairly wide range of soil base-status, e.g. *Succisa pratensis*, *Lotus corniculatus*, *Genista tinctoria*, *Saxifraga granulata*, *Carex panicea* and *Festuca rubra*.

For a longer list of vascular species and their associated soil conditions, see Table 18.

GEOGRAPHICAL LOCATION

Geographical differences in neutral grasslands depend mainly on a combination of climatic and geological factors, though there is also an element of chance in plant distribution which enhances spatial variability. Base-rich neutral grasslands in the north (groups 10 and 11) are on a relatively shallow calcareous drift soil derived from either Carboniferous Limestone or an ecologically closely allied calciferous sandstone. These conditions are absent in the south of England where a related type of grassland (group 7) is found on the much deeper alluvial soils of the flood plains and these are derived from either Jurassic limestones or Chalk. Some types of neutral grassland, notably the washlands and water meadows depend on a particular kind of land use which is limited to certain parts of lowland England. The more acidic types of neutral grassland are found mainly in western and northern Britain. Typical southern species of the base-rich grasslands, such as *Fritillaria meleagris*, *Orchis morio*, *Colchicum autumnale* and *Sanguisorba officinalis* are also characteristic of hay-cutting as a management factor. Northern hay meadows are distinguished by species such as *Trollius europaeus*, *Geranium sylvaticum*, *Crepis paludosa* and *Cirsium heterophyllum*, whilst the very local *Meum athamanticum* is a distinctive plant of grasslands on more acidic soils in certain northern districts. A number of species normally associated with woodlands are found in these traditional hay meadows; *Anemone nemorosa* and *Ranunculus auricomus* in the south; *Orchis mascula* in the north and *Platanthera chlorantha* in Wales.

Of the few areas seen in the limited survey of Wales, grasslands on similar soil types to those in northern England are of particular interest. The presence of *Trollius europaeus* and *Crepis paludosa* show marked similarities to the hill meadows of northern England. *Geranium sylvaticum* has recently been found in a species-rich meadow, but is a rare plant in Wales; on the other hand, *Vicia orobus* is a characteristic plant of upland hay meadows in north Wales, but is seldom seen elsewhere. New sites are still being discovered and a more extensive survey of central Wales is being carried out.

Grasslands on the calcareous boulder clays (group 8) are confined to southern Britain and most have been destroyed, particularly in eastern England where the local *Trifolium ochroleucon* meadows are nearly extinct.

Of the wetter neutral grasslands the base-poor (group 2) types are in the west and this is shown by the very strong westerly tendency of *Carum verticillatum*. The *Dactylorchis* spp. are characteristic of the corresponding base-rich areas (groups 1 and 3) and, within the genus, regional differences occur between the species. *D. praetermissa* has a southern distribution and its place in the north is taken by *D. purpurella*. The Welsh grasslands are again of interest in that both these species have recently been discovered on the same site.

CLASSIFICATION

Neutral grasslands have been classified into 14 groups according to a combination of environmental and floristic characteristics. Groups 1, 2 and 3 can be loosely lumped together as the *Carex–Juncus* communities of marshes and silty peats. They are not grasslands literally, but often pass into one or other of the true grassland groups on adjoining ground where the water table is lower, at least in the summer months; e.g. they often form a transition zone between an open water body and true grasslands of the alluvial meadow type (groups 4 to 7) on somewhat higher ground. A further, practical, reason for their inclusion here is that they are often incidentally managed in a similar manner to the nearby grasslands. Their soil consists of silt with a high proportion of organic matter rather than pure peat.

The remaining groups are the neutral grasslands *per se*. The sward is normally composed of five or six co-dominant grasses with a further six to 10 grass species and a wide range of forbs.

Groups 4, 5, 6 and 7 occur on alluvial soils associated with wide river valleys and consequently are more common in the south. Groups 8 and 9 are not associated directly with river systems, the former being on calcareous clays and the latter on lighter soils with much less clay and a greater proportion of silt and sand. Groups 10 and 11 are northern or western in distribution and show affinities with calcareous grasslands.

Groups 12, 13 and 14 are agriculturally unimproved or neglected grasslands in the sense that only sporadic attempts to increase production have taken place, e.g. by draining, fertilising or reseeding.

Neutral grasslands are the result of agricultural exploitation over the centuries and have acquired an agricultural nomenclature. This has been given to each group, not with any degree of significance, but as an *aide memoire*. Within each group the constant and distinctive species (list (*a*)) are shown together with those species (list (*b*)) which form recognisable associations within the group and which a more detailed classification would separate accordingly.

Group 1: Base-rich marshes

(a)	(b)
Caltha palustris	Carex hostiana
Eleocharis palustris	C. lepidocarpa
Galium palustre	Dactylorchis praetermissa
Juncus articulatus	Epipactis palustris
Lychnis flos-cuculi	Juncus acutiflorus
	J. subnodulosus

Group 2: Base-poor marshes

(a)	(b)
Carex rostrata	Carex curta
Hydrocotyle vulgaris	Carum verticillatum
Juncus acutiflorus	Eriophorum angustifolium
Menyanthes trifoliata	Equisetum fluviatile
Narthecium ossifragum	Pedicularis palustris
	Potentilla palustris

Groups 1 and 2 grade, respectively, into rich- and poor-fen. The grass component is sometimes high, with *Alopecurus pratensis*, *Holcus lanatus* and *Molinia caerulea* as co-dominants, and there may be summer grazing by cattle. Geographically, group 1 is more common in the south, following from the distribution of calcareous springlines and streams. Group 2 is normally associated with non-calcareous rivers which are more frequent in the north.

Group 3: Sedge-rich meadows

(a)	(b)
Carex nigra	Anagallis tenella
C. panicea	Carex hostiana
C. pulicaris	Cirsium dissectum
Dactylorchis spp.	Listera ovata
Molinia caerulea	Valeriana dioica

This group has similarities with Tansley's (1939) 'wet heath' but differs in the absence of *Erica tetralix*, *Drosera* and *Sphagnum*. It is a dwarf-grass/sedge community with *Carex nigra*, *C. panicea*, *Anthoxanthum odoratum*, *Holcus lanatus* dominant and *Molinia caerulea* occasional to frequent. Of the many forbs, the *Dactylorchis* spp. present a possible means of further subdivision of this group; *D. maculata* ssp. *ericetorum* and *D. praetermissa* are rarely found together, the former being an acidophilous species. Soil base-status mostly lies in the middle range between acidic and basic. Management is uniform throughout (i.e. summer grazing) and is therefore unlikely to account for any botanical differences.

Group 4: Tall grass washlands

(a)	(b)
Glyceria maxima	Stellaria palustris
Phalaris arundinacea	

This is a distinctive, but relatively infrequent group, found in areas subject to prolonged winter flooding. The dominant species is *Glyceria maxima* with the frequency of *Phalaris arundinacea* increasing as the water table falls. Similarly, management of this group is generally by summer grazing, but where conditions allow there is occasional cutting for hay.

This group is botanically poor, but the production of seed is important as a source of food for birds.

Group 5: Washlands and wet alluvial meadows

(a)	(b)
Alopecurus geniculatus	*Oenanthe fistulosa*
Carex hirta	*Polygonum hydropiper*
Glyceria fluitans	*P. minus*
Polygonum amphibium	*Ranunculus sceleratus*
	Rumex conglomeratus

The co-dominant grasses are *G. fluitans* and *A. geniculatus*, but unlike group 4, this group can be easily improved for agriculture by drainage, to give the ubiquitous *Alopecurus pratensis/Cynosurus cristatus/Holcus lanatus* community or, more frequently, a complete conversion to arable agriculture. Management is by summer grazing with cattle or, occasionally, by cutting for hay. Although botanically richer than group 4, the main ecological interest is still ornithological. *Rumex* and *Polygonum* spp. provide seed for wintering wildfowl and the summer grazing gives suitable nesting conditions for many species of waders and other ground nesting birds.

Group 6: Water meadows

(a)	(b)
Cardamine pratensis	*Bromus racemosus*
Festuca arundinacea	*Carex disticha*
F. pratensis	*Geum rivale*
× *Festulolium loliaceum*	*Myosotis scorpioides*
Lolium perenne	
Senecio aquaticus	

These specialised meadows were man-made between *c.* 1700 and 1850 to improve badly drained and non-productive alluvial meadows. The system consisted of interdigitating channels arranged on the ridge and furrow principle so that water was taken along a channel on the top of the ridge and spilled over the side of the ridge (= pane) into a channel cut along the bottom of the furrow. Water was directed into these channels by diversion from the adjacent river. After irrigating the meadow system, the water was returned to the river at a point further downstream. Land adjoining chalk streams was particularly suited to this arrangement, as water from such streams has a higher temperature than the land in late winter, thus encouraging grass growth for grazing. Water meadows were generally confined to the chalk streams of southern England.

Water meadows carry an example of the type of vegetation which will develop on a clay loam of alluvial nature overlying Chalk or gravel and subject to frequent controlled inundations by *running* water. They are grass-dominated with a low cover of forbs following selective control by the farmer, and are of special interest for the various hybrids between *Lolium* and *Festuca* which frequently occur. The absence of some moisture-demanding species is interesting, e.g. *Phalaris arundinacea*, which occurs along the water courses but not in the meadows.

Disused water meadows present a range of grassland types varying according to the regime of management after irrigation has ceased. Where management is intensive, with herbicides and moderate fertilisers, a *Lolium perenne–Trifolium repens* sward develops. If grazed but not otherwise managed, the sward develops a very diverse flora with similarities to group 5, but containing *Briza media*, *Leontodon hispidus* and *Cynosurus cristatus*, and thus showing affinities to group 7. Lack of management results in a *Salix* or *Alnus* carr.

Group 7: Alluvial meadows

(a)	(b)
Alopecurus pratensis	*Anemone nemorosa*
Briza media	*Bromus commutatus*
Filipendula ulmaria	*Fritillaria meleagris*
Ophioglossum vulgatum	*Oenanthe pimpinelloides*
Sanguisorba officinalis	*O. silaifolia*
Silaum silaus	*Ranunculus auricomus*
Thalictrum flavum	

The co-dominants of this group are *Agrostis stolonifera*, *Anthoxanthum odoratum*, *Cynosurus cristatus*, *Festuca pratensis*, *F. rubra*, *Holcus lanatus*, *Lolium perenne* and *Poa trivialis* with *Centaurea nigra*, *Plantago lanceolata* and *Trifolium pratense*. Management (hay-making/grazing) has been more or less constant over a long period but has never been as intensive as in group 6, i.e. weed-killing and artificial irrigation have not been practised. The result is a species-rich sward with no one species dominant. Geographically this is a southern group found mainly in the upper Thames, south Midlands and East Anglia.

Group 8: Calcareous clay pastures

(a)	(b)
Betonica officinalis	*Colchicum autumnale*
Briza media	*Genista tinctoria*
Helictotrichon pubescens	*Orchis morio*
Ophioglossum vulgatum	*Phleum pratense*
Primula veris	*Serratula tinctoria*
Sanguisorba officinalis	*Trifolium ochroleucon*
Senecio erucifolius	
Silaum silaus	

This group contains a similar set of co-dominants to group 7 but with *Festuca arundinacea* often replacing *F. pratensis*. Low soil fertility is frequent so that *Lolium perenne* is rarely one of the co-dominants; by contrast, *Rhinanthus minor* and *Centaurea nigra* often co-dominate. Possibly because of the drying out of these soils in summer, *Holcus lanatus* is more restricted than in group 7. This group differs from the last by reason of soil type and absence of flooding. The soils have a higher clay and lower organic content, which probably accounts for the presence of *Phleum pratense*, although the most striking difference between this group and the last is the presence of cowslip, often in large quantities. Management varies annually from hay-cutting to summer grazing, and is determined by the presence of *Colchicum officinale*. Swards containing this species are cut for hay, after the poisonous leaves have died down, and the aftermath grazed as in group 7. Geographically this is a southern group.

Group 9: Calcareous loam pastures

(a)	(b)
Briza media	*Cirsium acaulon*
Carex flacca	*Conopodium majus*
Galium verum	*Daucus carota*
Helictotrichon pubescens	*Pastinaca sativa*
Linum catharticum	*Saxifraga granulata*
Poterium sanguisorba	
Rumex acetosa	

Agrostis stolonifera, Anthoxanthum odoratum, Cynosurus cristatus, Festuca rubra, Dactylis glomerata and *Poa pratensis* form the basis of the sward, and the last two species indicate the drier soils of this group, compared with groups 7 and 8. Modern agriculture has taken full advantage of the easily-worked, free-draining soils characteristic of this group, and only fragments are known to persist, chiefly as small areas of common land. This group can be differentiated into acidic and basic types with, respectively, the two indicator species *Conopodium majus* and *Saxifraga granulata*. The basic types show close affinities with calcareous grasslands.

Group 10: Northern hay meadows

(a)	(b)
Alchemilla vulgaris agg.	*Cirsium heterophyllum*
Bromus mollis	*Geranium sylvaticum*
Crepis paludosa	*Orchis mascula*
Geum rivale	*Platanthera chlorantha*
Sanguisorba officinalis	*Tragopogon pratensis*
Trisetum flavescens	*Trifolium medium*
Trollius europaeus	

The major grass species are *Anthoxanthum odoratum, Bromus mollis, Dactylis glomerata, Festuca rubra, Holcus lanatus, Molinia caerulea* and *Poa trivialis*. This distinctive group of hay meadows occurs on Carboniferous Limestone or on calcareous sandstones between 200 and 300 m in northern England and central Wales, and on a variety of basic parent materials in Scotland. Preliminary survey has shown regional differences in the presence of *Platanthera chlorantha* and *Tragopogon pratensis* in Wales and of *Cirsium heterophyllum* and *Geranium sylvaticum* in England. Further survey is required, particularly in Wales and Scotland, where this community is known in meadows, on river banks and as a forb-dominated facies on mountain cliff ledges (see Chapter 9). To date, however, no meadow examples there have been surveyed. The meadows of this type are usually grazed by cattle during the autumn and winter, but otherwise little managed.

Group 11: Northern grazed meadows

(a)	(b)
Alchemilla vulgaris agg.	*Bartsia alpina*
Briza media	*Parnassia palustris*
Carex panicea	*Primula farinosa*
Lathyrus montanus	*Serratula tinctoria*
Pinguicula vulgaris	*Sesleria albicans*
Valeriana dioica	

These communities are especially associated with spring and flush conditions on upland and hill valley pastures of the

Carboniferous formations and other basic rocks in the north and west, and they include types described in Chapter 9. The soils are moist and often clayey, and grazing is by sheep and/or cattle; some species are favoured by the soil disturbance created by cattle poaching, if this is not too severe. There are often rapid transitions to drier grassland of a richer or poorer type, and choice of key examples of this group usually has to be within the context of selection of larger areas involving other groups or formations. The application of artificial fertiliser such as basic slag, and draining of these wet grasslands has deleterious effects on their flora, and many examples have been converted to *Juncus* pasture.

In addition to the above 11 groups, a further three widespread and often extensive groups are recognised. Small areas of these types occur within some of the grade 1 and 2 sites as bonuses, and specific sites have not been chosen for their intrinsic value within these three groups because:

1 They have a low nature conservation value.

2 They are abundant throughout Britain.

3 Given a suitable soil type it is thought possible to create these groups from one or other of the 11 main groups by appropriate management.

These three groups are included here because they are distinctive types and form an important part of the field of variation presented in the *Review*. Group 14 includes the colourful buttercup meadows which form a notable feature of the Pennine dales and fell bottoms; these have a high amenity value, but are usually otherwise poor floristically, having been much modified by management.

Group 12: Ordinary wet meadows

(a)	(b)
Deschampsia cespitosa	*Ranunculus ficaria*
Juncus inflexus	
Lysimachia nummularia	

This group occurs on heavy soils with impeded surface drainage and the larger examples provide feeding grounds for waders. Normally they are lightly grazed by cattle in summer, resulting in a tussocky vegetation.

Group 13: Ordinary damp meadows

(a)	(b)
Juncus effusus	*Ranunculus acris*
Holcus lanatus	*Stellaria graminea*
Poa trivialis	

This group occurs on peaty and/or lighter soils with a high water table but not impeded drainage. Management is similar to group 12.

Group 14: Ordinary dry meadows

(a)	(b)
Cynosurus cristatus	*Bellis perennis*
Dactylis glomerata	*Centaurea nigra*
Lolium perenne	*Cirsium arvense*
Trifolium repens	*Ranunculus acris*

This is the most widespread form of neutral grassland and one which commonly develops when sown grasslands are allowed to revert. Sporadic attempts to improve production from groups 4, 6, 7, 8 and 9 by drainage and application of fertilisers and herbicides, often result in the formation of this type. (The more usual management to increase production is to plough and reseed.) The fattening pastures of north Northumberland, Leicestershire and the Romney Marsh form part of this group. However, some of these pastures are of considerable age and have had very careful management, such as the *Lolium perenne*-dominated swards. The age of some of these pastures may make them suitable for the study of soil structure and also a useful source of genetic material for the development of future economic grass strains.

Flora

The list of species in Table 18 is somewhat arbitrarily chosen and includes those most characteristic of this class of vegetation, so that the number of widespread species is large and the number of rarities few. Many others, not listed, are also found in neutral grasslands. Neutral grasslands grade into unenclosed calcareous grassland in one direction, into scrub in another, and into the richer types of mire in yet a third. Species which overlap with neutral grasslands but belong more characteristically to these other vegetation classes are mostly omitted, as are many that belong mainly to rough uncultivated places, derelict land, roadside and railway verges, but find an occasional niche in neutral grasslands.

Neutral grasslands differ from calcareous downland grasslands on base-rich soils in the greater abundance of tall forbs, and in the general stature of the vegetation. These differences have dwindled with the decline of sheep-grazing on the calcareous lowland grasslands and with the great reduction in rabbit populations. Many of the forbs of neutral grasslands can persist under moderate grazing intensity or when grazed during only part of the year, but they disappear when grazing becomes heavy, e.g. *Agrimonia eupatoria, Genista tinctoria, Meum athamanticum, Silaum silaus, Sanguisorba officinalis, Serratula tinctoria, Geranium sylvaticum* and *G. pratense*. Others persist under heavy grazing as small, non-flowering rosettes and can grow to normal stature again if grazing is reduced or removed, e.g. *Trollius europaeus, Geum rivale, Filipendula ulmaria, Cirsium heterophyllum* and *Crepis paludosa*. Some species grow well and flower vigorously even when grazing is heavy, as do *Ranunculus acris, Cirsium palustre, C. vulgare, C. arvense, Conopodium majus* and *Senecio jacobaea*, which may be selectively avoided by animals. Abundance of rushes, such as *Juncus effusus, J. conglomeratus* and *J. inflexus* is often a sign of overgrazing of pastures, coupled sometimes with past disturbance, such as ploughing. Neutral grassland communities are often represented on roadside verges, which are mostly mown each year, and the characteristic meadow species may be even more abundant in the roadside habitats.

Neutral grasslands usually have a deep loam soil of moderate base status (pH 5.5–7.0). The more acidic examples are characterised by species such as *Conopodium majus, Carum verticillatum, Meum athamanticum, Rumex acetosa, Ononis repens, Lathyrus pratensis, Cirsium palustre, Hypochoeris radicata, Juncus effusus, Carex ovalis* and *Deschampsia cespitosa*. Where the soil is calcareous there is often an abundance of species commonly associated with unenclosed chalk or limestone grasslands, such as *Orchis mascula, Leontodon hispidus, Centaurea scabiosa, Filipendula vulgaris, Pimpinella major, Primula veris, Poterium sanguisorba, Helictotrichon pratense* and *H. pubescens*. Neutral grasslands with a flora of the second type are, however, becoming increasingly rare. Many of these enclosed grasslands have had their nutrient status boosted with manure or artificial fertiliser, or both. Some species may respond to the higher levels of nitrogen, potassium and phosphorus which often occur in these soils, compared with unenclosed grasslands, and some of the floristic differences between the two types may be accountable in this way. It is noticeable that the addition of basic slag to pastures has an extremely deleterious effect on some species, e.g. *Primula farinosa* and orchids generally, and usually causes a decrease in species-richness, especially of forbs. Drainage improvement work also tends to eradicate species which need damper soils.

The distribution data in Table 18 are based on presence/absence records on a purely geographical basis, and conceal the fact that many apparently widespread species are rare or local in Scotland and become abundant only south of the Border. Many of these may not, in fact, occur in neutral grasslands in their more northerly localities. The most varied neutral grassland flora is thus found in the southern half of England, and the rare species are mostly confined to this region. Other highly characteristic meadow plants are also found mainly or only in southern England, e.g. *Fritillaria meleagris, Trifolium ochroleucon, Oenanthe pimpinelloides, Colchicum autumnale* and *Juncus compressus*. There is, nevertheless, a characteristic group of northern meadow species, consisting of *Trollius europaeus, Geranium sylvaticum, Cirsium heterophyllum, Crepis paludosa, Meum athamanticum, Primula farinosa, Dactylorchis purpurella*. Only two species, *Vicia orobus* and *Carum verticillatum*, have a markedly western distribution.

Many of the species listed in Table 18 are widespread in Europe and do not fall into any of J. R. Matthews' (1937) more distinctive phytogeographical elements.

Fauna

For convenience, this is dealt with under lowland calcareous grasslands.

CRITERIA FOR SITE SELECTION

Comparative site evaluation

Most criteria used in selecting neutral grassland sites are linked with past management, and good sites occur only where there has been no drastic alteration in long-established practices. The criteria on p. 192 have been applied in descending order of priority.

Table 18. *Flora of neutral grasslands*

	Dry meadows	Damp meadows & fens	Roadside verges	Mountain cliff ledges	Sea cliffs & slopes	Grazed pastures	S. & S.E. England	East Anglia	S.W. England	S. Wales	N. Wales	Midlands	N. England	S. Scotland	E. Scotland	W. Scotland	Rare species	European distribution
	1	2	3	4	5	6	7	8	9	10	11	12	13	14	15	16	17	18
Equisetum arvense	+	—	+	—	—	—	+	+	+	+	+	+	+	+	+	+	—	—
E. palustre	—	+	+	—	—	+	+	+	+	+	+	+	+	+	+	+	—	—
Ophioglossum vulgatum	+	—	+	—	—	—	+	+	+	+	+	+	+	+	+	+	—	—
Trollius europaeus	+	+	+	+	+	+	—	—	—	+	+	+	+	+	+	+	—	—
Caltha palustris	—	+	+	—	—	—	+	+	+	+	+	+	+	+	+	+	—	—
Ranunculus acris	+	+	+	+	+	+	+	+	+	+	+	+	+	+	+	+	—	—
R. repens	+	+	+	+	—	+	+	+	+	+	+	+	+	+	+	+	—	—
R. bulbosus	+	—	+	—	—	+	+	+	+	+	+	+	+	—	—	—	—	—
R. ophioglossifolius	—	+	—	—	—	—	—	—	+	—	—	—	—	—	—	—	+	OS
Thalictrum flavum	—	+	—	—	—	—	+	+	—	—	—	+	—	—	—	—	—	—
Cardamine pratensis	—	+	+	—	—	+	+	+	+	+	+	+	+	+	+	+	—	—
Hypericum perforatum	+	—	+	—	—	—	+	+	+	+	+	+	+	+	+	+	—	—
H. tetrapterum	—	+	—	—	—	—	+	+	+	+	+	+	+	+	+	+	—	—
H. maculatum	+	—	+	—	—	—	+	+	+	+	+	+	+	+	+	+	—	CN
Lychnis flos-cuculi	—	+	—	—	—	—	+	+	+	+	+	+	+	+	+	+	—	—
Cerastium holosteoides	+	—	+	—	—	+	+	+	+	+	+	+	+	+	+	+	—	—
Stellaria palustris	—	+	—	—	—	—	+	+	—	—	—	—	+	—	—	—	—	—
S. graminea	—	+	+	—	—	—	+	+	+	+	+	+	+	+	+	+	—	—
S. alsine	—	+	+	—	—	—	+	+	+	+	+	+	+	+	+	+	—	—
Geranium pratense	+	—	+	—	—	—	+	+	+	+	+	+	+	+	+	+	—	—
G. sylvaticum	+	+	+	+	+	—	—	—	—	—	—	+	+	+	+	+	—	—
G. molle	+	—	+	—	—	+	+	+	+	+	+	+	+	+	+	+	—	—
Genista tinctoria	+	—	—	—	—	—	+	+	+	+	+	+	+	+	—	—	—	C
Ononis repens	+	—	+	—	+	—	+	+	+	+	+	+	+	+	+	—	—	—
O. spinosa	+	—	+	—	—	—	+	+	+	+	+	+	+	+	—	—	—	—
Medicago lupulina	+	—	+	—	—	—	+	+	+	+	+	+	+	+	+	+	—	—
Trifolium pratense	+	—	+	—	+	+	+	+	+	+	+	+	+	+	+	+	+	—
T. ochroleucon	+	—	—	—	—	—	—	+	—	—	+	—	—	—	—	—	—	C
T. medium	+	—	+	+	—	—	+	+	+	+	+	+	+	+	+	+	—	C
T. repens	+	+	+	—	+	+	+	+	+	+	+	+	+	+	+	+	—	—
T. fragiferum	+	—	—	—	—	+	+	+	+	+	+	+	+	—	—	—	—	—
T. campestre	+	—	+	—	—	—	+	+	+	+	+	+	+	+	+	+	—	—
T. dubium	+	+	—	—	—	—	+	+	+	+	+	+	+	+	+	+	—	—
Lotus corniculatus	+	+	+	—	+	+	+	+	+	+	+	+	+	+	+	+	—	—
L. pedunculatus	—	+	+	—	—	+	+	+	+	+	+	+	+	+	+	+	—	—
Vicia cracca	+	+	+	—	+	—	+	+	+	+	+	+	+	+	+	+	—	—
V. orobus	+	—	—	+	+	—	—	—	+	+	+	—	+	+	+	—	—	OW
V. sepium	+	—	+	+	+	—	+	+	+	+	+	+	+	+	+	+	—	—
Lathyrus nissolia	+	—	—	—	—	+	+	+	+	—	—	+	—	—	—	—	—	CS
L. pratensis	+	+	+	—	—	—	+	+	+	+	+	+	+	+	+	+	—	—
L. montanus	—	+	—	+	—	+	—	—	—	+	+	+	+	+	+	+	—	—
Filipendula ulmaria	+	+	+	+	+	+	+	+	+	+	+	+	+	+	+	+	—	—
Geum rivale	+	+	+	+	+	+	+	+	+	+	+	+	+	+	+	+	—	—
Potentilla erecta	+	—	+	—	—	+	+	+	+	+	+	+	+	+	+	+	—	—
Agrimonia eupatoria	+	—	+	—	—	—	+	+	+	+	+	+	+	+	+	+	—	—
Alchemilla vulgaris agg.	+	+	+	+	+	+	+	+	+	+	+	+	+	+	+	+	—	—
Sanguisorba officinalis	+	+	+	—	—	—	+	+	+	+	+	+	+	—	—	—	—	—
Saxifraga granulata	+	—	—	+	+	—	+	+	+	+	+	+	+	+	+	+	—	—
Parnassia palustris	—	+	—	—	—	+	—	+	—	—	—	—	+	—	—	+	—	—

Table 18 (*contd.*)

	1	2	3	4	5	6	7	8	9	10	11	12	13	14	15	16	17	18
Anthriscus sylvestris	+	−	+	+	+	−	+	+	+	+	+	+	+	+	+	+	−	−
Carum verticillatum	−	+	−	−	−	−	−	−	+	+	+	−	+	+	−	+	−	OW
Conopodium majus	+	−	+	−	−	+	+	+	+	+	+	+	+	+	+	+	−	OW
Oenanthe pimpinelloides	−	+	−	−	−	−	+	−	+	+	−	−	−	−	−	−	−	OS
O. fistulosa	−	+	−	−	−	+	+	+	+	+	+	+	+	−	−	−	−	−
O. silaifolia	−	+	−	−	−	−	+	+	−	−	−	+	−	−	−	−	+	OS
Silaum silaus	+	+	+	−	−	−	+	+	+	+	+	+	+	+	−	−	−	C
Meum athamanticum	+	−	+	−	−	+	−	−	−	+	−	+	+	+	+	+	−	CN
Selinum carvifolia	−	+	−	−	−	+	−	+	−	−	−	−	−	−	−	−	+	−
Angelica sylvestris	+	+	+	+	+	−	+	+	+	+	+	+	+	+	+	+	−	CN
Heracleum sphondylium	+	−	+	+	+	−	+	+	+	+	+	+	+	+	+	+	−	−
Polygonum amphibium	−	+	−	−	−	+	+	+	+	+	+	+	+	−	−	−	−	−
P. bistorta	−	+	+	−	−	−	+	+	+	+	+	+	+	+	+	+	−	−
Epilobium parviflorum	−	+	−	−	−	+	+	+	+	+	+	+	+	+	+	+	−	−
Rumex acetosa	+	+	+	+	+	+	+	+	+	+	+	+	+	+	+	+	+	−
Primula veris	+	−	+	−	+	+	+	+	+	+	+	+	+	+	+	+	−	−
P. farinosa	−	+	+	−	−	+	−	−	−	−	−	−	+	−	−	−	−	−
Anagallis tenella	−	−	+	−	−	−	+	+	+	+	+	−	+	−	−	−	−	−
Myosotis scorpioides	−	+	−	−	−	+	+	+	+	+	+	+	+	+	+	+	−	−
M. caespitosa	−	+	−	−	−	+	+	+	+	+	+	+	+	+	+	+	−	−
Pedicularis palustris	−	+	−	−	−	+	+	+	+	+	+	+	+	+	+	+	−	−
Rhinanthus minor	+	−	+	+	−	+	+	+	+	+	+	+	+	+	+	+	−	−
Prunella vulgaris	+	−	+	−	−	+	+	+	+	+	+	+	+	+	+	+	−	−
Betonica officinalis	+	−	+	−	−	+	+	+	+	+	+	+	+	+	−	−	−	−
Ajuga reptans	−	+	+	−	−	+	+	+	+	+	+	+	+	+	+	+	−	−
Plantago lanceolata	+	+	+	−	−	+	+	+	+	+	+	+	+	+	+	+	−	−
Galium verum	+	−	+	−	+	+	+	+	+	+	+	+	+	+	+	+	−	−
G. palustre	−	+	−	−	−	+	+	+	+	+	+	+	+	+	+	+	−	−
G. uliginosum	−	+	−	−	−	+	+	+	+	+	+	+	+	+	+	+	−	−
Valeriana officinalis	+	+	+	+	+	−	+	+	+	+	+	+	+	+	+	+	−	−
V. dioica	−	+	−	−	−	+	+	+	+	+	+	+	+	+	−	−	−	−
Succisa pratensis	+	+	+	+	+	+	+	+	+	+	+	+	+	+	+	+	−	−
Senecio jacobaea	+	+	+	+	+	+	+	+	+	+	+	+	+	+	+	+	−	−
S. aquaticus	−	+	−	−	−	+	+	+	+	+	+	+	+	+	+	+	−	−
Pulicaria dysenterica	−	+	+	−	−	−	+	+	+	+	+	+	+	+	−	−	−	−
Achillea millefolium	+	+	+	+	+	+	+	+	+	+	+	+	+	+	+	+	−	−
A. ptarmica	−	+	+	−	−	+	+	+	+	+	+	+	+	+	+	+	−	−
Chrysanthemum leucanthemum	+	+	+	+	+	+	+	+	+	+	+	+	+	+	+	+	−	−
Cirsium vulgare	+	−	+	−	+	+	+	+	+	+	+	+	+	+	+	+	−	−
C. arvense	+	+	+	−	−	+	+	+	+	+	+	+	+	+	+	+	−	−
C. palustre	+	+	+	−	−	+	+	+	+	+	+	+	+	+	+	+	−	−
C. dissectum	−	+	−	−	−	−	+	+	+	+	−	+	+	−	−	−	−	CN
C. heterophyllum	+	+	+	+	+	−	−	−	+	+	+	+	+	+	+	+	−	CN
Centaurea nigra	+	+	+	+	+	+	+	+	+	+	+	+	+	+	+	+	−	−
Serratula tinctoria	+	+	+	−	−	−	+	+	+	+	+	+	+	+	−	−	−	C
Hypochoeris radicata	+	−	+	−	−	+	+	+	+	+	+	+	+	+	+	+	−	−
Leontodon autumnalis	+	+	+	−	−	+	+	+	+	+	+	+	+	+	+	+	−	−
L. hispidus	+	−	+	−	−	+	+	+	+	+	+	+	+	+	+	+	−	−
L. taraxacoides	+	−	+	−	−	+	+	+	+	+	+	+	+	+	+	−	−	−
Tragopogon pratensis	+	−	+	−	−	−	+	+	+	+	+	+	+	+	+	+	−	−
Scorzonera humilis	−	+	−	−	−	−	−	−	+	−	−	−	−	−	−	−	+	C
Crepis capillaris	+	−	+	−	−	−	+	+	−	+	+	+	+	−	+	+	−	−
C. paludosa	−	+	+	+	−	−	−	−	+	+	+	+	+	+	+	+	−	CN
Taraxacum officinale agg.	+	+	+	+	+	+	+	+	+	+	+	+	+	+	+	+	−	−
Triglochin palustris	−	+	−	−	−	−	+	+	+	+	+	+	+	+	+	+	−	−
Fritillaria meleagris	−	+	−	−	−	−	+	+	+	−	−	−	+	−	−	−	−	C
Gagea lutea	+	−	−	−	−	−	+	+	+	−	−	+	+	+	+	−	−	C
Ornithogallum umbellatum	+	−	−	−	−	−	+	+	+	+	+	+	+	+	+	+	−	CS
Colchicum autumnale	+	+	−	−	−	−	+	+	+	+	+	+	+	−	−	−	−	CS
Juncus compressus	−	+	−	−	−	−	+	+	+	−	−	+	+	−	−	−	−	−

Table 18 (*contd.*)

	1	2	3	4	5	6	7	8	9	10	11	12	13	14	15	16	17	18
J. inflexus	+	+	+	−	−	+	+	+	+	+	+	+	+	+	+	+	−	−
J. conglomeratus	+	+	+	−	−	+	+	+	+	+	+	+	+	+	+	+	+	−
J. effusus	+	+	+	−	−	+	+	+	+	+	+	+	+	+	+	+	+	−
J. articulatus	−	+	−	−	−	+	+	+	+	+	+	+	+	+	+	+	+	−
Luzula multiflora	+	+	+	+	+	+	+	+	+	+	+	+	+	+	+	+	−	−
L. campestris	+	+	−	−	−	+	+	+	+	+	+	+	+	+	+	+	−	−
Leucojum aestivum	−	+	−	−	−	+	−	+	−	−	−	−	−	−	−	−	+	CS
Narcissus pseudonarcissus	+	−	−	−	−	+	+	+	+	+	+	+	+	−	−	−	−	−
Listera ovata	+	+	+	+	+	−	+	+	+	+	+	+	+	+	+	+	−	−
Epipactis palustris	−	+	−	−	−	+	+	+	+	+	+	+	+	−	−	−	−	−
Coeloglossum viride	+	−	+	+	+	+	+	+	−	+	+	+	+	+	+	+	−	CN
Gymnadenia conopsea	+	+	+	−	+	+	+	+	+	+	+	+	+	+	+	+	−	−
Platanthera chlorantha	+	+	+	−	−	+	−	−	+	+	+	+	+	+	+	+	−	−
P. bifolia	+	+	+	−	−	+	+	+	+	+	+	+	+	+	+	+	−	−
Orchis morio	+	−	−	−	−	+	+	+	+	+	+	+	+	−	−	−	−	−
O. mascula	+	−	+	+	+	+	+	+	+	+	+	+	+	+	+	+	−	−
Dactylorchis fuchsii	+	+	+	+	+	+	+	+	+	+	+	+	+	+	+	+	−	−
D. incarnata	−	+	+	−	−	+	+	+	+	+	+	+	+	+	+	+	−	−
D. praetermissa	−	+	+	−	−	+	+	+	+	+	+	+	+	−	−	−	−	OW
D. purpurella	−	+	+	−	+	+	−	+	+	+	+	+	+	+	+	+	−	−
Eriophorum latifolium	−	−	−	−	−	+	+	+	+	+	+	−	+	+	+	+	−	−
Eleocharis palustris	−	−	−	−	−	+	+	+	+	+	+	+	+	+	+	+	−	−
Blysmus compressus	−	+	−	−	−	+	+	+	+	+	+	+	+	−	−	−	−	−
Carex hostiana	−	+	−	−	−	+	+	+	+	+	+	+	+	+	+	+	−	−
C. lepidocarpa	−	+	−	−	−	+	+	+	+	+	+	+	+	+	+	+	−	−
C. rostrata	−	+	−	−	−	−	+	+	+	+	+	+	+	+	+	+	−	−
C. acutiformis	−	+	−	−	−	+	+	+	+	+	+	+	+	+	+	+	−	−
C. pallescens	+	+	+	+	−	+	+	+	+	+	+	+	+	+	+	+	−	−
C. filiformis	−	+	−	−	−	+	+	−	+	−	−	−	−	−	−	−	+	−
C. panicea	−	+	+	+	+	+	+	+	+	+	+	+	+	+	+	+	−	−
C. flacca	+	+	+	+	+	+	+	+	+	+	+	+	+	+	+	+	−	−
C. hirta	+	+	+	−	−	+	+	+	+	+	+	+	+	+	+	+	−	−
C. nigra	−	+	−	−	−	+	+	+	+	+	+	+	+	+	+	+	−	−
C. diandra	−	+	−	−	−	−	−	+	−	+	+	+	+	+	+	+	−	−
C. disticha	−	+	−	−	−	+	+	+	+	+	+	+	+	+	+	+	−	−
C. ovalis	+	−	+	−	−	+	+	+	+	+	+	+	+	+	+	+	−	−
C. pulicaris	−	+	−	−	−	+	+	+	+	+	+	+	+	+	+	+	−	−
Molinia caerulea	−	+	+	+	+	+	+	+	+	+	+	+	+	+	+	+	−	−
Sieglingia decumbens	+	−	−	−	−	−	+	+	+	+	+	+	+	+	+	+	−	−
Glyceria fluitans	−	+	−	−	−	+	+	+	+	+	+	+	+	+	+	+	−	−
G. maxima	−	+	−	−	−	+	+	+	−	−	−	+	+	+	+	+	−	−
Festuca pratensis	+	+	+	−	−	+	+	+	+	+	+	+	+	+	+	+	−	−
F. arundinacea	+	+	+	−	−	+	+	+	+	+	+	+	+	+	+	+	−	−
F. rubra	+	+	+	+	+	+	+	+	+	+	+	+	+	+	+	+	−	−
Lolium perenne	+	+	+	−	−	+	+	+	+	+	+	+	+	+	+	+	−	−
Poa pratensis	+	−	+	−	+	+	+	+	+	+	+	+	+	+	+	+	−	−
P. trivialis	+	+	+	−	−	+	+	+	+	+	+	+	+	+	+	+	−	−
Dactylis glomerata	+	+	+	+	+	+	+	+	+	+	+	+	+	+	+	+	−	−
Cynosurus cristatus	+	+	+	+	+	+	+	+	+	+	+	+	+	+	+	+	−	−
Briza media	+	+	−	−	−	+	+	+	+	+	+	+	+	+	+	+	−	−
Bromus mollis	+	−	+	−	+	+	+	+	+	+	+	+	+	+	+	+	−	−
B. racemosus	+	+	+	−	−	+	+	+	+	+	+	+	+	−	−	−	−	−
B. commutatus	+	+	+	−	−	+	+	+	+	+	+	+	+	+	+	+	−	−
Hordeum secalinum	+	+	+	−	−	+	+	+	+	+	+	+	+	−	−	−	−	−
Trisetum flavescens	+	−	+	−	−	+	+	+	+	+	+	+	+	+	+	+	−	−
Helictotrichon pubescens	+	+	+	−	−	+	+	+	+	+	+	+	+	+	+	+	−	−
Arrhenatherum elatius	+	+	+	+	+	−	+	+	+	+	+	+	+	+	+	+	−	−
Holcus lanatus	+	+	+	−	−	+	+	+	+	+	+	+	+	+	+	+	−	−
Deschampsia cespitosa	+	+	+	+	+	+	+	+	+	+	+	+	+	+	+	+	−	−
Agrostis stolonifera	+	+	+	+	+	+	+	+	+	+	+	+	+	+	+	+	−	−

Table 18 (*contd.*)

	1	2	3	4	5	6	7	8	9	10	11	12	13	14	15	16	17	18
Phleum pratense	+	—	+	—	—	+	+	+	+	+	+	+	+	+	+	+	—	—
Alopecurus pratensis	+	+	+	—	—	+	+	+	+	+	+	+	+	+	+	+	—	—
A. geniculatus	—	+	—	—	—	+	+	+	+	+	+	+	+	+	+	+	—	—
Anthoxanthum odoratum	+	+	+	+	+	+	+	+	+	+	+	+	+	+	+	+	—	—
Phalaris arundinacea	—	+	—	—	—	—	+	+	+	+	+	+	+	+	+	+	—	—
Total 174	111	122	116	42	50	109	157	158	160	156	154	160	162	146	135	132	6	

Notes
European distribution:
OS = oceanic southern   CN = continental northern
OW = oceanic west European   CS = continental southern
  C = continental

Diversity

This applies particularly to the grass component of the sward in that a site of high interest will contain five or six *co-dominant* grasses, with a wide selection of forbs. The first attempt at agricultural improvement immediately decreases the total number of species and quickly leads to a dominance of one or two grass species.

Rarity

Because of the wholesale destruction of old meadows in the past 30 years, many species which even 10 years ago were not considered rare have now become so. Species confined to meadows, e.g. *Fritillaria meleagris*, *Silaum silaus* and *Orchis morio* are particularly vulnerable. Aggregations of such rare and local species are rated highly.

Fragility

This connects with diversity and rarity since the element of fragility is integral in these factors. The grasslands with greatest diversity and abundance of rare species are most vulnerable to loss of interest through change in land use.

Recorded history

A few meadows have a very long history of known management and these are of great value in understanding ecological relationships and planning future management of neutral grasslands. Good documentation is thus a feature of some importance.

Research and educational value

Some areas have been selected for their research potential, as botanical study areas in particular. This links with the preceding criterion.

Position in an ecological series

Neutral grasslands show geographical diversity and examples were chosen when possible to represent notable regional features.

Representativeness

Certain meadow types, especially water meadows, have no particular floristic interest for rare or local species, but give especially good representation of the common Gramineae and so constitute examples of a typical community; they also represent an unusual ecological system, and so link with Research and educational value (above).

International interest

This is limited to winter wildfowl populations, but two sites (L.70 and L.142) were rated especially highly for this feature.

Requirements for the national series

In selecting a national series of neutral grasslands, emphasis has been placed on representation of the following features:

1. Regional floristic variants which show the least signs of deterioration through recent changes in management. This is mainly a climatic series determined especially by the south to north gradient of decreasing temperature.

2. Examples on base-rich soils, since these show the greatest floristic diversity.

3. A combination of faunal (especially ornithological) interest with good botanical features.

4. Communities and species of plant and animal which occur only or mainly in this type of ecosystem.

5. Communities and species which are most different from the related ecosystems of greatest similarity, namely, lowland calcareous grassland and flood-plain mire.

REGIONAL DIVERSITY AND SELECTION OF KEY SITES

GROUPS 1 AND 2: FRESHWATER MARSHES

Detailed survey of these groups is incomplete but examples are evidently widespread though scattered, since they show close relationships to both alluvial meadows (groups 4 to 7) and flood-plain mires. Base-rich marshes (group 1) are often associated with small, highly calcareous streams. Good examples occur on a chalk stream, Calceby Beck (L.83, gr. 2) in Lincolnshire, and near springs rising on Jurassic limestone at Brassey (L.109) in Gloucestershire, but the best yet seen is at Wintringham Marsh (L.141, gr. 1) in east

Yorkshire, where the vegetation approaches closely to that characteristic of eutrophic flood-plain mire. In the north of Scotland, an important and extensive area of base-poor marsh (group 2) occurs on the alluvial flood plain of the River Oykell (L.151, gr. 1). This is classified in group 2 since much of the vegetation has a hydrophilous character and approaches the northern mesotrophic type of flood-plain mire. There is, however, a range of variation from this type to the drier grasslands of groups 5 and 12. The marshes and meadows beside the River Ken in Kirkcudbrightshire (L.149, gr. 1) are of great interest for their wildfowl, and are also placed in group 2, though a few meadows show some affinity with those of southern England classified in group 7.

GROUP 3: SEDGE-RICH MEADOWS

This group is often found as a minor component of groups 1 and 7. At Wintringham (group 1) it forms a very narrow zone between the marsh and the surrounding grassland and at Sibson (group 7) it is found as an isolated community scattered within the site. At Bransbury Common (L.45, gr. 1) group 3 is the major community in an area showing considerable diversity with communities approaching those characteristic of flood-plain mires (fen). In Brecknock, preliminary survey has shown two good examples of this group: Glyn Perfedd (L.115, gr. 1) is of particular interest in that it also shows some affinities with the northern hay meadows of group 10; while Drostre Bank (L.118, gr. 2) is distinctive in being one of the few sites in Britain where the northern *Dactylorchis purpurella* and the southern *D. praetermissa* grow together.

GROUPS 4 AND 5: WASHES

Washes are a very specialised and local type of meadow system associated with long-established flood relief schemes in the Fenland basin of Cambridgeshire, Huntingdonshire and Lincolnshire. They have been developed along the four main Fenland rivers (Ouse, Nene, Welland and Witham) and their parallel artificial channels. The Nene and Welland washes were formerly of considerable biological interest but, as a result of improved drainage within these river systems, they are rarely used for flood relief and have mostly been ploughed and cropped, thus destroying most of their ecological interest. The largest remaining washes, and by far the most important biologically, are those along the two artificial channels of the River Ouse between Earith and Denver. The Ouse Washes (L.70, gr.1*) are botanically valuable for their range of meadow and wetland vegetation, but their greatest importance is ornithological; their winter wildfowl population (mainly duck and swans) is of international importance and the summer breeding bird population contains probably the largest single concentration of rare species in Britain, with black-tailed godwit, ruff, black tern, garganey and gadwall, as well as large numbers of snipe, redshank and lapwing. The much smaller area of Baston Fen (L.84, gr. 2) in Lincolnshire is the only other washland site which still has real biological value. Also acting as flood relief areas, although not as specialised as the Ouse Washes, are the alluvial meadows along the

River Derwent (L.142, gr. 1*). These show a wide range of grassland groups including transitions to flood-plain mire, and there are important winter populations of wildfowl. Coombe Hill Canal (L.114, gr. 2) in the Severn valley has less flooding leading to swards of group 5.

GROUP 6: WATER MEADOWS

This specialised variant of group 7 was developed mainly in association with the chalk streams of southern England. Working water meadows are now rare and will soon be extinct, as they are uneconomic under present agricultural conditions. Most of those that remain are in the Avon valley of Wiltshire and Hampshire. The most extensive yet found are between Britford and Downton in Wiltshire (L.57, gr. 2) but as a working unit the best is at Lower Woodford, Wiltshire (L.46, gr. 1).

GROUP 7: ALLUVIAL MEADOWS

These occur throughout lowland Britain but, owing to widespread reclamation for agriculture, only scattered biologically valuable examples now remain, mainly in southern and eastern England; their survival has been largely a matter of chance and so they show no particular distribution pattern. The *Fritillaria* meadows of the southern counties are an important and rapidly dwindling type of alluvial meadow; the best example now known is North Meadow at Cricklade in Wiltshire (L.43, gr. 1). In Oxfordshire, the bank of the River Thames at Pixey and Yarnton Meads/Port Meadow (L.47, gr. 1) has a grassland type similar to that of North Meadow, but more uniform. An outstanding feature of this site is the unbroken management over centuries by hay-cutting at Pixey compared with grazing at Port Meadow.

Alluvial meadows in East Anglia are best represented by those alongside the River Nene in Huntingdonshire. There are two main areas, between Sibson and Sutton, and between Chesterton and Castor (L.73), and these are together regarded as a grade 1 site. In places, these meadows again approach flood-plain mire in community composition. Port Holme, Huntingdonshire (L.85, gr. 2), like North Meadow at Cricklade, is Lammas land with attendant historical interest; *Fritillaria meleagris* is present but very rare. In Gloucestershire, a grade 2 system of alluvial meadows at Coombe Hill Canal is associated with a disused canal running from the River Severn. The only high grade alluvial meadows so far discovered in the Midlands are at Marston (L.125, gr. 1) which grade from various alluvial types to a few which are of 'permanent meadow' type (group 9).

GROUPS 8 AND 9: PERMANENT PASTURE

Both groups are found mainly in southern England; group 8 on the heavier boulder clay soils and group 9 on the lighter sandy soils.

Unimproved enclosed pastures were once the most widespread and extensive of meadow types, but they have so largely disappeared through ploughing, fertilising and reseeding that they now form a rather rare type of vegetation with a scattered distribution determined largely by chance.

A series of the best remaining sites has been chosen to represent the regional variation as far as it is known at present.

In the south of England, Clattinger Farm (L.44, gr. 1) at Oaksey in Wiltshire has a system of twelve meadows which has survived simply because the owner persists with time-honoured methods of management and refuses to 'improve' these grasslands. The flora contains a typically southern British element and there is a wide mixture of grass species, as is usual in an ancient pasture. In Huntingdonshire, Upwood Meadows (L.72, gr. 1) are a smaller but superbly rich example of old pasture with 112 vascular plants in 6 ha, again with several characteristic southern species. At Bratoft (L.86, gr. 2), in Lincolnshire, a system of five meadows has similarities with Upwood Meadows but is not quite so rich floristically. *Colchicum* meadows have been drastically reduced by ploughing but two of the better ones still remaining are Foster's Green Meadows in Worcester (L.126, gr. 1) and Monewden Meadows, Suffolk (L.74, gr. 1). The latter also contains one of the four remaining colonies of *Fritillaria meleagris* in East Anglia. The presence of this species gives an affinity with group 7. Cribb's Lodge Meadow in Leicestershire (L.128, gr. 2) is an old ridge and furrow meadow with similarities to Upwood but on a lighter soil and therefore shows the gradation between groups 8 and 9. Foulden Common (L.82, gr. 2) is a complex of habitats consisting of rich-fen, neutral grassland (groups 8 and 3) and calcareous grassland and scrub. With the loss of Worlaby meadows, Lincolnshire, by ploughing, in 1970, a grade 1 site has still to be found in group 9. It is hoped that the publicity now being given to old meadows will result in the discovery of another 'Worlaby'. Moor Closes in Lincolnshire (L.87, gr. 2) remains the only site in this group, although a small area of Port Meadow (L.47), Oxford, is representative of this type.

GROUPS 10 AND 11: NORTHERN MEADOWS

In northern England, the best examples of old enclosed pasture are on drift soils derived from Carboniferous Limestone in the upland valleys and lower hill slopes; here, the northern, submontane element in the flora is finely represented. The rich floral hay meadows described in the *Flora of Westmorland* (Wilson, 1937) for the country around Kendal, Orton, Kirkby Stephen and Upper Teesdale have been greatly reduced in number and extent, and good examples of this type are now rare everywhere. The best remaining examples of *Cirsium heterophyllum–Geranium sylvaticum–Trollius europaeus* communities may now be on ungrazed river banks, such as those of the Tees, South and North Tyne, Irthing, and, in Scotland, the Tay and Lochay. A system of four meadows alongside the Tees near High Force (L.144, gr. 1) has been chosen to represent this and other Pennine dales types of old pasture, and complements

the unenclosed submontane and montane grasslands of the Upper Teesdale NNR. A particularly fine surviving example of the above tall-herb community occurs at Gowk Bank (L.143, gr. 1) on the upper course of the River Irthing in north Cumberland. At Orton, Westmorland (L.139, gr. 1), a system of hill meadows also shows this type, plus a varied range of management practices. In the same area, the pasture at the head of Crosby Gill (L.140, gr. 1) has a fine complex of cattle-grazed but unimproved grasslands varying from slightly acidic to strongly calcareous. These show affinities with higher level unenclosed northern grasslands, of the type well represented on the higher part of Orton Fells (U.25), Ingleborough (U.23), Malham–Arncliffe (U.24), and Upper Teesdale (U.21) (all grade 1 upland sites).

Meadows of these groups have not been seen in Scotland (where they are believed to exist locally) but two sites have recently been found in Brecknock. Pen yr Hen Allt (L.116, gr. 1) has many similarities with some of the Orton meadows, and Boxbush (L.119, gr. 2) is provisionally included in group 10 pending a more detailed survey.

Since this review began, two grade 1 neutral grassland sites have been totally destroyed by ploughing; at Worlaby and Corby, in Lincolnshire. Ploughing has also destroyed part of Sibson meadows and part of the Upwood site has been treated with herbicides. Drainage schemes are taking place in the Derwent valley which will make possible agricultural improvement by ploughing etc. A major drainage scheme is proposed for the Avon valley south of Salisbury which will place in jeopardy not only the Britford water meadows but also much of the ecological interest outside the water meadows. Recently the farmer of the Pen yr Hen Allt applied artificial nitrogenous fertilisers for the first time and is likely to continue this substitute for farmyard manure to the detriment of the botanical interest of the sward.

Most of the grade 1 and 2 neutral grassland sites are being farmed by the older generation of farmers. A change of ownership or tenancy inevitably means destruction of this habitat and it can be predicted with great confidence that very few of these sites will remain by 1990, unless strenuous attempts are made to safeguard them. As a class, this is the most threatened of all British habitats with high nature conservation interest, but it is also the one which has been perhaps the most neglected in terms of actual conservation. The present list of grade 1 sites is probably not adequate in covering the range of variation in British neutral grasslands. Further survey, especially in northern and western Britain, may well disclose other sites of high national importance, so that the list of key sites should not be regarded as complete. In particular, the above-mentioned recent losses of important sites leave gaps in the national series which have still to be filled.

Table 19. **INDEX OF LOWLAND GRASSLAND, HEATH AND SCRUB SITES**

Region		Site	County	Acidic heath, grassland & scrub 1	Calcareous grassland & scrub 2	Mixed heath & rich grassland 3	Neutral grassland 4	Other formations 5
South-east England								
GRADE 1	L.1	ASHDOWN FOREST	SUSSEX	X	—	—	—	PW
	L.2	THURSLEY & HANKLEY COMMONS	SURREY	X	—	—	—	PW
	L.3	WYE & CRUNDALE DOWNS	KENT	—	Xs	—	—	W
	L.4	CASTLE HILL	SUSSEX	—	Xs	X	—	—
	L.5	MOUNT CABURN (LEWES DOWNS)	SUSSEX	—	X	—	—	—
	L.6	LULLINGTON HEATH	SUSSEX	—	s	XS	—	—
	L.7	BOX HILL–HEADLEY	SURREY	X	Xs	XS	—	—
	L.8	HARTING DOWN	SUSSEX	—	xS	—	—	—
GRADE 1*	L.9	KINGLEY VALE	SUSSEX	—	xS	—	—	W
GRADE 1	L.10	WOULDHAM–DETLING ESCARPMENT	KENT	—	xS	—	—	W
	L.11	HALLING–TROTTISCLIFFE	KENT	—	xS	—	—	—
	L.12	WHITE DOWNS	SURREY	—	xS	—	—	—
Grade 2	L.13	Iping & Ambersham Commons	Sussex	X	—	—	—	—
	L.14	Chobham Common[a]	Surrey	X	—	—	—	—
	L.15	Folkestone–Etchinghill Escarpment	Kent	—	Xs	—	—	—
	L.16	Heyshott Down	Sussex	—	Xs	—	—	—
	L.17	Purple Hill & Queendown Warren	Kent	—	X	—	—	—
	L.18	Therfield Heath	Hertfordshire	—	X	X	—	—
	L.19	Fulking Escarpment/ Newtimber Hill	Sussex	—	s	XS	—	—
South England								
GRADE 1*	L.20	NEW FOREST HEATHS	HAMPSHIRE	X	—	—	—	PW
GRADE 1	L.21	ASTON ROWANT	OXFORDSHIRE	—	XS	—	—	W
	L.22	ASTON UPTHORPE DOWNS	BERKSHIRE	—	XS	—	—	—
	L.23	COMPTON DOWN, ISLE OF WIGHT	HAMPSHIRE	—	X	—	—	—
	L.24	MARTIN DOWN	HAMPSHIRE	—	Xs	X	—	—
	L.25	OLD WINCHESTER HILL	HAMPSHIRE	—	Xs	—	—	W
	L.26	PEWSEY DOWNS[a]	WILTSHIRE	—	X	—	—	W
	L.27	WYLYE DOWN	WILTSHIRE	—	X	—	—	—
	L.28	PRESCOMBE DOWN	WILTSHIRE	—	X	—	—	—
	L.29	KNIGHTON DOWNS	WILTSHIRE	—	X	—	—	—
	L.30	STEEPLE LANGFORD, COW DOWN & CLIFFORD BOTTOM	WILTSHIRE	—	X	—	—	—
	L.31	WOODMINTON DOWN–KNOWLE HILL	WILTSHIRE	—	X	—	—	—

Table 19 (*contd.*)

Region		Site	County	1	2	3	4	5
GRADE 1	L.32	KNAPP DOWN	WILTSHIRE	—	X	—	—	—
	L.33	STARVEALL DOWN & STONY HILL[a]	WILTSHIRE	—	X	—	—	—
	L.34	PARSONAGE DOWN	WILTSHIRE	—	X	—	—	—
	L.35	SCRATCHBURY & COTLEY HILLS	WILTSHIRE	—	X	—	—	—
	L.36	PORTON DOWN	WILTSHIRE–HAMPSHIRE	—	XS	—	—	W
	L.37	TENNYSON DOWN, ISLE OF WIGHT	HAMPSHIRE	—	xs	XS	—	—
	L.38	ELLESBOROUGH WARREN	BUCKINGHAMSHIRE	—	xS	—	—	—
	L.39	BURGHCLERE BEACON	HAMPSHIRE	—	xS	—	—	—
	L.40	RUSHMORE DOWN	HAMPSHIRE	—	xS	—	—	—
	L.41	BULFORD DOWNS	WILTSHIRE	—	xS	—	—	—
	L.42	OLDBURY CASTLE & CHERHILL DOWNS	WILTSHIRE	—	X	—	—	—
	L.43	NORTH MEADOW, CRICKLADE	WILTSHIRE	—	—	—	X 7	—
	L.44	CLATTINGER FARM, OAKSEY	WILTSHIRE	—	—	—	X 7, 8	—
	L.45	BRANSBURY COMMON	HAMPSHIRE	—	—	—	X 3, 7	—
	L.46	LOWER WOODFORD WATER MEADOWS	WILTSHIRE	—	—	—	X 6	—
	L.47	PIXEY & YARNTON MEADS/PORT MEADOW	OXFORDSHIRE	—	—	—	X 5, 7, 9	—
Grade 2	L.48	Fyfield Down	Wiltshire	—	X	—	—	—
	L.49	Homington, Odstock & Coombe Bissett Downs[a]	Wiltshire	—	X	—	—	—
	L.50	Noar Hill	Hampshire	—	X	—	—	—
	L.51	Throope Down	Wiltshire	—	X	—	—	—
	L.52	Trow Down[a]	Wiltshire	—	X	—	—	—
	L.53	Well Bottom, Upton Lovell[a]	Wiltshire	—	X	—	—	—
	L.54	Stockbridge Down	Hampshire	—	xS	—	—	—
	L.55	Ivinghoe Hills, Steps Hill & Pitstone Hill	Buckinghamshire, Hertfordshire	—	xS	—	—	—
	L.56	Coombe Hill, Wendover	Buckinghamshire	—	xS	—	—	—
	L.57	Britford–Downton	Wiltshire	—	—	—	X 6	—
East Anglia GRADE 1	L.58	DUNWICH HEATHS & MARSHES	SUFFOLK	Xs	—	—	—	P
	L.59	ROYDON COMMON	NORFOLK	X	—	—	—	P
	L.60	STANFORD–WRETHAM HEATHS	NORFOLK					
		(a) STANFORD PRACTICAL TRAINING AREA		Xs	—	X	X	POW
		(b) EAST WRETHAM HEATH		Xs	—	x	—	Ow
		(c) BRIDGHAM–BRETTENHAM HEATHS		X	—	x	—	—
	L.61	ICKLINGHAM HEATHS	SUFFOLK					
		(a) CAVENHAM–TUDDENHAM HEATHS		Xs	—	x	—	PWA
		(b) ICKLINGHAM PLAINS & TRIANGLE		—	—	X	—	—
		(c) DEADMAN'S GRAVE		—	—	X	—	w
	L.62	LAKENHEATH–ELVEDEN HEATHS	SUFFOLK					
		(a) LAKENHEATH WARREN & ERISWELL HIGH & LOW WARRENS		X	—	X	—	—
		(b) WANGFORD WARREN–AIRFIELD LIGHTS		XS	—	—	—	p

Table 19 (*contd.*)

Region		Site	County	1	2	3	4	5
GRADE 1		(c) WANGFORD CARR		X	—	—	—	—
		(d) BERNER'S, HORN & WEATHER HEATHS		X	—	—	—	—
		(e) MAIDSCROSS HILL		xs	—	X	—	A
		(f) LORD'S WELL FIELD		—	—	X	—	A
	L.63	FOXHOLE HEATH	SUFFOLK	X	—	X	—	—
	L.64	WEETING HEATH	NORFOLK	x	—	Xs	—	—
	L.65	THETFORD HEATHS	SUFFOLK–NORFOLK					
		(a) THETFORD HEATH		X	—	X	—	—
		(b) SKETCHVAR HEATH		—	—	Xs	x	W
		(c) RAF BARNHAM		—	—	X	—	—
		(d) BARNHAMCROSS COMMON		—	—	X	—	—
		(e) LITTLE HEATH		—	—	X	—	—
	L.66	RISBY WARREN	LINCOLNSHIRE	X	x	X	—	—
	L.67	KNOCKING HOE	BEDFORDSHIRE	—	X	—	—	—
	L.68	BARTON HILLS	BEDFORDSHIRE	—	Xs	—	—	—
	L.69	BARNACK HILLS & HOLES	HUNTINGDON & PETERBOROUGH	—	X	—	—	—
GRADE 1*	L.70	OUSE WASHES	CAMBRIDGESHIRE–NORFOLK	—	—	—	$X_{4,\,5}$	O
GRADE 1	L.71	THOMPSON COMMON	NORFOLK	—	x	x	$X_{\underline{1,\,3}\,s}$	P
	L.72	UPWOOD MEADOWS	HUNTINGDON & PETERBOROUGH	—	—	—	$X_{\underline{8}}$	—
	L.73	SIBSON–CASTOR MEADOWS	HUNTINGDON & PETERBOROUGH	—	—	—	$X_{\underline{3,\,7}}$	p
	L.74	MONEWDEN MEADOWS	SUFFOLK	—	—	—	$X_{\underline{8}}$	—
Grade 2	L.75	Holt Lowes	Norfolk	XS	—	—	—	P
	L.76	Sandringham Warren (Dersingham Bog)	Norfolk	X	—	—	—	P
	L.77	Barnham Heath	Suffolk	Xs	—	X	—	w
	L.78	Thetford Warren	Norfolk	Xs	—	X	—	p
	L.79	Chalk Hill, Barton Mills	Suffolk	—	—	X	—	—
	L.80	Holywell Mound	Lincolnshire	—	X	—	—	—
	L.81	Castor Hanglands	Huntingdon & Peterborough	—	XS	—	—	W
	L.82	Foulden Common	Norfolk	—	x	—	$X_{\underline{9,\,3}\,s}$	P
	L.83	Calceby Beck	Lincolnshire	—	—	—	$X_{\underline{1}}$	—
	L.84	Baston Fen	Lincolnshire	—	—	—	$X_{\underline{5}}$	—
	L.85	Port Holme	Huntingdonshire	—	—	—	$X_{\underline{7}}$	—
	L.86	Bratoft Meadows	Lincolnshire	—	—	—	$X_{\underline{8}}$	—
	L.87	Moor Closes, Ancaster	Lincolnshire	—	—	—	$X_{\underline{9}}$	—
South-west England								
GRADE 1*	L.88	HARTLAND MOOR & ARNE HEATHS	DORSET	X	—	—	—	P
*	L.89	STUDLAND & GODLINGSTON HEATHS	DORSET	X	—	—	—	PCO
GRADE 1	L.90	MORDEN BOG	DORSET	X	—	—	—	Pw
	L.91	AYLESBEARE COMMON	DEVON	X	—	—	—	—
	L.92	NORTH DARTMOOR	DEVON	Xr	—	—	—	PU
GRADE 1*	L.93	ISLES OF SCILLY	CORNWALL	XR	—	x	—	C
GRADE 1	L.94	CHAPEL PORTH–ST AGNES	CORNWALL	XR	—	—	—	C
GRADE 1*	L.95	THE LIZARD	CORNWALL	xr	—	XR	—	Cp
GRADE 1	L.96	EGGARDON HILL, HAYDON & ASKERSWELL DOWNS	DORSET	—	X	—	—	—
	L.97	HOD & HAMBLEDON HILLS	DORSET	—	X	—	—	—
	L.98	BOXWELL	GLOUCESTERSHIRE	—	xS	—	—	—
	L.99	BARNSLEY WARREN	GLOUCESTERSHIRE	—	X	—	—	—
	L.100	RODBOROUGH COMMON	GLOUCESTERSHIRE	—	X	—	—	—
	L.101	CLEEVE HILL	GLOUCESTERSHIRE	—	X	—	—	—
	L.102	AVON GORGE	GLOUCESTERSHIRE–SOMERSET	—	XRs	—	—	W
	L.103	CHEDDAR GORGE	SOMERSET	—	XRs	—	—	—

Table 19 (*contd.*)

Region	Site	County	1	2	3	4	5
GRADE 1	L.104 BREAN DOWN & UPHILL CLIFF	SOMERSET	—	XRs	—	—	c
	L.105 BERRY HEAD	DEVON	—	XR	—	—	c
Grade 2	L.106 Creech–Grange–Povington Heaths	Dorset	X	—	—	—	—
	L.107 Dunkery Beacon	Somerset	X	—	—	—	—
	L.108 Park Bottom, Higher Houghton	Dorset	—	X	—	—	—
	L.109 Brassey	Gloucestershire	—	X	—	X 1	—
	L.110 Hornsleasow Roughs	Gloucestershire	—	X	—	—	—
	L.111 Minchinhampton Common	Gloucestershire	—	X	—	—	—
	L.112 Crook Peak	Somerset	—	Xs	x	—	—
	L.113 Dolebury Warren	Somerset	—	Xs	x	—	—
	L.114 Coombe Hill Canal	Gloucestershire	—	—	—	X 5, 7, s	—
South Wales							
GRADE 1	L.115 GLYN PERFEDD	BRECKNOCK	—	—	—	X 3, 1, 10	—
	L.116 PEN YR HEN ALLT	BRECKNOCK	—	—	—	X 10	—
Grade 2	L.117 Bannau Preseli & Chomin Carningli	Pembrokeshire	Xr	—	—	—	U
	L.118 Drostre Bank: Cefn Tros Dre	Brecknock	—	—	—	X 3	—
	L.119 Boxbush	Brecknock	—	—	—	X 10	—
North Wales							
GRADE 1	L.120 GLANNAU YNYS GYBI: HOLY ISLAND COAST	ANGLESEY	XR	—	—	—	C
	L.121 GREAT ORMES HEAD: PEN Y GOGARTH	CAERNARVONSHIRE	—	XRs	—	—	c
Grade 2	L.122 Yr Eifl	Caernarvonshire	XR	—	—	—	Uc
Midlands							
GRADE 1	L.123 STIPERSTONES	SHROPSHIRE	Xr	—	x	—	Wu
	L.124(i) DERBYSHIRE DALES GRASSLANDS	DERBYSHIRE–STAFFORDSHIRE					
	(a) DOVE VALLEY & BIGGIN DALE		—	XRS	—	—	W
	(b) LATHKILL DALE		—	XRS	—	—	W
	(c) CRESSBROOK DALE		—	XRS	—	—	W
	(d) MONK'S DALE		—	XRS	—	—	w
	(e) LONG DALE & GRATTON DALE		—	XRs	—	—	—
	L.125 MARSTON MEADOWS	STAFFORDSHIRE	—	—	—	X 7, 3, 9	—
	L.126 FOSTER'S GREEN MEADOWS	WORCESTERSHIRE	—	—	—	X 8	—
Grade 2	L.127 Bredon Hill	Worcestershire	—	XS	—	—	—
	L.124(ii) Derbyshire Dales Grasslands	Derbyshire					
	(a) Coombs Dale		—	XRS	—	—	—
	(b) Miller's Dale		—	XRS	—	—	—
	(c) Topley Pike & Deep Dale		—	XRS	—	—	—
	L.128 Cribb's Lodge Meadow	Leicestershire	—	—	—	X 8/9	—
North England							
GRADE 1	L.129 SKIPWITH COMMON	YORKSHIRE	X	—	—	—	pw
	L.130 WATERDALE	YORKSHIRE	—	X	—	—	—
	L.131 DUGGLEBY HIGH BARN WOLD	YORKSHIRE	—	X	—	—	—
	L.132 EAST DALE	YORKSHIRE	—	X	—	—	—
	L.133 HUMPHREY HEAD	LANCASHIRE	—	XRS	—	—	c
	L.134 GAIT BARROWS	LANCASHIRE	—	xRS	—	—	W
	L.135 HUTTON ROOF CRAGS & FARLETON KNOTT	WESTMORLAND	x	XRS	X	—	W
	L.136 WHITBARROW SCAR	WESTMORLAND	—	XRS	—	—	W
	L.137 SCOUT & CUNSWICK SCARS	WESTMORLAND	—	XRS	—	—	W
	L.138 THRISLINGTON PLANTATION	DURHAM	—	X	—	—	—
	L.139 ORTON MEADOWS	WESTMORLAND	—	—	—	X 10, 11	—

Table 19 (*contd.*)

Region	Site	County	1	2	3	4	5
GRADE 1	L.140 CROSBY GILL	WESTMORLAND	—	Xrs	—	X <u>11</u>	w
	L.141 WINTRINGHAM MARSH	YORKSHIRE	—	—	—	X <u>1</u>, 3	—
GRADE 1*	L.142 DERWENT INGS	YORKSHIRE	—	—	—	X <u>4/5</u>, 3, 7	—
GRADE 1	L.143 GOWK BANK	CUMBERLAND	—	—	—	X <u>10</u>	—
	L.144 UPPER TEESDALE MEADOWS	DURHAM–YORKSHIRE	—	—	—	X <u>10, 11</u>	—
Grade 2	L.145 Strensall Common	Yorkshire	X	—	—	—	—
	L.146 Lazonby & Wan Fells	Cumberland	Xr	—	—	—	p
	L.147 Arnside Knott & Warton Crag	Westmorland–Lancashire	—	XRS	—	—	W
	L.148 Cassop Vale	Durham	—	X	—	—	—
South Scotland							
GRADE 1	L.149 KEN–DEE MARSHES	KIRKCUDBRIGHTSHIRE	—	—	—	X <u>2</u>, 7	po
East Scotland							
GRADE 1	L.150 SANDS OF FORVIE	ABERDEENSHIRE	X	—	—	—	C
West Scotland							
GRADE 1	L.151 OYKELL MARSHES	ROSS–SUTHERLAND	—	—	—	X <u>2</u>, 5, 12, 13	p

Notes

* Internationally important sites.
X = major representation of types 1–4.
x = minor representation of types 1–4.
S = major representation of scrub within appropriate type.
s = minor representation of scrub within appropriate type.
R = major representation of rock habitat within appropriate type.
r = minor representation of rock habitat within appropriate type.
Other formations:

P = peatlands	C = coastlands
O = open waters	U = uplands
W = woodlands	A = artificial ecosystems

Capitals indicate major occurrence; lower case indicates minor occurrence.
Numbered suffix under Neutral grasslands entry indicates type. For description see pp. 185–8.
Underlining indicates main type.

[a] See Appendix.

7 OPEN WATERS

RANGE OF ECOLOGICAL VARIATION

Habitat factors, vegetation and invertebrate communities

Open waters include both fresh waters and those brackish waters in which the benthic fauna consists largely of insects and oligochaetes as opposed to marine and brackish conditions where crustaceans, molluscs and polychaetes predominate. Both running waters and standing waters are included, i.e. rivers, streams, canals, lakes, ponds and small pools. Open waters are certainly the most widespread of the natural or semi-natural habitats in Britain, although they cover only about 1% of the land surface. The deeper parts of some large oligotrophic lakes in the north are among the few habitats in Britain virtually unaffected by man's activities. In many areas nature conservation interests in open waters are increasingly threatened by water-based recreational activities, water abstraction, river regulation, drainage, hydro-electric schemes and pollution, including eutrophication, all of which may adversely affect wildlife. These threats are only partially offset by the creation of new open waters in the form of reservoirs and gravel pits. Hence the urgent need for the survey and description of intact open waters in Britain, and the selection of a series of sites to represent adequately the range of variation.

The most fundamental division of freshwater ecosystems is into standing and running waters. Although the difference between lakes and rivers is generally obvious, in a few running waters, such as the Fenland drains, current velocities may be so low in the summer months that they are effectively lakes, with a predominantly lacustrine flora and fauna. Conversely, physical conditions on the exposed wave-washed shores of large lakes may approach those in fast flowing rivers and components of a typical riverine flora and fauna may be present.

The major difference between non-tidal running waters and standing waters is that, in the former, currents are induced by gravity and, although variable in velocity, are constant in direction, while in the latter, currents are mainly induced by wind action and are very variable both in velocity and direction. The constancy of river currents assures a steady supply of particulate matter carried downstream in the drift, upon which a large assemblage of specialised filter-feeding invertebrates depends. These are absent from standing waters. The steady downstream current also prevents the growth of a true zooplankton and phytoplankton in many of our rivers. However, if a river is long enough or its flow slow enough a true plankton does develop. Running waters tend to be more aerated and to have a more constant temperature than neighbouring standing waters, so that a number of organisms dependent on low summer temperatures and high oxygen tensions are confined to them, while other species requiring high summer temperatures are restricted to small standing waters.

The following account of the major categories of open waters departs from the standardised treatment of other formations in the *Review*, in describing the invertebrate and phytoplankton fauna in terms of communities along with the vascular plant communities. This treatment is not conducive to easy reading by those unfamiliar with the invertebrates and phytoplankton (most of which can only be referred to by their scientific names), but it was felt to be the best way of dealing with the large amount of survey information available on these most important groups of aquatic organisms. Aquatic invertebrate and phytoplankton communities are highly diagnostic and therefore valuable in helping to categorise the different types of open water-body, and it is therefore desirable to discuss them in the account of habitat factors. The vertebrates are, however, dealt with in the usual way, as separate taxonomic groups.

STANDING WATERS

Standing waters occur either where the drainage is impeded, e.g. by glacial deposition or deepening in valleys, by the build-up of peat in mire systems, where water accumulates in kettle-holes and other depressions such as the Shropshire/Cheshire meres and the Norfolk Broads, or where man has created artificial dams or barriers of various kinds.

The overwhelming factor affecting the flora and fauna of standing waters is the chemical content of the water. A large number of elements and compounds are found dissolved in natural waters, and include trace elements and certain organic compounds which limit plant growth under culture conditions, but about which little is known in the field. In general, however, the primary production (and hence in most cases also the secondary production) of a waterbody is related to its alkalinity. This relationship is partially explained by the direct relationship between alkalinity and the concentration of dissolved major plant nutrients, nitrogen and phosphorus. Phosphate is commonly the factor limiting the algal primary production in fresh water in Britain. Alkalinity is a more convenient and constant measure of productive level, however, as the

Characteristics of lakes of different trophic status

Nutrient status	Alkalinity (p.p.m. CaCO₃)	Winter pH	Water colour	Productivity
Dystrophic	0–2	< 6.0	Brown, peat stained	Extremely low, plants limited by lack of nutrients and lack of light penetration
Oligotrophic	0–10	6.0–7.0	Clear	Low, plants limited by lack of nutrients
Mesotrophic	10–30	*c.* 7.0	Slight green algal colouration in summer	Moderate to high, some oxygen depletion may occur in the hypolimnion of deeper examples
Eutrophic	> 30	> 7.0	Often discoloured by algae	High, both for algae and macrophytes. Oxygen depletion occurs in hypolimnion of deep examples
Marl (calcareous)	> 100	> 7.4	Extremely clear	Extremely low phytoplankton production, but high macrophytic production
Brackish	(Conductivity > 500 μmhos. Sodium main cation)	Variable	Usually clear	Variable but phytoplankton generally sparse

dissolved plant nutrients (phosphate, nitrate, nitrites and ammonia) vary considerably in their concentrations over the seasons, depending upon their uptake by plants, sedimentation in organic form, and release from the sediment. Nitrogen and phosphorus also occur in organic and inorganic states in many different forms, thereby adding to the difficulties of chemical analysis and interpretation. Water pH has often been used as a measure of the productive level of water-bodies, but this can vary greatly according to photosynthetic activity, particularly during the summer months.

Summer pHs are not a reliable guide to the trophic status of lakes. Because of the low alkalinity of most oligotrophic lakes, any substantial algal growth will raise the pH far above 7; indeed 10 would be quite possible. The very reasons which permit wide fluctuations in pH in oligotrophic lakes during the summer tend to damp down the pH fluctuations in eutrophic lakes and there are few eutrophic lakes in which the pH is raised as high as 11 by photosynthesis.

Lakes have generally been classified into unproductive and productive types, to which the terms *oligotrophic* and *eutrophic*, respectively, have become applied. A third category of lake which has an intermediate alkalinity and productivity has been termed *mesotrophic*. Further categories are required to accommodate those lakes where, because of special chemical conditions, the relationship between alkalinity and nutrient content does not apply. Sodium rather than calcium may be the prevalent cation in some lakes, particularly in coastal regions, causing a high alkalinity, not necessarily accompanied by a high nutrient content. Lakes with a sodium concentration higher than that of calcium and a total ionic content and conductivity intermediate between that of fresh water and sea water, are termed *brackish*. In limestone regions, lakes have high

alkalinities but, since phosphorus is generally present only in insoluble form, primary production in the form of phytoplankton is generally very low. The phosphorus is precipitated together with a deposit of calcium carbonate, known as marl, which coats the bottom substrate, and hence these lakes are often termed *marl lakes*. A final category of lake distinguishes those where dissolved humic acids derived from acidic peat lower the pH to well below neutrality. Such lakes are termed *dystrophic* and are generally extremely unproductive, although the nutrient content may be relatively high.

Although there is general acceptance of these six categories of lake, the divisions between them are arbitrary and there is no general agreement as to their precise definition. For the purpose of this account they are defined in the table above.

Within each of these major divisions lakes may be divided into further categories using other physical attributes, including depth, area, nature of shoreline, altitude and latitude. These attributes are all to some extent interdependent (for instance large lakes in northern Britain tend to be oligotrophic, deep and have stony shorelines, while eutrophic lakes in southern Britain tend to be shallow and have organic shorelines) so that the theoretically large number of possible lake categories can be reduced in practice.

In shallow lakes, the depth to which light penetration enables plant growth to continue, the photic zone, may extend down to the bottom over the entire area. The exact depth of the photic zone depends on the clarity of the water, being greater for oligotrophic and marl lakes than for dystrophic and eutrophic waters. In general, the shallower the lake the more important are the benthic plant communities and the animal communities dependent on them, whereas in deeper lakes the major producers are plankton and dependent animal communities.

Depth is also important in relation to the establishment of thermal stratification. In deep lakes, a narrow transitional zone of relatively rapid temperature change occurs just below the depth to which the lake water is normally stirred by wind action. A density gradient is formed at this level which effectively prevents the transfer of water between the lower hypolimnion and the upper epilimnion until thermal stratification is broken down when the upper lake waters cool in autumn. This barrier, called the thermocline, forms at depths ranging from 5–25 m depending on the size of lake, and in large shallow lakes stable stratification does not occur. In shallow lakes, wave action can extend down to the bottom, bringing the substrate into suspension and so preventing the establishment of an undisturbed sediment. In the deeper lakes, there is a progression of substrate types from eroded shorelines to soft muds in deeper water. The depth at which the transition from erosion to deposition takes place depends on the size of the lake and its exposure to the wind.

In larger lakes, wind action becomes an increasingly important ecological factor, with its major effect upon the shallow littoral zone. Small, sheltered bodies of water generally have shorelines on which fine organic or mineral sediments are deposited, and here marginal vegetation may flourish. With increasing size and exposure, the shorelines become more eroding and thus more inhospitable for plant colonisation. With extreme wave action the shorelines may consist of barren storm beaches of unstable stones or gravel, or wave-washed stable bedrock. Mean wind speeds increase both with increasing altitude and latitude, so that a small lake in lowland southern Britain may have a depositing muddy shoreline with extensive reed-swamp development, while a lake of the same area and shape in the uplands of the north may be bounded by barren, stony, wave-washed shores. Mean water temperatures decrease with increasing altitude and latitude, and many species of aquatic plants and animals are restricted in their British distribution by their particular temperature requirements. In high-altitude lakes, ice scour at the time of melting restricts the colonisation of the shallow littoral by both plants and animals.

Within a deep lake there are four main habitat zones.

1. The open water, all depths inhabited by the plankton.

2. The profundal benthic zone which is in deep water beyond the depth of light penetration, where the bottom consists generally of fine organic mud, and where no plant production occurs.

3. The sublittoral benthic zone which is in shallower water and is the zone in which most macrophytes grow, the substrate being generally of fine sediments such as silt or mud.

4. The littoral benthic zone which is in the shallowest water at the margin of the lake where the effects of wave action are strong and the substrate consists of eroding mineral sediments such as sand, gravel, stones or boulders.

These divisions obviously grade into one another, but it is convenient to discuss the range of variation of the vegetation and invertebrate populations in terms of these zones, as each has its own distinctive communities. The depth at which the transition between the three benthic zones takes place is variable and depends on a number of factors such as water clarity, exposure and lake size. In shallow lakes the profundal may be absent, while in small sheltered waters where wave action is negligible, the sublittoral zone may extend up to the shoreline.

Because of the importance of depth and size to the physical characteristics of standing waters, it is practical to subdivide the above chemically based primary divisions into water-bodies with mean depths above and below 5 m, and with areas above and below 10 ha.

DYSTROPHIC STANDING WATERS

Dystrophic pools and lakes occur amongst or on oligotrophic mires or where a lake receives water draining largely from oligotrophic mire. The distribution of these waters in Britain therefore follows that of such mires. The most widespread oligotrophic mire type, blanket mire, is confined to the north and west of Britain, and contains a range of dystrophic waters from moderate-sized lakes to minute pools on patterned bogs. The mode of origin of small peat pools is still obscure, but many of the larger dystrophic waters occupy former glacial troughs (e.g. Loch Laidon). In the south and east of Britain dystrophic waters are far more scattered and many occupy former peat-cuttings on raised and basin mires: others have been formed by the encroachment of a *schwingmoor* on a eutrophic lake which thus becomes isolated from the ground water by the surrounding peat.

Peat pools and dubh lochans on blanket mire are the most widespread of dystrophic waters in Britain. Typically, these are small, shallow bodies of water less than a metre deep and with peat shorelines and bottoms. Littoral and profundal zones do not therefore exist, and the whole pool may be considered as a sublittoral habitat. The waters are generally acid (pH 4.0 to 6.0) and deficient in bases, although a number show surprisingly high phosphate and organic nitrogen contents, possibly resulting from the decay of allochthonous material carried into them. The water is normally stained brown by dissolved humic acids, though not invariably at all seasons.

The characteristic macrophytic plant species found in small bog pools are bryophytes such as *Sphagnum subsecundum* var. *auriculatum*, *S. subsecundum* var. *inundatum*, *S. cuspidatum* and *Drepanocladus fluitans*, and the angiosperms *Eriophorum angustifolium*, *Utricularia minor*, *Menyanthes trifoliata* and *Potamogeton polygonifolius*. Other angiosperms such as *Nymphaea alba* (including ssp. *occidentalis*), *Sparganium minimum*, *Juncus bulbosus*, *Eleocharis multicaulis* and *Carex limosa* also frequently occur in such situations together with certain leafy liverworts including *Gymnocolea inflata* and *Cephalozia fluitans*. The bottom is often covered by a dense layer of algae of which *Nostoc* spp., *Tribonema minus*, desmids, *Zygamales* and *Microspora* are characteristic, but phytoplankton production is low.

In small peat pools there is no true zooplankton but a

number of species of copepods and cladocerans are associated with the bottom peat and *Sphagnum*. These include the cladocerans *Streblocerus serricaudatus*, *Acantholeberis curvirostris* and *Chydorus sphaericus*, and the copepods *Cyclops (Acanthocyclops) venustus*, *Cyclops (Diacyclops) languidus*, *C. nanus* and *Bryocamptus weberi*.

Peaty-shored dystrophic lakes and peat pools have a very characteristic benthic invertebrate fauna in which some groups, such as molluscs, are typically absent, while others such as dragonflies, beetles and water bugs are very abundant. In small pools the invertebrate fauna often contains a preponderance of carnivorous species which must be largely dependent for food on terrestrial invertebrates that fall into the water.

The fauna consists predominantly of insects, and groups such as triclads, leeches, molluscs, Malacostraca and Hydracarina are poorly represented or absent. Molluscs are only found in the slightly richer sites when *Lymnaea (Radix) peregra*, *Pisidium casertanum*, *P. obtusale* and *P. personatum* occasionally occur, and in the larger dubh lochans *Valvata piscinalis* may be found in the deeper water. Tubificid and naidid worms are often abundant in the bottom deposits and vegetation of peaty pools, but leeches only occur in larger dubh lochans. The water spider *Argyroneta aquatica* is often plentiful in small pools where it spins its net amongst the submerged mosses and *Utricularia*. Mayflies and stoneflies are typically absent from the small waters, but species such as *Leptophlebia marginata* and *L. vespertina*, which are typical of oligotrophic lakes, are found in the larger dubh lochans.

One of the characteristic groups found in mire pools are the dragonflies which are represented by a wide range of species. The most widespread and abundant species found in such situations, but not necessarily confined to peat pools, are *Sympetrum danae*, *Aeshna juncea*, *Pyrrhosoma nymphula*, *Lestes sponsa* and *Libellula quadrimaculata*. Other widespread but rather uncommon mire species are *Leucorrhinia dubia* and *Coenagrion puella* while *Coenagrion hastulatum*, *Somatochlora arctica* and *Aeshna caerulea* are confined to the north (where they may all breed in dystrophic waters) but only *A. caerulea* is restricted to peat pools. *Somatochlora metallica* has an odd distribution, being found both in acidic waters in Scotland and in eutrophic waters in southern England, but not elsewhere.

Another characteristic group associated with peatland pools are the water bugs. The common species of acidic blanket mire pools in the north and west are *Callicorixa wollastoni*, *Hesperocorixa castanea*, *Arctocorisa carinata*, *Sigara scotti*, *Notonecta obliqua*, *Gerris costai*, *G. odontogaster*, *G. gibbifer* and, in the wet *Sphagnum* at the sides of the pools, *Hebrus ruficeps*. *Sigara lateralis* and *S. venusta* are less frequently found in these pools. *Glaenocorisa propinqua* and *Arctocorisa germari* are found in larger peat pools and dubh lochans. The water beetles are represented by a large number of species of *Hydroporus*, including particularly *H. nigrita*, plus *Agabus* spp., *Ilybius aenescens*, *Rantus exsoletus*, *R. bistriatus*, *Acilius sulcatus*, *A. canaliculatus* and *Gyrinus minutus* and *G. opacus*.

The alder fly *Sialis lutaria* is found in deeper dystrophic waters where there is a soft organic sediment and caddis flies also occur in peaty pools (usually in small numbers). Limnephilidae and Phryganeidae are characteristic, *Agrypnia varia*, *A. obsoleta* and *Oligotricha striata* being common and widespread, but the Limnephilidae of these waters are not well known. *Holocentropus* spp. are frequently found among thick moss in peat pools, but other Polycentropidae such as *Cyrnus flavidus* and *Polycentropus flavomaculatus* are only found in larger bodies of water where the shorelines are stony.

Chironomidae larvae are often extremely abundant, but little is known of the actual species found. The phantom midges are represented by *Chaoborus crystallinus*, *C. obscuripes* and *Mochlonyx martinii* and they may be extremely abundant in the deeper pools. In most peat pools various biting midges (Ceratopogonidae) and mosquitoes (*Culex*, *Aedes*, *Anopheles* and *Theobaldia*) also occur as larvae.

In lowland Britain, dystrophic waters are mainly found as residual open water in basin mires. Although acidic, they are usually richer than pools on blanket mire and may have calcium contents as high as 30 p.p.m. Such pools are often deeper than those on blanket mire and are invariably heavily peat-stained and plant growth is confined to shallow water. Since they are usually bounded by floating rafts of vegetation, a shallow littoral is absent, and submerged vegetation is restricted to a narrow fringe of *Sphagnum cuspidatum*, *S. subsecundum* var. *inundatum* and on occasions *Utricularia minor*. The marginal raft-forming vegetation generally comprises species such as *Potentilla palustris*, *Menyanthes trifoliata*, and a wide range of *Carex* spp. growing on a bed of *Sphagnum* spp., particularly *S. recurvum*. Algal production is also limited by lack of light penetration so that very little autochthonous primary production occurs in these waters. As a result, dissolved oxygen concentrations may be low and organic nitrogen and phosphate derived from the decay of allochthonous material may be present in relatively high concentrations.

The invertebrate fauna of lowland mire pools differs somewhat from that found in upland blanket mire pools, but whether these differences result from the different physical conditions within the pools, particularly water chemistry, or to restriction in geographical range of some species is difficult to ascertain.

The fauna of lowland mire pools consists primarily of insects, but non-insect groups may be more abundant than in upland pools. In addition to those species of mollusc found in blanket mire pools, soft-water species of gastropod such as *Lymnaea (Galba) palustris*, *Planorbis (Gyraulus) albus*, *P. (Armiger) crista* and *Potamopyrgus jenkinsi* may occur in the richer basin mire pools of the lowlands. Leeches such as *Helobdella stagnalis* also live in these conditions and in the most eutrophic pools the malacostracans *Asellus meridianus* and *Crangonyx pseudogracilis* may also occur. Stoneflies and mayflies are typically absent, but *Cloeon dipterum* has been found associated with the marginal vegetation of a few areas.

In addition to the widespread and abundant dragonflies

found in a variety of dystrophic waters, a number of species are restricted to the south of Britain where they occur in lowland peat pools, though not all of them are confined to base-poor waters. These include *Orthetrum coerulescens*, *O. cancellatum*, *Libellula fulva*, *Ischnura pumilio* and *Coenagrion mercuriale*, the last two being typical of *Sphagnum* flushes. The lowland pools have a different assemblage of water bugs from their upland counterparts and the common species are *Hesperocorixa castanea*, *H. linnei*, *H. sahlbergi*, *Notonecta glauca* and *Gerris odontogaster*. *Hesperocorixa moesta*, *Ilyocoris cimicoides* and *Hebrus pusillus* are found less frequently and *I. cimicoides* occurs in dense submerged bryophytes and *H. pusillus* in wet *Sphagnum* at the edges. Water beetles are usually abundant in lowland pools and a similar range of species to that found in upland situations is usually present, but a few species (e.g. *Haliplus variegatus* and *Ilybius fenestratus*) are confined to lowland Britain. The rare caddis flies *Oligotrichia clathrata* and *Rhadicoleptus alpestris* are confined to a few lowland peat pools in the Midlands, limnephilids such as *Micropterna lateralis* and *Limnephilus centralis* may be numerous and are more widespread. The phantom midge larvae *Chaoborus flavicans* and *C. crystallinus* are very characteristic of lowland dystrophic waters and may be extremely abundant especially where low oxygen concentrations prevail.

In larger dystrophic waters, as exposure to wind and wave action increases with increased fetch, there is a tendency for the peat shorelines to be replaced by coarser inorganic sediments of sand, gravel, stone or boulders. Dystrophic lakes of greater than 5 ha are seldom entirely bounded by shorelines of actively growing peat, and in the more exposed northerly sites, much smaller pools may have eroding mineral shorelines. The largest dystrophic lake found in this survey was Loch Laidon (465 ha) which receives drainage from Rannoch Moor, and all larger lakes in Britain appear to have a pH greater than 6.0. The vegetation of mineral shored dystrophic lakes is similar to that of oligotrophic lakes, but limited light penetration restricts macrophytic growth and phytoplankton production to a shallower photic zone. Stones in shallow water are often covered by thick mucilaginous growths of algae, of which *Batrachospermum* spp. is often conspicuous and these are not generally encountered in oligotrophic lakes.

The invertebrate fauna of the larger waters in this category is similar in composition to that of oligotrophic lakes. The extremely low primary production limits the production of the invertebrate fauna which is therefore very sparse. Molluscs are generally fewer than in typical oligotrophic lakes and only very adaptable species such as *Pisidium casertanum* and *Lymnaea* (*Radix*) *pereger* are found.

OLIGOTROPHIC STANDING WATERS

Most natural lakes in Britain belong to this category, and are mainly found in the base-poor upland areas of north Wales, the Lake District, Galloway and the Scottish Highlands and Islands. Most were formed by the processes of glacial erosion during the last glaciation, but many of the smaller examples are in areas of morainic deposition. In the main valleys occupied by the larger glaciers, long, narrow and generally very deep, fjord lakes were formed, and all the larger oligotrophic lakes in Britain are of this type. At higher altitudes many lakes were formed in corries and are usually roughly circular, deep and steep-sided. In more level areas, a combination of glacial erosion and deposition has often led to the formation of numerous small, shallow, irregularly shaped oligotrophic lakes. In lowland Britain oligotrophic lakes are very rare, being confined to areas of base-poor sandstones or drift where they have generally been formed as kettle-holes. South of the area of glaciation there are only a few artificial oligotrophic lakes and a few small natural rock basins.

The shorelines of these oligotrophic lakes almost invariably consist of coarse inorganic sediments, boulders, stones or gravel. With increasing depth these give way to finer material and in the deeper areas the bottom is covered by a mud deposit known as *dy*. This consists largely of allochthonous peaty material admixed with a gelatinous precipitate of ferric salts. Because of the low productivity of these lakes, the contribution of decaying phytoplankton and macrophytic remains to the deep water sediments is low, and the rate of decomposition in the *dy* is slow. Thus, this sediment and the overlying deep water of the lake (the hypolimnion) remains well oxygenated even during summer, when it becomes isolated from the surface of the lake by a stable layer of warmer water (the epilimnion) which occupies the upper 5–24 m of water. Phosphorus is only released from the sediments of lakes when these become anaerobic, so in oligotrophic lakes this element remains bound in the *dy* and the unavailability of phosphorus is generally the factor limiting phytoplankton production. The zooplankton and phytoplankton of these lakes are both sparse and generally lacking in diversity. The biomass of phytoplankton, as measured by the concentration of chlorophyll *a*, is much lower than in eutrophic lakes, with values from about 0.5 to 20 mg/m³. Maximum algal cell numbers reach concentrations of only hundreds per millilitre, except for the minute nannoplankton which may reach a few thousand per millilitre. Since light penetration is in part a function of algal abundance, a characteristic of oligotrophic lakes is the low phytoplankton production per unit volume of water down to great depths. This contrasts with eutrophic lakes where high production per unit volume of water limited to the upper water is typical. Production rates may not be correspondingly low per unit of biomass in oligotrophic lakes because nannoplankton, which often have higher production rates than the larger algae, commonly predominate. Typical values of phytoplankton production range from 5 to 25 g organic carbon/m² of lake surface per year.

As many algae are found in a wide variety of lakes, the major qualitative differences between the phytoplankton of oligotrophic and eutrophic lakes are in the relative abundance of the various groups. Discolouration of the water by blue-green or other abundant algae is very rare in oligotrophic lakes and few diatoms are found, the most abundant being species of *Cyclotella*, *Tabellaria*, *Rhizosolenia* and sometimes *Melosira distans*. *Asterionella* may be present but not in large numbers. Chrysophyta are prominent and are represented by a considerable variety of nannoplanktonic flagellates of which *Dinobryon* and occasionally *Uroglena* are characteristic genera. These two species may produce some turbidity or discolouration of the water.

Dinoflagellates such as *Peridinium*, *Gymnodinium* and *Ceratium cornutum* may be present especially in summer, but *C. hirundinella* is rare or absent. Among the Chlorophyta, desmids are not usually very numerous per unit volume of water. However, a wide variety of species is present, some of which are also benthic or come from boggy areas surrounding the lakes. Coccoid and colonial green algae are relatively common, especially in summer, including genera such as *Raphidonema*, *Chlorella*, *Sphaerocystis*, *Gloeocystis* and *Botryococcus*. There is a seasonal succession of plankton with diatoms and Chrysophyceae predominating from winter to midsummer, and green algae and dinoflagellates from midsummer to late autumn.

Few species of zooplankter are confined in Britain to oligotrophic waters, but the assemblage of species is generally very distinct from that of eutrophic waters. The cladocerans *Holopedium gibberum* and *Bythotrephes longimanus* and the copepods *Limnocalanus macrurus*, *Diaptomus (Mixodiaptomus) laciniatus* and *D. (Arctodiaptomus) laticeps* are only found in the plankton of oligotrophic lakes in the north of Britain. *Holopedium* has, however, disappeared from a number of lakes in the Lake District that have received increasing loads of sewage effluent, and *Limnocalanus*, which was previously recorded only in Ennerdale (where it was thought to be a glacial relict) may now be extinct in Britain.

The most common assemblage of species in the open water of these lakes comprises *Cyclops strenuus abyssorum*, *Diaptomus gracilis*, *Bosmina coregoni* (usually var. *obtusirostris*) and small numbers of *Leptodora kindti*. In all but the poorest lakes, *Daphnia hyalina* var. *lacustris* is also usually a constituent of the zooplankton. Variations on this basic community are frequent, for example *Cyclops strenuus* may be accompanied or replaced by other *Cyclops* spp. such as *C. agilis* or *C. leukharti* (the latter, a tropical species at the northerly edge of its range in Britain, is not found in Scotland). In some shallow oligotrophic waters *Diaptomus (Arctodiaptomus) wierzejskii* may replace *D. (Eudiaptomus) gracilis*, and in others one or more of the common species may be absent.

In the profundal zone of these lakes there is no autotrophic plant production and the flora consists only of bacteria and fungi whose production is limited by the relatively non-degradable nature of the peaty solids forming the organic fraction of the *dy*. The invertebrate fauna living in or on the *dy* mud consists of a few well-defined groups.

1. Filter feeders, such as sponges, lamellibranchs and some Chironominae and Orthocladiinae, which depend on fine particulate organic matter falling from the upper parts of the lake.

2. Burrowing forms feeding directly on the mud and its microflora and microfauna, e.g. oligochaetes and nematodes.

3. Largely carnivorous forms such as leeches, Tanypodinae, Chaoborinae and Hydracarina.

The sponge *Spongilla lacustris* may form large palmate colonies in still deep waters but is replaced by the encrusting species *Ephydatia fluviatilis* in more turbulent shallow water. Nematodes are often present but little is known about the biology of this group. Oligochaetes are little noted, but species such as *Peloscolex ferox*, *Tubifex tubifex* and the naidid *Arctonais lomondi* are recorded from the profundal of a few oligotrophic lakes in Britain. The most typical leech species of the deep-water zone is *Helobdella stagnalis*. *Glossiphonia complanata* and *Erpobdella octoculata* are also found in muddy conditions, usually in shallow water. Few gastropods extend to great depths: the pulmonate *Lymnaea (Radix) pereger* is restricted in Loch Lomond to depths of less than 6 m, but the opisthobranch *Valvata piscinalis* can go much deeper (down to at least 11 m in Loch Lomond) and is usually the most successful snail on a mud substrate in oligotrophic waters. *Planorbis (Gyraulus) albus*, *Potamopyrgus jenkinsi* and *Physa fontinalis* will also occur in the mud zone, but these snails are more typical of the shallower vegetation zones. *Pisidium* spp. generally form a considerable portion of the biomass of the deep water benthos. *Pisidium casertanum* the most widespread and adaptable member of this genus, *P. hibernicum*, *P. lilljeborgii* and *P. personatum*, are the most typical species and may be accompanied by the larger *Sphaerium corneum*. *Pisidium conventus* which is found in the mud of a number of cold-water northern lakes, is considered to be a glacial relict species.

Several genera of Hydracarina swim above the mud surface together with cladocerans such as *Latona setifera*, *Ilyocryptus acutifrons*, *I. sordidus* and various harpacticoid copepods. The glacial relict *Mysis relicta*, which was recorded from Ennerdale, is the only macrobenthic Crustacean found in the profundal of oligotrophic lakes in Britain. This species is partially benthic and partially planktonic.

A characteristic group of the deeper water is the Chironomidae of which Orthocladiinae may figure prominently, e.g. *Orthocladius* spp., *Cricotopus* spp. and *Metriocnemus* spp. Chironominae are less well represented than in nutrient-rich lakes and *Chironomus* spp. are not found, but *Cryptochironomus* spp., *Polypedilum* spp., *Pentapedilum* spp., and *Lauterborniella* spp. may occur together with *Tanytarsus* spp. These genera are mainly tube dwellers, unlike the carnivorous Tanypodinae which are free-living in the mud, feeding on chironomid larvae and oligochaetes. The genera *Procladius*, *Ablabesmyia* and *Anatopynia* are common in oligotrophic lakes. The phantom midge *Chaoborus flavicans* occurs widely in deeper water, and migrates between the mud and the water mass, where it is a specialist feeder on zooplankton. Small numbers of biting midge larvae, Ceratopogonidae, are also found in the deep-water mud.

The Trichoptera are not found in the deepest water but extend down into the aphotic zone. In oligotrophic lakes *Polycentropus flavomaculatus*, *Cyrnus flavidus*, *Athripsodes aterrimus*, *Mystacides azurea* and *Oxyethira* spp. are characteristic. Similarly the alder fly *Sialis lutaria* is a common predator in the mud zone of the slightly richer lakes but does not extend down into the deeper water.

Progressing into shallow water, the transition to the sublittoral zone is marked by the appearance of macrophytes such as *Nitella opaca*, *Isoetes lacustris* and occasionally *Fontinalis antipyretica*, usually growing in single-species stands. These may grow down to a depth of about 12 m, but the last two species can also occur in shallow water where competition from other plants is low. In shallower regions of this zone where the sediments are generally of fine inorganic material species such as *Myriophyllum alterniflorum*, *Juncus bulbosus*, *Callitriche hermaphroditica*, and occasionally *Potamogeton gramineus* and *P. perfoliatus* replace the deep-water species. In more sheltered situations floating-leaved communities of Nymphaceae, *Sparganium angustifolium* and *Potamogeton natans* may be found. In sheltered bays and along the margins of small oligotrophic lakes where peaty organic sediments accumulate and the sublittoral zone may extend up to the water's edge, emergent communities occur of species such as *Carex rostrata*, *Equisetum fluviatile*, *Schoenoplectus lacustris* and generally rather depauperate stands of *Phragmites communis*. In most cases these sparse reed-beds are not advancing with time and hydroseral progression is limited to areas around the mouths of inflow streams where reed-swamp progresses to poor-fen and wet alder–willow scrub growing on the deposited silt.

The benthic algae of the sublittoral zone of oligotrophic lakes are not well known. Desmids and diatoms, particularly certain species of *Frustulia* and *Pinnularia* are abundant on the surface of the mud, while the higher plants may be covered with a wide range of epiphytic diatoms and filamentous algae. The latter are more abundant, however, in the littoral zone where they attach to stones.

The fauna of the sublittoral benthic zone is more diverse than that of the profundal mainly because of the diversity of habitat provided by the presence of aquatic macrophytes and benthic algae. The carnivorous triclads appear where the bottom is firm enough to support them, or on vegetation. The only abundant species in these waters are *Polycelis nigra* and *P. tenuis* which feed on oligochaetes and insects. The oligochaetes in this zone are not well known but conspicuous species are *Lumbriculus variegatus* and *Stylaria lacustris*, the latter closely associated with macrophytes. Tubificidae and other Naididae are also present. The same species of leech found in deeper water may occur, and the fish leech *Piscicola geometra*. The firm substrates and greater variety of prey of this region favours a greater density of leeches than in the deeper mud zone. Gastropods also achieve their greatest abundance in this zone, though the variety of species is limited to those which are tolerant of low calcium concentrations. *Lymnaea* (*Radix*) *pereger*, *Valvata piscinalis* and *Planorbis* (*Gyraulus*) *albus* are the most abundant species in the vegetation zone but other species, such as *Planorbis* (*Bathyomphalus*) *contortus*, *P.* (*Gyraulus*) *laevis*, *P.* (*Anisus*) *leucostoma*, *Physa fontinalis* and the limpet *Acroloxus lacustris*, which are more typical and abundant in richer conditions, may also occur. *Sphaerium corneum* and

several *Pisidium* spp. are found in this zone, both climbing among the shoots of the vegetation, and burrowing in the sediment. Hydracarina may be plentiful and weed-dwelling Entomostraca such as *Sida crystallina* and *Eurycercus lamellatus* often occur in huge numbers amongst the submerged vegetation, but few large crustacea are found at this depth. *Gammarus* (*Gammaracanthus*) *lacustris* or *G.* (*Rivulogammarus*) *pulex* may be found among weed, but are more characteristic of the wave-washed littoral zone. *Asellus* spp. are found in small numbers in a few of the richer lakes but are not characteristic members of the fauna.

Where the bottom substrate is of silt or mud the mayfly nymph *Caenis horaria* is found, but is replaced by *C. moesta* where the substrate changes to sand. The typical mayfly fauna of weed-beds in oligotrophic lakes consists of *Centroptilum luteolum*, *Cloeon simile*, *Leptophlebia vespertina*, *Ephemerella ignita* and *Siphlonurus lacustris*. Few stoneflies are found in the silted conditions of this zone, *Nemoura* spp. perhaps being the most common.

Dragonflies are not usually found in the larger lakes in Britain but will occur where sheltered bays produce suitable conditions for emergence and breeding and in the smaller oligotrophic lakes. They are then usually associated with vegetation and in oligotrophic lakes the most frequent species are *Enallagma cyathigerum*, *Pyrrhosoma nymphula* and *Libellula quadrimaculata*, which are widespread and adaptable.

The aquatic Hemiptera must visit the surface to respire and are thus mostly restricted to shallow water. Of the submerging species *Glaenocorisa propinqua* extends to greater depths than others and is the characteristic species of the sublittoral zone of oligotrophic lakes. Shallow-water species such as *Sigara distincta* and *S. scotti* also occur. The aquatic beetles are also restricted to relatively shallow water but a few species, such as *Deronectes* (*Potamonectes*) *depressus* and *Haliplus fulvus*, will occur in deeper water among vegetation. The larvae of the alderfly *Sialis lutaria* are found throughout this zone wherever silt, mud or peat accumulates.

The net-spinning caddis larvae *Cyrnus flavidus* and *Polycentropus flavomaculatus* occur in vegetation, together with a variety of cased species. The latter include a number of Limnephilidae such as *Limnephilus lunatus* and *Anabolia nervosa*. The Leptoceridae are also well represented by *Mystacides azurea*, *Athripsodes aterrimus*, *Triaenodes bicolor* and others. Other caddises commonly found are the predatory *Phryganea* spp., and the small hydroptilid *Oxyethira costalis* which are associated with vegetation, and *Molanna angustata* which is typically found on sandy bottoms.

Several weed-dwelling Chironomidae occur, including tube-building forms such as *Stempellina*, *Cricotopus* and *Endochironomus*. In the underlying silty substrate there are several genera of Chironominae, though *Chironomus* itself is usually absent from oligotrophic waters. This is the typical *Tanytarsus* zone. Free-living *Procladius* and *Anatopynia* are found in both the weeds and mud and *Tipula* spp. occur in small numbers wherever organic muds accumulate.

The fauna of the sheltered shoreline, where fine deposits

are found and emergent vegetation such as *Carex rostrata* often occurs, differs little from that of the deeper sub-littoral. Dragonflies, corixids such as *Sigara scotti* and *S. distincta*, and some of the water beetles such as *Platambus maculatus* and several *Hydroporus* spp. are more frequent in the shallow water. In contrast to the open water the surface film is calm enough in this habitat to support surface dwelling insects such as Collembola, *Gerris lacustris*, *G. odontogaster*, *Gyrinus marinus* and *G. aeratus*.

As well as the true benthos, there is also a community of cladocerans and copepods which lives inshore swimming near the bottom or amongst macrophytes of the sublittoral zone. Even in oligotrophic lakes this community can be very varied with a large number of species. A typical constituent, especially in high-altitude, rock-shored lakes is *Alonopsis elongata*, a species with a northerly distribution. This community also contains several species such as *Chydorus sphaericus*, *Alona* spp., *Diaphanosoma brachyurum* and *Cyclops* (*Paracyclops*) *fimbriatus*, which are not selective in their choice of habitat and are consequently found in nearly every water-body. Where there is submerged vegetation, species such as *Sida crystallina*, *Eurycercus lamellatus*, *Ceriodaphnia* spp., *Peracantha truncata* and *Cyclops* (*Megacyclops*) *viridis* can be extremely abundant and form a major component of the fish diet. *Ophryoxus gracilis* and *Eurycercus glacialis* are Arctic species found in a few cold lakes in the north of Scotland.

In the littoral zone the nature of the flora and fauna is largely dependent upon the degree of exposure to wave action. On the relatively sheltered shores where the bottom consists of stones, gravel, or sand in depths of 1 m or less, the plant communities consist predominantly of rosette-leaved species such as *Isoetes lacustris*, *Littorella uniflora*, *Lobelia dortmanna* and *Subularia aquatica*, with emergent *Juncus bulbosus*, *J. articulatus* and *Ranunculus flammula* at the water's edge. On more exposed shores where the substrate is of stable boulders or bedrock, the macrophytic flora is restricted to bryophytes such as *Fontinalis antipyretica* and *Jungermannia cordifolia*. In both these situations the substrate is generally covered by a film of epilithic diatoms and desmids, while filamentous algae belonging to the genera *Mougeotia*, *Zygnema*, *Spirogyra*, *Microspora* and *Hormidium* may also be present. In the most exposed situations where the shorelines consist of unstable storm beaches, macrophytic vegetation cannot gain a footing and even the epilithic film of algae may be removed by abrasion in storms.

The physical conditions in the stable wave-washed stony shoreline of large oligotrophic lakes approximate to those of eroding rivers with moving, well-oxygenated water, and a clean silt-free substrate. This enables a number of riverine species of invertebrate to exist here also. The invertebrates of this zone consist mainly of grazers feeding on the epilithic algae, and predators, while a few species are filter feeders and rely on the waves to bring particulate matter to them.

Stones may be encrusted on their undersides with the filter-feeding sponge *Ephydatia fluviatilis* and ectoprocts such as *Cristatella mucedo* and *Plumatella repens*. The triclads *Polycelis tenuis* and *P. nigra* are most abundant in this zone and, in some cold-water lakes in the north, are joined by *Crenobia alpina* (which elsewhere is a stream species). The typical and often most abundant mollusc of the stony shore is the freshwater limpet *Ancylus fluviatilis*, but the other soft-water gastropod species, especially *Lymnaea* (*Radix*) *pereger*, may also be present. *Pisidium* spp. and *Sphaerium corneum* occur only in small numbers where there is sufficient gravel in which to burrow. Nematodes, and tubificid and naidid worms, are also present in small numbers in the gravel but the most conspicuous oligochaetes of this zone are the larger *Eiseniella tetraedra* and *Stylodrilus heringianus*. Among the leeches the horse leech *Haemopis sanguisuga* is confined, in oligotrophic lakes, to stones in shallow water where the more adaptable soft-water species *Glossiphonia complanata*, *Erpobdella octoculata*, *Helobdella stagnalis* and *Piscicola geometra* also occur. Some Hydracarina are also found swimming amongst the stones. The only common malacostracan Crustacea on the stony shores are *Gammarus* spp. *G.* (*Rivulogammarus*) *lacustris* is the typical lacustrine species in the north, but south of its range in Britain the stream species *G.* (*R.*) *pulex* may take over this habitat. The latter is also often found in oligotrophic reservoirs which it has colonised from the inundated river. In lakes where the two species occur together *G.* (*R.*) *pulex* is generally confined to the areas near the mouths of streams and appears to be unable to compete against *G.* (*R.*) *lacustris* within the lake itself.

The most characteristic insects of the stony lake shore are the mayflies and stoneflies. Many species live in this habitat and some, such as Ecdyonuridae and most stone-flies, are adapted to living in water currents. The mayfly species are *Ecdyonurus dispar*, *Heptagenia lateralis*, *Leptophlebia marginata*, *Ephemerella ignita*, *Centroptilum luteolum* and *Siphlonurus lacustris*. In the far north of Scotland *Ameletus inopinatus*, which is a high-altitude stream species, is found on stony lake shores down to sea-level. Other true stream species such as *Baetis* spp. are occasionally found on lake shores in small numbers.

The most abundant stoneflies are *Chloroperla torrentium*, *Leuctra fusca*, *L. inermis*, *Nemoura avicularis* and *Diura bicaudata*. The last species has a peculiar distribution in that it is found in lakes at all altitudes but in streams only above 300 m. The nymphs of *Capnia bifrons* and *C. atra* occur only in autumn and winter, and the former species is confined to Scotland. *Isoperla grammatica* and *Perlodes microcephala* are stream dwellers which, in Scotland, occur only on lake shores. *Nemoura cambrica*, *N. erratica* and *Leuctra hippopus* are also stream-dwelling species found occasionally in lakes.

Micronecta poweri often swims just above the bottom in large numbers, particularly in sandy areas, and *Sigara distincta* occasionally also occurs. The beetles of the stony lake shore are also found in rivers. The larvae and adults of helmids such as *Elmis aenea*, *Limnius volckmari* and *Oulimnius tuberculatus* are found in the gravel often several centimetres below the surface, while the adults of species such as *Oreodytes rivalis* and *Haliplus lineolatus* swim over the bottom, although their larvae are benthic.

The stony cases of *Agapetus fuscipes* frequently coat the stones of the littoral zone of oligotrophic lakes while other caddises such as *Tinodes waeneri* and *Lype phaeopa* live in silk tubes secreted on the surface of the stones. The adults of *Tinodes* often swarm in a band along the shores of large oligotrophic lakes. The Polycentropidae, of which *Plectrocnemia conspersa*, *P. geniculata* and *Polycentropus flavomaculatus* are the most frequent species occurring, live under and between the stones where they spin their nets. The mobile case-dwelling caddises of the exposed shore mostly have sturdy heavy cases of sand particles and include some Limnephilidae, *Sericostoma personatum* and *Molanna angustata*. The small *Hydroptila* spp. may also be found here.

Various chironomids inhabit the shoreline but little is known of the species composition. Orthocladiinae, Tanypodinae and Tanytarsini are amongst the groups present and the larvae of the tipulids *Dicranota* spp. and *Pedicia* spp. burrow deeply into the sand and gravel beneath stones.

On unstable storm beaches there is little organic matter on which invertebrates can feed; erosion and the frequent movement of the substrate makes it difficult for them to remain attached to the bottom and there is the danger of the animals being crushed. Most animals living in this habitat are therefore either deep burrowers, which escape the movement of the substrate by penetrating the more stable gravel below the mobile surface, or are strong swimmers living for the most part above the level of the stones. Included in the first category are the worms *Eiseniella tetraedra* and *Stylodrilus heringianus*, dipteran larvae such as *Dicranota*, *Pedicia* and certain chironomids, and adults and larvae of the helmid beetles *Oulimnius tuberculatus* and *Limnius volckmari*. The last two are small and have a strong hard exoskeleton which resists crushing by the stones, while the worms and diptera larvae are leathery and elastic. Among the species which swim over the substrate are *Gammarus*, *Micronecta poweri* and a number of beetles such as *Oreodytes rivalis*. A few stoneflies, mayflies and caddises of the stable stony shore may also cling precariously to the stones of the storm beach or wander over sandy areas.

MESOTROPHIC STANDING WATERS

Mesotrophic lakes are a relatively small series, intermediate in all respects between oligotrophic lakes and eutrophic lakes. In Britain they are frequently situated on the borders between uplands and lowlands where run off from base-poor rocks is slightly enriched by drainage from the more calcareous soils of the lower lying areas of the catchment. Drainage from the base-poor Tertiary sands of southern England also produces mesotrophic water.

The most productive large glacial trough lakes in Britain are mesotrophic, as are the least productive examples of kettle-hole lakes. In lowland Britain, a few mesotrophic lakes have been formed by coastal processes while others are of artificial origin. Mesotrophic lakes sometimes represent a successional stage between oligotrophic and eutrophic

conditions, but they may occasionally evolve into more oligotrophic waters where peripheral mire development isolates them from ground water.

Since mesotrophic lakes generally occur in regions of somewhat softer rocks than oligotrophic lakes, their shorelines tend to be of finer particles, often of gravel or sand instead of stones and boulders. They are frequently shallow and rarely have steeply shelving shorelines, so that emergent vegetation may extend well out into the water and some hydroseral progression may take place. Phytoplankton production is sufficiently high to cause discolouration of the water in summer and produces a significant contribution to the bottom mud in the form of dead algal cells. The deep-water mud is thus intermediate in character between the largely allochthonous *dy* muds of oligotrophic lakes and the largely autochthonous *gyttja* muds found on the bottom of eutrophic lakes. The sediment of mesotrophic lakes has thus been termed *dy–gyttja*. In the deeper examples, where thermal stratification takes place, the decay of the algal crop in the hypolimnion may cause some depletion of oxygen during the summer months. This may cause conversion of the ferric salts in the *dy–gyttja* to the ferrous state and thus allow the release of phosphorus from the sediment.

The phytoplankton of these lakes is also intermediate, in production and species composition between oligotrophic and eutrophic lakes, and species of algae characteristic of both types of lake may occur. Diatoms generally predominate in the spring, *Asterionella formosa* being a characteristic species, but the algal blooms produced by blue-green algae in late summer in eutrophic lakes do not generally occur.

The composition of the zooplankton community is similar to that of oligotrophic lakes except that species such as *Bythotrephes longimanus* and *Holopedium gibberum*, which are confined to the most nutrient-poor lakes, are absent. The zooplankton is, however, much denser and, in southern Britain, species characteristic of eutrophic conditions may be present. *Bosmina longirostris* replaces *B. coregoni*, a characteristic species of oligotrophic waters, although in some mesotrophic waters both species may exist. This change-over has occurred in recent years in a few oligotrophic lakes where the nutrient levels have been increased by man's activities.

The most striking qualitative change in the composition of the profundal benthic fauna of mesotrophic lakes, as compared to the oligotrophic situation, is the appearance of a number of species of invertebrate adapted to the somewhat anaerobic conditions which prevail in the *dy–gyttja* muds in the summer months. These include haemoglobin pigmented species such as the tubifid *Potamothrix hammoniensis* and *Chironomus* spp. such as *C. anthracinus*, *C. (Camptochironomus) tentans* and *C. cingulatus*. All these have appeared in recent years in oligotrophic lakes which have suffered from artificial eutrophication. Another characteristic species adapted to living in the oxygen-depleted hypolimnia of mesotrophic lakes is the phantom midge larva *Chaoborus flavicans* which lives partly in the plankton and partly in the bottom mud. *Asellus meridianus* and *A. aquaticus*, although more frequent in the sublittoral zone, may extend down into the profundal where they can survive very low oxygen concentrations. In quantitative terms the profundal fauna is much more abundant and productive in mesotrophic lakes.

Because of the restricted light penetration, the profundal zone extends into shallower water and submerged plants are confined to depths of 6 m or less. With increasing alkalinity and nutrient content the number of macrophyte species in a lake generally increases. Most of the species of oligotrophic lakes are also found under suitable conditions in mesotrophic lakes with the exception of the acidophilous *Sphagnum* spp., *Eriophorum angustifolium* and *Utricularia minor*. In addition there are a number of species more or less restricted to mesotrophic lakes together with those which are more characteristic of the eutrophic environment but which will tolerate relatively low ionic concentrations. Species characteristic of the mesotrophic condition include *Isoetes echinospora* (which may replace *I. lacustris*), *Pilularia globulifera*, *Elatine hexandra* and *E. hydropiper*, the last being far more common on sandy shores than was previously believed. Among the species also found in the eutrophic environment which will penetrate into mesotrophic lakes are the submerged species, *Chara* spp., *Elodea canadensis*, *Potamogeton praelongus*, *P. obtusifolius* and *P. alpinus*. Emergent marginal communities are usually more diverse in species and more vigorous in growth than those of oligotrophic lakes. Fen communities may develop at the inflows of streams or in sheltered bays, the hydroseral progression being very variable, and in sheltered or ungrazed conditions the most typical emergents are plants such as *Phragmites communis*, *Phalaris arundinacea*, *Typha* spp., various carices, and *Schoenoplectus lacustris*. Under certain conditions successions from floating-leaved communities through to *Menyanthes trifoliata*, *Potentilla palustris* and *Juncus* spp. occur. In conditions of heavy grazing, bryophyte-dominated communities may develop around the margins of mesotrophic lakes, with bryophytes such as *Acrocladium cuspidatum*, and low-growing herbs such as *Myosotis secunda*, *Hydrocotyle vulgaris* and *Galium palustre*. In more exposed conditions the marginal communities of mesotrophic lakes may be very similar to those of oligotrophic waters. One of the most characteristic communities of the moderately exposed shoreline with a substrate varying from gravel to a loam is a dense sward of *Littorella uniflora* which is often exposed at periods of low water. This community also extends into lakes belonging to the poorer end of the eutrophic spectrum.

Filamentous algae are more abundant than in oligotrophic lakes and may coat the submerged macrophytes, and *Cladophora*, the most abundant filamentous species in eutrophic lakes, may be present.

The fauna of the sublittoral zone is more diverse and much more abundant than in oligotrophic waters. The increased diversity arises mostly from the addition of species associated with richer conditions. These newcomers include the triclads *Dendrocoelum lacteum* and *Dugesia lugubris* which are restricted to waters whose calcium content is greater than 10 p.p.m. (This restriction is probably associated with the distribution of their prey organisms which

are respectively, *Asellus* and gastropods.) The soft-water mollusc species found in oligotrophic waters become more abundant and, as the calcium content increases, are joined by species such as *Acroloxus lacustris*, *Planorbis carinatus* and the duck mussel, *Anodonta anatina*. As with the triclads the distribution of the mollusc-feeding leech *Glossiphonia heteroclita* is linked to that of its prey. This species and the fish leech *Hemiclepsis marginata*, which are absent from oligotrophic waters, occur in mesotrophic lakes together with the leech species which extend into the poorer waters. The distribution of the Malacostraca is closely linked to the ionic content of water-bodies, species such as *Asellus aquaticus*, *A. meridianus* and the introduced American species, *Crangonyx pseudogracilis*, appearing in mesotrophic waters, and *Gammarus* spp. becoming more abundant.

In the Ephemeroptera there is an increased abundance of those species associated with macrophytes. The weed-dwelling *Cloeon dipterum* appears, and where there are silted conditions, *Ephemera danica* may be found and the numbers of weed-dwelling dragonfly nymphs such as *Ischnura elegans* and *Enallagma cyathigerum* increase. A number of species of water bug absent from the poorer lakes appear in mesotrophic waters. *Sigara falleni* and *Callicorixa praeusta* are associated with relatively open conditions amongst vegetation whilst *Hesperocorixa sahlbergi* is found in the thicker parts of the marginal vegetation and *Corixa punctata* is a typical species of weedy ponds. *Sigara scotti* and *S. distincta* decline in mesotrophic waters and are not found in rich lakes.

The weed-dwelling species of caddis generally increase in numbers and variety in mesotrophic waters. Most of the species of oligotrophic lakes are probably encountered. Phryganeidae, Limnephilidae, Leptoceridae and Hydroptilidae are often present in variety and abundance and large numbers and many species of Chironomidae occur, up to 100 species having been found in one small lake. *Chironomus* spp., *Ablabesmyia* spp. (particularly *A. cingulata*), *Procladius* spp. (particularly *P. choreus*), *Cricotopus* spp., *Psectrocladius* spp., *Dicrotendipes* spp., *Cryptochironomus* spp. *Endochironomus albipennis*, *Microtendipes chloris*, *Pentapedilum* spp. and Tanytarsini typically form the major components of the chironomid fauna.

The extent of the wave-washed littoral zone may be limited in mesotrophic lakes by their increased tendency to silting and by the encroachment of marginal vegetation around the shorelines. Storm beaches are generally absent and the bryophyte communities associated with stable exposed shores in oligotrophic lakes may be missing. The most exposed shores are often of gravel or sand, the pebbles being covered with growths of algae, particularly *Cladophora*, in which a layer of silt is trapped. *Littorella uniflora* often grows between the stones on this type of shoreline.

Because of the more silted nature of the shoreline in mesotrophic lakes, invertebrate species requiring a clean, firm, wave-washed substrate are scarce or absent. Species which are generally rare or absent include mayflies such as the Ecdyonuridae and *Ameletus inopinatus* and most of the stoneflies, including *Diura bicaudata* and *Capnia atra*, although *Chloroperla torrentium* may be plentiful even in relatively silted conditions in rich lakes.

Many of the species found in the sublittoral extend into the littoral, including especially the gastropods, leeches, malacostracans, caddises and chironomids. Polycentropid caddises are often very abundant under the stones of gravel shores, while *Molanna angustata* is characteristic where the shoreline is sandy. Even species such as *Chironomus* spp. and various tubificids which are more characteristic of the profundal may find a niche in the littoral zone by burrowing in the silt accumulated between stones.

EUTROPHIC STANDING WATERS

Most of the lakes of lowland Britain belong to this category and only a few examples in areas of upland limestone lie at altitudes over 300 m. They are found mostly in areas of glacial deposition where they were often formed as kettle-holes or as valleys dammed by moraines. Because of the generally calcareous nature of marine sediments nearly all lakes formed by coastal deposition and now cut-off from the sea are eutrophic. In eastern and southern England there were formerly extensive freshwater marshes and fens containing natural eutrophic lakes such as Whittlesea Mere, but these have virtually disappeared as a result of drainage. Their place has been taken by artificial water-bodies such as the Norfolk Broads and various reservoirs and gravel pits which are now the most common eutrophic lakes in this part of the country.

None of the large, deep, glacial trough lakes in the north and west of Britain is eutrophic and, as a group, eutrophic lakes tend to be both smaller and shallower than oligo-trophic lakes. Because of their generally small size (and therefore lack of exposure to wind action) and the rather soft rocks on which they are usually formed, the shorelines are normally of fine sediments of mud or silt. Only in the extremely exposed, large eutrophic lakes of northern Scotland (e.g. Loch Watten) do wave-washed rocky shores form an important part of the habitat. The deep surface deposits of glacial sands, silts and clays in the lowlands are more readily transported than the shallower and coarser deposits of the uplands. Lowland rivers thus carry far heavier silt loads, and the lakes into which they flow fill more rapidly with sediments. The progression of the hydrosere is therefore much more rapid since there is usually a continuous accretion of a suitable substratum for plant colonisation. Once areas of silt of suitable depth for colonisation by aquatic macrophytes have been deposited, the high productivity of eutrophic waters ensures a rapid build up of organic sediments derived from the decay of these plants and algae, in addition to organic material from the productive surrounding land.

In deeper eutrophic lakes phytoplankton is the main primary producer and the dense concentration of algae may so occlude the penetration of light that higher plants are confined to the shallowest water (sometimes less than 1 m). The bottom sediment in deep water is derived largely from the decay of autochthonous organic material, particularly phytoplankton but also invertebrates and macrophytes, and

generally consists of a black or brown flocculent *gyttja*-type mud. Its high organic content and the ready supply of nutrients encourages the development of a rich microflora which forms a plentiful food source for invertebrates. The bacterial activity causes deoxygenation within the mud, although the surface may be oxidised by contact with well-oxygenated water, leading to the development of a black sulphide horizon which may vary in depth from the surface. Few animals and plants can live in this black anaerobic layer because of the presence of toxic hydrogen sulphide. In deep eutrophic lakes where thermal stratification takes place in the summer months the bacterial activity of the mud causes the complete deoxygenation of the hypolimnion which is isolated from the surface of the lake by an overlying warmer aerobic epilimnion. Under these anaerobic conditions phosphate is released from the mud and with the breakdown of the stratification in the autumn becomes dispersed throughout the lake water. Thus this essential nutrient is recycled from sediment to water each year and is available for phytoplankton production in the spring. In the summer months the deoxygenated hypolimnion of deep eutrophic lakes may be virtually devoid of life, except anaerobic bacteria.

Deep eutrophic lakes which stratify are rare in Britain and in most eutrophic lakes the surface of the *gyttja* remains oxidised, and supports an abundant invertebrate fauna. Deoxygenation can, however, occur even in the shallowest of eutrophic lakes when the supply of oxygen at the water surface is cut-off during periods of prolonged ice cover, but this is relatively rare in Britain. In the most productive of eutrophic lakes particularly those artificially enriched by nutrients overnight deoxygenation may occur on rare occasions because of the respiration of heavy algal crops and this may lead to fish kills. Considerable quantities of phosphorus may be locked in the sediments of shallow eutrophic lakes and only be available to rooted plants within the photic zone. Wind action disturbing the bottom mud may be the major factor in recycling nutrients in these lakes.

Both the biomass and production of phytoplankton are much greater than in oligotrophic lakes, with chlorophyll *a* concentrations ranging from about 30 to 250 mg/m^3 and maximum cell numbers of the order of hundreds to thousands per millilitre, or in the case of nannoplankton even hundred thousands per millilitre. The gross primary production is of the order of 50 to 250 g organic carbon/m^2 of lake surface per year.

The phytoplankton is characterised by the abundance of diatoms in late winter or spring, notably species of *Stephanodiscus*, *Asterionella*, *Fragilaria*, *Melosira*, *Synedra* and *Diatoma*, and in summer also by the presence of the very characteristic *Melosira granulata* and *M. ambigua* which is especially associated with the Norfolk Broads.

The blue-green algae Cyanophyta are generally very abundant. In spring, or in winter under ice, *Oscillatoria* species are characteristic with, for example, *O. rubescens*, the famous indicator of eutrophication. But in Britain the *O. agardii* complex occurs much more commonly. These species retreat to the deeper water in late spring and early summer and may produce oxygen maxima there. *Oscillatoria redekei* is also characteristic (e.g. in Loch Leven, Kinross, and Lough Neagh, NI) but does not retreat to deeper water. In summer and autumn, water blooms of *Anabaena, Gomphosphaeria, Aphanizomenon* and *Microcystis* are common, the last being especially common in strongly eutrophic lakes. Dinoflagellates may also be abundant, notably *Ceratium hirundinella*, but *C. cornutum* is usually absent.

Chrysophyta are less prominent but species such as *Chrysochromulina parva* and *Prymnesium parvum* may be abundant, though *Dinobryon* and *Uroglena* are usually characteristic absentees. Chlorophyta too may be common, notably species of *Eudorina, Pandorina* and, especially in shallow waters such as the Norfolk Broads, *Scenodesmus* and other Chlorococcales. Desmids are rare with a restricted range of species (e.g. *Staurastrum chaetoceros*) and usually the more eutrophic the water the less prominent are the desmids.

Euglenophyta are found mainly in polluted waters but *Trachelomonas* is not uncommon in unpolluted eutrophic lakes in autumn, around the time of the overturn of stratification. Cryptophyta occur in all kinds of lakes and in eutrophic lakes they are at times very numerous and may be the dominant group.

As in oligotrophic lakes there is a seasonal succession of plankton with diatoms, often together with *Oscillatoria* and *Cryptophyta* predominating from late winter to summer, and blue-green algae, certain green algae and *Ceratium hirundinella* predominating in late summer and autumn. At times big growths of diatoms, notably *Melosira granulata* and *M. ambigua*, may also occur in the summer.

In lakes which are artificially enriched or polluted, the plankton is often dominated by nannoplankton, especially green algae, so that the water itself may be deep green. Plankton production is limited mainly by light, lack of carbon and high pH values produced by changes in the carbonate/bicarbonate equilibrium owing to excessive photosynthetic activity. Such waters are similar to sewage oxidation ponds. The summer biomass of phytoplankton lies at the upper limits given for eutrophic lakes, with maximum cell numbers in the thousands to millions per millilitre. Gross primary production is of the order of 300 to 700 g organic carbon/m² of lake surface per year.

In eutrophic lakes in the north of Britain the true open water zooplankton may not differ much in composition from that of oligotrophic waters although the quantity is greater. As one progresses south-east, certain new species appear and may replace those found in the more northerly waters. In lakes in the south *Cyclops vicinus* is the commonest planktonic *Cyclops* sp. and replaces *C. strenuus abyssorum*. Other species of *Cyclops* such as *C. (Mesocyclops) leuckarti* and *C. (Macrocyclops) fuscus* may replace *C. vicinus*, and in the Norfolk Broads *C. strenuus* s. str. and *C. (Thermocyclops) hyalinus* are the dominant copepods. *Diaptomus (Eudiaptomus) gracilis* is usually the commonest of the *Diaptomus* spp. but *D. (E.) vulgaris* may also be present. *Daphnia cucullata* var. *apicata* is the common daphniid, and *Cerio*

daphnia spp. occur alongside or replace *Daphnia hyalina*, and in a few weedy shallow lakes *D. magna* may be the dominant member of the Daphniidae.

In small ponds, if a true zooplankton exists, the species composition is very different from that of the larger eutrophic waters. *Daphnia hyalina* is usually absent from ponds and is replaced by *D. pulex, D. longispina, D. obtusa* or *D. magna*. The planktonic copepod fauna of similar situations includes *Cyclops (Acanthocyclops) vernalis, C. (Diacyclops) bisetosus, C. (Diacyclops) bicuspidatus* and *Diaptomus castor*, the last three being especially associated with temporary pools. *Simocephalus vetulus, S. exspinosus, Ceriodaphnia megalops, C. reticulata, C. laticaudata, Sida crystallina, Eurycercus lamellatus* and *Cyclops (Megacyclops) viridis* and various harpacticoids occur amongst weed-beds, both in ponds and the sheltered parts of larger eutrophic lakes.

The productivity of the profundal benthos is much greater than that of oligotrophic waters and is illustrated by comparing their standing crops. In the nutrient-rich Loch Leven, Kinross, the standing crop of the macrobenthos of the mud at 5 m is 100 times that at the same depth in the nutrient-poor Loch Rannoch (37 g/m² wet weight compared with 0.36 g/m²). Similarly the diversity of species is usually far greater in eutrophic lakes. This diversity also increases as one moves south in Britain since many species have been unable to disperse northwards. Eutrophic waters in the far north of Britain which are isolated from other eutrophic water-bodies by extensive tracts of unproductive upland may not have many more species than neighbouring oligotrophic waters. In deeper water of eutrophic lakes where anaerobic conditions develop during the summer, the fauna of the mud is restricted to specialised species, or the macro-benthos is absent (as in the deeper water of Rostherne Mere, where only dormant copepods are found in summer). The species tolerating these anaerobic conditions are often the same forms which can exist in organically polluted situations. Nematodes, haemoglobin-containing tubificids, *Chironomus* spp. and *Asellus aquaticus* are the characteristic forms of both sets of conditions.

Since eutrophic lakes tend to be smaller and more sheltered than oligotrophic lakes and are more turbid, plant growth does not extend into such deep water. Consequently the profundal zone normally extends into much shallower water. The invertebrate fauna of the profundal consists mainly of burrowing forms but some such as *Hydra*, which may on occasion be abundant, live on the mud surface. Mollusca are better represented in numbers and species than in the profundal zone of nutrient-poor lakes. Several species of *Pisidium* and *Sphaerium* may occur in the same water-body and in many of the lakes of southern England the introduced zebra mussel *Dreissena polymorpha* forms thick beds in the bottom muds. The most abundant snails in deeper water are the operculate species, *Potamopyrgus jenkinsi, Valvata piscinalis, V. cristata, Viviparus viviparus* and *V. fasciatus* plus a few pulmonate snails such as *Lymnaea (Radix) pereger, Segmentina complanata* and *Planorbis (Gyraulus) albus*. Oligochaetes are frequently the most abundant group and together with the chironomids form the bulk of the biomass. Among the commonest species are *Tubifex tubifex*, *Limnodrilus hoffmeisteri* and *Potamothrix hammoniensis*. *Helobdella stagnalis* is the most ubiquitous and abundant leech though several other species characteristic of the sublittoral zone may extend on to the mud. Hydracarina are often quite abundant, swimming at the mud–water interface. The only Malacostraca of this zone are *Asellus* spp. and in some places the introduced North American *Crangonyx pseudogracilis*. No stoneflies are found here and characteristically the only mayfly is *Caenis horaria* but, where the bottom consists largely of an inorganic silt, *Ephemera danica* may occur. Corixids and water beetles typical of the sublittoral may be found in the profundal zone where this extends into shallow water. The alderfly larva *Sialis lutaria* reaches its maximum abundance under these conditions. A few Trichoptera are found but mainly species straying from weed-beds.

The most abundant culicid is *Chaoborus flavicans* which is particularly plentiful in the larger deeper lakes where it migrates into the zooplankton at night. Biting midge larvae, Ceratopogonidae, occur in small numbers but are not very significant. Many species of chironomid found in mesotrophic conditions occur in eutrophic lakes but in greater quantities, *Chironomus* spp., such as *C. anthracinus*, *C. plumosus* and *C. riparius*, forming the bulk of the Chironomidae of the mud.

In these lakes the macrophytic vegetation of the sublittoral zone attains its maximum diversity and productivity. However, in some lakes receiving high nutrient loads, the growth of macrophytes may be poor, and rich growths of phytoplankton may develop. In several of the Norfolk Broads submerged macrophytes have recently disappeared. The mechanism of this change-over is imperfectly understood but once dense phytoplankton has established itself the return of macrophytes is unlikely as seedling growth from the bottom would be completely shaded out.

The plants reaching greatest depths are *Chara* spp., which may be shade-adapted, and tall-growing plants such as *Potamogeton praelongus* and *Myriophyllum spicatum* which reach towards the surface. A wide range of *Potamogeton* spp. such as *P. pectinatus*, *P. filiformis*, *P. lucens* and *P. berchtoldii* are restricted to eutrophic waters where together with species like *Zannichellia palustris*, *Ceratophyllum* spp., *Elodea canadensis*, *Callitriche stagnalis* and *Lemna trisulca* they often form dense stands, completely choking the shallow water. The free-floating aquatic flora is, in Britain, practically restricted to eutrophic waters especially in sheltered conditions in ponds, ditches, reedbeds and bays. These communities generally consist of single-species-dominated mats of *Lemna* spp., *Riccia fluitans*, *Ricciocarpus natans*, *Azolla filiculoides*, *Stratiotes aloides*, *Hydrocharis morsus-ranae* and *Wolffia arrhiza*. There are few floating attached species restricted to eutrophic water, but *Polygonum amphibium* and *Nymphoides peltata* are characteristic of these situations, the former on fairly exposed shores and the latter in more sheltered conditions. *Potamogeton coloratus* although mostly submerged has surface-floating leaves which

may cover the surface of the water in eutrophic fen conditions and the more ubiquitous floating-leaved species of the Nymphaceae and *P. natans* also frequently form extensive stands in shallow, relatively sheltered, waters. Most lakes in this category have at least a partial fringe of emergent vegetation which frequently encroaches rapidly on the open water, initiating a seral succession which progresses typically through rich-fen to alder carr and which may culminate in deciduous woodland. This succession is modified by the effects of land use, especially grazing pressure. Certain species of emergent macrophyte are restricted to the margins of eutrophic waters, these include *Hippuris vulgaris*, *Sparganium erectum*, *Glyceria maxima*, *Butomus umbellatus*, *Acorus calamus*, *Carex pseudocyperus*, *C. acutiformis*, *C. riparia* and *Rumex hydrolapathum*. Other species of emergent hydrophyte which are encountered in the oligotrophic or mesotrophic situation but which form their most vigorous and extensive stands in eutrophic water include reed-swamp species such as *Phragmites communis*, *Typha latifolia*, *T. angustifolia*, *Iris pseudacorus*, *Schoenoplectus lacustris* and *Cladium mariscus*.

The sublittoral zone supports the most diverse and often the most abundant invertebrate fauna found in standing waters. The great diversity of habitat within this zone allows invertebrates with a wide range of life forms to exist here. Burrowing species are found in the mud in deeper water and a wide range of species are associated with the submerged floating-leaved and emergent plants: swimming forms find cover among the macrophytes; and the surface of the water may be sufficiently calm to support species dwelling in or on the surface film. In those lakes where the aquatic macrophytes have gone into decline the fauna is greatly impoverished by the loss of those species dependent on the vegetation for food and shelter and may resemble that of the profundal zone.

Hydra spp. may be plentiful attached to the vegetation. All British species of triclad and mollusc, except those confined to rivers, can be found in this habitat but it is seldom that all these species occur in the same water-body and the composition of this fauna can vary considerably even between neighbouring water-bodies. Most of the molluscs range over the bottom and the plants, feeding either on the algal film or directly on the plants themselves, but *Anodonta* spp. and *Unio* spp. are almost completely submerged in the sediment, usually where this is sandy, and feed on suspended matter by filtering the water.

The tubificid worms of the deep-water sediments extend to the sediments of the plant zone but the commonest worms among the plants are the Naididae of which *Stylaria lacustris* is often present in large numbers. It is among the vegetation of eutrophic waters that the leeches reach their maximum abundance and most of the British species may be found here. *Dina lineata* is confined to small temporary pools, at least in the south of its range, while *Erpobdella testacea* is found where deoxygenation is likely to take place. The horse leech *Haemopis sanguisuga* is more often associated with a stony shore than with vegetation while *Trocheta viridis* and *T. bykowskii* are partly terrestrial and not normally found in lakes. Many species of Hydracarina are to be found swimming amongst vegetation together with a wide range of entomostracans including chydorids such as *Chydorus* spp., *Alona* spp., *Alonella* spp., *Pleuroxus* spp., *Acroperus harpae* and *Eurycercus lamellatus*; *Cyclops* spp. (including *C. (Tropocyclops) prasinus*); harpacticoids such as *Canthocamptus*; and ostracods such as *Candona* spp., *Cypris* spp., *Cyclocypris* spp. and *Eucypris* spp. *Scapholeberis mucronata* is a specialised cladoceran which feeds below the surface film of quiet ponds and lakes and *Moina rectirostris* inhabits small often turbid, temporary pools. Of the larger crustacea *Asellus* spp. and *Crangonyx pseudogracilis* are often numerous but *Gammarus* spp. are generally few in numbers and confined to areas where wave action ensures a high oxygen content.

Few species of mayfly are found here but those that are may be present in large numbers. *Cloeon dipterum* and *C. simile* are the most abundant species, the former more common in the south and the latter in the north. *Centroptilum luteolum* is the only other species found in the vegetation itself but *Caenis horaria, C. moesta* and *Ephemera danica* are often abundant in the underlying sediments. Many species of dragonfly require emergent vegetation on which to lay their eggs and for the nymphs to climb from the water to metamorphose into adults and the nymphs of most species are found in beds of dense submerged vegetation. The widespread and adaptable species, *Ischnura elegans, Enallagma cyathigerum, Libellula quadrimaculata* and *Lestes sponsa* are common; other species such as *Erythromma najas, Brachytron pratense, Coenagrion puella, C. pulchellum, Aeshna cyanea, A. grandis, Anax imperator, Sympetrum sanguineum* and *Libellula depressa* are more or less restricted to weedy eutrophic waters in the southern half of Britain whilst *Coenagrion armatum* and *Aeshna isosceles* are confined to the Norfolk Broads.

The commonest corixids are *Sigara falleni, S. dorsalis, Callicorixa praeusta* and occasionally *Cymatia bonsdorffi* and *C. coleoptrata*. In small ponds and ditches these may be replaced by *Sigara nigrolineata, S. fossarun* and *S. limitata*; and, particularly where the water is fouled by organic matter, *Sigara lateralis*. In sparse vegetation, particularly on a sandy bottom, *Arctocorisa germari* and *Sigara dorsalis* may be the most abundant species and in dense reed-beds *Hesperocorixa sahlbergi* is generally found. All four of the British species of *Notonecta* are found in eutrophic pond-like conditions but *N. maculata* is restricted to the south of England. *Plea leachii, Ilyocoris cimicoides* and *Ranatra linearis*, which are weed dwellers, are also confined to the south, but the water scorpion *Nepa cinerea* is widespread.

So many species of water beetle are found among vegetation that it is difficult to define the most characteristic species. Hydrophilidae (e.g. *Helophorus*), Haliplidae and Hydroporini are particularly well represented as both adults and larvae. The aquatic larvae of the amphibious *Donacia* spp., are also found and the surface-swimming Gyrinidae are often abundant in sheltered conditions. Similarly there are a large number of species of caddis present belonging chiefly to the families Leptoceridae, Limnephilidae,

Phryganeidae, Hydroptilidae and Polycentopidae. The larvae of a few Lepidoptera feed on the floating leaves of aquatic plants, *Nymphula (Nausinoe) nymphaeata* for example on the leaves of Nymphaceae and other floating-leaved plants.

A large number and a wide variety of chironomid species are found living on and in the weeds and the bottom sediment. Prominent among those living on the plants are the tube-dwelling Orthocladiinae. Many other groups of Diptera larvae are also found, particularly in sheltered conditions. These include Psychodidae such as *Pericoma* spp., Culicidae such as *Dixa* spp., *Culex* spp., *Aedes* and *Anopheles*, Stratiomyidae, Syrphidae, Empididae, Dolichopodidae and the Sciomyzidae.

In sheltered conditions among emergent vegetation and where the banks are overhung by trees, a thick layer of slowly decomposing plant remains usually accumulates. The decomposition of the litter causes local deoxygenation and at certain times of the year the bottom may be coated with fungi. This habitat has a limited fauna including *Asellus* spp., oligochaetes, *Erpobdella testacea, Pisidium* spp., corixids, a few caddises such as *Glyphotaelius pellucidus, Chironomus* spp., *Sialis lutaria* and Hydracarina.

The stony littoral zone rarely forms a large proportion of the shoreline of eutrophic lakes in Britain and the stones of the shoreline are usually covered with a layer of silt. *Hydra* spp. are sometimes found in very large numbers attached to the stones; and triclads, molluscs and leeches, all of which prefer a firm substrate for attachment, are usually abundant. The species of these groups are the same as for the sublittoral zone with the addition of the limpet *Ancylus fluviatilis* and the leech *Haemopis sanguisuga. Gammarus* spp. occur in larger numbers here than in any other lacustrine habitat and, in some limestone lakes in England and Wales, the stream-dwelling crayfish *Astacus pallipes* may be plentiful. The commonest mayflies here are the two *Caenis* spp., *C. moesta* and *C. horaria*. Other fairly plentiful species are *Centroptilum luteolum, Cloeon simile* and *C. dipterum*, the last two being probably associated with filamentous algae in this habitat. Small numbers of *Siphlonurus lacustris* and *Ephemerella ignita* may be found in upland limestone lakes. The stoneflies found in oligotrophic lakes can also occur in this habitat in the more exposed parts of the shore but, as the stones become more silted, the number of species diminishes leaving only the more tolerant species such as *Chloroperla torrentium* and *Leuctra fusca*. The waterbugs *Micronecta poweri* (and in the south *M. scholtzi*), *Arctocorisa germari* and *Sigara dorsalis* are all abundant on these shores where *Sigara falleni* and *Callicorixa praeusta* are also frequently found. The stone-dwelling caddises include a number of polycentropids, including *Tinodes waeneri* which lives in tubes attached to stones; leptocerids, such as *Mystacides* spp. and *Athripsodes* spp.; and the hydroptilids, *Agraylea* spp., which make their cases out of filamentous algae. Coleoptera belonging to the genera *Deronectes, Oreodytes* and *Haliplus* occur, including *D. depressus/ elegans, O. rivalis, H. lineolatus* and *H. fluviatilis*, which are also found on mesotrophic and oligotrophic lake shores.

The larvae and adults of the Helmidae are found in the gravel between the stones.

Chironomidae are usually extremely abundant on the stones, all the subfamilies being represented, particularly those species which spin tubes on the surface of the stones.

In some eutrophic lakes the most exposed shorelines consist of sandy storm beaches. This zone of unstable sand which generally contains little organic matter and may extend down to 3 m has a limited and rather sparse fauna. Burrowing forms such as tubificid and naidid oligochaete worms, nematodes, Ceratopogonidae and some chironomids predominate. The chironomid fauna consists of a few non-tube-forming species such as *Stictochironomus* spp. and *Cryptochironomus* spp., the former being particularly able to survive in shifting sand conditions. The lamellibranchs *Pisidium* spp. and *Anodonta* spp. are sometimes plentiful in this zone, their shells no doubt affording protection from the scouring action of the sand under windy conditions. The species of corixid, water beetles and amphipods found on the stony shores are also found in small numbers scudding over the sand but *Micronecta* is the most characteristic animal and is sometimes present in very large numbers.

MARL LAKES

Marl lakes are confined to scattered areas of soluble limestone and chalk where precipitation of calcium carbonate takes place. This precipitate, termed marl, is produced mainly as a result of the removal of carbon dioxide from the water by the photosynthetic activity of aquatic plants, both algae and macrophytes, which results in the shifting of the bicarbonate/carbonate equilibrium towards carbonate. As calcium carbonate is very insoluble it is precipitated in those lakes where calcium is by far the most abundant cation. The precipitation of marl also has other effects; phosphorus is precipitated in the form of various insoluble compounds and becomes unavailable to phytoplankton. The low levels of dissolved carbon dioxide may also limit the phytoplankton production and organic matter in suspension becomes bound to the marl and is sedimented out. As a result the water is the clearest of any category of lake in Britain and has a very characteristic blue tint. Although the phosphorus is unavailable to phytoplankton, rooted macrophytes are able to obtain it from the sediment, and they may be extremely abundant to great depths. The bottom sediment in deep water is generally very low in organic material, being composed largely of calcium carbonate, so there is little available food for benthic invertebrates. In shallower water in the macrophyte zone the marl deposit is mixed with a proportion of organic material derived from the decay of the plants and though this mud is generally anaerobic below the surface it may support a relatively abundant invertebrate fauna. The most productive invertebrate communities are those associated with the macrophytes and the littoral zone.

Unlike eutrophic lakes, marl lakes are found in both the upland and lowland areas of Britain, those in the upland areas may be stony shored, steep-sided and deep, thus, in morphometry, resembling oligotrophic lakes. Many marl lakes have been formed by karst erosion while others occupy small glacial troughs and some of these may be relatively deep. Shallower examples are found in areas of highly calcareous sand or shell marl, while in southern England only artificial examples occur. In many respects, although they are highly calcareous, marl lakes are oligotrophic in nature.

The phytoplankton is very sparse, but there are insufficient data to give figures for biomass. Judging from American work, however, gross production is of the order of 0.5–5 g of organic carbon/m² of lake surface per year (i.e. at the lower end of the range of oligotrophic lakes). The species composition of the phytoplankton is similar to that of mesotrophic or eutrophic lakes.

The zooplankton is also generally very sparse, but the species composition is rather variable. In the northern marl lakes species typical of oligotrophic lakes may be present (although not species such as *Holopedium* and *Bythotrephes*) while in lakes in southern Britain, species typical of eutrophic conditions are found. *Bosmina coregoni* has been found in Scottish marl lakes but *B. longirostris* is the species found in the lakes of southern England and Wales.

Where the bottom mud consists primarily of inorganic marl the biomass of invertebrates in the profundal zone may be very low, but where aquatic macrophytes contribute a significant quantity of organic material a relatively rich invertebrate fauna exists. In the latter case some deoxygenation may take place in the hypolimnion and species such as *Chironomus* spp., tubificids and *Chaoborus flavicans*, characteristic of the profundal of eutrophic lakes, are present. In the less productive marl lakes a profundal fauna similar to that of oligotrophic lakes is found, but *C. flavicans* appears to be a constant member of the deep-water fauna.

Aquatic vegetation colonises to greater depths than in lake types other than the clearest oligotrophic, and some marl lakes may be the most productive of all standing waters for higher plants. *Fontinalis antipyretica* has been recorded as growing down to 12 m in one such British lake but, generally, aquatic macrophytes are restricted to less than 6 m. *Chara* spp. attain their greatest importance and may dominate the submerged communities from the shoreline down to the limit of plant growth. A large number of *Chara* spp. occur but none appears to be restricted to this type of lake. Short-growing species such as *C. aspera* and *C. delicatula* may be found in the shallower water while in deeper water more robust species such as *C. aculeolata* and *C. hispida* may dominate. As well as the Characeae a wide range of submerged angiosperms may also be prolific, all the species found in eutrophic lakes being encountered. Since many marl lakes are rather steeper sided, and in the north more exposed and rocky than typical eutrophic lakes, the extent of the shallow-water marginal vegetation is generally rather limited and the rate of hydroseral progression is low. In extreme cases, as at the Durness lochs in Sutherland, the shorelines are of wave-washed limestone rocks with only very scattered growths of *Eleocharis palustris*, *Equisetum fluviatile* and *Cinclodotus fontinaloides*. In more sheltered examples aquatic transition successions more typical of eutrophic lakes occur, and in these situations a marl composed of fragments of aquatic gastropod shells may contribute to or largely form the accreted material on which plant colonisation takes place.

Associated with the rich growth of submerged macrophytes is an abundant and diverse invertebrate fauna containing many of the species found in the sublittoral zone of eutrophic lakes. In the isolated northern and upland marl lakes, however, the fauna tends to be somewhat impoverished and certain groups may be absent or represented by only a few adaptable species (e.g. mayflies in Malham Tarn and molluscs in the Durness lochs). Molluscs are generally extremely abundant and are represented by a wide range of species; *Potamopyrgus jenkinsi*, a recent maritime colonist of fresh water, is nowadays found in its greatest abundance in association with beds of *Chara* in marl lakes, where it may be present in enormous concentrations almost to the exclusion of other invertebrates. The beetle *Haliplus confinis* is another very typical associate of *Chara* in these conditions. The exposed littoral is a more important component of marl lakes than of eutrophic lakes, and whilst its stones are covered with encrustations of marl, they are usually relatively free from silt. Encrusting algae such as *Rivularia* and *Coleochaete*, which provide crevices and a relatively soft substrate for tunnel-forming invertebrates such as psychomyid caddises and orthoclad chironomids, are often prominent, as well as filamentous algae species found in eutrophic waters. Stoneflies and mayflies typical of exposed wave-washed shores in oligotrophic lakes may occur alongside invertebrates (including a wide variety of leeches and gastropods) of the littoral zone of eutrophic waters. *Gammarus* (*Rivulogammarus*) *lacustris* or *G.* (*R.*) *pulex* are frequently the most abundant invertebrates and the freshwater crayfish *Astacus pallipes* is characteristic of southern marl lakes and has been introduced farther north.

BRACKISH STANDING WATERS

Natural brackish standing waters in Britain are confined to coastal areas where fresh water mixes with sea water carried alternatively as sea spray, or ground water, or direct inflow via a tidal channel. Some artificial lakes in the Midlands are affected by discharge from salt mines and are distinctly brackish, while, in various parts of the country, there are a few, small, natural brackish springs in inland locations. As our climate has a large excess of rainfall over evaporation for most of the year none of our larger lakes evaporates sufficiently to become saline.

Because of the marine origin of all of our brackish lakes, the relative proportions of the major ions dissolved in this water are approximately the same as those for sea water, the only variations being those caused by differences in the chemical composition of the freshwater element of the water mix. Thus in areas of base-poor rocks the ratio of calcium to sodium is low, as generally is the concentration of dissolved plant nutrients, so that these might be termed oligotrophic brackish lakes. In areas of more soluble calcareous rocks the lakes are more alkaline and richer in nutrients and could be termed eutrophic brackish lakes. The differences between these two categories are only appreciable at the more dilute end of the salinity gradient; as the

salinity approaches that of sea water the chemical composition, physical properties and flora and fauna become more equivalent.

Although they comprise only a small group of lakes in Britain in many ways they are the most variable category of lake. Not only is there great variability in nutrient status and salinity but their morphology and origins are also diverse. In the north and west of Britain some relatively deep oligotrophic glacial troughs with only narrow openings to the sea are brackish at their inland ends. Other glacial lakes in this region are shallower and lie either on base-rich rocks, as do the brackish eutrophic lakes of Lochs Stenness and Harray on Orkney, or else lie on base-poor rocks as do the oligotrophic brackish lakes of the Outer Hebrides. All these northern lakes are stony shored but, in the south of Britain, shallow mesotrophic and eutrophic brackish waters occur which have muddy reed-fringed shorelines. These have mainly been formed by coastal deposition so that they have become semi-isolated from the sea by bars but some, such as the Norfolk Broads, are artificial in origin.

The phytoplankton of brackish lakes has been little studied in this country and it is impossible to give an account of the composition of this flora. *Prymnesium parvum*, belonging to the Chrysophyta, occurs fairly regularly in eutrophic waters where it can cause severe fish kills by the excretion of a powerful toxin. Phytoplankton production in brackish waters, even the base-rich examples, appears to be low and the water is generally fairly clear but the mechanism limiting production in these waters is not known.

As one progresses from fresh water into slightly brackish conditions many of the characteristic freshwater zooplankters disappear and are replaced by brackish and marine genera. With the exception of species with a wide range of tolerance, such as the ubiquitous *Chydorus sphaericus*, which may just extend to slightly saline conditions, Cladocera are absent from brackish waters. Several of the more versatile species of freshwater copepods, such as *Cyclops strenuus*, *C.* (*Megacyclops*) *viridis*, *C.* (*Tropocyclops*) *prasinus* and *C.* (*Paracyclops*) *fimbriatus*, extend into brackish waters, but the most characteristic zooplanktonic copepods of brackish water are members of the genera *Acartia*, *Eurytemora*, *Centropages*, *Cyclopina* and *Halicyclops* which also occur in the marine environment. Several genera of harpacticoids such as *Mesochra*, *Tachidius*, *Nitochra*, *Horsiella*, *Laophonte* and *Stenhelia* live in, and on, mud and vegetation in brackish conditions.

As salinity is the dominant habitat factor affecting organisms in this environment it is more convenient to discuss the range of variation of the macrobenthos and macrophytes in terms of this variable than in terms of zonation with depth.

As the salinity of a water-body increases with increasing marine influence there is a gradual transition from a freshwater macrophytic flora to a flora characteristic of the marine littoral. In salinities close to that of sea water, the characteristic flora consists of various seaweeds such as *Fucus serratus* and *Ascophyllum nodosum*. In somewhat less saline conditions these are replaced by other algal species such as *F. ceranoides* and *Enteromorpha intestinalis*. Of the angiosperms the most resistant to salinity are *Ruppia spiralis*, *R. maritima* and *Potamogeton pectinatus*, the last species occurring in waters of sodium content of at least 6000 p.p.m. Other submerged species relatively tolerant of high salinities, e.g. *Zannichellia palustris*, *Lemna trisulca* and *Ceratophyllum demersum*, while *Najas flexilis* and *N. marina* are generally only found in Britain in waters where the ionic content is raised slightly by infiltration of sea water. Where the brackish conditions grade into oligotrophic conditions the brackish water species are succeeded by species such as *Myriophyllum alterniflorum*, *Sparganium angustifolium*, *Lobelia dortmanna*, *Eleogiton fluitans* and *Littorella uniflora*, whereas, when they grade into eutrophic conditions, *Ranunculus baudotii*, *Myriophyllum spicatum*, *M. verticillatum*, *Hippuris vulgaris* and *Chara* spp. (particularly *C. baltica*) are among the first of the typical freshwater eutrophic plants to appear. In slightly brackish conditions it is not unusual to find seaweeds and freshwater angiosperms growing side by side.

The typical emergent species is *Scirpus maritimus*. Other species associated with slightly brackish conditions are *Schoenoplectus tabernaemontani* and, in the north-west of Britain, *Cladium mariscus*. *Phragmites communis* will also tolerate slightly brackish conditions and often grows to great heights in sheltered tidal waters.

As the salinity of a water-body increases sensitive freshwater invertebrate species are eliminated but, in areas of intermediate salinity, brackish and freshwater organisms are found together. The freshwater component of the fauna may be that of a typical oligotrophic or eutrophic water depending on the initial alkalinity of the water, but in the most marine areas of brackish lakes the brackish water component predominates and the fauna can be similar in both eutrophic and oligotrophic waters.

Among the Coelenterata, *Hydra* spp. are fairly resistant to brackish conditions but the colonial *Cordylophora lacustris* is the characteristic species in south-east England. The freshwater species of triclad are intolerant of saline conditions, but *Procerodes littoralis*, which is characteristic of streams on the sea shore, is also found on the stony shores of brackish lakes. A number of freshwater gastropods and lamellibranchs extend into brackish conditions, the number of species being greater in eutrophic brackish lakes than in oligotrophic lakes. The most abundant gastropod is *Potamopyrgus jenkinsi* which is often present in enormous numbers. This species was formerly a marine organism which is now found in fresh waters of all types and is still in the process of extending its range. In more saline conditions marine species of *Hydrobia*, *Littorina*, *Mytilus* and *Cardium* replace the freshwater molluscs.

A number of naidid and tubificid worms are confined to brackish waters and several of the freshwater species, such as *Stylaria lacustris*, are also found. Some of the more adaptable polychaetes, e.g. *Nereis diversicolor*, will extend into almost fresh water. Unlike worms, freshwater leeches are not tolerant of saline conditions and there are no brackish

water species. The widespread and adaptable species *Helobdella stagnalis* is probably the most tolerant and is found in very slightly brackish lakes. Insects are largely replaced by Crustacea as one progresses into more saline water. Where there is the slightest trace of sea water, *Gammarus* (*Rivulogammarus*) *pulex* and *G.* (*R.*) *lacustris* are replaced by *G.* (*R.*) *duebeni*, which is a freshwater species in Ireland, the Scottish islands and on the extreme west coast of mainland Scotland where the other species are absent. In more saline conditions *G.* (*R.*) *duebeni* may itself be replaced by *G. zaddachi* and *G. tigrinus*, the former especially where there is some water current and, in almost marine conditions, *Marinogammarus* spp. predominate. The shrimp *Neomysis integer* first appears at about the same salinity as *G.* (*R.*) *duebeni*, and extends into sea water. Other common brackish crustaceans are the amphipod *Corophium curvispinum* and isopods *Sphaeroma hookeri*, *S. rugicauda* and *Jaera nordmanni* and the true shrimp *Palaemonetes varians*, which is tolerant of fresh water when adult. Plecoptera and most of the Ephemeroptera are intolerant of brackish conditions. A number of species of widespread and highly adaptable dragonfly will breed in brackish water in Britain. They comprise *Enallagma cyathigerum*, *Pyrrhosoma nymphula*, *Ischnura elegans*, *Lestes sponsa*, *Sympetrum danae* and *Libellula quadrimaculata*. *Orthetrum cancellatum*, *Libellula depressa* and *Coenagrion pulchellum*, which are confined to the south of Britain, can also breed in these conditions. The water boatmen, *Sigara selecta* and *S. stagnalis*, are confined to brackish water. *S. lateralis* occurs here and in ponds, such as farm ponds, with organic pollution and *Notonecta viridis* occurs both in brackish and alkaline fresh waters, often far inland. On the other hand *S. concinna* is found in fresh water but almost always close to the sea. Other species of water boatman typical of fresh water may extend into slightly brackish conditions alongside the above mentioned species. A number of species of water beetle occur, and *Haliplus apicalis*, *Laccophilus variegatus*, *Hygrotus parallelogrammus*, *Agabus conspersus* (only found in the extreme south east of England), *Dytiscus circumflexus*, *Gyrinus caspius*, *Helophorus alternans*, some *Enochrus* spp. and some *Ochthebius* spp. are confined to such waters. A few caddis species extend into brackish water, especially limnephilids, including *Grammotaulius atomarius*. *Triaenodes reuteri* breeds in pools on salt marshes.

The Diptera are the most tolerant of the insect groups to marine conditions. Chironomids of the subfamily Clunioninae breed in the inter-tidal zone of the open sea. Several species of Tanypodinae such as *Anatopynia varia* and *Ablabesmyia barbitarsis*, Orthocladiinae such as *Corynoneura scutellata*, *Cricotopus sylvestris* and *Hydrobaenus rubicundus*, and Chironominae such as *Chironomus dorsalis*, *C. longistylus* and *Polypedilum nubeculosus* are able to breed in rock pools along the sea shore in near marine conditions as well as occurring in fresh water. Certain species of mosquito, e.g. *Aedes detritus* and *A. dorsalis*, and the larvae of some Ephydridae, e.g. *Ephydra riparia*, generally breed in brackish pools and ditches.

TEMPORARY STANDING WATERS

In Britain these are not an important category of water-body as the great excess of rainfall over evaporation ensures that only very small, shallow bodies of water ever dry out regularly. Temporary pools are more frequent in the low rainfall areas of the south and east where the rocks are mostly calcareous and they therefore tend to be mainly eutrophic in status. The principal feature of the flora and fauna of temporary waters is their ability to withstand periods of desiccation or their ability to colonise new habitats rapidly.

The macrophytic flora is characterised by species such as *Glyceria fluitans*, *G. plicata*, *Agrostis stolonifera*, *Polygonum amphibium*, *Oenanthe fistulosa* and, in less rich situations where the soil is of gravel or sand, *Littorella uniflora*. The bare soil left when the water of a pool recedes may be rapidly covered by common terrestrial weeds, while freshly created water is often quickly invaded by floating thallate plants such as *Lemna* spp. and *Riccia fluitans*. Algae too are successful colonisers of temporary pools which are frequently very turbid with planktonic forms, particularly Cyanophyta and Chlorophyta, while the bottom may be covered with filamentous algae, e.g. *Spirogyra* and *Anabaena*.

Triclads, mayflies, stoneflies and malacostracans are all absent from temporary pools but a number of molluscs are able to aestivate and are highly resistant to desiccation. *Lymnaea* (*Galba*) *glabra*, *L.* (*Galba*) *truncatula*, *Aplexa hypnorum*, *Planorbis* (*Anisus*) *leucostomus*, *Pisidium personatum* and *P. casertanum* are typical and may be very abundant in small pools in Britain. The amphibious leech *Dina lineata* is the only species generally found in such waters. The two rather uncommon crustaceans, the fairy shrimp *Cheirocephalus diaphanus* and *Triops cancriformis*, are restricted to small, rather turbid puddles in the south of England; these species have eggs resistant to desiccation. A large number of copepods and ostracods are directly resistant to drying out as adults while, under hostile conditions, the Cladocera lay resistant ephippial eggs. *Moina rectirostris* and *Daphnia obtusa* are characteristic and in the absence of many predators often abound in small pools. Among the insects a number of species have adapted to living in temporary pools by laying eggs which diapause throughout the summer and only hatch in the autumn. The larvae then feed and grow in the winter while the pool is full and the adults emerge in the spring before the pool dries out. These insects include the dragonfly *Lestes sponsa* and beetles such as *Agabus labiatus*. A number of other beetles, e.g. *Helophorus brevipalpis* which is a ready flier, utilise such pools as adults but may not be able to breed there. Adult corixids are also often found in large numbers in temporary pools but since the flightless nymphs grow during the dry summer months they are unlikely to be successful breeders. A number of opportunist Diptera, especially Culicidae and Chironomidae, will breed in small pools which dry out, the success of these groups being attributable to their very short life-cycle time. In the smallest and most ephemeral of pools which are likely to form and then dry out again in a matter of hours

the fauna may be restricted to a few highly resistant protozoa, rotifers, harpacticoids and tardigrades.

RUNNING WATERS

The velocity of the water current is the predominant ecological factor controlling the composition and abundance of the flora and fauna in running waters. The water current exerts its influence largely by determining the nature of the bed of the stream. In the fast upper stretches of streams, material is eroded from the bed, the faster the current the larger the particles moved, and in this zone only plants and animals capable of staying firmly attached to rocks or able to creep underneath them can survive. At slower current velocities, material eroded upstream is deposited, the slower the current the finer the sediment and, in this zone, rooted plants can gain a footing and burrowing animals predominate. As well as the indirect effect of current upon the flora and fauna the current may be responsible for directly dislodging animals and plants and thus preventing their colonisation. Planktonic organisms are only found in the longer or slower flowing of the British rivers, and floating plants, e.g. *Lemna* spp., are generally absent.

Streams with high current velocities and much turbulence remain saturated with oxygen while slower streams where much organic sediment collects may become partially anaerobic. Consequently many species of invertebrate and some fish which have high oxygen requirements are confined to fast-running waters while the fauna of slow-flowing rivers contains many species capable of withstanding low oxygen concentrations. Organic material carried downstream by the current forms the food for an association of filter-feeding animals which are restricted to areas where the velocity of the current is sufficient to ensure a ready supply of this material.

After current, the second most important ecological factor in running waters is water chemistry. Rivers, like lakes, can be divided according to their alkalinity into the same basic categories: dystrophic, oligotrophic, mesotrophic and eutrophic. Unlike most lakes, however, rivers may change their trophic status along their lengths. Many rivers start in base-poor upland areas and are oligotrophic in status; in their middle reaches they become mesotrophic, and in the lowermost stretches they enter more fertile land and are eutrophic. It is thus very difficult to classify river systems.

The faster the current the more important it becomes as a controlling factor and the less important is water chemistry. Thus the flora and fauna of base-rich torrential streams differs little from that of torrential base-poor streams, except that the former are more productive. Upland streams and rivers of an eroding nature are therefore dealt with as one group.

In the slower-flowing rivers, water chemistry becomes a more important ecological factor and a distinction must be made between dystrophic, oligotrophic and eutrophic rivers. Most oligotrophic rivers occur in upland areas but some occur in lowland areas where they form a distinct but small group. They are slower flowing and more silted than their upland counterparts and have a different flora and fauna both from these and from the lowland eutrophic streams.

The larger dystrophic streams and rivers differ little in flora and fauna from upland oligotrophic streams and rivers, but slow-flowing flushes and small streams have a characteristic flora and fauna which is basically similar to that of mire pools although there is generally a riverine component.

Within the eutrophic category of lowland rivers a further distinction can be made between chalk streams and rivers, and rivers draining other geological formations. The chalk streams form a category equivalent to marl lakes in standing waters, but the distinction between chalk streams and eutrophic streams is arbitrary and streams draining the more soluble limestones form a series intermediate in all respects between the two categories. Like marl lakes, chalk streams are characterised by their clear water and abundance of macrophytes. The porosity of the Chalk has a regulatory effect on river discharge and this absence of heavy spates allows the build up of silt in areas adjacent to eroding gravel and stones. Thus there is considerable structural diversity within a short stretch of chalk streams. During the spring and summer, the diverse substrate is stabilised by rich growths of rooted vegetation.

Typical eutrophic rivers, by contrast, may spate considerably and carry heavy loads of suspended silt which can occlude light penetration and restrict the growth of submerged plants. In faster stretches of these rivers, the bottom is much less stable than equivalent areas of chalk streams.

The slowest-flowing rivers and ditches, where the current practically ceases in the summer, form another distinct river type. Build-up of sediments allows the invasion of emergent species of plant which, without management, would rapidly cause progression to mire communities where restriction of water flow would cause flooding. These rivers are therefore all artificially managed but show a mixture of riverine and eutrophic lake species of plants and animals not found in natural waters.

Brackish running waters and estuaries have been largely omitted from this section although the lower tidal stretches of some rivers, e.g. the Wye, have been considered. Salinity is a dominant factor controlling the composition of the flora and fauna there and the range of variation is largely covered under the section dealing with brackish standing waters.

UPLAND OLIGOTROPHIC AND EUTROPHIC RIVERS AND STREAMS

Upland streams are the commonest and most widespread of all natural water-bodies in Britain. In altitude they range from over 1000 m to sea-level on the north and west coasts of Britain where the streams tend to be short and precipitous throughout their length. Streams draining eastwards from the uplands of Britain, especially Scotland, tend to form larger river systems with a slower-flowing lowland reach in the lower sections. The division between upland and lowland rivers is, however, arbitrary, but there is often a marked change in river character and flora and fauna at the point where a river enters the zone of arable cultivation.

Above this point the river tends to be fast flowing, eroding and, except in extensive upland limestone areas, oligotrophic, whereas below this point the river becomes richer, slower flowing, more subject to silting and often, in the lower reaches meandering. The upland river and stream as here defined is equivalent to the trout zone of Huet's (1954) classification of European rivers based on their fish populations.

The physical conditions in these streams and rivers are very variable depending on slope, geology and nature of run-off from the catchment. On the steepest upper slopes the bottom substrate is often stable with all loose material dislodged. The bottom may consist of large, tightly packed boulders or even bare rock. The turbulence of the torrential water results in the formation of a wet splash zone above the normal water level of the stream, in which hygrophilous plants abound. This zone is characterised by waterfalls. Below this area of extreme erosion the substrate consists of a mixture of bedrock, boulders, stones, gravel, sand and silt, the proportions varying with local conditions.

Because of the high rainfall and generally impervious soil of upland areas, run-off can be very rapid and subject to sharp variations in amount. Consequently most such streams and rivers are subject to spates when discharges of up to several hundred times that of normal dry weather flow may occur. During spates severe erosion of the bottom occurs and stones and gravel are dislodged and deposited further downstream. Those streams forming the outflows of lakes have a more uniform discharge, however, because of the regulating effect of the lake and may have quite stable bottom substrates. Rivers in porous limestone areas also tend to have more stable discharge rates since the effect of a heavy rainfall is spread over a longer period by the delay taken in percolating through the rock. The stability of the stream-bed is also dependent on the nature of the substrate particularly the particle size. Stability therefore varies between and within streams depending on a combination of slope, run-off and particle size.

In the eroding 'waterfall' zone, upland streams tend to consist of a series of runs and falls of rapidly flowing water with a few deep pools worn in the bedrock. As the slope of the ground decreases and the nature of the substrate changes the stream typically becomes a series of runs and pools. The runs are shallower, fast flowing and eroding, with clean stone and gravel bottoms, whereas the pools are deeper, the current is slower and there is deposition of sand and silt between or, in extreme conditions, over the stones. The composition of the flora and fauna varies between pool and run.

The torrential upper stretches of rivers and streams have a predominantly bryophyte flora where the substrate is stable but, where the bottom of the stream is covered with shifting unstable stones, the vegetation is limited to a thin coating of epilithic algae. Aquatic angiosperms are generally absent. The bryophyte communities of oligotrophic torrential streams include *Scapania undulata*, *Marsupella* spp., *Brachythecium rivulare* and *Fontinalis antipyretica*. Under more base-rich conditions the composition of these communities changes somewhat and species such as *Cinclodotus fontinaloides* may dominate. The algae of torrential streams are generally small diatoms, blue-green and green algae which attach to the rocks by mucilage, but in some limestone rivers encrusting marl-forming algae such as *Rivularia* and *Phormidium* form prominent growths on the stones.

In Britain nearly all high mountain streams above 700 m are base-poor and the fauna is limited by the climatic conditions. Naidid and enchytraeid worms and nematodes are found at high altitudes, the naids in large numbers, but leeches are absent. The only flatworm is the cold-adapted *Crenobia alpina* which is also found in cold springs at low altitudes. The mayfly *Ameletus inopinatus* is similarly confined, in streams, to high altitudes, but several other species which also occur at low altitudes, e.g. *Baetis rhodani, B. tenax* and *Rhithrogena semicolorata*, are present. Among the stoneflies *Protonemura montana* is confined to cold stony streams above 500 m and *Diura bicaudata* is only found in streams above 300 m but is also found in lower-altitude lakes. Short-winged forms of the adults of *Nemoura erratica, Leuctra hippopus, L. inermis* and *L. nigra* occur when these breed at high altitudes but normal adults are found in the lower parts of their range. *Protonemura praecox, P. meyeri, Nemurella picteti, Capnia bifrons* and *Chloroperla torrentium* are also found in, but not confined to, high-altitude streams Characteristic beetles of such streams are *Oreodytes borealis* and *Agabus bipustulatus*, the former an Arctic–alpine species and the latter widespread and adaptable. A number of caddis larvae are found including the Limnephilidae *Allogamus auricollis*, Philopotamidae (especially *Philopotamus montanus*), the Rhyacophilidae, *Plectrocnemia conspersa* and *P. geniculata*. Diptera are the most successful of the aquatic insects at high altitudes. Chironomidae, especially Orthocladiinae, are relatively abundant particularly among bryophytes. At altitudes over 650 m the only Simuliidae found are *Simulium monticola* and *Prosimulium inflatum*, the latter species being confined to streams above this altitude. Empidae (Hemerodromiinae) larvae are often abundant among the bryophytes of these streams where they are important predators, and *Dicranota* larvae are found among the gravel.

At lower altitudes both oligotrophic and eutrophic streams occur and the streams converge to form small rivers. Aquatic angiosperms are still absent and bryophyte and epilithic algae communities of similar composition to those at high altitudes are present. *Hydra* spp. may sometimes be present in considerable numbers particularly among thick growths of bryophytes and the triclad *Polycelis felina*, which is tolerant of slightly higher summer temperatures, appears alongside and eventually replaces *Crenobia alpina*. Leeches appear, but only small numbers of the three adaptable species *Erpobdella octoculata, Helobdella stagnalis* and *Glossiphonia complanata*. The freshwater limpet *Ancylus fluviatilis* which is adapted to clinging to stones in a fast current is the most abundant mollusc and, in the more base-rich streams, *Lymnaea (Radix) pereger, Potamopyrgus jenkinsi, Bithynia tentaculata* and *Pisidium* spp. are found in small numbers. *Gammarus (Rivulogammarus) pulex*

may be abundant in the richer hill streams but is absent from the poorest and Hydracarina may be numerous.

The most abundant and widespread mayfly nymph at all seasons is the ubiquitous *Baetis rhodani* which has several generations in a year. *B. pumilus* is also present throughout the year but is less abundant, while *B. scambus* and *Ephemerella ignita* are only plentiful as nymphs in the summer and *Rhithrogena semicolorata* is abundant in the winter. Other important but less abundant species are *B. tenax, Heptagenia lateralis, Ecdyonurus venosus, E. torrentis* and *Caenis rivulorum*.

Stonefly nymphs are generally more prominent in the winter and spring since most species emerge as adults in spring and early summer and in some species hatching of the eggs is delayed. The two most abundant stoneflies are *Leuctra inermis* and *L. fusca*; the nymphs of the former grow in the winter when those of *L. fusca* are not present and emerge as adults chiefly from April to June. The nymphs of *L. fusca* grow during the spring and summer and emerge mainly from August to October. The nymphs of the two species therefore avoid direct competition with each other by this temporal spacing but usually inhabit the same stream. The other abundant species of small streams are *Chloroperla torrentium, Brachyptera risi, Amphinemura sulcicollis* and *Isoperla grammatica. Protonemura meyeri, Leuctra hippopus* and *Chloroperla tripunctata* are widespread but less abundant. The three large species, *Perlodes microcephala, Perla bipunctata* and *Dinocras cephalotes* are found in small numbers but are important in terms of biomass.

In fast-flowing water the alderfly *Sialis lutaria* is replaced by *S. fuliginosa*. A number of dytiscid beetles, of which *Oreodytes rivalis* is the most abundant, swim over the gravel bottom. The larvae and adults of the helmid beetles *Limnius volckmari, Oulimnius tuberculatus, Elmis aenea* and *Esolus parallelopipedus*, live among gravel and moss where the adults of *Hydraena* spp. are also found. In Scotland *H. gracilis* is the common species. Where a thin film of water streams over rocks, and particularly where there are attached bryophytes, the flattened larvae of Helodidae are often found.

The caseless, net-spinning and free-living caddises of the families Hydropsychidae, Philopotamidae, Polycentropidae and Rhyacophilidae are well represented in the upland stream fauna. The most abundant members of these families are *Hydropsyche instabilis, Philopotamus montanus, Wormaldia occipitalis, Polycentropus flavomaculatus* and *Rhyacophila dorsalis*. The most abundant cased caddises are Limnephilidae and *Hydroptila* spp. Other species which occur frequently but less abundantly are *Plectrocnemia conspersa, P. geniculata, Hydropsyche fulvipes, H. angustipennis, Rhyacophila septentrionis* and *Oxyethira* spp. In the richer streams the stones may be encrusted with the cases of *Agapetus fuscipes*.

A varied community of Simuliidae larvae live attached to the stones or vegetation in current conditions varying from moderate to rapid. They often occur in dense single-species aggregations. *Prosimulium arvense, P. hirtipes, Simulium dunfellense, S. brevicaule, S. ornatum, S. tuberosum, S. variegatum, S. monticola, S. spinosum* and *S. reptans* generally form the bulk of this community. *Dicranota* spp. are the most common cranefly larvae living among sand and gravel and Empidae such as *Clinocera* and *Hemerodroma* may be abundant among bryophytes. Chironomidae are often extremely abundant particularly where there is a well-developed covering of epilithic algae. Orthocladiinae are generally the best represented of the chironomid subfamilies, and Tanytarsini, Diamesinae and Tanypodinae are important, but less numerous. A number of other dipteran larvae, such as Muscidae which inhabit the splash zone, and *Pericoma* associated with vegetation at the margins of streams, are represented.

Further downstream, the upland streams converge to produce fast-flowing upland rivers; conditions are still generally eroding but there is an increasing tendency for the bottom to be of finer sediments of sand and gravel. Chemically, these rivers are richer than the headwaters and their increased size offers a larger range of micro-habitats.

Where the current becomes less severe and the bottom is of a more or less stable gravel, aquatic angiosperms appear. In oligotrophic rivers the first submerged species to appear are *Myriophyllum alterniflorum, Callitriche* spp. and *Potamogeton perfoliatus*, while in more base-rich conditions *Ranunculus aquatilis* is characteristic. If marginal aquatic vegetation is present along the sides of these rivers it generally consists of a very sparse community of *R. flammula, Caltha palustris, Juncus articulatus, J. bulbosus, Myosotis* spp. and *Phalaris arundinacea*, similar to that found on exposed lake shores. Filamentous algae became more prominent under these conditions with genera such as *Zygnema* and *Batrachospermum* in oligotrophic rivers and *Cladophora* in eutrophic rivers.

The greater range of current speeds and bottom substrates in the larger rivers results in an increasing faunal diversity but some of the species of small streams are lost. *Crenobia alpina* disappears and *Polycelis felina* is joined in the slower reaches by *P. tenuis/nigra*. The gastropod fauna may be diversified by the addition of a few other species in small numbers and the pearl mussel *Margaritifera margaritifera* is characteristic of these waters. The leech *Theromyzon tessulatum*, which parasitises wildfowl, occasionally occurs. The mayfly *Baetis tenax* disappears and *Ecdyonurus dispar, Heptagenia sulphurea* and occasionally *Caenis macrura* appear, while species such as *Centroptilum luteolum, Ephemerella ignita* and *Leptophlebia marginata* occur in increasing numbers. Among the stoneflies *Nemoura* spp. are uncommon and *Leuctra nigra, L. hippopus* and *Capnia* spp. are generally absent but *L. geniculata* is confined to large stony rivers and *Nemurella picteti* is often abundant among the aquatic plants. *Brachyptera putata* is a rather rare species which is only known from the middle reaches of a few Scottish rivers.

There is a more diverse beetle fauna but *Oreodytes rivalis* is still the most abundant species over gravel, although amongst vegetation *Limnebius truncatellus* may be more numerous. Additions to the caddis fauna are *Brachycentrus*

subnubilus, Lepidostoma hirtum, Sericostoma personatum and *Odontocerum albicorne*, the first-named sometimes being extremely abundant attached to the stones, while in the slower reaches species such as *Anabolia nervosa* and *Cyrnus* spp. may occur. The cranefly *Pedicia* spp. occurs more frequently in rivers than in streams. *Prosimulium* spp. of blackfly are not found in large rivers where the characteristic species are *Simulium reptans* and *S. tuberosum* and, in the lower stretches, *S. latipes*.

In the deeper pools, current speeds are frequently slow enough to allow the deposition of silt in which burrowing species are found. *Sialis lutaria* is a characteristic species and replaces *S. fuliginosa* which occurs in the eroding sections. The mayflies *Ephemera danica* and *Caenis moesta* also occur in the silt and burrowing chironomids may be abundant.

DYSTROPHIC RIVERS AND STREAMS

Larger stony bottomed dystrophic rivers occur widely in areas draining upland blanket mire and are characterised by their brown, acidic, peat-stained waters. Peat-staining may, however, be a periodic phenomenon and many rivers are only seasonally dystrophic, having a pH near neutrality and clear water during some months. Particularly in areas where peat erosion and hagg formation is occurring, spates may carry downstream huge quantities of particulate peat which may be deposited when the discharge declines, smothering the fauna and flora of the stones. The flora and fauna of these rivers is very similar in composition to that of oligotrophic rivers, but the fauna may be even more sparse in quantity.

The impeded drainage of the more level areas in the uplands encourages the development of blanket mire through which slow-flowing, often deep, dystrophic rivers and streams with peat margins may run. The bottoms of these streams are usually composed of thick deposits of fine particulate peat but in the areas of slightly faster current the bottom may be of gravel or sand. *Microspora* is characteristic of streams in this category. The deeply coloured water restricts the penetration of light so that submerged vegetation is generally absent. Floating-leaved vegetation may however be abundant and even cover the entire surface. *Nymphaea alba* (especially ssp. *occidentalis*), *Nuphar pumila, Sparganium angustifolium* and *Potamogeton natans* are characteristic in the deeper water while at the margins, in shallower water, *P. polygonifolius* is usually present. The invertebrate fauna of these streams is generally extremely sparse. Many of the species found in dystrophic standing waters may be found in association with the vegetation but the bottom deposits only support a very limited fauna including naidid worms, *Pisidium* spp., *Sialis lutaria*, Ceratopogonidae and chironomids.

Slow-flowing trickles on upland soligenous mire have a characteristic aquatic plant community consisting of *Sphagnum subsecundum* var. *auriculatum, S. recurvum, Drepanocladus fluitans, Potamogeton polygonifolius, Molinia caerulea* and *Eleocharis multicaulis*, but little is known about the invertebrate fauna of such situations.

LOWLAND OLIGOTROPHIC RIVERS AND STREAMS

These are an uncommon category of water-body in Britain since most of the lowlands contain calcareous rocks. No large oligotrophic river systems are found in lowland Britain but small oligotrophic and mesotrophic streams occur in the base-poor Tertiary sands of the New Forest and Thames basin and on the Greensand of the Weald. They could be placed in the grayling or minnow zone of Huet's (1954) classification of rivers. These streams are generally slower flowing and thus more silted than their upland counterparts and aquatic vegetation may be more abundant, but the composition of the plant communities is similar.

The invertebrate fauna is basically similar to that of upland streams and contrasts noticeably with that of nearby calcareous streams draining other geological formations. Certain species such as the dragonflies *Agrion virgo* and *Gomphus vulgatissimus*, the amphipod *Niphargus aquilex* and the bug *Aphelocheirus montandoni*, which are restricted to the southern half of Britain, may also be present. The fauna is generally somewhat more diverse than upland streams and additional species of gastropod, mayfly and caddis may be present, while lowland species of *Simulium*, such as *S. latipes*, replace those of upland streams.

LOWLAND EUTROPHIC RIVERS AND STREAMS

The majority of rivers and streams in lowland Britain belong to this category, although their headwaters may be upland streams rising on high ground and their lower stretches may be sluggish rivers. The current in these rivers varies from moderately fast to slow and the bottom ranges from coarse gravel or stones to fine silt. Typically, there are alternate fast runs and quiet deeper pools and the river meanders through a fairly broad valley of rich farmland or woodland. These rivers constitute both the grayling or minnow zone and the barbel or chub zone of Huet's (1954) classification.

The nature of the discharge depends upon the porosity of the surrounding rock, those streams lying in clay areas being subject to the worst spates of any river in Britain when discharges of over a thousand times that of a dry weather flow may occur. Such rivers are generally steep-sided and fairly deep and, in dry weather, silt may accumulate on the bed but after spates this is washed away and the bottom may be of bare eroded clay or stones. Rivers on more porous rock formations such as sandstones tend to be broader and shallower and have predominantly gravel beds in the runs with silted pools between.

These rivers vary in nutrient status from mesotrophic examples which drain mostly upland areas and are closely linked to the upland rivers (e.g. the Tweed and Clyde), to extremely eutrophic examples which are of a lowland nature throughout (e.g. the Thames). Intermediate examples which are mainly lowland but have a short upland section at their headwaters include the Wye and the Severn. The nutrient content of most eutrophic lowland rivers has been increased in recent years by run-off from agricultural land and by discharge of sewage effluents, and none of the larger

eutrophic rivers in Britain is entirely intact in this respect. The lower stretches of many examples are severely polluted by domestic and industrial effluents, and some have been canalised by straightening and embankment and the construction of locks. Nearly all are subject to some water abstraction and in some the water regime is artificially regulated.

The growth of submerged macrophytes may be limited in some examples by the lack of light penetration caused by suspended material including sewage effluents and, in slow-flowing rivers, phytoplankton. The phytoplankton of the larger examples is characterised by the dominance of small centric diatoms, particularly *Stephanodiscus*, and green algae such as *Scenedesmus*. Particularly where the nutrient content has been raised artificially the filamentous alga *Cladophora* may cover the entire river bed and eliminate higher plants. In slow-flowing, highly enriched rivers, particularly where the salt content is relatively high, *Enteromorpha* may be a feature of the algal flora.

In other lowland eutrophic rivers the growth of aquatic angiosperms is prolific and weed-cutting is necessary in the summer months to maintain river flow. The composition of the vegetation depends very much upon the cutting regime. In moderately fast conditions the characteristic species is *Ranunculus aquatilis* which, together with other *Ranunculus* spp. such as *R. circinatus*, may achieve complete cover over the river bed. *Myriophyllum spicatum*, *Callitriche stagnalis*, *Potamogeton perfoliatus* and *P. pectinatus* are also found under reasonably fast currents, but the last only achieves dominance in the quieter waters. In quieter conditions most of the submerged macrophyte species which achieve their greatest abundance in chalk streams may occur but they are generally less abundant and the diversity in any one river is generally less than is the case for chalk streams. Floating-leaved species are often abundant and may be the most important component of the vegetation in deeper rivers such as those in clay areas where *P. natans*, *Sparganium emersum* and *Sagittaria sagittifolia* are frequently abundant. Except where grazing has eliminated it, a narrow belt of marginal reed-swamp species is usually present, *Sparganium erectum* being the most common dominant.

In general these river systems are more productive than upland rivers and non-insect groups become a more important component of the fauna, their density and number of species increasing. Triclads such as *Dendrocoelum lacteum* and *Dugesia lugubris* appear and may be quite abundant in the lower stretches while *Crenobia alpina* and *Polycelis felina* are restricted to the headwaters. Molluscs increase greatly both in numbers and species with the appearance of, for example, *Bithynia tentaculata*, *Physa fontinalis*, *Potamopyrgus jenkinsi*, *Theodoxus fluviatilis* and *Valvata piscinalis* with increasing alkalinity. The pearl mussel *Margaritifera margaritifera* is replaced by *Anodonta anatina*, *A. cygnea*, *A. minima*, *Unio pictorum* and *U. tumidus*. Oligochaetes are abundant and tubificids and *Stylaria lacustris* are a large component. As the alkalinity increases so does the number of leech species, probably related to the increasing abundance of molluscan and crustacean prey organisms. Among the latter *Asellus meridianus*, *A. aquaticus* and *Crangonyx pseudogracilis* appear and *Gammarus (Rivulogammarus) pulex* increases in numbers.

Most of the mayflies of base-poor rivers are present, but *Rhithrogena semicolorata* is confined to the upper reaches. *Baetis buceratus*, *Centroptilum pennulatum* and *Habrophlebia fusca* appear in the richer of these rivers. The rare *Ephemera lineata* has only been found in the Wye and Thames, while *Brachycercus harrisella* has been recorded from a number of such rivers on a few occasions. The stoneflies are generally restricted to the faster upper stretches where *Leuctra geniculata*, *L. inermis* and *L. fusca* are the most abundant species, and certain species, e.g. *Perlodes microcephala* and *Brachyptera risi*, are generally absent. A number of riverine dragonfly species such as *Agrion splendens* and *Gomphus vulgatissimus* may be present, especially in the southern rivers. The bug *Aphelocheirus montandoni* is found in the gravel, while corixids and *Micronecta* spp. may be found swimming in swarms in the slower stretches. The slower currents offer habitats for a more diverse haliplid and hydro-porine beetle fauna. The *Simulium* fauna differs from that of the upland rivers, *Simulium equinum* and *S. salopiense* being extremely abundant on submerged vegetation. *S. reptans* and *S. ornatum* are also abundant, but the upland species are confined to the headwaters.

CHALK STREAMS AND RIVERS

Chalk streams are confined to areas of south-east Britain from the Yorkshire Wolds to the Dorset Downs with one outpost in east Devon. In their present forms these are a largely artificial habitat maintained by dredging and weed-cutting, without which they would flood their banks in the lower stretches. Management is most intensive in the southern chalk streams of Hampshire and Berkshire where it is aimed at improving angling by stocking with trout and removal of coarse fish. 'Improvement' of the banks is in some cases carried out by removal of marginal vegetation and trees and the erection of wooden shuttering to retain the banks, which considerably reduces the conservation interest. Commercial water-cress beds have been constructed at the sources of many of these streams and, although artificial, they add diversity to the habitat. Modern management and the use of insecticides to control caddis larvae, however, can be detrimental. A recent threat to some of these streams and rivers is the proposal to pump water from Chalk aquifers in several parts of the country for domestic and industrial usage. The conservation implications of such proposals are being investigated.

Chalk streams are characterised by their clear waters and abundance of rooted vegetation and are thus analogous to marl lakes, and the chemical processes which limit the production of phytoplankton in marl lakes may also operate. The storage of water in the Chalk aquifer has a regulating effect on river flow which may be nearly constant through-out the year, but in the upper reaches seasonal changes in the level of the water table in the aquifer lead to the drying out of considerable lengths of river in the summer. These upper stretches, which are known as winterbournes, only flow in the winter when the water table once more reaches the surface. The more or less constant discharge produces a relatively stable bottom substrate even in areas of fairly fast current and allows the build-up of considerable quantities of silt among vegetation and in areas of slower current. In gravelly areas the bottom is further stabilised by the deposition of marl which cements the stones together.

Current velocities range from fast to slow or even sluggish but most frequently they are moderate flowing, forming broad, shallow, gravelly runs interspersed with deeper, slower-flowing pools.

Chalk streams derive almost all their flow from springs rather than direct run-off and this water is largely free from suspended material, well oxygenated and at a nearly constant temperature throughout the year. In the summer months the water temperature in the upper reaches is well below that of the air temperature, and a number of invertebrate species which are adapted to low temperatures and are found elsewhere in Britain only at high altitudes may occur here.

It is in the nutrient-rich, clear waters of chalk streams that the submerged angiosperms reach their greatest variety and maximum growth. Where plant cover is often complete, the communities of the open water consist of a patchwork of large clumps of vegetation each of a single species with no obvious zonation. The characteristic species found here are *Ranunculus aquatilis*, *R. penicillatus*, *R. circinatus*, *Callitriche stagnalis*, *Apium nodiflorum*, *Berula erecta*, *Oenanthe fluviatilis*, *Potamogeton pectinatus*, *Zannichellia palustris*, *Sagittaria sagittifolia*, *Sium latifolium*, *Elodea canadensis*, *Myriophyllum spicatum*, *Potamogeton crispus*, *P. friesii* and other linear-leaved *Potamogeton* spp., *Groenlandia densa*, *Veronica beccabunga* and *V. anagallis-aquatica*. The most typical marginal community is a band of *Rorippa nasturtium-aquaticum*, often with *Myosotis* spp., *Glyceria maxima* and *Mentha aquatica* grading into a tall, damp, herb community of which *Epilobium hirsutum* and *Lythrum salicaria* are prominent members, but often this last community is missing and trees or steep clay banks border the stream. Emergent *Rorippa* may also occur in midwater together with *Sparganium emersum*, *S. erectum* and the emergent shoots of many of the submerged species above. The dense beds of vegetation act as a trap for silt and during the summer months large quantities of fine inorganic and organic material build up in mounds within the vegetation clumps. These deposits which are very important to the invertebrates, are swept away during the winter. The structure of the angiosperm communities of the larger well-known trout streams such as the Hampshire Avon, Itchen and Test is dependent upon regular cutting of the weeds. This is normally done twice annually in May and August.

The most abundant and diverse invertebrate fauna found in British rivers occurs in chalk streams. Species associated with vegetation are particularly well represented but species requiring a firm rocky substrate for attachment may be absent since the stones are covered with soft incrustations of marl. Many of the species of lowland eutrophic river systems occur.

Hydra may be very abundant, attached to the submerged vegetation. The planarian *Crenobia alpina* is only found in the cool springs and the most abundant planarians are *Polycelis tenuis* and *P. nigra*. The molluscan fauna is extremely rich, and the species found in eutrophic lakes are usually abundant, but in the isolated chalk streams of Yorkshire the gastropod fauna is more limited. All the species of leech found in base-rich rivers are present and generally abundant, as are Hydracarina. The freshwater crayfish *Astacus pallipes* is confined in Britain to well-oxygenated calcareous water and is most abundant in chalk streams, where it is a characteristic species. *Gammarus* (*Rivulogammarus*) *pulex* occurs in every habitat in chalk streams, often in very high densities and in terms of total biomass is the dominant invertebrate. The ecdyonurid mayflies are practically absent except for small numbers of *Heptagenia sulphurea* and, in the northern streams, *Rhithrogena* spp. On the other hand, species which inhabit the weeds, e.g. *Baetis rhodani*, *B. vernus*, *B. bioculatus*, *Ephemerella ignita* and *Centroptilum luteolum*, abound, while in silted areas *Caenis horaria*, *Ephemera danica* and *E. vulgata* are found. Small numbers of *B. atrebatinus*, *Ephemerella notata* and *Paraleptophlebia cincta* which have a restricted distribution also occur. There is a big reduction in the number of species of stonefly and only small numbers of *Nemoura cambrica*, *Nemurella picteti*, *Leuctra fusca*, *L. inermis* and *L. nigra* occur commonly. In northern streams *Isoperla grammatica* also occurs and *N. picteti* may be abundant. A corixid and beetle fauna of similar species composition to that of eutrophic lakes may inhabit the slower stretches. Some beetles, e.g. *Agabus paludosus*, which lives in thick vegetation, and *Haliplus fluviatilis*, which is found over a gravelly bottom, are characteristic. A number of caddis which are normally found in eroding stretches of rivers are either absent or are restricted to the fastest reaches. Thus *Glossosoma* spp., *Tinodes waeneri* and some of the Philopotamidae are absent, whilst *Agapetus fuscipes* is found only here where it may be very abundant. *Hydropsyche instabilis* is replaced by *H. angustipennis* as the most common hydropsychid. *Athripsodes* spp. and *Molanna angustata* occur and Goerinae are possibly characteristic of chalk streams.

Dipteran larvae, such as *Dixa* and *Pericoma*, are found amongst the marginal vegetation. Larvae of the cranefly *Dicranota* are abundant in the gravel but those of *Pedicia* and *Atherix*, which are found in similar situations, with *Dicranota*, in upland streams, are absent. The upland blackfly larvae *Simulium monticola*, *S. variegatum* and *S. reptans* disappear whilst the common species of the base-rich river, *S. equinum*, *S. salopiense* and *S. ornatum*, are joined by *S. angustipes*, *S. erythrocephalum* and *S. angustitarse*. The latter two species are, in Britain, confined to chalk streams. *S. costatum* is the characteristic species found just below springs fed from the Chalk.

SLUGGISH LOWLAND RIVERS AND DITCHES

The lowermost stretches of many of the larger eutrophic rivers formerly ran to the sea through extensive freshwater marshes and fens as a series of diffuse channels with little perceptible flow. The fens have now been drained and the rivers are straightened and enclosed between embankments while the marshes themselves are drained by an intersecting network of drainage ditches. Although these waterways are entirely artificial and are only maintained in their present state by intensive management, they represent a type of running-water habitat not now found in a natural state in Britain. These rivers represent the Bream zone of Huet's (1954) classification.

Conditions in these rivers approximate to those of eutrophic lakes while the drainage ditches resemble small ponds. There is no appreciable flow in many during the summer, although in winter moderate flows may be experienced. The bottom is covered with a thick layer of silt which accumulates over the years, reducing the depth of the channel, and it is therefore periodically removed by dredging. This mud is frequently anaerobic below the surface but the slight current and shallowness of the river usually prevent complete deoxygenation of the water column except where organic pollution from an outside source enters the river. The rivers are invariably extremely rich in nutrients which, since the surrounding land is usually rich agricultural land, may be further increased by run-off of fertilisers. A dense phytoplankton may exist in the summer and this together with the heavy suspended solid load may reduce the penetration of light and thus limit the growth of submerged macrophytes. In some sluggish rivers and most drainage ditches however the growth of submerged macrophytes is prolific and weed-cutting is required to maintain the flow of water and the species composition is dependent upon this cutting.

The most typical submerged aquatic macrophytes in these rivers are *Potamogeton* spp., especially *P. pectinatus*, *P. crispus* and *P. lucens*, *Myriophyllum spicatum*, *Elodea canadensis* and *Zannichellia palustris*. In the shallows of such rivers emergent vegetation can frequently colonise the entire area, eventually restricting flow and causing silting so that they may need frequent dredging. The typical succession is from invasion by Nymphaceae or *P. natans*, or in the stillest conditions one of the free-floating species, through to emergent reed-swamp of which *Sparganium emersum* and *S. erectum* are the most prominent at first followed by *Glyceria maxima*. Eventually *Salix* spp. and *Alnus* spp. may invade the river course and so much restrict flow as to cause flooding of the surrounding land, but this succession is rarely allowed to go unchecked in Britain except in disused canals. The invertebrate fauna of these water-bodies is comparable to that of eutrophic lakes and most of the stream species are absent. The typical stream triclads, *Crenobia alpina* and *Polycelis felina*, are absent as are the riverine gastropods, *Ancylus fluviatilis* and *Theodoxus fluviatilis*. Lacustrine species such as the gastropods, *Viviparus fasciatus* and *V. viviparus*, and the introduced lamellibranchs, *Dreissena polymorpha* and *Sphaerium transversum*, which have spread throughout the English canal system, are plentiful. A characteristic species of the ditches is *Sphaerium lacustre* which is tolerant of adverse conditions. In the muds tubificid worms and Chironominae larvae are abundant and where the rivers are heavily polluted tubificids and *Chironomus* spp. may be the only macrobenthos present. *Helobdella stagnalis*, which is the most typical leech of lake muds, is the most common in lowland rivers although the other leeches of the faster stretches of base-rich rivers occur. In ditches, where there is not a strong current, *Glossiphonia heteroclita* is found. As the current decreases *Gammarus (Rivulogammarus) pulex* declines and is absent from drainage ditches, its place being taken by the introduced *Crangonyx pseudogracilis* which can tolerate mild pollution. The ponddwelling water spider *Argyroneta aquatica* is abundant in heavily weeded drains.

Most of the typical mayflies of streams such as *Baetis* spp., *Ephemerella ignita*, *Caenis moesta* and Ecdyonuridae are absent or present in small numbers where the current is more noticeable. The only abundant mayflies are the muddwelling *C. horaria* and species found amongst vegetation such as *Cloeon dipterum* and *Centroptilum luteolum*, and even the latter may be absent from the drains. *Ephemera danica* is found in small numbers among the silt of the larger rivers and *Paraleptophlebia tumida* is a characteristic, but rare, species of heavily weeded streams with little flow. Stoneflies are generally absent from slow-flowing rivers but some species, e.g. *Nemoura cinerea*, have been recorded from such waters in small numbers. Stoneflies are particularly prone to pollution and may have been more widespread in these rivers in the past. The dragonfly species of eutrophic lakes and ponds are found together with the riverine forms *Agrion splendens*, *Platycnemis pennipes* and *Oxygastra curtisi*. The latter now only occurs in one or two localities. These rivers and drains often have a rich corixid and *Notonecta* fauna similar to that of rich ponds. Riverine bugs such as *Aphelocheirus montandoni* and *Velia* spp. disappear and the latter are replaced by *Gerris* spp. In thickly weeded drains *Plea leachii* and *Ilyocoris cimicoides* are abundant. The pond species of water beetle are more numerous than in chalk streams and this is particularly so in drains where genera such as *Hydroporus*, *Hygrotus*, *Hyphydrus*, *Laccophilus*, *Haliplus*, *Ilyobius* and many others, including a variety of Hydrophilidae, are abundant, but Helmidae are absent. The larvae of the alderfly *Sialis lutaria* are plentiful in the bottom muds. Many of the species of caddis associated with running water or stony substrates, such as *Agapetus fuscipes*, *Brachycentrus subnubilus*, *Hydropsyche* spp., most *Hydroptila* spp., *Rhyacophila* spp., *Sericostoma personatum*, Goerinae and *Molanna angustata*, are absent. During the recent survey it was noticed that many species, such as Limnephilidae, Leptoceridae and *Oxyethira* spp., which are associated with submerged vegetation in standing water are notably absent from this habitat in slow-flowing waters, but the reason for this absence is unknown. *Polycentropus flavomaculatus* extends into slow-flowing rivers but not the drains where *Holocentropus picicornis* is the abundant species in thick vegetation. A few aquatic Lepidoptera of the families Acentropidae and Pyraustidae are found. *Simulium* larvae, which are dependent on a current in order to feed, are completely absent from slow-flowing rivers, as are the larvae of the gravel-dwelling cranefly *Dicranota* and the empids. *Pericoma* spp. are very abundant in the drains and the larvae of *Stratiomys*, Sciomyzidae and the phantom midge *Chaoborus crystallinus* and *C. flavicans* are also found here.

SUBTERRANEAN RIVERS AND STREAMS

Most subterranean waters occur in limestone areas where the rock is dissolved by the action of carbon dioxide in solution in the water. The form of these underground waters is very variable and can range from torrential streams and waterfalls to quiet pools and lakes. Subterranean water also exists in the interstices of gravel and in fissures in chalk and limestone where a highly specialised microflora and fauna is found.

In the absence of light in these situations, autotrophic plant production is limited to a few autochemotrophic bacteria which rely on exothermic inorganic chemical reactions for their energy. Most food chains in subterranean systems, however, rely on a supply of allochthonous organic material and the predominant flora consists of heterotrophic bacteria and fungi which live on this material.

The fauna of the underground waters of caves consists of a relatively few species of invertebrate which are ultimately dependent on food washed into the caves from outside. Many of these species are also found in the water trapped in interstitial habitats. The typical aquatic invertebrates of caves are the crustaceans *Asellus cavaticus*, *Crangonyx vejdovski*, *Niphargus aquilex*, *N. fontanus*, *N. kochianus* and *N. (Niphargellus) glennei*, the last being an endemic species so far recorded only from caves in Devon (apart from a single identification in south Wales). All these species are unpigmented and eyeless and are not usually found above ground. Preying on the crustaceans are the triclads *Phagocata vitta*, *Crenobia alpina* and *Polycelis felina*, and the leech *Trocheta subviridis* but none of these is confined to caves. In the interstitial water a variety of small crustacea are found including the cladoceran *Alona protzi*, copepods, such as *Cyclops (Acanthocyclops) sensitivus*, *C. (Paracyclops) fimbriatus*, *Canthocamptus (Bryocamptus) echinatus* and *C. (B.) pygmaeus*, and the primitive syncarid crustacean *Bathynella stammeri*. In addition specialised elongate species of oligochaete, nematode, rotifer, gastrotrich, coelenterate and protozoans are characteristic.

Flora

The aquatic flora is limited more by the habitat requirements of the individual species than by any geographical restriction of range. Most species are found almost throughout Britain wherever suitable habitats occur, and the restriction of some species to certain parts of the country reflects the localisation of suitable habitats. The habitat requirements and distribution of the British aquatic flora is summarised in Table 20.

In terms of their distribution in the British Isles the aquatic flora can be divided into five main groups:

WIDESPREAD COMMON

This is the largest group comprising about half of the British flora and consisting mainly of very adaptable species found in a wide range of situations. Many of these adaptable species are emergent or floating-attached plants such as *Caltha palustris*, *Phragmites communis*, *Eleocharis palustris*, *Potamogeton natans* and *Nymphaea alba* which also have a very wide world distribution, often cosmopolitan.

Also included in this group are species which are more restricted in their habitat requirements but which are such successful colonists that they have reached almost every suitable locality. They include *Rorippa nasturtium-aquatica*, *Hippuris vulgaris*, *Myriophyllum spicatum*, *Veronica anagallis-aquatica* and *Potamogeton pectinatus*, which are more or less confined to eutrophic waters and are found throughout the British Isles but are absent from many upland areas where suitable habitats do not exist. *Eleogiton fluitans* and *Potamogeton polygonifolius* and other species of mainly oligotrophic or dystrophic waters are abundant in the uplands of the north and west, but more scattered yet by no means rare in the south and east. A few brackish water species are sufficiently widespread to belong to this category; they include *Ruppia maritima* and *Scirpus maritimus*.

WIDESPREAD LOCAL

This group comprises 15 species which, although widely distributed in the British Isles and not ascribable to any particular region, are recorded from relatively few rather scattered localities. Some have rather precise habitat requirements and the wide dispersion of suitable sites may explain their distribution. These include brackish water species (*Ranunculus baudotii* and *Ruppia spiralis*), species which are more or less restricted to mesotrophic conditions (*Eleocharis uniglumis*, *Pilularia globulifera* and *Elatine hexandra*), and *Utricularia minor* which is confined to peat pools. *Limosella aquatica*, *Eleocharis acicularis* and *Baldellia ranunculoides* may have become restricted during the period of extensive forest growth by their requirements for rather open habitats, but it is not possible to explain the present scattered distribution of the other members of this group.

NORTHERN SPECIES

Thirteen species are more or less confined to the north and north-west of Britain, where they may be abundant, and are either absent or found in a few scattered localities in the south. With the exception of *Potamogeton filiformis*, they are all species of oligotrophic or dystrophic waters and their absence from the south may be largely explained by the lack of suitable habitats. Many have been recorded from Late-glacial deposits in the south of England so that temperature may also have been instrumental in causing their retreat northwards. A few (e.g. *Subularia aquatica*) are nowadays confined to cold-water lakes or to the cooler, deeper waters of lakes (e.g. *Isoetes lacustris*). Most of this group are submerged species, particularly rosette-leaved plants such as *Isoetes* spp., *Lobelia dortmanna* and *Subularia aquatica*, but

it also includes four species with floating leaves, *Nuphar pumila*, *Nymphaea alba* ssp. *occidentalis*, *Sparganium angustifolium* and *S. minimum*, and one emergent, *Myosotis secunda*, but there are no free-floating species.

Potamogeton filiformis is restricted to eutrophic lakes and, although recorded from Late-glacial deposits in southern Britain, all present-day records are north or west of the 14.4 °C July isotherm. Exposure may also be a factor controlling its present distribution since it is a plant of the wave-washed sandy littoral zone.

Most of this group are also of northerly world distribution, five belong to J. R. Matthew's (1937) continental northern element and two each to the northern montane and oceanic northern elements. Three of the remainder are of circumpolar distribution and one is found throughout most of Europe.

SOUTHERN SPECIES

Twenty-seven species are more or less confined to a line south of the Humber and Mersey and occur only in very few scattered localities farther north, although some (e.g. *Lemna trisulca* and *Sagittaria sagittifolia*) are plentiful in central Ireland. All these species are restricted to eutrophic waters and their northerly spread has evidently been halted by the scarcity of this habitat type in northern Britain. Their presence in Ireland indicates the calcareous nature of the central lowlands of that country. Most of these species are of very wide world distribution and many of them including *Ceratophyllum demersum*, *Myriophyllum verticillatum*, *Typha angustifolia* and *Lemna minor* are almost cosmopolitan. There are also two introduced North American species in this group, namely *Acorus calamus* and *Azolla filiculoides*, and a few species of fairly restricted European distribution of which *Oenanthe fluviatilis* is fairly common and widespread in the chalk streams of southern England, but is otherwise only known from a few localities in Denmark and Germany. A number of other species characteristic of chalk streams, e.g. *Groenlandia densa*, *Apium nodiflorum*, *Ranunculus circinatus*, *R. fluitans*, *R. tripartitus*, *Berula erecta* and *S. sagittifolia* also belong to this group. Free-floating species such as *L. trisulca*, *L. polyrrhiza*, *L. gibba*, *Wolffia arrhiza* and *Hydrocharis morsus-ranae*, although mostly of worldwide distribution, are in Britain confined to the south. The free-floating community is essentially tropical in distribution (e.g. the sudd communities of African lakes), and is restricted at high latitudes by the disruptive effects of ice action.

RARE SPECIES

A number of aquatic plants of apparently very restricted distribution in Britain are recorded from less than 15 10-km squares in the *Atlas of the British Flora*. Many of these species belong to very distinct phytogeographical groups.

One group comprises species which are very restricted in their European distribution but which are widely distributed in North America. These 'Irish–American' species are all confined to the west of Britain and are also found along

Table 20. *Habitat and distribution of open water vascular plants*

	Emergent	Floating-attached	Free-floating	Submerged littoral	Submerged deep-water	Base-rich	Base-poor	Mesotrophic	Dystrophic	Brackish	Standing water	Running water	Widespread common	Widespread local	Northern Britain	Southern Britain	Rare species	European/world distribution
	1	2	3	4	5	6	7	8	9	10	11	12	13	14	15	16	17	18
Isoetes lacustris	—	—	—	—	+	—	+	—	+	—	+	—	—	—	+	—	—	?CN
I. echinospora	—	—	—	—	+	—	+	+	—	—	+	—	—	—	+	—	—	?CN
Equisetum fluviatile	+	—	—	—	—	+	+	+	—	—	+	+	+	—	—	—	—	H
Pilularia globulifera	—	—	—	+	—	—	+	—	+	—	+	—	—	+	—	—	—	C
[a]*Azolla filiculoides*	—	—	+	—	—	+	—	—	—	—	+	—	—	—	—	+	—	NA
Caltha palustris	+	—	—	—	—	+	+	+	—	—	+	+	+	—	—	—	—	H
Ranunculus lingua	+	—	—	—	—	+	—	—	—	—	+	+	—	+	—	—	—	C(P)
R. flammula	+	—	+	—	—	+	+	+	+	—	+	+	+	—	—	—	—	P
R. reptans	+	—	+	—	—	+	+	+	—	—	+	—	—	—	—	—	+	NM
R. hederaceus	—	+	—	+	—	?	+	+	—	—	+	+	+	—	—	—	—	OW
R. omiophyllus	—	+	—	+	—	—	+	—	—	—	+	+	+	—	—	—	—	—
R. tripartitus	—	+	—	+	—	+	—	—	—	—	+	+	—	—	—	+	—	OW
R. fluitans	—	—	+	+	—	+	+	—	—	—	—	+	—	—	—	+	—	CS
R. circinatus	—	—	+	+	+	—	—	—	—	—	+	—	—	—	—	+	—	C
R. trichophyllus	—	—	+	+	+	?	?	—	—	—	+	+	+	—	—	—	—	H
R. aquatilis	—	—	+	+	+	+	+	—	—	—	+	+	+	—	—	—	—	C
R. baudotii	—	—	+	+	—	—	—	—	—	+	+	+	—	+	—	—	—	OS
Nymphaea alba	—	+	—	—	—	+	+	+	+	—	+	+	+	—	—	—	—	C
N. alba ssp. *occidentalis*	—	+	—	—	—	—	—	—	+	—	+	—	—	—	+	—	—	ON
Nuphar lutea	—	+	—	—	—	+	+	+	—	—	+	+	+	—	—	—	—	P
N. pumila	—	+	—	—	—	—	+	—	+	—	+	—	—	—	+	—	—	NM(P)
Ceratophyllum demersum	—	—	+	+	+	—	—	—	—	+	+	—	+	—	—	—	—	Cos.
C. submersum	—	—	+	+	+	—	—	—	—	—	+	—	—	—	—	+	—	P Et.
Subularia aquatica	—	—	—	+	—	—	+	—	—	—	+	—	—	—	+	—	—	NM(H)
Rorippa nasturtium-aquaticum	+	—	—	+	—	+	—	+	—	—	—	+	+	—	—	—	—	CS
R. microphylla	+	—	—	+	—	+	—	+	—	—	—	+	?	—	—	—	—	—
Elatine hexandra	—	—	—	+	—	+	+	—	—	—	+	—	—	+	—	—	—	C
E. hydropiper	—	—	—	+	—	+	+	—	—	—	+	—	—	—	—	—	+	H
Potentilla palustris	+	—	—	—	—	+	+	+	—	—	+	—	+	—	—	—	—	CN(H)
Ludwigia palustris	+	—	—	+	—	+	—	—	—	—	+	—	—	—	—	—	+	Cos.
Myriophyllum alterniflorum	—	—	+	+	—	+	+	+	—	—	+	+	+	—	—	—	—	H
M. verticillatum	—	—	+	+	+	—	—	—	—	+	+	—	—	—	—	+	—	Cos.
M. spicatum	—	—	+	+	+	+	—	—	—	—	+	—	+	—	—	—	—	H
Hippuris vulgaris	+	—	—	—	—	+	—	—	—	—	+	—	+	—	—	—	—	P
Callitriche truncata	—	—	+	+	+	—	—	—	—	—	+	—	—	—	—	—	+	OS
C. intermedia	—	—	+	+	—	+	+	+	—	—	+	+	—	—	—	—	—	C
C. hermaphroditica	—	—	+	+	—	+	+	+	—	—	+	+	—	—	+	—	—	C
C. obtusangula	—	—	+	+	+	—	—	—	—	—	+	—	—	—	—	+	—	OS
C. stagnalis & *C. platycarpa*	—	—	—	+	+	+	+	+	?	—	+	+	+	—	—	—	—	C
Hydrocotyle vulgaris	+	—	—	+	—	+	—	+	—	—	+	—	+	—	—	—	—	CS
Apium nodiflorum	+	—	—	+	—	+	—	—	—	—	+	+	—	—	—	+	—	CS
A. inundatum	—	—	+	+	—	+	+	+	—	—	+	—	+	—	—	—	—	—
Berula erecta	+	—	—	+	—	+	—	—	—	—	+	+	—	—	—	+	—	H
Oenanthe fistulosa	+	—	—	+	—	+	?	?	—	—	+	—	—	—	—	+	—	

Table 20 (*contd.*)

	1	2	3	4	5	6	7	8	9	10	11	12	13	14	15	16	17	18
O. lachenalii	+	−	−	−	−	+	−	−	−	+	+	−	+	−	−	−	−	—
O. crocata	+	−	−	−	−	+	+	+	−	−	+	+	+	−	−	+	−	OW
O. aquatica	−	−	−	+	−	+	−	−	−	−	+	+	−	−	−	+	−	C
O. fluviatilis	−	−	−	+	+	+	−	−	−	−	−	+	−	−	−	+	−	OW
Polygonum amphibium	−	+	−	−	−	+	?	+	−	−	+	−	+	−	−	−	+	H Et.
Rumex aquaticus	+	−	−	−	−	−	+	+	−	−	+	−	−	−	−	−	+	C
R. hydrolapathum	+	−	−	−	−	+	−	−	−	−	+	+	+	−	−	−	−	C
Hottonia palustris	+	−	−	+	−	+	−	−	−	−	+	−	−	−	−	+	−	CN
Menyanthes trifoliata	+	−	−	−	−	+	+	+	+	−	+	−	+	−	−	−	−	CN(H)
Nymphoides peltata	−	+	−	−	−	+	−	−	−	−	+	−	−	−	−	+	−	P
Myosotis scorpioides	+	−	−	+	−	+	+	+	?	−	+	+	+	−	−	−	−	H
M. secunda	+	−	−	+	−	−	+	−	+	−	+	+	−	−	+	−	−	?CN
M. caespitosa	+	−	−	+	−	+	+	+	?	−	+	+	+	−	−	−	−	P
Limosella aquatica	+	−	−	+	−	+	−	−	−	−	?	−	−	+	−	−	−	CN(P)
L. subulata	+	−	−	+	−	?	−	−	−	?	+	−	−	−	−	−	+	NA
Veronica beccabunga	+	−	−	+	−	+	+	+	−	−	−	+	+	−	−	−	−	H
V. anagallis-aquatica	+	−	−	−	−	+	−	−	−	−	−	+	+	−	−	−	−	Cos.
Utricularia vulgaris ⎫	−	−	−	+	+	+	?	+	−	−	+	−	+	−	−	−	−	—
U. neglecta ⎭																		
U. intermedia	−	−	−	+	−	−	+	−	+	−	+	−	−	−	+	−	−	CN(H)
U. minor	−	−	−	+	−	−	−	−	+	−	+	−	−	+	−	−	−	CN(H)
Mentha aquatica	+	−	−	+	−	+	+	+	−	−	+	+	+	−	−	−	−	P Et.
Littorella uniflora	−	−	−	+	−	+	+	+	+	−	+	+	+	−	−	−	−	CN
Lobelia dortmanna	−	−	−	+	−	−	+	+	+	−	+	−	−	−	−	+	−	ON/NA
Baldellia ranunculoides	+	−	−	−	−	+	+	+	−	−	+	−	−	+	−	−	−	?C
Luronium natans	−	+	+	−	−	+	+	+	−	−	+	−	−	*b*	*b*	−	−	?C
Alisma gramineum	+	−	−	−	−	+	−	−	−	−	+	−	−	−	−	−	+	—
A. plantago-aquatica	+	−	−	−	−	+	+	+	−	−	+	+	+	−	−	−	−	H Aus.
A. lanceolatum	+	−	−	−	−	+	?	?	−	−	+	−	−	−	−	+	−	H
Damasonium alisma	+	−	−	+	−	+	−	−	−	−	+	−	−	−	−	−	+	?CS
Sagittaria sagittifolia	+	+	−	+	−	+	−	−	−	−	−	+	−	−	−	+	−	H
Butomus umbellatus	+	−	−	−	−	+	−	−	−	−	+	+	−	−	−	+	−	P
Hydrocharis morsus-ranae	−	+	+	−	−	+	−	−	−	−	+	−	−	−	−	+	−	P
Stratiotes aloides	−	−	+	+	−	+	−	−	−	−	+	−	−	−	−	−	+	C
[a]*Elodea canadensis*	−	−	−	+	+	+	+	+	−	−	+	+	+	−	−	−	−	NA
E. nuttallii	−	−	−	−	+	−	−	+	−	−	+	−	−	−	−	−	+	NA
Potamogeton natans	−	+	−	−	−	+	+	+	+	−	+	+	+	−	−	−	−	Cos.
P. polygonifolius	−	+	−	−	−	−	−	−	+	−	+	+	+	−	−	−	−	H
P. coloratus	−	+	−	+	−	+	−	−	−	−	+	−	−	+	−	−	−	C
P. nodosus	−	+	−	+	−	−	−	−	−	−	−	+	−	−	−	−	+	OS
P. lucens	−	−	−	+	+	+	−	−	−	−	+	+	+	−	−	−	−	P
P. gramineus	−	−	−	+	+	+	+	+	−	−	+	+	+	−	−	−	−	H
P. alpinus	−	−	−	+	+	?	+	+	−	−	+	+	+	−	−	−	−	H
P. praelongus	−	−	−	−	+	+	−	+	−	−	+	+	+	−	−	−	−	CN(P)
P. perfoliatus	−	−	−	+	+	+	+	+	−	−	+	+	+	−	−	−	−	H Aus.
P. epihydrus	−	+	−	+	−	+	−	−	−	−	+	−	−	−	−	−	+	NA
P. freisii	−	−	−	+	+	+	−	−	−	−	+	−	+	−	−	−	−	H
P. rutilus	−	−	−	+	+	+	−	−	−	−	+	−	−	−	−	−	+	P
P. obtusifolius	−	−	−	−	+	+	+	+	−	−	+	−	+	−	−	−	−	CN(P)
P. pusillus	−	−	−	+	+	+	−	−	−	+	+	−	+	−	−	−	−	H Et.
P. berchtoldii	−	−	−	−	+	+	+	+	−	−	+	−	+	−	−	−	−	H
P. trichoides	−	−	−	+	+	+	−	−	−	−	+	−	−	−	−	+	−	H Et.
P. compressus	−	−	−	+	+	−	−	−	−	−	+	−	−	−	−	+	−	CN
P. acutifolius	−	−	−	+	+	−	−	−	−	−	+	−	−	−	−	+	−	C
P. crispus	−	−	−	+	+	+	−	+	−	−	+	+	+	−	−	−	−	P
P. filiformis	−	−	−	+	+	+	−	+	−	−	+	+	−	−	−	+	−	CN(P)
P. pectinatus	−	−	−	+	+	+	−	−	−	−	+	+	+	+	−	−	−	Cos.
Groenlandia densa	−	−	−	+	−	+	−	−	−	−	−	+	−	−	−	+	−	P Et.
Ruppia spiralis	−	−	−	+	+	−	−	−	−	−	+	+	−	−	+	−	−	Cos.
R. maritima	−	−	−	+	+	−	−	−	−	−	+	+	−	+	−	−	−	H Et.

Table 20 (*contd.*)

	1	2	3	4	5	6	7	8	9	10	11	12	13	14	15	16	17	18	
Zannichellia palustris	—	—	—	+	+	+	—	—	—	+	+	+	+	—	—	—	—	—	Cos.
Najas marina	—	—	—	+	+	+	—	—	—	+	+	—	—	—	—	—	—	+	Cos.
N. flexilis	—	—	—	—	+	+	—	+	—	—	+	—	—	—	—	—	—	+	ON/NA
Eriocaulon septangulare	+	—	—	—	—	—	—	—	+	—	+	—	—	—	—	—	—	+	NA
Juncus bulbosus	+	—	—	+	+	+	+	+	+	—	+	+	+	—	—	—	—	—	P
Iris pseudacorus	+	—	—	—	—	+	+	+	+	+	+	+	+	—	—	—	—	—	P
[b]*Acorus calamus*	+	—	—	—	—	+	—	—	—	—	+	+	—	—	—	—	+	—	NA
Lemna trisulca	—	—	+	+	—	+	—	—	—	—	+	—	—	—	—	—	+	—	Cos.
L. polyrrhiza	—	—	+	—	—	+	—	—	—	—	+	—	—	—	—	—	+	—	Cos.
L. minor	—	—	+	—	—	+	—	—	—	—	+	—	+	—	—	—	—	—	Cos.
L. gibba	—	—	+	—	—	+	—	—	—	—	+	—	+	—	—	—	+	—	Cos.
Wolffia arrhiza	—	—	+	—	—	+	—	—	—	—	+	—	—	—	—	—	+	—	Cos.
Sparganium erectum	+	—	—	—	—	+	—	—	—	—	+	+	+	—	—	—	—	—	P
S. emersum	+	+	—	+	—	+	—	—	—	—	+	+	+	—	—	—	—	—	H
S. angustifolium	+	+	—	—	—	—	+	—	+	—	+	+	—	—	+	—	—	—	CN(P)
S. minimum	+	+	—	—	—	—	—	+	—	+	+	—	—	—	+	—	—	—	H
Typha latifolia	+	—	—	—	—	+	—	+	—	—	+	—	+	—	—	—	—	—	almost Cos.
T. angustifolia	+	—	—	—	—	+	—	+	—	—	+	—	—	—	—	—	+	—	Cos.
Eleocharis acicularis	+	—	—	—	—	+	?	?	?	—	+	—	—	+	—	—	—	—	Cos. except Et.
E. multicaulis	+	—	—	—	—	—	—	—	+	—	+	—	+	—	—	—	—	—	CN
E. palustris	+	—	—	—	—	+	+	+	+	—	+	—	+	—	—	—	—	—	Cos.
E. uniglumis	+	—	—	—	—	+	—	—	—	+	+	—	—	+	—	—	—	—	P
Scirpus maritimus	+	—	—	—	—	+	—	—	—	+	+	+	+	—	—	—	—	—	Cos.
Schoenoplectus lacustris	+	—	—	—	—	+	+	+	—	—	+	+	+	—	—	—	—	—	Cos.
S. tabernaemontani	+	—	—	—	—	+	?	?	?	+	+	—	+	—	—	—	—	—	P
Eleogiton fluitans	—	—	+	+	—	—	+	—	+	—	+	—	+	—	—	—	—	—	P Et. Aus.
Cladium mariscus	+	—	—	—	—	+	—	—	—	—	+	—	—	+	—	—	—	—	Cos.
[c]*Carex* spp.																			
Phragmites communis	+	—	—	—	—	+	+	+	—	+	+	+	+	—	—	—	—	—	Cos.
Glyceria fluitans	—	+	—	+	—	+	+	+	+	—	+	+	+	—	—	—	—	—	H
G. plicata	—	+	—	+	—	+	?	?	?	—	+	+	+	—	—	—	—	—	H
G. declinata	—	+	—	+	—	+	+	+	+	—	+	+	+	—	—	—	—	—	—
G. maxima	+	—	—	—	—	+	—	—	—	—	+	+	+	—	—	—	—	—	P
Phalaris arundinacea	+	—	—	—	—	+	+	+	—	+	+	+	+	—	—	—	—	—	H Et.
Total 139	56	23	10	79	43	104	54	57	28	17	124	63	65	13	12	28	16		

Notes

World distribution	European distribution after Matthews
Cos. = cosmopolitan	CN = continental northern
H = holarctic	CS = continental southern
P = palaearctic	C = continental
Et. = Africa, south of Sahara	OW = oceanic west european
Aus. = Australasian	OS = oceanic southern
NA = North American	ON = oceanic northern
	NM = northern montane

The European distribution of many species is given by J. R. Matthews (1937) and for those with a wider distribution, the latter is given in parentheses after their European distribution

[a] Widespread introduced species.
[b] Midlands.
[c] See Peatlands.

the Atlantic seaboard of continental Europe. In Britain, *Elodea nuttallii* is known only from Esthwaite Water, while *Eriocaulon septangulare* is confined to the Ardnamurchan peninsula and Coll and Skye in the Hebrides. *Potamogeton epihydrus* is confined to South Uist and *Limosella subulata* to three coastal sites in Wales. *Najas flexilis* and *Lobelia dortmanna* also have some claims to belong to this group since they are both far more widespread in America than they are now in Europe, but they have contracted in distribution in Britain since Late-glacial times.

Another group consists of species which are widely distributed throughout the warmer parts of the world but which are on the edge of their range in Britain and northwest Europe. These are found only in the south or south-east of Britain. They comprise *Ludwigia palustris*, confined to one pond in the New Forest, *Najas marina*, restricted to the Norfolk Broads, *Potamogeton nodosus* in a few large rivers in central southern England (including the Thames, Loddon, Stour and Somerset Avon), and *Wolffia arrhiza*, found in ponds mostly south of the Thames.

A number of European species reach their most northerly or north-westerly location in Britain. *Alisma gramineum* occurs in Lincolnshire and Worcestershire, *Callitriche truncata* in a number of sites south from Lincolnshire (including Dungeness), *Stratiotes aloides* is a native in East Anglia and the north Midlands, but widely introduced elsewhere, and *Luronium natans* has a range extending from north Wales through the west Midlands to central northern England. Some of these species may be recent arrivals in Britain which are now in the process of extending their range.

Nuphar pumila which is fairly widely distributed north of the Highland Boundary Fault also occurs in Crose Mere in Shropshire where it is a glacial relict. Its hybrid *N. spennerana* (= *N. lutea* × *N. pumila*) also occurs as a relict in northern England outside the present range of *N. pumila*.

Potamogeton rutilus which is found in Shetland and in the Outer Hebrides is fairly widely distributed in north-west Europe including Scandinavia and Russia, as is *Rumex aquaticus* which in Britain is confined to Loch Lomond. The minute aquatic plant *Elatine hydropiper* is recorded from only 21 stations in Britain, but is probably widely overlooked as it has been recorded from a number of new localities during the survey for the *Review*.

Fauna

BIRDS AND MAMMALS

OLIGOTROPHIC AND DYSTROPHIC LAKES

Few aquatic birds frequent large oligotrophic lakes, but with increasing nutrient status both the numbers and variety of species increase. The most characteristic species of breeding duck of large, nutrient-poor lakes are goosander *Mergus merganser* and red-breasted merganser *M. serrator*, the latter on lakes nearer the sea; and small numbers of mallard *Anas platyrhynchos* and teal *A. crecca*, which are equally characteristic of peaty dubh lochans. Divers also breed on oligotrophic lakes but are restricted to Scotland. The red-throated diver *Gavia stellata* is found especially on small peaty lochans, mostly within flighting distance of the sea, where the adults prefer to feed, while the black-throated diver *G. arctica* is generally found on larger lochs with islands, often far inland. The common gull *Larus canus* is a characteristic breeding species on barren, stony-shored oligotrophic lakes and their islands in the north, but usually with only a few pairs on each water-body. In contrast, quite large colonies of black-headed gulls *L. ridibundus* are found on oligotrophic lakes throughout Britain, especially on peaty lakes amongst emergent *Carex rostrata*. The rare Slavonian grebe *Podiceps auritus* breeds in the marginal sedge swamp around rather oligotrophic lochs in the Highlands. Common sandpipers *Tringa hypoleucos* and dippers *Cinclus cinclus* are common and widespread around the margins of stony-shored lakes, but the greenshank *T. nebularia* which frequents similar habitats is confined as a breeder to the Highlands of Scotland. Certain species which are principally marine in habitat will also frequent oligotrophic lakes in small numbers. Of these the cormorant *Phalacrocorax carbo* is the most common. Herons *Ardea cinerea* are widespread throughout Britain and will feed on most types of water including the most nutrient-poor of lakes.

The indigenous breeding population of the greylag *Anser anser* is found mainly on the shallow rocky oligotrophic lakes of the Outer Hebrides where they breed on islands and feed on the rich calcareous grasslands of the nearby machair. Smaller numbers occur on the mainland of the northern Highlands either on large lochs, or the smaller tarns and dubh lochans of the great flows in east Sutherland and Caithness. Feral populations of this goose, in contrast, will breed on a wide variety of water-bodies including highly eutrophic lowland lakes. Common scoter *Melanitta nigra* breed on a small number of peaty hill lochans and larger lochs in Scotland; while the osprey *Pandion haliaetus* has recolonised the Highlands where it nests on trees in several widely scattered localities and fishes on the oligotrophic and mesotrophic lakes and rivers. Wigeon *Anas penelope* are fairly frequent breeders on oligotrophic lakes but also nest by mesotrophic and eutrophic waters.

Few species of aquatic mammals are found in oligotrophic lakes in Britain. The otter, which has declined in numbers in lowland Britain, is still a common species around the lakes and rivers of the upland areas, while the water shrew is found in all types of waters, but is absent from most of the Highlands of Scotland. As with birds, some marine animals are occasionally seen in the freshwater lochs of Scotland. For instance, grey seals are frequently encountered in Loch Shiel which is connected to the sea by a short river.

MESOTROPHIC LAKES

In mesotrophic lakes, as the nutrient content of the water and the productivity of the lake increases, the numbers of both breeding and wintering wildfowl follow suit. Diversity of species also increases, and birds such as the coot *Fulica atra* and mute swan *Cygnus olor* which are generally absent from oligotrophic waters, may appear.

EUTROPHIC AND MARL LAKES

It is only on eutrophic waters, generally large shallow lakes, that large concentrations of wintering waterfowl occur. These wildfowl concentrations are of two distinct groups of birds: those which use the lake merely as a roosting site, and flight out to feed in terrestrial or other aquatic habitats; and those birds which actually feed from the lake. The former group includes such geese as the pink-footed *Anser brachyrhynchus* which favours large lakes as a roost, and the greylag, more commonly found on smaller water-bodies. Several of the dabbling ducks, especially mallard, and some of the swans, roost by day and flight out at night to feed on surrounding land or water. Many of these lowland lakes are also used as roosts at night by huge numbers of gulls. These large concentrations of roosting birds are usually absent from oligotrophic water, presumably because extensive areas of farmland or estuarine water, which offer feeding to these birds, are not generally found in their vicinity. Roosting birds can have a major influence on the water chemistry of the smaller lakes by introducing large quantities of allochthonous nutrients in their droppings. This process of nutrient enrichment has been termed guanotrophy. (Rostherne Mere is considered to be a guanotrophic lake.) Species which feed mostly within the lake include diving ducks such as goldeneye *Bucephala clangula*, pochard *Aythya ferina* and tufted duck *Aythya fuligula*, dabblers such as the shoveler *Anas clypeata* (which is principally an invertebrate feeder), coot and mute swan which feed on aquatic macrophytes, and fish eaters such as great crested grebe *Podiceps cristata* and goosander. These species are more common on eutrophic waters since the production of food organisms is high compared with oligotrophic lakes. The latter are generally deep and therefore most of the bottom is inaccessible to wildfowl, which do not dive below about 8 m, while eutrophic waters holding large numbers of feeding wildfowl are generally shallow. Some wintering birds such as whooper and Bewick's swans (*Cygnus cygnus* and *C. bewickii*) feed on plants both from the lake and from surrounding farmland.

Of the breeding duck, pochard, tufted duck, gadwall *Anas strepera*, shoveler, pintail *A. acuta*, and garganey *A. querquedula* are associated with the richer lakes, whilst mallard, teal and wigeon which breed in higher concentrations around such waters also breed around oligotrophic lakes. Some of these ducks nest in swamp or close to the water edge but others breed well away from the lake. The great crested grebe and little grebe *Podiceps ruficollis* breed mainly on mesotrophic to eutrophic lakes amongst emergent or floating vegetation, and the rare black-necked grebe *P. nigricollis* appears to be confined to the richer lakes. The red-necked phalarope *Phalaropus lobatus* is confined as a breeder to small eutrophic lochs in the extreme north and west of Scotland.

As well as the truly aquatic birds, a large number of other bird species are associated with lowland eutrophic lakes. These include widespread fish-eating species such as the heron and the kingfisher *Alcedo atthis*. The swift *Apus apus* and members of the swallow family, Hirundinidae, may feed extensively on aquatic insects, especially chironomid midges, hatching from the surface of lakes. A number of species associated with the reed fringe surrounding many eutrophic lakes include the water rail *Rallus aquaticus*, reed bunting *Emberiza schoeniclus*, sedge warbler *Acrocephalus schoenabaenus*, and rarer species such as the bittern, *Botaurus stellaris*, bearded tit *Panurus biarmicus*, and marsh harrier, *Circus aeruginosus*, which are mostly confined to the extensive *Phragmites* beds of East Anglia and south-east England and to one outpost in Lancashire. The more exposed shores of eutrophic lakes where vegetation is sparse offer feeding to wagtails, pipits and a variety of waders, the latter mostly as passage migrants. In lowland England the little ringed plover *Charadrius dubius* has nested inland in recent years on unvegetated gravel beside gravel pits and reservoirs.

One species of aquatic mammal confined in Britain to eutrophic waters is the introduced coypu *Myocastor coypus*, which is restricted to the Norfolk Broads and dykes in East Anglia where it causes extensive damage by burrowing into the banks and may cause flooding. Their numbers have been effectively controlled by trapping. Water voles *Arvicola amphibius* and water shrews are also found in eutrophic lakes but both these species are more frequently associated with running waters.

RIVERS

Birds principally associated with running waters in Britain include the dipper which is found in the more torrential parts of upland rivers, the grey wagtail *Motacilla cinerea*, which occurs in similar habitats but is more widespread, and the kingfisher which is mainly found on lowland rivers. Many birds characteristic of standing waters are also found in smaller numbers on rivers. The commonest species associated with the faster-flowing stretches include common sandpiper, ringed plover *Charadrius hiaticulus* and oystercatcher *Haematopus ostralegus*, which often nests on shingle banks. The last two extend well up rivers in Scotland but are mainly coastal in England. The greenshank feeds along rivers and lake shores in the central and north-western Highlands. The red-breasted merganser and heron are also found on moderately fast and slow rivers. The slower stretches may hold small numbers of wintering wildfowl, and the flats between the loops of the river may provide a safe refuge for large numbers of wintering geese. The moorhen *Gallinula chloropus* is a common breeding bird of slower rivers and, where there are steep alluvial banks, colonies of sand martins *Riparia riparia* often breed.

The commonest aquatic mammal found by running waters is the water vole which is found throughout mainland Britain, the type species being replaced, in the Scottish Highlands, by a melanic race *Arvicola amphibius reta*. Otters and water shrews are also found by running waters of all types. Many marine mammals travel considerable distances up tidal estuaries and may penetrate well into fresh water (common porpoises *Phocaena phocaena* sometimes travel up the Thames as far as London).

FISH

Fish are by far the most important vertebrates inhabiting fresh waters. In Britain, they are more widely distributed and more abundant than other aquatic vertebrates and their value both in terms of human food and sporting interest runs into millions of pounds annually. Relatively few fresh waters in Britain are fishless though many isolated lakes must owe their present fish stocks to man-made introductions in the past. Fish are not found in Britain in lakes above 850 m in altitude and although attempts have been made to introduce fish to lakes above this level the stocks soon died out. Waters that frequently dry out in summer months are also fishless, as no British species is truly resistant to desiccation, although certain cyprinids, such as the tench

Tinca tinca, may survive for short periods in wet mud. Very acidic peat pools are also generally without fish, as pH values of less than about 4.5 are directly toxic to most fish species. Fish are now absent from the most grossly polluted stretches of rivers running through industrialised Britain, and from a small number of lakes where ancient mine workings cause unusually high concentrations of toxic heavy metals in the water.

The habitat preferences of the British freshwater fish are somewhat obscured by the uneven geographical distribution of several species. With the exception of those which can tolerate sea water and can enter the sea, the powers of natural dispersal of freshwater fish are very limited. Eels *Anguilla anguilla*, salmon *Salmo salar*, brown trout *Salmo trutta* (and its sea-going race the sea trout), flounder *Platichthys flesus*, three-spined stickleback *Gasterosteus aculeatus*, ten-spined stickleback *Pungitius pungitius*, marine lamprey *Petromyzon marinus*, and river lamprey *Lampetra fluviatilis*, frequently enter the sea and have become distributed in much of the British Isles in suitable waters. Apart from these, few fish have spread further north than the central lowlands of Scotland after their recolonisation of south-east England in the last interglacial, while Britain was still connected to the Continent. The two most successful colonists are the minnow *Phoxinus phoxinus*, which has been largely spread by man as fish bait, and the perch *Perca fluviatilis*, which lays long sticky ribbons of eggs which attach to wildfowl. Until man recently assisted their dispersion by canal-building and deliberate introductions, some species (e.g. barbel *Barbus barbus*, bleak *Alburnus alburnus*, ruff or pope *Gymnocephalus cernua*, white (or silver) bream *Blicca bjoerkna* and burbot *Lota lota*) were more or less restricted to those British rivers which flowed into the Rhine when the landbridge between Britain and the Continent was intact. Gudgeon *Gobio gobio*, dace *Leuciscus leuciscus*, chub *Squalius cephalus*, rudd *Scardinius erythrophthalmus*, tench *Tinca tinca* and bream *Abramis brama*, have extended as far north as the Scottish Border. Some species have crossed the barrier of the Southern Uplands of Scotland and have colonised lowland Scotland and some have just penetrated the Highlands. This group comprises grayling *Thymallus thymallus*, roach *Rutilus rutilus*, stone loach *Noemacheilus barbatulus*, and bullhead *Cottus gobio*. The pike *Esox lucius* extends north as far as Ross but its natural distribution is obscured by its introduction as a food fish in the past. Other species such as the *Coregonus* spp., *C. lavaretus* and *C. albula*, and charr *Salvelinus alpinus*, are glacial relicts and are now restricted to generally deep waters in the north and west.

OLIGOTROPHIC LAKES

In Britain such waters generally have a fish fauna dominated by salmonids. In those lakes containing fish, brown trout are invariably present and, where the outflow gives uninterrupted access to the sea, these are joined by salmon and sea trout. These species of salmonid require a clean gravel through which a current of water is flowing in which to spawn. Many such lakes, particularly those that are large and deep, contain charr, and a few in Wales, the Lake District and South Scotland contain white fish *Coregonus lavaretus* or vendace *C. albula*. Charr can seldom survive in competition with *Coregonus* spp. and few lakes in Britain contain both. Oligotrophic lakes also contain the ubiquitous eel and three-spined stickleback as well as one or more of the three lamprey species (*Lampetra planeri*, *L. fluviatilis* and *Petromyzon marinus*). Minnows are not found in Scotland much further north than the Great Glen but are widespread in stony-shored lakes further south. Perch and pike are also found in many oligotrophic lakes but become more dominant in slightly richer waters. In lakes within the range of the cyprinid fishes (south of Loch Lomond) species such as roach may be found but only become abundant in more eutrophic waters. Stream-dwelling fish such as stone loach and bullhead may extend out from stream mouths into oligotrophic lakes.

MESOTROPHIC LAKES

In mesotrophic lakes in England and Wales perch, pike and various cyprinid fishes, especially roach, may begin to replace the salmonid fishes. Thus, in Esthwaite Water with increasing nutrient enrichment, roach and rudd have greatly increased in numbers in recent years at the expense of the trout population. Small numbers of roach and rudd have been caught more recently in the south basin of Windermere. Esthwaite is the most evolved of the larger Lake District lakes and is the only one which does not contain either *Coregonus* spp. or *Salvelinus alpinus*. Charr are generally only found in oligotrophic lakes in Britain, though they were formerly found in Loch Leven (alkalinity = 35–70 p.p.m. $CaCO_3$), Kinross, and occur in one marl lake, Loch Borralie (alkalinity = 140–150 p.p.m. $CaCO_3$). The richest water in which *Coregonus* is now found in Britain is the Mill Loch, Lochmaben (alkalinity = 50–60 p.p.m. $CaCO_3$), and they have disappeared from the neighbouring shallower and more enriched Castle Loch.

EUTROPHIC LAKES

Cyprinids are usually the most abundant fish in eutrophic lakes in England and Wales but, in Scotland, outside the range of this family the fish fauna may be very similar to that of oligotrophic waters. In eutrophic waters in Scotland self-maintaining populations of fast-growing brown trout may exist. On the other hand, the silted conditions of the inflows in many eutrophic waters in the south of Britain may prevent natural spawning and the maintenance of a trout fishery will depend on regular re-stocking. In such cases rainbow trout *Salmo gairdneri* are often stocked instead of the native brown trout. The murky phytoplankton-laden waters of many eutrophic lakes militate against visual feeders such as the salmonids and favour fish such as the cyprinids which use their sense of smell to locate food. The latter also require weed-beds in which to spawn and these are generally more abundant in eutrophic lakes. Consequently, where there is natural competition between

Table 21. *A classification of European rivers into zones, based upon their fish populations (adapted from Huet, 1954)*

Trout zone: current rapid, gradient very steep	Grayling or minnow zone: current fast, gradient steep	Barbel or chub zone: current moderate, gradient gentle	Bream zone: current slow to sluggish, gradient very gentle	Flounder or mullet zone: current tidal, no gradient, brackish water

Fish species present (those in italics are most abundant and those in parentheses when present are found in small numbers)

Trout	*Trout*	Barbel	*Bream*	*Flounder*
Salmon	*Salmon*	Chub	*White bream*	*Thick-lipped mullet*
	Minnow	Dace	*Carp*	*Thin-lipped mullet*
Minnow	*Bullhead*	Gudgeon	*Tench*	*Golden mullet*
Bullhead	*Stone loach*	Bleak	*Three-spined stickleback*	*Three-spined stickleback*
Stone loach	*Grayling*	Roach	*Ten-spined stickleback*	*Ten-spined stickleback*
		Rudd	*Roach*	*Common goby*
	Barbel	Perch	*Rudd*	
	Chub	Pope	*Perch*	
	Dace	Pike	*Pope*	
	Gudgeon	Eel	*Pike*	
	Bleak		*Eel*	
		(Trout)		Smelt
		(Salmon)		Allis shad
(Perch)		(Grayling)		Twaite shad
(Pike)		(Minnow)		Trout
(Eel)		(Bullhead)	(Barbel)	
(Roach)		(Stone loach)	(Chub)	(Perch)
(Rudd)		(Tench)	(Dace)	(Salmon)
		(Bream)	(Gudgeon)	(Eel)
		(White bream)	(Bleak)	(Roach)
		(Carp)		
		(Three-spined stickleback)		
		(Ten-spined stickleback)		

these two groups, the cyprinids are usually favoured in eutrophic waters and the salmonids often eliminated.

Of the few species of fish which only occur in abundance in enclosed standing waters, carp and tench are bottom feeders, and rudd feed at the surface. Many other species found in standing waters also occur in the slower stretches of lowland rivers (the so-called bream zone (see Table 21)).

A few exotic species have been introduced into small lakes and ponds in southern England. These include the wels *Silurus glanis*, which came into Britain with the aquarium trade and has since been spread by anglers, the pike-perch *Stizostedion lucioperca*, and various American bass belonging to the Centrarchidae. The carp was originally introduced into Britain by monks in the sixteenth century and is now widely distributed in scattered localities throughout lowland Britain, but is abundant only in the southern half of England. The bitterling carp *Rhodeus sericeus* is now fairly widely distributed in canals and slow-flowing rivers in England, where it has been introduced by aquarists.

RIVERS

Some fish in Britain are wholly or mainly confined to running water. These are grayling, barbel, burbot, bleak, dace, spined loach *Cobitis taenia*, chub and bullhead.

In running waters there is a progression from the gener-ally fast-flowing upper reaches, through the slower-flowing middle reaches, to the slow or sluggish lower stretches and the estuary. Different communities of fish occur in these zones as shown in Table 21 based on the classification of Huet (1954) for European rivers. Such a classification cannot be applied generally to British rivers because of the northerly limits of distribution of many species. Thus, in the north of Scotland, brown trout may be the dominant species throughout from the most torrential to the most sluggish stretches of river. Many lowland rivers have no fast upper reaches and species of the chub zone extend throughout the river.

AMPHIBIANS AND REPTILES

In Britain there are only six native species of Amphibia, but in addition two species of frog have recently been introduced from the continent and survive in southern England. One species of reptile, the grass snake, is partially aquatic, and the adder sometimes takes to water.

The newts are the most aquatic of the British Amphibia. The warty or crested newt *Triturus cristatus* is found throughout mainland Britain and breeds mainly in deep ponds. The smooth newt *T. vulgaris* (which is the only species found in Ireland), is mainly a lowland species frequenting weedy ponds, while the palmate newt *T. helveticus* is the only species found at high altitudes where it may occur in quite large corrie lakes. This species is also found at low altitudes and may even occur in brackish pools at sea-level.

The common frog and common toad, both found throughout mainland Britain, may breed in the same water-body, but toads are generally found in deeper water and do not breed in extremely shallow pools as do frogs. Frogs also extend to higher altitudes and can occur in Britain at up to 1000 m. Both species may be found breeding in waters ranging from peat pools to highly calcareous lowland lakes and even, in the case of toads, brackish pools. The natterjack toad is mainly a coastal species in Britain but is also found in sandy heathland areas inland. Its scattered distribution is probably a result of its requirement for mobile sand into which to burrow. Its breeding sites are usually small, often temporary, and frequently brackish pools and dune slacks. The edible frog *Rana esculenta* has been introduced into some ponds around London and the marsh frog *R. ridibunda* into Romney Marsh, the Pevensey Levels and the Somerset Levels where it breeds in weed-choked, calcareous or slightly brackish dykes, in which it appears to have displaced the common frog.

The grass snake, distributed throughout lowland England and Wales, is usually found near water. It is a powerful swimmer and much of its prey consists of fish and amphibians.

CRITERIA FOR KEY SITE ASSESSMENT AND SELECTION

Comparative site evaluation

The general criteria used in the comparative evaluation of key sites are described in Chapter 2. In addition the following special factors have been taken into account in the selection of key open water sites.

Naturalness

Open waters are more likely to be altered by man's activity than completely destroyed, and few open water sites in Britain have disappeared entirely. The modification of open waters can be so profound however that they become valueless to nature conservation, and in extreme cases (e.g. heavily polluted rivers) they may be virtually lifeless. Pollution, including eutrophication, is the major modifying factor affecting open waters, and chemical and biotic tests for different forms of pollution play a part in the comparative evaluation of sites. Since most sources of pollution originate at points within the catchment remote from the water-body, naturalness of the catchment, as well as intactness of the water-body itself, is important. In the case of oligotrophic sites the effects of slight pollution or enrichment are more drastic and the degree of intactness demanded of the catchment is much greater than that demanded of eutrophic sites. Fortunately most oligotrophic waters are in the relatively unpopulated uplands, but aerial applications of fertilisers may pose a threat to them.

The hydrology of open waters may also be affected by man's activities. Many natural lakes have been converted to storage reservoirs in which rapid and large-scale fluctuations in water level cause severe impoverishment of the littoral and sublittoral fauna and flora. The greater and more rapid the drawdown in a reservoir the less is it likely to be of value for conservation, and in this respect hydro-electric reservoirs are usually of less value than water supply reservoirs. In rivers, the hydrology is modified by the construction of locks, weirs and dams, and by regulation of discharge, embankment and straightening as well as water abstraction and effluent discharge. Most of these modifications lead to a deterioration in the structural and biological diversity of river systems.

In lowland Britain increased recreational activity on many open waters is destroying much aquatic wildlife and the presence of the more destructive forms of recreation on a water-body has counted against that site in the overall assessment.

Natural water-bodies are normally preferable to those artificially constructed, particularly in relation to the stratigraphical history depicted in their sediments, and artificial water-bodies have only been chosen where no natural alternative exists. However, some types of water-body such as the shallow fenland meres (e.g. the former Whittlesea Mere) are no longer found in a natural state in Britain and, since many of the interesting invertebrate species are now extinct in this country, this ecosystem is irretrievably lost and artificial waters now form the nearest alternative. In many parts of lowland Britain, particularly in the chalk and limestone areas, there are very few natural standing water-bodies, and artificial types, such as Tring Reservoirs and the Cotswold Water Park gravel pits, are habitats not previously found in Britain, yet have high conservation value. Many rivers, particularly the chalk streams of southern England, which are often thought of as a natural part of the British scene, are highly modified and only maintained in their present form by intensive management involving dredging, weed-cutting, removal of coarse fish, and stocking with trout. They nevertheless represent a diverse habitat not found in a natural state in Britain.

In spite of the modifications to many British freshwater stystems, some of these, including a high proportion of Scottish Highland lochs and streams, are probably the habitats least changed by man in inland Britain.

Structural diversity

This is an extremely important criterion in the assessment of open waters, since, probably more than for any other formation, chemistry and morphology are the most critical factors controlling the flora and fauna. Diversity of shoreline is particularly important in the case of lakes and, since the coarser sediments only occur in exposed situations, larger lakes are more diverse than smaller ones. Similarly, the presence of deep water gives additional diversity. Oligotrophic lakes are naturally rather uniform in structure, and examples of extreme oligotrophy are often chosen for their rather uniform shoreline, but great depth and size are desirable features.

In rivers, gradients of such factors as water chemistry, current, nature of substrate, size and depth as one progresses downstream are desirable features. On this account large river systems, especially those running over a wide altitudinal range are of particular value. Similarly in a brackish situation grading to fresh water, a wide range of salinities and associated flora and fauna scores highly.

Floristic and faunal diversity

Oligotrophic waters have a naturally rather impoverished fauna and flora, and diversity is not a highly desirable feature in these habitats: the presence of certain additional species is often indicative of nutrient enrichment or pollution. Thus, the ideal features of an extreme oligotrophic lake are a flora and fauna restricted to a few highly characteristic groups, and a uniformity of habitat.

Eutrophic waters, on the other hand, are characterised by their diversity of flora and fauna, and diversity is the most important criterion in the selection of these sites. Modifications such as nutrient enrichment, pollution and artificial manipulation of water level, lead to a loss of biological diversity in eutrophic waters, and biotic changes are often more sensitive indicators of chemical and physical changes in a water-body than the measurement of the chemical and physical parameters themselves. Nutrient enrichment in eutrophic lakes frequently leads to the development of a dense phytoplankton and a decline in the abundance and variety of submerged macrophytes. As many aquatic invertebrates are dependent on the submerged macrophytes, nutrient-enriched waters are generally poor both in plant and invertebrate species, and this lack of diversity may also adversely affect vertebrate groups such as fish and wildfowl. Thus the conservation value of such waters is low.

Rarities

The occurrence of rare species, or species outside their normal range within a site adds to its value, but is not sufficient to give a high grading to a site which is unsatisfactory on other criteria. The conservation of species which have their headquarters in Britain and are rare abroad is especially important. Some sites have therefore been chosen largely because they are principal autumn–winter haunts of certain wildfowl species. The British whitefish species belonging to the genus *Coregonus* differ at least subspecifically from their European counterparts and survive as isolated rather vulnerable populations in a few lakes; the presence of these species and their races has influenced the choice of a few key sites. Similarly the presence of the relatively uncommon charr *Salvelinus alpinus*, which occurs in Britain as a number of isolated distinct races mainly in oligotrophic lakes, has influenced the choice of such sites.

Some aquatic sites in the south of England are noted for the occurrence of a large number of nationally rare invertebrate species which are on the edge of their range in Britain. The presence of such rarities (e.g. dragonflies in the Moors River in Hampshire and water beetles at the Pevensey Levels, Sussex) adds greatly to the value of these sites.

Research

Some sites are included principally on the grounds of their interest as sites of prolonged scientific research. In these sites complete intactness is not necessary, and nutrient-enriched lakes such as Loch Leven are included.

Ecological–geographical continuity

Because survey of some of the more widespread categories of open water is incomplete, notably in the case of oligotrophic lakes and upland streams, it has been assumed that typical examples of these habitats are provided by the standing and running water bodies which happen to be present on many upland and peatland key sites.

Requirements for the national series

The overall requirement of the series of key open water sites is that it should adequately represent the range of variation described in pp. 200–33. Initially open waters have been classified into major physical types and a number of sites selected within each type to represent the variation in geographical distribution, chemistry, structural habitat, flora and fauna. The number of sites included within each type depends on the range of variability of that type and its range of distribution. Particular attention has been given to the following features:

1. Representation of sites covering the complete natural range of nutrient status found in British waters. Extreme cases of oligotrophy and eutrophy have been selected as well as a whole range of intermediate types. In the case of marl lakes and brackish waters the number of sites from which a selection could be made is small, and a large proportion of the existing intact sites has been selected.

2. Representation of the altitudinal range of each type of water-body has been attempted. Oligotrophic lakes and rivers have the greatest range from over 1200 m in the Cairngorms to sea-level, but eutrophic lakes and chalk streams are confined to the lowlands, and marl lakes to altitudes less than 380 m, while all brackish waters are at or near sea-level.

3. A range of water-bodies of various sizes and depths has been selected within each category since size and depth are important factors controlling the environmental conditions and flora and fauna of open waters. Some combinations of nutrient status, size and depth (e.g. small, deep, eutrophic lakes) are not represented in Britain, while others (e.g. large, deep, eutrophic lakes) are so rare that nearly all existing natural examples have been selected.

4. In order to cover those groups which are of restricted distribution in the British Isles (particularly fish, dragonflies, water beetles and some caddises and aquatic macrophytes) similar sites have been selected from widely ranging localities in Britain. Some water-body types (e.g. the oligotrophic brackish water lochs of the Outer Hebrides) are of such restricted distribution in Britain, however, that no

geographically separated similar types were available for selection.

5. Oligotrophic waters are mainly northern and north westerly in distribution while eutrophic waters are mainly found in south-eastern Britain. Isolated examples of one type within the province of another are therefore of especial importance (e.g. the Durness Lochs in the far north-west of Scotland).

6. As well as selecting unusual and extreme types of water-body it is important to include representatives of the more common types from a wide range of localities. The commonest types, small oligotrophic lakes and small upland streams, are well represented in sites selected for their upland value on which they are of bonus interest.

7. Because of the greater diversity of eutrophic waters (as compared to oligotrophic), a larger series of key sites is required to represent their range of variation.

8. The series of key sites is intended to reflect adequately the importance of certain open waters in Britain as wintering grounds for European wildfowl.

REGIONAL DIVERSITY AND SELECTION OF KEY SITES

Dystrophic standing waters

These have not been well covered in this review and, in general, it has been assumed that a representative range of small dystrophic waters is included within peatland and upland sites. This is particularly the case with dystrophic waters on upland blanket mire, but in the case of the richer lowland dystrophic waters a series of open water sites has been selected which represents the most outstanding examples of this type of habitat. One very large dystrophic water, Loch Laidon, has also been chosen as no other comparable dystrophic water is known to occur in sites selected for their peatland or upland interest.

Dystrophic waters are rare in southern Britain where they are confined to areas of base-poor rocks and to areas of impeded drainage where topogenous mire systems have developed. The main concentration of such mires is on the Tertiary sands which extend from Surrey through the New Forest in Hampshire to Dorset. Most of these mires however contain very little open water and only in some of the New Forest Valley Mires (P.3)[1] such as Cranesmoor is there extensive pool development. These pools are similar to those found on many patterned blanket mires in the north west of Britain and contain a similar range of flora and fauna. The range of variation of such pools has not however been adequately covered in this review and they are regarded as bonus to the peatland interest. Woolmer Pond, Hampshire (OW.7, gr. 1), also lying on the Tertiary sands, is a much larger dystrophic water which may be an ancient peat-cutting. This very shallow lake of 25 ha is of interest on account of its rich invertebrate fauna associated with dense

[1] Cross references to key sites are identified by an initial letter (indicating habitat) and number.

beds of submerged bryophytes, particularly *Drepanocladus fluitans*.

East Anglia is geologically mostly calcareous, and natural dystrophic waters are only represented by tiny pools in a few oligotrophic mire systems (e.g. Dersingham Bog (P.23)) which occur along the narrow belt of non-calcareous Greensand in west Norfolk. One of the Norfolk Broads, Calthorpe Broad (OW.16, gr. 1), has recently and dramatically become highly dystrophic, at least seasonally. Prior to 1970 this Broad was highly calcareous and was one of the few Broadland sites which retained the characteristic flora and fauna of the area. In that year, however, a drop in the water table resulted in temporary chemical changes which brought about a fall in pH to pH 3.0–3.4.

In the upland areas of south-west England and south and north Wales dystrophic waters are represented by pools and small lakes in areas of blanket mire on sites such as North Dartmoor (P.25), Cors Goch, Radnorshire (P.34), and Y Berwyn (U.13), where they are of bonus interest. Raised mires such as Shapwick Heath, Somerset (P.24), Cors Fochno, Cardiganshire (P.29) and Cors Goch glan Teifi, Cardiganshire (P.30), generally contain very little natural standing open water, but peat-cuttings may contain pools which are chemically richer than those on upland blanket mire and have a different invertebrate fauna.

Within the Cheshire–Shropshire–Staffordshire plain many kettle-holes have developed into basin mires surrounding areas of dystrophic open water, which typically become cut-off from the surrounding drainage and are very acidic and base-poor. The Gull Pool on the basin mire of Abbots Moss, Cheshire (P.46), has a thick carpet of the moss *Drepanocladus fluitans* and a fauna similar to that of Woolmer Pond and is a grade 2 alternative (OW.46), while the pools on the south of the Moss have a more limited fauna. Other very acidic peat-stained pools formed within a basin mire *schwingmoor* are found on Chartley Moss, Staffordshire (P.42). These have an interesting aquatic fauna containing a number of rare caddis species, and are chosen as the grade 1 example of an acidic basin mire open water site (OW.42). At Clarepool Moss (P.43) the open water formed at the periphery of the mire is influenced by outside drainage and is therefore both base-rich and dystrophic. Despite the extremely acidic dystrophic condition, the invertebrate fauna contains a large proportion of species associated with eutrophic conditions as well as carnivores typical of peat pools. Because of this interesting dual nature the area is given grade 1 status as an open water site (OW.40). At Sweat Mere, Shropshire, the drainage of the mire has been affected by the cutting of ditches draining from the nearby larger eutrophic lake, Crose Mere, and the pool is now base-rich (alkalinity = 160 p.p.m. $CaCO_3$) and neutral, with a fauna typical of a base-rich pond. This site, in association with Crose Mere, is rated grade 1 mostly on account of the well-developed hydroseral succession (OW.39). A series of partially interconnected ponds at Brown Moss (OW.45), Shropshire, show a range of trophic conditions ranging from acidic, base-poor pools to eutrophic ponds with a wide range of associated flora and fauna. They are of great potential research interest and deserve grade 2 status.

From northern England northwards, blanket mire becomes an increasingly common habitat in upland areas and with the increasing rainfall in the west, peat pools and dystrophic tarns and lochans become more abundant, reaching their greatest concentration in the extreme north-west of Scotland where they cover a high proportion of the land surface. Dystrophic pools, tarns and lochans occur as a bonus on most of the grade 1 blanket mire peatland and upland sites in northern England and Scotland, e.g. on Irthinghead Mires (P.49), Moor House (P.50), Silver Flowe (P.71), Rannoch Moor (P.85) and Inverpolly (U.66). Larger dystrophic waters are more uncommon and the largest known example in Britain of a dystrophic lake is Loch Laidon, Perthshire/Argyll (OW.71, gr. 1) which adjoins Rannoch Moor and is one of the most unproductive lakes in Britain.

Oligotrophic standing waters

These are by far the most abundant type of standing waterbody in Britain and information is available only for a small proportion of them. Fortunately, however, the range of variation of oligotrophic waters is more limited than that of richer waters, and the commonest types, with their very limited and uniform flora and fauna, are already well represented in sites selected for their upland interest. In the selection of oligotrophic lakes, therefore, only those showing extreme characteristics (e.g. Arctic–alpine lakes, very large deep lakes and isolated lowland lakes) have been included as key open water sites.

Oligotrophic lakes are virtually confined to the high rainfall, base-poor upland areas of north Wales, the Lake District, Galloway and the Scottish Highlands, where intense erosion during the last glaciation was the major factor in their formation. The only known oligotrophic lake in lowland England is Oakmere in Cheshire (OW.43, gr. 1) which is a kettle-hole occupying a pocket of base-poor glacial drift. Despite its very low alkalinity it contains calcicoles such as *Typha angustifolia* and *Asellus meridianus* alongside a flora and fauna more typical of oligotrophic conditions. In south-west England the upland areas of Dartmoor, Exmoor and Bodmin Moor contain very few standing open waters since they lie south of the area of glaciation. A few small pools do occur, however, the largest of these being Dozmary Pool on Bodmin Moor which is not, however, sufficiently distinctive for inclusion within the series.

The most southerly areas of glacial erosion occurred in south Wales where small examples of lakes occupying glacial troughs and corries are found. Llyn y Fan Fawr (OW.31, gr. 2) is the largest and most southerly of the corrie lakes. In north Wales these lakes are more abundant (although some are polluted by drainage from old copper mines) and a number are represented on existing National Nature Reserves (NNRs), e.g. Llyn Cau on Cader Idris and Llyn

Glaslyn (OW.35, gr. 2) below Y Wyddfa. The latter is a high-altitude example showing some affinities to those in the Cairngorms in its very sparse fauna and absence of aquatic angiosperms. Llyn Idwal (OW.33) on the northern side of Glyder Fawr represents the mesotrophic end of this series of upland corrie lakes and has a diverse relict aquatic flora for which it is given grade 1 status. A few large oligotrophic glacial trough lakes are also found in north Wales. Llyn Tegid (OW.32, gr. 1), Merioneth, represents the richer end of the spectrum and contains the white fish *Coregonus lavaretus pennanti*, while Llyn Cwellyn (OW.34, gr. 2), Caernarvonshire, is more barren and oligotrophic, and contains the Welsh race of the charr *Salvelinus alpinus*. Llyn Padarn is similar to Llyn Cwellyn and also contains charr, but is less intact.

In northern England natural oligotrophic lakes are confined to the Lake District: although there are a number of artificial oligotrophic reservoirs in the Millstone Grit areas of the Pennines, none of these is of great conservation value. The two extreme ends of the range of variation of the larger Lake District lakes are represented by Wastwater (OW.56, gr. 1) which is in most respects the most oligotrophic, and Esthwaite Water (OW.48, gr. 1*) which is the most productive and is mesotrophic. Buttermere (OW.59, gr. 2) is similar to Wastwater, but is a less extreme case in that it is smaller and shallower and has a somewhat richer fauna. Many of the lakes of nutrient status intermediate between that of Esthwaite and Wastwater are now more or less modified, either by enrichment, e.g. Windermere, or by water abstraction, e.g. Ullswater, Ennerdale and Thirlmere. Smaller lakes in the Lake District are represented by high-altitude corrie lakes and lower-lying small glacial trough lakes and tarns. Among the former, Red Tarn lies within the upland site of Helvellyn and Fairfield (U.19) and contains an isolated population of skelly *Coregonus lavaretus*, while Blea Water (OW.58, gr. 2) is an extremely deep, barren type. Among the lowland tarns, Blelham Tarn (OW.52, gr. 1) and the tarns on Claife Heights which are included within the Esthwaite Water site are selected primarily for the considerable research already invested in them by the Freshwater Biological Association.

In Galloway, the larger oligotrophic fjord lochs such as Loch Doon and Loch Ken have been converted into reservoirs and have very little conservation value although the marshes surrounding the latter are important for wildfowl, particularly bean geese (see L.149, gr. 1). There are also numerous smaller shallow lochs in this area, but none are considered sufficiently distinct from examples in the Highlands for inclusion within the series of key sites. A few examples (Loch Enoch and Loch Neldricken), however, lie within the upland site of the Merrick–Kells (U.35, gr. 1). Further north in the Southern Uplands the high-altitude corrie loch, Loch Skene, lies within the Moffat Hills upland site (U.36, gr. 1), but has only been rated grade 3. Loch Lomond (OW.60, gr. 1*) is the largest oligotrophic lake in Britain and has been selected because of its unique dual trophic nature. The deep, narrow northern end is morphologically oligotrophic (although chemically it is at the lower end of the mesotrophic scale) whereas to the south of the Highland Boundary Fault the loch broadens and becomes shallower and chemically much richer. It has an exceptionally diverse fish population and is also a research site for Glasgow University.

In the Highlands and Islands, oligotrophic lochs abound, and in the intensely glaciated, high rainfall areas of gneiss in the extreme north-west of Scotland and the Outer Hebrides the land surface is densely studded with a multitude of lochs and lochans which in places occupy much of the land surface. Many of these lochs are included in areas selected for their upland interest as at Inverpolly (U.66), Rhum (U.71) and Cairngorms (U.44). Thus, in the Highlands, only oligotrophic lochs showing outstanding features have been selected as key sites. The highest-altitude lakes in Britain are found in the Cairngorms where lakes such as Loch Etchachan (altitude 930 m) and Loch Coire an Lochain (altitude 995 m) are of an Arctic–alpine character. In these clear-water lakes ice cover may last for six months and the summer temperature of the epilimnion rarely exceeds 10 °C. The shores are very steep and consist of large stones and boulders worn smooth by the action of the ice and remaining relatively free from algae. There are no aquatic angiosperms or fish and the flora consists of a few species of bryophyte while the scanty invertebrate fauna has a few adaptable or high-altitude species. Because of their unique qualities, their isolation from other Arctic–alpine lakes in Europe, and their location within a high-grade upland area, they are graded as of international importance (see OW.68, gr. 1*). The most extreme oligotrophic lake in Britain is Loch Morar (OW.86, gr. 1*) which is not only the deepest lake in Britain, maximum depth 310 m, but is seventeenth deepest in the world. For a large lake it also has an extremely low dissolved mineral content and very clear water. Many of the other large, deep oligotrophic lochs of Scotland have been severely modified by hydro-electric schemes, but Loch Shiel (OW.95), is still relatively intact and is a grade 2 alternative for Loch Morar. It is not as deep nor as chemically poor as the latter, however, and its catchment has been partially afforested. Loch Stack (OW.97, gr. 2) is a typical shallower, slightly richer oligotrophic fjord loch, somewhat similar to Llyn Tegid in north Wales.

Large, shallow, very exposed oligotrophic lochs in north-west Scotland are represented by Loch Druidibeg (see OW.88, gr. 1*) on South Uist, on whose numerous islands the largest colony of indigenous greylag geese breeds. The influence of sea spray on this site is reflected in the presence of brackish water invertebrates such as *Gammarus (Rivulogammarus) duebeni* and *Neomysis integer*. The flora and fauna of Druidibeg contrast strongly with the neighbouring calcareous machair lochs, a'Mhachair and Stilligarry, which lie even nearer the sea and are influenced by blown shell sand. On the mainland, Loch Sionascaig (OW.92, gr. 1) on the Inverpolly NNR is an example of an extremely barren, irregularly shaped loch in which large areas of the bottom, even in deeper water, consist of bedrock or sand.

Mesotrophic standing waters

Such lakes are relatively infrequent in the British Isles, and are mostly situated along the margins of upland areas. No examples are known in south-east England or East Anglia where the rocks are mainly too calcareous to produce lakes of this trophic status, but a few examples are found in the areas of base-poor Tertiary sands in southern England. Hatchet Pond (OW.10, gr. 2) is the largest of the ponds in the New Forest belonging to this category. It contains isolated populations of species normally found in oligotrophic lakes in the north of Britain alongside a flora and fauna typical of southern Britain. Little Sea Mere (OW.21, gr. 1), on the Studland Heath NNR in Dorset, is another isolated mesotrophic lake formed in recent times from a coastal lagoon. Most coastal lagoons in this country develop on calcareous sand and are consequently base-rich, e.g. Loch of Strathbeg, Kenfig Pool and Lochs Spiggie and Brow. The development of such a system in an area of mineral-leached sand to produce a mesotrophic lake is very unusual in Britain. The mere contains species typical of mesotrophic lakes alongside species of richer waters (e.g. *Asellus*) and has a very varied dragonfly population. Looe Pool in Cornwall is another example of a coastal mesotrophic lake formed by the damming of a drowned river valley by a shingle bar. This lake receives the effluent of the town of Helston, and, although the flora and fauna is very diverse the site is not included in the series of key sites on account of its lack of intactness. Nearby on the Lizard (L.95) the tiny Ruan Pool is also mesotrophic, but it is so infilled with vegetation that it is best regarded as a bonus to the heathland site.

Examples of kettle-hole mesotrophic lakes are Llyn Ebyr in mid-Wales and Gormire at the foot of the Hambledon Hills escarpment in the North Riding of Yorkshire, but neither has been graded higher than 3. Esthwaite Water (OW.48), which is contiguous with North Fen NNR, is the richest of the larger Lake District lakes. It is the largest and best example of a mesotrophic lake in England and Wales and has been the site of extensive research by the Freshwater Biological Association especially on aspects of lake enrichment. It is also one of the few sites in Britain for the two North American plants *Najas flexilis* and *Elodea nuttallii*.

Gladhouse Reservoir (OW.63, gr. 1) lying at the foot of the Moorfoot Hills in Midlothian, is an artificial mesotrophic lake whose main interest is the largest overwintering population of pink-footed geese ($9\frac{1}{2}$% of the world population). Loch Lomond (OW.60) (see also Oligotrophic lakes, p. 236), where it broadens out south of the Highland Boundary Fault, changes from a deep oligotrophic loch into a shallow mesotrophic one.

Loch Insh (OW.74, gr. 1), an unusual lake for Britain, lies within the course of the River Spey, and has a very short retention time. It is an example of a more sandy type of mesotrophic loch with abundant submerged vegetation. It is contiguous with the Loch Insh Fens (P.87). Lochs Kinord (OW.76, gr. 1) and Davan are two mesotrophic kettle-hole lochs lying in the granite drift of the Dee valley. Despite the relatively low alkalinity and nutrient content they have a diverse flora and extensive hydroseral communities grading into fen, features which are very unusual for Highland lochs. Loch Eye (OW.91, gr. 1) in east Ross represents the top end of the mesotrophic scale and compares with Loch Leven prior to enrichment. Its diverse aquatic flora has components usually associated with both base-rich and base-poor situations, a combination not found in other lakes. The loch lies between two important wintering wildfowl sites, the Lower Dornoch Firth (C.123) and Cromarty Firth (C.112) and is itself an important wildfowl roost.

Eutrophic standing waters

These are almost entirely confined to the lowlands but, south of the area covered by the last glaciation, natural examples are very uncommon. The Oppen Pits (OW.1, gr. 1) were formed by the deposition of coastal shingle at Dungeness, and show different stages in the hydroseral succession. Elsewhere in south-east England eutrophic standing waters are only represented by artificial waterbodies. These include Stodmarsh in Kent (P.1) which is of considerable ornithological and peatland interest. It contains a lake too polluted by run-off from a coal tip and by inflow from the River Stour for inclusion within the national series. Some of the Metropolitan Water Board Reservoirs are also of considerable wildfowl value but are too artificial for inclusion as key open water sites.

A series of natural eutrophic waters in the Breckland of East Anglia were formed as kettle-holes in the calcareous drift which largely covers this region. These waters, known as the Breckland Meres (OW.14, gr. 1) are noted for irregular fluctuations in water level which are not directly related to rainfall. They have a very rich aquatic flora, but a fauna composed mainly of species resistant to desiccation. The large pump-storage reservoir at Abberton (OW.13, gr. 1) in Essex is of national importance for wintering wildfowl.

Much of south Lincolnshire, Cambridgeshire and west Norfolk were once covered by extensive fens and shallow eutrophic lakes. In the seventeenth century, Dutch engineers initiated large-scale drainage operations and the amounts of standing water in these areas have since become progressively less. The habitat is now represented only by a few situations, such as the Ouse Washes and Wicken Fen, which are artificially maintained and contain only small relics of the old fenland open waters. The greatest extent of fen and eutrophic open water in East Anglia is found in the Norfolk Broads which are derived from mediaeval peatcuttings but, as a result of pollution, increasing recreational activity and changes in land management, the Broads are less interesting biologically than they were 50 years ago. Some, such as Surlingham and Rockland, are so polluted that all submerged vegetation has disappeared and the fauna is limited to a few pollution-resistant species. These

areas still retain considerable peatland interest however. The only freshwater Broads still known to retain the characteristic Broadland fauna and flora are the rather small and isolated Upton Broad (OW.15, gr. 1) and Calthorpe Broad (OW.16) which complement each other. Even the latter, however, has undergone drastic and rapid changes during the course of this review, and may no longer be a viable Broadland habitat. Further survey is required to determine whether other intact fragments of open water remain in this area. Reports indicate that Martham Broad is still relatively intact, but this may be a brackish rather than a eutrophic site.

Elsewhere in East Anglia artificial fenland conditions exist in the Ouse Washes (OW.17, gr. 1) where extensive alluvial meadows are inundated in winter to form large impermanent lakes. In summer these largely dry out to leave only small pools and dykes which nevertheless have a rich and diverse flora and fauna. The Ouse Washes are of great ornithological importance both for wintering wildfowl and for breeding marsh birds, and they also contain areas of running water interest.

In south-west England natural eutrophic waters are rare, the only large example being Slapton Ley in Devon (OW.22, gr. 1), which is a fine example of a lake impounded by a coastal shingle beach. It is used for research and education by the nearby Field Studies Centre and is selected as the most southerly example of a series of maritime lakes in this category.

The tiny eutrophic pond known as Priddy Pool, on the Mendips, is included mainly for its research interest as one of the key freshwater sites for the study of biological production during the International Biological Programme. Together with two adjacent caves of running water interest, it is considered as part of a single complex open water site (OW.24, gr. 2). Chew Valley and Blagdon Reservoirs (OW.23, gr. 2) at the foot of the Mendips, are included as representatives of large eutrophic lakes which do not naturally occur in this part of the country. They are also of considerable interest as sites for the study of eutrophication in lowland lakes and as wildfowl wintering areas.

During the last glaciation the ice sheet reached its most southerly extent in Britain in south Wales, and in the lower-lying areas of glacial deposition kettle-holes were formed as the ice retreated. The largest of these is now occupied by Llyn Syfaddan (OW.28, gr. 1). It is now one of the most intact of the large British eutrophic lakes which so far appears to have escaped the changes which have occurred elsewhere, and which have been attributed to eutrophication, but it is threatened by recreational activities.

Kenfig Pool (OW.30, gr. 2) is a dune slack pool lying south of the area of glaciation on the Glamorgan coast. It has a very diverse flora and fauna and is similar to other dune-system eutrophic lakes such as the machair lochs on the west coast of Scotland.

In north Wales, eutrophic lakes are found mainly on the island of Anglesey where they contrast strongly with the oligotrophic lakes of Snowdonia. Llyn Coron (OW.36, gr. 2) is a large, shallow example formed behind coastal dune systems and is comparable with Loch of Strathbeg in Aberdeenshire. It is also an important wildfowl site.

The greatest concentration of natural standing water-bodies in lowland Britain is found in the Cheshire–Shropshire–Staffordshire plain where many kettle-holes, known locally as meres, have developed in the thick deposits of glacial drift. Most of these meres are eutrophic. One, Oakmere, is oligotrophic, while others such as Clarepool Moss have become infilled with basin mire and are now dystrophic. Of the eutrophic meres Rostherne Mere (OW.38, gr. 1*), Cheshire, is the deepest, and one of the very few lakes in Britain in which summer stratification leads to deoxygenation of the hypolimnion. As a consequence the deep-water benthos is practically non-existent. In addition this site is receiving natural nutrient enrichment from the droppings of the large number of gulls and wildfowl which frequent it. Crose Mere is more typical of the meres in general and also contains relict populations of *Gammarus (Rivulogammarus) lacustris* and *Nuphar pumila* outside the main areas of their range in Britain. This site is closely associated with the nearby dystrophic Sweat Mere and the two are considered as one site (OW.39). Some of the complex of pools at Brown Moss (OW.45) are eutrophic while others are dystrophic, and the area shows a great range of trophic status and flora and fauna. The Prees Branch of the Shropshire Union Canal (OW.41, gr. 1) has a range of alkalinity along its length although it is eutrophic through-out. The site exhibits a complete successional sequence from wet woodland at the more eutrophic closed end, to diverse open water submerged plant communities at the less eutrophic end.

There are no eutrophic lakes in the Lake District, and in northern England natural examples are relatively few and scattered. Hornsea Mere (OW.49) is one of the largest natural water-bodies in lowland England. Despite persistent algal blooms it has a rich and varied submerged aquatic flora. Tubificids and snails abound in this lake but there are indications that deleterious changes, resulting from nutrient over-enrichment, may be taking place. Because of this lack of intactness, it is not of national importance on limnological grounds, but when its considerable wildfowl interest is taken into account it is regarded as a grade 1 site. In the Pennines, Semer Water (OW.51, gr. 1) is a limestone lake, with no marl formation, which experiences great fluctua-tions in water level because of flash floods. These have the effect of producing an element of a typical riverine fauna within the invertebrate fauna of the stony shores, including at least six species of mayfly and crayfish – a phenomenon not found in any other lake in Britain. Further north in the Pennines, Tarn Dub (OW.57, gr. 2) on the Upper Teesdale NNR is a fine example of a large temporary pool which dries out regularly and has an interesting flora and fauna resistant to desiccation. The tarn lies at the base of a Whin Sill escarpment on Carboniferous sediments and is moderately eutrophic. A number of lakes occur in similar geological settings in Northumberland; these include Broomlee Lough, Greenlee Lough, Grindon Lough and Crag Lough, but none is considered sufficiently intact or distinctive for in-clusion within the national series.

In Scotland, eutrophic lochs are confined to the central lowlands and the coastal plain. A number of kettle-hole lochs occur on the plain bordering the north coast of the Solway Firth, most of which are shallow, but Mill Loch, Lochmaben (OW.61, gr. 1), is a relatively deep example which is of particular interest as containing a relict popula-tion of the vendace *Coregonus albula*, known elsewhere in Britain only in the Lake District where a different race occurs. Farther west in Wigtownshire a number of shallow lochs are important mainly for their wildfowl populations. Of these, the White Loch of Lochinch (OW.64, gr. 2) is particularly important as a roost for greylag geese. Dud-dingston Loch (OW.65, gr. 2) in Midlothian is also of interest as a large winter roost of pochard, but it has little limnological value.

Between the Firth of Forth and the Highland Boundary Fault numerous kettle-hole lochs have formed in drift largely originating from the Highlands; the trophic status of these lochs varies according to the nature of the drift, but most are eutrophic. The largest is Loch Leven (OW.67, gr. 1*), Kinross, which is also the largest natural eutrophic water in Britain. This is a very important site both for breeding and wintering wildfowl and has one of the densest nesting populations of tufted duck and mallard recorded. It is also a main site for the study of the productivity of fresh-water ecosystems as part of the International Biological Programme. In recent years there have been very many changes in the flora and fauna associated with increasing nutrient content and this is now a key site for the study of eutrophication and conservation management of fresh waters. Kilconquhar Loch (OW.79, gr. 2), Fife, is a much smaller eutrophic kettle-hole loch, also of some ornitho-logical importance but, unlike Loch Leven, it has extensive marginal and submerged vegetation.

A whole series of kettle-hole lochs occurs in a line just to the south of the Highland Boundary Fault from the Lake of Menteith in the south-west to Lochs Rescobie and Bal-gavies in the north-east. In general, the productivity of these lochs increases from west to east and Lochs Rescobie and Balgavies (OW.81) represent the most eutrophic end of the series, but artificial enrichment has led to a loss of floristic diversity. They are, however, important for wintering wild-fowl and it is mainly for this interest that they are given grade 2 status. A number of other kettle-hole lochs here have also been selected mainly for their wildfowl interest, particularly as pink-footed and greylag roosts, but little is known about the freshwater interest of these sites. These lakes are Carsebreck Lochs (OW.70, gr. 1), Drummond Pond (OW.80, gr. 2), Loch of Kinnordy (OW.82, gr. 2) and Loch of Lintrathen (OW.83, gr. 2). The artificially con-structed Dupplin Lochs in Perthshire (OW.69, gr. 1) also come into this category and are examples of lochs enriched by bird droppings. They are, however, very poor in floristic and faunal diversity.

North of the Highland Boundary Fault eutrophic lakes are restricted to the coast where they are influenced by wind-blown calcareous sand, and to areas of base-rich rocks in Caithness, Orkney and small isolated areas in the uplands. Loch of Strathbeg (OW.77, gr. 1) on the north-east coast of Aberdeenshire is the largest dune slack lake in Britain with an area of 200 ha. It is very exposed and shallow and the flora and invertebrate fauna are influenced by sea spray and contain a few brackish water species. It is also of outstanding importance as a wintering wildfowl resort for a wide range of species including particularly whooper swan and geese. The much smaller Loch Spynie on the Moray coast (OW.84) is more sheltered, with more abundant submerged vegetation and a completely freshwater fauna. It is an important greylag roost but as the loch has been partially drained by a canal it is only given grade 2 status.

Farther north, on the Old Red Sandstone of east Ross, Caithness and Orkney, eutrophic lochs, mainly kettle-holes, are frequent. Loch Eye in east Ross (OW.91, gr. 1) is intermediate between mesotrophic and eutrophic conditions. The largest of these northern eutrophic lochs is Loch Watten (OW.93, gr. 1): a shallow exposed kettle-hole which, as it has a largely non-agricultural catchment, is probably the least modified large eutrophic lake in Britain. It has a very diverse submerged and marginal aquatic flora, a prolific invertebrate fauna and is a well-known trout fishing loch. On Orkney the northern end of the Loch of Harray (OW.78, gr. 1) is eutrophic, very similar to Loch Watten, but most of this loch and the neighbouring Loch of Stenness are brackish and are dealt with on p. 241. The Shetlands are composed mainly of base-poor rocks and eutrophic lakes are mainly confined to coastal areas. The largest are Lochs of Spiggie and Brow (OW.85) at the southern end of the Mainland where they are formed behind coastal calcareous sand dunes. Because of their extreme isolation these lochs lack a rich invertebrate fauna, but the maritime influence and low summer temperatures are indicated by the presence of brackish and cold-water species. These lochs are also important for wintering wildfowl, particularly whooper swan.

In the western Highlands and the Hebrides eutrophic lochs are very rare. A few examples occur in areas where the Durness Limestone outcrops, as at the Inchnadamph NNR, where the small shallow Loch Mhaolach-coire (OW.96, gr. 2) is found. The limestone surrounding this loch is largely covered with blanket mire, giving a highly alkaline loch with periodically peat-stained water which has a flora and fauna very similar in composition to oligotrophic lakes. It has dense beds of submerged vegetation, however, and the invertebrate fauna is very prolific and supports a population of fast-growing brown trout.

Along the western seaboard of Scotland, and particularly on the Outer Hebrides, a coastal fringe of flat machair grassland (in places up to about 2 km wide) grows on calcareous shell sand of marine origin, and contains a number of shallow eutrophic lochs. On South Uist these lochs characteristically have a rich, submerged vegetation and a brackish element in the invertebrate fauna, particularly *Potamopyrgus jeninksi*, *Neomysis integer* and *Gammarus duebeni*. Loch Stilligarry and Loch a'Mhachair (see OW.88)

on the Druidibeg NNR, are excellent examples. The former has a well-developed reed-swamp and shows a good hydroseral progression. The Royal Society for the Protection of Birds' reserve at Balranald on North Uist contains a small machair loch, Loch nam Feithean (OW.99, gr. 2) which is very overgrown with emergent vegetation and is important as a nesting site for red-necked phalarope.

Marl lakes

This is the rarest category of standing water in Britain and is confined to areas of highly calcareous soluble limestone and chalk, or fluvio-glacial deposits derived from these rocks. Since they are so rare and have a great floristic and faunal diversity, a large proportion has been accorded key site status.

The Chalk of south and south-east England is devoid of natural standing waters, but the Tring Reservoirs (OW.3, gr. 1) are situated at the foot of the Chalk escarpment of the Chilterns. Of these, only Wilstone has been surveyed. It is a clear-water marl lake with extensive growths of submerged macrophytes. The high ionic content of the water coming from the Chalk may account for the presence of species such as *Notonecta viridis* and *Sigara concinna* which are mainly of coastal distribution.

Natural standing water-bodies are also absent from the permeable Jurassic limestones of southern England, but excavation of fluvio-glacial deposits of gravel derived from this rock in the upper Thames valley is producing a series of artificial lakes known as the Cotswold Water Park (OW.9) which will constitute by far the largest marl lakes in Britain. A lake of about 100 ha and a few smaller lakes, some of which are still to be excavated, have been proposed as a nature reserve area. The flora and fauna of neighbouring existing pits is already quite diverse and despite much disturbance, the park attracts increasing numbers of wildfowl. It is likely that, with suitable management, these could become one of the most important areas of open water in southern England. On its potential value the Cotswold Water Park has, therefore, been given grade 1 status. Four small artificial marl ponds and associated limestone streams (OW.11, gr. 2) are found within the Wychwood NNR. These ponds show very different floristics but a similar fauna characteristic of calcareous conditions. In south-west England, Chew Valley and Blagdon Reservoirs (OW.23) are fed from the Carboniferous Limestone of the Mendips, but neither is a true marl lake, and they are probably influenced by drainage from the Keuper Marl on which they lie. Both have relatively high phosphate contents, and Chew Valley has dense algal blooms on occasions.

The Carboniferous Limestone of south Wales lies south of limits of glaciation and has very few standing waters. Bosherston Lake: Llyn Bosier (OW.29, gr. 1) occupies a drowned limestone river valley which has become isolated from the sea by a coastal sand dune. No other British marl lake has been formed in this manner. Submerged vegetation is extremely profuse and shows a transition from a community in which *Chara hispida* predominates, nearer the coast, to a community dominated by *Potamogeton* spp., and finally to reed-swamp.

In north Wales the extensive Carboniferous Limestone has natural lakes only on Anglesey, where there are a number of limestone lakes now largely invaded by valley mire. Llyn yr Wyth Eidion (OW.37, gr. 2) lies within the valley mire of Cors Erddreiniog (P.35) and similar-sized but un-surveyed water-bodies occur in the nearby Cors Goch (P.36). The Llyn, which lies on deposits of lacustrine shell mud, is deep for its size and unusual for British marl lakes in that it stratifies in summer. Submerged vegetation is not abundant in this lake which is made somewhat turbid by drainage from the surrounding peatland.

In the Midlands there are no natural standing waters on either the Jurassic limestone or on the Carboniferous Lime-stone of the Peak District but, further north in the Pennines, Malham Tarn (OW.47(a), gr. 1*), at an altitude of 380 m, is the highest and largest marl lake in Britain. It shows an exceptional range of plant and animal communities associ-ated with the base-rich tarn, the fen at its inflow and the marginal raised mire. The presence of a Field Studies Centre on the shores of the lake make this the best known British marl lake. Sunbiggin Tarn (OW.54, gr. 1) is another much smaller example on the limestone of the Pennines lying within a grade 1 peatland site (P.53). The tarn itself has a diverse flora and fauna compared to an impoverished nearby pool which is receiving nutrient enrichment from a colony of black-headed gulls. Hawes Water (OW.53, gr. 1) lies within thick lacustrine shell marl deposits near the north Lancashire coast. It has well-developed marginal vegetation which grades into a eutrophic flood-plain mire. Like Llyn yr Wyth Eidion, it is deep and undergoes thermal stratification in summer.

No natural marl lakes are known in southern Scotland and they are exceedingly rare in the Highlands. None is known in the areas of Dalradian limestone in the eastern Highlands but three small examples occur on this formation on the island of Lismore in Argyll. These lochs (OW.94, gr. 2) are similar to those at Durness for which they are a substitute. The Durness Lochs (OW.89, gr. 1*) in the extreme north-west of Scotland are probably the finest examples of marl lakes in Britain. They are larger and more diverse than those on Lismore and because of their extreme isolation from other calcareous lakes have a fauna that con-tains only a few of the species associated with base-rich conditions farther south. Loch Borralie is the only marl lake in Britain now containing charr.

On the Scottish islands the only known marl lake is a tiny pool on the limestone peninsula of Whiteness on the Main-land of Shetland, but this does not merit inclusion in the national series.

Brackish standing waters

Brackish lakes are rare in Britain since the conditions required to produce such water-bodies are rather precise. In England the best examples are found in the Norfolk Broads where some slight tidal influence and seepage of sea

water through the low-lying soil combine to produce brackish water in a few of the Broads lying near the sea. Of these, Hickling Broad and Horsey Mere (OW.12, gr. 1*) are the most intact and still preserve the unique Broadland flora and fauna which includes rare plants such as *Najas marina* and breeding birds such as the bittern and marsh harrier. Martham Broad is similar, but probably contains no features not found in Hickling and Horsey.

Elsewhere in Britain brackish lakes occur mainly on the islands of Scotland where complex glacial basins connect to the sea via narrow tidal outflows which allow a limited in-flow of sea water at high tide. These lakes are very different from the Broads in having rocky exposed shorelines. On Orkney, the inter-connected brackish lochs of Harray and Stenness (OW.78) show a transition from sea water in the lower end of Loch of Stenness to base-rich fresh water in the northern end of Loch of Harray, with an associated gradient of fauna and flora. In the more fresh-water areas animals and plants typical of eutrophic lakes are found alongside brackish water species. On the Outer Hebrides many brackish lochs grade from sea water to oligotrophic freshwater conditions. The finest example is Loch an Duin (OW.87, gr. 1*), and Lochs Roag and Fada and the Howmore Estuary (part of the Grogarry Lochs grade 1* site (OW.88) in South Uist) which extend from brackish conditions into oligotrophic fresh water. These lakes are similar in floral and faunal composition, in the more saline parts, to Loch of Stenness but are completely different in the more freshwater areas where animals and plants typical of oligotrophic lakes are found alongside brackish water species.

Upland streams and rivers

These are by far the most common type of open water habitat remaining intact in Britain and, as they are already well represented as bonus sites in the majority of the key sites chosen for their upland interest, only a few examples showing outstanding features have been selected as key open water sites.

Since most of the uplands are base-poor, eutrophic up-land streams are rather uncommon and are of particular interest. The Peak District is drained by a series of streams and rivers which are intermediate in character between true upland limestone streams and the chalk streams of lowland England. The River Lathkill (OW.44, gr. 1) is a fairly intact example with abundant submerged and emergent vegeta-tion and alternating slow-flowing pools and faster stretches where it cascades over natural tufa dams.

Farther north in the Pennines there are a number of spectacular limestone streams in the Malham–Arncliffe grade 1* upland site. These include the slow-flowing weedy outflow of Malham Tarn itself, which disappears under-ground about 1 km away from the tarn, the moderately flowing Gordale Beck, which plunges in a series of water-falls over Gordale Scar, and the fast flowing Cowside Beck in its steep-sided limestone valley. These three streams form a complementary series (see OW.47, gr. 1*), each with a slightly different flora and fauna, which represents the range of variation of alkaline stream types in this part of the Pennines. Even more precipitous limestone streams occur at the extreme north-western end of the Pennines. Knock-Ore Gill (OW.55, gr. 1) on the Moor House NNR is one of the highest and most precipitous, and contains alpine species such as the stonefly *Protonemura montana*. On the other side of the Pennine watershed, both on the Moor House and Upper Teesdale NNRs, many of the streams which flow into the River Tees are base-rich, although most are also heavily peat-stained. Some flow first over base-poor rocks, often covered with a substantial thickness of blanket peat, before flowing over or, in the case of the White Well on Teesdale, under a limestone outcrop. Downstream of the limestone this stream is considerably richer in such groups as molluscs and *Gammarus*.

The Cairngorms NNR contains the highest streams in Britain forming the headwaters of the River Dee and River Avon at an altitude of 1220 m, just below the summit of Ben MacDhui. These Arctic–alpine streams with their very restricted flora and fauna form part of the River Dee grade 1 site (OW.75).

Alkaline upland streams are scattered widely among the isolated pockets of limestone in the Highlands of Scotland. The River Traligill (OW.96, gr. 2) in Inchnadamph NNR is a fine example of an upland limestone stream showing many features of karst topography such as swallow holes, caves with underground streams and temporary, surface flood-water channels. At a much lower altitude and with a slower current are the streams flowing into and from the Durness Lochs (OW.89, gr. 1*). Unlike most Highland streams they have abundant submerged and marginal vegetation and abundant and diverse associated invertebrate fauna. The nearby Smoo Cave has a fine limestone stream with brown trout living in the lower part of the cave. The River Strontian (OW.90, gr. 1) is a typical example of a short, west-coast, spating, oligotrophic river. The Old Red Sandstone areas of Orkney, Caithness and Moray have a large number of base-rich streams with a fauna basically similar in composition to that of poor Highland streams but more abundant. The Burn of Latheronwheel (OW.98, gr. 2) in Caithness is an example of one of these species-rich streams.

Base-poor lowland streams

These are mainly confined to the Greensands of the Weald and the Tertiary sands of southern England. They are well represented within the New Forest, the Oberwater (OW.6, gr. 1) being a particularly good example with fauna similar to that of many upland streams. Moors River (OW.8, gr. 1) lies just outside the boundaries of the New Forest, and although it runs mainly through base-poor sands and gravels it rises on the Chalk of Cranborne Chase. Consequently this stream is intermediate between chalk streams and the base-poor streams of the New Forest, and its base-status may vary seasonally depending on the relative proportions of its drainage deriving from the sand and the

Chalk. It has an exceedingly rich flora and associated fauna and is a breeding site for a large number of species of dragonfly. Small base-poor, fairly fast-flowing streams are found in the Weald within the Ashdown Forest grade 1 heathland site (L.1), where they contribute a bonus.

Lowland eutrophic streams and rivers

This category of water-body has suffered more modification from human activities than any other in Britain. Such watercourses are mainly distributed in the heavily populated and industrialised areas of south-east England, the Midlands, south Wales and the central Lowlands of Scotland, and as a consequence the great majority are polluted at least in a part of their length. Those which have largely escaped pollution are much sought after as a source of water supply and are increasingly being regulated by the construction of reservoirs, while the lower stretches of many have been modified for navigation or flood control. As this type of river is now very rare in an unmodified state in Britain, only a few, large, relatively intact river systems have been selected as key sites.

In south-east England no river is considered sufficiently intact for inclusion within the national series, while in southern England most rivers are either chalk streams or drain the Tertiary sands and are oligotrophic. Moors River (see previous section) drains both formations and is intermediate in character. In East Anglia many rivers are very slow flowing and are dealt with under the section on sluggish river systems (p. 244). Others such as the River Lark (OW.19, gr. 2) drain Chalk or calcareous till and are chalk streams. The largest relatively unpolluted and unmodified rivers in southern Britain are the Severn and the Wye (OW.26, gr. 1), which both drain the uplands of central Wales but become typical large eutrophic rivers in their lower courses. Of these, the Wye is the more intact as the Severn receives some effluent from the industrial Midlands and is used more for water abstraction and navigation. The Wye has four distinct sections, an upland oligotrophic fast-flowing section, a moderately flowing eutrophic section where it runs as a broad gravelly stream through a wide valley of Old Red Sandstone, a slow-flowing lower section where it cuts through a limestone gorge and becomes highly calcareous, and a long meandering silted tidal section. Related to these physical and chemical changes along its length are changes in the flora and fauna.

The rivers draining the Midlands plain, particularly the Trent, are all polluted to various degrees, and the only relatively unmodified rivers in this region drain the lightly populated upland area of the Peak District. These rivers are eutrophic and intermediate between upland and lowland streams. Lathkill Dale (OW.44) is a slower-flowing example (see Upland streams, p. 241).

Most of the large rivers draining the Pennines are eutrophic, at least in their lower reaches, but few are intact and most are either seriously polluted or are modified by other means such as canalisation or water abstraction. Rivers within the Mersey and Yorkshire Ouse basins are polluted intermittently throughout their lengths but the Tyne, Tees and Wear are badly polluted only in the lower stretches.

The large river systems of the Southern Uplands of Scotland which drain the somewhat calcareous Ordovician and Silurian rocks are moderately eutrophic. The two largest systems are the Clyde and Tweed of which the former is badly polluted and severely modified in its lower stretches. The Tweed (OW.62, gr. 1) is moderate to fast flowing throughout its length but is chemically somewhat poorer than the Wye. The Teviot is chemically the richest of the tributaries, and this is reflected in the composition and quantity of its flora and fauna. In the upper stretches of the Tweed the flora and fauna is typical of upland streams while in the lower stretches the flora and fauna is intermediate between that of base-poor rivers (e.g. the Aberdeenshire Dee) and the richer lowland rivers (e.g. the Wye). Submerged vegetation is more abundant and varied in composition than in most Scottish rivers, and the short estuarine reach is intact and has a typical brackish water fauna. Part of the Tay–Isla Valley (OW.72, gr. 1) is treated in this section for its outstanding importance for wintering greylag geese (although the four areas concerned include alluvial meadows and freshwater marsh as well as three areas of open water).

The River Endrick (OW.66, gr. 2) is one of the least modified of the eutrophic rivers draining the central Lowlands of Scotland. The lowermost section where it enters Loch Lomond is very slow flowing and is important as a wildfowl site. The middle reaches are more moderately flowing and eutrophic with a relatively rich fauna, but the upper reaches are typical oligotrophic upland streams.

No large eutrophic rivers occur north of the Highland Boundary Fault.

Chalk streams and rivers

These are confined to areas where Chalk reaches the surface and are distributed from east Devon to south-east Yorkshire. The extensive areas of Chalk in East Anglia are largely covered by glacial deposits so that the largest and finest examples of chalk rivers are found in central southern England. Those most renowned for their trout fishing are the Test, Itchen and the Hampshire Avon which rise on the Chalk of the Hampshire Downs and flow south into the English Channel, passing over base-poor Tertiary sands in their lower courses. The major sources of the Avon are located in the clay of the Vale of Pewsey, so this river passes over three distinct rock formations along its course. These rivers are noted for their water meadows, most of which have now fallen into disuse. The engineering of the river to provide water and drainage for the meadows has produced a series of channels with very varying current conditions and depths which add greatly to the ecological diversity of the river system. Parts of the Test and Itchen have been greatly modified for fishing and the lower stretches of these rivers pass through Southampton. Compared to these the Avon (OW.5) is relatively intact. Its invertebrate fauna is the most diverse found in any chalk stream system and it has one of the most diverse fish faunas of any water in Britain, with at least 24 species. The flora also contains all those species associated with chalk streams and certain species of limited distribution such as *Potamogeton nodosus* and *Ranunculus tripartitus*. The upper tributaries of the Avon, such as the Wylye, Nadder, Bourne and Ebble, and the main stream itself, are typical chalk streams and rivers whereas the tributaries of the lower reaches draining from the New Forest, such as the Docken's Water and Ripley Brook, are good quality lowland base-poor streams. Some components of the fauna of these latter streams extend into the main stream. The whole Avon System is a grade 1* open water site. In order to maintain the full range of diversity of the system a stretch of water meadow should be safeguarded and managed in the traditional manner.

The rivers cutting through the North and South Downs in south-east England originate on the clays of the Weald and are not typical chalk streams, for the impervious nature of the clay tends to make them spate heavily. The chalk streams flowing south from the Chilterns into the London Basin are mostly modified or polluted especially in their lower sections and do not justify inclusion in the national series. Several fine chalk streams drain northwards into the Thames from the Hampshire Downs, including the Kennet, Lambourne, Blackwater and Whitewater. The source of the last is the grade 2 peatland site, Greywell Fen, for which the river provides bonus interest, though it has been highly modified by ponding. In general, these rivers duplicate habitats found in the more diverse River Avon System, except that the snail *Planorbis acronicus* is confined to the Thames basin.

In south-west England three rivers, the Stour, Piddle and Frome, rise on or cut through the Dorset Downs, the Stour itself rising on the clay of the Vale of Blackmoor. In their lower reaches they leave the Chalk and flow through the Tertiary sands and gravels to the sea. Although good chalk streams, they do not provide any habitat of major conservation interest not adequately represented in the Avon System.

In East Anglia some streams flowing over the drift have the properties of streams draining solid Chalk, but because of the low lying nature of the countryside are generally slow flowing. The lowest stretch of the River Lark (OW.19, gr. 2) is a deep Fenland drain with turbid water and a very sluggish flow (see previous section). In its middle stretches it more closely resembles a chalk river and has abundant vegetation, but it has been canalised by the construction of locks, now long disused, and by deepening as far as the town of Bury St Edmunds. The fauna is largely lacustrine with a few typical riverine species in the faster stretches and it falls, therefore, between the true chalk streams of southern England (e.g. the Avon) and the Fenland drains. Part of the middle section of the Lark adjoins the Cavenham Heath–Tuddenham NNR part of the Icklingham Heaths grade 1 Breckland site (L.61). Biological surveys of this river were published in the 1930s and give it additional value. An unnamed tributary of the Wissey (OW.20, gr. 2), most of whose catchment lies within the Stanford Practical Training

Area site (L.60(*a*)), is smaller and faster flowing in stretches than the Lark and has lower nitrate and phosphate concentrations, possibly associated with its largely non-agricultural Breckland catchment. Along its length the stream widens out into a series of shallow meres. The submerged aquatic flora is not very diverse but emergent communities are well represented and the fauna is very varied.

A number of chalk streams are found in north-east Lincolnshire on the Wolds. The River Great Eau (OW.18, gr. 1) shows a transition from a small, fast-flowing chalk stream with little vegetation in its upper reaches to a sluggish calcareous lowland drain. Between these two sections it is broad and shallow, with a moderate flow and appreciable amounts of submerged vegetation, and resembles the chalk streams of southern England. The lower drain-like stretches are rich in aquatic plant species and the stream passes through the freshwater marsh site of Calceby Beck (L.83, gr. 2).

Of the northerly Yorkshire chalk streams the Scampston Beck which runs through the grade 1 freshwater marsh site of Wintringham (L.141) shows some features characteristic of upland limestone streams. The submerged vegetation is very sparse, consisting only of a few clumps of *Callitriche*, and the fauna is very restricted in species compared to typical chalk streams farther south. The source is tapped as a local water supply and the stream itself does not merit a high grade but the section passing through the Wintringham marsh can be regarded as a bonus.

Lowland, sluggish eutrophic ditches and rivers

These rivers are characteristic of lowland England particularly East Anglia. The river channels are usually artificial having been constructed during the draining of the Fenlands and other low-lying land. They are generally deep and steep sided and are maintained by dredging, the spoil being used to form levees to prevent flooding of the surrounding ground. The channels have often been straightened and have a very uniform flow over the whole length which may cease entirely in summer.

In south-east England the dykes to the east of the Lampern Wall on the Stodmarsh NNR in Kent are rich botanically but this type of habitat is better represented on Pevensey Levels (OW.2, gr. 1) and on the Romney Marsh (OW.4), its grade 2 alternative. These two sites, which were once extensive freshwater marshes, now consist of grazing land intersected by numerous dykes which retain much of the flora and fauna of the former marsh. Of the two, Pevensey Levels scores higher on its diversity of fauna, especially water beetles, which include a number of rare species. The sites are similar botanically but Pevensey has a number of rather local species. The main drains at Romney Marsh suffer to some extent from spraying with herbicides to control emergent vegetation and there are pressures from arable farmers for the water table to be lowered.

The lowermost sections of a number of rivers in southern England, including key sites such as the River Avon (OW.5) just above Christchurch, are sluggish and resemble Fenland drains. In south-west England extensive raised mires and intervening alluvial flood-plain mires formerly occurred on the Somerset Levels, where the Shapwick Heath NNR is a remnant, but many of the dykes now draining this area are polluted and none shows any features not better represented in East Anglia.

The most extensive areas of fens and freshwater marshes existing in historic times were to the south of the Wash and in the coastal areas of East Anglia. These have been almost completely drained and in the surviving fragments there is now very little open water, but the rivers and dykes which drain these areas contain relics of the former aquatic flora and fauna of the Fens.

The artificial rivers which flank the Ouse Washes (OW.17) and flood them in winter are good examples of Fenland drains. The New Bedford River on the east is brackish and tidal, while the Old Bedford River and River Delph on the west are fresh water and very slow flowing. The freshwater rivers are very clear, and have an abundance of submerged plant species and a relatively intact invertebrate fauna. The lower reaches of many of the chalk rivers of East Anglia are very slow flowing, a factor which determines their ecology: for example the River Great Eau (OW.18) becomes a weedy Fenland drain, but the lower reaches of the Lark (OW.19) are deep and turbid with very little submerged vegetation.

The lower reaches of the Yare, Waveney, Bure and Ant are very turbid, largely devoid of submerged vegetation, and have very little nature conservation value. The slightly brackish channels connecting Hickling Broad and Horsey Mere (OW.12) are intact and biologically similar to the standing water areas and are included in the same key site.

In northern Britain, areas of flat alluvial marshland are rare and there are few eutrophic sluggish rivers of any length. On Anglesey, the Afon Ffraw a short, slow-flowing, weed-choked stream, comes into this category and is included within the site boundary of Llyn Coron (OW.36) of which it is the outflow. Small dykes are present in the extensive area of *Phragmites* swamp at Leighton Moss on the Lancashire coast but are not sufficiently diverse for inclusion in the national series.

In Scotland, sluggish rivers are even more infrequent. The lowermost section of the River Endrick (OW.66) has already been mentioned as a very slow-flowing lowland eutrophic river. The section of the River Spey (OW.73, gr. 1) flowing through the Loch Insh Fens does not fit easily into any classification of river systems since, although it is very slow flowing and has the appearance of an East Anglian river, it lies at an altitude of about 300 m and is mesotrophic, with species characteristic of both base-poor and base-rich conditions.

Subterranean systems

All the major cave systems in Britain, except those formed by coastal erosion, are found in limestone areas where they have originated by solution of the rock by running water; they are thus absent from south-east and southern England and East Anglia. In south-west England, Pridhamsleigh

Cave (OW.25, gr. 2) in Devon is important as a site for the endemic crustacean *Niphargus glennei*. Farther north the limestone hills of the Mendips have numerous caves. Those of the Cheddar Gorge, e.g. Gough's Cave, are the best known, but show no features not found in the more extensive Ogof Ffynnon Ddu systems in south Wales although those at Priddy, including Swildon's Hole, have a slightly different fauna. The Priddy caves are adjacent to the International Biological Programme's open water research site of Priddy Pool and the whole area is a grade 2 open water site (OW.24). The largest cave systems in Britain are found in south Wales in the Carboniferous Limestone of Fforest Fawr where two cave systems Ogof Ffynnon Ddu (OW.27, gr. 1*) and Dan yr Ogof contain a diverse aquatic subterranean fauna. Much research is being carried out on the ecology and geology of these caves which are geological sites of international importance. In the limestone of the Pennines the largest cave systems (OW.50, gr. 1) are found within the grade 1* upland site of Ingleborough (U.23). The cave-dwelling crustacean *Bathynella stammeri* has been recorded from here but other subterranean malacostracan species found in caves further south are absent. The Smoo Cave on the Durness Limestone and the subterranean River Traligill and its caves (OW.96) at Inchnadamph, have already been mentioned, but freshwater organisms confined to caves have not been recorded from either site.

Table 22. INDEX OF OPEN WATER SITES

* Internationally important sites.

Region		Site	County	Type of water-body
South-east England				
GRADE 1	OW.1	OPPEN PITS	KENT	ES
	OW.2	PEVENSEY LEVELS	SUSSEX	SR
	OW.3	TRING RESERVOIRS	HERTFORDSHIRE	MaS
Grade 2	OW.4	Romney Marsh	Kent	SR
South England				
GRADE 1*	OW.5	RIVER AVON SYSTEM	HAMPSHIRE/WILTSHIRE	CR, OR
GRADE 1	OW.6	OBERWATER	HAMPSHIRE	OR
	OW.7	WOOLMER POND*a*	HAMPSHIRE	DS
	OW.8	MOORS RIVER	HAMPSHIRE/DORSET	OR, ER
	OW.9	COTSWOLD WATER PARK	WILTSHIRE/GLOUCESTERSHIRE	MaS
Grade 2	OW.10	Hatchet Pond	Hampshire	MeS
	OW.11	Wychwood Ponds	Oxfordshire	MaS
East Anglia				
GRADE 1*	OW.12	HICKLING BROAD & HORSEY MERE	NORFOLK	BS
GRADE 1	OW.13	ABBERTON RESERVOIR	ESSEX	ES
	OW.14	BRECKLAND MERES	NORFOLK	
		(*a*) LANG MERE		ES, TS
		(*b*) RING MERE		ES, TS
		(*c*) FOWL MERE		ES, TS
	OW.15	UPTON BROAD*a*	NORFOLK	ES, BS
	OW.16	CALTHORPE BROAD	NORFOLK	DS, ES
	OW.17	OUSE WASHES	NORFOLK/CAMBRIDGESHIRE	TS, SR
	OW.18	RIVER GREAT EAU	LINCOLNSHIRE	CR, SR
Grade 2	OW.19	River Lark	Cambridgeshire/Suffolk	CR, SR
	OW.20	Tributary of River Wissey	Norfolk	CR
South-west England				
GRADE 1	OW.8	MOORS RIVER (PART)	DORSET See under South England	
	OW.21	LITTLE SEA MERE	DORSET	MeS
	OW.22	SLAPTON LEY	DEVON	ES
	OW.9	COTSWOLD WATER PARK (PART)	GLOUCESTERSHIRE See under South England	
	OW.26	RIVER WYE (PART)	GLOUCESTERSHIRE See under South Wales	
Grade 2	OW.23	Chew Valley & Blagdon Reservoirs	Somerset	ES
	OW.24	Swildons Hole, Priddy Caves & Priddy Pool	Somerset	SuR, ES
	OW.25	Pridhamsleigh Cave	Devon	SuR

Table 22 (*contd.*)

Region	Site	County	Type of water-body
South Wales			
GRADE 1	OW.26 RIVER WYE: AFON GWY	GLOUCESTERSHIRE, MONMOUTHSHIRE, HEREFORDSHIRE, RADNOR, BRECKNOCK & MONTGOMERYSHIRE	UR–ER
GRADE 1*	OW.27 OGOF FFYNNON DDU	BRECKNOCK	SuR
GRADE 1	OW.28 LLYN SYFADDAN: LLANGORSE LAKE	BRECKNOCK	ES
	OW.29 BOSHERSTON LAKE: LLYN BOSIER	PEMBROKESHIRE	MaS
Grade 2	OW.30 Kenfig Pool	Glamorgan	ES
	OW.31 Llyn y Fan Fawr	Brecknock	OS
North Wales			
GRADE 1	OW.26 RIVER WYE (PART)	MONTGOMERYSHIRE See under South Wales	
	OW.32 LLYN TEGID: BALA LAKE	MERIONETH	OS
	OW.33 LLYN IDWAL	CAERNARVONSHIRE	OS
Grade 2	OW.34 Llyn Cwellyn	Caernarvonshire	OS
	OW.35 Llyn Glaslyn	Caernarvonshire	OS
	OW.36 Llyn Coron & Afon Ffraw	Anglesey	ES, SR
	OW.37 Llyn yr Wyth Eidion	Anglesey	MaS
Midlands			
GRADE 1	OW.26 RIVER WYE (PART)	HEREFORDSHIRE See under South Wales	
GRADE 1*	OW.38 ROSTHERNE MERE	CHESHIRE	ES
GRADE 1	OW.39 CROSE MERE & SWEAT MERE	SHROPSHIRE	ES, DS
	OW.40 CLAREPOOL MOSS	SHROPSHIRE	DS
	OW.41 SHROPSHIRE UNION CANAL, PREES BRANCH	SHROPSHIRE	ES
	OW.42 CHARTLEY MOSS	STAFFORDSHIRE	DS
	OW.43 OAK MERE	CHESHIRE	OS
	OW.44 LATHKILL DALE	DERBYSHIRE	ER, UR
Grade 2	OW.45 Brown Moss	Shropshire	ES, MeS, DS
	OW.46 Abbots Moss	Cheshire	DS
North England			
GRADE 1*	OW.47 MALHAM–ARNCLIFFE	YORKSHIRE	
	(a) MALHAM TARN		MaS
	(b) OUTFLOW OF MALHAM TARN		UR
	(c) GORDALE BECK		UR
	(d) COWSIDE BECK		UR
*	OW.48 ESTHWAITE WATER	LANCASHIRE	MeS
GRADE 1	OW.49 HORNSEA MERE	YORKSHIRE	ES
	OW.50 INGLEBOROUGH CAVE SYSTEMS	YORKSHIRE	SuR
	OW.51 SEMER WATER	YORKSHIRE	ES
	OW.52 BLELHAM TARN	LANCASHIRE	MeS
	OW.53 HAWES WATER, SILVERDALE	LANCASHIRE	MaS
	OW.54 SUNBIGGIN TARN	WESTMORLAND	MaS
	OW.55 KNOCK-ORE GILL	WESTMORLAND	UR
	OW.56 WASTWATER	CUMBERLAND	OS
	OW.62 RIVER TWEED (PART)	NORTHUMBERLAND See under South Scotland	
Grade 2	OW.57 Tarn Dub	Yorkshire	ES, TS
	OW.58 Blea Water	Westmorland	OS
	OW.59 Buttermere	Cumberland	OS

Table 22 (*contd.*)

Region	Site	County	Type of water-body
South Scotland			
GRADE 1*	OW.60 LOCH LOMOND	DUNBARTONSHIRE/ STIRLINGSHIRE	OS, MeS
GRADE 1	OW.61 MILL LOCH, LOCHMABEN	DUMFRIES-SHIRE	ES
	OW.62 RIVER TWEED	BERWICKSHIRE/PEEBLESHIRE/ SELKIRKSHIRE/ ROXBURGHSHIRE/ NORTHUMBERLAND	UR, ER
	OW.63 GLADHOUSE RESERVOIR	MIDLOTHIAN	MeS
Grade 2	OW.64 White Loch, Lochinch	Wigtownshire	ES
	OW.65 Duddingston Loch	Midlothian	ES
	OW.66 River Endrick	Dunbartonshire/Stirlingshire	UR, ER, SR
East Scotland			
GRADE 1*	OW.67 LOCH LEVEN	KINROSS	ES
*	OW.68 CAIRNGORM LOCHS	ABERDEENSHIRE,	
	(a) LOCH ETCHACHAN	INVERNESS-SHIRE,	OS
	(b) LOCH COIRE AN LOCHAIN	BANFFSHIRE	OS
	(c) LOCHAN UAINE, BEN MACDHUI		OS
	(d) LOCH EINICH		OS
	(e) LOCH AVON		OS
GRADE 1	OW.69 DUPPLIN LOCHS	PERTHSHIRE	ES
	OW.70 CARSEBRECK LOCHS	PERTHSHIRE	ES
	OW.71 LOCH LAIDON	PERTHSHIRE/ARGYLL	DS
	OW.72 TAY–ISLA VALLEY	PERTHSHIRE	ES
	OW.73 RIVER SPEY	INVERNESS-SHIRE	UR, SR
	OW.74 LOCH INSH	INVERNESS-SHIRE	MeS
	OW.75 RIVER DEE	ABERDEENSHIRE/ KINCARDINESHIRE	UR
	OW.76 LOCH KINORD	ABERDEENSHIRE	MeS
	OW.77 LOCH OF STRATHBEG	ABERDEENSHIRE	ES
	OW.78 LOCHS OF HARRAY & STENNESS	ORKNEY	ES–BS
Grade 2	OW.79 Kilconquhar Loch	Fife	ES
	OW.80 Drummond Pond	Perthshire	ES
	OW.81 Lochs Rescobie & Balgavies	Angus	ES
	OW.82 Loch of Kinnordy	Angus	?ES
	OW.83 Loch of Lintrathen	Angus	?ES
	OW.84 Loch Spynie	Morayshire	ES
	OW.85 Lochs of Spiggie & Brow	Shetland	ES, BS
West Scotland			
GRADE 1*	OW.86 LOCH MORAR	INVERNESS-SHIRE	OS
*	OW.87 LOCH AN DUIN, NORTH UIST	INVERNESS-SHIRE	OS–BS
*	OW.88 GROGARRY LOCHS, SOUTH UIST	INVERNESS-SHIRE	
	(a) LOCH DRUIDIBEG		OS
	(b) LOCH A'MHACHAIR & LOCH STILLIGARY		ES
	(c) HOWMORE ESTUARY, LOCH ROAG & LOCH FADA		BS
*	OW.89 DURNESS LOCHS & STREAMS	SUTHERLAND	MaS
GRADE 1	OW.90 RIVER STRONTIAN	ARGYLL	UR
	OW.71 LOCH LAIDON (PART)	ARGYLL See under East Scotland	
	OW.91 LOCH EYE	ROSS	ES

Table 22 (*contd.*)

Region	Site	County	Type of water-body
GRADE 1	OW.92 LOCH SIONASCAIG	ROSS	OS
	OW.93 LOCH WATTEN	CAITHNESS	ES
Grade 2	OW.94 Lismore Lochs	Argyll	MaS
	OW.95 Loch Shiel	Argyll/Inverness-shire	OS
	OW.96 Loch Mhaolach-coire & River Traligill	Sutherland	ES, UR, SuR
	OW.97 Loch Stack & River Laxford	Sutherland	OS, UR
	OW.98 Burn of Latheronwheel	Caithness	UR
	OW.99 Loch nam Feithean, Balranald, North Uist	Inverness-shire	ES

Notes

Standing waters	Running waters
DS = dystrophic	UR = upland
OS = oligotrophic	OR = oligotrophic (lowland)
MeS = mesotrophic	ER = eutrophic (lowland)
ES = eutrophic	CR = chalk
MaS = marl	SR = sluggish
BS = brackish	SuR = subterranean
TS = temporary	

[a] See Appendix.

8 PEATLANDS

RANGE OF ECOLOGICAL VARIATION

Habitat factors and vegetation

Peatlands are ecosystems in which vegetation of wet ground builds up organic deposits over the underlying mineral substratum, under conditions of waterlogging that are usually anaerobic. The depth and degree of decomposition of a peat deposit vary according to the behaviour of the water regime during the total period of peat formation at the site. In general, the more complete and permanent the degree of waterlogging, the lower the rate of humification and more rapid the peat formation, so that the deepest peats tend to occur on the wettest sites. The stratigraphy of a peat deposit therefore contains a record of hydrological conditions during the whole period of its formation, and typically shows variations in rate of growth. In general, too, the more acidic and base-deficient the water supply, the slower the humification, and in many situations the onset of peat formation appears to have been associated with acidification of the ground surface, often accompanied by a growing independence from mineral-rich ground water.

The differences in vegetation which accompany these changes in water regime and nutrient supply are also involved in the differences in rate of peat formation. This is especially true in regard to changes in abundance of the genus *Sphagnum* (bog-moss) which has such an important role in the formation of peat in Britain. The Cyperaceae also contribute notably to peat formation. Both these are moisture-loving groups of plants which decrease if water tables fall and the ground surface begins to dry out.

Peatlands may be classified either according to their different physical (especially hydrological) characteristics or their present range of vegetation, or by a combination of these two inter-related criteria. Nomenclature of peatlands in Britain has become a little confused because certain terms defined according to one criterion have acquired meaning for the other through looser usage. The term bog (in raised bog and blanket bog) has become synonymous with 'peat moss' as meaning an acidic peatland usually with abundant *Sphagnum*. However, it has also been used in valley bog, where conditions are often strongly alkaline. The term fen has been used to denote the swampy peatlands associated with transitions to open water or occupying wide flood plains; as these typically support eutrophic vegetation, fen has also come to indicate a particular range of plant communities, especially those dominated by tall grasses, sedges and forbs. The term has then been extended to

similar vegetation in quite different topographic situations (e.g. valley bog), and also qualified (as in poor-fen) to indicate certain communities intermediate between fen and bog. Because of these confusions, it has seemed best to follow Scandinavian practice, and apply the term mire to all peatlands, as a simple name with no further connotation, and to classify these mires first according to their topographic and hydrological features.

The permanently high water table which induces peat formation may result from different environmental conditions. Land forms such as basins, channels and flat-bottomed valleys naturally collect and hold water which falls as rain or drains into these situations from elsewhere, so that suitable topography is one basic factor in mire development. Permeability of the substratum also interacts with topography to determine degree of waterlogging, and depends largely on the physical and chemical properties of rocks and their derived soils. Superimposed on both these conditions is the overall availability of water, determined basically by the balance between precipitation and evapotranspiration, i.e. effective wetness of climate. The wetter the climate the wider is the range of topographic situations which allow peat formation. The strongly oceanic (i.e. cool, humid) conditions of western Britain, and especially the high orographic rainfall of the uplands, favour the development of extensive, continuous areas of peat-forming vegetation over most flat or gently sloping ground.

A primary division of mire types has long been recognised according to these major environmental differences (Tansley, 1939). Mires that are formed in topographic situations which allow peat formation only when effective wetness of climate is high, are described as *ombrogenous* (i.e. originating through rainfall). Other mires are restricted to topographic situations which obviously favour the collection of water. Such situations occur either where superficial moving drainage water becomes localised along definite tracks (often in sloping terrain) or where local relief results in a permanently high water table as in depressions or on extensive flat areas such as coastal plains. It has become customary to refer to the first of these conditions as *soligenous* and the second as *topogenous*.

These three classes intergrade and are not always truly separable. For instance, the frequency of occurrence and extent of soligenous mire is strongly influenced by the supply of run-off water, which in turn depends on wetness of climate, as well as on the nature of the ground. On some topogenous mires, too, upward growth of the peat has gradually raised the mire surface above the influence of ground water, so that the living vegetation eventually becomes dependent on the atmosphere for its water and nutrients (i.e. it becomes ombrogenous). Further examples of such intergradation are the distinct water-tracks within ombrogenous mires which can be regarded as small-scale soligenous components. The concepts of topogenous, soligenous and ombrogenous mire nevertheless express different degrees of interaction of important factors, and the extreme types diverge considerably in gross morphology, floristics and distribution. Topogenous mires can occur in any region but are the major type represented in the dry lowlands of southern and eastern England, whereas active ombrogenous mires are now largely confined to the humid west and north of Britain.

The topographic situation, hydrology and gross morphology of mires vary considerably and some workers have produced a more elaborate classification of mire types based on variations in these features. The disadvantage of such a scheme is that it involves features which can only be identified by careful stratigraphical surveys and water studies, and thus is of limited use during rapid field survey. The more conservative classification adopted here is based on six major topographic or structural mire types.

Ombrogenous mires are subdivided into *blanket mires* (blanket bogs), which are predominantly upland and restricted to the north and west, and *raised mires* (raised bogs), which occur mainly in lowland situations north-west of a line from the Severn to the Wash. Topogenous mires are of three main types: *open water transition* and *flood-plain mires* (fens), *basin mires*, and *valley mires* (valley bogs). These are mainly lowland but geographically widespread. *Soligenous mires* (flush bogs) can occur in association with some of the other main types, but are most distinctively developed on the uplands of the north and west.

Although certain types of vegetation show a particular association with certain classes of mire, the classification of mire vegetation does not run closely parallel to the above subdivision of mires based on physical characteristics. Detailed characterisation of mire vegetation in terms of particular floristic assemblages (noda) has not yet been comprehensively worked out in Britain, so that a phytosociological classification cannot be given here, and a descriptive system which takes account of ecological factors is used. The range of vegetational variation within these peatlands is best analysed in terms of the major controlling factors, namely, height of the mire water table and chemical composition of the water.

Some plant species have a very limited range of moisture tolerance/requirement and thus are good indicators of water table, whereas others with a wider range occur in a variety of communities from wet to dry. Mires as a whole show a tendency to an ecological succession whereby open water is colonised by strongly hydrophilous plants which build up a peat surface until it can be invaded by other, less hydrophilous species, and so on, until the ground becomes so dry that mire plants largely disappear and peat formation and upward growth cease. Such hydroseral development occurs especially in mires containing pools or those fringing larger bodies of open water, but may become arrested at any stage. In ombrogenous mires, in particular, upward growth of a *Sphagnum* carpet usually draws up the water table, and, though hydroseral development proceeds continuously, the early, wet stages persist or redevelop and there is at any one time a mosaic pattern of different stages (the regeneration complex); there is thus a steady state overall and the mire surface remains generally wet and spongy. A fall in water table and consequent surface drying, with reduction in hydrophyte cover, often results from climatic change and human activity, but some ecologists believe that it may sometimes also represent a natural termination of bog growth with no change in other conditions. Ombrogenous mires, with a water table often lifted far above mineral soil level, are especially susceptible to drying out through peat cutting, draining, burning and grazing, which often tap the edges first and initiate degeneration of the whole peat system, ending frequently in erosion. As the water table falls, either laterally along an environmental gradient or through succession in time at any one place, there is an increasing tendency to invasion by tall shrubs and trees to form scrub or woodland. Scots pine can invade wet *Sphagnum* carpets but, unless there is appreciable drying, the small saplings remain stunted (checked) and eventually die in this state. Succession to woodland usually depends on the water table falling appreciably below the mire surface, either through upward growth or external change in hydrology. The type of woodland which then develops depends on the chemical nature of the peat and water, and also on geographical location.

Although much studied, the relationships between water chemistry and floristic composition of mire vegetation are still imperfectly understood. Acidity/alkalinity levels are known to be of great importance and are most easily measured as pH and calcium carbonate content. The oxygen content and level of oxidising or reducing conditions of mire waters are also important, and various chemical factors are influenced by and interact with physical conditions such as rate of water movement and amplitude of water table fluctuation. The physical and chemical characteristics of the peat itself are important, and though they are essentially dependent on the water regime, they may affect it, as by buffering effects and by drawing up the water table. It is perhaps best to think of the peat and mire water as a single system with complex cause/effect relationships which involve some degree of circularity.

Acidity/alkalinity has been much used as an index of nutrient status of waters, and the terms oligotrophic, mesotrophic and eutrophic have become generally accepted terms for different nutrient levels (their original meaning was not quite the same), though there is no general agreement about their quantitative definition. In the present account they are defined and applied as follows on p. 251.

The nutrient requirements of individual plant species and communities may be described in terms of these three levels, which thus give a simple but useful means of analysing and classifying mire vegetation in one direction. A

Nutrient status	pH	Alkalinity (p.p.m. CaCO$_3$)
Oligotrophic (poor)	4.0–7.0	10.0
Mesotrophic (moderate)	7.0–7.5	10.0–30.0
Eutrophic (rich)	7.5–9.5	30.0

number of mire species have a very wide range of tolerance/ requirements in regard to nutrient status, and so cannot be regarded as diagnostic of any particular trophic level of mire vegetation. They include *Carex rostrata*, *C. nigra*, *C. limosa*, *C. lasiocarpa*, *Eriophorum angustifolium*, *Juncus acutiflorus*, *Menyanthes trifoliata* and *Myrica gale*. A few species show marked regional change in adaptation to nutrient status, being strongly basiphilous in the south and east of Britain, but much less so or even indifferent in the north and west, e.g. *Cladium mariscus*, *Schoenus nigricans*, *Drosera anglica*, *Phragmites communis*, *Carex dioica*, *Utricularia vulgaris*, *Scorpidium scorpioides* and *Drepanocladus revolvens*.

The pH values of peat tend to be lower than those of mire water, by up to one unit, and the more acidic peats are prone to seasonal variation in pH, as the greater amount of oxidation under drier, summer conditions increases the level of acidity.

Peat varies in nature according to the factors which produce differences in the vegetation of the mire surface, i.e. acidity/alkalinity and height of water table, both of which are affected by degree of human disturbance. Peat formed by acidophilous vegetation tends to have certain common features regardless of the type of mire. With a high water table, *Sphagnum* spp. are typically the important peat-forming plants, producing a fast-growing, loose-textured deposit known to peat-cutters as moss-litter. Where the mire surface is drier but still wet enough to prevent high humification, *Sphagnum* cover is reduced, and mono-cotyledonous plants such as *Eriophorum vaginatum*, *E. angustifolium*, *Trichophorum cespitosum* and *Molinia caerulea* are important peat-formers, producing a dense fibrous material. In former ages, the now very rare *Scheuchzeria palustris* locally contributed a good deal to the formation of this fibrous peat, under conditions of high water table which were usually transitory. On still drier mire surfaces, dwarf shrubs such as *Calluna vulgaris*, *Erica tetralix* and *Empetrum nigrum*, along with *Eriophorum vaginatum* and *Rhacomitrium lanuginosum* contribute significantly to peat formation, but the greater rate of oxidation produces a more highly humified, amorphous deposit in which it is frequently more difficult to identify the remains of particular species.

In general, on ombrogenous mires, the shallower the depth of peat, the greater the degree of humification (and vice versa), and there is a gradual transition to the mor surface horizons of wet heaths as drainage improves. The peat most valued for fuel is that of relatively shallow, well-humified deposits. The peat of raised mires is often deep (up to 10 m), but the acidic material sometimes passes below into a fen peat laid down under mesotrophic or eutrophic conditions, and this in turn may overlie lake,

fluvio-glacial or marine sediments. The remains of trees and shrubs, varying in size from twigs to large trunks, may occur at various levels, indicating periods when forest or scrub cover developed on the site. Though there is a general tendency for humification to increase towards the bottom of a deposit the deeper profiles of acidic peat are often stratified into layers of markedly differing humification, indicating changes in water table which may or may not be related to drier or wetter climatic phases. Often, too, deep peat-cuttings reveal the past small-scale surface structure of the mire, with systems of hummocks and hollows, either corresponding in position to similar features of the present day, or differing somewhat in their spatial relationships. The complete profile of a raised mire thus provides a unique record of the developmental history of the site, dating back in many instances to the period immediately following the end of the last Ice Age.

The peat of blanket mires differs from that of raised mires mainly in being shallower (not usually more than 5 m and most often from 2–4 m), and thus often more humified and generally in lacking underlying deposits formed under fen or open water conditions. Blanket mire is, however, variable in age; in many districts it evidently began to form widely at the onset of the Atlantic Period (around 5000 B.C.) as ground which carried forest or heath became waterlogged and soils impoverished under the wetter climate following the dry Boreal Period. Yet in many places, blanket mire did not begin to develop until much later; and topography, through its influence on drainage, appears to have been a crucial factor in the initiation of the process. There is also some evidence that blanket mire formation was accelerated in Neolithic times by human activities of forest clearance and stock grazing. Many blanket mires have peat with a basal layer containing remains of trees and tall shrubs which grew on the underlying mineral soil, typically of glacial drift. Some deposits contain tree remains at higher levels in the profile and, as in raised mires, the peat is usually stratified, with layers of differing humification reflecting vegetational change according to variations in wetness of bog surfaces over long periods. These changes may sometimes be climatic, but it is again possible that some apparent changes in wetness may be the result of early human disturbance. Patterns of surface structure are again shown by the undulations of the horizons exposed in cut profiles. In many districts upland blanket peat is now subject to severe and widespread erosion, resulting in breakdown of the mire as a continuous system. This may be due to changing climatic conditions, or to inherent instability in the growth of blanket mire, but there is abundant stratigraphical evidence that heavy grazing and attendant land-use practices, especially burning, have played a part in initiating peat erosion.

Basin mires have often developed over kettle-holes and tend to have underlying deposits which are very deep, especially in relation to surface area. Some have basal lake sediments, and quite often the mire surface is a floating raft of vegetation (*schwingmoor*) overlying open water or semi-fluid peat. Where there is a deeper layer of more solid peat it tends to be like that of raised mires, except in the rather rare mesotrophic or eutrophic basin mires. The oligotrophic valley mires and soligenous mires tend to have rather shallow peats overlying the fluvial, fluvio-glacial or drift deposits of the channels, hollows and depressions where they occur. The peat is nevertheless often the unhumified moss-litter type, except at the shallow edges of a mire where there is a transition to the podsolic soils of dry ground. In some examples, especially of soligenous mires, there are good examples of peaty gley soils, and where periodic flooding of the surface occurs there may be varying mixtures of mineral sediment.

The open water transition and flood-plain mires, basin mires, valley mires and soligenous mires with poor-fen vegetation have peat formed from sedges or *Sphagnum* spp., or mixtures of these, varying again in humification between different places, and within the same profile. The mesotrophic and eutrophic examples with rich-fen vegetation generally have a distinctive peat formed from sedges and their allies, *Phragmites communis* and other tall grasses, forbs and 'brown mosses', in varying proportion. This peat tends to be moderately to highly humified, probably because higher pH allows some decomposition even under anaerobic conditions, but in open water transition and flood-plain mires the deposits are often quite deep (up to 8 m). When drained these rich-fen peats give agricultural soils of high fertility, as in the East Anglian Fenlands, but drying is accompanied by rapid oxidation and a tendency to wind-blow, so that over much of this district the land surface has shrunk by a depth of several metres, and in places the underlying clay is exposed. Conversely, the undrained remnants of the old Fenlands appear now as isolated blocks of peat forming more elevated islands, which can only be kept moist by artificial methods of maintaining water tables. Fen peat often contains the remains of alder and willow, indicating phases of carr development. In some localities, nuclei of oligotrophic vegetation amongst areas of rich-fen on the present surface may indicate incipient acidification of the kind which occurred on a large scale where flood-plain mire changed into raised mire.

The detailed description of mire vegetation is presented under the account of the six topographic/hydrological classes of mire which now follows.

RAISED MIRE

Raised mires occur on more or less level flood plains of mature river systems, and more especially on alluvial deposits of estuaries, where they owe their origin to the absence of slope which first favoured extensive development of topogenous mire (i.e. open water transition or flood-plain mire). With upward growth, and possibly influenced by changing climatic conditions, the original mesotrophic or eutrophic mire vegetation became increasingly isolated from and independent of ground water influence, with the result that vegetation of truly ombrogenous character became established and has persisted. Some of the most extensive British raised mires cover an area of 20 km² or more (e.g. Flanders Moss, Perthshire; Lochar Moss, Dumfries-shire; Thorne

Waste, Yorkshire), though the best active examples now are much smaller. The mire expanse is typically bounded by clearly defined features including a drier, steeply sloping margin (rand) and an adjacent stream course (lagg) with richer water which limits the lateral extension of acidophilous communities. Although raised mires are characterised by a convex profile the surface gradient from the centre to the edges is very low (often less than 1 m in 0.5 km) so that run-off rates are low and these mires do not depend on such a high precipitation/evaporation ratio as blanket mires. One of the most extensive raised mires, Thorne Waste, has developed in an area of very low rainfall (58 cm per annum) and remnants of raised mires are known from other low rainfall areas, e.g. Huntingdonshire and Norfolk, so that rainfall does not appear to be limiting in Britain.

Raised mires have a very localised distribution in Britain, reflecting a dependence on suitable geomorphological conditions for their formation. The majority occur on coastal lowlands especially adjoining large estuaries, but some occur in areas of suitable topography, usually broad river valleys, far inland. Important areas of coastal raised mires include the Somerset Levels, estuaries around Cardigan Bay and Morecambe Bay, the Vale of Trent, the Solway, the upper Forth valley and isolated situations along the western seaboard of Scotland. In all cases these mires lie below 15 m. The inland raised mires are less numerous and vary considerably in altitude. Some of the largest examples are in Wales and the Welsh border land (e.g. Fenns Moss 90 m, Cors Goch glan Teifi 170 m and Rhos Goch 270 m) whilst smaller examples occur at higher altitudes elsewhere, e.g. Malham Tarn Moss at 380 m in the Craven Pennines. Raised mire is increasingly replaced towards the north-west of Britain by blanket mire, which smothers plain and slope alike, and in some northern areas where morphological features are not clear, the distinctions between blanket and raised mires become somewhat tenuous with intermediate types occurring frequently. This is especially true of Southern Scotland where discrete raised mires occur on flat ground at low altitudes, but similar mires merge into the surrounding blanket mire at higher levels (i.e. above 60 m). The ombrogenous mires of such areas may be viewed as a continuous series, the components of which vary according to the relative importance of climatic and topographic factors in any one situation.

Raised mire vegetation varies considerably throughout Britain. The main differences correspond to the type and degree of surface relief developed on any particular site and the relative height of the water table. Climate is the most important single factor determining type of surface microtopography, but the size of any single raised mire also seems to be important. The usual type of raised mire in lowland Britain has a large scale but shallow hummock–hollow mosaic within a predominantly *Spagnum*-covered surface (e.g. Cors Fochno, Cardiganshire, and Glasson Moss, Cumberland). These are extensive mires over a kilometre in diameter developed in areas of moderate rainfall (76–114 cm per annum). Smaller raised mires developed in similar climatic conditions often have a more pronounced surface microtopography with steep-sided pools set in a relatively dry mire surface which is dominated by *Calluna* or *Erica tetralix* (e.g. Rhos Goch, Radnor; Wem Moss, Shropshire). Such features are accentuated in areas of low and infrequent rainfall (Penmanshiel Moor, Berwickshire). At the other extreme are the oceanic raised mires of western Scotland (e.g. Claish Moss, Argyll) with very pronounced surface patterns consisting of extensive shallow pools separated by narrow waterlogged ridges, the vegetation being relatively hydrophilous compared with that of more southerly sites. This type occurs in areas of high rainfall (150–230 cm with over 200 wet days per annum).

In addition to this variation in surface morphology there are broad geographical differences in floristics such as the abundance of *Rhacomitrium lanuginosum*, *Pleurozia purpurea* and *Carex limosa* in northern oceanic situations and dominance of *Vaccinium oxycoccus* and *Andromeda polifolia* in more southerly sites. Probably no plant species is confined to British raised mires, though the rare moss *Dicranum bergeri* is a characteristic species. Communities of *A. polifolia* with *Sphagnum magellanicum* and *Rhynchospora alba* with *S. pulchrum* are best developed in raised mire, though all four species are abundant in other types. The northern oceanic raised mires of Europe are characterised by an association of *R. fusca* and *S. pulchrum*, but this is rare in Britain.

Marginal communities such as *Myrica–Molinia* mire and *Betula–Carex* carr form an integral part of raised mire systems. Raised mires differ from valley, basin and blanket mires in that large-scale soligenous water tracks and associated communities do not occur on the central mire surface, though these mires have numerous small water tracks between adjacent pool systems, which are best developed on the oceanic raised mires with a pronounced surface pattern such as Claish Moss.

In the more normal development of raised mire in Britain the mire expanse is typically covered with a *Sphagnum*-dominated vegetation showing a gently undulating surface with a large-scale hummock and hollow pattern, usually of small vertical amplitude. The hollows seldom contain open water and are usually spongy carpets of *Sphagnum* spp. which need constant saturation, such as *S. cuspidatum* and *S. pulchrum*, which grade into flat 'lawns' and then low hummocks, through the appearance and increase of other species, notably *S. magellanicum*. Vascular plants typical of the wettest *Sphagnum* communities include *Eriophorum angustifolium*, *Rhynchospora alba*, *Drosera anglica*, *D. rotundifolia* and *Narthecium ossifragum*, whilst *Andromeda polifolia* and *Vaccinium oxycoccus* are often abundant on lawns and low hummocks, and undisturbed Sphagnetum contains a variety of small leafy liverworts. Upward growth of the low hummocks is associated with the appearance of *S. rubellum*, and a wider range of vascular plants such as *Eriophorum vaginatum*, *Trichophorum cespitosum*, *Calluna vulgaris* and *Erica tetralix*, which increase in cover and luxuriance with height above the water table. Some species have a wide vertical range in the hollow and hummock system, but the tallest and driest hummocks are quite different from the

hollows and lawns in appearance – *Sphagnum* spp. are largely replaced by tussocky growths of *Eriophorum vaginatum* and *Trichophorum* with small bushes of *Calluna*, and there is often an abundance of heathland mosses and lichens, such as *Pleurozium schreberi*, *Cladonia impexa* and *C. sylvatica*.

The more sloping and therefore better drained margin (rand) of these raised mires has a drier vegetation resembling that of the central surface hummocks, with the vascular plants more important than *Sphagnum* spp., and often an abundance of species such as *Myrica gale* and *Molinia caerulea*. Various forms of human disturbance (e.g. peat-cutting, burning) which lower the water table also reduce *Sphagnum* cover although *S. compactum* and *S. tenellum* may be favoured by conditions following a fire. Drying of the surface promotes increased growth and tussock or bush formation in the vascular plants, which increase to dominance. The vegetation then comes to resemble wet heath, or even, when drying is severe, dry heath. The marginal rand where the water table is usually lower than in the mire centre is particularly susceptible to this disturbance and drying. Old peat-cuttings, characteristic of raised mire edges, are often recolonised to form pockets of Sphagnetum with other hydrophilous mire plants, but are typically dominated by *S. recurvum*, which seldom occurs in undisturbed central mire communities. The original lagg bounding the outer edge of a raised mire has usually been destroyed or completely modified in British examples. Where it remains, there is usually a heterogeneous vegetation ranging from wet *Molinia* grassland or poor-fen to birch–willow carr.

On the oceanic raised mires along the western Scottish seaboard the vegetation is quite distinct and more akin to that of western blanket mire. The mire expanse has a pronounced surface pattern of linear pools and ridges aligned parallel to the surface contours. The pools usually hold open water and there is a greater vertical amplitude between hollow and hummock than on the more southerly raised mires. The pools range from deep, bare types containing only algae and open growths of *Menyanthes trifoliata*, *Eriophorum angustifolium* and *Carex limosa* to others showing varying degrees of infilling by *Sphagnum* spp. mainly *S. cuspidatum* and *S. subsecundum* var. *auriculatum*. Lawn and low hummock communities are dominated by *S. magellanicum*, *S. papillosum* and *S. pulchrum* whilst the taller hummocks are composed of *S. rubellum* and *Rhacomitrium lanuginosum*. The oceanic liverwort *Pleurozia purpurea* is constantly present and the moss *Campylopus atrovirens* often occurs in association with algae-covered peat surfaces. The vascular plants of the lawns and hummocks are similar to those of more southerly raised mires but *Molinia caerulea* is abundant whilst *Vaccinium oxycoccus* and *Andromeda polifolia* are absent. A feature of these northern raised mires is the abundance of *Rhynchospora fusca* and *Eleocharis multicaulis* in shallow pools. The rand is largely dominated by *Molinia* with *Myrica gale* whilst lagg channels are occupied by tussocky Molinietum.

Many raised mires have been totally reclaimed by agricultural improvement; others have been considerably modified by drainage attempts, resulting often in an extensive development of birch and pine woodland, especially around the mire edges, as at Kirkconnell Flow, Kirkcudbrightshire. At Holme Fen, Huntingdonshire, virtually the whole of the original raised mire has gone over to mature birchwood, and the cut-over surface of the huge Thorne Waste in Yorkshire shows extensive birch colonisation. Peat exploitation has taken place on many sites both on a local domestic scale (often only peripherally) and more extensively in the case of commercial peat winning – an industry which has evolved mainly over the last 25 years. Even the few remaining actively growing raised mires are largely covered with a vegetational mosaic which reflects varying degrees of drying and modification resulting from disturbance (mainly fire and drainage).

BLANKET MIRE

Blanket mire is the extreme climatic type of mire and the most oceanic of the whole European series. It is not only the most extensive type of mire in Britain, but is also better represented in this country (and Ireland) than in any other part of Europe. Indeed, few areas in the world show such a spectacular development of ombrogenous peatland, and many of the best British examples are thus of great international importance. Blanket mire is confined to the wetter parts of Britain, but an even distribution of rainfall is more important to its development than total amount, and the apparent limiting precipitation frequency of 160 wet days (a wet day = 1 mm of rain in 24 hours) is probably a meaningful expression of this relationship with wetness of climate. Effective humidity for plants depends on the evaporating power of the atmosphere, and the relative coolness and cloudiness of the oceanic climate are important factors in promoting peat formation.

Blanket mire formation depends also on a suitable topography and substratum giving impeded surface drainage and pronounced acidity. It is inhibited by steep slopes, porous substrata and soil parent materials of high base-status (especially limestone), but these limitations are increasingly over-ridden as effective wetness of climate increases. Thus, under the tremendously humid climate of the western and northern Scottish Highlands and islands, blanket mire mantles all but the steepest slopes and alpine summits, irrespective of substratum, almost down to sea-level. While deep deposits are everywhere confined to slopes of less than 15°, in the very wettest parts of this region, shallow blanket mire occurs on slopes of up to 30°. Blanket mire is especially characteristic of broad, flat upland watersheds, but reaches an upper altitudinal limit at about 1070 m in the Cairngorms. It is extensive in most moorland areas where gentle slopes and large plateaux prevail, as on Dartmoor, some of the Welsh mountains (especially in the east and south), the Pennines, Cheviots, Southern Uplands and eastern Highlands. In the south, blanket mire occurs mainly above 300 m, but shows altitudinal descent with distance north. Types intermediate between raised and blanket mire occur in northern England and southern Scotland at 90–300 m, and blanket mire reaches its most extensive development in

Britain on the great flow country of east Sutherland and Caithness, where a vast area (approximately 2500 km²) of plain and gently sloping terrain from 0 to 500 m is covered by this type of peatland.

Two major types of blanket mire vegetation can be recognised each with various facies. One of these is the predominant type in western situations generally below 460 m and it is usually this vegetation type which intergrades with that of raised mires. This western blanket mire is characterised by dominance of *Trichophorum* spp., *Molinia* spp. and *Eriophorum* spp., together with abundance of pools and *Sphagnum*-dominated hollows. The second is essentially an upland type, often dominated by *Calluna* and *E. vaginatum*, which occurs mainly above 300 m and is best developed on the Pennines and eastern uplands of Scotland. Although these two types can be separated on a broad geographical basis it is also apparent that in some districts local variations in topography can cause both types to occur in close proximity. An example is the northern Pennines where the main blanket-mire vegetation is Calluneto–Eriophoretum. In this area localised pockets of mire, closely comparable with the western Trichophoreto–Eriophoretum, are found wherever blanket mire has developed on flat areas such as the hillside terraces on Yoredale sandstones. Other good examples occur in Y Berwyn of north Wales, and in east Sutherland this juxtaposition of the two types is associated with two major morphological mire types, flat valley-side flows and convex watershed flows.

There is strong evidence that closely similar vegetation types can result from the interaction between climatic and topographic conditions in different regions. For example the type of vegetation developed on level blanket mire in parts of the northern Pennines under moderate rainfall (152 cm per annum) is closely comparable with that developed on distinctly sloping blanket mire under a higher rainfall regime (230 cm) in south-west Scotland, whilst flat-lying blanket mire in the latter area has closer affinities with the oceanic blanket mires of north-west Scotland. At present there is insufficient information to make a critical appraisal of the relationship between climate, topography and variations in blanket mire vegetation. A more detailed investigation is required.

The western *Trichophorum–Molinia–Eriophorum* mire is especially well developed in Scotland but facies of this complex also occur in northern England, Wales and Dartmoor. In Scotland this type covers all gently sloping blanket mire in the west up to about 460 m. The flattest and wettest surfaces have a characteristic linear pattern of pools and hummocks aligned parallel to the surface contours. Pools range from deep (20–50 cm), bare types containing only algae and open growths of *Menyanthes trifoliata* and *Eriophorum angustifolium*, to others showing varying degrees of infilling by *Sphagnum* spp. mainly *S. cuspidatum* and *S. subsecundum* var. *auriculatum*, often with *Eleocharis multicaulis* and *Carex limosa*. Lawn and low hummock communities are dominated by *S. papillosum* (contrasting with the dominance of *S. pulchrum* and *S. magellanicum* in the northern raised mires) and taller hummocks of *S. rubellum* are usually abundant. *S. imbricatum* probably attains its greatest abundance on these surfaces, typically forming tall domed hummocks. The vascular plants are *Molinia caerulea, Trichophorum cespitosum, Narthecium ossifragum, Erica tetralix, Eriophorum angustifolium, E. vaginatum, Drosera anglica, D. rotundifolia, Myrica gale* and *Rhynchospora alba.* Certain species are especially characteristic of the northwestern blanket mire such as *S. plumulosum, Campylopus atrovirens* and the oceanic liverwort *Pleurozia purpurea.* Others which have a wider distribution in Britain are usually associated with higher nutrient status, e.g. *Carex limosa, Eleocharis multicaulis, Melampyrum pratense* and *Schoenus nigricans. Betula nana* is a frequent component of these mires in northern Scotland and both *Andromeda polifolia* and *Vaccinium oxycoccus* occur in southern districts. A conspicuous feature of tall hummocks and drying surfaces more generally in the western blanket mire is the occurrence of dense crowns or patches of the moss *Rhacomitrium lanuginosum.* As well as constituting a major element of actively growing mires in the north-west this moss characterises degenerating pool and hummock systems on the blanket mire in many southern districts including the flat spurs of Y Berwyn (north Wales) and extensive areas on Dartmoor.

The second blanket mire vegetation complex is best developed on upland and eastern plateaux generally above 300 m. The typical community has few pools or hollows and *Sphagnum* spp. are mainly of the hummock-forming group (*S. papillosum, S. rubellum, S. capillaceum* and *S. fuscum*). The vascular plant dominants are usually *Calluna* and *Eriophorum vaginatum* whilst the most characteristic species is the montane *Rubus chamaemorus. Molinia caerulea* is normally absent, and *Trichophorum cespitosum* shows a patchy or local abundance. Where extensive level areas with a permanently high water table occur there are well-developed *Sphagnum* communities with obvious similarity to those of raised mires and western blanket mire. Transitional types with pronounced pool systems occur locally, especially in northern Scotland where they form the watershed flows of Caithness and Sutherland.

Several distinctive facies of this Calluneto–Eriophoretum can be recognised. A *Sphagnum*-rich facies occurs on flat-lying blanket mire which has not been subject to erosion, and this is especially well represented in the moorlands of the Scottish Borders. The more typical and most widespread community (perhaps produced partly by human influence) has a lower cover of *Sphagnum*, more *Vaccinium myrtillus* and *V. vitis-idaea,* and a greater abundance of hypnaceous mosses, such as *Pleurozium schreberi, Hylocomium splendens, Plagiothecium undulatum* and *Rhytidiadelphus loreus.* In some districts, notably parts of the Pennines, heavy sheep-grazing and repeated burning have not only severely reduced *Sphagnum* cover but have also locally eradicated *Calluna,* to give *Eriophorum vaginatum*-dominated blanket mires. In the Peak District, atmospheric pollution has eliminated *Sphagnum* and may possibly be involved in the characteristic replacement here of *Calluna* by luxuriant *Empetrum nigrum.*

From their topographic position, the upland plateau blanket mires are especially vulnerable to marginal drying and erosion, and the majority show some degree of erosion by gullying, which may spread to dissect the whole of a mire surface, and often develops into sheet erosion, involving complete destruction of the whole peat cover. Such peat wastage leads to the exposure of tree remains which have lain preserved in the peat for up to thousands of years, and also causes a marked drying of the adjoining peat surface. This drying is reflected by an increase in dwarf shrubs (especially *Empetrum nigrum* and *Vaccinium myrtillus*) and locally of *Rhacomitrium lanuginosum* and/or lichens. However, in the Scottish Highlands (especially the east) there are distinctive facies of undisturbed blanket mire rich in both dwarf shrubs and lichens of the *Cladonia sylvatica* group. The dwarf shrubs here include montane species such as *Betula nana, Arctostaphylos uva-ursi, Arctous alpinus, V. uliginosum* and *E. hermaphroditum* (which replaces *Calluna* at high levels). Finally, in northern Scotland, particularly Shetland, an unusual facies includes *Erica cinerea* and *Carex binervis.*

Although blanket mires are not floristically rich, their vegetation is thus diverse, and the wide range of surface structure is a most interesting feature. The patterned mires of western and northern Scotland are regarded as especially important scientifically. Yet despite the great extent of blanket mire in Britain, few areas appear to have escaped some degree of modification by man. Those which have – perhaps largely by chance – are outstandingly valuable. Damage has been caused mainly by heavy grazing and burning, but during the last 30 years subsidised hill farm improvement has resulted in extensive draining of blanket mires. Commercial afforestation has destroyed many other areas, though in places where particularly wet areas have been left undisturbed among the new forests, they now have a higher degree of protection than before, as in the Kielder Forest area of northern England. Large-scale working of the blanket mire peat as a source of power, on the great flows of Caithness, was abandoned as uneconomic in this country. However, the steady destruction of both raised and blanket mires for this purpose in Ireland enhances the conservation value of the comparable examples remaining in Britain.

The more distinctive types of blanket mire association are listed in the classification of upland vegetation, p. 297.

OPEN WATER TRANSITION AND FLOOD-PLAIN MIRE

These are essentially topogenous mires, familiarly described as fen. Open water transition mire refers to the shallow edges of both lakes and rivers, which show colonisation by emergent aquatic vegetation to form swamp communities. An arbitrary separation has to be made in defining the limits of open water transition mire, as distinct from open water. The limits drawn here are at the outer edge of the zone of emergent swamp vegetation, composed mainly of monocotyledons which rise well above normal water level. Aquatic plants with leaves floating on the surface, and submerged aquatics are considered to belong to the open water class of habitats, e.g. macrophytes such as *Potamogeton* spp., *Myriophyllum* spp., *Callitriche* spp. and *Nymphaea* spp., and the majority of freshwater algae. Species which belong essentially to the open water of rivers and ditches will also be excluded from the present account.

Flood-plain mire describes lowland alluvial plains traversed by (usually) sluggish rivers and subject both to permanently impeded drainage and periodic flooding; there is development of a similar and sometimes identical range of hydrophilous vegetation to that of the open water transition mires. Where shallow lakes occur on alluvial flood plains the two types of mire form a single continuous system. Both occur especially in the lowlands, where drainage water is from a mature river system and tends to be base-rich, and they may persist indefinitely only in regions where the rainfall is too low to allow the development of ombrogenous mire; both types have frequently been the precursors to raised mires which have developed in western Britain. The occurrence of oligotrophic nuclei amongst certain of the East Anglian fens has been interpreted as the initiation of raised mire development. However, some of these mires probably persist indefinitely because topographic and hydrologic features of the site and catchment ensure that the surface can never outgrow the influence of base-rich drainage water. Conversely, the extensive cutting of certain raised mires, e.g. Shapwick Heath in Somerset and Thorne Waste in Yorkshire, has created depressions and channels influenced by base-rich water, with subsequent redevelopment of eutrophic mire vegetation, juxtaposed with acidophilous communities.

The nutrient status of the water varies considerably within this class of mires, the more oligotrophic types being characteristic of the predominantly hard and acidic ancient rocks of northern and western Britain, whereas the eutrophic types are found mainly within the base-rich catchments on the younger horizons of the south and east, especially East Anglia. The parallel climatic contrast, as between oceanicity and continentality, also enhances the effects of this geological contrast. Eutrophic examples nevertheless occur in virtually all regions and are well represented in the central Lowlands and east of Scotland; even in the oceanic western Highlands and islands there are eutrophic mires of this type associated with wet ground and lochs on the shell sand machair.

At the oligotrophic end of the series these topogenous mire communities intergrade with the still more markedly acidophilous types belonging to ombrogenous mire, and it is thus convenient to begin description with this.

Compared with raised and blanket mires, the mire water of the topogenous mires at the oligotrophic end of the series is slightly less acidic and poor in nutrients, and is evidently associated with lateral movement or other ground water influence, giving a different type of vegetation, sometimes known as poor-fen. A *Sphagnum* carpet is typically present, but with a different spectrum of species, mainly *S. papillosum*, *S. palustre*, *S. recurvum*, *S. cuspidatum*, *S. fimbriatum*, *S. squarrosum* and *S. subsecundum* vars. *auriculatum* and *inundatum*, and there are Bryalean mosses such as *Aula-comnium palustre*, *Drepanocladus exannulatus* and *Acrocladium stramineum*. The vascular plants forming a layer above the *Sphagnum* carpet have some species in common with the previous, more strongly acidophilous range of communities, but are characterised by dominance of carices, notably *Carex rostrata*, *C. lasiocarpa*, *C. nigra*, *C. echinata*, *C. curta* and *C. limosa*. *C. aquatilis* and *C. paupercula* are typical plants of northern poor-fen. Other characteristic species include *Equisetum palustre*, *E. fluviatile*, *Eriophorum angustifolium*, *Narthecium ossifragum*, *Juncus kochii*, *Agrostis stolonifera*, *Molinia caerulea*, *Caltha palustris*, *Menyanthes trifoliata*, *Potentilla palustris*, *Ranunculus flammula*, *Drosera rotundifolia*, *Vaccinium oxycoccus*, *Potamogeton polygonifolius*, *Viola palustris* and *Dactylorchis maculata*. Often, the growth of sedges and other plants excludes the *Sphagnum* spp., and in some of these mires, the *Sphagnum* carpet is fragmentary or absent. Where this type of mire dries out sufficiently to allow colonisation by shrubs, *Salix cinerea* and *S. aurita* are usually the most abundant species. Where *Myrica gale* is present and ungrazed, it also may become abundant and form a shrubby growth several feet tall. Birch commonly invades and becomes more abundant if the surface dries, though the *Sphagnum* spp. often continue to form a carpet and *Polytrichum commune* often becomes very abundant. *Molinia* may become dense and *Dryopteris carthusiana* often becomes abundant. Alder sometimes appears but is more typically associated with richer conditions. Some extensive examples of this poor-fen occur in Scotland (e.g. the Insh Marshes in Inverness-shire), but it is more widespread as small patches fringing the shallow edges of lakes and tarns.

As nutrient status of the mire water increases to a level within the lower edge of the mesotrophic range there are marked floristic changes. If a *Sphagnum* carpet persists, it is usually composed of the relatively basiphilous species *S. teres*, *S. subsecundum*, *S. contortum*, *S. warnstorfianum* and *S. squarrosum*. *Carex rostrata*, *C. nigra* and some of the poor-fen species remain abundant, but there is an addition of others such as *C. vesicaria*, *C. elata*, *C. paniculata*, *Phragmites communis*, *Phalaris arundinacea*, *Galium palustre*, *Myosotis secunda*, *Veronica scutellata*, *Lythrum salicaria*, *Epilobium palustre*, *Pedicularis palustris*, *Lychnis flos-cuculi*, *Hydrocotyle vulgaris* and *Senecio aquaticus*. The Bryalean mosses typically include *Acrocladium cuspidatum* and *Mnium seligeri*, and the liverworts *Lophocolea bidentata* and *Marchantia polymorpha* var. *aquatica* are sometimes abundant. Colonising shrubs are again mainly *Salix cinerea* and *S. aurita*, but *S. pentandra* and *Frangula alnus* are locally abundant, and alder often appears in the developing carr. *Sphagnum* carpet may persist, some of the herbs remain in the field layer, and there is often an abundance of *Juncus acutiflorus*, *Deschampsia cespitosa*, *Angelica sylvestris*, *Dactylorchis fuchsii* and *Calamagrostis epigejos*. This intermediate kind of fen is widespread in Britain, especially on rock formations which give moderately fertile but non-calcareous soils.

Where richness of water lies within the upper range of mesotrophic and passes into eutrophic, *Sphagnum* spp.

Plate 9. *Tuddenham Heath, Suffolk (L. 61(a))* (see p. 139). The acidic heathlands of southern England are typically dominated by heather, with varying amounts of gorse, and show invasion by birch to form woodland. Burning and grazing formerly resisted this succession, but other management techniques, such as cutting woody growth, now have to be used. (Photo: D. A. Ratcliffe.)

Plate 10. *Porton Down, Wiltshire/Hampshire (L.36)* (see p. 161). This Ministry of Defence area contains probably the largest remaining continuous expanse of uncultivated chalk grassland in Britain. The chalk sward in the foreground has large patches of *Anthyllis vulneraria*. Other facies include a more open, flint-strewn breck area in the middle distance, and a tall-grass sward beyond, with scattered growths of juniper, yew and hawthorn, other shrubs and trees, and blocks of woodland. (Photo: D. A. Ratcliffe.)

Plate 11. *Weeting Heath, Norfolk (L. 64)* (see p. 181). One of the best remaining fragments of the once-vast brecks which covered the poor chalky and sandy soils of this district, but have been extensively replaced by conifer plantations. The aerial view reveals the system of peri-glacial soil nets and stripes situated on, respectively, the plateau and slope. The surface has an open, flint-strewn sward of Grassland B type (*see p.* 175), heavily grazed by rabbits, with variable invasion by bracken, and scattered trees, especially Scots pine at the north end. (Photo: Cambridge University Collection, copyright reserved.)

Plate 12. *Wasdale Screes and Wastwater, Cumberland (U.18 and OW.56)* (see p. 316). A crumbling line of precipice carved in the Borrowdale Volcanic Series, feeds huge fans of unstable scree beneath. Deep gullies and hollows have formed along bands of faulted rock (shatter-belts), and here the iron-stained, calcite-bearing rock supports a fairly rich upland flora. There was probably once at least a partial woodland cover, now represented by a few scattered bushes and trees, and its destruction may have helped to expose scree. The lower slopes and rocks have relics of a woodland flora mingling with plants seeding downwards from higher levels. Wastwater is a typical example of a deep, oligotrophic lake, with clear water, low nutrient content, a stony, gravelly shore, and low

disappear and the vegetation is often dominated by vascular plants almost to the exclusion of bryophytes. The outer colonising zone of this swamp vegetation often has dense, tall growths of *Schoenoplectus lacustris*, *Phragmites communis*, *Typha latifolia* and *T. angustifolia*. The characteristic sedges include *Cladium mariscus*, *Carex riparia*, *C. acutiformis*, *C. diandra*, *C. disticha*, *C. acuta*, *C. elata*, *C. pseudocyperus*, and other typical vascular plants are *Ranunculus lingua*, *Iris pseudacorus*, *Galium uliginosum*, *Scutellaria galericulata*, *Oenanthe fistulosa*, *Berula erecta*, *Rumex hydrolapathum*, *Myosotis scorpioides*, *M. caespitosa*, *Stellaria palustris*, *Veronica anagallis-aquatica*, *Bidens cernua*, *Juncus subnodulosus*, *Sparganium erectum* and *Schoenus nigricans*. In some mires the grass *Glyceria maxima* becomes completely dominant, forming a floating raft. Communities of the above type are known under the general term of rich-fen, and are probably best represented in the Norfolk Broads.

In mires where the water is strongly calcareous, another type of moss carpet often develops, with a more open growth of vascular plants, and is composed of the 'brown mosses' *Campylium stellatum*, *C. elodes*, *Acrocladium giganteum*, *Scorpidium scorpioides*, *Drepanocladus revolvens* var. *intermedius*, *Cratoneuron filicinum*, *C. commutatum* and *Ctenidium molluscum*. Many of the above named plants of rich-fen are present, including especially the monocotyledons, but characteristically there are also additional species such as *Parnassia palustris*, *Pedicularis palustris*, *Valeriana dioica*, *Epipactis palustris*, *Dactylorchis praetermissa* (southern), *D. purpurella* (northern), *D. incarnata*, *Eriophorum latifolium*, *Triglochin palustris*, *Juncus articulatus*, *Eleocharis quinqueflora*, *Carex lepidocarpa*, *C. pulicaris* and *C. dioica*. Vegetation of this kind is especially associated with drainage from Chalk and limestone, and is well developed though seldom extensive from the south to the north of Britain.

The rich-fens show hydroseral development by the invasion of alder and willows to form carr. *Salix cinerea* remains a common constituent, but other willows such as *S. pentandra*, *S. viminalis*, *S. fragilis*, *S. triandra*, *S. purpurea* and *S. alba* are all locally abundant. In the East Anglian Fens both *Frangula alnus* and *Rhamnus catharticus* have locally become abundant and there is a good deal of *Prunus padus*, *Ribes sylvestre* and *R. nigrum*. Within the carr, many of the swamp species are killed by shade, and the peat surface often decomposes to a rather treacherous open mud. Some species are able to flourish under the willows, where shade is not too dense, e.g. *Iris* and *Carex paniculata*, and others are especially associated with this habitat, e.g. *Thelypteris palustris*, *Eupatorium cannabinum* and *Crepis paludosa*. Where the water table falls but there is no invasion by woody species, tall herbs such as *Filipendula ulmaria*, *Valeriana officinalis*, *Angelica sylvestris*, *Epilobium hirsutum*, *Lythrum salicaria*, *Lysimachia vulgaris*, *Senecio aquaticus* and *Phalaris arundinacea* often form dense growths, and the woody climber *Solanum dulcamara* is sometimes abundant. In the Norfolk Broads and the remaining fragments of the East Anglian Fenlands, this kind of succession continually reduces the extent of the earlier swamp communities, and

has to be kept in check deliberately if these are not to disappear.

A related vegetation type is the brackish swamp sometimes found fringing salt marshes and the upper reaches to estuaries, coastal lagoons, or river valleys which have recently become sealed off from the sea, as on the Suffolk coast. Typically, there are dense beds of *Phragmites*, but in places a mixed community of more or less halophytic species such as *Scirpus maritimus*, *Juncus maritimus*, *Carex otrubae* and *Oenanthe lachenalii*, is mixed with plants of rich fen such as *Iris pseudacorus*, *Sparganium ramosum*, *Carex disticha* and *Dactylorchis* spp. The swamps of the lochs and waterlogged flats on the shell-sand machair, in the Outer Hebrides, have a good deal in common with the rich-fens of southern England, except that their predominantly herbaceous swards are mostly shorter in stature.

Vegetation in this type of mire shows a certain tendency, noted also in the herbaceous field layer of woodlands, towards development of societies, i.e. patchy dominance of single species, such as *Menyanthes trifoliata* and *Potentilla palustris*, in a heterogeneous pattern that shows no superficial correspondence to variation in habitat. This may represent an effect of random spread and chance arrival of species in an essentially immature and unstable kind of vegetation.

There are especially close relationships between flood-plain mires and valley mires and in some cases the differences between the two are rather arbitrary. Flood-plain mires occupy broad valleys or extensive plains usually with a central stream or river, whereas valley mires occupy much narrower valleys and often lack an actual open, flowing stream. Similarly there can be difficulty in separating open water transition mires from basin mires which still contain a central open pool. However, there is again usually a difference in size, the basin mires being much smaller and with more obviously internal drainage. Any one flood-plain or open water transition mire tends to have vegetation belonging to a single trophic level, and varying mainly according to wetness of ground, whereas both valley and basin mires tend to show large variations in trophic level of vegetation within a small area. Oligotrophic nuclei occur in a few flood-plain or open water transition mires, but strongly acidophilous Sphagnetum is usually absent, whereas it is very well developed in many valley and basin mires.

Open water and flood-plain mires have probably been more extensively destroyed by man in Britain than those of any other class. This is especially true of the once vast swamps and marshes of the East Anglian Fenlands, occupying the large shallow basin of the three main rivers draining to the Wash. Many others have been reclaimed for agriculture, since the richer types of fen peat give a very fertile soil when dried out, and a great many have been partly drained or modified by human activity. By way of compensation, the best remaining examples, in the Norfolk Broads, owe their present existence mainly to the large-scale cutting of peat during the Middle Ages, forming extensive hollows which developed numerous hydroseral complexes from open water to rich-fen and carr.

BASIN MIRE

Topogenous mire develops in enclosed waterlogged depressions which have become colonised by peat-forming vegetation and which show no obvious unidirectional movement of water at the mire surface. The essentially level and usually stagnant water table is a fundamental feature and affords the major distinction from valley mire. Such sites occur most frequently in areas of glacial deposition where local irregularities of relief such as kames and kettle-holes provide the necessary geomorphological environment of hollows with enclosed drainage. In northern and western areas such mire pockets have largely been obliterated by the general growth of ombrogenous mire over the whole area, so that basin mires are most characteristic of lowland Britain. They are, however, found mainly in the Midlands, northern England and southern Scotland, where suitable fluvio-glacial topography is best developed. Basin mires are usually small in area (less than 50 ha) but are often very deep in relation to their size, and some are underlain by deposits of Late-glacial age.

Mires of this type vary from oligotrophic to eutrophic, and although there is a preponderance of the former this is more a reflection of the inherent successional tendency towards an oligotrophic surface than an actual prevalence of base-poor ground water. Usually, either the whole basin becomes filled with peat or a floating raft becomes established across the original water-body. As the surface of the mire grows above the direct influence of ground water, conditions favouring the development of central oligotrophic communities are initiated. In such mires, relatively base-rich facies are restricted to the margins, where succession to fen carr often occurs. Analogy with raised mire is clear, but basin mire development is determined and restricted by the hydromorphology of the basin. Furthermore, in view of the limited extent of such mires and the relatively dry climate under which many are developing, it is doubtful if the central oligotrophic communities can be regarded as truly ombrogenous. More probably the mire water budget is supplemented to some extent by ground water which is effectively buffered during movement through the acidic peat-body.

The vegetation of basin mire is composed very largely of communities already described under raised mire or the topogenous series from poor to rich fen. Open spongy areas of *Sphagnum* lawn communities are most typical of basin mires, but a distinction is made between those sites exhibiting varied *Sphagnum* communities (including *S. rubellum*, *S. magellanicum* and *S. papillosum*) with numerous leafy liverworts and a hummocky surface, in association with *Erica tetralix*, *Vaccinium oxycoccus* and *Andromeda polifolia*, and those which show a floristically poorer *Sphagnum* lawn association dominated largely by *S. recurvum* and *Eriophorum angustifolium*. This latter type (which is apparently spreading in some sites) may be a result of eutrophication, and the connection with disturbance is shown by its usual occurrence in old peat-cuttings. The more varied type of *Sphagnum* surface often has hollows and hummocks and

very closely resembles the surface of many undamaged raised mires. A common feature of many oligotrophic basin mires is their relatively recent colonisation by Scots pine often as a result of local seeding from plantations, but with persistent depauperate checked growth where the water table is high. Though tiny by comparison, these pine-grown mires bear a striking resemblance in general appearance to the great forest mires of Scandinavia.

Poor-fen of *Sphagnum* lawn and *Carex* layer (mainly *C. rostrata–C. lasiocarpa*) occurs in some basin mires. Strongly eutrophic basin mires are infrequent, being limited by the chance association of calcareous rocks and soils in conjunction with a suitable topographical environment. Instead of *Sphagnum* lawns, there are typically 'brown moss' carpets and succession to willow carr is a feature of such mires, the vegetation being of the rich-fen type. Some basin mires show a range of vegetation types from strongly acidophilous *Sphagnum* surface, through poor-fen to rich-fen, and there is seldom uniformity of water conditions over the whole surface. Where small lakes and tarns in enclosed basins are undergoing marginal succession, the resulting open water transition mire may eventually extend over the whole surface, and would then be regarded as a basin mire. Clarepool Moss in Shropshire, although regarded as a basin mire, still contains a large pool representing the last stage of infilling of an original lake.

VALLEY MIRE

This type of mire occurs in small, shallow valleys or channels which are not enclosed, so that movement of water along the long axis is possible even though ground slope in that direction may be very slight. Such topography is characteristic of the soft and relatively young rocks in many parts of southern England and East Anglia. Valley mires are especially associated with wet, elongated depressions in the acidic heathlands of these regions, and were first described in the New Forest, where they are numerous. Although widespread in Britain and not confined to the lowlands, valley mires are most distinct in low rainfall districts. In the uplands, their distinctness is often lost through the general occurrence of blanket mire over more gently undulating terrain, or by transitions to various types of soligenous mire. Valley mires could, in fact, be regarded as lowland soligenous mires but, from their dependence on a particular kind of topography it seems best to regard them as a separate class. Valley mires are typically larger than basin mires, but seldom exceed 300 ha. The valley sides vary from 1–150 m or more in vertical height but are usually under 10 m, and they range from gentle to steep in angle of slope. The peat is often very shallow, but in the case of certain northern glacial overflow channels is extremely deep and fluid.

As in basin mires, the vegetation of valley mires consists largely of communities described under the mire classes on pp. 252–60, and ranges from oligotrophic to eutrophic according to the base content of substrata within the catchment. Valley mires often show marked differences in water chemistry and vegetation within a small space, indicating hydrological complexities within a single mire system. A characteristic feature of oligotrophic examples is a relatively base-rich central watercourse or soakway, with lateral zonation of communities associated with decreasing base-status towards the valley sides. At the edges there is often a transition to dry heath through zones of wet heath and humid heath varying in width according to steepness of the valley sides. Some oligotrophic valley mires contain communities virtually identical with those of ombrogenous bog, but more typically there are species which appear to need lateral water movement, and the vegetation is of the poor-fen type.

Mesotrophic to eutrophic valley mires are restricted to areas where base-rich substrata occur within the catchment, and are best developed in East Anglia. Nearly all the major types of rich-fen occur in valley mires, and 'brown moss' carpets are often especially well represented in the calcareous types. Most of the communities of lowland mires in Britain, from the poorest to the richest, are in fact represented in valley mires. Some examples contain spectacular contrasts between acidophilous *Sphagnum* carpets and rich herb fen, and many show great vegetational diversity and richness of flora. Many valley mires also show degrees of hydroseral development to carr and woodland, with birch, pine, willow and alder according to varying conditions. As many acidic valley mires are situated within extensive areas of uncultivated heathland, they are less threatened by eutrophication than some basin mires with similar vegetation. This is, nevertheless, a class of habitats rather vulnerable to disturbance in various forms.

The separation between some of the larger and richer valley mires (e.g. Redgrave–South Lopham Fen in Norfolk and Suffolk) and typical flood-plain mires is perhaps rather tenuous, but the smaller acidic valley mires are very distinct. The distinction between valley and basin mires is also rather fine at times, and both types may be fed either by springs or a more extensive inflow of water from the catchment; but the first type tends to show a more particular direction of water movement than the second. Vegetationally, valley and basin mires show a similar range of variation, taking the country as a whole; but few basin mires individually approach the degree of diversity shown by many valley mires, and there is a preponderance of acidophilous vegetation in basin mires generally. Where raised mires have well-developed laggs, these have certain affinities with valley mire in both form and vegetation. In the uplands, extensive complexes of blanket mire may contain soakways or other areas of obvious lateral water seepage (often, but not always, associated with depressions or channels) where poor-fen communities suggest a clear analogy with lowland valley mire. Unlike typical valley mires, however, these seepage areas have no clear limits defined by transitions to dry mineral soils, for they merge laterally into deep ombrogenous mire. Valley mire in these situations tends to be a vegetational rather than a topographic concept, for many shallow valleys are filled by the general mantle of ombrogenous mire, and the only distinguishing feature may be a higher water table (sometimes with a patterned surface) compared with the surrounding mire.

SOLIGENOUS MIRE

Uplands invariably have areas of localised surface water seepage with mire vegetation which usually contrasts strongly with that of the blanket mires. These areas are often associated with emergent drainage water from springs, rills or flushes, and they occur on slopes of varying steepness and amongst a wide range of other vegetation, from dry grasslands and heaths to blanket mire. Soligenous mires of this kind are often especially well developed on the lower glacial drift-covered slopes and on the valley floors of the steeper mountains, but they occur high up into the montane zone where they are often associated with prolonged snow cover. Individual examples are usually small (less than 5 ha) but in the aggregate they sometimes cover quite large areas of an upland massif. The underlying peat is usually shallow (less than 1 m) and many examples have peaty gley soils rather than true mire peats. Though widespread all over the hill country of northern and western Britain, soligenous mires are better developed and more varied in high rainfall areas than on some of the dry eastern moorlands.

As acidic, base-poor rocks predominate in the British uplands, the commonest types of soligenous mire are oligotrophic, typically with a *Sphagnum* lawn composed of species (e.g. *S. recurvum*) which need moving water, and a *Carex* sward with species such as *C. echinata*, *C. nigra*, *C. curta* and *Carex rostrata*. This bears obvious resemblances to lowland poor-fen communities of other mires. High-altitude Highland examples locally have montane species such as *Carex aquatilis*, *C. rariflora*, *C. bigelowii* and *Sphagnum lindbergii*. The most widespread type of soligenous mire, occurring in nearly all the British uplands, is one dominated by *Juncus effusus*, with variable ground cover of *Sphagnum recurvum*, *S. palustre* and *Polytrichum commune*. Oligotrophic *Juncus acutiflorus* mires with *Sphagnum* carpet occur in parts of western Scotland, and grade into a still more widespread community with *Myrica gale* and tussocky *Molinia caerulea*; whilst *Molinia caerulea* occurs still more widely as a dominant of flush mires without *Myrica*, and with a variable cover of *Sphagnum*. *Juncus squarrosus–Sphagnum* flush communities occur widely on acidic mountains.

The mesotrophic soligenous mires typically have a moss layer composed of the relatively basiphilous *Sphagnum* spp. (e.g. *S. teres*, *S. contortum*, *S. squarrosum*, *S. subsecundum*, *S. warnstorfianum*) and/or Bryalean mosses such as *Acrocladium cuspidatum*, *Aulacomnium palustre*, *Mnium pseudopunctatum* and *Bryum pseudotriquetrum*, with a mixed sedge–forb sward containing *Carex nigra*, *C. demissa*, *C. panicea*, *C. pulicaris*, *C. hostiana*, *Leontodon autumnalis*, *Prunella vulgaris*, *Ranunculus acris* and *Euphrasia officinalis* agg. *Carex rostrata* may be the dominant sedge and *Juncus acutiflorus* sometimes replaces the carices as dominant vascular plant; *J. squarrosus* also does so on some of the basic Scottish mountains. These mesotrophic communities occur widely on the more basic mountains but are somewhat local. They grade into markedly eutrophic mires on calcareous mountains, notably those of Carboniferous Limestone in northern England and Dalradian mica-schists and limestones in central Scotland. The calcareous soligenous mires typically have a carpet of 'brown mosses' usually containing the same mixture of species (e.g. *Scorpidium scorpioides*, *Campylium stellatum*) as those of the lowland rich-fens but with northern species (e.g. *Cinclidium stygium*) often present. There is a variable development of a sedge–forb sward, containing many of the species found in the mesotrophic examples, but greater constancy of others such as *Carex lepidocarpa* and *Eleocharis quinqueflora*. In western Scotland these upland rich-fen communities merge into lowland counterparts, as on the wet machairs, and on both shell sand and limestone there is a characteristic type dominated by *Schoenus nigricans*, with few other species. At high levels, both the mesotrophic and eutrophic soligenous mires often occur in complexes with basic flushes and springs, the whole being an especially favourable habitat for many montane base-demanding plants of wet ground.

An interesting feature of soligenous mires is that various kinds of mixtures of poor and rich communities frequently occur. Sometimes there are fairly obvious spatial changes in nutrient content of the water supply, giving a sudden separation of contrasting communities. The more puzzling examples are various types of mosaic pattern of poor and rich communities, especially those involving a vertical separation of the different components.

Soligenous mires differ from the topogenous lowland mires in having a vascular plant sward of much lower stature; usually this appears to be the result of the heavy grazing by sheep, deer or cattle which characterises the British uplands. On the poorer mountains, such flushed sites often carry the most palatable vegetation and are selectively grazed. As well as reducing the stature of the sward, this grazing tends to suppress completely the shrub and tree growth so usually present in Scandinavian counterparts (within the altitudinal limits of shrubs and trees). Probably most British soligenous mires, except the high-altitude examples, would carry growths of willow and perhaps birch in the absence of grazing. Grasses and sedges also probably tend to increase in abundance at the expense of forbs and bryophytes. Some soligenous mires have been modified by deliberate draining, which promotes conversion to grassland or heath, or allows the planting of trees, but on the whole these mires are not deliberately altered. Some examples become so heavily charged with water during exceptional rainfall that landslips occur and destroy them.

Soligenous mires obviously intergrade with the seepage areas often found within or along the edges of blanket mires, and the wetter types of community which sometimes regenerate in the gullies of eroding blanket mires are best regarded as soligenous mire. Similarly, there is no distinct line of demarcation between this class and valley mires, although the latter are more typically lowland and southern, with usually a rather larger area and deeper peat. In hill country the placing of a particular mire in one of these two classes is sometimes an arbitrary procedure.

The more distinctive types of soligenous mire association are listed in the classification of upland vegetation, p. 297.

Flora

The preceding account of mire vegetation types has indicated a range of floristic diversity in relation to water nutrient status. Table 23 gives the ecological distribution of each British vascular mire species according to the major divisions of water pH and nutrient status, as far as these are known at present. Species which occur widely in other habitats besides mires are omitted, as are woody species above the size of medium shrub (i.e. most of the willows) as these belong more properly to woodland or lowland scrub classifications. The true hydrophytes belonging essentially to open water are treated under that habitat formation, though the limits of this group have had to be arbitrarily defined, and species characteristic of ombrogenous mire pools are included here.

A few general features emerge from this study of edaphic relationships. Few species appear to be confined to eutrophic fen, but there is a large group of broadly basiphilous species whose tolerances/requirements range from mesotrophic to eutrophic. This could perhaps reflect an inadequacy of data on water chemistry for some species or a badly chosen boundary between the two trophic levels, but it suggests that above a certain level, further increase in nutrient status has no effect on many species. There is a much smaller number of species confined to oligotrophic mire waters, compared with those in the two higher trophic levels. Only a few species show a complete range of tolerance to acidity/alkalinity of mire waters.

There is insufficient information to record the distribution of each species in relation to the six main morphological types of mire. However, chemical factors, and thus species distribution, tend to vary independently of mire morphology, except in ombrogenous mires (raised and blanket mires), for these have only oligotrophic conditions. It is more meaningful to separate oligotrophic ombrogenous from oligotrophic topogenous as there appears to be a real difference between these two in both chemical and floristic terms; some plants belong to raised and/or blanket mire, but not to poor-fen, and vice versa, and the controlling differences may include rate of movement and aeration of the water.

Geographical distribution of mire plants is also shown in Table 23. There is a certain degree of parallelism between ecological and geographical distribution of mire species. The restriction of ombrogenous mire to the west and north ensures that species confined to or occurring mainly in this class of peatland have a similar distribution while the strong representation of mesotrophic and eutrophic fen in southern Britain (especially in East Anglia) is matched by the restriction of some strongly basiphilous species to this part of the country. Since lowland mires have been so widely drained and destroyed in the interests of farming and building, many of their characteristic species have suffered great reduction in range or even extinction. Many widespread mire species are much less common and generally distributed in the south and east of Britain than in the north and west because of this effect, and the patchy distribution of some largely reflects the present restricted occurrence of suitable habitats.

To give examples of this retreat, the East Anglian *Senecio palustris* is extinct while *S. paludosus* is known in a single ditch in this region: the northern *Scheuchzeria palustris* is known only on Rannoch Moor in Scotland; and the once rather widespread *Carex elongata* is now quite rare. Other restricting factors may operate and it has been suggested that the decline of the rare fern *Dryopteris cristata* is partly the result of introgressive hybridisation with *D. carthusiana*, accompanied by selection in favour of the hybrid forms.

As an analysis of mire species geographical distribution according to presence or absence in particular regions often fails to indicate distinctive patterns, a different and more meaningful treatment has been adopted. Study of mire species distribution maps suggested that eight main patterns of scatter could be recognised; these have been chosen subjectively and arbitrarily but nevertheless enable a useful analysis to be made. These distribution classes (see Table 23) are defined as follows:

WIDESPREAD/COMMON

Species occurring over virtually the whole of Britain, and limited mainly by lack of suitable habitats. These naturally tend to be species with wide ecological amplitude, but the group which find their optimum water nutrient status in the upper oligotrophic to lower mesotrophic range are especially well represented, as waters of this type are probably the most widespread in Britain. Typical examples are *Caltha palustris*, *Lychnis flos-cuculi*, *Juncus articulatus* and *Phalaris arundinacea*.

WIDESPREAD/LOCAL

Species occurring in most districts of Britain, but much less abundantly than the last group, and often absent from apparently suitable localities. These appear to show no particular ecological bias as a group. Typical examples are *Ranunculus lingua*, *Utricularia vulgaris*, *Dactylorchis incarnata*, *Carex vesicaria* and *C. acuta*.

SCATTERED/VERY LOCAL

Species showing a highly discontinuous scatter, absent from a great many apparently suitable localities, but widely spread and showing an irregular pattern with no single geographical bias. These certainly show no particular ecological bias as a group. They are *Dryopteris cristata*, *Cicuta virosa*, *Pyrola rotundifolia*, *Naumburgia thyrsiflora*, *Dactylorchis traunsteineri*, *Eriophorum gracile*, *Cladium mariscus*, *Carex flava*, *C. elongata* and *Calamagrostis stricta*.

SOUTHERN

Species which become increasingly widespread and abundant with distance south in Britain; they belong essentially to England and Wales, but especially southern England, and though some reach Scotland they are local or rare there.

This group includes a high proportion belonging to mesotrophic and eutrophic mire, e.g. *Thalictrum flavum*, *Berula erecta*, *Oenanthe fistulosa*, *Rumex hydrolapathum*, *Cirsium dissectum*, *Epipactis palustris*, *Dactylorchis praetermissa*, *Carex pseudocyperus* and *C. riparia*.

OCEANIC

Species occurring mainly in coastal districts, but especially along the south and/or west coasts. The most localised is the thermophilous southern oceanic *Hypericum undulatum*, only in south-west England and west Wales, which contrasts with the northern oceanic *Drosera anglica*, most abundant in the north-west Highlands. Other characteristic members are *Hypericum elodes*, *Drosera intermedia*, *Pinguicula lusitanica*, *Scutellaria minor*, *Rhynchospora alba* and *R. fusca*. *Osmunda regalis*, *Oenanthe crocata*, *Eleocharis multicaulis* and *Schoenus nigricans* show the same general pattern but occur more widely away from coastal districts. If the Irish–American *Spiranthes romanzoffiana* can be regarded as a mire plant in Britain, it belongs here. It is perhaps significant that the majority of species in this group grow also on acidic wet heathland, a characteristic oceanic British vegetational formation.

EAST ANGLIAN

Species found mainly in eastern England from Suffolk to the Humber, but especially in East Anglia. The rare or very local species which occur in very few places outside this belt are *Viola stagnina*, *Lathyrus palustris*, *Peucedanum palustre*, *Sonchus palustris*, *Liparis loeselii* and *Carex appropinquata*. More widespread and plentiful species which could be regarded as southern, but are more abundant in the Suffolk–Humber region than elsewhere include *Thelypteris palustris*, *Sium latifolium*, *Juncus subnodulosus*, *C. elata* and *Calamagrostis canescens*. These are without exception plants of rich-fen.

NORTHERN

Species which become increasingly widespread and abundant with distance north in Britain and have their headquarters north of the Midlands, but are confined to fairly low altitudes. This includes extreme rarities such as *Carex buxbaumii*, *C. chordorrhiza*, *Scheuchzeria palustris* and *Ledum groenlandicum*, and local species such as *Listera cordata*, *C. paupercula*, *C. pauciflora*, *C. aquatilis* and *Corallorhiza trifida*. Most of these could be regarded as submontane as they occur mainly in upland districts. Many northern species have a wide distribution in Britain, reaching to the extreme south of England, where they are, however, rare or very local. These include *Vaccinium oxycoccus*, *Utricularia intermedia*, *Hammarbya paludosa*, *Carex limosa*, *C. lasiocarpa*, *C. curta* and *C. dioica*.

Nearly all the northern species so far mentioned belong to oligotrophic mire, especially of the topogenous kind (poorfen), thus reflecting the general edaphic trend towards increasing prevalence of base-poor waters in northern Britain. Strongly basiphilous and widespread northern species include *Parnassia palustris*, *Dactylorchis purpurella*, *Eriophorum latifolium* and *Carex lepidocarpa*.

Andromeda polifolia is essentially a northern species in mainland Europe, but has a curious British distribution, for it does not reach the Highlands and occurs mainly in northern England and southern Scotland, where it is locally abundant in oligotrophic mires (cf. *Primula farinosa* in calcareous habitats). *Calamagrostis stricta* could be regarded as a northern species, but is included in Table 23 as scattered, local. *Eriophorum vaginatum* and *Trichophorum cespitosum* occur in the extreme south of England but are regarded as northern as they become really abundant only from Wales northwards.

MONTANE

Species with a northern distribution which are found mainly at high altitudes and are most abundant in or confined to the Scottish Highlands. These are necessarily restricted to the only kinds of mire found at high levels, namely, blanket and soligenous mires. The montane species of blanket mire are *Betula nana*, *Arctostaphylos uva-ursi*, *Arctous alpinus*, *Vaccinium uliginosum*, *V. microcarpum*, *Empetrum hermaphroditum* and *Rubus chamaemorus*. Those of oligotrophic soligenous mire are *Carex rariflora*, *C. lachenalii*, *C. bigelowii* and *Saxifraga stellaris*. The montane species belonging to mesotrophic or eutrophic soligenous mire are *S. hirculus*, *Thalictrum alpinum*, *Polygonum viviparum*, *Kobresia simpliciuscula*, *Juncus castaneus*, *C. atrofusca*, *C. capillaris*, *C. microglochin* and *C. norvegica*. A few species in this group appear to be indifferent to mire water base-status, e.g. *C. saxatilis*, *C. vaginata*, *Alopecurus alpinus* and *Phleum alpinum*. Most of these species of montane soligenous mire are omitted from Table 23 as they belong to a wider range of habitats, including flushes, rills, springs and rock ledges, and they are dealt with under the flora of uplands (Chapter 9).

Some northern submontane species also occur in montane mires up to considerable elevations, e.g. *Vaccinium vitis-idaea* and *Empetrum nigrum*. It is noteworthy that the northern and montane mire flora has a strong representation of acidophilous dwarf shrubs (mainly Ericaceae) which belong mainly or entirely to ombrogenous mire.

Of the 161 peatland species listed in Table 23 only about half are classified into phytogeographical elements by J. R. Matthews (1937). A few more species have been tentatively classified from literature records and added, but distribution of most of the remainder could not be judged accurately enough and they have been left blank. These classifiable species give the following representation in the various elements:

oceanic southern (1), oceanic west European (7), continental southern (2), continental (8), continental northern (43), northern montane (4), oceanic northern (3), Arctic-subarctic (2), Arctic-alpine (9).

The northern continental element thus constitutes over half the total list. The remaining unclassified peatland species would seem to belong either to this or to the continental element, or to be so widespread in Europe that no definite distribution pattern is discernible within this continent.

European and British distributions of mire species show some parallelism but there are certain discrepancies. Most of the oceanic western species in Europe have a western and coastal distribution here, but *Drosera anglica*, *D. intermedia*, *Rhynchospora fusca* and *R. alba* (all somewhat oceanic and with a western bias in Britain) are either continental or continental northern in Europe. All the European Arctic-alpine or Arctic–subarctic species are northern, and most are montane, in Britain; and the four northern montane species are northern and submontane here. Several continental northern species show no particular northern bias in Britain, and many British southern species are widely distributed in Europe.

The British vascular mire flora contains 13 rare species (present in 1–15 10-km grid squares) fairly well spread through the different ecological and geographical groupings.

Fauna

In considering the fauna, peatlands are best divided into two groups, namely, the strongly oligotrophic peat mosses (mainly raised and blanket mires) with abundant *Sphagnum* and dwarf shrubs, and the mesotrophic to eutrophic rich-fens (mainly open water transition and flood-plain mires) typically with a tall-herb sward grading from swamp to damp meadow. In this context, valley and basin mires are best referred to one of these two broad peatland classes according to their predominant vegetation. The fauna of soligenous mires is considered in Chapter 9, pp. 301ff.

MAMMALS, REPTILES AND AMPHIBIANS

Ombrogenous mire species

The upland blanket mires form an important part of the habitat of many vertebrates considered under uplands in general. In Scotland, red deer range and feed widely over blanket mires, avoiding only the very wettest ground where, like sheep, they may become bogged-down and perish. Their treading and grazing helps to dry the ground and promote increased tussock formation in plants such as cotton grass and deer sedge, but also tends to suppress dwarf shrubs. Where they occur, feral goats *Capra hircus* frequent these peatlands, and many mountain hares *Lepus timidus* appear to live entirely in such habitats, making their forms in drier patches or on hummocks. Foxes range over the upland mires but usually breed and lie up in drier places. Of the smaller mammals, the short-tailed field vole is widespread and may be abundant, at least periodically, on drier ground where vascular plants give a dense cover. The common frog sometimes breeds in the bigger mire pools but appears to prefer those with richer waters. The palmate newt is known to be abundant in some acid peat pools. The adder is locally plentiful on blanket mires up to 500 m, and the common lizard is generally distributed and common.

Some of these creatures are also found on the lowland, acidic raised, valley and basin mires. This is particularly so

Table 23. *Habitat and distribution of peatland vascular plants*

	Oligotrophic ombrogenous	Oligotrophic	Mesotrophic	Eutrophic	Widespread/common	Widespread/local	Scattered/very local	Southern	Oceanic	East Anglian	Northern	Montane	Rare species	European distribution
	1	2	3	4	5	6	7	8	9	10	11	12	13	14
Equisetum fluviatile	—	+	+	—	+	—	—	—	—	—	—	—	—	
E. palustre	—	—	+	+	+	—	—	—	—	—	—	—	—	—
Osmunda regalis	+	+	+	—	—	—	—	—	+	—	—	—	—	OW
Dryopteris cristata	—	+	+	—	—	—	+	—	—	—	—	—	+	C
D. carthusiana	—	+	+	—	—	+	—	—	—	—	—	—	—	—
Thelypteris palustris	—	—	+	+	—	—	—	+	—	—	—	—	—	—
Caltha palustris	—	—	+	+	+	—	—	—	—	—	—	—	—	—
Ranunculus lingua	—	—	+	+	—	+	—	—	—	—	—	—	—	C
R. flammula	—	+	+	—	+	—	—	—	—	—	—	—	—	—
Thalictrum flavum	—	—	+	+	—	—	—	+	—	—	—	—	—	—
Viola stagnina	—	—	+	+	—	—	—	—	—	+	—	—	+	CN
V. palustris	—	+	+	—	+	—	—	—	—	—	—	—	—	CN
Hypericum elodes	—	+	+	—	—	—	—	—	+	—	—	—	—	OW
H. undulatum	—	+	+	—	—	—	—	—	+	—	—	—	—	OW
Lychnis flos-cuculi	—	—	+	+	+	—	—	—	—	—	—	—	—	—
Myosoton aquaticum	—	—	+	+	—	—	—	+	—	—	—	—	—	—
Stellaria palustris	—	—	+	+	—	+	—	—	—	—	—	—	—	CN
Lotus pedunculatus	—	+	+	—	+	—	—	—	—	—	—	—	—	CS
Lathyrus palustris	—	—	+	+	—	—	—	—	—	+	—	—	+	CN
Rubus chamaemorus	+	—	—	—	—	—	—	—	—	—	—	+	—	AS
Potentilla palustris	—	+	+	—	+	—	—	—	—	—	—	—	—	CN
Saxifraga hirculus	—	—	+	—	—	—	—	—	—	—	—	+	+	AA
Parnassia palustris	—	—	+	+	—	—	—	—	—	—	+	—	—	CN
Drosera rotundifolia	+	+	—	—	+	—	—	—	—	—	—	—	—	CN
D. anglica	+	+	+	+	—	—	—	—	+	—	—	—	—	CN
D. intermedia	+	+	—	—	—	—	—	—	+	—	—	—	—	CN
Lythrum salicaria	—	—	+	+	—	—	—	+	—	—	—	—	—	—
Epilobium parviflorum	—	—	+	+	—	—	—	+	—	—	—	—	—	—
E. obscurum	—	—	+	+	—	+	—	—	—	—	—	—	—	—
E. palustre	—	+	+	+	+	—	—	—	—	—	—	—	—	—
E. hirsutum	—	—	+	+	—	—	—	+	—	—	—	—	—	—
Hippuris vulgaris	—	—	+	+	—	+	—	—	—	—	—	—	—	—
Hydrocotyle vulgaris	—	+	+	—	+	—	—	—	—	—	—	—	—	—
Cicuta virosa	—	—	+	+	—	—	+	—	—	—	—	—	—	CN
Sium latifolium	—	—	+	+	—	—	—	—	—	+	—	—	—	—
Berula erecta	—	—	+	+	—	—	—	+	—	—	—	—	—	—
Oenanthe fistulosa	—	—	+	+	—	—	—	+	—	—	—	—	—	—
O. lachenalii	—	—	+	+	—	—	—	+	—	—	—	—	—	CS
O. crocata	—	—	+	—	—	—	—	—	+	—	—	—	—	OW
Peucedanum palustre	—	—	+	+	—	—	—	—	—	+	—	—	—	CN
Polygonum amphibium	—	—	+	+	+	—	—	—	—	—	—	—	—	—
Rumex hydrolapathum	—	—	+	+	—	—	—	+	—	—	—	—	—	C
Myrica gale	+	+	+	—	—	—	—	—	+	—	—	—	—	ON
Betula nana	+	+	—	—	—	—	—	—	—	—	—	+	—	AA
Salix repens	—	+	+	—	—	+	—	—	—	—	—	—	—	—
Ledum groenlandicum	+	—	—	—	—	—	—	—	—	—	+	—	—	CN
Andromeda polifolia	+	+	—	—	—	—	—	—	—	—	+	—	—	CN
Arctostaphylos uva-ursi	+	—	—	—	—	—	—	—	—	—	—	+	—	AA
Arctous alpinus	+	—	—	—	—	—	—	—	—	—	—	+	—	AA
Erica tetralix	+	+	+	—	+	—	—	—	—	—	—	—	—	OW

Table 23 (*contd.*)

	1	2	3	4	5	6	7	8	9	10	11	12	13	14
Vaccinium uliginosum	+	—	—	—	—	—	—	—	—	—	—	+	—	AA
V. vitis-idaea	+	—	—	—	—	—	—	—	—	—	+	—	—	AA
V. oxycoccus	+	+	—	—	—	—	—	—	—	—	+	—	—	CN
V. microcarpum	+	+	—	—	—	—	—	—	—	—	—	+	—	—
Pyrola rotundifolia	—	—	—	+	—	—	+	—	—	—	—	—	—	CN
Empetrum nigrum	+	—	—	—	—	—	—	—	—	—	+	—	—	AA
E. hermaphroditum	+	—	—	—	—	—	—	—	—	—	—	+	—	AA
Lysimachia vulgaris	—	—	+	+	—	—	—	+	—	—	—	—	—	—
Naumbergia thyrsiflora	—	—	+	+	—	—	+	—	—	—	—	—	—	CN
Menyanthes trifoliata	+	+	+	+	+	—	—	—	—	—	—	—	—	CN
Myosotis scorpioides	—	—	+	+	+	—	—	—	—	—	—	—	—	—
M. secunda	—	—	+	—	—	+	—	—	—	—	—	—	—	CN
M. caespitosa	—	—	+	+	+	—	—	—	—	—	—	—	—	—
Solanum dulcamara	—	—	+	+	—	—	—	+	—	—	—	—	—	—
Scrophularia aquatica	—	—	+	+	—	—	—	+	—	—	—	—	—	OS
Veronica anagallis-aquatica	—	—	+	+	—	+	—	—	—	—	—	—	—	—
V. scutellata	—	—	+	+	—	+	—	—	—	—	—	—	—	—
Pedicularis palustris	—	+	+	+	+	—	—	—	—	—	—	—	—	—
Pinguicula lusitanica	—	—	+	+	—	—	—	—	+	—	—	—	—	OW
P. vulgaris	—	+	+	+	—	—	—	—	—	—	+	—	—	CN
Utricularia vulgaris	—	+	+	+	—	+	—	—	—	—	—	—	—	—
U. intermedia	—	+	—	—	—	—	—	—	—	—	+	—	—	CN
U. minor	+	+	+	—	—	+	—	—	—	—	—	—	—	CN
Mentha aquatica	—	—	+	+	+	—	—	—	—	—	—	—	—	—
Lycopus europaeus	—	—	+	+	—	—	—	+	—	—	—	—	—	—
Stachys palustris	—	—	+	+	—	+	—	—	—	—	—	—	—	—
Scutellaria galericulata	—	—	+	+	—	—	—	+	—	—	—	—	—	—
S. minor	—	+	+	—	—	—	—	—	+	—	—	—	—	OW
Galium palustre	—	+	+	+	+	—	—	—	—	—	—	—	—	—
G. uliginosum	—	—	+	+	—	+	—	—	—	—	—	—	—	CN
Valeriana dioica	—	—	+	+	—	—	—	+	—	—	—	—	—	—
Bidens cernua	—	—	+	+	—	—	—	+	—	—	—	—	—	—
B. tripartita	—	—	+	+	—	—	—	+	—	—	—	—	—	—
Senecio aquaticus	—	—	+	+	+	—	—	—	—	—	—	—	—	—
Eupatorium cannabinum	—	—	+	+	—	—	—	+	—	—	—	—	—	—
Cirsium dissectum	—	+	+	+	—	—	—	+	—	—	—	—	—	OW
Sonchus palustris	—	—	+	+	—	—	—	—	—	+	—	—	+	C
Alisma plantago-aquatica	—	—	+	+	—	—	—	+	—	—	—	—	—	—
Scheuchzeria palustris	+	+	—	—	—	—	—	—	—	—	+	—	+	CN
Triglochin palustris	—	—	+	+	—	+	—	—	—	—	—	—	—	—
Potamogeton polygonifolius	—	+	+	—	—	+	—	—	—	—	—	—	—	—
Narthecium ossifragum	+	+	—	—	—	—	—	—	—	—	+	—	—	ON
Juncus squarrosus	+	+	+	—	—	—	—	—	—	—	+	—	—	ON
J. effusus	—	+	+	—	+	—	—	—	—	—	—	—	—	—
J. subnodulosus	—	—	+	+	—	—	—	+	—	—	—	—	—	—
J. acutiflorus	—	+	+	+	+	—	—	—	—	—	—	—	—	—
J. articulatus	—	—	+	+	+	—	—	—	—	—	—	—	—	—
J. bulbosus (incl. *J. kochii*)	—	+	+	—	+	—	—	—	—	—	—	—	—	—
Iris pseudacorus	—	—	+	+	+	—	—	—	—	—	—	—	—	—
Epipactis palustris	—	—	—	+	—	—	—	+	—	—	—	—	—	C
Listera cordata	+	—	—	—	—	—	—	—	—	—	+	—	—	NM
Hammarbya paludosa	—	+	—	—	—	—	—	—	—	—	+	—	—	CN
Liparis loeselii	—	—	+	+	—	—	—	—	—	+	—	—	+	C
Corallorhiza trifida	—	—	+	+	—	—	—	—	—	—	+	—	—	CN
Dactylorchis fuchsii	—	—	+	+	+	—	—	—	—	—	—	—	—	—
D. maculata	+	+	—	—	+	—	—	—	—	—	—	—	—	—
D. praetermissa	—	—	—	+	—	—	—	+	—	—	—	—	—	—
D. purpurella	—	—	+	+	—	—	—	—	—	—	+	—	—	—
D. incarnata	—	—	—	+	—	+	—	—	—	—	—	—	—	—
D. traunsteineri	—	—	—	+	—	—	+	—	—	—	—	—	+	—
Sparganium erectum	—	—	+	+	—	—	—	+	—	—	—	—	—	—
S. emersum	—	—	+	+	—	+	—	—	—	—	—	—	—	—

Table 23 (*contd.*)

	1	2	3	4	5	6	7	8	9	10	11	12	13	14
Typha latifolia	—	—	+	+	—	—	—	+	—	—	—	—	—	—
T. angustifolia	—	—	+	+	—	—	—	+	—	—	—	—	—	—
Eriophorum angustifolium	+	+	—	—	+	—	—	—	—	—	—	—	—	CN
E. gracile	—	+	—	—	—	—	+	—	—	—	—	—	+	CN
E. vaginatum	+	+	—	—	—	—	—	—	—	—	+	—	—	CN
E. latifolium	—	—	+	+	—	+	—	—	—	—	—	—	—	CN
Trichophorum cespitosum	+	+	+	—	—	—	—	—	—	—	+	—	—	CN
Eleocharis quinqueflora	—	—	+	+	—	—	—	—	—	—	+	—	—	CN
E. multicaulis	—	+	+	—	—	—	—	—	+	—	—	—	—	CN
E. palustris	—	+	+	—	+	—	—	—	—	—	—	—	—	—
Schoenus nigricans	+	+	+	+	—	—	—	—	+	—	—	—	—	C
Rhynchospora alba	+	+	—	—	—	—	—	—	+	—	—	—	—	C
R. fusca	+	+	—	—	—	—	—	—	+	—	—	—	—	CN
Cladium mariscus	—	+	+	+	—	—	+	—	—	—	—	—	—	—
Carex flava	—	—	—	+	—	—	+	—	—	—	—	—	+	—
C. lepidocarpa	—	—	+	+	—	+	—	—	—	—	—	—	—	—
C. pseudocyperus	—	—	+	+	—	—	—	+	—	—	—	—	—	—
C. rostrata	+	+	+	+	—	—	—	—	—	—	+	—	—	—
C. vesicaria	—	—	+	+	—	+	—	—	—	—	—	—	—	—
C. riparia	—	—	+	+	—	—	—	+	—	—	—	—	—	—
C. acutiformis	—	—	+	+	—	—	—	+	—	—	—	—	—	—
C. limosa	+	+	+	—	—	—	—	—	—	—	+	—	—	CN
C. paupercula	+	+	—	—	—	—	—	—	—	—	+	—	—	NM
C. rariflora	—	+	—	—	—	—	—	—	—	—	—	+	+	AS
C. lasiocarpa	—	+	+	+	—	—	—	—	—	—	+	—	—	CN
C. buxbaumii	—	+	—	—	—	—	—	—	—	—	+	—	+	CN
C. elata	—	—	+	+	—	—	—	—	—	+	—	—	—	—
C. acuta	—	—	+	+	—	+	—	—	—	—	—	—	—	—
C. aquatilis	—	+	+	+	—	—	—	—	—	—	+	—	—	—
C. nigra	—	+	+	+	+	—	—	—	—	—	—	—	—	—
C. bigelowii	+	+	—	—	—	—	—	—	—	—	—	+	—	AA
C. paniculata	—	+	+	+	—	—	—	+	—	—	—	—	—	—
C. appropinquata	—	—	+	+	—	—	—	—	—	—	+	—	—	CN
C. diandra	—	—	+	+	—	+	—	—	—	—	—	—	—	CN
C. otrubae	—	—	+	+	—	—	—	+	—	—	—	—	—	—
C. disticha	—	—	+	+	—	+	—	—	—	—	—	—	—	CN
C. chordorrhiza	—	+	—	—	—	—	—	—	—	—	+	—	+	NM
C. elongata	—	+	+	—	+	—	+	—	—	—	—	—	—	CN
C. echinata	—	+	+	—	+	—	—	—	—	—	—	—	—	CN
C. curta	—	+	—	—	—	—	—	—	—	—	+	—	—	CN
C. pauciflora	+	+	—	—	—	—	—	—	—	—	+	—	—	NM
C. pulicaris	—	—	+	+	+	—	—	—	—	—	—	—	—	CN
C. dioica	—	+	+	+	—	—	—	—	—	—	+	—	—	CN
Phragmites communis	+	+	+	+	+	—	—	—	—	—	—	—	—	—
Glyceria maxima	—	—	+	+	—	—	—	+	—	—	—	—	—	—
Calamagrostis epigejos	—	—	+	+	—	—	—	+	—	—	—	—	—	—
C. canescens	—	—	+	+	—	—	+	—	—	+	—	—	—	—
C. stricta	—	—	+	+	—	—	+	—	—	—	—	—	—	NM
Phalaris arundinacea	—	+	+	+	+	—	—	—	—	—	—	—	—	—
Total 161	37	68	123	99	34	23	10	34	13	9	28	10	13	

Notes

For definition of trophic levels see p. 251.
For definition of British distribution classes see p. 262.
European distribution:

OS = oceanic southern   OW = oceanic west European
CS = continental southern   C = continental
CN = continental northern   NM = northern montane
ON = oceanic northern   AS = Arctic–subarctic
AA = Arctic–alpine

Species' vertical amplitude in relation to water table is not sufficiently well known to be indicated.

for the adder which usually resorts to damp habitats during the summer and for the grass snake, a more southern species with similar habits. In central Wales, the polecat (now found mainly in this part of Britain) frequents and perhaps breeds on the lowland raised mires such as Cors Fochno (Borth Bog) and Cors Goch glan Teifi, and was formerly found in these habitats on the plains of the Solway. Roe deer range over and feed on the drier parts of these lowland mires but avoid the wettest ground.

Topogenous fen species

While small mammals occur at times on the acidic mires, these habitats are less consistently productive for vertebrates than lowland fens. The Norfolk Broads and their associated fens are perhaps the richest examples of this kind of peatland for vertebrates in general. Here, the species which has the greatest impact on its habitat is the introduced coypu, which not only lives and breeds in the reeds and sedge-swamps and river banks, but also has a considerable effect on the vegetation. Ellis (1965) has described the effects of coypu in the Broads, including the cutting back of large areas of reed, sedge and reed-mace, the great depletion of sensitive species such as *Cicuta virosa* and *Rumex hydrolapathum*, and the spread of others such as the resistant *Lythrum salicaria*. In many places, hydroseral succession has been interrupted, modified or reversed, and even developing willow carr may be destroyed. Sometimes, fen has been converted to black mud and shallow water, and some 'coypu-lows' have proved attractive to duck and waders in autumn and winter and nesting black-headed gulls and common terns in summer. The coypus breed on platforms in swamp or in tunnels in the banks of dykes and rivers, and sometimes make raids on farmland crops from their fen sanctuaries. Coypu flourish in the Broads, except during unusually cold winters, when their numbers are greatly reduced, and it is conceivable that a winter of exceptional severity could exterminate the species in Britain.

The water vole is a widespread species in fens but is associated more with the open water and banks of ditches, dykes and rivers, where it burrows and breeds in tunnels. The common, pygmy and water shrews are widespread in fen systems, though the last is associated more particularly with wet conditions. The short-tailed vole occurs abundantly in a wide range of fen vegetation, including the drier reed swamps, and flourishes in the generally dense vegetational cover. The bank vole and wood mouse are found on the drier edges of fens, embankments, hedgerows, and the latter also occurs in alder–willow carrs. In the south of England, the harvest mouse finds a natural habitat in beds of *Phragmites*, *Phalaris* and *Carex*, and makes its nest from the leaves of these plants.

These small mammals, but especially the short-tailed field vole, are important as prey for various predators, including short-eared owl, marsh and Montagu's harrier, heron, bittern, weasel and stoat. The last two species also take birds, and their eggs and young, and both of them often breed in fens in situations clear of flood level, such as banks,

holes in trees and even tall-sedge tussocks. The otter is associated with the open water of lakes and rivers, but also frequents the swamplands and sometimes breeds in dense sedge-beds or under fallen trees in carr. Both fox and badger locally include these habitats among their hunting grounds, though they usually have their dens on drier ground.

The brown hare sometimes frequents fen, but is more at home in marshy grasslands and meadows, and though the roe deer may feed in fen vegetation, it too has a preference for the drier ground. Within their range, sika deer will also frequent fen at times.

The abundance of insects over lowland fens is an attraction to bats, and various species feed over such ground, though they need hollow trees, buildings or caves for roosting and breeding. The species seen over swampy ground include the noctule, serotine, Daubenton's bat, Natterer's bat and barbastelle, pipistrelle and whiskered.

Of the reptiles both the adder and grass snake resort to fens in summer but in the autumn return to drier places above water level to hibernate during the winter. The adder is now less commonly found in fen than in peat mosses, but was once numerous in parts of the Norfolk Broads. Both the common lizard and slow-worm may be found at times in fen, but are much more characteristic of drier ground.

The amphibians have obvious associations with wetlands, and both frog and common toad are often abundant in fens, where they breed in the open water, though the toad tends to make for drier ground after spawning. Both species are taken as prey by birds such as the heron and bittern, and have recently declined considerably in many areas, especially in the southern half of England. There is little information about the ecological distribution of newts, but the smooth newt widely inhabits many open waters which pass into fen, and the palmate and great crested newts evidently occur in fen locally.

BIRDS

Birds of peatlands are best considered in conjunction with those of open waters, for some species belong to both habitats at once, e.g. many ducks, which feed on the open water of lakes and nest in the surrounding marsh. This account is, however, limited to species which breed within the range of vegetation already considered in this Chapter. The grebes, which all build floating nests in very open emergent aquatic vegetation, have been mentioned in Chapter 7. Reference should also be made to that Chapter and to Chapter 6 for information on the populations of birds, both wintering species and passage migrants, which frequent all kinds of wetlands, permanent and temporary, during that part of the year outside the breeding season.

Ombrogenous mire birds

Lowland raised mires have a rather limited breeding avifauna, consisting of sparse populations of red grouse, meadow pipit, skylark, cuckoo, reed bunting, and curlew, with the occasional addition of merlin, linnet, twite, snipe, teal, mallard and shelduck. A few raised mires had colonies of black-headed, lesser black-backed and even great black-backed gulls, but these seem mostly to have disappeared in recent years. Still farther back, some of the northern England examples were nesting places of the hen harrier, and in Scotland raised mires may have been recolonised during the general recent spread of this species. Golden plover appear no longer to nest on these mires, despite the suitability of the terrain and dunlin seem to have gone also, despite their fidelity to certain coastal salt marshes adjoining some sites. Raised mires are locally, and at times, the winter feeding place of some species of grey geese which appear to have a fondness for the stem bases of *Rhynchospora alba*.

The birds of blanket mire are dealt with also in Chapter 9. There is a characteristic group of moorland species which nests and feeds just as typically on the wet peatland as on the dry dwarf-shrub heath or grassland. Of these, the golden plover is the blanket mire bird *par excellence*, and is usually accompanied by dunlin (in smaller numbers, mostly), red grouse, curlew, meadow pipit and skylark. Dunlin and teal are especially associated with pool systems on blanket mires, and black-headed gull colonies, ranging from a few to 2000 pairs, breed on some blanket mires, especially where there are swampy pools or tarns. There are a few lesser black-backed gull colonies, and occasional pairs of great black-backed, on large level expanses of blanket mire (flow) in some moorland areas.

Ornithologically, the most productive blanket mires in species diversity are the great flows of Sutherland and Caithness. Here, where there are often extensive pool systems and peaty lochans of varying size, the usual species nest rather sparsely, but there are also greenshank, red-throated divers, greylag geese, wigeon, common scoters, Arctic skuas and common gulls, widely but thinly distributed. All these except the skua are associated with open water on the moors. The greenshank feeds beside pools, lochs and rivers but nests on a mire hummock or dry, stony moraine, sometimes far distant. Red-throated diver, greylag, wigeon and scoter spend much time on the open water of moorland tarns and nest by preference on islands, but where there are no islands they breed on the surrounding flow. Common gulls prefer tarns with islands or swampy edges for nesting. The Arctic skua parasitises this species and the black-headed gull, and its distribution is limited by that of its victims; the nesting site is usually a hummock or dry place on the flow. The colonies are small compared with those in Orkney and Shetland. In the Highlands, the boreal wood sandpiper has appeared in recent years as a nesting bird in several widely separated localities, favouring swamp-edged lochs for feeding and the surrounding blanket mire for its nesting place.

A few other species nest sporadically on blanket mire. There are a few snipe but this species favours richer marshes and wet grassland. The merlin, hen harrier, short-eared owl, lapwing and redshank, all nest at times in this habitat, but are typically on drier or more productive moorland. The scaup which occasionally breeds in northern Scotland may also favour the peaty moorland lochs and surrounds. Although the peregrine has long been known to nest widely on hummocks in the great peat mires of Finland, it is not known to do so in Britain, where it would be too vulnerable to foxes and humans. Blanket mires are among the least productive of all British habitats in terms of bird population density, but they support a wide spectrum of species, and are interesting as the nearest equivalent to the tundra of the Arctic.

Topogenous mire (fen) birds

The dense beds of reed *Phragmites communis* so extensive in many rich fens are one of the most important habitats for birds, and form the chief nesting place of the marsh harrier, bittern, bearded tit and reed warbler. The first three species need reed beds and are rarities confined to places where these occur, in inland fens and brackish marshes, mainly in East Anglia, though the marsh harrier formerly bred regularly in Dorset and a few other scattered places in England and the bittern nests in Anglesey and at Silverdale in north Lancashire. The reed warbler also nests in reed fringes along riversides, and occurs widely through England, reaching almost to Scotland. Montagu's harrier also sometimes nests in large reed-beds and is partly a fen and brackish marsh species, breeding in a few scattered English localities; it is a species which has decreased again after a recovery during the 1940s.

Other types of dense herbaceous fen vegetation, with sedges, tall grasses, *Iris*, *Sparganium*, *Typha*, *Epilobium* and *Filipendula*, sometimes tangled with willows or brambles, provide the cover required for nesting by sedge warbler, reed bunting, water rail, spotted crake, marsh warbler and Savi's warbler. The first two species are widespread and numerous, but the water rail is more thinly scattered, and the others are extreme rarities. The spotted crake evidently breeds sporadically and unpredictably in swamps widely scattered over the whole country; there are probably only a few pairs in any one year and the nest is very seldom found. The marsh warbler is a diminishing southern England species especially associated with managed osier beds, and is best known in the Severn Vale. Savi's warbler has been found breeding in Kent since about 1960 and may be on the point of colonising eastern England.

The wetter kind of mixed swamp, with standing water usually visible, is the nesting place of the pochard and coot, and some of these places, especially those least accessible to humans and foxes, have large breeding colonies of black-headed gulls. Duck such as the mallard, teal, wigeon, shoveler, tufted duck, gadwall, pintail and garganey usually nest in rather drier kinds of fen vegetation, and some of them breed far from the open water, on rough uncultivated ground or even moorland. The last three species are all rare as breeders in Britain, the wigeon is mainly northern and only the mallard is common and present in almost all parts of the country.

The moorhen nests widely in a variety of fen vegetation from wet to dry and is perhaps the most widespread of all wetland nesting birds in Britain. The grasshopper warbler nests in the drier types of dense fen, widely but rather sparingly. Other species breeding widely in drier fen, but most characteristic of habitats other than wetland include whitethroat, wren and pheasant *Phasianus colchicus*. Drier sedge fen, grazed short by cattle or mown, and grading into seasonally wet meadow grassland, is a favourite nesting place of snipe and redshank. This transitional range of vegetation from real fen to the damper type of permanent grassland is exemplified by the Ouse Washes, Cambridgeshire, which have recently regained as nesters three marshland species long lost to the Fenlands, the black-tailed godwit, ruff and black tern.

INSECTS

The Lepidoptera and Odonata of peatlands are fairly well known, but information about other insect groups is too erratic to justify presentation here.

Lepidoptera

Two butterflies occur in each broad class of mire, the large heath and silver-studded blue being found on peat mosses and the swallowtail and large copper on rich-fens. The number of fen moths, however, exceeds that of peat moss species. Only a few species are found in both classes of mire. A few, such as the rosy marsh moth evidently belong to intermediate types of mire, e.g. poor-fen. The peat moss species include all seven dwarf-shrub feeders and the fen species show a general preference for Gramineae. A large group of moths is associated with *Phragmites communis* and other fenland grasses, and many, e.g. the wainscots *Archanara* spp. and *Photedes* spp., have stem-boring larvae.

The rich-fen Lepidoptera are predominantly species of southern Britain, and especially East Anglia – a pattern which reflects the distribution of their habitat. These species have lost most ground during recent times, for their habitat has been more extensively destroyed by drainage operations than the peat mosses. The extinction of the British race of the large copper *Lycaena dispar dispar* by the draining of the Fenlands is the best known of these impacts. The reintroduced Dutch race *L. d. batavus* is maintained at Woodwalton Fen by rather artificial methods of management, and it is apparent that there are no longer areas of suitable habitat large enough to support a viable wild population of this species in Britain. Other extinctions in the Fenlands include the reed tussock *Laelia coenosa*, many-lined moth *Costaconvexa polygrammata*, orache *Trachea atriplicis*, and rosy marsh moth, but the last species has been discovered at Cors Fochno, Cardiganshire. The swallowtail is now restricted to the Norfolk Broads but formerly had a wider distribution in the southern half of England, and some moths such as the concolorous and Fenn's wainscot are now extremely rare and local.

Some of the peat moss moth species are fairly widespread, e.g. the marsh oblique barred and silver hook but even within this group many species are far less widespread than their vegetational habitat, and are evidently limited by other factors. The silver-studded blue butterfly is a southern species, which formerly occurred as a distinctive separate race in its northernmost stations on the Morecambe Bay peat mosses, where it became extinct apparently in the 1920s. The large heath is a widespread northern peat moss butterfly showing a latitudinal cline of variation in which three geographical races are distinguished; subspecies *philoxenus* in Shropshire and Cheshire, *tullia* in northern England and southern Scotland, and *scotica* in the Highlands. There is some overlap, with two subspecies occurring in certain districts.

Odonata

In their larval stage dragonflies are essentially creatures of open water, and so the group as a whole is considered in detail in Chapter 7. Adult dragonflies are found in nearly all types of habitat but since open water is usually surrounded by mire vegetation, adult dragonflies are a more important component of mires than of other terrestrial habitats. The widespread *Aeshna juncea* and the rare and local *A. caerulea* frequently lay their eggs in *Sphagnum* peat pools where no surface water is visible. A number of other species breed in waters which appear to be mires rather than ponds, although close inspection always reveals at least small areas of surface water.

SPIDERS

The spiders of peatlands are most easily described under two main headings, namely acidic or oligotrophic mires (bogs) and mesotrophic or eutrophic mires (fens). Of the 76 species listed here which are confined to or most abundant in peatlands, 31 are typical of mesotrophic or eutrophic conditions, 21 are typical of oligotrophic mires, and the remaining 24 species may be found in either group. The spiders thus tend not to be so rigidly confined to a particular type of mire as are the Lepidoptera, probably because they are not restricted by specific food-plants.

Many of the fen species are largely confined to East Anglia, the most notable rarities in this category being *Dolomedes plantarius*, known only from Redgrave Fen, *Glyphesis servulus*, recorded only from Wicken Fen and Chippenham Fen, *Clubiona rosserae*, from Chippenham and Tuddenham Fens only, and *Centromerus incultus*, once known from Wicken Fen and recently discovered at Woodbastwick marshes. Slightly less rare species which occur mainly in East Anglia are *Neon valentulus*, recorded from Wicken, Chippenham and Redgrave Fens, Foulden Common and Box Hill; *Zora armillata*, known from Wicken and Woodwalton Fens, and from Morden Bog; *Entelecara omissa*, recorded from a number of East Anglian fens, Ham Fen and Stodmarsh in Kent, and Askham Bog; *Hypomma fulvum*, recorded from Wicken Fen, various localities in eastern Norfolk and Suffolk and from Romney Marsh; *Hygrolycosa rubrofasciata*, widespread in the Fens and with a few scattered records elsewhere, including one from Matley Bog in the New Forest; *Maso gallica* (records include Wicken and Chippenham Fens, Foulden Common and Castor Hanglands); and *Marpissa pomatia*, which is widespread in the Fens and Broads and known elsewhere from Shapwick Heath and a few other scattered old records.

Other noteworthy rare fen species are *Maro sublestus*, recorded only from Wicken and Woodwalton Fens and

Table 24. *Habitat and distribution of typical peatland Lepidoptera[a]*

		Mesotrophic & eutrophic mire	Oligotrophic mire	Dwarf shrubs	Forbs	Grasses	S. & S.E. England	S.W. England	East Anglia	Midlands	Wales	N. England	S. Scotland	Highlands
		1	2	3	4	5	6	7	8	9	10	11	12	13
Butterflies														
Large heath	*Coenonympha tullia*	—	+	—	—	+	—	—	—	+	+	+	+	+
Large copper	*Lycaena dispar*	+	—	—	+	—	—	—	+	—	—	—	—	—
Silver-studded blue	*Plebejus argus*	—	+	+	+	—	+	+	+	+	+	—	—	—
Swallowtail	*Papilio machaon*	+	—	—	+	—	—	—	+	—	—	—	—	—
Moths														
Dotted footman	*Pelosia muscerda*[b]	+	—	—	—	—	+	—	+	—	—	—	—	—
Goodson's footman	*P. obtusa*[b]	+	—	—	—	—	—	—	+	—	—	—	—	—
Speckled footman	*Coscinia cribraria*	—	+	+	—	—	—	+	—	—	—	—	—	—
Rosy marsh moth	*Eugraphe subrosea*	—	+	+	—	—	—	—	—	—	+	—	—	—
Fen square spot	*Diarsia florida*	—	+	—	+	—	—	—	+	—	—	+	—	—
Heath rustic	*Xestia agathina*	—	+	+	—	+	+	+	+	+	+	+	+	+
Neglected	*X. castanea*	—	+	+	—	—	+	+	+	+	+	+	+	+
Flame wainscot	*Senta flammea*	+	—	—	—	+	—	—	+	—	—	—	—	—
Striped wainscot	*Mythimna pudorina*	+	+	—	—	+	+	+	+	—	+	+	—	—
Obscure wainscot	*M. obsoleta*	+	—	—	—	+	+	—	+	—	—	—	—	—
Light knot grass	*Acronycta menyanthidis*	—	+	+	—	—	—	—	—	—	—	+	+	+
Reed dagger	*Simyra albovenosa*	+	—	—	—	+	—	—	+	—	—	—	—	—
Marsh moth	*Athetis palustris*	+	—	—	+	—	—	—	+	—	—	+	—	—
Crescent	*Celaena leucostigma*	+	+	—	—	+	—	—	+	—	—	+	+	+
Large wainscot	*Rhizedra lutosa*	+	+	—	—	+	+	—	+	+	+	+	+	+
Small wainscot	*Photedes pygmina*	+	+	—	—	+	+	+	+	+	+	+	+	+
Concolorous	*P. extrema*	+	—	—	—	+	—	—	+	—	—	—	—	—
Mere wainscot	*P. fluxa*	+	—	—	—	+	—	—	+	—	—	—	—	—
Fenn's wainscot	*P. brevilinea*	+	—	—	—	+	—	—	+	—	—	—	—	—
Fen wainscot	*Arenostola phragmitidis*	+	+	—	—	+	+	—	+	—	—	—	—	—
Rush wainscot	*Archanara algae*	—	—	—	—	+	—	—	+	—	—	—	—	—
Webb's wainscot	*A. sparganii*	+	—	—	—	+	+	+	+	—	—	—	—	—
Twin-spotted wainscot	*A. geminipuncta*	+	—	—	—	+	+	+	+	—	—	—	—	—
Brown-veined wainscot	*A. dissoluta*	+	—	—	—	+	+	+	+	—	—	+	—	—
White-mantled wainscot	*A. neurica*	+	—	—	—	+	—	—	+	—	—	—	—	—
Bulrush wainscot	*Nonagria typhae*	+	—	—	—	+	+	+	+	+	—	+	—	—
Small rufous	*Coenobia rufa*	+	—	—	—	+	+	+	+	—	+	+	+	—
Silky wainscot	*Chilodes maritimus*	+	—	—	—	+	+	+	+	—	—	—	—	—
Silver barred	*Deltote bankiana*	+	—	—	—	+	—	—	+	—	—	—	—	—
Silver hook	*Eustrotia uncula*	+	+	—	—	+	+	+	+	+	+	+	+	+
Scarce burnished brass	*Diachrysia chryson*	+	—	—	+	+	—	—	—	—	+	—	—	—
Pinion-streaked snout	*Schrankia costaestrigalis*	+	+	—	+	—	+	+	+	+	+	+	+	—
Marsh oblique-barred	*Hypenodes turfosalis*	—	+	—	+	+	+	+	+	+	+	+	+	+
Smoky wave	*Scopula ternata*	—	+	—	+	—	—	+	—	—	+	+	+	+
Purple-bordered gold	*Idaea muricata*	+	+	—	—	+	+	—	+	—	—	—	—	—
Oblique carpet	*Orthonama vittata*	+	—	—	+	—	+	+	+	+	+	+	+	—
Marsh carpet	*Perizoma sagittatum*	+	—	—	+	—	—	—	+	—	—	—	—	—
Manchester treble-bar	*Carsia sororiata*	—	+	+	—	—	—	—	—	—	—	+	+	+
Dentated pug	*Anticollix sparsata*	+	—	—	+	—	—	+	+	—	—	+	—	—

Table 24 (*contd.*)

		1	2	3	4	5	6	7	8	9	10	11	12	13
Reed leopard	*Phragmataecia castaneae*	+	—	—	—	+	—	—	+	—	—	—	—	—
	Catoptria margaritella	—	+	—	—	+	—	+	—	—	—	+	+	+
	Chilo phragmitella	+	—	—	—	+	+	+	+	+	—	—	—	—
Total 46		33	20	7	12	27	21	20	39	12	15	23	15	12

Notes

'Grasses' includes all monocotyledons growing in mires.

[a] The nomenclature of the Lepidoptera follows that of Kloet & Hincks (1972) but the arrangement follows the conventional order used by previous authors, viz. Butterflies, Macrolepidoptera and Microlepidoptera.

[b] Algal feeders.

Dubh Lochan (Stirling); *Lycosa paludicola*, which has been recorded from six widely scattered localities including Woodwalton Fen and Shapwick Heath; and *Donacochara speciosa*, the few scattered localities for which include Horsey Mere.

Among the commonest and most characteristic fen species are *Clubiona stagnatilis*, *C. phragmitis*, *Gnathonarium dentatum*, *Hypomma bituberculatum*, *Lophomma punctatum*, *Porrhomma pygmaeum*, *Kaestneria pullata* and *Bathyphantes approximatus*. Some other species are about equally abundant in fens and in oligotrophic mires, e.g. *Pirata piraticus*, *P. hygrophilus*, *Antistea elegans*, *Diplocephalus permixtus* and *Centromerus expertus*.

Among the species characteristic of oligotrophic mires, there is a group of eight which are mainly northern or submontane in distribution and are described in Chapter 9. These are *Walckenaera clavicornis*, *Erigone capra*, *Eboria caliginosa*, *Hilaira excisa*, *H. nubigena*, *H. pervicax*, *Maro lepidus* and *Clubiona norvegica*. The last named is also one of a small group of rarities which appear to be centred on the north Midlands. Abbots Moss is the only known site in Britain for both *Sitticus floricola* and *Centromerus laevitarsis*, although *S. floricola* also occurs in a few sites in western Ireland. *Carorita limnaea*, a recently discovered British spider, is known only from *Sphagnum* in Wybunbury Moss.

An interesting southern species is *Glyphesis cottonae* which is common in *Sphagnum* in valley mires at Thursley, the New Forest and in Dorset, but has not been found anywhere else in Britain, and thus has perhaps the most clearly defined habitat of any peatland species.

Apart from those already mentioned as being abundant in fens as well as oligotrophic mires, some of the most characteristic species of lowland oligotrophic mires, although not restricted to them, are *Arctosa leopardus*, *Dolomedes fimbriatus*, *Theonoe minutissima*, *Walckenaera nodosa*, *Hypselistes jacksoni*, *Trichopterna thorelli* and *Aphileta misera*. Species most abundant in northern oligotrophic mires but also occurring in the south are *Silometopus elegans*, *Notioscopus sarcinatus* and *Drepanotylus uncatus*.

Two species whose habitat perhaps comes nearer to open water than to mires are *Argyroneta aquatica* and *Tetragnatha striata*. *A. aquatica*, the water spider, is widespread in Britain but local, and occurs in a wide range of habitats, including valley mires, well-vegetated ponds and ditches, and even brackish water on Romney Marsh. *T. striata* is unusual in that it lives mainly among *Phragmites* standing in open water, well away from the shore of lakes. Its apparent rarity may be linked to its inaccessible habitat; it has been recorded from a number of widely scattered localities, including Horsey Mere.

A number of characteristic peatland species also occur in coastal habitats, especially salt marshes and sand dunes, widespread examples being *Clubiona phragmitis*, *Arctosa leopardus*, *Pirata piraticus*, *Gnathonarium dentatum* and *Hypomma bituberculatum*.

Historical significance

Peat deposits and the lake sediments which sometimes underlie them have enormous value as historical records of conditions, both physical and biological, going well back into the Quaternary Period. Both direct stratigraphical studies, involving examination of subfossil plant and animal remains, and pollen analysis, supported by the technique of radio-carbon dating, have built up the ecological history of the British Quaternary as summarised by Godwin (1956, 1975).

Soligenous mires are of negligible historical interest, for their peat is usually very shallow and much influenced by downwash of material or other disturbance. Valley mires are mostly of relatively little value, for similar reasons, though some examples with deep peats and underlying Post-glacial sediments are notable exceptions. Most blanket mires began to form at the onset of the wet Atlantic Period or later, and the deepest deposits contain particularly good records of vegetational history during this part of the Post-glacial Period. The peat of blanket mires often contains abundant buried tree remains, especially of pine, birch and willow, at various horizons, giving valuable direct evidence of former forest composition and tree growth at the particular sites. The most valuable stratigraphic sequences are in certain basin mires and raised mires which formed on the sites of ancient lakes and contain basal Late-glacial and Post-glacial sediments, often overlain by fen peat, and finally by a thick layer of acidic mire peat, usually rich in *Sphagnum* remains.

Table 25. *Habitat and distribution of peatland spiders*

	Mesotrophic & eutrophic	Oligotrophic	Other habitats	S. & S.E. England	S.W. England	East Anglia	Midlands	Wales	N. England	S. Scotland	Highlands	Ireland
	1	2	3	4	5	6	7	8	9	10	11	12
Clubiona stagnatilis	+	—	—	+	+	+	+	+	+	+	+	+
C. norvegica	—	+	—	—	—	—	+	—	+	—	+	—
C. rosserae	+	—	—	—	—	+	—	—	—	—	—	—
C. phragmitis	+	—	+	+	+	+	+	+	+	+	+	+
Agraecina striata	+	+	—	+	+	+	+	—	—	—	—	+
Zora armillata	+	+	—	—	+	+	—	—	—	—	—	—
Xysticus ulmi	+	—	—	+	+	+	+	+	+	+	+	+
Marpissa pomatia	+	—	—	—	+	+	—	—	—	—	—	—
Neon valentulus	+	—	+	+	—	+	—	—	—	—	—	—
Sitticus caricis	+	+	—	+	+	+	+	—	+	—	—	+
S. floricola	—	+	—	—	—	—	+	—	—	—	—	+
Evarcha arcuata	+	+	+	+	+	+	+	—	—	—	—	—
Hygrolycosa rubrofasciata	+	—	—	+	—	+	+	—	—	—	—	—
Pardosa paludicola	+	—	+	+	+	+	+	—	—	—	—	—
Trochosa spinipalpis	+	+	—	+	+	+	+	+	+	—	—	—
Arctosa leopardus	+	+	+	+	+	+	+	+	+	+	+	+
Pirata piraticus	+	+	+	+	+	+	+	+	+	+	+	+
P. hygrophilus	+	+	+	+	+	+	+	+	+	+	+	+
P. latitans	+	+	+	+	+	+	+	+	+	+	—	+
P. piscatorius	+	+	—	+	+	+	+	+	+	+	—	+
P. uliginosus	—	+	+	+	+	—	+	+	+	—	+	—
Dolomedes fimbriatus	—	+	—	+	+	+	+	+	+	—	+	+
D. plantarius	+	—	—	—	—	+	—	—	—	—	—	—
Argyroneta aquatica	+	+	+	+	+	+	+	+	+	+	+	+
Antistea elegans	+	+	—	+	+	+	+	+	+	+	+	+
Hahnia pusilla	—	+	+	+	+	—	+	+	+	—	—	+
Crustulina sticta	+	—	+	+	+	+	+	—	—	—	—	+
Theridion instabile	+	—	—	+	+	+	+	—	+	—	—	+
Theonoe minutissima	—	+	+	+	+	—	+	+	+	+	+	+
Tetragnatha striata	+	—	—	+	+	+	+	+	+	—	—	+
Theridiosoma gemmosum	+	—	+	+	+	+	—	—	—	—	—	+
Walckenaera nodosa	—	+	+	+	+	+	+	+	+	+	+	+
W. clavicornis	—	+	—	—	—	—	—	+	+	+	+	—
W. vigilax	+	+	+	+	+	+	+	+	+	+	+	+
Entelecara omissa	+	—	—	+	—	+	—	—	+	—	—	—
Gnathonarium dentatum	+	—	+	+	+	+	+	+	+	+	+	+
Tmeticus affinis	+	—	—	+	+	+	+	+	+	—	—	+
Hypomma bituberculatum	+	—	+	+	+	+	+	+	+	+	+	+
H. fulvum	+	—	—	+	—	+	—	—	—	—	—	—
Maso gallica	+	—	—	+	—	+	—	+	—	—	—	—
Hypselistes jacksoni	—	+	+	+	+	—	+	+	+	—	+	—
Trichopterna therelli	+	+	+	+	+	+	+	—	+	+	+	+
Silometopus elegans	+	+	+	+	+	+	+	+	+	+	+	+
Lophomma punctatum	+	—	—	+	+	+	+	+	+	+	+	+
Carorita limnaea	—	+	—	—	—	—	+	—	—	—	—	—
Gongylidiellum murcidum	+	+	—	+	+	+	—	—	—	—	+	+
Notioscopus sarcinatus	+	+	—	+	—	+	+	—	+	—	+	—
Glyphesis cottonae	—	+	—	+	+	—	—	—	—	—	—	—

Table 25 (*contd.*)

	1	2	3	4	5	6	7	8	9	10	11	12
G. servulus	+	—	—	—	—	+	—	—	—	—	—	—
Erigonella ignobilis	+	+	—	+	+	+	+	+	+	—	—	+
Diplocephalus permixtus	+	+	+	+	+	+	+	+	+	+	+	+
Araeoncus crassiceps	+	+	—	+	+	+	+	+	+	+	+	+
Collinsia distincta	+	—	—	+	+	+	+	+	+	+	—	—
Erigone capra	+	+	—	—	—	—	—	+	+	—	+	+
Eboria caliginosa	—	+	—	—	—	—	—	—	+	—	+	—
Donacochara speciosa	+	—	—	+	—	+	—	—	—	—	—	+
Leptorhoptrum robustum	+	—	—	+	+	+	+	+	+	+	+	+
Drepanotylus uncatus	—	+	—	+	+	+	+	+	+	+	+	+
Hilaira excisa	—	+	—	+	+	—	+	+	+	+	+	+
H. nubigena	—	+	—	—	—	—	—	—	+	—	+	—
H. pervicax	—	+	—	—	—	—	—	+	+	—	+	—
Aphileta misera	+	+	—	+	+	+	+	+	+	+	+	+
Porrhomma pygmaeum	+	—	+	+	+	+	+	+	+	+	+	+
Syedra gracilis	—	+	+	+	+	—	+	—	+	+	—	—
Maro sublestus	+	—	—	—	—	+	—	—	—	+	—	—
M. lepidus	—	+	—	—	—	—	—	—	+	—	—	—
Centromerus expertus	+	+	—	+	+	+	+	+	+	+	+	+
C. laevitarsis	—	+	—	—	—	+	—	—	—	—	—	—
C. incultus	+	—	—	—	—	+	—	—	—	—	—	—
Sintula cornigera	—	+	+	+	+	+	+	—	+	—	+	—
Kaestneria pullata	+	—	+	+	+	+	+	+	+	+	+	+
Bathyphantes approximatus	+	—	—	+	+	+	+	+	+	+	+	+
B. setiger	—	+	—	+	+	+	+	—	+	+	+	+
Taranucnus setosus	+	+	—	+	+	+	+	+	+	—	—	—
Microlinyphia impigra	+	—	—	+	+	+	+	—	+	—	—	+
Allomengea warburtoni	+	—	—	+	—	+	+	—	+	—	+	+
Total 76	55	45	26	59	53	59	56	40	54	33	40	44

It is therefore necessary to ensure that the peat deposits of greatest historical significance are included in the series of nationally important peatland sites. In some cases, these peats are associated with underlying mineral deposits which represent an integral and earlier part of the stratigraphic sequence. The scientific value of sediments in their own right will, however, be considered in a separate and subsequent evaluation of geological and geomorphological features. Many of the peatlands which are of outstanding importance for their morphological and surface features are also valuable for their historical content, so that the lists to be presented take account of this interest to a considerable extent.

CRITERIA FOR KEY SITE ASSESSMENT AND SELECTION

Comparative site evaluation

In addition to the general criteria for assessment of key sites described in Chapter 2, certain criteria have been used in particular to evaluate the scientific quality of peatland sites. These are as follows.

(1) Degree of intactness of the mire structure in terms of both morphological features and associated vegetation zones. This applies especially to raised mires, where marginal encroachment by peat-cutting or other disturbance has often destroyed the characteristic marginal features of lagg and rand, and produced an artificial edge to the mire, e.g. East Flanders Moss, Perthshire. Erosion of peat, either by gullying or surface stripping, under the influence of water, wind and frost, produces very direct damage to a mire surface and profound changes to the vegetation. Enlargement of pools by marginal scouring is also usually a symptom of retrogression of a mire surface. Retrogressive changes of this kind lower the value of a mire system.

(2) Lack of disturbance of the mire hydrology. Such disturbance is often associated with (1) above but may occur also when there is no alteration in gross morphology of a mire, as when the water table is lowered by drainage operations or erosion some distance from the mire itself. Some flood-plain mires have been so much affected by reclamation of surrounding peatland that they are no longer viable as mires unless the water table is artificially maintained by pumping. In these circumstances, a mire has to have very high intrinsic scientific value to be rated as of national importance. Burning of the surface vegetation may also help to lower the water table, and occasionally subterranean erosion may do so without first modifying the surface structure.

Plate 13. *Calthorpe Broad, Norfolk (OW.16, P. 10)* (see p. 238). This small mere is one of the few remaining Norfolk Broads which has not shown a dramatic loss of its macrophyte vegetation during the last two decades. The surface is still covered largely with sheets of yellow water lily *Nuphar lutea*, and the picture also shows marginal communities of bogbean *Menyanthes trifoliata*, sweet flag *Acorus calamus*, yellow flag *Iris pseudacorus* and reed *Phragmites communis* passing into carr of alder *Alnus glutinosa* and willow *Salix cinerea*. (Photo: D. A. Ratcliffe.)

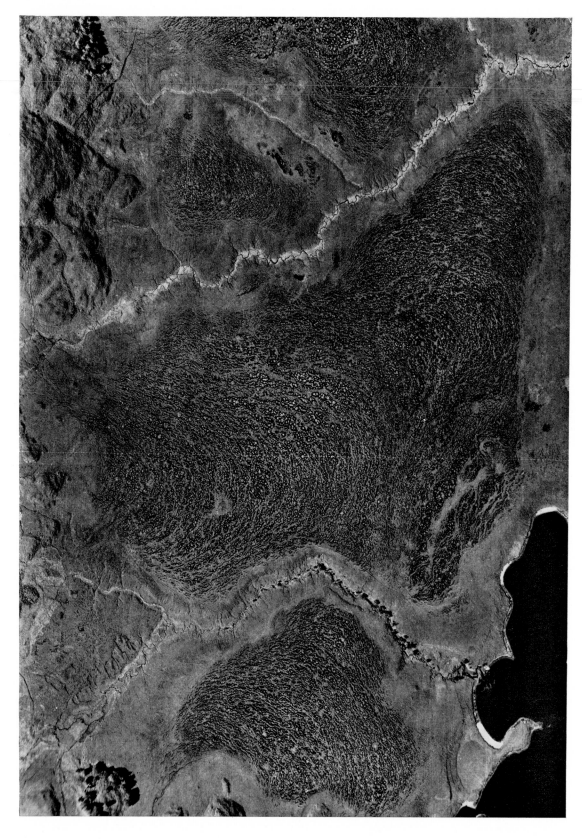

Plate 14. *Claish Moss, Argyll (P.94)* (see p. 276). An aerial view of the chain of patterned raised mires lying along Loch Shiel in the western Highlands. Each mire is eccentrically domed in vertical section and has a surface system of pools and ridges aligned parallel to the contours. The complex is dissected by transverse Molinetum flanking their courses; and transitional rand communities lie between these and the pool–ridge systems. (Photo: Crown copyright.)

Plate 15. *Denny Bog, New Forest, Hampshire (P.3(b))* (see p. 282). This fine example of oligotrophic valley mire has extensive *Sphagnum* carpets, poor-fen swamp and central carr, occupying a shallow channel in the Tertiary deposits of the New Forest. The edges pass through transitional wet and humid heath into dry heath with heather and bracken (foreground). Beyond are the extensive birch, pine, oak and beech woods of Denny Lodge Inclosure, Frame Wood and Stubbs Wood. (Photo: D. A. Ratcliffe.)

Plate 16. *Rannoch Moor, Argyll/Perthshire (P.85)* (see p. 277). This moorland is a complex of lochs, blanket mires, valley mires and drier moraines. The blanket mires vary from *Sphagnum*-dominated flows with patterned surfaces (Plate 18) to eroded peat areas in which the remains of numerous ancient Scots pines are exposed (*see picture*). The edges of these erosion hollows, and drier parts of the mire surfaces have a profusion of dense hummocks of the woolly fringe moss *Rhacomitrium lanuginosum*. (Photo: D. A. Ratcliffe.)

Sites with a catchment which can be readily protected are valuable, as in the case of valley mires set in an area of acidic heathland.

Changes to the water table result from physical disturbance, but disturbance to mire hydrology also includes chemical modification. This applies particularly to eutrophication resulting from run-off of chemical fertilisers (especially nitrogenous kinds) from agricultural land, and from pollution by sewage. This problem is generally more serious in the case of open water-bodies, but it affects a number of basin, valley, open water transition and floodplain mires, and in some instances appears to have caused virtually irreversible loss of quality.

(3) Lack of modification of the vegetation, i.e. naturalness. Vegetational changes invariably follow disturbance to mire morphology and hydrology, though there may be a time lag. Any changes which involve lowering of the water table cause increase in cover of less hydrophilous mire species at the expense of more hydrophilous species. In oligotrophic mires this usually involves reduction in *Sphagnum* cover and increase in abundance and performance of vascular plants such as *Eriophorum vaginatum*, *Trichophorum cespitosum* and *Calluna vulgaris*. In western Scotland, *Rhacomitrium lanuginosum* increases greatly in drying blanket mire and may become dominant. In the Highlands, the more local montane dwarf shrubs such as *Betula nana*, *Arctostaphylos uva-ursi* and *Arctous alpinus* decrease as a result of burning; and in all regions burning accompanied by heavy grazing tends to suppress the dwarf shrubs as a whole. Severe peat erosion may be accompanied by profound vegetational change, giving dry heath-like communities on the residual peat, and there may be recolonisation and succession on eroded ground to restore a vegetation cover. In many mires, surface drying is the prelude to invasion of shrubs and trees, to give eventually a carr or woodland.

While these various forms of modification give new types of vegetation and thus increase diversity, there is a strong tendency to regard this derived vegetation as much less important than the original types, and to select accordingly for mires showing the least modification. Most derived communities are incidentally represented (often repeatedly) during the selection of sites for other features. Occasionally it happens that severe disturbance leads to renewal of surface mire growth, as when peat-cutting is so extensive that it produces large, water-filled hollows in which hydrophilous communities regenerate spontaneously. This has happened at Moorthwaite Moss, Cumberland, where superb Sphagnetum has regenerated after most of the original mire surface was removed. Undisturbed Sphagnetum is highly valued in whatever type of mire it occurs.

(4) Diversity in nutrient status of mire water within a site is regarded as an interesting and valuable feature and is especially characteristic of valley mires. Calcareous mires with 'brown moss' carpet and low–medium herb sward have been highly rated, as a rare and fragile type. Open water transition and flood-plain mires which are contiguous with important open waters (both lakes and rivers) are regarded as more valuable than those with little or no open water; this is another aspect of diversity.

(5) Representation of individual plant species characteristic of the particular mire type, i.e. floristic richness. This links with (3) above, as species may be lost through anthropogenic modification of the vegetation. Small areas of undamaged mire may, however, lack certain species largely as a result of chance, as smallness of size reduces chances of colonisation, e.g. Abbots Moss, Cheshire. Species/area effects of this kind are especially likely in districts where the extent of mire vegetation has always been limited.

(6) Stratigraphical importance of the site. The peat and any underlying mineral substrata are an integral part of a mire system, and have provided the bulk of the material for the unravelling of the vegetational and climatic history of the Late Quaternary Period. The most valuable deposits are those with the greatest time span, and examples which extend back to the early Late-glacial (Late Weichselian) Period are especially valued. The deposits under some mires have become classic Quaternary sites and there is a need to preserve the most important against the need for further investigations of their sequences. Since destruction of a mire often involves the removal or erosion of the deposits underlying the surface, National Nature Reserve (NNR) status is usually necessary to secure conservation of such sites. In a few cases, the Quaternary historical value of a site greatly outweighs its living surface interest, but in many mires the two run more or less parallel.

Requirements for the national series

In selecting the series of key mire sites, an attempt has been made to include representative examples of the range of variation within each of the six main categories of peatland, balancing the numbers and areas chosen against the frequency of occurrence and general extent of each of the six types. In addition, special attention has been given to representation of the following features:

1. The marked differences in flora and fauna which are associated with change in geographical position from south to north and east to west, in each main category of peatland. Efforts have been made to include good populations of all the more characteristic or exclusive mire species.

2. The wide range of nutrient status of water and peat (from oligotrophic to eutrophic) and associated biological differences found in the topogenous mires (valley, basin, open water transition–flood plain, and soligenous mire).

3. The marked variations in surface structure of blanket mires and, to a lesser degree, raised mires. Blanket mire is a type of peatland especially associated with the oceanic British climate, and is thus of considerable international importance. It is by far the most extensive major type of peatland now remaining in Britain but the best (i.e. least disturbed) examples are all in Scotland or the extreme north of England, so that there is bias towards selection of sites in these districts. The range of altitudinal variation in this class of mire has also been represented.

4. Undisturbed Sphagneta in various types of mire. Dis-

turbance here includes not only factors which cause drying out and reduction of *Sphagnum* cover, but also chemical changes produced by inflow of fertilisers and sewage.

5. The important breeding bird communities especially associated with the larger open water transition and flood-plain mires, where not covered by 1 above.

6. Mires known to be important for their invertebrate fauna, where not covered by 1 above.

7. The range of stratigraphic sequences characteristic of British mires, especially those extending back to the Late Weichselian Period.

REGIONAL DIVERSITY AND SELECTION OF KEY SITES

Raised mire

Raised mire is an extremely local type in Britain, restricted to those areas where conditions have allowed topogenous flood-plain mires to develop ombrogenous surfaces. The former occurrence of raised mire at Holme Fen in the Huntingdonshire Fenlands suggests that this type can develop even under low rainfall when the original topogenous mire begins to grow above the influence of nutrient-rich ground water. Extensive peat-cutting has destroyed the raised mires of the Somerset Levels, but areas of secondary vegetation have developed in cut-over areas at Shapwick Heath and adjacent areas, especially Westhay Moor. These vary from small areas of ombrogenous communities, through *Molinia–Myrica* types to remnants of rich-fen. The whole complex (P.24)[1] merits grade 1 status on entomological, floristic and ornithological grounds. Similar conditions are found at Thorne and Crowle Waste in Yorkshire. At one time very extensive raised mires occurred there and at Hatfield Moors but these have been destroyed or severely modified by peat-cutting and have lost their former importance as intact raised mires. However, the variety of habitats represented within the parts of Thorne and Crowle Waste cut over during the nineteenth century makes this an important peatland site (P.60, gr. 2). It has considerable floristic and entomological interest and bird populations are particularly important because of the large extent of semi-natural vegetation.

The most southerly raised mires in Britain which are reasonably undamaged are in south Wales. On the south side of the Dyfi estuary, in Cardiganshire, Cors Fochno (Borth Bog) (P.29, gr. 1*) has developed over estuarine sediments and has the largest and most important area of undamaged raised mire surface now remaining in Britain. Extensive Sphagneta occur here and the characteristic raised mire features of drier rand and more base-rich lagg are well represented. The mire flora is rich and contains a blend of southern and northern elements. Farther south-east and inland, Cors Goch glan Teifi (P.30) in the same county is an extensive raised mire system overlying an ancient Late-glacial lake which once occupied the broad Teifi valley. The

---

[1] Cross-references to key sites are identified by an initial letter (indicating habitat) and number.

---

largest patch of raised mire lies to the west of the Teifi, and is sufficiently different from Cors Fochno to merit grade 1 status as well. The classical raised mire features of central cupola, with marginal rand and laggs are finely developed here, and the stratigraphy shows an equally classical developmental history. Locally there are pool and tall hummock systems giving a patterned surface not found on Cors Fochno, and the range of communities is greater, probably because of local drying.

Still farther inland and at a higher elevation (260 m), Rhos Goch in Radnor (P.31) differs from the previous two mires and is also placed in grade 1. It is smaller, with well-developed lagg, but has a pool–hummock system of unusually large vertical amplitude and shows an interesting association with valley mire, with continuity between the two systems. The whole complex is floristically rich. There are a few other raised mires of regional importance in Wales, such as Arthog Bog on the Mawddach estuary in Merioneth, but north Wales is on the whole too mountainous to give a terrain favouring the formation of this kind of mire.

In the west Midlands, the drift-covered Shropshire–Cheshire plain, with its important concentration of basin mires, also has at least two notable raised mires. The extensive Fenns Moss is worked commercially for its peat and is no longer of national importance. By contrast, the rather small Wem Moss (P.40) in Shropshire is important for its remaining area of undamaged surface with large amplitude pool–hummock system, and finely developed mesotrophic lagg; there is also a rich mire flora. Wem Moss resembles Rhos Goch in some of these features, but is regarded as sufficiently important to rate as grade 1 in addition.

North-western England is one of the most important regions in Britain for raised mires. Inland, in Craven, Tarn Moss at Malham forms an ombrogenous component in an important complex of predominantly calcareous wetlands and, on its own, merits only bonus ranking. The main areas of raised mire are coastal. At the head of Morecambe Bay on coastal flats beside the estuaries of the Kent and Lune are a number of raised mires, all more or less severely disturbed and somewhat degenerate. Foulshaw Moss has dried out and is now partially afforested. Some remaining raised mires, notably those along the east side of the Leven estuary, are nevertheless important entomologically, especially for Lepidoptera, and this feature is partly related to their geographical position. Thus, although it has been strongly modified, the raised mire complex adjoining Roudsea Wood (Fish House, Deer Dyke and Stribers Mosses (P.47)) is regarded as a grade 1 site.

Farther inland and to the north, Meathop Moss has similar entomological interest, but is rated grade 3. In the same area of southern Lakeland the existing NNR of Rusland Moss is a partly dried-out raised mire thickly grown with Scots pine. Since its notable features would seem to be duplicated by the larger and more important Kirkconnell Flow in southern Scotland, grade 3 is the appropriate status for this site. From its proximity to Merlewood Research Station, however, Rusland Moss may have considerable potential as a woodland and mire research site.

On both sides of the Solway Firth, extensive series of raised mires have developed over plains of former marine sediment. On the Cumberland side the main areas are around Kirkbride to the west of Carlisle. Reclamation and peat-cutting have caused marginal contraction of remaining areas and destroyed most of the original natural boundaries with laggs. Until about 30 years ago, several separate patches of raised mire retained a largely undisturbed *Sphagnum*-covered surface, but since then repeated fires and commercial peat winning have destroyed these surfaces to the point where only two good examples remain.

The best remaining raised mire on the Cumberland side of the Solway is Glasson Moss north of Kirkbride. The southern part of this mire was cut commercially for peat and has dried out to give a heather-dominated vegetation. Despite occasional fires, the northern part still has a fine area of undamaged Sphagnetum with small amplitude hollow–hummock system, and a rich mire flora. There is some resemblance to Cors Fochno but the southern element in the mire flora is lacking, and undamaged lowland Sphagnetum is now so rare in Britain that Glasson Moss is also regarded as a grade 1 site (P.48). Wedholme Flow to the south of Kirkbride, the other area with undamaged Sphagnetum, is now smaller than at Glasson and so surrounded by a cut or modified peat surface that its viability is less certain. Nevertheless, it is of some national importance and is given grade 2 status (P.62). Bowness Common (P.61) is a large raised mire system immediately west of and once continuous with Glasson Moss. It has been repeatedly burned and, although some parts of the surface have a high *Sphagnum* cover, it cannot be rated as more than grade 2. (But see Appendix regarding all the above sites.)

Drumburgh and Fingland Moss to the east and Oulton Moss to the south are too modified to merit selection (but see Appendix). Orton Moss, just west of Carlisle, was probably originally a raised mire in part, but is now a complex of dry to wet woodland with much poor-fen and fragments of acidophilous mire communities mainly in old peat-cuttings. East and north of Carlisle, Scaleby Moss and Todhills Moss are much cut and severely dried raised mires with Sphagnetum only in old peat-cuttings, and Solway Moss near Gretna has been so ravaged by commercial peat-cutting that virtually no undamaged surface is left; pine colonisation is also widespread here. Scaleby Moss has an important Quaternary sequence to which the technique of radio-carbon dating was first applied in Britain, and it is thus a classic site in this field. Farther inland and at slightly higher levels (90 m) around Hethersgill in north Cumberland, are acidic peat mires which appear to be transitional between raised mire and blanket mire. These have deteriorated in recent years, mainly through large-scale peat-cutting, and though there are still good areas of Sphagnetum locally, they cannot be rated more highly than grade 3. Bolton Fell is the best of these intermediate mires.

The parallel series of raised mires on the Scottish side of the Solway has also undergone extensive deterioration in recent years. Much of the large Lochar Moss near Dumfries has dried out through repeated burning and the best remaining area, Racks Moss, has been afforested. Mosses east of Annan, such as Nutberry Moss, are degenerate also. The best remaining example of these Scottish Solway raised mires is Kirkconnell Flow on the Kirkcudbrightshire side of the Nith estuary. It is extensively colonised by pine and birch, and the former has spread greatly in recent years. Despite local drying, much of the bog centre is wet and *Sphagnum*-dominated, though its surface structure is quite different from that of Glasson Moss. Kirkconnell Flow is regarded as a grade 1 site (P.70) mainly for the interesting combination and relationships which it shows between the two quite different formations, woodland and raised mire.

Farther west, Auchencairn Moss in Kirkcudbrightshire and Moss of Cree in Wigtownshire are too strongly modified to rate highly but several small raised mires in this area are of grade 3 status, e.g. Carsegown Moss near Wigtown.

In the central Lowlands of Scotland many mosses are intermediate between raised and blanket mire in their morphology. Most have been severely modified by human disturbance but two examples merit grade 2. These are Blawhorn Moss, West Lothian (P.76), which still has an active *Sphagnum* surface, and Dogden Moss within the grade 2 site known as Greenlaw Moor (P.78). This site is rather more modified by grazing but has a good chance of recovering a *Sphagnum*-dominated surface under suitable management.

In the upper Forth valley between Stirling and the Highland Boundary Fault there was at one time a vast area of raised mire development, two large areas of which still remain intact, the remainder having been cut away in the past. A complex of mires known as West Flanders Moss is now largely planted with conifers but the single area known as East Flanders Moss (P.89) still has characteristic raised mire vegetation. It has suffered to some extent from drainage and periodic burning and the communities are considerably more modified than those of Cors Fochno and Glasson Moss. This site is considered to be nationally important morphologically and appropriate conservation measures could probably restore the *Sphagnum* cover so that grade 2 status is indicated. Other smaller Mosses to the south of the Forth are rated grade 3. In Loch Lomond the island of Inch Moan has a covering of peat which can be regarded as an unusual type of raised mire, bounded by the rocky shores. Typical communities have re-established themselves after further peat removal. This site is best regarded as another unit in the grade 1 island complex of Loch Lomond and is treated as a bonus to the woodland site (W.169).

In eastern Scotland, areas of lowland peat moss on the plains of Angus and Aberdeenshire evidently represent former raised mires or intermediates between this type and blanket mire. Nearly all are severely modified and many have dried out through excessive disturbance. There is, however, a most unusual example of high-altitude raised mire, Dun Moss at 350 m in the Forest of Alyth, Perthshire. This site (P.84) shows a classic raised mire developmental history and has a well-developed lagg; the surface has a *Sphagnum*-dominated hummock–hollow mosaic and a greater abundance of lichens than any other raised mire in Britain. Dun Moss thus has some features of blanket mire, reflecting its altitude and geographical position, and is an extreme type in the national series, meriting grade 1.

In the western Highlands, on the borders of northern Argyll and Inverness-shire, there is a fine series of raised mires known as Claish Moss (P.94) on level ground beside Loch Shiel. There are striking surface patterns of aligned pools with intervening ridges on the individual mires, and many of the pools are in a mature phase, showing signs of linking up with each other. Well-developed marginal rands are present and lagg streams separate the individual mires. This is one of the most spectacular mire systems in Britain, and amply deserves grade 1* status. Kentra Moss (P.102) is best regarded as a westward extension of Claish Moss on coastal flats, but is in a more modified state and, though important, is regarded as grade 2. Farther north along the west coast, Blar na Caillich Buidhe (P.103) has developed on low ground adjoining Loch Morar. This area has a patterned surface similar to that of Claish Moss but has been more disturbed and is rated as grade 2.

Blanket mires

As blanket mire development depends not only on a cool, wet climate, but also on suitable topography, it is best developed in those parts of western and northern Britain where the uplands are gently contoured, with broad, flat watersheds falling away very gradually into the low country. Many upland sites have, in fact, been given grade 1 or 2 rating partly for the blanket mires which they contain; in some instances these mires rate as nationally important in their own right, though most are to be regarded as bonus in value, and an integral part of total site diversity. For convenience, most of these blanket mires are described in Vol. 2 under the upland key sites to which they belong.

In southern England, the only blanket mires are on the moorlands of the south-west peninsula; those of Exmoor and Bodmin Moor are shallow in peat depth, relatively dry and unimportant, but the plateau land of Dartmoor at over 430 m has a large expanse of this peatland. It seems necessary to represent this most southerly British occurrence of blanket mire in the national series of key sites, and an area of north Dartmoor around East Dart Head and Cranmere Pool has been chosen for its range of diversity as a grade 1 site (P.25). This area falls within the North Dartmoor site rated as grade 1 for its range of variation from lowland heath to upland moor. On the southern part of Dartmoor, the area of blanket mire around Cater's Beam is less varied but is still regarded as nationally important (P.28, gr. 2).

In south Wales many of the upland plateaux have a covering of blanket mire, but this is mainly rather shallow and dry, and has no particular ecological interest. A good example of patterned blanket mire occurs, however, within the Cwm Ystwyth grade 1 upland site at Gors Lwyd, and other areas of mire between there and Teifi Pools rate as bonus. The plateau mire of Cors Goch (P.34) in Radnor is one of the best examples of this peatland in the region and is given grade 2 rating. Within the Mynydd Du grade 2 upland site there are also quite good areas of typical Pennine blanket mire. In north Wales, the eastern upland massif of Y Berwyn (U.13) contains a varied range of high-level blanket mire, also of the Pennine *Calluna–Eriophorum* type, with the southernmost stations for *Rubus chamaemorus*. The Carneddau, within Eryri (U.10) have quite large areas of *Juncus squarrosus* mire on shallow peat, a distinctive oceanic type. There are numerous patches of *Sphagnum*-rich mire within Rhinog (U.12) which probably complete the range of variation for this formation in north Wales. The Migneint and Denbigh moors have quite extensive areas of blanket mire, but these are only of regional importance.

In the Midlands, the gritstone moors of the High Peak have large areas of blanket mire, and this covers a significant part of the Kinder–Bleaklow grade 1 upland site, ranking here as a nationally important example of a regional facies of Calluneto–Eriophoretum in its own right (P.41, gr. 1). These Peak District mires are characterised by the great depths of peat, local severity of erosion and abundance of dwarf shrubs other than *Calluna*. The Pennines farther north have huge expanses of blanket mire though much of this is eroded or severely modified, with dominance of *Eriophorum vaginatum* and low cover of *Sphagnum*. The once fine blanket mires of Stainmore have been much damaged in recent decades, and no longer have large areas of *Sphagnum* carpet. The best remaining areas nevertheless appear to lie within the Alston Block, and four grade 1 upland sites here have important blanket mires. Moor House with its outlying extension of Yad Moss (P.50, gr. 1*) shows a wide range of high level facies, from those with continuous *Sphagnum* carpet to others severely degraded by erosion: these rate as nationally important. Appleby Fells and Upper Teesdale also contain significant areas of blanket mire and Mallerstang–Swaledale Head is interesting for its evidence of the full cycle of peat erosion and regeneration.

By far the best undamaged *Sphagnum*-dominated blanket mires outside Scotland are on the great flat and gently undulating moors lying between the River North Tyne in Northumberland and the River Irthing in Cumberland, at the south-western end of the Cheviot Hills. The altitude here is considerably lower than at Moor House. Although these moors have been extensively afforested in recent years, several of these flows (level expanses of mire) have remained undisturbed and, because of the widespread disappearance of such ecosystems elsewhere, are now of the highest national importance. Each of these Border flows differs from the others in some noteworthy feature, and to represent the range of topographical, structural, hydrological and vegetational variation, a group of five have been rated as an aggregate grade 1* site (P.49): Butterburn Flow, Haining Head Moss, Hummel Knowe Moss, Coom Rigg Moss and Felecia Moss. Of the many others, two, Falstone Moss (P.63) and Gowany Knowe Moss (P.64), are designated alternative grade 2 sites. Elsewhere in Northumberland, the flow of Boddle Moss in the Simonside Hills, the watersheds of Kielderhead Moors, pockets of mire on the Harbottle

Moors and the peat-covered summit of the Cheviot itself are bonus areas of blanket mire in grade 2 upland sites.

In the Southern Uplands, a broad valley in the Galloway hills contains a fine linear series of *Sphagnum*-dominated *Trichophorum–Eriophorum* mires with patterned surfaces, ranging from a type approaching raised mire to typical blanket mire. This complex, known as the Silver Flowe (P.71, gr. 1*) and contiguous with the Merrick–Kells (U.35) upland site, is one of the most important mire systems in Britain. Farther west in Galloway the extensive peat-covered areas of Wigtownshire have a vegetation intermediate between that of raised and blanket mire (see Appendix). Much of this district has been afforested in recent years and few good quality blanket mires remain. Two grade 2 sites are selected which include the range of conditions in this area. These are Kilquhockadale Flow (P.79) and the blanket mires around Mochrum Lochs (P.77). The Cairnsmore of Fleet grade 1 upland site contains typical examples of western blanket mire with abundant *Molinia* and *Trichophorum*, mostly on shallower peat. On the watersheds of the Moorfoot Hills at the eastern end of the Southern Uplands are good examples of little disturbed *Sphagnum*-rich Calluneto–Eriophoretum mire with abundant *Rubus chamaemorus*; these merit grade 1 status in their own right (P.72). Adjoining the western end of the Cheviots, the Langholm–Newcastleton Hills (U.38) also have a very similar complex of watershed blanket mire. In the same district, the much lower-lying Fala Flow (P.80, gr. 2) in Midlothian is an isolated area of rather dry blanket mire with considerable wildfowl interest.

Pennine-type Calluneto–Eriophoretum blanket mire is very extensive in the eastern Highlands, and high level examples are well represented in the series of upland key sites, e.g. Drumochter Hills (U.45) and Monadhliath (U.58). Really montane examples, in which *Empetrum hermaphroditum* replaces *Calluna*, are present in the Cairngorms (U.44) and Caenlochan–Clova (U.42). The most distinctive vegetational feature of blanket mire in this district is the occurrence of a lichen-rich facies of Calluneto–Eriophoretum, and the large mire-crowned plateau of Carn nan Tri-tighearnan 16 km east of Inverness, has been chosen as a grade 1 site (P.86) specifically to represent this feature; the Ladder Hills (P.90) much farther east are regarded as a grade 2 alternative. The great basin of Rannoch Moor on the borders of the eastern and western Highlands, in Perthshire and Argyll, contains an extremely wide range of variation, not only in blanket mire but also in valley, basin and soligenous mires. The blanket mire here is of the low-level, western type (Trichophoreto–Eriophoretum). Part of this complex has been selected as a grade 1* site (P.85). Gull Nest (P.91) in Moray is included as an eastern grade 2 example of a mire system with markedly western features, notably a patterned surface.

The Highlands west and north of the Great Glen have the largest continuous areas of blanket mire in Britain. Owing to the extremely wet climate over all but the far eastern parts of this region, blanket mire is extensively developed at low levels (down to sea-level locally). By contrast, many of the higher mountains, especially in the west, are characterised by sharp relief, so that high-level blanket mire is less well represented than in the eastern Highlands. Some of the islands, notably Lewis and Shetland, are covered largely by blanket mire, but the biggest expanses are in the flow country of east Sutherland and Caithness, where an area of roughly 2500 km² from Strath Naver eastwards is covered mainly by this type of peatland. This last district has the largest areas of undamaged *Sphagnum*-rich blanket mire in Britain, and the conservation of representative examples of the range of variation is of the highest importance.

Within the Sutherland–Caithness flow country two morphological types of blanket mire have been distinguished, namely, peat-covered watersheds and valley-side mires which exhibit marginal features resembling those of raised mire. The watershed flows are by far the most extensive and typically show numerous irregularly shaped deep peat pools on their relatively level surfaces. The second type occurs marginally to these but has a more restricted occurrence; it is a gently sloping mire surface with linear patterns of ridges and hollows aligned parallel to the contours. Two vegetation types have been distinguished in these flows, the western Trichophoreto–Eriophoretum and a representative of the higher level and more eastern Calluneto–Eriophoretum, locally rich in northern dwarf shrubs and lichens, but usually lacking *Rubus chamaemorus*. On strongly modified ground there are locally extensive *Trichophorum cespitosum* communities.

The finest example of watershed patterned mire is the great flow of Blar nam Faoileag (P.95) in Caithness, covered with the eastern type of vegetation and with a spectacular development of pool-and-hummock patterned surface. This is one of the most important mire sites in Britain, and rates as grade 1*. The nearest equivalent is the flow a few kilometres to the east, containing the Dubh Lochs of Shielton. The pools here are less numerous than on Blar nam Faoileag, and the site as a whole is less extensive and varied in floristics, and it is regarded as an alternative grade 2 site (P.104). A third, more dissected system of typical watershed mire, still in a relatively undisturbed state, occurs on the moorlands west of Forsinard (P.105) at the head of Strath Halladale. Separate patches of pool and hummock mire occur in a general expanse of drier and more disturbed blanket mire. This area contains the grade 2 upland site of Ben Griam More and Ben Griam Beag. The most extreme type of watershed blanket mire occurs slightly to the east on the other side of Strath Halladale. The Knockfin Heights (P.98) on the marches of Sutherland and Caithness are a moorland tract with a large area of plateau watershed studded with pools and dubh lochans of larger size than usual. In places, maze-like systems of peat lochans have developed by the breakdown of the ridges between separate pools; the intervening mire is mostly in a senescent phase of growth, and the whole complex may represent a final stage of development of blanket mire. Part of this watershed is rated as grade 1.

The best examples of valley-side flow yet found are near the head of the Strathy River (P.96) where a group of four relatively undisturbed sites has been chosen as an aggregate grade 1* site. These four areas are essentially undamaged pool and hummock systems in a continuous expanse of more disturbed blanket mire which contains degraded examples of similar type, and a boundary has been chosen to include this intervening ground as a buffer zone against further damage. All four mire areas differ in morphology, including pool–hummock features. The same area also contains a good example of watershed flow which should be included in the site. Another example of valley-side mire and an associated mire of intermediate type near Loch Badanloch in the same district might be regarded as a less varied alternative site to the Strathy River Bogs, and is linked to the Forsinard grade 2 site (P.105).

An area of moorland in the Southern Parphe (P.97, gr. 1) in the extreme north-west corner of Sutherland, has been chosen to represent the most oceanic facies of the range of patterned blanket mire. It includes good examples of watershed and valley side flows, and several areas of sloping mire surface with pronounced linear patterns. The area also contains an important example of northern valley mire, and forms part of a larger site rated as grade 1 for its upland interest, especially the marked altitudinal descent of montane vegetation. The coastal margin of the area, with extensive cliffs and dunes at Sandwood, is also regarded as a grade 1 coastal site. Farther east in Sutherland, on the large tongue of moorland known as A'Mhoine between Loch Eriboll and the Kyle of Tongue, are areas of patterned watershed mire with numerous peat lochans. The ground is *Sphagnum*-rich in places but, more unusually, some areas show local dominance of lichens, a feature usually associated with continental conditions. There are also patches of dwarf-shrub-rich mire and low-level occurrences of montane dwarf-shrub heath on Ben Hutig. The site (P.106) is rated as grade 2.

Several grade 1 upland sites in the western and northern Highlands have significant areas of blanket mire which fall into the bonus category. The island of Rhum has extensive areas of western Trichophoreto–Eriophoretum which locally contain a good deal of *Schoenus nigricans* and thus show a similarity to the blanket mires so characteristic of western Ireland. The Inchnadamph and Beinn Dearg–Seana Bhraigh areas have a good deal of blanket mire, especially the Calluneto–Eriophoretum type. The Inverpolly and Foinaven–Meall Horn areas have extensive but somewhat dissected complexes of low-level Trichophoreto–Eriophoretum, including numerous patches of patterned mire. The Hermaness coastal grade 1 site has a good deal of the Shetland type of blanket mire with a facies of Calluneto–Eriophoretum on rather shallow peat. Finally, Ben Wyvis has some of the best examples of blanket mire rich in montane dwarf shrubs, and these are regarded as having grade 1 importance in their own right (P.99).

Flood-plain and open water transition mires

Flood-plain mire is not well represented in the extreme south of England, probably as the result of draining the river valleys of their original swampland, but a good example occurs at Stodmarsh (P.1, gr. 1) in Kent, where coal-mining subsidence has caused extensive flooding along the valley of the Great Stour, and produced an area of open water and rich fen with especially high ornithological interest. The best examples of these types of mire are concentrated in two districts of East Anglia, the Norfolk Broads and the Fenlands. Broadland is a low-lying district in eastern Norfolk where several shallow river valleys contain extensive tracts of fen and carr which represent the most important area (c. 3300 ha) of flood-plain mire now remaining in Britain. By contrast, the once vast mire system of the Fenlands south of the Wash has been drained almost out of existence.

The Norfolk Broads fenland has survived mainly as a result of continued exploitation for various fen products. Indeed, much of the present habitat diversity, unique in British ecosystems, is due to various forms of exploitation in the past. Peat was cut extensively along the Norfolk river valley fens during the twelfth and thirteenth centuries. A gradual rise in sea-level of about 3 m during the fourteenth century caused periodic and increasing tidal inundation of the peat workings, which were regularly 3–3.5 m deep. In the face of this adversity, the industry waned and the flooded peat-cuttings were eventually abandoned, thereby forming the Broads. Subsequent peat extraction produced extensive shallow turf-ponds, generally less than 1 m deep, a large number being of relatively recent origin. Many of the shallower areas of open water have silted up to the critical point where reed-swamp can spread throughout, and in many places the succession proceeds to alder carr. Only the deeper broads remain as sheets of open water.

Although very large areas of the flood plain, especially in the lower sections of the river valleys, have been reclaimed for summer pasture, much of the fenland has been retained and exploited for reed (*Phragmites communis*), sedge (*Cladium mariscus*) and marsh-litter consisting of mixed fen (tall herb and sedge) communities. Many areas which would normally progress to carr were maintained as open fen by these practices. However, this industry has declined considerably during the last 40 years, with the result that large areas of mowing marsh and fen have changed to carr and woodland. Ellis (1965) has emphasised that almost all the specialised insects and other invertebrates, as well as the plants of the Cambridgeshire Fens are represented in the artificially-maintained communities of Broadland. There is a very real danger that, should the present trend continue, much of the ecological value of this area will be lost under a blanket of alder carr.

Open fen and carr communities show considerable floristic differences from one river system to the next, the most pronounced distinction being between the Yare and the northern rivers. These and other differences such as the extent of tidal influence and even the local effect of salinity, and the variation in past land-use on a local scale are in some cases so great that no single site can be regarded as representative of the Broadland ecosystem as a whole. The total variation is such that four grade 1 sites are chosen to include a reasonable representation of both the range of edaphic and other habitat conditions, vegetation, flora and the specialised fauna for which the area is famous. The open waters and aquatic macrophyte communities are considered in Chapter 7.

The four areas selected are the upper section of the Bure Marshes (P.7), the Surlingham–Rockland section of the Yare valley (P.8), Sutton Broad (P.9) on the Ant and the Hickling–Horsey area on the Thurne (P.6). The first three are primarily selected on vegetational grounds whilst the Hickling–Horsey system is an internationally important complex of habitats including some large tracts of rather uniform and floristically poor reed-beds which provide the necessary habitat for many marshland birds and insects. It is also important for its open water broads, and there are nuclei of acidic mire with *Sphagnum*. In addition, Calthorpe Broad (P.10), which is isolated from the main river systems and therefore less polluted, is also chosen as a grade 1 mire/open water site. Barton Broad and Reedham Marsh (see Appendix) (P.20) on the River Ant are an alternative site to the Bure Marshes. Upton Broad is a grade 1 open water broad and has bonus interest for its fringing reed-swamp (see Appendix). Many other areas of high scientific interest are scattered throughout Broadland and the whole must be regarded as a nationally important wetland complex.

The Fenland is an area of almost completely flat land covering 3800 km² at about mean-tide level, south of the Wash, in Huntingdon and Peterborough, Cambridgeshire, Lincolnshire and Norfolk. Essentially this is a shallow basin filled on the northern side with silts and clays of estuarine origin and on the landward side with peat which is the only visible evidence of a once vast flood-plain mire. The area was almost completely drained by Dutch engineers during the seventeenth–nineteenth centuries, and only fragments of the former mire vegetation remain. Because of shrinkage of the surrounding drained peatland, these isolated fragments now lie above the general level of the land and are therefore subject to a hydrological regime quite different from that which caused their development. Wicken Fen (P.14) and Woodwalton Fen (P.12) are the two most extensive areas of relict fenland now surviving. Holme Fen is another such area, where ombrogenous raised mire surface has developed, but become almost completely colonised by birch, so that only fragmentary mire communities remain. Chippenham Fen (P.13), on the fringe of the true Fenland at a slightly higher level (26 m), is springfed and so has a hydrological regime quite different from that of the first two sites.

The present condition of these surviving fen areas is entirely the result of human activity. Chippenham Fen is the least dependent on artificial maintenance of the water table, but even here succession to ash woodland has occurred over much of the site. Nevertheless these areas are nationally important since they form refugia for relict populations of plants and invertebrate species which have a very restricted distribution in Britain. The invertebrates (especially insects) have been investigated in detail, so that the fauna is unusually well known. In view of their all-round

ecological and historical importance Woodwalton Fen, Wicken Fen and Chippenham Fen are all rated grade 1. The periodically flooded grade 1 neutral grassland complex of the Ouse Washes in the Cambridgeshire Fenlands also has reed-swamp in places, and there are intentions of creating more swamp within existing reserves here, so that the area has bonus value in regard to flood-plain and open water transition mire. Similarly, the grade 1 site of Sibson Meadows (L.73) on the flood plain of the River Nene in Huntingdon and Peterborough has rich-fen communities in places.

In Breckland, many of the meres and smaller ponds have fringing fen vegetation with bonus interest, and on the flood plain of the River Lark, an extensive rich-fen and willow carr adjoin the Cavenham–Tuddenham Heath grade 1 site (L.61(*a*)). On the Suffolk coast on either side of Dunwich, at Minsmere and Walberswick, two river valleys dammed by coastal accretion at their mouths have developed extensive reed-beds which are of outstanding importance for breeding birds, and are associated with areas of acidic heath, scrub and woodland in a composite grade 1* site (P.11).

Vegetationally, there is a good deal in common between all the East Anglian mires which are influenced by base-rich water, regardless of their morphological type. Mesotrophic to eutrophic basin, valley, open water transition and flood-plain mires overlap a great deal in range of plant communities, but certain vegetation types belong mainly to a particular morphological type of mire, e.g. the calcareous 'brown moss' carpets with low-herb sward are found mainly in valley mires.

Elsewhere, open water transition mire is widespread, occurring wherever there are lakes and tarns, and so is best represented in north Wales, northern England and Scotland. Flood-plain mire is more local and usually of limited area, for many former examples have been drained out of existence, and are now represented mainly by seasonally wet meadowland. While there are a number of bonus areas very few sites in the present class outside East Anglia merit grade 1 status in their own right.

Natural sheets of water are extremely scarce in the southern half of England, but some river valleys outside East Anglia formerly had extensive flood-plain mires. One of the most important remnants is on the extensive plain of the River Brue draining to Bridgwater Bay in Somerset. Here, the large area known as the Somerset Levels is a former complex of raised mire and flood-plain mire, now largely cut away through long-continued removal of peat. Shapwick Heath (P.24) contains remnants of both mire types which together merit grade 1 status. Just to the south, the area of Sedgemoor is now mainly seasonally wet meadowland drained by numerous dykes, but some parts remain swampy in a particularly wet season. On the south side of Poole Harbour, Dorset, the grade 1 lagoon of Little Sea (OW.21) has marginal reed-swamp which may be regarded as a bonus.

In south Wales, the coastal dune system at Oxwich, Glamorgan, passes into a hinterland of extensive reed-swamp and species-rich mesotrophic to eutrophic low sward mire communities. This is the best known example of rich-fen in south Wales and, together with the maritime interest, gives a site (P.32) of grade 1 quality. North Wales has a number of mountain lakes and many tarns. Some of these are interesting open water sites, but they generally have little fringing swamp. Certain mesotrophic to eutrophic lowland lakes in Anglesey have a fairly good development of marginal swamp, but none has been investigated from this angle, although Llyn Coron is regarded as a grade 2 open water site. In Caernarvonshire, two flood-plain mires, Cors Geirch in Lleyn and Ystumllyn near Criccieth, have been so modified by drainage operations that they can no longer be regarded as nationally important sites.

The meres of the west Midlands plain have variable amounts of marginal swamp. Of the grade 1 open water sites here, Sweat Mere, Shropshire, has well developed fringing mire vegetation which represents a bonus, but Rostherne Mere, Cheshire, has relatively little.

In northern England, the grade 1 open water site of Hornsea Mere in Holderness, east Yorkshire has fringing mire worthy of mention as a bonus and, in the Vale of York, Skipwith Common has been given grade 1 status for its combination of dry heathland, colonising birchwood and patches of flood-plain mire (cf. Cavenham–Tuddenham Heath). Within the Malham–Arncliffe grade 1 upland site in the Craven Pennines, Yorkshire, Malham Tarn has an associated eutrophic fen (P.52, gr. 1) of northern character which merits this status in its own right, and adds to the astonishing diversity of wetland types in the Malham complex. Sunbiggin Tarn Fen (P.53) within the Orton Fells grade 1 upland site has marginal calcareous swamp which forms part of the wetland complex at this site, including additionally open water and soligenous mire. On the edge of Morecambe Bay, Lancashire, the artificially flooded valley known as Leighton Moss in Silverdale is an important outlying northern reed-swamp with some of the characteristic breeding birds of the Norfolk Broads. This is a grade 1 site (P.51) adjoining the limestone complex which includes the grade 1 open water of Haweswater (with its marginal swamp providing bonus interest).

The Lake District has by far the largest sheets of open water in Britain outside Scotland, but these are mainly oligotrophic mountain lakes in character, with steep, hard and often rocky edges which do not favour the development of marginal swamp. There are some fringing fens and carrs around the edges of Derwentwater and Bassenthwaite Water (e.g. The Ings – see W.133) but the best examples are around some of the smaller lakes, notably Esthwaite Water and the adjoining Priest Pot. Here, the existing North Fen NNR is a tiny but high quality area of mesotrophic fen which rates as a bonus area within the Esthwaite Water grade 1 open water site. In the same area, Blelham Bog NNR is a poor-fen developed over a kettle-hole on one side of Blelham Tarn, but its vegetation is of too limited value to merit more than grade 3. Again the tarn itself is of grade 1 status and so it is appropriate to regard the NNR as a bonus area. In addition it has considerable value as a site for Quaternary studies.

Scotland has numerous lakes of all sizes, many of which (especially in the lowlands) show development of marginal swamp. These are, however, the least studied of all peatland types during the review, and much further survey remains to be done. Many of the open waters rated as nationally important have marginal fen likely to be worth including in the bonus category. This is particularly true of the base-rich examples which occur widely in Galloway and the central Lowlands, and thence through the eastern plains from east Perthshire to Aberdeenshire. Rich water sites where the surrounding mire is regarded as at least grade 3 in value in its own right include Black Loch, Kilconquhar Loch (OW.79, gr. 2) and Lindores Loch, Fife; Duddingston Loch, Midlothian; Carlingwark Loch, Kirkcudbrightshire; Loch Rescobie (OW.81, gr. 2), Angus; Lochs Clunie and Lowes, Perthshire; and Loch Avich, Argyll. The machair swamps at Loch Hallan, South Uist, and Balranald, North Uist, belong to the eutrophic class of mires vegetationally but are treated under coastlands (Chapter 4). Many northern poor-fens remain to be investigated, but here floristic variation is more limited, and it may well be that existing key sites are adequately representative of this class of mires. Adjoining the south end of Loch Lomond, on either side of the Endrick mouth are freshwater marshes and a eutrophic flood-plain mire, Aber Bogs (P.73), which has affinities with both northern and southern types; this complex is identified as grade 1 within the Loch Lomond composite grade 1 site. In Galloway, the neutral grassland grade 1 site known as Ken–Dee marshes passes into mesotrophic fen fringing the edge of this long, open water system, and there is thus a bonus peatland interest here.

The eastern Highlands have the distinction of possessing the largest flood-plain mire in Britain outside the Norfolk Broads. The Insh Fens (P.87, gr. 1*) between Kingussie and Loch Insh cover an area of almost 780 ha in the middle Spey Valley, Inverness-shire. This great expanse of mire was once partly drained but has been rejuvenated by the construction of a railway embankment on one side and artificial banks to the River Spey. The vegetation is predominantly the characteristic northern poor-fen contrasting with the eutrophic types of the Broads, and there is a rich avifauna with a distinctly northern element. Loch Insh itself rates as a grade 1 open water site, and within the fens are small tarns and flooded oxbows. Altogether this is one of the most important peatland sites in the country. The previously-mentioned grade 1 ecosystem complex known as the Moor of Dinnet (P.88) on Deeside includes two large tarns, Lochs Davan and Kinord (OW.76), with fringing oligotrophic swamp and acidic Sphagnum mire grading into poor-fen and valley mire.

North of the Great Glen, the lower reach of the River Fleet in east Sutherland has developed a large area of flood-plain mire and alder–willow carr after it was disconnected from the sea by an estuarine embankment (the Mound) built in 1816. The influence of the sea is still sufficient to give saline conditions just inside the embankment and brackish effects for some distance upstream, but most of the mire system is a mesotrophic fen. The Mound swamps represent a northern counterpart to the Minsmere–

Walberswick coastal flood-plain mires in Suffolk (P.11), but have had longer in which to progress to carr. The area does not have the same degree of ornithological interest as the Suffolk sites, and the carr woodland (grade 1) is more important than the mire component, which is therefore regarded as a bonus. Slightly farther south, the flood plain of the River Oykell between Sutherland and Ross has a general appearance rather similar to that of the Spey at Insh Fens. Incomplete survey suggests, however, that most of the Oykell site is better placed in alluvial meadow and freshwater marsh, though some parts may prove to be sufficiently wet to rank as mire. The site is at present rated as a grade 1 neutral grassland and described under these as it is inappropriate to attempt to grade the various parts separately.

Basin mires

This is a very local type of mire with few examples in the southern half of England or Wales. An area of eutrophic fen vegetation in Breckland, known as Cranberry Rough, is best classified as basin mire since it has developed over and replaced a small lake basin (Hockham Mere). It is regarded as a grade 2 site (P.19).

An isolated basin mire in Radnor called Llyn (P.33) has an undisturbed central *schwingmoor* with open Sphagnetum and pine-grown margins, surrounded by birch carr. This is rated grade 1* since it has the best representation of oceanic mire vegetation found in any single basin mire and also has a classical stratigraphical sequence.

The most important examples of basin mire are concentrated in three districts, all in the northern half of England. The first district is the drift-covered Shropshire–Cheshire plain in the Midlands, where some of the hollows containing basin mires are probably of glacial origin, but others are believed to have been formed by subsidence following solution and wastage of the underlying thick layers of rock salt within the Triassic succession. The largest and in many ways most typical of these Midland basin mires is Chartley Moss (P.42, gr. 1) in Staffordshire, where there is a classical *schwingmoor* or floating raft of Sphagnetum containing pools over a considerable depth of open water in the basin. Characteristic colonisation by Scots pine is well represented, and one area shows the influence of base-rich ground water.

Clarepool Moss (P.43) near Ellesmere in Shropshire is another partly pine-grown basin mire with oligotrophic lawn communities, including a *schwingmoor*, but compared with Chartley Moss has a more extensive development of mesotrophic fen and carr, in association with a large open pool containing base-rich water. The pool is one of the few examples of a small, deep and nutrient-rich open water body, and for its combination of interests the site is given grade 1 status. A further stage in the ecological series is represented by Wybunbury Moss (P.44, gr. 1) near Crewe, Cheshire, where mesotrophic fen and carr occupy a large and increasing proportion of the whole basin. The phenomenon of eutrophication is evident here, and the Sphagnetum *schwingmoor* is only partly of a truly acidophilous type.

Wybunbury Moss is the most varied and closely studied of British basin mires and the data on stratigraphy, hydrology and floristics give a firm basis for evaluating present and future changes. The inclusion of Sweat Mere and Crose Mere, Shropshire, as an open water grade 1 site (OW.39) completes the main range of ecological variation in the Midland basin mire series, for Sweat Mere has peripheral zones consisting entirely of the hydroseral sequence from rich-fen swamp to carr and damp mixed woodland. On their own, these fen communities are perhaps not of first national importance, but they are appropriately included as bonus areas.

The Abbots Moss (P.46) basin mire complex in Cheshire is regarded as a grade 2 alternative to Chartley Moss, with predominantly acidophilous Sphagneta and a high potential for hydrological research. Cranberry Bog (P.45) in Staffordshire has a superb example of a rich fen lagg surrounding an acidophilous central *Sphagnum* lawn, but is so small and vulnerable to marginal influence that it cannot rate higher than grade 2.

The inclusion of a raised mire, Wem Moss (P.40), gives a grade 1 series adequately representative of the very varied complex of west Midlands mires.

The other two important districts for basin mires in England are both in the far north, on the coastal plain of Northumberland and in the lowlands of the Cumberland Plain and low lying coastal strip south of St Bees. In Northumberland there are a number of basin mires, ranging from oligotrophic to eutrophic, but only one, Newham Fen (P.54) near Bamburgh, merits grade 1 status. This basin mire contains a fine example of a vegetation type not represented in the Midlands series, namely, highly calcareous fen with extensive 'brown moss' communities and their associated vascular calcicoles. Such vegetation shows close parallels with that of calcareous valley mires in the south, such as Cothill Fen, Berkshire, and Scarning Fen, Norfolk. Much farther inland in Northumberland, Caw Lough (P.68) is a basin mire near the Roman Wall, and has fragments of calcareous fen, but mainly a mixture of oligotrophic to mesotrophic fen of a type well represented in many northern mires. As this site seems to have no outstanding features, but is a good basin mire with a wide range of vegetation, it is rated grade 2.

In Cumberland, the most important basin mire is Moorthwaite Moss (P.56) east of Carlisle, which appears to be the only example left of this mire type with a highly acidophilous Sphagnetum. This site thus adds to the grade 1 series the opposite vegetation extreme to Newham Fen. The *Sphagnum* hummock and hollow communities are also an especially fine and actively growing example of regeneration-complex mire surface. The peripheral belt of pinewood increases rather than detracts from the range of vegetational interest. Farther south in Cumberland, on the northern fringe of the Lake District, Tarn Moss (P.55) near Troutbeck is an example of basin mire covered with a northern type of poor-fen vegetation not represented in the other grade 1 basin mires so far described, and merits this grade. It is more nearly allied in floristics to such sites as the Insh

Fens (flood-plain mire) and the valley mires of Rannoch Moor and Inverpolly.

Newton Reigny Moss (P.65) west of Penrith is the only calcareous fen in Cumberland. It is a western counterpart to Newham Fen for which it is a grade 2 alternative, but hydroseral development has progressed further, giving a greater extent of carr and a lesser area of 'brown moss' carpets. Several characteristic rich-fen species have declined or disappeared in recent years, and the site has tended to dry out considerably. East of Penrith, another basin mire, Cliburn Moss (P.66) is intermediate between Moorthwaite Moss and Newton Reigny Moss in ecological character. It is a pine-grown poor-fen, with local development of meso-trophic communities. The floristic combination is unusual but the site does not merit more than grade 2. On the narrow plain fringing the south-west Cumberland coast are several interesting but small basin mires. The largest of these is Hallsenna Moor (P.67) near Drigg, a complex of acidic heathland, basin mire and carr. The mire is largely poor-fen basically similar in type to that at Tarn Moss, Troutbeck, and though there are certain floristic differences, these are not sufficient to warrant a grading higher than 2.

In southern Scotland, the Whitlaw Mosses (P.75) near Selkirk consist of four separate though closely adjacent mires grading from valley to basin mire. The most obvious basin mire in the group, Beanrig Moss, contains an unusual weakly mesotrophic Sphagnetum different from the eutrophic fen communities occupying the other three sites. The whole group forms a grade 1 complex of very great ecological interest. Adderstonlee Moss (P.74) also in Selkirkshire, has a varied range of communities from the northern poor-fen type to calcareous fen. This combination is unusual in the north and the site is considered to be sufficiently different from any other mire to merit grade 1. Of the numerous other basin mires in southern Scotland none of those examined is sufficiently different from the basin mires already mentioned to be regarded as of first national importance. One interesting though small site, Barmufflock Dam (P.81) in Renfrewshire, is another particularly good example of mixed poor- and rich-fen, and merits grade 2 status.

In Aberdeenshire, Wartle Moss (P.92) has been chosen as another grade 2 example of a northern mesotrophic basin mire. Basin mires occur in various other parts of the Highlands and are associated with valley mires on Monadh Mor (P.100, gr. 1) and in Abernethy Forest (P.93, gr. 2) but no further examples have yet been seen that are sufficiently important or different from more southern basin mires to warrant national status. Basin mires in this region tend to be obscured by the general development of blanket mire, giving a continuous spread of peat over all but steep ground.

Valley mires

Two regions, both in the lowlands of the southern half of England, contain the best examples of valley mire. The first stretches from Surrey, through the New Forest in Hampshire, to Dorset, and has mainly oligotrophic valley mires associated with acidic heathlands on base poor sands and gravels. The second, in Norfolk and Suffolk, has mainly eutrophic types associated particularly with chalky boulder clay. The national mire series should represent adequately the range of variation within these two regions, and any distinctive geographical variants in other regions farther north.

Of the numerous valley mires on the Greensand of southeast England, the finest example occurs on Thursley Common (P.2) in Surrey and has an exclusively oligotrophic range of vegetation, set in an area of grade 1 heathland. Areas of valley mire within the Ashdown Forest grade 1 heathland complex rate only as bonus.

The New Forest, rated as a whole as a large grade 1 complex of woodland, heathland and mire, is the most important single area in Britain for valley mires (P.3), and the *locus classicus* for this mire type. These valley mires occupy shallow, broad channels in a low plateau of Tertiary sandstones and clays capped by gravels. They show a great range of variation, and especially good examples of vegetational zonation parallel to the long axis, with the beginnings of mesotrophic mire (sometimes with carr) along the central drainage track, and well-developed undamaged *Sphagnum* lawns to each side. Cranesmoor is probably the finest example of acidic valley mire in Britain, and has particular interest in its oceanic flora and aligned pool system which links it with western and northern blanket mires. The Denny Bog–White Moor complex contains several distinct valley mires with central carr and oligotrophic *schwingmoor* showing gradation into wet heath. Further variation is included in the Wilverley, Holmsley and Thorney Hill group, which all form part of a single mire system. The first two sections have mesotrophic centres, finely developed *Sphagnum* lawns and an especially rich flora, while the Thorney Hill section is unusual for the area in being a calcareous fen, with calcicolous 'brown mosses' and vascular plants. Hincheslea Bottom is regarded as a good typical site for the area. These four systems are regarded as fully representative of the very large range of diversity in the New Forest valley mires but this large area contains a number of other examples.

In Dorset, Morden Bog (P.27) north-west of Poole Harbour has a large valley mire which forms an integral part of the grade 1 complex of dry and wet heathland partly grown with Scots pine. The vegetation is rather different from that of the preceding valley mires and has affinities with certain northern poor-fen communities, and the insect fauna is outstanding. In the Isle of Purbeck, the once continuous but now dissected area of acidic heathland has two grade 1* areas, Hartland Moor (L.88) and Studland Heath (L.89) which contain well-developed valley mires. The Hartland mire rates as grade 1 in its own right (P.26) as it shows an interesting combination of oligotrophic and mesotrophic communities, and has an outstandingly rich invertebrate fauna. The valley mires of Studland Heath are more limited in diversity, being mainly acidic, but they have considerable interest especially in their unusually steep surface gradients and strongly patterned surfaces.

The contrasting calcareous valley mires in Norfolk and north Suffolk occur mainly in valley-head situations at the sources of certain rivers. Because of the national rarity of calcareous mires of any type, three really high-quality examples in this district have been rated as grade 1 although two of these are small in size. Scarning Fen (P.17) on the outskirts of East Dereham, and Smallburgh Fen (see Appendix) (P.15) in the headwaters of one of the Broadland streams are the most outstanding in their development of 'brown moss' carpets, though both have a range of other eutrophic mire communities dominated by vascular plants, including carr, and a remarkably rich flora for such small areas. At the head of the Waveney between Thetford and Diss is a more extensive valley mire, Redgrave–South Lopham Fen (P.18) which has extensive areas of reed-swamp and other tall-herb, rich-fen vegetation of a kind especially associated with East Anglian hydroseres. There is a variety of communities ranging from lower herb swards to developing carr and the area has a rich invertebrate fauna. Thelnetham and Blo' Norton Fens (P.21) at the head of the Little Ouse to the west have examples of the 'brown moss'–herb carpets and there is a luxuriant development of mixed tall herbaceous vegetation. This site is sufficiently important to be rated grade 2 despite deterioration following recent adjacent drainage improvement.

Roydon Common (P.16) near King's Lynn is different from the other Norfolk sites described in that its valley mire occupies a shallow valley in an area of acidic heathland (itself regarded as grade 1). As in some of the New Forest examples there is a gradation from wet heath to calcareous fen and carr and the whole site is of outstanding interest. Buxton Heath (P.22) nearer Norwich has a similar complex of acidic heathland and calcareous fen, which could be regarded as a grade 2 alternative to Roydon Common. Dersingham Bog (P.23) north of King's Lynn, is interesting as a completely acidic valley mire in the grade 2 heathland area of Sandringham Warren. It has unusual surface features but is not regarded as of first national importance. Interesting mixed valley mires with much *Sphagnum* also occur as a bonus within the grade 2 acidic heathland site of Holt Lowes west of Cromer.

Elsewhere in the southern half of England, Cothill Fen (P.4) near Oxford is a small but very fine grade 1 example of calcareous valley mire on Jurassic limestone, and has been much used as a research site. Greywell Fen (P.5) in north Hampshire is a rather different type of eutrophic valley mire, but as its main features are represented on other sites, grade 2 status is appropriate. On the south-western granite moorlands of Dartmoor and Bodmin Moor a number of acidic mires bridge the gap between valley and upland soligenous mire, but these are probably adequately represented within the North Dartmoor upland and blanket mire grade 1 site, and key examples elsewhere in Devon or Cornwall have not been identified.

In south Wales, Rhos Goch, Radnor, is important mainly as a raised mire, but contains an example of somewhat acidic valley mire which is of interest as a bonus. Cors Graianog (P.39) at the foot of the mountains of south Caernarvonshire and Cors y Sarnau (P.38) in Merioneth, are more upland acidic valley mires of a type represented elsewhere, but are both felt to be of grade 2 quality.

Anglesey in north Wales has some affinities with East Anglia in its strong representation of eutrophic fens and open waters. Most of the former are valley mires, and two closely adjacent examples on Carboniferous Limestone, Cors Goch (Anglesey) (P.36) and Cors Erddreiniog (P.35) are unusual in being western and oceanic examples of calcareous mire, for most examples of this type are rather eastern and continental. Also on Anglesey, Cors Bodeilio and Cors y Farl (P.37) are regarded as an aggregate grade 2 alternative for the above two grade 1 sites.

Three grade 1 valley mires are recognised in northern England. In the North Riding of Yorkshire a deep glacial overflow channel in the North York Moors contains a valley mire known as Fen Bogs (P.59) which has developed an ombrogenous surface in places, and otherwise has poor-fen communities of a northern type. This is an extreme topographic form of valley mire. In Northumberland the Muckle Moss (P.58) near Haltwhistle is a particularly good example of a *Sphagnum*-dominated *schwingmoor* and has especial floristic interest, though the communities are entirely acidophilous. Cumwhitton Moss (P.57, gr. 1) near Carlisle is important for its highly unusual combination of ecological features, with variable colonisation of mixed acidic and mesotrophic mire by birch and pine. It is a floristically rich site giving an interesting contrast with the acidic basin mire of Moorthwaite Moss less than a kilometre away. West of Carlisle, Biglands Bog (P.69) is a mesotrophic valley mire in which the rich-fen is interrupted very strikingly by a small area of ombrogenous *Sphagnum* surface having strong similarity to the adjacent raised mires of the Solway. This is an important site, but recent deterioration through sewage contamination of the ground water has reduced its scientific value, and it is regarded as grade 2. The grade 1 woodland site of Roudsea Wood, Lancashire, contains an interesting example of eutrophic valley mire.

In southern Scotland a small aggregate group of four mires known as Whitlaw Mosses (P.75) near Selkirk includes three eutrophic valley mires with a wide range of vegetation from swamp to carr. There is a rich flora, with a strongly northern element, and the group is regarded as the best example (grade 1) of northern rich valley mire. Dunhog Moss (P.82) in the same district is a grade 2 example of northern poor-fen of a widespread type. Heart Moss (P.83, gr. 2) in Kirkcudbrightshire is a valley mire with a wide range of communities from oligotrophic to mesotrophic, but is rather similar vegetationally to certain basin mires.

In the Highlands, valley mires occur widely, but in uplands are largely replaced by types regarded as soligenous mires, on ground with more definite slope. On Rannoch Moor (P.85), an important area of blanket mire on the borders of Perthshire and Argyll, are numerous examples of mire affected by ground water seepage and many of these could be regarded either as valley or soligenous mires. Their vegetation is of a northern poor-fen type and grades into blanket mire or into swamp fringing the numerous tarns. The area selected as grade 1* for its blanket mires contains valley mires which are of similar quality in their own right. The important grade 1 complex of open water, mire moorland and woodland known as the Moor of Dinnet, to the east of the Cairngorms in Aberdeenshire, has good examples of northern valley mires (P.88) with poor-fen (Black Moss and Ordie Moss) in a much more continental area. In Abernethy Forest (W.187(e), gr. 1) in the Cairngorm foothills of Inverness-shire, a grade 2 complex of valley and basin mires (P.93) gives a wide range of vegetation types, from strongly acidophilous to weakly mesophilous, and forms an interesting (though smaller) northern counterpart to the New Forest valley mires. The Kinrara section of the Aviemore birchwoods grade 1 site contains a good bonus example of oligotrophic valley mire with northern poor-fen resembling that of the Loch Insh Fens.

In the Black Isle of east Ross, the area of glacial deposition known as the Monadh Mor (P.100), has a complex of pinewood on dry ridges and hillocks with acidic valley mires and lochans in channels and hollows. Northern poor-fen is well represented and the complex has Scandinavian affinities. There are similarities to the Abernethy Forest mires, but this system is regarded as more important and rated as grade 1. Elsewhere in the Highlands, valley mires are particularly well developed in the coastal belt of Lewisian Gneiss. A very fine example lies immediately west of Loch Sionascaig within the present Inverpolly NNR (Inverpolly Valley Mire, P.101, gr. 1). This has an oceanic mixed mire vegetation including northern poor-fen and well-developed *Sphagnum* hummocks which grade laterally into marginal blanket mire. Another example of this type at Little Loch Roag on Lewis (P.107) is included as a grade 2 alternative.

Soligenous mires

Soligenous (flush) mires are represented in virtually all the upland grade 1 and 2 sites and are described under these as it is inappropriate to attempt to grade them separately.

There follows a list of the upland sites which contain the more noteworthy examples of soligenous mire.

Oligotrophic soligenous mires

These are especially widespread and occur within the majority of upland sites listed, but the following are the notable examples:

North Dartmoor, Devonshire; Rhinog, Merioneth; Eryri, Caernarvonshire; Moor House and Cross Fell, Westmorland–Cumberland; Mallerstang–Swaledale Head, Westmorland–Yorkshire; Cairnsmore of Fleet, Kirkcudbrightshire; Caenlochan–Clova, Angus; Cairngorms, Inverness-shire–Aberdeenshire–Banffshire; Rhum, Inverness-shire; Beinn Dearg and Seana Bhraigh, Ross; Ben Wyvis, Ross; Foinaven and Meall Horn, Sutherland; Inverpolly, Ross. Rannoch Moor, Perthshire, is a grade 1 blanket mire and soligenous mire site.

Mesotrophic and eutrophic soligenous mires

These are much more local and do not occur on all upland key sites. Their distribution depends on the occurrence of strongly calcareous rock and soils, so they are best developed on the Carboniferous Limestone of northern England, Dalradian limestone and calcareous schist in the eastern Highlands, and dolomitic Durness Limestone in the western Highlands. The following are notable examples within grade 1 upland sites.

Malham–Arncliffe, Yorkshire; Orton Fells, Westmorland; Moor House and Cross Fell, Westmorland–Cumberland; Upper Teesdale, Durham–Yorkshire; Ben Lawers–Meall nan Tarmachan, Perthshire; Caenlochan–Clova, Angus; Tulach Hill, Perthshire; Morrone, Aberdeenshire; Rhum, Inverness-shire; Strath Suardal, Skye, Inverness-shire; Inchnadamph, Sutherland; Durness, Sutherland; Invernaver, Sutherland.

Table 26. INDEX OF PEATLAND SITES

			Site	County	Mire type
Region			* Internationally important sites.		
South-east England					
GRADE 1		P.1	STODMARSH	KENT	F
		P.2	THURSLEY COMMON	SURREY	V
South England					
GRADE 1*		P.3	NEW FOREST VALLEY MIRES	HAMPSHIRE	
			(a) CRANESMOOR		V
			(b) DENNY BOG & WHITE MOOR		V
			(c) WILVERLEY, HOLMSLEY & THORNEY HILL		V
			(d) HINCHESLEA BOTTOM		V
GRADE 1		P.4	COTHILL FEN & PARSONAGE MOOR	BERKSHIRE	V
Grade 2		P.5	Greywell Fen	Hampshire	V
East Anglia					
GRADE 1*		P.6	HICKLING & HORSEY AREA	NORFOLK	F
*		P.7	BURE MARSHES	NORFOLK	F

Table 26 (*contd.*)

Region		Site	County	Mire type
GRADE 1*	P.8	SURLINGHAM MARSHES, WHEATFEN & ROCKLAND BROAD	NORFOLK	F
GRADE 1	P.9	SUTTON BROAD	NORFOLK	F
	P.10	CALTHORPE BROAD	NORFOLK	F
GRADE 1*	P.11	DUNWICH HEATHS & MARSHES	SUFFOLK	
		(a) MINSMERE		F
		(b) WALBERSWICK		F
GRADE 1	P.12	WOODWALTON FEN	HUNTINGDON & PETERBOROUGH	F
	P.13	CHIPPENHAM FEN	CAMBRIDGESHIRE	F
	P.14	WICKEN FEN	CAMBRIDGESHIRE	F
	P.15	SMALLBURGH FEN[a]	NORFOLK	V
GRADE 1*	P.16	ROYDON COMMON	NORFOLK	V
GRADE 1	P.17	SCARNING FEN	NORFOLK	V
	P.18	REDGRAVE–SOUTH LOPHAM FEN	NORFOLK–SUFFOLK	V
Grade 2	P.19	Cranberry Rough	Norfolk	Ba
	P.20	Barton Broad & Reedham Marsh[a]	Norfolk	F
	P.21	Thelnetham & Blo' Norton Fens	Suffolk	V
	P.22	Buxton Heath	Norfolk	V
	P.23	Sandringham Warren (Dersingham Bog)	Norfolk	V
	P.60	Thorne & Crowle Waste (part)	Lincolnshire	See under North England

South-west England

GRADE 1	P.24	SHAPWICK HEATH & ADJACENT AREAS	SOMERSET	RF
	P.25	NORTH DARTMOOR	DEVON	Bl, S
	P.26	HARTLAND MOOR	DORSET	V
	P.27	MORDEN BOG	DORSET	V
Grade 2	P.28	Cater's Beam, Dartmoor	Devon	Bl

South Wales

GRADE 1*	P.29	CORS FOCHNO (BORTH BOG)	CARDIGANSHIRE	R
GRADE 1	P.30	CORS GOCH GLAN TEIFI	CARDIGANSHIRE	R
	P.31	RHOS GOCH	RADNOR	R, V
	P.32	OXWICH	GLAMORGAN	F
GRADE 1*	P.33	LLYN	RADNOR	Ba
Grade 2	P.34	Cors Goch	Radnor	Bl

North Wales

GRADE 1	P.35	CORS ERDDREINIOG	ANGLESEY	V
	P.36	CORS GOCH	ANGLESEY	V
Grade 2	P.37	Cors Bodeilio & Cors y Farl	Anglesey	V
	P.38	Cors y Sarnau	Merioneth	V
	P.39	Cors Graianog	Caernarvonshire	V

Midlands

GRADE 1	P.40	WEM MOSS	SHROPSHIRE	R
	P.41	KINDER–BLEAKLOW	DERBYSHIRE/YORKSHIRE	Bl
	P.42	CHARTLEY MOSS	STAFFORDSHIRE	Ba
	P.43	CLAREPOOL MOSS	SHROPSHIRE	Ba
	P.44	WYBUNBURY MOSS	CHESHIRE	Ba
Grade 2	P.45	Cranberry Bog	Staffordshire	Ba
	P.46	Abbots Moss	Cheshire	Ba

North England

GRADE 1	P.41	KINDER–BLEAKLOW (PART)	YORKSHIRE	See under Midlands
	P.47	ROUDSEA MOSSES & STRIBERS MOSS	LANCASHIRE	R
	P.48	GLASSON MOSS[a]	CUMBERLAND	R

Table 26 (*contd.*)

Region		Site	County	Mire type
GRADE 1*	P.49	IRTHINGHEAD MIRES	CUMBERLAND/ NORTHUMBERLAND	
		(a) BUTTERBURN FLOW		Bl
		(b) HAINING HEAD MOSS		Bl
		(c) HUMMEL KNOWE MOSS		Bl
		(d) COOM RIGG MOSS & FELECIA MOSS		Bl
GRADE 1*	P.50	MOOR HOUSE–CROSS FELL	WESTMORLAND/ CUMBERLAND/DURHAM	Bl, S
	P.51	LEIGHTON MOSS	LANCASHIRE	F
	P.52	TARN FEN, MALHAM	WEST YORKSHIRE	F
	P.53	SUNBIGGIN TARN FEN	WESTMORLAND	F
	P.54	NEWHAM FEN	NORTHUMBERLAND	Ba
	P.55	TARN MOSS, TROUTBECK	CUMBERLAND	Ba
	P.56	MOORTHWAITE MOSS	CUMBERLAND	Ba
	P.57	CUMWHITTON MOSS	CUMBERLAND	V
	P.58	MUCKLE MOSS	NORTHUMBERLAND	V
	P.59	FEN BOGS	NORTH YORKSHIRE	V
Grade 2	P.60	Thorne & Crowle Waste	West Yorkshire, Lincolnshire	R
	P.61	Bowness Common[a]	Cumberland	R
	P.62	Wedholme Flow[a]	Cumberland	R
	P.63	Falstone Moss	Northumberland	Bl
	P.64	Gowany Knowe Moss	Northumberland	Bl
	P.65	Newton Reigny Moss	Cumberland	Ba
	P.66	Cliburn Moss	Westmorland	Ba
	P.67	Hallsenna Moor	Cumberland	Ba
	P.68	Caw Lough	Northumberland	Ba
	P.69	Biglands Bog	Cumberland	V
South Scotland				
GRADE 1	P.70	KIRKCONNELL FLOW	KIRKCUDBRIGHTSHIRE	R
GRADE 1*	P.71	SILVER FLOWE	KIRKCUDBRIGHTSHIRE	Bl
GRADE 1	P.72	MOORFOOT HILLS	PEEBLES-SHIRE/MIDLOTHIAN/ SELKIRKSHIRE	Bl, S
	P.73	ABER BOGS & LOCH LOMOND MARSHES	STIRLINGSHIRE/ DUNBARTONSHIRE	F
	P.74	ADDERSTONLEE MOSS	ROXBURGHSHIRE	Ba
	P.75	WHITLAW MOSSES	SELKIRKSHIRE/ ROXBURGHSHIRE	Ba
		(a) BEANRIG MOSS		Ba
		(b) BLACKPOOL MOSS		V
		(c) MURDER MOSS		V
		(d) NETHER WHITLAW MOSS		V
Grade 2	P.76	Blawhorn Moss	West Lothian	R/Bl
	P.77	Mochrum Lochs	Wigtownshire	R/Bl
	P.78	Greenlaw Moor	Berwickshire	R/Bl
	P.79	Kilquhockadale Flow[a]	Wigtownshire	R/Bl
	P.80	Fala Flow	Midlothian	Bl
	P.81	Barmufflock Dam	Renfrewshire	Ba
	P.82	Dunhog Moss	Selkirkshire	V
	P.83	Heart Moss	Kirkcudbrightshire	V
East Scotland				
GRADE 1	P.84	DUN MOSS	PERTHSHIRE	R
GRADE 1*	P.85	RANNOCH MOOR	ARGYLL/PERTHSHIRE	Bl, V
GRADE 1	P.86	CARN NAN TRI-TIGHEARNAN	NAIRN/INVERNESS-SHIRE	Bl
GRADE 1*	P.87	LOCH INSH FENS	INVERNESS-SHIRE	F
GRADE 1	P.88	MOOR OF DINNET	ABERDEENSHIRE	F, V
Grade 2	P.89	East Flanders Moss	Perthshire	R

Table 26 (*contd.*)

Region		Site	County	Mire type
Grade 2	P.90	Ladder Hills	Aberdeenshire, Banffshire	Bl
	P.91	Gull Nest	Moray	Bl
	P.92	Wartle Moss	Aberdeenshire	Ba
	P.93	Abernethy Forest Mires	Inverness-shire	Ba, V
West Scotland				
GRADE 1*	P.85	RANNOCH MOOR (PART)	ARGYLL	See under East Scotland
*	P.94	CLAISH MOSS	ARGYLL	R
*	P.95	BLAR NAM FAOILEAG	CAITHNESS	Bl
*	P.96	STRATHY RIVER BOGS	SUTHERLAND	Bl
GRADE 1	P.97	SOUTHERN PARPHE	SUTHERLAND	Bl
	P.98	KNOCKFIN HEIGHTS	SUTHERLAND/CAITHNESS	Bl
	P.99	BEN WYVIS	ROSS	Bl, S
	P.100	MONADH MOR	ROSS	Ba, V
	P.101	INVERPOLLY VALLEY MIRE	ROSS	V
Grade 2	P.102	Kentra Moss	Argyll	R
	P.103	Blar na Caillich Buidhe	Inverness-shire	R
	P.104	Dubh Lochs of Shielton & the Flows	Caithness	Bl
	P.105	Forsinard–Badanloch Flows	Sutherland	Bl
	P.106	A'Mhoine	Sutherland	Bl
	P.107	Little Loch Roag Valley Mire, Lewis	Inverness-shire	V

Notes

R = Raised mire   Ba = Basin
Bl = Blanket mire   V = Valley
F = Flood-plain and open water transition   S = Soligenous

^a See Appendix

9 UPLAND GRASSLANDS AND HEATHS

RANGE OF ECOLOGICAL VARIATION

Habitat factors and vegetation

DIAGNOSTIC FEATURES OF THE BRITISH UPLANDS

If any single factor could be described as paramount in the upland environment, it is the low temperature associated with high altitude, and coldness of climate is a condition which, more than any other, is implied by the terms alpine or montane. Heavy precipitation, high atmospheric humidity and windiness are also important conditions associated with mountain topography. The extreme oceanicity of British mountains, compared with those of mainland Europe, is expressed notably in a strongly hygrophilous component in the vegetation, marked altitudinal zonation of vegetation and, with increasing oceanicity, an altitudinal depression of these vegetation zones through severity of wind and lack of summer warmth or sunshine. The strongly oceanic character of British mountains, as reflected in their soils, vegetation, flora and fauna, is a feature of international importance, as it is not duplicated exactly anywhere else in the world.

The uplands of Britain show a greater ecological similarity to those of Scandinavia than to the Alpine ranges of Europe. They have much in common with the coastal mountains of south-west Norway (e.g. Sogn) and may be regarded as insular, oceanic outliers of these ranges, with biota limited by the relatively small extent of really high land, and impoverished or severely modified by Post-glacial change, including especially warming of climate and human influence. Although the highest Scottish hills have a few semi-permanent snow-beds, and the extent of late snow cover in summer has increased here since 1960, the British mountains now lack the great snow fields and glaciers which distinguish the Alps and the mountains of northern Europe. The mountain flora is poor compared with that of these great continental ranges, some widespread and characteristic species being scarce (e.g. *Oxytropis campestris*) or absent (e.g. *Ranunculus glacialis*) here, as a result of Post-glacial depletion or extinction. On the other hand, no continental European mountains have a comparable extent of vegetation dominated by *Calluna vulgaris*, *Juncus squarrosus* or *Ulex gallii*, and the abundance of strongly Atlantic ferns (e.g. *Hymenophyllum wilsonii*) and bryophytes (a large number of species, but especially *Rhacomitrium lanuginosum*) is also unparalleled except perhaps in coastal south-west Norway and the Faeroes. The extent of blanket mire in the British

uplands is another unique feature, and although it is sometimes loosely compared to the Arctic tundra, this is not an accurate description. The British hill country is in addition one of the main European strongholds of birds such as the peregrine falcon and golden eagle.

The rather arbitrary criteria for separating the upland from the lowland zone are discussed in Chapter 3, p. 23. Many of the characteristic dominant and constant plant species of the lowland grasslands and heaths extend upwards to considerable altitudes, and it is only the gradual appearance and disappearance of certain other species which reveal a change. Some of the characteristic lowland and upland plants are decidedly local, and this floristic separation is as much geographical as altitudinal, i.e. southern–northern. The transition from lowland to upland grasslands and heaths is indicated by the general increase in presence and abundance of widespread submontane species such as *Empetrum nigrum*, *Vaccinium vitis-idaea*, *Lycopodium clavatum*, *Antennaria dioica* and *Viola lutea*, and of montane species which descend to low levels, e.g. *Alchemilla alpina*, *Lycopodium alpinum*, *Saxifraga stellaris*, *S. aizoides*, *Thalictrum alpinum* and *Festuca vivipara*. There are, however, quite large areas of rather low and floristically dull hill country in which all these species are sparse or absent. The presence of the red grouse *Lagopus lagopus scoticus* could be regarded as the best single diagnostic feature distinguishing the upland heather moors from the comparable lowland heaths, but this is not an infallible guide, and there is no such common differential species for the grasslands. It therefore seems best to acknowledge that there is an altitudinal/geographical transition zone within which any separation into lowland and upland must usually be arbitrary. The transition from the submontane to the montane grasslands and heaths is also often ill defined and arbitrary, and only two strictly montane plant species, *Carex bigelowii* and *Salix herbacea*, are sufficiently widespread to be regarded as diagnostic of the montane zone. The range of habitats included in this Chapter is obviously wide, but the emphasis here is particularly on the range of hill grasslands, heaths and rock communities. Peatlands and open waters of the mountains and moorlands have already been considered in the appropriate Chapters, and upland woods and scrub are dealt with in Chapter 5.

Although all ground above 460 m lies to the north and west of a line from Start Point to Flamborough Head, uplands are the most extensive of the semi-natural habitats in Britain. In southern England they are confined to a few relatively low moorlands in the west, but uplands are extensive in northern England, and cover a large part of Wales and Scotland. From their wide distribution, the British mountains experience certain regional differences in climate, associated particularly with the south to north decrease in mean temperature, and the east to west increase in oceanicity. These two main gradients of climate produce parallel ecological gradients in the upland ecosystems, both through their effects on other habitat factors and more directly on organisms. With increasing distance north there is a decreasing representation of southern, thermophilous elements of flora and fauna, and a parallel increase in northern, montane types. In passing from east to west there is a gradual exchange of continental for oceanic elements, and an increasing prevalence of peat-forming and hygrophilous vegetation. In combination, these two climatic gradients give a resultant orientated in a south-east to north-west direction, and most noticeably reflected in the downward altitudinal shift in limits of the vegetation zones.

The characteristic mountain or orographic climate involves local (as distinct from regional) gradients related to topography, especially altitude and aspect. Within a single upland massif there is decrease in temperature and insolation, and increase in windspeed, rainfall, snowfall and cloud cover with altitude, whilst atmospheric humidity varies according to aspect, though the effect depends on steepness of slope. These local topographic effects may either override or reinforce the regional gradients of climate, especially where differences in altitude occur between the mountains of separate regions. For instance, while there are substantial areas of montane ground (above 600 m) in Wales, northern England and the Southern Uplands, the only appreciable extent of really high mountain (above 900 m) lies in the Scottish Highlands. When this uneven distribution of high land is combined with the south to north temperature decrease, it becomes obvious that the most extreme Arctic conditions, shown most clearly in duration of snow cover, must obtain in the Scottish Highlands. However, the highest mountains are in the centre and not the north of the Highlands, so that the most northerly mountains experience less prolonged snow cover than many of those much farther south. Topography is also important to local climate through its influence on wind exposure and snow depth. Actual duration of snow cover depends not only on regional climate and altitude, but also configuration of the ground, with its effects on extent of snow gathering grounds, drift-formation, and degree of shelter from the sun.

TOPOGRAPHY, GEOLOGY AND SOILS

Topography has profound effects on drainage and soil development, and may exert a considerable influence on land-use. It is the expression of geomorphological processes which may themselves be much affected by underlying rock type. Certain types of mountain landform predominate in particular districts. Snowdonia, Lakeland, and many parts of the western Highlands contain heavily glaciated mountain systems formed mainly of hard igneous and metamorphic rocks, and show a prevalence of rugged terrain, with steep slopes, cliffs and corries, narrow watershed ridges and sharply peaked summits. The Cairngorms have numerous corries and U-shaped valleys, but their summits and high watersheds are rounded and massive, giving a large area of ground above 600 m. In Sutherland, isolated mountains and massifs rise abruptly from large tracts of low-lying though often uneven moorland. Gently contoured moorland with broad valleys and large plateaux is exemplified by the Cheviots and Pennines, where cliffs are mostly low and consist of characteristic gritstone edges and limestone scars. The predominantly sedimentary hills of Wales and the Southern Uplands are typically steep but smooth sided, with rounded tops, and show dissection by deep, much-branched valleys carved by water. These topographic tendencies have strong influence in determining regional extent of certain major classes of vegetation.

Mountain soils have a number of characteristic general features, reflecting climatic severity in particular. The high precipitation/evaporation ratio promotes leaching of exchangeable ions, whilst the low temperatures slow down chemical weathering and humus decomposition, so that there is a general tendency for soils to be acidic and base-deficient, with acidic humus horizons. The development of the surface humus layer depends on angle of slope, so that there is a range of podsolic types from deep blanket peat over buried mineral horizons on flat or gently sloping ground to skeletal brown semi-podsols with only a thin surface litter on steep slopes. Steepness of slope promotes instability and this is enhanced by solifluction effects. Wind-blasting and the erosive power of heavy rain also cause redistribution of finer material. The lower slopes of mountains are typically covered with a variable layer of glacial drift, and this sometimes extends to considerable heights. Steeper ground at all levels usually has a gravitational accumulation of weathered material (colluvium) on which a finer surface layer of soil has formed, and this is often exposed again as scree through erosion and gravitational movement. Higher mountain summit areas frequently have a deep layer of frost-shattered rock debris and this may remain exposed as extensive block-litters and boulder fields.

Soils in the montane zone thus tend to be shallow, immature and raw. Shallow alpine podsols occur in more stable places, but the more common types are mountain tundra (rawmark) soils, rankers and skeletal brown soils. The mountain tundra soils can be divided into patterned types in which solifluction has produced networks and stripes of larger stones in a matrix of finer material, or systems of terraces; and *Hamada* types in which there is an unsorted stony surface with variable amounts of finer material. At the lower levels there is a greater development of podsols, semi-podsols and thin iron pan soils, gleyed soils of various types, brown earths, alluvial soils, and blanket peats. Rendzinas are rare, since limestone is so localised. Soil erosion is often marked in the uplands, not only because of climatic severity, but also through human influence (i.e. deforestation, moor burning, heavy animal stocking, draining and, more recently and locally, recreational pressures), and varies from truncation of profiles to complete denudation except for larger rock fragments. Redistribution of material can produce buried horizons or variable banding of profiles, and on some high mountain tops there are cyclical alternations of ablation and accumulation.

Parent material affects soil type and vegetation chiefly according to the inter-related factors of hardness, texture and chemical composition. Hardness of rock is probably more important in determining the amount of soil formed, rather than its base-status and fertility, at least in the British uplands. Rocks such as granite and some sandstones give coarse-textured, porous soils, whereas materials such as slate, shale and limestone give less permeable soils of higher silt and clay content, and these are often the more affected by solifluction. Glacial drift soils are also often more compacted and less permeable than those formed on colluvium or mountain top detritus. According to present knowledge, the calcium carbonate content of the parent rock and drainage water is the most critical chemical factor in determining vegetational composition on upland soils, but insufficient is known about the influence of rock type on available phosphate, nitrogen and potassium, which are certainly significant for animal production. Calcium in chemically combined and less available form (e.g. hornblende) has less influence, though its effect may appear more strongly where ground is affected by water (flushed) draining from such materials. Magnesium-rich rocks such as serpentine and peridotite also exert a considerable influence on mountain vegetation, though this cation is apparently toxic to many plants which grow on calcareous rocks (the true calcicoles). Calcium and magnesium are the chief cations responsible for maintaining base-saturation and high pH in upland soils, and when leaching results in marked unsaturation (i.e. high acidity), soils become biologically inactive, and deficient in anions such as nitrate and phosphate.

The greater part of the British uplands is composed of non-calcareous rocks, such as granite, rhyolite, quartzite, acidic sandstones, schists, granulites and slates which, under the cool, wet climate, give predominantly acidic and base-deficient soils. Here, richer soils are mostly confined to local flushed areas, and even where there are occurrences of base-rich rock, leaching is often so prevalent that base saturation is maintained only where there is pronounced instability, either as gravitational movement exposing unweathered parent material on steep ground or water seepage, giving redistribution of particles and dissolved nutrients, or both. Peat can form even over limestone in stable situations, and this tendency increases as the climate becomes wetter. As leaching increases in intensity, so the process of flushing becomes more important in maintaining base-status, though it can only do so locally, and is inevitably a redistribution of nutrients in a downhill direction. Richness of flora and diversity of vegetation tend to increase with base-status (especially calcium) of the substratum, so that the most floristically important uplands are those composed of calcareous parent materials. Whilst most hill districts have at least some basic rocks, the two most extensive tracts of calcareous upland in Britain are in the Pennines (Carboniferous Limestone) and south-central Highlands (Dalradian

limestones and calcareous schists) but there are important occurrences in Snowdonia (Ordovician pumice-tuff) and the north-west Highlands (Durness Limestone). The Moine Series of the Highlands and Old Red Sandstone of Scotland and Wales are locally strongly calcareous, and the greywackes and shales of the Ordovician and Silurian have numerous calcite-bearing beds, especially in the Southern Uplands. Many igneous rocks such as basalt, dolerite, andesite and epidiorite (but not gabbro) are calcareous, and the crushed rock of fault zones is often heavily charged with calcite.

Nevertheless, despite the general relationship between base-richness and soil fertility, some highly calcareous rocks and soils are deficient in other available nutrients. This applies to the Ben Lawers schist (Ferreira, 1959), celebrated for its rich montane flora, and the floristically rich montane communities on the Teesdale 'sugar' limestone are associated with soils rich in calcium, lead and barium, but poor in nitrogen and phosphorus (Jeffrey & Pigott, 1973). Floristic richness can thus be related to poverty in major nutrients apart from calcium, and is often marked by low productivity (i.e. standing crop).

THE PATTERN OF HABITAT AND VEGETATION

The original pattern of vegetation and animal communities of the British uplands, as determined by climatic, topographic and edaphic factors, has been profoundly altered during the last 2000 years by the increasing impact of man, mainly through his utilisation of the hill country as grazing land. It is simplest to consider this original pattern first (some notion of its character can be gained by a visit to the mountains of south-western Norway), and then to deal with the modifications which have come about. Except on very wet ground, the lower levels of our mountains were once evidently virtually all forest clad, though to a variable elevation, since the present limits of tree growth vary from about 600 m in south Wales and the eastern Highlands to 300 m or less on the exposed moorlands of the north-west Highlands and islands. The upper limits of tree growth are marked by a zone of tall scrub, often composed of the same tree species (mainly oak, birch and pine) which dominate the forest below, but giving way with increasing altitude to medium shrubs of other species (especially juniper and willows), and then to dwarf-shrub heath (ericoids). The upper limits of tall scrub (shrubs 1.5–5.0 m tall) may conveniently be taken as the boundary between the submontane and montane zones, though nowadays these limits are nearly everywhere potential rather than actual, and revealed mainly by scattered woody growth on cliff faces. On the predominantly acidic rocks and soils of the British mountains, the zone of dwarf-shrub heath consists largely of ling heather, decreasing gradually in stature with altitude, until at around 840 m (460 m or less in north-west Scotland) it exists as a dense wind-flattened carpet of prostrate ecotypes, and then gives way at about 900 m either to *Rhacomitrium lanuginosum* moss heath, lichen heath, or bare, stony erosion surface with the sparsest growth of plants, including especially *Juncus trifidus*.

This simple pattern of zonation determined by wind exposure, cloud cover and temperature is diversified by the separate yet interacting influences of varying snow cover and drainage. There is increasing modification of vegetation pattern in those topographic situations which favour the winter accumulation of snow and thus support long-lasting snow patches into the spring and summer. Within the zone of dwarf-shrub heath the first indications of longer than average snow cover are given by local replacement of heather heath by *Vaccinium myrtillus* or *Vaccinium–Empetrum hermaphroditum* heath. With increasing length of snow-lie, communities of monocotyledonous plants, chiefly *Nardus stricta*, sometimes with *Trichophorum cespitosum*, replace the snow-tolerant dwarf shrubs. Locally, especially on richer soils protected from grazing, there are communities of herbs and ferns. In the longest-lasting snow patch hollows, dominance of vascular plants gives way to dominance of bryophytes, though there is usually a sparse growth of montane grasses, sedges and herbs in these moss and liverwort carpets. At higher levels of the Scottish mountains, moderately chionophilous (snow-loving) communities are often the prevailing type of vegetation on all but strongly wind-exposed ground.

With increasing drainage impedance there is a gradual development of raw humus and then peat horizons in the soil, and increasing proportions of hygrophilous and peat-forming species in the vegetation. Dwarf shrubs, especially *Calluna*, usually remain abundant in the mire communities, but monocotyledonous vascular plants such as *Eriophorum vaginatum*, *E. angustifolium*, *Trichophorum cespitosum*, *Molinia caerulea* and *Narthecium ossifragum* are more characteristic, and on the wettest ground bog mosses (*Sphagnum* spp.) are dominant, forming a living surface to the peat. The blanket mires fed by rain water (ombrogenous) and covering badly drained ground in large expanses, grade into the peatland types of lowland such as raised mire, and in northern Scotland occupy vast areas of moorland at extremely low levels. Blanket mire is virtually an azonal type of vegetation, for it suppresses tree growth and thus occurs at all levels within the forest zone and at altitudes far above. Many flat-topped mountains are peat covered and blanket mire formation appears to cease only above 1070 m, where climatic severity inhibits its development. Extent of blanket mire is naturally dependent on wetness of climate, and on topography; it is thus most extensive where flat or gently sloping moorland prevails in the north and west of Britain (see also Chapter 8).

Wherever drainage water emerges at the ground surface, as springs, rills, streams or diffuse seepage areas (flushes), there is wetland vegetation of a specialised kind. These habitats are topographically determined, and occur at all levels on all uplands. Where water seepage is copious and extensive, there is an intermediate type of wetland between blanket mire and flush which is usually termed soligenous (or flush) mire and which has affinities with lowland fens. Flush mires typically show a peat horizon over gleyed mineral soil, and within the woodland zone they may be grown with alder, birch and willow as well as mire plants. *Sphagnum* spp. and hydrophilous vascular plants, especially Carices, may be dominant, but are species associated with moving rather than stagnant water. Flushes and springs typically have a saturated mineral soil mixed with varying amounts of humus, and they are often dominated by bryophyte carpets. Rills and streams are essentially small scale and linear open water habitats with fringing, island and submerged vegetation, but most of the hill examples fall into the eroding rather than the depositing types of moving water-body. Standing open water-bodies of all sizes, including pools or lochans in mire systems, corrie tarns, and large valley lakes, are well represented in many upland areas, but are nearly all characterised by base-poor waters.

On base-rich mountains there is, or was, the same general pattern of life-form zonation according to altitude, with local modification according to variation in snow cover and drainage, but the species differ from those of the acidic hills. Above the forest limits there was once a characteristic zone of medium willow scrub, passing at higher levels into growths of low willows and calcicolous dwarf shrubs, notably *Dryas octopetala* (most of the British montane willows are calcicolous, e.g. *Salix lanata*, *S. reticulata*, *S. arbuscula*, *S. myrsinites* and, to a lesser extent, *S. lapponum*). These woody plants are typically associated with a large number of herbs, varying in stature, but including tall species typical of the field layer of undisturbed submontane woodland, e.g. *Trollius europaeus*, *Geranium sylvaticum*, *Cirsium heterophyllum*, *Crepis paludosa*, *Geum rivale* and *Angelica sylvestris*. With increasing altitude, whether involving greater wind exposure or snow cover, these communities are replaced by others with a predominance of small montane herbs, including various grasses as well as numerous dwarf forbs, giving alpine meadows.

Ericoids may be abundant on basic soils, especially *Empetrum hermaphroditum*, *Arctostaphylos uva-ursi* and *Vaccinium uliginosum*, but *Calluna* is more limited in its occurrence. Nevertheless, within the altitudinal range of heather, there is a variety of species-rich *Calluna* heaths on base-rich brown earths soils in which this shrub is intimately associated with numerous basiphilous herbs and mosses. This is a northern and upland equivalent of the calcareous heaths of the lowland chalk and limestones of southern Britain. Although, in comparable situations, the montane communities of the basic soils tend to be richer in species (especially forbs) than their counterparts on the acidic soils, there is increasing similarity of vegetation towards the mountain summits regardless of parent material, for leaching becomes increasingly prevalent and base-rich soils correspondingly scarce. Blanket mires are an essentially acidophilous complex of vegetation, but soligenous mires, flushes, rills and streams show wide floristic variations according to base content of the drainage water, and those with high base-status typically have an abundance of hypnaceous 'brown mosses' instead of *Sphagnum* spp. Small, shallow tarns and pools within strongly calcareous catchments may have base rich waters, but on the whole this is a rare condition in the upland standing water-bodies.

On mountains in general, open, unstable habitats such as cliffs and broken slopes, screes and fell-field, solifluction ground, erosion features, flushes and rills, provide the habitat required by many small, competition-sensitive montane and submontane plants. Factors such as severe wind-blasting, prolonged snow cover and frost heaving are important in maintaining instability and incomplete vegetation cover, and as they tend to increase with altitude, so does the extent of bare ground. This upland flora of open habitats is, however, very much richer on the calcareous formations, compared with similar situations on acidic substrata. South of the Highlands this flora is best represented on cliff faces and their ungrazed ledges, notably on Y Wyddfa and the Glyder, the Helvellyn range and the Moffat Hills, but in Upper Teesdale a rich and unusual calcicolous flora occurs mainly in short limestone turf and calcareous flushes or mires. In the Highlands, the high-lying calcareous cliffs have a wealth of montane species, but many species here are less restricted to cliffs than in hill districts farther south, and high-lying slopes and stony summits are often rich in 'alpines'.

This is the general pattern of habitat and vegetation in the British uplands. In many districts the full altitudinal sequence has always been truncated since the Climatic Optimum by lack of really high land and even the highest mountains of Wales, England and the Southern Uplands lack the extent and diversity of montane vegetation found in the Highlands. Snow bed communities are poorly developed, *Juncus trifidus* heath is absent, and the montane flora is much fewer in species in these uplands south of the Highlands, so that much of their vegetation is submontane. Many of the lower moorlands lie within the present potential tree-limit, so that montane vegetation is entirely absent.

There is considerable original diversity within the Highlands, and within this region, the mountains with the greatest variety of vegetation are those with the greatest range of altitude and rock type, namely the Cairngorms and Breadalbane mountains. From their combination of continental cold winters, massive land forms and high elevation, the Cairngorms carry a greater extent of snow-influenced and acidophilous montane vegetation than any other mountain system. The mica-schist and limestone mountains of Breadalbane have the largest area of calcicolous montane vegetation, and the richest montane flora. In some districts, especially north of the Great Glen, the montane *Calluna* heaths are notably rich in other species of dwarf shrub. Bryophyte-rich or dominated communities are best developed in the oceanic west and lichen heaths in the continental east.

HUMAN INFLUENCE

Human impact has further diversified this originally complex pattern of upland vegetation. The general deforestation of the last 2000 years has caused a vast expansion of heather heath within the submontane zone, so that on many hills this community occurs in continuous sweeps from base to summit, and the change to montane Callunetum is marked imperceptibly by a slow alteration in growth form with altitude. Where heavy grazing by goats, cattle or sheep coincided with or followed forest clearance, and perhaps even without such grazing on the more base-rich soils, there was evidently a change from woodland to grassland rather than heather moor, and today there is perhaps an even greater extent of submontane grassland. Whether the original change was from forest to dwarf-shrub heath or to grassland, it is clear that the present distribution of these two contrasting derivatives of forest is the outcome largely of recent and present differences in land-use, often related in turn to variations in geology and soils.

Most of the British uplands are now managed for sheep, red grouse and red deer, either separately or in combination. Use for water catchment, afforestation and military training have also recently affected substantial areas. With the exception of Exmoor, Lakeland and Galloway, deer forests are confined to the Scottish Highlands. Grouse-moors are now mainly in the Pennines, Cheviots, parts of the Southern Uplands and the eastern Highlands. Sheep are kept almost universally over the British uplands, except on a few of the remoter Highland deer forests and grouse-moors, and on certain moorlands within State Forests. Moor-burning is nearly everywhere an integral part of the management regime; on grouse-moors it aims at maintaining a rotational system of heather communities of different age classes, but where large herbivore grazing is heavy it usually results (whether intentionally or not) in the gradual conversion of *Calluna* heath into *Festuca–Agrostis* grassland, often with abundance or even dominance of bracken, and sometimes with an intermediate *Vaccinium myrtillus* stage; on wetter ground the change is usually to dominance of *Nardus stricta*, *Juncus squarrosus*, *Trichophorum cespitosum*, *Molinia caerulea* or *Eriophorum vaginatum*. Within the montane zone, the dwarf *Calluna* heaths are even more readily converted to grassland by these influences, and even *Rhacomitrium* heath becomes replaced by grasses where sheep density is high. Locally, the depredations of heather beetle and horse-hair fungus may also be contributory factors in the decline of heather, and frost can be especially damaging when other adversities are operating already. Deforestation, moor-burning and heavy grazing have also caused substantial physical effects, especially soil erosion and scree formation on steep slopes; and the widespread degeneration and erosion of blanket bogs is thought to be connected with these influences.

Sheep-walks thus tend to be grassland dominated, but deer forests which are run with few or no sheep often have a high proportion of heather ground, as grazing is usually less heavy. In many upland districts, especially south of the Highlands, there is a continuing loss of *Calluna* heath and replacement by bilberry, grassland and bracken. This tendency is most pronounced on the richer rocks and soils, which are selectively grazed in preference to ground of low fertility where grazing pressure often remains light. Many of the large remaining areas of heather moor are on uplands formed of predominantly acidic rock, whereas nearly all the hills with extensive occurrences of basic rock have a prevalence of grasslands within the submontane zone. The conversion of dwarf-shrub heath to monocotyledonous vegetation is more marked in the west than the east, partly because the wetter climate of the west gives the grasses and grass-allies a competitive advantage over the woody species, and partly because the combination of more suitable terrain and climate in the east has favoured grouse and their management.

Removal of grazing may be followed by some degree of reversal of these changes. Where grazed remnants of dwarf shrubs persist in grasslands, they recover and may regain dominance, but where they have been eradicated, the grassland may persist as a fairly stable community for a considerable time, though with some readjustment between the herbaceous species. There may be a slow invasion by tree seedlings, especially of birch and rowan, but the lack of a good seed source nearby and the luxuriance of the ungrazed vegetation, can make the natural restoration of a woodland cover a slow process.

The overall result of human exploitation has been to produce a large total extent of submontane grassland and heath, and in areas where these effects have spread into the montane zone, virtually all the hill vegetation, up to the highest summits, is in a modified condition. This is true of Snowdonia and Lakeland, where grasslands predominate and heather heath is found mainly on the most acidic or rugged mountains; almost the only natural vegetation is on ungrazed cliff faces and ledges, and some of the original communities of base-rich soils (notably tall-herb meadows) survive here as mere fragments. Many of the uplands of England, Wales and southern Scotland are, in fact, rather uninteresting in their vegetation and flora, and are characterised by large areas of relatively uniform communities, poor in species, and showing little difference from one massif to the next. One could argue that the only mountains of real importance to nature conservation in Britain are in the Highlands, and that those of other regions are insignificant by comparison. However, while the Highlands must take precedence, some of the mountain systems farther south are sufficiently different and interesting in their own right to have national importance (notably the northern Pennines); and though many of these southern hills are botanically dull (especially the sheep-walks), their fauna is often of considerable interest.

Even within the Highlands, many of the original communities of base-rich soils survive only as fragments in ungrazed situation, such as inaccessible cliff ledges. The calcareous mountains have all been heavily grazed by deer and sheep, and vegetation such as montane willow scrub, *Dryas* heath and growths of tall forbs has mostly been converted to species-rich grassland. The full altitudinal sequence described on p. 290 cannot be seen in Britain today, though its former widespread distribution can be clearly inferred from the fragmentary occurrence of the various communities, and by reference to the mountains of Scandinavia, where this kind of zonation is so characteristic. Probably the most acidic mountains of the Highlands, and

in particular the Cairngorms, have the least modified vegetation; within the montane zone here, the extremely low fertility of soils has discouraged heavy grazing, and there is probably a relatively large extent of more or less natural vegetation. However, some of the thin, peaty soils and their communities on acidic mountains in the western Highlands are extremely fragile, and in many instances it is apparent that a single fire has completely destroyed large areas of dwarf-juniper scrub and caused irreversible, adverse changes in the physical and chemical properties of the soils. Even under the most favourable conditions, conservation measures are unlikely to produce any rapid restoration of the original ecosystems.

VEGETATION TYPES

The range of ecological variation outlined above is analysed and classified more fully, in terms of a hierarchical system of vegetation units, in the phytosociological treatment of British uplands which follow. This is based on the classification given by McVean & Ratcliffe (1962), simplified, but also extended in part to take account of mountain regions south of the Highlands. Chapter 8 should be consulted for a fuller account of the blanket mire complex, while Chapter 7 gives detailed treatment of upland lakes and rivers. Further details of the geographical differentiation of upland vegetation are also given on pp. 312–25.

CLASSIFICATION OF UPLAND VEGETATION TYPES

SUBMONTANE GRASSLANDS AND HEATHS

Essentially anthropogenic communities derived from forest and tall scrub, and therefore lying within the potential altitudinal limits of these life forms. Prone to fairly rapid change if the management regime alters.

Dwarf-shrub heaths

Acidic

(i) *Ulex gallii* heath
Calluna vulgaris is often co-dominant, and there are other transitions to acidic grassland. Widespread in south-western uplands, especially in south-west England and Wales.

(ii) *Calluna vulgaris* heath
Includes seral stages after burning, which locally have dominance of *Erica cinerea*, *E. tetralix* or *Vaccinium myrtillus*. In some areas *Genista anglica* is a characteristic species. Widespread and especially extensive on eastern grouse-moors. In the western Highlands, includes an open community on moraines, transitional to wet heath, with sparse *Molinia*, *Trichophorum*, *Rhacomitrium lanuginosum*, *Antennaria dioica* and *Lycopodium selago*.

(iii) *Vaccinium myrtillus* heath
Often derived from *Calluna* heath, and similar to woodland *Vaccinium* communities. Widespread and often extensive in England, Wales, the Southern Uplands and southern Highlands; very local further north.

(iv) *Vaccinium vitis-idaea* heath
Grades into (iii) above. Local, but especially well developed

in the Peak District and certain moorlands in north Wales.

(v) *Empetrum nigrum* heath

Usually mixed with other heaths and grasslands. Very local, mainly in the Peak District and south Wales.

(vi) *Arctostaphylos uva-ursi* heath

Most commonly co-dominant with *Calluna vulgaris*. Virtually confined to the Scottish Highlands and there found mainly in the eastern half.

Types (ii) and (iii) above, in particular, often have a ground carpet of the common woodland and heath mosses, such as *Hypnum cupressiforme, Pleurozium schreberi, Rhytidiadelphus loreus, R. squarrosus, Hylocomium splendens, Plagiothecium undulatum, Dicranum scoparium, D. majus, Polytrichum commune* and *Mnium hornum*. On dry ground, during regeneration after burning, or beneath dense, younger growths of *Calluna*, this moss cover may be much reduced. Conversely, in damp ground, and steep but shaded aspects, it is often richer in liverworts such as *Barbilophozia floerkii, Lophozia ventricosa, Diplophyllum albicans, Lophocolea bidentata* and *Calypogeia muellerana*: and there may be variable replacement by *Sphagnum* spp. such as *S. nemoreum, S. quinquefarium, S. russowii* and *S. girgensohnii*.

Basic

On moderately base-rich soils, most of the above heath types have counterparts in which the dwarf shrubs are associated with a variety of grasses and forbs characteristic of the corresponding grasslands, to which they are converted by heavy grazing and burning. These herb-rich, dwarf-shrub heaths are all very local and found mainly on the calcareous rock formations; the *Calluna* type is the most widespread and extensive, and the others are mainly fragmentary, in scattered localities. The only approach to a calcicolous submontane dwarf-shrub heath yet found is a community rich in *Helianthemum chamaecistus* and *Arctostaphylos uva-ursi* on Dalradian 'sugar' limestone in Perthshire.

Grasslands

Acidic

(i) *Festuca ovina–Agrostis canina–A. tenuis* grassland

This includes examples rich in *Deschampsia flexuosa*. *Festuca* is usually dominant in more southerly regions, but *Agrostis* spp. often have a higher cover in the Highlands. Depauperate *Vaccinium myrtillus* is often present, and *Galium saxatile* and *Potentilla erecta* are constant. Widespread, but extensive mainly to the south of the Highlands, and on sheep-walks.

(ii) *Nardus stricta* grassland

Grades into (i) but typically on damper soils. Extensive in Wales, northern England, Southern Uplands and the southern Highlands, where it grades into snow-bed *Nardus* communities at higher levels.

(iii) *Juncus squarrosus* 'grassland'

Grades into (ii) but typically on still wetter soils. Locally extensive in Wales, northern England, Southern Uplands

and widespread in smaller stands in the Highlands, especially the west.

(iv) *Molinia caerulea* grassland

Grades into *Calluna–Molinia* wet heath. Widespread and often extensive in the west (Dartmoor, central and south Wales, Galloway, western Highlands) but less so in the east.

Basic

(i) Forb-rich grassland with mixed dominance of grass species (*Festuca ovina, F. rubra, Agrostis* spp., *Anthoxanthum odoratum, Sieglingia decumbens, Cynosurus cristatus*) and species such as *Plantago lanceolata, Achillea millefolium, Lotus corniculatus* and *Trifolium repens*. On limestone and other calcareous soils, the number of species increases, e.g. grasses such as *Briza media, Koeleria cristata, Helictotrichon pratense*; and a much larger variety of forbs. This grades into lowland calcareous grassland. Species-rich *Festuca–Agrostis* grasslands are widespread on basic rocks and extensive on the calcareous formations, especially Carboniferous Limestone.

(ii)–(iv) Forb-rich examples of *Nardus, Juncus squarrosus* and *Molinia* grasslands occur on basic soils; the first two are local, but extensive in the Breadalbane mountains of Perthshire, while rich *Molinia* grasslands are more widespread, especially along the west Highland coast.

(v) *Deschampsia cespitosa* grassland

Some stands are rich in forbs. Local and not usually extensive, mainly on damp, clayey soils, tending towards acidic.

(vi) *Luzula sylvatica* 'grassland'

Local and usually in fairly small stands. Mainly on low hills along the seaboard of the western Highlands and islands, but also in scattered localities inland, e.g. Ben Loyal and parts of the Southern Uplands. Soils basic to acidic.

(vii) *Sesleria albicans* grassland

Confined to Carboniferous Limestone in the Pennines, but there locally extensive.

Fern and tall-forb communities

Acidic

(i) *Pteridium aquilinum* dominant

This is typically *Festuca–Agrostis* grassland invaded by *Pteridium* in varying density, the extreme condition being total dominance of bracken. It is widespread and extensive, especially to the south of the Highlands, and grades into woodland Pteridietum. There are transitions also to *Calluna* heath.

(ii) *Thelypteris oreopteris*

This also is typically *Festuca–Agrostis* grassland invaded by the fern. Stands are much smaller and more local, but this is a fairly widespread community, at least in fragmentary form.

(iii) *Cryptogramma crispa* on scree

This is an essentially open community. Sometimes seral to *Festuca–Agrostis* grassland, but perhaps more often represents an 'arrested' successional stage. Widespread in north Wales, northern England and parts of the Southern Uplands.

Basic

(i) *Pteridium aquilinum* communities are sometimes associated with the more species-rich types of *Festuca–Agrostis* grassland on basic soils, including limestone. This is a widespread type of bracken community, but less extensive than those on acidic soils.

(ii) Mixed medium–tall forbs, grasses and ferns are characteristic of ungrazed situations with basic soils, mainly on the bigger cliff ledges or on islands of mountain lakes. There are usually many species, but among the most constant are *Angelica sylvestris, Filipendula ulmaria, Succisa pratensis, Solidago virgaurea, Rumex acetosa, Silene dioica, Geum rivale, Luzula sylvatica, Deschampsia cespitosa, Athyrium filix-femina* and *Dryopteris filix-mas.* There are often characteristic northern and submontane species such as *Trollius europaeus, Geranium sylvaticum, Cirsium heterophyllum, Galium boreale* and *Crepis paludosa.* Such communities are virtually identical with those found in the less modified northern hay meadows and on river banks, and they were probably once widespread in submontane woodlands on richer soils. They are widespread in Britain but fragmentary. Heavy grazing usually converts them to species rich *Festuca–Agrostis* grassland, in which grazed-down rosettes of some of the taller forbs persist.

MONTANE GRASSLANDS AND HEATHS

Dwarf-shrub heaths

Acidic

(i) Montane *Calluna vulgaris* heath
Contains species such as *Rubus chamaemorus, Empetrum hermaphroditum, Arctostaphylos uva-ursi* and *Vaccinium uliginosum.* It is widespread and often extensive in the Highlands, but only fragmentary farther south. There is often an abundance of mosses and a western Highland facies on damp, shady slopes has a carpet of large, leafy liverworts such as *Herberta hutchinsiae* and *Pleurozia purpurea.*

(ii) Prostrate *Calluna vulgaris* heath
The flattened carpet on windswept ground as *Calluna* approaches its altitudinal limits. Widespread and often quite extensive in the Highlands but only fragmentary farther south. Within the Highlands, several facies can be distinguished. The typical community is dominated by *Calluna,* with *Empetrum hermaphroditum* and sometimes *Loiseleuria procumbens, Arctostaphylos uva-ursi* and *Salix herbacea* but is usually rather poor in species. In the western Highlands this is often replaced by one in which *Rhacomitrium lanuginosum* is co-dominant; in the east there is often a high cover of reindeer moss (*Cladonia sylvatica* group) lichens, giving lichen heath. North of the Great Glen, *Calluna* is more frequently accompanied by other prostrate dwarf shrubs, especially *Arctous alpina* and *Juniperus communis* spp. *nana* as well as those named above. A fire-sensitive dwarf *Juniperus–Calluna* community now survives only on a few scattered quartzite mountains in this region.

(iii) *Empetrum hermaphroditum–Vaccinium* spp. heath
Replaces *Calluna* heath with increasing snow cover and altitude. All three *Vaccinium* spp. occur though *V. myrtillus*

generally has the highest cover. Western *Rhacomitrium*-rich and eastern lichen heath facies may also be distinguished from the typical community, rich in hypnaceous mosses. Widespread in the Highlands, but only fragments occur farther south, in the Moffat Hills and Snowdonia.

(iv) *Vaccinium myrtillus* late snow-bed heath
Related to the previous, but restricted to areas of prolonged snow cover. *Empetrum hermaphroditum* has lower cover, but other montane spp., e.g. *Vaccinium uliginosum, Chamaepericlymenum suecicum* and *Lycopodium annotinum* are often present. Widespread in the eastern Highlands, but replaced by a mixed type with much *Nardus stricta, Rhacomitrium lanuginosum* and *Empetrum* in the west. Reaches the Southern Uplands and northern England but very local there.

Basic

Basiphilous montane dwarf-shrub heath of any kind is extremely local and mainly fragmentary.

The main types are:

(i) Low willow scrub, mostly of *Salix lapponum, S. myrsinites* or *S. arbuscula,* occasionally with *S. lanata.* Found mainly on cliff ledges or rocky slopes and stream sides, and confined to the Scottish Highlands. Mostly converted to grassland in grazing situations.

(ii) *Dryas octopetala* heath occurs as fragments in the Pennines, but mainly in the Highlands, and the most extensive occurrences are on blown shell sand and Durness Limestone in the far north-west. *Salix reticulata* is very locally present on high mountains in the Highlands.

(iii) There are fragmentary and very scattered occurrences of species-rich montane *Calluna* and *Vaccinium–Empetrum* heath in the Highlands.

Grasslands

Acidic

(i) Montane *Festuca vivipara–Agrostis canina* grassland
A derivative of montane dwarf-shrub heath in the southern mountains and often species poor. In the Highlands *Alchemilla alpina* is often present, along with other montane species, in a more natural community, and has transitional types with much *Vaccinium* spp., *Rhacomitrium lanuginosum* or reindeer moss lichens. Widespread and locally extensive.

(ii) Montane *Nardus stricta* grasslands
Associated with prolonged snow cover, occurring extensively in the Highlands but only as fragments farther south. Various facies, with abundance of *Trichophorum cespitosum, Rhacomitrium lanuginosum* or hypnaceous mosses. An extreme form with few species other than montane lichens occurs on the high plateaux of the Cairngorms.

(iii) Montane *Juncus squarrosus* communities
Probably also associated with prolonged snow cover. Species poor, but contain *Carex bigelowii,* and widespread in western mountains as far south as Wales.

(iv) *Deschampsia cespitosa* grassland
Confined to the corries and high slopes of the Scottish Highlands but widespread and often extensive there. Associated with moderately prolonged snow cover and may often

be derived by grazing from communities in which forbs or ferns were dominant.

(v) *Carex bigelowii* communities

This sedge is dominant, but there may be a high cover of *Dicranum fuscescens*, *Polytrichum alpinum* or lichens. Confined to the central and eastern Highlands, but locally extensive there.

(vi) *Juncus trifidus* communities

Best developed *Juncus trifidus* heaths on coarse granite and quartzite soils on plateaux at well over 900 m in the central Highlands. Dense *Juncus* tussocks are associated with *Rhacomitrium lanuginosum* or crustaceous lichens, but vegetation cover is usually patchy. In the western Highlands, *J. trifidus* is a characteristic species of still more open communities of high-level ablation surfaces.

Basic

(i) Forb-rich *Festuca–Agrostis* grassland with montane species such as *Polygonum viviparum*, *Saxifraga hypnoides*, *Potentilla crantzii* and *Carex capillaris*. A Pennine limestone facies contains *Sesleria albicans*, *Gentiana verna* and *Myosotis alpestris*. A widespread and locally extensive type on calcareous mountains.

(ii)–(iv) Forb-rich facies of montane *Nardus*, *Juncus squarrosus* and *Deschampsia cespitosa* grasslands occur locally on calcareous mountains in the Highlands, and fragments of the first two are found farther south.

Tall-herb and fern communities

Acidic

(i) *Athyrium alpestre–Cryptogramma crispa* fern communities

Confined to the Highlands, in high corries where snow lies late. Other ferns such as *Dryopteris abbreviata* and *D. assimilis* sometimes present.

(ii) *Luzula sylvatica* ledge communities with montane species such as *Athyrium alpestre*, *Salix lapponum*, *Vaccinium uliginosum*, *Chamaepericlymenum suecicum* and, very locally, *Cicerbita alpina*. These occur mainly in the Highlands.

Basic

(i) Montane facies of the mixed medium to tall-forb–grass–fern communities of cliff ledges are similar to those at lower levels, but more constantly contain montane species such as *Sedum rosea*, *Oxyria digyna*, *Saussurea alpina* and *Cochlearia officinalis* ssp. *alpina*. Widespread in the Highlands but very local farther south; and in the Breadalbane mountains, species such as montane willows, *Pyrola rotundifolia*, *Carex atrata*, *Helictotrichon pratense* and *Polystichum lonchitis* often occur.

Dwarf-forb communities

These intergrade with grassland and are usually in grazed situations, though actual grazing intensity is often low.

Acidic

(i) *Alchemilla alpina* communities on fairly base-poor soils

Thymus drucei is often abundant. Confined to Lakeland and the Highlands.

(ii) *Sibbaldia procumbens* communities

Found mainly in situations with prolonged snow cover and confined to the Highlands. *Gnaphalium supinum* is often abundant and may occasionally be dominant.

Basic

(i) *Alchemilla vulgaris* communities

One or more micro-species of this aggregate taxon (generally *A. vestita*, *A. filicaulis* or *A. xanthochlora*) are abundant, with other montane species. Found widely but usually as fragments, mainly in the Highlands.

(ii) *Silene acaulis–Cherleria sedoides* communities

Rich in montane species. Confined to the Highlands, and found especially on the higher levels of calcareous mountains, where snow lies late.

(iii) *Saxifraga* communities

Mainly of *S. aizoides*, *S. hypnoides* or *S. oppositifolia* on steep, rocky banks on calcareous mountains. Small in area but widespread, especially in the Highlands.

Bryophyte heaths

Acidic

(i) *Rhacomitrium lanuginosum* heath

A widespread summit community from north Wales northwards, typically with *Carex bigelowii* and *Salix herbacea*. On sheep-grazed mountains south of the Highlands a facies with abundant *Festuca vivipara* is usually present, whilst north of the Great Glen, the *Rhacomitrium* heaths often have an abundance of cushion herbs, e.g. *Silene acaulis*, *Cherleria sedoides* and *Armeria maritima*.

(ii) *Rhytidiadelphus loreus* heath

This species is accompanied by other pleurocarpous mosses and dwarfed *Deschampsia cespitosa* in areas of late snow-lie in the northern and western Highlands.

(iii) *Dicranum starkei* heath

This moss becomes abundant in situations where snow cover is longest, but the areas involved are small in Britain. Two main facies: (*a*) species of *Rhacomitrium* (other than *R. lanuginosum*) have a high cover, and (*b*) *Polytrichum norvegicum* is abundant. Both confined to high mountains in the Highlands. Gradations to *Alchemilla–Sibbaldia* communities are frequent.

(iv) *Gymnomitrium–Salix herbacea* heath

An hepatic crust on soils at high elevations, both on windswept ground and where snow lies late, in the Highlands only.

(v) On high rocks, earthy banks and gullies, there are often very heterogeneous bryophyte communities containing many species more or less restricted to ground with late snow cover. These intergrade with spring and flush communities in other habitats.

Basic

(i)–(ii) Species-rich facies of both *Rhacomitrium lanuginosum* and *Rhytidiadelphus loreus* heaths occur very locally in the Highlands.

PEATLANDS: (See also Chapter 8.)

Blanket mire and wet heath

Trichophorum cespitosum–Eriophorum vaginatum
(i) Vascular plants dominant.
(ii) *Sphagnum* cover high, vascular plants reduced.
(iii) Hummock–hollow surface pattern (hollows either *Sphagnum*-grown or water-filled and mainly bare).
(iv) *Rhacomitrium lanuginosum* cover high.
(v) Lichen cover high.

Calluna vulgaris–Trichophorum cespitosum
(i) Vascular plants dominant.
(ii) *Sphagnum* cover high.
(iii) *Rhacomitrium lanuginosum* cover high.
(iv) Lichen cover high.
(v) *Trichophorum* dominant, *Calluna* sparse or absent.

Calluna vulgaris–Molinia caerulea
(i) Vascular plants dominant.
(ii) *Sphagnum* cover high.

Calluna vulgaris–Eriophorum vaginatum
(i) Vascular plants dominant.
(ii) *Sphagnum* cover high.
(iii) Hummock–hollow surface pattern (hollows either *Sphagnum*-grown or water-filled and mainly bare).
(iv) *Rhacomitrium lanuginosum* cover high.
(v) Lichen cover high.
(vi) *Eriophorum* dominant, *Calluna* sparse or absent.
(vii) *Empetrum nigrum* replacing *Calluna*.
(viii) Montane dwarf shrubs present (*Betula nana, Arctous alpina, Arctostaphylos uva-ursi, Vaccinium uliginosum*).
(ix) *Empetrum hermaphroditum* replacing *Calluna*.

Juncus squarrosus
(i) Typical.
(ii) *Sphagnum*-rich.

Some facies of these blanket mire associations occur over a wide range of altitude, but *Trichophorum cespitosum–Eriophorum vaginatum* is largely submontane, and only (viii) and (ix) under *Calluna vulgaris–Eriophorum vaginatum* are distinctively montane.

Soligenous mire

The floristics and distribution of the various types are discussed more fully in Chapter 8.

Acidic
(i) *Molinia caerulea–Myrica gale*
Myrica is sometimes absent, especially in eastern districts. *Sphagnum* cover may be high.
(ii) *Erica tetralix*
Facies rich in *Sphagnum, Carex* spp. or *Trichophorum* occur.
(iii) *Juncus effusus–Sphagnum recurvum*
Polytrichum commune can replace *Sphagnum* in some examples.
(iv) *Juncus acutiflorus–Sphagnum* spp.
Some examples have much *Myrica*.
(v) *Juncus squarrosus–Sphagnum* spp.
Intergrades with *Juncus squarrosus* blanket mire.
(vi) *Carex rostrata–Sphagnum recurvum*

(vii) *Carex echinata–C. nigra–Sphagnum* spp.
(viii) *Carex curta–Sphagnum* spp.
(ix) *Carex aquatilis–C. rariflora*

Basic
(i) *Juncus acutiflorus–Acrocladium cuspidatum*
Often herb-rich or with basiphilous *Sphagnum* spp. A western, coastal facies widespread in the Highlands is dominated by *Juncus acutiflorus × articulatus*.
(ii) *Myrica gale*
Basiphilous species.
(iii) *Carex rostrata*
Distinctive facies with a bryophyte layer either of basiphilous *Sphagnum* spp. or 'brown mosses' occur.
(iv) *Carex nigra–C. panicea*
Basiphilous *Sphagnum* or 'brown moss' facies occur.
(v) *Carex panicea–C. hostiana–C. flava* agg.
'Brown mosses' and numerous herbs usually present.
(vi) *Eleocharis quinqueflora*
(vii) *Schoenus nigricans*
(viii) *Kobresia simpliciuscula*
(ix) *Carex saxatilis*

Some of these soligenous mire associations are mainly submontane (Acidic, (i)–(iv); Basic, (i), (ii) and (vii)) but others occur over a wide range of altitude and show montane facies. Only Acidic, (ix), and Basic, (viii) and (ix), are exclusively montane.

Spring and flush vegetation

Acidic
(i) *Sphagnum recurvum*
(ii) *S. auriculatum*
A *Campylopus atrovirens* facies occurs in western districts.
(iii) *Philonotis fontana–Saxifraga stellaris*
A variety of bryophytes are present and may assume dominance – *Scapania undulata, S. uliginosa, Dicranella squarrosa, Drepanocladus exannulatus* and *Bryum weigelii*.
(iv) *Anthelia julacea–A. juratzkana*
(v) *Pohlia albicans* var. *glacialis*, sometimes *P. ludwigii*

Basic
(i) *Cratoneuron commutatum* springs
(ii) Other 'brown moss' flushes with small herbs, e.g. *Sedum villosum, Thalictrum alpinum, Saxifraga hirculus*
(iii) Open *Carex demissa–Saxifraga aizoides* flushes. High-altitude examples are rich in montane species, e.g. *Saxifraga oppositifolia, Juncus triglumis, Acroladium trifarium, Meesia uliginosa*.

Flora

The British upland flora may be divided into the following four ecological/geographical groups:
1. Montane (alpine), occurring more plentifully above the tree limit than below, and with a markedly northern distribution.
2. Submontane (subalpine), occurring more plentifully or vigorously below the tree limit (some species often within woods) than above, and with a markedly northern distribution.

298 Upland grasslands and heaths

Table 27. *Habitat and distribution of montane vascular plants*

	High montane	Dry	Moist	Wet	Acidic	Medium base	Calcareous	Special	Open	S.W. England	S. Wales	N. Wales	Midlands	N. England	S. Scotland	E. Highlands	W. Highlands	Rare species	European distribution
	1	2	3	4	5	6	7	8	9	10	11	12	13	14	15	16	17	18	19
[a]*Lycopodium selago*	—	+	+	—	+	—	—	—	—	+	+	+	+	+	+	+	+	—	NM
L. annotinum	—	+	+	—	+	—	—	—	—	—	—	—	—	+	—	+	+	—	NM
L. alpinum	—	+	—	—	+	—	—	—	—	+	+	+	+	+	+	+	+	—	NM
[a]*Cryptogramma crispa*	—	+	—	—	+	—	—	—	+	+	+	+	+	+	+	+	+	—	NM
[a]*Asplenium viride*	—	+	—	—	—	—	+	—	—	—	+	+	+	+	+	+	+	—	AA
Athyrium alpestre	+	+	+	—	+	+	—	—	—	—	—	—	—	—	—	+	+	—	AA
Cystopteris montana	+	+	+	—	—	—	+	—	—	—	—	—	—	+	—	+	+	+	AA
Woodsia ilvensis	—	+	—	—	—	+	—	—	—	—	—	+	—	+	+	+	—	+	NM
W. alpina	+	+	—	—	—	—	—	—	—	—	—	—	—	—	—	+	+	+	AA
[a]*Dryopteris abbreviata*	—	+	—	—	+	—	—	—	—	+	+	+	—	+	+	+	+	—	NM
Polystichum lonchitis	—	+	—	—	—	+	+	—	—	—	—	—	—	+	+	+	+	—	AA
Juniperis communis ssp. *nana*	—	+	+	—	+	+	—	—	—	—	—	—	—	+	+	+	+	—	NM
Thalictrum alpinum	—	+	+	+	—	+	+	—	—	—	—	—	—	+	+	+	+	—	AA
Thlaspi alpestre	—	+	—	—	—	+	+	+	—	+	+	+	+	+	—	—	—	—	A
Cochlearia officinalis ssp. *alpina*	—	+	+	+	+	+	+	—	—	—	—	+	+	+	+	+	+	—	AA
Draba norvegica	+	+	—	—	—	+	+	—	—	—	—	—	—	—	—	+	+	+	AS
D. incana	—	+	—	—	—	+	+	—	—	—	—	+	+	+	—	+	+	—	AA
Cardaminopsis petraea	—	+	—	—	+	+	—	?	+	—	—	+	—	—	—	+	+	—	AA
Arabis alpina	+	+	—	—	—	—	—	—	—	—	—	—	—	—	—	—	+	+	AA
[a]*Viola rupestris*	—	+	—	—	—	+	—	—	+	—	—	—	+	—	—	—	—	+	NM
[a]*Polygala amara*	—	+	—	—	—	+	—	—	+	—	—	—	+	—	—	—	—	+	CN
Silene acaulis	—	+	—	—	+	+	+	—	—	—	—	+	—	+	—	+	+	—	AA
Lychnis alpina	+	+	—	—	—	—	—	+	—	+	—	—	—	+	—	+	—	+	AA
Cerastium cerastoides	+	—	+	+	—	+	+	—	—	—	—	—	—	—	—	+	+	—	AA
C. alpinum	+	+	+	—	—	+	+	—	+	—	—	+	—	+	+	+	+	—	AA
C. arcticum	+	+	+	—	+	+	+	—	+	—	—	+	—	—	—	+	+	—	AS
C. nigrescens	—	+	—	—	—	—	—	+	—	—	—	—	—	—	—	+	+	+	AS
Sagina saginoides	+	+	—	—	+	+	+	—	+	—	—	—	—	—	—	+	+	—	AA
S. normaniana	+	—	+	+	—	+	+	—	+	—	—	—	—	—	—	+	—	+	AA
S. intermedia	+	+	—	—	—	+	—	—	+	—	—	—	—	—	—	+	—	+	AS
Minuartia verna	—	+	—	—	—	+	+	+	+	+	—	+	+	+	+	—	—	—	AA
[a]*M. stricta*	—	—	+	+	—	+	—	—	+	—	—	—	+	—	—	—	—	+	AA
M. rubella	+	+	—	—	—	+	—	—	+	—	—	—	—	—	—	+	—	+	AS
Cherleria sedoides	—	+	+	—	+	+	+	—	—	—	—	—	—	—	—	+	+	—	A
Arenaria norvegica ssp. *norvegica*	—	+	+	—	—	+	—	+	+	—	—	—	—	—	—	+	+	+	AS
Astragalus alpinus	+	+	—	—	—	+	—	+	—	—	—	—	—	—	—	+	—	+	AA
Oxytropis campestris	—	+	—	—	—	+	—	+	—	—	—	—	—	—	—	+	+	+	AA
Rubus chamaemorus	—	—	+	+	+	—	—	—	—	—	—	+	+	+	+	+	+	—	AS
[a]*Potentilla fruticosa*	—	+	+	—	—	+	+	—	—	—	—	—	—	+	—	—	—	+	NM
P. crantzii	—	+	—	—	—	+	+	—	—	—	—	+	—	+	+	+	+	—	AA
Sibbaldia procumbens	+	+	+	—	+	+	+	—	—	—	—	—	—	+	—	+	+	—	AA
Dryas octopetala	—	+	—	—	—	—	+	+	—	—	—	—	—	+	—	+	+	—	AA
Alchemilla alpina	—	+	+	—	+	+	+	—	—	—	—	—	—	+	—	+	+	—	AA
Sedum rosea	—	+	+	—	—	+	+	—	—	—	+	+	—	+	+	+	+	—	AA
S. villosum	—	—	+	+	—	+	—	—	+	—	—	—	—	+	+	+	—	—	CN
Saxifraga nivalis	—	+	—	—	—	+	+	—	+	—	—	—	—	+	+	+	+	—	AA
S. stellaris	—	+	+	+	—	+	+	—	+	—	—	+	—	+	+	+	+	—	AA
[a]*S. hirculus*	—	—	+	—	+	+	—	—	—	—	—	—	—	+	+	+	+	+	AA
S. cernua	+	+	—	—	—	+	—	—	+	—	—	—	—	—	—	+	+	+	AA
S. rivularis	+	+	+	—	+	+	—	—	+	—	—	—	—	—	—	+	+	+	AS

Table 27 (*contd.*)

	1	2	3	4	5	6	7	8	9	10	11	12	13	14	15	16	17	18	19
S. cespitosa	+	+	−	−	−	−	+	−	+	−	−	+	−	−	−	+	+	+	AS
S. hypnoides	−	+	+	+	−	+	+	−	+	+	+	+	+	+	+	+	+	−	NM
S. aizoides	−	+	+	+	−	+	+	−	+	−	−	−	−	+	+	+	+	−	AA
S. oppositifolia	−	+	+	+	−	+	+	−	+	−	+	+	−	+	+	+	+	−	AA
Epilobium anagallidifolium	−	−	+	+	+	+	−	−	+	−	−	+	−	+	+	+	+	−	AA
ªE. alsinifolium	−	−	+	+	−	+	−	−	+	−	−	+	−	+	+	+	+	−	AA
Chamaepericlymenum suecicum	−	+	+	−	+	−	−	−	−	−	−	−	−	+	+	+	+	−	AS
Polygonum viviparum	−	+	+	+	−	+	+	−	−	−	−	+	−	+	+	+	+	−	AA
Koenigia islandica	+	+	+	+	−	+	−	−	+	−	−	−	−	−	−	−	+	+	AS
Oxyria digyna	−	+	+	−	−	+	+	−	−	−	−	+	−	+	+	+	+	−	AA
Betula nana	−	−	+	+	+	−	−	−	−	−	−	−	−	−	−	+	+	−	AA
Salix lapponum	+	+	+	−	−	+	+	−	−	−	−	−	−	+	+	+	+	−	AA
S. lanata	+	+	+	−	−	+	+	−	−	−	−	−	−	−	−	+	+	+	AS
Salix arbuscula	+	+	+	−	−	+	+	−	−	−	−	−	−	−	−	+	+	+	AA
S. myrsinites	−	+	+	−	−	+	+	−	−	−	−	−	−	−	+	+	+	+	AA
S. reticulata	+	+	−	−	−	−	+	−	−	−	−	−	−	−	−	+	+	+	AA
S. herbacea	−	+	+	−	+	+	−	−	+	−	−	+	−	+	+	+	+	−	AA
Loiseleuria procumbens	+	+	−	−	−	+	−	−	−	−	−	−	−	−	−	+	+	−	AA
Phyllodoce caerulea	+	+	−	−	−	+	−	−	−	−	−	−	−	−	−	+	+	+	AA
Arctostaphylos uva-ursi	−	+	+	−	+	+	+	−	−	−	−	−	+	+	+	+	+	−	AA
Arctous alpinus	−	+	+	−	+	−	−	−	−	−	−	−	−	−	−	+	+	−	AA
Vaccinium uliginosum	−	+	+	+	+	+	+	−	−	−	−	−	−	+	+	+	+	−	NM
V. microcarpum	−	−	+	+	+	−	−	−	−	−	−	−	−	−	−	+	+	−	NM
Diapensia lapponica	+	+	−	−	+	−	−	−	+	−	−	−	−	−	−	−	+	+	AS
Empetrum hermaphroditum	−	+	+	−	+	+	+	−	−	−	+	−	−	+	+	+	+	−	AA
ªGentiana verna	−	+	−	−	−	−	+	−	+	−	−	−	−	+	−	−	−	+	A
G. nivalis	+	+	−	−	−	+	+	−	+	−	−	−	−	−	−	+	−	+	AA
Myosotis alpestris	+	+	−	−	−	+	+	−	+	−	−	−	−	+	−	+	−	+	AA
Veronica fruticans	+	+	−	−	−	+	+	−	+	−	−	−	−	−	−	+	+	+	AA
V. alpina	+	+	+	+	−	+	+	−	+	−	−	−	−	−	−	+	+	+	AA
Bartsia alpina	−	+	+	−	−	+	+	−	−	−	−	−	−	+	−	+	−	+	AA
Homogyne alpina	−	−	+	−	−	−	+	−	−	−	−	−	−	−	−	+	−	+	A
Gnaphalium norvegicum	+	+	+	−	+	+	−	−	−	−	−	−	−	−	−	+	+	+	AA
G. supinum	−	+	−	−	+	−	−	−	−	−	−	−	−	−	−	+	+	−	AA
Erigeron borealis	+	+	−	−	−	−	+	−	−	−	−	−	−	−	−	+	−	+	AS
Artemisia norvegica	+	+	−	−	+	+	−	−	−	−	−	−	−	−	−	−	+	+	AS
Saussurea alpina	−	+	+	−	+	+	+	−	−	−	+	−	+	+	+	+	−	AA
Cicerbita alpina	+	+	+	−	−	+	+	−	−	−	−	−	−	−	−	+	−	+	AA
Tofieldia pusilla	−	+	+	+	−	+	+	−	−	−	−	−	−	+	+	+	+	−	AA
Lloydia serotina	+	+	−	−	−	+	+	−	+	−	−	+	−	−	−	−	+	−	AA
Juncus trifidus	+	+	−	−	+	+	−	+	+	−	−	−	−	+	+	+	+	+	NM
ªJ. alpino-articulatus	−	−	+	+	−	+	+	−	+	−	−	−	−	+	+	+	+	−	AA
J. castaneus	+	−	+	+	−	+	+	−	+	−	−	−	−	−	−	+	+	−	AA
J. biglumis	+	−	+	+	−	+	+	−	+	−	−	−	−	−	−	+	+	+	AA
J. triglumis	−	−	+	+	−	+	+	−	+	−	−	+	−	+	+	+	+	−	AA
Luzula spicata	−	+	−	−	+	+	−	−	+	−	−	−	−	−	−	+	+	−	AA
L. arcuata	+	+	−	−	+	−	−	−	+	−	−	−	−	−	−	+	+	+	AS
Kobresia simpliciuscula	−	+	+	+	−	−	+	−	−	−	−	−	−	+	+	+	+	−	AA
Carex capillaris	−	+	+	−	−	−	+	−	−	−	−	+	−	+	+	+	+	−	AA
Carex stenolepis	+	−	+	−	+	−	−	−	−	−	−	−	−	−	−	+	−	+	?
C. saxatilis	+	−	+	+	+	+	+	−	−	−	−	−	−	−	−	+	+	−	AS
C. vaginata	+	+	+	+	−	+	−	−	−	−	−	−	−	−	+	+	+	−	AA
C. rariflora	+	−	+	+	+	−	−	−	−	−	−	−	−	−	−	+	+	+	AS
C. norvegica	+	−	+	−	−	+	−	−	−	−	−	−	−	−	−	+	−	+	AA
C. atrata	+	+	+	−	+	+	−	−	+	−	−	+	−	+	+	+	+	−	AA
C. atrofusca	+	−	+	+	−	−	−	−	−	−	−	−	−	−	−	+	+	+	AA
C. bigelowii	−	+	+	+	+	+	−	−	−	−	−	+	−	+	+	+	+	−	AA
C. lachenalii	+	+	+	−	+	−	+	−	+	−	−	−	−	−	−	+	+	+	AA
C. rupestris	−	+	−	−	−	+	−	−	+	−	−	−	−	−	−	+	+	+	AA
C. microglochin	+	−	+	+	−	+	+	−	+	−	−	−	−	−	−	+	−	+	AA

Table 27 (*contd.*)

	1	2	3	4	5	6	7	8	9	10	11	12	13	14	15	16	17	18	19
Festuca vivipara	—	+	+	+	+	+	—	—	—	—	+	+	+	+	+	+	+	—	AA
Poa alpina	+	+	+	—	—	+	+	—	+	—	—	+	—	+	—	+	+	—	AA
P. flexuosa	+	+	+	—	+	—	—	—	+	—	—	—	—	—	—	+	+	+	AS
P. glauca (P. balfourii)	—	+	—	—	—	+	+	—	+	—	—	+	—	+	+	+	+	—	AA
Agropyron donianum	—	+	—	—	—	—	+	—	+	—	—	—	—	—	—	+	+	+	AS
Deschampsia alpina	+	+	+	+	+	+	—	—	+	—	+	—	—	—	—	+	+	—	AS
Phleum alpinum	+	+	+	+	—	+	+	—	—	—	—	—	—	+	—	+	+	+	AA
Alopecurus alpinus	+	—	+	+	+	+	—	—	+	—	—	—	—	+	+	+	+	+	AS
Total 118	53	96	73	36	45	69	74	5	73	6	11	42	12	61	41	106	93	54	

Notes

Categories:
High montane: most stations situated above 600 m.

Dry ⎫
Moist ⎬ subjectively assessed moisture content of soil.
Wet ⎭

Acidic: soil pH < 4.8, < 30 mg exchangeable calcium/100 g.
Medium base: soil pH 4.8–6.0, 30–300 mg exchangeable calcium/100 g.
Calcareous: soil pH > 6.0, > 300 mg exchangeable calcium/100 g.
Special: soils with either prominence of a cation other than Ca^{++}, or with an unusual balance of cations.
Open: habitats lacking 100 % vegetation cover of substratum surface; or extremely close grazed swards. This is a relative term, for many montane species which grow in closed communities can only persist in vegetation of less than a certain stature and luxuriance.
European distribution:

AA = Arctic–alpine   CN = continental northern
AS = Arctic–subarctic   C = continental
A = alpine   B = British endemic
NM = northern montane   [a]Could also be regarded as submontane.

3. Widespread species with a major niche on mountains.
4. Species mainly of other habitats, sparingly represented on mountains.

The first two groups are obviously the most distinctive, and the accompanying Tables 27 and 28 summarise some of the main features of the ecological and geographical distributions of the vascular element of the two, excluding the 'critical' groups, *Alchemilla vulgaris* agg., *Euphrasia officinalis* agg. and *Hieracium*. The separation between montane and submontane is often difficult, involving arbitrary decisions based on knowledge of the bias of altitudinal distribution; species in Table 27 marked *a* could equally be placed in Table 28. The data given are not claimed to be final, and further work both field and analytical may lead to revision of statements about the ecological and geographical ranges of some species. Soil preferences and tolerances, in particular, need much further study. Nevertheless, existing knowledge in these fields is sufficiently adequate and reliable for broad trends to be discussed.

Both montane and submontane groups show a tendency to increase northwards, in response to the gradient of falling mean temperature. This general trend is, however, modified by the varying extent, between different regions, of suitable topographic and edaphic habitats. In both groups, the majority of species are calcicolous in some degree, i.e. they require soils from mildly to strongly calcareous. The montane species are thus best represented in the southern and eastern Highlands, where calcareous rocks occur most extensively above the tree limit, and where there is more really high ground of any kind than elsewhere in Britain. The Highlands as a whole have almost twice the number of montane species found in the richest region farther south (northern England). High montane species, including those associated with prolonged snow cover, are mostly confined to the Highlands, only 14 out of 53 species being known in regions farther south. Of 54 rare montane species, 48 occur in the Highlands, and only 15 in the next richest region, northern England. Conversely, the submontane group attains its greatest numbers in northern England, where calcareous rock is most extensive at lower levels. Of 11 rare submontane species, seven occur in the Highlands and seven in northern England.

The small number of species of both groups in south-west England probably reflects unfavourable regional climate and absence of ground above 600 m, as well as scarcity of calcareous rock. The heavier sheep-grazing pressure to which uplands south of the Highlands have been subjected may have depleted the montane and submontane flora still further, but is more likely to have caused reduction in populations of some species, rather than complete extinctions. Burning, in combination with grazing, has probably helped to reduce the abundance of montane ericoid shrubs in these more southerly regions.

Post-glacial restriction and extinction have greatly fragmented and reduced the flora of the British mountains, both climatically and through human influence. The montane flora as a whole may thus be regarded as relict, but the different species show all degrees of relictness, from those which are widespread, occurring in almost all suitable localities, to the few which are known only in one or a very few, scattered stations, e.g. *Diapensia lapponica, Homogyne alpina, Cerastium nigrescens, Arabis alpina, Minuartia stricta, Phyllodoce caerulea, Koenigia islandica, Lychnis alpina, Artemisia norvegica, Oxytropis campestris, Astragalus alpinus, Viola rupestris, Polygala amara* and *Cicerbita alpina*. The submontane group shows similar variations in discontinuity, and the rare, highly disjunct species here are *Arenaria norvegica* ssp. *anglica, Schoenus ferrugineus* and *Potentilla rupestris*.

Some species in both groups show a high degree of localisation, but are fairly plentiful, with many stations, within these distribution centres. Wales has only one species which occurs nowhere else in Britain, *Lloydia serotina* which grows on several different cliffs in Snowdonia. By contrast, northern England has a number of species which occur widely there but are either confined to that region or occur elsewhere only in southern Scotland, namely, *Potentilla fruticosa, Gentiana verna, Dryopteris villarii* (also north Wales), *Primula farinosa, Polemonium caeruleum, Myosotis brevifolia, Carex ornithopoda*. All of these except the *Myosotis* are markedly calcicolous and their concentration in northern England is probably the result of the extensive occurrence there of Carboniferous Limestone, which gave a large area of suitable habitat at the time when this flora was undergoing Post-glacial spread. The species which appear to need special soil conditions chemically have a highly disjunct distribution: they are *Lychnis alpina, L. viscaria, Cerastium nigrescens, Asplenium septentrionale*, and, perhaps, *Arabis alpina, Koenigia islandica* and *Potentilla rupestris*. A few species grow on special soils only in part of their range, e.g. *Minuartia verna* and *Thlaspi alpestre* (both locally on lead mine refuse), *Cardaminopsis petraea* and *Oxytropis halleri*.

Many relict species do not, however, appear to be limited in distribution by the lack of suitable habitats; this is especially true of calcifuge or indifferent species such as *Diapensia lapponica* and *Artemisia norvegica*. There may for some relict species be cryptic limiting conditions which remain undetected, but for many the extent of suitable but unoccupied habitat is very large. For the second group, it seems that factors, including chance in particular, which operated during past periods of climatically initiated spread or retreat have been responsible for the highly disjunct pattern which we see today.

The majority of British montane vascular plant species are Arctic–alpine (77), with smaller numbers in the Arctic–subarctic (22) and alpine (4) elements. A few species which are somewhat montane here, e.g. *Potentilla fruticosa, Viola rupestris* and *Polygala amara*, are less so in Europe as a whole, and could equally well be placed in the submontane group. The majority of our submontane species belong to J. R. Matthews' (1937) continental northern (13) and northern montane (19) elements; a few species which belong to these elements but are found in maritime or low-lying peatland habitats are omitted from the accompanying lists (Table 28), but included in the appropriate habitat accounts. A few critical species cannot be satisfactorily placed as regards European distribution. Whilst the British mountains may be regarded as an impoverished outpost of the continental European mountains, the combination of different phytogeographical groupings is of considerable interest. *Alopecurus alpinus* and several bryophytes are unknown elsewhere in Europe, and the close juxtaposition of certain cold-adapted northern with warmth-loving southern species in western Britain is an unusual ecological feature.

Fauna

MAMMALS, REPTILES AND AMPHIBIANS

The largest wild mammal of the British uplands is the red deer, which has become adapted to the treeless mountain terrain and is now much more characteristic of such country than of the forests, which are its chief habitat in mainland Europe. Red deer are managed, as an exploitable resource, for game and food, and most herds are culled annually in the autumn and winter.

The most southerly upland haunts of the species as a native animal are Exmoor and the Quantock and Brendon hills of south-west England, but here the deer live partly in woodland. There are no other upland herds south of the Lake District, where they are found mainly in the Ullswater and Haweswater hills, but have also increased to considerable numbers in the conifer forests between Coniston and Windermere. In southern Scotland there are red deer over much of the higher hill country of Galloway, while in the Scottish Highlands, red deer are widespread, with a population estimated at around 184000. They are sparse or absent on some intensively stocked sheep walks, mainly in the south and west, and on some of the eastern grouse-moors. Deer forests occur on most of the larger Hebridean islands, but not in Orkney or Shetland. The majority of upland key sites in the Highlands carry red deer, and many are primarily deer forests managed for this species. Many deer forests also carry sheep, and some are managed as grouse-moor too. Roe deer, although essentially forest animals, range onto many areas of upland.

There are no other large wild herbivores on the uplands, but the feral goat has lived wild and unmanaged for so long in many places that it has some claims to be considered with the native fauna. To many naturalists this animal is certainly an interesting and attractive addition to the wildlife of upland country, though it is culled locally (especially in the interests of afforestation). One objection to goats, that they cause further impoverishment of vegetation and flora by grazing cliff ledges inaccessible to sheep, is not usually relevant today. Feral goats have a fairly static distribution over long periods, and in the areas where they occur, they have probably long since done all the damage they are likely to do to vegetation of precipitous ground. Their main occurrences are in north Wales, the Cheviots, the Galloway and Moffat Hills, and scattered places in the Highlands and

Table 28. *Habitat and distribution of submontane vascular plants*

	Dry	Moist	Wet	Acidic	Medium	Calcareous	Special	Open	S.W. England	S. Wales	N. Wales	Midlands	N. England	S. Scotland	E. Highlands	W. Highlands	Rare species	European distribution
	1	2	3	4	5	6	7	8	9	10	11	12	13	14	15	16	17	18
Equisetum hyemale	+	+	+	—	+	+	—	—	—	+	—	+	+	+	+	+	—	C
E. variegatum	+	+	+	—	+	+	—	—	—	+	—	+	+	+	+	+	—	NM
E. pratense	—	+	—	—	+	+	—	—	+	+	+	+	+	+	+	+	—	NM
Asplenium septentrionale	+	—	—	+	—	—	+	+	—	—	—	+	—	+	+	+	+	NM
Dryopteris villarii	+	—	—	—	—	+	+	—	—	—	+	—	+	—	—	—	+	A
Thelypteris robertiana	+	—	—	—	+	+	—	+	+	+	+	+	—	—	—	—	—	NM
Trollius europaeus	+	+	+	—	+	+	—	—	+	+	+	+	+	+	+	+	—	NM
Viola lutea	+	—	—	+	+	—	—	—	—	+	+	+	+	+	+	+	—	A
Lychnis viscaria	+	—	—	—	—	+	+	—	+	+	—	+	+	+	—	+	+	CN
Arenaria norvegica ssp. *anglica*	+	—	—	—	+	+	—	+	—	—	—	+	—	—	—	—	+	E
Geranium sylvaticum	+	+	—	—	+	+	—	—	—	+	+	+	+	+	+	+	—	CN
Oxytropis halleri	+	—	—	+	+	?	+	—	—	—	—	—	+	+	+	+	+	A
Vicia orobus	+	—	—	+	+	—	—	—	+	+	+	+	+	+	+	+	—	NM
Rubus saxatilis	+	—	—	—	—	+	—	+	+	+	+	+	+	+	+	+	—	NM
Potentilla rupestris	+	—	—	—	—	+	?	+	—	+	+	—	—	—	—	+	+	NM
Circaea alpina	+	—	—	+	+	—	—	—	+	+	—	+	—	—	+	+	+	CN
Meum athamanticum	+	—	—	+	+	—	—	—	+	+	+	+	+	+	+	+	—	CN
Salix nigricans	—	+	+	—	+	+	—	—	—	—	—	+	+	+	+	+	—	CN
S. phylicifolia	+	+	+	—	+	+	—	—	—	—	—	+	+	+	+	+	—	NM
Andromeda polifolia	—	+	+	+	—	—	—	—	—	+	+	+	+	+	+	—	—	CN
Vaccinium vitis-idaea	+	+	+	+	—	—	—	+	+	+	+	+	+	+	+	+	—	AA
Orthilia secunda	+	—	—	+	+	—	—	—	—	+	+	+	+	+	+	+	—	CN
Pyrola media	+	+	—	+	+	—	—	—	—	+	+	+	+	+	+	+	—	CN
Empetrum nigrum	+	+	—	+	—	—	—	+	+	+	+	+	+	+	+	+	—	AA
Primula farinosa	—	+	+	—	+	+	—	+	—	—	—	+	—	—	—	—	—	NM
P. scotica	—	+	+	—	+	+	—	+	—	—	—	—	—	+	—	+	—	B
Trientalis europaea	+	+	—	+	—	—	—	—	—	+	+	+	+	+	+	+	—	NM
Polemonium caeruleum	+	—	—	—	+	—	—	—	—	—	+	+	—	—	—	—	+	NM
Myosotis brevifolia	—	+	+	—	+	—	—	+	—	—	—	+	+	—	—	—	—	B
Melampyrum sylvaticum	+	—	—	+	—	—	—	+	—	—	+	—	+	+	+	+	+	CN
Ajuga pyramidalis	+	—	—	+	+	—	—	+	—	—	+	+	+	+	+	+	—	NM
Galium boreale	+	+	—	—	+	+	—	—	—	+	+	+	+	+	+	+	—	CN
Antennaria dioica	+	—	—	+	+	—	—	+	+	+	+	+	+	+	+	+	—	NM
Cirsium heterophyllum	+	+	—	—	+	+	—	—	—	+	+	+	+	+	+	+	—	CN
Leucorchis albida	+	—	—	+	—	—	—	—	—	+	+	+	+	+	+	+	—	NM
Listera cordata	+	+	—	+	—	—	—	—	—	+	+	+	+	+	+	+	—	NM
Schoenus ferrugineus	—	+	+	—	—	+	—	+	—	—	—	—	—	+	—	—	+	CN
Carex paupercula	—	—	+	+	—	—	—	—	—	—	+	+	+	+	+	+	—	NM
C. ornithopoda	+	—	—	—	—	+	—	+	—	—	—	+	+	—	—	—	+	CN
C. aquatilis	—	—	+	+	+	—	—	—	+	+	—	+	+	+	+	+	—	AS
C. pauciflora	—	+	+	+	—	—	—	—	—	—	—	+	+	+	+	+	—	NM
Melica nutans	+	—	—	—	+	+	—	—	—	+	+	+	+	+	+	+	—	NM
Sesleria albicans	+	—	—	—	—	+	—	—	—	—	—	—	+	—	+	—	—	A
Total 43	33	21	14	16	28	23	2	16	8	21	24	20	38	32	32	33	11	

Note

Categories: see under Table 27, p. 300.   E = endemic

islands; one of the largest herds is on the island of Rhum. Feral goats seem able to flourish in various types of upland for their haunts range from gentle grouse-moor country to high, steep and precipitous mountains.

Rabbits were formerly widespread and locally numerous at the lower levels of the uplands, flourishing best in areas of basic soil, as on limestone. They were in most places greatly reduced or exterminated by myxomatosis after 1954, and though there has been some local recovery, in most places they have failed to regain their former numbers or even to reappear. One isolated colony which has escaped unscathed is on the 'sugar' limestone plateau of Cronkley Fell in Upper Teesdale, where the close grazing and erosion created by the dense rabbit population are posing a serious threat to some of the most interesting plants of the site. The common buzzard is the predator most affected by the decline of the rabbit, and in general it has either stayed at reduced numbers or maintained its population through adaptation to alternative prey.

The mountain hare is a widespread animal in the Scottish Highlands, and has become established through introduction in other places such as the Hebrides, Orkney, Shetland, Southern Uplands, the Cheviots and Peak District. It has evidently declined greatly over much of western Scotland, and is now most numerous on the heathery eastern grouse-moors. High density of hares and grouse often seem to go together and presumably are a parallel effect of good upland productivity. Locally in the eastern Highlands, this is an important prey species of the golden eagle, fox and wild cat.

Of the small rodents, only the short-tailed field vole is particularly associated with uplands. This is a widespread and often numerous species over most of the hill country of Britain, though on some of the Scottish islands its niche is occupied by insular races of the wood mouse, and on Orkney by a race of the European common vole *Microtus arvalis orcadensis*. The field vole needs cover and flourishes best in some of the rank *Molinia* grasslands and *Juncus* communities extensive in many areas. Where these are fenced and planted with young conifers, the grasses and dwarf shrubs become extremely luxuriant, and during the several years which elapse before the young trees grow big enough to suppress this lush growth, the voles often reach very high densities. Their numbers then become a great attraction to predators such as fox, stoat, kestrel, short-eared owl, buzzard and hen harrier, and these species often increase in parallel. The cyclical fluctuations of vole numbers and dependent predators are well known, and are most obvious in these young plantations. Field voles occur up to considerable elevations (900 m or over), as is evidenced by finding their droppings and chopped-up fodder where late snowbeds have melted out, and they are the most ubiquitous mammal of the uplands.

The bank vole and wood mouse occur up to high elevations on some British mountains, but appear to be much less common than *Microtus*, and there is little information about the niches they occupy in the uplands. Water voles are thinly distributed but widespread among the hills, frequenting mainly the slower stream courses where there are deep alluvial or drift banks in which they can tunnel, and rather stagnant pools. They occur at surprisingly high elevations, reaching at least 1030 m.

Moles are widespread in most uplands of mainland Britain, Mull and Skye, showing an invariable association with the better soils (usually grassland-covered brown loams with earthworms) which are often revealed by the molehills on the surface. The animal is thus especially numerous on soils derived from limestone or other calcareous rock, and has been recorded up to 900 m, sometimes in small, completely isolated pockets of such material, well away from the next nearest occurrences, which may be separated by large expanses of peat or other quite unsuitable ground. Conversely, it is absent from soils derived from granite or quartzite, except where these rocks contain beds of more basic material. Moles appear at times in the dietary of some of the hill predators. Both common shrew and pygmy shrew occur up to high levels on mountains, but little is known in detail of their habitats.

While several predatory mammals are to be found in hill country, the fox is the only really widespread species, and occurs almost everywhere except on some of the Scottish islands. Although generally regarded as a pest and destroyed relentlessly, the hill fox is an extraordinarily resilient animal, and maintains its numbers remarkably well. Clearly, enough cubs are reared annually in the remoter or more inaccessible dens to make good the losses. Conversely, territorialism prevents the animal from exceeding a certain density of population, though this varies regionally, being high in much of the sheep country of Wales, northern England and southern Scotland, and low in the barren parts of the west Highland deer forests. The breeding places are mostly in holes tunnelled in deep soils, or in large crevices deep in block-litters, usually below 600 m. Foxes prey on the smaller mammals within their habitat, and at times take the young of deer, goats and sheep, birds of many species, and their eggs and young. Carrion, especially deer and sheep, is an important part of their food locally.

The stoat is widespread on lower moors and the weasel occurs in places, but is mainly a lowland animal. In its very local haunts, in Wales and the Welsh borders, the polecat also frequents the lower hills but is evidently more a creature of uncultivated land in the valleys. The pine marten is typically a hill woodland mammal, but within its range, in north Wales, Lakeland and the Highlands, some pairs frequent and breed in treeless situations among the hills, making their dens in deep rock crannies, in block-litter or cliffs. The pine marten is widespread in the Highlands, mainly north of the Great Glen nowadays, but is common nowhere. The wild cat *Felis silvestris* is essentially a Highland animal, though it has spread in recent years to the Campsie Fells, Stirlingshire. This carnivore is at home in quite treeless country, but usually on the lower mountain slopes, where it breeds in holes amongst block litters or less often on a cliff ledge. Wild cats are much persecuted but evidently manage to hold their own, and have increased in some areas.

Some badgers live and breed on the open hillsides and

moorlands well away from the woods which are their more typical haunt, though it is not clear how widespread this animal is as an upland dweller; but it is not found at higher levels and occurs mostly within the tree limit. Otters live by many hill streams and lakes, at the lower levels, but are thinly distributed in most districts.

Although bats roost and hibernate in rock crevices and caves, they are essentially creatures of low levels in Britain and are seldom seen on mountains. Some species probably occur at the foot of rocky hills, but there is little information about the bats of this habitat.

The reptiles and amphibians of uplands are few. The common lizard is a widespread species, though perhaps most common on heathery moorlands where it occurs up to 760 m. The slow-worm is not really an upland creature, but occurs in places on the lower moors, and so qualifies for inclusion. Although it is a widespread species in upland country, the adder has a curiously local distribution. It is common on Dartmoor, parts of the Cheviots, some but not all of the Galloway moors, and in certain parts of both eastern and western Highlands; but absent or scarce in such areas as Snowdonia, Lakeland, the Pennines, other parts of the Highlands, and some of the Scottish islands. Adders occur on both grasslands and dwarf-shrub heaths, and on blanket mires; they are especially associated with *Molinia* grasslands and heather moors, but their habitat varies seasonally. Adders occur up to 600 m in places, but are essentially creatures of the lower hill ground.

The Amphibia of the uplands are represented chiefly by the common frog which is widespread and common in most districts and has shown nothing of the extensive decline affecting lowland frog populations in recent years. Frogs occur up to at least 900 m, breeding in pools and wet places, but occurring otherwise on all kinds of ground, including precipitous slopes and even cliff ledges. While they occur on acidic mountains and breed in some base-poor waters, the largest frogs would appear to be consistently met with on calcareous hills, such as the mica-schist and limestone Breadalbane range in the Highlands. One or more species of newt may occur on the lower moorlands but information on this group is lacking.

The British fauna of mammals, reptiles and amphibia is singularly deficient in species belonging to the uplands. Nearly all species occur in other habitats as well, and only the mountain hare could be regarded as a montane animal.

BIRDS

Only three species in the British avifauna, the snow bunting *Plectrophenax nivalis*, ptarmigan *Lagopus mutus* and dotterel *Eudromias morinellus*, are montane or alpine types. The first two are confined to the Scottish Highlands as breeding birds, and the dotterel now nests only sporadically in other upland districts farther south. All three breed almost exclusively above 760 m in the central Highlands, but all three have nested down to 300 m in the far north-west of Scotland. The dotterel breeds on exposed plateaux and ridges, and the snow bunting in the crevices of block screes or boulder fields, whilst the ptarmigan nests in a wide variety of high mountain habitats. The snow bunting is at present very much a fringe species, nesting in a very few places, and the dotterel is local, being found mainly in the eastern Highlands. The ptarmigan is more widespread, occurring on nearly all the higher hills of the mainland.

The mountain cliffs are the breeding refuges of a characteristic group of predators, consisting of the golden eagle, peregrine, raven, common buzzard and kestrel. All of these nest also on sea cliffs, but the golden eagle only does so where moorlands run down to the sea, and may be regarded as an upland species in Britain, breeding occasionally as high as 900 m. They all have a large territory size so that it needs a considerable area to contain a reasonably large sample of their populations. The golden eagle was for many years confined to the Scottish Highlands as a breeding bird, but since 1945 has become firmly established in Galloway, and a pair (3 pairs in 1976) has bred in northern England from 1969 onwards. The other four species are widespread in the British uplands, though the peregrine and, to a lesser extent, the raven are locally limited in numbers by scarcity of suitable cliffs, which can include old quarries. Apart from the kestrel, which shows cyclical population fluctuations in parallel with changes in vole numbers, all these predators maintain fairly constant populations in many uplands. The peregrine declined seriously in hill country south of the Highlands between 1956–63, but is now showing a strong recovery in the uplands of southern Scotland and northern England, and evidently also in Wales. Buzzards declined locally after myxomatosis and ravens have done so where sheep-walks have been extensively afforested. In north Wales the chough *Pyrrhocorax pyrrhocorax* breeds among the mountains, singly or in small groups, but these inland birds nearly always use disused quarries or mines for their nest sites.

The lower, gently contoured moorlands, typically with mixtures of Callunetum and *Calluna–Eriophorum* blanket mire, are the main haunt of northern, submontane birds such as the red grouse *Lagopus lagopus*, golden plover *Pluvialis apricarius*, dunlin *Calidris alpina* and merlin. The grouse is a bird of some economic importance, and large areas of moorland, especially in northern England and eastern Scotland are managed for this species and the sport it provides. Grouse management has considerable impact on both vegetation and fauna, largely beneficial (by comparison with sheep-farming) but deleterious in the case of predators. The golden plover breeds on moors at all elevations down to nearly sea-level, but also shares mountain top haunts at 900 m or more with the dotterel, especially where there is peaty ground, and the dunlin breeds also by the sea on salt and machair marshes. The merlin is especially a bird of the heather moors up to around 600 m, but locally breeds in bracken, on cliffs (including coastal rocks), in old tree nests of other species on moorland, and on sand dunes; having declined over several decades, it is now a relatively rare bird, thinly distributed over the uplands and seems now to be more numerous in Orkney and Shetland than anywhere else. These species extend as far south as Dartmoor, but they do not become well represented until central Wales is

Plate 17. *Borralie, Sutherland (U.68)* (see p. 325). The outcrops of Durness Limestone around Loch Borralie at Durness have the best areas of *Dryas octopetala* heath in Britain, developed at elevations of less than 50 m above sea-level. This is a particularly good example of the altitudinal descent of montane vegetation in a north-westerly direction, corresponding to marked increase in oceanicity of climate from east to west, and latitudinal decrease in temperature from south to north. (Photo: D. A. Ratcliffe.)

Plate 18. *Scar Close, Ingleborough, Yorkshire* (U.23) (see p. 317). A fine example of a limestone pavement, characteristic of this Pennine area. The deep vertical fissures contain shade-loving woodland plants, while the pavement surface has a mixture of typical calcicolous plants in a very open community and areas of acidophilous heath on a thin layer of non-calcareous drift soil. There is a patchy development of scrub woodland with a variety of trees and shrubs. The higher peak and plateau of Ingleborough behind have alternating bands of gritstone and limestone, the latter notable for montane calcicolous plants. (Photo: D. A. Ratcliffe.)

Plate 19. *Cairnsmore of Fleet, Kirkcudbrightshire (U.34)* (see p. 319). This massif carries a range of vegetation types representative of the Galloway granite uplands, and has an especially varied fauna, including characteristic Highland elements near or at their southern limits. It is one of the few hill areas in Galloway not planted with conifers, and its value increases as blanket commercial afforestation advances over the Southern Uplands. (Photo: D. A. Ratcliffe.)

Plate 20. *Beinn a'Bhuird, Cairngorms, Aberdeenshire (U.44)* (see p. 322). The deep, ice-carved corries of the higher Scottish mountains hold snow until late in the year; this photograph was taken on 6 June 1975. The cold, clear water of the corrie lake (lochan), the great block litters and boulder fields, and the high flanking cliffs are all important habitats for the montane plants and animals living in these inhospitable places. The elevation of the lochan is 1000 m. (Photo: D. A. Ratcliffe.)

Plate 21. *Lodore Falls, Cumberland (W.133(d))* (see p. 107). The block-filled bed of this wooded waterfall ravine adjoining Derwentwater is a celebrated locality for mosses and liverworts with a markedly Atlantic distribution, and has many species which have their European headquarters in western Britain. (Photo: D. A. Ratcliffe.)

Plate 22. *Berriedale Cliffs, Caithness* (see Appendix and p. 359). The great breeding seabird colonies of the rocky coasts are one of the outstanding wildlife features of Britain. The picture shows the horizontally stratified Old Red Sandstone cliffs of Inver Hill at Berriedale, with massive concentrations of guillemots spread all the way along the precipice, and kittiwake ledges above. These great throngs of seafowl are now especially at risk to oil spill hazards resulting from North Sea oilfield developments. (Photo: D. A. Ratcliffe.)

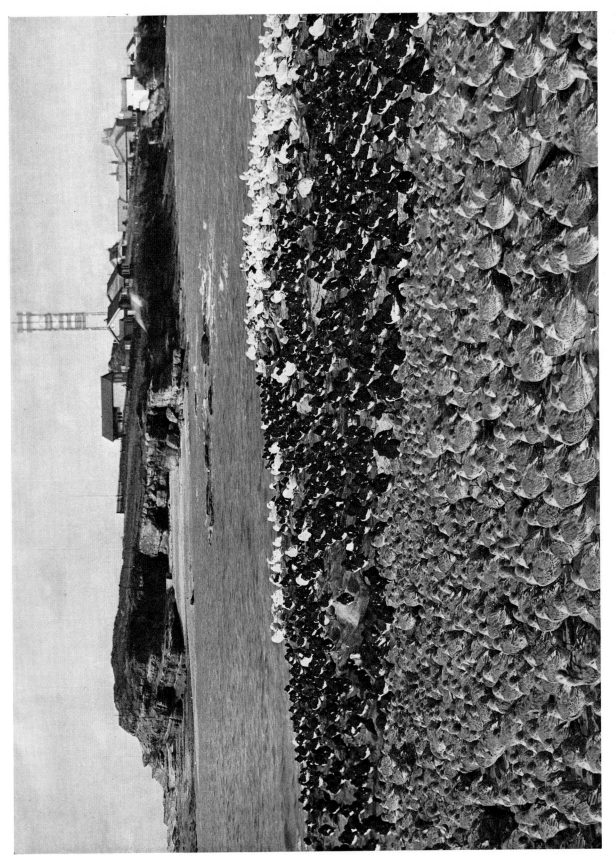

Plate 23. *Wader flocks on Hilbre Island, Cheshire* (C.55) (see p. 369). The low, rocky island of Hilbre is famous as the resting place for large concentrations of wading birds displaced by the high tides from the great sand banks and mud flats of the Dee estuary. This great western sea inlet, between the Welsh coast and the Wirral peninsula, is one of the internationally important haunts of waders during autumn and winter, with peak counts of about 125,000 birds, but is threatened by proposals for a barrage and freshwater impoundments. The picture shows knot, oystercatchers and herring gulls. (Photo: E. Hosking.)

Plate 24. *Cairngorms, Aberdeenshire (U.44)* (see p. 322). The high dissected plateau of the Cairngorms, seen here in the view from Beinn a'Bhuird to Ben Macdhui, is the closest approach in this country to truly Arctic terrain. The scene, taken on 15 June 1968, with the fell-field barrens in the foreground, the great snow-fields lying at over 1000 m, and the ice-carved corries below, bears strong resemblance to those typical of wilderness country in the high latitudes of the world. (Photo: D. A. Ratcliffe.)

reached, and the golden plover and dunlin are numerous only from the Pennines northwards. Hen harriers have two main habitats; heathery grouse-moors, where they are usually persecuted, and young forestry plantations where they are mostly protected. This species has increased greatly since 1945 and now breeds widely in Scotland, and has re-colonised certain moorlands in northern England and north Wales. The twite *Acanthis flavirostris* is nowadays encountered less often on the moors than on the rocky coastal areas of the western Highlands and islands.

A few species are widely distributed over various types of upland. The meadow pipit *Anthus pratensis*, skylark *Alauda arvensis*, wheatear *Oenanthe oenanthe* and ring ouzel *Turdus torquatus* breed up to 900 m and the cuckoo follows the first species as its host on the lower moorlands and hills. The meadow pipit is the most widespread of all upland birds, occurring in almost all kinds of terrain. The wren is a characteristic bird of rocky places in the hills and breeds on many of the crags up to around 900 m. The stock dove is a fairly widespread though not common bird nesting in crevices and holes of the lower cliffs, and many of these less elevated escarpments have colonies of jackdaws. Species such as the carrion crow, hooded crow (Highlands only), lapwing *Vanellus vanellus*, black grouse, curlew *Numenius arquata*, snipe *Gallinago gallinago*, redshank *Tringa totanus*, woodcock, short-eared owl, mallard, teal *Anas crecca*, nightjar, stonechat and whinchat all have a moorland niche, but are equally or more characteristic of other habitats; some are more especially birds of the marginal land, where the moor passes into permanent grassland, or where there is a transition to woodland. The tree pipit overlaps with the meadow pipit where there is open tree growth on the moor.

Some hill birds are associated with water. The dipper *Cinclus cinclus* breeds along the rocky sections of most hill streams, but the grey wagtail *Motacilla cinerea* has decreased and is now less numerous in similar habitats. The common sandpiper frequents rivers and lake margins and is a widespread species, but the greenshank, which feeds in these places (and by small tarns or even pools) and breeds on the moors, is confined to the Scottish Highlands, where it is most numerous in the north-west. In contrast to their preference for forest mires and heaths in Arctic and Subarctic Europe, greenshanks in the Highlands nest mainly on barren, treeless moors and blanket mires, though they occupy the former habitats on Speyside. The black-throated and red-throated divers are entirely Scottish birds, too, but extend as far south as Galloway. The black-throated diver *Gavia arctica* is a bird of the bigger lochs, where it usually breeds on islands, and occurs mainly in the north-west Highlands; whereas the red-throated diver *G. stellata* often breeds on small peaty lochans on the moors, but prefers to be within flight of the coast, where it often feeds. The goosander and red-breasted merganser are birds of both upland and lowland rivers, mainly in Scotland, but have spread south in recent years. Wildfowl such as the greylag goose *Anser anser*, wigeon *Anas penelope* and scoter *Melanitta nigra* breed on islands or around the shores of some Scottish hill lochs, mainly at low levels, but are very local.

A few birds which can be regarded as moorland breeders occur mainly on flat blanket mires or flows, often with pool and hummock systems, and lying mostly below 460 m. These include some of the species already mentioned, especially dunlin, golden plover, red grouse and teal, together with others such as the black-headed *Larus ridibundus* and lesser black-backed *L. fuscus* gulls, both of which may occur in large colonies. Some colonies of lesser black-backs have smaller numbers of great black-backed gulls *L. marinus* nesting amongst them, but both species have declined as inland nesting birds. The common gull *L. canus* is a largely Scottish breeder, but has isolated nesting places in England and Wales, mainly on loch islands, but sometimes on flows, and the black-headed gull is a still more widespread moorland species, nesting in swamps or flows. In the far north of Scotland, Orkney and Shetland, there are moorland colonies of great skua *Catharacta skua* and Arctic skua *Stercorarius parasiticus*, which parasitise the colonies of gulls and other seabirds for food.

Two rare Scottish breeders may be regarded as lower moorland species. The whimbrel *Numenius phaeopus* occurs mainly in Shetland and the wood sandpiper *Tringa glareola* at scattered places around the Highlands, where it seems to favour lakes, tarns and blanket mire lochans with well-developed marginal swamp vegetation, at least for feeding.

INSECTS

Lepidoptera

The ecological and geographical distribution of upland Lepidoptera is indicated in the accompanying Table 29. As might be expected in country where sunshine is greatly reduced, butterflies are few, there being only five species, nearly all of the 'brown' family. Conversely, because of the low temperature at night, some normally nocturnal moths have evolved diurnal upland forms, e.g. *Diarsia mendica* ssp. *conflua*. Some upland moths, e.g. *Lasiocampa quercus* ssp. *callunae* and *Xestia alpicola*, have a two-year life cycle and overwinter as larvae.

Few species appear to be adapted to a single larval food plant (although *Erebia epiphron* is said to feed only on *Nardus*), and even those montane moths which feed on certain montane plant species are mostly known to eat a wider selection, including submontane plants. For this reason, food plants have been classified into three broad groups: dwarf shrubs, forbs and grasses. A few species, such as *Zygaena exulans* and *Z. purpuralis*, are adapted to food plants which need base-rich soils, so that their distribution is related to underlying geology, but the majority are associated with food plants which are either calcifuge or indifferent to base-status.

For many local or disjunct montane Lepidoptera, the distribution of food plants is far more widespread than that of the insect, so that other factors evidently limit the occurrence of the latter, e.g. *Erebia epiphron* on *Nardus*, and *Xestia alpicola* on various dwarf shrubs. However, the eradication of dwarf-shrub heaths by heavy sheep-grazing and burning has obviously had the effect of reducing and fragmenting the

Table 29. *Habitat and distribution of upland Lepidoptera*[a]

		Dwarf shrubs	Forbs (dicot. herbs)	Grasses	Widespread	Submontane	Montane	S.W. England	S. Wales	N. Wales	Midlands	N. England	S. Scotland	E. Highlands	W. Highlands
		1	2	3	4	5	6	7	8	9	10	11	12	13	14
Butterflies															
Small heath	*Coenonympha pamphilus*	—	—	+	+	—	—	+	+	+	+	+	+	+	+
Large heath	*C. tullia*	—	—	+	—	+	—	—	+	—	+	+	+	+	+
Scotch argus	*Erebia aethiops*	—	—	+	—	+	—	—	—	—	—	+	+	+	+
Mountain ringlet	*E. epiphron*	—	—	+	—	—	+	—	—	—	—	—	—	+	+
Dark green fritillary	*Argynnis aglaja*	—	+	—	+	—	—	+	+	+	+	+	+	+	+
Moths															
Pale oak eggar	*Trichiura crataegi*	+	—	—	+	—	—	+	+	—	+	+	+	+	+
Oak eggar	*Lasiocampa quercus*	+	—	—	+	—	—	+	+	+	+	—	—	+	—
Northern eggar	*L. quercus* ssp. *callunae*	+	—	—	—	—	—	+	—	+	—	+	+	+	+
Fox moth	*Macrothylacia rubi*	+	—	—	+	—	—	+	+	+	+	+	+	+	+
Emperor	*Saturnia pavonia*	+	+	—	+	—	—	+	+	+	+	+	+	+	+
Clouded buff	*Diacrisia sannio*	—	+	—	+	—	—	+	+	+	+	+	+	+	—
Ruby tiger	*Phragmatobia fuliginosa*	—	+	—	+	—	—	+	+	+	+	+	+	+	+
Wood tiger	*Parasemia plantaginis*	—	+	—	+	—	—	+	+	+	+	+	+	+	+
Transparent burnet	*Zygaena purpuralis*	—	+	—	—	+	—	—	+	—	—	+	—	—	+
Scotch burnet	*Z. exulans*	+	—	—	—	—	+	—	—	—	—	—	—	+	—
Slender Scotch burnet	*Z. loti*	—	+	—	—	+	—	—	—	—	—	—	—	—	+
New Forest burnet	*Z. viciae*	—	+	—	—	+	—	—	—	—	—	—	—	—	+
True lover's knot	*Lycophotia porphyrea*	+	—	—	+	—	—	+	+	+	+	+	+	+	+
Ingrailed clay	*Diarsia mendica*	+	+	—	+	—	—	+	+	+	+	+	?	?	?
	D. mendica ssp. *conflua*	+	+	—	+	—	—	—	—	—	—	+	+	+	+
Heath rustic	*Xestia agathina*	+	—	—	+	—	—	+	+	+	+	+	+	+	+
Northern dart	*X. alpicola*	+	—	—	—	—	+	—	—	—	—	+	—	+	+
Ashworth's rustic	*X. ashworthii*	+	+	—	—	—	+	—	—	+	—	—	—	—	—
Neglected rustic	*X. castanea*	+	—	—	+	—	—	+	+	+	+	+	+	+	+
Cousin German	*Paradiarsia sobrina*	+	—	?	—	—	+	—	—	—	—	—	—	+	—
Beautiful yellow underwing	*Anarta myrtilli*	+	—	—	+	—	—	+	+	+	+	+	+	+	+
Small dark yellow underwing	*A. cordigera*	+	—	—	—	+	—	—	—	—	—	—	—	+	+
Broad bordered white underwing	*A. melanopa*	+	—	—	—	—	+	—	—	—	—	—	+	+	+
Antler	*Cerapteryx graminis*	—	—	+	+	—	—	+	+	+	+	+	+	+	+
Northern arches	*Apamea exulis*	—	—	+	—	—	+	—	—	—	—	—	—	+	+
Haworth's minor	*Celaena haworthii*	—	—	+	+	—	—	+	?	?	?	+	+	+	+
Sweet gale	*Acronicta euphorbiae*	+	+	—	—	+	—	—	—	—	—	—	+	+	+
Golden-rod brindle	*Lithomoia solidaginis*	+	—	—	+	—	—	—	—	—	+	+	+	+	+
Scarce silver Y	*Syngrapha interrogationis*	+	—	—	—	+	—	—	—	+	+	+	+	+	+
Weaver's wave	*Idaea contiguaria*	+	+	—	—	+	—	—	—	+	—	—	—	—	—
Yellow-ringed carpet	*Entephria flavicinctata*	—	+	—	—	—	—	—	—	—	—	+	+	+	+
Red carpet	*Xanthorhoe munitata*	—	+	—	—	—	+	—	+	—	+	+	+	+	+
Grey mountain carpet	*Entephria caesiata*	+	+	—	—	+	—	—	+	+	+	+	+	+	+
Pretty pinion	*Perizoma blandiata*	—	+	—	—	+	—	—	—	+	—	+	+	+	+
Heath rivulet	*P. minorata*	—	+	—	—	+	—	—	—	—	—	+	+	+	+
Manchester treble bar	*Carsia sororiata*	+	—	—	—	+	—	—	—	—	+	+	+	+	+
Slender-striped rufous	*Coenocalpe lapidata*	—	+	—	—	+	—	—	—	—	—	+	+	+	+
Small autumnal moth	*Epirrita filigrammaria*	+	—	—	—	+	—	—	—	—	+	+	+	+	+
Rannoch brindled beauty	*Lycia lapponaria*	+	—	—	—	+	—	—	—	—	—	—	—	+	+
Scotch annulet	*Gnophos obfuscatus*	+	—	—	—	+	—	—	—	—	—	—	+	+	+
Black mountain moth	*Psodos coracina*	+	—	—	—	—	+	—	—	—	—	—	—	+	+

Table 29 (*contd.*)

		1	2	3	4	5	6	7	8	9	10	11	12	13	14
Netted mountain moth	*Semiothisa carbonaria*	+	—	—	—	—	+	—	—	—	—	—	—	+	+
Rannoch looper	*S. brunneata*	+	—	—	—	+	—	—	—	—	—	—	—	+	+
Common heath	*Ematurga atomaria*	+	+	—	+	—	—	+	+	+	+	+	+	+	+
Grey scalloped bar	*Dyscia fagaria*	+	—	—	+	—	—	+	+	+	+	+	+	+	+
	Eudonia alpina	—	—	?	—	—	+	—	—	—	—	—	—	+	+
	Crambus ericella	—	—	+	—	—	+	—	—	—	+	—	+	—	+	+
	Catoptria furcatellus	—	—	+	—	—	+	—	—	+	—	+	—	+	+
Total 53		31	19	9	20	18	13	19	21	25	25	35	33	46	45

Note
[a] The nomenclature of the Lepidoptera follows that of Kloet & Hincks (1972) but the arrangement follows the conventional order used by previous authors, viz. Butterflies, Macrolepidoptera and Microlepidoptera.

populations of moorland species which depend on this group of food plants; this effect is described more particularly under the site account of Skiddaw Forest (U.17).

The Lepidoptera of uplands are divided into three ecological groups in the table: widespread species occur at various levels of the mountains, but mainly below 600 m, and are present also in the lowlands away from the hills, as in southern England; submontane species are confined to northern and hilly areas but also occur mainly or wholly below 600 m; and montane species occur mainly over 600 m on southern mountains but descend lower towards the north-west. As with plants, the number of submontane and montane species tends to increase with distance north, along the gradient of falling mean temperature, so that the Scottish Highlands are the richest region. While the number of species of upland Lepidoptera is small, some occur in considerable numbers. An interesting feature is that a number of moths, including upland species such as *Apamea exulis*, are represented on Shetland mainly by dark forms. On the other hand, *Parasemia plantaginis* has a white form, var. *hospita*, in the north.

Odonata

The Odonata are essentially tropical insects at the edge of their range in the British Isles. The larvae of most British species require static or slow-moving water. Much of upland Britain is, therefore, either climatically or ecologically unsuitable for dragonflies and damsel flies. However, dragonflies have great powers of dispersal, and some species, notably *Aeshna juncea*, *Sympetrum* spp., are quite often seen flying in upland habitats where they do not and cannot breed.

Of the few species of British Odonata which breed in fast-moving streams, only *Cordulegaster boltoni* is a truly upland species. This large insect is locally common in England, Wales and Scotland. In addition, ten other species (*Aeshna juncea*, *A. caerulea*, *Somatochlora arctica*, *Sympetrum striolatum*, *S. nigrescens*, *S. danae*, *Lestes sponsa*, *Libellula quadrimaculata*, *Pyrrhosoma nymphula* and *Enallagma cyathigerum*) breed in mire pools, ponds, lakes and slow streams in upland country, but mainly at the lower levels (i.e. up to 300 m). Of these species *A. juncea* and *L. sponsa* are characteristic

insects of lower upland habitats in many areas of Britain. The three boreo-alpine species *A. caerulea*, *Somatochlora arctica* and *Coenagrion hastulatum* are confined to upland country in Scotland; the first two are local and the last is very rare even in the Highlands. Even these northern species are not characteristic of the higher ground, though *A. caerulea* occurs on boggy terrain up to at least 460 m.

SPIDERS

Some species occurring in woodlands and peatlands at high altitudes are included in this Chapter, as well as in Chapters 5 and 8; a northern spider which occurs only in Highland pinewoods is really more typical of upland than woodland, and there is a considerable overlap of occurrence of upland and peatland spiders.

The 61 upland species listed on p. 308 are arbitrarily divided into three categories: (*a*) montane (17 species) characteristically found at high altitudes and in open habitats in the mountains of Scotland, northern England and Wales, but occasionally occurring at lower altitudes, especially in the extreme north; (*b*) submontane (30 species) including species of woodlands in the Scottish Highlands, and species occurring elsewhere frequently at lower altitudes than the montane group, a number of peatland species found in northern England also being included here; (*c*) widespread (14 species) not restricted to uplands, but most abundant in the north or on moderately high ground.

Montane species

The most extreme montane spiders, which occur only in the Scottish Highlands in Britain, are *Tricca alpigena*, *Collinsia holmgreni*, *Erigone tirolensis*, *E. psychrophila*, *Rhaebothorax paetulus*, *Centromerus parkeri* and *Lepthyphantes umbraticola*, of which only *C. holmgreni*, *E. tirolensis* and *L. umbraticola* are widespread and common in this region. *R. paetulus* and *C. parkeri* are known only from Ben Lawers, while *T. alpigena* and *E. psychrophila* are confined to the Cairngorms massif. Other typical Scottish Highland species are *Meioneta nigripes*, which has also been recorded once from Snowdonia, and *Tiso aestivus*, also found but less frequent in Snowdonia and the Lake District. The only montane species confined to Snowdonia are *Micaria alpina* and *Typhochrestus*

Table 30. *Habitat and distribution of upland spiders*

	Open moorland	Wetlands, upland bogs	Woods	S.W. England	S. & S.E. England	East Anglia	Midlands	S. Wales	N. Wales	N. England	S. Scotland	Highlands	N. Scotland	Ireland
	1	2	3	4	5	6	7	8	9	10	11	12	13	14
Montane														
Micaria alpina	+	—	—	—	—	—	—	—	+	—	—	—	—	—
Pardosa trailli	+	—	—	—	—	—	—	—	+	+	—	+	—	—
Tricca alpigena	+	—	—	—	—	—	—	—	—	+	—	+	—	—
Theridion bellicosum	+	—	—	—	—	—	—	—	+	+	—	+	—	—
Entelecara errata	+	—	—	—	—	—	—	—	+	+	—	+	+	+
Tiso aestivus	+	—	—	—	—	—	—	—	+	+	—	+	+	—
Typhochrestus simoni	+	—	—	—	—	—	—	—	+	—	—	+	+	—
Collinsia holmgreni	+	—	—	—	—	—	—	—	—	—	—	+	+	—
Erigone tirolensis	+	—	—	—	—	—	—	—	—	—	—	+	+	—
E. psychrophila	+	—	—	—	—	—	—	—	—	—	—	+	—	—
Rhaebothorax paetulus	+	—	—	—	—	—	—	—	—	—	—	+	—	—
Hilaira frigida	—	—	—	—	—	—	—	—	+	+	+	+	+	+
Meioneta nigripes	+	—	—	—	—	—	—	—	+	—	—	+	+	—
Centromerus parkeri	+	—	—	—	—	—	—	—	—	—	—	+	—	—
Oreonetides vaginatus	+	—	—	—	—	—	+	—	+	+	+	+	+	+
Lepthyphantes whymperi	+	—	—	—	—	—	+	+	+	+	+	+	+	+
L. umbraticola	+	—	—	—	—	—	—	—	—	—	—	+	—	—
Submontane														
Haplodrassus soerenseni	—	—	+	—	—	—	—	—	—	—	—	+	—	—
Clubiona subsultans	—	—	+	—	—	—	—	—	—	—	—	+	—	—
Dipoena torva	—	—	+	—	—	—	—	—	—	—	—	+	—	—
Robertus scoticus	—	—	+	—	—	—	—	—	—	—	—	+	—	—
Walckenaera clavicornis	—	+	—	—	—	—	—	—	+	+	+	+	—	—
Dismodicus elevatus	—	—	+	—	—	—	—	—	—	—	—	+	+	—
Trichopterna mengei	+	—	—	+	—	—	+	—	+	+	+	+	—	+
Pelecopsis elongata	—	—	+	—	—	—	—	—	—	—	—	+	—	—
Lessertiella saxetorum	—	+	—	—	—	—	+	—	—	+	—	+	—	—
Diplocephalus connatus	—	+	—	—	—	—	—	—	—	+	—	—	—	—
D. protuberans	—	+	+	—	—	—	—	—	—	+	+	—	—	—
Caledonia evansi	+	—	—	—	—	—	+	—	—	+	+	+	+	—
Diplocentria bidentata	+	+	—	—	—	—	+	+	+	+	—	+	—	+
Erigone capra	—	+	—	—	—	—	—	+	—	+	—	+	—	+
Rhaebothorax morulus	+	+	—	—	—	—	+	+	+	+	+	+	+	+
Eboria fausta	+	+	—	—	—	—	+	+	+	+	+	+	—	+
E. caliginosa	—	+	—	—	—	—	—	—	—	+	—	—	+	+
Hilaira nubigena	—	+	—	—	—	—	—	—	—	+	—	—	+	—
H. pervicax	—	+	—	—	—	—	—	—	+	+	—	+	+	—
Porrhomma montanum	+	—	—	—	—	—	—	—	+	+	—	+	+	—
Meioneta gulosa	+	—	—	—	—	—	+	+	+	+	+	+	—	—
Centromerus persimilis	+	—	—	—	—	—	—	—	—	—	+	—	—	+
Maro lepidus	—	+	—	—	—	—	—	—	—	—	+	—	—	—
Macrargus carpenteri	+	—	—	—	—	—	—	—	—	—	+	+	—	—
Bolyphantes alticeps	+	—	—	—	—	—	+	—	—	+	+	+	+	—
Lepthyphantes pinicola	+	—	—	—	—	—	+	—	+	+	+	+	—	—
L. angulatus	+	—	—	—	—	—	—	—	+	+	+	+	—	—
L. expunctus	—	—	+	—	—	—	—	—	—	+	+	+	—	—
Linyphia marginata	—	—	+	—	—	—	—	—	—	—	—	+	+	—
Clubiona norvegica	—	+	—	—	—	—	+	—	—	+	—	+	—	—

Table 30 (*contd.*)

	1	2	3	4	5	6	7	8	9	10	11	12	13	14
Widespread species														
Zora nemoralis	+	—	+	+	—	—	—	—	+	+	—	+	—	—
Euophrys erratica	+	—	—	+	—	+	+	+	+	+	+	+	—	+
Pardosa agricola	—	+	—	—	—	—	+	+	—	+	+	+	—	+
Arctosa cinerea	—	+	—	—	—	—	—	+	+	+	—	+	—	+
Coelotes atropos	+	—	—	+	+	—	+	+	+	+	+	—	—	—
Cryphoeca silvicola	+	—	+	+	—	+	+	+	+	+	+	+	+	+
Walckenaera capito	+	—	—	+	+	+	+	—	+	+	+	+	—	+
Dicymbium tibiale	+	—	—	+	—	—	+	+	+	+	+	+	+	+
Evansia merens	+	—	—	+	—	—	+	+	+	+	+	+	—	+
Tapinocyba pallens	—	—	+	—	+	—	+	+	+	+	+	+	+	+
Monocephalus castaneipes	+	—	+	+	+	—	+	—	+	+	+	+	+	+
Hilaira excisa	—	+	—	+	+	—	+	+	+	+	+	+	+	+
Bolyphantes luteolus	+	—	—	+	+	+	+	+	+	+	+	+	+	+
Allomengea scopigera	+	+	—	+	+	+	+	+	—	+	+	+	+	+
Total 61	38	17	13	12	7	5	23	18	32	44	28	53	24	22

simoni, the latter known only from Lliwedd, while the former occurs on several of the highest peaks. The other montane species listed, *Pardosa trailli*, *Theridion bellicosum*, *Entelecara errata*, *Hilaira frigida*, *Oreonetides vaginatus* and *Lepthyphantes whymperi*, are all widespread in Scotland, the Lake District and north Wales, the last two species also occurring occasionally at lower altitudes in northern England and the Midlands.

Submontane species

These are a more mixed assemblage of species. Eight are more or less confined to Scottish woodlands, *Haplodrassus soerenseni*, *Clubiona subsultans* and *Dipoena torva* all being confined to the Black Wood of Rannoch and the Rothiemurchus/Abernethy Forest region, while *Robertus scoticus* is known only from the Black Wood and one other site in Perthshire, and *Pelecopsis elongata* only from Rothiemurchus/Abernethy and near Loch Rannoch. *Dismodicus elevatus* has been found in Sutherland in addition to Rothiemurchus/Abernethy and the Black Wood. *Linyphia marginata* and *Lepthyphantes expunctus* are more widespread species of woodland on high ground in Scotland, the latter also occurring in northern England.

The most widespread and characteristic submontane species are *Trichopterna mengei*, *Caledonia evansi*, *Diplocentria bidentata*, *Rhaebothorax morulus*, *Meioneta gulosa* and *Bolyphantes alticeps*. All of these are found in dry montane habitats, but some occur also in peatland. Other characteristic submontane species of more restricted range are *Walckenaera clavicornis*, *Eboria fausta*, *E. caliginosa*, *Hilaira pervicax*, *Porrhomma montanum*, *Macrargus carpenteri*, *Lepthyphantes pinicola* and *L. angulatus*.

Rarities among this group are *Erigone capra*, known only from three widely separated sites, Malham, Ben Lawers and Traeth Mawr, near Brecon, all in very wet habitats; *Hilaira nubigena*, known from four peatland sites in northern England and from Ben Hope; *Centromerus persimilis*, the only British record of which is from Malham Cove; *Maro*

lepidus, a peatland species recorded at Malham, Pen y Ghent and Rusland Moss; *Diplocephalus protuberans*, known from moorland and woodland in a few sites in Yorkshire, and in Durham and Ayrshire; and *Clubiona norvegica*, known only from Rannoch Moor, Abbots Moss and near Rosedale Abbey (Yorkshire).

Two submontane species with an unusual habitat requirement are *Diplocephalus connatus* and *Lessertiella saxetorum*, both of which are confined to the stony banks of upland rivers, the former being known only from two sites in Northumberland, while the latter is recorded from south Wales, northern England and Scotland, including Abernethy Forest.

Widespread species

Among the commonest and most widespread northern and upland species are *Bolyphantes luteolus*, *Allomengea scopigera*, *Dicymbium tibiale*, *Cryphoeca silvicola* and *Hilaira excisa*, the last-named being confined to peatland or other wet habitats; also abundant on high ground in England and Wales, but rare in Scotland, is *Coelotes atropos*. All of these species are sometimes found at relatively low altitudes in the south, but are never abundant except on high ground. Less common upland species are *Evansia merens*, which is associated with ants, *Walckenaera capito* and *Euophrys erratica*. Possibly two of the most characteristic species of woodland on high ground or in the north are *Tapinocyba pallens* and *Zora nemoralis*, especially the former.

Species with unusual habitat requirements are *Pardosa agricola* and *Arctosa cinerea*, both of which are found on the stony banks of upland or northern rivers, the former being much more widespread and common than the latter. *Monocephalus castaneipes* was formerly thought to be an almost exclusively upland species, occurring in open grassland and stony habitats, but it has recently also been found abundantly in several places in the south of England in moss on the branches and trunks of trees.

CRITERIA FOR KEY SITE ASSESSMENT AND SELECTION

Comparative site evaluation

The following criteria have been given particular weight in the assessment of upland key sites.

Size

Preference has been given to sites which show the greatest range of altitude, i.e. vertical size, which especially affects the range of local climate. In general, the greater the altitude, the greater the extent and variety of montane vegetation, but much depends on the actual form of the summits. The massive plateaux and broad watersheds of the Cairngorms give a much greater *area* for montane vegetation than the relatively small summits and narrow ridges of the Ben Nevis range. There is thus an inclination to select for high mountains of massive form, with flat or rounded summits. The problem of obtaining an area of adequate size applies only to the higher levels of the uplands, where the montane habitats are mostly of small extent in Britain. At lower levels, submontane habitats are so extensive that the problem more often lies in keeping the size of area chosen within reasonable limits.

Diversity

Assessment has favoured sites which show the greatest variation in topography (which especially affects local climate and drainage) and geology (which especially affects soil conditions and land-use). Variations in angle of slope are important in giving a range of soil types from wet to dry; steep slopes accentuate aspect differences as well, and their gravitational instability tends to maintain the open habitats which many upland plants need. Cliffs in any situation are important habitats – at high levels as montane plant refugia, and at lower levels as nesting places for various predatory birds. Corries, with cliffs, screes and (usually) tarns, add greatly to the diversity of a mountain, and are highly rated features. Too much steep and rocky ground does, however, tend to limit the development of a full range of upland vegetation, and it is desirable that in addition to these somewhat unstable habitats there should be a range of more gently sloping or even level ground. Well-developed solifluction features also add greatly to the interest of a mountain.

The occurrence of calcareous rocks and soils is regarded as a particularly desirable feature. Not only do these (and their dependent organisms) have a certain rarity value, in being much more localised than non-calcareous substrata, but they carry a far richer flora, of both montane and submontane plants, and give much greater productivity for many animals. Moreover, because of the general tendency towards podsolisation under the oceanic British climate, areas of calcareous substrata nearly always carry some leached and acidic soils, and thus inevitably have a wider range of soil and vegetation types than an area composed entirely of non-calcareous substrata. High edaphic diversity thus tends

to be associated with the occurrence of calcareous rocks and soils. The presence of rocks, such as serpentine, which give soils with an unusual cation balance, is advantageous, for when they occur within a site valued mainly for other features it may be possible to avoid the necessity of selecting another site especially to deal with this habitat. For example, lead mine spoil at Moor House, and non-calcareous serpentine in Caenlochan–Clova, represent these unusual soil habitats.

In many places, good examples of other formations, such as woodland, peatland, open water and coastland, lie within or are contiguous with sites valued highly for upland features, giving sites of considerable diversity. Examples are the woods of oak on North Dartmoor, Cothi Tywi, Cwm Ystwyth and Rhinog; ash on the Appleby Fells; alder on the Simonside Hills; pine in the Cairngorms and at Beinn Eighe; and birch on Inverpolly and Foinaven. The majority of upland key sites contain some open water; streams are present on most sites and lakes are especially well represented on Inverpolly (Loch Sionascaig and other lochs) and in the Cairngorms (Loch Einich and numerous corrie lakes). Important blanket mires within or adjoining upland sites are found on Dartmoor, Y Berwyn, Kinder–Bleaklow, Moor House, Merrick–Kells (Silver Flowe), Moorfoot Hills, Langholm–Newcastleton Hills, the Cairngorms, Ben Wyvis, Inverpolly, Foinaven–Meall Horn and Southern Parphe. Complexes of soligenous mire occur on most upland sites but are especially varied and important on some of the calcareous upland sites. Good coastal sections occur within several northern and western Scottish upland sites, notably Inverpolly, Durness, Southern Parphe, Invernaver, Rhum and North Hoy, where the altitudinal descent of vegetation zones brings uplands and coastlands together. One site, the Moor of Dinnet, has been chosen not for any one outstanding feature, but for its interesting combination of moorland, woodland, open water and peatland.

Contrasting regimes of land management are not often found within the same upland area, but are instructive when they occur. The best example yet found is in Skiddaw Forest. Differences in grazing pressure are, however, characteristically associated with variations in the base-status of parent rocks and derived soils.

Floristic and faunal richness, in terms of number of species, are another form of diversity to which a good deal of attention has been paid in key site selection. As already explained, floristic richness is often a measure of the presence and extent of calcareous rock, but not always so, as in the group of Atlantic plants, many of which grow on base-poor substrata.

Naturalness

Human disturbance may increase diversity at first, but has to be considered separately, for it is often an undesirable feature. As virtually all uplands have been disturbed, the matter is one of degree. Plant communities showing the least modification, such as those with tall herbs and ferns, or montane dwarf shrubs, are regarded as the most valuable, partly because they are relatively uncommon and represent surviving fragments of once more widespread vegetation types. Many upland plants which are sensitive to fire (especially dwarf shrubs) or grazing (especially tall forbs) have been eradicated locally by these influences, and a few have evidently been brought to the verge of complete extinction, e.g. *Cicerbita alpina*, *Salix lanata*. It seems especially important to conserve the relics of communities with such species, and others which are still declining.

By contrast, the grasslands derived by burning and heavy grazing of original vegetation are mostly so widespread and uniform that the choice of representative sites is extremely wide. These anthropogenic communities are often well represented on sites which show other, more valuable features and can often be included incidentally when making a choice on other grounds. The uplands least disturbed by man lie in the Highlands, and some massifs there have a good deal of evidently unmodified vegetation at the higher levels.

The criterion of *fragility* is also involved in these considerations.

Rarity

This criterion has already been mentioned in connection with the occurrence of calcareous rocks, and the effects of human disturbance. The highly valued Arctic–alpine plant refugia contain concentrations of rare species, but the presence of a single rare plant species in small quantity has, however, been only an additional and usually minor factor in assessing key sites. Large populations of rare species and rare community dominants are rated highly, e.g. *Dryas* heath, *Salix myrsinites* scrub and *Juniperus communis* ssp. *nana* scrub, which contribute to the high valuation placed on certain western Highland sites. Some rare habitats have special importance. Limestone pavement with clint and grike structure, and a characteristic flora and fauna, is regarded as a very local and valuable feature, and one which is essentially fragile and in need of conservation.

Typicalness

Assessment of sites according to the previous criteria tends to single out the best features, which can sometimes lead to choosing the atypical rather than the typical features, though both are often combined within the same site. Sometimes, however, it is necessary to value more highly those features which are ordinary and widespread, and would otherwise be under-represented. The majority of upland key sites contain at least some typical features, especially within the sub-montane zone, as well as any special and unusual features which they may possess. In a few cases, however, ordinary areas have been chosen to represent the characteristic range of upland communities in certain areas.

The foregoing discussion of criteria has been concerned with habitat and vegetational features, but applies very largely to the zoological component of the ecosystem, too. The main difference is that botanical and zoological qualities do not necessarily run parallel, i.e. a site with a rich and diverse flora, including many rare species, is not necessarily similarly endowed faunally. To the extent that they diverge, flora and fauna may need to be assessed separately and due allowances made in selecting sites to represent both features.

Requirements for the national series

The overall aim in selecting a series of key sites within this formation is to give an adequate representation of the field of variation in British upland ecosystems, in terms of diversity of climate, topography, geology and pedology, and land-use, with their associated biological features, on both the regional and local scales. A series of typical regional representatives of upland along the main south–north temperature gradient has been made and examples of typical upland key sites include Cader Idris, Y Berwyn, Skiddaw Forest, Moor House, Langholm–Newcastleton Hills, Cairnsmore of Fleet, Drumochter Hills and Inverpolly. Emphasis has also been placed on representation of the following features.

1. The marked east to west gradient in oceanicity.
2. The greater development of the montane zone and its associated biota in the Highlands, compared with regions farther south.
3. The marked altitudinal descent of vegetation zones in the western Highlands.
4. The profound influence of calcareous rock on vegetational and floristic richness, notably basic igneous rocks in Snowdonia and Lakeland, Carboniferous Limestone in northern England, Dalradian mica-schist and limestone in the eastern Highlands, and Durness Limestone in the western Highlands.
5. The effects of rocks, such as serpentine, which give unusual cation balance in the derived soils.
6. Diversity in pattern of land-use, and associated effects on vegetation, flora and fauna.
7. The lesser deterioration, from human disturbance (i.e. greater naturalness), shown by some parts of the Highlands, compared with districts farther south.
8. Richness of flora, determined mainly by 2, 4 and 7 above. Montane and oceanic elements are regarded as especially important.
9. Richness of fauna, determined mainly by 2, 4 and 7 above, but not necessarily showing a parallel with richness of flora within the same area. Special recognition is given to birds, as the best known faunal group.
10. Aggregation of rare species; this is often closely connected with 8 and 9 above, but not always. An effort has been made to include the most notable montane plant refugia in all regions, e.g. Snowdonia, Upper Teesdale, Ben Lawers, Caenlochan–Clova and the Cairngorms.

It will be clear from this brief analysis, that selection of key sites has had to favour the Scottish Highlands and, to a lesser extent, northern England, for these are the most important upland regions of Britain, according to the principles defined. Features of the British uplands regarded as internationally important are mainly the extremely oceanic character of vegetation (especially in the west), the highly

anthropogenic nature of much of the vegetation, the unusual biogeographical combinations of flora and fauna in
many areas and the large population size of certain animal
species rare or local in Europe as a whole. Sites have been
chosen to ensure that all these features are well represented
in the national series.

REGIONAL DIVERSITY AND SELECTION OF KEY SITES

Although the account of the field of variation and the
classification of upland vegetation is based on a broadly
ecological analysis of the range of upland ecosystems, the
selection of key sites will be considered on a geographical
basis within each of eight regions of Britain. This does,
however, allow us to follow perhaps the most important
direction of ecological variation, that of decreasing mean
temperature, by examining the regional distribution of uplands in a south to north direction. The representation of
both regional and local ecological variation is considered
next, and a final table attempts to integrate the selection of
key sites with the major elements of the ecological/vegeta-
tional classification.

SOUTH-WEST ENGLAND

The only significant areas of upland in southern England
are Dartmoor (Devon), Exmoor (Devon and Somerset) and
Bodmin Moor (Cornwall). The highest ground, on Dartmoor, only just tops 600 m, though there is an extensive
plateau-land at over 460 m. The terrain is mostly undulating
moorland, and there are none of the features, such as
corries, which are so characteristic of the heavily glaciated
mountains of northern Britain. Much of the vegetation is
referable to other formations, mainly peatland or lowland
acidic heath and grassland, and the only upland communities represented are submontane types (e.g. Callunetum,
Vaccinetum, Molinietum, Trichophoreto–Eriophoretum)
widespread and much more extensive in other parts of
Britain. There are distinctive floristic features such as the
abundance of *Agrostis setacea* and *Wahlenbergia hederacea*,
but these are not upland plants; and while submontane
species such as *Empetrum nigrum*, *Vaccinium vitis-idaea*, *V.
oxycoccus*, *Lycopodium clavatum* and *L. selago* are represented, true montane species are absent. The occurrence of
the thermophilous *Hymenophyllum tunbrigense* at over 460 m
is an indication of the mildness of the upland climate in
this region.

Several northern birds, such as merlin, ring ouzel, red
grouse, black grouse, golden plover and dunlin, breed
sparingly on these southern moorlands, and Exmoor is a
notable stronghold of red deer. The granite tors and clitters
(block screes) of Dartmoor and Bodmin Moor have geomorphological importance, and the extensive blanket mires
and soligenous mires of Dartmoor have considerable
ecological interest.

These three moorland areas are the southernmost
outposts in Britain of northern and upland elements of
vegetation and fauna, and it is appropriate to identify

a grade 1 site within one of them, particularly as there
are additional claims for such status on the grounds of
representing important peatland and lowland heath–
acidic grassland complexes. The omission of a south-west
England upland grade 1 site would mean that one end of
an important ecological gradient was unrepresented, but
it would be difficult to justify more than one such site in
this region.

Dartmoor has the strongest claims for the site representing the upland ecosystem of south-west England. It has the
greatest elevation, the largest upland area, the most interesting geomorphological features, the most varied plant
communities and by far the most important blanket mires
in the region. North Dartmoor (U.1, gr. 1)[1] is regarded as
the most important area, for it contains the highest ground,
reaching 600 m, and has a better development of certain
upland vegetation types than the southern part of the area.
Bodmin Moor is geologically similar, consisting of granite,
but much lower (highest point 420 m), with a less varied
range of vegetation, the most important types being soligenous mires and *Ulex gallii* grass heaths. Exmoor reaches
an intermediate elevation (520 m) on Dunkery Beacon
(U.2, gr. 2) and has less mire, its most important vegetational feature being a wide range of dwarf-shrub heath and
acidic grassland grading from lowland to submontane upland. It is composed of Old Red Sandstone, a softer rock
than granite, and there are no tors or clitters. The smaller
and lower areas of the Brendon and Quantock hills to the
east are so similar to Exmoor that they are not considered
separately; they cannot properly be regarded as upland and
their lowland grassland and heath communities are well
represented elsewhere.

SOUTH WALES

All the counties of south Wales contain uplands, and this
habitat is extensive in some of them. However, apart from
doleritic intrusions in the rather low Bannau Preseli
(540 m) in Pembrokeshire (which are regarded as a grade 2
lowland acidic heath site with upland affinities, and have
interesting glacial and fluvio-glacial features), nearly all the
uplands of south Wales are composed of sedimentary rocks,
and much of the high ground consists of rather dull dissected plateau land with an undistinguished flora and fauna.
There are great areas of uninteresting *Molinia* grassland and
shallow mire and the Forestry Commission have locally
established extensive conifer plantations on the slopes and
across the plateaux, up to relatively high elevations (460–
490 m). The climate of the region is moderately oceanic but
less so in the east than in the west.

The uplands of this region belong to three major geological formations, lying in well-defined tracts. In the south,
mainly in Glamorgan, but extending into south Brecknock
is a block of Carboniferous rocks with a central mass of Coal
Measures forming the South Wales coalfield and dissected
by the parallel, southward-draining mining valleys. Around
the Coal Measures is Millstone Grit, extensively exposed in

[1] Cross-references to key sites are identified by an initial letter
(indicating habitat) and number.

the north on the watershed with the Usk Valley, and surrounding this is an outermost peripheral and discontinuous band of limestone, outcropping here and there as cliffs, steep scree slopes and, more locally, as pavement. This is an important karst area second only to that in the Craven Pennines. Where the limestone is exposed extensively there is calcicolous vegetation and a rich flora, but as the elevation is only moderate, montane species are very poorly represented; the area is, however, remarkable for its number of endemic species of *Sorbus* and *Hieracium*. The most important exposure is the Craig y Ciliau National Nature Reserve (NNR) which, together with the adjoining Millstone Grit area of Mynydd Llangatwg, is regarded as a grade 1 site (U.3) representative of this geological formation.

Immediately north of the Carboniferous block is a belt of Old Red Sandstone, broadening from west to east and containing, in the same direction, the Carmarthenshire Black Mountain, the Brecon Beacons and the Mynydd Du (Brecknock and Monmouth). These massifs, containing several peaks exceeding 760 m, form the highest ground in south Wales; the first two, in particular, contain a good deal of sharply contoured ground, with well-developed, north-facing corries bounded by cliffs. These precipices, formed of somewhat calcareous sandstone, are the southernmost British refugium for certain Arctic–alpine plants. There is a wide range of acidic grassland and shallow blanket mire communities, but basic grasslands are also well represented. The limits of tree growth lie high in this district, and the rather high limits of farmland probably also reflect a relatively favourable climate, as well as fairly fertile soils. The Brecon Beacons, containing the Craig Cerrig Gleisiad NNR and Pen y Fan (U.4, gr. 1), are chosen as the most important site, with the Mynydd Du (Brecknock, Carmarthenshire) (U.7, gr. 2) as a similar alternative. The Mynydd Du (Brecknock and Monmouth) (U.8) is less heavily glaciated than these two massifs, and while this Welsh high moorland ecosystem of slightly continental character deserves to be represented in the national series, the rather similar Y Berwyn (U.13) in north Wales is the preferred choice, with the former regarded as a grade 2 alternative. The more northerly and low-lying Mynydd Epynt (475 m) belongs also to this sandstone block, but is not regarded as an area with outstanding ecological features.

Between Llandovery (Carmarthenshire) in the south and Machynlleth (Montgomeryshire) in the north, and stretching eastwards to the Welsh borders, is the largest upland block in Wales, consisting almost entirely of Ordovician and Silurian grits and shales. This is a dissected plateau, giving rise to several large rivers, the Severn, Wye, Teifi and Tywi. This 'slate' block is botanically the least interesting of the south Wales uplands. The prevailing land forms are fairly extensive plateaux, drained and cut by radiating deep and steep-sided valleys containing variable amounts of native woodland. The rock is soft, and while some of the bigger valleys have long, broken lines of crag, there is on the whole a scarcity of cliffs. Distinct corries are developed only in the northern massif dominated by Plynlimon (752 m), the

highest summit of the 'slate' block, and even here they are not particularly good examples. The range of vegetational diversity is limited, with a preponderance of acidic grasslands, especially Molinietum, but also *Nardus*, *Juncus squarrosus* and *Festuca–Agrostis* types, according to drainage. *Calluna* and *Vaccinium* communities are patchy in distribution and usually of limited extent, and the generally intensive exploitation of the area as sheep-walk is reflected also in the prevalence of bracken on drier slopes. There is little if any truly montane vegetation, and few notable local or rare plants, though the Plynlimon area provides the most southerly British localities for *Saxifraga stellaris*. Radnor Forest, in the extreme east of the 'slate' block, has at least regional importance in the persistence of extensive dwarf shrub communities, especially on Black Mixen (660 m). There is a good deal of *Calluna* and *Vaccinium myrtillus* heath, locally with abundant *V. vitis-idaea*, and *Empetrum nigrum*.

Ornithologically the 'slate' block is important: it is the last refuge in Britain of the red kite, which breeds mainly in the hanging oakwoods on the valley sides, but hunts chiefly over the open slopes and plateaux above. There are also outposts of northern birds such as merlin, ring ouzel, red grouse, golden plover and dunlin, and the area is a stronghold of the buzzard and raven which, like the kite, forage over the open sheep-walks. There was formerly a very large rabbit population in many places, and the breeding density of the buzzard was then extremely high; though buzzard numbers are now fewer, this is still a relatively numerous bird. Until the post-1955 'crash' there was a good population of peregrine falcons. Of the mammals, the polecat has its British headquarters in this part of central Wales, and though it is largely a lowland species, its range extends over the uplands.

This is an appropriate area in which to consider the need to conserve a complete hill farm unit, containing the whole range of variation from valley bottom to hill top, with river, meadows and enclosed land, woodland and sheep-walk. The old-style hill farm, geared to a sheep economy and important as a wildlife habitat, especially for carrion-feeding predators such as the raven, buzzard and red kite, could eventually disappear or become everywhere profoundly changed. The valleys of central Wales have a particular conservation value in this respect. Despite increasing invasion by reservoir and forestry schemes, there remain here some of the most sequestered human communities in Britain, and hill farms are managed essentially by time-honoured methods. The threat of further reservoir construction and afforestation is considerable, and the survival of the sheep-walk ecosystem, with its interesting fauna, is problematical and subject to the vagaries of economic trends. The conservation of the red kite, in particular, involves maintenance of a favourable pattern of land use.

At least three sites could be chosen as representative examples of this submontane ecosystem. The existing Nant Irfon NNR (U.9) with its nucleus of oakwood and upland sheep-walk, forms part of a larger site chosen to include Drygarn Fawr (641 m). A second area has been chosen in the headwaters of the Cothi and Tywi valleys (U.6), containing the Royal Society for the Protection of Birds' Reserve at Gwenffrwd and the woodland NNR at Allt Rhyd y Groes, but extending over a wider area of moorland to the north (Carn Nant-yr-ast 440 m). The last of the three areas is farther north near the head of the River Ystwyth, and includes a tract of moorland rising to 593 m on Carn-yrhyrddod, with a number of tarns (including the Teifi Pools) and patches of oakwood on the steep, lower slopes. This Cwm Ystwyth site (U.5) is probably the most diverse ecologically, but the Cothi Tywi area has better representation of woodland and valley bottom farmland; so that both of these sites are regarded as worth grade 1 status, while Nant Irfon is rated as grade 2.

NORTH WALES

The rest of Wales, lying north of the Dyfi estuary, is largely an upland region and contains the highest mountains in Britain south of the Scottish Highlands. This region is geologically more complex than south Wales, but the mountains fall into fairly distinctive topographic groups. The highest and most rugged areas all lie in the west. Snowdonia proper, in Caernarvonshire and Merioneth north of Ffestiniog, contains the most spectacular mountains in Wales, with the ranges of Y Wyddfa, the Glyder and the Carneddau all rising well above 900 m, and the lesser massifs with Moel Siabod, Moel Hebog, the Moelwyn and the Manod. This district consists of an assemblage of sedimentary and igneous rocks, the latter giving rise to the most rugged landforms. It is a heavily glaciated block of upland, with deep U-shaped valleys, truncated spurs, sharp peaks and ridges, and deep corries, often with tarns.

In west Merioneth, between Maentwrog and the Mawddach estuary, lies a lower but especially rugged upland massif, the Rhinog, composed of hard grits. South of the Mawddach is the fine range of Cader Idris, about 900 m in elevation, and with especially well-developed corries and escarpments; the rocks here are a complex mixture of sedimentary and igneous units. North-east of Cader Idris is the similarly elevated Aran range, with fine east facing corries, formed of andesite.

The eastern part of north Wales has, for the most part, more gently contoured moorlands, with fewer cliffs and corries. The two Arenigs in north Merioneth are isolated, rocky hills rising out of a large area of undulating moorland which includes the level expanse of blanket mire called Migneint. In mid-Denbighshire are extensive low moors, with both dry Callunetum and blanket mire, now partly afforested; and where the counties of Denbigh, Montgomery and Merioneth meet, moorlands rise gradually to form the high, broad whaleback ridge of Y Berwyn, which has rounded summits lying within the montane zone. Montgomeryshire, in particular, has a lot of lower, rather undistinguished hill country, rather like that of the 'slate' block in south Wales, though there are some precipitous hillsides around Llangynog and Lake Vyrnwy. The rather low Clwydian range in east Denbighshire is composed of Silurian slates and shales and limestone which are exten-

sively exposed as scarps at the southern end, on Mynydd Eglwyseg, above Llangollen.

The uplands of north Wales show a pronounced climatic gradient from west to east, notably in decreasing precipitation, but also in the tendency towards a more continental temperature regime. In the Y Wyddfa massif, mean annual rainfall exceeds 430 cm locally, though there are steep gradients, and rainfall in the lowlands barely 16 km away is only 114 cm. The ground in Snowdonia is mostly too steep for extensive peat formation, but soligenous mires are very well represented. The humidity and mildness of climate in the western part of the region is best reflected in the large number of plants, especially bryophytes and ferns, which need oceanic conditions. In particular, there is a strong representation of species which have their European headquarters in south-west Ireland; most of these are confined to the lower hill slopes, mainly in woods and ravines but the geographical proximity of thermophilous species such as *Trichomanes speciosum* and *Hymenophyllum tunbrigense* to cold-adapted plants such as *Silene acaulis* and *Saxifraga oppositifolia* is a most interesting ecological feature. This convergence of highly contrasting phytogeographical elements becomes possible only under extreme oceanic conditions, which satisfy the climatic requirements of both groups.

North Wales is the southernmost part of Britain where a really rich Arctic–alpine flora and a significant extent of montane vegetation have survived the adversities of the Post-glacial Period. Within the region, it is the highest mountains and those with the greatest extent of suitable habitat which are most important in this respect, and many of the lower massifs are as undistinguished in flora and vegetation as much of the uplands of south Wales. Heavy grazing may have obscured the effects of prolonged snow cover by producing large areas of *Nardus* grassland and *Vaccinium* heath which resemble the snow-bed communities with these dominants, but it is possible that this region is too far south to show any definitely snow-influenced vegetation. With the exception of the Rhinog, which have extensive areas of heather, most of the western uplands are managed as sheep-walk and are predominantly grassy. In the east, probably largely because of the more suitable topography, there are, or were until recently, extensive heathery grousemoors. The drier climate and prevalence of poor, peaty soils may also have encouraged this form of land-use. The western part of north Wales was formerly a stronghold of peregrines, but these are at present very few, having been almost exterminated by the effects of pesticides. There is still a large breeding population of ravens in the hills, and this district has several herds of feral goats. Choughs nest among the hills, mainly in old quarries and mines, and there are still a few pine martens. Moorland birds such as grouse and golden plover are found mainly in the east, and here there are breeding hen harriers. The upland invertebrate fauna is rich, especially in the higher mountains.

It is felt that at least four grade 1 sites should represent the range of variation in upland ecosystems in north Wales. In Snowdonia proper (Caernarvonshire), an area extending over parts of three of the central massifs, Y Wyddfa, Glyder (Cwm Idwal) and Carneddau, is needed to encompass all the major features of this most important mountain system. This composite area, Eryri, is the most important upland site in Wales (U.10) and has features which qualify for its inclusion as a site of international importance; it is outstandingly rich in montane plants as a result of the extensive occurrence of calcareous cliffs at high elevations. In Merioneth, Rhinog (U.12) and Cader Idris (U.11) are important sites sufficiently different from the mountains of Caernarvonshire and south Wales to merit grade 1 status; and in the east, Y Berwyn (U.13) has been preferred to Mynydd Du (Brecon–Monmouth) as an example of high moorland of relatively continental character.

Whilst some of the other north Wales ranges have considerable interest, they can hardly be regarded as having first national importance. However, the outlying range of Yr Eifl in Lleyn (U.15) has different and distinctive features (mainly its maritime dwarf-shrub heaths) which qualify the site for grade 2 rating. Mynydd Eglwyseg is included as a grade 2 site (U.14) as it is the only extensive exposure of Carboniferous Limestone in the uplands of this part of Britain, but botanically it is less important than limestone hills in northern England. Migneint and the Denbigh Moors (Mynydd Hiraethog) are regionally important areas, but their range of vegetation is largely represented within Y Berwyn.

MIDLANDS

Although the Pennines are best regarded as a single upland system, their southern extremity, the Peak District of Derbyshire, is usually regarded as belonging to the north Midlands of England. It is the Millstone Grit of the High Peak which will be considered here; the limestone dales of southern Derbyshire are treated as lowland habitats in the *Review*. The limestone area around Castleton, near the junction of the two formations occupies an intermediate ecological position and is of outstanding geological interest.

The prevailing grits and associated beds of shale give mostly soils of very low base-status with much heather moor, and on the more gently contoured moorlands there are large areas of blanket mire. The Peak District has one major feature of special ecological significance – an enormous fall-out from nearby industrial centres of atmospheric pollution both as solid matter and dissolved substances (notably sulphur dioxide) in rain water. The result has been to produce an extremely high level of acidity in the blanket mire peat and kill-off virtually all the *Sphagnum* spp. in this habitat; some soligenous mires on the slopes and in the valleys, however, still have a *Sphagnum* carpet. The lichen flora has been adversely affected, though this is more noticeable in the case of arboreal species. The moorlands of the High Peak are an example of an acidophilous vegetation complex found widely on acidic rock formations but, perhaps from the particular and intense kind of human influence, they show features not found elsewhere and a representative area has been included in the list of grade 1

sites. Interesting vegetational features include the abundance of *Vaccinium myrtillus* and *Empetrum nigrum* in blanket mires, and the occurrence of heaths dominated by *V. vitis-idaea*.

The area with the greatest range of altitude is that containing the two 600 m plateaus of Kinder Scout and Bleaklow Hill, and this probably contains most of the characteristic vegetation, flora and fauna of the High Peak; this area is therefore regarded as the grade 1 upland site (U.16) for the Midlands. In Shropshire, the two lower ranges of the Long Mynd and Stiperstones have extensive heather and bilberry moor, bracken, and some acidic grassland but little peatland. The Stiperstones have been regarded as a good northern example of lowland acidic heath, with transitions to upland heath, and are rated as grade 1 on these grounds (L.123) with bonus value in regard to uplands.

NORTHERN ENGLAND

The uplands of this region form four main blocks: the Lakeland fells, the Pennines, the Cheviots and the North York Moors, with the smaller massifs of Bowland fells, Howgill fells and Shap fells. The Lake District of Cumberland, Westmorland and north Lancashire has a system of steep, heavily glaciated and often rugged mountains, formed of both igneous and sedimentary rocks, and dissected into fairly well-defined massifs by the deep valleys radiating out from the central area. The Pennines form a broad north–south upland tract lying across all the northern England counties; they are composed of Carboniferous Limestone, locally covered by shales and grits, with Coal Measures on their flanks, and though steep and rocky locally, they show a prevalence of gently contoured moorland and plateau summits. The Cheviots lie chiefly in Northumberland, though their main watershed forms the border between England and Scotland. This is another moorland tract composed largely of Carboniferous rocks, especially sandstones and shales, but extrusive and intrusive igneous rocks of Old Red Sandstone age make a considerable spread at the north-east end. The North York Moors consist of a moorland plateau of Jurassic rocks, drained by deep valleys running mainly north–south.

Northern England has a richer montane flora than Wales, but a lesser representation of thermophilous southern species, a difference reflecting the lower mean temperatures of the first region. Northern England also has definite occurrences of chionophilous vegetation though, as in north Wales, heavy grazing has disturbed any original patterns caused by prolonged snow cover. Heather moor and blanket mire are better represented than in Wales, largely because of the greater extent of suitable topography. There is again a quite pronounced gradient of decreasing oceanicity from west to east, the Lake District being strongly oceanic, and the eastern Pennines, Cheviots and North York Moors relatively continental; this climatic gradient is most clearly reflected in the bryophyte flora. The preponderance of heathery grouse-moors in the east is probably the result not only of a lower rainfall, but also of a greater prevalence of suitable moorland terrain and extremely base poor rocks. Another important difference compared with Wales is the much more extensive occurrence in northern England of Carboniferous Limestone, and a correspondingly better representation of calcicolous vegetation, though calcareous cliffs are less extensively exposed within the montane zone (over 600 m) than in Eryri.

The rugged Lakeland mountains are strongholds of crag nesting birds such as peregrine, raven and buzzard, and there are several herds of red deer; the pine marten still holds out here and the area was formerly notable as a southern breeding haunt of dotterel. On the moorlands of the Pennines there are large populations of red grouse, golden plover, dunlin, curlew, sandpipers and ring ouzels; the same was once true of the Cheviots, but here large-scale afforestation has greatly reduced the area of open moorland which these birds need. The Cheviots have herds of feral goats, and hen harriers have recently recolonised this district, whilst the merlin is still fairly well distributed over the whole region. Lakeland is famous entomologically as the southernmost area for the mountain ringlet butterfly *Erebia epiphron*, and the region as a whole has a rich northern invertebrate fauna.

The Lakeland fells closely resemble Eryri in ecological features. The highest ground (Scafell Pike, 978 m) is slightly lower than that in Snowdonia, but the greater distance north probably compensates to give a similar temperature regime on the main summits. There is a parallel assemblage of mainly acidic igneous and sedimentary rocks, which give a similar range of largely base-poor soils in the two regions. Submontane vegetation complexes in Snowdonia and Lakeland are essentially similar, with a preponderance of acidic grasslands, and differences between the two are mainly in detailed composition of flora; a notable difference is the abundance in Lakeland of the Arctic–alpines *Alchemilla alpina* and *Saxifraga aizoides*, both of which are absent from Wales. Because of the much more limited occurrences of calcareous rock in Lakeland, there is not the profusion of calcicolous montane plants which occurs on the cliffs of Y Wyddfa and Cwm Idwal, but Helvellyn actually has a larger number of montane species than any mountain in Wales.

Because of this general vegetational similarity between the two districts, many upland massifs in Lakeland repeat the essential features of mountain systems in north Wales. Thus, while it is felt that the Lakeland fells should be adequately represented in the list of grade 1 sites, the Pennines are regarded as the more important upland district, for they show a greater contrast when compared with the mountains of north Wales. The higher fells of Lakeland are formed mainly of two rock formations; the Borrowdale Volcanic Series which is largely acidic but locally quite strongly calcareous, and the Skiddaw Slate which is almost everywhere acidic. Probably partly because of nutrient differences in the derived soils, the Skiddaw Slate fells have been less heavily exploited as sheep pasturage than those of the Borrowdale Volcanic Series, and so as a whole have retained a much larger extent of dwarf shrub (mainly heather

and bilberry) heath than the latter. Floristically rich ground is, conversely, confined to those of the Borrowdale Volcanic fells which have calcareous rocks.

The Skiddaw group in northern Lakeland shows the widest range of acidophilous vegetation types found in this district, and probably also has the most varied fauna; and in many respects is intermediate in character between the central Lakeland fells and typical Pennine uplands. Part of this massif has been chosen as a grade 1 site (U.17) representing the Skiddaw Slate fells. The next most important area on this geological formation, though not really an alternative site, is the group of hills east of Buttermere and Crummock Water, and known as the Buttermere Fells (U.27, gr. 2).

Of the Borrowdale Volcanic fells, the most unusual site botanically is Wasdale Screes (U.18) and, although it does not quite reach 600 m, several montane species are represented. The physiographic interest of the site is also high and it is given grade 1 rating. The Helvellyn–Fairfield range is over 300 m higher, with a richer montane flora, and represents the best high-level refugium for these plants in England. The chief habitats of the montane flora are cliff faces and ledges, screes and flushes on steep ground, so that there is a contrast with the other main English refugium, in Upper Teesdale – a difference reflected also in composition of the flora. Helvellyn and Fairfield are regarded as sufficiently important in the series of south to north montane refugia to rank as a grade 1 site (U.19). An area of the moorland known as Armboth Fells west of Thirlmere has been recognised as a grade 2 site for its varied complex of mainly acidic soligenous mire, and is described (U.29); this site includes also the wooded waterfall ravine of Launchy Gill.

The Pennines contain most of the main upland communities found in Lakeland, but, while the acidic grassland complex is extensive in some areas, heather and bilberry heaths cover large expanses of moorland and there is a much greater development of blanket mire than in Lakeland. There are also much more extensive outcrops of strongly calcareous rock, and in the Pennines, lime-rich soils occur in a wide variety of topographic situations, instead of being confined largely to steep rock faces and wet flushes, as they are in Lakeland. Calcicolous vegetation is therefore more widely developed in the Pennines, but some characteristic Lakeland species, notably *Alchemilla alpina*, do not occur; the Pennine flora is also much poorer in Atlantic species of plants. Moorland breeding birds, especially waders, are much better represented than in Lakeland, though crag-nesting predators are sparser.

The Pennines are best subdivided into the northern Pennines lying between the Tyne Gap and the Stainmore (Bowes Moor) road (the Alston Block), the central Pennines between Stainmore and the River Aire (the Askrigg Block) and the southern Pennines between the Aire and the Derbyshire border. The northern Pennines form a continuous mass of high moorland reaching 890 m on Cross Fell. There is a steep scarp slope, broken in places by outcropping limestone edges and drained by the swift streams of deeply cut dales, falling to the Eden valley on the south-west side, but on the dip slope a great sweep of gently inclined moorland falls away eastward and gives rise to the headwaters of the Tees and south Tyne.

The Cross Fell range between Hartside and Stainmore is biologically the most important upland massif in England and a large part of it has claims to grade 1 status. Not all the ground is equally interesting, for there are large areas of uniform *Nardus*, *Juncus squarrosus* and *Eriophorum vaginatum* ground, and the most valuable parts are well scattered. Three contiguous areas have been chosen as grade 1 sites, as a compromise between a single very large area with much low quality ground and a larger number of well scattered high-quality sites. Cross Fell–Moor House (U.20) has the main area of high ground (above 760 m) and the most fully representative range of typical vegetation, flora and fauna; Upper Teesdale (U.21) contains the internationally famous Arctic–alpine plant refugium and has the most unusual habitats, e.g. 'sugar' limestone outcrops, open calcareous flushes and unstable river banks; and the Appleby Fells (U.22) have the greatest extent of cliff and scree, both of Whin Sill and unaltered limestone. Together the three contain almost the whole extent of high-level (700–760 m) grassland on limestone to be found south of the Scottish Highlands. The Moor House NNR was originally chosen as a representative expanse of typical Pennine *Calluna–Eriophorum* blanket mire, with a wide range of biotically derived hill acidic grasslands and more local basic grasslands typical of northern England. It was regarded, and has been much used, as a typical site with high research value for basic ecological studies of the upland ecosystem and for work on moorland hydrology.

The other parts of the northern Pennines, including the group between Hartside and the Tyne Gap, and the massifs drained by the rivers Wear, Derwent and the Allens, are mainly grouse-moor country with extensive blanket mire, often containing abundance of *Rubus chamaemorus* and locally with large expanses of dry heather and bilberry moor, as well as the usual acidic grassland complex. Most of this kind of upland ecosystem is well represented on the Moor House and Upper Teesdale sites (see Appendix).

The central Pennines, situated mainly in Yorkshire, consist of a more dissected mountain system, drained by the rivers Swale, Ure, Wharfe, Ribble and Aire. The northern part has a predominance of grits and shale, giving generally acidic upland areas, but the Craven district from Ingleton to Wharfedale is famous for its karst features, with massive exposures of limestone, especially of tabular pavement fissured with grikes, at up to 600 m. Together with the rather low limestone hills around Kendal and Arnside, this is the headquarters in Britain for this very local habitat. The extent of steep limestone hillsides with cliff and scree is also greater than in any other upland area of Britain. This limestone complex is of great scientific interest; two areas are regarded as outstandingly important sites, the well-defined massif of Ingleborough (U.23, gr. 1*) and the tract of upland lying between Malham and Arncliffe (U.24, gr. 1). Both these sites differ from the three grade 1 sites in the Alston Block in having a great deal more exposed limestone,

as pavement, cliff and scree, and much less acidophilous vegetation, especially ericoid heath and blanket mire. Ingleborough is higher than Malham–Arncliffe and has a greater range of vegetation on dry ground, but Malham has an important wetland complex (including Malham Tarn) which forms an integral part of this limestone area. The limestone exposures, including large potholes, in Ease Gill, near Kirkby Lonsdale are floristically rich. At the northern end of the central Pennines, the fells lying between the Mallerstang valley and Swaledale Head have an interesting range of calcareous and acidic habitats, some of which are absent or less well represented on other grade 1 sites. There is a large limestone plateau covered with hummocky grassland, a complete cycle of blanket mire erosion and recolonisation, and a large extent of slightly alpine dwarf-shrub heath. Part of this area including Tailbridge Hill, Mallerstang Edge and Great Shunner Fell thus merits grade 1 status (U.26).

The southern Pennines contain little of interest until the Peak District is reached, most of the moors having suffered too severely from the proximity of industrial Lancashire and Yorkshire. One of their few interesting biological features is the persistence of a relict population of twites in the neighbourhood of Halifax, but the once flourishing merlin has declined greatly in this district during recent decades. Although the Kinder–Bleaklow grade 1 site overlaps slightly into Yorkshire, it is dealt with in the Midlands section.

A rather low-lying belt of limestone runs westwards from Kirkby Stephen to Shap, bridging the gap between the Pennines and the eastern Lakeland fells. Around Orton, on this limestone tract, is an important complex containing calcareous open water (Sunbiggin Tarn), flush, soligenous and topogenous mire, grassland, scar and pavement, which together carry a rich flora with some montane species. This area, designated Orton Fells, lies just above and below the 300 m contour and has some lowland affinities, but is regarded as mainly an upland site (U.25), of grade 1 quality. The steep sided Howgill Fells to the south are composed of Silurian rocks and have a cover largely of acidic grassland. There are two waterfall gorges and flanking crags at Cautley Spout and Black Force, and a few northern or montane plants, but this massif has little which is not better represented in Lakeland.

The Cheviots begin as rather low moorlands (490 m) in the Bewcastle fells on the Cumberland–Northumberland border, and in the area south of North Tyne are mainly of importance for their undisturbed expanses of blanket mire (Irthinghead Mires), though great areas of the moorlands in this district have been planted with conifers by the Forestry Commission. An area of moorland around the head of Caudbeck has been rated as grade 2 for its soligenous mires and is described (U.32). North-eastwards, the altitude of the watersheds rises gradually, reaching 580 m on Carter Fell, and then culminates in the large plateau of Cheviot at 815 m. This end of the range is composed largely of igneous rocks which have supported a heavy grazing pressure, so that the acidic grassland complex prevails on the uplands, and dwarf-shrub heaths are still dwindling. The

Cheviot itself is the most important area of this type and has a number of features, including a large summit plateau covered with blanket mire, which merit its inclusion as a grade 2 site (U.33). Elsewhere in the Northumberland Cheviots there are areas of acidic sandstone-floored moorland similar to those of the southern Pennines, but especially notable for their extent of pure Callunetum, grading into blanket mire on wet ground. Coniferous afforestation of these moorlands also proceeds steadily. In view of the steady disappearance of heather moor in this district and the contiguous Southern Uplands, it is felt essential to select key sites in which this typical eastern upland ecosystem is represented. The most diverse examples in this climatic region are however in the Southern Uplands, and only grade 2 representatives of heather moor have been chosen in Northumberland – Simonside Hills (U.28), Harbottle Moors (U.30) and Kielderhead Moors (U.31); all three have good examples of blanket mire as well as heather moor, and the first two have alderwoods as well.

The North York Moors consist of a large Jurassic plateau drained and dissected by mainly north–south oriented valleys. The plateau and upper slopes have extensive areas of dry heather moor, with much bracken and some bilberry heath, but rather little *Eriophorum vaginatum*. While limestone outcrops in the valleys, the higher ground seems to be mainly composed of sandstones and shales which give base poor soils. At Ingleby Greenhow there is an outcrop of Liassic shale with the second British station for the 'copper moss' *Mielichoferia elongata*. This massif has not been properly examined but, although it was rated as a Scientific Area worthy of conservation in Cmd 7122 (Ministry of Town and Country Planning, 1947), no particular area worthy of grade 1 or 2 status has become known. While there might be a case for choosing a typical example of this grouse-moor country which characterises these dry eastern uplands, the range of diversity is rather limited, and there are no outstanding differences compared with key sites containing heathery moorland in other eastern regions.

The Bowland fells west of the Pennines have also remained unexplored during the *Review*, but evidently resemble the North York Moors in principal upland vegetational features. From their geographical position, the flora is likely to have a stronger oceanic element than the latter area.

SOUTHERN SCOTLAND

Although this is the least mountainous region of Scotland, it contains extensive tracts of hill country of submontane character. The Southern Uplands stretch from near the Firth of Forth to the Clyde, as a series of dissected ranges formed mainly of Ordovician and Silurian grits with subsidiary shales, which are roughly constant in hardness and gives a characteristic topography of smooth though often steep-sided hills with rounded summits and deeply carved glens. The greywackes and shales of the prevailing sedimentary formations vary from acidic to strongly calcareous, as do the more local occurrences of igneous rock, and there is a wide range of soil types in which base-rich brown earths

are extensively represented, giving a good deal of hill land of relatively high fertility. Formerly many of the lower moors were managed as grouse preserves, and though this interest is still strong locally (mainly in the east) it has declined in many areas, and the Southern Uplands are now mainly sheep-walk. Heather moor is still extensive in places but there is thus a predominance of acidic grasslands with a good deal of quite rich hill pasture locally. There is again a strong gradient of decreasing oceanicity from west to east. Despite the limited extent of the montane zone, the Southern Uplands are an important mountain region, somewhat neglected in scientific studies but with considerable ecological diversity, and great potential for investigations in various fields, especially the effects of changes in hill land-use.

The Southern Uplands contain two districts with high summits, exceeding 820 m, the first being in Kirkcudbrightshire and southern Ayrshire (Galloway and Carrick). In this district, large intrusive masses of granite and their surrounding metamorphic aureoles have given rise to some extremely rugged hills, similar in appearance to some of the Lewisian Gneiss uplands of the western Highlands and islands. The highest tops are composed of metamorphosed sedimentary rocks; and are mostly rounded, but the district has fine corries, high cliffs, numerous tarns and several larger lakes. The wetness of the climate has led to a prevalence of peaty soils, and there is a great deal of wet Molinietum, often with abundant *Myrica gale*, and blanket mire or soligenous mire where the water table is permanently high. There is rather little calcareous rock in the Galloway hills, so that the montane flora is rather limited, but oceanic bryophytes are well represented. The more gently contoured lower moorlands of Wigtownshire to the west are covered with still larger expanses of blanket mire, down to levels as low as 90–120 m above sea-level.

In ecological character the Galloway and Carrick hills are important as a southern outlier of the western Highland upland ecosystem and they are quite unlike the rest of the Southern Uplands or any of the uplands in England or Wales. This is the southernmost part of Britain where certain typical Highland species are well established, and as such it is a key area for studying factors controlling the distribution limits and powers of spread of organisms at the edge of their range. At least four pairs of golden eagles attempt to breed regularly, and show interesting evidence of competition with peregrines, ravens and buzzards, which have a major stronghold in this district. Of other Highland species, the dotterel has bred on the high tops during the last few years; red-throated and black-throated divers and common gulls breed on the hill lochs; the dragonfly *Aeshna caerulea* is resident; the Scotch argus butterfly is widespread and locally abundant; mountain hares occur though in smaller numbers than formerly; *Schoenus nigricans* grows locally in rather acidic flushes, and the distinctive northern Atlantic bryophytes *Sphagnum strictum* and *Pleurozia purpurea* occur in local abundance. There are quite large herds of red deer and feral goats, though these have been reduced in the interests of forestry. Galloway also has the most southerly examples of the distinctive patterned ombrogenous mires, with aligned systems of pools and hummocks, so characteristic of the western and northern Highlands.

The lower parts of this upland district have been and are being extensively afforested with conifers, to the point where there will soon cease to be any ground which shows the complete altitudinal range of ecosystem from the limits of enclosed land to the montane zone of the higher summits. It is highly undesirable that this complete sequence should be entirely lost, and there now remain only two areas where it is well represented. These two areas are different from each other and are both regarded as grade 1 sites, namely the granite Cairnsmore of Fleet massif (U.34) with a grousemoor, and the group of sedimentary and granite hills including the Merrick, Craignaw and Corserine (U.35), which is richer floristically. The second area contains the important patterned mire system of the Silver Flowe (P.71). Cairnsmore of Fleet is less rich in moorland birds such as the golden plover than the adjoining area of Grobdale a few kilometres to the east, but it has a greater variety of upland habitat and a more varied fauna overall.

The uplands eastwards are of less interest until the second area of high hills is reached, namely that between Moffat and Tweedsmuir, on the borders of Dumfries-shire, Peebles-shire and Selkirkshire, where there are several large, rounded summits over 760 m. The rock here is sedimentary and, as it is both locally calcareous and also exposed extensively as crags within the steep-sided catchment of Moffat Water, this is the most important area in the Southern Uplands for calcicolous montane plants. This is also probably the most southerly upland area in Britain where the effects of prolonged snow cover on vegetation are clearly shown, and it has a more continental climate than the Galloway hills. The Dumfries-shire portion of the Moffat Hills is rated as grade 1 (U.36), but the less rocky and botanically rich Tweedsmuir Hills immediately to the north are rated as grade 2 (U.39). These uplands are covered mainly by a range of acidic grasslands similar to those of northern England and Wales, but locally there are fairly rich grasslands which give good grazing, and on the whole, the sedimentary rocks of the Southern Uplands give better soils than the igneous or sedimentary formations of the other two regions. A notable feature here is the local abundance of *Luzula sylvatica* in the hill grasslands, for this is usually a species which heavy grazing tends to eradicate except in inaccessible places.

There is a good deal of bilberry heath on Moffat Water, and patchy heather heath as well on the Tweedsmuir Hills, and the same is true of the lower uplands farther east. However, it is not until the grouse-moors of the Moorfoot Hills and Lammermuirs are reached that heather communities become the predominant upland vegetation. The Moorfoot Hills just exceed 600 m and are not notable floristically, but faunally these are one of the best areas of grouse-moor yet encountered, and there are quite important examples of undisturbed blanket mire on the watersheds. Part of the area has been chosen as a grade 1 site (U.37), as the best representative example of the less modified grouse-moor ecosystem of the sedimentary hills of the Southern Uplands.

Both the Lammermuirs and Pentland Hills are less interesting biologically than the Moorfoots, and cannot really be regarded as providing an alternative site, or having national importance. However, closer to the English border, and adjoining the south-west end of the Cheviots, an area of hills surrounding the Tarras Water between Langholm and Newcastleton has been chosen as another grade 1 site (U.38). There is a southern tract of heathery grouse-moor on acidic Carboniferous sandstone which represents the type mentioned for the Northumberland Cheviots, while the rest of the area is thoroughly representative of the less spectacular type of sheep-walk/grouse-moor country found over much of the Southern Uplands, and has good areas of richer pasture. It is lower than the Moffat or Moorfoot Hills, but geologically more diverse, with a wide range of soil types and submontane vegetation, and contains a sizeable stream and interesting fragments of woodland.

Immediately north of the central Lowlands of Scotland, the rather low basaltic plateaux of the Kilpatrick and Fintry (Campsie) hills are mainly sheep-walk with a grassland complex. They have a good deal of Molinietum and Nardetum on damper ground, and though there are a few floristically interesting cliffs, such as the Balglas Corrie, they have only regional importance.

THE SCOTTISH HIGHLANDS

The Highlands contain by far the largest area of upland in Britain, and only the more important tracts can be mentioned here. In this large region there is such an *embarras de richesses* that key site selection is often difficult, and many sites which are intrinsically superior to some grade 1 upland sites south of the Highlands have had to be given lower status. There are important differences in topography and climate within the Highlands. Steep-sided, rugged mountains, rising to narrow ridges and small, peaked summits tend to prevail in the west, while more massive and gently contoured hills with broad ridges and large summit plateaux are more characteristic of the east. There is a pronounced gradient of decreasing oceanicity from west to east, and along the south-western seaboard conditions are mild enough to support a bryophyte and fern flora containing many southern Atlantic species which have their European headquarters in south-west Ireland. By contrast, the eastern hills belong to that part of Britain experiencing the lowest winter temperatures, where markedly thermophilous species cannot grow.

This oceanicity gradient, in combination with that of decreasing mean temperature from south to north, is reflected in a marked altitudinal descent of the vegetation zones with increasing distance north-west. In the relatively continental Cairngorms area, fragments of pine and birch wood still occur up to 600 m, whereas in north-west Sutherland the limits of tree growth appear to be about 300 m lower, and on the most exposed coast are reduced to pockets of scrub in sheltered places. Similarly, even on the most exposed spurs, prostrate montane dwarf-shrub heath does not occur below 600 m in the Cairngorms, but in north-west Sutherland it is found even below 300 m. This downward shift of vegetation zones is probably a response particularly to the severity of wind and lack of summer warmth or sunshine which are associated with extreme oceanicity. The gradient of oceanicity is marked also by the greater extent in the north and west of ombrotrophic mire, which covers great areas of the gentler moorlands, down to sea-level; and by the increased abundance of hygrophilous plants, notably leafy liverworts and *Rhacomitrium lanuginosum*. In the east, *Rhacomitrium* is dominant on some hill tops, but in the west it occurs in the greatest profusion in a wide range of communities from sea-level upwards. Vegetation rich in lichens of the reindeer moss (*Cladonia sylvatica*) type show in general a reverse trend and, with a few exceptions, reach their greatest development on the continental eastern hills.

Another broad geographical trend is the increasing abundance in a north-westerly direction of *Rhacomitrium* summit heath with an abundance of the cushion herbs, *Silene acaulis*, *Cherleria sedoides* and *Armeria maritima*, which gradually change from basiphilous to indifferent in their soil requirements. Where the moss heath is flushed intermittently a still richer community with *Polygonum viviparum*, *Thalictrum alpinum*, *Saussurea alpina* and *Aulacomnium turgidum* is found. In parallel with this trend, there is an increasing occurrence of erosion (ablation) surfaces with much bare soil and stone, in the *Rhacomitrium* heaths, and this bare ground typically has a sparse cover of *Juncus trifidus*, *Festuca ovina* and small herbs.

The greater extent of ground above 900 m, and of calcareous rock at high levels, gives the eastern Highlands a greater extent of montane (especially calcicolous) vegetation and a richer montane flora than the western Highlands. Nevertheless, the trends associated with increasing oceanicity give some compensation for the lesser extent of suitable habitat in the west, in regard to development of montane vegetation and flora. Several peat alpines, notably *Arctous alpinus* and *Betula nana*, show increasing abundance with distance north, and a few montane plants occur only in the northern Highlands (see Table 27, p. 298). *Dryas* heath, especially the low-level type, reaches its greatest development in the north-west; whereas vegetation dependent on prolonged snow cover is best represented in the Cairngorms and thereafter decreases with distance north. Some regional ecological differences between north and south, or east and west, are the result of topographic or geological differences, but others seem referable to the overall climatic gradients.

Human exploitation of the uplands has been intensive throughout the Highlands, but the effects are more marked in some districts than others. There has been general deforestation and widespread replacement of woodland by subalpine upland vegetation, but the latter shows differences between east and west. In general, much of the ground within the potential woodland and dwarf-shrub zones in the west is occupied by mixed grass heath communities in which *Calluna* shares dominance with *Trichophorum cespitosum* and *Molinia caerulea* or, more locally, with *Nardus* and *Juncus squarrosus*. Where grazing by domestic animals and burning have been especially heavy in the west, *Calluna* has often been severely reduced or even eliminated, leaving the grasses and their allies as dominants. Heather-dominated moors are more characteristic of the drier eastern Highlands, but they occur locally in the west, which suggests that their absence on suitable terrain reflects a combination of suboptimal climate and adverse land-use effects.

The western Highlands appear to have suffered greater degradation of habitat and loss of productivity than the eastern Highlands. The excessively wet and cool climate of the west has probably been partly responsible for this difference, by reducing the capacity of the ecosystem for withstanding exploitation, but there are likely to have been other contributory factors, connected with differences in upland management. Whatever the cause, much of the western Highlands could today be regarded as semi-desert in productivity (i.e. wet desert), and this sterility is most obviously reflected in the vertebrate populations. There is documentary evidence that during the last 100 years, the western populations of moorland species, such as mountain hare, red grouse, golden plover, curlew and snipe, have suffered substantial decline, and that numbers of dependent predators such as the peregrine have fallen in parallel. By contrast, the golden eagle has increased, for this species feeds on carrion as well as living prey and has benefited from the increase in sheep stocks (and of mortality among these). The greenshank is, however, more numerous in the west and is the most characteristic bird of the barren moorlands of Ross and Sutherland.

The drier eastern Highlands have, on the whole, a much higher productivity for animals. Except in areas managed primarily as sheep-walk, red grouse and mountain hares are generally abundant on heather moorland, and there is often a relatively high density of other moorland species such as golden plover, lapwing, snipe and curlew, some of which are associated partly with richer grassland feeding places within or adjoining the moors. Golden eagles in this region take a much higher proportion of live wild prey, and peregrines occur at higher density than in the west. The main Scottish populations of the three montane birds, dotterel, snow bunting and ptarmigan, are also in the eastern Highlands, but this may be largely an effect of the greater extent of suitable habitat, i.e. ground above 900 m, compared with the west. The productivity of the calcareous mountains, such as the Breadalbane range, for both sheep and deer, is far higher than that of the prevailing acidic mountain ranges of the west.

Compared with upland regions farther south, the Highlands as a whole are distinguished by their much more extensive montane plant communities and much richer montane flora and fauna. Many distinctive vegetation types of the Highlands, especially those associated with high altitude and/or prolonged snow cover, do not occur in regions to the south. Certain Highland community dominants such as *Juncus trifidus*, *Athyrium alpestre*, *Arctostaphylos uva-ursi*, *Dryas octopetala*, *Empetrum hermaphroditum* and *Dicranum starkei* are either absent or rare outside this region. The montane flora of the Ben Lawers range alone contains 32 species unknown in Britain outside the Highlands, whereas the Southern Uplands, northern

England and north Wales possess between them only six species not found in the Highlands, and five of these are in Upper Teesdale. Moreover, perhaps as a result of the less extreme grazing pressure, as well as the more extensive calcareous habitats, many species show a lesser restriction to cliff faces in the Highlands than elsewhere. Table 27 (p. 298) gives further details of these regional floristic differences.

The biotically produced *Vaccinium* heaths, *Festuca–Agrostis*, *Nardus* and *Juncus squarrosus* communities so typical of regions from the Southern Uplands southwards are rather poorly represented in the Highlands, and occur there mainly in the south, especially Perthshire and Angus. Submontane *Vaccinium* heath is particularly local and the dry grasslands have more *Agrostis* than *Festuca*. *Rhacomitrium* heaths of southern British mountains usually have abundance or co-dominance of *F. ovina*, evidently as a result of heavy sheep-stocking, and the true *Rhacomitrium*-dominated community of the Highlands does not occur now. Sheep and fire have also virtually eliminated the characteristic Highland prostrate montane Callunetum in other regions, and only fragments remain in the Southern Uplands and Pennines. Scree colonisation by *Cryptogramma crispa* is one feature characteristic of southern hills, especially Lakeland and north Wales, but extremely local in the Highlands, and there found mainly in the south. However, effective humidity in even Lakeland and north Wales seems to be insufficient to allow development of the mixed community of northern Atlantic leafy liverworts, which is so notable a feature of hills along the western seaboard of the Highlands. *Schoenus nigricans* communities in largely acidophilous moorland vegetation are virtually confined to the Highlands and Galloway.

Comparison of fauna shows parallels, with many northern and montane species confined to the Highlands, or rare in regions to the south. Red deer forests belong mainly to the Highlands, along with species such as golden eagle, dotterel, red-throated diver, black-throated diver, common gull and pine marten, whilst ptarmigan, snow bunting, greenshank and wild cat occur nowhere else. Similar trends in the invertebrate fauna are exemplified by the Lepidoptera (Table 29, p. 306).

The Highlands are the only uplands of Britain which show any strong similarity to mountains of continental Europe and they most closely resemble those of oceanic south-west Norway (e.g. Sogn). The differences are referable mainly to the heavier exploitation for grazing animals suffered by the Highlands, which has so generally destroyed woodlands, scrub and tall herbaceous communities and caused a great extension of grassland and dwarf-shrub heath. Other differences are the result of the more extreme oceanic climate of the Highlands, especially in the west.

The Nature Conservancy's administrative subdivision of the Highlands between East and West Regions (see Map 2) is ecologically artificial and inconvenient for present purposes, as the East includes western Inverness-shire, Orkney and Shetland, which are climatically all strongly oceanic and therefore western in character. A better ecological division into eastern and western Highlands has been made in the present account, so that the especially important contrast between the continental east and the oceanic west is more clearly illuminated. Within each region, further subdivision will be made according to ecologically important differences in climate, geology, topography and land-use.

EASTERN HIGHLANDS

This region includes the counties of Perth, Aberdeen, Angus, Kincardine, Banff, Moray, and that part of east Inverness-shire (Vice-county 96) to the south of the Great Glen. It has a large total area of upland and contains the highest mountains in Britain, in regard to both calcareous and non-calcareous rocks. It also contains the most continental uplands and thus the areas where late snow-bed vegetation is most extensively developed. While sheep-farming is an important activity, it is practised mainly in the south of the region. Management of uplands as deer forest and/or grouse-moor is general, and this region contains the largest area of grouse-moor in Britain.

The geology of the region is complex, but in essence there are two major Series of metamorphic rocks, the Dalradian in the south and the Moine to the north. Both Series consist of schists, gneisses and quartzites and contain large granitic intrusions. Ecologically, these may be regarded as predominantly hard, acidic rocks, but with locally extensive occurrence of calcareous materials. In the north-east, mainly in Aberdeenshire, there are limited areas of serpentine.

One of the most important upland tracts lies along the broad belt of Dalradian rocks, notably calcareous mica-schists and limestones, which runs north-eastwards from Argyll through Perthshire to Angus and south Aberdeenshire. At the south-west end is the botanically famous district of Breadalbane, and the tract as a whole is by far the richest area in the British Isles for calcicolous Arctic–alpine plants. There are many hills, almost equally rich, though Ben Lawers has always been celebrated for its particular concentration of rarities. From the relatively high fertility of their soils, most of these hills have been heavily exploited as grazing land, especially for sheep, and grasslands rather than dwarf-shrub heaths are the prevailing type of vegetation within the submontane zone. There is a wide range of alpine calcicolous communities and types associated with prolonged snow cover.

An attempt has been made to select an adequate series of grade 1 sites along the Dalradian tract, having regard to the climatic gradient and floristic variation involved. This has meant relegating to grade 2 several hills of virtually equal richness, as these duplicate the interest of the areas chosen as the outstanding sites. The grade 1 Dalradian hills are Beinn Laoigh (U.40), which lies partly in Argyll (i.e. the western Highlands) at the oceanic end of the tract, the combined massifs of Ben Lawers and Meall nan Tarmachan (U.41) in the centre, and the area which includes the heads of Glens Caenlochan, Clova and Callater (U.42), in the east, at the continental end. Ben Lawers is regarded as internationally important. The much lower area containing Tulach Hill near Killiecrankie (U.43, gr. 1) is also included for its unusual limestone and calcareous wetland habitats; and Morrone (U.48, gr. 1) above Braemar has calcareous montane habitats mixed with interesting birchwood and juniper scrub. The grade 2 series includes Creag Mhor and Ben Heasgarnich (U.49), Meall Ghaordie (U.50), Meall na Samhna (U.51), Carn Gorm and Meall Garbh (U.52) in Breadalbane; the area containing Glen Tilt, Glen Loch and Beinn a'Ghlo (U.55); Ben Vrackie (U.56) above Pitlochry; Ben Chonzie (U.54) near Crieff; Ben More, Stobinian and Cruach Ardrain (U.53) near Crianlarich. Nearly all these hills are floristically much richer than any to the south of the Scottish Highlands.

The other upland district of major importance in the region is the large granite mass of the Cairngorms, lying on the marches of Inverness-shire, Banffshire and Aberdeen-shire, and forming the watershed between the Rivers Spey and Dee. The Cairngorms are higher than the Breadalbane-Clova ranges and provide a strong contrast in showing a prevalence of base-poor soils and acidophilous vegetation, with dwarf-shrub heath more extensive than grassland. Cal-careous rocks outcrop locally around the flanks of the massif and their influence on vegetation and flora is especially marked by comparison with the granite. Late-snow-influenced vegetation is also more extensively developed here than anywhere else in Britain. The Cairngorms are regarded as the most important mountain system in the country, with the rating 1*. Tourist developments have reduced the conservation value of the north-west slopes of Cairn Gorm, but apart from the Inverness-shire section between the Lairig Ghru and Bynack More (which contains the area developed for skiing), the whole of the massif is rated as a single grade 1* site (U.44) – the largest in the country (nearly 39 200 ha) though it is not of uniform scientific value throughout. The glens and lower slopes con-tain important remnants of the original pine forests and birch woods, and this is one of the few places in Britain where a natural upper tree limit is still represented.

The only area comparable to the Cairngorms is the granite massif of Lochnagar south of the River Dee, which con-nects by a high watershed with the Caenlochan-Clova hills still farther south. On intrinsic merits, Lochnagar would rate as a top grade site, but as it largely duplicates the range of variation found in the Cairngorms and is far less exten-sive, it is given grade 2 status (U.57).

The eastern Highlands contain a large number of other mountain systems which together form the ill-defined dis-trict known as the Grampians. North of the Spey, and forming the catchment of the Findhorn River is the great undulating plateau-land of the Monadhliath, which rises only just above 900 m but contains a fairly large total area between 760 and 900 m. Similar tracts of high rounded hills comparable in altitude surround the Pass of Drumoch-ter and extend far eastwards through the Forest of Atholl to join up with the Caenlochan-Clova range east of the Devil's Elbow. These hills are composed of rocks of the Moine Series in the north and west, but change to the pedo-genically similar Dalradian Series in the east. It is thought desirable to include in the upland grade 1 series a site

representative of the central Grampians, and the rather low hills around the Pass of Drumochter have accordingly been chosen (U.45). The Drumochter hills lie midway between Breadalbane and the Cairngorms, and have a climate transi-tional between the two extremes of oceanic and continental; they are more oceanic than the Caenlochan-Clova group, but more continental than Beinn Laoigh, and the differences are reflected in the vegetation. The southern part of the Monadhliath, around the head of Glen Banchor, is regarded as an alternative site (U.58, gr. 2) to the Drumochter Hills, but shows slightly more continental features in places. An important continental feature which should be represented in the series of key sites is the dominance in dry ericoid heath and blanket mire of lichens of the reindeer moss group. Dry lichen heath is well represented in the Cairn-gorms and Caenlochan-Clova massifs, but lichen-rich mire is not strongly developed in either, so that the moorland plateau of Carn nan Tri-tighearnan, only 16 km east-south-east of Inverness, has been included to fill this gap. This is predominantly an area of blanket mire (see Chapter 8), but has bonus interest in regard to other upland features. An alternative area with well-developed, lichen-rich blanket mire is the more easterly Ladder Hills (U.59, gr. 2) sur-rounding the Lecht road between Cock Bridge and Tomin-toul.

In the eastern Highlands, the complex of low-level, dry moorland, mire, open water and birch wood known as the Moor of Dinnet (U.46) is an important research and educational area, and is rated as grade 1. The Hill of Towanreef (U.47, gr. 1) near Rhynie, Aberdeenshire, is regarded as the most important of the serpentine outcrops in this part of Scotland, and the more elevated Coyles of Muick in the Lochnagar massif are rated as a grade 2 site (U.60).

Although grouse-moor is represented on several of these key sites, no really typical example of this most character-istic eastern Highland ecosystem has been chosen for the national series. These extensive moorlands have not yet been adequately surveyed but the rationale of safeguarding a truly representative series of upland types requires that attention be given to this matter.

WESTERN HIGHLANDS

This region includes Arran, Argyll, Stirlingshire north of the Highland Boundary Fault, Dunbartonshire, west Inverness-shire (Vice-county 97) south of the Great Glen, the whole of the mainland north of the Great Glen, all the Western Isles, Orkney and Shetland. Climatically, it is characterised above all by extreme oceanicity, but with a contrast between the relative warmth of Knapdale and Kintyre, compared with the cool conditions of Sutherland, Orkney and Shetland. Thus, while there is a strong oceanic element in the flora of the west generally, southern Atlantic species are best represented in Argyll and northern Atlantic species in west Ross and Sutherland. Arable farming is con-fined largely to the strip of east coast lowland, and acidic moorland and even blanket mire extend down to sea-level over much of the west and north coast. Along this barren western and northern seaboard, crofting communities still persist at intervals, especially where shell sand deposits have been a means of enriching the poor soils, either by natural windblow to form machair, or by artificial transport, along with seaweeds, by the human settlers.

Numerous areas of old 'lazy bed' cultivation, showing varying degrees of reversion to moorland communities, indicate that the human population was once much greater, and many of the western hills show extensive suppression or reduction of dwarf-shrub heaths in favour of grassland. Moreover, only fragments of the once extensive forests now remain. Most of these western uplands have some sheep today, but numbers vary locally, from high density on limestone ground and in some of the islands, such as Lewis, to complete absence on some of the Sutherland deer forests. Much of the region is managed as deer forest, and the red deer is perhaps the only large herbivore which can flourish on this poor terrain without management other than periodic culling. Most of the present-day grouse-moors lie in the extreme east of the region, and this bird is now at low density through much of the western Highlands.

The western Highlands south of the Great Glen consist mainly of rocks of the Dalradian and Moine Series interrupted by large intrusive masses of granite, and with smaller areas of more basic igneous rock. The Dalradian forms the western end of the Breadalbane range which just penetrates the borders of Argyll. Beinn Laoigh, representing the oceanic, western end of the massive belt of calcareous Dalradian mica-schist and limestone has already been described under the eastern Highlands, though its Argyll face carries perhaps the richest of all the cliff vegetation on the mountain. The other western Breadalbane hills in Argyll, such as Beinn Dorain, Beinn an Dothaidh and Beinn Achaladair, have a rich flora, but contain little if anything not represented on the Breadalbane key sites already described. Rannoch Moor (partly in Argyll) is of great ecological interest, but is treated essentially as a peatland site. The mountains around Glen Coe and Glen Etive, e.g. Buachaille Etive Mor (andesite), Black Mount (granite and Moine Schists), Ben Starav (granite) and Ben Cruachan (granite), are rather limited in their range of vegetation, and most of their interesting biological features are represented on other Grampian key sites. However, the spectacular craggy andesite mountain of Bidean nam Bian, and its limestone outlier Meall Mor, both flanking the south side of Glen Coe, have sufficient floristic richness and vegetational diversity to warrant grade 2 status (U.81).

There is no area of national importance in the extensive hill country stretching from Ben Lomond and the Trossachs, on the borders of Perthshire and Stirlingshire, through Dunbartonshire and the districts of Cowal and Lorne in Argyll. Some of the higher hills have moderately rich montane floras, and certain basic igneous outcrops in Lorne have interesting botanical features, but all these are better represented elsewhere. Farther south, in Knapdale and Kintyre, there is rather low moorland, but near the Mull of Kintyre is an interesting occurrence of montane plants on the sea cliffs of Dun Ban (U.82, gr. 2), representing

the southernmost occurrence in Britain of an Arctic–alpine-type refugium in this situation. In the Hebrides belonging to this part of the Highlands, the only high hills are the Dalradian quartzite Paps of Jura, but the notable ecological features of these are much better represented on the Cambrian quartzite mountains of the north-west. Likewise, the granite mountains of Arran in the Clyde have no noteworthy ecological features which do not occur on key sites elsewhere.

North of Kinlochleven, there is a change to Moine rocks. The hills of Mamore Forest are largely quartzite and of limited interest, but farther north still lies the Ben Nevis range, with the highest summit in Britain (1343 m), and the only 1220 m tops outside the Cairngorms. There is here an assemblage of granite, andesite and schist, some of which is calcareous, supporting a rich montane flora in places, while prolonged snow cover gives a wide range of chionophilous vegetation. Farther east are two other high massifs of the Moine Series reaching 1130 m, Creag Meagaidh north of Loch Laggan, and Ben Alder and Aonach Mor between Lochs Laggan and Ericht; both of these lie on the borderline between west and east Inverness-shire, but are western rather than eastern in climatic and ecological character. These three massifs of the western Grampians form an important group and vegetationally are sufficiently different from the Drumochter Hills to the east, the Breadalbane hills to the west and the nearest grade 1 Moine hills to the north, to justify the inclusion of one of them in the grade 1 series. The Ben Alder–Aonach Mor massif (U.61) has been selected for grade 1 status having a great diversity of vegetation types, while the Ben Nevis range (U.79) has smaller summits and Creag Meagaidh (U.80) has lesser occurrences of calcareous rock. The last two sites have lost more of their dwarf-shrub heaths through heavy grazing and burning on the lower slopes, and both are rated as grade 2. All three of these massifs have fine examples of the vegetation complexes associated with really prolonged snow cover.

The geology of the western Highlands north of the Great Glen is complex and has international fame. Most of the region is composed of metamorphic schists and gneisses, but locally there are large igneous intrusions, of peridotite, gabbro and granite, and extrusions of basalt, while the north-west has a considerable tract of Torridonian Sandstone and the north-east has a large area of Old Red Sandstone. These different rock formations have given rise to varied land forms, and soils varying widely in base-status, but as they are mostly hard and non-calcareous, the derived substrata are mostly base-poor and acidic. Strongly calcareous soils are limited to a rather narrow band of dolomitic limestone and mudstone in the west; restricted areas of blown shell sand by the sea; certain of the igneous rocks, mainly basalt; small occurrences of Triassic limestone; and locally base-rich exposures of gneiss, schist and sandstone. The Old Red Sandstone is often calcareous but the Torridonian Sandstone in the west is mainly acidic and, at best, has thin shale bands which give a richer seepage water. The Lewisian Gneiss and Moine Schist can both be strongly calcareous, but are more usually poor in available lime, and some of the Moine granulites can be almost as siliceous as the Cambrian Quartzite (which extends from Whiten Head to Sleat), which is about the most sterile of all Scottish rocks in its soil-forming capabilities. Many massifs in the western Highlands contain mixtures of these different rocks, so that a series of areas representative of the range of variation in climate, topography, soils and land-use features may show some geological duplication.

The Moine Series of rocks covers the largest area in the north-west Highlands, and contains the mountain system regarded as having the widest range of plant communities and species, namely, the Beinn Dearg–Seana Bhraigh massif (U.62, gr. 1*) at the head of Loch Broom in west Ross. This massif has larger summit areas and higher watersheds than is usual in this district, and more extensive exposures of calcareous rock with a richer flora at high elevations than any other mountain group to the north of the Great Glen; it is also the most northerly British mountain system with a full sequence of late snow-bed communities. The nearest alternative to this area is the Fannich Hills (U.84, gr. 2) immediately to the south, but the summits here cover a smaller area and calcareous rock is less extensive. The rather lower range with Meall Horn, next to Foinaven in the Reay Forest (U.65, gr. 1*), Sutherland, is somewhat similar, but has less late snow-bed vegetation. Ben Hope (U.86, gr. 2), an isolated mountain in Sutherland also has a rich calcicolous flora but covers a smaller area and has a rather more limited range of plant communities. The Moine Series has the highest mountains north of the Great Glen, lying at the head of Glens Affric and Cannich (Carn Eige, 1182 m), on the borders of Inverness-shire and Ross; these hills have a large extent of late snow-bed vegetation and good dwarf-shrub heaths but very little calcareous rock and rather small summit areas, so they are rated only as gr. 2 (U.83). The rather lower tops of Monar Forest (U.85) farther north are also rated as grade 2 because of the especially interesting range of summit vegetation.

Ben Wyvis in east Ross (U.63) lies in an area of more continental climate than Beinn Dearg and is regarded as sufficiently different in major vegetational features to merit grade 1* status in addition. It has little calcareous rock but has a very large summit area and carries an extremely full range of acidophilous vegetation, including latest snow-bed types. The only other comparable eastern hill on the Moine Series is Ben Klibreck (U.87, gr. 2) in Sutherland, but this is lower than Ben Wyvis and has a much smaller summit area. The Affric–Cannich Hills also show similarities but are more oceanic than Wyvis. The extensive tract of mountain land along the western seaboard from Loch Sunart to Loch Carron is composed mainly of Moine rocks and contains many high peaks, such as Ladhar Bheinn, Beinn Fhada, A'Chralaig and Sgurr Fhurain. Some of these hills are interesting, but most of their important features are adequately represented in the key sites already mentioned.

On their west side the Moine rocks are bounded by the Moine Thrust Plane, and close to this line lies a discontinuous band of dolomitic limestone. This Durness Limestone is exposed as major outcrops, usually with scarps and fragmented areas of pavement, in Strath Suardal in southern Skye, at Glas Cnoc and elsewhere in Kishorn, at Knockan near Elphin, at Inchnadamph on Loch Assynt, at Durness itself, and along the east side of Loch Eriboll. Of these, the exposures at Strath Suardal (U.73), Knockan (U.66), Inchnadamph (U.67) and Durness (U.68) are vegetationally the most important and are regarded as sufficiently different for each to warrant grade 1 status, whilst that at Glas Cnoc (see Appendix) (U.93) is regarded as grade 2. The outcrop in Strath Suardal gives another complex of limestone habitats including exposed bedrock, grassland, soligenous mire, as a more northerly counterpart to those at Malham, Orton Fells and Tulach Hill; and it has additionally a substantial area of birch–ash–hazel woodland and a coastal margin. The limestone at Durness itself also contains other habitats, including the grade 1* group of four calcareous lochs (Loch Borralie etc.), and calcareous mire. To the west of the Moine Thrust Plane, the Lewisian Gneiss and Torridonian Sandstone both form high mountains, but in many places there is a vertical sequence of these rock formations often accompanied by the overlying Cambrian Quartzite.

The chief quartzite mountain systems are the hills of Coulin Forest and Beinn Eighe in west Ross, and the Foinaven–Arkle and Conival–Breabag ranges in Sutherland. Beinn Eighe (U.64, gr. 1*) is perhaps the most varied of these, for it has more extensive exposures of the associated calcareous Serpulite Grit and Fucoid Beds (mudstones) than anywhere else, and the Torridonian Sandstone is also well represented. The important pine and birch wood of Coille na Glas-Leitire lies on its lower slopes. The much more northerly Foinaven–Arkle massif (U.65) is, however, rated as a grade 1* site because of its distinctive features. The higher part of the range is flanked by a lower area of rugged gneiss country with considerable faunal interest, and passes to the south-east into the Moine range of Meall Horn. The massif of Conival–Breabag (U.91) adjoining the Inchnadamph limestone is rated as grade 2. The Torridonian Sandstone mountains are represented by Cul Mor and Cul Beag in the existing Inverpolly NNR, which is rated as grade 1 overall (U.66), from the combined interest of its high and low ground. Of the high Torridonian Sandstone peaks, Liathach in Glen Torridon (adjoining Beinn Eighe) is probably the best in range of vegetation, but Beinn Bhan (U.88, gr. 2) in Applecross and An Teallach (U.89, gr. 2) above Dundonnell are almost equally good. Along western coastal areas the Lewisian Gneiss forms a great deal of rugged low-lying country, with innumerable lochs and outcropping bosses of rock, but in a few places it rises into high summits. The hills of the Letterewe (U.90) and Fisherfield Forests in West Ross, Ben More Assynt (U.91) in Sutherland and North Harris (U.92) in the Outer Hebrides are composed wholly or largely of Lewisian Gneiss, but in biological features are not regarded as sufficiently different from the high Moine hills to justify more than grade 2 status; the first two are, however, quite rich floristically. The knobbly and lochan-studded plains of the lower gneiss country are well represented in the Inverpolly NNR and in the ground adjoining the Foinaven–Arkle massif. An important complex of soligenous mire has been recognised as a grade 2 site on the Lewisian moorlands south of Laxford Bridge but is described here (U.99).

On the west coast of northern Argyll and in the Inner Hebrides are massive Tertiary igneous intrusions and lava plateaux of which the most important biologically are in the Trotternish peninsula of Skye (U.72, gr. 1) and on Rhum (U.71, gr. 1), with those in western Mull (Ardmeanach (U.95, gr. 2)), Morvern (Beinn Iadain and Beinn na h-Uamha – U.96, gr. 2), and Ardnamurchan rated lower. The gabbro of Skye gives scenically magnificent mountains, but the Black Cuillin are mostly dull biologically. Of the other igneous rocks, the syenite of Ben Loyal (U.94, gr. 2) gives interesting botanical differences compared with adjacent hills, and the outlying island group of St Kilda, though chosen largely for importance as a coastal site, has ground which must be regarded as bonus upland.

The Old Red Sandstone of the north-east rises high nowhere, but gives two interesting lower hill groups; the locally calcareous Ben Griam More and Ben Griam Beag (U.97, gr. 2), rising out of the flow country of east Sutherland, and the more acidic Morven–Scarabens range (U.98, gr. 2) still farther east in Caithness.

A few ecological features are not adequately covered by the above series – in particular, the extreme examples of altitudinal descent of plant communities in response to severe wind exposure on the north-west coast. In north-west Sutherland, the limestone ground at Durness and the sandstone headland immediately to the west, Sgribhis Bheinn, show fine examples of this effect, and are together regarded as a grade 1* site (U.68); this site has a seaward boundary which includes the magnificent bird cliffs of Clo Mor and the dunes north of Durness, rated separately as a grade 1* coastal site (C.108). A second sandstone hill farther to the south, Creag Rhiabhach, is included and connects with the interesting blanket mire and coastal habitats at Sandwood, the whole forming the Southern Parphe key site (U.69, gr. 1). To the east of Loch Eriboll the low hill of Ben Hutig has interesting montane vegetation at low elevations rising above an important type of blanket mire on A'Mhoine (P.106, gr. 2). To complete this series the blown shell sand area at Bettyhill, Invernaver (U.70, gr. 1), is included for its exceptional ecological interest, including *Dryas* heaths almost at sea-level, but also rates as a coastal key site (C.109). The island of Rhum in the Inner Hebrides is important not only for its geological and biological diversity, but also for the exceptional opportunities it offers in the field of management research; it too has a diverse range of coastal habitats. Orkney and Shetland, the two northernmost groups of Scottish islands, have a cool oceanic climate. Actual precipitation is not high, but there is a large annual number of days with overcast skies, and even low mist, and effective wetness is reflected in the strong representation of northern Atlantic bryophytes. *Pleurozia purpurea*, a good indicator of humid climate, is widespread in suitable habitats, and *Rhacomitrium lanuginosum* attains dominance in a variety of grassland communities. Marked oceanicity is also indicated by the low levels at which distinctly montane vegetation occurs, and by the extensive development of blanket mire. Orkney is composed almost entirely of Old Red Sandstone, which gives soils of reasonable fertility so that although blanket mire and wet heath cover much of the higher ground, there is also a good deal of farmland. The predominant Dalradian schists and gneisses of Shetland give poorer soils, and here blanket mire covers a high proportion of the total land surface.

Both Orkney and Shetland have each only one area with ground exceeding 300 m in elevation, and neither has any high montane habitat, though both (especially Shetland) have large areas of lower moorland. North Hoy (U.74, gr. 1) in the south of Orkney has been chosen as an area which represents most of the important higher-level plant communities of both groups of islands, and for its altitude has a remarkably varied range of vegetation, with certain montane types and plant species occurring at unusually low altitudes. It also has a magnificent cliff coast. The only comparable area, Ronas Hill (U.100), in the north mainland of Shetland, has a more limited range of habitat and vegetation and is rated, though its peri-glacial features are of great interest, as grade 2 (see Appendix). A lower-lying tract of upland, Milldoe and Starling Hill (U.75, gr. 1) on Mainland Orkney, has been chosen for its more 'typical' vegetational features representing the Orkney moorlands, and for its unusually high ornithological interest. The Orkney uplands have long been famous as the classic British breeding haunt of the hen harrier, and are rich in other ground nesting birds of prey, as well as non-predatory species. The area includes the Royal Society for the Protection of Birds' reserve at Dale of Cottascarth. The distinctive serpentine outcrops of northern Shetland, with their unusual plant communities and flora, are represented by the Keen of Hamar (U.76, gr. 1) and adjacent ground in Unst, whilst other serpentine ground in North Fetlar (U.77) is rated as grade 1 for its high bird interest, and contains further examples of heaths which characterise this rock formation. A more typical Shetland range of acidophilous moorland and blanket mire, with strong ornithological interest, is contained in the existing NNR of Hermaness (U.78, gr. 1), which has still greater importance as a coastal site, with cliffs, stacks and seabird colonies. The island of Noss, also chosen for its coastal bird interest, has a still smaller representation of moorland communities, but merits mention here as another coastal site with bonus upland interest.

Table 31. *Main ecological features of grade 1 upland sites*

Grade 1 site	Acidic submontane	Calcareous submontane	Acidic montane	Calcareous montane	Unusual soils	Continental features	Oceanic features	Altitudinal descent	Regional refugium	Floristic interest	Faunal interest	Sheep-walk	Grouse-moor	Deer forest
	1	2	3	4	5	6	7	8	9	10	11	12	13	14
North Dartmoor	3	—	—	—	—	—	3	—	1	2	2	3	1	—
Craig y Ciliau	2	3	—	—	—	1	—	—	1	3	1	3	—	—
Pen y Fan	3	1	1	1	—	1	1	—	2	3	1	3	—	—
Cwm Ystwyth	3	—	—	—	—	—	—	—	1	3	3	—	—	—
Cothi Tywi	3	—	—	—	—	—	1	—	1	3	3	—	—	—
Eryri	3	2	2	2	1	—	3	—	3	3	3	3	1	—
Cader Idris	3	1	1	1	—	—	3	—	2	3	2	3	—	—
Rhinog	3	—	1	—	—	—	3	—	—	2	2	1	1	—
Y Berwyn	3	—	1	—	—	2	—	—	1	2	3	2	3	—
Kinder–Bleaklow	3	—	—	—	1	2	—	—	1	2	3	2	3	—
Skiddaw Forest	3	—	2	—	—	1	1	—	1	1	3	3	3	—
Wasdale Screes	2	1	1	1	1	—	2	2	2	3	2	3	—	—
Helvellyn–Fairfield	2	1	2	1	—	—	1	—	3	3	2	3	—	—
Moor House–Cross Fell	3	2	2	2	1	1	—	—	2	3	3	3	2	—
Upper Teesdale	3	2	1	2	1	2	—	—	3	3	3	3	3	—
Appleby Fells	3	3	1	2	1	1	—	—	2	3	2	3	1	—
Ingleborough	2	3	1	2	—	—	—	—	2	3	1	3	—	—
Malham–Arncliffe	2	3	—	1	1	1	—	—	2	3	1	3	—	—
Orton Fells	2	3	—	—	—	1	—	—	1	3	1	3	—	—
Mallerstang–Swaledale	3	2	1	1	—	2	—	—	1	2	3	3	2	—
Cairnsmore of Fleet	3	—	2	—	—	—	2	2	1	1	3	3	3	3
Merrick–Kells	3	—	2	1	—	—	2	1	2	2	2	2	1	3
Moffat Hills	3	2	2	2	1	2	—	—	3	3	3	3	1	—
Moorfoot Hills	3	1	1	—	—	2	—	—	1	1	3	3	3	—
Langholm–Newcastleton Hills	3	2	1	—	—	2	—	—	1	2	3	3	3	—
Beinn Laoigh	2	1	3	3	—	—	3	2	3	3	1	3	2	—
Ben Lawers	3	2	3	3	—	1	2	—	3	3	3	3	2	1
Caenlochan–Clova	3	3	3	3	2	3	—	—	3	3	3	2	2	3
Tulach Hill	2	3	—	2	—	1	—	—	1	2	1	3	1	—
Cairngorms	3	2	3	2	—	2	2	—	3	3	3	1	3	3
Drumochter Hills	3	1	3	1	—	1	2	—	1	2	3	2	3	3
Moor of Dinnet	3	—	—	—	—	2	—	—	1	2	1	3	—	—
Hill of Towanreef	1	1	1	1	3	1	—	—	1	2	—	2	2	—
Morrone	1	3	1	2	—	1	—	—	1	2	1	2	—	2
Ben Alder–Aonach Mor	3	1	3	2	—	1	2	—	3	3	2	1	2	3
Beinn Dearg–Seana Bhraigh	3	2	3	2	—	—	3	1	3	3	3	2	1	3
Ben Wyvis	3	1	3	1	—	2	2	—	2	2	2	2	2	3
Beinn Eighe & Liathach	3	1	2	1	—	—	3	1	2	3	2	1	1	3
Foinaven & Meall Horn	3	1	2	1	—	—	3	2	2	3	3	1	1	3
Inverpolly & Knockan	3	1	1	2	—	—	3	1	1	3	3	1	1	3
Inchnadamph	2	3	1	2	—	—	2	2	3	3	2	2	2	3
Durness	3	2	2	2	—	—	2	3	2	3	3	2	—	1
Southern Parphe	3	—	2	—	—	—	2	3	2	2	1	2	—	3
Invernaver	2	2	1	2	—	—	2	3	2	3	2	1	1	1
Rhum	3	2	2	2	3	—	3	2	2	3	3	—	1	3
Trotternish Ridge	2	2	2	2	2	—	3	2	2	3	2	3	—	2
Strath Suardal	2	3	1	2	—	—	2	3	2	3	2	3	—	2
North Hoy	3	1	2	2	—	2	3	3	2	3	3	3	1	—
Milldoe & Starling Hill	3	1	1	—	—	—	2	2	—	1	3	3	—	—

Table 31 (*contd.*)

Grade 1 site	1	2	3	4	5	6	7	8	9	10	11	12	13	14
Keen of Hamar	1	1	1	2	*3*	—	2	*3*	*3*	*3*	1	*3*	—	—
North Fetlar	3	1	1	1	*3*	—	2	2	1	1	*3*	*3*	—	—
Hermaness	*3*	—	—	—	2	—	*3*	2	—	1	*3*	*3*	—	—

Notes

Each feature is given a subjective rating on a 0–3 point scale. Features 1–4 are a measure of actual extent, whereas 5–8 involve greater weighting of the quality of these features. Unusual soils are those which have an unusual balance of cations, notably with magnesium, lead, copper, iron or other metal in excess of calcium. Numbers 9–11 concern the *regional* importance of the features, e.g. floristic interest is not simply a matter of number of species, but involves questions of phytogeography, rarity, abundance, floristic combination and ecological significance. Features 12–14 give a rating of emphasis of interest in land use.

N.B. The different features carry different weight, so that it is not valid to add them together to give an aggregate score and then to assess the comparative value of sites on this basis. The features which were regarded as most important in qualifying a site for grade 1 rating are indicated by italic figures; they are not necessarily scored as 3, as regional significance is also considered.

Table 32. **INDEX OF UPLAND SITES**

Region	* Internationally important sites. Site	County
South-west England		
GRADE 1	U.1 NORTH DARTMOOR	DEVON
Grade 2	U.2 Dunkery Beacon	Somerset
South Wales		
GRADE 1	U.3 CRAIG Y CILIAU & MYNYDD LLANGATWG	BRECKNOCK
	U.4 PEN Y FAN (including CRAIG CERRIG GLEISIAD)	BRECKNOCK
	U.5 CWM YSTWYTH	CARDIGANSHIRE
	U.6 COTHI TYWI	CARMARTHENSHIRE
Grade 2	U.7 Mynydd Du: Black Mountain (Carmarthen)	Brecknock–Carmarthenshire
	U.8 Mynydd Du: Black Mountains (Brecknock & Monmouth)	Brecknock–Monmouthshire
	U.9 Nant Irfon	Brecknock
North Wales		
GRADE 1*	U.10 ERYRI: MOUNTAINS OF SNOWDONIA (*a*) Y WYDDFA: SNOWDON (*b*) GLYDER (*c*) CARNEDDAU	CAERNARVONSHIRE
GRADE 1	U.11 CADER IDRIS	MERIONETH
	U.12 RHINOG	MERIONETH
	U.13 Y BERWYN	MERIONETH–DENBIGHSHIRE–MONTGOMERYSHIRE
Grade 2	U.14 Mynydd Eglwyseg	Denbighshire
	U.15 Yr Eifl	Caernarvonshire
Midlands		
GRADE 1	U.16 KINDER–BLEAKLOW	DERBYSHIRE–YORKSHIRE
North England		
GRADE 1	U.16 KINDER–BLEAKLOW (PART)	YORKSHIRE See under Midlands
	U.17 SKIDDAW FOREST	CUMBERLAND
	U.18 WASDALE SCREES	CUMBERLAND
	U.19 HELVELLYN & FAIRFIELD	WESTMORLAND

Table 32 (*contd.*)

Region		Site	County
GRADE 1*	U.20	MOOR HOUSE & CROSS FELL	WESTMORLAND–CUMBERLAND–DURHAM
*	U.21	UPPER TEESDALE	DURHAM–YORKSHIRE
GRADE 1	U.22	APPLEBY FELLS	WESTMORLAND
GRADE 1*	U.23	INGLEBOROUGH	YORKSHIRE
GRADE 1	U.24	MALHAM–ARNCLIFFE	YORKSHIRE
	U.25	ORTON FELLS	WESTMORLAND
	U.26	MALLERSTANG–SWALEDALE HEAD	WESTMORLAND–YORKSHIRE
Grade 2	U.27	Buttermere Fells	Cumberland
	U.28	Simonside Hills	Northumberland
	U.29	Armboth Fells	Cumberland
	U.30	Harbottle Moors	Northumberland
	U.31	Kielderhead Moors	Northumberland–Roxburghshire
	U.32	Caudbeck Flow	Cumberland
	U.33	The Cheviot	Northumberland
South Scotland			
GRADE 1	U.34	CAIRNSMORE OF FLEET	KIRKCUDBRIGHTSHIRE
	U.35	MERRICK–KELLS	KIRKCUDBRIGHTSHIRE
	U.36	MOFFAT HILLS	DUMFRIES-SHIRE
	U.37	MOORFOOT HILLS	MIDLOTHIAN–PEEBLES-SHIRE–SELKIRKSHIRE
	U.38	LANGHOLM–NEWCASTLETON HILLS	DUMFRIES-SHIRE–ROXBURGHSHIRE
Grade 2	U.31	Kielderhead Moors (part)	Roxburghshire See under North England
	U.39	Tweedsmuir Hills	Peebles-shire–Selkirkshire
Eastern Highlands			
GRADE 1	U.40	BEINN LAOIGH (BEN LUI)	PERTHSHIRE–ARGYLL
GRADE 1*	U.41	BEN LAWERS–MEALL NAN TARMACHAN	PERTHSHIRE
GRADE 1	U.42	CAENLOCHAN–CLOVA	ANGUS–PERTHSHIRE–ABERDEENSHIRE
	U.43	TULACH HILL	PERTHSHIRE
GRADE 1*	U.44	CAIRNGORMS	INVERNESS-SHIRE–ABERDEENSHIRE–BANFFSHIRE
GRADE 1	U.45	DRUMOCHTER HILLS	INVERNESS-SHIRE–PERTHSHIRE
	U.46	MOOR OF DINNET	ABERDEENSHIRE
	U.47	HILL OF TOWANREEF	ABERDEENSHIRE
	U.48	MORRONE	ABERDEENSHIRE
Grade 2	U.49	Creag Mhor & Ben Heasgarnich	Perthshire
	U.50	Meall Ghaordie	Perthshire
	U.51	Meall na Samhna	Perthshire
	U.52	Carn Gorm & Meall Garbh	Perthshire
	U.53	Ben More & Stobinian	Perthshire
	U.54	Ben Chonzie	Perthshire
	U.55	Beinn a'Ghlo	Perthshire
	U.56	Ben Vrackie	Perthshire
	U.57	Lochnagar	Aberdeenshire
	U.58	Monadhliath	Inverness-shire
	U.59	Ladder Hills	Aberdeenshire–Banffshire
	U.60	Coyles of Muick	Aberdeenshire
Western Highlands			
GRADE 1	U.61	BEN ALDER & AONACH MOR	INVERNESS-SHIRE
GRADE 1*	U.62	BEINN DEARG & SEANA BHRAIGH	ROSS
*	U.63	BEN WYVIS	ROSS
*	U.64	BEINN EIGHE & LIATHACH	ROSS
*	U.65	FOINAVEN & MEALL HORN	SUTHERLAND
GRADE 1	U.66	INVERPOLLY & KNOCKAN	ROSS
	U.67	INCHNADAMPH	SUTHERLAND
GRADE 1*	U.68	DURNESS	SUTHERLAND

Table 32 (*contd.*)

Region		Site	County
GRADE 1	U.69	SOUTHERN PARPHE	SUTHERLAND
	U.70	INVERNAVER	SUTHERLAND
	U.71	RHUM	INVERNESS-SHIRE
	U.72	TROTTERNISH RIDGE, SKYE	INVERNESS-SHIRE
	U.73	STRATH SUARDAL, SKYE	INVERNESS-SHIRE
	U.74	NORTH HOY	ORKNEY
	U.75	MILLDOE & STARLING HILL	ORKNEY
	U.76	KEEN OF HAMAR, UNST	SHETLAND
	U.77	NORTH FETLAR	SHETLAND
	U.78	HERMANESS, UNST	SHETLAND
Grade 2	U.79	Ben Nevis	Inverness-shire
	U.80	Creag Meagaidh	Inverness-shire
	U.81	Bidean nam Bian	Argyll
	U.82	Dun Ban, Kintyre	Argyll
	U.83	Affric–Cannich Hills	Inverness-shire–Ross
	U.84	Fannich Hills	Ross
	U.85	Monar Forest	Ross
	U.86	Ben Hope	Sutherland
	U.87	Ben Klibreck	Sutherland
	U.88	Beinn Bhan, Applecross	Ross
	U.89	An Teallach	Ross
	U.90	Letterewe Forest	Ross
	U.91	Ben More Assynt & Breabag	Sutherland
	U.92	North Harris	Inverness-shire
	U.93	Glas Cnoc[a]	Ross
	U.94	Ben Loyal	Sutherland
	U.95	Ardmeanach, Mull	Argyll
	U.96	Beinn Iadain & Beinn na h-Uamha	Argyll
	U.97	Ben Griam More & Ben Griam Beag	Sutherland
	U.98	Morven & Scarabens	Caithness
	U.99	Laxford Moors	Sutherland
	U.100	Ronas Hill[a]	Shetland

[a] See Appendix.

10 ARTIFICIAL ECOSYSTEMS

This category comprises those habitats so completely created and maintained by human activity that they cannot be termed semi-natural but which nevertheless have a considerable wildlife and nature conservation interest, especially as they cover so large a part of Britain. This most intensively managed kind of land consists of arable farmland, horticultural land, or urban–industrial land; the last in the broad sense, includes that with buildings of all kinds, gardens, town parks, roads, railways, airfields, sewage farms and rubbish dumps. There is also a variety of land left derelict from human activities. The populations of species which these habitats incidentally support are large and of obvious national importance, not least in their proximity to human populations; these are the plants and animals most readily seen and appreciated by the majority of people. Yet this is also probably the most vulnerable and threatened element of British wildlife, in that there is an increasing effort to maximise the use of such land for economic purposes, at the expense of all extraneous components.

This is particularly noticeable in the arable farming areas, where intensification of agricultural practice is tending steadily to eliminate organisms and habitats other than the crop species and their soils. Land is such a valuable commodity in many lowland areas that the idea of allowing even tiny areas to remain as unproductive waste ground is becoming increasingly unacceptable, and there is a growing tendency to make every square metre yield some measurable return to someone. As well as the inroads into semi-natural ecosystems already discussed, the use of man-made habitats themselves is being intensified; quarries and disused railway cuttings are being used for tipping waste; waste ground for building; and places such as disused canals and gravel pits for intensive recreation. Hedges and their trees are being removed, field edges ploughed, ponds filled in, and even road verges encroached upon, in the interests of increased farm production.

These man-made habitats are mostly small individually, discontinuous or linear, and the nature conservation problems they pose cannot be dealt with adequately by the selection of a series of the most important sites. It is seldom that any one site within this range could be regarded as nationally important: their interest is geographically dispersed and assumes this degree of importance only when whole districts are considered. While it is certainly possible to identify examples of some of these habitats as locally, or even regionally, important and to safeguard them on a site basis, even this is usually only a token effort at conservation. Such sites may be valuable in conserving rare species, but they usually do little towards safeguarding significant portions of the populations of more common species. It may well be necessary, for instance, to set aside small areas within which to perpetuate populations of certain declining arable weed communities, if the species concerned are to survive in Britain at all. For some of these man-made habitats, the practical problems of safeguarding are often difficult and/or expensive, especially in relation to the nature conservation value involved.

Since this range of habitats does not lend itself to the key site approach, its inclusion may seem somewhat anomalous within the *Review*. Nevertheless, it is felt that since a basic purpose of the *Review* is to identify the field of nature conservation interest in Britain, in terms of habitats, communities and species, it is relevant to describe this interest for man-made habitats, at least in outline, and to indicate the practical problems for conservation. For brevity, the description of interest and analysis of problems will be presented together. No attempt is made to suggest what proportions of these habitats, communities and species should be safeguarded.

RANGE OF ECOLOGICAL VARIATION

The range of artificial ecosystems has been identified as primarily agricultural and non-agricultural, but the separation is not clear-cut. Some of the habitats (e.g. road and railway verges, ditches and canals) are obviously not on farmland, but are often set in an agricultural environment, and are thus affected to some degree by farming practices.

Hedges of essentially similar or identical character occur on farms and away from farms, and along roadsides they form the boundary between the two classes of land. The distinction between these overlapping habitats is, however, important in terms of management: farm habitats are the responsibility of individuals, tenant farmers or landowners; others are the responsibility either of local or national government agencies and utilities (transport and river authorities, and water boards) or of other large organisations. Habitats of an obviously urban–industrial character are much more clearly distinct from those of agricultural land, but management responsibilities here are divided between individuals and bodies. A list of artificial habitats is given in Table 33.

Within the range of agricultural habitats, the steady elimination of non-productive land, and the increased effi-

Table 33. *Types of artificial habitat*

	Agricultural	Non-agricultural
	Productive land Arable Grazing Orchards	
	Non-productive land	

Dry land	Hedges
	Headlands
	Fallow
	Green lanes and access roads
	Stackyards and areas near buildings
	Uncultivated field corners, fallow and marginal
	  uncultivated land
	Walls
		Road verges and hedges. Motorway banks
		Green lanes, trackways
		Railway verges and disused railway tracks
		Station and goods yards
		Sea and airports, airfields (including disused)
		Retaining banks of reservoirs
		Parks, recreational land and golf courses, gardens,
		  shrubberies and roadside trees
		Cemeteries/churchyards
		Dumps and sewage farms
		Industrial sites; mineral workings and spoil heaps
		Individual areas of waste land
		Buildings and walls

Riparian	Dry ditches Wet ditch edges Pond edges Farm reservoirs Marsh land	Banks of rivers, canals, dykes and main drainage ditches Banks of reservoirs (with and without drawdown of water) Flooded and gravel pit banks
Aquatic[a]	Ditches Streams Ponds Reservoirs	Rivers Canals Main drainage ditches Reservoirs Gravel pits and flooded mineral workings

[a] Dealt with generally in Chapter 7.

ciency of production itself, pose a considerable threat to nature conservation interest. There is also encroachment by urban–industrial development or other human pressure on both agricultural and non-agricultural land. Even where non-agricultural habitats remain undeveloped, they are often subject to management in order to control vegetation growth, increasingly involving chemical methods which often pose a considerable threat to floristic and invertebrate interest.

Agricultural habitats

The greater area of England (but not of Wales or Scotland) supports productive agriculture and horticulture, i.e. 9.7 million out of 13.0 million ha of which about half (5.3 million ha) is arable land (*Agricultural Returns*, Nov. 1971, MAFF). The intensity of agricultural production and types of cultivation vary widely according to soils, climate and other factors but essentially some 8.4 million ha in England (the area of arable land and improved grassland) are managed for maximum production from relatively few cultivated plant species, involving regular disturbance of soil and addition of plant nutrients. The balance of 1.3 million ha is categorised as rough grazing and belongs largely to the less modified, semi-natural grassland types dealt with in Chapters 6 and 9.

PRODUCTIVE FARMLAND
Arable

Cultivated land in Britain is concentrated where there is the greatest summer warmth and sunshine, and the lowest rainfall and windspeed. Arable farming is also favoured by low elevation, flat relief, and high soil fertility. These conditions obtain most strongly in eastern England, where climate is relatively continental, topography generally low and rather flat, and the soils predominantly base-rich, since leaching is not marked and the parent materials are mostly soft superficial and recent deposits. With increasing distance westward there is a steady decrease in extent of arable land in the lowlands, as the climate becomes more oceanic, the ground more undulating and elevated, and the soils damper and less base-rich. This decrease is marked by a corresponding increase in permanent grassland on farms. As the ground rises into the uplands of western England and Wales, arable land becomes confined to valleys or coastal plains, and enclosed grasslands give way to unenclosed rough grazings on hill grassland and moorland. Like Wales, Scotland is so mountainous that arable land is restricted, but there are rich areas on the eastern coastal plains, in the central Lowlands and, to a lesser extent, on the north side of the Solway Firth. An interesting feature is the high elevation (at least 300 m) to which arable land rises on the continental eastern foothills of the Highlands in the counties of Aberdeen, Banff, Moray and Nairn.

Of the cereals, wheat (1.1 million ha) is grown mainly in eastern England, especially from Lincolnshire through the Fenlands to Essex. The pattern of arable crops is not static, however, and barley has become much more important than hitherto. Since 1940, many old pastures in southern and eastern England (especially chalk and neutral grasslands) have been ploughed for barley growing. In 1955, the distribution of this crop was similar to that of wheat, but with a greater westward spread. Since then, the development of fast-maturing strains of barley has revolutionised the cultivation of this crop, and it is now grown in western districts such as Lakeland where the summers were formerly too wet and sunless. Barley (2.2 million ha) has increased at the expense of oats and mixed cereals.

Potatoes (0.24 million ha) are widespread, with concentrations in the Fenlands, west Midlands, Lincolnshire, east Yorkshire, west Lancashire and eastern Scotland, while sugar beet (0.2 million ha) is grown mainly in eastern England, from Yorkshire to the Thames, with a lesser belt in the west Midlands. Fodder crops and green crops (rape, fodder beet, vetches, tares, turnips, mangolds, swedes, cabbage, kale and kohlrabi) are widespread in the arable lowlands of most districts and cover about 0.24 million ha. Fruit-growing (0.08 million ha), as orchards and small fruit, is highly localised and scattered, mainly in the Fenlands, Kent, Somerset and east Devon, Herefordshire and Worcestershire, and the Carse of Gowrie in eastern Scotland. Vegetables, flowers and nursery stock (0.2 million ha) are also widespread but local, mainly in England and more in the east than the west, and especially in a belt from the Fenlands to Bedfordshire. Temporary (ley) grass (2.1 million ha) is widespread and extensive, especially in western England, Wales, and all arable districts of Scotland.

Within this basic pattern there is considerable fluctuation from year to year more especially with changes in support for break crops such as field beans (24 000 ha in 1963 and 60 000 ha in 1971). Unusual crops such as flax, chicory and maize have not become popular, and though there have been major trends (notably the increase in barley and oil seed rape), there has been little significant change from the patterns in the maps of crop distribution in the *Atlas of Britain and Northern Ireland* (Anon., 1963).

The wildlife content of arable lands is considerable but decreasing. Between 150 and 200 species of plant can be described as weeds in arable land but many of these are sufficiently frequent in other habitats to need no further consideration here. Only about 90 species are significant in the present context, in that they are mainly dependent on

arable land and are infrequent or decreasing in abundance and distribution.

Particularly long-established and interesting but local arable weeds include the following:

Adonis annua	*Melampyrum arvense*
Myosurus minimus	*Stachys arvensis*
Fumaria purpurea	*Galeopsis angustifolia*
F. bastardii	*G. speciosa*
F. martinii	*Legousia hybrida*
F. muralis	*Galium tricornutum*
F. micrantha	*Valerianella locusta*
F. parviflora	*V. dentata*
Agrostemma githago	*V. rimosa*
Chenopodium ficifolium	*Filago spathulata*
C. hybridum	*Chrysanthemum segetum*
Scandix pecten-veneris	*Centaurea cyanus*
Bupleurum rotundifolium	*Arnoseris minima*
Euphorbia platyphyllos	*Bromus interruptus*
Antirrhinum orontium	*B. secalinus*
Veronica praecox	*Avena ludoviciana*
V. verna	*Apera spica-venti*
V. triphyllos	

The exact present status of many of these species is unknown. A current survey of weeds in arable land, organised by the Botanical Society of the British Isles and the Weed Research Organisation, should give some information on many of these species and others, but does not include many of the most common species such as *Papaver rhoeas* or *Agropyron repens*. It is, however, apparent that a number of arable weeds have declined considerably, including *Lolium temulentum* darnel, *Agrostemma githago* corncockle, *Centaurea cyanus* cornflower and *Chrysanthemum segetum* marigold (which were listed as amongst the most common weeds in the sixteenth century) together with species such as *Bromus interruptus*, *Arnoseris minima* and *Filago spathulata*, which have been dwindling over the last 50 years, to a point where less than a dozen localities are known for each. The once familiar and colourful displays of poppies in the cornfields of eastern England have largely disappeared, though there are still occasional spectacular occurrences. Annual weeds are prone to considerable fluctuations in their appearance, and plants such as poppies still have relatively 'good' years, e.g. 1971.

Little is known of the animal life dependent on these weed species or on arable land in general. A few species of Lepidoptera are restricted to one or two plant species (e.g. *Endothenia ericetana* on *Stachys arvensis*) but most are polyphagous within a group of food plant species (e.g. about a dozen species of Lepidoptera on *Atriplex* and *Chenopodium*) so that the extinction of a rare arable weed may be of less overall significance to insects than the reduction in population size of a group of related plants which remain relatively common. About 25 species of Lepidoptera and 25 of Coleoptera are known to be relatively restricted to weeds as food plants, and certain other species which seem to depend on crop situations and structures, such as *Zabrus tenebrioides* in the Carabidae which is found in cornfields, and *Oxytilus insecatus* on rotting potatoes. Larvae and pupae of the migratory death's head hawk-moth seem to be found less often nowadays in potato fields, possibly because the haulms are chemically sprayed.

Among vertebrates no single species is entirely dependent on arable land but many farmland birds would suffer some population decline if arable fields were devoid of weeds; they include notably linnet, greenfinch, goldfinch, yellow-hammer, corn bunting, stock dove and turtle dove. Whilst many birds feeding on arable land breed in habitats such as hedges, trees, woods and verges (e.g. pigeons, finches, blackbirds and thrushes), some have become adapted to nesting actually on ploughed land (e.g. lapwing, oyster-catcher, common curlew, stone curlew, skylark and reed bunting), and most of the corn buntings and quail breeding in Britain nest in hay and cereal crops. Some of these adaptations to arable land are very recent, and in Holland, since 1950, the dotterel has shown a remarkable colonisation of this habitat, breeding in fields of flax and sugar beet. On the other hand, some species have apparently been unable to cope with the increasing mechanisation and other methods of modern agriculture. The decline of the corncrake is attributed to the earlier and more rapid mechanical harvesting of hay crops, and many nests of corn bunting are cut out in hay and cereal fields. Current studies by G. R. Potts have shown that the widespread and substantial decline of the grey partridge is correlated with the decrease in insect food vital for the chicks, through use of herbicides and reduction of undersowing of cereals.

Apart from the mechanical hazards to ground-nesting birds, the main threats to wildlife on arable land are the efficient cleaning of crop seeds and the widespread use of herbicides to eradicate weeds, and equally general use of insecticides as seed-dressings and sprays. Some distinctive weeds of cereal crops could well become extinct unless deliberate efforts are made to retain sample populations. An area adjoining the Weeting Heath National Nature Reserve (NNR) has been set aside as a reserve for the perpetuation, through appropriate management, of populations of the notable Breckland plants which belong to ancient arable or fallow land; such reserves may be the only answer to the general problem of conserving these weed floras.

Less is known about the interest of the insect fauna of arable land, but insecticides, being largely unselective, kill pests and harmless species alike, and the indirect effects on other animals (e.g. grey partridge) have been noted. The accidental effects of the persistent organochlorine insecticides (especially dieldrin, aldrin and heptachlor) on wildlife are well known. After catastrophic direct kills of seed-eating birds of many species, and heavy indirect mortality of predators (notably raptors, owls and carnivores) feeding on these granivorous birds, voluntary restrictions on the use of these insecticides have resulted in considerable improvement in the wildlife situation. Nevertheless, once widespread species such as the sparrowhawk and kestrel are still scarce breeders (or absent) over much of eastern England, and the peregrine remains absent as a breeding bird in those of its former haunts closest to large areas of arable land.

NON-PRODUCTIVE FARMLAND

Headlands

These are areas round a cultivated field which are left un-cropped, usually to give a turning space for machinery and access round the edge, and sometimes to provide a buffer zone between one crop and another or between the crop and the field boundary. Normally they are seasonal features but when a field is similarly cropped in successive years, head-lands will tend to persist. These verges of arable fields are decreasing as field sizes grow and as modern machinery becomes increasingly manoeuvrable. Headlands too are often deliberately sprayed with herbicides.

Headlands have essentially a weed flora, developed in the absence of competition from the crop. The ground is often considerably trampled, rutted and generally disturbed, with plants such as *Poa annua*, *Lolium perenne*, *Plantago major*, *Coronopus squamatus*, *Chenopodium* spp. and *Matricaria* spp. Headlands adjoining hedges are much used by hedge-row birds for feeding, but their fauna is not known to have any special interest. Headlands have some conservation interest in supporting a variant of the field flora often merging into the field boundary grassland flora. The plant communities of headlands are in general well represented in other situations, however, and this is not a habitat in which deliberate conservation measures are practicable.

Fallow

The practice of resting arable land between crops is no longer economic, and fallow ground is now found mainly where land has been taken out of cultivation by farmers concentrating on intensive stock-rearing indoors. This is particularly the case where soils are of marginal agricultural fertility, and in the Breckland such ground often produces spectacular displays of colourful weeds such as *Echium vulgare*. Ancient fallow ground has been an important factor in the persistence of the peculiar Breckland weed flora (see Chapter 6).

Hedges

The extent of hedges is not accurately known. According to the Forestry Commission census in the mid 1950s, there were then in Britain 612000 miles (984000 km) of hedge, which represents 445000 acres (180000 ha) assuming an average width of *c.* 2 m. Random samples, each of 1 sq. mile (2.56 km²) in area across England and Wales give a mean hedgerow mileage of 14 per sq. mile (22.4 km per km²), which (assuming 24 million acres (9.7 million ha) of hedged land) gives a total mileage of 546000 (874000 km). Hedges vary in three important ways: linear extent (i.e. km per km²), management and shrub species content. They are least frequent and extensive in the arable east of England and most common in the western lowlands. Typical eastern areas now have between 8 and 13 km of hedgerow per km², while in the west 24 to 29 km/km² is usual and up to 40 km/km² is known. Management of hedgerows also varies according to type of farming. In the east, hedges are usually either intensively managed by mechanical means and kept at or below 1.0 m in height, or intermittently cut or burnt down to ground level. In stock areas, hedges are usually higher and thicker and more frequently managed by manual techniques such as cutting and laying. Shrub species content varies with soil type and age of the hedge: the soil determines which species occur but age affects the number of species in any one length. In general, the number of shrub species increases with the age of the hedge. Most hedges in the stock areas are richer in species than those in arable areas but there are significant exceptions, particularly in Norfolk, Suffolk, Essex and Kent where rich hedges occur in arable country. Ancient hedges, especially those delimiting parish boundaries, are of particular interest.

About 500 vascular plant species occur in hedges but half of these are more common in woodland and grassland, and the rest also grow in these situations. Nevertheless, in certain areas where woodland and scrub are scarce, hedges are important habitats for many shrubs and trees such as *Thelycrania sanguinea, Euonymus europaeus, Malus sylvestris, Pyrus communis, Rhamnus catharticus, Sorbus torminalis* and *Viburnum lantana*; climbers such as *Bryonia dioica, Clematis vitalba, Lonicera periclymenum* and *Tamus communis*; and herbs such as *Viola odorata, Zerna ramosa* and *Poa nemoralis*. There are also three important genera, *Ulmus, Rosa* and *Rubus*, which have a major habitat in hedgerows. All species of *Ulmus* (apart from *U. glabra*) are found mainly in hedges and the recent serious epidemic of Dutch elm disease has necessitated wholesale removal of infected trees. In *Rosa* and *Rubus* the assessment of nature conservation value is complicated by taxonomic questions. In *Rosa* (a genus subject to 'lumping') there are perhaps five 'species' dependent on hedges, but in *Rubus* (subject to 'splitting') perhaps 40 'species' are dependent on hedges.

Hedgerow plants have considerable importance as hosts for animals, although it is difficult to assess what proportions of total populations depend on hedges. For instance, although no *Ulmus* spp. may be entirely removed from the British landscape by the combined forces of disease and hedgerow destruction, the genus is a basic food for 100 or so species of insect; these must decrease in total abundance and, as the trees become scarce, survival of some dependent insect species may become critical. Many invertebrates feeding on the more common trees and shrubs have important secondary habitats in hedges containing their host plants, and their total populations must be considerable. It is thought that many insect species are dependent largely or entirely on hedges, but as with plants, the relative importance of hedges as habitat varies locally according to the occurrence of the primary habitat of woodland and scrub.

It is estimated that very approximately 10 million birds breed in hedges but no species is confined to this habitat, for this is secondary to woodland for most of them. Nevertheless in unwooded areas at least 20 species may be dependent on hedges, and these decline in due proportion as hedges are removed. When hedges are compared with woodland and scrub on an area basis, they show an unusually high density of breeding birds, because territorial spacing is operating only in a linear dimension. The hedge bottom or verge is also important for some breeding birds. Although a significant proportion of British mammal species occur in hedges, too little is known of their relative frequency in this and other habitats to do more than suggest tentatively that the populations of a few species such as hedgehog and bank vole may be appreciably affected by changes in hedgerow area.

As farms increasingly become entirely arable or keep stock in specialised environments, hedges become redundant as stock barriers and are removed. Another important factor is the increasing cost of labour for manual management of hedges. To a lesser extent the increasing use of large machinery has led to hedge removal for field enlargement, but as the optimum field size is about 20 to 24 ha and hence some 10 or 11 km of boundary are required per km^2, this factor alone is probably not of major importance. Hedgerow removal has greatly accelerated since 1945, and some arable districts (e.g. Huntingdonshire) have now lost a substantial proportion. The rate of removal varies greatly geographically and its significance must be related to the total length of hedge and extent/number of woodlands in the particular district. The conservation of hedgerows for wildlife has most urgency in areas where deciduous woodland is absent or nearly so. Hedges also have landscape and archaeological value, and are thus important to conservation of the countryside in a general sense. They are an integral and vital part of the rural scene, and the maintenance of scenic beauty requires that some limit be placed on the extent of hedgerow removal.

Farm and village ponds

Farm ponds were originally used for watering animals and are therefore more numerous in stock-farming districts than in arable country. Sample surveys in traditional cattle areas give frequencies of one pond to between 8 and 28 ha, and a mean area of nearly 100 m^2 for each pond. Village ponds are less numerous, but are sometimes fairly large.

Ponds are a type of standing open water body, but only the largest examples are considered in Chapter 7. Farm ponds are mostly shallow (46–76 cm depth) and base-rich, with water pH in the range of 6.5–8.5. Ponds form a wildlife habitat of mainly local interest, most of their characteristic and abundant plants and animals being widespread and fairly common species. The list of higher plants associated with farm ponds is short, the most frequent species being *Juncus inflexus, J. effusus, J. articulatus, Glyceria fluitans, Potamogeton natans, Epilobium hirsutum, Lemna trisulca, L. polyrrhiza, L. minor, Sparganium erectum, Rorippa nasturtium-aquaticum, Alisma plantago-aquatica* and *Ranunculus aquatilis*. Some species grow only in the larger, deeper ponds and could be considered as lake plants. The nationally rare *Ranunculus ophioglossifolius, Pulicaria vulgaris* and *Alopecurus aequalis* are confined to pond margins, especially where trodden by cattle.

Farm ponds are a most significant habitat for invertebrates, e.g. the Dytiscidae (Coleoptera) and Corixidae

(Hemiptera). Several corixids seem to depend on or be adapted to the discontinuity in space and time which ponds provide, e.g. *Corixa nigrolineata, C. lateralis, C. punctata, C. sahlbergi, C. fallini* and *C. striata*. Similar adaptation is probably shown by Crustaceans such as *Cyclops vernalis* which is very common in small ponds and ditches but rare in large open waters; *C. strenuus* and *C. gracilis* are also recorded only from ponds. In the Cladocera, species apparently confined to small ponds include *Daphnia longispina* (common) and *D. alkinsonii* and *Moina macrocopa* (both rare). The Odonata are among the more 'popular' aquatic groups, and although again no species is entirely dependent on farm ponds, the relative frequency of perhaps 10 species might be decreased significantly by substantial loss of these habitats, e.g. *Aeshna cyanea, Anax imperator, Libellula quadrimaculata, L. depressa, Sympetrum striolatum* and *Ischnura elegans*. Although the vertebrates of ponds are few and lacking in rarities, large proportions of the British populations of common frog, common toad, the three newt species and moorhen must depend permanently on these habitats, and a larger number of species may use them at times.

Ponds are steadily disappearing in many areas through deliberate infilling. In areas still used for stock, ponds are filled and piped water supplies laid on to fields because of the risk, particularly to young cattle, of Johne's disease. A Leicestershire survey showed that 12.5% of ponds on dairy farms have been filled in since 1930. In areas converted from stock to arable, ponds are redundant and are filled in and ploughed-over whenever drainage conditions allow. In the Leicestershire area 37% of ponds on arable land have been filled in since 1930. When the field containing a pond is converted to arable (without infilling) or if cattle are fenced off to prevent disease, the pond margin is colonised by scrub (commonly *Crataegus monogyna, Solanum dulcamara, Urtica dioica, Rubus* spp. and *Rosa* spp.) which can cast heavy shade and leaf litter onto the pond, and thus destroy much of the wildlife interest.

Ponds, especially in villages, are frequently used for dumping rubbish, which is unsightly and often contains toxic materials. Of 67 farm ponds examined in detail 16 were contaminated by dumping of chemical containers (8 were contaminated with herbicide, 1 with insecticide, 5 with fertiliser and in 10 were various other substances). Although farm ponds are obviously vulnerable to run-off of fertilisers and pesticides, in a Huntingdonshire survey only one pond in 30 examined for organochlorine insecticide residues was found with detectable amounts of pp-TDE and pp-DDT in the water. Some invertebrates depend on the pollution of ponds by cattle.

Farm and estate roads

These vary from muddy tracks to high-class roads with all-weather surfaces, and are generally private although there may be public rights of passage over some. They are complementary to the public road system and perhaps more common in upland and marginal areas. The vegetation associated with them often merges into the surrounding land, though there may sometimes be hedges or walls.

The flora and fauna are similar to that of public roads (see below), and they are subject to the same threats, especially the uncontrolled and haphazard use of chemical sprays such as paraquat. Their conservation importance depends on their nature, use and management, and is generally similar to that of minor public roads and green lanes, though there is less chance of influencing management for wildlife in the medium and long term. When boundary features (hedges/walls/ditches) are present the conservation interest is likely to be greater because of the complete discontinuity with the surrounding land-use; but when these features are absent the trampled-ground grassland communities of plants will often be different from those of the surrounding land, even if it is also grassland.

Stackyards and areas around farm buildings

Changes in farm practice have led to gradual changes in these habitats, especially in arable districts. Stackyards of unthreshed corn hardly exist now, and farmyard animals are now mostly kept under cover. The virtual demise of the farm horse and disappearance of associated stables, feed lofts, grazing fields and dung-heaps have caused loss of habitat in some cases, and perhaps a temporary increase in others when buildings stand unused and decaying.

Except for some aliens, the flora of stackyards and areas around farm buildings is generally undistinguished, with *Urtica dioica, Chenopodium* spp., *Malva* spp., *Polygonum* spp. and other weed plants predominating. But many older buildings and walls, especially where limestone and mortar with lime have been used, support communities of rather specialised plants of greater interest. Although the ground flora is seldom of much botanical interest, many of the plants are valuable for a wide range of insects and their associated predators, and litter, sheds, barns and outbuildings provide favoured habitats for vertebrates and invertebrates. Stackyards used to be an important source of winter food for chaffinches and other granivorous birds.

These farm habitats are disappearing or changing through tidying up, including use of insecticides and herbicides (especially 'total' herbicides) for control of pests, plant diseases and weeds, and reduction of fire risks. Old buildings made of traditional materials are gradually disappearing and being replaced by modern concrete, galvanised iron or asbestos-bound structures on metal frameworks. Chemical control of house sparrows with alpha-chloralose is increasing – its misuse could be hazardous to other species. The prospects for practical conservation measures within these habitats are probably poor. They are, nevertheless, one of the more important wildlife habitats on many farms.

Non-agricultural habitats

Road verges on public roads

The extent of verges associated with public roads in Britain has been estimated at 210 000 ha, of which 4000–4800 ha abut existing or proposed motorways. A further 4000 ha can be estimated for green lanes in England and Wales. The road network covers virtually the whole country, though some northern upland areas have very few roads, except on ground planted by commercial forestry interests; the wildlife interest of the verges varies, but is considerable in the aggregate. For the purposes of nature conservation, road verges are best considered with the hedge, bank, wall or other boundary feature, which forms part of the available habitat. Habitats represented on road verges vary from sand dune and salt marsh to moorland and rock face, but by far the most common are forb-rich grassland communities, with varied floristics.

Commonly associated with the grass verge over about half the total length of roads in the country are hedges representing a scrub/woodland-edge habitat. Width of verges varies considerably: along many minor roads and lanes there may be little or no verge, the boundaries consisting of steep earth banks or walls, or mixtures of these, nevertheless representing a significant area of often species-rich habitat. Road verges on chalk and limestone are often wider than usual because the clay soils of these rock formations were readily 'puddled' by domestic stock and rutted by traffic before they were metalled, so that users tended to spread the trampling pressure more evenly and the highway became widened.

Management of roadside verges is a comparatively recent development since, except for the major routes, most roads were unmetalled until the late nineteenth century and consolidation of road surfaces only took place in the 1920s and 1930s. Although many roads are of considerable antiquity, road verges as a distinct habitat have really only come into existence with the development of motor transport. Most road verges have been managed by cutting, which represents a form of simulated but low-intensity grazing, and it is under this regime that the characteristic floristic composition of the swards have developed. Only along minor roads in more sequestered country districts are verges still regularly grazed by domestic stock.

The prevailing grassland communities of road verges are mostly neutral or basiphilous in character and their soils are often more base-rich than on surrounding land. In areas of acid heath and in unfenced uplands, grass verges may show some degree of contrast with the surrounding vegetation according to drainage, grazing factors and effects of road dust, salt and disturbance. About 400 species of higher plants were recorded in a random survey of road verges covering the major geographical and ecological (except maritime) regions of Britain. At least another 250 species might reasonably be expected and the overall figure of 650 species could be a minimum for the total flora associated with roads in lowland and inland districts. The survey has revealed a continuous range of associations of vascular plants, with the following grasses predominant: *Arrhenatherum elatius, Agropyron repens, Agrostis stolonifera, Bromus erectus, Dactylis glomerata, Festuca rubra, F. pratensis, Holcus lanatus, Lolium perenne, Poa annua, P. pratensis* (agg.) and *P. trivialis*. The relative proportions of these and of accompanying forbs depend to a large extent on management.

The roadside verge grasslands are usually forb-rich and this is probably their most interesting wildlife feature. Lack of stock-grazing allows full growth and vigorous flowering of many attractive and colourful forbs which, though often widespread and common, are much more restricted and still decreasing in predominantly arable districts. In counties such as Cambridgeshire, roadside verges are among the most important of botanical habitats, and in the country as a whole they support many rare and local species (see Table 34). Umbelliferae are especially well represented, with *Anthriscus sylvestris, Heracleum sphondylium, Chaerophyllum temulentum, Torilis japonica, Pastinaca sativa* and, in the north, *Myrrhis odorata* and the very local *Meum athamanticum*. Other noteworthy common species include *Geranium pratense, Vicia cracca, Centaurea nigra, Alliaria petiolata, Agrimonia eupatoria, Artemisia vulgaris, Filipendula ulmaria, Rubus idaeus, R. caesius, Achillea millefolium, Ranunculus acris, Hypericum* spp., *Malva* spp., *Galium cruciata, G. mollugo* and *Knautia arvensis*. Acidic soils have fewer and different species, e.g. *Digitalis purpurea, Hypochaeris radicata*, while in western and northern districts there is often a profusion of ferns such as *Dryopteris borreri, D. filix-mas, Athyrium filix-foemina, Thelypteris oreopteris* and *Polypodium vulgare*.

On calcareous soils there are sometimes shorter grass–forb swards resembling those of the semi-natural calcareous grasslands, with species such as *Briza media, Carex flacca, Leontodon hispidus, Primula veris, Poterium sanguisorba* and, occasionally, rarities such as *Linum anglicum* and *Orchis ustulata*. In northern England, this type of sward often has *Dactylorchis fuchsii, Listera ovata, Gymnadenia conopsea, Platanthera chlorantha, P. bifolia, Coeloglossum viride, Trifolium medium, Silaum silaus*, and, locally, *Primula farinosa* and *Sesleria caerulea*. In northern England and Scotland, there are assemblages of medium–tall forbs such as *Geranium sylvaticum, Cirsium heterophyllum, Trollius europaeus, Crepis paludosa, Geum rivale* and *Alchemilla vulgaris* agg. which locally give verge communities approximating to those of ungrazed northern hay meadows and mountain cliff ledges. Lanes in Devon and perhaps coastal districts more generally are notable for their floral banks and earthed walls, with *Silene dioica, Endymion non-scriptus, Cotyledon umbilicus, Stellaria holostea, Primula vulgaris* and the common ferns. In Devon and Cornwall there are local oceanic ferns such as *Dryopteris aemula* and *Asplenium obovatum* in these habitats, and characteristic flowering plants such as *Rubia peregrina* and *Allium triquetrum*.

Newly created verges tend to have ephemeral communities, including colourful seasonal displays of dandelions and poppies. Though scrub invasion is deliberately arrested on narrow verges, the broader examples and larger embankments often show considerable development of scrub with gorse, broom, willows, hawthorn, blackthorn and other shrubs, according to soil conditions.

Many plants occurring in road verges, especially the Papilionaceae, Compositae and Umbelliferae, are valuable food plants for insects or provide habitats for other animals. Figures for species breeding on roadside verges include 20 out of 50 mammals, all 6 reptiles, 40 out of 200 birds, 25 out of 60 butterflies, and 8 out of 17 bumble bees. Some birds e.g. tree pipit and corn bunting, have declined as verge nesters, but verges are still quite important breeding habitats for species such as yellowhammer, robin, hedge sparrow, common whitethroat, willow warbler, pheasant, partridge, mallard and, locally, common sandpiper. Kestrels commonly hunt over the broad verges of some trunk roads and motorways, where dense growths of herbage support good numbers of small mammals. Scavengers such as carrion crows and gulls feed on the remains of animals killed on roads, and even insectivorous species such as the pied wagtail are attracted by the numbers of dead and moribund insects.

There are numerous threats to the nature conservation interest of road verges. Certain engineering works associated with road improvements are unavoidable, but even these may not be entirely harmful – disturbance can sometimes promote variety and open habitats. Dumping of spoil on verges should, however, be avoided. The growth of verge vegetation must be kept down in the interests of road safety, but adverse management, such as the wrong chemicals or unsympathetic cutting programmes, can cause damage to the flora whilst achieving little or nothing for the engineer. Unfavourable agricultural activities on road verges, include dumping, ditch cleaning with spoil spread on the verge, irresponsible use of chemicals in the name of weed control, fires from stubble burning and disturbance by farm traffic. Statutory undertakings, such as trenching for water, sewage and telephone services can also cause a good deal of disturbance.

Casual disturbance and dumping pose as big a threat to persistence of a stable forb-rich grassland sward as indiscriminate use of chemicals or bad management. Although only a comparatively small area may be affected each year, this can add up to quite a large area over the course of a decade. Moreover, even if an area is only disturbed once every 10 years this would be sufficient to prevent long-term development of stability. Many of the richest grass-forb communities of the neutral and calcareous grassland types may be hundreds of years old, and once the more local species have been lost through disturbance, the lack of another seed source in the same area often prevents recolonisation. Only the more common and easily dispersed species usually colonise newly disturbed ground.

Animals living on the edge of roads could be poisoned by lead derived from the anti-knock ingredient of petrol. Many mammals, birds, reptiles, amphibians and insects are killed by motor vehicles, but there is no evidence that numbers lost have more than local significance. Species tend to be killed according to their abundance, though some may be more at risk than others, e.g. moths may be drawn towards vehicle headlights.

The importance of road verges to wildlife conservation lies both in the particular local interest of individual sites and in the far greater national value in providing a widely dispersed network of habitats (totalling 200 000 ha) on land for which no alternative land-use is proposed. Opportunities should therefore be explored for promoting a general policy of management of road verges in which the maximum wildlife interest is retained, consistent with the need to manage these habitats for other purposes, notably road safety. Particular opportunities for favourable arrangements are possible on the protected banks of the motorways where there is a very real chance to practise creative conservation. Likewise, the verges of minor roads often have a high wildlife interest at present in areas where there is often little need for intensive management for road safety.

Railways

At the time of nationalisation in 1948, there were approximately 28 800 km of railway track occupying about 24 000 ha (assuming an average width of 5.5 m). A further large area would be taken up by stations and ancillary land. Up to 1970, 8989 km of track representing about 8000 ha had been closed and between half and a third of the land sold off, mostly to neighbouring landowners: it can be assumed that the management of most of this land has changed.

Railways are less extensive than roads but their verges and banks have been subject to less disturbance and probably greater uniformity of management for a longer period. Because of the need to maintain gentle, even gradients, railways have a great many embankments and cuttings which greatly increase the extent and diversity of their verges. Most railway verges were probably burnt accidentally at some time or another but with the passing of the steam engine this important ecological factor is now reduced.

Railways tend to follow the low ground and valleys: they traverse a wide variety of geological formations, and their verges have a correspondingly wide range of soils. In many places railway embankments cause an impoundment of water on surrounding land and may be an important factor in promoting the development and persistence of wet meadow or even fen.

Much less is known about the botanical interest of railway verges than about road verges. Railway verges are completely ungrazed by large herbivorous mammals and, apart from intentional burning, chance fires and periodic cutting of scrub, they are relatively undisturbed habitats in which plant communities have developed under a fairly stable management regime over 100 years or more. The vegetation is essentially similar to that of road verges, consisting largely of a forb-rich grassland showing a continued and rapid tendency to invasion by scrub. In northern and moorland areas there may be an acidophilous, heathy vegetation. Many of the communities and species are the same as those of road verges. There is a preponderance of common grasses and forbs characteristic of base-rich soils, and the total flora is rich, especially on the calcareous formations.

The following local species, representing wide phytogeographical diversity, illustrate the floristic interest of railway verges: *Ophrys insectifera, Allium scorodoprasum, Geranium sanguineum, Astragalus glycyphyllos, Ononis spinosa, Lathyrus sylvestris, Vicia sylvatica, Campanula glomerata, Melampyrum cristatum, Cirsium acaulon, C. heterophyllum, Antennaria dioica, Lycopodium selago, Alchemilla alpina* and *Arctostaphylos uva-ursi*. The scrub plants include a variety of *Rubus* spp. and *Rosa* spp., hawthorn, blackthorn, willows, guelder rose, gorse, broom and some of the less common shrubs of calcareous soils, such as *Rhamnus catharticus*, *Thelycrania sanguinea* and *Viburnum lantana*. Climbers include *Tamus communis* and *Clematis vitalba*. More disturbed ground on railway verges often has an abundance of species such as *Anthyllis vulneraria*, *Lotus corniculatus*, *Trifolium campestre*, *Medicago lupulina*, *Fragaria vesca*, *Potentilla reptans*, *Crepis capillaris*, *Hieraceum pilosella* and *Geranium robertianum*. A few, such as *Linaria repens*, grow on railway ballast and may become dispersed by following the tracks. Many weeds, both native and alien, flourish on the waste ground associated with railway verges, sidings and stations, and *Senecio squalidus* is especially associated with these habitats.

The fauna of railway verges has not been studied in detail, but is of considerable interest. Many mammals live and breed in the embankments, and include large predators such as the fox and badger. The bird population is considerable and quite varied in species, the majority being small-to-medium passerines breeding in rough grassland, banks or low/open scrub. Railway embankments beside lakes are a favourite nesting place of the common sandpiper, and other breeding birds include both partridges, pheasant, mallard, woodpigeon, turtle dove, stock dove and cuckoo. They were also favoured formerly by red-backed shrikes. Railway bridges and viaducts provide nesting places for some species, mainly hole breeding birds including the kestrel, but exceptionally also for cliff-nesters such as the raven and buzzard. Locally, sheltered railway cuttings and embankments are favoured habitats for reptiles, including the rare sand lizard. The insect fauna is rich and varied, and the habitat is ideal for many Lepidoptera, with an abundance of food plants for both larvae and adults, and a considerable degree of shelter in the deeper cuttings. In the more intensively agricultural districts of eastern England, railways (and especially disused lines) are notable havens for butterflies. The 'browns' with larvae feeding on grasses, flourish here, and the adult gatekeeper is especially favoured by the frequent profusion of brambles. The fritillaries (larvae on *Viola* spp.) are represented locally, and the 'blues' (larvae on Papilionaceae) include the uncommon small blue. Migrant vanessids are attracted by the abundance of flowers produced by the shrubs and ungrazed forbs. The other invertebrate groups have not been studied, but could be expected to show considerable diversity and interest too.

Two main threats to the nature conservation interest of railway verges are (1) change of management policy leading to the use of herbicides on the banks, and (2) change of management resulting from closure of lines. Soon after the closure of a line the wildlife interest may well increase, but where the ground is not managed, scrub soon invades and thickens, so that much of the botanical interest disappears, with parallel effects on the fauna. When closed lines are sold and the land-use changed to some more productive form there is usually a consequent loss of wildlife interest. Because of the continuity of favourable management over a period of 100 years or more, and the relative lack of soil disturbance, railway land has a considerable nature conservation interest, although, as with roads, there are likely to be quite large areas with comparative uniformity. Railway verges provide habitats for large numbers of (at present) common plants and animals which quickly diminish when drastic changes in management are introduced. Their importance is relatively greater in urban areas and the intensively farmed areas of southern and eastern England, where they are often among the most significant wildlife habitats. No section of railway verge has been identified as nationally important, but a number of examples have been established as nature reserves by voluntary bodies for nature conservation.

Managed river banks, canal and ditch banks, reservoir banks

The extent of these riparian habitats is not known but they are extremely widespread in Britain. Some idea of their range of diversity can be obtained from the account of the field of ecological variation for open waters (Chapter 7). The flora is a mixture of species of open damp habitats maintained by wave action, and emergent aquatic species. One native grass, *Leersia oryzoides*, is confined to canal and river banks and is a national rarity. Very little information is available about the fauna of these habitats, but they are the main breeding place of species such as the water vole and kingfisher, and are important emergence and resting places for dragonflies.

The flora of river banks is more at risk from management activities in low-lying parts of the country where flow of water is comparatively slow, than in the faster moving rivers. In flat areas of the Fens and Lincolnshire, Romney Marsh and the Somerset Levels, cleaning out of the river-bed and control of vegetation on the banks is a continuing process to prevent flooding. The rare *Sonchus palustris* has recently spread markedly in the Norfolk Broads through extensive dyke-dredging involving dumping of mud on the banks, and Fenland banks have large populations of local species such as *Dipsacus fullonum* and *Carduus nutans*. In agricultural districts there is, however, always pressure to control weeds on river banks. The principal threat to wildlife on river-beds comes from the increasing use of selective herbicides and growth retarders applied from boat, land or helicopter. Canal banks are managed for access and in the interest of weed control, while reservoir banks may be managed for amenity and weed control; in all cases the threat from herbicides is considerable.

River banks, like road and rail verges, provide a wide range of habitats from woody to marshy ground, but are obviously subject to the influence of the river itself. Canal banks represent a slightly different ecological situation as there is practically no movement of water vertically or horizontally. River banks may have paths, but canals always have a tow path and, between this and the boundary, a further strip of land, often very rich in rough grassland and scrub habitats. Reservoir banks are often separated from the water by a more or less sterile drawdown zone created by fluctuations in the water level. On some artificial reservoirs in southern England the vegetation is entirely on the outer retaining earthwork slope, unconnected with the water. These reservoir banks cover quite large areas altogether and are likely to remain inviolate for the foreseeable future. At present many of the external banks are managed by sheep grazing or mowing. The habitats represented vary from coarse grassland to high quality turf; scrub and woody growth is generally controlled except on the lower banks.

Old quarries, mines and gravel pits

Disused mineral workings of various kinds often have a considerable biological nature conservation interest. Old quarries, especially on chalk or limestone, sometimes develop a varied range of plant communities and a rich flora, and some plants (e.g. the bee orchid) particularly favour this habitat. They also locally provide nesting places for rock-breeding birds, including peregrine and raven, and virtually all the choughs nesting inland in north Wales nest in old quarries or mine shafts. These habitats are, however, of greatest value in providing breeding and roosting places for bats, and some rare species are almost entirely dependent on them (see Chapter 12, pp. 356–7). Old quarries often have considerable geological value in exposing stratigraphic sequences and fossil-bearing rocks. Abandoned mine tips sometimes have an interesting flora, and lead mine spoil associated with calcite in certain upland areas is notable for its distinctive assemblage of northern species, with *Minuartia verna*, *Thlaspi alpestre*, *Cochlearia alpina*, *Viola lutea* and an inland form of *Armeria maritima*.

The most valuable of such habitats are the numerous disused gravel workings which have become flooded and allowed to develop a natural vegetation. Aquatic and marsh plants usually colonise quite rapidly, and varied hydroseres may develop. Apart from their ecological interest in demonstrating natural processes of plant dispersal, colonisation and succession, these places attract birds of various kinds, including wildfowl and species of swamp and shore. They have been the main factor in the widespread colonisation of England by the little ringed plover, a bird not known to breed here before 1938. Flooded gravel workings are also valuable habitats for aquatic invertebrates, especially mobile species such as dragonflies. At least one complex of old gravel pits is regarded as having national importance, and identified as having grade 1 status – the Cotswold Water Park (site OW.9).

These man-made habitats are increasingly likely to be put to other uses after mineral extraction ceases. Old quarries and mines are much used for tipping waste material, and this has ruined the nature conservation interest of many. Flooded gravel pits attract recreational activities, especially boating, and the disturbance and pollution may severely reduce the wildlife value. There is also a growing pressure to fill in old workings and restore the land for agriculture or other use.

Other artificial habitats

This category includes the remaining miscellany of non-agricultural habitats listed in Table 33, situated mainly in the lowlands and associated with centres of urban population.

The waste ground of ports, railway yards and sidings and urban areas generally has long had a considerable interest for its alien flora, containing many colourful herbs and showy grasses, some of which have spread more widely from their original places of introduction. There is also a large variety of native species, contributing to the often colourful displays of flowers which have much aesthetic appeal.

The old-fashioned type of sewage farm was important as a habitat for migrating waders and other birds; a few still exist, but they are disappearing (see Chapter 12, p. 367). Old buildings and walls have a certain wildlife interest. Some large, old houses and churches have attics and towers with considerable colonies of bats, including rare species (p. 357). Most of the swallows, swifts and house martins in Britain nest in or on buildings, and other species such as kestrel, barn owl, little owl, jackdaw, spotted flycatcher, pied wagtail, stock dove, tree sparrow and redstart have breeding niches here. The rare black redstart is confined to buildings as a breeder. Walls have an interesting flora, with characteristic species; ferns are especially well represented, some species occurring more abundantly and luxuriantly than in natural habitats, e.g. *Ceterach officinarum*, *Asplenium trichomanes* and *A. ruta-muraria*. Walls also provide a habitat for numerous bryophytes and lichens. Mortared walls usually have a richer flora than drystone walls, but are often disturbed by re-pointing. The walls of old buildings have several noteworthy plants which may be long-established introductions, such as *Cheiranthus cheiri*, *Centranthus ruber* and *Erinus alpinus*.

Golf courses, with their considerable areas of rough ground, are often quite valuable wildlife areas, especially in intensively farmed or developed districts where little semi-natural habitat remains. The grassland and scrub communities, with their associated animals, belong to types described under Chapter 6. Parks, with their grasslands, variety of shrub and tree habitats, and often lakes, are interesting areas, too, and in the aggregate churchyards and cemeteries support considerable wildlife populations. Gardens are especially rich in birds, and the breeding populations in some suburban areas are higher than in many natural or semi-natural habitats.

Studies and surveys by London naturalists have shown that the wildlife interest of this great city is considerable, especially with regard to birds and insects; ranging from the central parks where various native birds (e.g. tufted duck and pochard) live and breed alongside exotic introductions, to the extensive suburban areas and railway banks, which have large predators such as the fox, kestrel and carrion crow. The lepidopterous fauna of London is especially rich in moths, large species such as the privet hawk and lime hawk finding their larval food plants in abundance in garden hedges, roadside trees and parks. Wildlife interest of this kind persists in spite of the most intensive development of land, and the role of nature conservation here is probably to spread and increase awareness of this interest, and of the ways in which it might be enhanced by suitable management.

Table 34. *The ecological distribution of vascular plant species in artificial habitats*

Species	Rapidly declining species	Agricultural			Non-agricultural								
		Cultivated	Non-cultivated	Aquatic	Road verge & hedgerow	Railways	River banks	Ports	Sewage	Spoil & quarries	Urban waste	Parks & churchyards	Walls
	+	1	2	3	4	5	6	7	8	9	10	11	12
Asplenium adiantum-nigrum	—	—	—	—	×	—	—	—	—	×	—	—	X
A. ruta-muraria	—	—	—	—	—	—	—	—	—	×	—	—	X
A. trichomanes	—	—	—	—	—	—	—	—	—	×	—	—	X
Ceterach officinarum	—	—	—	—	—	—	—	—	—	×	—	—	X
[a]Eranthis hyemalis	—	—	—	—	×	—	—	—	—	—	—	X	—
Ranunculus arvensis	+	X	×	—	×	×	×	—	—	—	×	—	—
R. sardous	+	×	X	×	×	×	—	—	—	—	—	—	—
R. parviflorus	+	×	X	—	×	×	—	—	—	—	—	—	—
R. OPHIOGLOSSIFOLIUS	+	—	—	X	—	—	—	—	—	—	—	—	—
[a]Adonis annua	—	X	×	—	×	—	×	×	—	—	—	—	—
Myosurus minimus	+	X	×	×	×	—	—	—	—	—	—	—	—
Berberis vulgaris	+	—	—	—	X	×	—	—	—	—	—	—	—
Papaver rhoeas	+	X	×	—	×	×	—	—	—	×	×	—	—
P. dubium	—	X	×	—	×	×	—	—	—	×	×	—	—
P. lecoqii	—	×	X	—	X	×	—	—	—	×	X	—	—
P. hybridum	—	X	×	—	×	—	—	—	—	—	—	—	—
P. argemone	—	X	×	—	×	—	—	—	—	×	—	—	—
[a]P. somniferum	—	×	×	—	×	×	×	—	—	X	—	—	—
Chelidonium majus	—	—	—	—	×	—	—	—	—	—	×	×	X
[a]Corydalis lutea	—	—	—	—	—	—	—	—	—	—	—	—	X
FUMARIA OCCIDENTALIS	—	×	X	—	—	—	—	—	—	—	—	—	—
F. capreolata	—	×	×	—	X	—	—	—	—	—	—	—	—
F. purpurea	—	X	×	—	×	—	—	—	—	—	—	—	—
F. bastardii	—	X	×	—	×	—	—	—	—	—	—	—	—
F. MARTINII	—	×	—	—	×	—	—	—	—	—	—	—	—
F. muralis	—	X	×	—	×	×	—	—	—	—	—	—	—
F. micrantha	—	X	—	—	×	×	—	—	×	—	—	—	—
F. officinalis	—	×	×	—	×	—	—	×	—	×	×	—	—
F. vaillantii	—	X	—	—	—	—	—	—	—	—	—	—	—
F. parviflora	—	X	—	—	—	—	—	—	—	—	—	—	—
[a]Brassica napus	—	×	×	—	×	×	×	—	×	×	X	—	—
[a]B. rapa	—	×	×	—	×	—	X	—	—	—	—	—	—
B. nigra	—	—	×	—	×	—	X	—	—	—	×	—	—
[a]Erucastrum gallicum	—	×	—	—	×	—	×	×	×	X	—	—	—
[a]Rhynchosinapis cheiranthos	—	—	—	—	×	×	—	×	—	—	X	—	—
Sinapis arvensis	—	X	×	—	×	—	×	—	—	×	×	—	—
[a]S. alba	—	×	—	—	×	—	—	—	—	×	X	—	—
[a]Diplotaxis muralis	—	×	—	—	×	X	×	×	—	×	×	—	×
D. tenuifolia	—	—	—	—	×	×	×	×	—	×	X	—	×
Raphanus raphanistrum	—	X	×	—	×	×	—	—	—	—	—	—	—
[a]Rapistrum rugosum	—	×	—	—	×	×	×	×	—	—	X	—	—
Lepidium campestre	—	X	—	—	×	×	—	—	—	×	×	—	—
L. heterophyllum	—	—	—	—	X	×	—	—	—	—	—	—	×
[a]L. ruderale	—	—	—	—	X	×	×	—	—	×	X	—	—
Coronopus squamatus	—	×	X	—	×	—	—	—	—	—	×	—	—
[a]C. didymus	—	×	—	—	×	—	—	—	—	—	X	—	—
[a]Cardaria draba	—	×	—	—	X	X	×	×	—	—	—	—	—
Thlaspi arvense	—	X	×	—	×	×	×	×	—	×	×	—	—

Table 34 (*contd.*)

	+	1	2	3	4	5	6	7	8	9	10	11	12
ᵃ*T. alliaceum*	—	—	X	—	—	—	—	—	—	—	—	—	—
ᵃ*Bunias orientalis*	—	×	—	—	X	X	×	—	—	×	X	—	—
ᵃ*ALYSSUM ALYSSOIDES*	—	×	—	—	—	×	—	×	—	—	×	—	—
ᵃ*Lobularia maritima*	—	—	—	—	—	×	—	×	—	×	×	—	—
Draba muralis	—	—	—	—	—	—	—	—	—	—	—	—	X
ᵃ*Armoracia rusticana*	—	—	—	—	×	—	X	—	—	—	×	—	—
Barbarea stricta	—	—	—	—	—	—	X	—	—	—	—	—	—
ᵃ*B. intermedia*	—	×	—	—	X	—	—	—	—	—	×	—	—
ᵃ*B. verna*	—	—	—	—	X	—	—	—	—	—	×	—	—
Turritis glabra	+	—	—	—	X	×	—	—	—	×	×	—	—
ᵃ*RORIPPA AUSTRIACA*	—	—	—	—	×	×	—	×	—	—	×	—	—
ᵃ*Hesperis matronalis*	—	—	×G	—	×	×	×	—	—	×	×	—	×
Erysimum cheiranthoides	—	×	X	—	—	×	—	×	—	—	×	—	—
ᵃ*Cheiranthus cheiri*	—	—	—	—	—	—	—	—	—	—	—	—	×
ᵃ*Sisymbrium irio*	—	×	×	—	—	×	—	×	—	—	X	—	—
ᵃ*S. orientale*	—	×	×	—	×	×	—	×	—	×	X	—	×
ᵃ*S. altissimum*	—	—	—	—	×	×	×	×	—	×	X	—	—
Descurainia sophia	—	×	×	—	×	—	—	×	—	—	X	—	—
Viola tricolor ssp. **tricolor**	—	X	—	—	×	×	×	—	—	—	×	—	—
V. arvensis	—	X	—	—	×	×	—	—	—	—	×	×	—
ᵃ*Hypericum elatum*	—	—	—	—	—	—	—	—	—	—	×	X	—
ᵃ*H. hircinum*	—	—	—	—	×	—	×	—	—	—	—	—	—
ᵃ*H. calycinum*	—	—	—	—	X	—	—	—	—	×	×	×	—
Silene conica	—	X	—	—	×	—	—	×	—	—	×	—	—
S. gallica	—	X	—	—	×	×	—	—	—	—	×	—	—
ᵃ**S. italica**	—	—	—	—	—	—	—	×	—	—	×	—	—
S. noctiflora	—	X	—	—	×	×	—	—	—	—	×	—	—
S. alba	—	—	×	—	X	×	—	—	—	—	×	—	—
ᵃ*Agrostemma githago*	+	X	—	—	—	—	—	×	—	—	×	—	—
ᵃ*Saponaria officinalis*	—	—	—	—	X	×	×	—	—	—	×	—	—
Cerastium arvense	—	—	—	—	×	×	×	×	—	×	—	—	×
ᵃ*C. tomentosum*	—	—	—	—	X	—	—	—	—	—	×	—	—
ᵃ*C. BRACHYPETALUM*	—	—	—	—	—	X	—	—	—	—	—	—	—
Sagina apetala	—	—	XG	—	×	X	—	—	—	—	×	—	X
Minuartia hybrida	—	×	—	—	×	X	—	×	—	×	—	×	×
ᵃ*Arenaria balearica*	—	—	×G	—	—	—	—	—	—	—	—	—	X
POLYCARPON TETRAPHYLLUM	—	—	×G	—	—	—	—	×	—	—	X	—	—
CORRIGIOLA LITTORALIS	—	—	—	—	—	X	—	—	—	—	—	—	—
Scleranthus annuus	—	X	—	—	×	—	—	—	—	×	—	—	×
ᵃ*Montia perfoliata*	—	×	×G	—	X	—	—	—	—	—	×	×	×
ᵃ*M. sibirica*	—	—	×G	—	X	—	X	—	—	—	—	—	—
ᵃ*Chenopodium bonus-henricus*	—	—	×	—	X	—	—	—	—	—	—	×	—
C. polyspermum	—	X	—	—	×	—	—	×	—	—	×	—	—
C. vulvaria	—	×	—	—	×	—	×	×	—	—	X	—	—
C. album	—	X	×	—	—	×	×	×	—	—	×	—	—
C. ficifolium	—	X	×	—	×	×	×	×	—	—	×	—	—
C. murale	—	×	×	—	×	×	—	×	—	—	X	—	—
ᵃ*C. urbicum*	—	—	X	—	—	—	—	×	—	—	×	—	—
ᵃ*C. hybridum*	—	X	—	—	×	×	—	×	—	—	×	—	—
Chenopodium rubrum	—	×	×	X	×	×	×	×	×	—	×	×	—
ᵃ*C. glaucum*	—	×	×	×	×	—	—	×	—	—	X	—	—
Atriplex patula	—	X	—	—	×	×	—	—	—	—	×	—	—
A. hastata	—	×	—	—	×	—	—	—	—	—	X	—	—
Malva sylvestris	—	×	—	—	×	—	—	—	—	—	X	—	—
M. neglecta	—	×	×	—	×	—	×	×	—	—	X	—	—
LAVATERA CRETICA	—	×	—	—	—	×	—	×	—	—	×	—	—
ᵃ*ALTHAEA HIRSUTA*	—	×	—	—	—	—	×	—	×	×	×	—	—
ᵃ*Geranium endressii*	—	×	—	—	X	×	×	—	—	—	—	×	—
ᵃ*G. versicolor*	—	—	—	—	X	—	—	—	—	—	—	×	—
ᵃ*G. phaeum*	—	—	—	—	X	—	—	—	—	—	×	×	—
G. pyrenaicum	—	—	—	—	×	×	×	—	—	—	—	×	—

Table 34 (*contd.*)

	+	1	2	3	4	5	6	7	8	9	10	11	12
G. rotundifolium	—	×	—	—	X	×	×	—	—	×	×	—	×
Erodium moschatum	—	×	—	—	×	×	—	—	—	—	X	—	×
[a]*Oxalis corniculata*	—	—	XG	—	×	—	—	—	—	—	×	×	×
[a]*O. europaea*	—	—	XG	—	×	—	—	—	—	—	×	×	×
[a]**Impatiens capensis**	—	—	—	—	×	—	X	×	—	—	—	—	—
[a]**I. parviflora**	—	×	—	—	×	×	×	—	—	×	X	—	—
[a]**I. glandulifera**	—	—	×	×	×	—	X	—	—	—	×	—	—
[a]**Lupinus arboreus**	—	—	—	—	×	X	×	—	—	—	—	—	—
[a]*Medicago sativa*	—	×	—	—	×	×	—	—	—	—	X	—	—
[a]*Melilotus altissima*	—	×	—	—	×	×	—	×	—	×	X	—	—
[a]*M. officinalis*	—	×	—	—	×	×	×	—	—	×	X	—	—
[a]*M. alba*	—	—	×	—	×	×	×	×	—	×	X	—	—
[a]*M. indica*	—	—	×G	—	×	×	—	×	—	—	X	—	—
Trifolium ochroleucon	—	—	—	—	X	×	×	—	—	×	—	—	—
[a]*T. STELLATUM*	—	—	—	—	—	—	×	—	—	—	X	—	—
[a]*T. hybridum*	—	×	—	—	X	—	—	—	—	—	×	—	—
[a]*Coronilla varia*	—	—	—	—	—	X	—	×	—	—	×	×	—
Vicia hirsuta	—	×	×	—	×	X	×	—	—	×	×	—	—
[a]*Lathyrus tuberosus*	—	—	×	—	×	X	—	—	—	×	×	—	—
[a]*Spiraea salicifolia*	—	—	—	—	X	—	—	—	—	—	×	—	—
[a]*Potentilla recta*	—	×	—	—	X	×	—	—	—	×	—	—	×
[a]*P. norvegica*	—	—	—	—	×	×	—	×	—	—	X	—	—
[a]*Fragaria ananassa*	—	—	—	—	×	X	—	—	—	—	×	—	—
Aphanes arvensis (*sensu strictu*)	—	X	×	—	×	×	—	—	—	×	×	—	×
[a]*Poterium polygamum*	—	X	—	—	×	×	—	—	—	—	×	—	—
[a]**Acaena anserinifolia**	—	—	—	—	X	—	—	—	—	—	—	—	—
Rosa canina agg.	—	—	—	—	X	—	—	—	—	—	—	—	—
R. villosa agg.	—	—	—	—	X	—	—	—	—	—	—	—	—
[a]*Prunus domestica*	—	—	—	—	X	—	—	—	—	—	—	—	—
[a]*P. cerasifera*	—	—	—	—	X	—	—	—	—	—	—	—	—
[a]*P. cerasus*	—	—	—	—	X	×	—	—	—	—	—	—	—
[a]**Pyrus communis**	—	—	—	—	X	—	—	—	—	—	—	—	—
P. CORDATA	—	—	—	—	X	—	—	—	—	—	—	—	—
[a]*Sedum spurium*	—	—	—	—	—	—	—	—	—	×	×	—	X
[a]*S. dasyphyllum*	—	—	—	—	—	—	—	—	—	—	—	—	X
[a]**S. album**	—	—	—	—	—	—	—	—	—	—	—	—	X
[a]*S. reflexum*	—	—	—	—	—	—	—	—	—	—	—	—	X
Umbilicus rupestris	—	—	—	—	×	—	—	—	—	×	—	—	X
[a]*Escallonia macrantha*	—	—	—	—	X	—	—	—	—	—	—	—	—
LYTHRUM HYSSOPIFOLIA	—	—	—	X	—	—	—	—	—	—	—	—	—
LUDWIGIA PALUSTRIS	—	—	—	×	—	—	—	—	—	—	—	—	—
Epilobium lanceolatum	—	—	×	—	X	×	—	×	—	×	×	—	×
E. roseum	—	—	×G	×	×	×	×	×	—	—	X	—	×
[a]*E. adenocaulon*	—	—	×G	×	×	X	×	×	×	×	X	—	×
E. tetragonum	—	—	×G	X	×	×	×	—	×	×	×	—	×
[a]*E. nerterioides*	—	—	×	×	×	×	×	—	—	X	—	×	×
[a]*Oenothera biennis*	—	—	—	—	×	×	—	—	—	X	×	—	—
[a]*O. erythrosepala*	—	—	—	—	×	×	—	—	—	×	X	—	—
[a]*O. stricta*	—	—	×	—	—	×	—	—	—	—	×	×	—
[a]*O. parviflora*	—	—	—	—	—	×	×	—	—	—	×	—	—
Fuchsia magellanica	—	—	—	—	X	—	—	—	—	—	—	—	—
Anthriscus caucalis	—	×	—	—	X	—	×	—	—	×	×	—	—
Scandix pecten-veneris	+	X	×	—	×	—	—	—	—	—	—	—	—
[a]**Myrrhis odorata**	—	—	×	×	X	×	×	—	—	×	×	—	—
Torilis arvensis	+	X	—	—	×	—	—	—	—	×	—	—	—
T. nodosa	—	×	×	×	X	—	—	—	—	—	—	—	—
[a]*Caucalis platycarpos*	+	X	—	—	—	×	—	×	—	×	×	—	—
[a]*C. latifolia*	+	X	×	—	—	×	—	×	—	—	×	—	—
[a]**Smyrnium olusatrum**	—	—	—	—	X	—	—	—	—	—	—	×	—
Bupleurum rotundifolium	+	X	—	—	×	—	—	—	—	—	×	—	—
[a]*Petroselinum crispum*	—	—	—	—	—	×	—	—	—	×	×	—	X

Table 34 (*contd.*)

	+	1	2	3	4	5	6	7	8	9	10	11	12
P. segetum	—	X	—	×	×	×	—	—	—	—	—	—	—
Sison amomum	—	—	—	×	X	—	—	—	—	—	—	×	—
[a]**Carum carvi**	—	×	—	×	×	×	×	×	—	×	×	—	—
BUNIUM BULBOCASTANUM	—	—	X	—	—	—	—	—	—	×	—	—	—
Pimpinella major	—	—	—	—	X	—	×	—	—	—	—	×	—
[a]**Aegopodium podagraria**	—	—	X	—	×	—	—	—	—	—	×	×	—
Aethusa cynapium	—	X	—	—	×	—	×	—	—	—	—	—	—
[a]*Foeniculum vulgare*	—	—	×	—	×	×	×	—	×	×	X	—	—
[a]*Peucedanum ostruthium*	—	—	×	—	×	—	X	—	—	—	×	×	—
[a]*Heracleum mantegazzianum*	—	—	×	—	×	×	X	—	—	—	×	×	—
Bryonia dioica	—	—	—	—	X	—	—	—	—	—	—	×	—
[a]*ASARUM EUROPAEUM*	+	—	×	—	×	—	×	—	—	—	—	X	—
[a]*ARISTOLOCHIA CLEMATITIS*	+	—	×	—	X	—	—	—	—	—	—	×	—
Mercurialis annua	—	—	×G	—	—	×	—	×	—	×	X	×	—
Euphorbia lathyrus	—	—	×G	—	×	—	—	—	—	—	×	—	—
E. platyphyllos	+	X	—	—	×	—	—	—	—	—	—	—	—
E. helioscopia	—	X	—	—	—	—	—	—	—	—	—	—	—
E. peplus	—	×	XG	—	×	—	—	—	—	—	×	—	—
E. exigua	—	X	—	—	—	×	—	—	—	—	—	—	—
[a]**E. cyparissias**	—	—	—	—	×	X	—	—	—	—	×	—	—
[a]**E. esula × uralensis**	—	—	—	—	×	—	×	×	—	—	X	—	—
Polygonum aviculare	—	×	X	—	×	—	—	—	—	—	×	—	—
P. persicaria	—	×	X	—	×	—	×	—	×	—	×	—	—
P. lapathifolium	—	×	X	—	×	—	×	—	—	—	×	—	—
P. convolvulus	—	X	×	—	—	—	—	—	×	—	×	—	—
[a]**P. cuspidatum**	—	—	×	—	×	×	×	—	—	—	X	×	—
[a]**P. sachalinense**	—	—	—	—	×	×	×	—	—	—	X	×	—
[a]**P. polystachyum**	—	—	—	—	X	—	×	—	—	—	—	×	—
[a]*Fagopyrum esculentum*	—	×	—	—	×	×	—	×	—	—	X	—	—
[a]**Rumex alpinus**	—	—	—	—	X	—	×	—	—	—	×	—	—
[a]*R. patientia*	—	—	—	—	×	×	×	—	—	—	X	—	—
R. pulcher	—	—	×	—	×	—	—	×	—	—	X	×	—
Parietaria diffusa	—	—	—	—	—	—	—	—	—	—	—	×	X
[a]*Helxine soleirolii*	—	—	×G	—	×	—	—	—	—	—	—	—	X
Urtica urens	—	—	X	—	—	—	—	—	—	—	—	—	—
Humulus lupulus	—	—	—	—	X	×	×	—	—	—	—	—	—
Ulmus procera	—	—	—	—	X	—	—	—	—	—	—	×	—
U. carpinifolia	—	—	—	—	X	—	—	—	—	—	—	×	—
Anagallis arvensis	—	×	X	—	×	—	—	—	—	—	—	—	—
[a]**Buddleja davidii**	—	—	—	—	×	×	—	—	—	×	X	—	—
[a]*Symphytum orientale*	—	—	—	—	X	×	×	—	—	—	×	×	—
[a]**S. × uplandicum**	—	—	—	—	X	×	×	—	—	—	×	×	—
[a]*Pentaglottis sempervirens*	—	—	—	—	X	—	—	—	—	—	—	×	—
Anchusa arvensis	—	X	—	—	×	×	—	—	—	×	×	—	—
Myosotis discolor	—	×	—	—	X	×	—	—	—	—	—	—	—
Lithospermum arvense	—	X	—	—	×	×	—	×	—	—	×	—	—
ECHIUM LYCOPSIS	—	×	—	—	—	—	—	×	—	—	X	—	—
Convolvulus arvensis	—	×	XG	—	×	×	—	—	—	—	×	—	—
[a]**Calystegia sepium** ssp. *pulchra*	—	—	—	—	X	×	×	—	—	—	—	×	—
[a]*C. sepium* ssp. *silvatica*	—	—	×G	—	X	×	—	—	—	×	×	—	—
[a]*Lycium halimifolium*	—	—	—	—	×	—	—	—	—	—	×	—	—
Hyoscyamus niger	—	×	X	×	×	—	×	—	—	×	×	—	—
Solanum nigrum	—	×	X	—	—	—	—	—	—	—	×	×	—
[a]*Datura stramonium*	—	×	×G	—	×	—	—	—	—	—	×	—	—
[a]*Verbascum phlomoides*	—	—	×	—	—	—	—	—	—	×	X	—	—
[a]**V. lychnitis**	—	—	×	—	×	×	×	—	—	X	×	×	×
V. PULVERULENTUM	—	—	—	—	X	—	—	—	—	—	—	—	—
V. nigrum	—	—	×	—	X	×	—	—	—	×	×	—	×
[a]*V. blattaria*	—	—	×	—	×	—	×	×	—	×	X	—	×
V. VIRGATUM	—	—	×	—	×	—	×	×	—	×	X	—	×
Antirrhinum orontium	—	X	×	—	×	×	—	—	—	—	×	—	—

344 Artificial ecosystems

Table 34 (contd.)

Species	+	1	2	3	4	5	6	7	8	9	10	11	12
[a]*A. majus*	—	—	—	—	—	—	—	—	—	×	×	×	X
[a]*LINARIA SUPINA*	—	—	—	—	—	X	—	—	—	×	—	—	—
[a]*L. purpurea*	—	—	—	—	×	X	—	—	—	—	×	—	X
L. repens	—	—	×	—	×	X	—	—	—	—	—	—	×
L. vulgaris	—	—	×	—	X	×	—	—	—	—	×	—	—
Chaenorhinum minus	—	×	—	—	×	X	—	—	—	—	—	—	×
Kickxia spuria	—	X	×G	—	×	—	—	—	—	—	—	—	—
K. elatine	—	X	—	—	—	×	—	—	—	—	×	—	—
[a]*Cymbalaria muralis*	—	—	—	—	—	—	—	—	—	—	—	—	X
SCROPHULARIA SCORODONIA	—	—	—	—	X	—	—	—	—	×	—	—	×
[a]*S. vernalis*	—	—	×	—	X	×	—	—	—	—	—	×	×
[a]**Mimulus guttatus**	—	—	—	X	—	—	×	—	—	—	—	—	—
[a]**M. luteus**	—	—	—	X	×	—	X	—	—	—	—	—	—
[a]**M. moschatus**	—	—	—	X	—	×	—	—	—	—	—	—	—
Limosella aquatica	+	—	—	X	—	—	×	—	—	—	—	—	—
[a]*Erinus alpinus*	—	—	—	—	—	×	×	—	—	—	—	×	X
VERONICA PRAECOX	—	X	—	—	—	—	—	—	—	—	—	—	—
[a]*V. peregrina*	—	—	XG	—	—	—	—	—	—	—	—	—	—
V. VERNA	—	X	—	—	—	—	—	—	—	—	—	—	—
V. TRIPHYLLOS	+	X	—	—	—	—	—	—	—	×	—	—	—
V. hederifolia	—	×	X	—	×	—	—	—	—	—	×	—	—
[a]*V. persica*	—	X	×	—	—	—	—	—	—	—	—	—	—
V. polita	—	×	X	—	×	×	—	—	—	×	×	—	—
V. agrestis	—	×	×	—	×	×	—	—	—	×	—	—	—
MELAMPYRUM ARVENSE	+	X	×	—	—	—	—	—	—	—	—	—	—
[a]*Acanthus mollis*	—	—	—	—	×	×	×	—	—	—	X	—	—
Verbena officinalis	—	—	—	—	X	—	×	—	—	—	—	—	—
Mentha arvensis	—	X	×	×	×	—	×	—	—	—	×	—	—
[a]**M. spicata**	—	—	—	—	×	×	×	—	—	×	X	—	—
[a]**M. longifolia**	—	—	×	×	×	×	×	—	—	×	X	—	—
[a]**M. rotundifolia**	—	—	×	—	X	—	×	—	—	—	×	×	—
Calamintha ascendens	—	—	—	—	X	×	—	—	—	×	—	×	—
C. nepeta	—	—	—	—	X	—	—	×	—	—	—	×	—
[a]*Melissa officinalis*	—	×	—	—	X	—	—	—	—	—	×	—	—
Salvia horminoides	—	—	—	—	X	—	—	—	—	×	×	×	—
MELITTIS MELISSOPHYLLUM	—	—	—	—	X	—	—	—	—	—	—	—	—
Stachys arvensis	—	X	×	—	×	×	—	—	—	—	—	—	—
Ballota nigra	—	—	—	—	×	—	—	—	—	—	X	—	×
Lamium amplexicaule	—	X	×	—	×	—	—	—	—	—	×	—	—
L. moluccellifolium	—	X	×	—	—	—	—	—	—	—	—	—	—
L. hybridum	—	X	×	—	×	—	×	—	—	×	—	—	×
L. purpureum	—	×	X	—	×	×	—	—	—	—	—	×	—
L. album	—	—	×	—	X	×	—	—	—	—	×	×	×
[a]*Leonurus cardiaca*	+	—	—	—	X	—	—	×	—	—	×	—	—
Galeopsis angustifolia	—	X	—	—	×	×	—	—	—	—	—	—	—
G. speciosa	+	X	×	—	×	—	—	×	—	×	—	—	—
G. SEGETUM	—	×	X	—	—	—	—	—	—	—	—	—	—
Nepeta cataria	—	—	×	—	X	—	—	—	—	×	—	×	—
Marrubium vulgare	—	—	—	—	×	×	—	—	—	—	X	×	—
TEUCRIUM CHAMAEDRYS	—	—	—	—	—	—	—	—	—	×	—	—	X
Ajuga chamaepitys	+	X	×	—	—	—	—	—	—	—	—	—	—
Legousia hybrida	+	X	—	—	—	×	—	—	—	—	×	—	—
Sherardia arvensis	—	X	—	—	×	—	—	—	—	—	—	—	—
Galium mollugo	—	—	—	—	X	×	—	—	—	×	×	—	—
G. tricornutum	+	X	—	—	—	×	—	×	—	—	×	—	—
[a]*G. SPURIUM*	—	×	XG	—	—	×	—	×	—	—	×	—	—
G. parisiense	—	—	×	—	—	×	—	—	—	×	—	—	X
Sambucus ebulus	—	—	—	—	X	—	×	—	—	—	—	×	—
[a]*Lonicera caprifolium*	—	—	—	—	X	—	×	—	—	×	—	—	—
Valerianella locusta	—	X	×	—	×	×	—	—	—	—	—	—	×
V. carinata	—	—	×	—	×	×	—	×	—	—	—	—	×

Table 34 (*contd.*)

	+	1	2	3	4	5	6	7	8	9	10	11	12
V. rimosa	—	X	—	—	×	×	—	—	—	—	—	—	×
[a]*V. ERIOCARPA*	—	X	×	—	×	—	—	×	—	—	—	—	×
V. dentata	+	X	×	—	—	—	—	—	—	—	—	—	—
[a]**Valeriana pyrenaica**	—	—	—	—	×	×	X	—	—	—	—	—	—
[a]**Centranthus ruber**	—	—	—	—	×	×	—	—	—	×	×	×	X
[a]*Galinsoga ciliata*	—	×	X	—	×	×	—	×	×	×	×	×	—
[a]*G. parviflora*	—	—	XG	—	×	—	—	×	—	—	×	×	—
[a]**Senecio squalidus**	—	×	×	—	×	X	×	—	—	×	×	—	×
S. viscosus	—	—	×	—	×	X	×	×	×	×	×	—	—
S. vulgaris	—	×	X	—	×	×	—	—	—	×	×	—	—
[a]**Doronicum pardalianches**	—	—	—	—	X	×	×	×	—	×	×	×	—
[a]*Petasites albus*	—	—	—	—	X	×	×	—	—	—	—	×	—
[a]*P. fragrans*	—	—	×	—	X	×	—	—	—	—	×	×	—
[a]**Inula helenium**	—	—	—	—	X	×	×	—	—	×	—	—	—
PULICARIA VULGARIS	+	—	—	X	×	—	—	—	—	×	—	—	—
Filago spathulata	+	×	×	—	×	—	—	—	—	×	—	—	—
F. APICULATA	+	X	—	—	—	—	—	—	—	—	—	—	—
[a]*F. gallica*	+	×	×	—	—	—	—	—	—	—	—	—	—
GNAPHALIUM LUTEO-ALBUM	—	X	×	—	×	—	—	×	×	×	—	—	—
[a]**Anaphalis margaritacea**	—	—	—	—	×	—	—	—	—	X	—	—	—
[a]*Erigeron mucronatus*	—	—	—	—	×	—	—	—	—	—	—	—	X
[a]*Conyza canadensis*	—	—	×	—	×	×	—	×	—	×	X	—	—
Anthemis cotula	—	X	—	—	×	—	×	×	—	×	—	—	—
A. arvensis	—	X	×	—	×	×	—	—	—	×	×	—	—
Tripleurospermum maritimum ssp. *inodora*	—	X	×	—	×	—	—	—	—	×	—	—	—
Matricaria recutita	—	X	×	—	×	—	—	—	×	×	—	—	—
[a]*M. matricarioides*	—	—	X	—	×	×	—	—	—	×	—	—	—
Chrysanthemum segetum	+	X	—	—	×	—	—	—	—	×	—	—	—
[a]*C. parthenium*	—	—	×	—	×	×	—	—	—	—	×	X	×
Tanacetum vulgare	—	—	—	—	X	×	×	—	—	×	—	—	—
Artemisia vulgaris	—	—	×	—	×	—	—	—	—	×	X	—	—
[a]*A. verlotorum*	—	—	×	—	×	×	×	—	—	×	X	—	—
A. absinthium	—	—	—	—	×	—	—	—	—	—	X	—	—
Arctium lappa	—	—	—	—	X	—	×	—	—	×	×	—	—
Carduus crispus	—	—	—	—	X	×	×	—	—	×	×	—	—
Cirsium vulgare	—	×	×	—	×	×	×	—	—	×	×	×	—
C. arvense	—	×	X	—	×	×	×	×	—	×	×	×	—
[a]*Silybum marianum*	—	—	X	—	×	×	—	—	—	×	×	×	—
Onopordum acanthium	—	—	×	—	×	×	—	—	—	×	×	×	—
Centaurea cyanus	+	X	×	—	×	×	—	—	—	×	—	—	—
C. calcitrapa	+	×	—	—	×	—	—	×	—	X	—	—	—
[a]*C. solstitialis*	+	×	X	—	—	×	—	×	—	×	—	—	—
Cichorium intybus	—	×	×	—	X	—	—	×	—	×	—	—	—
ARNOSERIS MINIMA	+	X	—	—	—	—	—	—	—	—	—	—	—
[a]*Tragopogon porrifolius*	—	—	—	—	×	×	—	—	—	—	X	—	—
Lactuca serriola	—	—	—	—	×	×	—	×	—	—	X	—	—
L. virosa	—	—	×	—	×	×	—	—	—	X	—	—	—
L. saligna	—	—	—	—	—	×	—	×	—	—	×	—	X
Sonchus arvensis	—	×	X	—	×	—	—	—	—	×	—	—	—
S. oleraceus	—	X	×	—	×	×	—	—	—	×	—	—	×
S. asper	—	X	×	—	×	×	—	—	—	×	—	—	—
[a]*Cicerbita macrophylla*	—	—	—	—	X	—	×	—	—	×	×	×	—
[a]*Crepis vesicaria*	—	—	—	—	X	×	—	—	—	×	×	—	—
C. biennis	—	×	—	—	X	×	—	—	—	×	—	—	—
Ornithogalum umbellatum	—	—	—	—	X	—	—	—	—	—	—	×	—
O. pyrenaicum	—	—	—	—	X	—	—	—	—	—	—	—	—
MUSCARI ATLANTICUM	—	—	—	—	X	×	—	—	—	—	—	—	—
Allium vineale	—	×	—	—	X	×	—	—	—	—	—	×	—
A. oleraceum	—	—	—	—	X	—	×	—	—	—	×	—	×
[a]*A. carinatum*	—	—	×	—	×	×	X	—	—	—	—	×	—
[a]*A. paradoxum*	—	—	—	—	X	—	×	—	—	×	—	—	—

Table 34 (*contd.*)

	+	1	2	3	4	5	6	7	8	9	10	11	12
[a]**Crocosmia × crocosmiflora**	—	—	—	—	×	—	X	—	—	×	×	—	—
Tamus communis	—	—	—	—	X	—	—	—	—	—	—	—	—
Ophrys apifera	—	—	—	—	×	×	—	—	—	X	—	—	—
Lemna polyrhiza	—	—	—	X	—	—	—	—	—	—	—	—	—
Wolffia arrhiza	—	—	—	X	—	—	—	—	—	—	—	—	—
Eleocharis acicularis	—	—	—	X	—	—	×	—	—	—	—	—	—
CYPERUS FUSCUS	+	—	—	X	—	—	—	—	—	—	—	—	—
CAREX DEPAUPERATA	+	—	—	—	X	—	—	—	—	—	—	—	—
C. vulpina	—	—	—	X	—	—	—	—	—	—	—	—	—
C. divulsa	—	—	—	×	X	—	—	—	—	—	×	×	—
C. polyphylla	—	—	—	—	X	—	—	—	—	×	—	—	—
C. spicata	—	—	×	—	X	×	×	—	—	—	×	—	×
C. muricata	—	—	—	—	X	×	—	—	—	×	×	—	×
LEERSIA ORYZOIDES	—	—	—	—	—	—	X	—	—	—	—	—	—
[a]*Lolium temulentum*	—	×	—	—	—	—	—	×	—	—	X	—	—
Vulpia myuros	—	×	—	—	×	×	—	×	—	×	×	—	×
[a]*V. megalura*	—	—	—	—	—	—	—	—	—	×	X	—	—
Catapodium rigidum	—	—	—	—	×	×	—	—	—	×	—	—	X
NARDURUS MARITIMUS	—	—	—	—	—	×	—	—	—	X	—	—	—
Poa annua	—	×	X	×	×	×	—	—	—	×	×	×	—
P. compressa	—	—	×	—	×	×	—	—	—	×	×	—	X
[a]*Cynosurus echinatus*	—	×	—	—	X	×	—	×	—	×	×	—	—
BRIZA MINOR	—	X	×	—	—	—	—	—	—	—	—	—	—
[a]**Zerna inermis**	—	—	—	—	×	×	×	—	—	×	×	—	—
Anisantha sterilis	—	—	×G	—	X	×	—	—	—	×	—	—	×
A. MADRITENSIS	—	—	—	—	—	—	X	—	—	—	×	—	×
A. diandrus	—	—	×	—	X	×	—	×	—	×	—	—	—
A. rigidus	—	—	—	—	×	×	—	×	—	—	×	—	—
[a]*A. tectorum*	—	—	—	—	—	×	—	X	—	×	×	—	—
BROMUS INTERRUPTUS	+	X	×	—	—	—	—	—	—	—	—	—	—
[a]*B. arvensis*	—	×	—	—	×	×	×	×	—	—	X	—	—
[a]*B. secalinus*	+	X	×	—	—	×	—	×	—	—	×	—	—
[a]*Ceratochloa carinata*	—	×	—	—	—	—	X	×	—	—	×	—	—
[a]*C. unioloides*	—	—	×	—	×	×	—	×	—	—	X	—	—
Agropyron repens	—	×	—	—	X	—	—	—	—	—	×	—	—
Hordeum murinum	—	—	—	—	X	×	—	—	—	—	×	—	—
Avena fatua	—	X	—	—	×	—	—	—	—	—	—	—	—
[a]*A. ludoviciana*	—	X	—	—	—	—	—	—	—	—	×	—	—
[a]*A. strigosa*	—	X	—	—	×	—	—	—	×	—	×	—	—
Agrostis gigantea	—	X	×	×	×	—	—	—	—	×	×	—	—
[a]*Polypogon semiverticillatus*	—	—	×	—	—	—	—	×	—	—	X	—	—
Apera spica-venti	—	X	—	—	×	×	—	×	×	—	×	—	—
A. interrupta	—	×	—	—	×	×	—	×	×	—	×	—	—
Gastridium ventricosum	—	×	—	—	—	—	—	×	—	—	X	—	—
Alopecurus myosuroides	—	X	×	—	×	×	—	×	—	—	×	—	—
A. aequalis	—	—	—	X	—	—	×	—	—	—	—	—	—
[a]*ANTHOXANTHUM PUELII*	+	X	—	—	—	—	—	×	—	—	×	—	—
[a]*Phalaris canariensis*	—	—	×	—	—	×	—	—	—	—	X	—	—
CYNODON DACTYLON	—	—	—	—	—	—	—	×	—	—	X	—	—
[a]*Echinochloa crus-galli*	—	×	×	—	—	×	—	×	—	—	X	—	—
[a]*Setaria viridis*	—	×	×	—	—	×	—	×	—	—	×	—	—
[a]*S. verticillata*	—	—	X	—	—	×	—	—	—	—	×	—	—
[a]*S. lutescens*	—	—	X	—	—	×	—	—	—	—	×	—	—

[a] Non-native species.
G Gardens.
× Occurs in this habitat.
X Main habitat.
Ceterach officinarum Species in bold type would survive without regular disturbance by man.
F. MARTINII Species in capitals are national rarities.

Flora

The number of species of vascular plants in Britain is debatable. If native species which occur in natural or semi-natural vegetation alone are counted the number might be as low as 1000; but if one includes all species which have grown successfully in the wild, even if only ephemerally on a rubbish dump, the number could be well over 2000, and if the micro-species of *Rosa*, *Rubus* and other critical genera are added, the total might exceed 3000. In this survey native species and frequent or well-established introductions are included, but casuals and micro-species omitted. The number of species is then about 1700 and it is probably these which are primarily in need of conservation: the conservation of rare ephemeral casuals would hardly be possible even if it were desirable.

Of the 1700 species, 406 (24%) are wholly or mainly dependent on man-made habitats or human activity for their survival in Britain. The criteria applied in selecting this species list rule out many species which are also characteristic of man-made habitats, e.g. common umbellifers of roadside and railway verges. In Table 34 the habitat requirements of these 406 species are presented according to an analysis of data held by the Biological Records Centre at Monks Wood, Huntingdon. The analysis is summarised in Table 35.

The status of each species is indicated: 229 (56%) are regarded as native, the remaining 177 species (44%), as introductions. The species are divided into those entirely dependent on man-made or man-influenced habitats (267: 66%); and those which, dependent as they are on man's activity, could nevertheless survive in his absence though undoubtedly in much reduced numbers (137: 34%). Of the 406 species, 45 (11%) are national rarities, i.e. species which since 1950 have been recorded in 15 or fewer 10-km squares in Britain. The total number of British rarities is only about 280, of which approximately one-sixth are dependent on man-made habitats. Some species not yet nationally rare by our definition are declining so rapidly that they must be regarded as potential national rarities. There are 40 such species (10%), mostly weeds of arable land which were formerly widespread but now are extremely local, e.g. *Agrostemma githago*, *Bupleurum rotundifolium*, *Galium tricornutum*, *Galeopsis speciosa*, *Ranunculus arvensis* and *Torilis arvensis*.

If the broad division of species between the two major categories of land-use is examined, it appears that 267 (66%) are recorded in agricultural and 380 (94%) in non-agricultural man-made habitats. The number of species completely confined to agricultural land is therefore small, but for many (142) this is the most important habitat, and for 26 species it is the only suitable habitat. The fumitories (*Fumaria* spp.) are almost entirely dependent on arable fields, as are most of the rapidly declining species listed above. The most important habitats for plants on non-agricultural land are roadside verges with their associated hedges, urban waste ground, building sites and rubbish dumps. Nearly 75% of the 405 species have been recorded

Table 35. *Summary of distribution of vascular plant species of the British flora in artificial habitats*

	No.	%
Native	229	56
Non-native	177	44
Agricultural habitats	267	66
Non-agricultural habitats	380	94
Rapidly declining	40	10
National rarities	45	11
Survive without man	137	34
Total of species	406	

			Main habitat	
	No.	%	No.	%
Agricultural				
Cultivated land	180	44	88	22
Non-cultivated land	166	41	39	10
Aquatic	33	8	15	4
Non-agricultural				
Road verge & hedgerow	300	74	101	25
Railways	194	48	19	5
River banks	103	25	15	4
Ports	103	25	2	0.5
Sewage	13	3	0	0.0
Spoil & quarries	120	30	7	2
Urban waste	235	58	69	17
Parks & churchyards	69	17	4	1
Walls	72	18	28	7

on roadside verges and this is the main habitat for 101 of these. Just under 60% have occurred on urban waste ground and for 69 species this is the most important habitat. Golf courses should perhaps be considered with lowland grasslands and heaths or coastal grasslands and sand dunes. Railway verges and river banks each have a large flora, but only a few near-exclusive species, whilst ports, sewage farms, quarries, parks and churchyards mainly provide alternative habitats for species more widespread elsewhere. The flora of walls is, however, much more distinct: although the number of species is not large (72) a considerable number (28) have this as their most important habitat. There is a strong case for the preservation of the flora of the walls of ancient buildings as well as the buildings themselves, so long as the two aspects are compatible.

These data suggest that to conserve the greatest number of vascular plant species in man-made habitats attention should be focussed particularly on arable fields, roadside verges and hedges, and walls. No doubt urban waste ground will continue to contribute its quota to species conservation without intervention so long as public desire for tidiness does not become overwhelming.

Knowledge of the fauna of artificial habitats is at present too fragmentary to present as a separate account, but this interest is indicated for some better known groups in agricultural and non-agricultural habits (see above).

GENERAL REQUIREMENTS FOR NATURE CONSERVATION

There are two distinct conservation problems connected with artificial ecosystems:

1. The need to ensure survival of species, e.g. certain arable weeds, which are restricted to crop lands.

2. The need to maintain reasonably large populations, nationally and locally, of the many species which are found in this range of habitats as well as in those represented on key sites and undeveloped semi-natural land generally.

Woodlands and wetlands are often scarce in the lowlands and are tending to decrease, so that their counterparts associated with agricultural land, notably small copses, hedges and ponds, may provide important additional habitats for woodland and wetland species, especially in the south-eastern half of Britain. The national requirement is to maintain enough artificial habitats, especially on farms, to reinforce conservation measures elsewhere. In practice, this task is made difficult by inadequate knowledge of this element of the total wildlife resource and by the complexity and subjectivity of the value judgements involved in putting an actual figure on the national requirement. The relative importance of the secondary man-made habitats compared to the primary semi-natural ones for any species has been little studied; the national importance of farmlands as a habitat for wildlife is thus not accurately known, though their local value may be fairly obvious in general terms. Hedgerows, for example, undoubtedly provide habitats for thousands of woodland, scrub and grassland organisms, and though it is unlikely that they are essential for the survival of many species they are nevertheless obviously important in maintaining local diversity and total quantity of wildlife, which is desirable for local amenity and educational reasons, especially in the agricultural 'prairie' districts of eastern England.

The linear habitats – hedges, railway embankments, road verges and canals – may be important on the national scale because they may provide dispersal pathways for certain organisms, e.g. some plants and molluscs; but for more mobile groups, e.g. most insects and birds, they are probably unimportant in this respect. Relatively little is known, too, about the minimum extent of habitat required for the survival of most species of plant and animal, or about the long-term significance of new ecological factors, e.g. the cumulative effects of herbicides as the reservoir of weed seeds in the soils gradually becomes exhausted over a long period.

By definition, conservation measures are not required to safeguard those species which can successfully exploit artificial habitats such as the extensive unstable croplands under modern methods of cultivation. On the other hand a number of plants, the invertebrates associated with them, and other animals depend on obsolete or obsolescent methods of land use, especially in agriculture. The need for arable weed reserves to ensure the survival of certain species in Britain has been mentioned. The intensive pest control practised in orchards nowadays and the disappearance of the old-style sewage farms are other examples of changes which have had markedly adverse effects on wildlife, especially birds.

The wildlife of artificial habitats is on the whole vulnerable to the changes produced by technological development and shifting economic policy. The extent of these habitats will always depend on current patterns of land-use and will be subject to the vagaries of change in these. The future course of agriculture in Britain depends very much on the agricultural policies of the European Economic Community. There are likely to be significant changes in use of farmland, and in human impact on the environment more generally. The present trend of rapid increase in land values may lead to a general intensification of use which could adversely affect many artificial habitats. The best chance for successfully promoting nature conservation in the whole range of artificial ecosystems would seem to come from

1. acquiring adequate background ecological knowledge of the distribution and abundance of wildlife species and the factors controlling these;

2. developing a predictive capacity in which this knowledge is integrated with forecasts of land-use change;

3. promoting sympathetic attitudes to wildlife among all users of land, public and private, corporate and individual, and providing appropriate advice based on 1 and 2 above.

The provision of wildlife habitats on farmland, both for local conservation reasons, and to increase the viability of national populations, can best be done by encouraging landowners to retain small woods, hedges, ponds, etc. wherever economically possible, and manage them so as to produce suitable conditions for wildlife. Similarly, those in charge of road verges, railway embankments and other non-agricultural land should be encouraged to manage these habitats in order to provide a rich flora and fauna. By these means total national populations can be reinforced and the chances of survival of many species which are not present in nature reserves today can be increased. Wildlife is a national resource, but needs to be conserved on a geographically dispersed, local scale, so that as much interest as possible is retained – consistent with over-riding economic dictates – even in those areas where human influence is greatest and most adverse.

11 THE CONSERVATION OF FLORA

The choice of key sites in the *Review* has been primarily according to the representation of vegetation types, for their intrinsic interest and as animal habitats. A selection based on plant communities does not, however, necessarily take adequate account of other aspects of botanical interest, including the representation of the plant species which together constitute the *flora* of a district. The botanical interest represented within the national series has, in fact, to provide for taxonomy and systematics, phytogeography, genetics and plant breeding, physiology and biochemistry, field studies and any other aspects of this science where concern is with species and individuals. The problems of representing floristic assemblages in this way, as well as plant communities, are considerable. Many of the less common species occupy small, specialised or transitional habitats which may not occur on a site chosen for the quality of its major vegetation types. Moreover, the low numbers and erratic distribution of many rarer plants reduce the chances of their inclusion within key sites unless there is deliberate selection for them. It has thus been necessary to use floristic richness (i.e. number of plant species in relation to area and habitat) and presence of rare or local species as additional criteria in site selection.

Common and widespread native species, especially community constants and dominants, tend to be well represented in the key site series, and aggregations of rare and local species, as in well-known plant refugia such as Upper Teesdale, are also adequately dealt with. Representation is much affected by dispersion pattern and habitat. Uncommon species which are concentrated in a few localities and occur in important habitats are often strongly represented, whereas others which are widely dispersed and belong to less distinctive habitats tend to be under-represented. No attempt has been made to include rare species which occur singly in localities undistinguished for any other features, e.g. *Diapensia lapponica*. Plants characteristic of artificial habitats are especially poorly represented on key sites.

Representation of flora is not only a matter of the presence of species within key sites, but is also concerned with proportions of the total British populations thus included. Inevitably, there are wide variations in regard to this second aspect; for some species a large proportion of the total British population occurs within key sites, whereas for others only an insignificant fraction is included. It is still not possible to say exactly what proportion of the total number of vascular plant macro-species in the total British flora occurs on at least one key site, but the figure probably exceeds

80%. The assessment of the proportions of the total populations of these species occurring on key sites presents still greater difficulties, though some relevant data for a few species are given in the site accounts.

The *Review* has acknowledged the varying weight of interest, both professional and amateur, in different taxonomic groups, as a factor influencing the choice of the key site series. The greatest emphasis is thus given to the most popular plants, i.e. the vascular flora, but the bryophytes and lichens have received a good deal of attention. Less well-known groups, such as algae and fungi, have perforce been neglected in the *Review*; it is hoped that their incidental representation in key sites is adequate, though rarities will inevitably tend to be omitted. It is, moreover, only realistic to take account of the variations in fragility (i.e. intrinsic vulnerability and foreseeable degree of threat) shown by different species, and to emphasise the representation within key sites of the essentially fragile and threatened species.

The representation of the different families of plants has not been analysed in detail, but the fact that some show a stronger representation on key sites than others is largely a matter of their ecological bias, e.g. Ericaceae and Saxifragaceae belong largely to natural and semi-natural communities, whereas a relatively large proportion of Cruciferae and Umbelliferae belong to man-made habitats.

The attention given to critical groups has varied. Because of their rarity, limited number and association with woodland, the various species within the genus *Sorbus* have mostly been represented on key sites. While *Alchemilla vulgaris* agg. has not been specifically considered, most of its segregates are probably present on at least one selected site, and the same is probably true for *Euphrasia officinalis* agg. However, the very large number of micro-species in *Rubus fruticosus* agg. and *Hieracium* can only be represented haphazardly and largely according to chance, e.g. the Cairngorms are especially rich in montane *Hieracia*.

It is of concern to geneticists, plant breeders, agriculturalists and foresters that adequate samples of the range of genetic variation within populations of species be maintained, especially in the case of species with an economic value, such as grasses, legumes and trees. Polymorphic taxa are also of great interest in more academic taxonomic, cytogenetic and evolutionary studies, for much work has still to be done in this field. Selection of key sites has not specifically taken account of these requirements, but it is hoped that, in representing the British flora according to other criteria, a

Table 36. *Representation on key sites of species characteristic of the major formations*

Habitat	Total listed species	Number present	%	Species not known to be present in any key site of the habitat type
1. Coastlands (see Table 1)	215	206	95.8	*Cystopteris dickieana, Rhynchosinapis wrightii, Lepidium latifolium, Polygonum maritimum, Centaurium tenuiflorum, C. portense, ᵃOtanthus maritimus, Carduus pycnocephalus, Cyperus longus*
2. Woodlands (see Table 5)	236	229	97.0	*Aconitum anglicum, ᵃEuphorbia pilosa, E. esula, Calamintha sylvatica, Campanula patula, Lonicera xylosteum, Epipogium aphyllum*
3. Lowland acidic heaths and grasslands (see Table 11)	97	96	99.0	*Hypericum undulatum*
4. Lowland calcareous grasslands (see Table 12)	154	148	96.1	*Bunium bulbocastanum, Orobanche reticulata, O. picridis, Stachys germanica, Ajuga chamaepitys, Orchis simia*
5. Lowland calcareous scrub (see Table 15)	129	117	90.7	*Berberis vulgaris, Vicia bithynica, Ribes spicatum, Polygonum dumetorum, Orobanche rapum-genistae, Campanula patula, Ornithogalum pyrenaicum, Leucojum aestivum, Iris foetidissima, Orchis simia, Carex divulsa, Hordelymus europaeus*
6. Mixed heaths and grasslands (see Chapter 6, pp. 174–83)	17	17	100.0	
7. Neutral grasslands (see Table 18)	174	164	94.3	*Ranunculus ophioglossifolius, Lathyrus nissolia, Carum verticillatum, Meum athamanticum, Orobanche minor, Salvia horminoides, Crepis biennis, Gagea lutea, Leucojum aestivum, Scorzonera humilis*
8. Open waters (see Table 20)	139	136	97.8	*Alisma gramineum, Eriocaulon septangulare, Limosella subulata*
9. Peatlands (see Table 23)	161	157	97.5	*Hypericum undulatum, Carex buxbaumii, C. chordorrhiza, Eriophorum gracile*
10. Upland grasslands and heaths				
(a) Montane (see Table 27)	118	116	98.3	*Arabis alpina, Diapensia lapponica*
(b) Submontane (see Table 28)	43	42	97.7	*Lychnis viscaria* (see Appendix)

Note
ᵃ Species now apparently extinct in Britain.

wide range of genotypic variability has incidentally been included.

The conservation of the British flora will now be examined in relation to those aspects considered under the separate formations, namely habitat requirements, geographical distribution and abundance classes. The representation of vascular species according to these categories will be examined separately. A fourth aspect, which may be termed historical significance, deals with the question of native status and its importance.

The conservation of flora is, however, a much broader issue than that dealt with in the *Review*. It is greatly to be hoped that the proportion of the British native flora, in both species and populations, which is conserved in practice will be far larger than that confined within key sites. The present analysis draws attention to the deficiencies and limitations of the key site approach in safeguarding our wild plants, and points to the need for a more comprehensive countrywide policy for achieving this desirable end.

FLOWERING PLANTS, FERNS AND FERN ALLIES (VASCULAR PLANTS)

Habitat requirements

The flora of each major formation type has already been considered, and a tabular list of vascular species given for each, in the appropriate Chapters. Table 36 indicates the representation within key sites of those species considered to be characteristic of the various major formations, and shows that the proportions are mostly high. The lists of characteristic species for the different formations have been drawn up from the taxa included in the *Atlas of the British Flora* (excluding the *Critical Supplement*) and total 1483 out of 1700 different forms, i.e. 87%. The remaining 217 taxa are those which do not fit easily into the range of natural and semi-natural formations considered. Many of these ecologically unclassified taxa are, in fact, represented on key sites, but the exact number is not yet known. However, it is equally certain that many of these taxa are not represented.

The least well represented on key sites of any of the ecological groups of British plants is that associated with entirely artificial habitats, i.e. roadside and railway verges, waste ground, uncultivated field edges and cultivated land. These habitats were excluded from the site selection process of the *Review*, and are represented only as bonus areas, to a very limited extent on some lowland grassland, heath and woodland sites, as in the Breckland. The number of herbaceous vascular species which they carry is large, the families Cruciferae, Umbelliferae and Compositae being especially well represented. Many species occur in no other habitat, but a high proportion of these are aliens and relatively recent introductions, some of which may find only an ephemeral foothold in this country. Plants in this class tend to be lumped together as weeds, but they are often of considerable interest to botanists. In particular, the forbs of arable (especially cereal) crops are of ecological interest as well as aesthetic value. The interest of artificial ecosystems and problems associated with their conservation are discussed in Chapter 10.

Phytogeography

The analysis of the British flowering plants into 16 phytogeographical elements by J. R. Matthews (1937) gives a comprehensive framework for reviewing the conservation of this portion of our flora on a distributional basis. While corresponding groupings may be recognised within the pteridophytes, bryophytes, lichens, algae and fungi, a comparable analysis is not yet available for these orders. As phytogeographical groupings mostly have some ecological validity in addition (i.e. in relating to various climatic patterns), the selection of a series of key sites primarily according to ecological criteria has automatically ensured a good degree of representation of species within these groupings. In some instances, phytogeographical importance has been used as a further criterion for conferring key site status, e.g. to Upper Teesdale and many western woods.

On the international scale, probably the most important of Matthews' phytogeographical elements in Britain are the oceanic southern and oceanic west European (which contains the 'Lusitanian' element). These together fall within a group loosely known as 'Atlantic' or 'oceanic' which includes also a number of ferns. Britain is the European headquarters for some of these species, and a particular effort has been made to include a strong representation of these plants within the series of key sites (see also Bryophytes and Lichens, below). The ferns are especially well represented in woodland and on coastal or upland rocks, and the flowering plants especially on heaths and coastlands. The ferns as a whole are an oceanic group, and are extremely well represented on key sites; only one of the 45 species occurring in Britain does not occur on at least one key site, namely *Cystopteris dickieana*.

The Arctic–alpine, Arctic–subarctic and alpine elements belong mostly to the montane or submontane flora, and are

extremely well represented on upland sites, whilst the northern montane and continental northern elements include a number of species which are northern and submontane in Britain, in a variety of habitats, including coastlands and woodlands. The continental and continental southern elements include a large number of species which have a southern distribution (though marked in varying degree) in Britain, and so contain some which are especially characteristic of lowland grasslands on Chalk and Oolitic limestone. Most of the noteworthy Breckland plants belong to these two groups.

Matthews' wide Eurasian and European elements have not been analysed in the present context. They include species widespread in Britain, and others with more limited distribution patterns suggestive within this country of one of the more restricted elements. Again, the best represented species are those which fall clearly into the major formations which have been recognised, while the most poorly represented are those which belong to rather nondescript habitats, especially the arable farm and urban environments of the lowlands.

Abundance classes

The validity of 'rarity' as a criterion in assessing scientific value has been accepted (Chapter 3). The rare species of British plants thus have a particular importance, especially when they are also rare in Europe or the world as a whole. Rarity, or any other qualitative term of abundance, can only be defined more precisely in terms of numbers with arbitrarily chosen limits. The *Atlas of the British Flora* has given quantitative information for such definition, on the basis of vascular species' occurrence in the 10-km squares of the National Grid. After due consideration of the total range of data available, the following definitions have been adopted:

A *Very rare*: present in only 1–2 10-km squares. This includes single-station plants.

B *Rare*: present in 3–15 10-km squares.

C *Very local*: present in 16–100 10-km squares.

The occurrence of vascular species in these three abundance classes on key sites is summarised in Table 37. Species surveys of many key sites are not yet complete, and the position of species in classes A and B changes as new localities are found, old ones rediscovered, or present ones lost. Furthermore, unknown and often widely varying sizes of population go to making a single 10-km grid square record, so that the system is not an absolute measure of species' rarity, but a conventional index. This problem is being studied and it may soon be possible to define the actual population sizes of the rare British vascular plants with greater accuracy, and to indicate what proportions are represented on key sites.

The montane and northern group is by far the best represented of species in abundance classes A–C, with those of lowland grasslands and heaths, and coastlands next in order. There are several reasons for the preponderance of upland rarities – they tend to be aggregated in refugia;

Table 37. *Percentage occurrences of uncommon species in grade 1 and 2 sites*

Category	Total extant	No. species in key sites	Grade 1	Grade 2 (only)	No. species not in key sites
A	71 (13)	47 (66)	43 (60)	4 (6)	24 (34)
B	201 (36)	165 (82)	157 (78)	8 (4)	36 (18)
C	279 (51)	252 (90)	243 (87)	9 (3)	27 (10)
Overall total	551	464 (84)	443 (80)	21 (4)	87 (16)

Note

Figures in parentheses are percentages.

upland sites are probably the best recorded botanically; and upland sites cover the largest area (i.e. there is a species/area effect). Since sites have not been chosen for the presence of single rarities, the widely dispersed rare species tend to be less well represented than those which are aggregated with each other.

Historical status

Species have appeared in the British flora at different points in historical time. As a result they can be grouped in relation to the various time zones of the Late- and Post-glacial Periods when they appeared. These would, however, tend to be largely climatic groupings and so fall within the ecological subdivision of the flora which has been considered earlier. Relict or newly arrived species also represent historical classes, but they are best treated as geographical types.

The subdivisions which are most suitably considered here are the native and introduced species. These two classes represent concepts rather than hard and fast categories. The boundary between them is vague and ill defined, and any sharp distinction which might be made would involve arbitrary limits. There is a general feeling that plants deliberately introduced (i.e. carried from one place and planted in another) into a country, or even a new locality within a country, have lower status than those which arrived of their own accord, and that they have no particular claims in regard to conservation. However, even the term 'deliberately introduced' cannot be applied easily to particular species within the British flora. Some were brought here so long ago that it will never be known what part deliberate human intervention played in their appearance; some have spread widely of their own accord since original introduction, so that the degree of human influence is difficult to assess; others were probably introduced accidentally, and many have escaped from cultivation. Others again are native species whose numbers and distribution have been increased by introduction.

There have been attempts to categorise degrees of 'non-nativeness', and various terms have been introduced, such as alien, denizen, adventive, casual and exotic. The conservationist's view of these plants needs to be realistic, judging each case on its merits. Many introduced species have become so widespread of their own accord that they have claims to be accepted along with natives as part of the British flora, e.g. *Myrrhis odorata*, *Rumex alpinus*, *Montia perfoliata*, *Erinus alpinus* and *Senecio squalidus*. Where these are now decreasing through destruction of habitat, there is reason to conserve them. It may be noted, however, that many introduced species belong to artificial habitats, such as road and railway verges, farmland, urban–industrial waste land and spoil heaps, which are mostly not involved in key site selection. Scientific value is further reduced when a site is invaded by a rapidly spreading and vigorously competitive introduction, e.g. *Rhododendron ponticum*, *Acaena anserinifolia*, *Hippophaë rhamnoides*, *Spartina anglica* (hybrid between *S. maritima* and introduced *S. alterniflora*), which seriously reduces the native flora.

In the *Review* human influence has been accepted as an integral factor in producing ecosystem diversity. On the whole, long-established introductions, and especially species whose origins are now obscure (e.g. *Allium schoenoprasum*), have been regarded in the same way as true natives. However, application of the accepted criterion of 'naturalness' causes many introduced species to be rated rather low in the scale of scientific value. The representation of introduced plants in key sites tends to be largely a matter of chance, as they seldom influence the actual choice of site, but their presence is not regarded as undesirable unless there is definite evidence of this in the form of competition with more highly valued natives.

BRYOPHYTES AND LICHENS

The geographical and ecological distribution of mosses, liverworts and lichens in Britain have received a great deal of attention. The general patterns are fairly well known, distribution records for many of the less conspicuous and taxonomically more difficult species continue to increase rapidly, and knowledge of lichens probably lags behind that of the bryophytes. In these groups, only certain acrocarpous mosses and thallose liverworts have their main or only habitats in artificial ecosystems. Many species in such genera as *Bryum, Dicranella, Tortula, Barbula, Pottia, Phascum, Weissia* and *Ephemerum* among the mosses, and *Anthoceros, Sphaerocarpos, Riccia* and *Fossombronia* among the liverworts, have their main or only occurrences in man-made habitats, such as arable or much disturbed land, banks and ditches, walls and buildings. These are the groups least well represented in the series of key sites, though many species are probably contained by the chance inclusion of bonus habitats.

A few of the very rarest bryophytes in Britain are not known to occur in any key site, but most of the species belonging to natural and semi-natural habitats are represented within at least one grade 1 or 2 site.

Britain is the European headquarters for many Atlantic bryophytes, and a number of species are unknown on the mainland of Europe. Many have a highly disjunct and relict world distribution and are of special phytogeographical interest. The choice of key sites has deliberately included a good selection of habitats and localities important for these plants, especially woodlands, coastlands and uplands in western Britain, and the northern, southern and widespread subgroups are all well represented. The upland sites tend to be rich in bryophytes and, for some species in the high montane calcicole and late snow-bed groups, a substantial proportion of the total British populations is probably thus included.

The lichens, too, are probably well represented as regards presence of species within key sites. A considerable effort has been made to include examples of lichen-rich woodland, and importance for lichens has been a significant criterion in assessing national value of sites, especially in the case of old park woodland. Some of the very rarest species are at present unknown within key sites, and when lichenological interest is somewhat dispersed over a large area as it is within the very important Loch Sunart area, there are difficulties in including the whole of this interest within a site of reasonable size. The Atlantic element of the British lichen flora is parallel in importance to that in the bryophytes, and is likewise strongly represented in western woodlands, coastlands and uplands. The threats to lichens from atmospheric pollution, and from such activities as the steady felling of old but scattered trees, create obvious extra difficulties for the conservation of lichens by means of key sites.

A detailed analysis of the occurrence of the bryophyte and lichen floras within key sites has not been made. With present incompleteness of survey information for these groups on many sites, such an analysis could only be inaccurate and would almost certainly under-represent the true figure. Virtually all the communities dominated by bryophytes and lichens are represented in the series of key sites, and some of the best British examples of these distinctive vegetation types are included.

FUNGI AND ALGAE

A good deal is known about the fungi and algae of certain areas and sites, but in the time available, it seemed impossible to organise a countrywide survey which could give a consistent assessment of the value of sites for either group. Knowledge of the mycological importance of certain sites, and of the contribution of algae to the limnological value of some open waters, has been a factor in assessment and selection. Nevertheless, it has to be said that, in general, the only assured representation of fungi and algae is for those species which occur fairly widely in natural and semi-natural habitats.

12 THE CONSERVATION OF FAUNA

It has been explained earlier that the selection of key sites is based on assessment of scientific interest defined primarily in vegetational terms, and that only a minority are chosen because of the high value placed on fauna (or animal communities in a loose sense). The distribution of emphasis accorded to faunal features has been partly a measure of acknowledged public interest and partly of the special and often local interests of individual scientists concerned in the *Review*. Thus, special weight has been given to representation of birds in general, and to Lepidoptera, as the most popular groups of animals; while there is a lesser and more random emphasis on spiders in East Anglia, weevils in southern calcareous habitats, dragonflies in southern Britain, insects associated with calcicolous scrub, and various invertebrate groups of open waters.

Although a good deal is known about some animal groups neglected in the *Review*, most of the information is not readily translatable into the kind of analysis needed in conservation assessments. For many faunal groups, adequacy of coverage in the national series of key sites at present thus depends on the degree of parallelism between botanical and zoological interest. Close parallelism certainly often exists, but there are a good many known instances in which it does not. Whilst selection for these known faunal sites has been made, as appropriate, it is necessary to allow for the important zoological sites as yet unknown (i.e. in the little-studied groups) by conceding that further key sites may need to be added to the present list as knowledge of other animal groups increases.

The inclusion of sections for all the major invertebrate groups would also have made the present document impossibly lengthy. Sections on weevils and spiders have been included as examples of groups which have not, for the most part, significantly influenced the choice of key sites; the accompanying analyses show that they are nevertheless well represented on these sites. This encourages confidence that for most other, neglected, invertebrate groups in natural and semi-natural habitats, the series of key sites may well give a reasonably adequate representation of species. It is felt that, as fuller knowledge of other invertebrate groups on key sites becomes available, it may be published in supplementary accounts.

The problems of conserving animal species closely parallel those discussed under plants (Chapter 11). True, bats, birds and insects are particularly mobile, with many species regularly migratory; they can thus, in theory, more readily spread to new localities or recolonise lost ones. For all their apparent mobility, however, many animal species are nevertheless very limited and conservative in distribution and movements, and have great difficulty in spreading from established localities. Some insects are extremely sedentary and unable to recolonise lost ground even within a short distance. For the rarer species it is thus important to protect minimum populations by means of safeguarded sites.

The key site series contains substantial proportions of the total British population of many rare animal species; for a few rare species, the whole known British population is included. The rarities not present on key sites remain a problem to be dealt with by the safeguarding of lower grade sites on the regional or local scale, or by other appropriate conservation measures. The more widespread and numerous species tend to be represented as a matter of course on key sites, but with increasing abundance and scatter there is a tendency for decrease in the proportion of the total British population thus represented, unless the species is highly aggregated in a few localities. As with the majority of plants, for most animal species the key site series provides a means of conserving only relatively small population samples. The remaining and larger portions of their populations are vulnerable to change in land-use and other human impact, and require more general conservation measures outside key sites.

A good many animals are regarded as pests, at least by some people, and the continued abundance of some is a reflection of their resistance to adverse pressures. Others, especially some mammals and birds, have been less successful in withstanding deliberate persecution and have decreased or even disappeared from Britain. Whether a species presents a conservation problem thus depends on the human standpoint and on the present status of the animal concerned. Many of the more widespread and widely adapted animal species are likely to remain fairly numerous in the future, despite foreseeable environmental change, and there is no need for undue concern about those which will look after themselves. The important task is to identify those whose future security of status is less assured, and to consider the measures required to promote their conservation.

The rest of this section will attempt to assess adequacy of coverage in the *Review*, i.e. representation on key sites, for the vertebrates and a few invertebrate groups.

MAMMALS

The conservation of British mammals has received less attention than that of birds. This is partly because many species are either game animals, often managed as a resource by landowners and protected by law in varying degree, or pests which are generally disliked and killed at least in some parts of their range. Some animals belong to both categories, according to the human viewpoint or to varying conditions of place and time. The rabbit and many small mammals are important prey species of Carnivora and birds of prey, and their numbers and distribution greatly affect those of the related predators.

The red deer is the principal mammalian game species and perhaps the only British mammal which now has economic value in a positive sense. Many people believe that management of red deer is the only realistic way of utilising much of the poor hill land of Scotland, and the red deer forest is now a traditional form of land-use through much of the Highlands. In places and at certain times, the numbers of this animal have to be kept drastically in check to prevent marauding on arable farmlands and damage to young forests, but on the whole it is conserved as a crop species and a cull of the population is taken annually, with varying degrees of selection. Red deer forests are well represented in the list of Scottish grade 1 upland sites, and include Cairnsmore of Fleet and Merrick–Kells in southern Scotland; the Cairngorms, Drumochter Hills and Caenlochan–Clova in the eastern Highlands; and Ben Alder–Aonach Mor, Rhum, Inverpolly, Beinn Dearg–Seana Bhraigh, Beinn Eighe–Liathach, and Foinaven–Meall Horn in the western Highlands.

The roe deer is a widespread species which has increased in recent decades, probably as a result of the general increase in area of afforested land in Britain. It can accommodate itself well in coniferous plantations and is something of a nuisance in young commercial forests, where it is fairly strictly controlled, but it holds its own and may still be spreading. Roe deer occur in very many woodland key sites and on some heathland sites which also have woodland in association. The other species of deer (fallow, sika and muntjac) are established locally, mainly through escapes from parks, and different people have different views about their place in the natural scene. They are quite widespread whether one likes it or not, and their conservation does not as yet present problems, though their control may do so locally. In particular, the introgressive hybridisation of the introduced sika with native red deer in areas such as the southern Lake District is causing considerable concern, for the resulting genetic dilution of the native stock is difficult to control.

Feral goats are also disliked by foresters and their numbers have been drastically reduced in some areas of recently afforested uplands. Herds of these goats are represented on a number of grade 1 upland sites, though their populations vary in size. Goats are still plentiful on Cairnsmore of Fleet and Merrick–Kells, Eryri (fewer), and Rhum. Though goats may increase on grounds from which sheep are removed, they appear to maintain a fairly constant population and distribution in most places where they are not molested, but are a very local animal and do not occur in many upland areas. Feral goats have strong claims to be treated as a

native animal and to be conserved as such, for they are considered by many people to be an attractive and interesting addition to a habitat which is usually singularly deficient in large wild mammals.

Before the advent of myxomatosis in 1953, the rabbit was important locally for human food, and certain areas had been managed as rabbit warrens for some considerable time. Probably the most famous of these warrens were those of the Breckland, where large areas of the dry, sandy soils were given over to rabbits, which exerted a profound influence on the vegetation and other wildlife. Other large rabbit populations were found especially on calcareous and sandy soils, such as the chalk downlands of southern England, the limestone pastures of various districts, and dune systems in many coastal areas. Rabbits were also common over much of the agricultural lowlands but were here increasingly regarded as a pest. In many parts of the country, the rabbit was an important prey species for certain wild predators, notably the common buzzard, golden eagle, badger, fox, stoat and weasel.

Myxomatosis drastically reduced the rabbit population over much of Britain, and has shown repeated recurrences in most places where the rabbits made any significant recovery. As a result, the total British rabbit population has shown a depression in numbers, with only very local recovery up to 1973. The reduced grazing pressure has had a marked effect on vegetation once kept close-grazed, as on the chalk downlands, where there has been extensive invasion by scrub, and on the grass heaths of Breckland, where the swards are now relatively luxuriant. Some of the changes in balance between plant species have been unfavourable to the conservation of the flora of these grasslands and heaths. Perhaps the densest rabbit population now remaining in Britain is at Weeting Heath in the Suffolk Breckland, where an experimental enclosure has allowed a high density of rabbits to develop, and the breck is maintained in an extremely open condition. Over most of the country the rabbit now survives in much reduced numbers. On the whole this is a useful animal to nature conservation, but any general increase in its numbers is bound to be opposed by the agricultural community, even on non-agricultural land, which is regarded by many people as a reservoir of 'vermin'.

Brown hares remain widespread and moderately numerous animals of agricultural and marginal land. They are still valued by some as a game species and are not usually at high enough density to be regarded as a serious pest. Blue hares are widespread in Scotland and also thrive in some places, such as the Peak District, where they have been introduced. Their numbers seem to show some relationship to those of the red grouse, presumably because of parallel effects of differences in moorland productivity, and blue hares are found at high density mainly on the heathery moorlands of the drier, eastern parts of Scotland, e.g. the Moorfoot Hills, Midlothian–Peebles-shire. In at least some areas they are subject to fluctuations in numbers.

Most of the remaining species of British mammal are regarded as pests and treated accordingly, at least by some people. The widespread carnivores, e.g. fox, badger, otter, stoat and weasel survive in some numbers regardless of persecution, which varies a good deal from place to place. The otter is said to be suffering a substantial decline, at least in the south, and some badgers have been poisoned by dieldrin residues absorbed from prey living in the agricultural environment. The populations of animals of this kind are influenced mainly by broad changes in human impact through the country as a whole, though reasonable samples (except perhaps for the otter) are represented in the national series of key sites.

The rarer terrestrial carnivores, the polecat, pine marten and wild cat, are restricted to the remoter and more sparsely populated parts of the country; and the last two are now confined to upland areas, though they inhabit the lower level of the hills. Despite much persecution, the polecat and wild cat have increased and spread recently in, respectively, their Welsh and Scottish haunts. The same may be true of the pine marten in the western Highlands, but it remains scarce in other parts of its range, such as Lakeland and Snowdonia, and there requires strict protection. The pine marten and wild cat are well represented in upland and woodland grade 1 sites in the Highlands and the polecat occurs on peatland, coastland and probably woodland grade 1 sites in central and west Wales.

Perhaps the most vulnerable British mammals to adverse influences are the two maritime carnivores, the grey and common seals, which in the breeding season have a restricted distribution through their habit of assembling in large colonies. The grey seal crowds together in large numbers on low rocky islands to produce its young and the common seal gathers likewise in shallow coastal waters with sandbanks or rocks. Four of the largest British colonies of the grey seal are located on the coastal grade 1 sites of the Isles of Scilly, the Ynsoedd Preseli, the Farne Islands and North Rona. However, the numbers of grey seals have increased to a level where serious damage to fishery interests is alleged, and even damage to habitat occurs on the Farnes, so that many people feel that some measure of control on these breeding grounds is desirable. Culls have been made in Orkney and on the Farnes in recent years. The position for the common seal is less clear, for this species has less need still than the other for dry land above high-tide mark; the large population of the Wash and North Norfolk Coast probably overlaps considerably in distribution with the grade 1 coastal sites of this region.

Apart from bats, which are treated separately below, the remaining British mammals consist either of species which the naturalist, at least, regards as having a rightful place in the native fauna, or of species which virtually everyone regards as out-and-out pests and whose extinction would cause few regrets in any quarters. In the last category are the black and brown rats, house mouse, coypu and, perhaps, the grey squirrel. The others occur mostly in large numbers despite varying degrees of control, and their position in Britain seems to depend largely on the grosser kinds of change in land-use patterns throughout the country. Short-tailed field voles, for instance, usually thrive during the

early stages of growth of young conifer forests, when the ground is fenced against the larger grazing animals, but they largely disappear as the forest canopy closes. The species most in need of conservation in this group of mammals are the red squirrel, dormouse, Orkney vole, Skomer bank vole and certain insular races of the wood mouse. The red squirrel occurs in some key woodland sites from East Anglia northwards, and the dormouse is probably represented in some southern woodland sites. St Kilda National Nature Reserve (NNR) has *Apodemus sylvaticus hirtensis*, Rhum NNR has *A. s. hebridensis*, the Shetland NNRs have *A. s. fridariensis* and the Isles of Scilly have the Scilly (white-toothed) shrew *Crocidura suaveolens cassiteridum*; the Orkney vole is present in the area around the grade 1 open water site of Lochs Harray and Stenness on Mainland Orkney. The Skomer vole is confined to Skomer NNR.

The conservation of bats presents quite different problems. Bats in Britain are not known to be directly harmful to human interests, though, as with the carnivores, there are anxieties about their potential role as carriers of the rabies at present spreading westwards through Europe. As bats feed on insects it is sometimes presumed that their influence is favourable to agriculture and forestry, though they probably eat beneficial as well as harmful insects. Like many other animals, bats are profoundly affected indirectly by human activity, and changes in land use are of great consequence to them. Hibernation and other roost requirements of bats are highly specific and these animals are extremely vulnerable to any change or loss affecting the habitats concerned. Bats, being insectivorous, are also vulnerable to changes in flying insect populations.

Historically, there is no information indicating the size of populations or detailed distribution of bat species within Britain, but recent observations indicate that certain species at least are declining in southern Britain. There are many reasons to account for this. Reduced insect populations as a result of changes in farming methods and more directly through the use of pesticides must together have had the greatest effect. Felling hollow trees, either in woodlands or hedgerows is one cause of continuing loss of roosts, and another is the further quarrying and filling in by farmers and local councils of caves, mine tunnels and quarries. Within the caves and tunnels speleologists are an increasing source of disturbance to bat colonies and only three to four disturbances per winter will often result in deaths of bats through loss of food reserves. Bats are also exploited both within Britain and on an international scale for use by universities and research institutions and are sold by biological supply companies. Fumigation of buildings, against both wood-boring insects and bats, kills many hundreds of bats each year. It is not known, however, what proportion of existing bat populations is affected in this way.

Sixteen species of bats are known in Britain, of which 14 are resident with breeding populations:

The greater horseshoe *Rhinolophus ferrumequinum* is the only British species for which there are data on total population size. It is one of the most cave-dependent species in winter and the greater part of the population congregates in certain distinct areas, namely the caves and mines around the southern periphery of Dartmoor, the Purbeck quarries and the Mendip caves. These three distinct regions support an estimated 75% of Britain's population, totalling approximately 1400 bats. The Purbeck quarries give shelter to *R. ferrumequinum* from a catchment of about 2600 km² including much of Dorset, south Wiltshire and west Hampshire. The Mendips catchment is about 4100 km² including east Somerset, west Wiltshire and much of Gloucestershire. The extent of the south Devon catchment is unknown but it covers at least 1550 km² and includes part of east Cornwall, and lies almost completely outside the Dartmoor National Park.

The mouse-eared *Myotis myotis*, another cave-dependent species, spread to Britain in the 1950s and was only found in the Isle of Purbeck. By the late 1960s it died out there, but a new larger colony of about 40 individuals has recently been found in a tunnel in West Sussex. Once plentiful on the Continent, this species is very vulnerable to human interference and is now in danger of extinction in much of north-west Europe. Bechstein's *Myotis bechsteini*, Daubenton's *M. daubentoni*, Natterer's *M. nattereri*, whiskered *M. mystacinus* and lesser horseshoe *Rhinolophus hipposideros* are all semi-dependent on caves in winter, although other sites, e.g cellars, are used. *M. bechsteini* is very rare in Britain and throughout its entire range. Most British records for this species are from the Purbeck quarries.

The grey long-eared *Plecotus austriacus* (new to science in 1957), has only one known roost in Britain, at Furzebrook Research Station. It is likely that this bat is confined to, at most, a few roosts in the extreme south of England, and its survival must be considered problematical. *P. austriacus* and the widespread and common long-eared *P. auritus* are non-migratory 'house' bats, whereas the other British species, with the possible exceptions of *R. hipposideros* and some pipistrelle *Pipistrellus pipistrellus*, are migratory.

The remaining four species, noctule *Nyctalus noctula*, Leisler's *N. leisleri*, serotine *Eptesicus serotinus* and barbastelle *Barbastella barbastellus*, roost in hollow trees and houses, but although they are fairly widespread, little is known of their status in Britain.

The conservation of bats presents special difficulties, and cannot in general be dealt with on a key site basis. The more widespread species are vulnerable to land-use effects which may influence large areas, and so could only be safeguarded by wide control over adverse changes and practices in the more important districts – the concept of the Conservation Area presented in Cmd 7122 (Ministry of Town and Country Planning, 1947) but never adopted. The rare species roost in highly localised habitats, notably caves, and disused mines and quarries; while these are fairly well concentrated in certain districts they are mostly too numerous and separate, yet too small, to be treated as distinct key sites, either in groups or individually. A few such habitats of importance lie within key sites (e.g. the Purbeck coast), but the majority do not. There is an additional problem – that many of the rare bats would suffer even more from deliberate collecting if their whereabouts were more generally known,

so that exact localities of many roosts cannot be disclosed in the *Review*. All that can be done here is to indicate the general nature of the problem, and the districts specially important for bats, and to hope that measures of a particularly individual and local kind can be implemented to protect as many of the vital roosts as possible. The question of legislation to protect bats is also outside the scope of the *Review*. It can, however, point to the need for critical research on the impact of land-use on bat populations in Britain; and stress the importance of broad environmental change to our native fauna. In a negative sense, this issue illuminates the general problem that key sites do not, on their own, cover the needs for adequate national representation of nature conservation interest.

Some bats have large home ranges (*c*. 1300 km²), but the following five areas contain all British species and include viable population units.

1. Isle of Purbeck–New Forest (quarries). Linked to include parts of the Avon and Stour river valleys. All British species occur in this area and probably in the highest density of anywhere in Britain.

2. South Devon (caves, mines and quarries, south of approximate line from Tavistock to Newton Abbot). Again probably all British species are included.

3. Mendips–Cotswolds–Forest of Dean east to Cirencester (caves and mines). The main centre for *Rhinolophus ferrumequinum*, but also including most British species.

4. Norfolk Broads–East Suffolk: A representative section with eight resident species.

5. Peak District (mostly the National Park area): The caves and mines of this area provide winter roosts for several species and seven (possibly eight) species are resident.

Nothing is known of the status of bats in Scotland, although seven species are found in the south and five extend up to the extreme north including many of the large islands.

BIRDS

The conservation of birds has been the focus of much interest and effort in this country, and this is the only faunal group covered by comprehensive protective legislation. The present report is, however, concerned chiefly with the conservation of birds through safeguarding of selected areas. From a practical angle it is best to consider bird populations in two groups, namely the spring and summer populations of breeders and the autumn and winter populations.

Breeding populations

The total number of species breeding in Britain is not large (about 200), but covers a wide range of geographical and ecological elements. These consist of relatively sedentary species (e.g. golden eagle, raven, red grouse), partial migrants (e.g. merlin, golden plover, auks); and summer visitors (e.g. swallow, hobby, dotterel). Such categories are convenient but not rigid; the surplus young of even sedentary species disperse to seek new territories and species such as the peregrine may be sedentary or partial migrants according to local conditions.

The rare British breeding birds are regarded as important and, in particular, the Royal Society for the Protection of Birds (RSPB) has endeavoured, latterly by means of reserves, to protect the populations of many such species, the red kite and avocet being among the most notable examples. A number of NNRs have also been established mainly for their ornithological interest. In the case of certain species trying to maintain a foothold in this country, guard has been kept on the nests of individual pairs, e.g. osprey and snowy owl. The rare British breeding birds may be thought of as species with spring and summer populations of less than 1000 pairs; these are mostly included in Schedule 1 of the Protection of Birds Acts, 1954–67, but this also includes a few species with greater numbers and a few not yet found breeding or not breeding regularly in Britain. The conservation of rare birds often requires the creation of a 'single-species reserve', although many areas have considerable value beyond the species in question. Occasionally it happens that several rare species occur together, as in the Ouse Washes, Cambridgeshire. However, a general problem here is that many rare species are so widely dispersed and have such large territories and home ranges that a considerable area is required to contain a single pair, as with the golden eagle. A few rare species, such as the greenshank, dotterel and red kite are sufficiently aggregated locally to make it possible to define a single key site containing a population of reasonable size. Estimates of the populations of rare breeding birds contained within key sites are available for only a few easily counted species.

Breeding birds that can be most satisfactorily conserved by means of key sites are those with large but colonial populations, giving an irregular but locally highly aggregated distribution. This is especially true of seabirds, at least for those which nest on cliffs, offshore islands and sand dune or shingle shores. For most of these species, a relatively small number of sites contains a large proportion of the total British populations.

For the bulk of British breeding birds, the position lies somewhere between the above two extremes. A representative series of areas chosen on vegetational grounds is likely to contain reasonable populations of the spectrum of common and widespread breeding birds appropriate to the habitat, but varying in numbers according to their normal species densities. Efforts have been made to ensure that at least one good population of most of the more local species is represented in the list of grade 1 sites.

The following is a review of the representation of breeding birds on grade 1 and 2 sites throughout Britain. RSPB and other bird reserves are not mentioned unless they merit this key site status, but their valuable contribution to the conservation of birds in this country has to be remembered, and a list is appended.

COASTAL BIRDS

Internationally, one of the most important of these elements is the group of sea birds breeding on coastal cliffs and rocky shores, notably the razorbill, guillemot, puffin, black guillemot, kittiwake, herring gull, lesser black-backed gull, great black-backed gull, gannet, shag, cormorant, fulmar, Manx shearwater, storm petrel and Leach's petrel. Some of these species have an extremely restricted world distribution and for several the British Isles are the European headquarters. These sea cliff and slope stations support the largest and most spectacular concentrations of nesting birds of any kind in Britain, despite the fact that many of the huge auk colonies of 60 years ago have declined considerably. The puffin especially has declined seriously in several of the once immense colonies in the north-west Scottish islands, and the guillemot and razorbill are much reduced in some of the more southerly colonies, including Bempton and Ailsa Craig. Some species such as the kittiwake and fulmar have, however, increased greatly and spread, and the herring and great black-backed gulls and the gannet have shown large population increases.

Colonies of over 10000 pairs of all but the *Larus* gulls, shags and cormorants have been regarded as nationally important, and rated as grade 1 or 2 sites, as follows:

The Ynysoedd Preseli (1*); Bempton–Speeton (1*), Yorkshire; Farne Islands (1*), Northumberland; Ailsa Craig (1*), Ayrshire; St Abb's Head (1*), Berwickshire; the Bass Rock (2), East Lothian; the Isle of May (1), Fife; Fowlsheugh (1*), Kincardineshire; Troup Head–Pennan Head (see C.88, 1), Banffshire and Aberdeenshire; Handa (2), and Clo Mor (1), Sutherland; Mingulay–Berneray (2); St Kilda (1*), Flannan Isles (2), and Shiant Isles (2), Outer Hebrides; North Rona and Sula Sgeir (1*); Foula (2), Noss (1*), and Hermaness–Muckle Flugga (1*), Shetland. In addition, several seafowl cliff stations of lesser size are included in the following coastal or other grade 1 sites: Purbeck coast; Isles of Scilly; Glannau Ynys Gybi, Anglesey; Great Ormes Head, Caernarvonshire; Mull of Galloway, Wigtownshire; Rhum, Inverness-shire and North Hoy, Orkney.

This total includes seven existing NNRs and four other reserves. Together, these sites probably support over three-quarters of the British populations of the species mentioned above, with the possible exception of the three *Larus* gulls, cormorant, shag and black guillemot. Several coastal key sites have been identified as such largely for their cliff seafowl interest, and the strong representation of these stations in the national series is considered entirely justifiable in view of the need for a contribution to the conservation of this internationally important group of British birds. Many of these cliff breeding stations are in remote and inaccessible places, however, and the main threat to their bird populations comes from the pollution of the sea, especially by oil. The impending exploitation of oil fields off the north-east coast of Scotland, and along the Atlantic seaboard, now poses serious threats to seabird colonies which were once well removed from oil spill risks. After the initial choice of cliff seafowl sites was made, Operation Seafarer has provided up-to-date population figures for British breeding stations and revision of the key site series is required accordingly. New sites and revised gradings are given in the

Table 38. *Sites of national importance for breeding seabirds of cliffs and rocky slopes or islands*
Figures are numbers of pairs, mainly 1969 or 1970

Site	Gannet	Guillemot	Razorbill	Puffin	Kittiwake	Fulmar
Ynysoedd Preseli	16 000	4 800	2 450	Order 4	1 500	100
Glannau Ynys Gybi	—	1 300	500	10	—	20
Bempton cliffs	35	12 700	1 500	—	40 000	500+
Farne Islands	—	3 000	7	6 800	2 200	44
Ailsa Craig	13 000	4 200	2 300	20	7 700	32
St Abb's Head	—	6 500	200	20	18 500	350
Isle of May	—	9 000	300	2 500	3 000	46
Bass Rock	9 000	500	?	?	1 600	51
Fowlsheugh	—	33 000	5 500	10	35 000	100
Buchan Coast	—	3 000	400	300	10 000	800
Pennan Head–Macduff	—	9 000	600	250	11 200	1 000
Berriedale cliffs	—	31 000	8 000	Order 3	15 500	6 000
Duncansby Head	—	7 500	2 300	Order 4	6 800	2 500
Dunnet Head	—	6 000+	Order 4	Order 5	15 000	5 000
Noss	4 300	24 000	Order 4	c. 1 000	10 500	2 100
Hermaness	6 000	16 000	2 000	15 000	4 600	8 200
Fetlar	—	200	100	Order 4	700	13 000
North Hoy	—	2 500	Order 3	Order 4	1 000	Order 4–5
Marwick Head	—	Order 5	1 000	40	Order 5	400
Westray & Papa Westray	—	73 000	Order 4	400	60 000	3 000
Copinsay	—	9 000	300	50	10 200	680
Foula	—	Order 5	Order 3	Order 5	4 000	Order 5
Fair Isle	—	c. 10 000	1 200	15 000	12 000	17 300
St Kilda	52 000	21 000	Order 4	163 000	11 500	22 000+
Shiant Isles	—	8 000	Order 4	78 500	1 000	3 500
North Rona & Sula Sgeir	9 000	Order 4–5	Order 4	6 000	?	Order 4
Sule Skerry & Sule Stack	4 000	300	100	60 000	300	250+
Cape Wrath (Clo Mor)	—	Order 5	Order 4	Order 5	Order 5	5 000
Mingulay & Berneray	—	12 800	7 400	1 300	4 000	7 500
Handa	—	30 000	6 000	300	8 300	2 400
Flannan Isles	16	10 000	7 250	6 000	2 000	2 600

Notes

Population data by courtesy of Dr W. R. P. Bourne, D. Saunders, S. Cramp and the Seabird Group.
Order 3 = 100–999 pairs; order 4 = 1000–9999 pairs; order 5 = 10 000–99 999 pairs.
Dash indicates data unavailable; question mark indicates data uncertain.

Appendix, but the accompanying Table gives the data on which this revision is based (Table 38).

The coastal sites with sea cliffs contain a large number of nesting places of the cliff-nesting raptors and corvids. For the raven, grade 1 coastal sites include an estimated total of about 80 pairs, with another 13 in grade 2 sites. A total of 63 pre World War II peregrine territories lies within grade 1 coastal sites, though only 16 of these are believed to be tenanted at present; for grade 2 sites the figures are 10 known and four tenanted territories. Probably no more than four pairs of golden eagles breed regularly on grade 1 coastal sites and only two more on those in grade 2. The numbers of kestrels and common buzzards represented in these sites cannot be estimated, but must be considerable. The chough no longer breeds in Cornwall and Devon, but is nesting in Pembrokeshire coastal sites and on Bardsey–Aberdaron (2) and Yr Eifl (2), both in Caernarvonshire, and inland on the grade 1 site of Y Wyddfa. The conservation of this extremely local species poses considerable problems, for it ranges fairly widely from its nesting haunts during the non-breeding season, and the reasons for its extinction in south-west England and earlier general decreases in south Wales and west Scotland are not understood.

The coastal tern colonies on sand dunes or rocky islands are well represented in key sites. The main Sandwich tern colonies at Havergate (1), Minsmere (1*), Scolt Head–Blakeney Point (1*), Walney Island–Drigg Point (1–2), Coquet Island (2), Farne Islands (1*), Forth Islands (2), Sands of Forvie (1*) and Morrich More (1*) are at present mostly protected as reserves of some kind. The largest roseate tern colonies on the Farne Islands, Coquet Island and Forth Islands, as well as the small colonies in the Isles of Scilly (1*), are all in grade 1 or 2 sites. The little tern is much more scattered, mainly in small colonies, round our coasts, but important nesting stations at Chesil Beach, Foulness, Blakeney Point, and several other lesser colonies, are located on grade 1 sites. The common tern and Arctic tern breed on many coastal key sites, and are well represented, and the large concentration in Orkney is included. Major coastal colonies of black-headed gulls occur at North Solent Marshes (2) and Drigg Point (2); of herring and lesser black-backed gulls at Walney Island (1), and Isle of May (1); and of great black-backed gulls on North Rona (1*) and North Hoy (2), and in the Isles of Scilly (1*). The herring gull has increased so much as to be regarded as a nuisance in many places, and there is concern to reduce the size of some of its largest colonies on key sites and elsewhere. Widespread species such as ringed plover, oystercatcher, shelduck, rock pipit, wheatear and stock dove breed on many key sites and adequate samples of their populations are thus represented.

The machair sites of Grogarry and Askernish coast (1), South Uist; Monach Isles (1), North Uist; Balranald (1), North Uist; Barrapoll and Ballevullin (2), Tiree, contain all the breeding birds of machair including good populations of dunlin and most of the few pairs of red-necked phalaropes which nest in the Hebrides. Balranald RSPB reserve is also one of the few British nesting places of the gadwall. The most important salt marshes for nesting birds are those of the Solway, Morecambe Bay and Ribble Estuary, as these contain the only extensive areas of this ecosystem which are not flooded frequently by high tides. In this region, salt marsh nesting populations of lapwing, redshank, oystercatcher, dunlin, skylark, common tern, black-headed gull and lesser black-backed gull are smaller than formerly, but are still well represented on Caerlaverock–Kirkconnell Merses, Dumfries-shire–Kirkcudbrightshire; Rockcliffe–Burgh Marshes, Cumberland; Longnewton–Skinburness Marshes, Cumberland – all within the Upper Solway grade 1* site; Morecambe Bay marshes (1*), Lancashire; and Southport–Ribble (1*), Lancashire. By contrast, salt marsh nesting populations of black-headed gulls in north Kent and Hampshire have greatly increased during the last two decades. The reclaimed grazing marshes behind sea walls typically have many of the salt marsh breeding birds, and this habitat is represented especially on the four key sites of the north Kent coast and on the Ribble Estuary (1*). It is, however, a rapidly disappearing habitat for most of these nesting birds, as conversion to arable land proceeds increasingly.

Among the paramaritime nesting birds, the great and Arctic skuas have large colonies on the Shetland sites of Hermaness (1*), Noss (1*) and Foula (2) and occur in smaller numbers on several other northern Scottish key sites. Red-throated divers are particularly well represented on Hermaness (1*), Shetland; Milldoe and Starling Hill (1), Orkney; and Rhum (1*), Inner Hebrides; and nest on several upland and peatland key sites on the Scottish mainland. The twite breeds on St Kilda (1*), Outer Hebrides; Rhum (1), and Cape Wrath–Aodann Mhor (1*), Sutherland; and probably on several other coastal or inland sites in north-west Scotland.

WOODLAND BIRDS

The list of key woodland sites contains population samples of all the widespread birds which either belong exclusively to woodland or include this habitat within their ecological range. For most of these species these samples represent only a very small fraction of their total British populations, and the conservation of these is thus dependent on national trends in forestry and other land-use practices. The sparrowhawk has declined severely in the south and east through the use of persistent pesticides outside woods, but the species remains a fairly constant inhabitant of all but the smallest woods in the north and west, and is even more suited by non-indigenous coniferous than by native broad-leaved woods. The numbers and distribution of the common buzzard as a woodland breeder are probably more limited by gamekeeper persecution than by any other factor, and the species occurs mainly in the west. Tree-nesting ravens may be limited similarly, though this species shows an especially close association with sheep-farming (i.e. sheep carrion) and may be geographically limited accordingly.

The increase in afforestation on formerly treeless land during the past few decades has obviously allowed the spread and increase of some of the less selective woodland species, including the black grouse, but the gradual replacement of broad-leaved woods by coniferous plantations is slowly reducing the populations of those birds which do not favour conifers or, at least, the conditions of close canopy under which they are usually grown. Some birds, such as the three woodpeckers, nightingale, redstart, pied flycatcher, blackcap, garden warbler, chiffchaff, willow warbler, wood warbler, willow tit, marsh tit, tree creeper, nuthatch and hawfinch, do not usually occur in coniferous woods. All the hole-excavating nesters need some dead or moribund timber, which is not usually found in conifer plantations, and some of the warblers need dense undergrowth which is also usually absent under the heavy shade of these artificial woods.

The two woodland areas which have a distinctive bird fauna, namely the New Forest and the pine forests of the middle Spey Valley, are regarded as key sites partly because of this feature. In both, particular blocks of woodland have been singled out as having special all-round interest, but it is important that the conservation of the whole areas of these forests is achieved by management which has regard for wildlife and ecological interest. With the exception of the Scottish crossbill (on Scots pine), no British birds are specific to a particular tree dominant, and most of the rare or local woodland species are limited in distribution and numbers not through availability of suitable habitat, but for quite different reasons. This does not, however, reduce the necessity of conserving the particular woodlands in which the rare species are to be found. The best example of this is probably the red kite, restricted to the upland valleys of central Wales, but for this species woodland is only the breeding habitat, and the hill farmland and open moorland where the bird feeds also have to be conserved. A number of the designated key sites include some recent or former kite breeding places. The still rarer honey buzzard breeds regularly in the New Forest, but this is a migratory species which might spread more rapidly than the kite if conditions allowed. Probably about a third of the British breeding population of hobbies nest in key sites, notably the New Forest, but this is a species which often nests in small clumps or lines of trees, or even scattered individuals, and its main need is for the right kind of heathland or open country over which to hunt.

LOWLAND GRASSLANDS AND HEATHLAND BIRDS

The Breckland key sites probably contain a good sample of the remaining (and still decreasing) stone curlew population of East Anglia, though this species is also said to breed quite widely on the stony arable fields of the area and on the broad rides of the conifer forests. Another population is represented in the chalk grassland sites of Wiltshire, notably at Porton Down. The other Breckland species, such as the ringed plover, stonechat and woodlark, have declined partly because of destruction of habitat, but the first now has little suitable ground, because there are few rabbits to maintain bare areas, and the other two have evidently suffered from hard winters. The nightjar still occurs in reduced numbers on most of the southern acidic heather and bracken-grown heathland key sites, but the red-backed shrike is limited to those with tall scrub and seems to be disappearing steadily even where suitable habitat remains. The bulk of the population of the extremely local Dartford warbler is contained within the key heathland sites of the Isle of Purbeck and the New Forest, and a substantial population of hobbies and woodlarks are represented on heathland sites in the extreme south of England.

The more common and widespread birds of acidic heathland are present on many key sites, but most of them occur also in a wider range of habitat, including the varied agricultural–urban environment. However, many of these birds depend on the maintenance of at least some habitat apart from actual crops or cultivated gardens, i.e. hedges, shrubberies, rough field corners or verges.

The draining and ploughing of many damp, rough meadows have resulted in the local decline of birds such as the snipe and redshank, but there is still a large extent of this habitat in the north and west of Britain. The curlew has increased in recent years as a breeding bird on agricultural land, though the lapwing has declined and the corncrake become quite rare, except in the extreme north-west. The most important of the periodically flooded meadow systems as a breeding haunt for rare birds, the Ouse Washes (1*), is the main breeding place in Britain of black-tailed godwits and perhaps of garganey, shoveler and pintail.

WETLAND BIRDS

Aquatic birds

Of the birds which live mostly on open water and nest round its edges, only the Slavonian grebe, scaup and scoter are evidently not represented on key sites. Loch Leven (1*) in Kinross and the Ouse Washes (1*) in Cambridgeshire are

probably the most important single breeding places for waterfowl in Britain, in both the variety of species and size of their populations. Rare breeding ducks such as the gadwall and pintail are represented here as well as the more common dabbling ducks, and on Loch Leven there is a strong breeding population of tufted duck. The Ouse Washes are the British headquarters of the garganey as a nesting species, and Minsmere (1*) has a high concentration of duck, including this species and the gadwall. The north Kent marshes of High Halstow (2) and Allhallows (2) are important for pochard and have a few pairs of pintail. The total numbers of breeding ducks represented on key wetland sites is considerable but is for most species (excepting the mallard and possibly teal) only a small proportion of the wintering population and an insignificant fraction of the total European numbers. Conservation of duck in Britain is thus much more concerned with their wintering haunts than with breeding places, though the summer breeding populations are of considerable interest to British ornithologists.

The largest native colony of breeding greylag geese is at Loch Druidibeg (1*) in South Uist, Outer Hebrides, already an NNR. This is otherwise a thinly spread nesting bird in northern Scotland occurring on a few other key sites, but distribution has been extended in recent years by the establishment of feral colonies in various parts of Britain. Canada geese are well established breeders on many lowland lakes and marshes and have also been introduced in many localities by wildfowlers, who are actively concerned in conservation of this species. The whooper swan is an extreme rarity, nesting sporadically in a very few places (none of them key sites) in the Highlands. Mute swans are numerous and in some wildfowl breeding haunts are regarded as something of a nuisance to other species, whose young they often destroy. Black-throated and red-throated divers breed on several key sites, but the numbers involved are small. Of the grebes, the black-necked is a rarity, breeding on at least two key lake sites, but in extremely small numbers. The great crested and little grebes are widespread species well represented on the more eutrophic lakes and tarns graded 1 or 2. Coots and moorhens are the most numerous aquatic breeding birds on wetlands as a whole and their conservation gives no anxieties.

Fen or swamp birds

The breeding birds of Phragmites swamp, such as the reed warbler, bittern and marsh harrier, are favoured by the inclusion of some of the largest British stands of this community in key sites, as at Hickling–Horsey Mere (1*), Dunwich Marshes (1*), North Norfolk Coast (1*), Poole Harbour (1) and Leighton Moss (1). A large proportion of these three species are now located within the four sites. The bearded tit is fairly numerous on the East Anglian fen sites but its numbers are depressed by hard winters, after which it spreads again and breeds sparingly in widely scattered localities outside this district. Savi's warbler is present at Stodmarsh (1) in Kent, and a few other places, but the marsh warbler is not known to be represented on any key site, and is a species requiring special conservation measures (the RSPB have one reserve for this species). The spotted crake is a sporadic nester and could appear on a good many sites which have suitable swamp vegetation; it has nested on some key sites. Water rails probably breed on many wetland key sites, but are elusive birds and not easy to count.

Samples of the populations of the more common fen or swamp species are well represented on the sites listed, but the total populations of these birds are especially vulnerable to the continuing drainage and reclamation of wetlands. The Ouse Washes (1*) are an example of a periodically flooded grassland and marsh system with large populations of breeding ducks, and waders such as the lapwing, snipe and redshank, and they have recently become famous as the nesting place of black-tailed godwit, ruff and black tern, species once present in East Anglia but lost to Britain as breeders for many years. The Ouse Washes are one of the most important breeding bird sites in Britain, and a valuable winter haunt of wildfowl.

Ombrogenous peat-mire birds

The raised mires of Britain have rather limited bird populations, but some of the northern blanket mires have a wide spectrum of moorland birds. The key blanket mire sites from Derbyshire northwards contain significant population samples of breeding species such as golden plover, dunlin, curlew, red grouse, skylark and meadow pipit. Teal are represented more sparingly, and in the Scottish Highlands such species as the wood sandpiper, wigeon, greylag goose and Arctic skua breed on at least one key blanket mire site, while the greenshank and red-throated diver breed on several.

Riparian birds

Most of the birds which breed along riversides, especially the hill streams, occur on key sites, but for all of these only a very small fraction of the total number is included. The goosander and red-breasted merganser are not protected species in Scotland, and in some areas they are a good deal persecuted by fishermen. The kingfisher and sand martin are birds of the larger, slower-flowing, lowland rivers, and the kingfisher in particular is in some need of protection, although it seems to have recovered in numbers locally after the severe winter of 1963, when there was a serious decline. The little ringed plover is perhaps best included here; the fate of this species is largely bound up with that of the gravel pits beside or in which it nests.

UPLAND BIRDS

The series of key upland sites selected on other grounds includes good population samples of many species. The following estimates of breeding populations refer to totals on grade 1 and 2 sites respectively: peregrine 23 and 16 pairs, with an additional 13 and 6 deserted territories, mainly in Wales; raven, 54 and 40 pairs; golden eagle, 23 and 27 pairs. The numbers of breeding kestrels, common buzzards and merlins on key sites cannot yet be estimated, but all three species are well represented. Probably few hen harriers breed on key sites, and the conservation of this species

in general presents some problems, for its young forest habitat is ephemeral, and its grouse-moor habitat is usually guarded by gamekeepers who dislike the bird more than any other species of predator. On Orkney the RSPB has established a moorland raptor reserve at Dale of Cottasgarth which includes hen harriers, merlins, short-eared owls and ground-nesting kestrels; this has been rated, with a larger surrounding area of moorland, as a grade 1 site, Milldoe and Starling Hill.

The three high montane species are especially favoured in the selection of key sites. The only regular nesting places of the snow bunting in Britain lie within the existing Cairngorms NNR, and the eastern Scotland upland grade 1 and 2 sites probably hold well over half the British breeding population of dotterel. The numbers of ptarmigan on the high ground of Highland upland sites is also considerable. The densest populations of golden plover and greenshank known in Britain today are included within grade 1 sites, and all the widespread moorland species are well represented in the national series. Some upland areas such as Kinder–Bleaklow, Mallerstang–Swaledale Head, Upper Teesdale, Moor House and Cross Fell, Skiddaw Forest, Cairnsmore of Fleet, Moorfoot Hills, North Hoy and Hermaness are especially rich in moorland birds and have been given grade 1 status partly for this ornithological interest. The Loch Druidibeg NNR was established largely as the site of the biggest truly wild nesting colony of greylag geese in Scotland, and the colonies of great and Arctic skuas on Hermaness and Noss are an important part of the scientific interest of these sites. For some species, such as the red grouse, the sites listed give substantial population samples living under a range of different conditions.

Whilst colonies of the moorland breeding gulls are all represented on upland key sites, the lesser black-backed and black-headed gulls are regarded by some people as pest species. The goosander and red-breasted merganser breed on many of the Scottish sites listed. Of the other species which belong really to aquatic habitats, the black-throated diver has breeding stations on the moorland lochs of the Inverpolly and Foinaven grade 1 sites, and the red-throated diver has good populations on the moors of Rhum and Hermaness, but in neither is more than a tiny fraction of the total population represented. The whimbrel, red-necked phalarope and the only British snowy owls breed on the submontane island of Fetlar. The northern part of this Shetland island is an RSPB reserve and is rated as grade 1 on its ornithological interest.

The avifauna of the British uplands is threatened in various ways. Perhaps the most serious changes are the extensive conversion of the lower moorlands to coniferous forest by planting. Reclamation for farmland is so far on a much more local scale but could perhaps become a more general process as the pressure on land increases. The conversion of grouse-moor to sheep-walk has continued steadily in many southern areas and has probably caused the decline of species such as the red grouse and merlin, which depend on heather communities, although the associated decline in grouse preservation has reduced the impact on predators. High stocking density with sheep and wide-spread burning may have run down the productivity of moorlands for some birds, but for others it may be land-use changes or other increased adversities in the wintering haunts which have reduced numbers.

The use of persistent pesticides within the upland environment has had an unfavourable impact on some species (e.g. dieldrin sheep dips on golden eagles), whereas for others the use of these chemicals in areas far distant has had still more serious consequences (e.g. organochlorine seed dressings on peregrines). Human recreational pressures are causing increasing disturbance on remote mountain tops and may perhaps affect some species there (but evidently not ptarmigan), and rock-climbing is becoming an increasing nuisance to crag-nesting birds in Snowdonia, Lakeland and elsewhere. The flooding of glens or raising of lake levels in the Highlands has destroyed, at least for a time, the feeding places of some greenshanks, and submerged some nesting islands of black-throated divers. On the whole, however, the deer forest country of the western Highlands is the least changed of all our upland districts and will provide a refuge for most forms of wildlife as long as this form of land-use continues. But in some parts of northern Scotland human pressures related to oil developments may become locally serious in the next few years.

BIRDS OF AGRICULTURAL AND URBAN LAND

As these habitats are for the most part explicitly excluded from our consideration of key sites, their avifauna is represented on such sites only to the extent that certain species have a niche in the range of semi-natural habitats. Many species are, in fact, well represented, either in woodland or lowland grassland and heath sites. Some, such as the starling and house sparrow are widely regarded as pest species, and others such as the rook, magpie and jackdaw could be placed in this category, at least in some areas. The birds of urban areas, and especially the building-nesters, are in no danger of reduction, but hedgerow and verge-nesters are decreasing and will continue to do so in parallel with the destruction of these habitats. The birds of permanent grassland (mostly mentioned under Lowland grasslands and heathlands, p. 152) will also decline as this type of land is ploughed and converted to arable ground. Some species, including recently the reed bunting and sedge warbler, have shown a remarkable adaptation to arable land, but on the whole this is not a rich habitat for breeding birds. The effect of cleaning crops with herbicides is not yet adequately known, though Potts (1970) has established that it is an important factor in the marked decline of the grey partridge; and the advanced mechanisation now used for harvesting crops is generally blamed for the widespread and catastrophic decline of the corncrake, and may have affected species such as the lapwing, oystercatcher and stone curlew, where these nest on ploughed land. The corn bunting is potentially one of the most vulnerable species, for it is now largely confined as a breeder to crops of hay and cereals. The wryneck is even more a problem species in south-eastern England, as it is declining fast for reasons unknown, and belongs to rather

nondescript tree-grown habitats which come mostly under the present group but have little protection under modern systems of land use. This species is, however, colonising native woodland in the central Highlands and a distinct northern population may well become established.

Table 39 gives a rough indication of the representation of British breeding birds on key sites, with species grouped under the different abundance classes recognised by Parslow (1973). Only species with an 'A' rating can be regarded as adequately taken care of through key site selection, and they are in the minority, consisting mainly of the rarest and most colonial species. For the majority of our breeding species, the safeguarding of key sites will clearly not be a sufficient conservation measure; the bulk of their populations will inevitably lie outside the final total of grade 1 and 2 sites, and only rather small samples will be represented on reserves of any kind. Moreover, the organochlorine pesticide problem has shown that even sedentary species breeding on nature reserves may be seriously and uncontrollably affected by events far distant geographically, and for migratory species this is even more of a problem. The numbers of breeding summer visitors could well be influenced largely by factors operative within their winter ranges, i.e. outside Britain, so that conservation of these species is essentially an international problem.

The gradings in Table 39, both for abundance and key site occurrence, are based on the data available at the moment (1973), but are liable to change with time. Few bird species show constant populations, and within a breeding avifauna, numbers and distribution are continually changing. Birds are mobile creatures and during the present century many British breeding species have shown marked changes in status and distribution, sometimes for reasons not yet understood. The puffin, for instance, was one of our most numerous species, but has declined during the last 15 years to no more than class 6 abundance, though the causes are still unknown. Britain is evidently climatically marginal for many European species, which are thus at or close to the natural limits of range here. For such birds, climatic change can be critical in determining spread or retreat and is a factor beyond control. The present trend towards colder springs is reflected in the southwards shift in distribution limits of certain northern birds.

Most of our rare and sporadic breeders are fringe species which in Britain represent the edges of large continental populations. Their rarity is thus only local on the European scale, and the conservation of such birds is not an international problem, except for certain species which are showing a consistent downward trend on the continent as well as in Britain. Not all fringe species are constrained by climatic factors, and some may be held back by adverse human influence (e.g. goshawk) or lack of suitable habitat (e.g. avocet, stilt). Some of these, especially the sporadic breeders, may establish a stronger foothold with appropriate conservation measures, including protection enforcement and provision of suitable habitat. Others, such as the collared dove, may arrive and flourish of their own accord, as part of a general expansion of range. Some species are

Table 39. *Analysis of British breeding birds according to abundance class and representation on key sites*

Table 39 (*contd.*)

Class 1
(1–9 pairs)

Honey buzzard	A	Snowy owl	A
Marsh harrier	A	Firecrest	A
Montagu's harrier	B	Ruff	A
Osprey	B	Black tern	A
Goshawk	B	Snow bunting	A

Class 2 (10–99 pairs)

Black-throated diver	B	Whimbrel	B
Slavonian grebe	O	Black-tailed godwit	A
Black-necked grebe	A	Wood sandpiper	B
Bittern	A	Avocet	A
Garganey	A	Red-necked phalarope	A
Pintail	B	Wryneck	O
Common scoter	O	Redwing	B
Red kite	B	Black redstart	O
Hobby	B	Savi's warbler	A
Dotterel	A	Dartford warbler	A
		Red-backed shrike	B

Class 3
(100–999 pairs)

Red-throated diver	B	Corncrake	B
Gadwall	A	Little ringed plover	B
Wigeon	B	Greenshank	B
Pochard	B	Stone curlew	A
Goosander	B	Arctic skua	A
Greylag goose	B	Woodlark	B
Golden eagle	B	Chough	B
Hen harrier	B	Crested tit	B
Peregrine	B	Bearded tit	A
Merlin	B	Marsh warbler	O
Quail	O	Cirl bunting	O

Class 4
(1000–9999 pairs)

Great crested grebe	B	Dipper	B
Little grebe	B	Common buzzard	B
Leach's petrel	A	Sparrowhawk	B
Cormorant	B	Water rail	B
Heron	B	Ringed plover	B
Teal	B	Dunlin	B
Shoveler	B	Great skua	A
Tufted duck	B	Roseate tern	A
Eider	B	Little tern	A
Red-breasted merganser	B	Sandwich tern	A
Canada goose	B	Turtle dove	B
Mute swan	B	Collared dove	B
Little owl	B	Stonechat	B
Long-eared owl	B	Redstart	B
Short-eared owl	B	Grasshopper warbler	B
Nightjar	B	Reed warbler	B
Kingfisher	B	Lesser whitethroat	B
Lesser spotted		Yellow wagtail	B
woodpecker	B	Hawfinch	B
Raven	B	Siskin	B
Marsh tit	B	Twite	B
Willow tit	B	Crossbill	B
Long-tailed tit	B	Corn bunting	B
Nuthatch	B		

Class 5
(10 000–99 999 pairs)

Gannet	A	Sedge warbler	B
Shag	B	Blackcap	B
Shelduck	B	Tawny owl	B
Kestrel	B	Green woodpecker	B
Ptarmigan	A	Greater spotted	
Black grouse	B	woodpecker	B
Capercaillie	B	Sand martin	B
Coot	B	Magpie	B
Oystercatcher	B	Jay	B
Golden plover	B	Coal tit	B
Snipe	B	Treecreeper	B
Woodcock	B	Mistle thrush	B
Curlew	B	Ring ouzel	B
Common sandpiper	B	Wheatear	B
Redshank	B	Garden warbler	B
Cuckoo	B	Wood warbler	B
Barn owl	B	Goldcrest	B
Whinchat	B	Spotted flycatcher	B
Nightingale	B	Pied flycatcher	B
Great black-backed		Tree pipit	B
gull	B	Rock pipit	B
Lesser black-backed		Pied wagtail	B
gull	B	Goldfinch	B
Common gull	B	Redpoll	B
Common tern	B	Bullfinch	B
Arctic tern	B	Reed bunting	B
Black guillemot	B	Tree sparrow	B
Stock dove	B	Grey wagtail	B
Rock dove	B		

Class 6
(100 000–999 999 pairs)

Storm petrel	A	Puffin	A
Manx shearwater	A	Swift	O
Fulmar	A	Skylark	B
Mallard	B	Swallow	B
Red grouse	B	House martin	B
Red-legged partridge	B	Carrion crow	B
Partridge	B	Hooded crow	B
Pheasant	B	Jackdaw	B
Moorhen	B	Great tit	B
Lapwing	B	Blue tit	B
Herring gull	B	Willow warbler	B
Black-headed gull	B	Chiffchaff	B
Kittiwake	A	Greenfinch	B
Razorbill	A	Linnet	B
Guillemot	A		

Class 7
(over 1 000 000 pairs)

Wood pigeon	B	Dunnock	B
Rook	B	Meadow pipit	B
Wren	B	Starling	B
Song thrush	B	Chaffinch	B
Blackbird	B	Yellowhammer	B
Robin	B	House sparrow	B
Whitethroat	B		

Sporadic breeders

Great northern diver	Whooper swan
Little bittern	Scaup

Table 39. *Sporadic breeders* (cont.)

Goldeneye	Green sandpiper
Spotted crake	Bee-eater
Temminck's stint	Bluethroat
Hoopoe	Golden oriole
Fieldfare	Brambling

Notes

O = unknown on a grade 1 or 2 site.

B = present, but only a small proportion of total population on grade 1 and 2 sites.

A = a substantial proportion, probably approaching 50% or more, of the total population present on grade 1 and 2 sites.

This list does not include all species which have been known to breed in Britain in recent years, nor those which are now extinct. A number of additional species may be on the point of colonising Britain.

more adaptable to new habitats or changed conditions than others, and it is the less resilient species which have to be identified in working out conservation needs.

Natural adverse environmental change, especially of climate, can over-ride attempts to conserve a declining species. On the whole, though, with natural changes, the losses and gains of species are fairly well balanced over a period. During the last hundred years, several British birds have declined or disappeared, but several species have recently appeared or reappeared, mostly by expansion of their continental range. It is the species declining through human influence, and especially the international rarities among these, which represent the main conservation problem. Broad conservation measures are particularly needed for the more threatened British species which are inadequately represented within the key site series.

CONCLUSIONS ON CONSERVATION OF BREEDING BIRDS

The rare species of breeding birds are in general in need of protection against human predators, and the RSPB devotes a good deal of time and resources to looking after such species in various ways, including its own series of nature reserves (see Table 40). Yet even when they are granted freedom from deliberate disturbance, rare birds may pose considerable conservation problems. This is especially true of the rare woodland breeding raptors such as the kite, honey buzzard, osprey and hobby, which hunt largely or exclusively outside the woods; for these species the total range of habitat must be safeguarded. It is therefore often necessary to think in terms of composite sites in which woodlands are only one component; this approach has been taken in recommending some of the key sites designated in central Wales for the conservation of the kite. The future of the hobby in Britain probably depends on the maintenance of the right kind of open country, especially heath and downland, with an adequate food supply for the bird.

The problem of the persistent organochlorine and organomercury pesticides and their impact on birds, especially the raptors, is now well understood, and there has been improvement through voluntary restrictions on use. The present Pesticides Safety Precautions Scheme seems to work reasonably well in preventing the marketing of new pesticides with a serious wildlife hazard. There are, however, anxieties about the effects of industrial toxic chemical pollutants, such as the parachlorobenzoates, mainly discharged as waste into rivers or the sea, and thence accumulated in considerable quantities by both sea- and landbirds. The solution to these problems of toxic chemicals lies in administrative changes which could reduce or even eliminate such residues from the environment. The problem of marine oil pollution and sea-birds, notably the auks, is one of the most serious and difficult to handle, but until it is solved satisfactorily, by international action, the great seafowl colonies on coastal cliff reserves are all at considerable risk.

The future of bird populations in Britain is closely bound up with trends in land-use. Increasing simplification is now apparent within the agricultural ecosystem complex, through the steady elimination of all competitors for living space, to give maximum production by the crop species; this may be expected to continue in the lowlands, at least. The replacement of grouse-moor and deer forest by sheep-walk continues locally, and the improvement of marginal land, at present limited largely by the cost of fertilisers and draining, could become greatly extended. Drainage of wetland is also likely to continue. In commercial forestry the recent trend

Table 40. *List of RSPB reserves*

Arne, Dorset; Barfold Copse, Surrey; Bempton Cliffs, Yorkshire; Blacktoft Sands, Yorkshire; Chapel Wood, Devon; Church Wood, Buckinghamshire; Coombes Valley, Staffordshire; Coquet Island, Northumberland; Cowpen Marsh, Durham; Dungeness, Kent; East Wood, Cheshire; Elmley Marshes, Kent; Fairburn Ings, Yorkshire; Havergate Island, Suffolk; Hornsea Mere, Yorkshire; Leighton Moss, Lancashire; The Lodge, Sandy, Bedfordshire; Minsmere, Suffolk; Moreton Vallence, Gloucestershire; Morecambe Bay, Lancashire; Nagshead, Gloucestershire; Northward Hill (High Halstow), Kent; North Warren, Suffolk; Ouse Washes, Cambridgeshire; Radipole Lake, Dorset; Rye House Marsh, Hertfordshire; St Bees Head, Cumberland; Snettisham, Norfolk; Strumpshaw Fen, Norfolk; Sutton Fen, Bedfordshire; Tetney Marshes, Lincolnshire; Titchwell, Norfolk; Wolves Wood, Suffolk; Grassholm Island, Pembrokeshire; Gwenffrwd/Dinas, Carmarthenshire; Ynys Feurig, Anglesey; Ynys-hir, Cardiganshire; Balranald, North Uist, Outer Hebrides; Birsay Moors, Orkney; Copinsay, Orkney; Cottasgarth, Orkney; Eyebroughty, Fidra and the Lamb, East Lothian; Fetlar, Shetland; Fowlsheugh, Kincardineshire; Handa, Sutherland; Hobbister, Orkney; Horse Island, Ayrshire; Inchmickery, Midlothian; Insh Marshes, Inverness-shire; Loch Garten, Inverness-shire; Loch of Strathbeg, Aberdeenshire; Lochwinnoch, Renfrewshire; Mull of Galloway, Wigtownshire; Noup Head, Orkney; Ramna Stacks, Shetland; Vane Farm, Kinross.

has been to replace deciduous woods with conifers, and to plant moorland and heathland almost exclusively with conifers. New towns, roads and industrial undertakings will continue to eat into the countryside, and human recreational needs will create increasing pressure, especially on coastlands, heathlands, lakes and rivers, and mountains and moorlands. Estuarine barrages are likely to destroy for ever the present character of certain inter-tidal flat and salt marsh systems, as will reclamation for other purposes, such as airport construction.

Some future trends, especially in agriculture and forestry are not wholly predictable, as they are subject to technological, economic, political and social developments, in Britain and the European Economic Community. It is nevertheless clear that adverse pressures on bird life can only increase.

Passage migrants, autumn and winter populations

After the breeding season there are considerable changes in the distribution and composition of bird populations. Comparatively few species of British birds are completely sedentary. The majority migrate or move about after the breeding season, but the proportion of the population doing so and the distance they move varies from species to species. The summer visitors emigrate in autumn and some species regarded as resident may undertake considerable movements within this country. Many other species which do not breed in Britain come to spend the winter here, and the numbers of some breeders are considerably augmented by continental immigrant populations in autumn. Yet other species pass through Britain twice a year, spending only a short period each time, as they migrate between breeding and wintering haunts in autumn and spring.

Conservation of bird populations outside the breeding season presents some of the same general problems which affect the breeders, i.e. the more widely dispersed and numerous the species the more difficult does it become to conserve a reasonable proportion of the population by means of a limited number of safeguarded areas, and vice versa. The more sedentary residents are represented on key sites outside the breeding season to much the same extent as when they are nesting, except that their numbers may be increased by the juveniles of the year. These sites may also contain bird populations which have moved in at this time of year. However, in considering the conservation of bird populations outside the breeding season, it is again realistic to focus effort, in the form of protected areas, on the places and habitats with the greatest concentration of birds, namely, the open waters and marshes inland, and the inter-tidal flats and salt marshes of the estuaries and coasts. The large aggregations of birds of these habitats fall mainly into the two groups, waders and wildfowl, and these will be considered separately. The key sites chosen to represent these groups also support adequate samples of other birds found in the particular range of habitats. In addition, the passage migrants, which may be considerably aggregated (for some species and some localities), will be considered separately.

This section is mainly concerned with the conservation in Britain of three groups of longer distance migrants: (i) those which breed here but winter much farther south, often in Africa; (ii) similar species which breed in northern Eurasia, also Iceland and Greenland, and which pass through Britain on migration; and (iii) those which come to Britain for the winter, mainly from northern Europe.

Birds in the first two groups comprise mainly the trans-equatorial migrant passerines and near-passerines such as the cuckoo, turtle dove, swift, hirundines, tree pipit, yellow wagtail and various kinds of warblers, flycatchers and chats. Despite the occasional occurrence under certain (adverse) weather conditions of large 'falls' of many of these species on certain headlands and islands, notably in southern England, it is probable that most immigrants in spring do not alight at the coast but make straight for their breeding quarters in Britain. The involvement of continental breeding birds in falls at this season is probably slight, although appreciable numbers of transient migrants, such as wheatears and white wagtails, making for Iceland and/or Greenland pass through Britain, especially in the west. Falls of night-migrants also occur on many headlands and islands around Britain in autumn. These are often larger than in spring and they frequently include appreciable numbers of drifted or off-course, continental passerine migrants, including a high proportion of juvenile birds.

In conservation terms it is difficult to assess the national significance of the coastal sites at which these concentrations of passerine and near-passerine migrants occur. At most mainland sites, particularly in spring, many immigrants move on inland within a few hours of making landfall. On some island sites, however, migrants may stay for some days or weeks before moving on, particularly in autumn. Even so, the proportion of the total populations of the species concerned which occur at these sites must be very small. At many of these places bird observatories or ringing stations have been established by groups of amateur enthusiasts, and their research has added much to our knowledge of bird migration. The more important of these sites are listed in Table 41.

The passage of these migrants through Britain in autumn tends to be more leisurely than in spring and the conservation requirements of the species concerned are more demanding. Swallows and sand martins, for example, require relatively large, undisturbed osier or *Phragmites* beds in which to roost. Over one million sand martins – which must represent a very substantial part of the British population – have been recorded at an osier bed roost on the Ouse Washes, while other especially large hirundine roosts occur regularly at Chichester gravel pits, Sussex (sand martins), beside the Humber and at Fairburn Ings, Yorkshire (swallows). A network of such roosts, close to rich feeding areas, is an obvious requirement of these species in autumn.

Many passerine long-distance migrants need to put on much migratory fat before setting off on autumn migration. A sedge warbler for instance almost doubles its weight

Table 41. *Coastal and insular 'bird observatories' at which concentrations of passerine migrants occur in spring and/or autumn*

Site	British summer visitors		Continental transient migrants		Iceland/Greenland migrants		Winter visitors	
	Spring	Autumn	Spring	Autumn	Spring	Autumn	Spring	Autumn
Fair Isle, Shetland (C.97, gr. 2)	+	+	+ +	+ + +	+	+ +	+	+ + +
Isle of May, Fife (C.81, gr. 1)	+	+	+	+ +	−	−	−	+ +
Spurn Point, Yorkshire	+	+	−	+ +	+	+	+	+ + +
Gibraltar Point, Lincolnshire (See C.20, gr. 1*)	+	+	−	+ +	−	+	+	+ + +
North Norfolk Coast (C.19, gr. 1*)	+	+	−	+ +	−	+	+	+ +
Sandwich Bay, Kent (See C.4, gr. 1)	+ +	+ +	+	+	−	−	+	+ +
Dungeness, Kent (C.3, gr. 1*)	+ + +	+ + +	+	+ +	−	−	+	+ +
Beachy Head, Sussex (See C.1, gr. 1)	+ +	+ +	+	+	−	−	+	+
Portland Bill, Dorset	+ +	+ +	+	+ +	+	+	+	+ +
Isles of Scilly (C.28, gr. 1*)	+ +	+	+	+ +	+	+ +	+	+
Lundy, Devon	+ +	+ +	+	+	+	+ +	+	+ +
Skokholm, Pembrokeshire (See C.45, gr. 1*)	+ +	+ +	−	+	+	+ +	−	+ +
Ynys Enlli; Bardsey, Caernarvonshire (See C.53, gr. 2)	+ +	+ +	−	+	+	+	−	+ + +

Notes

Sites are listed clockwise round the coast.

Number of pluses denotes approximate order of importance.

before it sets out. This species, and the reed warbler, feed mainly in wet, marshy areas, particularly in the muddy bottoms of *Phragmites* beds, in autumn. The conservation of such areas, particularly in southern England, is therefore critical for these species. Considerable autumn concentrations of reed and sedge warblers occur at such places as Chew Valley Lake (2), Somerset; Slapton Ley (1), Devon; Christchurch Harbour, Hampshire; Minsmere (1*), Suffolk and on the Norfolk Broads. In many inland counties in southern England, an increasing number of flooded gravel pits provides suitable wetland vegetation for these species and must help compensate for the loss of many marshy areas through drainage.

Other passerine and near-passerine long distance migrants which occur in aggregations on passage include the yellow wagtail which occurs mainly in damp meadows (e.g. the Ouse Washes) and the turtle dove, which occurs widely on agricultural land and on gravel pit borders, rubbish dumps and other places with an abundance of seed-producing weeds, especially fumitory. Most other species migrate singly and do not become aggregated except accidentally on coastal headlands and islands. The proportions of the populations which utilise key sites are therefore small, and the conservation of these species while on passage presents similar problems to those in the breeding season.

Another important group of transient migrants are the northern Eurasian waders, many of which pass through Britain, particularly in autumn. The numbers of some species, such as the little stint and curlew sandpiper are variable and depend on weather conditions while they are

migrating. Others, such as the ruff and several species of coastal waders, occur regularly in larger numbers. Many European dunlin halt in Britain in autumn to moult before moving on southwards; the Wash is particularly important in this respect. The conservation requirements for these passage waders are similar to those which winter here (see Wintering waders, p. 368) except that proportionately rather more of them are inland or freshwater species. In this respect the role of sewage farms has hitherto been important: a considerable proportion of the numbers of species like the green, wood and curlew sandpipers, little stint and ruff, which occur on passage in Britain, are found at sewage farms. Many of the more famous of these farms, such as the one at Nottingham, have now been modernised and are unsuitable for waders. Others, like those at Wisbech, Cambridgeshire, and Perry Oaks, Middlesex, still attract large numbers of waders but are due to be modernised in the near future. It is difficult to make out a scientific case for the conservation of any one sewage farm on ornithological grounds – but taken together the contribution they have made in providing an inland network of safe, food-rich places at which waders and other wetland birds can feed and rest on migration must have been considerable during the period they have been in existence.

The conservation of wintering waders and wildfowl in Britain is dealt with in the following two sections. There remain, however, several other groups of birds which migrate to Britain for the winter. Many of the most numerous of these are also species which are resident in Britain, such as the black-headed, common, herring and great black-backed gulls, heron, starling, blackbird, song thrush and chaffinch. For all these the conservation requirements are much as they are for the resident populations of the same species. All are numerous and many of them frequent agricultural land. Several north European species which do not breed in Britain (or breed only in very small numbers) come here for the winter. Redwings and fieldfares occur commonly on agricultural land – especially grassland; bramblings also occur on farmland but in years when mast is abundant they feed mainly in beech woods; flocks of snow buntings occur in many sandy coastal areas, notably on the British east coast, such as at Spurn Point, Yorkshire, and in north Norfolk, and also on northern hills; the rarer shore lark is exclusively coastal and is restricted to certain sites on the east coast.

WINTERING WADERS (LIMICOLAE)

Of nearly 30 species of waders which may be found in Britain in winter, eight or nine are irregular or extremely rare (e.g. stone curlew, great snipe) or occur only in very small numbers (e.g. common sandpiper, green sandpiper, whimbrel). Of the remaining 21, four species (spotted redshank, greenshank, ruff and avocet) occur regularly in small numbers in a few restricted localities, while the other 17 are common.

The wader population which winters in Britain is made up of birds of many different origins. The bulk of the British breeding populations of nine species remain with us through the winter, although some emigrate to the Continent or Ireland, especially during cold weather. These species include birds with such diverse habitat preferences as the woodcock (mainly woodlands), redshank (flood meadows and coastal grasslands in summer, coasts in winter), and curlew (mainly upland moors in summer, coasts or low-lying farmland in winter).

These British residents are augmented in winter by others of the same species from northern Europe and by large numbers of seven northern Eurasian breeding species (grey plover, turnstone, jack snipe, bar-tailed godwit, knot, purple sandpiper and sanderling); small numbers of an eighth species, the spotted redshank, also winter in Britain. The populations of knot and turnstone which winter here include birds from Greenland and north-east Arctic Canada, while Britain, together with Ireland, forms one of the main wintering areas for the Icelandic race of the black-tailed godwit. Norwegian and Icelandic oystercatchers also winter in Britain, the former in large numbers especially on the east coast, and the latter in western Britain and Ireland (and probably no further south or east).

From a conservation viewpoint the five common species of waders which winter mainly in inland localities in Britain pose greater problems than do the majority of species which are essentially coastal at this season. The most numerous and widespread of these inland species is the lapwing, which is found mainly on low-lying farmland of various kinds, but particularly on grassland. Golden plover, though more local than the lapwing, are also found in winter on flood meadows and coastal and other low-lying grasslands. The snipe and jack snipe require damp meadows and soft muddy ground into which they can probe for worms and other invertebrates. The woodcock is a widely dispersed woodland species – in the breeding season – which occurs in other, more open habitats during hard weather.

A feature of all these species is that during hard weather, whenever the ground becomes frozen, large numbers are forced to move southwards and westwards, and many emigrate to Iberia or Ireland. In very hard winters, for example, practically no lapwings remain in Britain, whereas during mild ones many thousands do so. Their conservation in hard winters is therefore an international concern. Most of these species, particularly the snipe and jack snipe, must have suffered from the drainage of many damp rough meadows and small marshy places, particularly in southern England. Some of the largest aggregations of snipe in Britain are still found on the old-fashioned, field-type sewage farms which were once located on the peripheries of most inland large towns and cities in England; in total, the numbers of snipe found in such places must at one time have been considerable. In the last 20–25 years, however, many of these farms have been modernised and this unique – if completely artificial habitat – is fast disappearing. These five species are represented on many grade 1 sites in winter, though in terms of the total wintering populations the proportion must be relatively small. As in the breeding season, the most important of the periodically flooded meadow grasslands is the Ouse Washes, where the four open country species all occur in some numbers. This is also a winter haunt of a sixth mainly inland wader, the ruff – a scarce species otherwise found at this season mainly on the coast, especially the Thames estuary, Solent and Poole Harbour. In the north some 15–20% of oystercatchers and redshank also feed in fields near the coast during mild spells in midwinter.

Of the remaining 15 wader species which regularly winter in Britain all except one, the curlew (which is also found on farmland), are exclusively coastal in winter. The sanderling is restricted to sandy beaches, and is adequately represented on several grade 1 sites from the Hebrides and Holy Island south to the Isles of Scilly. The purple sandpiper is confined to rocky coasts, while another, the turnstone, is found mainly on them; both species are frequent on key coastal sites, particularly in northern and western Britain.

All the other coastal species are found in winter in greatest numbers in shallow estuarine areas. A pilot survey of estuaries of importance for waders was carried out by the British Trust for Ornithology (BTO), with A. J. Prater as organiser, in the winter of 1969/70 and was repeated during 1970/71. The results of these surveys are given in Tables 42 and 43, and are averages for the two years. Only part of some estuaries were counted and in some areas coverage did not extend throughout the winter period. The figures given are therefore approximate and minimal.

A total of 70 000 waders has been taken as representing an estuary of international importance. All estuaries which fall into this category have 30 000 or more knot and over 2000 bar-tailed godwits (see Table 42). The importance of British estuaries for these species may be gauged by the totals of

Table 42. *Estuaries of international importance for waders (grade 1*)*

	Averages of peak counts[a] of selected species, winters 1969/70 and 1970/71				
	Morecambe Bay	Wash	Dee	Solway	Ribble
Oystercatcher	45	10	20	30	1
Ringed plover	7	1	+	3	+
Grey plover	+[b]	2	+	+	+
Curlew	14	12	3	12	1
Bar-tailed godwit	8	3	6	3	6
Redshank	12	5	6	7	5
Black-tailed godwit	+	+	1	1	+
Knot	80	85	50	29	60
Dunlin	44	40	30	17	13
Sanderling	14	3	6	1	3
Grand total	225 000	161 000	123 000	103 000	90 000

Notes

[a] The peak counts are presented in thousands and are rounded to the nearest thousand.

[b] + = present in numbers below 500.

Table 43. *Estuaries of national importance for waders*

		Peak counts of wader species 1969/71	
Grade	Site	County	Numbers
1	Burry Inlet	Glamorgan/Carmarthenshire	45 000
2	Severn	Somerset/Gloucestershire/Monmouthshire	45 000
1*	Humber	Lincolnshire/Yorkshire	40 000
1*	Firth of Forth	Fife/Lothians	34 000
1/2/3	Thames	Kent/Essex (excl. Foulness)	33 000
1	Lindisfarne	Northumberland	30 000
1*/2/3	Moray Firth Basin	incl. Moray, Beauly, Cromarty and Dornoch Firths	30 000
1	Chichester Harbour	Sussex/Hampshire	24 000
2	Duddon	Cumberland/Lancashire	24 000
2	Teesmouth	Durham/Yorkshire	24 000
1*	Blackwater/Dengie	Essex	22 000
2	Exe	Devon	22 000
1	Langstone Harbour	Hampshire	22 000
3/4	Firth of Clyde		20 000
1*	Foulness–Maplin	Essex	20 000
1	The Swale	Kent	20 000

Note

Population data by courtesy of A. J. Prater and the BTO/RSPB/Wildfowl Trust Birds of Estuaries Enquiry.

130 000 knot and 25 000 bar-tailed godwits obtained by an international count on the coasts of Germany, the Netherlands, Belgium and France during the winter of 1966/67. All British estuaries so far examined contain a diversity of species and no estuary is important for one species alone.

Estuaries supporting more than 20 000, but less than 70 000 waders have been termed of national importance (see Table 43). Several other estuaries, particularly in Scotland, were not included in this pilot survey and some of them may well qualify as of national importance when counts of their wader populations have been made.

Several other estuaries are of considerable interest for holding high densities of waders within a relatively small area (e.g. Poole Harbour C.23, gr. 1) or because they hold a substantial proportion of the wintering population of uncommon species (e.g. the Beaulieu Estuary (see C.11, gr. 2) is the regular wintering haunt of spotted redshanks, and the Tamar estuary has the only winter flock of avocets in Britain).

As well as forming winter haunts, estuaries are a vital habitat for waders at other seasons. In particular they afford safe, food-rich areas for migrant waders passing through Britain in spring and autumn.

Estuaries in Britain are threatened in several different ways. Impoundment schemes, for the reclamation of land or the provision of freshwater reservoirs, have been proposed for several estuaries, including the four holding the greatest concentrations of waders in Britain – Morecambe

Bay, the Wash, the Solway, and the Cheshire Dee. Industrial development elsewhere, e.g. at Teesmouth, has diminished the wildlife interest of some estuaries and is a potential threat to others. Estuarine ecosystems are also particularly sensitive and vulnerable to pollution, though no detailed studies have been made to indicate the effects that such pollution may be having on waders.

Internationally, the coastal wintering waders together with the breeding seabirds and the wintering wildfowl, form perhaps the most important elements of the British avifauna. The conservation of estuaries is thus particularly urgent, especially in view of the great changes which have already taken place in estuarine areas elsewhere in western Europe – notably in the Netherlands – and the increasing likelihood that further demands will be made on such areas by many different interests, most of which will conflict with nature conservation aims. Because of this special, international significance, all the wader estuaries with peaks of over 20 000 birds – not just a sample of these – have been rated as grade 1 or 2 sites, and those with over 70 000 birds have been graded 1*. In a few instances, the BTO wader counts refer to estuarine complexes which the *Review* has to regard as composed of two or more distinct sites (e.g. Severn, Thames, Moray Firth basin and Firth of Clyde); when the wader numbers for the individual components of such estuaries then fall below 20 000, a lower grading than 1 or 2 is given.

WILDFOWL (ANATIDAE)

During the past 20 years, the Wildfowlers' Association of Great Britain and Ireland, the Wildfowl Trust and the Nature Conservancy laid the foundations of a national policy for wildfowl conservation. This included the planning and partial establishment of a countrywide series of wildfowl refuges, provision for control of shooting and disturbance at certain sites, and the acceptance by wildfowlers of a voluntary ban on shooting during periods of hard weather.

The conservation requirements of wildfowl in Britain in terms of site protection were the subject of a survey by Atkinson–Willes (1963), on behalf of the Wildfowl Conservation Committee of the Nature Conservancy. The data contained in his report are quoted here extensively and are incorporated in the accounts of key sites where wildfowl populations are a feature of particular interest.

Most wildfowl are migratory, and pass through many different countries in the course of each year. Their conservation is therefore a matter for international co-operation, each country sharing in the responsibility. This principle is clearly recognised in the Ramsar *Convention on wetlands of international importance, especially as waterfowl habitat* (Foreign and Commonwealth Office, 1973), to which the British Government is a signatory.

In this context, Britain is important primarily as a terminal wintering ground for migrants breeding in Iceland, Scandinavia and the north-western districts of the USSR. From October–March a substantial proportion of the north-west European population of many species is concentrated here, notably greylag (65 %), shelduck (45 %), Bewick's swan, teal and wigeon (30–35 %), mallard, scaup and pochard (20–25 %) and whooper swan, European white-fronted goose, pintail and shoveler (10–15 %). Above all, Britain is important as a wintering ground for a large proportion of the world population of four species or races of goose, the Greenland white-fronted goose (25 %), the pink-footed goose (85 %), the barnacle goose (50 %) and the dark-bellied brent goose (50 %).

The native breeding stocks of most species are too small to contribute significantly to the winter populations, even within Britain. Exceptions are mallard, tufted duck, eider, red-breasted merganser, goosander, shelduck, mute swan and possibly teal. Even among these, breeding populations are widely dispersed, and relatively few sites hold enough pairs to warrant high status for this reason alone. Although the breeding populations of other species such as gadwall, wigeon, pintail, shoveler, pochard and greylag goose are nationally insignificant in terms of winter numbers, quite large colonies occur locally and are of considerable interest.

Large concentrations of moulting ducks are rare in Britain but are nonetheless important, both nationally and internationally. During the flightless period (usually July/ August) the birds are extremely vulnerable to disturbance, and any interference on traditional sites is likely to disrupt the native population for a wide area around. The moulting concentrations of the common breeding species, such as shelduck, eider, mallard and tufted duck, are more important than the gatherings of species which do not breed freely, such as pochard and common scoter, but both deserve attention.

The conservation of a highly mobile group such as wildfowl poses special problems that can only be partially solved by safeguarding a representative series of key sites. Over a period of years the distribution and numbers of a species may change markedly, for various reasons. The potential (as well as the actual) value of certain types of habitat is therefore an important consideration. Some sites, where wildfowl numbers are at present low, might become vastly more important, with suitable management, and there is thus a good deal of scope for creating new habitats for certain species to offset the destruction of existing sites, e.g. by drainage and other development.

Several important wildfowl sites are or have been under threat of severe disturbance from proposed development, notably Foulness, Langstone and Chichester Harbours and the Cromarty Firth. The major estuaries of the Wash, the Cheshire Dee, Morecambe Bay and the Solway Firth are possible sites for impoundment schemes that would radically alter the habitat and create large freshwater lakes, over parts if not the whole of each of these areas. This type of development would seriously affect some species, but might well benefit others, especially if provision is made for nature reserves on the new waters, as was planned at Morecambe Bay. Many big artificial inland reservoirs are already important for wildfowl (e.g. Gladhouse, Abberton, Grafham Water, Chew Valley Lake) and others now planned could prove equally valuable, provided that a reasonable compromise is reached between the wildfowl interest and the steadily increasing demand for recreational facilities. This also applies to many flooded gravel workings and mining subsidences which have come into being in recent years, and which in the aggregate provide a great deal of potentially valuable habitat.

Some species are in more urgent need of conservation than others, depending on their status and distribution, the pressures to which they and their habitats are subjected, and the extent to which they are able to adapt to changing conditions and alternative food supplies. Species most in need are those with specialised requirements, restricted to a small number of sites; in such cases the loss of even one resort might prove disastrous. Species least in need are those widely distributed, and well adapted to a broad range of conditions. In this case the pressures on the bird itself are likely to be greater than those on its habitat, and if added protection were required it would best be applied by shortening the shooting season.

In some cases it is possible to delineate individual sites of special importance to wildfowl. Where these lie close together, they are often complementary to each other: the local distribution of flocks may vary from day to day, or from month to month, according to weather, fluctuation in disturbance, or availability of food. Furthermore, the roosting and feeding areas are often some distance apart, spread over several distinct sites. In these circumstances, the loss of any one component site within the whole district can reduce to a quite disproportionate extent the number of birds that the district can support. It follows that the safeguarding of individual sites is not sufficient in these circumstances, and the whole district should be treated as one unit for conservation to be effective. In other situations, the mobility of the populations makes it difficult, if not impossible, to define the limits of important sites: this is particularly true of certain coastal areas, including estuaries, e.g. Solway Firth, Tay–Isla Valley, the Essex coast, Dornoch and Cromarty Firths, Chichester and Langstone harbours, the North Kent Marshes and the North Norfolk Coast. This problem of delineation applies also to wading bird interest and is discussed in Chapter 4.

During their stay in Britain, most migratory wildfowl are located on coastlands, wetlands (open waters and peatlands) and meadow grasslands, in that order of importance. The conservation of these populations thus depends in large measure on appropriate management of sites and habitats which often have considerable conservation importance in other respects.

For the purpose of the *Review*, the most important sites in terms of wildfowl are those supporting an appreciable proportion of the world, or north-west European population of one or more species, or which hold a total of at least 10 000 wildfowl. The time of year at which these concentrations occur is immaterial; in fact most of the sites selected are important only during winter. The Atkinson–Willes (1963) report defines strict criteria for 'international' and 'national' importance. Because of the need to balance the gradings of sites according to a wider range of nature conservation interest than ornithological, there has been a more

Table 44. *Sites of international importance for wildfowl*

	Approximate wildfowl population
Ouse Washes, Cambridgeshire (L.70, gr. 1*)	34 000
Loch Leven, Kinross (OW.67, gr. 1*)	24 000 +
Upper Solway Flats & Marshes, Cumberland, Dumfries-shire, Kirkcudbrightshire (C.61, gr. 1*)	23 000 +
Firth of Forth, Midlothian–Fife (C.76, gr. 1*)	19 000
Wash Flats & Marshes, Lincolnshire (C.20, gr. 1*)	18 500 +
Loch Gruinart/Loch Indaal, Islay, Argyll (C.99, gr. 1*)	18 000
Cromarty Firth, Ross (C.112, gr. 1*)	17 000
Stour Estuary, Essex (C.16, gr. 1)	14 000
Lindisfarne, Northumberland (C.65, gr. 1)	13 000
Dupplin Lochs, Perthshire (OW.69, gr. 1)	13 000
Tay–Isla Valley, Perthshire (OW.72, gr. 1)	12 000
Chichester/Langstone Harbours, Sussex, Hampshire (C.5, gr. 1*)	11 500
Sands of Forvie & Ythan Estuary, Aberdeenshire (C.86, gr. 1*)	11 000
Loch of Strathbeg, Aberdeenshire (OW.77, gr. 1)	11 000
Abberton Reservoir, Essex (OW.13, gr. 1)	10 000
Eden Estuary, Fife (C.93, gr. 2)	10 000
Medway Marshes & Estuary (C.7, gr. 1)	10 000 +
Blackwater Flats & Marshes, Essex (C.14, gr. 1*)	10 000 +

The following nine sites also have special value in that they are of international importance to at least one species. The total number of wildfowl exceed 8000 at all these sites, except the last two which hold *c.* 6500 and 3000, respectively.

New Grounds, Slimbridge, Gloucestershire (C.35, gr. 1); Gladhouse Reservoir, Midlothian (OW.63, gr. 1); Tentsmuir Point, Fife (C.82, gr. 1); Mersey Estuary, Cheshire (C.56, gr. 2); Carsebreck Lochs, Perthshire (OW.70, gr. 1); Foulness & Maplin Sands, Essex (C.13, gr. 1*); Ribble Estuary, Lancashire (C.58, gr. 1*); Lower Dornoch Firth, Ross/Sutherland (C.123, gr. 2); Ken–Dee Marshes, Kirkcudbrightshire (L.149, gr. 1).

Note

Population data by courtesy of G. Atkinson-Willes and the Wildfowl Trust.

conservative application of these terms to wildfowl sites in this review.

Of the key sites listed in the *Review*, 18 (10 in Scotland) hold a peak of at least 10 000 wildfowl in an average winter, *and* attract internationally important concentrations of at least one species. These are given in Table 44.

All these 27 localities are regarded as key sites, and all but three are rated as grade 1. Most of the estuaries important for wildfowl are also valuable wader areas, and the grading of some sites has depended on the weight of this additional interest. A further 31 sites are of national or regional importance for wildfowl. Between them, these 58 listed sites hold more than half the British winter population of at least

11 species or subspecies of wildfowl (European white-fronted goose, Greenland white-fronted goose, pink-footed goose, bean goose, barnacle goose, dark-bellied brent goose, pale-bellied brent goose, Bewick's swan, pintail, scaup and shelduck). The same sites also hold at least 20% of the British population of a further seven species (greylag goose, whooper swan, teal, wigeon, gadwall, goldeneye and smew). Mallard, shoveler, pochard, tufted duck, eider and mute swan are less well represented in proportion to their populations, but enough of their main resorts are listed in the *Review* to satisfy both the national and international conservation requirement in these cases. The remaining five species of wildfowl which winter regularly in Britain cannot feasibly be protected by safeguarding sites, though all would benefit from other conservation measures. Three – the long-tailed duck, common scoter and velvet scoter – live almost entirely on the open sea and are much more threatened by oil pollution than by loss of habitat. The other two – the goosander and red-breasted merganser – seldom concentrate in large numbers for any length of time, and the most effective measure of protection, if one were needed, might be to introduce a close season in Scotland.

If the key sites listed in the *Review* are adequately safeguarded, this will go a long way towards meeting the needs of a national policy for wildfowl conservation; additional arrangements may still be needed, however, to provide some measure of protection in other areas. Many other key sites, chosen largely for quite different features, have wildfowl in small numbers, either during the breeding season or outside it, and their presence often adds significantly to the overall nature conservation interest.

REPTILES AND AMPHIBIANS

There are only twelve indigenous species of reptiles and amphibians in Britain – three snakes, three lizards, three newts, a frog and two toads. The British Herpetological Society has recently set up a conservation committee, but in general the reptiles and amphibians are not popular with amateur naturalists: they are relatively unknown and, until recently, unprotected by any law. Their scientific value is nevertheless considerable: they are survivors of primitive groups of the vertebrate stock; several of the British species are at or near the limit of their world range; and the common frog is extensively used in the teaching of biology. Three species, the sand lizard, the smooth snake and the natterjack toad, are sufficiently rare and restricted in their distribution to be in danger of possible extinction in Britain.

Consideration of the conservation of both groups is severely handicapped by lack of knowledge. The three above-mentioned rare species are all well represented on grade 1 sites, but their population size and distribution within these sites is not usually known. The smooth snake occurs on Thursley Common, and the heaths of the New Forest and Dorset, while the sand lizard is also in these localities and at Ainsdale Dunes in Lancashire. The natterjack toad is represented in various coastal sites from the Norfolk coast to the Solway. The grass snake occurs on many heathland and wetland key sites in England, and the adder is even better represented as it occurs on various northern moorland sites as well. The common lizard is probably present on most heath and upland sites, but the distribution of the newts, frog and toad on keysites is not properly known. The common frog has declined considerably over much of lowland England and is probably now more numerous on some upland sites in northern Britain (up to 900 m in the Highlands) than on many lowland sites in the south.

Irrespective of numbers on key sites, the bulk of the populations of the reptiles and amphibians is at risk to general adverse pressures. Most of the changes which have so greatly affected heathland during the last 30 years are detrimental to the reptiles. Building on heathland destroys many reptiles, and survivors are usually eliminated by children and domestic cats. Heavier public pressure increases the frequency of heath fires, and the risk grows as the heaths become smaller in area. A severe fire will kill most of the reptiles present and render the habitat unsuitable for several years; if there are no adjoining areas with surviving populations, recolonisation cannot take place even when the habitat recovers. On the important sand dunes of the Dorset and west Lancashire coasts, disturbance by sheer numbers of people is in danger of overwhelming the sand lizard and natterjack toad areas. Collecting of frogs and other species for teaching purposes may now be inimical in areas where there has already been marked decline. There is probably less deliberate destruction nowadays of species such as the adder, though this snake is killed in large numbers during afforestation work. The afforestation of heath and moorland is itself sooner or later unfavourable to reptiles, which cannot tolerate the deep shade of conifer plantations or survive the frequent mowing or ploughing of the fire-breaks. Drainage of waterlogged areas has also reduced the extent of suitable habitat for species (e.g. natterjack toad) which need wet ground during part of the year.

The conservation of reptiles and amphibians on safeguarded areas will depend on gaining increased knowledge of their ecology and managing such areas accordingly. It has been found that snakes can travel considerable distances (2 km or more) and may regularly make seasonal movement between different habitats; here it is necessary to safeguard an area of sufficient size and diversity. On some of the Dorset heaths, populations of toads, newts and grass snakes are associated with artificial ponds, clay diggings and bomb-holes; this points to the value which may derive from creating new habitats. Some preliminary studies suggest that reptiles can be deliberately transported considerable distances and reintroduced into appropriate areas. Many species can also be bred in captivity for subsequent release into the wild. However, work of this kind depends on fairly precise knowledge of habitat needs and limiting factors.

For the amphibians, the recent widespread loss of lowland freshwater habitat may have had a substantial adverse effect, as through urbanisation and filling-in of field ponds. Other habitat modifications associated with modern agriculture may have been inimical, such as mechanical cutting of ditches, conversion of pasture land to arable, and possibly the local contamination of waterways by pesticide residues. Probably only the adder is deliberately persecuted, and this is largely an educational problem. Apart from the three rarest species mentioned the conservation of this group is likely to depend on the trend of influences in the countryside mostly outside key sites.

FRESHWATER FISH

Of the 54 species of freshwater fish found in Britain none is endemic; three of them occur only as vagrants and 11 species have been introduced by man. Many of the remaining 40 indigenous species are common and widespread, but several are declining in numbers or restricted in distribution and confined to a few waters. As a group, fish occur in almost all types of open water except extremely acidic peat pools, high-altitude waters, grossly polluted waters and those which dry out periodically. Although the general distribution of most freshwater species in the British Isles is quite well known, information is still needed from a number of key sites which it has not yet been possible to examine in detail and the present assessment must be partly provisional.

In general, the number of fish species decreases from south to north in Britain: many species are confined to the south and east of the country and only a few to the north and west. Thus the maximum number of species which could be expected to occur in any key site decreases as one moves north. Some species are represented in a number of key sites, well distributed over a large part of the country and including standing and running open waters, e.g. salmon, trout, pike, minnow, roach, eel, three-spined stickleback, ten-spined stickleback and perch. In a somewhat similar category are those which are common in many sites in the southern half of the country (possibly a few elsewhere) but mostly restricted to standing or very slow-flowing waters (crucian carp *Carassius carassius*, tench, bream *Abramis brama*, silver-bream, rudd and chub) or to running waters (sea lamprey, river lamprey, brook lamprey, grayling, gudgeon, bleak, dace, stone loach, ruff, bullhead and flounder).

The barbel *Barbus barbus* is somewhat restricted in its distribution by its requirements for clean, well-oxygenated fast-flowing waters which are now rare in the range of its distribution in Britain. It is a highly prized fish, however, and attempts are being made by angling societies to stock suitable waters with this species. It is present in the grade 1 open water site, the Hampshire Avon. The charr has a much more restricted, northern and western distribution, but is found in several lakes in all the major upland areas of Britain. Many of these isolated populations are racially distinct, so much so, that many were described as separate species in the past. Charr have disappeared from a number of lakes, e.g. Loch Leven, Kinross, as a result of increased eutrophication, impoundment or drainage. The Welsh race is found in only three localities, of which two, including the grade 2 Llyn Cwellyn, are now threatened by reservoir or pump storage schemes.

In order to safeguard this race it may be necessary to establish populations elsewhere in Wales, at least until the effects of the proposals can be judged. In the Lake District, charr occur in all the larger lakes, except Bassenthwaite, Ullswater and the mesotrophic Esthwaite, but these populations are not at present threatened. In Scotland, charr are widespread in the Highlands as far north as Loch Girlsta in Shetland, and are also found in a few lochs in Galloway. Charr are present in six of the grade 1 or 2 open water sites in Scotland and the future of the Scottish populations does not appear to be in jeopardy at the moment. The spined loach is a more restricted species confined to the Midlands and south-east England, and is not known to occur in any of the existing key sites.

The status of many estuarine species is rather doubtful though most of them could be expected to occur in the larger estuaries and some coastal areas and, with two notable exceptions, there is no reason yet to suppose that any could be classified as rare or endangered. The following can be included in this category: allis shad *Alosa alosa*, twaite shad *A. fallax*, smelt *Osmerus eperlanus*, sea bass *Dicentrarchus labrax*, common goby *Pomatoschistus microps*, thick-lipped mullet *Crenimugil labrosus*, thin-lipped mullet *Chelon ramada*, and golden mullet *Chelon auratus*. Two other species, the houting *Coregonus oxyrinchus* and the sturgeon *Acipenser sturio*, are either extinct or extremely rare in this country. Occasional specimens of the latter turn up in estuarine waters, but this declining species is at the edge of its range in Britain. The houting has probably been completely wiped out by overfishing and pollution of the southern North Sea.

Three freshwater fish species can be considered rare in Britain, and may be endangered as they are very sensitive to pollution and eutrophication. The vendace *Coregonus albula* is restricted to Bassenthwaite and Derwentwater in the Lake District and the grade 1 Mill Loch, Lochmaben in Dumfries-shire, the two populations being racially distinct. The Lochmaben vendace also formerly occurred in the nearby Castle Loch but is now thought to be extinct there. The other *Coregonus* sp. found in Britain, the powan, schelly or gwyniad, *C. lavaretus*, is still present in the grade 1 open water site of Llyn Tegid, Merioneth, in the grade 1 Loch Lomond, and in three Lake District lakes, Ullswater, Haweswater and Red Tarn (within the Helvellyn grade 1 site). At present this species is under no threat, even though most of its localities in Britain are now used as reservoirs. The status of the burbot *Lota lota* is extremely doubtful at the moment, and it has been suggested from time to time that the species is extinct, probably as a result of pollution. Occasional specimens still turn up in some of the larger south-eastern English rivers, including the Ouse and Wissey, but no locality for any firmly established population is known.

The main human pressures on existing fish stocks can be considered under the headings of fisheries, pollution and changing land-use. Threats from direct exploitation by fishing are mainly to those species which have no interest for anglers, and which may be deliberately eliminated by management. The recent practice of treating a water-body with a piscicide to kill off 'worthless' species, and re-stocking with highly valued fish, is having adverse effects on the native fish fauna. There have been considerable and often successful attempts to reduce pollution, especially from industry and in rivers, to the benefit of both kinds of fish. It is more difficult to influence changing land-use, which may also involve a pollution aspect. Conservation of freshwater fish species of commercial or angling value, is the statutory responsibility of the River Authorities in England and Wales (now RWAs and WNWDA), and the River Purification Boards in Scotland. In addition, angling societies and private landowners carry out their own schemes of stocking and water management aimed at improving the populations of freshwater fishes. As a consequence, despite the many kilometres of fishless polluted rivers, most of the widespread species of fish angled for are now well protected. In fact, many of the lakes and rivers in lowland Britain are greatly overstocked with fish. Because of the increasing transfer of fish and water from one catchment to another the natural distribution of many of the fish species is becoming obscured. The major trends in the country are away from natural stable mixed fish populations towards artificially maintained, unstable stocks of a few species (e.g. brown trout and rainbow trout) of sporting or commercial value. In particular, the rarer, more sensitive fish stocks with poor powers of dispersal are being eradicated and replaced by commoner, more robust forms with greater powers of dispersal. The rarer species and genetic races are likely to survive only if constructive conservation projects are initiated now at a variety of levels.

Thus active work is necessary on the conservation of these rare species, as well as valuable stocks of common species, by protecting the ecosystems in which they occur and by transferring selected stock to appropriate waters in the same area. Even with common fish species there should be action to reintroduce species to waters, including estuaries, from which they have disappeared (if conditions are appropriate) and to establish suitable mixed communities in water-bodies. The new stocks used for such introductions should be chosen carefully. Also, it should not be thought necessary for every water to have a fish population: it is highly desirable that among the diversity of water-bodies in this country there should be some which have no fish species, thus allowing the development there of the interesting natural communities which exist in the absence of fish. These would complement the varied populations of native fish species in other waters which, if conserved intelligently, must form a valuable natural resource for the country as a whole.

A more detailed account of the conservation of British freshwater fishes has been given by Maitland (1974).

BUTTERFLIES AND MOTHS (LEPIDOPTERA)

During the last 25 years, Lepidoptera have been subjected increasingly to adverse changes in the environment, some general and others more local. Some of the butterflies (e.g. fritillaries) are obviously less widespread and numerous than before 1950, and there has been much argument about causes – whether this is a natural decline or one resulting at least partly from human influence. Butterflies are warmth- and sun-loving creatures notoriously sensitive to weather, and certain species (e.g. comma, white admiral) have long been known to be prone to change in distribution for no obvious reason. Migratory species are especially subject to year-by-year variations in their appearance, and the numbers of some species in Britain may depend on immigration from the Continent to an even greater extent than has generally been realised. In Britain, butterflies increase in species diversity and abundance with distance south, and the warm south-western counties are more productive than the east coast districts. Cool, wet summers have an adverse effect on numbers of most species, and a succession of bad years may result in the cutting back of range for some. The apparent decline of species such as the purple emperor and certain fritillaries may be the result of such factors, but may be simply a downward phase in a normal long-term cyclical fluctuation between expansion and retreat.

On the other hand, human influence during recent years is likely to have had deleterious effects on many butterflies and moths, and may have reinforced natural adversities for some species. For instance, habitat changes may lead to an increase of predators and parasites which can locally reduce populations below levels critical for survival.

For many species the agricultural revolution has caused a considerable loss of habitat, especially through the almost universal weeding of crops with herbicides and widespread destruction of hedgerows and rough corners. Chemical weed killers have also been widely used in a variety of other habitats. It is uncertain whether insecticides have had any direct effect in reducing populations of these insects. The species belonging to lowland meadow grasslands and way-sides have been the most affected by these changes. A considerable extent of lowland permanent grassland and heath has been lost through arable cultivation or ploughing and reseeding, especially on the Chalk, and the 'blue' butter-flies in particular have lost ground. Afforestation of unculti-vated ground has caused changes in species composition, but here there is a replacement of open ground insects by woodland species. However, extensive replacement of heath and grassland by conifers has often given a rather limited and uniform insect fauna, and it is often the more interesting species which have declined, as in the Breckland. The widespread replacement of deciduous woods by coni-fers has, on balance, been deleterious. Draining of wetlands over the past 150 years has caused loss or decline of many species, especially in the East Anglian Fenlands, the classic case being the large copper, but several moths have also disappeared or become extremely rare in this district. Even now, the general drying out of many fens, which is accom-panied by encroachment of carr woodland, is greatly reducing the extent of habitat for many species; this is especially noticeable in the Norfolk Broads. Post-myxomato-sis changes, involving increased luxuriance and cover of grasses, and invasion of shrubs, with corresponding decrease in many small food plant species, may well have contributed to the further decline of calcareous grassland insects, and it has been suggested that the large blue has suffered in this way.

There are still very large areas of mountain, moorland and peat moss (basin, raised and blanket mire) in the west and north of Britain, and the populations of Lepidoptera here are less affected by change than in many lowland situations. However, in this range of habitats, the conversion of heather-dominated moorland to sheep-walk grassland by heavy sheep-grazing and repeated burning has, over a long period, caused a decline of those butterflies and moths whose larvae feed on dwarf shrubs. Coastal habitats are also relatively little changed on the whole, and many sand-dune and cliff slope areas are still extremely productive for these insects. Afforestation of some dune areas may have caused local decline of some species. Finally, over-collecting may have reduced the numbers and distribution of some rare species, and grows in seriousness as species become rarer and more restricted.

These growing environmental pressures make it necessary to think in terms of conserving minimum populations of Lepidoptera on selected areas where conditions can be carefully controlled. A great deal has still to be learned, however, about the ecological requirements and population dynamics of Lepidoptera, and at present it may not be possible to assess properly the needs for conservation of these insects, in terms of adequate size of areas and the exact vegetational and environmental composition of the habitats involved. It is nevertheless hoped that the series of key sites recommended gives a basis for the conservation of many species, and that appropriate management will in time increase the value of many sites. The problem of rare species not present on any key site, and occurring mostly in widely scattered localities, may have to be tackled by conservation action at regional or local level. The question of introductions or reintroductions is beyond the scope of the *Review*, but a precedent has been set in the instance of the Dutch race of the large copper *Lycaena dispar batavus* at Woodwalton Fen, Huntingdonshire.

The representation of Lepidoptera on key sites will be examined only for the *characteristic* species, i.e. those listed in the fauna sections for each main habitat formation. These lists omit most species which occur here only as migrants. Particular notice has been taken of the *rare* species among these groups, namely those not known to occur recently in more than six 10-km squares of the National Grid. The completion of current surveys is likely to lead to revision of the provisional list of 13 rare butterflies and 92 rare moths thus recognised: these include some species not yet assigned to a particular formation type and thus not identified as characteristic Lepidoptera.

The following are the rare characteristic species not known to occur on any key site:

Coastlands
Portland ribbon wave *Idaea degeneraria* at Portland Bill; the Welsh form of the transparent burnet *Zygaena purpuralis* ssp. *segontii* at Abersoch.

Woodlands
Large tortoiseshell *Nymphalis polychloros* scattered in eastern England and probably a migrant in part; netted carpet *Eustroma reticulata* scattered localities mainly in Lakeland.

Uplands
Slender Scotch burnet *Zygaena loti*, Argyll, exact locality undisclosed.

Artificial ecosystems
Four-spotted *Tyta luctuosa*, only known from one site in south-east London.

All the other characteristic butterflies and moths, except possibly the conformist *Lithophane furcifera* (woodlands), are represented on at least one key site. At present, 13 of the non-characteristic rare moth species are not thus represented, but all the rare butterflies are present.

The list of key sites includes a number of areas (some of them already declared NNRs) which have long been famous for their butterflies and moths, both for variety of species and presence of rarities. There follows a list of the most celebrated of these localities, with the number of known rare species (if any) given in brackets.

Woodlands
Southern oak and mixed deciduous woodland
Blean Woods (1), and Ham Street Woods, Kent; the New Forest, Hampshire.

Midlands oak and mixed deciduous woodland
Waterperry Wood (1), Oxfordshire; Castor Hanglands (2) and Monks Wood (1), Huntingdon and the Soke of Peterborough; Wyndcliff Wood (2), Monmouthshire; Wyre Forest (1), Worcestershire.

Northern oak and mixed deciduous woodland
Roudsea Wood (1), Lancashire; Witherslack Woods (1), Westmorland.

Highland birchwood
Craigellachie Wood (1), Inverness-shire.

Highland pine wood
Black Wood of Rannoch (2), Perthshire.

Coastlands
Sand dunes, salt marsh and shingle
Dungeness (8), Kent; Foulness and Maplin Sands (2) and Blackwater Flats and Marshes (1), Essex; Winterton Dunes (1), Norfolk; North Norfolk Coast (3); Braunton Burrows (1), Devon; Ainsdale Dunes (2), Lancashire.

Cliff and undercliff, grassland, heath and scrub
Folkestone Warren (4), Kent; Needles to St Catherine's Point (2), Isle of Wight; Durlston Head–Ringstead Bay,

Dorset; Axmouth–Lyme Regis (2), Devon; The Lizard (2), Cornwall; Steeple Point to Blackchurch Rock (1), Cornwall–Devon; Rhum (1), Inverness-shire.

Lowland grasslands, heaths and scrub

Southern calcareous grasslands

Wye and Crundale Downs (2), Kent; Mount Caburn, Sussex; Martin Down (1), Hampshire; Porton Down, Wiltshire; Avon Gorge (2), Somerset.

Northern calcareous grasslands

Great Ormes Head, Caernarvonshire; Arnside Knott, Lancashire; Whitbarrow Scar (1), Westmorland.

Mixed basic grasslands and heaths

Various Breckland key sites (5), Suffolk–Norfolk.

Acidic heaths

Thursley and Hankley Common, Surrey; Ashdown Forest, Sussex; New Forest, Hampshire; Hartland–Arne Heaths and Studland–Godlingston Heaths, Dorset.

Peatlands

Eutrophic valley and flood-plain mire (fen)

Hickling and Horsey (8), and Bure Marshes (4), Norfolk; Redgrave–South Lopham Fen (2), Norfolk–Suffolk; Wicken Fen (6), Cambridgeshire; Chippenham Fen (3), Cambridgeshire; Woodwalton Fen (4), Huntingdonshire; Walberswick (3), Suffolk.

Oligotrophic basin, valley, raised and blanket mires (peat moss)

Morden Bog (1), Dorset; Cors Fochno (1), Cardiganshire; Wem Moss and Clarepool Moss, Shropshire; Chartley Moss, Staffordshire; Abbots Moss, Cheshire; Roudsea and Stribers Moss, Lancashire; Glasson Moss, Bowness Common, Wedholme Flow and Orton Moss (1), Cumberland; Rannoch Moor, Perthshire–Argyll.

Uplands

Wales

Eryri (2), Caernarvonshire; Y Berwyn, Merioneth–Denbighshire–Montgomeryshire.

Northern England

Ingleborough and Malham–Arncliffe, Yorkshire; Moor House and Cross Fell, Westmorland–Cumberland; Skiddaw Forest, Cumberland.

Highlands

Ben Lawers and Meall nan Tarmachan, Perthshire; Cairngorms, Inverness-shire–Aberdeenshire–Banffshire; Clova–Caenlochan, Angus–Perthshire–Aberdeenshire; Ben Wyvis, Ross; Hermaness and Fetlar, Shetland.

These sites hold a high proportion of the total number of British Lepidoptera. Many other key sites are also rich in Lepidoptera, but less famous, and further study could well reveal that some of these are more important than has been suspected hitherto. The total series of key sites contains substantial populations of many of the more common and widespread species, and some sites which apparently lack rarities are nevertheless remarkable for the abundance of both common and local butterflies and/or moths, e.g. Porton Down, Wiltshire.

Many of the less common butterflies and moths found in Britain are immigrants from the Continent, and these vary greatly in their regularity of occurrence and actual numbers from year to year. Immigration occurs over a wide sector of the south and east coasts of England, but there are some especially favoured landfalls, and five of these on the south coast are included as grade 1 sites, namely Folkestone Warren, Sandwich/Pegwell Bay and Dungeness, Kent; the south coast of the Isle of Wight, Hampshire; and the Dorset coast from Durlston Head to Ringstead Bay.

Many artificial ecosystems are rich in Lepidoptera, especially migrant species; and roadside and railway verges, hedges, arable fields and headlands, gardens and parks are often highly productive. In some of these habitats there have been declines and further losses are likely. Here the educational approach may be the most successful conservation measure. There has already been a favourable response to showing the public the interest and beauty of these insects, and encouraging the leaving of larval food plant weeds such as nettle, and the planting of flowering species attractive to the adults, such as buddleia.

WEEVILS (CURCULIONOIDEA (COLEOPTERA) – EXCLUDING SCOLYTIDAE AND PLATYPODIDAE)

The *Review* has been only partly successful in including those sites known to be especially important for the British Curculionoidea. This is inevitable, for many species belong to disturbed and marginal land associated with certain forms of agriculture, and to other habitats not well represented in the key site series. The weevils are an underworked faunal group in which knowledge of distribution is patchy and incomplete. New localities for many of the rarer species will probably yet be found or old records reconfirmed. Survey of weevils on many key sites has not been possible in the time available so that knowledge of the representation of species is inadequate. The following account is thus only a provisional analysis, indicating a minimum proportion of the British weevil fauna which could be conserved by the safeguarding of key sites.

The weevils have a predominantly southerly distribution in Britain. The rather few montane species appear to occur fairly frequently and to be well represented in key sites. The species of the Caledonian pine forests are more numerous and their status less secure, but many of them, too, are well represented, as are the more widespread northern weevils. Most of the rare British weevils occur in southern lowland England and their extremely limited distribution represents the fringe of the European population. All these species are more common on the Continent and many are abundant there, so that there is seldom an international case for conserving British populations of any species. On the other hand, the interest of the British species to amateur and professional workers is considerable, especially in zoogeographical aspects, and ecologically because of the many different kinds of plant/animal relationships which they exemplify.

In this account, species have been assigned subjectively to one of four groups: Group I contains those species which are recognised as national rarities, though not in the formal sense used to define the rare Macrolepidoptera. The conservation of the species in this list may be regarded as of importance nationally. Group II contains local and uncommon species which are not, however, rare enough to merit consideration on a national scale. Regionally, and at a county level the conservation of such species might include specific considerations of reserve acquisition and management. Group III contains all those species of common occurrence and wide distribution whose conservation does not constitute any problem. Group IV contains those species which are taxonomically doubtful, extinct, have no known recent locality or for some other reason cannot be considered at the present time. Some of these may be rediscovered; and qualify for Group I.

For the purposes of the *Review* only the 53 Group I species will be considered; this is about 10% of the British weevil fauna, and the high proportion reflects the zoogeographical 'edge effect' so typical in the British Isles. Some 2500 species of weevil are known from France, about 530 from Britain, and about 220 from Ireland. Many Group I species have been relatively well known in Britain for 150 years at least and on the whole their populations appear to be much less transient than those of many Macrolepidoptera with a similar distribution. The rare weevils do not seem to be limited in distribution by the occurrence of their food plants, which do not include any rarities, and other factors are evidently responsible.

Below is a tentative separation of the Group I species into their appropriate 'habitats':

	No. of species
Agricultural ecosystems	6
Woodlands	14
Lowland grasslands and heaths	10
Upland grasslands and heaths	2
Coastlands	19
Wetlands	18

The total number is 69 and not 53 because several species need to be classified into more than one 'habitat', e.g. species of wetland and heath habitats within the New Forest, or grassland species which occur on the coast. It seems best to discuss these weevils under the primary ecological grouping of the site in which they occur, but to indicate their other habitat in brackets.

Not much can be said about species inhabiting *artificial ecosystems* in the context of the *Review* (*Apion lemoroi*, *A. semivittatum*, *Anthonomus chevrolati*, *A. cinctus*, *A. humeralis* and *Gymnetron collinum*). The six species are almost equally divided among agricultural weeds in waste land, roadside verges and fruit trees in orchards. Of the last, some also inhabit native and naturalised trees in such areas as the New Forest, and could be represented on key sites.

The *woodland* key sites noted as important for their Lepidoptera include several of first national importance for weevils and other Coleoptera. The most notable woods, with their rare species are the New Forest (*Apion armatum* (grassland), *Nanophyes gracilis* (wetland), *Aoromius quinquepunctatus*, *Bagous longitarsus* (wetland), *Bagous czwalinai* (wetland) and *Bagous frit* (wetland)); Windsor Forest (*Dryophthorus corticalis*); Ham Street Woods (*Dorytomus affinis*); Blean Woods (*Ceuthorhynchus pervicax*); Monks Wood (*D. affinis*); Roudsea Wood (*Anthonomus rufus*); Moccas Park and the Beinn Eighe pinewood (*Pissodes validirostris*) (upland). The rare woodland weevils not known on key sites are *Anchonidium unguiculare* (Gweek, Cornwall), *Polydrusus sericeus* (East Malling, Kent), and *Rhynchaenus decoratus* (wetland) in Hampshire.

Five important entomological coastland sites are known to contain 10 species of rare weevil, namely: Sandwich–Pegwell Bay (*Limobius mixtus*, *Lixus vilis*); Dungeness (*Smicronyx coecus*); Needles–St Catherine's Point (*Otiorhynchus ligustici* (grassland), *Mononychus punctumalbum*); Axmouth–Lyme Regis (*Pachytychius haemotocephalus* (grassland)); and the Lizard (*Cathormiocerus attaphilus*, *C. britannicus*, *Miarus micros* and probably the taxonomically obscure *M. salsolae*). Of the remaining species, *Lixus algirus* (grassland) occurs within the Pevensey Levels grade 1 wetlands site, *Ceuthorhynchus parvulus* possibly occurs within the Braunton Burrows grade 1 site, and *Baris scolopacea* possibly within the High Halstow/Cliffe grade 2 site. Four rare species are not known on any key site: *Cathormiocerus socius* occurs at Culver Cliff, outside the Isle of Wight grade 1 coastland site, whilst *Hypera pastinacae* is known only from St Margaret's Bay, Kent. *Ceuthorhynchus pilosellus* and *Procas armillatus* cannot be located at the moment.

The rare *wetland* weevils include species from a wide range of habitats. The New Forest Valley mire and open water species have been mentioned under woodlands above. The fresh and brackish dykes of reclaimed salt marshes in south-east England are important, particularly in Pevensey grade 1 site and Pett Levels (with *Bagous binodulus*, *B. nodulosus* (coastland)) and the marshes of the north Kent coast (with *B. cylindrus* (wetland)) and the last two species possibly within one of the key sites. *Tapinotus sellatus* and *Ceuthorhynchus querceti* may still occur in the Norfolk Broads, though presence within one of the key sites here is still more problematical, and *Lixus paraplecticus* may still be in the East Anglian fens such as Wicken Fen. *Hylobius transversovittatus* (coastland) has been recorded from localities which may lie within the Axmouth–Lyme Regis and Shapwick Heath key sites, and there is an old record of *Bagous lutosus* (grassland) from East Wretham Heath. The remaining wetland species *Bagous brevis*, *B. collignensis*, *B. diglyptus* and *Hypera arundinis* are not known to occur on any key site.

The *grasslands* share some species of rare weevil with

other habitats, especially coastlands, and have rather few species of their own. Of these, *Ceuthorhynchus moelleri* occurs within the Aston Rowant and Halling to Trottis-cliffe sites, and *C. unguicularis* within a Breckland key site, but *C. pilosellus* and *Baris analis* are not known within any key sites. *Lixus algirus* is perhaps best regarded as a grass-land species, and occurs on Pevensey Levels, breeding on *Cirsium palustre*; it could thus also be regarded both as a coastland and a wetland insect.

Only one rare weevil is confined to *uplands* namely *Otiorhynchus auropunctatus*, which is widespread on the east coast of Ireland, but found in Britain only on the Inverpolly grade 1 site (U.66).

Thus, of the 53 rare species, 24 are certainly known to occur on at least one grade 1 or 2 site, and at least another 10 species may be present.

DRAGONFLIES (ODONATA)

The common British dragonflies are represented on a large number of key sites, well distributed over the country, and include standing and running open waters, peatlands and heathlands with pools or wet valleys. Species in this class include *Aeshna cyanea, A. juncea, Libellula quadrimaculata, Sympetrum striolatum, S. danae, Lestes sponsa, Pyrrhosoma nymphula, Ischnura elegans* and *Enallagma cyathigerum*. A number of other species are well represented on key sites in this range of habitats in the southern half of Britain: these include *A. grandis, Anax imperator, Libellula depressa, Orthetrum cancellatum, Agrion virgo, A. splendens, Coena-grion puella* and *C. pulchellum*. The remaining species show varying degrees of localisation, and some are much less well represented on key sites, while a few appear to be absent altogether. The dragonflies of all key sites have not yet been fully surveyed, however, and the assessment made here must be provisional.

Certain areas are particularly rich in variety of species. The Norfolk Broads are an especially favoured area, with large populations of most of the above species, except *Aeshna juncea*, and other species locally common include *Libellula fulva, Erythromma najas* and *Brachytron pratense*. The two very rare species *A. isosceles* and *Coenagrion arma-tum* are confined to the Norfolk Broads in Britain. Probably, but not certainly, all the above mentioned dragonflies occur within at least one grade 1 site in the Norfolk Broads, though the latter rare species is extremely localised and has not been seen recently.

The slow rivers and other remaining wet areas of the fen-lands in Cambridgeshire and Huntingdonshire and of Kent and Sussex are another important haunt of these southern dragonflies which breed in eutrophic waters. Many of the species referred to above are present; *Platycnemis pennipes* is also common in suitable localities, and there are two other very local dragonflies, *Lestes dryas* and *Libellula fulva*. It is not known how many species occur in the Ouse Washes grade 1 site, but at least 16 are recorded from Woodwalton Fen.

In southern England, the acidic heaths of Dorset and the New Forest, with their spongy valley mires and numerous pools, are another important haunt of dragonflies. In addi-tion to many of the above species (but not those which need water of high pH), some very local dragonflies are quite numerous on at least one grade 1 site, and often on several; these species are *Sympetrum sanguineum, Ischnura pumilio, Coenagrion mercuriale, Ceriagrion tenellum, Orthetrum coerulescens* and *Cordulea aenea*. The similar heaths of Surrey have all these species, and Thursley Common (P.2) contains one of the few British stations for *Leucorrhinia dubia* (also in at least three northern peatland/upland sites). At least 26 species of dragonfly have been recorded from Thursley Common, including the very rare *Somatochlora metallica*, which also occurs in a pond on the edge of the acidic heath-land district of Ashdown Forest in Sussex.

The Basingstoke Canal in Hampshire is another interest-ing dragonfly haunt, and has the last-named species, while the West Moors River (OW.8) in the same county has an extraordinary concentration of rarities. These include *Libellula fulva, Gomphus vulgatissimus, Coenagrion mer-curiale, Ischnura pumilio* and *Oxygastra curtisii*. The last is a Lusitanian species of very restricted world distribution. This classic locality is reported to have been adversely affected in recent years by a sewage works up-river, and it is thought that *Oxygastra* may now be extinct there. This species above all is in need of protection, and it is hoped that unconfirmed reports of its occurrence in south-west Eng-land will prove correct.

The mountains and moorlands of the west and north, with their streams and blanket mire pools, provide habitats for large populations of *Aeshna juncea, Libellula quadri-maculata, Sympetrum danae* and *Pyrrhosoma nymphula*. *Cordulegaster boltonii* is locally common in the western up-lands, as is *S. nigrescens* in parts of the Scottish Highlands. Three species are confined to Scotland and appear to be rare even there. *A. caerulea* occurs on blanket mire key sites, in-cluding Rannoch Moor, Perthshire/Argyll (P.85). *Somato-chlora arctica* is present on grade 1 sites in Perthshire and Ross, and *Coenagrion hastulatum* occurs in tarns and pools in the Speyside foothills of the Cairngorms within one of the grade 1 woodland sites.

The British dragonflies are threatened chiefly by drainage and reclamation of peatlands, river drainage improvement schemes, and pollution of remaining lakes, ponds and waterways. Rarer species which occur in standing waters on key sites are perhaps the easiest to protect, but those breed-ing in rivers may be affected by environmental changes occurring many kilometres upstream. Dragonflies living in upland habitats are in general the least threatened, but those in the lowlands of England face considerable pressures; the commoner and more widespread species less so than the rare and local dragonflies, which face greater chances of serious depletion or extinction as their relatively few localities suffer degradation or destruction. The survival in Britain of the rarest species of all, *Oxygastra curtisii*, is problematical. Several other rarities are doubtfully represented on key sites, e.g. *Somatochlora metallica* and *Coenagrion armatum* and *C. hastulatum*. Some of our dragonflies are summer immigrants, and a few do not regularly breed in Britain, i.e.

Aeshna mixta, Sympetrum flaveolum, S. fonscolombii and *S. vulgatum*, which frequent various types of habitat, including fields and woodland edges, as well as wet places. Only the first is a regular visitor. Conservation of these immigrants rests mainly on developments in the parts of Europe where they regularly breed.

SPIDERS (ARACHNIDA)

There is a high representation of the British spider fauna on key sites (see the accounts of spiders for separate formations).

Out of the total of 609 species of spiders which have been recorded from the British Isles, 90% have been recorded from at least one key site. A further 4% occur in or near buildings or in other artificial habitats which are unlikely to be represented, leaving only 6% of the British spider fauna of natural and semi-natural habitats which is, as far as is known, unrepresented on key sites. Because of incomplete knowledge of spider distribution, especially in woodlands and grasslands, this last figure is probably nearer 2 or 3% in fact. Uplands and peatlands probably have the most complete representation, most of the absentees being found in heathlands, grasslands or woodlands. The factors affecting spider populations and their conservation are broadly similar to those mentioned under Lepidoptera above, and many famous entomological sites are also notable for their rare spiders. Many of these localities are mentioned in the descriptions of the spider fauna of the various habitat formations, but some of the more notable arachnological sites are listed here.

Woodlands
The New Forest, Blean Woods, Burnham Beeches, Black Wood of Rannoch, Rothiemurchus and Abernethy Forest.

Peatlands
Wicken Fen, Chippenham Fen, Woodwalton Fen, Redgrave Fen, Norfolk Broads, New Forest, Abbots Moss, Shropshire Mosses, Rannoch Moor.

Coastlands
Orfordness and Havergate, Dungeness, Sandwich, Dorset coast including Portland and Chesil, Braunton, Whiteford, Ainsdale.

Heathlands
Ashdown Forest, Thursley and Hankley, Chobham Common, New Forest, Dorset heaths, West Lizard.

Grasslands
Box Hill, Heyshott Down, Breckland grass heaths.

Uplands
Cader Idris, Snowdonia, Malham, Cheviot, Ben Nevis, Ben Lawers, Cairngorms, Caenlochan–Clova.

Although most rare species have been recorded from at least one key site, the proportion of their population involved varies, and in many cases is difficult to assess. An example of possibly almost complete representation is the peatland species *Glyphesis cottonae*, which has been recorded from *Sphagnum* bogs only at Thursley, four sites in the New Forest, Morden, Hartland and Studland; the other member of the same genus, *G. servulus* is known in this country only from Wicken and Chippenham Fens. Of those rare species which have been recorded from only three sites or less, about 30 (c. 35% of the total) are known only from key sites. To some extent this must reflect the disproportionate amount of collecting which has been done on these places, but it must also serve to indicate the value of such sites.

Only three out of 40 coastal species listed have not been recorded from at least one key site, these being *Silometopus incurvatus*, *Trichopterna cito* and *Heliophanus auratus*. The last two occur at Colne Point, near the Colne estuary marsh, and it is possible that *T. cito* at least may be present on other east or south-east coastal sites, e.g. Orfordness or Dungeness. All the heathland and grassland species listed have been recorded from at least one key site, except for *Bianor aenescens* and *Lepthyphantes insignis*. All peatland spiders are represented, and in the upland group only the submontane *Linyphia marginata*, *Diplocephalus connatus* and *D. protuberans* are not known to be present on a key site.

13 APPRAISAL AND CONCLUSIONS

This final section will attempt to assess how far the *Review* is likely to serve the needs of nature conservation in Britain and to consider some of the implications for policy for safeguarding sites.

FIELD COVERAGE

First, it is necessary to examine and define deficiencies in the basic survey on which the whole process of site selection depends. In a collective project of this kind there is always a risk that the different individuals and teams involved may have differed in their emphasis on certain criteria and in standards of judgement, so that all sites rated under a particular grade might not be of equivalent quality. It is believed that this has not in fact been a serious short-coming, as a deliberate effort has been made to ensure that all teams worked to the same standards, and all reports have been scrutinised by the Scientific Assessor with this issue in mind. Inconsistencies of treatment within the *Review* lie mainly in the variable degree of field survey.

A truly comprehensive survey and assessment of all natural and semi-natural ecosystems in Britain would require far more time and resources than were actually available for this task. The *Review* has been something of a compromise between the desirability of achieving complete coverage of all formations and geographical areas, and the need to produce as quickly as possible a recommended list of key sites for safeguarding.

The survey teams for the different major habitat groups started with varying advantage. In particular, lowland calcareous grasslands and uplands had been the subjects of both extensive and intensive field survey and description for some time before the *Review* was launched, whereas for other major habitats such study had been more sporadic and the teams involved less geared to the kind of work involved. Indeed, the group newly formed to deal with open waters was starting virtually from scratch in regard to a conservation-oriented survey of their habitat. Moreover, the different major formations pose different problems as indicated below.

Coastlands

The coast presents rather different survey problems from the other major formations. Together with the montane zone of the higher mountains, it is in general the least disturbed of the major habitats and, except where completely built up, most of the coastline is potentially of interest to conservation. Interest has long focussed upon sand-dune systems, which are extremely localised and are probably the best known of all coastal habitats, though the strong interest of some Scottish sites was not known before the present survey. The very local Hebridean machairs have also been fairly thoroughly investigated, and the larger systems have mostly been assessed. Salt marshes and coastal flats have received special attention as the most important of all wildfowl habitats in Britain, and their national interest in this respect has been fully assessed by the Wildfowl Trust, and discussed by the Wildfowl Conservation Committee whose report to the Conservancy has been of great value to this review. The value of estuaries to autumn and winter populations of wading birds has also been the subject of special study by the British Trust for Ornithology, and is now well documented. The botanical importance of salt marsh is less completely known, especially towards the north and west. Vegetated shingle beaches are rather local and the best examples are probably mostly well known.

From the conservation viewpoint, the least studied of coastal habitats is the sea cliff and rocky shore type; not only is there an enormous length of coastline of this kind (especially in western Scotland) but also considerable physical difficulties of investigation are usually created by the precipitous nature of the ground. Most of the sea cliffs with large concentrations of breeding seafowl are well known, especially through recent censuses made by the Seabird Group, and have considerable international importance, but these are often the least interesting sites botanically. Much further botanical survey of sea cliffs is required in the north and west, and for the present an attempt has been made to select representative sections of rocky coast from available information on geology and floristics. The inter-tidal zone of rocky shore has specifically been ignored, during field survey, though examples of this type of coastal habitat are incidentally included in rocky coast sites chosen for other features. Brackish habitats of any appreciable extent are rather local in occurrence, and types such as coastal lagoons are few and fairly well known. There is, however, much less information about certain para-maritime communities, such as coastal heaths and grasslands, and certain of the local but decidedly maritime vegetation which occurs on exposed rocky coasts of western Scotland, where spray and sand are driven some distance uphill and inland during storms. A selection of these last habitats and communities has been made, but may yet prove to be inadequate.

Woodlands

Certain difficulties are inherent in woodland survey. Not least is the unfortunate circumstance that it is not usually possible to assess the conservation value of a wood without actually going inside and walking about a good deal. The surveyor of woodlands is thus immediately at a disadvantage compared with his colleague in open country. The quality of a woodland from a conservation viewpoint usually depends very largely on its past treatment, and this can only be ascertained by a site inspection or enquiry into the history of management. One cannot take any short cuts on site assessment here, as may sometimes be done for other major ecosystems, for instance, in the straightforward use of large-scale maps and air photographs.

However, the biggest problem lies in the degree of fragmentation and the very large number of separate sites involved. Although woodland is the climatic climax over much of the country, it is the most fragmented of all habitats. Some idea of the scale of the problem may be gauged from the fact that a substantial increase in the number of key woodland sites has been made since the first draft of this report was written. For certain local woodland types such as ashwoods and native pinewoods, survey information is probably fairly complete, but beechwoods and northern Scottish birchwoods are still not fully known, and a large number of lowland oak and mixed deciduous woods (including the park woodland variants of these) has yet to be examined. The great extent of woodland in Sussex has still not been adequately surveyed. Many gorge woodlands in Scotland are also quite unknown at present. It is, however, probable that the existing selection of key sites covers the range of variation in British woodlands reasonably well, and that further survey would not result in any fundamentally new discoveries from the botanical viewpoint, although it might produce some better examples of certain woodland types. Allowance will certainly have to be made for the inclusion of further woodlands of faunal importance.

Lowland grasslands, heaths and scrub

The lowland grasslands and heaths are another highly fragmented group, but are geographically limited and belong mainly to England and Wales. The acidic heaths are the most easily located as they are usually marked on maps as uncultivated land and, although some outlying examples in the north and west have not been examined, the major areas have been visited and assessed. Some areas transitional between lowland and upland acidic heath in south-west England are, however, less fully known but appear to show a rather limited range of variation and may well be covered by the sites selected. The Breckland is a rather circumscribed and well-known district of lowland heaths and grasslands in which survey is virtually complete in broad outline, although some details have locally still to be filled in.

Of the calcareous lowland group, the chalk grasslands, in particular, have been the subject of a thorough and detailed survey, and the only areas not yet properly examined are those of Salisbury Plain where access is restricted for military and defence reasons. Knowledge of lowland grasslands becomes less complete with distance north, though the most important sites on Carboniferous Limestone have probably become known through a long history of botanical focus upon them. The Jurassic limestones are probably the least surveyed of the northern calcareous formations. The ecologically interesting calcareous heaths are fairly well known in the south, but have received much less attention in the north, where examples have mostly been found incidentally during examination of limestone sites. Calcareous scrub is both a seral and a persistent vegetation type, and efforts have been made to locate and examine the longer-standing examples, which are rather local in distribution, but usually associated with grassland or heath; again, knowledge of these is more complete in the south and many areas of northern scrub, including some examples on key sites, have yet to be examined properly.

Neutral grasslands are in some ways the most difficult of all habitats to survey, but the problem lies mainly in the initial locating of sites. Present occurrence is almost a matter of accident and there are few clues to guide the search. Undiscovered high-quality examples probably still exist in various districts, especially of Wales, northern England, and Scotland but they are likely to be disappearing rapidly. The present selection of sites is a bare minimum and could need enlarging considerably if other important examples are discovered.

Open waters

Although much work has been done on open waters in Britain, this is probably the least well known of the major ecosystems from the nature conservation angle. Standing open waters have been partially surveyed, but many sites are still unknown. An attempt has been made to visit and assess the lakes known to be important in England and Wales, where their number is limited, and a good deal of information is sometimes available, as in the Lake District. However, changing environmental conditions, including the now widespread process of eutrophication, are so fundamentally altering the hydrological regime of many freshwater systems that earlier information may no longer be relevant, and re-investigation is required. In Scotland the number of lochs is extremely large and vast resources would be needed to complete a full survey. However, the majority of these lochs belong to a small number of major types, and a representative range within this limited field of variation has been examined and chosen as key sites. There is a still greater lack of information about rivers, and although an attempt has been made to select a representative series of important examples, a good deal of further survey is still required. Because survey information for open waters is so limited, it has seemed sensible to identify key examples of different types within or adjacent to sites rated as grade 1 or 2 for other interest.

Peatlands

Peatlands overlap with other formations, especially uplands, but present rather different problems to the surveyor for here it is often essential to examine the ground carefully before a promising site can be located. However, an extensive survey of peatlands in parts of the country had already been made by an informally constituted Mires Research Group, and a good deal of information about the occurrence and nature of important sites was available at the beginning of the review. A large number of sites was examined during the present survey, and several hitherto unknown but extremely valuable mires were found, especially in the extensive blanket mire systems of northern Britain. The vast areas of blanket mire in northern Scotland and its islands are still incompletely explored, especially in Sutherland and Caithness, and the expanding commercial afforestation of this type of peatland makes it imperative to define the areas of greatest importance to conservation. The remaining good examples of raised mire are also threatened by moss-litter exploitation (and afforestation), but the important areas of this type are all well known.

The group of mires least adequately known is the aquatic transition–flood-plain type (lowland fen), which is widely distributed in Britain, and represented by a large number of separate sites. A good deal of further survey remains to be done for this type, especially in the lowlands of Scotland.

It is, however, felt that the range of variation within the six main types is now fairly fully defined, and that while new sites may well give other important examples, these will probably lie within the known framework.

Uplands

Uplands cover a far larger total area than any other ecosystem, yet the field of attention is immediately narrowed by the fact that, in general, the most important areas are those which reach the highest altitudes, and are thus rapidly identified on a topographic map. The uniformity of much upland country formed of hard, acidic rocks again allows the surveyor to save much time by using geological maps and concentrating on the more varied and important areas. The very continuity and openness of upland ecosystems is also an advantage during field survey. The nature conservation value of virtually all the high montane upland massifs is fairly well known, and while many lower moorland areas have still to be examined, it is unlikely that these will contain any important elements of vegetation, flora or fauna not represented within the series of grade 1 sites listed in this report. The least-known areas are in some of the less spectacular parts of the Scottish Highlands, such as the Monadhliath in Inverness-shire, and the eastern moorlands of Ross, Sutherland and Caithness, where much of the terrain belongs more to peatland. Parts of southern Argyll, in Kintyre, Knapdale, Lorne and Cowal, have yet to be examined and, in the Hebrides, the island of Mull is probably the least known of the islands with substantial areas of upland. On the other hand, some habitats which are transitional between upland and lowland may not be adequately represented in the existing series, especially if research needs are considered.

Artificial ecosystems

The various types of artificial habitat have been considered in the *Review*, but since it is felt that nature conservation needs here do not involve safeguarding key sites at national level, except perhaps by provision for arable weed habitats, no attempt at full countrywide survey has been made.

Flora and fauna

The variable representation of plant and animal species within and between main taxonomic groups on key sites has been discussed in Chapters 11 and 12. It is obvious that many of the lower orders of plants and animals are represented mainly by chance, and that a good deal of further survey and assessment (and probably inclusion of new sites) is needed to ensure that cover for these is adequate.

Conclusion

Survey has been more complete, and site selection therefore more satisfactory, in some formations and areas than others; in woodlands and wetlands, in particular, coverage has been less than might be desired, and on the whole, Scotland is probably the least explored region. However, except in rocky inter-tidal coastlands (which are deliberately excluded), and perhaps some types of lake and river, and neutral grasslands, the *Review* has produced a reasonably comprehensive and systematic body of knowledge of British ecosystems. In compiling a national inventory of key sites, few of a really new type or outstanding importance are likely to have been missed. It is also believed that the standards of site survey, assessment and selection have been reasonably consistent throughout.

THE NUMBERS AND AREAS OF KEY SITES

Table 45 shows the distribution and hectarages of key sites according to regions and formations. Uplands cover by far the greatest total area amongst the major formations, but in general, the largest sites naturally tend to be on land with the lowest agricultural value, since this is the most likely to have escaped development for farming. In the uplands, it is often important to include relatively large areas in key sites, for there is usually a wide range of diversity spread over a considerable extent of ground, and the inclusion of a complete topographic unit, from the base to the summit of a particular mountain system, involves a fairly considerable minimum area. Moreover, some of the vertebrates, such as red deer, pine marten, predatory birds, greenshank and dotterel have large home ranges which could not be contained in a small area. One is dealing here with scale of a much larger order than in most other formations, and the representative areas selected must accordingly be larger than usual.

The number of key woodland sites is substantially larger than for any other major formation; this comes about for several reasons. First, as the prevailing climatic climax type, woodland is the most widespread and well represented of all the formations in each of the geographical regions of Britain. Secondly, the very high degree of fragmentation which woodlands have received has produced a situation where it is

Table 45. *Distribution and hectarages of key sites according to regions and formations*

Region	Coasts Gr. 1	Gr. 2	Woodland Gr. 1	Gr. 2	Lowland grass Gr. 1	Gr. 2	Open water Gr. 1	Gr. 2	Peatland Gr. 1	Gr. 2	Upland grass Gr. 1	Gr. 2	Total numbers of sites Gr. 1	Gr. 2	Total hectares (×10³) Gr. 1	Gr. 2
England																
South-East	7	2	15	6	12	7	3	1	2	0	0	0	34	16	23.9	4.3
South	1	2	6	5	28	10	5	2	2	1	0	0	37	20	36.7	5.8
East Anglia	9	1	13	14	17	13	7	2	13	5	0	0	51	34	81.6	5.1
South-West	13	5	17	12	18	9	2	3	4	1	1	1	43	30	29.4	24.8
Midlands	1	1	7	11	4	3	7	2	5	2	1	0	20	18	27.0	8.2
North	9	6	13	21	16	4	10	3	13	10	10	7	53	47	98.0	25.7
Total	40	17	71	69	95	46	34	13	39	19	12	8	238	165	296.6	73.9
Wales																
South	6	3	8	7	2	3	4	2	5	1	4	3	25	15	29.8	16.5
North	3	2	7	5	2	1	2	4	2	3	4	2	16	15	27.7	2.4
Total	9	5	15	12	4	4	6	6	7	4	8	5	41	30	57.5	18.9
Scotland																
South	5	4	5	8	1	0	4	3	6	8	5	1	21	24	33.3	13.4
East	12	5	8	2	1	0	12	7	5	5	14	15	43	32	117.2	61.7
West	15	11	23	17	1	0	8	6	8	6	13	19	52	56	122.5	118.4
Total	32	20	36	27	3	0	24	16	19	19	32	35	116	112	273.0	193.5
Britain	81	42	122	108	102	50	64	35	65	42	52	48	395	307	627.1	286.3
Hectares (×10³)	207.9	55.4	51.5	15.5	53.8	11.3	24.0	4.0	48.8	14.2	241.1	185.9	627.1	286.3		
Total	263.3		67.0		65.1		28.0		63.0		427.0		913.4			

Notes

Table 45 takes into account the amalgamation/duplication of certain sites (i.e. an area or its components may be listed as sites under more than one formation; for practical purposes and in geographical terms, however, only one site is involved). In the case of some composite sites, hectarages have been arbitrarily distributed between the component formations in the absence of more accurate measurement. For this reason the sum of the six formations in this table is usually greater than the total number of sites.

In Chapter 9, the subdivision of the Scottish Highlands between east and west regions ignores the artificial divisions adopted for the formations (see p. 321). In this Table, however, the sites are allocated according to the artificial division so as to allow comparison with other formations.

Areas *below* Mean Low Water are excluded from coastland site hectarages, which are, in most cases, only an approximation.

Hectarages given for open waters are often greater than the actual area of open water so as to include a buffer zone.

Running-water sites are not measured and no hectarage has been included.

seldom possible to find a single woodland site covering more than a rather small part of the local range of variation, and several sites may be needed in order to represent this variation adequately. Thirdly, the structural and man-induced diversity of woodlands gives added dimensions to the range of variability within this formation, and there is thus a large number of woodland types with claims for representation in any series covering the national field of variation.

There is a certain disparity between different formations in ratio of grade 1 to grade 2 sites. This arises not through varying standards, but from differences in availability of sites, criteria for selection and national requirements, and completeness of survey. Coastlands have only half as many grade 2 as grade 1 sites because survey of 'hard' coasts is inadequate, whilst much of the remaining undeveloped 'soft' coast is of first national importance, requiring that a majority of sites be placed in grade 1. Uplands, however, have about equal numbers of grade 1 and grade 2 sites because survey has been fuller, and there are very many and large tracts of mountain country with considerable nature conservation interest, especially in Scotland, so that it would be unreasonable to place a majority of these in grade 1.

ATTAINMENT OF OBJECTIVES

This review has been concerned with survey and assessment of *existing* habitats and ecosystems which have conservation value. Although some key sites are wholly artificial in origin (e.g. Cotswold Water Park) there is virtually no attempt to deal with the question of the deliberate creation of new conservation areas by planned intervention and manipulation of both environment and species. This is a relatively new and exciting aspect of nature conservation which will occupy attention increasingly in the future, as the pressures on certain types of semi-natural habitat continue to grow and as new, large-scale developments in land use open up fresh possibilities. The Morecambe Bay Feasibility Study has already made allowance for the creation of new wetland habitat for aquatic plants and wildfowl, as some compensation for the loss of estuarine flats and saltings. If certain important key sites cannot for practical reasons be safeguarded from destruction or serious modification, careful thought will have to be given to the possibility of creating comparable ecosystems elsewhere as opportunity allows. The potential value of various kinds of derelict land as wildlife habitat should be considered. It is accepted that woodland in Britain is to a large degree man-made, and that a good deal of careful management of woodland nature reserves is usually necessary to produce and maintain an ecosystem of desired constitution. It would seem only one step further in starting from scratch and re-creating a woodland in a deforested habitat such as grassland; there should, however, be especially cogent reasons for such projects and their success will depend largely on a detailed knowledge of what is wanted and of the ways of achieving this. These new-style key sites might be especially suitable as research and educational areas.

Key sites are intended to serve a variety of needs, not all of which are predictable at any one moment or in any one area. Requirements may change or develop, and in a dynamic situation such as this, a national series judged adequate for the present may not remain so indefinitely. Nor can present knowledge of the occurrence of important sites or representation of species be regarded as adequate. The present list of key sites is thus in no way final, but is believed to be the best that circumstances allow. Indeed, it is undesirable ever to think in terms of a final list, and there should always be scope for additions or deletions. Some grade 1 sites may prove impossible to safeguard or may deteriorate seriously before suitable measures can be implemented; whenever

possible these will have to be replaced, often through upgrading of a lower grade site. There will be good reason to review the situation periodically and to recommend such changes as are necessary to meet new requirements and changed conditions, as well as to cope with any deficiencies which remain through incompleteness of field survey and taxonomic 'cover'.

The production of *A Nature Conservation Review* is a means to an end and not an end in itself. Its declared objective is only a proximate goal and the final purpose will be fulfilled only if and when adequate safeguards have been achieved for as many as possible of the nationally important sites. Even if all the key sites could be protected and managed as desired, however, it would still not follow that the ends of nature conservation in Britain had been attained in full; and it is hoped that this report will not distract attention from the need to pursue more general measures for wildlife conservation, throughout the country.

This involves the still more difficult problem that safeguarded areas of any category can inevitably be only one part of the total nature conservation effort, and there remains the large residue of wildlife interest which lies outside not only the key sites, but also those in grades 3 and 4. There is some measure or overlap between the two, in that safeguarded areas can provide refuge at times for mobile species outside, and for some organisms they can also act as reservoirs which supply and repopulate the country beyond. Safeguarded areas should be regarded as the essential hard core of nature conservation interest, and thus the keystone for national strategy in this field.

No more can be done here than to draw attention to this larger problem. Clearly, a great deal will depend on the future pattern of land use throughout the country, and its impact on the environment and wildlife. In turn, promotion of nature conservation as one aspect of land use in a changing Britain will depend on the existence of a store of accurate ecological knowledge relating to all ecosystems. It is felt that the present review has contributed significantly to this fund of knowledge, but that a great deal more remains to be added, through field survey and study of processes and relationships, especially those concerned with change, in natural and semi-natural ecosystems.

APPENDIX: INTRODUCTION

The *Nature Conservation Review* has involved a compromise between the desirability of making a truly comprehensive survey of habitats and the need to produce a definitive report for action within a reasonable time. It is inevitable that during the interval between the completion of a manuscript report and its appearance as a published document, there should have been changes to some of the existing key sites, and additional information to suggest new ones. A few sites have been destroyed or badly damaged and replacements have been made. Some others are judged so vulnerable to damage that alternatives have been added as a sensible precaution. Several completely new sites of obvious national importance have become known, and additional information about others requires that they be upgraded or extended.

There follows a synopsis of the changes which have been made. Detailed accounts of the completely new sites, those with major extensions, and those upgraded on the basis of extensive new information are given in vol. 2.

Coastlands

The recent census of breeding seabirds by the Seabird Group has provided new data (summarised in Cramp, Bourne & Saunders, 1974) which allow a reappraisal of the choice of key sites to take account of this outstanding ornithological feature. The criterion of national importance is still defined as a minimum total population of 10000 breeding pairs (other than *Larus* gulls), and the new census data show a number of additional sites to qualify for this label (Table 38). A notable feature of the survey is that the Orkneys have been shown to hold the largest concentration of guillemots and kittiwakes in the British Isles. Three Scottish breeding stations gave total population counts exceeding 100000 pairs. St Kilda (C.105), with its huge gannetry and total of 15 breeding species, is confirmed as one of the most important seabird stations in the North Atlantic. Foula (C.96) has 16 breeding species, some in massive numbers and must clearly be regraded as a grade 1* site. The hitherto little-known islands of Westray and Papa Westray in Orkney have 19 breeding species with probably the largest colonies of guillemots, kittiwakes and Arctic terns in Britain; this is regarded as a new grade 1* site. Marwick Head in the north-west mainland of Orkney has guillemot and kittiwake colonies approaching those of Westray in size and is regarded as a new grade 1 site, and the same grading is given to the Berriedale cliffs in Caithness which also have immense concentrations of these two species. New grade 2 sites, identified mainly because of their large numbers of cliff seabirds, are Copinsay in Orkney; Sule Skerry and Sule Stack off the north coast of Sutherland; Dunnet Head and Duncansby Head in Caithness; and the Buchan cliffs in Aberdeenshire. The Bass Rock (C.79) and Shiant Isles

(C.120) have been regraded as grade 1, and North Hoy (C.94) and Fetlar (U.77) have been confirmed as nationally important for their seabird interest alone.

In southern England, the North Solent Marshes (C.11), now known to have the largest black-headed gull colony in Britain (15000 pairs) have been upgraded from 2 to 1.

In addition, Carmarthen Bay in south Wales and the Montrose Basin in eastern Scotland have been included as new grade 1 and 2 sites for, respectively, their widely dispersed populations of seaducks and estuarine wildfowl, waders and other birds. Two important salt marsh systems at opposite ends of the country, Berrow Marsh in Somerset and the Wick River Marshes in Caithness, have been added as new grade 1 sites for their vegetational features, which extend the range of variation represented in the coastal key sites.

Woodlands

In Pembrokeshire, Tycanol Wood on the lower slopes of the Bannau Preseli appears to be a surviving fragment of original sessile oak–ash woodland and is outstandingly rich in oceanic lichens, bryophytes and ferns; this is a new grade 1 site. The Carn Gafallt woodland complex in Brecknock has been upgraded from grade 2 to grade 1, and the site extended to include an important meadow system. In southern England, the grade 1 oak–ash woodland of Wychwood, Oxfordshire, has been extended by adding the compartments outside the existing National Nature Reserve (NNR). This extension, which includes grassland and old quarries, is described in an additional site account.

Further survey in the Midlands Region has led to the identification of an important mixed oak–birch–lime wood, Swithland Wood in Leicestershire, and this has been added as a new grade 2 site. In the same region, further study has led to the view that Brampton Bryan Park (W.124) in Herefordshire should be regraded from grade 2 to 1 as a fine example of park woodland with rich arboreal lichen communities and invertebrate fauna. The ravine wood of Hanley Dingle on the borders of Herefordshire and Worcestershire has been added as a grade 2 Midland example of a species-rich mixed deciduous wood. The other Herefordshire ravine woodland of Hill Hole Dingle (W.118) has, however, been down-graded from grade 1 to 2. On the Welsh borders, the botanically famous dolerite outcrops of Stanner Rocks form a new grade 1 site with an exceptional rocky woodland edge flora; there is a patchy growth of trees, but the distinctive communities of open rock habitats could also be regarded as belonging to the lowland grassland and scrub formation. In the north Region of England (see map 2), further damage to the interesting woodland–peatland complex of Orton Woods in north Cumberland has made it desirable to include an alternative, and the rather similar area of Finglandrigg Woods farther west of Carlisle is added as a grade 2 site. In the western Highlands, the combination of pine and birch wood at Shieldaig, Loch Torridon, west Ross, is now regarded as grade 1 instead of 2. The grade 2 birchwood at Loch a' Mhuillin, Sutherland, has been found to contain a fair amount of pedunculate oak, here at its northern limit, and for this important feature, it also has been elevated to grade 1.

Lowland Grasslands, Heaths and Scrub

Predictions about the probable loss of key sites within this vulnerable group of habitats have been borne out in practice. In the southern counties of England, heathland continues to be lost, especially through building. In Dorset, where so much heathland has been lost since 1945, a group of three heathland sites, Horton Common, Holt Heath and Parley Common, lying between the New Forest and the Purbeck heathlands, has been rated as grade 2. The important area of heathland around Woolmer Pond (OW.7) in east Hampshire has been added as an extension to the grade 1 site. In Surrey, further examination of heathlands within the military training areas of Pirbright and Bisley has indicated the national importance of these, and they have been grouped with Chobham Common (L.14) as a large aggregate site, the Chobham–Pirbright Heaths.

In Wiltshire the grade 1 chalk grassland site of Pewsey Downs (L.26) has been extended by the addition of adjacent areas. Four chalk grassland sites in Wiltshire have so deteriorated through the application of artificial fertiliser since their selection that they may no longer be of key site quality: they are Starveall Down and Stony Hill (L.33, gr. 1), Coombe Bissett Down (part of L.49, gr. 2), Trow Down (L.52, gr. 2) and Well Bottom, Upton Lovell (L.53, gr. 2). In the Midlands, Clehonger Meadow, Herefordshire (gr. 1), and Draycote Meadows, Warwickshire (gr. 2), have been included to extend the series of the vanishing old meadow grasslands.

In south Wales, the Dryslwyn Meadows on the alluvial flats of Afon Tywi in Carmarthenshire have been rated grade 2 for their wintering flock of European white-fronted geese; and the Carn Gafallt meadows in Brecknock are regarded as a grade 1 extension to the woodland site (W.97) for their forb-rich grasslands.

Peatlands

In the Norfolk Broads, further survey has disclosed that some of the extensive fens surrounding Barton Broad (as distinct from the open water Broad itself) are of very high nature conservation value. The peatland site of Barton Broad–Reedham Marshes (P.20) has therefore been enlarged and regraded as grade 1 under the name Ant Marshes. Similarly, the fens and carr surrounding the open water areas of the grade 1 Upton Broad (OW.15) are of high quality, and the site has been extended to include these. By contrast, Smallburgh Fen

(P.15) has been subject to deterioration, and is downgraded from grade 1 to 2, as an alternative site to the Ant Marshes.

In the Lleyn peninsula of Caernarvonshire, the eutrophic valley mire of Cors Geirch is a good example of this very local type of peatland and is rated as grade 2. Deterioration of raised mires throughout Britain during the last decade has enhanced the value of the least-damaged examples which remain. In particular, two recent catastrophic fires have seriously damaged the *Sphagnum* cover of Glasson Moss (P.48, gr. 1), the best example in northern England in 1968. In compensation, two grade 2 raised mires in the same area of the Solway Plain as Glasson Moss, Bowness Common (P.61) and Wedholme Flow (P.62), are elevated to grade 1; both still have good areas of *Sphagnum*-dominated surface, despite peat-cutting or drying over other parts. Drumburgh Moss, slightly to the south-east of Glasson Moss, has recovered from earlier fires to the extent of being judged worthy of inclusion as a grade 2 site. Also in northern England, Austwick Moss in north-west Yorkshire is regarded as worthy of inclusion as a grade 2 raised mire. In southern Scotland, many of the low-lying transitional raised-blanket mires of Wigtownshire have been afforested, and Kilquhockadale Flow (P.79, gr. 2) has been destroyed as a result. In the same district, Dergoals Flow has been substituted as an alternative site (grade 2). A newly discovered site in the eastern Highlands, Pitmaduthy Moss in east Ross, is regarded as a grade 1 example of the very local, pine-grown, mixed, raised valley mire. In the north-west Highlands, Cnoc na Moine near Tongue has been added as an unusual peatland–open water complex with high ornithological interest, ranking as grade 1. Another new site, the Dee of Dirkdale in Orkney, is included as a grade 1 example of calcareous valley mire, an unusual type in the far north of Scotland.

Another new site is an important eutrophic fen at Loch Tallant on the island of Islay; this grade 1 mire has affinities with Malham North Fen, and is extremely rich floristically.

Upland Grasslands and Heaths

At the extreme northern end of the Pennines, the Geltsdale–Tindale Fells area, with its combination of upland, marginal hill land and woodland habitats, has proved to have outstandingly diverse and large bird populations, and for this ornithological interest has been added as a grade 1 site.

The high-lying outcrop of Durness limestone at Glas Cnoc, Kishorn (U.93) is now regarded as of major botanical importance equivalent to the other floristically rich exposures of this rock type in the north-west Highlands, and has accordingly been uprated from grade 2 to 1.

In Shetland, further examination of the lochan-studded moorlands of North Roe to the north of Ronas Hill (U.100) has led to their addition to this grade 2 site, and the whole has been upgraded to grade 1 as a diverse and important upland complex of habitats.

Table A. 1. **INDEX OF APPENDIX SITES**

* Internationally important sites.

Formation and site no.ᵃ	Site	County	New site grade	Extension (E)	Regraded site grade
Coastlands					
C.11	NORTH SOLENT MARSHES	HAMPSHIRE	—	—	1
C.124	BERROW MARSH (BRIDGWATER BAY)	SOMERSET	1	—	—
C.125	CARMARTHEN BAY	CARMARTHEN/ GLAMORGAN/ PEMBROKE	1	—	—
C.79	BASS ROCK	EAST LOTHIAN	—	—	1
C.126	MARWICK HEAD	ORKNEY	1	—	—
C.127	WESTRAY AND PAPA WESTRAY	ORKNEY	1*	—	—
C.96	FOULA	SHETLAND	—	—	1*
C.120	SHIANT ISLES	ROSS	—	—	1
C.128	WICK RIVER MARSHES	CAITHNESS	1	—	—
C.129	BERRIEDALE CLIFFS	CAITHNESS	1	—	—
C.130	Montrose Basin	Angus	2	—	—
C.131	Buchan Cliffs	Aberdeenshire	2	—	—
C.132	Copinsay	Orkney	2	—	—
C.133	Sule Skerry and Sule Stack	Orkney	2	—	—
C.134	Dunnet Head	Caithness	2	—	—
C.135	Duncansby Head	Caithness	2	—	—
Woodlands					
W.24	WYCHWOOD FOREST	OXFORDSHIRE	—	E	—
W.230	STANNER ROCKS	RADNOR	1	—	—
W.231	TYCANOL WOOD	PEMBROKESHIRE	1	—	—
W.124	BRAMPTON BRYAN PARK	HEREFORDSHIRE	—	—	1
W.222	OB MHEALLAIDH, SHIELDAIG	ROSS	—	E	1
W.226	LOCH A' MHUILLIN WOOD	SUTHERLAND	—	—	1
W.232	Hanley Dingle	Herefordshire	2	—	—
W.118	Hill Hole Dingle	Herefordshire	—	—	2
W.233	Swithland Wood	Leicestershire	2	—	—
W.234	Finglandrigg Woods	Cumberland	2	—	—
Lowland grasslands, heath and scrub					
L.14	CHOBHAM AND PIRBRIGHT COMPLEX	SURREY	—	E	1
L.152	WOOLMER POND (OW.7) AND FOREST	HAMPSHIRE	—	E	—
L.26	PEWSEY DOWNS	WILTSHIRE	—	E	—
L.153	CARN GAFALLT MEADOWS (W.97)	BRECKNOCK	—	E	1
L.154	CLEHONGER MEADOW	HEREFORDSHIRE	1	—	—
L.155	Parley Common	Dorset	2	—	—
L.156	Horton Common	Dorset	2	—	—
L.157	Holt Heath	Dorset	2	—	—
L.158	Dryslwyn Meadows	Carmarthenshire	2	—	—
L.159	Draycote Meadows	Warwickshire	2	—	—

Table A. 1 (*contd.*)

Formation and site no.[a]	Site	County	New site grade	Extension (E)	Regraded site grade
Peatlands					
P.108	UPTON BROAD (OW.15)	NORFOLK	—	E	—
P.20	ANT MARSHES (Barton Broad and Reedham Marsh)	NORFOLK	—	E	1
P.61	BOWNESS COMMON	CUMBERLAND	—	—	1
P.62	WEDHOLME FLOW	CUMBERLAND	—	—	1
P.109	DEE OF DIRKADALE AND GLIMS MOSS	ORKNEY	1	—	—
P.110	LOCH TALLANT, ISLAY	ARGYLL	1	—	—
P.111	PITMADUTHY MOSS	ROSS	1	—	—
P.112	CNOC NA MOINE	SUTHERLAND	1	—	—
P.15	Smallburgh Fen	Norfolk	—	—	2
P.113	Cors Geirch	Caernarvonshire	2	—	—
P.114	Drumburgh Moss	Cumberland	2	—	—
P.115	Austwick Moss	Yorkshire	2	—	—
P.116	Dergoals Flow	Wigtownshire	2	—	—
Uplands					
U.93	GLAS CNOC	ROSS	—	—	1
U.100	RONAS HILL AND NORTH ROE	SHETLAND	—	E	1
U.101	GELTSDALE–TINDALE FELLS	CUMBERLAND	1	—	—

[a] Regraded and extended sites retain their site number.

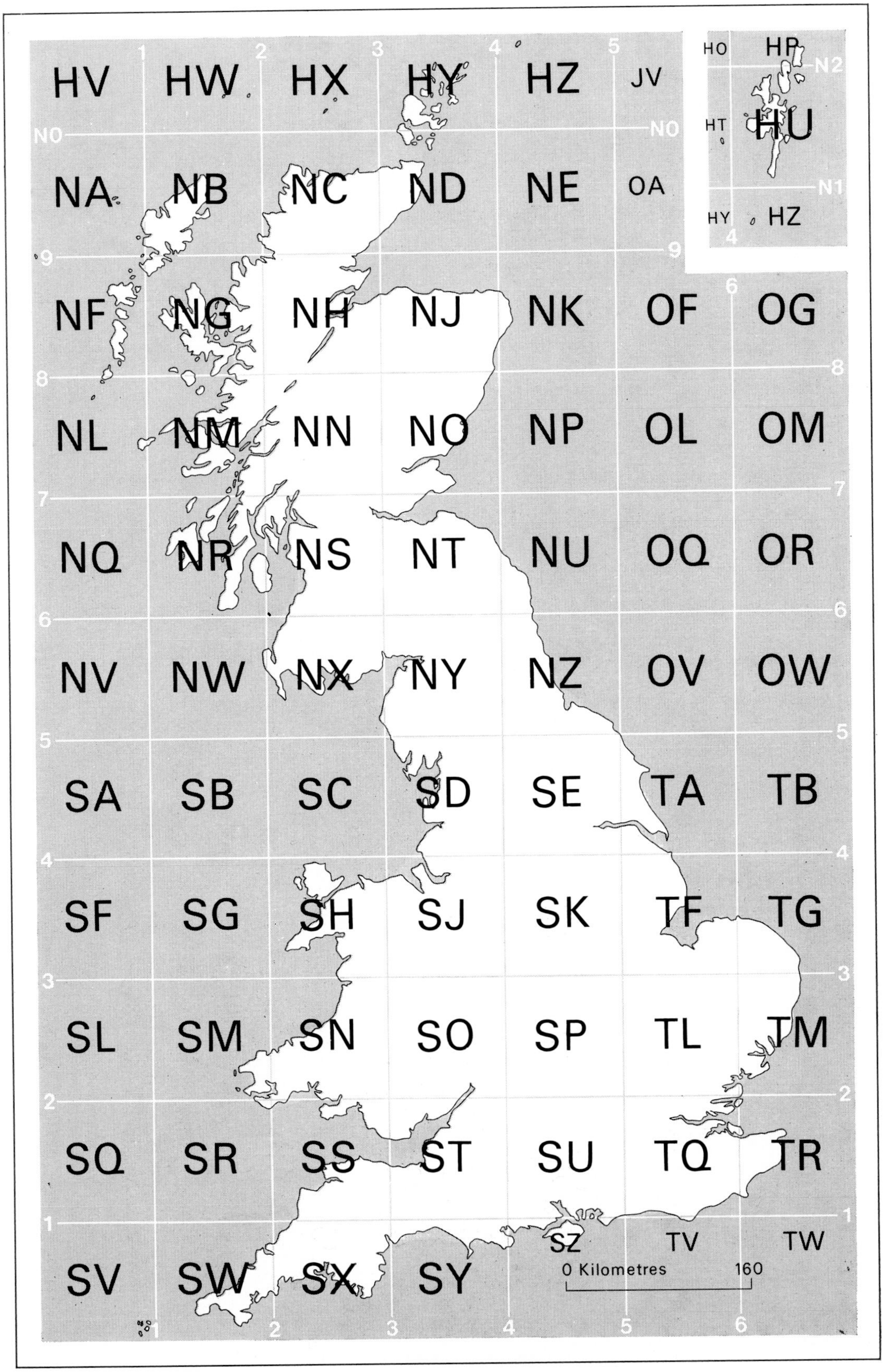

Map 1. National Grid prefixes

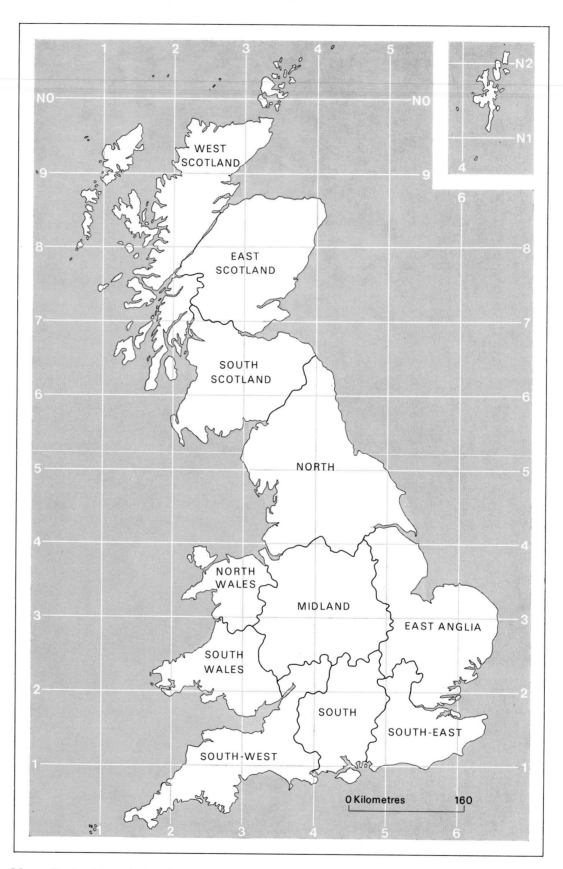

Map 2. Regional boundaries of the Nature Conservancy

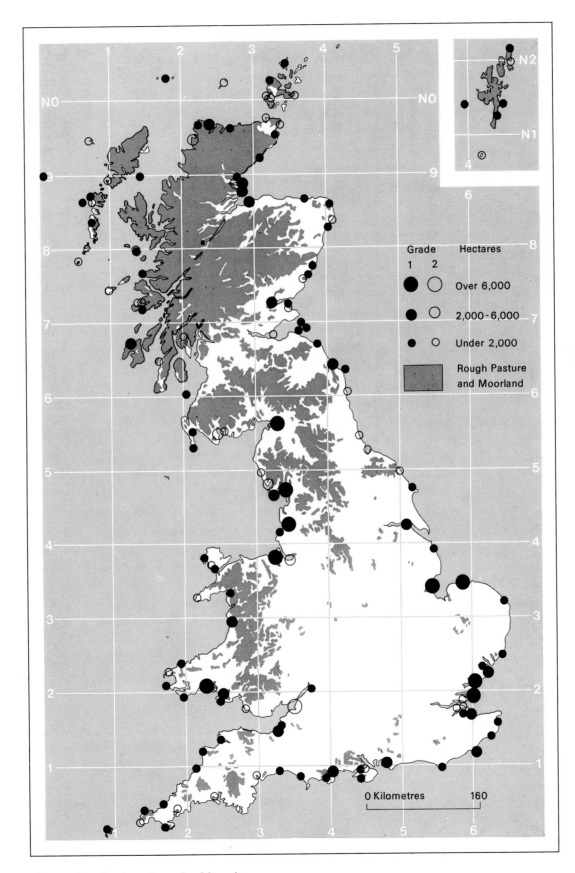

Map. 3. Distribution of coastland key sites

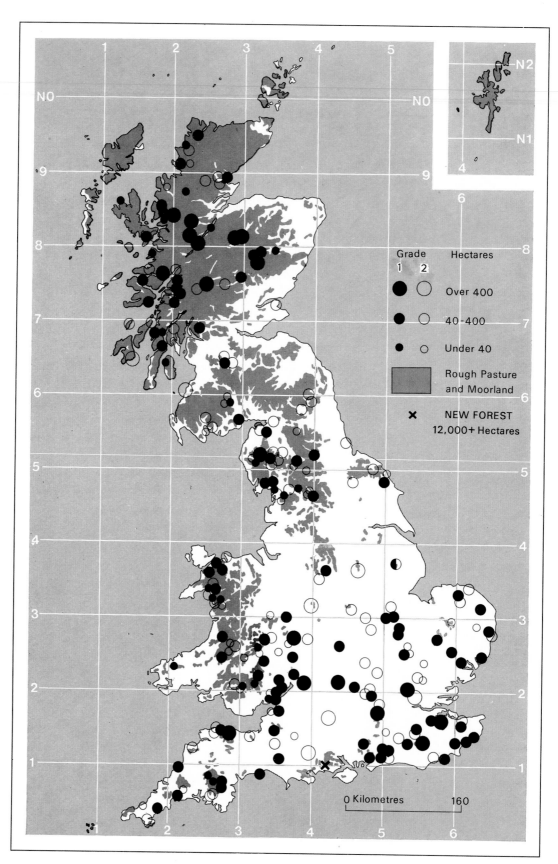

Map 4. Distribution of woodland key sites

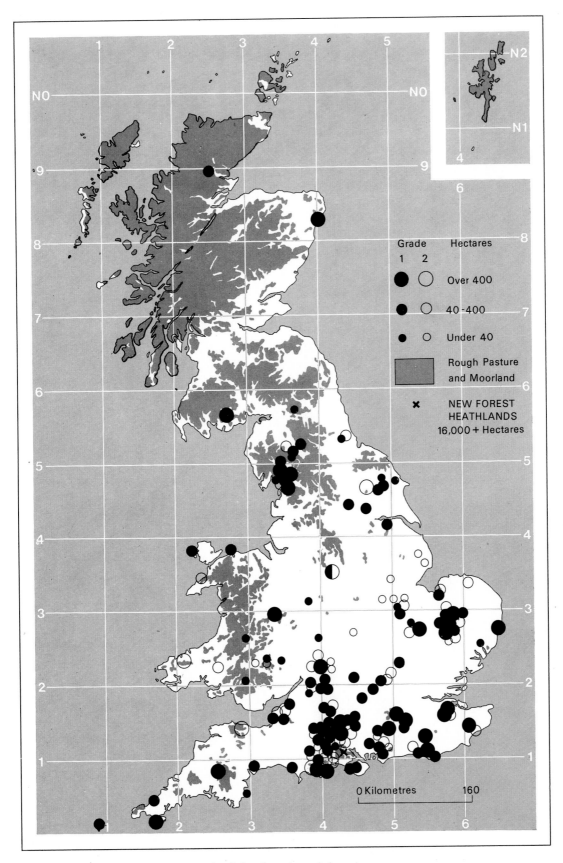

Map 5. Distribution of lowland grassland, heath and scrub key sites

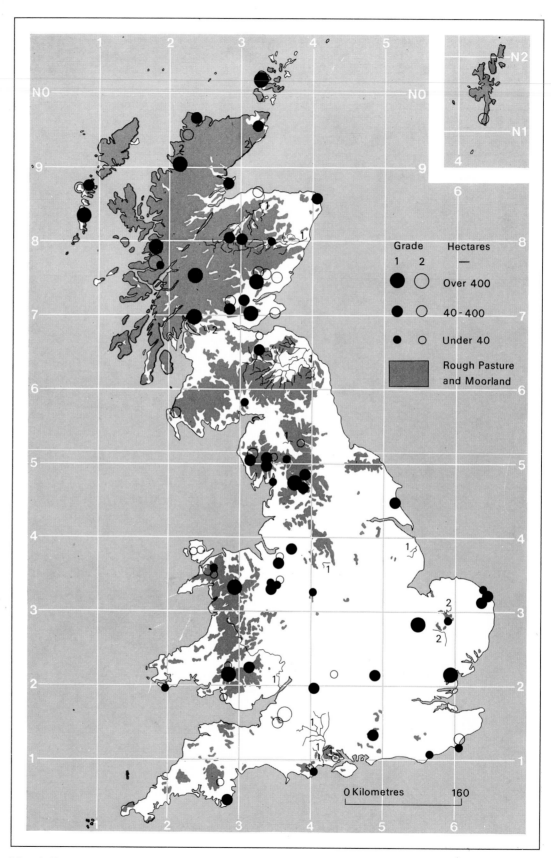

Map 6. Distribution of open water key sites. Numbers by rivers indicate grade 1 or 2 running water sites

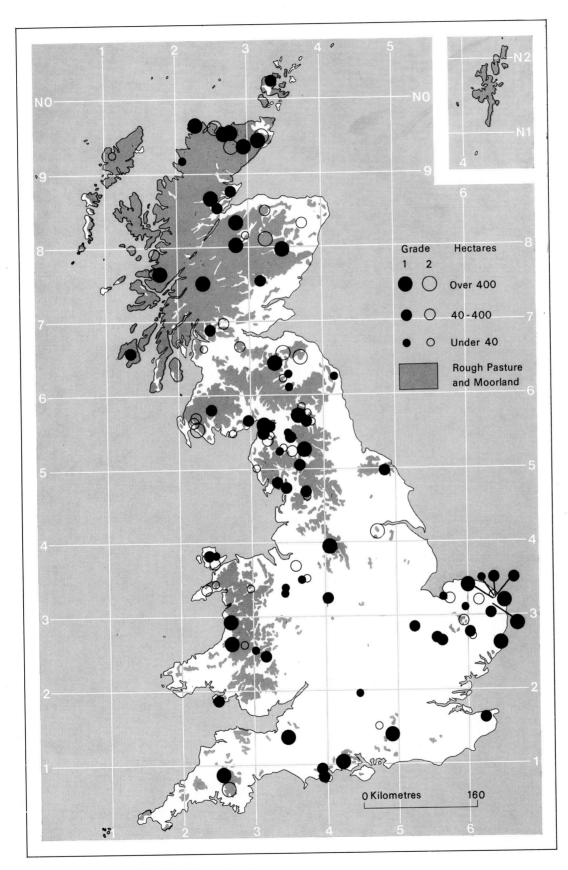

Map 7. Distribution of peatland key sites

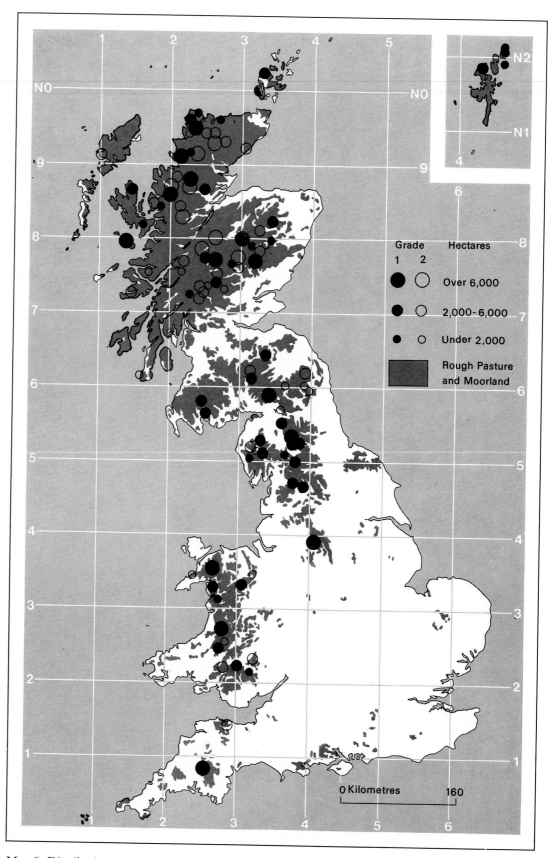

Map 8. Distribution of upland grassland and heath key sites

BIBLIOGRAPHY

No attempt has been made to provide a comprehensive bibliography to the *Review*, for it would be vast. References in the text to specific published work have also been kept to the minimum but where an exception has been made full bibliographic reference is listed below. A short selection of material to give background reading, together with nomenclature authorities, is also given. Attention is drawn to the volumes of the *New Naturalist Series* which are valuable for general background reading and of which a selection is included.

Allen, E. J. & Todd, R. A. (1902). Fauna of the Exe estuary. *Journal of the Marine Biological Association, UK*, **6**, 295–335.

Anon. (1963). *The Atlas of Britain and Northern Ireland*. Oxford, Clarendon Press.

Atkinson-Willes, G. L. (ed.) (1963). *Wildfowl in Great Britain: a survey of the winter distribution of the Anatidae and their conservation in England, Scotland and Wales*. Monographs of the Nature Conservancy, no. 3. London, HMSO.

Baker, H. (1937). Alluvial meadows: a comparative study of grazed and mown meadows. *Journal of Ecology*, **25**, 408–420.

Benson-Evans, K., Fisk, D., Pickup, G. & Davies, P. (1964–68). The natural history of Slapton Ley Nature Reserve. 2. Preliminary studies on the freshwater algae. *Field Studies*, **2**, 493–519.

Birks, H. J. B. (1973). *Past and present vegetation of the Isle of Skye: a palaeoecological study*. London, Cambridge University Press.

Blackwood, J. W. & Tubbs, C. R. (1970). A quantitative survey of chalk grassland in England. *Biological Conservation*, **3**, 1–5.

Bowen, H. C. (1970). Historical monuments of the County of Dorset. In *An Inventory of the historical monuments in the County of Dorset*, **3** (2). Royal Commission on Historical Monuments (England).

Bristow, W. S. (1971). *The world of spiders*, revised edn. (New Naturalist Series.) London, Collins.

Burnett, J. H. (ed.) (1964). *The vegetation of Scotland*. Edinburgh & London, Oliver & Boyd.

Butcher, R. W. (1954). *Colchicum autumnale* L. *Journal of Ecology*, **42**, 249–257.

Butcher, R. W., Pentelow, F. T. K., Woodley, J. W. A. (1931). A biological investigation of the River Lark. *Fisheries Investigations Series*, **3**, no. 3.

Clarke, W. G. (1925). *In Breckland wilds*. London, Scott.

Condry, W. M. (1966). *The Snowdonia National Park*. (New Naturalist Series.) London, Collins.

Coombe, D. E. & Frost, I. C. (1956). The heaths of Cornish Serpentine. *Journal of Ecology*, **44**, 226–256.

Corbet, P. S., Longfield, C. & Moore, N. W. (1960). *Dragonflies*. (New Naturalist Series.) London, Collins.

Cramp, S., Bourne, W. R. P. & Saunders, D. (1974). *The seabirds of Britain and Ireland*. London, Collins.

Crampton, C. B. (1911). *The vegetation of Caithness considered in relation to the geology*. Committee for the Survey and Study of British Vegetation.

Darling, F. F. & Boyd, J. M. (1969). *The Highlands and Islands*, 2nd edn. (New Naturalist Series.) London, Collins.

Davidson, J. M. (1961). *An ecological study of Risby Warren*. Dissertation, University College London.

Donisthorpe, H. St J. K. (1939). *A preliminary list of the Coleoptera of the Windsor Forest*. London, Lloyd.

Dutt, W. A. (1906). *Wild life in East Anglia*. London, Methuen.

Edwards, K. C., Swinnerton, H. H. & Hall, T. H. (1962). *The Peak District*. (New Naturalist Series.) London, Collins.

Ellis, E. A. (ed.) (1965). *The Broads*. (New Naturalist Series.) London, Collins.

Farrow, E. P. (1941). Notes on vegetational changes on Cavenham Heath, Breckland. *Journal of Ecology*, **29**, 215–216.

Ferreira, R. E. C. (1959). Scottish mountain vegetation in relation to geology. *Transactions of the Botanical Society of Edinburgh*, **37**, 229–250.

Ford, E. B. (1957). *Butterflies*, 3rd edn. (New Naturalist Series.) London, Collins.

Ford, E. B. (1972). *Moths*, 3rd edn. (New Naturalist Series.) London, Collins.

Foreign and Commonwealth Office (1973). *Final act of the international conference on the conservation of Wetlands and Waterfowl, Ramsar, Iran . . . 1971, and, Convention on wetlands of international importance especially as waterfowl habitat, Paris . . . 1972*. (Cmnd 5483.) London, HMSO.

Frohawk, F. W. (1934). *The complete book of British butterflies*. London, Ward Lock.

Gillham, M. E. (1957). Vegetation of the Exe estuary in relation to water salinity. *Journal of Ecology*, **45**, 735–756.

Godwin, H. (1956). *The history of the British flora: a factual basis for phytogeography* (1975, 2nd edn). London, Cambridge University Press.

Godwin, H. & Conway, V. M. (1939). The ecology of a raised bog near Tregaron, Cardiganshire. *Journal of Ecology*, **27**, 313–359.

Graham, E. H. (1944). *Natural principles of land use*. New York, Oxford University Press.

Grubb, P. J., Green, H. E. & Merrifield, R. C. J. (1969). The ecology of chalk heath, its relevance to the calcicole calcifuge and similar soil acidification problems. *Journal of Ecology*, **57**, 175–212.

Helliwell, D. R. (1973). Priorities and values in nature conservation. *Journal of Environmental Management*, **1**, 85–127.

Holme, N. A. (1949). Fauna of sand and mud banks near the mouth of the Exe estuary. *Journal of the Marine Biological Association, UK*, **28**, 189–237.

Hope-Simpson, J. F. (1940–41). Studies of the vegetation of the English chalk. *Journal of Ecology*, **28**, 386–402 (1940); **29**, 107–116, 217–267 (1941).

Huet, M. (1954). Biologie profile en long et en traverse des eaux courantes. *Bulletin français de Piscie*, no. **175**, 41–53.

Jeffrey, D. W. & Pigott, C. D. (1973). The response of grasslands on sugar-limestone in Teesdale to application of phosphorus and nitrogen. *Journal of Ecology*, **61**, 85–92.

Kubiena, W. L. (1953). *The soils of Europe.* London, Thomas Murby.

Landsberg, S. Y. (1955). The morphology and vegetation of the Sands of Forvie. Ph.D. thesis, University of Aberdeen.

Leach, W. (1930). A preliminary account of the vegetation of some non-calcareous British screes (Gerolle). *Journal of Ecology*, **18**, 321–332.

Longfield, C. (1949). *The dragonflies of the British Isles*, 2nd edn. London, Warne.

Lousley, J. E. (1969). *Wild flowers of chalk and limestone*, 2nd edn. (New Naturalist Series.) London, Collins.

MacGillivray, W. (1855). *The natural history of Deeside and Braemar.* London.

McVean, D. N. & Ratcliffe, D. A. (1962). *Plant communities of the Scottish Highlands: a study of Scottish mountain, moorland and forest vegetation.* Monographs of the Nature Conservancy, no. 1. London, HMSO.

MacVicar, S. M. (1926). *The students handbook of British hepatics.* Eastbourne, V. V. Sumfield. (Reprinted, 1961, by Wheldon & Wesley.)

Maitland, P. S. (1966). *Studies on Loch Lomond. 2. The fauna of the river Endrick.* (Glasgow University Publications.) London, Blackie.

Maitland, P. S. (1974). The conservation of freshwater fishes in the British Isles. *Biological Conservation*, **6**, 7–14.

Manley, G. (1952). *Climate and the British scene.* (New Naturalist Series.) London, Collins.

Matthews, J. R. (1937). Geographical relationships of the British flora. *Journal of Ecology*, **25**, 1–90.

Matthews, J. R. (1955). *Origin and distribution of the British flora.* London, Hutchinson's University Library.

Matthews, L. H. (1968). *British mammals.* (New Naturalist Series.) London, Collins.

Meteorological Office (1952). *Climatological atlas of the British Isles.* London, HMSO.

Ministry of Town and Country Planning (1947). *Conservation of nature in England and Wales: Report of the Wild Life Conservation Special Committee (England and Wales).* (Cmd 7122.) London, HMSO.

Moss, C. E. (1913). *Vegetation of the Peak District.* London, Cambridge University Press.

Nethersole-Thompson, D. & Watson, A. (1974). *The Cairngorms: their natural history and scenery.* London, Collins.

Parslow, J. L. F. (1973). *Breeding birds of Britain and Ireland: a historical survey.* Berkhamsted, T. & A. D. Poyser.

Pearsall, W. H. (1971). *Mountains and moorlands*, revised edn. (New Naturalist Series.) London, Collins.

Perring, F. H. & Walters, S. M. (ed.) (1962). *Atlas of the British flora.* London, Nelson for Botanical Society of the British Isles.

Potts, G. R. (1970). Recent changes in the farmland fauna with special reference to the decline of the grey partridge. *Bird Study*, **17**, 145–166.

Ragge, D. R. (1965). *Grasshoppers, crickets and cockroaches of the British Isles.* London, Warne.

Ratcliffe, D. A. (1968). An ecological account of Atlantic Bryophytes in the British Isles. *New Phytologist*, **67**, 365–439.

Ratcliffe, D. A. (1974). Ecological effects of mineral exploitation in the United Kingdom and their significance to nature conservation. *Proceedings of the Royal Society of London A*, **339**, 355–372.

Raven, J. & Walters, M. (1956). *Mountain flowers.* (New Naturalist Series.) London, Collins.

Salisbury, E. J. (1918). The ecology of scrub in Hertfordshire: a study of colonisation. *Transactions of the Hertfordshire Natural History Society*, **17**, 53–64.

Shimwell, D. W. (1968). 'The vegetation of the Derbyshire Dales: a report to the Nature Conservancy and Supplement.' Unpublished report available from the Nature Conservancy Council.

Smith, M. (1964). *The British amphibians and reptiles*, 3rd edn. London, Collins.

Southern, H. N. (ed.) (1964). *The handbook of British mammals.* Oxford, Blackwell Scientific Publications.

Stamp, L. D. (1967). *Britain's structure and scenery*, 6th edn. (New Naturalist Series.) London, Collins.

Steers, J. A. (1964). *The coastline of England and Wales*, 2nd edn. London, Cambridge University Press.

Steers, J. A. (1973). *The coastline of Scotland.* London, Cambridge University Press.

Steven, H. M. & Carlisle, A. (1959). *The native pinewoods of Scotland.* Edinburgh, Oliver & Boyd.

Tansley, A. G. (1939). *The British Islands and their vegetation.* London, Cambridge University Press.

Water Resources Board (1972). *Morecambe Bay estuary storage: report by the Water Resources Board.* London, HMSO.

Watt, A. S. (1936–40). Studies in the ecology of Breckland. *Journal of Ecology*, **24**, 117–138 (1936); **25**, 91–112 (1937); **26**, 1–37 (1938); **28**, 42–70 (1940).

Watt, A. S. (1971). Rare species in Breckland: their management for survival. *Journal of Applied Ecology*, **8**, 593–609.

West, G. (1910). An epitome of a comparative study of the dominant phanerogamic and higher cryptogamic flora of aquatic habitat, in seven lake areas of Scotland. *Bathymetrical Survey of the Scottish Freshwater Lochs*, **1**, 156–260.

Williams, C. B. (1964). *Patterns in the balance of nature and related problems in quantitative ecology.* London, Academic Press.

Wilson, A. (1938). *Flora of Westmorland.* Arbroath, Buncle.

Witherby, H. A., Jourdain, F. C. R., Ticehurst, N. F. & Tucker, B. W. (1943–44). *The handbook of British Birds*, 2nd revised edn. London, Witherby.

NOMENCLATURE AUTHORITIES

Mammals

Corbet, G. B. (1964). *Identification of British mammals.* London, British Museum (Natural History).

Birds

British Ornithologists' Union (1971). *The status of birds in Britain and Ireland.* Oxford, Blackwell.

Amphibians and reptiles

Smith, M. (1964). *The British amphibians and reptiles*, 3rd edn. (New Naturalist Series.) London, Collins.

Fish

Maitland, P. S. (1972). A key to the freshwater fishes of the British Isles. *Scientific Publications of the Freshwater Biological Association*, **27**.

Wheeler, A. C. (1969). *The fishes of the British Isles and north-west Europe*. London, Macmillan.

Insects

Kloet, G. S. & Hincks, W. D. I. (1964–72). *A check list of British insects*, 1st & 2nd edns. London, Royal Entomological Society.

Spiders

Locket, G. H., Millidge, A. F. & Merrett, P. (1951–74). *British spiders*, 3 vols. London, Ray Society.

Aquatic invertebrates (excluding gastropods)

Illies, J. (1967). *Limnofauna Europea*. Stuttgart, Fischer.

Gastropods

Macan, T. T. (1969). A key to the British fresh and brackish-water gastropods, 3rd edn. *Scientific Publications of the Freshwater Biological Association*, **13**.

Flowering plants

Clapham, A. R., Tutin, T. G. & Warburg, E. F. (1962). *Flora of the British Isles*, 2nd edn. London, Cambridge University Press.

For English names see

Dony, J. G., Rob, C. M. & Perring, F. H. (1974). *English names of wild flowers*. London, Butterworths.

Lichens, liverworts and mosses

Paton, J. A. (1965). *Census catalogue of British hepatics*, 4th edn. Sutton, British Bryological Society.

Warburg, E. G. (1963). *Census catalogue of British mosses*, 3rd edn. Sutton, British Bryological Society.

Watson, W. (1963). *Census catalogue of British lichens*. London, Cambridge University Press.

Fungi

Ainsworth, G. C. & Bisby, G. R. (1971). *Dictionary of the fungi*, 6th edn. Kew, Commonwealth Mycological Institute.

Algae

Bourrelly, P. (1966–70). *Les algues d'eau douce*, 3 vols. Paris, Boubée.

Fritsch, F. E. (1945–48). *The structure and reproduction of the algae*, 2 vols. London, Cambridge University Press.

Pascher, A. (ed.) (1930). *Die Süsswasserflora Mitteleuropas*. Heft **10**, *Bacillariopliyta (Diatomeae)*, ed. by F. Hustedt. Jena, Fischer.

SITE INDEX